# Central Asia

Kazakhstan, Tajikistan, Uzbekistan, Kyrgyzstan, Turkmenistan

Bradley Mayhew

Greg Bloom, John Noble, Dean Starnes

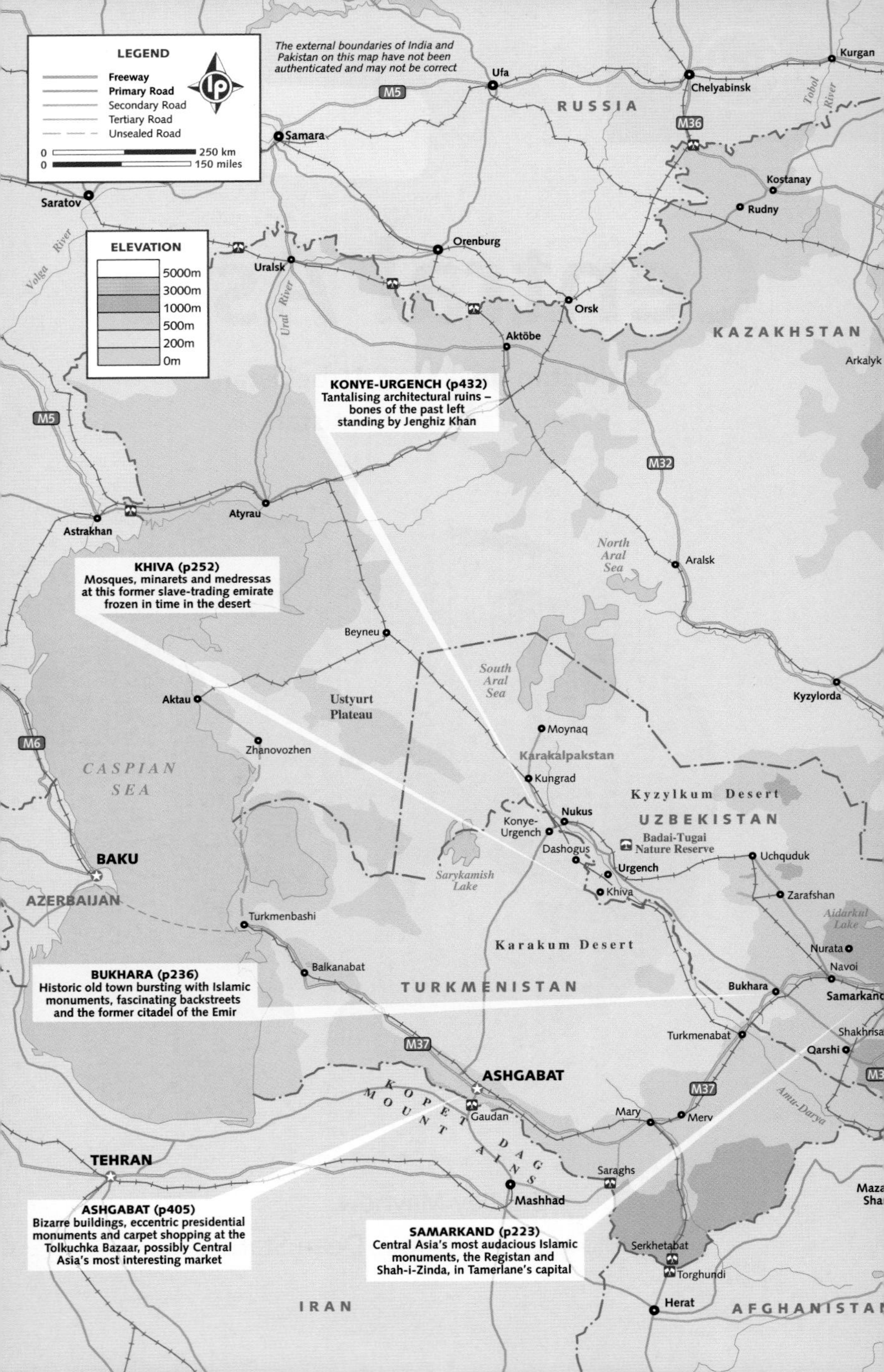

LEGEND
Freeway
Primary Road
Secondary Road
Tertiary Road
Unsealed Road
0 250 km
0 150 miles
ELEVATION
5000m
3000m
1000m
500m
200m
0m
The external boundaries of India and Pakistan on this map have not been authenticated and may not be correct
KONYE-URGENCH (p432)
Tantalising architectural ruins – bones of the past left standing by Jenghiz Khan
KHIVA (p252)
Mosques, minarets and medressas at this former slave-trading emirate frozen in time in the desert
BUKHARA (p236)
Historic old town bursting with Islamic monuments, fascinating backstreets and the former citadel of the Emir
ASHGABAT (p405)
Bizarre buildings, eccentric presidential monuments and carpet shopping at the Tolkuchka Bazaar, possibly Central Asia's most interesting market
SAMARKAND (p223)
Central Asia's most audacious Islamic monuments, the Registan and Shah-i-Zinda, in Tamerlane's capital
RUSSIA
KAZAKHSTAN
UZBEKISTAN
TURKMENISTAN
AZERBAIJAN
IRAN
AFGHANISTAN
CASPIAN SEA
North Aral Sea
South Aral Sea
Sarykamish Lake
Aidarkul Lake
Ustyurt Plateau
Kyzylkum Desert
Karakum Desert
Karakalpakstan
Badai-Tugai Nature Reserve
KOPET DAG MOUNTAINS
Volga River
Ural River
Tobol River
Amu-Darya
M5
M36
M32
M6
M37
Ufa
Kurgan
Chelyabinsk
Samara
Saratov
Kostanay
Rudny
Orenburg
Uralsk
Orsk
Aktöbe
Arkalyk
Astrakhan
Atyrau
Aralsk
Beyneu
Aktau
Zhanovozhen
Kyzylorda
Moynaq
Kungrad
Nukus
Konye-Urgench
Dashogus
Urgench
Khiva
Uchquduk
Zarafshan
Nurata
Navoi
Samarkand
Bukhara
Turkmenabat
Shakhrisabz
Qarshi
BAKU
Turkmenbashi
Balkanabat
ASHGABAT
Gaudan
Mary
Merv
Saraghs
TEHRAN
Mashhad
Serkhetabat
Torghundi
Herat

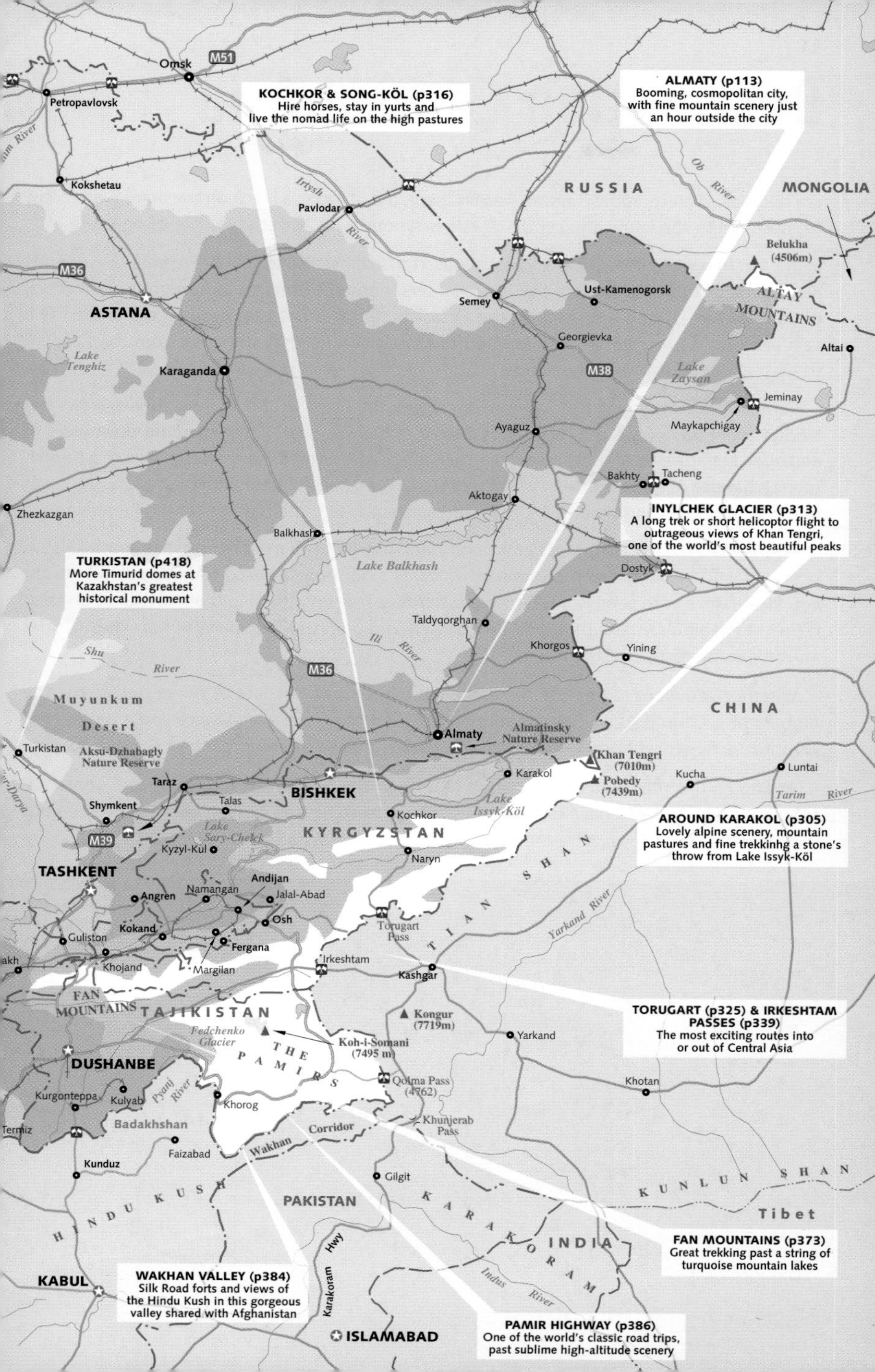
KOCHKOR & SONG-KÖL (p316)
Hire horses, stay in yurts and live the nomad life on the high pastures
ALMATY (p113)
Booming, cosmopolitan city, with fine mountain scenery just an hour outside the city
INYLCHEK GLACIER (p313)
A long trek or short helicoptor flight to outrageous views of Khan Tengri, one of the world's most beautiful peaks
TURKISTAN (p418)
More Timurid domes at Kazakhstan's greatest historical monument
AROUND KARAKOL (p305)
Lovely alpine scenery, mountain pastures and fine trekkinhg a stone's throw from Lake Issyk-Köl
TORUGART (p325) & IRKESHTAM PASSES (p339)
The most exciting routes into or out of Central Asia
FAN MOUNTAINS (p373)
Great trekking past a string of turquoise mountain lakes
WAKHAN VALLEY (p384)
Silk Road forts and views of the Hindu Kush in this gorgeous valley shared with Afghanistan
PAMIR HIGHWAY (p386)
One of the world's classic road trips, past sublime high-altitude scenery
RUSSIA
MONGOLIA
CHINA
KYRGYZSTAN
TAJIKISTAN
PAKISTAN
INDIA
Tibet
ASTANA
BISHKEK
TASHKENT
DUSHANBE
KABUL
ISLAMABAD
Omsk
M51
Petropavlovsk
Kokshetau
Pavlodar
Irtysh River
Ob River
Belukha (4506m)
ALTAY MOUNTAINS
Semey
Ust-Kamenogorsk
Georgievka
M38
M36
Lake Zaysan
Altai
Jeminay
Maykapchigay
Lake Tenghiz
Karaganda
Ayaguz
Bakhty
Tacheng
Aktogay
Zhezkazgan
Balkhash
Lake Balkhash
Dostyk
Taldyqorghan
Ili River
Khorgos
Yining
Shu River
Muyunkum Desert
Almaty
Almatinsky Nature Reserve
Khan Tengri (7010m)
Pobedy (7439m)
Turkistan
Aksu-Dzhabagly Nature Reserve
Karakol
Kucha
Luntai
Tarim River
Taraz
Talas
Lake Issyk-Köl
Shymkent
Kochkor
M39
Lake Sary-Chelek
Kyzyl-Kul
Naryn
TIAN SHAN
Andijan
Namangan
Jalal-Abad
Angren
Osh
Kokand
Fergana
Guliston
Torugart Pass
Yarkand River
Margilan
Khojand
Irkeshtam
Kashgar
FAN MOUNTAINS
Kongur (7719m)
Fedchenko Glacier
Koh-i-Somani (7495 m)
Yarkand
THE PAMIRS
Qolma Pass (4762)
Khotan
Kurgonteppa
Kulyab
Pyanj River
Khorog
Khunjerab Pass
Termiz
Badakhshan
Corridor
Wakhan
Faizabad
Kunduz
Gilgit
KUNLUN SHAN
HINDU KUSH
KARAKORAM
Karakoram Hwy
Indus River

# Destination Central Asia

For decades, even centuries, Central Asia has been out of focus, a blank on the map. Even today, to those not in the know, the centre of Asia is synonymous with the middle of nowhere.

Yet for two millennia, known variously as Transoxiana, Turkestan or Tartary, these lands were a major thoroughfare for Silk Road traders, nomadic empires and migrating invaders, tying together Europe and Asia on the Eurasian steppes. The backdrop to this drama is a vast arena of desert, steppe and knotted mountain ranges that stretches from the Caspian to China, Siberia south to the Hindu Kush.

Central Asia's storybook history, from Alexander the Great to the khans of Khiva, litters the land at every turn. You'll get more than a whiff of the Silk Road when standing downwind of an Uzbek kebab seller and glimpse more than a hint of a nomadic past in the eyes of a Kazakh moneychanger. At times the caravan stops of Samarkand and Bukhara, with their exotic skyline of minarets, mosques and medressas, seem lifted directly from the days of Timur (Tamerlane).

Further east the snowcapped Pamirs and Tian Shan mountains of Kyrgyzstan and Tajikistan host fantastic trekking and mountain adventures. Community-based tourism projects bring you face to face with semi-nomadic Kyrgyz herders, meeting them in their yurts and on their terms. The region's little-visited oddities, namely Turkmenistan and parts of Kazakhstan, offer an offbeat interest all of their own.

Whether you want to explore the architectural gems of Bukhara or horse trek across the high Pamirs, Central Asia offers something for everyone. And everywhere you'll be greeted with instinctive local hospitality, offering a shared meal, a helping hand or a place to stay.

Add to all this the intrinsic fascination of a forgotten region fast emerging as a geopolitical pivot point and you have one of Asia's most absorbing and hidden corners. Even if your friends don't quite know where it is.

ANTHONY PL

# Kazakhstan

ANTHONY PLUMMER

Stroll through Panfilov Park (p118), making sure to stop by the colourful Zenkov Cathedral, Almaty

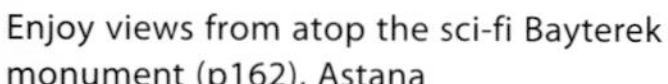

Enjoy views from atop the sci-fi Bayterek monument (p162), Astana

IAN TROWER/PHOTOLIBRARY

BERNARD O'KANE/PHOTOLIBRARY

Join the pilgrimage to Yasaui Mausoleum (p149), resting place of the revered Sufi teacher, Turkistan

# Uzbekistan

DEAN STARNES

Lament the environmental disaster of the Aral Sea, amid remains of abandoned fishing vessels, Moynaq (p260)

Marvel at the intricate tiled patterns of the Ulugbek Medressa (p225) at the Registan, Samarkand

MARTIN MOOS

Admire the striking blue façade of Mir-i-Arab Medressa (p241), Bukhara

BRADLEY MA

MARTIN MOOS

Take in the Guri Amir Mausoleum, Samarkand (p226)

DEAN STARNES

Look up towards the attractively decorated roof at Tosh-Hovli Palace (p255), Khiva

Visit both the Ichon-Qala (p254) and Kalta Minor Minaret (p255), Khiva

MARTIN MOOS

# Kyrgyzstan

BRADLEY M

Purchase an *ak kalpak* (Kyrgyz white felt hat) from Jayma Bazaar (p337), Osh

Trek through the picturesque Karakol Valley (p307)

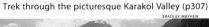

BRADLEY MAYHEW

ANTHONY PLUMMER

Take a breather and look out over the rolling hills, outside of Kochkor (p317)

# Tajikistan

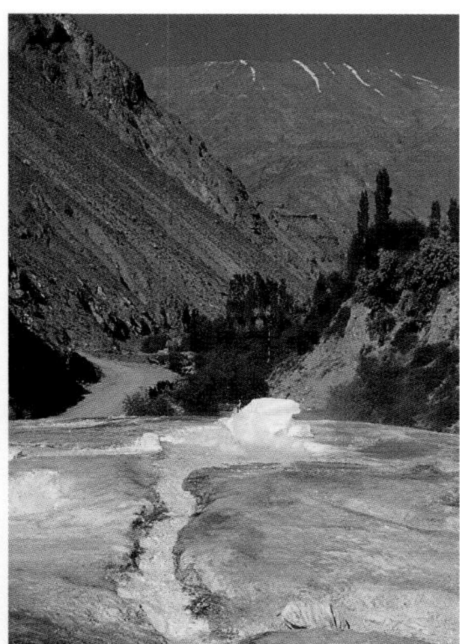

JOHN MOCK

Relax in hot springs at Garam Chashma (p385), Wakhan Valley

Follow the footsteps of Marco Polo through the high-altitude desert and mountains of Kara-Kul (p391), in the Pamirs

BRADLEY MAYHEW

Pitch a tent along the scenic Alauddin lakes, Fan Mountains (p374)

BRADLEY MAYHEW

# Turkmenistan

MARTIN MOOS

Take advantage of the healing properties of the Nejameddin Kubra Mausoleum and the Sultan Ali Mausoleum (p433), Konye-Urgench

Pay tribute to the late and 'great' Turkmenbashi, Independence Park (p410), Ashgabat

THOMAS LEHNE/PHOTOLIBRARY

Gaze up at the giant calendar mosaic on the Turabeg Khanym Complex (p433), Konye-Urgench

MARTIN

# Tradition

ANDREW PEACOCK

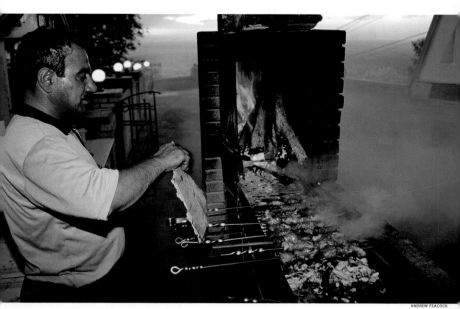

Indulge in Central Asia's finest cuisine, the shashlyk. Almaty (p123), Kazakhstan

Uzbek man, Bukhara (p236)

MARCO BRIVIO/PHOTOLIBRARY

ANTHONY PLUMMER

Enjoy a good night's sleep in a yurt (p273), Kyrgyzstan

# Activities

ANDREW PEACOCK

Head to the summit of Uchityel peak, Ala-Archa region (p292), Kyrgyzstan

Surround yourself in the greenery of Karakol Valley (p307), Kyrgyzstan

ANTHONY PLUMMER

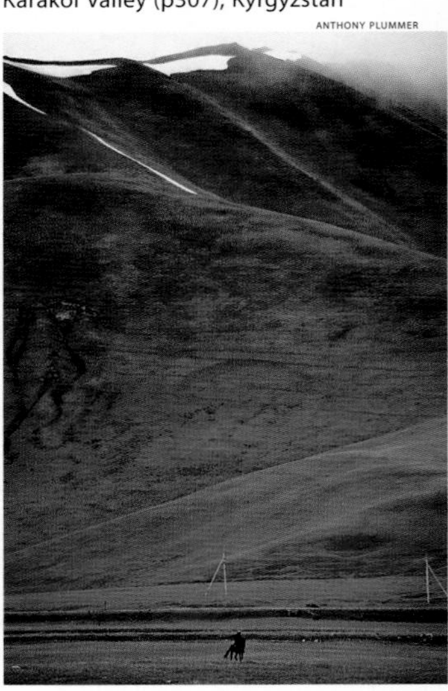

Trek through Ak-Say Canyon (p292), the Ala-Archa region, Kyrgyzstan

ANDREW P

# Contents

# Regional Map Contents

# The Authors

## BRADLEY MAYHEW **Coordinating Author, Tajikistan**

It must be a taste for mutton that has driven Bradley repeatedly to almost every corner of Inner Asia since spending six months in Uzbekistan writing the *Odyssey Guide to Uzbekistan*. He has coordinated the last three editions of *Central Asia* and is also the co-author of Lonely Planet guides *Tibet, Nepal, Bhutan, China, Jordan* and *Yellowstone & Grand Teton National Parks*. He has lectured on Central Asia to the Royal Geographical Society and contributed chapters to *Silk Road: Monks, Warriors and Merchants on the Silk Road* and the Insight Guide to the Silk Road. An expat Brit, Bradley lives in Yellowstone County, Montana.

### Life on the Road

Research, like any travel in Central Asia, is an intriguing mix of the exotic and banal. Sure, there are some world-class sights here, but what really makes travel in Central Asia such a riot are the eccentricities of the region. If Central Asians had bumper stickers, they would read '(weird) sh*t happens'.

Every Central Asian research trip has its moments of insanity. After four hours in the back of a snub-nosed bus to Sary-Chelek, with no other passengers left on board, my wife and I were still swinging wildly on the hand bars like a pair of demented monkeys, eyes rolled up in our heads, with the driver looking at us nervously through the rear-view mirror.

The high Pamirs offered challenges of a more cloak-and-dagger nature. Once the local KGB got whiff that I was a writer, plain-clothes security officers suddenly appeared out of the woodwork in even the smallest town and my name magically appeared on blacklists at several military checkpoints. All of which made arriving in Shaimak, and later Zor-Kul, thrilling moments. Score one for the guidebook writers.

## GREG BLOOM **Uzbekistan**

On his previous mission to Tashkent, Greg trained Uzbek newspaper reporters in Western journalism techniques for the International Centre for Journalists (ICFJ), an American NGO. That was in 2003, before the ICFJ's partner, Internews, was kicked out of Uzbekistan in the wake of the bloodshed at Andijon. Returning to Uzbekistan three years later, Greg reports that surprisingly, despite Uzbekistan's well-publicised political troubles, the country remains an ideal destination for individual travel – safe, hospitable, (relatively) hassle-free and utterly fascinating. Formerly the editor of Ukraine's *Kyiv Post*, Greg is now based in Manila and writes frequently for Lonely Planet about the Philippines and former Soviet countries.

**LONELY PLANET AUTHORS**

Why is our travel information the best in the world? It's simple: our authors are independent, dedicated travellers. They don't research using just the internet or phone, and they don't take freebies in exchange for positive coverage. They travel widely, to all the popular spots and off the beaten track. They personally visit thousands of hotels, restaurants, cafés, bars, galleries, palaces, museums and more – and they take pride in getting all the details right, and telling it how it is. For more, see the authors section on www.lonelyplanet.com.

## JOHN NOBLE

**Kazakhstan**

John, with colleague John King, pioneered Lonely Planet's coverage of the Soviet Union with *USSR* (1991). After Soviet disintegration, John worked on the first editions of several LP guides to the successor states, including *Central Asia* (1996), for which he covered Kazakhstan and parts of Uzbekistan and Turkmenistan. He then took a 10-year breather before returning to Kazakhstan for this edition. He found the country as big, bleak and beautiful as ever, its people just as warm but more open, travel getting steadily easier, and the restaurants and hotels unrecognisable. He hopes this book will somehow encourage more travellers to get acquainted with one of the world's last unknown gems.

## DEAN STARNES

**Kyrgyzstan**

A one-time English teacher in Japan, children's palaeontology presenter and now a travel writer and part-time graphic designer in New Zealand, Dean first came across the 'stans' of Central Asia while travelling to India from Iran. His unjustified aversion to flying (why fly over what you can travel through?) and a deep-rooted desire to improve his shoddy geography (how long have these been here?) meant it was only a matter of time until he ended up lost in Kyrgyzstan. An unfortunate visa error (long story – but he assures us he's innocent) and an unnatural taste for *kymys* (fermented mare's milk) meant that he stayed long enough to see the wrong side of a Kyrgyz winter, but the right side of everything else. Photographs and travel stories from this and other trips can be viewed at his website www.deanstarnes.co.nz.

## ANONYMOUS

**Turkmenistan**

The author of the Turkmenistan chapter has chosen to remain anonymous to protect the people who helped him/her during research.

# Getting Started

Central Asia isn't the easiest place to travel through. You'll need to invest some serious time tracking down visas, permits and the latest travel information, preferably months before you depart. You won't meet many travellers on the road and there are certainly no video cafés serving banana muesli. But this is part of the attraction of a land that has been largely off-limits to travellers for the last 2000 years.

Travel today is generally getting easier every year, with new accommodation options, vastly improved food and a network of shared taxis that will shuttle you around cheaply and in relative comfort. Do your research on Central Asian epic history in particular and you'll find the region quickly addictive. The more you put in, the more you'll get out of this Asian heartland.

## WHEN TO GO

At lower elevations spring and autumn are the overall best seasons, in particular April to early June and September through October. In March/April the desert blooms briefly and the monotonous ochre landscapes of Turkmenistan, Uzbekistan and Kazakhstan become a Jackson Pollock canvas of reds, oranges and yellows. Autumn is harvest time, when market tables heave with freshly picked fruit.

See Climate Charts (p446) for more information.

Summer (mid-June to early September) is ferociously hot in the lowlands of Tajikistan, Uzbekistan and Turkmenistan, with sizzling cities and desert temperatures as high as 40°C or more. Winters (November to March) are bitterly cold even in the desert.

July through August is the best time to visit the mountains of Kyrgyzstan, Tajikistan and southeast Kazakhstan, and to trek (earlier and later than that, herders and other summer residents will have returned to the lowlands). Snow starts to fall in November and mountain passes fill with snow until April or even May. Bishkek and Almaty might have snow in April. Northern Kazakhstan is comfortable right through the summer but freezes in the sub-Siberian winter.

For more details see the Climate and When to Go sections of the individual country chapters.

### 'STANS AT A GLANCE

**Kazakhstan** One of the last great blanks in the map, with interesting and quirky sites separated by vast amounts of nothing. Good hiking in the southeast and increasingly popular ecotourism options. Sub-Siberian Russian cities in the north.

**Kyrgyzstan** Vowel-challenged republic of Alpine mountains, yurts and high pastures. The best place in Central Asia for hiking and horse riding. Community tourism programmes and a wide network of homestays give you a grass-roots adventure on the cheap. Plus it'll give you a gazillion points at Scrabble.

**Tajikistan** The region's most outlandish high-altitude scenery, home to Central Asia's best road trip, the stunning Pamir Hwy. This is the cutting edge of adventure travel. Obtaining permits requires some preparation. Fabulous trekking and the region's most humbling hospitality.

**Turkmenistan** The 'North Korea of Central Asia'. Hard to get into (tourist visas require you to hire a guide) but fascinating once you are there, not least for the bizarre personality cult of Turkmenbashi. An uncertain future follows the death of President Niyazov in December 2006 and the election of Gurbanguly Berdimuhammedow on 11 February 2007, though reforms are promised.

**Uzbekistan** Home to historic Silk Road cities, epic Islamic architecture and the region's most stylish private guesthouses. The heart of Central Asia. Don't miss it.

You might want to time your visit with the region's two major celebrations – Navrus (around 21 March) and the various independence days (around September/October). See p449 for details.

## COSTS & MONEY

By travelling with a friend, staying in homestays, eating in *chaikhana* (teahouses) and hiring the odd taxi when there is no public transport, you can get around Central Asia for around US$15 to US$20 per person per day (more like US$20 to US$40 in Kazakhstan). For a minimum of comfort you'll probably have to part with US$20 for a hotel in bigger towns. In order of expense, the cheapest countries are Kyrgyzstan, Uzbekistan, Tajikistan, Kazakhstan and (most expensive) Turkmenistan. Budget accommodation costs are highest in Kazakhstan, transport costs are highest in the Pamirs of Tajikistan.

You can shave down costs further by self-catering in shops and bazaars, staying in private homes and the occasional bottom-end place, sharing hotel rooms with other travellers, getting around town by local bus instead of taxi, riding overnight trains to save hotel costs, and spending less time in (expensive) cities.

Trekking trips start at around US$50 per person per day with professional trekking agencies but you can arrange a trip for a fraction of this through community tourism organisations such as Community Based Tourism (CBT) in Kyrgyzstan (p277) and Murgab Ecotourism Association (META) in the Pamir region of Tajikistan (p388).

For midrange travel in Uzbekistan, you'll be looking at spending US$15 to US$30 per person for a stylish B&B; throw in US$10 per day for taxi hire between towns. Where there are any, four-star hotels run to around US$100 per double.

Don't forget to factor in visa costs, which can mount up, especially in Tajikistan and Turkmenistan, and of course long-haul transport to get you to and from Central Asia.

Money is best brought in a combination of cash in US dollars (perhaps around two-thirds of your funds), a credit card (and PIN) and a few emergency travellers cheques (which are the least useful form of currency in this destination).

### HOW MUCH?

Snickers bar US$0.40 to US$0.50

100km bus ride US$0.40 (Turkmenistan) to US$2 (Kazakhstan)

One minute phone call to the US US$0.50 (Tajikistan) to US$2 (Kazakhstan)

Internet connection per hour US$0.75 (Kyrgyzstan) to US$1.75 (Kazakhstan)

Traditional hat US$2 (Tajikistan) to US$10 (Kazakhstan)

### LONELY PLANET INDEX

Litre of bottled water US$0.25 to US$0.50

Bottled beer US$0.20 (Turkmenistan) to US$1 (Kazakhstan)

Shashlyk US$0.30 (Uzbekistan) to US$1 (Kazakhstan)

Litre of petrol US$0.50 (Uzbekistan) to US$1.50 (Turkmenistan)

## TRAVEL LITERATURE

See the directories in the individual country chapters for recommended books on specific republics.

Lonely Planet's coverage of neighbouring countries includes *China; Pakistan & the Karakoram Highway; Afghanistan; Iran; Georgia, Armenia & Azerbaijan; The Trans-Siberian Railway;* and *Russia & Belarus*. Lonely Planet also produces a dedicated *Central Asia phrasebook*.

*Beyond the Oxus; Archaeology, Art & Architecture of Central Asia* by Edgar Knobloch is an oddly appealing book for a specialist cultural history

### TRAVELLING SAFELY IN CENTRAL ASIA

In general Central Asia is a pretty safe place to travel despite the media's presentation of the region as a hot spot of environmental disaster, human rights violations and Islamic insurgency.

Most travellers eventually come face to face with crooked officials, particularly policemen, as checks are endemic throughout the region. You shouldn't have any problems as long as your documents are in tip-top shape. You will find specific safety information about each country at the start of each individual country chapter.

**DON'T LEAVE HOME WITHOUT...**

- A fistful of visas (see p456 and the Visas sections of the individual country chapters) and plans set in motion for any travel permits (p456) you might need.
- The latest government travel warnings (p447).
- A sun hat, sunglasses and sunscreen for the strong desert and mountain sun, plus a torch (flashlight) for overcoming iffy electricity supplies in the countryside.
- Water purification – essential if you plan to get off the beaten track.
- Slide film – impossible to find in Central Asia.
- Maps – hard to find in Central Asia.
- A sleeping bag – very useful for winter or for rural Kyrgyzstan and Tajikistan in summer.
- Mementos from home (eg postcards and photos) and gifts to help break the ice at homestays and yurtstays.
- Long, loose, nonrevealing clothes. These will win you friends in Islamic Central Asia, particularly in rural areas and the Fergana Valley of Uzbekistan. Leave the singlets and shorts behind.
- A Russian phrasebook.

of Central Asia, perhaps because it's so rich in all the background information, reconstructions, floor-plans and close-ups that nobody in Central Asia seems to know about any more.

*Central Asia; A Travellers' Companion* by Kathleen Hopkirk is a handy and very readable historical background on the region (although not half as entertaining as her husband Peter's books). It's an excellent companion book for those keen to know more about the places they're seeing. Half the book covers Chinese Central Asia.

*The Great Game* by Peter Hopkirk is a fast-paced, very readable history of the Great Game – the 19th-century cold war between Britain and Russia – as it unfolded across Europe and Asia. It's carried along in Hopkirk's trademark style, in a series of personal stories – all men, all Westerners, all resolute and square-jawed, with Victoria Crosses for everybody – real *Boys' Own* stuff; melodramatic, but essentially true.

*Setting the East Ablaze,* also by Peter Hopkirk, takes up where *The Great Game* stops – a gripping cloak-and-dagger history of the murderous early years of Soviet power in Central Asia, and Communist efforts to spread revolution to British India and China.

*The Lost Heart of Asia* by Colin Thubron is a worthwhile read – the author is deservedly praised for his careful research, first-hand explorations, delicate observations and baroque prose. *Shadow of the Silk Road* is Thubron's follow-up a decade later, covering a transcontinental trip from Xi'an to Antioch, via Kyrgyzstan and Uzbekistan.

From the Peter Hopkirk school of history, *Tournament of Shadows* by Karl E Meyer looks at some lesser-known Great Game characters and brings the Game up to date with the present scramble for oil in the Caspian Sea. A modern regional follow-up by the same author is *Dust of Empire*.

If you fancy some fiction, try Tom Bissell's *God Lives in St Petersburg,* a collection of six well-crafted short stories set in Samarkand, Tashkent, Kazakhstan and Kyrgyzstan. Also check out Hamid Ismailov's recent novel *The Train Station* (see p71) or something by the Kyrgyz writer Chinghiz Aitmatov (p275). Pack Dostoyevsky's hefty *The Brothers Karamazov* for the long train trip up to Semey in northeastern Kazakhstan, where the author was exiled for two years and began his famous novel.

*Land Beyond the River: The Untold Story of Central Asia* by Monica Whitlock, the BBC's former Central Asia correspondent, pieces together the history of Soviet Central Asia through the lives of half a dozen witnesses. It's strong on modern Tajikistan but can make for dry reading in places.

By contrast, *Silk Road to Ruin* by Ted Rall is a rollicking, subversive and satirical portrait of the region that is part travelogue, part graphic novel. It's fresh and edgy and neatly captures the realities of travel in the region.

## INTERNET RESOURCES

Some of the best Central Asian websites are those of the major local travel agencies (see p457), Central Asian embassies abroad (see also p457) and US embassies in Central Asia.

For country-specific sites see the Internet Resources headings in the relevant country Directory.

**Central Asia News** (www.centralasianews.net) Regional news service. Also try www.ferghana.ru.

**Discovery Central Asia** (http://silkpress.com) An excellent quarterly tourism magazine full of interesting articles and cultural details from across Central Asia.

**EurasiaNet** (www.eurasianet.org) News and cultural articles, with resource pages for each country.

**Lonely Planet** (www.lonelyplanet.com) The dedicated Central Asia branch of the Thorn Tree is one of the best places anywhere to get up-to-date info on visas, border crossings and more.

**Oriental Express Central Asia** (www.orexca.com) Lots to explore in this virtual travel guide focusing on Uzbekistan, Kyrgyzstan and Kazakhstan.

### PERSONAL HIGHS & LOWS OF CENTRAL ASIA *Bradley Mayhew*

#### Favourites

- Sitting in a teahouse with a cold Tian-Shansky beer, a round of kebabs and hot nan bread – magic!
- Shared taxis, when you score the front seat
- Finally crossing the Torugart Pass
- White-bearded *aksakals* (literally 'white beard', revered elders) resplendent in stripy cloaks and turbans
- Turquoise-blue domes and mesmerising Timurid tilework
- Trekking, almost anywhere
- Central Asian handshakes, with a slight bow and a hand on the heart
- Overnighting in a yurt in Kyrgyzstan or Tajikistan or a traditional courtyard house in Uzbekistan
- Central Asian melons and grapes, and Kyrgyz *kaimak* (cream) and honey (for breakfast)

#### Pet Peeves

- The taste of congealed mutton fat on the roof of your mouth
- Local bus trips that take seven hours to go 100km, when you don't have a seat and there are sweaty armpits in your face
- Getting turned back at the Torugart Pass
- Aggressive drunks who think you are Russian
- Soviet hotel architecture
- Bride of Frankenstein receptionists with dyed cherry-red hair, all mysteriously called Svetlana
- The fifth vodka toast to 'international friendship', with the sixth lined up behind it…
- Visa hassles and *militsia* (police) checks
- The smell of Soviet canteens

**Pamirs** (www.pamirs.org) Superb travel site on the Pamir Mountains of Tajikistan.
**Radio Free Europe/Radio Liberty** (www.rferl.org) Click on 'News by Country' for a range of interesting reports. There's also a weekly news report on Central Asia at http://rfe.rferl.org/reports/centralasia/, which you can get by email.
**Registan.net** (www.registan.net) News and views on Central Asia.
**Roberts Report** (www.roberts-report.com) Biting political blog from US Central Asia expert Sean Roberts, with an emphasis on Kazakhstan.
**Turkic Republics & Communities** (www.khazaria.com/turkic/index.html) Music, books and excellent links for the entire Turkic world.
**Unesco** (www.unesco.kz) Website of the Unesco regional office for Central Asia, with lots of cultural info.

## RESPONSIBLE TRAVEL

Tourism is still relatively new to Central Asia, so please try to keep your impact as low as possible and create a good precedent for those who follow you.

One of the best ways to ensure your tourist dollars make it into the right hands is to support community tourism projects, such as CBT (p277) in Kyrgyzstan, META (p388) in Tajikistan and several programmes in Kazakhstan (see p112). Elsewhere try to engage local services and guides whenever possible and choose companies that follow ecofriendly practice (eg Ecotour in Bishkek, see p282).

The following are a few tips for responsible travel:

- Be respectful of Islamic traditions and don't wear singlets, shorts or short skirts in rural areas or the Fergana Valley.
- Don't hand out sweets or pens to children on the streets, since it encourages begging. Similarly, doling out medicines can encourage people not to seek proper medical advice. A donation to a project, health centre or school is a far more constructive way to help.
- You can do more good by buying your snacks, cigarettes, bubble gum etc from the enterprising grannies trying to make ends meet rather than state-run stores.
- Don't buy items made from endangered species, such as Marco Polo sheep and snow leopards. Don't accept Marco Polo sheep meat in the Pamirs.
- Don't pay to take a photo of someone and don't photograph someone if they don't want you to. If you agree to send someone a photo, make sure you follow through with it.
- Discourage the use of scarce fuels such as firewood and *tersken* in the eastern Pamirs (see p359).
- If someone offers to put you up for the night make sure you don't put your host under financial burdens. Don't let them sacrifice an animal in your honour (common in the Pamirs) and try to offer money or a gift in return for your host's hospitality. See also p63 for more hints on responsible travel.
- Don't let your driver drive too close to archaeological sites and try to stick to existing tracks when driving off road.
- Try to give people a balanced perspective of life in the West. Point out that you are only temporarily rich in Central Asia and that income and costs balance out in Amsterdam just as they do in Almaty. Try also to point out the strong points of the local culture – strong family ties, comparatively low crime etc.
- Make yourself aware of the human rights situation in the countries you travel through; don't travel blindly.

**'A donation to a project, health centre or school is a far more constructive way to help'**

For hints on trekking responsibly see p94.

# Itineraries

## CLASSIC ROUTES

### SILK ROAD CITIES OF UZBEKISTAN — 10 to 14 Days

Fly into **Tashkent** (p194) and get a feel of the big city before taking a domestic flight to Urgench and then a short bus or taxi ride to **Khiva** (p252), comfortably seen in a day. Then take a taxi for an overnight trip to one or two of the **desert cities** (p251) around Urgench.

From Urgench take the long bus or taxi ride down to **Bukhara** (p236), which deserves the most time of all the Silk Road cities. Try to budget a minimum of three days to take in the sights and explore the backstreets.

From here take the golden (actually tarmac) road to **Samarkand** (p223) for a day or two. Soak in the glories of the Registan and Shah-i-Zinda and, if you have time, add on a day trip to **Shakhrisabz** (p232), Timur's birthplace.

An alternative to this route is to tack on Turkmenistan, visiting **Konye-Urgench** (p432) from Khiva before crossing the desert to **Ashgabat** (p405) and then travelling to Bukhara via the Mausoleum of Sultan Sanjar at **Merv** (p426).

**This loop route through Uzbekistan and Turkmenistan, starting and finishing in Tashkent, is a historical and architectural tour that links Central Asia's most popular tourist sites. You'll need at least 14 days if you tack on Turkmenistan.**

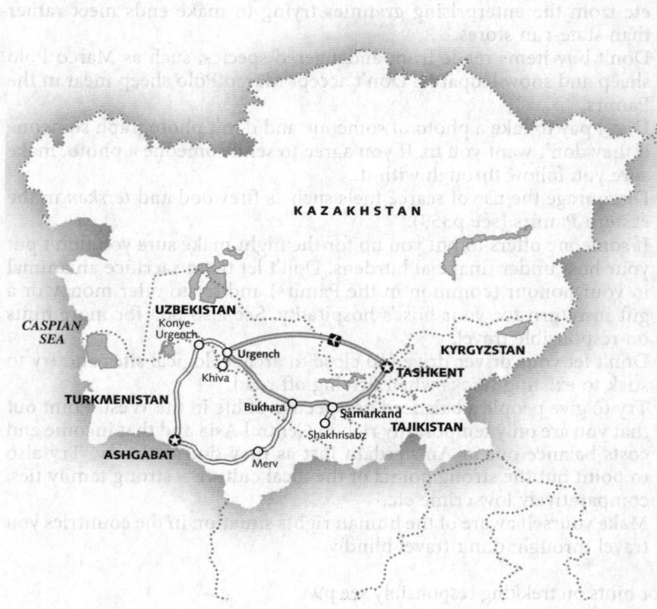

## OVER THE TORUGART – LAKES, HERDERS & CARAVANSERAIS

**Two Weeks**

This trip takes in fabulous mountain scenery, a taste of life in the pastures and the roller-coaster ride over the Torugart Pass to Kashgar. There are lots of opportunities for trekking or horse riding on this route.

From easy-going **Bishkek** (p278) head east to the blue waters and sandy beaches of **Issyk-Köl** (p294), the world's second-largest alpine lake. Take in a couple of days' trekking or visiting the alpine valleys around **Karakol** (p300). The idyllic valley of **Altyn Arashan** (p306) offers great scope for horse riding or a short trek to alpine Ala-Köl and the glorious Karakol Valley. If you have time you can explore the little-visited southern shore en route to Kochkor. If you are low on time head straight to Kochkor from Bishkek.

In small and sleepy **Kochkor** (p316) take advantage of the Community Based Tourism (CBT) programme and spend some time in a yurt or homestay on the surrounding *jailoos* (summer pastures). This is one of the best ways to glimpse traditional life in Kyrgyzstan. Try to allow three days to link a couple of yurtstays by horse, although most can be visited in an overnight trip. The most popular trip is to the herders' camps around the peaceful lake **Song-Köl** (p318), either by car or on a two-day horseback trip. The pastures are popular with herders and their animals between June and August.

From here head to **Naryn** (p319) and then the Silk Road caravanserai of **Tash Rabat** (p323), where you can stay overnight in yurts and even take a difficult horse trip to a pass overlooking Chatyr-Köl. From Tash Rabat it's up over the Torugart Pass *(insha'Allah)* to wonderful Kashgar.

KAZAKHSTAN
Bishkek
Issyk-Köl
Karakol
Altyn Arashan
Kochkor
KYRGYZSTAN
Song-Köl
Naryn
Tash Rabat
Chatyr-Köl
Torugart Pass
Kashgar
UZBEKISTAN
TAJIKISTAN
CHINA

**If you want to experience traditional life in the high pastures while enjoying stunning scenery, take this trip through Kyrgyzstan from Bishkek to Kashgar, over the Torugart Pass.**

## CENTRAL ASIA OVERLAND – THE SILK ROAD Three Weeks

There are dozens of different route options for traversing Central Asia. Much of this itinerary follows ancient Silk Road paths.

Western roads into Central Asia lead from Mashhad in Iran to Ashgabat in Turkmenistan, or from Baku in Azerbaijan (by boat) to Turkmenbashi, also in Turkmenistan. If you only have a three-day transit visa for Turkmenistan you can travel from Mashhad to Mary (to visit the World Heritage–listed ruins of Merv) in one long day via the crossing at Saraghs, giving you more time at Merv and bypassing Ashgabat.

From **Ashgabat** (p405) the overland route leads to **Merv** (p426) and the Silk Road cities of **Bukhara** (p236), **Samarkand** (p223) and **Tashkent** (p194). From here head into the Fergana Valley and swing north along the mountain road to relaxed **Bishkek** (p278). From Bishkek cross the border into Kazakhstan to cosmopolitan **Almaty** (p113) and make some excursions from the city before taking the train (or bus) to Ürümqi in China.

An alternative from Bishkek is to arrange transport to take you over the **Torugart Pass** (p325) visiting the *jailoos* (summer pastures) around **Kochkor** (p316) and Song-Köl and the caravanserai at **Tash Rabat** (p323), before crossing the pass to Kashgar. You can then continue down into Pakistan to join the main overland trail into India and Nepal.

A third alternative if you are in a hurry is to travel from Tashkent to Andijon, cross the border to **Osh** (p334) and then take a bus or a combination of bus and taxi over the **Irkeshtam Pass** (p340) to Kashgar.

**The trip from Mashhad/Baku to Ürümqi/Kashgar fits nicely into an overland route from the Middle East to Asia. Much of this trip follows ancient Silk Road paths and can be completed in three weeks.**

## TASHKENT TO BISHKEK (THE LONG WAY) Three Weeks

From **Tashkent** (p194) take in the sights of **Samarkand** (p223), and maybe also Bukhara, before taking a shared taxi across the border into Tajikistan. Check out the Sogdian archaeological site of **Penjikent** (p372) and maybe hire a car for the day trip to the Marguzor Lakes. The next day take a taxi through the mountains to lake **Iskander-Kul** (p373), which offers a great base for trekking or just relaxing on the lake shore.

Continue the taxi ride through and then over some really stunning vertical scenery to Tajikistan's capital **Dushanbe** (p359) to pick up your Gorno-Badakhshan (GBAO) permit. Day trip to the deserted fort and medressas of **Hissar** (p367) while waiting. From Dushanbe follow the Pamir Hwy to **Osh** (p334), stopping in Khorog and Murgab (see the Pamir Highway itinerary, p28). Try to do the road trip from Dushanbe to Khorog in daylight as the scenery is superb. Osh deserves a day of sightseeing for its bustling bazaar and city comforts.

From Osh take the mountain road to **Kazarman** (p322), visiting Central Asia's most spectacular petroglyphs at **Sailmaluu Tash** (p323), a rough overnight trip from Kazarman. From here continue to Naryn and see the sights of central Kyrgyzstan (see the Over the Torugart – Lakes, Herders & Caravanserais itinerary, p25) before heading to Bishkek. If you have less time you can shoot from **Jalal-Abad** (p332) to Bishkek directly in a day, or take a three-day detour to **Lake Sary-Chelek** (p329).

**A three-week wild, untrammelled and scenically splendid route through the heart of Central Asia's mountains, from Tashkent (Uzbekistan) to Bishkek (Kyrgyzstan).**

# ROADS LESS TRAVELLED

## PAMIR HIGHWAY **10 to 14 Days**

The stretch from **Khorog** (p379) to Murgab could be done in a day, although there are lots of interesting detours. In a reliable 4WD you could go up to the lake of Turuntai-Kul. The Murgab Ecotourism Association (META) can arrange a yurt or homestay for you in gritty Bulunkul, where you can explore the banks of Yashil-Kul, or in a Kyrgyz yurt in the Alichur Valley. From the latter an adventurous 4WD excursion leads to the archaeological site of Bazar-Dara.

The **Wakhan Valley** (p384) is well worth tacking on for its stunning scenery and rich collection of historical sights. Marco Polo travelled through this valley in 1275. Make sure you visit the 12th-century Yamchun Fort (and the nearby Bibi Fatima Springs) and Abrashim Qala, another fort that offers amazing views across to Afghanistan and the Hindu Kush. From **Langar** (p385), with your own transport, you can connect with the Pamir Hwy and continue to Khorog. If hitching you probably have to return to Khorog and take the main highway.

There are loads of side trips to be made from **Murgab** (p387), so try to budget a few days here. Lake **Kara-Kul** (p391) is a scenic highlight. From **Sary Tash** (p339) it's worth detouring 40km to **Sary Moghul** (p341) for its fine views of towering Pik Lenin (Koh-i-Istiqlal). From here you can continue to **Osh** (p334). Exit Kyrgyzstan via **Irkeshtam** (p340) for Kashgar and then continue down the Karakoram Hwy to Gilgit in Pakistan.

**One of the world's most beautiful and remote mountain road trips, through Tajikistan from Dushanbe to Osh, this is not one to rush; hire a vehicle for at least part of the way.**

## JOURNEY TO SHAMBHALA

**Two to Three Weeks**

This little-travelled itinerary through Kazakhstan is a good one for explorers, trekkers and fans of the road *much* less travelled.

Start off in **Almaty** (p113), picking up the necessary invitations for permits required later. Take in some hiking or a short trek in the mountains south of the city (p130) and maybe even splurge on a helicopter flight round **Khan Tengri** (p137).

From here head northeast by shared taxi to **Taldyqorghan** (p138), which you can use as a jumping-off point for the surrounding areas. Take advantage of the homestay programme at **Lepsinsk** (p139) for some hiking in the glacier- and fir-covered Zhungar Alatau.

Head north to **Semey** (p173), a memorial to its nuclear-test victims and place of exile for famed Russian writer Fyodor Dostoevsky. From here you can take a train further along the Turk–Sib railway line to Barnaul in the Russian Altay. A better option is to head east to the pleasant sub-Siberian city of **Ust-Kamenogorsk** (p169) and then explore the foothills of 4506m Mt Belukha from the health resort of **Rakhmanovskie Klyuchi** (p172).

From here, remote Asian border junkies will get a kick out of determining a way to cross the border between Ridder and Gorno-Altaisk in Russia's Altay Republic and then taking the road east, to cross the equally remote border post at Tashanta into Mongolia's ethnically Kazakh and scenically spectacular Bayan-Ölgii region.

Alternatively take a bus or train into Russia from Ust-Kamenogorsk. It's also possible to take the weekly flight between Ust-Kamenogorsk and Ölgii in Mongolia or the equally offbeat border crossing via Maykapshagay to Altai in China's Xinjiang province.

**This Kazakhstan itinerary, from Almaty to the Altay, will suit those who love to explore off the tourist trail. You'll need to apply for a border zone permit a month in advance for Taldyqorghan, Lepsinsk and the Altay.**

## TRANSCASPIA

**Two Weeks**

There are three major excursions inside Turkmenistan; to the north, to the west and to the east. For a shorter trip, pick just one of the following three spokes.

Headed from **Bukhara** (p236), make first for Mary and base yourself there for day trips to **Merv** (p426) and Gonur. Budget a couple of days in **Ashgabat** (p405), visiting the various monuments, gold statues of the president and the National Museum. Don't miss **Tolkuchka Bazaar** (p411) and the new cable car into the **Kopet Dag Mountains** (p411). Then visit an Ahal Tekke farm for a day of horse riding.

From Ashgabat, visit **Nissa** (p416), **Gypjak** (p417) and the **Köw Ata Underground Lake** (p418) before visiting **Nokhur** (p418), a friendly and photogenic village that offers good hiking in the mountains. Most visitors spend two nights here, sleeping in a guesthouse. From Nokhur, continue west to the pilgrimage site of **Parau Bibi** (p419), and then remote **Dekhistan** (p420), one of many cities decimated by the Mongols. From the city of Balkanabat, head north to scenic **Yangykala Canyon** (p420), before driving back to the capital. Alternatively continue to the sleepy port town of **Turkmenbashi** (p421) and fly or train back from there.

The third leg leads into northern Turkmenistan. From Ashgabat travel to the spectacular **Darvaza Gas Crater** (p418). If you are well-equipped it's possible make a desert excursion to some remote Turkmen villages, such as Damla, overnighting in a yurt. From Darvaza, continue north to see the ruins of **Konye-Urgench** (p432), once capital of Khorezm, before heading into **Khiva** (p252), Uzbekistan (or flying back to Ashgabat).

**This route through Turkmenistan begins and ends in Uzbekistan. You can easily do it in reverse or even exit at Turkmenbashi on the ferry to Azerbaijan. If you fly in and out of Ashgabat you'll have to do some backtracking but domestic flights are cheap.**

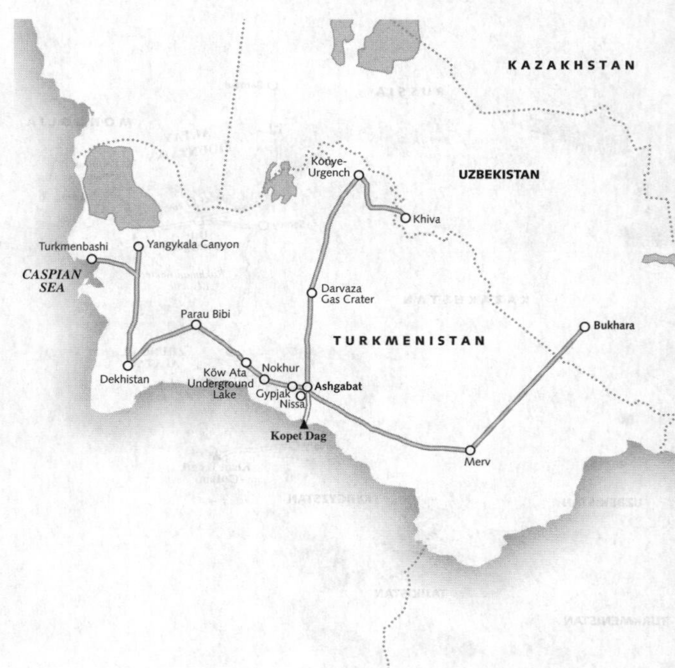

# TAILORED TRIPS

## COMMUNITY TOURISM

Kyrgyzstan leads the world in small-scale ecotourism projects that connect travellers with local families, guides and shepherds.

**Kochkor** (p316) is a fine place to find a homestay, watch your host make *shyrdaks* (felt carpets) and arrange a horse and guide for the two-day trek to **Song-Köl** (p318), where real shepherds will put you up in a real yurt.

In the little-visited pastures of the **Talas Valley** (p328) and **Suusamyr Valley** (p328) are two other ecotourism projects; hardy travellers are guaranteed to have these to themselves.

From Talas you can arrange a great five-day trek to **Lake Sary-Chelek** (p329). The nearby valley has a CBT coordinator who can organise yurts and guides for a two-day hike to the lake. At **Arslanbob** (p330) you can make a multiday trek to a chain of holy lakes or blaze some mountain trails.

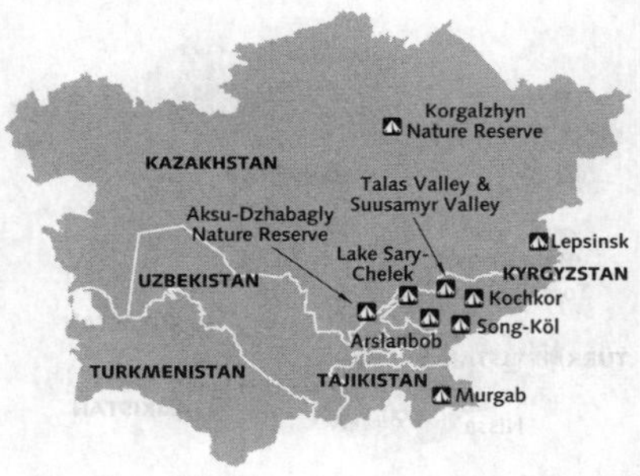


In spectacular high-altitude Tajikistan, **Murgab** (p387) has a great tourism programme that can arrange homestays and jeep hire for trips to local archaeological sites, petroglyphs and lakes.

Kazakhstan's best ecotourism option is probably **Aksu-Dzhabagly Nature Reserve** (p146) in the south of the country. Overnight horse trips into the mountains, past springtime tulips are very pleasant. Other homestay and hiking options are at **Lepsinsk** (p139) and **Korgalzhyn Nature Reserve** (p165), which offers the opportunity to spot the world's northernmost community of pink flamingos.

## OFFBEAT CENTRAL ASIA

First stop is wacky Turkmenistan, 'the North Korea of Central Asia'. In **Ashgabat** (p405), watch the golden statue of Turkmenbashi revolve with the sun, then stroll past the 'Ministry of Fairness' and pick up your own Niyazov bust in the Ministry of Culture shop.

The dinosaur footprints at **Kugitang Nature Reserve** (p431) are off the wall, but nothing compares to the burning desert around the **Darvaza Gas Craters** (p418), especially at night. Bizarre future Turkmen attractions include an ice palace/skating rink in the mountains and a huge US$9 billion artificial lake in, where else, the middle of the desert. Until then (or if someone comes to their senses), you'll have to settle for a surreal swim in the underground lake of **Köw Ata** (p418).

In **Moynaq** (p260) or, better, outside **Aralsk** (p150), see beached fishing boats 150km from what's left of the Aral Sea. And if the mind-numbing steppes of Kazakhstan appeal, go to **Aktau** (p155), 300km from…anywhere. From here track down the underground mosques of **Mangistau** (p157). Alternatively, visit the new Kazakh capital, **Astana** (p159; Kazakh for, er, 'capital'), and stare open-mouthed at the world's largest tent (150m tall) after dining in Kazakhstan's only Jamaican Restaurant. You know we couldn't make this stuff up!

## JOURNEYS THROUGH HISTORY

At every turn in Central Asia you will face multiple layers of history on a breathtaking scale. The following are just a few historical highpoints.

Amateur archaeologists should not miss the five overlapping historic cities of **Merv** (p426) in Turkmenistan, the 'Queen of the World' and the world's most populous city in the 12th century. If you've made it this far it would be a shame not to visit the former Parthian capital of **Nissa** (p416).

Up in the far northwest of Uzbekistan you can add a pinch of fun to your history lesson by staying at a yurt camp in the desert near the ruined 2500-year-old desert citadels of **Toprak-Qala** (p251) and **Ayaz-Qala** (p251).

Fans of the Great Game era will want to visit **Bukhara** (p236), which was visited by everyone from Alexander 'Bokhara' Burnes to the British officers Arthur Conolly and Charles Stoddart (who were held in a pit for two years before being executed in front of the Ark). Don't miss the Kalon Minaret that so awed Jenghiz Khan in 1220.

Timur's capital **Samarkand** (p223) still glitters, but fewer travellers make it to the frescoes of **Afrosiab** (p227), the city visited by Alexander the Great. The archaeologically dedicated can pop over the border to glimpse ancient Sogdian remains at **Penjikent** (p372).

Slightly less tangible sites include **Otrar** (p147) in Kazakhstan, where the pivotal murder of 450 Mongol envoys fatefully deflected Mongol rage from China to Central Asia, forever changing the face of the region, and where Timur breathed his last.

## ACTIVITIES

The austere **Fan Mountains** (p373) have long been one of Central Asia's premier trekking destinations, easily visited from Samarkand, and offering a wide range of route options. Donkey hire is possible here.

The lush, forested alpine valleys of the Tian Shan around **Karakol** (p300) also offer great versatility for both trekking and horse trips and are probably the most popular trekking destination in Central Asia. The **Zailiysky Alatau range** (p134) south of Almaty also has great trekking just an hour from the city.

One of the easiest and yet most scenic hikes in the western Pamirs is up the **Geisev Valley** (p383) in Tajikistan, where you can stay and eat in local villages. And yes, the scenery looks better without the 20kg backpack.

Horse riding is the natural way to traverse the pastures around **Kochkor** (p316), where community-based tourism groups can arrange multi-day horse treks to places such as Song-Köl.

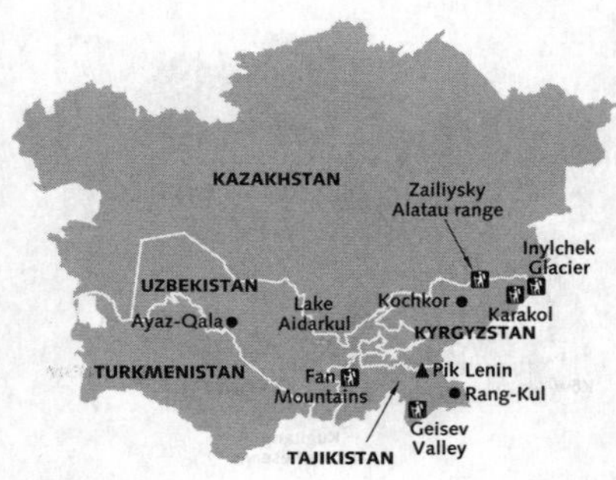


Nothing conjours up the spirit of the Silk Road like travelling by camel. For the desert experience try **Lake Aidarkul** (p236) or **Ayaz-Qala** (p251) in Uzbekistan; for Bactrian camel trekking on the roof of the world try **Rang-Kul** (p389) in the Pamirs.

Mountaineers who know what they are doing can tackle **Pik Lenin** (Independence Peak; p375), one of the world's easier 7000m peaks. Few mountain amphitheatres can compare to base-camp on the **Inylchek Glacier** (p313), where ascents can be made to peaks around Khan Tengri.

# Snapshot

Since independence from the USSR in 1991, the Central Asian republics have forged differing paths, while facing many shared challenges. All have grappled with population shifts and economic migration. All have weathered economic difficulties and resurgent Islam and are attempting to modernise while maintaining and redefining their national character. All have reinvented their past and rehabilitated historical heroes, while reinforcing their national languages. All are feeling pressure from Russia seeking to reassert its interests, while opening themselves, more or less, to new spheres of influence from Turkey, Iran, China and the industrialised West. The initial rush of post-independence joy has been replaced everywhere by a yearning for stability and the search for new ideals.

The Caspian region of Central Asia is sitting atop an estimated 200 billion barrels of crude oil.

Politically speaking, many of the faces remain familiar, even from the Soviet era. Presidents Nazarbaev (in power since 1989), Karimov (1990) and Rakhmanov (1993) continue to rule without active opposition. President Niyazov (Turkmenbashi) of Turkmenistan upped the ante further, proclaiming himself 'president for life' in 1999. Only his death in December 2006 forced him out of office; he was replaced by his former dentist (and health minister) Gurbanguli Berdymukhadedov.

Only in Kyrgyzstan has 'people power' made any real headway, sweeping President Akyev from power during the 'Tulip Revolution' of 2005 and forcing curbs on the new president's power in 2006. Contrast this to the Andijon (Andijan) massacre of May 2005, when hundreds of government troops, some in helicopters, shot up to 1000 unarmed Uzbek protestors in the streets (see p191).

Rates of HIV/AIDS infections are doubling annually in Kazakhstan.

A lack of economic and political reform hampers the entire region but no more so than in suffocating Uzbekistan and Turkmenistan. Despite attempts to portray independence as 'a new golden age', isolated Turkmenistan limped through the last decade in a cycle of Stalinesque purges and appointments. The recent replacement of health care professionals with military conscripts has merely sped up the dismantling of health and education facilities. Tajikistan in particular suffers from chronic unemployment; 70% of the population lives under the poverty line and more than one million Tajiks have left the country to find work in Russia.

Yet there are major differences within the region. Turkmenistan and Kazakhstan are the only republics which seem to have bright economic possibilities - sitting pretty on enormous reserves of oil and gas. Tajikistan is the only country which has experienced the nightmare of ethnic violence and civil war. The iron-fisted regimes of Uzbekistan and Turkmenistan have completed their slide into pariah states, where political abductions, torture and trumped-up charges are commonplace and where stagnation is regularly confused for stability. What will happen in a post-Turkmenbashi Turkmenistan is anyone's guess. Optimists see an opening for a transition to democracy; pessimists fear a chaotic struggle for power in the energy-rich state.

Central Asia now has an estimated half a million drug users.

Tensions remain among the Central Asian nations. Tajikistan and Uzbekistan are no great friends. Disputes over water and gas supplies bubble just under the surface, and the lack of regional cooperation means that regional issues such as the Aral Sea, the drug trade and economic cooperation rarely even make it onto the agenda. Drug smuggling is a particular regional problem and the soaring rise in domestic drug use is fuelling some of the world's fastest growing rates of HIV/AIDS, especially in Kazakhstan.

Islamic fundamentalism is the bogeyman which the majority of Central Asia, especially Uzbekistan, uses to justify its increasing repressive policies. Bombings in Uzbekistan in 2004 and an alleged assassination attempt against President Niyazov in 2002 underscored this, although in reality the fall of the Taliban in Afghanistan seriously diminished the growth of fundamentalist activities in the region. Yet as long as the issues of reform, poverty and corruption remain unaddressed by Central Asian regimes, the region will be a fertile breeding ground for dissent of all kinds.

The Turkmen government supplies its citizens with free natural gas, electricity, water and salt and has committed to doing so until 2030!

The US 'War on Terror' temporarily raised the strategic importance of Central Asia, as the US used bases in Uzbekistan, Kyrgyzstan and Tajikistan to launch bombing raids on Afghanistan. In a remarkable turnaround, relations with the West have soured in recent years and favour has swung back towards the Russian, as foreign NGOs and American military personnel leave Uzbekistan in droves. All the republics are busy balancing the security interests of the US with the energy needs of China and their historical ties to Russia, while all the time trying to score the best deals for themselves. There are few clearer symbols of the struggle for Central Asia's soul than the two rival military bases that face off at each other in Bishkek, one Russian, the other American.

But it's not all political dictatorships and environmental disaster. Life has settled for many Central Asians. Economies are finally growing and standards of living are slowly rising. Grassroots community tourism projects are flourishing in much of the region. International crossings have been retied with China, Afghanistan and Iran, opening up new opportunities for both trade and tourism.

Investment and nationalism are reshaping the very face of Central Asia. Kazakhstan has built an entire new capital, Astana, from scratch. Impressive new state buildings and surreal statues have transformed Ashgabat. Cities across the region have been brought up to date by the arrival of Turkish supermarkets, new restaurants and international-standard hotels.

Looking to the future, the region is a mother lode of energy and raw materials and has a potential for great wealth, a fact which quietly drives many countries' Central Asian policies. All eyes are on Kazakhstan, Central Asia's brightest economy, sitting pretty on what is estimated to be the world's third-largest oil reserves (see p107), but don't forget Turkmenistan, which boasts the world's fourth-largest reserves of natural gas. Kazakhstan and Uzbekistan also have major natural gas reserves. New pipelines to Turkey and China and proposed routes through Iran and Afghanistan are just the beginning of the economic turnaround. This superpower scramble for oil and gas in the region – dubbed 'round two of the Great Game' – is a drama that will unfold in the decades ahead.

Some 5km below the surface of the Caspian Sea, Kazakhstan's Kashagan oil field holds probably the world's second-largest concentration of oil, some 30 million barrels.

Following the pipelines are grand plans for a new Eurasian transport corridor, with transcontinental rail links extending down into Afghanistan, with transit on to Karachi and the Persian Gulf.

As Central Asia's new economic and cultural ties strengthen, oil routes open and Silk Roads are redrawn, this little-understood region will undoubtedly become increasingly important to the security, economy and politics of Russia, Asia and even the world. The Central Asian governments look set to continue to tread a dangerous tightrope between authoritarianism and Islamisation as they face the long-term challenge of meeting the religious, secular and economic desires of their people. Whatever happens, one thing is sure; Central Asia matters.

# History

Central Asia is perhaps the best place on earth to explore the reality of the phrase 'the sweep of history'. Populations, conquerors, cultures and ideas have traversed the region's steppes, deserts and mountains for millennia. Central Asia's role as a conduit between cultures is symbolised by the Silk Road, through which the great civilisations of the East and the West first made contact. But Central Asia was, and is, more than just a middle ground, and its cultural history is far more than the sum of the influences brought from the East and the West.

Here in the heart of the largest landmass on earth, vast steppes provided the one natural resource – grass – required to build one of this planet's most formidable and successful forms of statehood, the nomadic empire. The grass-fed horses by the millions and mounted archers remained the unstoppable acme of open-ground warfare for more than 2500 years. How the settled civilisations on the periphery of Eurasia interacted with successive waves of mounted nomadic hordes is the main theme of the story of Central Asia.

For more on the Silk Road, including recommended books, see p53.

See www.orientarch.uni-halle.de/ca/bud/bud.htm for more on the archaeology of southeastern Central Asia.

## PREHISTORY & EARLY HISTORY

In the Middle Palaeolithic period, from 100,000 to 35,000 years ago, people in Central Asia were isolated from Europe and elsewhere by ice sheets, seas and swamps.

Cultural continuity begins in the late 3rd millennium BC with the Indo-Iranians, speakers of an unrecorded Indo-European dialect related distantly to English. The Indo-Iranians are believed to have passed through Central Asia on their way from the Indo-European homeland in southern Russia. From Central Asia, groups headed southeast for India and southwest for Iran. These peoples herded cattle, went to battle in chariots, and probably buried their dead nobles in burial mounds *(kurgans)*. The Tajiks are linguistic descendants of these ancient migrants. One of these subsequent Indo-European groups was the Sakas (also known as Scythians), who have left *kurgans*, rock carvings and other remains across Central Asia. For more

### UNEARTHING THE AMAZONS

As early as the 5th century BC the Greek historian Herodotus knew of an army of women warriors, known as the Amazons, who were so dedicated to warfare that they allegedly cut off their own right breast in order to improve their shot with bows and arrows. Recent excavations of Saka (Scythian)burial mounds *(kurgans)*, on the Kazakh border with Russia, are unearthing some intriguing links to these perhaps not-so-mythical warrior women.

Archaeologists have discovered skeletons of women, bow-legged from a life in the saddle, buried with swords, daggers and bronze-tipped arrows, indicating warrior status. Others appear to be priestesses, buried with cultic implements, bronze mirrors and elaborate headdresses.

The finds indicate that women of these early steppe civilisations were trained from the outset to be warriors, fighting alongside men, perhaps even forming an elite social group. The status of these steppe women seems far higher than that of sedentary civilisations of the same time, challenging the stereotypical macho image of the Central Asian nomad.

**TIMELINE**

**100,000–40,000 years ago**

Remains of Neanderthal man found at Aman-Kutan cave near Samarkand

**2nd millennium BC**

Saka/Scythian tombs in the Pamirs and the tomb of Sarazm (western Tajikistan) date from this period

For a detailed chronicle of Central Asian history try *Empire of the Steppes* by Rene Grousset, *A History of Inner Asia* by Svat Soucek or the excellent (but hard to find) *Central Asia* by Gavin Hambly.

on Kazakhstan's famous 'Golden Man' find, dating from a 5th-century Saka (Scythian) *kurgan* outside Almaty, see p119.

Central Asia's recorded history begins in the 6th century BC, when the large Achaemenid empire of Persia (modern Iran) created client kingdoms or satrapies (provinces), in Central Asia: Sogdiana (Sogdia), Khorezm (later Khiva), Bactria (Afghan Turkestan), Margiana (Merv), Aria (Herat), Saka (Scythia) and Arachosia (Ghazni and Kandahar). Sogdiana was the land between the Amu-Darya and Syr-Darya, called Transoxiana by the Romans and Mawarannhr by the Arabs (both names mean 'Beyond the Oxus'). Here Bukhara and Samarkand later flourished. Khorezm lay on the lower reaches of the Amu-Darya, south of the Aral Sea, where one day the 19th-century khans of Khorezm would lord it from the walled city of Khiva. Saka (also

**329–327 BC**
Alexander the Great in Central Asia

**250 BC–AD 226**
Kushan empire

called Semireche by the Russians), extending indefinitely over the steppes beyond the Syr-Darya and including the Tian Shan range, was the home of nomadic warriors until their way of life ended in the late 19th century.

## ALEXANDER THE GREAT

In 330 BC this former pupil of Aristotle, from Macedonia, led his army to a key victory over the last Achaemenid emperor, Darius III, in Mesopotamia. With the defeat of his Persian nemesis, Alexander (356–323 BC) developed a taste for conquest. By 329 BC he had reached modern Herat, Kandahar and Kabul. Crossing the Hindu Kush he pressed northward to Bactria, crossed the Oxus (Amu-Darya) on inflated hides and proceeded via Cyropol/Cyropolis (Istaravshan) and Marakanda (Samarkand) and towards the Jaxartes (Syr-Darya), which he crossed in order to crush Saka defenders. Perhaps in celebration he founded his ninth city, Alexandria Eskhate (Farthest Alexandria), on the banks of the Jaxartes where today's Khojand stands.

Central Asia is strewn with ancient petroglyphs, some of the best of which can be visited at Saimaluu Tash in Kyrgyzstan (p323) and Tamgaly in Southeastern Kazakhstan (p138).

Alexander met the most stubborn resistance of his career in the Sogdians, who in concert with the Massagetes, a Saka clan, revolted and under the leadership of Spitamenes held the mountains of Zerafshan (Zeravshan) until 328 BC. After an 18-month guerrilla war, the rebels' fall was a poignant one: attacked and defeated after Greek troops scaled the cliffs of their last redoubt the 'Rock of Sogdiana' (its location today in the Hissar Mountains remains a mystery), their leader yielding his daughter, the beautiful Bactrian princess Roxana, into captivity and marriage to Alexander.

Alexander the Great, known locally as Iskander or Sikander, is a popular figure in Central Asia, after whom several lakes and mountains are named. His troops are blamed for the occasional blond-haired, blue-eyed Tajik, although this is probably more the result of Aryan influence.

The brilliant Macedonian generalissimo's sojourn in Central Asia was marked by a growing megalomania. It was at Marakanda that Alexander murdered his right-hand general, Cleitus. He tried to adopt the dress and autocratic court ritual of an Oriental despot; however his Greek and Macedonian followers refused to prostrate themselves before him.

When he died in Babylon in 323 BC, Alexander had no named heir. But his legacy included nothing less than the West's perennial romance with exploration and expansion.

## EAST MEETS WEST

The aftermath of Alexander's short-lived Macedonian empire in Central Asia saw an increase in East–West cultural exchange and a chain reaction of nomadic migrations. The Hellenistic successor states of the Seleucid empire disseminated the aesthetic values of the classical world deep into Asia; trade brought such goods as the walnut to Europe.

Legend has it that the biblical prophet Daniel (of the Lion's Den fame) was buried in Samarkand, where he is known as Daniyar. Another legend says the bones of St Matthew lie buried underneath a recently discovered Armenian monastery on the shores of Issyk-Kul.

Several thousand kilometres east, along the border of Mongolia and China, the expansion of the warlike Xiongnu (Hsiung-nu) confederacy (probably the forebears of the Ephalites, or Huns) uprooted the Yüeh-chih of western China (the Yüeh-chih ruler was slain and his skull made into a drinking cup). The Yüeh-chih were sent packing westward along the Ili River into Saka, whose displaced inhabitants in turn bore down upon the Sogdians to the south.

The Xiongnu were also irritating more important powers than the Yüeh-chih. Although protected behind its expanding Great Wall since about 250 BC, China eagerly sought tranquillity on its barbarian frontier. In 138 BC, the Chinese emperor sent a brave volunteer emissary, Zhang Qian, on a secret mission to persuade the Yüeh-chih king to form an alliance against the Xiongnu.

**138–119 BC**

Voyage of Chinese Zhang Qian from Xi'an to Central Asia

**107 BC**

Chinese armies arrive in the Fergana Valley

Hellenistic cities and Buddhist monasteries of the 2nd century BC, such as Ai-Khanum, Takht-i-Sangin, Kobadiyan and Khalchayan, on the southern borders of Tajikistan, Uzbekistan and Afghanistan, reveal a fascinating mixture of Greek, Persian and local art forms.

When he finally got there, 13 years later, Zhang found that the Yüeh-chih had settled down in Bactria/Tokharistan (southern Tajikistan and northern Afghanistan) to a peaceable life of trade and agriculture, and no longer had an axe to grind with the Xiongnu. But Zhang Qian's mission was still a great success of Chinese diplomacy and exploration and the stage had been set for the greatest of all East-West contacts; the birth of the Silk Road (see p53).

## THE KUSHANS

The peaceable, put-upon Yüeh-chih finally came into their own in the 1st century BC when their descendants, the Kushan dynasty, converted to Buddhism. The Kushan empire controlled northern India, Afghanistan and Sogdiana from its base at Kapisa, near modern-day Bagram in Afghanistan. At its height in the first three centuries after Christ, it was one of the four great powers of the world, along with Rome, China and Parthia.

Vigorous trade on the Silk Road helped spread Kushan culture. The rich Kushan coinage is concrete testimony to this classic Silk Road power's lively religious ferment: the coins bear images of Greek, Roman, Buddhist, Persian and Hindu deities. The art of the empire fused Persian imperial imagery, Buddhist iconography and Roman realism. It was carried out from Gandhara over the mountainous maze of deepest Asia to the furthest corners of Transoxiana, Tibet and the Tarim Basin. Indian, Tibetan and Chinese art were permanently affected.

## SASSANIDS, HUNS & SOGDIANS

The Silk Road's first flower faded by about AD 200, as the Chinese, Roman, Parthian and Kushan empires went into decline. Sogdiana came under the control of the Sassanid empire of modern-day Iran. As the climate along the middle section of the Silk Road became drier, Central Asian nomads increasingly sought wealth by plundering, taxing and conquering their settled neighbours. The Sassanids lost their Inner Asian possessions in the 4th century to the Huns, who ruled a vast area of Central Asia at the same time that Attila was scourging Europe.

Check out www.kroraina.com/ca for a run-down on obscure medieval kingdoms such as Tokharistan and Sogdiana.

The Huns were followed south across the Syr-Darya by the western Turks (the western branch of the empire of the so-called Kök Turks or Blue Turks), who in 559 made an alliance with the Sassanids and ousted the Huns. The western Turks, who had arrived in the area from their ancestral homeland in southern Siberia, nominally controlled the reconquered region.

The mixing of the western Turks' nomadic ruling class with the sedentary Sogdian elite over the next few centuries produced a remarkable ethnic mix and beautiful artwork in cities such as Penjikent, Afrosiab and Varakhsha, much of which is still visible in museums across the region.

## THE ARRIVAL OF ISLAM

When the western Turks faded in the late 7th century, an altogether new and formidable kind of power was waiting to fill the void – the religious army of Islam. Exploding out of Arabia just a few years after the Prophet Mohammed's death, the Muslim armies rolled through Persia in 642 to set up a military base at Merv (modern Turkmenistan) but met stiff resistance from the Turks of Transoxiana. The power struggle between the Amu-Darya

**AD 226–651**
Sassanid empire

**630**
Buddhist pilgrim Xuan Zang travels to Issyk-Köl, Chuy Valley, Tashkent, Samarkand, Balkh and Kashgar in search of Buddhist texts

**LOST BATTLE, LOST SECRETS**

The Chinese lost more than just a fight at the Battle of Talas in 751. The defeat marked the end of Chinese expansion west and secured the future of Islam as the region's foremost religion. But to add insult to injury, some of the Chinese rounded up after the battle were no ordinary prisoners: they were experts at the crafts of papermaking and silkmaking. Soon China's best-kept secrets were giving Arab silkmakers in Persia a commercial advantage all over Europe. It was the first mortal blow to the Silk Road. The spread of papermaking to Baghdad and then Europe sparked a technological revolution; the impact of this on the development of civilisation cannot be underestimated.

and Syr-Darya ebbed and flowed, while Arab armies spread to take Bukhara in 709 and Samarkand in 712.

China, meanwhile, had revived under the Tang dynasty and expanded into Central Asia, murdering the khan of the Tashkent Turks in the process. It was perhaps the most costly incident of skulduggery in Chinese history. The enraged Turks were joined by the opportunistic Arabs and Tibetans; in 751 they squeezed the Chinese forces into the Talas Valley (in present-day Kazakhstan and Kyrgyzstan) and sent them flying back across the Tian Shan, marking the limits of the Chinese empire for good (see the boxed text, above).

Medieval Merv (in modern Turkmenistan) may well have been the setting for Scheherazade's tales in *The Thousand and One Nights*.

After the Battle of Talas, the Arab's Central Asian territories receded in the wake of local rebellions. By the 9th century, Transoxiana had given rise to the peaceful and affluent Samanid dynasty. It generously encouraged development of Persian culture while remaining strictly allied with the Sunni caliph of Baghdad. It was under the Samanids that Bukhara grew into a the vanguard of Muslim culture and garnered the epithet 'The Pillar of Islam'. Some of the Islamic world's best scholars were nurtured in its 113 medressas and the city became one of the world's main centres of intellectual development (see the boxed text 'Shining Stars', p40).

## KARAKHANIDS TO KARAKITAY

By the early 10th century, internal strife at court had weakened the Samanid dynasty and opened the door for two Turkic usurpers to divide up the empire: the Ghaznavids in Khorasan and modern-day Afghanistan, south of the Amu-Darya; and the Karakhanids in Transoxiana and the steppe region beyond the Syr-Darya. The Karakhanids are credited with finally converting the populace of Central Asia to Islam. They held sway from three mighty capitals: Balasagun (now Burana in Kyrgyzstan) in the centre of their domain, Talas (now Taraz in Kazakhstan) in the west, and Kashgar in the east. Bukhara continued to shine, and Karakhanid Kashgar was the home of rich culture and science. The Ghaznavids ruled Afghanistan, Samarkand and Bukhara at their height and are credited with snuffing out Buddhism in the region and introducing Islam to India.

The Karakitay lent their name to both Cathay (an archaic name for China) and Kitai (the Russian word for China).

The Karakhanids and Ghaznavids coveted each other's lands. In the mid-11th century, while they were busy invading each other, they were caught off guard by a third Turkic horde, the Seljuqs, who annihilated both after pledging false allegiance to the Ghaznavids. In the Seljuqs' heyday their sultan had himself invested as emperor by the caliph of Baghdad. The empire was

**642–712**
Arab conquest of Central Asia brings Islam

**751**
Battle of Talas

**SHINING STARS**

In the 9th to 11th centuries Samanid Central Asia produced some of history's most important thinkers:

**Al-Khorezmi** (Latinised as Algorismi; 787–850) A mathematician who gave his name to algorithm, the mathematical process behind addition and multiplication. The title of another of his mathematical works, Al-Jebr, reached Europe as algebra.

**Al-Biruni** (973–1046) From Khorezm, he was the world's foremost astronomer of his age, who knew 500 years before Copernicus that the earth rotated and that it circled around the sun. He estimated the distance to the moon to within 20km.

**Abu Ali ibn-Sina** (Latinised as Avicenna; 980–1037) From Bukhara, the greatest medic in the medieval world, whose *Canon of Medicine* was the standard textbook for Western doctors until the 17th century.

vast: on the east it bordered the lands of the Buddhist Karakitay, who had swept into Balasagun and Kashgar from China; to the west it extended all the way to the Mediterranean and Red Seas.

An incurable symptom of Inner Asian dynasties through the ages was their near inability to survive the inevitable disputes of succession. The Seljuqs lasted a century before their weakened line succumbed to the Karakitay and to the Seljuqs' own rearguard vassals, the Khorezmshahs. From their capital at Gurganj (present-day Konye-Urgench), the Khorezmshahs burst full-force into the tottering Karakitay. The Khorezmshahs emerged as rulers of all Transoxiana and much of the Muslim world as well.

The English word 'horde' comes via French from the Turkic word *orda*, meaning the yurt or pavilion where a khan held his court.

And so Central Asia might have continued in a perennial state of forgettable wars. As it is, the Khorezmshahs are still remembered primarily as the unlucky stooge left holding the red cape when the angry bull was released.

## MONGOL TERROR, MONGOL PEACE

Jenghiz Khan felt he had all the justification in the world to ransack Central Asia. In 1218 a Khorezmian governor in Otrar (in modern-day Kazakhstan) received a delegation from Jenghiz to inaugurate trade relations. Scared by distant reports of the new Mongol menace, the governor assassinated them in cold blood. Up until that moment Jenghiz, the intelligent khan of the Mongols who had been lately victorious over Chung-tu (Beijing), had been carefully weighing the alternative strategies for expanding his power: commerce versus conquest. Then came the crude Otrar blunder, and the rest is history.

In early 1219 Jenghiz placed himself at the head of an estimated 200,000 men and began to ride west from his stronghold in the Altay. By the next year his armies had sacked Khojand and Otrar (the murderous governor was dispatched with savage cruelty in Jenghiz' presence), and Bukhara soon followed.

It was in that brilliant city, as soldiers raped and looted and horses trampled Islamic holy books in the streets, that the unschooled Jenghiz ascended to the pulpit in the chief mosque and preached to the congregation. His message: 'I am God's punishment for your sins'. Such shocking psychological warfare is perhaps unrivalled in history. It worked and news reached Europe of the 'Devil's Horsemen'.

**9th–10th centuries**

Samanid heyday in Bukhara

**998–1030**

Mahmud of Ghazni rules Central Asia

Bukhara was burned to the ground, and the Mongol hordes swept on to conquer and plunder Samarkand, Merv, Termiz, Kabul, Balkh, Bamiyan, Ghazni and, eventually under Jenghiz' generals and heirs, most of Eurasia. No opposing army could match them.

Settled civilisation in Central Asia took a serious blow, from which it only began to recover 600 years later under Russian colonisation. Jenghiz' descendants controlling Persia favoured Shiite Islam over Sunni Islam, a development which over the centuries isolated Central Asia even more from the currents of the rest of the Sunni Muslim world.

But there was stability, law and order under the Pax Mongolica. In 20th-century terms, the streets were safe and the trains ran on time. The resulting modest flurry of trade on the Silk Road was the background to many famous medieval travellers' journeys, including the greatest of them all, Marco Polo's (see the boxed text, p56).

On Jenghiz Khan's death in 1227, his empire was divided among his sons. By tradition the most distant lands, stretching as far as the Ukraine and Moscow and including western and most of northern Kazakhstan, would have gone to the eldest son, Jochi, had Jochi not died before his father. They went instead to Jochi's sons, Batu and Orda, and came to be known collectively as the Golden Horde. The second son, Chaghatai, got the next most distant portion, including most of Kazakhstan, Uzbekistan, Afghanistan and western Xinjiang; this came to be known as the Chaghatai khanate. The share of the third son, Ogedei, seems to have eventually been divided between the Chaghatai khanate and the Mongol heartland inherited by the youngest son, Tolui. Tolui's portion formed the basis for his son Kublai Khan's Yüan dynasty in China.

For more on the Mongols see the excellent book *Storm from the East* by Robert Marshall.

Unlike the Golden Horde in Europe and the Yüan dynasty, the Chaghatai khans tried to preserve their nomadic lifestyle, complete with the khan's roving tent encampment as 'capital city'. But as the rulers spent more and more time in contact with the Muslim collaborators who administered their realm, the Chaghatai line inevitably began to settle down. They even made motions towards conversion to Islam. It was a fight over this issue, in the mid-14th century, that split the khanate in two, with the Muslim Chaghatais holding Transoxiana and the conservative branch retaining the Tian Shan, Kashgar and the vast steppes north and east of the Syr-Darya, an area collectively known as Moghulistan.

## TIMUR & THE TIMURIDS

The fracturing of the Mongol empire immediately led to resurgence of the Turkic peoples. From one minor clan near Samarkand arose a tyrant's tyrant, Timur ('the Lame', or Tamerlane). After assembling an army and wresting Transoxiana from Chaghatai rule, Timur went on a spectacular nine-year rampage which ended in 1395 with modern-day Iran, Iraq, Syria, eastern Turkey and the Caucasus at his feet. He also despoiled northern India.

All over his realm, Timur plundered riches and captured artisans and poured them into his capital at Samarkand. The city grew, in stark contrast to his conquered lands, into a lavish showcase of treasure and pomp. Much of the postcard skyline of today's Samarkand dates to Timur's reign, as do many fine works of painting and literature. Foreign guests of Timur's, including the Spanish envoy Ruy Gonzales de Clavijo, took home stories

**1220**
Jenghiz Khan destroys Bukhara, killing 30,000

**1405**
Timur (Tamerlane) dies, his huge Bibi Khanum Mosque unfinished

of enchantment and barbarity which fed the West's dreams of remote and romantic Samarkand.

Timur claimed indirect kinship with Jenghiz Khan, but he had little of his forerunner's gift for statecraft. History can be strange: both conquerors savagely slaughtered hundreds of thousands of innocent people, yet one is remembered as a great ruler and the other not. The argument goes that Timur's bloodbaths were insufficiently linked to specific political or military aims. On the other hand, Timur is considered the more cultured and religious of the two men. At any rate, Timur died an old man at Otrar in 1405, having just set out in full force to conquer China.

For more on the extraordinary life of Timur see *Tamerlane: Sword of Islam, Conqueror of the World* by Justin Marozzi.

Important effects of Timur's reign can still be traced. For instance, when he pounded the army of the Golden Horde in southern Russia, Timur created a disequilibrium in the bloated Mongol empire which led to the seizure of power by its vassals, the petty and fragmented Russian princes. This was the predawn of the Russian state. Like the mammals after the dinosaurs, Russia arose from small beginnings.

For a scant century after Timur's death his descendants ruled on separately in small kingdoms and duchies. A Timurid renaissance was led by Timur's son Shah Rukh (1377–1447) and his remarkable wife Gowhar Shad, who between them established a cultured Timurid capital in Herat, populated by fine architects, musicians, miniature painters and poets (including Jami). From 1409 until 1449, Samarkand was governed by the conqueror's mild, scholarly grandson, Ulugbek (Ulugh Bek). Gifted in mathematics and astronomy, he built a large celestial observatory and attracted scientists who gave the city a lustre as a centre of learning for years to come.

Timur's (Tamerlane) campaigns resulted in the deaths of more than one million people and he became infamous for building towers or walls made from the cemented heads of a defeated army.

In addition to Persian, a Turkic court language came into use, called Chaghatai, which survived for centuries as a Central Asian lingua franca.

## UZBEKS & KAZAKHS

Modern Uzbekistan and Kazakhstan, the two principal powers of post-Soviet Central Asia, eye each other warily across the rift dividing their two traditional lifestyles: sedentary agriculture (Uzbeks) and nomadic pastoralism (Kazakhs). Yet these two nations are closely akin and parted ways with a family killing.

The family in question was the dynasty of the Uzbek khans. These rulers, one strand of the modern Uzbek people, had a pedigree reaching back to Jenghiz Khan and a homeland in southern Siberia. In the 14th century they converted to Islam, gathered strength, and started moving south. Under Abylqayyr (Abu al-Khayr) Khan they reached the north bank of the Syr-Darya, across which lay the declining Timurid rulers in Transoxiana. But Abylqayyr had enemies within his own family. The two factions met in battle in 1468, and Abylqayyr was killed and his army defeated.

The Great Horde roamed the steppes of the Jeti-Suu region (Russian: Semireche), north of the Tian Shan; the Middle Horde occupied the grasslands extending east from the Aral Sea; and the Little Horde took the lands west of there, as far as the Ural River.

After this setback, Abylqayyr's grandson Mohammed Shaybani brought the Uzbek khans to power once more and established Uzbek control in Transoxiana; modern-day Uzbekistan. Abylqayyr's rebellious kinsmen became the forefathers of the Kazakh khans.

The Uzbeks gradually adopted the sedentary agricultural life best suited to the fertile river valleys they occupied. Settled life involved cities, which entailed administration, literacy, learning and, wrapped up with all of these, Islam. The Shaybanid dynasty, which ruled until the end of the 16th cen-

**1424–29**

Ulugbek builds observatory, before he is beheaded in 1449 as part of a religious backlash

**15th century**

Shah Rukh rules the Timurid empire from Herat

tury, attempted to outdo the Timurids in religious devotion and to carry on their commitment to artistic patronage. But the Silk Road had disappeared, usurped by spice ships, and Central Asia's economy had entered full decline. As prosperity fell, so did the region's importance as a centre of the Islamic world.

The Kazakhs, meanwhile, stayed home on the range, north of the Syr-Darya, and flourished as nomadic herders. Their experience of urban civilisation and organised Islam remained slight compared with their Uzbek cousins. By the 16th century the Kazakhs had solidly filled a power vacuum on the old Saka steppes between the Ural and Irtysh Rivers and established what was to be the world's last nomadic empire, divided into three hordes: the Great Horde, the Middle Horde and the Little Horde.

## THE ZHUNGARIAN EMPIRE

The Oyrats were a western Mongol clan who had been converted to Tibetan Buddhism. Their day in the sun came when they subjugated eastern Kazakhstan, the Tian Shan, Kashgaria and western Mongolia to form the Zhungarian (Dzungarian) empire (1635–1758). Russia's frontier settlers were forced to pay heavy tribute and the Kazakh hordes, with their boundless pasturage beyond the mountain gap known as the Zhungarian Gate, were cruelly and repeatedly pummelled until the Oyrats were liquidated by Manchu China.

Memory of the Oyrat legacy has been preserved in epic poetry by the Kazakhs and Kyrgyz, who both suffered under the Oyrats' ruthless predations.

Reeling from the Zhungarian attacks, the Kazakhs (first the Little Horde, then the Middle Horde, then part of the Great Horde) gradually accepted Russian protection over the mid-18th century.

The Russians had by this time established a line of fortified outposts on the northern fringe of the Kazakh Steppe. However, it appears that there was no clear conception in St Petersburg of exactly where the Russian Empire's frontier lay. Slow on the uptake, Russia at this stage had little interest in the immense territory it now abutted.

## THE KHANATES OF KOKAND, KHIVA & BUKHARA

In the fertile land now called Uzbekistan, the military regime of a Persian interloper named Nadir Shah collapsed in 1747, leaving a political void which was rapidly occupied by a trio of Uzbek khanates.

The three dynasties were the Kungrats, enthroned at Khiva (in the territory of old Khorezm), the Mangits at Bukhara and the Mins at Kokand; all rivals. The khans of Khiva and Kokand and the emirs of Bukhara seemed able to will the outside world out of existence as they stroked and clawed each other like a box of kittens. Boundaries were impossible to fix as the rivals shuffled their provinces in endless wars.

Unruly nomadic clans produced constant pressure on their periphery. Bukhara and Khiva vainly claimed nominal control over the nomadic Turkmen, who prowled the Karakum desert and provided the khanates with slaves from Persia and the Russian borderlands. Kokand expanded into the Tian Shan mountains and the Syr-Darya basin in the early 19th century.

The khans ruled absolutely as feudal despots. Some of them were capable rulers; some, such as the last emir of Bukhara, were depraved and despised tyrants. In the centuries since Transoxiana had waned as the centre of Islam, the mullahs had slipped into hypocrisy and greed. The level of education and

**1592**
Khiva made capital of Khorezm

**1635–1758**
Zhungarian empire terrorises Kazakhstan, Kyrgyzstan and China

literacy was low, and the *ulama* (intellectual class) seems to have encouraged superstition and ignorance in the people.

It was no dark age, however – trade was vigorous. This was especially true in Bukhara, where exports of cotton, cloth, silk, karakul wool and other goods gave it a whopping trade surplus with Russia. Commerce brought in new ideas, with resulting attempts to develop irrigation and even to reform civil administrations. European travellers in the 19th century mentioned the exotic architectural splendour of these distant glimmering capitals.

In none of the three khanates was there any sense among the local people that they belonged to a distinct nation – whether of Bukhara, Khiva or Kokand. In all three, *sarts* (town dwellers) occupied the towns and farms, while clans who practised nomadism and seminomadism roamed the uncultivated countryside. *Sarts* included both Turkic-speaking Uzbeks and Persian-speaking Tajiks. These two groups had almost identical lifestyles and customs, apart from language.

In many respects, the three khanates closely resembled the feudal city-states of late-medieval Europe. But it is anybody's guess how they and the Kazakh and Kyrgyz nomads might have developed had they been left alone.

## THE RUSSIANS ARE COMING!

By the turn of the 19th century Russia's vista to the south was of anachronistic, unstable neighbours. Flush with the new currents of imperialism sweeping Europe, the empire found itself embarking willy-nilly upon a century of rapid expansion across the steppe.

'Russia has two faces, an Asiatic face which looks always towards Europe, and a European face which looks always towards Asia.'

BENJAMIN DISRAELI

The reasons were complex. The main ingredients were the search for a secure, and preferably natural, southern border, nagging fears of British expansion from India, and the boldness of individual tsarist officers. And probably, glimmering in the back of every patriotic Russian's mind, there was a vague notion of the 'manifest destiny' of the frontier.

The first people to feel the impact were the Kazakhs. Their agreements in the mid-18th century to accept Russian 'protection' had apparently been understood by St Petersburg as agreements to annexation and a few decades later Tatars and Cossacks were sent to settle and farm the land. Angered, the Kazakhs revolted. As a consequence, the khans of the three hordes were, one by one, stripped of their autonomy, and their lands were made into bona fide Russian colonies, sweet psychological revenge, no doubt, for centuries of invasion by nomadic tribes from the east. In 1848, as the USA was gaining land stretching from Texas to California, Russia abolished the Great Horde. Theirs was the last line of rulers in the world directly descended, by both blood and throne, from Jenghiz Khan. Kokand was the first of the three Uzbek khanates to be swamped, followed by Bukhara (1868) and then Khiva (1873).

The last and fiercest people to hold out against the tsarist juggernaut were the Tekke, the largest Turkmen clan. Of all nomad groups, the Tekke had managed to remain the most independent of the khanates. Some Turkmen clans had asked to be made subjects of Russia as early as 1865, for convenient help in their struggle against the Khivan yoke. But none were in a mood to have their tethers permanently shortened as Russia expanded into their territory. To add rancour to the pot, the Russians were anguished by the Tekkes' dealings in slaves, particularly Christian ones.

**1758**

Oyrats defeated by Manchu China and Kyrgyzstan nominally under Chinese rule

**1832**

Alexander 'Bokhara' Burnes visits Bukhara

Much blood was spilled in the subjugation of the Tekke. The Russians were trounced in 1879 at Teke-Turkmen, but returned in 1881 with a huge force under General Mikhail Dmitrievich Skobelev (who famously rode a white horse and dressed only in white). The siege and capture of Geok-Tepe, the Tekkes' last stronghold, resulted in up to 16,000 Tekke and only 268 Russians dead.

With resistance crushed, the Russians proceeded along the hazily defined Persian frontier area, occupying Merv in 1884 and the Pandjeh Oasis on the Afghan border in 1885. It was the southernmost point they reached. Throughout the conquest, the government in St Petersburg agonised over every advance, while their hawkish generals in the field took key cities first and asked for permission later.

When it was over, Russia found it had bought a huge new territory – half the size of the USA, geographically and ethnically diverse, and economically rich – fairly cheaply in terms of money and lives, and in just 20 years. It had not gone unnoticed by the world's other great empire further south in British India.

'I hold it as a principle that in Asia the duration of peace is in direct proportion to the slaughter you inflict upon the enemy. The harder you hit them the longer they will be quiet afterwards.'

GENERAL SKOBELEV, TSARIST RUSSIAN COMMANDER IN CENTRAL ASIA

## THE GREAT GAME

What do two expanding empires do when their fuzzy frontiers draw near each other? They scramble for control of what's between them, using a mix of secrecy and stealth.

The British called it the Great Game; in Russia it was the Tournament of Shadows. Its backdrop was the first cold war between East and West. All the ingredients were there: spies and counterspies, demilitarised zones, puppet states and doom-saying governments whipping up smokescreens for their own shady business. All that was lacking was the atom bomb and a Russian leader banging his shoe on the table. Diplomatic jargon acquired the phrase 'sphere of influence' during this era.

The story of the Great Game would be dull as dishwater except that its centre arena was some of the world's most exotic and remote geography. The history of Central Asia from the beginning of the 19th century to the present day must be seen in the context of the Great Game, for this was the main reason for Russian interest in the region.

The phrase 'Great Game' was first coined by British officer Arthur Conolly (later executed in Bukhara) and immortalised by Kipling in his novel *Kim*.

The Russian occupation of Merv in 1884 immediately raised blood pressures in Britain and India. Merv was a crossroads leading to Herat, an easy gateway to Afghanistan which in turn offered entry into British India. The British government finally lost its cool when the Russians went south to control Pandjeh. But the storm had been brewing long before 1884.

By 1848 the British had defeated the Sikhs and taken the Peshawar valley and Punjab. With a grip now on the 'Northern Areas' Britain began a kind of cat-and-mouse game with Russia across the vaguely mapped Pamir mountain range and Hindu Kush. Agents posing as scholars, explorers, merchants – even Muslim preachers and Buddhist pilgrims – crisscrossed the mountains, mapping them, spying on each other, courting local rulers, staking claims like dogs in a vacant lot.

For more on that quintessential Great Gamester, Francis Younghusband, read Patrick French's excellent biography *Younghusband*.

In 1882 Russia established a consulate in Kashgar. A British agency at Gilgit (now in Pakistan), which had opened briefly in 1877, was urgently reopened when the *mir* (hereditary ruler) of Hunza entertained a party of Russians in 1888. Britain set up its own Kashgar office in 1890.

**1842**

British officers Conolly and Stoddart beheaded by the Emir of Bukhara

**1862–84**

Tsarist Russia takes Bishkek (1862), Aulie-Ata (1864), Tashkent (1865), Samarkand (1868), Khiva (1873), Kokand (1877) and Merv (1884)

Also in 1890, Francis Younghusband (later to head a British incursion into Tibet) was sent to do some politicking with Chinese officials in Kashgar. On his way back through the Pamirs he found the range full of Russian troops, and was told to get out or face arrest.

This electrified the British. They raised hell with the Russian government and invaded Hunza the following year; at the same time Russian troops skirmished in northeast Afghanistan. After a burst of diplomatic manoeuvring, Anglo-Russian boundary agreements in 1895 and 1907 gave Russia most of the Pamirs and established the Wakhan Corridor, the awkward finger of Afghan territory that divides the two former empires.

The Great Game was over. The Great Lesson for the people of the region was: 'No great power has our interests at heart'. The lesson has powerful implications today.

## COLONISATION OF TURKESTAN & SEMIRECHE

In 1861, the outbreak of the US Civil War ended Russia's imports of American cotton. To keep the growing textile industry in high gear, the natural place to turn to for cotton was Central Asia. Other sectors of Russian industry were equally interested in the new colonies as sources of cheap raw materials and labour, and as huge markets. Russia's government and captains of industry wisely saw that their own goods could not compete in Europe but in Central Asia they had a captive, virgin market. Gradually, Russian Turkestan was put in line with the economic needs of the empire.

In the late 19th century, Europeans began to flood the tsar's new lands, a million in Kazakhstan alone. The immigrants were mostly freed Russian and Ukrainian serfs who wanted land of their own. Central Asia also offered a chance for enterprising Russians to climb socially. The first mayor of Pishpek (Bishkek) left Russia as a gunsmith, married well in the provinces, received civil appointments, and ended his life owning a mansion and a sprawling garden estate.

The Trans-Caspian railway was begun at Krasnovodsk in 1880 and reached Samarkand in 1888. The Orenburg–Tashkent line was completed in 1905. This was also the golden age of Russian exploration in Central Asia, whose famous figures including Semenov, Przhevalsky and Merzbacher, are only today getting credit abroad.

The Kazakh army officer Shoqan Ualikhanov, a friend of Dostoevsky, was the first man to record a fragment of the Kyrgyz epic *Manas* and, as a spy, managed to make his way in disguise into Kashgar in 1858, risking death if discovered.

The Russian middle class brought with them straight streets, gas lights, telephones, cinemas, amateur theatre, charity drives, parks and hotels. All these were contained in enclaves set apart from the original towns. Through their lace curtains the Russians looked out on the Central Asian masses with a fairly indulgent attitude. The Muslim fabric of life was left alone, as were the mullahs, as long as they were submissive. Development, both social and economic, was initially a low priority. When it came, it took the form of small industrial enterprises, irrigation systems and a modest programme of primary education.

In culture it was the Kazakhs, as usual, who were the first to be influenced by Russia. A small, Europeanised, educated class began for the first time to think of the Kazakh people as a nation. In part, their ideas came from a new sense of their own illustrious past, which they read about in the works of Russian ethnographers and historians. Their own brilliant but short-lived scholar, Shoqan Ualikhanov, was a key figure in Kazakh consciousness-raising.

**1890**
Captain Francis Younghusband thrown out of the Pamirs by Russians

**1917**
Russian Revolution

The Uzbeks were also affected by the 19th-century cultural renaissance of the Tatars. The Jadidists, adherents of educational reform, made small gains in modernising Uzbek schools. The Pan-Turkic movement found fertile ground among educated Uzbeks at the beginning of the 20th century and took root.

## THE 1916 UPRISING

Resentment against the Russians ran deep and occasionally boiled over. Andijan in Uzbekistan was the scene of a rebellion, or holy war, from 1897 to 1898, which rocked the Russians out of complacency. After the insurrection was put down, steps were taken to Russify urban Muslims, the ones most under the influence of the mullahs and most likely to organise against the regime.

More than 200,000 Kazakhs fled to China in 1916 after an uprising over forced labour conscription during WWI, and more fled in the wake of forced collectivisation in the 1920s.

The outbreak of WWI in 1914 had disastrous consequences in Central Asia. In Semireche (Saka), massive herds of Kazakh and Kyrgyz cattle were requisitioned for the war effort, whereas Syr-Darya, Fergana and Samarkand provinces had to provide cotton and food. Then, in 1916, as Russia's hopes in the war plummeted, the tsar demanded men. Local people in the colonies were to be conscripted as noncombatants in labour battalions. To add insult to injury, the action was not called 'mobilisation' but 'requisition', a term usually used for cattle and materiel.

Exasperated Central Asians just said no. Starting in Tashkent, an uprising swept eastwards over the summer of 1916. It gained in violence, and attracted harsher reprisal, the further east it went. Purposeful attacks on Russian militias and official facilities gave way to massive rioting, raiding and looting. Colonists were massacred, their villages burned, and women and children carried off.

The central district of Karakol, on Lake Issyk-Köl in Kyrgyzstan, is probably the best-preserved relic of the Russian colonial environment.

The resulting bloody crackdown is a milestone tragedy in Kyrgyz and Kazakh history. Russian troops and vigilantes gave up all pretence of a 'civilising influence' as whole Kyrgyz and Kazakh villages were brutally slaughtered or set to flight. Manhunts for suspected perpetrators continued all winter, long after an estimated 200,000 Kyrgyz and Kazakh families had fled towards China. The refugees who didn't starve or freeze on the way were shown little mercy in China.

But not all unrest among Muslims was directed against Russia. The Young Bukharans and Young Khivans movements agitated for social self-reform, modelling themselves on the Young Turks movement which had begun transforming Turkey in 1908.

## REVOLUTION & CIVIL WAR

For a short time after the Russian Revolution of 1917, which toppled the tsar, there was a real feeling of hope in some Central Asian minds. The society which the West, out of ignorance and mystification, had labelled backward and inflexible had actually been making preparations for impressive progress. The Bolsheviks made sure, however, that we will never know how Central Asia might have remade itself.

*Mission to Tashkent,* by FM Bailey, recounts the derring-do of this British intelligence officer/spy in 1918 Soviet Tashkent. At one stage, under an assumed identity, he was employed as a Bolshevik agent and given the task of tracking himself down!

In 1917 an independent state was launched in Kokand by young nationalists under the watchful eye of a cabal of Russian cotton barons. This new government intended to put into practice the philosophy of the Jadid movement: to build a strong, autonomous Pan-Turkic polity in Central Asia by modernising the religious establishment and Westernising and educating the people. Within a year the Kokand government was smashed by the Red

| 1920 | 1921 |
|---|---|
| Soviet troops seize Khiva and Bukhara, ending the respective khanate and emirate | Creation of Turkestan Soviet Socialist Republic (SSR) |

Army's newly formed Trans-Caspian front. More than 5000 Kokandis were massacred after the city was captured. Central Asians' illusions about peacefully coexisting with Bolshevik Russia were shattered as well.

### Bolshevik Conquest

Like most Central Asians, Emir Alim Khan of Bukhara hated the godless Bolsheviks. In response to their first ultimatum to submit, he slaughtered the Red emissaries who brought it and declared a holy war. The emir conspired with White (ie anti-Bolshevik) Russians and British political agents, while the Reds concentrated on strengthening party cells within the city.

For more on Nazaroff's cat-and-mouse exploits on the run in Central Asia from the Bolsheviks, read his *Hunted Through Central Asia*.

In December 1918 a counter revolution broke out, apparently organised from within Tashkent jail by a shadowy White Russian agent named Paul Nazaroff. Several districts and cities fell back into the hands of the Whites. The bells of the cathedral church in Tashkent were rung in joy, but for the last time. The Bolsheviks defeated the insurrection, snatched back power, and kept it. Nazaroff, freed from jail, was forced to hide and flee across the Tian Shan to Xinjiang, always one step ahead of the dreaded secret police.

The end came swiftly after the arrival in Tashkent of the Red Army commander Mikhail Frunze. Khiva went out with barely a whimper, quietly transforming into the Khorezm People's Republic in February 1920. In September, Frunze's fresh, disciplined army captured Bukhara after a four-day fight. The emir fled to Afghanistan, taking with him his company of dancing boys but abandoning his harem to the Bolshevik soldiers.

## THE SOVIET ERA

From the start the Bolsheviks ensured themselves the universal hatred of the people. Worse even than the tsar's bleed-the-colonies-for-the-war policies, the revolutionaries levied grievous requisitions of food, livestock, cotton, land and forced farm labour. Trade and agricultural output in the once-thriving colonies plummeted. The ensuing famines claimed nearly a million lives; some say many more.

### Forced Collectivisation

'The Communist Party is the mind, honour and conscience of our era.'

VLADIMIR ILYCH LENIN

Forced collectivisation was the 'definite stage of development' implicit in time-warping the entire population of Central Asia from feudalism to communism. This occurred during the USSR's grand First Five Year Plan (1928–32). The intent of collectivisation was first to eliminate private property and second, in the case of the nomadic Kazakhs and Kyrgyz, to put an end to their wandering lifestyle.

The effect was disastrous. When the orders came down, most people simply slaughtered their herds and ate what they could rather than give them up. This led to famine in subsequent years, and widespread disease. Resisters were executed and imprisoned. Millions of people died. Evidence exists that during this period Stalin had a personal hand in tinkering with meagre food supplies in order to induce famines. His aims seem to have been to subjugate the people's will and to depopulate Kazakhstan, which was good real estate for Russian expansion.

The *basmachi* (Muslim guerrilla fighters; see the boxed text, p367), in twilight for some time, renewed their guerrilla activities briefly as collectivisation took its toll. It was their final struggle.

**1928–30**

Latin script replaces Arabic script in Central Asia, to be replaced again by Cyrillic script in 1939–40

**1930s**

Stalin's genocidal collectivisation programmes strike the final blow to nomadic life

## Political Repression

Undeveloped Central Asia had no shortage of bright, sincere people willing to work for national liberation and democracy. After the tsar fell they jostled for power in their various parties, movements and factions. Even after they were swallowed into the Soviet state, some members of these groups had high profiles in regional affairs. Such a group was Alash Orda, which was formed by Kazakhs and Kyrgyz in 1917. Alash Orda even held the reins of a short-lived autonomous government.

By the late 1920s, the former nationalists and democrats, indeed the entire intelligentsia, were causing Stalin serious problems. From their posts in the communist administration they had front-row seats at the Great Leader's horror show, including collectivisation. Many of them began to reason, and to doubt. Stalin, reading these signs all over the USSR, foresaw that brains could be just as dangerous as guns. Throughout the 1930s he proceeded to have all possible dissenters eliminated. Alash Orda members were among the first to die, in 1927 and 1928.

Thus began the systematic murder, called the Purges, of untold tens of thousands of Central Asians. Arrests were usually made late at night. Confined prisoners were rarely tried; if any charges at all were brought, they ran along the lines of 'having bourgeoisie-nationalist or Pan-Turkic attitudes'. Mass executions and burials were common. Sometimes entire sitting governments were disposed of in this way.

## Construction of Nationalities

The solution to the 'nationality question' in Central Asia remains the most graphically visible effect of Soviet rule: it drew the lines on the map. Before the revolution the peoples of Central Asia had no concept of a firm national border. They had plotted their identities by a tangle of criteria: religion, clan, location, way of life, even social status. The Soviets, however, believed that such a populace was fertile soil for Pan-Islamism and Pan-Turkism. These philosophies were threats to the regime.

So, starting in about 1924, nations were invented: Kazakh, Kyrgyz, Tajik, Turkmen, Uzbek. Each was given its own distinct ethnic profile, language, history and territory. Where an existing language or history was not apparent or was not suitably distinct from others, these were supplied and disseminated. Islam was cut away from each national heritage, essentially relegated to the status of an outmoded and oppressive cult, and severely suppressed throughout the Soviet period.

Ultimately, each nation became the namesake for a Soviet Socialist Republic (SSR). Uzbek and Turkmen SSRs were proclaimed in 1924, the Tajik SSR in 1929, and the Kazakh and Kyrgyz SSRs in 1936.

Some say that Stalin personally directed the drawing of the boundary lines. Each of the republics was shaped to contain numerous pockets of the different nationalities, and each with long-standing claims to the land. Everyone had to admit that only a strong central government could keep order on such a map. The present face of Central Asia is a product of this 'divide and rule' technique.

## World War II

'The Great Patriotic War Against Fascist Germany' galvanised the whole USSR and in the course of the war Central Asia was drawn further into the fold. Economically the region lost ground from 1941 to 1945 but a sizable boost came in the form of industrial enterprises arriving ready-to-assemble

**1948**
Ashgabat destroyed in an earthquake; 110,000 perish

**1954**
Virgin Lands campaign in Kazakhstan

in train cars: evacuated from the war-threatened parts of the USSR, they were relocated to the remote safety of Central Asia. They remained there after the war and kept on producing.

Do a search for 'Central Asia' at www.loc.gov/exhibits/empire for wonderful old photos of Central Asia from the Prokudin-Gorskii collection.

Other wartime evacuees – people – have made a lasting imprint on the face of Central Asia. These are the Koreans, Volga Germans, Chechens and others whom Stalin suspected might aid the enemy. They were deported from the borderlands and shuffled en masse. They now form sizable minority communities in all the former Soviet Central Asian republics.

For many wartime draftees, WWII presented an opportunity to escape the oppressive Stalinist state. One Central Asian scholar claims that more than half of the 1.5 million Central Asians mobilised in the war deserted. Large numbers of them, as well as prisoners of war, actually turned their coats and fought for the Germans against the Soviets.

## Agriculture

The tsarist pattern for the Central Asian economy had been overwhelmingly agricultural; so it was with the Soviets. Each republic was 'encouraged' to specialise in a limited range of products, which made their individual economies dependent on the Soviet whole. Tajik SSR built the world's fourth-largest aluminium plant but all the aluminium had to brought in from outside the region.

Independent Uzbekistan is still the world's second-largest producer of cotton.

Uzbek SSR alone soon supplied no less than 64% of Soviet cotton, making the USSR the world's second-largest cotton producer after the USA. Into the cotton bowl poured the diverted waters of the Syr-Darya and Amu-Darya, while downstream the Aral Sea was left to dry up. Over the cotton-scape was spread a whole list of noxious agricultural chemicals, which have wound up polluting waters, blowing around in dust storms, and causing serious health problems for residents of the area. For further details, see p77.

Another noxious effect of cotton monoculture was the 'cotton affair' of the Brezhnev years. A huge ring of corrupt officials habitually over-reported cotton production, swindling Moscow out of billions of roubles. When the lid finally blew off, 2600 participants were arrested and more than 50,000 were kicked out of office. Brezhnev's own son-in-law was one of the fallen.

From the Mongol destruction of irrigation canals to the Russian harnessing of water for cotton production and the death of the Aral Sea, the control of water in the deserts of Central Asia has been central to the region for centuries and will continue to be a source of future contention.

In 1954 the Soviet leader Nikita Khrushchev launched the Virgin Lands campaign. The purpose was to jolt agricultural production, especially of wheat, to new levels. The method was to put Kazakh SSR's enormous steppes under the plough and resettle huge numbers of Russians to work the farms. Massive, futuristic irrigation schemes were drawn up to water the formerly arid grassland, with water taken from as far away as the Ob River in Siberia. The initial gains in productivity soon dwindled as the fragile exposed soil of the steppes literally blew away in the wind. The Russians, however, remained.

## Benefits of the Soviet Era

In spite of their heavy-handedness, the Soviets made profound improvements in Central Asia. Overall standards of living were raised considerably with the help of health care and a vast new infrastructure. Central Asia was provided with plants, mines, farms, ranches and services employing millions of people (never mind that no single republic was given the means

**1966**
Tashkent destroyed in earthquake

**1979**
USSR invades Afghanistan

for a free-standing economy, and that most operations were coordinated through Moscow). Outside the capitals, the face of the region is still often a Soviet one.

Education reached all social levels (previously education was through the limited, men-only network of Islamic schools and medressas), and pure and applied sciences were nurtured. Literacy rates hit 97% and the languages of all nationalities were given standard literary forms. The Kyrgyz language was even given an alphabet for the first time.

Soviet women had 'economic equality' and although this meant that they had the chance to study and work alongside men *while* retaining all the responsibilities of homemakers, female literacy approached male levels, maternity leave was introduced and women assumed positions of responsibility in middle-level administration as well as academia.

Artistic expression was encouraged within the confines of communist ideology and cinemas and theatres were built. The Central Asian republics now boast active communities of professional artists who were trained, sometimes lavishly, by the Soviet state. And through the arts, the republics were allowed to develop their distinctive national traditions and identities (again, within bounds).

If the Central Asian republics were at all prepared when independence came, they were prepared by the Soviet era.

Central Asia's old Arabic alphabet was replaced by the Soviets with a Latin one, and later with a Cyrillic script. Several republics (Turkmenistan and Uzbekistan) have shifted back to a Latin script, meaning older people are using alphabets incomprehensible to the youth.

### The Afghan War

In 1979 the Soviet army invaded Afghanistan, determined to prop up a crumbling communist regime on their doorstep. In retrospect, someone should have consulted the history books beforehand, for the lessons of history are clear; no-one wins a war in Afghanistan. Central Asian Muslims were drafted into the war to liberate their backward relatives, while the Afghan mujaheddin said a prayer for the souls of their godless Central Asian kin.

In the end, after 10 years of brutal guerrilla war that ended the lives of 15,000 Soviets and 1.5 million Afghans, the Soviets finally pulled out, limping back over the Amu-Darya to Termiz. They weren't quite massacred to a man as were the British before them but the strains of war indelibly contributed to the cracking of the Soviet empire.

In the last years of the USSR, official reports revealed that Central Asia was home to 16% of the USSR's population, and 64% of its poor.

## POST-SOVIET CENTRAL ASIA

One Russian humorist has summed up his country's century in two sentences: 'After titanic effort, blood, sweat and tears, the Soviet people brought forth a new system. Unfortunately, it was the wrong one'.

By the spring of 1991 the parliaments of all five republics had declared their sovereignty. However, when the failure of the August coup against Gorbachev heralded the end of the USSR, none of the republics was prepared for the reality of independence.

On 8 December the presidents of Russia, the Ukraine and Belarus met near Brest in Belarus to form the Commonwealth of Independent States (CIS). Feeling left out, the Central Asian presidents convened and demanded admission. On 21 December, the heads of 11 of the former Soviet states (all except the three Baltic states and Georgia) met in Almaty and refounded the CIS. Gorbachev resigned three days later.

The collapse of the Soviet Union sent the Central Asian republics into an economic collapse estimated at three times greater than the Great Depression of 1930s America.

**8 December 1991**
Collapse of the Soviet Union, formation of the Commonwealth of Independent States

**1992–97**
Civil War in Tajikistan claims 60,000 lives and displaces 500,000

*Sons of the Conquerors: The Rise of the Turkic World* by the journalist Hugh Pope is a modern portrait of the entire Turkic world.

With independence suddenly thrust upon them, the old Soviet guard was essentially the only group with the experience and the means to rule. Most of these men are still in power today. All the Central Asian governments are still authoritarian to some degree, running the gamut from pure *ancien regime*–style autocracy (Turkmenistan), to a tightly controlled mixture of neocommunism and spurious nationalism (Uzbekistan), to a marginally more enlightened 'channelled transition' to democracy and a market economy (Kazakhstan and Kyrgyzstan).

In some ways, not much changed. In most of the republics the old Communist Party apparatus simply renamed itself using various combinations of the words 'People', 'Party' and 'Democratic'. Political opposition was completely marginalised (Turkmenistan), banned (Uzbekistan), or tolerated but closely watched (Kazakhstan, Kyrgyzstan and Tajikistan). Kazakhstan suddenly found itself with nuclear weapons and a space programme. All the republics swiftly formed national airlines from whatever Aeroflot planes happened to be parked on their runways on the day after independence.

For an account of the 2005 Tulip Revolution in Kyrgyzstan visit www.eurasianet.org/kyrgyzstan.

Yet in most ways, everything changed. The end of the old Soviet subsidies meant a decline in everything from economic subsidies to education levels. The deepest economic trauma was/is in the countryside, but even many urbanites are just scraping by, with wages for many professionals as low as US$35 a month in the cities. Most heart-rending are the pensioners, especially the Slavs whose pensions were made worthless overnight with the devaluation of the rouble. Throughout the 1990s, one of the most common sights across Central Asia was watery-eyed *babushkas* (old women) sitting quietly on many street corners, surrounded by a few worthless possessions for sale, trying not to look like beggars. Suddenly the Soviet era began to look like a golden age.

**13 May 2005**
Massacre of between 200 and 1000 unarmed protestors in Andijon, Uzbekistan

**2006**
President Niyazov (Turkmenbashi) of Turkmenistan dies

# The Silk Road

> The history of the Silk Road is neither a poetic nor a picturesque tale; it is nothing more than scattered islands of peace in an ocean of wars.
>
> *Luce Boulnois,* Silk Road: Monks, Warriors & Merchants on The Silk Road

Silk Road Foundation (www.silk-road.com) has articles on Silk Road cities and travel, as well as information on workshops, lectures and music.

No-one knows for sure when the miraculously fine, light, soft, strong, sensuous fabric spun from the cocoon of the *Bombyx* caterpillar first reached the West from China. We do know that Chinese silk strands have been found in the hair of a 3000-year-old Egyptian mummy. In the 4th century BC, Aristotle described a fibre that may have been Chinese silk. The Romans probably first laid eyes on silk when the Parthians unfurled great blinding banners of the stuff on the battlefield. Cool in summer, warm in winter and impervious to rot, it soon caught on.

Writing a short while after the time of Christ, Pliny the Elder was scandalised by the luxurious, transparent cloths, which allowed Roman women to be 'dressed and yet nude'. He fell wide of the mark in describing silk's origin and processing, though, believing silk to literally grow on trees in a land called Seres or Serica. The Chinese, had they known, would most likely have done little to disillusion him.

One major Silk Road industry rarely mentioned is the trade in slaves. Slaves dominated the global workforce between the 8th and 11th centuryiesand nomadic Turkmen slave raiders kept the slave markets of Khiva and Bukhara well stocked into the 18th and 19th centuries.

Parthia, on the Iranian plateau, was the most voracious foreign trader and consumer of Chinese silk at the close of the 2nd century BC, having supposedly traded an ostrich egg for its first bolt of silk. In about 105 BC, Parthia and China exchanged embassies and inaugurated official bilateral trade along the caravan route that lay between them. With this the Silk Road was born – in fact, if not in name – to flourish for another 800 years.

## THE SILK ROUTES

Geographically there's no such thing as a single 'Silk Road', but rather a fragile network of shifting intercontinental caravan tracks that threaded through some of Asia's highest mountains and bleakest deserts.

At any given time any portion of the network might be beset by war, robbers or natural disaster: the northern routes were plagued by nomadic horsemen and a lack of settlements to provide fresh supplies and mounts; the south by fearsome deserts and frozen mountain passes.

Though the road map expanded over the centuries, the network had its main eastern terminus at the Chinese capital Ch'ang-an (modern Xi'an). West of there, the route reached the oasis town of Dunhuang and exited China through the Jade Gate. Here it divided, one branch skirting the dreaded Taklamakan Desert to the north through Loulan, Turfan, Kucha and Aksu,

### THE SECRET OF SILK

For centuries China guarded the secret of silk-making jealously, making it illegal to transfer silkworm eggs or mulberry seeds out of the country.

Some people give credit for history's first great industrial espionage coup to a Chinese princess who was departing to marry a Khotanese king: the legend goes that she hid live worms and cocoons in her elaborate hairstyle, in order to fool customs agents so she would be able enjoy the luxury of silk in her 'barbarian' home. Others give the credit to Nestorian monks who allegedly hid silkworm eggs in their walking sticks as they travelled from Central Asia to Byzantium.

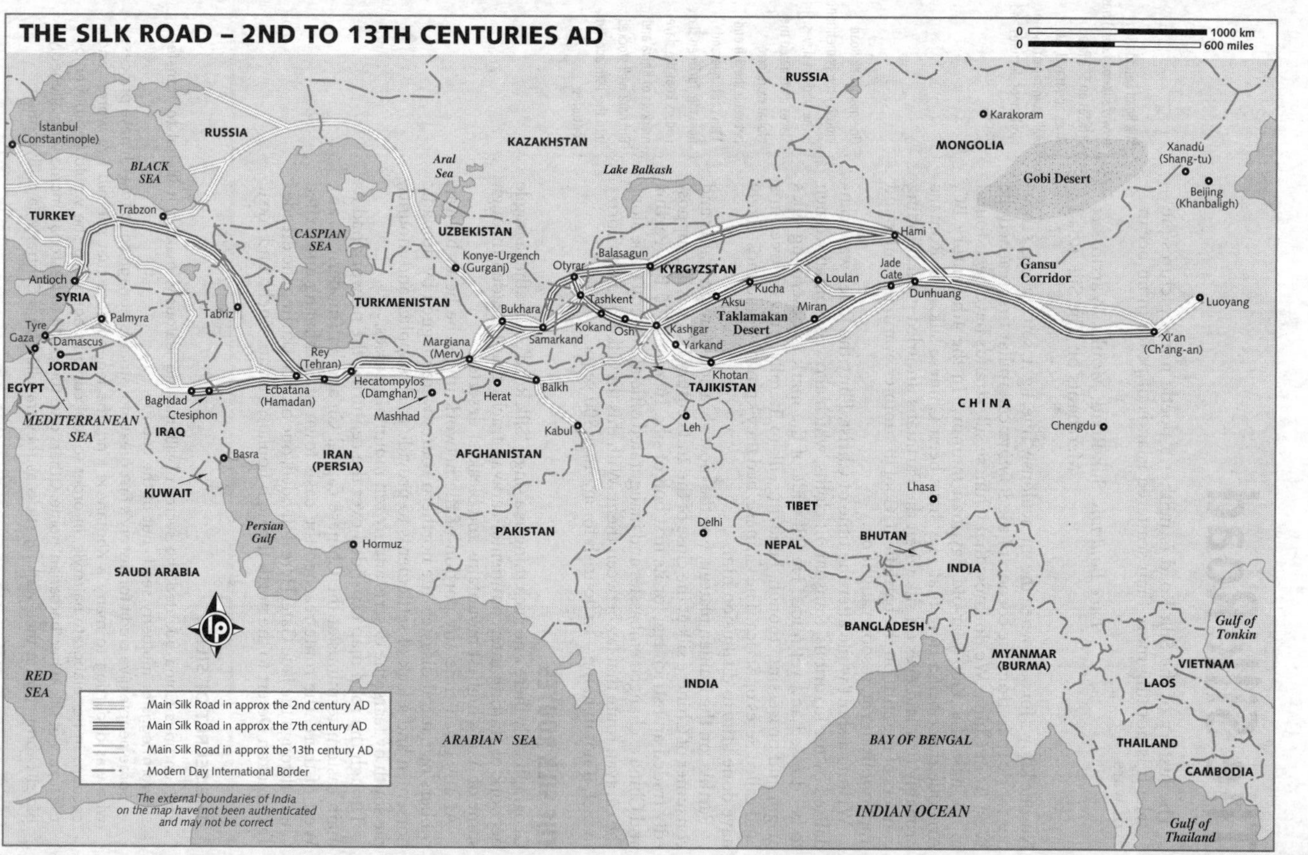
THE SILK ROAD – 2ND TO 13TH CENTURIES AD
0 1000 km
0 600 miles
Main Silk Road in approx the 2nd century AD
Main Silk Road in approx the 7th century AD
Main Silk Road in approx the 13th century AD
Modern Day International Border
The external boundaries of India on the map have not been authenticated and may not be correct
İstanbul (Constantinople)
TURKEY
BLACK SEA
RUSSIA
Trabzon
Antioch
SYRIA
Palmyra
Damascus
Tyre
Gaza
JORDAN
EGYPT
MEDITERRANEAN SEA
IRAQ
Baghdad
Ctesiphon
Basra
KUWAIT
SAUDI ARABIA
RED SEA
Tabriz
Ecbatana (Hamadan)
Rey (Tehran)
IRAN (PERSIA)
Persian Gulf
Hormuz
CASPIAN SEA
Hecatompylos (Damghan)
Mashhad
TURKMENISTAN
Margiana (Merv)
Aral Sea
UZBEKISTAN
Konye-Urgench (Gurganj)
Bukhara
Herat
AFGHANISTAN
Balkh
Kabul
PAKISTAN
ARABIAN SEA
KAZAKHSTAN
Samarkand
Otyrar
Tashkent
Kokand
Osh
Balasagun
Lake Balkash
KYRGYZSTAN
TAJIKISTAN
Kashgar
Yarkand
Aksu
Khotan
Kucha
Taklamakan Desert
Leh
Delhi
INDIA
RUSSIA
Loulan
Miran
NEPAL
TIBET
Jade Gate
Dunhuang
Hami
Lhasa
BHUTAN
BANGLADESH
MONGOLIA
Karakoram
CHINA
INDIA
BAY OF BENGAL
INDIAN OCEAN
Gobi Desert
Gansu Corridor
MYANMAR (BURMA)
Chengdu
Xanadu (Shang-tu)
Beijing (Khanbaligh)
Xi'an (Ch'ang-an)
Luoyang
LAOS
THAILAND
VIETNAM
CAMBODIA
Gulf of Tonkin
Gulf of Thailand

while the other headed south via Miran, Khotan (Hotan) and Yarkand. The two forks met again in Kashgar, from where the trail headed up a series of passes into and over the Pamirs and Tian Shan (two such passes in use today are the Torugart and Irkeshtam, on the Chinese border with Kyrgyzstan).

Beyond the mountains, the Fergana Valley, long famed for its horses, fed westward through Kokand, Samarkand and Bukhara, past Merv and on to Iran, the Levant and Constantinople. Another route wound through the Pamirs and Badakhshan, through Bactria (Balkh) and Aria (Herat) to Iran. Goods reached transhipment points on the Black and Mediterranean Seas, where caravans took on cargo for the march back eastward over the same tracks. In the middle of the network, major branches headed south over the Karakoram range to India and north via the Zhungarian Gap and across the Saka (Scythia) steppes to Khorezm and the Volga.

In the course of his archaeological expeditions in neighbouring Xinjiang (Chinese Turkestan), Albert von Le Coq brought back examples of 17 different languages written in 24 different scripts.

## CARAVANS & TRADE

Goods heading west and east did not fall into discrete bundles. In fact there was little 'through traffic'; caravanners were mostly short- and medium-distance haulers who marketed and took on freight along a given beat according to their needs and inclinations. The earliest exchanges were based on mercantile interactions between the steppe nomads and settled towns, when barter was the only form of exchange. Only later did a monetary economy enable long-distance trade routes to develop.

Nor was silk the only trade, though it epitomises the qualities required for such a long-distance trade; light, valuable, exotic and greatly desired. In fact China's early need for horses was a major reason for the growth of the Silk Road.

Though heavily stacked in favour of China, traffic ran both ways. China received gold, silver, ivory, lapis, jade, coral, wool, rhino horn, tortoise shell, horses, Mediterranean coloured glass (an industrial mystery originally as inscrutable to the Chinese as silk was in the West), cucumbers, walnuts, pomegranates, golden peaches from Samarkand, sesame, garlic, grapes and wine, plus – an early Parthian craze – acrobats and ostriches. Goods arriving at the western end included silk, porcelain, paper, tea, ginger, rhubarb, lacquerware, bamboo, Arabian spices and incense, medicinal herbs, gems and perfumes.

Silk Road Seattle (http://depts.washington.edu/uwch/silkroad) has online maps, virtual art, historical texts and articles on traditional culture, architecture and more.

And in the middle lay Central Asia, a great clearing house that provided its native beasts – horses and two-humped Bactrian camels – to keep the goods flowing in both directions. The cities of Bukhara and Samarkand marked the halfway break, where caravans from Aleppo and Baghdad met traders from Kashgar and Yarkand. *Rabat* (caravanserais) grew up along the route, offering lodgings, stables and stores. Middlemen such as the Sogdians amassed great fortunes, much of which went into beautifying cosmopolitan and luxuriant caravan towns such as Gurganj, Merv and Bukhara. The cities offered equally vital services, such as brokers to set up contracts, banking houses to set up lines of credit, and markets to sell the goods.

Ruined Silk Road cities in Kyrgyzstan's Chuy Valley include Ak-Beshim, Balasagun and Navekat, all dating from the 6th to 8th centuries AD. The last of these is to be restored by Unesco.

## THE CULTURAL LEGACY OF THE SILK ROAD

The Silk Road gave rise to unprecedented trade, but its true legacy was the intellectual interchange of ideas, technologies and faiths that formed the world's first 'information superhighway'.

Religion alone presents an astounding picture of diversity and tolerance that would be the envy of any modern democratic state. Manichaeism, Zoroastrianism, Buddhism, Nestorian Christianity, Judaism, Confucianism, Taoism and the shamanism of grassland nomads all coexisted and in some cases mingled, until the coming of Islam. Ironically as the bulk of trade headed west, religious ideas primarily travelled east.

Uzbekistan is the world's third-largest producer of silk. For the opportunity to see traditional silk production in Uzbekistan, see p220.

Buddhism spread along the trade routes to wend its way from India to China and back again. It's hard to imagine that Buddhist monasteries once dominated cultural life in Central Asia – today only the faintest archaeological evidence remains in ex-Soviet Central Asia, at Adjina-Tepe in Tajikistan, Kuva in the Fergana Valley, Termiz in Uzbekistan and Ak-Beshim in Kyrgyzstan.

Musical styles and instruments (including the lute) crossed borders as artists followed in the wake of traders, pilgrims and missionaries. The spread

### THE TRAVELLING POLOS (1271–98)

In the 1250s, Venice was predominant in the Mediterranean and looking for new commercial routes. In this context the Venetian brothers Nicolo and Mafeo Polo set out to do some itinerant trading; sailing from Constantinople with a cargo of precious stones, they made their way to the Crimea. Choice business deals followed and took them gradually up the Volga (they stayed a year at the Mongol khan's encampment at Sarai), eastward across the steppes, south to Bukhara (for an enforced three-year stay), then across Central Asia in the company of a Mongol envoy to Karakoram (now in Mongolia), the seat of Kublai Khan, grandson of Jenghiz.

Kublai welcomed the Europeans warmly and questioned them at length about life and statecraft in Europe. Such was the style of hospitality on the steppe that the khan couldn't bear to let them go (modern travellers know similar treatment!). The Polos remained at court for some four years.

In the end Kublai made them ambassadors to the pope in Rome, requesting that the pope send him 100 of his most learned priests to argue the merits of their faith over others. If they succeeded, Kublai said, his whole empire would convert to Christianity. It took the Polos three difficult years to get home; when they arrived, no-one believed where they had been.

Marco Polo, the teller of the world's most famous travel tale, was not yet born when his father Nicolo and uncle Mafeo set out on their journey. When they returned he was a motherless teenager. A couple of years later the elder Polos set off once more for Kublai's court, this time taking the 20-year-old Marco.

The pope had supplied only two monks, and they stayed behind in Armenia, perhaps after their first taste of shashlyk. (It is tempting to conjecture how the fate of Eurasia might have been different if the requested 100 doctors of religion had shown up at Karakoram and converted the entire Mongol empire.)

The Polos made their way to Balkh, and on through the Hindu Kush, Badakhshan and the Pamirs (stopping by Kara-Kul lake, now in Tajikistan, on the way), then on past Kashgar, Yarkand and the southern route around the Taklamakan Desert, reaching China via Dunhuang and the Gansu Corridor. They found the khan dividing his time between Khanbaligh (now Beijing) and his nearby summer capital of Shangdu (the Xanadu of Samuel Taylor Coleridge's poem).

Marco was exceptionally intelligent and observant, and Kublai took a great liking to him. He was soon made a trusted adviser and representative of the ageing khan. The three Polos spent about 16 years in China; Marco travelled far afield and brought the khan news of his far-flung and exotic empire, little of which he had seen.

The Polos were only allowed to go home when they agreed to escort a Mongol princess on her way to be married in Persia. To avoid long hardship the party took the sea route from the east coast of China around India and up the Gulf. Back in Venice, in 1295, still no-one believed the Polos' tales.

Many years later, during a war with Genoa, Marco Polo was captured in a naval battle. While in prison he dictated the story of his travels. The resulting book has become the world's most widely read travel account, though some question its authenticity. If Marco really did travel to China, why did he omit any mention of the Great Wall and the customs of drinking tea and binding feet? And why do Chinese imperial records fail to make any mention of Polo?

Hounded all his life by accusations that the exotic world he described was fictitious, Marco Polo was asked to recant on his deathbed. His answer: 'I have not told the half of what I saw.'

**SILK ROAD READING**

*Life along the Silk Road,* by Susan Whitfield, is a scholarly yet intriguing book that brings alive the Silk Road through a variety of characters (including a Sogdian merchant from Penjikent). Think the *Canterbury Tales* set in Central Asia. It's required reading for Silk Road obsessives.

*Silk Road: Monks, Warriors & Merchants on The Silk Road,* by Luce Boulnois, is a wonderful new reworking of a classic text. It has chapters on Silk Road museum collections, websites and travel information, all set in an attractive package.

*The Silk Road,* by Frances Wood, author of *Did Marco Polo Go To China?,* is another good overview, with fine illustrations.

*The Silk Road: Art & History,* by Jonathon Tucker, is a large-format art book for the connoisseur.

of Buddhism caused Indian, Chinese, Greek and Tibetan artistic styles to merge and fuse to form the exquisite Serindian art of Chinese Turkestan and the Gandharan art of Pakistan and Afghanistan.

To religion and art, add technology. The Chinese not only taught Central Asia how to cast iron but also how to make paper. Prisoners from the Battle of Talas (see p39) established paper production in Samarkand and then Baghdad, from where it spread into Europe, making it culturally the most important secret passed along the Silk Road.

Marco Polo's writings inspired Columbus to sail westwards to explore a new route to Asia, in doing so 'discovering' America by accident.

## THE DEATH OF THE SILK ROAD

The Silk Road was delivered a major body blow when China turned its back on the cosmopolitanism of the Tang dynasty (618–907) and retreated behind its Great Wall. The destruction and turbulence wreaked by Jenghiz Khan and Timur (Tamerlane) dealt a further economic blow to the region, and the literal and figurative drying-up of the Silk Road lead to the abandonment of a string of cities along the southern fringes of the Taklamakan Desert. The metaphoric nail in the Silk Road's coffin was the opening of more cost-effective maritime trading routes between Europe and Asia.

Central Asia remained largely forgotten by the East and the West until the arrival of Russian and British explorers in the 19th century and the rediscovery of the glory of Xinjiang's Silk Road cities. Ironically, it was only then, 20 centuries after the first Chinese missions to the West, that the term 'Silk Road' was thought up, coined for the first time by the German geographer Ferdinand von Richthofen.

The Sogdians (from modern Tajikistan and Uzbekistan) were the consummate Silk Road traders and their language became the lingua franca of the Silk Road.

## REBIRTH

The fall of the USSR has seen a minirevival in all things Silk Road in Central Asia. The re-establishment of rail links to China and Iran, the growth of border trade over the Torugart and Khunjerab Passes and the increase in oil piped along former silk routes have all offered the 'stans a means to shake off ties with Moscow. Camel trains have been replaced by Kamaz trucks and silk replaced by scrap metal, but the Silk Road remains as relevant as it ever was.

# People

From gold-toothed Turkmen in shaggy, dreadlocked hats to swarthy skull-capped Uzbeks and high-cheekboned Kazakh and Kyrgyz herders whose eyes still carry the glint of nomadism in their eyes, Central Asia presents a fascinating collection of faces and peoples. The total population of the former Soviet Central Asia is about 57 million, with a 2.4% annual growth rate. Few areas of its size are home to such tangled demographics and daunting transitions.

Each republic has inherited an ethnic grab bag from the Soviet system. Thus you'll find Uzbek towns in Kyrgyzstan, legions of Tajiks in the cities of Uzbekistan, Kazakhs grazing their cattle in Kyrgyzstan, Turkmen in Uzbekistan – and Russians and Ukrainians everywhere. Given the complicated mix of nationalities across national boundaries, Central Asia's ethnic situation is surprisingly tranquil. The most noticeable divide (and a largely amicable one) is between the traditionally sedentary peoples, the Uzbeks and Tajiks, and their formerly nomadic neighbours, the Kazakhs, Kyrgyz and Turkmen.

Kazakhs are the most Russified of Central Asians, due to their long historical contact with Russia, although some still maintain a seminomadic existence.

## PEOPLES OF THE SILK ROAD

Centuries of migrations and invasions have added to Central Asia's ethnic diversity. A trip from Ashgabat to Almaty reveals an absorbing array of faces from Turkish, Slavic, Chinese and Middle Eastern to downright Mediterranean – surmounted, incidentally, by an equally vast array of hats.

Before the Russian Revolution of 1917, Central Asians usually identified themselves 'ethnically' as either nomad or *sarts* (settled), as Turk or Persian, as simply Muslim, or by their clan. Later, separate nationalities were 'identified' by Soviet scholars as ordered by Stalin. Although it is easy to see the problems this has created, some Kazakhs and Kyrgyz at least will admit that they owe their survival as a nation to the Soviet process of nation building.

The following sections are a summary of the peoples of Central Asia.

**KAZAKHS**

Kazakhstan: 8.4 million

China: 1.1 million

Uzbekistan: 900,000

Russia: 740,000

Turkmenistan: 90,000

Western Mongolia: 70,000

Kyrgyzstan: 50,000

Afghanistan: 30,000

### KAZAKHS

The Kazakhs were nomadic horseback pastoralists until the 1920s; indeed the name Kazakh is said to mean 'free warrior' or 'steppe roamer'. Kazakhs trace their roots to the 15th century, when rebellious kinsmen of an Uzbek khan broke away and settled in present-day Kazakhstan. They divide themselves into three main divisions, or *zhuz*, corresponding to the historical Great (southern Kazakhstan), Middle (north and east Kazakhstan) and Little (west Kazakhstan) Hordes (p105). To this day family and ancestry remain crucial to Kazakhs. 'What *zhuz* do you belong to?' is a common opening question.

Most Kazakhs have Mongolian facial features, similar to the Kyrgyz. Most wear Western or Russian clothes, but you may see women – particularly on special occasions – in long dresses with stand-up collars or brightly decorated velvet waistcoats and heavy jewellery. Some men still wear baggy shirts and trousers, sleeveless jackets and wool or cotton robes. This outfit may be topped with either a skullcap or a high, tasselled felt hat resembling nothing so much as an elf's hat.

Kazakh literature is based around heroic epics, many of which concern themselves with the 16th-century clashes between the Kazakhs and Kalmucks, and the heroic *batyrs* (warriors) of that age. Apart from various equestrian

**BUZKASHI**

In a region where many people are descended from hot-blooded nomads, no-one would expect cricket to be the national sport. Even so, *buzkashi* (literally 'grabbing the dead goat') is wild beyond belief. As close to warfare as a sport can get, *buzkashi* is a bit like rugby on horseback in which the 'ball' is the headless carcass of a calf, goat or sheep (whatever is handy).

The day before the kickoff the *boz* (carcass)has its head, lower legs and entrails removed and is soaked in cold water for 24 hours to toughen it up. The game begins with the carcass in the centre of a circle at one end of a field; at the other end is a bunch of wild, adrenaline-crazed horsemen. At a signal it's every man for himself as they charge for the carcass. The aim is to gain possession of the *boz* and carry it up the field and around a post, with the winning rider being the one who finally drops the *boz* back in the circle. All the while there's a frenzied horsebacked tug-of-war going on as each competitor tries to gain possession; smashed noses and wrenched shoulders are all part of the fun.

Not surprisingly, the game is said to date from the days of Jenghiz Khan, a time when it enforced the nomadic values necessary for collective survival – courage, adroitness, wit and strength, while propagating a remarkable skill on horseback. The point of the game used to be the honour, and perhaps notoriety, of the victor, but gifts such as silk *chapans* (cloaks), cash or even cars are common these days.

*Buzkashi* takes place mainly outside of the pastoral season, in the cooler months of spring and autumn, at weekends, particularly during Navrus or to mark special occasions such as weddings or national days. Mazar-e-Sharif in Afghanistan is the place to find authentic *buzkashi* but if you are lucky you might catch local versions in Tajikistan (in Hissar), Kyrgyzstan (where it's known as *ulak-tartysh*) and Kazakhstan (where it's called *kökpar*). Navruz is the best time to find a game on, especially in Hissar (outside Dushanbe) or the hippodrome at Shymkent in Kazakhstan.

sports (see above and p275), a favourite Kazakh pastime is *aitys*, which involves two people boasting about their own town, region or clan while running down the other's, in verses full of puns and allusions to Kazakh culture. The person who fails to find a witty comeback loses.

Kazakhs make up 56% of Kazakhstan, Tajiks 65% of Tajikistan, Kyrgyz 66% of Kyrgyzstan, Uzbeks 80% of Uzbekistan and Turkmen 85% of Turkmenistan.

Kazakhs adhere rather loosely to Islam. Reasons for this include the Kazakhs' location on the fringe of the Muslim world and their traditionally nomadic lifestyle, which never sat well with central religious authority. Their earliest contacts with the religion, from the 16th century, came courtesy of wandering Sufi dervishes or ascetics. Many were not converted until the 19th century, and shamanism apparently coexisted with Islam even after conversion.

Kazakh women appear the most confident and least restricted by tradition in Central Asia. All this is despite the lingering custom of wife stealing, whereby a man may simply kidnap a woman he wants to marry (often with some collusion, it must be said), leaving the parents with no option but to negotiate the *kalym* (bride price).

The eight or so million Kazakhs have only recently become a majority in 'their' country, Kazakhstan.

## KYRGYZ

The name Kyrgyz is one of the oldest recorded ethnic names in Asia, going back to the 2nd century BC in Chinese sources. At that time the ancestors of the modern Kyrgyz are said to have lived in the upper Yenisey Basin (Ene-Sai, or Yenisey, means 'Mother River' in Kyrgyz) in Siberia. They migrated to the mountains of what is now Kyrgyzstan from the 10th to 15th centuries, some fleeing wars and some arriving in the ranks of Mongol armies.

**KYRGYZ**

Kyrgyzstan: three million

Tajikistan: 300,000

Uzbekistan: 180,000

China: 143,000

Afghanistan: 3000

Many Kyrgyz derive their name from *kyrk kyz*, which means '40 girls' and goes along with legends of 40 original clan mothers. Today, ties to such clans as the Bugu (the largest clan), Salto (around Bishkek), Adigine (around Osh) and Sary-Bagysh remain relevant and politicised. Clans are divided into two federations, the Otuz Uul (30 Sons) of the north and the Ich Kilik of southern Kyrgyzstan. The southern and northern halves of the country remain culturally, ethnically and politically divided.

During special events older Kyrgyz women may wear a large white wimple-like turban (known as an *elechek*) with the number of windings indicating her status. Kyrgyz men wear a white, embroidered, tasselled (and slightly silly-looking) felt cap called an *ak kalpak*. In winter, older men wear a long sheepskin coat and a round fur-trimmed hat called a *tebbetey*.

Traditions such as the *Manas* epic (see p275), horseback sports and eagle hunting remain important cultural denominators.

**TAJIKS**

Tajikistan: 4.4 million

Afghanistan: 3.5 million

Uzbekistan: 630,000

Kazakhstan: 100,000

China: 33,000

## TAJIKS

With their Mediterranean features and the occasional green-eyed redhead, Tajiks like to tell visitors that their land was once visited by Alexander the Great and his troops, who are known to have taken local brides. Whether that blood is still visible or not, the Tajiks are in fact descended from an ancient Indo-European people, the Aryans, making them relatives of present-day Iranians. The term 'Tajik' is a modern invention. Before the 20th century, *taj* was merely a term denoting a Persian speaker (all other Central Asian peoples speak Turkic languages).

Tracing their history back to the Samanids, Bactrians and Sogdians, Tajiks consider themselves to be the oldest ethnic group in Central Asia and one that predates the arrival of the Turkic peoples. Some Tajik nationalists have even demanded that Uzbekistan 'give back' Samarkand and Bukhara, as these cities were long-time centres of Persian culture.

There are in fact many Tajik subdivisions and clans (such as the Kulyabis and Khojandis), which is one reason why the country descended into civil war after the fall of the USSR.

Most Tajiks are Sunni Muslims, but Pamiri Tajiks of the Gorno-Badakhshan region belong to the Ismaili sect of Shiite Islam, and therefore have no formal mosques.

Badakhshani or Pamir Tajik (sometimes called mountain Tajiks) are a quite distinct group, speaking a mix of languages quite distinct from Tajik and following a different branch of Islam. Most Badakhshani define themselves primarily according to their valley (Shugni, Rushani, Yazgulami, Wakhi and Ishkashimi), then as Pamiris, and finally as Tajiks.

Traditional Tajik dress for men includes a heavy, quilted coat *(chapan)*, tied with a sash that also secures a sheathed dagger, and a black embroidered cap *(tupi)*, which is similar to the Uzbek *doppilar*. Tajik women could almost be identified in the dark, with their long, psychedelically coloured dresses *(kurta)*, matching headscarves *(rumol)*, striped trousers worn under the dress *(izor)* and bright slippers.

There are around 3.5 million Tajiks in Afghanistan and around 33,000 Sarikol and Wakhi Tajiks in China's Tashkurgan Tajik Autonomous County. Wakhi Tajiks also live in northern Pakistan.

**TURKMEN**

Turkmenistan: 3.6 million

Iran: one million

Afghanistan: 650,000

## TURKMEN

Legend has it that all Turkmen are descended from the fabled Oghuz Khan or from the warriors who rallied into clans around his 24 grandsons. Most historians believe that they were displaced nomadic horse-breeding clans who in the 10th century drifted into the oases around the Karakum desert (and into Persia, Syria and Anatolia) from the foothills of the Altay Mountains in the wake of the Seljuq Turks.

Turkmen men are easily recognisable in their huge, shaggy sheepskin hats *(telpek)*, either white (for special occasions) or black with thick ringlets resembling dreadlocks, worn year-round on top of a skullcap, even on the hottest days. As one Turkmen explained it, they'd rather suffer the heat of their own heads than that of the sun. Traditional dress consists of baggy trousers tucked into knee-length boots, and white shirts under the knee-length *khalat*, a cherry red cotton jacket. Older men wear a long, belted coat.

Turkmen women wear heavy, ankle-length velvet or silk dresses, the favourite colours being wine reds and maroons, with colourful trousers underneath. A woman's hair is always tied back and concealed under a colourful scarf. Older women often wear a *khalat* thrown over their heads as protection from the sun's rays.

Turkmenistan's population is now 85% Turkmen, giving it the highest proportion of the titular nationality of any Central Asian republic.

The Turkmen shared the nomad's affinity for Sufism, which is strongly represented in Turkmenistan alongside the cult of sheikhs (holy men), amulets, shrines and pilgrimage. The Turkmen language (also called Turkmen) is closest to Azeri. Interestingly, there was a Turkmen literary language as early as the mid-18th century.

## UZBEKS

The Uzbek khans, Islamised descendants of Jenghiz Khan, left their home in southern Siberia in search of conquest, establishing themselves in what is now Uzbekistan by the 15th century, clashing and then mixing with the Timurids. The Uzbek Shaybanid dynasty oversaw the transition from nomad to settler, although the original Mongol clan identities (such as the Kipchak, Mangits and Karluks) remain.

**UZBEKS**

Uzbekistan: 18 million

Tajikistan: 1.6 million

Afghanistan: 1.3 million

Kyrgyzstan: 690,000

Kazakhstan: 334,000

Turkmenistan: 396,000

China: 14,700

Uzbek neighbourhoods *(mahalla)* and villages *(kishlak)* are coherent and solid, both physically and socially. Houses are built behind high walls, sometimes with handsome gates.

Uzbek men traditionally wear long quilted coats tied by a bright-coloured sash. Nearly all wear the *dopy* or *doppilar*, a black, four-sided skullcap embroidered in white. In winter, older men wear a furry *telpek*. Uzbek women are fond of dresses in sparkly, brightly coloured cloth *(ikat)*, often as a knee-length gown with trousers of the same material underneath. One or two braids worn in the hair indicate that a woman is married; more mean that she is single. Eyebrows that grow together over the bridge of the nose are considered attractive and are often supplemented with pencil for the right effect. Both sexes flash lots of gold teeth.

There are around 1.3 million Uzbeks in northern Afghanistan.

Check out http://www.oxuscom.com/Uzbeks.pdf for more information on the Uzbek people.

## SLAVS

Russians and Ukrainians have settled in Central Asia in several waves, the first in the 19th century with colonisation, and the latest in the 1950s during the Virgin Lands campaign. Numerous villages in remoter parts of Central Asia, with names such as Orlovka or Alexandrovka, were founded by the early settlers and are still inhabited by their descendants.

Many Slavs, feeling deeply aggrieved as political and administrative power devolves to 'local' people, have emigrated to Russia and the Ukraine. At the height of the migration more than 280,000 Russians left Kazakhstan and

### HOLY SMOKE

In markets, stations and parks all over Central Asia you'll see gypsy women and children asking for a few coins to wave their pans of burning herbs around you or the premises. The herb is called *isriq* in Uzbek, and the smoke is said to be good medicine against colds and flu (and the evil eye), and a cheap alternative to scarce medicines. Some people also burn it when they move into a new home.

### BODY LANGUAGE

A heartfelt handshake between Central Asian men is a gesture of great warmth, elegance and beauty. Many Central Asian men also place their right hand on the heart and bow or incline the head slightly, a highly addictive gesture that you may find yourself echoing quite naturally.

Good friends throughout the region shake hands by gently placing their hands, thumbs up, in between another's. There's no grabbing or Western-style firmness, just a light touch. Sometimes a good friend will use his right hand to pat the other's. If you are in a room full of strangers it's polite to go around the room shaking hands with everyone. Don't be offended if someone offers you his wrist if his hands are dirty. Some say the custom originates from the need to prove that you come unarmed as a friend.

Women don't usually shake hands but touch each others' shoulders with right hands and slightly stroke them. Younger women in particular will often kiss an elder woman on the cheek as a sign of respect.

200,000 left Tajikistan in a single year, most of them well-educated professionals. Some have returned, either disillusioned with life in the motherland or reaffirmed in the knowledge that Central Asia is their home, like it or not.

## OTHER PEOPLES

Dungans are Muslim Chinese who first moved across the border in 1882, mainly to Kazakhstan and Kyrgyzstan, to escape persecution after failed Muslim rebellions. Few still speak Chinese, though their cuisine remains distinctive.

You'll come across the occasional village in Central Asia with a German name, such as Rotfront in Kyrgyzstan, the legacy of forced German immigration.

Over half-a-million Koreans arrived in Central Asia as deportees in WWII. They have preserved little of their traditional culture. They typically farm vegetables and sell their pickled salads in many bazaars.

A further half-a-million Germans were deported in WWII from their age-old home in the Volga region, or came as settlers (some of them Mennonites) in the late 19th century. Most have since departed to Germany but pockets remain. Likewise, Jews, an important part of Bukharan commerce since the 9th century, have mostly already made for Israel (and Queens, New York).

Meskhetian Turks have groups in the Fergana (the largest concentration), Chuy and Ili Valleys.

Karakalpaks occupy their own republic in northwest Uzbekistan and have cultural and linguistic ties with Kazakhs, Uzbeks and Kyrgyz (see p258).

Kurds are another WWII-era addition to the melting pot, with many living in Kazakhstan. Estimates of their numbers in Central Asia range from 150,000 to over a million.

Bukhara's once famous community of Jews have largely left the region for a new life in Israel, though the chief rabbi of Central Asia remains in Bukhara – see p237.

It is estimated that there are half-a-million Uyghurs in the former Soviet Central Asian republics (having moved there from Xinjiang after heavy Chinese persecution in the late 19th century).

You may see colourfully dressed South Asian–looking women and children begging or working as fortune-tellers. These are Central Asian gypsies, called *luli (chuki),* who number around 30,000, speak Tajik and originate from areas around Samarkand, southern Tajikistan and Turkmenistan.

# DAILY LIFE

It's been a social rollercoaster in Central Asia: the overall birth rate is down, deaths from all causes are up, economies have plummeted, crime has skyrocketed, life expectancies have dropped and migration (most especially emigration) is on the rise. Many older Central Asians lost their social and cultural bearings with the fall of the Soviet Union. Health levels are plum-

**DOS & DON'TS**

- Dress codes vary throughout Central Asia. The main place where you should dress conservatively is Uzbekistan's Fergana Valley (see p214). Western-style clothes are acceptable in the capital cities and in large towns such as Samarkand, which see a lot of tourist traffic.
- Working mosques are closed to women and often to non-Muslim men, though men may occasionally be invited in. When visiting a mosque, always take your shoes off at the door, and make sure your feet or socks are clean. It is polite to refer to the Prophet Mohammed as such, rather than by his name alone. Never walk in front of someone praying to Mecca.
- When you visit someone's home, take your shoes off at the door unless you are told not to. You will often find a pair of undersized flip-flops waiting for you at the door. (Traditional Central Asian footwear consists of overshoes, which can be taken off without removing the *massi,* soft leather under-boots.) Avoid stepping on any carpet if you have your shoes on. See p87 for tips on food etiquette.
- Central Asian society devotes much respect to its elderly, known as *aksakals* (white beards). Always make an effort to shake hands with an elder. Younger men give up their seats to *aksakals,* and foreigners should certainly offer their place in a crowded chaikhana (teahouse). Some Central Asians address elders with a shortened form of the elder's name, adding the suffix 'ke'. Thus Abkhan becomes Abeke, Nursultan becomes Nureke, and so on.

meting, drug addiction is up and alcoholism has acquired the proportions of a national tragedy.

But it's not all bad news. Traditional life is reasserting itself in today's economic vacuum and tourism projects are encouraging traditional crafts, sports and music. Communities remain strong and notions of hospitality remain instinctual despite the economic hardships. After 15 years of uncertainty, most people have started to find their way in the new order.

Kazakhs and Kyrgyz share many customs and have similar languages, and in a sense they are simply the steppe (Kazakh) and mountain (Kyrgyz) variants of the same people.

## TRADITIONAL CULTURE

In Islam, a guest – Muslim or not – has a position of honour not very well understood in the West. If someone visits you and you don't have much to offer, as a Christian you'd be urged to share what you had; as a Muslim you're urged to give it all away. Guests are to be treated with absolute selflessness.

For a visitor to a Muslim country, even one as casual about Islam as Kazakhstan or Kyrgyzstan, this is a constant source of pleasure, temptation and sometimes embarrassment. The majority of Central Asians, especially rural ones, have little to offer but their hospitality, and a casual guest could drain a host's resources and never know it. And yet to refuse such an invitation (or to offer to bring food or to help with the cost) would almost certainly be a grave insult.

Uzbeks resisted Russification and have emerged from Soviet rule with a strong sense of identification and their rich heritage.

All you can do is enjoy it, honour their customs as best you can, and take yourself courteously out of the picture before you become a burden. If for some reason you do want to decline, couch your refusal in gracious and diplomatic terms, allowing the would-be host to save face. As an example, if you are offered bread, you should at least taste a little piece before taking your leave.

If you are really lucky you might be invited to a *toi* (celebration) such as a *kelin toi* (wedding celebration), a *beshik toi* (nine days after the birth of a child), or a *sunnat toi* (circumcision party). Other celebrations are held to mark the birth, name giving and first haircut of a child.

# Religion

With the exception of rapidly shrinking communities of Jews and Russian Orthodox Christians, small minorities of Roman Catholics, Baptists and evangelical Lutherans, and a few Buddhists among the Koreans of the Fergana Valley and Kyrgyzstan, nearly everyone from the Caspian Sea to Kashgar is Muslim, at least in principle. The years since independence have seen a resurgence of a faith that is only beginning to recover from 70 years of Soviet-era 'militant atheism'.

The word Islam translates loosely from Arabic as 'the peace that comes from total surrender to God'.

## ISLAM

### History & Schisms

In AD 612, the Prophet Mohammed, then a wealthy Arab of Mecca in present-day Saudi Arabia, began preaching a new religious philosophy, Islam, based on revelations from Allah (Islam's name for God). Islam incorporated elements of Judaism, Christianity and other faiths (eg heaven and hell, a creation story much like the Garden of Eden, stories similar to Noah's Ark), but treated their prophets simply as forerunners of the Prophet Mohammed. These revelations were eventually to be compiled into Islam's holiest book, the Quran.

The world's oldest Quran, the Osman Quran (Othman Koran), is kept in a library museum at the Khast Imom Mosque in Tashkent (see p200). The Quran was written just 19 years after the death of the Prophet Mohammed and was later brought to Central Asia by Timur (Tamerlane).

In 622 the Prophet Mohammed and his followers were forced to flee to Medina due to religious persecution (the Islamic calendar counts its years from this flight, known as Hejira). There he built a political base and an army, taking Mecca in 630 and eventually overrunning Arabia. The militancy of the faith meshed nicely with a latent Arab nationalism and within a century Islam reached from Spain to Central Asia.

Succession disputes after the Prophet's death soon split the community. When the fourth caliph, the Prophet's son-in-law Ali, was assassinated in 661, his followers and descendants became the founders of the Shiite sect. Others accepted as caliph the governor of Syria, a brother-in-law of the Prophet, and this line has become the modern-day orthodox Sunni sect. In 680 a chance for reconciliation was lost when Ali's surviving son Husain and most of his male relatives were killed at Karbala in Iraq by Sunni partisans.

About 80% of all Central Asians are Muslim, nearly all of them Sunni (and indeed nearly all of the Hanafi school, one of Sunnism's four main schools of religious law). The main exception is a tightly knit community of Ismailis in the remote western Pamirs of Gorno-Badakhshan in eastern Tajikistan (see p377).

To learn more about Ismailism, try the scholarly *Short History of the Ismailis: Traditions of a Muslim Community*, or *The Isma'ilis: Their History and Doctrines*, both by Farhad Daftary.

A small but increasingly influential community of another Sunni school, the ascetic, fundamentalist Wahhabi, are found mainly in Uzbekistan's Fergana Valley.

### Practice

Devout Muslims express their faith through the five pillars of Islam (see the boxed text, opposite)

Devout Sunnis pray at prescribed times: before sunrise, just after high noon, in the late afternoon, just after sunset and before retiring. Prayers are preceded if possible by washing, at least of the hands, face and feet. For Ismailis the style of prayer is a personal matter (eg there is no prostration), the mosque is replaced by a community shrine or meditation room, and women are less excluded.

Just before fixed prayers a muezzin calls the Sunni and Shiite faithful, traditionally from a minaret, nowadays often through a loudspeaker. Islam

**FIVE PILLARS OF ISLAM**

- The creed that 'There is only one god, Allah, and Mohammed is his prophet'
- Prayer, five times a day, prostrating towards the holy city of Mecca, in a mosque (for men only) when possible, but at least on Friday, the Muslim holy day
- Dawn-to-dusk fasting during Ramadan
- Making the haj (pilgrimage to Mecca) at least once in one's life (many of those who have done so can be identified by their white skullcaps)
- Alms giving, in the form of the *zakat*, an obligatory 2.5% tax

has no ordained priesthood, but mullahs (scholars, teachers or religious leaders) are trained in theology, respected as interpreters of scripture, and are sometimes quite influential in conservative rural areas.

The Quran is considered above criticism: it is the word of God as spoken to his Prophet Mohammed. It is supplemented by various traditions such as the Hadith, the collected acts and sayings of the Prophet Mohammed. In its fullest sense Islam is an entire way of life, with guidelines for doing nearly everything, from preparing and eating food to banking.

The melancholy sounding Arabic azan (call to prayer) translates roughly as 'God is most great. There is no god but Allah. Mohammed is God's messenger. Come to prayer, come to security. God is most great.'

## Islam in Central Asia

Islam first appeared in Central Asia with Arab invaders in the 7th and 8th centuries, though it was mostly itinerant Sufi missionaries who converted the region over the subsequent centuries (see Sufism, below).

Islam never was a potent force in the former nomadic societies of the Turkmen, Kazakhs and Kyrgyz, and still isn't. Islam's appeal for nomadic rulers was as much as an organisational and political tool as a collection of moral precepts. The nomad's customary law, known as *adat*, was always more important than Islamic sharia.

The Central Asian brand of Islam is also riddled with pre-Islamic influences – just go to any important holy site and notice the kissing, rubbing and circumambulation of venerated objects, women crawling under holy stones to boost their fertility, the shamanic 'wishing trees' tied with bits of coloured rag, the cult of Pirs (holy men) and the Mongol-style poles with horse-hair tassels set over the graves of revered figures. Candles and flames are often burned at shrines and graves, and both the Tajiks and Turkmen jump over a fire during wedding celebrations or the Qurban (Eid al-Azha) festival, traditions that hark back to Zoroastrian times. The Turkmen place particular stock in amulets and charms. At Konye-Urgench Turkmen women even roll en masse down a hillside in an age-old fertility rite.

The percentage of practising Muslims ranges from 47% in Kazakhstan to 75% in Kyrgyzstan, 85% in Tajikistan, 88% in Uzbekistan and 89% in Turkmenistan.

There is also a significant blurring between religious and national characteristics. The majority of Central Asians, although interested in Islam as a common denominator, seem quite happy to toast your health with a shot of vodka.

Some archaeologists believe that the Bronze Age site of Gonur Depe (see p428) was the birthplace of Zoroastrianism.

## Sufism

The original Sufis were simply purists, unhappy with the worldliness of the early caliphates and seeking knowledge of God through direct personal experience, under the guidance of a teacher or master, variously called a sheikh, Pir, *ishan*, *murshid* or *ustad*. There never was a single Sufi movement; there are manifestations within all branches of Islam. For many adherents music, dance or poetry were routes to trance, revelation and direct union with God. Secret recitations, known as *zikr*, and an annual 40-day retreat, known as the *chilla,* remain cornerstones of Sufic practice. This mystical side of Islam parallels similar traditions in other faiths.

Before the arrival of Islam, Central Asia sheltered strong pockets of Zoroastrianism, Manichaeism and Nestorian Christianity, as well as a long tradition of Buddhism. In the 8th century there were even Nestorian bishoprics in Samarkand and Merv.

Sufis were singularly successful as missionaries, perhaps because of their tolerance of other creeds. It was largely Sufis, not Arab armies, who planted Islam firmly in Central Asia and the subcontinent. The personal focus of Sufism was most compatible with the nomadic lifestyle of the Kazakh and Kyrgyz in particular. Although abhorred nowadays in the orthodox Islamic states of Iran and Saudi Arabia, Sufism is in a quiet way dominant in Central Asia. Most shrines you'll see are devoted to one Sufi teacher or another.

When Islam was itself threatened by invaders (eg the Crusaders), Sufis assumed the role of defenders of the faith, and Sufism became a mass movement of regimented *tariqas* (brotherhoods), based around certain holy places, often the tombs of the *tariqas'* founders. Clandestine, anti-communist *tariqas* helped Islam weather the Soviet period, and the KGB and its predecessors never seemed able to infiltrate.

The moderate, non-elitist Naqshbandiya *tariqa* was the most important in Soviet times, and probably still is. Founded in Bukhara in the 14th century, much of its influence in Central Asia perhaps comes from the high profile of Naqshbandi fighters in two centuries of revolts against the Russians in the Caucasus. In 1944 large Chechen and Ingush communities were deported to Siberia and Kazakhstan. When, after Stalin's death, the survivors were permitted to return to their homeland, they left behind several well-organised Sufi groups in Central Asia. A number of well-known 1930s *basmachi* (Muslim guerrilla fighters) leaders were Naqshbandis.

The Bakhautdin Naqshband Mausoleum in Bukhara is Central Asia's most important Sufi shrine.

Another important Sufi sect in Central Asia is the Qadiriya, founded by a teacher from the Caspian region. Others are the Kubra (founded in Khorezm, see p432) and Yasauia (founded in the town of Turkistan in Kazakhstan). All these were founded in the 12th century.

## The Soviet Era

The Soviet regime long distrusted Islam because of its potential for coherent resistance, both domestically and internationally. Three of the five pillars of Islam (the fast of Ramadan, the haj and the zakat) were outlawed in the 1920s. Polygamy, the wearing of the *paranja* (veil), and the Arabic script in which the Quran is written were forbidden. Clerical (Christian, Jewish and Buddhist as well as Muslim) land and property were seized. Medressas and other religious schools were closed down. Islam's judicial power was curbed with the dismantling of traditional sharia courts (which were based on Quranic law).

By 1940, after Stalin's attacks on religion, only 1000 of Central Asia's 30,000 mosques remained standing and all 14,500 Islamic schools were shut.

From 1932 to 1936 Stalin mounted a concerted antireligious campaign in Central Asia, a 'Movement of the Godless', in which mosques were closed and destroyed, and mullahs arrested and executed as saboteurs or spies. By the early 1940s only 2000 of its 47,000 mullahs remained alive. Control of the surviving places of worship and teaching was given to the Union of Atheists, which transformed most of them into museums, dance halls, warehouses or factories.

During WWII things improved marginally as Moscow sought domestic and international Muslim support for the war effort. In 1943 four Muslim Religious Boards or 'spiritual directorates', each with a mufti (spiritual leader), were founded as administration units for Soviet Muslims, including one in Tashkent for all of Central Asia (in 1990 one was established for Kazakhstan). Some mosques were reopened and a handful of carefully screened religious leaders were allowed to make the haj in 1947.

But beneath the surface little changed. Any religious activity outside the official mosques was strictly forbidden. By the early 1960s, under Khrushchev's 'back to Lenin' policies, another 1000 mosques were shut. By the beginning of the Gorbachev era, the number of mosques in Central Asia was down to between 150 and 250, and only two medressas were open – Mir-i-Arab in Bukhara (p241) and the Imam Ismail al-Bukhari Islamic Institute in Tashkent (p200).

Perhaps the most amazing thing though, after 70 years of concerted Soviet repression, is that so much faith remains intact. Credit for any continuity from pre-Soviet times goes largely to 'underground Islam', in the form of the clandestine Sufi brotherhoods (and brotherhoods they were, being essentially men-only), which preserved some practices and education – and grew in power and influence in Central Asia as a result.

## Islam Today

Since independence, Central Asia has seen a resurgence of Islam, and mosques and medressas have sprouted like mushrooms across the region, often financed with Saudi or Iranian money. Even in more conservative Uzbekistan and Tajikistan, those new mosques are as much political as religious statements and the rise of Islam has as much to do with the search for a Central Asian identity as it does with a rise in religious fervour.

Most Central Asians are torn between the Soviet secularism of the recent past and the region's deeper historical ties to Muslim world, but few have a very deep knowledge of Islam. Only the Fergana Valley regions of Uzbekistan and southern Kyrgyzstan can be considered strongly Muslim, and only here do women commonly wear the *hejab* (headscarf).

All the Central Asian governments have taken great care to keep strict tabs on Islam. Only state-approved imams and state-registered mosques are allowed to operate in most republics. Tajikistan's Islamic Revival Party is the only Islamist party in the region not to be outlawed.

Central Asia has experienced Islamic extremism, in the form of the Islamic Movement of Uzbekistan, which launched a series of armed raids and kidnappings in 1999–2001 in an attempt to establish an Islamic state in Uzbekistan. However, the movement largely disappeared when its Al-Qaeda–supplied bases in Afghanistan were destroyed and its enigmatic leader Juma Namangani killed.

Under the cloak of the 'War on Terror', the Uzbek government has arrested thousands of Muslims as 'extremists', most of them from the Fergana Valley. Some, but not all, are members of the peaceful but radical organisation Hizb-ut-Tahrir (Movement of Liberation), which hopes to establish a global Islamic caliphate and has support across the region.

Turkmenistan also keeps tight controls on Islam. Turkmen mosques have quotations from former President Niyazov's book the *Ruhnama* engraved next to quotations from the Quran. The former chief cleric of Turkmenistan was charged with treason and sentenced 22 years in prison after refusing to accept the Turkmen president as a messenger of God.

With the old communist ideals discredited, democracy suppressed and economic options stagnating, the fear is that radical Islam will provide an alluring alternative for a Central Asian youth left with few remaining options.

www.muslimuzbekistan.com for pro-Islam website on religious and human-rights abuses in Uzbekistan

*Jihad: The Rise of Militant Islam in Central Asia,* by Ahmed Rashid, is an incisive journalistic review of how and why Islamic militant groups, such as the Islamic Movement of Uzbekistan (IMU) and Hizb ut-Tahrir (HUT), rose in the Fergana Valley from the ashes of the Soviet Union.

# Arts

Set astride millennia-old trade and migration routes, Central Asia has long blended and fused artistic traditions from the Turkic and Persian, Islamic and secular, settled and nomadic worlds to create an indigenous Central Asian aesthetic.

*Uzbekistan: Heirs to the Silk Road,* by Johannes Kalter and Margareta Pavaloi, is a beautiful hardback look at the art of the region.

Whether it be the architectural glories of Samarkand, the other-worldly performance of a Kyrgyz bard, the visual splendour of a Turkmen carpet or the exotic musical sounds blasting from your taxi driver's stereo, artistic expression lies at the heart of the Central Asian identity and will follow you on your travels through the region.

## ARCHITECTURE

Central Asia's most impressive surviving artistic heritage is its architecture. Some of the world's most audacious and beautiful Islamic buildings grace the cities of Bukhara, Khiva and especially Samarkand; all in Uzbekistan. Few sights evoke the region better than the swell of a turquoise dome, a ruined desert citadel or a minaret framed black against a blazing sunset.

Thanks in the main to the destructive urges of Jenghiz Khan, virtually nothing has survived from the pre-Islamic era or the first centuries of Arab rule. The Bolsheviks further destroyed many of Central Asia's religious buildings, except those of architectural or historical value.

*Monuments of Central Asia: A Guide to the Archaeology, Art and Architecture of Turkestan,* by Edgar Knobloch, is an excellent overview of the region's architectural heritage.

### Early Influences

Central Asian architecture has its roots in the Parthian, Kushan and Graeco-Bactrian desert citadels, whose structure was defined by the demands of trade, security and water. Iranian, Greek and Indian art blended in the 2000-year-old sites of Topraq-Qala, Nissa and Termiz, among others.

Environmental constraints naturally defined building construction. The lack of wood and stone forced Central Asian architects to turn to brickwork as the cornerstone of their designs. Tall portals, built to face and catch the prevailing winds, looked fabulous but also had a cooling effect in the heat of summer. The influence of a nomadic lifestyle is particularly relevant in Khiva, where you can still see the brick bases built to house the wintertime yurts of the khans.

Several important technological advances spurred the development of architectural arts, principally that of fired brick in the 10th century, coloured tilework in the 12th century and polychrome tilework in the 14th century.

Without the seemingly insignificant squinch (the corner bracketing that enables the transition from a square to an eight-, then 16-sided platform), the development of the monumental dome would have stalled. It was this tiny technology that underpinned the breathtaking domes of the Timurid era.

### Timurid Architecture

For an in-depth look at the Timurid architecture of Samarkand try www.oxuscom.com/timursam.htm.

Most of the monumental architecture standing today dates from the time of the Timurids (14th to 15th centuries); rulers who combined barbaric savagery with artistic sophistication. During his campaigns of terror Timur (Tamerlane) forcibly relocated artisans, from Beijing to Baghdad, to Central Asia, resulting in a splendid fusion of styles in textiles, painting, architecture and metal arts.

The Timurid's architectural trademark is the beautiful, often ribbed and elongated, azure-blue dome. Other signature Timurid traits include the

### ARCHITECTURAL HIGHLIGHTS

Merv and Konye-Urgench (both in Turkmenistan), Khiva's Ichon-Qala, the old towns of Bukhara, Samarkand and Shakhrisabz (all in Uzbekistan) and Turkistan's Kozha Akhmed Yasaui Mausoleum (in Kazakhstan) are all Unesco World Heritage sites. These archaeological sites have been included in the list of the 100 most endangered sites in the world: Merv (2000 and 2002) and Nissa (2004), both in Turkmenistan, and Bukhara's Abdul Aziz Khan Medressa (2000) in Uzbekistan.

The following are our picks of the architectural highlights of Central Asia.

**Ismail Samani Mausoleum** (900-1000) In Bukhara: mesmerising brickwork (p242).
**Kalon Minaret** (1127) In Bukhara: Central Asia's most impressive minaret, 48m high (p241).
**Sultan Sanjar Mausoleum** (1157) In Merv: huge double-domed Seljuq monument (p427).
**Shah-i-Zinda** (1300-1400) In Samarkand: features Central Asia's most stunning and varied tilework (p226).
**Bibi-Khanym Mosque** (1399-1404) In Samarkand: Timur's intended masterpiece, so colossal that it collapsed as soon as it was finished (p226).
**Guri Amir Mausoleum** (1404) In Samarkand: exquisite ribbed dome, sheltering the tomb of Timur (p226).
**Ak-Saray Palace** (1400-50) In Shakhrisabz: tantalising remains of Timur's once-opulent palace (p233).
**Registan** (1400-1600) In Samarkand: epic ensemble of medressas; the Sher Dor (1636) flaunts Islamic tradition by depicting two lions chasing deer, looked down upon by a Mongol-faced sun (p225).
**Lyabi-Hauz** (1600) In Bukhara: featuring a pool, *khanaka* (pilgrim resthouse) and medressa (p240).
**Char Minar** (1807) In Bukhara: quirky ex-gateway, resembling a chair thrust upside down in the ground (p243).
**Islom-Huja Minaret** (Islam Khoja; 1910) In Khiva: reckoned by Central Asian archaeological specialist Edgar Knobloch to be the last notable architectural achievement of the Islamic era in Central Asia; we'd expand that to say the last notable architectural achievement in Central Asia, period (p255).

tendency towards ensemble design, the monumental *pishtak* (arched entrance portal) flanked by tapering minarets, and exuberant, multicoloured tilework, all evident in the quintessential Timurid showpiece, the Registan Square in Samarkand (see p225).

## Architectural Design

Khiva and Bukhara reveal the most about traditional urban structure, highlighting the distinction between *ark* (fortified citadel), *shahristan* (inner city with wealthy residential neighbourhoods, bazaars and city wall) and outlying *rabad* (suburbs), that has formed the structure of settlements since the first Central Asian towns appeared 4000 years ago. A second outer city wall surrounded most cities, protecting against desert storms and brigands.

The best surviving caravanserai in Central Asia is the Tash Rabat (Stone Caravanserai), high in the pastures of central Kyrgyzstan, near the border with China (see p325).

Apart from the Islamic monuments mentioned below, secular architecture includes palaces (such as the Tosh-Khovli in Khiva), *ark* or *bala hissar* (forts), *hammam* (multidomed bathhouses), *rabat* (caravanserais), *tim* (shopping arcades), *tok* (covered crossroad bazaars) and the local *hauz* (reservoirs) that supplied the city with its drinking water.

### MOSQUES

Islam dominates Central Asian architecture. *Masjid* (mosques) trace their design back to the house of the Prophet Mohammed, though later designs vary considerably. Common to most is the use of the portal, which leads into a colonnaded space and a covered area for prayer. The entrance of many Central Asian mosques, such as the Bolo-Hauz Mosque in Bukhara, have, instead, a flat, brightly painted roof, supported by carved wooden columns. Other mosques, such as the Juma Mosque in Khiva, are hypostyle, that is with a roofed space, divided by many pillars.

Whether the place of worship is a *guzar* (local mosque), serving the local community, a *jami masjid* (Friday mosque), built to hold the entire city congregation once a week, or a *namazgokh* (festival mosque), the focal point is always the mihrab, a niche that indicates the direction of Mecca. Central Asia's largest modern mosque is at Gypjak in Turkmenistan (see p417).

#### MEDRESSAS

These are Islamic colleges, normally two-storeys high and set around a cloistered central courtyard, punctuated with *aiwan* (arched portals) on four sides. Rows of little doors in the interior façades lead into *hujras* (cell-like living quarters for students and teachers) or *khanakas* (prayer cells or entire buildings) for the ascetic wandering dervishes who stayed there. Most medressas are fronted by monumental portals. On either side of the entrance you will normally find a *darskhana* (lecture room) to the left, and mosque to the right.

The niches in the medressas' front walls were once used as shopkeepers' stalls.

#### MAUSOLEUMS

The *mazar* (mausoleum) has been popular for millennia, either built by rulers to ensure their own immortality or to commemorate holy men. Most consist of a *ziaratkhana* (prayer room), set under a domed cupola. The actual tomb may be housed in a central hall, or underground in a side *gurkhana*. Popular tombs offer lodging, washrooms and kitchens for visiting pilgrims. Tombs vary in design from the classic domed cupola style or the pyramid-shaped, tentlike designs of Konye-Urgench (p432) to whole streets of tombs as found at the glorious Shah-i-Zinda in Samarkand (p226).

*The Arts and Crafts of Turkestan*, by Johannes Kalter, is a detailed, beautifully illustrated historical guide to the nomadic dwellings, clothing, jewellery and other 'applied art' of Central Asia.

#### MINARETS

These tall, tapering towers were designed to summon the faithful during prayer time, so most have internal stairs for the muezzin to climb. They were also used as lookouts to spot invaders, and even, in the case of the Kalon Minaret in Bukhara, as a means of execution. Some minarets (eg at Samarkand's Registan) exist purely for decoration.

### Decoration

Tilework is the most dramatic form of decoration in Central Asia, instilling a light, graceful air into even the most hulking Timurid building. The deep cobalts and turquoise ('colour of the Turks') of Samarkand's domes have moved travellers for centuries. Each of Uzbekistan's historic cities has its own colour; greens are most common in Khorezm, khakis in Bukhara and blues in Samarkand.

Decoration almost always takes the shape of abstract geometric, floral or calligraphic designs, in keeping with the Islamic taboo on the representation of living creatures. Geometric and knot *(girikh)* designs were closely linked to the development of Central Asian science – star designs were a favourite with the astronomer king Ulugbek. Calligraphy is common, either in the square, stylised Kufic script favoured by the Timurids or the more scrolling, often foliated thulth script.

Tiles come in a variety of styles, either stamped, faïence (carved onto wet clay and then fired), polychromatic (painted on and then fired) or jigsaw-style mosaic. Take time also to savour the exquisite details of Central Asia's carved *ghanch* (alabaster), patterned brickwork, and intricately carved and painted wood.

Some of the best examples of Central Asian folk art can be seen at Tashkent's Museum of Applied Arts (p201).

## FOLK ART

Central Asian folk art developed in tune with a nomadic or seminomadic way of life, focusing on transport (horses) and home (yurts). Designs followed the natural beauty of the environment: snow resting on a leaf, the elegance of an ibex horn, the flowers of the steppe. Status and wealth were apparent by the intricacy of a carved door or a richly adorned horse. Yet art was not merely created for pleasure; each item had a practical function in everyday life. From brightly coloured carpets used for sleeping and woven reed mats designed to block the wind, to leather bottles used for carrying *kumys* (fermented mare's milk), many of what are today souvenirs in Kyrgyzstan and Kazakhstan are remnants of a recent nomadic past.

With such emphasis on equestrian culture it is not surprising that horses donned decorative blankets, inlaid wooden saddles, and head and neck adornments. Men hung their wealth on their belts with daggers and sabres in silver sheaths, and embossed leather purses and vessels for drink. Even today the bazaars in Tajikistan and the Fergana Valley are heavy with carved daggers and *pichok (*knives).

Nomads required their wealth to be portable and rich nomadic women wore stupendous jewellery, mostly of silver incorporating semiprecious stones, such as lapis lazuli and carnelian (believed to have magical properties).

To remain portable, furnishings consisted of bright quilts, carpets and *aiyk kap* (woven bags), which were hung on yurt walls for storing plates and clothing. *Kökör* (embossed leather bottles) were used for preparing, transporting and serving *kumys*; these days empty Coca Cola bottles suffice.

Most Central Asian peoples have their own traditional rug or carpet styles. The famous Bukhara rugs – so called because they were mostly sold, not made, in Bukhara – are made largely by the Turkmen. The Kyrgyz specialise in *shyrdaks* (felt rugs with appliquéd coloured panels or pressed wool designs called *ala-kiyiz*); see p276. Kazakhs specialise in *koshma* (multicoloured felt mats).

Uzbeks make silk and cotton wall hangings and coverlets such as the beautiful *suzani (suzan* is Persian for needle). *Suzanis* are made in a variety of sizes and used as table covers, cushions and *ruijo* (a bridal bedspread), and thus were important for the bride's dowry. Generally using floral or celestial motifs (depictions of people and animals are against Muslim beliefs) an average *suzani* requires about two years to complete. Possibly the most accessible Kazakh textile souvenir is a *tus-kiiz* (*tush-kiyiz* in Kyrgyzstan), a colourful wall hanging made of cotton and silk.

The colourful psychedelic tie-dyed silks known as *ikat* or *khanatlas* are popular throughout the region. Take a close-up tour of how the cloth is made at the Yodgorlik Silk Factory in Margilon (Margilan) (p220). For more on silk production, see p220.

If you are into carpets, don't miss a visit to Ashgabat's Carpet Museum (see p410), which also features the world's largest carpet.

Central Asian film isn't high profile, but two films well worth checking out are *Luna Papa,* by Tajikistan's Bakhtyar Khudojnazarov, and *Beshkempir,* by Kyrgyz director Aktan Abdykalykov.

## LITERATURE

The division into Kazakh literature, Tajik literature, Uzbek literature and so on, is a modern one; formerly there was simply literature in Chaghatai Turkic (pioneered by the poet Alisher Navoi) and literature in Persian. With most pre-20th-century poets, scholars and writers bilingual in Uzbek and Tajik, literature in Central Asia belonged to a shared universality of culture.

For example, Abu Abdullah Rudaki, a 10th-century Samanid court poet considered the father of Persian literature, stars in the national pantheons of Afghanistan, Iran and Tajikistan (he is buried in Penjikent) and is also revered by Uzbeks by dint of being born in the Bukhara emirate. Omar Khayam, famed composer of *rubiayyat* poetry, although a native of what is now northeast Iran, also has strong, if indistinct, ties to Tajikistan and to Samarkand where he spent part of his early life at the court of the Seljuq emir.

For a fictional account of Omar Khayam's life, check out Amin Maalouf's imaginative novel *Samarkand*, partially set in Central Asia.

A strong factor in the universal nature of Central Asian literature was that it was popularised not in written form, but orally by itinerant minstrels in the form of songs, poems and stories. Known as *bakshi* or *dastanchi* in Turkmen and Uzbek, *akyn* in Kazakh and Kyrgyz, these storytelling bards earned their living travelling from town to town giving skilled and dramatic recitations of crowd-pleasing verse, tales and epics to audiences gathered in bazaars and chaikhanas. With their rhythms, rhymes and improvisation, these performers share much in common with rap artists in the West (but with fewer women in thongs/g-strings and considerably less bling).

To listen to DJ Andy Kershaw's musical travels through Turkmenistan visit www.bbc.co.uk/radio3/worldmusic/onlocation/turkmen.shtml.

The most famous epic is Kyrgyzstan's *Manas* (p275), said to be the world's longest, and recited by a special category of *akyn* known as *manaschi*, though other epics include the Uzbek *Alpamish* and Turkmen *Gorkut*. Certain bards are folk heroes, regarded as founders of their national literatures, and memorialised in Soviet-era street names (eg Toktogul, Zhambyl and Abay, see p173). Soviet propagandists even used *akyns* to praise Lenin or popularise the latest directive from party central. Bardic competitions are still held in some rural areas, these days with cash prizes.

It was only with the advent of Bolshevik rule that literacy became widespread. Unfortunately, at the same time, much of the region's classical heritage never made it to print because Moscow feared that it might set a flame to latent nationalist sentiments. Instead writers were encouraged to produce novels and plays in line with official Communist Party themes. While a number of Central Asian poets and novelists found acclaim within the Soviet sphere, such as the Tajik, Sadruddin Ayni (1878–1954), and the Uzbeks, Asqad Mukhtar and Abdullah Kodiri, the only native Central Asian authorto garner international recognition has been the Kyrgyz, Chinghiz Aitmatov, who has had novels translated into English and other European languages (see p275). His works have also been adapted for the stage and screen, both in the former USSR and abroad.

The art of the Kyrgyz bards and the classical Uzbek music known as *shash maqam* are both included on Unesco's list of 28 'Masterpieces of the Oral and Intangible Heritage of Humanity'.

One interesting recent work is the exiled Uzbek writer Hamid Ismailov's *The Railway* (2006), a satirical novel that mixes anecdote and fantasy to depict life in the fictional end-of-the-line town of Gilas in Soviet Uzbekistan. The novel was swiftly banned in Uzbekistan.

## MUSIC

Although visual arts and literature succumbed to a stifling Soviet-European influence (which they're presently struggling to shrug off), the music of Central Asia remains closely related to the swirling melodies of Anatolia and Persia. The instruments used are similar to those found in this region; the *rabab* (*rubab*; six-stringed mandolin), *dutar* (two-stringed guitar), *tanbur* (long-necked lute), *dombra/komuz* (two-stringed Kazakh/Kyrgyz guitar), *kamanche* (Persian violin, played like a cello) and *gijak* (upright spiked fiddle), *ney* (flute), *doira* (tambourine/drum) and *chang* (zither). Most groups add the ubiquitous Russian accordion.

Anyone interested in the music of the region should pick up *The Hundred Thousand Fools of Gold: Musical Travels in Central Asia,* by Theodore (Ted) Levin, one of the world's foremost experts on Central Asian music. The book is part travel, part ethnomusicology and comes with a CD of on-site recordings.

In the past the development of music was closely connected with the art of the bards, but these days the traditions are continued by small ensembles of musicians and singers, heavily in demand at weddings and other festivals. In Uzbek and Tajik societies there's a particularly popular form of folk music known as *sozanda,* sung primarily by women accompanied only by percussion instruments such as tablas, bells and castanets. There are also several forms of Central Asian classical music, such as the courtly *shash maqam* (six modes) tradition of Uzbekistan. Central Asia has a strong tradition of the performer-composer, or *bestekar,* the equivalent of the singer-songwriter, who mixed poetry, humour, current affairs and history into music.

One Uzbek group that has successfully mixed Central Asian and Middle Eastern folk melodies and poetry with modern pop and dance influences is Yalla.

### CENTRAL ASIAN DISCOGRAPHY

The following recordings offer a great introduction to Central Asian music and are our personal favourites.

**City of Love** (Real World; www.realworld.co.uk) By Ashkabad, a five-piece Turkmen ensemble. Superb and lilting, with a Mediterranean feel. Recommended.

**Yol Boisin** (Real World; www.realworld.co.uk) By Sevara Nazarkhan. Uzbek songstress given a modern feeling by producer Hector Zazou. In 2003 Nazarkhan played at the Womad festival and supported Peter Gabriel on tour. She won a BBC Radio 3 World Music Award in 2004.

**Rough Guide to the Music of Central Asia** (World Music Network) Excellent introduction to the sounds of the Silk Road, from Tajik rap to Kyrgyz folk melodies. Artists include Munadjat Yulchieva, the Kambarkan Folk Ensemble, Sevara Nazarkhan, Ashkabad, Yulduz Usmanova and Uzbek tanbur player Turgun Alimatov, among others.

**A Haunting Voice** (Network; www.networkmedien.de) By Munadjat Yulchieva, the classical *maqam* Uzbek music star recently nominated for a BBC Radio 3 World Music Award. Alternatively, try *Asie Centrale Traditions Classique* (World Network).

**The Selection Album** (Blue Flame; www.blueflame.com) By Yulduz Usmanova. Career retrospective from the Uzbek pop superstar.

**Secret Museum of Mankind, The Central Asia Ethnic Music Classics: 1925–48** (Yazoo; www.shanachie.com) Twenty-six scratchy but wonderfully fresh field recordings of otherwise lost music.

**The Silk Road – A Musical Caravan** (Smithsonian Folkways; www.folkways.si.edu) 'Imagine if Marco Polo had a tape recorder' runs the cover note for this excellent two-CD collection of traditional recordings by both masters and amateurs, from China to Azerbaijan.

**Music of Central Asia Vol. 1: Mountain Music of Kyrgyzstan** (Smithsonian Folkways; www.folkways.si.edu) Collection of evocative Kyrgyz sounds by Tengir-Too, featuring the *komuz* and jew's harp, with a section from the *Manas*. The other volumes in this series are also worth looking into.

## PAINTING

Rendered in a style that foreshadows that of Persian miniature painting, some splendid friezes were unearthed in the excavations of the Afrosiab palace (6th to 7th centuries), on the outskirts of Samarkand, depicting a colourful caravan led by elephants. Similar Silk Road–era wall frescoes were discovered at Penjikent and Varakhsha, depicting everything from panthers and griffins to royal banqueting scenes.

The Musical Nomad (www.bbc.co.uk/nomad) is an interesting interactive website chronicling a musical journey through the region in 1997.

The Arab invasion of the 8th century put representational art in Central Asia on hold for the better part of 1300 years. Islam prohibited the depiction of the living, so traditional arts developed in the form of calligraphy, combining Islamic script with arabesques, and the carving of doors and screens. Textiles and metalwork took on floral or repetitive, geometric motifs.

Painting and two-dimensional art were only revived under the Soviets who introduced European ideas and set up schools to train local artists in the new fashion. Under Soviet tutelage the pictorial art of Central Asia became a curious hybrid of socialist realism and mock traditionalism – Kyrgyz horsemen riding proudly beside a shiny red tractor, smiling Uzbeks at a chaikhana surrounded by record-breaking cotton harvests. You'll see a good selection of these at most regional museums.

Art lovers should not miss the collection of 'lost' Soviet art at the Savitsky Museum (p259) in remote Nukus.

# Environment

## THE LAND

The Central Asia of this book includes Kazakhstan, which in Soviet parlance was considered a thing apart. It is true that Kazakhstan's enormous territory actually extends westward across the Ural River, the traditional boundary between Europe and Asia, but Kazakhstan still shares many geographic, cultural, ethnic and economic similarities and ties with Central Asia 'proper'.

A quick spin around the territory covered in this book would start on the eastern shores of the oil-rich Caspian Sea. Then dip southeast along the low crest of the Kopet Dag mountains between Turkmenistan and Iran. Follow the Amu-Darya river along the desert border with Afghanistan up along its headstream, the Pyanj, into the high Pamir plateau. Round the eastern nose of the 700m snow peaks of the Tian Shan range; skip northwestward over the Altay Mountains to float down the Irtysh River and then turn west to plod along Kazakhstan's flat, farmed, wooded border with Russia, ending in the basin of the Ural River and the Caspian Sea.

Central Asia, as defined by this book, occupies 4 million sq km, of which almost 70% belongs to Kazakhstan.

The sort of blank which is drawn in the minds of many people by the words 'Central Asia' is not entirely unfounded. The overwhelming majority of the territory is flat steppe (arid grassland) and desert. These areas include the Kazakh Steppe, the Betpak Dala (Misfortune) Steppe, the Kyzylkum (Red Sands) desert and the Karakum (Black Sands) desert. The Kyzylkum and Karakum combined make the fourth-largest desert in the world.

Central Asia's mountains are part of the huge chain which swings in a great arc from the Mongolian Altay to the Tibetan Himalaya. Central Asia's high ground is dominated by the Pamirs, a range of rounded, 5000m to 7000m mountains known as the 'Roof of the World', which stretch 500km across Tajikistan. With very broad, flat valleys, which are nearly as high as the lower peaks, the Pamirs might be better described as a plateau (*pamir* roughly means 'pasture' in local dialects). The roof of the Pamir, Tajikistan's 7495m Koh-i-Samani, is the highest point in Central Asia and was the highest in the USSR (when it was known as Kommunizma). The Pamirs is probably the least explored mountain range on earth.

Uzbekistan is only one of two countries in the world defined as double landlocked, ie surrounded by countries which are themselves landlocked.

Varying from 4000m to more than 7400m, the crests of the Tian Shan form the backbone of eastern Central Asia. Known as the Celestial Mountains, the Chinese-named Tian Shan (the local translation is Tengri Tau) extend over 1500km from southwest Kyrgyzstan into China. The summit of the range is Pobedy (7439m) on the Kyrgyzstan–China border. The forested alpine valleys and stunning glacial peaks of the range were favourites among such Russian explorers as Fedchenko, Kostenko, Semenov and Przewalski.

These two mountain ranges hold some of the largest glaciers and freshwater supplies on earth (around 17,000 sq km) and are one of the region's most significant natural resources. The 77km-long Fedchenko Glacier (the longest in the former USSR) allegedly contains more water than the Aral Sea.

The Caspian Sea is called either the world's biggest lake or the world's biggest inland sea. The Caspian Depression, in which it lies, dips to 132m below sea level. Lake Balkhash, a vast, marsh-bordered arc of half-saline water on the Kazakh Steppe, is hardly deeper than a puddle, while mountain-ringed Lake Issyk-Köl in Kyrgyzstan is the fourth-deepest lake in the world. Other glacially fed lakes dot the mountains, including Song-Köl in Kyrgyzstan and stunning Kara-Kul, first described by Marco Polo, in Tajikistan.

Most of Central Asia's rainfall drains internally. What little water flows out of Central Asia goes all the way to the Arctic Ocean, via the Irtysh River. The Ili River waters Lake Balkhash; the Ural makes a short dash across part of Kazakhstan to the Caspian Sea. Numerous rivers rise as cold streams in the mountains only to lose themselves on the arid steppes and sands below. The region's two mightiest rivers, the Syr-Darya (Jaxartes River) and Amu-Darya (Oxus River), used to replenish the Aral Sea until they were bled dry for cotton. There is evidence that the Amu-Darya once flowed into the Caspian Sea, along the now-dry Uzboy Channel.

Some residents of massive Kazakhstan live about as far away from Vienna as they do from Almaty. Tashkent is closer to Kashgar and Tehran than to Moscow or Kiev.

## GEOLOGY

The compact, balled-up mass of mountains bordering Tajikistan, Kyrgyzstan and China is often called the Pamir Knot. It's the hub from which other major ranges extend like radiating ropes: the Himalaya and Karakoram to the southeast, the Hindu Kush to the southwest, the Kunlun to the east and the Tian Shan to the northeast. These young mountains all arose (or more correctly, are arising still) from the shock waves created by the Indian subcontinent smashing into the Asian crustal plate more than a hundred million years ago. Amazing as it seems, marine fossils from the original Tethys Sea have been found in the deserts of Central Asia as a testament to the continental collision. The Tian Shan are currently rising at the rate of around 10mm per year.

Central Asia is therefore unsurprisingly a major earthquake zone. Ashgabat was destroyed by earthquake in 1948 and Tashkent was levelled in 1966. More recently, devastating earthquakes hit the Tajikistan–Afghanistan border in 1997 and 1998.

*Realms of the Russian Bear*, by John Sparks, is an elegant, beautifully illustrated work focusing on the flora and fauna of the old Soviet empire, including 80-plus pages on the Tian Shan and Central Asia's steppes, deserts and seas.

## WILDLIFE

Central Asia is home to a unique range of ecosystems and an extraordinary variety of flora and fauna. The region comprised only 17% of the former USSR's territory, but contained over 50% of its variety in flora and fauna.

The mountains of Kyrgyzstan, Kazakhstan and Tajikistan are the setting for high, summer pastures known as *jailoo*s. In summertime the wild flowers (including wild irises and edelweiss) are a riot of colour. Marmots and pikas provide food for eagles and lammergeiers, while the elusive snow leopard preys on the ibex, with which it shares a preference for crags and rocky slopes, alongside the Svertsov ram. Forests of Tian Shan spruce, ash, larch and juniper provide cover for lynxes, wolves, wild boars and brown bears. Lower down in the mountains of southern Kyrgyzstan, Uzbekistan, Tajikistan and Turkmenistan are ancient forests of wild walnut, pistachio, juniper, apricot and apple.

The steppes (what's left of them after massive Soviet cultivation projects) are covered with grasses and low shrubs such as saxaul. Where they rise to meet foothills, the steppes bear vast fields of wild poppies (including some opium poppies) and several hundred types of tulip.

Roe deer and saiga (see Poaching on p80), a species of antelope, have their homes on the steppe. The ring-necked pheasant, widely introduced to North America and elsewhere, is native to the Central Asian steppe, as are partridges, black grouse, bustards, and the falcons and hawks that prey on them. Korgalzhyn Nature Reserve in Kazakhstan is home to the world's most northerly colony of pink flamingos.

*Chiy*, a common bullrush-like grass with whitish, canelike reeds, is used by nomads to make decorative screens for their yurts.

Rivers and lake shores in the flatlands create a different world, with dense thickets of elm, poplar, reeds and shrubs known as *tugai*, where wild boar, jackal and deer make their homes. A carplike fish called the *sazan* is the most popular catch.

**HEAVENLY HORSES**

Central Asia has been famed for its horses for millennia. The earliest Silk Road excursions into the region were made to bring back the famous blood-sweating (due to parasites or skin infection) horses of Fergana (based in the ancient kingdom of Davan, near modern-day Osh) to help Han China fight nomadic tribes harassing its northern frontier. Much of the highly coveted silk that made its way into Central Asia and beyond came from the trade of steeds the Chinese believed were descended from dragons.

Today's most famous horses are the Akhal-Teke of Turkmenistan, the forefather of the modern Arab thoroughbred. The Roman-era historian Appian praised the horses of Parthian Nissa for their beauty. Today there are only around 2000 thoroughbred Akhal-Teke in the world, of which 1200 are in Turkmenistan. Turkmenistan's state emblem and banknotes feature an Akhal-Teke and there's even a national holiday named after them. Akhal-Teke are regularly handed out as diplomatic gifts (François Mitterrand and Boris Yeltsin each received one), much as they were 2000 years ago. It's possible to ride Akhal-Tekes in several stables outside Ashgabat (see p411).

Other regional breeds include the stocky Lokai of Tajikistan and Karabair of Uzbekistan, which are used in sports such as *buzkashi* (a traditional pololike game played with a headless goat/sheep/calf carcass) and are descendants of horses that played a pivotal role in the Mongol conquest of Eurasia.

*Extremes along the Silk Road,* by Nick Middleton, is a geographical travelogue through the region by the Oxford professor turned TV star.

In the barren stony wastes of the Karakum and Kyzylkum you'll need a sharp eye to catch a glimpse of the goitred gazelle *(zheyran)*. Gophers, sand rats and jerboas feed various reptiles, including (in Turkmenistan) vipers and cobras.

Turkmenistan's wildlife has a Middle Eastern streak, understandable when you consider that parts of the country are as close to Baghdad as they are to Tashkent. Leopards and porcupines inhabit the parched hills. The *zemzen* or *varan* (desert crocodile) is actually a type of large lizard that can grow up to 1.8m long (see p404).

## Endangered Species

Locals have blamed Vozrozhdenia, a former island used to store bioweapons (see p79) for the terrifying sudden deaths, in less than an hour, of half a million saiga antelope on the Turgay Steppe, northeast of the Aral, in 1988.

The mountain goose, among other rare species, nests on the shores of Kyrgyzstan's mountain lakes, but the population has shrunk over the years to fewer than 15 pairs worldwide.

The population of snow leopards in Central Asia and the Russian Altay is estimated at about 1000, out of a global population of around 7000. Only 5% of the snow leopard's habitat is currently protected.

Tragically the last Turan (Caspian) tiger was killed in the Amu-Darya delta in 1972. Wild Bactrian camels, once the quintessential Silk Road sight, are now only found in remote areas of Afghanistan, though you can sometimes see them from the Tajikistan side of the Wakhan Valley. Perhaps 1000 remain.

There has been some good news, though: eight Przewalski's horses were recently reintroduced into Kazakhstan's Altyn-Emel National Park after being extinct in the region for 60 years.

# NATIONAL PARKS

Many of the region's approximately two-dozen nature reserves *(zapovednik)* and protected areas *(zakazniki)* and nine or so national parks *(gosudarstvenny prirodny park)* are accessible for tourists.

The existing system of national parks and protected areas, one of the positive legacies of the USSR, is nevertheless antiquated and inadequate. Unfortunately all suffer from a chronic lack of government funding and are under increasing pressure from grazing, poaching, firewood gathering and even opium-poppy plantations.

In Kyrgyzstan and Kazakhstan just 2.5% of the country's area is dedicated to land conservation, of which most is only semiprotected and commercially managed, often as hunting reserves. This is well below the minimum 10% recommended by the World Conservation Union.

The most easy to visit protected areas include the following:

**Aksu-Dzhabagly Nature Reserve** (p146) In southern Kazakhstan, famed for its beautiful tulips, it also has a fledgling ecotourism programme.
**Ala-Archa National Park** (p292) Offers fine hiking and climbing just outside Bishkek.
**Almatinsky Nature Reserve** Outside Almaty, with big-horned sheep, gazelle and hiking trails.
**Badai-Tugai Nature Reserve** (p252) In Karakalpakstan, it protects a strip of *tugai* riverine forest on the eastern bank of the Amu-Darya. Once off limits, today it welcomes foreign tourists, as the entry fee pays for food for a Bukhara deer-breeding centre.
**Karakol Valley** (p307) Alpine ecosystem in the Tian Shan, southeast Issyk-Köl, with superb scenery and fine trekking routes.
**Kugitang Nature Reserve** (p431) The most impressive of Turkmenistan's nature reserves, focused around the country's highest peak, is home to the rare markhor mountain goat and several hundred dinosaur footprints.
**Sary-Chelek Biosphere Reserve** (p329) Remote trekking routes cross this Unesco-sponsored reserve, centred on a large mountain lake.
**Ugam-Chatkal National Park** (p211) Unesco-sponsored, with juniper forests, wild boars, bears and snow leopards, plus some fine hiking and rafting.

## ENVIRONMENTAL ISSUES

Central Asia's 'empty' landscapes served as testing grounds for some of the worst cases of Soviet megalomania. Land and water mismanagement and the destruction of natural habitat were part of a conscious effort to tame nature ('harness it like a white mare', as the propaganda of the day had it). The results are almost beyond belief and on a staggering scale.

Even casual students of the region are familiar with some of the most infamous catastrophes of Soviet environmental meddling: the gradual disappearance of the Aral Sea and the excessive levels of radiation around the Semey (Semipalatinsk) nuclear testing site. Add to this the consequences of Khrushchev's Virgin Lands scheme, which was planned to boost grain production but which ended up degrading tens of millions of hectares of Kazakh steppe. For information on these last two issues see p111.

In the economic malaise of the post-Soviet years, the environment has taken a back seat. Whether it is poaching, hunting tours or pollution from gold-mining operations, the promise of hard-currency in an otherwise bleak economic landscape means that nature is often the victim.

The extreme continental climate of Central Asia is particularly susceptible to global climate change and locals can expect even colder winters and even hotter summers in the years ahead. Glaciers in the Pamirs and Tian Shan are already starting to shrink and you can expect water issues to become increasingly pressing over the next few decades. Central Asia's future will be defined by two of nature's greatest gifts: oil and water.

For news articles on environmental issues click on the Environment Department of www.eurasianet.org.

For reports on the state of Central Asia's environment search the website of the United Nations Environment Programme (www.grida.no).

### The Aral Sea

One of the most amazing things about the Aral Sea disaster is that it was no accident. The Soviet planners who fatally tapped the rivers that fed the Aral Sea, in order to irrigate new cotton fields, expected the sea to dry up. They also wanted to bring water to Central Asia by a huge canal from Siberia, not to replenish the Aral Sea but to expand cotton production still further. They either didn't understand that drying up the world's fourth-largest lake would wreck a whole region's climate and ecology, and cause untold suffering to its people, or didn't care.

The Aral Sea was once the world's fourth-largest lake. It is now recognised as the world's worst manmade ecological disaster.

The Aral Sea, or rather seas, since it split into two in 1987, straddles the border between western Uzbekistan and southern Kazakhstan. It's fed (in the years that they actually reach it) by the Syr-Darya and Amu-Darya rivers, flowing down from the Tian Shan and Pamir mountain ranges. Back in the 1950s these rivers brought an average 55 cubic km of water a year to the Aral Sea, which stretched 400km from end to end and 280km from side to side, and covered 66,900 sq km. The sea had, by all accounts, lovely clear water, pristine beaches, plenty of fish to support a big fishing industry in the ports of Moynaq and Aralsk, and even passenger ferries crossing it from north to south.

The best place to view the Aral disaster is Moynaq (p260), where you can see rusty fishing trawlers beached 150km from the sea.

Then the USSR's central planners decided to boost cotton production in Uzbekistan, Turkmenistan and Kazakhstan, to feed a leap forward in the Soviet textile industry. But the thirsty new cotton fields, many of them on poorer desert soils and fed by long, unlined canals open to the sun, required much more water per hectare than the old ones. The irrigated area grew by only about 20% between 1960 and 1980, but the annual water take from the rivers doubled from 45 to 90 cubic km. By the 1980s the annual flow into the Aral Sea was less than a tenth of the 1950s supply.

Production of cotton rose, but the Aral Sea sank. Between 1966 and 1993 its level fell by more than 16m and its eastern and southern shores receded by up to 80km. In 1987 the Aral divided into a smaller northern sea and a larger southern one, each fed, sometimes, by one of the rivers.

The two main fishing ports, Aralsk (Kazakhstan) in the north and Moynaq (Uzbekistan) in the south, were left high and dry when efforts to keep their navigation channels open were abandoned in the early 1980s. Of the 60,000 people who used to live off the Aral fishing industry (harvesting 20,000 tons of fish a year), almost all are gone. These days the rusting hulks of beached fishing boats lie scattered dozens of miles from the nearest water.

In parts of Karakalpakstan (far-west Uzbekistan) more than one baby in 10 dies (compared to one in 100 or more in Britain or the USA), a rate largely attributable to health problems caused by the Aral Sea disaster.

In any case there are hardly any fish left in the Aral Sea: the last of its 20-odd indigenous species disappeared in about 1985, wiped out by the loss of spawning and feeding grounds, rising salt levels and, very likely, residues of pesticides, fertilisers and defoliants used on the cotton fields, which found their way into the sea. Only introduced species such as the Black Sea flounder remain, though there is some hope for future shrimp cultivation in the increasingly briny waters.

The Aral Sea's shrinkage has devastated the land around it. The climate around the lake has changed: the air is drier, winters are colder and longer, and summers are hotter. The average number of rainless days has risen from 30 to 35 in the 1950s to between 120 and 150 today. Salt, sand and dust from the exposed bed is blown hundreds of kilometres in big salt-dust sandstorms, which also pick up residues of the chemicals from cultivated land. Locals talk of a new Akkum (White Sands) desert forming an unholy trinity with the Kyzylkum (Red Sands) and Karakum (Black Sands) deserts. A visit to anywhere near the sea is a ride into a nightmare of blighted towns, blighted land and blighted people.

www.cawater-info.net has info on Aral Sea and other water-related issues in Central Asia.

In human terms, the worst-affected areas are those to the Aral Sea's south – as far as northern Turkmenistan – and east (the areas north and west of the Aral Sea are very sparsely populated). The catalogue of health problems is awful: salt and dust are blamed for respiratory illnesses and cancers of the throat and oesophagus; poor drinking water has been implicated in high rates of typhoid, paratyphoid, hepatitis and dysentery; and the area has the highest mortality and infant mortality rates in the former USSR, as well as high rates of birth deformities. In Aralsk, tuberculosis is common.

Humans are not the only ones affected. Of the 173 animal species that used to live around the Aral Sea, only 38 survive. Especially devastating has been the degradation of the big Amu-Darya and Syr-Darya deltas, with their diverse flora and fauna. The deltas have supported irrigated agriculture for many centuries, along with hunting, fishing, and harvesting of reeds for building and papermaking. The dense *tugai* forests, unique to the valleys of these desert rivers, have shrunk to a fifth of their old size, causing a catastrophic drop in the once-abundant water bird population.

The local name for the Aral is the Aral Tenghiz, or Sea of Islands. Barsakelmes (the Place of No Return) Island, a nature reserve protecting the saiga antelope and the rare Asiatic wild ass, has reportedly become an unviable habitat because it is now so arid.

Nor can matters have been helped by the use of Vozrozhdenia Island as a Soviet biological warfare testing site (anthrax and plague were both released on the island) until it was abandoned in 1992. In 2002 the island's secrets were joined to the mainland by the exposed seabed. Ironically, the island's name in pious Russian means 'rebirth'.

The Aral isn't the only body of water drying up. Lake Balkhash in Kazakhstan, which gets its water from the Ili River of Xinjiang, has shrunk by 2000 sq km in recent years.

### LONG-TERM SOLUTIONS

Dozens of inquiries, projects and research teams have poked and prodded the Aral problem; locals joke that if every scientist who visited the Aral region had brought a bucket of water the problem would be over by now. The initial outcry over the disaster seems to have largely evaporated, along with the sea, and the focus has shifted from rehabilitating the sea, to stabilising part of the sea and now stabilising the environment around the sea.

To restore the Aral would require irrigation from the Amu-Darya and Syr-Darya to cease for three years, or at least a slashing of the irrigated area from over 70,000 to 40,000 sq km; in other words, a complete restructuring of the economies of Uzbekistan and Turkmenistan. No-one is seriously considering this.

A 600-year-old mausoleum recently discovered on the dried-out bed of the Aral Sea has indicated that Aral levels might be cyclical to some degree.

Finally in 1988 a gradual increase in water flow to the sea was ordered, to be achieved by more efficient irrigation and an end to the expansion of irrigation. However, early promises of cooperation and money from the Central Asian leaders bore little fruit. The now annual Aral Sea convention of Central Asian leaders has achieved little, except to highlight conflicting claims to sections of the Amu-Darya. A US$250-million World Bank scheme aims to clean up water supplies, improve sanitation and public health, restore some economic viability and biodiversity to the Amu-Darya delta, and stabilise the Aral's northern sea.

In 2003 the little channel still connecting the northern and southern seas was blocked by a 12.8km-long dike, preventing further water loss from the northern sea (see the boxed text, p151), but condemning the southern sea to oblivion. The northern sea is now expected to rise almost 3.5m and should reach a state of equilibrium, with an area of 3500 sq km, by about 2025. But if recent rates of depletion continue, the southern sea is expected to split again into western and eastern parts. The eastern part will receive the Amu-Darya and is expected eventually to stabilise into three lakes with the construction of small dikes, but the western part will go on shrinking.

*The Devil and The Disappearing Sea*, by Robert Ferguson, gives a recent (2003) look at the politics of aid and corruption in Central Asia, with a car chase and murder accusation thrown in for good measure.

Longer-term efforts may focus on building more dikes around parts of the sea, rehabilitating the blighted region around the sea and stabilising its fragile environment, improving water management and building up local institutions to manage these projects. Whether the will exists among Central Asia's politicians to introduce less water-intensive irrigation methods, or even less thirsty crops than cotton, remains to be seen.

## Overgrazing

Overgrazing and soil degradation are major problems affecting all the Central Asian republics. The steady rise in livestock grazing has unhinged delicate ecosystems and accelerated desertification and soil erosion. From 1941 to

**RETAIL THERAPY FOR SNOW LEOPARDS**

At Ak Shyrak and Inylchek (Engilchek), two villages in Kyrgyzstan's remote Central Tian Shan, a US-based organisation called the Snow Leopard Trust is trying to help people increase their household income in a way that also helps protect snow leopards and their habitat.

Together with local partners, the Snow Leopard trust provides herders with training and equipment to produce handicrafts like felt rugs, handbags and slippers, using wool from their livestock. These products are marketed at stores in the US and through the Snow Leopard Trust's website (www.snowleopard.org). Members pledge not to kill snow leopards or wild sheep and goats (the snow leopard's most important large prey) and to follow sustainable herding practices. About half of households in Ak Shyrak, bordering the Sarychat-Ertash Reserve, currently participate in the programme.

1991 the population of sheep and goats more than doubled to 5.5 million in Turkmenistan and quadrupled to 10 million in Kyrgyzstan, while a third of Kyrgyzstan's available grasslands have disappeared.

In Kazakhstan much of the semiarid steppe, traditionally used as pasture over the centuries, was put to the plough under the Virgin Lands campaign (see p111). Wind erosion in the steppes of north Kazakhstan has accelerated soil depletion.

Soil degradation is also activated by failure to rotate crops and by excessive use of chemicals, and aggravated by irrigation-water mismanagement. In Kazakhstan, 40% of rangeland is considered to be overused, and will need 10 to 50 years to be restored to its original fertility. In Kyrgyzstan an estimated 70% of pastureland suffers erosion above acceptable levels. In Tajikistan the productivity of summer pastures in the mountains has dropped by 50% over the last 25 years and large areas of the Pamirs are threatened by desertification.

In the last few years the number of saiga (antelope) has dropped from over one million to less than 40,000.

## Pollution

Cotton is to blame for many of Central Asia's ills. Its present cultivation demands high levels of pesticides and fertilisers, which are now found throughout the food chain – in the water, in human and animal milk, in vegetables and fruit, and in the soil itself. In the Osh region of Kyrgyzstan 94% of soils contain DDT.

Kazakhstan, the third-largest industrial power in the Commonwealth of Independent States (CIS), suffers particularly from industrial pollution, the worst culprits being power stations running on low-grade coal, and metallurgical factories. Lake Balkhash has been polluted by copper smelters established on its shores in the 1930s; bird and other lake life is now practically extinct. An added threat comes from a planned nuclear power station on the shores of the lake. There are also concerns about oil and other pollution draining into the Caspian Sea (see p111) and radioactive seepage from Soviet-era uranium mines in Kyrgyzstan (p278).

Marco Polo sheep are named after the Italian traveller who first wrote of them, 'There are... wild sheep of great size, whose horns are a good six palms in length.'

Mining techniques are inefficient, outdated and environmentally hazardous. In 1998 almost two tonnes of sodium cyanide destined for the Kumtor gold mine in Kyrgyzstan was spilled into the Barskoön River, which made its way into Issyk-Köl.

## Poaching

The unfortunate combination of economic hardship, a sudden crisis in funding for wildlife protection and the opening of borders with China (the region's main market for illegal trafficking in animal parts) saw a huge rise in poaching after the fall of the Soviet Union, both as a food source and for trophies to sell for hard currency.

Tens of thousands of critically endangered saiga antelope are killed every year by poachers, who sell their horns to Chinese medicine makers. Musk deer, currently found in Kyrgyzstan, Uzbekistan and Russia, are killed for their musk glands. Around 160 deer are killed for every 1kg of musk, making the musk worth three to four times its weight in gold. Tens of thousands of the deer have been killed in the last 20 years and numbers in Russia have fallen by 50%.

Several private and government travel agencies run hard-currency hunting expeditions. The high prices charged for trophies (US$7500 for a Marco Polo sheep) can, in theory, fund wildlife protection and discourage local poaching by adding broader value to local endangered species. Ironically, one of the few places in Tajikistan not to have seen a dramatic drop in the number of ibex and Marco Polo sheep in recent years is the Jarty-Gumbaz hunting camp, where local poaching has almost completely ceased.

# Food & Drink

The Central Asian culinary experience is unlikely to be a highlight of your trip. Most restaurants and cafés serve only standard slop, which somehow seems to taste (and smell) indelibly of the old USSR. The situation has improved in recent years, particularly in the cities, with a rush of pleasant open-air cafés, fast-food joints and particularly Turkish restaurants. The best way to appreciate regional cuisines, and the region's extraordinary hospitality, is still at a meal in a private home.

In the heavily Russian-populated cities of northern Kazakhstan and in all the Central Asian capitals, the dominant cuisine is Russian.

For country-specific food-and-drink information, see the Food & Drink entries in each individual country chapter.

## STAPLES & SPECIALITIES

Central Asian food resembles that of the Middle East or the Mediterranean in its use of rice, savoury seasonings, vegetables and legumes, yogurt and grilled meats. Many dishes may seem familiar from elsewhere – *laghman* (similar to Chinese noodles), pilau or *plov* (similar to Persian rice pilafs), nan (flat breads found all over Asia), and *samsa* (the samosa of India). Others are more unusual, such as Kazakh horsemeat sausage.

*Food Culture in Russia & Central Asia*, by Glenn Mack & Asele Surina, is a detailed look at everything from *plov* (pilaf) to *piroshki* (fried potato or meat pies).

The cuisine falls into three overlapping groups. First, there's the once-nomadic subsistence diet found in large areas of Kazakhstan, Kyrgyzstan and Turkmenistan – mainly meat (including entrails), milk products and bread. Second, there's the diet of the Uzbeks and other settled Turks, which includes pilafs, kebabs, noodles and pasta, stews, elaborate breads and pastries. The third group is Persian, ranging from southern Uzbekistan to Tajikistan, which is distinguished by subtle seasoning, extensive use of vegetables, and fancy sweets.

Seasoning is usually mild, although sauces and chillies are offered to turn up the heat. Principal spices are black cumin, red and black peppers, barberries, coriander and sesame seeds. Common herbs are fresh coriander, dill, parsley, celeriac and basil. Other seasonings include wine vinegar and fermented milk products.

### Ingredients

Mutton is the preferred meat. Big-bottomed sheep are prized for their fat, meat and wool, and fat from the sheep's tail costs more than the meat. The meat-to-fat ratio is generally stacked heavily in favour (and flavour) of the fat, and you will soon find that everything smells of it. Sheep's head is a great delicacy, which may be served to honoured guests in some homes.

Produce is at its most bountiful around September. In general, May is the best time for apricots, strawberries and cherries, June for peaches, and July for grapes and figs. Melons ripen in late summer, but are available in the markets as late as January.

You can find caviar and seafood dishes in western Kazakhstan, near the Caspian Sea. Dried and smoked fish are sold near Issyk-Köl.

### Standards

The ubiquitous shashlyk – kebabs of fresh or marinated mutton, beef, minced meat *(farsh* or *lyulya kebab)* or, in restaurants, chicken – is usually served with nan and vinegary onions. The quality varies from inedible to addictively delicious. Liver kebabs are known in Turkic as *jiger*.

*Plov* (*pilau* in Tajikistan) consists mainly of rice with fried and boiled meat, onions and carrots, and sometimes raisins, chickpeas or fruit slices, all cooked up in a hemispherical cauldron called a *kazan*. *Plov* is always the *pièce de résistance* when entertaining guests and Uzbekistan is the *plov* capital of Central Asia.

Stout noodles *(laghman)* distinguish Central Asian cuisine from any other. *Laghman* is served everywhere, especially as the base for a spicy soup (usually called *laghman* too), which includes fried mutton, peppers, tomatoes and onions. Korean, Uyghur and Dungan noodles are generally the best.

Other soups include *shorpa (shurpa* or *sorpo)*, boiled mutton on the bone with potatoes, carrots and turnips; *manpar* (noodle bits, meat, vegetables and mild seasoning in broth); and Russian borsht (beetroot soup).

Nan (*non* to Uzbeks and Tajiks; *lepyoshka* in Russian), usually baked in a *tandyr* (tandoori) oven, is served at every meal. Some varieties are prepared with onions, meat or sheep's-tail fat in the dough; others have anise, poppy or sesame seeds placed on top. Nan also serves as an impromptu plate for shashlyks. Homemade breads are often thicker and darker than normal nan. Boring, square, white-flour Russian loaves are known simply as *khleb*.

Salads are a refreshing break from heavy main courses, although you'll soon tire of the dreaded salat tourist (sliced tomatoes and cucumbers). Parsley, fresh coriander, green onions and dill are served and eaten whole.

## Snacks

There are four other variations on the meat-and-dough theme – steamed, boiled, baked and fried. *Manty* (steamed dumplings) are a favourite from Mongolia to Turkey. *Chuchvara (tushbera* in Tajik, *pelmeny* in Russian) are a smaller boiled cousin of *manty*, served plain or with vinegar, sour cream or butter, or in soups. Both are sometimes fried.

One of the most common and disappointing street foods are *piroshki*, greasy Russian fried pies filled with potatoes or meat.

Fruits are eaten fresh, cooked, dried or made into preserves, jams and drinks known as *kompot* or *sokh*. Central Asians are fond of dried fruits and nuts, particularly apricots and apricot stones, which when cracked open have a pith that tastes like pistachios. At any time of year you'll find delicious walnuts, peanuts, raisins and almonds, plus great jams (sea-buckthorn jam is a real treat) and wonderful mountain honey.

A favourite snack is the *samsa* (*sambus*a in Tajik), a meat pie made with flaky puff pastry, and baked in a tandoori oven – at their best in Kyrgyzstan..

## Milk Products

Central Asia is known for the richness and delicacy of its fermented dairy products, which use cow, sheep, goat, camel or horse milk. The milk itself is probably unpasteurised, but its cultured derivatives are safe if kept in hygienic conditions.

The fresh yogurt served up to guests in the mountain pastures of Kyrgyzstan and Tajikistan will be the best you've ever tasted. Yogurt can be strained to make *suzma*, which is like tart cottage or cream cheese, and used as a garnish or added to soups. *Ayran* is a salty yogurt/water mix, the Russian equivalent is called *kefir*; don't confuse this with the Russians' beloved *smetana* (sour cream). *Katyk* is a thinner, drinkable yogurt. Many doughs and batters incorporate sour milk products, giving them a tangy flavour.

Central Asians of every ethnic group love ice cream *(marozhnoe* in Russian). You'll find a freezer of the stuff almost anywhere.

The final stage in the milk cycle is *kurut*, which is dried *suzma* (often rolled into marble-size balls), a rock hard travel snack with the half-life of uranium. Scrape away the outer layer if you're uneasy about cleanliness.

*Tvorog* is a Russian speciality, made from soured milk, which is heated to curdle. This is hung in cheesecloth overnight to strain off the whey. The closest Central Asian equivalent is *suzma*. *Kaimak* is pure sweet cream, skimmed

**NASVAI**

You might notice some men chewing and copiously spitting, or talking as if their mouth is full of saliva. *Nasvai* (also known as *nasvar* or *noz)* is basically finely crushed tobacco, sometimes cut with spices, ash or lime. As a greenish sludge or as little pellets, it's stuffed under the tongue or inside the cheek, from where the active ingredients leach into the bloodstream, revving up the user's heart rate. Amateurs who fail to clamp it tightly in place, thus allowing the effluent to leak into the throat, might be consumed with nausea.

Before you try it, bear in mind that *nasvai* is sometimes cut with opium and can be quite potent.

from fresh milk that has sat overnight. This wickedly tasty breakfast item, wonderful with honey, is available in many markets in the early morning, but sells out fast, usually by sunrise.

### Turkish Food

Turkish restaurants are popping up everywhere in Central Asia and most are excellent value. *Pides* are similar to thin-crust pizzas; *lahmacun* is a cheaper, less substantial version. Kebabs are popular, especially Adana kebabs (mincemeat patties) and delicious Iskander kebabs (thinly sliced mutton over bread, with yogurt and rich tomato sauce). *Patlıcan* (aubergine) and *dolma* (stuffed peppers) are the most common vegetable dishes. *Çaçık* is a delicious yogurt, cucumber and mint dip and makes a great snack with *lavash*, a huge bread similar to nan but lighter. Desserts include baklava (light pastry covered in syrup) and *sütlaç* (rice pudding).

### Holiday Food

A big occasion for eating is Navrus (see p450), a celebration of the spring equinox. Along with *plov* and other traditional fare, several dishes are served at this time in particular. The traditional Navrus dish, prepared only by women, is *sumalak* – wheat soaked in water for three days until it sprouts, then ground, mixed with oil, flour and sugar, and cooked on a low heat for 24 hours. *Halim* is a porridge of boiled meat and wheat grains, seasoned with black pepper and cinnamon, prepared just for men. *Nishalda (nishollo* in Tajik) – whipped egg whites, sugar and liquorice flavouring – is also popular during Ramadan. To add to this, seven items, all beginning with the Arabic sound 'sh', are laid on the dinner table during Navrus – wine *(sharob)*, milk *(shir)*, sweets *(shirinliklar)*, sugar *(shakar)*, sherbet *(sharbat)*, a candle *(sham)* and a new bud *(shona)*. Candles are a throwback to pre-Islamic traditions and the new bud symbolises the renewal of life.

Uzbek men usually stay out of the kitchen but are almost always in charge of preparing *plov*; an *oshpaz*, or master chef, can cook up a special *plov* for thousands on special occasions.

A special holiday dish in Kazakhstan and Kyrgyzstan is *beshbarmak* (*besbarmak* in Kazakh, *shilpildok* in Uzbek, *myasa po-kazakhskiy* in Russian), large flat noodles with lamb and/or horsemeat and cooked in vegetable broth (the Kazakh version serves the broth separately). It means 'five fingers' since it was traditionally eaten by hand.

## DRINKS

### Tea

*Chay* (чай; *choy* to Uzbeks and Tajiks, *shay* to Kazakhs) is drunk with reverence. Straight green tea (*kok* in Turkic languages; *zelyonnyy* in Russian) is the favourite; locals claim it beats the heat and unblocks you after too much greasy *plov*. Black tea *(kara* in Turkic languages; *chyornyy chay* in Russian) is preferred in Samarkand and Urgench, and by most Russians. Turkmen call green tea *gek* and black tea *gara*.

**TEAHOUSES**

The *chaikhana* or teahouse *(chaykhana* in Turkmen, *chaykana* in Kyrgyz, *choyhona* in Uzbek and Tajik, *shaykhana* in Kazakh) is male Central Asia's essential sociogastronomic institution, especially in Uzbekistan. Usually shaded, often near a pool or stream, it's as much a men's club as an eatery – although women, including foreigners, are tolerated. Old and young congregate to eat or to drink pot after pot of green tea and talk the day away.

Traditional seating is on a bedlike platform called a *tapchan*, covered with a carpet and topped with a low table. Take your shoes off to sit on the platform, or leave them on and hang your feet over.

Western Turkmen brew tea with *chal* (camel's milk) and Pamiris use goat's milk. Kazakh tea is taken with milk, salt and butter – the nomadic equivalent of fast food – hot, tasty and high in calories.

## Nonalcoholic Drinks

Don't drink the tap water. Cheap bottled mineral water is easy to find, but it's normally gassy and very mineral tasting. Modern joint-venture brands are more expensive but taste a lot better, though most are carbonated. Companies such as Coca-Cola have factories in all the republics and their products are everywhere.

Tins of cheap imported instant coffee can be found everywhere; hot water *(kipitok)* is easy to drum up from a hotel floor-lady or homestay.

## Alcoholic Drinks

### VODKA & BEER

Despite their Muslim heritage, most Central Asians drink. If you don't enjoy hard booze and heavy drinking, make your excuses early. Like the Russians who introduced them to vodka, Central Asians take their toasts seriously and a foreign male guest may be expected to offer the first toast.

Given the depth of Central Asian hospitality it's impolite to refuse the initial 'bottoms up' (Russian – *vashe zdarovye!*), and/or abstain from at least a symbolic sip at each toast. But there's usually heavy pressure to drain your glass every time – so as not to give offence, it is implied – and the pressure only increases as everybody gets loaded. It's worth knowing that while Russian dictionaries define *chut chut* as 'a little bit', when applied to a shot of vodka it would appear to mean 'up to the rim'.

Apart from the endless array of industrial-strength vodkas, you'll find a wide range of Russian and European beers *(pivo)* for around US$1 to US$2 a can. The St Petersburg's Baltika is the brew of choice and comes in a wide range of numbers from 0 (nonalcoholic) to 9 (very strong). Baltikas 3 and 6 are the most popular. Popular beers on tap include Tian-Shansky, Shimkent (both Kazakh) and Siberian Crown (Russian). The first time you order a local Berk Beer in Turkmenistan always seems to raise a smile.

### KUMYS & OTHER ATTRACTIONS

*Kumys* (properly *kymys* in Kyrgyz; *qymyz* in Kazakh) is fermented mare's milk, a mildly (2% to 3%) alcoholic drink appreciated by Kazakhs and Kyrgyz, even those who no longer spend much time in the saddle (nonalcoholic varieties are also made). It's available only in spring and summer, when mares are foaling, and takes around three days to ferment. The milk is put into a *chelek* (wooden bucket or barrel) and churned with a wooden plunger called a *bishkek* (from where that city derives its name).

Locals will tell you that *kumys* cures anything from a cold to TB but drinking too much of it may give you diarrhoea. The best *kumys* comes from the herders themselves; the stuff available in the cities is sometimes diluted with cow's milk or water.

Kazakhs and Kyrgyz also like a thick, yeasty, slightly fizzy concoction called *bozo*, made from boiled fermented millet or other grains. Turkmen, Kazakh and Karakalpak nomads like *shubat* (fermented camel's milk).

## WHERE TO EAT & DRINK

Don't misread meat prices on menus in fancier restaurants – they are often given as per 100g, not per serving (which is often more like 250g to 400g).

You can eat in streetside stalls and cafés, private and state-run restaurants and chaikhanas and, best of all, in private homes. There has recently been an explosion of private restaurants in larger towns and you can now eat well and cheaply, a great improvement on a few years ago. In smaller towns, restaurants, if they exist at all, can be pretty dire, and hotels may have the only edible food outside private homes.

A few restaurants *(askhana* in Kazakh and Kyrgyz, *oshhona* in Uzbek) in bigger cities offer interesting Central Asian, Turkish, Chinese, Georgian, Korean or European dishes and earnest service.

Outside the cities, Russians and Russified locals don't expect good food from restaurants. What they want at midday is a break. What they want in the evening is a night out – lots of booze and gale-force techno music or a variety show. Even if there's no music blasting when you come in, the kind staff will most likely turn on (or turn up) the beat especially for the foreigners.

The canteen (столовая; *stolovaya*) is the ordinary citizen's eatery – dreary but cheap, with a limited choice of cutlet or lukewarm *laghman*.

Bear in mind that many Russian main dishes are just that and you'll have to order garnishes (rice, potatoes or vegetables) separately.

Certain old-town neighbourhoods of Tashkent and Samarkand have home restaurants offering genuine home-style cuisine. There is rarely a sign; family members simply solicit customers on the street, and the competition can be intense.

Midrange and top-end restaurants are limited to Tashkent, Bishkek, Dushanbe and Almaty. The food is generally well-prepared European cuisine, with the occasional Siberian salmon or black caviar to liven things up.

### Self-Catering

Every sizable town has a colourful bazaar *(rynok* in Russian) or farmers market with hectares of fresh and dried fruit, vegetables, walnuts, peanuts, honey, cheese, bread, meat and eggs. Private shops now sell a decent range of European and Russian goods.

Perhaps the best opportunity to sample authentic Kyrgyz, Dungan and Tartar specialities is Kyrgyzstan's Festival of National Cuisine and Folklore, held near Issyk-Köl in July – see p310.

Korean and Dungan vendors sell spicy *kimchi* (vegetable salads), a great antidote for mutton overdose. Russians flog *pelmeny, piroshki* (deep-fried meat or potato pies) and yogurt. Fresh honey on hot-from-the-oven nan makes a splendid breakfast.

Don't be afraid to haggle (with a smile) – everybody else does. As a foreigner you may be quoted twice the normal price or, on the other hand, given a bit extra. Insist on making your own choices or you may end up with second-rate produce. Most produce is sold by the kilo.

The odd state food store *(gastronom)* exists here and there, stocked with a few bits of cheese and dozens of cans of Soviet-made 'Beef in its own Juice' stacked up along the windowsill.

## VEGETARIANS & VEGANS

Central Asia can be difficult for vegetarians; indeed the whole concept of vegetarianism is unfathomable to most locals. Those determined to avoid meat will need to visit plenty of farmers markets.

In restaurants, you'll see lots of tomato and cucumber salads. *Laghman* or soup may be ordered without meat, but the broth is usually meat-based. In private homes there is always bread, jams, salads, whole greens and herbs on the table, and you should be able to put in a word to your host in advance. Even if you specifically ask for vegetarian dishes you'll often discover the odd piece of meat snuck in somewhere – after a while it all seems a bit of a conspiracy.

'Without meat' is *etsiz* in Turkmen, *atsiz* in Kazakh and Kyrgyz, *goshsiz* in Uyghur, *gushtsiz* in Uzbek, and *bez myasa* in Russian.

## HABITS & CUSTOMS

There are a few social conventions that you should try to follow.

Devout Muslims consider the left hand unclean, and handling food with it at the table, especially in a private home and with communal dishes, can be off-putting. At a minimum, no-one raises food to the lips with the left hand. Try to accept cups and plates of food only with the right hand.

Bread is considered sacred in Central Asia. Don't put it on the ground, turn it upside down or throw it away (leave it on the table or floor cloth). If someone offers you tea in passing and you don't have time for it, they may offer you bread instead. It is polite to break off a piece and eat it, followed by the *amin* (see the boxed text, below). If you arrive with nan at a table, break it up into several pieces for everyone to share.

The *dastarkhan* is the central cloth laid on the floor, which acts as the dining table. Never put your foot on or step on this. Try to walk behind, not in front of people when leaving your place at the *dastarkhan* and don't step over any part of someone's body. Try not to point the sole of your shoe or foot at anyone as you sit on the floor. Don't eat after the *amin*. This signals thanks for and an end to the meal.

### Hospitality

If you're invited home for a meal this can be your best introduction to local customs and traditions as well as to local cuisine. Don't go expecting a quick bite. Your host is likely to take the occasion very seriously. Uzbeks, for example, say *mehmon otanda ulugh*, 'the guest is greater than the father'.

It's important to arrive with a gift. Something for the table (eg some fruit from the market) will do. Better yet would be something for your hosts' children or their parents, preferably brought from your home country (eg sweets, postcards, badges, a picture book). Pulling out your own food or offering to pay someone for their kindness is likely to humiliate them (although some travellers hosted by very poor people have given a small cash gift to the eldest child, saying that it's 'for sweets'). Don't be surprised if you aren't thanked: gifts are taken more as evidence of God's grace than of your generosity.

You should be offered water for washing, as you may be eating with your hands at some point. Dry your hands with the cloth provided; shaking the water off your hands is said to be impolite.

Wait until you are told where to sit; honoured guests are often seated by Kyrgyz or Kazakh hosts opposite the door (so as not to be disturbed by traffic through it, and because that is the warmest seat in a yurt). Men (and foreign women guests) might eat separately from women and children of the family.

The meal might begin with a mumbled prayer, followed by tea. The host breaks and distributes bread. After bread, nuts or sweets to 'open the appetite', business or entertainment may begin.

**AMIN**

After a meal or prayers, or sometimes when passing a grave site, you might well see both men and women bring their cupped hands together and pass them down their face as if washing. This is the *amin*, a Muslim gesture of thanks, common throughout the region.

**TEA ETIQUETTE**

Tea is the drink of hospitality, offered first to every guest, and almost always drunk from a *piala* (small bowl). From a fresh pot, the first cup of tea is often poured away (to clean the *piala*) and then a *piala* of tea is poured out and returned twice into the pot to brew the tea. A cup filled only a little way up is a compliment, allowing your host to refill it often and keep its contents warm (the offer of a full *piala* of tea is a subtle invitation that it's time to leave).

Pass and accept tea with the right hand; it's extra polite to put the left hand over the heart as you do this. If your tea is too hot, don't blow on it, but swirl it gently in the cup without spilling any. If it has grown cold, your host will throw it away before refilling the cup.

The meal itself is something of a free-for-all. Food is served, and often eaten, from common plates, with hands or big spoons. Pace yourself – eat too slowly and someone may ask if you're ill or unhappy; too eagerly and your plate will be immediately refilled. Praise the cook early and often; your host will worry if you're too quiet.

The cuts of meat served are often symbolic; the tongue is served to someone who should be more eloquent and children get the ears, to help them be better listeners.

Traditionally, a host will honour an important guest by sacrificing a sheep for them. During these occasions the guest is given the choicest cuts, such as the eyeball, brain or meat from the right cheek of the animal.

If alcohol consumption is modest, the meal will end as it began, with tea and a prayer.

## EAT YOUR WORDS

We have used mostly Russian words and phrases in this section.

### Useful Phrases in Russian

**I can't eat meat.**
*ya ni em maysnovo* Я не ем мясного.

**I'm a vegetarian.**
*ya vegetarianka* (female)/*ya vegetarianets* (male) Я вегетарианка./Я вегетарианец.

**Can I have the menu please?**
*daytye, pazhalsta, myenyu* Дайте, пожалуйста, меню?

**How much is it/this?**
*skol'ka eta stoit* Сколько это стоит?

**May I have the bill?**
*schyot, pazhalsta* Счёт, пожалуйста?

The prize for 'Most Surreal Place to Eat' goes to the Hound Dog Hole in the US embassy in Almaty (guests only), where food is prepared in Elvis Presley's kitchen (he bought it while serving in the military).

### Menu Decoder

A typical menu is divided into *zakuski* (cold appetisers), *pervye* (first courses, ie soups and hot appetisers), *vtorye* (second or main courses) and *sladkye* (desserts). Main dishes may be further divided into *firmennye* (house specials), *natsionalnye* (national, ie local, dishes), *myasnye* (meat), *rybnye* (fish), *iz ptitsy* (poultry) and *ovoshchnye* (vegetable) dishes.

Don't be awed by the menu; they won't have most of it, just possibly the items with prices written in.

#### SALADS

**agurets** (огурец) – cucumber
**chuisky salat** (чуйский салат) – spicy carrot salad in vinaigrette
**Frantsuzky salat** (Французский салат) – beetroot, carrots and French fries
**gribi** (грибы) – mushrooms
**kapustiy salat** (капустный салат) – cabbage salad
**kartoshka** (картошка) – potato
**mimosa salat** (салат мимоза) – fish and shredded-potato salad

**morkovi salat** (морковный салат) – carrot salad
**olivye salat** (салат оливье) – potato, ham, peas and mayonnaise
**pomidor** (помидор) – tomato
**salat iz svezhei kapusty** (салат из свежей капусты) – raw cabbage salad
**salat tourist** (салат турист) – sliced tomatoes and cucumbers
**stolichny** (столичный) – beef, potatoes, eggs, carrots, mayonnaise and apples

### MEAT, POULTRY & FISH
**antrecot** (антрекот) – steak
**befstroganov** (бефстроганов) – beef stroganoff
**bifshteks** (бифштекс) – 'beefsteak', glorified hamburger
**bitochki** (биточки) – cutlet
**farel** (форель) – trout
**frikadela** (фрикаделька) – fried meatballs
**galuptsi** (голубцы) – cabbage rolls stuffed with rice and meat
**gavyadina** (говядина) – beef
**gulyash** (гуляш) – a dismal miscellany of meat, vegetables and potatoes
**kotleta po-Kievski** (котлета по-киевски) – chicken Kiev
**kuritsa** (курица) – chicken
**lyulya kebab** (люля кебаб) – beef or mutton meatballs
**ragu** (рагу) – beef stew
**shashlyk iz baraniny** (шашлык из баранины) – mutton kebabs
**shashlyk iz okorochkov** (шашлык из окорочков) – chicken kebabs
**shashlyk iz pecheni** (шашлык из печени) – liver kebabs
**sosiski** (сосиски) – frankfurter sausage
**sudak zharei** (судак жареный) – fried pike or perch

### SNACKS
**chuchvara** (чучвара) – dumplings
**kolbasa** (колбаса) – sausage
**laghman** (лагман) – noodles, mutton and vegetables
**nan** (нон) – bread
**pelmeni** (пельмени) – small dumplings in soup
**samsa** (самса) – samosa (meat pie)

### GARNISHES
**grechka** (гречка) – boiled barley
**kartofel fri** (картофель фри) – French fries, chips
**kartofel pure** (картофельное пюре) – mashed potato
**makarony** (макароны) – macaroni, pasta
**ris** (рис) – rice

### SOUPS
**borsht** (борщ) – beetroot and potato soup, often with sour cream
**okroshka** (окрошка) – cold or hot soup made from sour cream, potatoes, eggs and meat
**rassolnik s myasam** (рассольник с мясом) – soup of marinated cucumber and kidney
**shorpa** – soup of boiled mutton on the bone with potatoes, carrots and turnips
**manpar** – noodle bits, meat, vegetables and mild seasoning in broth

## Food Glossary
### FRUIT & VEGETABLES
| | |
|---|---|
| *agurets* | cucumber |
| *pomidor* | tomato |
| *gribi* | mushrooms |
| *kartoshka* | potato |

### MEAT, POULTRY & FISH

*beshbarmak* chunks of meat served atop flat squares of pasta. The broth from the meat is drunk separately.
*farel* trout
*gavyadina* beef
*karta* horsemeat sausage
*kazy* smoked horsemeat sausage
*kolbasa* sausage
*kuurdak* fatty stew of meat, offal and potato
*kuritsa* chicken
*shashlyk* kebab

### DAIRY & FARM PRODUCE

*ayran* salty yogurt/water mix
*kurut* dried suzma (see below)
*kaimak* sweet cream
*marozhenoe* ice cream
*sir* cheese
*smetana* sour cream
*suzma* strained yogurt, similar to tart cottage or cream cheese
*yitso* egg

### SNACKS

*samsa* samosa (meat pie)
*manty* steamed dumplings
*myod (assal* in Turkic) honey
*nan* bread
*nahud sambusa* chickpea samosas
*nahud shavla* chickpea porridge
*barsook* fried bits of dough

### PASTA, RICE, NOODLES & GRAINS

*laghman* noodles, mutton and vegetables*
*plov* rice pilaf
*Tuhum barak* egg-filled ravioli coated with sesame-seed oil

### DRINKS

*bozo* beverage made from fermented millet
*chay* tea
*katyk* thin, drinkable yogurt
*kompot* juice/fruit squash
*kumys* fermented mare's milk
*mineralnaya vada* mineral water
*piva* beer
*sok* juice
*shubat* fermented camel's milk

# Activities

The soaring peaks, rolling pasturelands and desert tracts of Central Asia offer some of the region's finest active adventures. Make like the Kazakh hordes and ride horses across the Tian Shan, explore the Pamirs on foot like the first Russian imperial explorers, or live the Silk Road dream on a camel trek across the Kyzylkum desert – these are just some of the ways to get under the skin and into the landscapes of Central Asia.

With few facilities, tricky paperwork and modest traveller infrastructure, the 'stans aren't the easiest place for do-it-yourself adventurers. The good news is that the ever-increasing network of community-based tourism projects offers thrilling new opportunities to get off the map and meet locals on their own terms. Once the exclusive playing fields of Soviet scientists and Eastern European alpinists, these days you are almost guaranteed to have these magical places to yourself. See the Itineraries chapter (p24) for a variety of trips available throughout the region.

For an overview of trekking options in Tajikistan check out the excellent trekking section of www.pamirs.org.

## TREKKING

Central Asia is not only one of the world's great trekking destinations but also one of its best kept secrets. Kyrgyzstan, Tajikistan and southeastern Kazakhstan hold the cream of the mountain scenery thanks to the mighty spurs of the Tian Shan and Pamir ranges. See the 'Top Trekking Areas' boxed text (below) for a list of the most popular trekking destinations and cross-references to coverage in the text.

With many established routes and excellent trekking companies, Kyrgyzstan is the best republic for budget trekking. Treks here have the added bonus of adding on a visit to a eagle-hunter or a night or two in a yurt en route.

Tajikistan packs a double whammy, with the Fan Mountains in the west and high Pamirs in the east. The former offers a wide range of route options and difficulties, plus dozens of turquoise lakes. Treks in the Pamirs are more hardcore and anyone but the most experienced trekkers will really need professionals with them for these remote, demanding routes. See p391 for a list of the easier Pamir trek options.

In Kazakhstan, the mountains south of Almaty conceal some great mountain scenery, just an hour's drive from the city. Other less-visited regions in Kazakhstan include the Zhungar Alatau range east of Taldyqorghan and the Altay Mountains in the far northeast.

For some off-the-beaten-treks in Kyrgyzstan, not covered in this guide, try the three-day trek from Sokuluk Canyon to Suusamyr Valley; from Shamsy

### TOP TREKKING AREAS

- Fan Mountains (p374), Tajikistan
- Tian Shan (p308), around Karakol, Kyrgyzstan
- Around Arslanbob (p331), Kyrgyzstan
- Geisev Valley (p383), western Pamirs, Tajikistan
- Khan Tengri and Inylchek Glacier – from Kyrgyzstan (p313) or Kazakhstan (p312)
- Around Almaty, Kazakhstan – either from Bolshoe Almatinskoe Lake (see p133 and p136) and Medeu (p131), or around the Kolsay Lakes (p134).
- Ala-Archa National Park (p292), Kyrgyzstan

to yurtstays at Sarala-Saz; or from Kyzyl-Oi to Köl Tör lakes. Another option is the trek from Chong-Kemin Valley to Grigorievka or to Jasy-Köl and back; arrange horses in Kaindy (p293).

## What Kind of Trek?

Self-supported trekking is possible but not easy in Central Asia. There are no trekking lodges like the ones you'd find in Nepal and few porters, so you will have to carry all your own food for the trek. Public transport to the trail heads can be patchy, slow and uncomfortable so it's generally worth shelling out the extra money for a taxi. Some trekking areas are at the junction of several republics, requiring you to carry multiple simultaneous visas and a fistful of different currencies. It is possible to hire donkeys at many trail

### COMMUNITY-BASED TOURISM IN CENTRAL ASIA

At the end of the 1990s, with few economic options left to Kyrgyzstan, development organisations started to look to a new form of tourism to support remote communities. The idea was to help connect intrepid tourists to a series of service providers, from drivers to herders, in a fair and equitable way, while supporting local craft production and sustainable tourism practices.

The phenomenon started in Kochkor in central Kyrgyzstan with Swiss help (Helvetas) and has since rapidly spread throughout the region. Today these community-based tourism organisations offer you some of Central Asia's best and most exciting experiences, at fantastic value. The bottom line is that you'll sleep better in your yurtstay at night knowing that your money is going directly to the family you are staying with, rather than a middleman in Bishkek or abroad.

**Community Based Tourism** (CBT; p277; www.cbtkyrgyzstan.kg) in Kyrgyzstan is the region's leader, with a network across the country in a dozen locations, sometimes overlapping with original organisation Shepherd's Life. Most towns in Kyrgyzstan have CBT-inspired homestays and the organisation now offers everything from homestays and horse treks (see 'Horse Trips' in this chapter) to folk music concerts and horse-racing festivals. See the boxed text on opposite for a rundown of the best CBT adventures in Kyrgyzstan.

In Tajikistan, **Murgab Ecotourism Association** (META; p388; http://phiproject.free.fr) offers fantastic adventure in the Pamirs and can put you in touch with remote yurtstays, fixed price 4WD hire and English-speaking guides in a region devoid of any formal tourist infrastructure. **Mountain Societies Development and Support Project (MSDSP)** in Khorog has helped establish homestays in the eastern Pamir and recently initiated a homestay and hiking programme in the Geisev Valley (see p383).

The hub for ecotourism in Kazakhstan is the **Ecotourism Information Resource Centre** (EIRC; p117; www.ecotourism.kz), which offers similar grassroots adventures and homestays, from flamingo-watching at Korgalzhyn Nature Reserve to horse riding in Sayram-Ugam National Park, though at higher prices than elsewhere in the region. See p112 for a run down of ecotourism options in Kazakhstan, including horse treks and nature trips at Lepsinsk and Aksu-Zhabaghly Nature Reserve.

Community-based tourism is even starting to make its way into Uzbekistan through a Unesco-supported programme in the Nuratau-Kyzylkum Biosphere Reserve (see the boxed text, p236).

In addition to gung-ho adventures, most community-tourism organisations offer a range of cultural activities. CBT can organise displays of felt-making or eagle-hunting. EIRC arranges fun *kumys*-making workshops and concerts of traditional Kazakh music.

Programme coordinators in CBT or META sustain themselves through a 15% commission or, in the case of Shepherd's Life a small coordinator's fee. A few teething problems remain to be addressed, including issues with nepotism and service providers breaking away and founding their own rival businesses, and most of the organisations are not yet financially self-supporting. Remember also that these are not professional tourism companies, so pack a sense of humour and expect some delays and schedule changes during your trip.

Community-based tourism projects are a fantastic resource for independent travellers and deserve your support. Expect the experience to rank amongst the highlights of your travels.

**TOP COMMUNITY TOURISM ADVENTURES IN KYRGYZSTAN**

The following adventurous trips can be arranged by the various CBT branches in Kyrgyzstan and offer exciting ways to get off-the-beaten track without blowing your budget.

- Two- or three-day horse trip across the *jailoo* (summer pasture) from Kyzart or Jumgal to Song-Köl (p318).
- Four-day trek from Arslanbob to the holy lakes of the Köl-Mazar (p331).
- Trekking in the alpine valleys behind Karakol (see the boxed text, p308).
- Trek through a Unesco Biosphere from Talas to Sary-Chelek (five days) or from Kara-Suu to Sary-Chelek (two to three days; p329).
- Excursion to Chatyr-Köl from Tash Rabat – day hike/horse trip or overnight at the lake (p325).
- Overnight horse trek from Kazarman to petroglyphs at Sailmaluu Tash (p323).
- Intrepid seven-day horse trek from Echki-Bashy (near Naryn) to Bokonbayevo or four-days to Song-Köl (p321).
- Three-day trip from Kochkor to Köl Ükök lake (p317).
- Eagle hunting in Bokonbayevo (p312).

heads (eg in the Fan Mountains) and hire horses (around US$10 per day) in Kyrgyzstan. Companies such as CBT and META (see the boxed text, opposite) can often offer logistical support.

You can hire tents, sleeping bags and stoves from Bishkek and Karakol but in general, good gear, particularly sleeping bags, is hard to find in the region. A multifuel (petrol) stove is most useful, though you will need to clean the burners regularly as local fuel is of extremely poor quality. Camping gas canisters are generally available in Karakol.

Karakol is the main centre of trekking. The tourist information centre here sells 1:100,000 topo maps and has a folder detailing trekking routes. Several companies here offer a range of logistical support.

Trustworthy local knowledge, and preferably a local guide, are essential for trekking in Central Asia. The various branches of CBT (p277) in Kyrgyzstan can put you in touch with a guide for US$10, though for someone with a guaranteed knowledge of mountain routes you are better off arranging this with a trekking agency for between US$15 and US$20 per person per day.

*Trekking in Russia & Central Asia* by Frith Maier is an unrivalled guide to the former USSR's wild places. It has 77 pages of Central Asia route descriptions, plus chapters of useful background and planning info. Unfortunately it's now seriously dated, as it was written in 1994.

There are lots of competent trekking agencies in Central Asia who can arrange a full service trek. See the Adventure Travel Operators in Central Asia list, p100, for the most reliable. Treks organised through local trekking agencies cost from US$50 per person per day, far cheaper than international companies.

Foreign trekking companies such as **Himalayan Kingdoms** (www.himalayankingdoms.com), **Explore Worldwide** (www.explore.co.uk), **Exodus** (www.exodus.co.uk), **KE Adventure** (www.keadventure.com) and **World Expeditions** (www.worldexpeditions.com) run treks in the Inylchek/Khan Tengri region and the Fan Mountains.

## When to Go

The best walking season is June to September, but be ready for bad weather at any time. Most high-altitude treks or climbs take place in July or August; lower areas can be scorching hot during these months.

## Trekking Permits & Problems

Permits are needed in some areas of Kazakhstan, including Lepsinsk, the Altay region and the Zhungar Alatau. These take up to three weeks to procure (see p181) so apply ahead of time if you plan to trek in these regions.

## RESPONSIBLE TREKKING

To help preserve the ecology and beauty of Central Asia, consider the following tips when trekking.

### Rubbish

- Carry out all your rubbish. Don't overlook easily forgotten items, such as silver paper, orange peel, cigarette butts and plastic wrappers. Empty packaging should be stored in a dedicated rubbish bag. Make an effort to carry out rubbish left by others.
- Never bury your rubbish: digging disturbs soil and ground cover, and encourages erosion. Buried rubbish will likely be dug up by animals, who may be injured or poisoned by it. It may also take years to decompose.
- Minimise waste by taking minimal packaging and no more food than you will need. Take reusable containers or stuff sacks.
- Sanitary napkins, tampons, condoms and toilet paper should be carried out despite the inconvenience. They burn and decompose poorly.

### Human Waste Disposal

- Contamination of water sources by human faeces can lead to the transmission of all sorts of nasties. Where there is a toilet, please use it. Where there is none, bury your waste. Dig a small hole 15cm (6in) deep and at least 100m (320ft) from any watercourse. Cover the waste with soil and a rock. In snow, dig down to the soil.
- Ensure that these guidelines are applied to a portable toilet tent if one is being used by a large trekking party. Encourage all party members, including porters, to use the site.

### Washing

- Don't use detergents or toothpaste in or near watercourses, even if they are biodegradable.
- For personal washing, use biodegradable soap and a water container (or even a lightweight, portable basin) at least 50m (160ft) away from the watercourse. Disperse the waste water widely to allow the soil to filter it fully.
- Wash cooking utensils 50m (160ft) from watercourses using a scourer, sand or snow instead of detergent.

### Erosion

- Hillsides and mountain slopes, especially at high altitudes, are prone to erosion. Stick to existing tracks and avoid short cuts.
- If a well-used track passes through a mud patch, walk through the mud so as not to increase the size of the patch.
- Avoid removing the plant life that keeps topsoils in place.

### Fires & Low-Impact Cooking

- Don't depend on open fires for cooking. The cutting of wood for fires in popular trekking areas can cause rapid deforestation. Cook on a light-weight kerosene, alcohol or Shellite (white gas) stove and avoid those powered by disposable butane gas canisters.
- Fires may be acceptable below the tree line in areas that get very few visitors. If you light a fire, use an existing fireplace. Don't surround fires with rocks. Use only dead, fallen wood. Remember the adage 'the bigger the fool, the bigger the fire'. Use minimal wood, just what you need for cooking. In huts, leave wood for the next person.
- Ensure that you fully extinguish a fire after use. Spread the embers and flood them with water.

In Kyrgyzstan any place within 50km of the Chinese border (such as the Inylchek Glacier, the Alay Valley, the Turkestan range or Pik Lenin) requires a military border permit which are fairly easy to obtain through a trekking agency.

When trekking over the Zailiysky Alatau range between Kazakhstan and Kyrgyzstan, the lack of border posts (and thus a visa entry stamp) can cause potential problems when you leave the country. Travel agencies can usually smooth over the problem, otherwise you'll have to hike back over into the republic you started from.

While most commonly used trekking routes are quite safe, there have been problems in the past with bandits in the mountains between Almaty and Lake Issyk-Köl. Some trekking routes, especially those in southern Kyrgyzstan and Tajikistan, traverse some remote areas that are prime opium-growing territory. American climbers were kidnapped in this region in 2000. Discuss your route with a trekking agency before you wander off into these hills and, if possible, take a local guide.

The website http://mountains.czweb.org/foto_all.html offers general information and photos of treks in the Pamir, Khan Tengri, Pik Lenin and Fan Mountains.

## Maps

The following trekking/climbing maps for Central Asia are published and available abroad:

**Central Tian Shan** (EWP; www.ewpnet.com) 1:150,000; Inylchek Glacier and surroundings.
**Fan Mountains** (EWP; www.ewpnet.com) 1:100,000; Fan Mountains in Tajikistan.
**Pamir Trans Alai Mountains** (EWP; www.ewpnet.com) 1:200,000; Pik Lenin and the Fedchenko Glacier.
**Pik Lenin** (Gecko Maps; www.geckomaps.com) 1:100,000; topographical map of the mountain.

Geoid (see p279) in Bishkek sells useful maps of major central Tian Shan trekking regions for the equivalent of about US$3 each.

Firma Geo (see p116) in Almaty sells a wide variety of topographic and trekking maps from 1:25,000 to 1:100,000, as well as more general maps.

Asia Travel in Tashkent (p199) can often supply good 1:100,000 Uzbek topographical maps, printed in 1992, which are essential for trekking. These include:

**Bisokiy Alay** Treks from Shakhimardan, Khaidakan and the Sokh Valley in southern Kyrgyzstan.
**Fannsky Gory** Tajikistan's Fan Mountains.
**Matcha Palmiro-Alay Tsentralnaya Chast** Treks from Vorukh and Karavshin Valley, southern Kyrgyzstan.

Note that on Russian maps, passes marked Unclassified (N/K) or 1A are simple, with slopes no steeper than 30°; glaciers, where they exist, are flat and without open crevasses. Grade 1B passes may have ice patches or glaciers with hidden crevasses and may require ropes. Passes of grade 2A and above may require special equipment and technical climbing skills.

Robert Craig's *Storm and Sorrow in the High Pamirs* chronicles the tragic 1974 climbing season on Pik Lenin, during which all eight members of a Soviet women's climbing team perished on the mountain.

## Hiking

Hiking (as opposed to trekking, which is multiday) is a major outdoor pursuit for Almaty residents and there are fine hikes from Medeu (p131), among others. The Sayram-Ugam National Park and Aksu-Zhabaghly Nature Reserve are two beautiful areas of hiking country on the fringes of the Tian Shan between the southern Kazakhstan cities of Shymkent and Taraz. Rakhmanovskie Klyuchi in far north Kazakhstan is the starting point for hikes up the sublimely beautiful Altay valleys that fall off the slopes of Mt Belukha.

You can make nice day-hikes from bases in Ala-Archa National Park, near Bishkek, and Altyn Arashan, near Karakol, both in Kyrgyzstan. The Wakhan

Valley in the Pamirs of Tajikistan offers superb valley walks, as does the Geisev Valley (p383), where you can overnight in village homestays.

Uzbekistan has less potential, though Chimgan has some nice hikes. Walks in the mountains around Nokhur are possible in Turkmenistan. Most of the trekking regions mentioned earlier offer fine day-hikes.

## HORSE TRIPS

Kyrgyzstan is the perfect place to saddle up and join the other nomads on the high pastures. CBT and Shepherd's Life coordinators (p277) throughout the country arrange overnight horse treks to *jailoos* (summer pastures) around central Kyrgyzstan, or longer expeditions on horseback lasting up to two weeks. Horse hire costs the equivalent of around US$11 per day, or around US$30 per person per day with a guide, yurtstay and food.

If you know what you're doing, there's nothing at all to stop you buying your own horse.

Horseback is the perfect way to arrive at Song-Köl. Trips can depart from either Jangy Talap, Chayek, Jumgal or Chekildek and take around three days, staying in yurts en route. The six-day horse trek from Song-Köl to Tash Rabat via the Mazar Valley is an adventurous choice.

There are also good horse treks from Karakol (Altyn Arashan offers some lovely day trips) and Tamga (on the southern shores of Issyk-Köl), as well as Naryn, Arslanbob, Kazarman and Ak-Terek north of Özgön. Kegeti canyon, east of Bishkek, is another popular place for horse riding. See the boxed text, p93, for longer horse-trek ideas.

For organised trips in Kyrgyzstan, the following private local companies are also recommended:

**AsiaRando** (☎ 3132-47710/47711, 517-73 97 78; www.asiarando.com; Padgornaya 67, Rot Front, Chuy Oblast) Horse-riding trips to Song-Köl from their base in Rotfront village. Contact Gérard and Dominique Guillerm.

**Pegasus Horse Trekking** (p297) Trip from Choplan-Ata into the mountains on the north side of Issyk-Köl, including the Ornok Valley and Grigorievka.

**Shepherds Way** (www.kyrgyzstrek.com; p310) Excellent treks into the Terskey Ala-Tau south of Barskoön.

Foreign companies that offer horse-riding trips in Kyrgyzstan include **Wild Frontiers** (www.wildfrontiers.co.uk), **The Adventure Company** (www.adventurecompany.co.uk), **High and Wild** (www.highandwild.co.uk) and **Alexandra Tolstoy** (www.alexandratolstoy.com).

If you know what you're doing, there's nothing at all to stop you buying your own horse, though you'll be haggling with some wily horse traders. You can buy a horse in Karakol's animal bazaar for around US$400 to US$500.

For a classy ride, you can't do better than astride a thoroughbred Akhal-Teke in Turkmenistan. A couple of stables in the Geok-Depe region outside Ashgabat (see p411) offer short rides and some travel agencies can arrange multiday horse treks. **DN Tours** (www.ridingholidays.com) offers an 11-day desert ride on Akhal-Tekes, camping and staying in local villages. **Stan Tours** (www.stantours.com) offers a week-long horse-riding trip through the Kopet Dag Mountains.

Kan Tengri (see p100) offers horse treks through the desert landscapes of Altyn-Emel National Park and also in the central Tian Shan. There are further horseback options in the ecotourism centres of Aksu-Dzhabagly Nature Reserve and Sayram-Ugam National Park (ride between them in three days) and at the Kolsay Lakes in southeast Kazakhstan. These are generally more expensive than in neighbouring Kyrgyzstan.

The German company **Kasachstan Reisen** (http://kasachstanreisen.de) offers interesting horse riding and trekking trips in Kazakhstan.

## CAMEL TREKKING

If you've got Silk Road fever and imagine a multiday caravan across the wastes of Central Asia, you could be in for a disappointment. Bukhara travel agencies arrange camel treks north of Nurata around Lake Aidarkul (p236) and there are also possibilities at Ayaz-Qala in northwest Uzbekistan (p251) but these are mostly short jaunts from comfortable tourist yurts (with electricity, plumbing and three-course meals). The best time for low-altitude desert camel trekking is from March to May, when the spring rains turn the floor of the Kyzylkum into a Jackson Pollock canvas.

For the full-on 'Marco Polo' experience, META in Tajikistan offers one- to three-day treks on Bactrian camels in the high-altitude Rang-Kul region of the eastern Pamirs (see p389).

## MOUNTAIN BIKING

Several tour companies offer supported biking trips over the Torugart Pass, although die-hard do-it-yourselfers will find the Irkeshtam crossing logistically easier. The Kegeti canyon and pass in northern Kyrgyzstan is another biking location favoured by adventure-travel companies. In the past Dostuck Trekking (p100) has offered an amazing mountain-biking itinerary to Merzbacher Lake in the central Tian Shan.

In Kyrgyzstan the Karkara Valley offers a quiet country backroads. From here you can cycle around the southern shore of Issyk-Köl and then up into central Kyrgyzstan. Karakol's Guide and Porters Association (p302) arranges five-day mountain bike trips from Karakol. The dirt road from Almaty to Kyrgyzstan looks like serious fun but you may have visa problems (see p93).

A few die-hards bring their mountain bikes to Central Asia. The most popular route is probably the Pamir Hwy in Tajikistan. For accounts of bicycling around Central Asia see www.tandemtoturkestan.com and www.trans-tadji.info.

You can rent mountain bikes for local trips in Bishkek, Naryn and, possibly, Murgab. You can get some bike parts in Bishkek (see p289).

The website www.mountain.ru/eng has some articles on climbing in Central Asia. The Kyrgyz Alpine Club (www.kac.centralasia.kg) is another good resource.

## RAFTING

A good venue for rafting and kayaking at all skill levels is Tashkent, where you can find flat water on the Syr-Darya and Angren rivers, and more exciting stretches on the Ugam, Chatkal and Pskem. The best season is September through to October. **Asia Raft** (Map pp196-7; ☎ 71-360 09 18; http://asiaraft.netfirms.com/eng; Mavlono Rieziy 77) in Tashkent can arrange trips.

There is easy rafting and canoeing on the Ili River, between Lake Kapshaghay and Lake Balkhash, north of Almaty, from mid-April to mid-October. You could also try the Uba and Ulba Rivers near Ust-Kamenogorsk.

In Kyrgyzstan rafting is possible on the Kokomoron, Chuy (p344), Naryn and Chong-Kemin Rivers (grades II to V). The season runs from 25 June until 15 September and wetsuits are essential in the glacial melt water. Contact **Silk Road Water Centre** (p282; www.rafting.com.kg) to take the plunge.

Great Game Travel in Tajikistan (p362) can help with information on kayaking and rafting in Tajikistan.

## MOUNTAINEERING & ROCK CLIMBING

Central Asian 'alpinism' was very popular during the Soviet era, when climbers dragged their crampons from all over the communist bloc to tackle the region's five impressive 'Snow Leopards' (peaks over 7000m).

Top of the line for altitude junkies are Khan Tengri, Pik Pobedy and other peaks of the central Tian Shan in eastern Kyrgyzstan (p312) and southeast

Kazakhstan (p137). Khan Tengri is a stunningly beautiful peak. Massive Pobedy is the world's most northern 7000m-plus peak and the hardest of Central Asia's 7000m-plus summits.

Several Almaty and Bishkek tour agents can arrange trips to this region, including helicopter flights to the base camps during the climbing season from the end of July to early September. There are two approaches, via the northern Inylchek Glacier from Kazakhstan and along the southern Inylchek Glacier from Kyrgyzstan. Even if you aren't a climber, these are fine treks that lead into a breathtaking mountain amphitheatre. There are no peak fees in Kyrgyzstan but you will need a border zone permit (see p347). Peaks in Tajikistan require a US$100 permit.

The website http://mountains.tos.ru/kopylov/pamir.htm is an excellent climbing resource, with route descriptions, plans and schematic maps. This link is for the Pamir mountain range, follow the index links for other Central Asian regions.

The other prime high-altitude playground is the Pamir in southern Kyrgyzstan and eastern Tajikistan, especially Pik Lenin (Koh-i-Istiqlal), accessed from Achik Tash base camp (p342). Lenin is a non-technical climb and is considered one of the easiest 7000m summits, yet one which has claimed the most lives. The season is July and August. Peaks Koh-i-Samani (Kommunizma; 7495m) and Korzhenevskaya (7105m) are much less known and both accessed from Moskvin Glade base camp to the west.

The most accessible climbing is in Ala-Archa National Park, just outside Bishkek, where popular routes from the Ak-Say glacier require just a couple of days. Mt Korona and Mt Free Korea are the most popular peaks here. The **Alpine Fund** (p282; www.alpinefund.org) in Bishkek is a good resource for this region.

Other 4000m-plus peaks include Mt Sayramsky in the Aksu-Zhabaghly Nature Reserve and Mt Belukha in east Kazakhstan's northern Altay Mountains. Experienced climbers will find that plenty of unclimbed summits await, especially in the Kokshal-Tau range near the border with China.

Some of the best rock climbing is in the Turkestan range in Kyrgyzstan's southern arm, in particular the Karavshin and Liailiak regions, often called 'the Patagonia of Central Asia' due to its towering rock spires. The action focuses on Mt Pyramid (5509m) and the 2km vertical wall of Mt Ak Suu (5335m). Trips to this once volatile region are best organised by a travel company.

*Kyrgyzstan: A Climber's Map & Guide,* by Garth Willis and Martin Gamache, and published by the American Alpine Club, is a map that covers Ala-Archa, the western Kokshal-Tau and Karavshin regions. See p95 in this chapter for more climbing maps.

**Jagged Globe** (www.jagged-globe.co.uk) is one foreign company that offers supported climbs on Khan Tengri. Most of Almaty and Bishkek's trekking agencies arrange mountaineering expeditions, as does Moscow-based **RusAdventure** (www.rusadventure.com).

For more on summits in Central Asia visit www.summitpost.com and start with a search for 'Snow Leopards'.

Mountaineering equipment is hard to find in the region and you should really bring your own gear, though you might find basic equipment at the Leader office in Karakol (no rope).

## WINTER SPORTS

Central Asia's ski season is approximately November to April, with local variations. The region's best-known and best-equipped downhill area is **Chimbulak** (Shymbulak; p130; www.chimbulak.com), a day-trip from Almaty. February is the best time to be there. A lift pass here costs US$31 to US$40 per day. The luxury new Ak Bulak resort near Talgar is due to open winter 2006/7. Almaty made an unsuccessful bid to host the 2014 Winter Olympics.

Skiing is still in its infancy in Kyrgyzstan, but there are options in the Kyrgyz Alatau valleys (especially Ala-Archa), south of Bishkek (p292) and at Karakol (p309). It's possible to rent skis and boards in Bishkek through

Extreme Plus (p289) and ITMC Tien Shan (p284). Nearby Kashka-Suu has a chairlift and 'ski lodge'. Kashka-Suu (www.karakol-ski.kg) in Karakol has pulls and rental equipment between November and March and was revamped in 2005.

Nearly every sports-related agency in Central Asia offers heli-skiing, in which old Aeroflot MI-8 helicopters drop you off on remote high peaks and you ski down. Most guarantee from 3000 to 4000 vertical metres per day for descents of up to 5km but require a group of 12 to 15 people. The Kyrgyz Alatau range behind Bishkek is one of the cheapest places to do this (p293).

Heli-skiing is also awesome in Uzbekistan's Chimgan and Chatkal ranges behind Tashkent from January to May. While the Chatkals aren't huge, they are blanketed in some of the driest, fluffiest powder you'll find anywhere and the winter weather is relatively stable, lessening the chances of getting grounded for days on end. But the best part is the price – US$355 per day for about 6000 vertical metres, which is little more than half of what you'll pay in North America. Book heli-skiing through Asia Travel (p199), as most other agencies go through them.

Kazakhstan's pristine Altay Mountains are renowned for cross-country skiing; the best place to do this is Rakhmanovskie Klyuchi (p172).

A few travel firms in Kazakhstan and Kyrgyzstan offer ski-mountaineering trips in central Tian Shan in July and August, and in the Zailiysky Alatau and Küngey Alatau ranges, between Almaty and Lake Issyk-Köl, from February to April. In Tajikistan contact the **Dushanbe Ski Federation** (p362; www.tajiktraveller.com) for this.

The Medeu ice rink (p130) just outside Almaty is one of the largest speed-skating rinks in the world; it's open to the public on weekends from about November to March. There's also some winter skating at football grounds in Kazakhstan, including at Almaty and Karaganda.

For more on the issues behind community-based tourism see www.unesco.org/culture/ecotourism.

## FOUR-WHEEL DRIVE TRIPS

The back roads of Kyrgyzstan, and particularly Tajikistan's Badakhshan region, offer great scope for adventure travel in an indestructible Russian UAZ 4WD. Four wheel drives can be hired for around US$0.25 to US$0.40 per kilometre in both countries.

In Kyrgyzstan one possible 4WD itinerary leads from Talas over the Kara Bura Pass into the Chatkal river valley and then around to Lake Sary-Chelek. Other tracks lead from Naryn to Barskoön, and Barskoön to Inylchek, through the high Tian Shan.

It's well worth hiring a 4WD from Murgab in the eastern Pamirs for trips out to such gorgeously remote places as Shaimak, Jalang and Zor-Kul (see p389).

More 4WD fun, of a slightly sandier nature, is possible in Turkmenistan. One exciting itinerary is the trip from Yangykala Canyon across the Karakum desert to the Darvaza Gas Craters. Expect plenty of dune bashing, sleeping under starry skies and stops for tea in remote Turkmen villages.

**Kasachstan Reisen** (☎ 030-4285 2005; http://kasachstanreisen.de; Schönhauser Allee 161, Berlin) operate interesting 4WD trips in Kazakhstan.

## OTHER ACTIVITIES

Several companies organise caving trips, especially around Osh in Kyrgyzstan and Chimgan, north of Tashkent in Uzbekistan. It's possible to scuba dive in Lake Issyk-Köl, but some of the equipment used looks like props from a 1960s Jacques Cousteau documentary.

There are some fine opportunities for nature spotting. Kazakhstan's Korgalzhyn Nature Reserve is a water-bird habitat of major importance and offers

In 1990 an earthquake-induced avalanche killed 43 people on Pik Lenin in mountaineering's worst single accident.

the world's most northerly flamingo habitat (between April and September). The tulips of Aksu-Dzhabagly Nature Reserve are world famous and several local and foreign companies run tours to this area in spring. **Kan Tengri** (see below) offers bird-watching and botanical tours in Kazakhstan and **East Line Tours** (www.birdwatching-uzbekistan.com, www.eastlinetour.com) runs bird-watching trips in Uzbekistan. The website www.kazakhstanbirdtours.com is a great resource for bird-watching in Kazakhstan. Foreign companies include **Naturetrek** (www.naturetrek.co.uk), which runs botanical and bird-watching tours of Kazakhstan, and **Wings** (www.wingsbirds.com), which offers a 'Birding the Silk Road' tour of Uzbekistan and Kazakhstan in May. All these websites have good background info on the type of birds you might spot.

**Odyssey Travel** (www.odysseytravel;com.au), in Australia, operates archaeological tours to the Khorezm region of Uzbekistan, during which you'll spend two weeks on an archaeological dig, followed by a short general tour of the country.

Sport fishing is an option in the Ili delta in Kazakhstan p138.

## ADVENTURE TRAVEL OPERATORS IN CENTRAL ASIA

The following travel companies all offer adventure trips in the region, whether it be a full tour or partial logistical support for your own trip.

### Kazakhstan

**Altai Expeditions** (p169; altai_expeditions@dvn.kz) Wide range of active trips and nature tours in the Altay. Email for the current trip list.

**Asia Discovery** (p118; www.asia-discovery.nursat.kz) Experienced agency offering treks, horse riding, rafting and bird-watching tours lasting one to two weeks for €400 to €1100.

**Kan Tengri** (p118; www.kantengri.kz) Kazakhstan's top adventure travel company, offering trekking and heli-skiing in the central Tian Shan (including Mt Khan Tengri) and the ranges between Almaty and Lake Issyk-Köl. Also offers horse treks, mountain biking, heli-skiing, snowboading, sport fishing, bird-watching and botanical tours. A two-week trekking tour typically costs around €1000 per person from Almaty. The company's director is Kazbek Valiev, the first Kazakh to scale Mt Everest.

**Karlygash (Karla) Makatova** (p118; kmakatova@yahoo.com) Independent one-woman operator who offers day hikes, treks and climbs, plus kayaking.

**Rakhmanovskie Klyuchi** (p172; www.altaytravel.ru) This travel firm owns the Rakhmanovskie Klyuchi health resort near Mt Belukha, and offers foot and horse treks in the Altay, plus rafting, skiing and snowboarding elsewhere in the region.

**Tour Asia** (p118; www.tourasia.kz) Long-established company offers trekking and mountaineering in the central Tian Shan, the mountains south of Almaty and the Pamirs, plus horse riding, mountain bike trips and horse treks in Aksu-Dzhabagly

### Kyrgyzstan

Unless otherwise specified, the following companies are based in Bishkek:

**Ak Sai** (p284; www.ak-sai.com) Trekking, mountaineering, biking and heli-skiing. Operates base camps at Inylchek, Pik Lenin and the Red Fox camping store (p289).

**Alp Tour Issyk Köl** (p303; khanin@infotel.kg; Karakol) Contact Stas & Igor. A range of treks around Karakol and further afield, including Kazakhstan and Khan Tengri base camp. They can arrange border permits in a day (US$25), supply guide/cooks (US$25/35 per day), porters (US$18) and climbing guides for Khan Tengri (US$40 to US$50). They will also resupply your own long-distance treks and arrange daily transport on request to the ski base in winter.

**Alptreksport** (p336; Osh) Contact Yury Lavrushin. Two brothers, veterans of the Soviet sports agency Sovintersport's Pamir International Mountaineering Camp (IMC), organise mountaineering, trekking and caving trips, including some around Sary-Chelek, Achik, Jiptik Pass (4185m) and Sary Moghul in the Alay Valley. Yury speaks English and prefers advance bookings.

**Asia Mountains** (p285; www.asiamountains.co.uk) A well-organised agency charging US$25 to US$55 per person per day, depending on the programme. Can get border permits for the Central

Tian Shan, even if you aren't trekking with them. Runs a base camp at Achik Tash and a guesthouse in Bishkek; (p285).

**Dostuck Trekking Ltd** (p284; www.dostuck.com.kg) Offers ascents to peaks, including base camps near Khan Tengri, Pobedy and Lenin as well as less specialised, fixed date treks including yurt camps in the Suusamyr Valley and Tash Rabat. Can arrange helicopter transport and border permits.

**Edelweiss** (p284; www.edelweiss.elcat.kg) Trekking, mountaineering, heli-skiing, horse tours, ski trips and visa support. Contact Slava Alexandrov.

**International Mountaineering Camp Pamir** (IMC Pamir; p284; www.imcpamir.netfirms.com) Trekking and mountaineering programmes and operates the Achik Tash base camp at the foot of Pik Lenin. Contact Bekbolot Koshoev.

**ITMC Tien-Shan** (p284; www.itmc.centralasia.kg) Competent adventure-travel operator offering package and piecemeal help, including mountaineering, with base camps at Khan Tengri, Achik Tash (for Pik Lenin/Independence Peak) and Koh-i-Samani; trekking' heli-skiing and mountain biking.

**Kyrgyz Travel** (p311; ☎ 67 99 75; www.kyrgyz-travel.com; 237 Bakinskaya, Bishkek) Based in Tamga, with horse riding, trekking and biking in mountains south of Issyk-Köl.

**Neofit** (p303; www.neofit.kg/Kyrgyzstan.htm; Karakol) All kinds of trekking support including outfitting and border permits; based in the Neofit guesthouse.

**Novinomad** (p282; www.novinomad.com) Horse treks, mountain bikes and trekking with an environmentally responsible company. Can book CBT trips.

**Tien-Shan Travel** (p284; www.tien-shan.com) Ex-cartographers with expedition gear and a menu of set group tours into the mountains, but unaccustomed to walk-in clients. Contact Vladimir Birukov.

**Top Asia** (p285; www.topasia.kg) Trekking, mountaineering and horse riding.

**Turkestan** (see p302; www.karakol.kg; Karakol) Professionally-run treks and mountaineering trips to Khan Tengri, horse treks into the Küngey Alatau mountains north of Issyk-Köl. In winter they operate heli-skiing trips (eight-day package for 14 skiers, US$2250 per person). Contact Sergey Pyshnenko.

For useful but dated info on Sokuluk, Suusamyr, Kyzyl-Oi and the Chong-Kemin Valley see www.kirgistan-reisen.de

## Tajikistan

**Great Game Travel Co** (p362; www.greatgame.travel; Dushanbe) Treks to the interesting Yagnob region and to Sarez Lake, plus the Fan Mountains and support for most other adventures you can dream up. British-run and contactable in the UK or Dushanbe.

**Pamir Adventure** (☎ 223 54 24; surat@pamir-adventure.com, www.pamir-adventure.com; Dushanbe) Pamir treks operated by the experienced English-speaking trekking guide Surat Toimastov.

**Pamir Travel** (☎ 2240906; www.travel-pamir.com; Rudaki 154-8, Dushanbe) Good for Fan Mountain treks.

**Yevgeny and Elena Lourens** (☎ 237 91 76; lem_camp@mail.ru; Dushanbe;) English-speaking trekking and adventure guides who run the base camp for Peak Koh-i-Samani.

## Turkmenistan

**Ayan Travel** (p408; www.ayan-travel.com; Ashgabat) Wildlife watching, horse treks, hikes, camel trek, 4WD desert tours.

**DN Tours** (p408; www.dntours.com; Ashgabat) Horse riding.

## Uzbekistan

**Asia Travel** (p199; www.asia-travel.uz; Tashkent) Trekking and climbing specialists, with mountain biking and camel trekking in central Uzbekistan, horse riding from Arkit, heli-skiing.

**Elena Tour** (p199; www.elenatour.uz; Tashkent) Trekking, horse treks, rafting, camel treks around Nurata, heli-skiing in Chimgan and mountain-bike trips, with a focus on the Chimgan and Chatkat area, northeast of Tashkent.

**Orient Star** (p225; www.tour-orient.com; Samarkand) Trekking in the Zerafshan, Hissar and Fan Mountains.

# Kazakhstan Казахстан

The world's ninth-biggest country is one of its last great travel unknowns. Though the outside world is gradually becoming aware of Kazakhstan, largely thanks to its oil and the antics of that pseudo-Kazakh Borat Sagdiyev, few have explored this country of vastly varied attractions.

The most economically advanced of the 'stans', post-Soviet Kazakhstan is reinventing itself as a uniquely prosperous and modern Eurasian nation. The leafy commercial and social hub, Almaty, has an almost European feel with its quality hotels, slick boutiques, chic cafés and luxurious cars. Astana, in the north, is being transformed at quickfire speed into a 21st-century capital with a mix of Islamic, Western, Soviet and wacky futuristic architecture. President Nazarbaev, who's ruled Kazakhstan since Soviet times, doesn't encourage political opposition but is managing to forge a peaceful, multiethnic nation – which makes him on the whole pretty popular.

Around the great steppes where the once nomadic Kazakh people – still famed for their horse skills – used to roam, Kazakhstan presents an array of adventures. You can trek on foot or horse in the spectacular Tian Shan or Altay Mountains, watch flamingos on steppe lakes or discover mysterious underground mosques near the Caspian Sea. Ecotourism programmes in some of the most beautiful areas enable travellers to stay with village families at affordable cost.

With travellers still rare here, a foreign guest is usually treated not as just another tourist but with real hospitality, and locals will often go out of their way to help you. Enjoy it while it lasts!

**FAST FACTS**

- **Area** 2.7 million sq km
- **Capital** Astana
- **Country Code** ☎ 7 (the same as Russia)
- **Famous For** oil, steppe, Borat
- **Languages** Kazakh, Russian
- **Money** tenge (T); US$1 = 128T; €1 = 177T
- **Phrases** *salemetsiz be* (hello); *rakhmet* (thanks).
- **Population** 15 million

**HOW MUCH?**

- Snickers bar US$0.50
- 100km bus ride US$2
- One-minute phone call to the US/UK US$2
- Internet per hour US$1.75
- Traditional hat US$10
- 1L of bottled water US$0.50
- Bottle of local beer US$1
- Shashlyk US$1
- 1L of petrol US$0.70

## HIGHLIGHTS

- **Almaty** (p113) Leafy, sophisticated metropolis at the foot of the Tian Shan.
- **Aksu-Dzhabagly Nature Reserve** (p146) Hikes, homestays and horse rides amid gorgeous mountain scenery.
- **Zailiysky Alatau & Central Tian Shan** (p130, p134 and p137) Great mountain trekking, hiking and climbing.
- **Astana** (p159) Twenty-first-century fantasy architecture in a brand-new capital.
- **Turkistan** (p148) Magnificent Timurid architecture at the country's holiest site.

## ITINERARIES

- **Three days** Explore Almaty by foot, taking in Panfilov Park, the Arasan Baths, the Central State Museum and the Kök-Töbe cable car, and make a one- or two-day trip into the mountains south of the city. If you're travelling on to Kyrgyzstan in summer, use the Karkara Valley crossing.
- **One week** Extend the three-day itinerary with time in southern Kazakhstan – Shymkent, lovely Aksu-Dzhabagly Nature Reserve and the splendour of Turkistan – or head for the spectacular central Tian Shan in Kazakhstan's far southeastern corner.
- **Two weeks** The extra week allows for a more leisurely exploration of the south and east, adding hiking in the Zhungar Alatau mountains (from Lepsinsk) or the Altay, and a visit to Kazakhstan's capital-under-construction, Astana.
- **One month** You can get around the whole country, taking in more adventurous destinations such as the Aral Sea and the strange underground mosques and dramatic rock formations of the deserts outside Aktau.

## CLIMATE & WHEN TO GO

Like the rest of Central Asia, Kazakhstan has hot summers and very cold winters. During the hottest months, July and August, average daily maximums reach the high 20°Cs in Almaty and Astana.

During the tourist low-season months of November to March, frosty mornings are typical in Almaty and temperatures there typically remain below freezing for much of December, January and February. The ground is snow-covered for an average 111 days a year. In sub-Siberian Astana there's frost from October to April, with temperatures lurking between -10°C and -20°C from December to February.

Annual precipitation ranges from less than 100mm a year in the deserts to 1500mm in the Altay Mountains.

You can travel any time of year with the right preparation and logistics, but the most comfortable months are May to September. July, August and September are best for trekking in the southeastern and eastern mountains. See p446 for an Almaty climate chart.

## HISTORY

The early history of Kazakhstan is a shadowy procession of nomadic empires, most of whom swept into the region from the east and left few records. Recurring themes down the millennia include a great deal of large-scale slaughter and a contrast between Kazakhstan's far south, which was within the ambit of the settled Silk Road civilisations of Transoxiana (between the Syr-Darya and Amu-Darya rivers), and the rest of the country, which remained the domain of nomadic horseback animal herders until the 20th century.

### Early Peoples

By around 500 BC southern Kazakhstan was inhabited by the Saka (Scythian), a nomadic people who are considered part of the vast network of Scythian cultures that stretched across the steppes from the Altay to Ukraine. The Saka left many burial mounds, in some of which fabulous relics have been found – above all, the Golden Man (see p119), a superb warrior's costume discovered near Almaty which has become a national symbol.

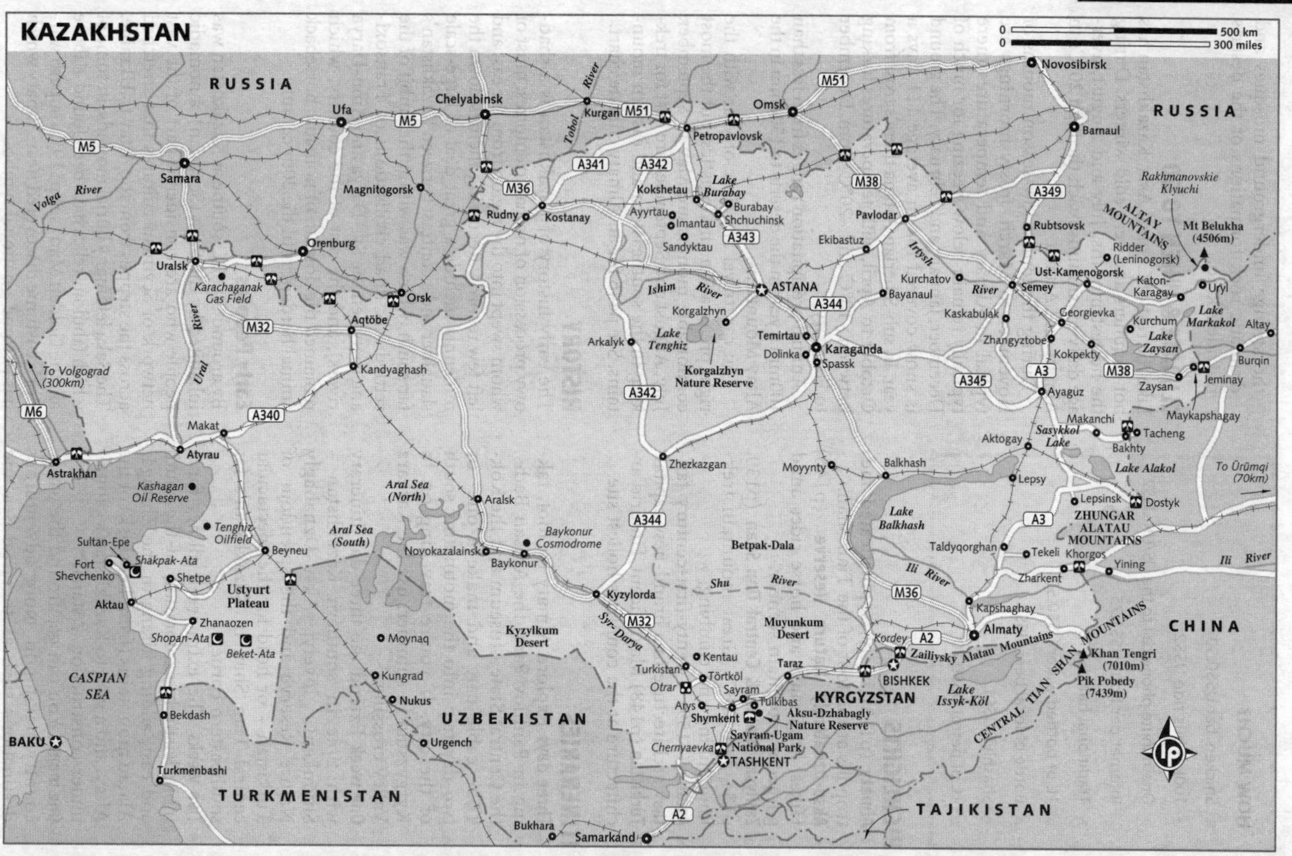
KAZAKHSTAN
0 500 km
0 300 miles
RUSSIA
CHINA
KYRGYZSTAN
UZBEKISTAN
TURKMENISTAN
TAJIKISTAN
ASTANA
BISHKEK
TASHKENT
BAKU
CASPIAN SEA
Aral Sea (North)
Aral Sea (South)
Lake Balkhash
Lake Alakol
Sasykkol Lake
Lake Zaysan
Lake Markakol
Lake Issyk-Köl
Lake Tenghiz
Lake Burabay
ALTAY MOUNTAINS
ZHUNGAR ALATAU MOUNTAINS
CENTRAL TIAN SHAN MOUNTAINS
Zailiysky Alatau Mountains
Mt Belukha (4506m)
Khan Tengri (7010m)
Pik Pobedy (7439m)
Rakhmanovskie Klyuchi
Ustyurt Plateau
Betpak-Dala
Muyunkum Desert
Kyzylkum Desert
Korgalzhyn Nature Reserve
Aksu-Dzhabagly Nature Reserve
Sayram-Ugam National Park
Baykonur Cosmodrome
Karachaganak Gas Field
Tenghiz Oilfield
Kashagan Oil Reserve
Beket-Ata
Shopan-Ata
Shakpak-Ata
Irtysh River
Ishim River
Ili River
Shu River
Syr-Darya
Ural River
Tobol River
Volga River
To Ürümqi (70km)
To Volgograd (300km)
Novosibirsk
Barnaul
Rubtsovsk
Ust-Kamenogorsk
Ridder (Leninogorsk)
Semey
Katon-Karagay
Uryl
Burqin
Altay
Jeminay
Maykapshagay
Kurchum
Zaysan
Kokpekty
Georgievka
Zhangyztobe
Ayaguz
Makanchi
Tacheng
Bakhty
Dostyk
Lepsinsk
Aktogay
Lepsy
Tekeli
Khorgos
Yining
Zharkent
Taldyqorghan
Kapshaghay
Almaty
Kordey
Balkhash
Moyynty
Omsk
Pavlodar
Ekibastuz
Kurchatov
Kaskabulak
Bayanaul
Karaganda
Spassk
Dolinka
Temirtau
Petropavlovsk
Kokshetau
Burabay
Shchuchinsk
Imantau
Sandyktau
Ayyrtau
Korgalzhyn
Arkalyk
Zhezkazgan
Kurgan
Kostanay
Rudny
Chelyabinsk
Magnitogorsk
Orsk
Aqtöbe
Kandyaghash
Ufa
Orenburg
Samara
Uralsk
Makat
Atyrau
Astrakhan
Beyneu
Zhanaozen
Shetpe
Aktau
Fort Shevchenko
Sultan-Epe
Aralsk
Novokazalainsk
Baykonur
Kyzylorda
Turkistan
Otrar
Kentau
Törtköl
Sayram
Arys
Shymkent
Chernyaevka
Tulkibas
Taraz
Moynaq
Kungrad
Nukus
Urgench
Bukhara
Samarkand
Bekdash
Turkmenbashi
M51
M38
M36
M32
M5
M6
A349
A345
A344
A343
A342
A341
A340
A3
A2

**TRAVELLING SAFELY IN KAZAKHSTAN**

Kazakhstan is a safe country to travel in, provided you maintain normal safety precautions (p447). The oil towns of Atyrau and Aktau have seen a few violent incidents and robberies.

Try to avoid the police, who are often only interested in foreigners as possible sources of bribes for minor 'infringements'.

The former nuclear testing area outside Semey, the Polygon, still has extreme levels of radiation in unmarked areas.

From 200 BC the Huns, followed by various Turkic peoples, migrated here from what are now Mongolia and northern China. The early Turks left totemlike carved stones known as *balbals,* bearing the images of honoured chiefs, at burial/worship/sacrifice sites. These can be seen in many museums in Kazakhstan today. From about AD 550 to 750 the southern half of Kazakhstan was the western extremity of the Kök (Blue) Turk empire, which reached across the steppe from Manchuria.

The far south of Kazakhstan was within the sphere of the Bukhara-based Samanid dynasty from the mid-9th century and here cities such as Otrar and Yasy (now Turkistan) developed on the back of agriculture and Silk Road trade. When the Karakhanid Turks from the southern Kazakh steppe ousted the Samanids in the late 10th century, they took up the Samanids' settled ways (as well as Islam) and constructed some of Kazakhstan's earliest surviving buildings (in and around Taraz).

## Jenghiz Khan

Around AD 1130 the Karakhanids were displaced by the Khitans, a Buddhist people driven out of Mongolia and northern China. The Central Asian state set up by the Khitans, known as the Karakitay empire, stretched from Xinjiang to Transoxiana but in the early 13th century it became prey to rising powers at both extremities. To the west was the Khorezmshah empire, based in Khorezm, south of the Aral Sea. In 1210 the Khorezmshah Mohammed II conquered Transoxiana.

To the east was Jenghiz Khan, who sent an army to crush the Karakitay in 1218, then turned to the Khorezmshah empire, which had misguidedly rebuffed his relatively peaceable overtures by murdering 450 of his merchants at Otrar. The biggest Mongol army in history (150,000 or more) sacked Samarkand, Bukhara and Otrar, then carried on westwards to Europe and the Middle East. All of Kazakhstan, like the rest of Central Asia, became part of the Mongol empire.

On Jenghiz Khan's death in 1227, his enormous empire was divided between his sons. The lands most distant from the Mongol heartland – from the Aral Sea to Ukraine and Moscow – went to the descendants of his eldest son Jochi and came to be known as the Golden Horde. The bulk of Kazakhstan went to Jenghiz Khan's second son Chaghatai, and became known as the Chaghatai khanate. In the late 14th century far southern Kazakhstan was conquered by Timur from Samarkand.

## The Kazakhs

The Kazakh people, descendants of the Mongols and of peoples who survived their conquest, did not emerge as a distinct group until the 15th century. The story actually starts with the Uzbeks, a group of Islamised Mongols named after a 14th-century leader Özbeg (Uzbek), who were left in control of northern Kazakhstan as the Golden Horde disintegrated in the 15th century.

In 1468 an internal feud split the Uzbeks into two groups. Those who ended up south of the Syr-Darya ruled from Bukhara as the Shaybanid dynasty and ultimately gave their name to modern Uzbekistan. Those who stayed north remained nomadic and became the Kazakhs, taking their name from a Turkic word meaning free rider, adventurer or outlaw.

In the late 15th and 16th centuries the Kazakhs established one of the last great nomadic empires, stretching across the steppe and desert north, east and west of the Syr-Darya. They even briefly ruled a chunk of Siberia from Sibir (modern Tobolsk) from 1563 to 1582.

The three Kazakh hordes that had emerged – with which Kazakhs today still identify – were the Great (or Elder) Horde in the south, the Middle Horde in the centre and northeast, and the Little (or Young or Lesser) Horde in the west. Each was ruled by a khan and composed of a number of clans whose leaders held the title *axial, bi* or *batyr*.

Despite their military prowess, the three clans failed to unite against danger, and were defeated first by the Zhungars (Oyrats), a warlike Mongol clan who subjugated eastern Kazakhstan between 1690 and 1720 (the 'Great Disaster'), and later by the Russians.

## The Russians Arrive

Russia's expansion across Siberia ran up against the Zhungars, against whom they built a line of forts along the Kazakhs' northern border. The Kazakhs sought tsarist protection from the Zhungars, and the khans of all three hordes swore loyalty to the Russian crown between 1731 and 1742. Russia later chose to interpret these oaths as agreements to annexation, and gradually extended its 'protection' of the khanates to their ultimate abolition. Despite repeated Kazakh uprisings, notably by Abylay Khan's grandson Kenisary Qasimov in the 1840s, Russia steadily tightened its grip.

The revolts were brutally suppressed. By some estimates one million of the four million Kazakhs died in revolts and famines before 1870. Meanwhile, movement of peasant settlers into Kazakhstan was stimulated by the abolition of serfdom in Russia and Ukraine in 1861. The tsarist regime also used Kazakhstan as a place of exile for dissidents – among them Fyodor Dostoevsky and the Ukrainian nationalist writer and artist Taras Shevchenko.

In 1916 Russian mobilisation of Kazakhs as support labour behind the WWI front caused a widespread uprising. It was brutally quashed, with an estimated 150,000 Kazakhs killed and perhaps 200,000 fleeing to China.

## The Communist Takeover

In the chaos following the Russian Revolution of 1917, a Kazakh nationalist party, Alash Orda, tried to establish an independent government. Alash Orda's leader was Ali Khan Bukeykhanov, a prince and descendant of Jenghiz Khan, and ultimately a victim of Stalin's 1930s purges.

As the Russian civil war raged across Kazakhstan, Alash Orda eventually sided with the Bolsheviks who emerged victorious in 1920 – only for Alash members soon to be purged from the Communist Party of Kazakhstan (CPK). Meanwhile many thousands more Kazakhs and Russian peasants had died in the civil war, which devastated the land and economy, and several hundred thousand fled to China and elsewhere.

The next disaster to befall the Kazakhs was denomadisation, which began in the late 1920s. The world's biggest group of seminomadic people was pushed one step up the Marxist evolutionary ladder to become settled farmers in new collectives. They slaughtered their herds rather than hand them over to state control and, unused to agriculture, died in their hundreds of thousands from famine and disease. Those who opposed collectivisation were sent to labour camps or killed. Kazakhstan's population fell by more than two million between 1926 and 1933.

## 'Development' & Unrest

In the 1930s and '40s more and more people from other parts of the USSR, prisoners and otherwise, were sent to work in new industrial towns and labour camps in Kazakhstan. Camp inmates included entire peoples deported en masse from western areas of the USSR around the time of WWII. A further wave of around 800,000 migrants arrived in the 1950s when Nikita Khrushchev decided to plough up 250,000 sq km of north Kazakhstan steppe to grow wheat in the Virgin Lands scheme (see p111).

Although the labour camps were wound down in the mid-1950s, many survivors stayed on. Yet more Russians, Ukrainians and other Soviet nationalities arrived to mine and process Kazakhstan's reserves of coal, iron and oil. The population of Kazakhs in Kazakhstan dwindled to less than 30%.

The CPK's leader from 1964 to 1986 was a Kazakh named Dinmukhamed Kunaev. Although he was corrupt, Kunaev's replacement by a Russian, Gennady Kolbin, in 1986 provoked big demonstrations and violent riots in many cities.

During the Cold War the USSR decided Kazakhstan was 'empty' and 'remote' enough to use for its chief nuclear bomb testing ground (the Semipalatinsk Polygon; see p111) and its space launch centre (the Baykonur Cosmodrome, see p150). In 1989 Kazakhstan produced the first great popular protest movement the USSR had seen: the Nevada-Semey (Semipalatinsk) Movement, which forced an end to nuclear tests in Kazakhstan.

## Independence

Nursultan Nazarbaev, born into a rural Kazakh peasant family in 1940, began to rise up the CPK ranks in the 1970s. A protégé of Kunaev, he became first secretary (party leader) in 1989 and has ruled Kazakhstan ever since. In 1991 Nazarbaev did not welcome the break-up of

### KAZAKHSTAN'S OIL

Kazakhstan's proven oil reserves are about 35 billion barrels, enough to supply the whole world for a year at current consumption rates. The government expects this figure to rise to more than 100 billion barrels by 2015, putting Kazakhstan in the world's top five nations for oil reserves. These riches are not only key to Kazakhstan's development but also a magnet to foreign governments and oil companies.

Tenghiz, southeast of Atyrau, is one of the world's 10 biggest oilfields, with reserves of at least six billion barrels and possibly 15 billion. It's being pumped by Tengizchevroil, a joint venture whose main partners are the Kazakhstan government and the US oil giant Chevron. Chevron's gamble in striking this deal way back in 1992, in the turbulent aftermath of the Soviet collapse, bought it some of the cheapest oil of modern times. The Kashagan field, 400m below the Caspian seabed, is three times as big as Tenghiz – it's the world's richest oil find since Prudhoe Bay, Alaska, in 1967, and is likely to come on stream in 2010 (Italy's Eni is the operator heading a multicompany international consortium).

Kazakh oil production in 2005 was 1.3 million barrels a day, making it one of the world's top 20 producers. This is scheduled to at least double (to about 3% of world consumption) by 2015.

Where Kazakh oil goes is a geopolitical issue. Most currently runs through pipelines into Russia, including a major pipe to the Black Sea port of Novorossiysk. Increasing amounts, however, now avoid Russia by being shipped across the Caspian to Baku (Azerbaijan), to feed into the Baku-Tbilisi-Ceyhan (BTC) pipeline, opened in 2005, which takes oil to the Turkish Mediterranean port of Ceyhan. A new Kazakh oil port is being built at Kuryk, 76km south of Aktau, for trans-Caspian tankers. The first oil pipeline from Kazakhstan not to go through Russia was also inaugurated in 2005, from Atasu in central Kazakhstan to western China. This will eventually be linked to the Caspian oilfields, where oil-thirsty China has been buying up reserves.

Kazakhstan also has at least three trillion cubic metres of gas, of which 500 billion are in the Karachaganak field east of Aqtöbe. These figures are modest compared with neighbouring Russia and Turkmenistan, but a massive trans-Caspian gas pipeline is under discussion to feed Kazakh gas to Europe – something Russia is unhappy about since it would be bypassed. Kazakh gas production is due to rise from 25 billion cubic metres a year to 45 billion by 2105.

the USSR and Kazakhstan was the last Soviet republic to declare independence. He soon renounced the opportunity for Kazakhstan to become a nuclear power by transferring all 1410 Soviet nuclear warheads on Kazakh soil to Russia. Kazakhstan's first multiparty elections, in 1994, returned a parliament favourable to Nazarbaev, but were judged unfair by foreign observers. There were complaints of arbitrary barring of some candidates, ballot rigging and media distortion.

The parliament, however, turned out to be a thorn in Nazarbaev's side, obstructing his free-market economic reforms, which one deputy called 'shock surgery without anaesthetics'. Nazarbaev dissolved parliament in 1995 and soon afterwards won an overwhelming referendum majority to extend his presidential term until 2000. New parliamentary elections returned a new assembly favourable to Nazarbaev.

In 1997 Nazarbaev moved Kazakhstan's capital from Almaty to Astana, then a medium-sized provincial city in the central north, citing Astana's more central location and greater proximity to Russia. He may also have wanted to mollify Kazakhstan's restive Russian population, concentrated in the north of the country. Despite incredulity at first, the new capital is there to stay and Astana is being transformed at great cost with impressive, sometimes spectacular, new buildings.

Nazarbaev's free-market economic policies won the support of Western governments and companies, some of which paid vast amounts to get a slice of Kazakhstan's large oil and gas reserves, mainly near and beneath the Caspian Sea. In 1999 Nazarbaev had a virtual walkover in new presidential elections after the main opposition leader, Akezhan Kazhegeldin, was barred from standing.

## CURRENT EVENTS

Nazarbaev continues to rule Kazakhstan with an iron hand, but enjoys broad popularity as the country posts 9% to 10% economic growth year after year and maintains broad ethnic harmony. He argues openly that democratic reform can only succeed on the back of economic progress. He won yet another seven-year presidential term with over 90% of the vote in the 2005 elections. International observers denounced the vote as unfair, as they have done every election held in post-Soviet Kazakhstan. Nazarbaev's political rivals and critics are frequently sacked, jailed and even, in two cases in 2005 and 2006, found shot dead. (The government denied any involvement in the deaths.)

Even Nazarbaev's commitment to *eventual* democracy is under question: his eldest daughter Dariga Nazarbaeva, a powerful media owner and previously a mild critic of her father, merged her own political party, Asar, with his, Otan, in 2006. Nazarbaev is reckoned one of the world's richest men and his family circle is said to have at least a finger in every important enterprise in the country.

Many in the growing middle class want to see more genuine democracy and less corruption, and while the elite are unbelievably rich, by Nazarbaev's own admission almost 16% of the population still live below the poverty line. Rural migrants live in illegal settlements on the fringes of Almaty and Astana, and the country's health-care system is woefully antiquated.

Nazarbaev's long-term strategy for Kazakhstan is to use its natural-resource wealth to build a diversified, hi-tech economy by the year 2030. He sees Kazakhstan as 'a Central Asian snow leopard, creating a model to be followed by other developing countries'. He admires Lee Kuan Yew of Singapore and Margaret Thatcher, and has forged warm relationships with the main Western powers while remaining on good terms with Russia and China (also eager customers for Kazakh oil) and rubbing along OK with Kazakhstan's Central Asian neighbours.

Taking Norway's successful use of its North Sea oil as a model, Kazakhstan salts away some of its oil revenue in a national oil fund, worth US$8 billion by 2005, which is designed to accumulate wealth for the future and reduce Kazakhstan's vulnerability to oil price swings. As the oil and gas are pumped ever faster it's not easy to see where Kazakhstan can go wrong, on the economic front at least.

With a vision of a trilingual populace speaking Kazakh, Russian and English by 2030, Nazarbaev is also considering a change from the Cyrillic to the Latin alphabet.

## PEOPLE

Whereas rural Kazakhs have maintained some old traditions, particularly on display during festivals or weddings, most modern Kazakhs have mixed long enough with Slavs to make them seem almost European in their dress, work habits and home life. Their former nomadic lifestyle, however, has bequeathed a certain laid-back and open attitude which separates them from their Russian brethren.

Quality of life for most people in Kazakhstan has improved since the difficult years following independence. A middle class has emerged and in places such as Almaty and Astana their incomes are fuelling the opening of ever more leisure complexes, malls, car showrooms, nightclubs and restaurants.

While the rich, who earn salaries comparable to middle-income Europe, build themselves mansions up in the valleys around Almaty, home life for others hasn't changed much. Several generations of a family are still accustomed to living under one roof, with grandparents often caring for children while parents go to work. Kazakh homes tend to be decorated with colourful carpets and tapestries, a tradition inherited from brightly decked yurts.

In precommunist Kazakhstan, when most homes were one-room yurts, women occupied an important place in maintaining the home while husbands were out in the pastures, sometimes for extended periods. Islamic tendencies, however, gave ultimate domination to men. Following independence, economic depression forced many women to abandon careers in favour of less sophisticated jobs such as working in bazaars. Women occupy 20% of ministerial positions in the government.

Family and ancestry remain very important to Kazakhs. They determine both a person's *zhus* (horde) and clan. The best ancestor of all is Jenghiz Khan, and right up to the 20th century the Kazakh nobility consisted of those who could trace their lineage back to him.

### Population

Southern areas are about 90% Kazakh; this figure declines the further north one travels; in many northern towns the majority population is Russian. An estimated 40% of people live in rural areas.

### KAZAKHSTAN READING LIST

As Kazakhstan becomes more important to the Western world, more books in English are helping outsiders to understand the country.

- *Once in Kazakhstan: The Snow Leopard Emerges* by Keith Rosten (2004). Lively account of life in Kazakhstan against the backdrop of its current affairs and history.
- *Modern Clan Politics and Beyond: The Power of "Blood" in Kazakhstan* by Edward Schatz (2005). Investigates the ongoing influence of the traditional Kazakh *zhus* (hordes).
- *The New Great Game: Blood and Oil in Central Asia* by Lutz Kleveman (2004). Very readable introduction to Caspian oil and its politics.
- *The Silent Steppe* by Mukhamet Shayakhmetov (published in English 2006). First-hand account of the horrors of collectivisation and WWII.
- *Kazakhstan: Unfulfilled Promise* by Martha Brill Olcott (2002). Edgy commentary on independent Kazakhstan, heavily critical of its democratic failings.
- *The Kazakhs* by Martha Brill Olcott (1995). Authoritative tome of several hundred detailed pages that will keep you quiet for many a long evening on the steppe.

To understand Kazakh current affairs, keep a check on the **Roberts Report** (www.roberts-report.com) and **Eurasianet** (www.eurasianet.org).

About 56% of the 15 million population are Kazakhs – a big upward swing from Soviet times, aided by emigration of Russians, Germans and Ukrainians since independence and the arrival of hundreds of thousands of *oralman* (ethnic Kazakhs repatriating from other countries). The numbers of *oralman* are much higher than the government planned for and many have found themselves without decent housing or proper jobs. The total population is down by over two million since the early 1990s.

Other main ethnic groups are Russians (27%), Ukrainians and Uzbeks (3% each), and Germans, Tatars and Uyghurs (about 1.5% each). There are more than 100 other nationalities. Despite occasional incidents of unrest and some resentment among Russians over laws enshrining Kazakh as the country's official language, on the whole Kazakhstan's diverse ethnic groups rub along well with each other.

## RELIGION

Kazakhstan as a nation has never been deeply religious and extremism is notable by its absence. Islam, the leading faith among Kazakhs, is at its strongest in the south, especially around Taraz, Shymkent and Turkistan. Pilgrimages to the mausoleum of Kozha Akhmed Yasaui at Turkistan and the desert shrine of Beket-Ata, east of Aktau, are important ways for Kazakh Muslims to affirm their faith. Most Muslims are of the Sunni denomination, while the Russian Orthodox Church is the major Christian denomination. The government trumpets Kazakhstan's tradition of religious tolerance.

## ARTS

The new Kazakhstan is forging an identity based on old traditions, monuments and cultural icons. Some of the most inspiring symbols, such as the Scythian-style Golden Man costume (see p119) or the Kozha Akhmed Yasaui Mausoleum (p149), were actually not Kazakh in origin but left on the territory by earlier inhabitants. Other elements, such as the writings of the national bard Abay Kunanbaev (1845–1904; see p173), or the riveting *aitys* (song duels) between skilled bards, are purely Kazakh.

The national musical instrument is the *dombra*, a small two-stringed lute with an oval box shape. Other instruments include the *qobyz* (a two-stringed primitive fiddle), the playing of which is said to have brought Jenghiz Khan to tears, and the *sybyzgy* (two flutes made of reed or wood strapped together like abbreviated pan pipes). The best place to catch Kazakh musical concerts is Almaty's State Philharmonia (see p126).

The music is largely folk tunes, handed down like the area's oral literature through

**NOMAD**

As Kazakhs continue to reassert their identity, the government invested almost US$40 million in the Hollywood-style epic *Nomad* (*Koshpendiler* in Kazakh, *Kochevnik* in Russian), about 18th-century Kazakh resistance to the invading Zhungars and unification under Abylay Khan. This all-action, lavishly filmed production was the most expensive Kazakh film ever made. An entire 18th-century town was built on the steppe near the Ili River, and the cast included Hollywood stars Jay Hernandez, Jason Scott Lee, Kuno Becker, Ron Yuan and Mark Dacascos. *Nomad* proved a big hit on release in Kazakhstan in 2006. Release in the West was pending at time of writing. The film was based on part of a celebrated historical novel of Kazakh nation-building, *Nomads,* by Ilyas Yesenberlin (1915–83).

the generations. The most skilled singers or bards are called *akyns*. Undoubtedly the most famous and important form of Kazakh art is the *aitys,* a duel between two *dombra* players who challenge each other in poetic lyrics. This may be seen during Nauryz (Navrus or 'New Days', the main Islamic spring festival on 22 March; see p179) and possibly other holidays, including 9 May (Victory Day) and 16 December (Independence Day). Meanwhile, Kazakh pop music is enjoying its greatest popularity, largely thanks to talent contests such as SuperStar KZ, the local version of Pop Idol. Stars like Madina Sadvaqasova, Roman Kim and Makpal Isabekova, who may sing in Russian, Kazakh or English, are all products of this trend.

As a nation of nomads, Kazakhs have little architectural or artistic tradition, but some of the new buildings going up in Astana display a uniquely Kazakhstani mix of Asian, Western and Russian styles – undeniably spectacular in some cases – and beautiful new mosques have been built in Pavlodar, Almaty and Astana.

High skills were developed in the crafts associated with nomadic life, such as brightly woven carpets and wall-hangings for yurts, jewellery, ornate horse tackle and weaponry, and splendid costumes for special occasions. You can admire these in almost any museum in the country.

## ENVIRONMENT

### The Land

Except for strings of mountains along its southern and eastern borders, Kazakhstan is almost as flat as a pancake. At 2.7 million sq km, it's the ninth-biggest country in the world, about the size of Western Europe. It borders Russia to the north, Turkmenistan, Uzbekistan and Kyrgyzstan in the south, and China in the east. It has lengthy shorelines on the Caspian Sea (1894km) and on the Aral Sea, which it shares with Uzbekistan.

Southeast Kazakhstan lies along the northern edge of the Tian Shan; Mt Khan Tengri (7010m) pegs the China–Kazakhstan–Kyrgyzstan border. Kazakhstan's eastern border, shared with China, is a series of mountain ranges culminating in the Altay where some peaks top 4000m.

The north of the country is flat, mostly treeless steppe, as much akin to Siberia as to Central Asia, with much of its original grassland now turned over to wheat or other agriculture. Further south and west the steppe is increasingly arid, becoming desert or semidesert. A surprising number of lakes break up the steppe, especially in the north.

The most important rivers are the Syr-Darya, flowing across the south of Kazakhstan to the Little Aral Sea; the Ural, flowing from Russia into the Caspian Sea; the Ili, flowing out of China into Lake Balkhash; and the Irtysh, which flows across northeast Kazakhstan into Siberia. Lake Balkhash in the central east is the fourth-largest lake in Asia (17,400 sq km) but very shallow – only 26m at its deepest point.

### Wildlife

Kazakhstan's mountains are rich in wildlife, including bear, lynx, argali sheep, ibex, wolves, wild boar, several types of deer, the goitred gazelle (known locally as the zheyran), and the elusive snow leopard, of which about 30 remain in the Altay, the mountains south of Almaty and the Aksu-Dzhabagly Nature Reserve. The saiga antelope population has been reduced from two million to 40,000 in 20 years, chiefly by poaching: its horns are considered an aphrodisiac in China. The saiga survives in Kazakhstan only in the Betpak-Dala desert west of Lake Balkhash and in an area near Uralsk. The antlers of the large maral deer are also believed to have aphrodisiac properties and the animal is farmed for this reason in the Altay. In the Altyn-Emel National Park, Przewalski's horses, extinct in Kazakhstan since 1940, have been reintroduced from zoos in Europe.

The golden eagle on Kazakhstan's flag is a good omen for ornithologists. Hundreds of bird species are to be seen, from the paradise flycatcher of Aksu-Dzhabagly to the Himalayan snowcock and the relict gulls of Lake Alakol. More spectacular to the casual traveller are the thousands of flamingos which spend summer at Korgalzhyn Nature Reserve, 150km southwest of Astana. See www.kazakhstanbirdtours.com for good bird background.

## Environmental Issues

Because of its vast size and relative emptiness, Kazakhstan, more than any other Central Asian country, was forced to endure the worst excesses of the Soviet system – a fearful legacy it is still grappling with. The Aral Sea catastrophe (p151) is well known, but the country also continues to suffer from the fallout, both literal and metaphorical, of Soviet nuclear tests conducted mainly near Semey in eastern Kazakhstan. The Caspian Sea is another environmental flashpoint, as oil and gas exploitation has an increasing impact. Industrial air pollution, especially from metallurgical plants, is still bad in cities such as Karaganda, Ust-Kamenogorsk, Ekibastuz and Kostanay.

### NUCLEAR TESTS

During the Cold War, far from both Moscow and the eyes of the West, some 460 nuclear tests were carried out at the Polygon, as the testing ground near Semey was known. Although looking empty on the map, the region around the Polygon certainly wasn't uninhabited: villagers living close by were given virtually no protection or warning of the dangers.

The end for the Polygon came about as a result of the Nevada-Semey Movement, a popular protest launched in the wake of two particular tests in 1989. Within a few days more than a million signatures had been collected on Kazakhstan's streets calling for an end to the tests. The Communist Party of Kazakhstan called for the closure of the Polygon, and President Nazarbaev closed the site in 1991 after the collapse of the USSR, announcing compensation for the victims. The tragic effects linger, however: genetic mutations, cancers, weakened immune systems and mental illness continue to destroy lives and occupy hospitals and clinics in and around Semey, and may do so for generations to come. The website of Kazakhstan's embassy in the USA (www.kazakhembus.com) issues a heartfelt plea for assistance and an appeal on behalf of the Semey Oncology Centre where cancers are treated. The UN Development Programme says the number of irradiated people in the area has reached half a million. According to the Karaganda Ecological Museum, there is a shortfall of about US$100 million in compensation payments.

### THE VIRGIN LANDS CAMPAIGN

In 1954 under Khrushchev, the Soviet government undertook to expand arable land on a massive scale by irrigating the steppes and deserts of Kazakhstan and Uzbekistan. The water was to come via canals from the Amu-Darya and Syr-Darya, and certain Siberian rivers would be tapped or even reversed.

The Siberian part was dropped but the rest went ahead with great fanfare. Only under *glasnost* (openness) did the downside become clear. In some areas of the Kazakh steppe, soil has become degraded or is so over-fertilised that local rivers and lands are seriously polluted. By some measures, the problems of erosion, aridity and salinity are on a larger scale than those associated with the Aral Sea (p77). One UN report estimates that the country has lost 1.2 billion tonnes of topsoil.

### THE CASPIAN SEA

As the Kashagan underwater oilfield is being prepared for exploitation, and other fields around the Caspian are already being pumped, the environmental future of the world's largest lake hangs in the balance.

An estimated 2000 sq km of land has been contaminated by oil accidents, spills and leak, and flaring-off of unwanted gas has caused air pollution and health problems in the area of the Tenghiz oilfield.

Signs of trouble are also visible among the sea's 415 species of fish, including the famous beluga (white) sturgeon, source of the world's best caviar. A beluga can grow 6m in length and the 100kg of caviar that it might yield can sell for a quarter of a million dollars. The

### ECOTOURISM IN KAZAKHSTAN

Ecotourism is still finding its feet in Kazakhstan, but, with the country's great wealth of varied natural attractions, it surely has a bright future. Your first stop should be the Ecotourism Information Resource Centre (EIRC) in Almaty (see p117) – it's a good idea to look at its website when you're planning your Kazakhstan trip. The helpful, English-speaking EIRC is the focal point for community-based ecotourism in Kazakhstan, providing travellers with information, bookings and organisational help for visiting half-a-dozen ecotourism programmes around the country.

These programmes, situated in some of the country's most attractive natural areas, offer welcoming homestays with local families, guided hikes, treks and horse rides, and a variety of other activities from bird-, animal- and plant-spotting to concerts of traditional Kazakh music and even *kumys*-making sessions. At some sites you can spend your nights in yurts. Average homestay prices are US$25 to US$30 per person per night including three meals – pretty good value. You'll typically spend about the same again on guides, park fees, horses, vehicle transfers and other expenses.

Top sites:

**Aksu-Dzhabagly Nature Reserve** (p146) Beautiful mountain country at the northwest extremity of the Tian Shan, with high biodiversity.
**Sayram-Ugam National Park** (p147) Near Aksu-Dzhabagly, with similar attractions.
**Lepsinsk** (p139) Quaint village at the foot of Zhungar Alatau mountains: great hikes and rides.
**Korgalzhyn Nature Reserve** (p165) Steppe lakes and exciting bird-watching; the world's most northerly flamingo habitat.
**Kokshetau** (p166) Village life, walks and rides amid unspoiled northern countryside with lakes, woodlands and rocky hills.

Some sites including Lepsinsk are in border zones which require a special permit that can take a month or more to get. Plan ahead!

Caspian is the source of 90% of the world's caviar, yet catches of all types of sturgeon have dropped dramatically since 1990, as over-harvesting, water pollution and poaching all take their toll. Caviar yields for Kazakh fishing boats have dwindled to almost nothing. There's also concern for the endemic Caspian seal: outbreaks of disease and death among the seal population in recent years have been blamed partly on sea pollution.

## FOOD & DRINK

The food culture of Kazakhstan is one of the strongest indications of the Kazakhs' nomadic roots. Nomads eat the food most readily available, and in most cases this meant horses and sheep. Across the country you'll also find ubiquitous Central Asian dishes such as shashlyk, *laghman* (noodles), *manty* (steamed dumplings) and *plov* (Central Asian pilaf of rice and mixed vegetables). In the main cities and northern Kazakhstan, Russian cuisine is prevalent, reflecting the tastes of the immigrant culture – and today is supplemented by an international range of restaurants ranging from Italian and Tex-Mex to Chinese and Korean.

The Kazakh national dish is *besbarmak*, chunks of long-boiled beef, mutton or perhaps horse meat and onions, served in a huge bowl atop flat squares of pasta. The broth from the meat is drunk separately.

In bazaars and a few restaurants, it is likely that you'll come across *kazy* (a smoked horse-meat sausage, though beef is sometimes substituted); when served on special occasions sliced with cold noodles it is called *naryn*. *Karta* (literally 'horse intestines', which is used as the casing) and *chuchuk* are two other kinds of horse-meat sausage. *Kuurdak* is a fatty stew of meat, offal (including lungs and heart) and potato, boiled in a pot for two to three hours.

Kazakhs make a sweet *plov* with dried apricots, raisins and prunes, while *plov askabak* is made with pumpkin. *Zhuta* is pasta shaped like a Swiss roll with a carrot and pumpkin filling.

A local snack is *baursaki*, fried dough balls or triangles, not unlike heavy doughnuts. Kazakh apples are also famous in Central Asia (Almaty and its old name, Alma-Ata, literally mean 'father of apples').

As in Kyrgyzstan, *kumys* (fermented mare's milk) is popular. On the steppes and in the desert regions, you'll even come across *shubat* (fermented camel's milk) which has a somewhat less salty taste.

Most midrange and top-end restaurants add a 10% service charge to the bill, and most main dishes on menus do not include any 'garnish' such as potatoes, rice or vegetables. If main dishes cost between 400T and 700T, a full meal with a salad, bread, garnish, dessert, a couple of drinks and service charge can easily add up to 2000T.

One way to eat economically is to go for the 'business lunch' *(biznes lanch, kompleksny obed)* offered by many city restaurants. This is a good-value set meal, typically comprising soup or salad, a main course, a dessert and a drink.

# ALMATY АЛМАТЫ

☎ 327 / pop 1.3 million

Kazakhstan's economic prosperity is most palpable here in its biggest city, where at times you could almost believe you are in Europe, such are the numbers of glitzy international shops lining the streets and of Mercedes, Audis, Volkswagens and BMWs negotiating the peak-hour jams. This leafy city with a backdrop of the snow-capped Zailiysky Alatau (a spur of the Tian Shan) has always been one of the most charming Russian creations in Central Asia. Today Almaty's fast-growing middle class also have expensive suburban housing, well-stocked 24-hour supermarkets, Western-style coffee lounges, fine restaurants, chic bars, dance-till-dawn nightclubs and even new ski resorts to help them enjoy life to the full.

The ethnic Kazakh presence is gradually getting stronger in what was always a heavily Russian-influenced city, but everyone seems to rub along fine. No-one even seems too bothered that Astana has replaced Almaty as Kazakhstan's capital – except those who have had to move to Astana.

Almaty is Kazakhstan's main transport hub and a place many travellers pass through rather than linger, but if you do stay a few days you'll find – as several thousand Western expats have – that Almaty is a place for enjoying many green parks and colourfully illuminated fountains, for visiting excellent museums, theatres, shops and markets, and for eating, drinking and dancing in Central Asia's best selection of restaurants, bars and clubs. It's also a starting point for great hikes, drives, treks and skiing in the Zailiysky Alatau between here and Kyrgyzstan (the border is just 25km south) and it's the obvious jump-off point for the magnificent central Tian Shan in Kazakhstan's far southeastern corner.

The best times to visit Almaty are mid-April to late May, and mid-August to mid-October, when it's neither too cold nor too hot.

## HISTORY

Almaty was founded in 1854, when the Kazakhs were still nomads, as a Russian frontier fort named Verny on the site of the Silk Road oasis Almatu which had been laid waste by the Mongols. Cossacks and Siberian peasants settled around it, but the town was twice almost flattened by earthquakes, in 1887 and 1911. In the late 19th and early 20th centuries it was a place of exile, its best-known outcast being Leon Trotsky.

Renamed Alma-Ata (Father of Apples), it became the capital of Soviet Kazakhstan in 1927, and was connected to Siberia by the Turksib (Turkestan–Siberia) railway in 1930. The railway brought big growth and so did WWII, as factories were relocated here from Nazi-threatened western USSR, and many Slavs came to work in them. Large numbers of ethnic Koreans, forcibly resettled from the Russian Far East, arrived at the same time.

In the 1970s and early '80s Kazakhstan's leader Dinmukhamed Kunaev, the only Central Asian member of the Soviet Politburo, managed to steer lots of money southeast from

### ALMATY MUST-SEES

**Kök-Töbe cable car** Smooth ride to the best views in town (p120).

**Central State Museum** All Kazakhstan's history under one roof (p119).

**Chimbulak** Fresh powder snow a 40-minute drive from your door (p130).

**Abay State Opera & Ballet Theatre** High-quality theatre at a bucket shop price (p125).

**Barakholka** This market is a vast melange of junk and gems (p127).

ALMATY
0 1 km
0 0.5 miles
A
B
C
D
1
2
3
4
5
6
To Hippodrome (3km); Almaty-I Train Station (7km); Ural Airlines Office (8km); Kapshagay (70km); Taldyqorghan (265km)
To Airport (10km)
To Talgar (25km); Issik (47 km); Charyn Canyon (210km); Kegen (250km)
Almaty-II Train Station
Suyinbay
Stanislavsky
Malaya Almatinka River
To Barakholka (5km); Bishkek (275km); Taraz (575km)
Rayymbek
Central Mosque
Pushkin
Mametova
Zelyony Bazar (Green Market)
Seyfullin
Maqataeva
Silk Way Mall
Zhibek Zholy
Abdullindar
Karibekov
Baibaev
Central (Gorky) Park
Nauryzbay Batyr
Zheltoqsan
Gogol
Kaldayakov
Zenkov
Panfilov Park
Bayturysnuly
Shagabutdinov
Muratbaev
Abylay Khan (Kommunistichesky)
Panfilov
Furmanov
Ayteke Bi (Oktyabrskaya)
Qazybek Bi (Sovietskaya)
Kazakh-British Technical University
Tölebaev
Qonaev (Karl Marx)
Ualikhanov
Dostyq (Lenina)
To Khan Tengri (350m)
Töle Bi (Komsomolskaya)
Karasay Batyr
Qabanbay Batyr (Kalinian)
Bögenbay Batyr (Kirova)
To Sayran Bus Station (4km)
Market
Masanchi
Dosmukhamedov
Zhambyl
Adi Sharipov
Mukanov
Shevchenko
Bayseyitova
Academy of Sciences
Kurmanghazy
Kök-Töbe Cable-Car
Lugansky
To Turkmenistan Consulate (500m); XXX (5km)
Abay
Satpaev
Respublika alanghy
Mikrorayon Samal-1
Circus
Musrepov
To GEO (200m)
Zhandosov
Timiryazev
Zholdasbekov
Mikrorayon Samal-2
To Hotel Dan (200m); Mongolian Embassy (5km)
Bukhar Zhirau bulvary
Bayzaqov
Esentay River
Markova
Al-Farabi
To Medeu (14km); Chimbulak (21km)
Qazhy Muqan
To Tour Asia (3.5km); Mega Center Alma-Ata (3.5km)
To Tajik Embassy Office (4km); GES-2 (12km); Bolshoe Almatinskoe Lake (27km)

Moscow to transform Alma-Ata from a provincial town into a worthy capital of a Soviet republic. Hence the number of buildings in relatively adventurous late-Soviet styles such as the Arasan Baths and Hotel Kazakhstan, and the stately piles such as the Academy of Sciences and the old parliament, now the Kazakh-British Technical University.

Almaty saw the first unrest unleashed in Central Asia by the Gorbachev era of *glasnost*. Thousands took to the streets in December 1986 to protest against Kunaev's replacement as head of the Communist Party of Kazakhstan by the Russian Gennady Kolbin. A counterdemo of workers armed with metal bars turned the protest into riots,

**INFORMATION**
ACS.......1 D6
Akademkitap No 1.......2 C3
Akademkitap No 2.......3 C4
Alai.......4 C3
Asia Discovery.......5 B5
Australian Consulate.......6 D6
British Council.......7 C5
Cafemax.......8 C2
Cafemax.......9 C5
Canadian Embassy.......10 D3
Central Asia Tourism Corporation.......11 D3
Central Post Office.......12 C3
Chinese Embassy Office.......13 D4
Coffeedelia.......(see 72)
DHL.......14 A5
Ecotourism Information Resource Centre.......15 B3
French Embassy.......16 C4
German Embassy.......(see 16)
Global Air.......17 C3
Goethe Institute.......18 A5
Hotel Otrar1.......(see 58)
InterContinental Almaty.......(see 66)
International SOS.......19 D5
Interteach.......20 B3
Iranian Embassy.......21 D5
Japanese Embassy Office.......22 D3
Jibek Joly.......(see 64)
Kazkommertzbank.......23 C5
Kyrgyz Consulate.......24 D5
Migration Police.......25 A4
Netherlands Embassy.......26 B4
Pakistani Embassy.......27 C2
Qazaqtelekom.......28 C3
Qazaqtelekom.......29 C4
Russian Consulate.......30 A5
Silk Way City.......(see 87)
Stalker.......31 D3
Troy Internet Café.......32 C3
Trus, Balbes, Byvaly.......33 C4
Turan-Asia.......34 C3
UK Embassy Office.......(see 16)
US Embassy Office.......35 D5
Uzbek Embassy.......36 D3

**SIGHTS & ACTIVITIES**
Almaty City History Museum & Museum of Repression.......37 B4
Arasan Baths.......38 C3
Central (Gorky) Park (Main Entrance).......39 D2
Central State Museum.......40 C5
City Government Building.......41 C5
Dinamo Stadium.......42 B4
Fantasy World.......43 A5
Geology Museum.......44 D4
Kazakhstan Museum of Arts.......45 A5
Monument to Independence.......46 C5
Museum of Kazakh Musical Instruments.......47 D3
Presidential Residence.......48 C5
Rakhat Fitness.......49 A5
St Nicholas Cathedral.......50 B4
War Memorial.......51 D3
Zenkov Cathedral.......52 C3

**SLEEPING**
Gostinitsa.......53 B1
Hotel Almaty.......54 C4
Hotel Ambassador.......55 B4
Hotel Kazakhstan.......56 D4
Hotel Kazzhol.......57 B3
Hotel Otrar.......58 C3
Hotel Saulet.......59 C5
Hotel Tranzit.......60 B2
Hotel Turkistan.......61 C2
Hotel Tyan-Shan.......62 C4
Hotel Uyut.......63 B3
Hotel Zhetisu.......64 B2
Hyatt Regency Almaty.......65 A5
InterContinental Almaty.......66 C5
Saya Hotel.......67 C4
Third Dormitory.......68 D5
Tien Shan Grand Hotel.......69 C3

**EATING**
American Bar & Grill.......70 C3
Biskvit.......71 D4
Coffeedelia.......72 C4
Dastarkhan.......73 B4
Inara.......74 D3
Kafe Keruen.......75 C3
Kishlak.......76 B5
Mad Murphy's.......(see 96)
Mama Mia.......77 C3
Namaste.......78 B5
Pomodoro Caffé.......79 C3
Printsessa Turandot.......80 A5
Qorqyt Ata.......81 C3
Ramstor.......82 D5
Restoran Printsessa.......83 C3
Safran.......84 D3
Shi Bon Kha.......85 C3
Shvabsky Domik.......86 C4
Silk Way City Gipermarket.......87 B3
SM Market.......88 C2
Stolichny.......89 C4
Thai.......90 D4
Traktir Zhili-Byli.......91 C4
Yubileyny.......92 C3
Zheti Qazyna.......93 C2

**DRINKING**
Dublin Pub.......94 C5
Guinness Pub.......95 D4
Mad Murphy's.......96 D3
San Siro.......97 C3
Shtab.......98 C4
Soho.......99 C3
Tinkoff.......100 B5
Vogue.......101 C5

**ENTERTAINMENT**
Abay State Opera & Ballet Theatre.......102 C4
Auezov Kazakh Drama Theatre.......103 A5
Central Stadium.......104 B5
Crystal.......105 B6
Cuba.......106 D3
Da Freak.......107 D3
Gas.......(see 112)
Kazkontsert Hall.......108 C3
Kinoteatr Tsezar.......109 C3
Members Bar.......(see 66)
Mostafterpartyclub.......110 B2
Nice Bar.......(see 105)
Palace of the Republic.......111 D4
Petroleum.......112 B4
Real Club.......113 B2
State Philharmonia.......114 D3
Stereo.......115 B5

**SHOPPING**
Megasport.......116 C2
Meloman.......117 C3
Ramstor1.......(see 82)
Republican Palace of Schoolchildren.......118 D5
Silk Way City.......(see 87)
Sport Land.......119 B3
Tengri Umai.......120 C3
TsUM.......121 C3

**TRANSPORT**
Air Astana.......(see 58)
Asiana Airlines.......(see 56)
British Airways.......122 D4
Europcar.......123 C4
Georgian National Airlines.......(see 125)
Gorodskoy Aerovokzal.......124 B3
Imair.......125 B3
KLM.......(see 58)
Kras Air.......(see 44)
Lufthansa.......(see 65)
Pulkovo Airline.......126 C2
Sayakhat Bus Station.......127 C2
Transaero.......128 C2
Turkish Airlines.......129 C3
Uzbekistan Airlines.......130 C3

police opened fire and possibly as many as 250 people were killed.

In 1991 Almaty was the venue for the meeting at which the USSR was finally pronounced dead, when all five Central Asian republics, plus Azerbaijan, Armenia and Moldova, joined the CIS (Commonwealth of Independent States), founded by Russia, Ukraine and Belarus. The name Almaty, close to that of the original Silk Road settlement, replaced Alma-Ata soon after.

Almaty lost its status as Kazakhstan's capital in 1998 but remains the country's commercial, social and cultural hub. In an ongoing property boom, ever more office towers, apartment blocks and shopping centres are pushing skyward, especially in the south of the city. The tarnished side of this shiny middle-class coin is represented by the shabby settlements of rural migrants and Kazakh returnees on the city's outskirts.

## ORIENTATION

Some find Almaty's long, straight streets easy to navigate once you get to know the key north–south and east–west arteries; others find a lack of landmarks confusing. Keep in mind that the mountains are to the south, and the city slopes upward from north (650m) to south (950m).

Posted street names are generally Kazakh spellings but local people are often equally familiar with the old Soviet names, so you'll find the most important of these given in brackets on the Almaty map.

The airport is 13km north of the centre and the Sayran long-distance bus station is 5km west. The main train station, Almaty-II, and the Sayakhat regional bus station are on the northern edge of the central area.

In the centre, the main north–south streets are Dostyq (Lenina), Qonaev (Karl Marx), Furmanov, Abylay Khan (Kommunistichesky) and Seyfullin. The key east–west streets are Zhibek Zholy (Gorkogo; partly pedestrianised), Gogol, Töle Bi, Abay and Satpaev.

### Maps

An unpredictable selection of city maps in English and Russian is available for a few hundred tenge each at hotels and the Akademkitap bookshops (right). For public transport routes, get *Almaty Marshruty Gorodskogo Transporta,* in Russian.

For topographical maps of parts of Kazakhstan, head to GEO (below). Akademkitap has some Almaty-area hiking maps.

## INFORMATION

### Bookshops

**Akademkitap** (⌚ 10am-8pm Mon-Fri, 10am-7pm Sat & Sun) No 1 (☎ 273 78 18; Furmanov 91) No 2 (☎ 272 79 81; Furmanov 139) Has a range of dictionaries, phrasebooks, books; No 1 is good for city and hiking maps.

**GEO** (☎ 243 75 88; Satpaev 30B; ⌚ 9.30am-6pm Mon-Fri) Sells topographical maps of regions of Kazakhstan published at various times from the 1970s onwards; 1:200,000 maps are 700T, 1:500,000 are 800T.

**Hotel Otrar** (☎ 250 68 48; Gogol 73) The newsstand here has a good map selection.

**InterContinental Almaty** (☎ 250 50 00; Zheltoqsan 181) Has a reasonably well-stocked bookshop.

### Cultural Centres

**British Council** (☎ 250 66 48, www.britishcouncil.kz; Respublika alanghy 13; ⌚ library noon-7pm Mon-Thu, 10am-4pm Fri & Sat) Organises exhibitions, concerts, dance and drama performances, and has an English library with internet (per hr 400T, British sites free).

**Goethe Institute** (☎ 247 27 04;www.goethe.de/almaty; Zhandosov 2; ⌚ 9am-5pm Mon-Fri, library 1-6.15pm Mon-Thu, 10am-2pm Fri)

### Emergency

**Ambulance** (☎ 03)
**Fire service** (☎ 01)
**Police** (☎ 02)

### Internet Access

Internet cafés generally offer much better prices than hotel business centres.

**Cafemax** Silk Way (☎ 273 95 53; 2nd fl, Silk Way Mall, Zhibek Zholy 70; per hr 350T; ⌚ 10am-9pm); Timiryazev (☎ 260 99 99; Timiryazev 1A; per hr 350T; ⌚ 24hr) Bright, modern facilities with fast connections on lots of computers, and good cafés on the spot. Also copies CDs, sends faxes and makes photocopies.

**Coffeedelia** (☎ 272 64 09; Qabanbay Batyr 79; ⌚ 8am-midnight Mon-Thu, 8am-1am Fri, 9am-1am Sat, 9am-midnight Sun) Free wi-fi at this great coffee house (see p123).

**Qazaqtelekom** (☎ 233 11 50; Zhibek Zholy 100; per hr 122T; ⌚ 8am-10pm) Cheap net in a phone office.

**Silk Way City** (Töle Bi 71; per hr 300T; ⌚ 24hr) Good facility upstairs in this mall.

**Stalker** (☎ 291 20 46; Töle Bi 20; per hr 300T; ⌚ 11am-1am Mon-Thu, 11am-2am Fri, 11am-1pm Sat &

Sun) Slow connections but there's a cosy café-bar on the premises.

**Troy Internet Café** (Zhibek Zholy 68; per hr 250T; 10am-1am) Medium-speed connections and convenient location next to Silk Way Mall.

### Laundry

Many hotels will do your laundry but it will take at least 24 hours.

**Trus, Balbes, Byvaly** (261 66 38; Qabanbay Batyr 96; 8am-8pm Mon-Fri, 9am-7pm Sat) Charges 200T to 400T per shirt, T-shirt or trousers, ironing included. Normal service is 24 hours.

### Medical Services

Pharmacies (Kazakh: *darikhana*, Russian: *apteka*) all over Almaty sell many Western medicines.

**Alai** (cnr Furmanov & Gogol; 24hr) This pharmacy never closes.

**International SOS** (258 19 11; www.internationalsos.com; Lugansky 11; 9am-7pm Mon-Fri, 9am-1pm Sat) International-standard clinic with 24-hour emergency service; very expensive for nonmembers.

**Interteach** (/fax 258 81 00; www.interteach.kz; Ayteke Bi 83; 8am-8pm Mon-Fri, 9am-6pm Sat & Sun, ambulance 24hr) Private polyclinic charging €17 for a normal consultation, €52 for an ambulance. Also does remote-area medical assistance.

### Money

There are exchange kiosks on all main streets. Avoid kiosks in other very public places, such as the Zelyony Bazar (Green Market), to minimise the risk of theft.

An ATM is never too far away: look for 'Bankomat' signs. All shopping malls, the TsUM department store, most banks and some supermarkets and smaller shops have them. To change travellers cheques look for branches of Kazkommertsbank or Halyk Bank (there are many all over the city).

**Global Air** (258 50 59; www.globalair-kz.com; Qonaev 85) The Amex agent.

**Kazkommertzbank** (258 51 23; Bayseyitova 49; www.kkb.kz; 9am-12.30pm & 1.30-7pm Mon-Fri, 9am-3.30pm Sat) This bank's main branch.

### Post

**Central post office** (Bögenbay Batyr 134; 8am-7pm Mon-Fri, 9am-5pm Sat & Sun)

**DHL** (258 85 88; Zhandosov 1/1; 9am-7.30pm Mon-Fri, 10am-2pm Sat)

**FedEx** (250 35 66; Tölebaev 38; 9am-6pm Mon-Fri, 10am-1pm Sat)

### Registration

**Migration Police** (254 41 45; Baytursynuly; 9am-7pm Mon-Wed & Fri) If for some reason you have missed out on registration when you entered the country, try here. Located between Bögenbay Batyr and Karasay Batyr.

### Telephone & Fax

Card payphones are located all over the city. See p180 for how to operate them.

**Qazaqtelekom** Panfilov (297 56 03; Panfilov 129; 8am-7pm Mon-Fri, 10am-4pm Sat); Zhibek Zholy (233 11 50; Zhibek Zholy 100; 8am-10pm) You can phone from these offices. The Panfilov branch has fax and photocopying too, and there's cheap internet at the Zhibek Zholy branch.

### Tourist Information

**Ecotourism Information Resource Centre** (EIRC; 278 02 89, 279 81 46; www.ecotourism.kz; Zheltoqsan 71; 10am-7pm daily May-Sep, 9am-6pm Mon-Fri Oct-Apr) Helpful, English-speaking, information and booking centre for community ecotourism programmes in Kazakhstan (p112); can help with travel arrangements to ecotourism villages and also offers weekend day trips by bus to places of interest outside Almaty (with Russian-speaking guides) for around 1100T to 1500T per person.

### Travel Agencies

There are a number of general travel agencies useful for air and train tickets, hotel bookings, visa support, day and two-day outings to places of interest within reach of Almaty, and longer tours.

**ACS** (264 49 49; www.polet.kz; Dom 63, Mikrorayon Samal-2) English-speaking staff. Excursions to Uzbekistan offered. Has other offices in Astana and Aktau.

**Central Asia Tourism Corporation** (CATC; 250 10 70; www.centralasiatourism.com; Qazybek Bi 20½; 9am-6.30pm Mon-Fri, 9am-1pm Sat) Very experienced agency with branches in eight other Kazakhstan cities plus Dushanbe, Tajikistan. Staff speak several European languages. Services include ticketing for trains and all airlines flying in and from Kazakhstan, visa arrangements (including for other Central Asian countries), tours and accommodation. Day trips from Almaty cost around 35,000T to 40,000T for up to seven people.

**Jibek Joly** (250 04 15; www.jibekjoly.kz; Hotel Zhetisu, Abylay Khan 55) Offers tours, accommodation in and around Almaty, visa support and ISIC cards (900T).

**Stantours** (297 70 72, 705-1184619; www.stantours.com) Low-key operation with excellent personal service; offers reliable free advice on Central Asia travel and is a specialist in visas for the whole region. Also provides air and train tickets, and can book accommodation and tours throughout Central Asia, including Turkmenistan tours and active tours to offbeat locations. Prices are reasonable. Contact Stantours by email (info@stantours.com) or phone.

**Turan-Asia** (☎ 273 46 21; www.turanasia.kz; Office 8, Abylay Khan 66) Accommodation, visa support, ticketing and tours.

The following agencies specialise in mountaineering, trekking and active tours, but can usually also organise visa support and accommodation:

**Kan Tengri** (☎ 291 60 06, 291 08 80; www.kantengri.kz; Kasteev 10) Kazakhstan's top adventure-travel company, highly experienced and respected in mountain tourism. Kan Tengri focuses on climbs, trekking and heli-skiing in the central Tian Shan (including Mt Khan Tengri) and the ranges between Almaty and Lake Issyk-Köl. Also offers horse treks, mountain biking, sport fishing, bird-watching and botanical tours. Most trips last between one and three weeks. A two-week trekking tour typically costs around €1000 per person from Almaty. Small groups, including solo travellers, can be catered for. The company's director is Kazbek Valiev, the first Kazakh to scale Mt Everest.

**Tour Asia** (☎ 248 25 73; www.tourasia.kz; Radostovets 359) This long-established company offers trekking and mountaineering in the central Tian Shan, the mountains south of Almaty and the Pamirs, plus ticketing, accommodation and visa support. Located 6km south from the centre.

**Asia Discovery** (☎ 260 13 93; www.asia-discovery.nursat.kz; Abay 61) Experienced agency offering treks, horse-riding, rafting and bird-watching tours lasting one to two weeks for €400 to €1100.

**Karlygash (Karla) Makatova** (☎ 273 21 09, 271 26 17, 701-7552086; kmakatova@yahoo.com) Independent one-woman operator who has long organised trips for the expat community and offers day hikes, treks and climbs from one day up, drives, kayaking, helicopter flights, night-time tours of Almaty's fountains and more. Her trips are spirited, not too expensive, and a good way to meet locals and expats. Karlygash has no office: contact her by email or phone.

## DANGERS & ANNOYANCES

Almaty is a pretty safe town, but you should still exercise the usual precautions (see p447). The commonest emergencies for Westerners here concern late-night activities – people robbed in taxis after emerging inebriated from bars and nightclubs, or passports and money stolen by prostitutes.

Though police harassment is less common these days, it can still happen. It's best not to carry much cash around, and you certainly wouldn't want to let your wallet into police hands. If you are stopped on the street, show only a photocopy of your passport and visa (preferably one certified by your embassy or consulate; see p182). Writing down a name and badge number helps keep police honest (and may unmask impostors).

### Scams

One thing you do have to be wary of is the 'Wallet Full of Dollars' scam. Someone finds a wallet lying on the ground as you pass, opens it and finds hundreds of dollars inside. They draw your attention to it and if you stop, it becomes clear there's nothing in the wallet to identify its owner. The person offers to share the loot with you and if you start to get involved, another person appears, claiming the wallet is theirs and that it originally contained much more money. They demand compensation or threaten to take you to the police, in the hope of intimidating you into making them a payment. Another less subtle ruse is for people to say they have lost their wallet and ask to see the contents of your pockets or bag to prove that you don't have it. This is an opportunity for them to filch your valuables.

To avoid trouble, ignore anyone who 'finds' or 'loses' a wallet, and keep walking without hesitation.

There have also been reports of drivers from the airport taking new arrivals to the Almaty outskirts and threatening to strand them. Only large sums of money could persuade them otherwise. To avoid complications, jot down your vehicle's licence number, give the exact address of the place you want to go, and try not to let on that you are an Almaty novice.

Be wary of accepting invitations to stay with strangers. One traveller's 'hosts' demanded a large amount of money to let her leave with her luggage.

## SIGHTS

### Panfilov Park

Located between Gogol and Qazybek Bi, this large and popular rectangle of greenery, first laid out in the 1870s, is focused on the candy-coloured **Zenkov Cathedral**, Almaty's nearest (albeit distant) rival to St Basil's Cathedral. Designed by AP Zenkov in 1904, the cathedral is one of Almaty's few surviving tsarist-era buildings (most of the others were destroyed in the 1911 earthquake). Although at first glance it doesn't look like it, the cathedral is built entirely of wood (including the nails). Used as a museum and concert hall in the Soviet era, then boarded up, it was returned to the Russian Orthodox Church in 1995 and has been restored as a functioning place of worship, with colourful icons and murals. Services are held at 8am and 5pm Monday to Saturday, and 7am, 9am and 5pm Sunday.

The park is named for the Panfilov Heroes, commemorated at the fearsome **war memorial** east of the cathedral. This represents the 28 soldiers of an Almaty infantry unit who died fighting off Nazi tanks in a village outside Moscow in 1941. An eternal flame commemorating the fallen of 1917–20 (the Civil War) and 1941–45 (WWII), flickers in front of the giant black monument of soldiers from all 15 Soviet republics bursting out of a map of the USSR.

The park is on the routes of trolleybus 1, 11 and 12, tram 4 and 6, and bus 63 and 94, among others.

## Central (Gorky) Park

Almaty's biggest **recreational area** (admission 25T; 24 hr), at the eastern end of Gogol, is still known as Gorky Park. It has boating lakes, funfair rides, an **Aquapark** (adult/child 2000/1500T; noon-10pm Jun-Sep), a rather sad **zoo** (adult/child 300/50T; 9am-7pm), and several cafés, and shashlyk and beer stands. It's busiest on Sunday and holidays. Trolleybus 1 and 12 and bus 65, 94 and 166 run along Gogol to the entrance.

## Museums

In a striking 1908 wooden building (also the work of cathedral architect Zenkov) at the east end of Panfilov Park is the **Museum of Kazakh Musical Instruments** (☎ 261 63 16; Zenkov 24; admission 200T; 9am-1pm & 2-6pm Tue-Sun), the city's most original museum. It has a fine collection of traditional Kazakh instruments – wooden harps and horns, bagpipes, the lutelike two-stringed *dombra* and the viola-like *qobyz*. If you're there at the same time as a tour group you'll hear tapes of the instruments and see the attendant strum the *dombra*.

The intriguing **Geology Museum** (☎ 261 58 83; Dostyq 85; admission 100T; 10am-5pm Mon-Fri) is in the bowels of a building opposite the Hotel Kazakhstan. The country's mineral wealth is on display, with relief maps and touch-screen computers to provide quick geology lessons in English.

The city's best museum stands 300m up Furmanov from Respublika alanghy (square). The **Central State Museum** (☎ 264 23 90; Mikrorayon Samal-1, No 44; admission 80T; 9.30am-6pm Wed-Mon) takes you through Kazakhstan's history from bronze-age burial mounds to telecommunications and the transfer of the capital to Astana, with many beautiful artefacts. A large replica of the Golden Man (see below) stands in the entrance hall. The downstairs rooms cover archaeological finds and early history up to Jenghiz Khan (with models of some of Kazakhstan's major monuments); the ethnographic display upstairs features a finely kitted-out

### THE GOLDEN MAN

The Golden Man (Zolotoy Chelovek in Russian, Altyn Adam in Kazakh) is a warrior's costume from about the 5th century BC that was found in 1969 in a Saka (Scythia) tomb about 60km east of Almaty, near Issik. It is made of more than 4000 separate gold pieces, many of them finely worked with animal motifs, and has a 70cm-high headdress bearing skyward-pointing arrows, a pair of snarling snow leopards and a two-headed winged mythical beast. Though the person who wore this costume may have no genetic connection with modern Kazakhs, the Golden Man has become modern Kazakhstan's favourite national symbol. Replicas adorn museums all over the country and a stone version stands atop the Independence Monument on Almaty's Respublika alanghy (square). A copy was even unveiled by President Nazarbaev in front of the Kazakhstan embassy in Washington, DC, in 2006.

Some, however, believe that Kazakhstan's adopted symbol of warrior strength wasn't a man at all. Archaeologist Jeannine Davis-Kimball, in *Warrior Women* (2002), argues that the skeleton in the grave was too badly damaged for its gender to be determined, and that other goods found there suggest the Golden Man was in fact a Golden Woman. Apparently 20% of graves with armaments from the Scythian cultures, of which the Saka were one, were of women.

The current whereabouts of the original treasure are not publicised. Staff in the President's Culture Centre in Astana told us the original was kept there – but not on view.

yurt and some beautifully worked weaponry and horse and camel gear, plus musical instruments and exotic costumes going back to the 18th century. The upper floors cover the 20th and 21st centuries, with exhibits on some of Kazakhstan's many ethnic groups, independent Kazakhstan and a special section on the pilgrimage town of Turkistan (p148). Get there by bus 2 or 63 or marshrutka 526, 528 or 537 up Furmanov.

The **Kazakhstan Museum of Arts** (☎ 247 83 56; Satpaev 30A; admission 100T; ⌚ 10am-6pm Tue-Sun, closed last day of month) has the best art collection in the country, including works of artists banned during the Soviet period. There are also collections of Russian and Western European art. Particularly interesting are the room of modern Kazakh handicrafts and the large collection of paintings by Abylkhan Kasteev (1904–73), to whom the museum is dedicated. Kasteev's clear portraits, landscapes and scenes of Soviet progress (railways, hydroelectricity, collective farming) obviously toed the party line but his technique is fabulous. Marshrutkas heading west on Satpaev, including the 520, will stop here.

The combined **Almaty City History Museum & Museum of Repression** (Nauryzbay Batyr 108) was closed for renovations at the time of writing but is well worth checking on. The Repression Museum goes into haunting detail about the fate of thousands who earned Stalin's ire.

### Kök-Töbe Cable Car

This smooth, gleaming and recently renovated **cable car** (one-way 300T; ⌚ 11am-midnight Mon, Wed & Thu, 4pm-midnight Tue, 11am-1am Fri-Sun) runs from beside the Palace of the Republic on Dostyq up to Kök-Töbe (Green Hill) on the city's southeast edge. The hill is crowned by a 372m-high **telecommunications tower**. Near the top station are a viewing platform, crafts stalls and a cafeteria doing good shashlyk. If you go during the day, the walk back down to Dostyq is a pleasant one.

### Respublika Alanghy

This broad ceremonial square at the high southern end of Almaty, created in Soviet times, is a block uphill from Abay. The focal point is the attractive **Monument to Independence**. The stone column is surmounted with a replica of the Golden Man standing on a winged snow leopard, and is flanked at its base by fountains and two bas-relief walls depicting scenes from Kazakhstan's history. Overlooking the square from the south is the neoclassical-style **city government building** and, at the southeast corner opposite the Central State Museum, a large official **Presidential Residence** (Furmanov 205). You can reach the square on bus 2 or 63 or marshrutka 526, 528 or 537 going up Furmanov from Gogol.

### St Nicholas Cathedral

The pale turquoise Nikolsky Sobor, with its gold onion domes, stands out west of the centre near the corner of Qabanbay Batyr and Baytursynuly. The cathedral was built in 1909 and later used as a stable for Bolshevik cavalry, before reopening about 1980. It's a terrifically atmospheric place, like a corner of old Russia, with icons, candles and restored frescoes inside and black-clad old supplicants outside. For the best impression visit at festival times such as Orthodox Christmas Day (7 January) or Easter for the midnight services.

## ACTIVITIES

At the **Arasan Baths** (☎ 272 40 18; cnr Ayteke Bi & Qonaev; admission until 2pm Tue-Fri 500T, other times 800T, 20-min massage 2000T; ⌚ sessions start every 2hr, 8am-8pm Tue-Sun) you can choose from Russian *(Russkaya)*, Finnish *(Finskaya)* and Turkish *(Vostochnaya)* baths, the latter with three different temperatures of heated stone platforms plus a plunge pool. Each part has men's and women's sections. Take along soap, a towel and some flip-flops for walking around in. Go with a friend or two and you'll find it's an enjoyable and truly relaxing experience. If you don't have any bathing gear handy, there's a shop in the lobby. Sellers with *veniki* (bunches of oak and birch leaves) wait outside, if you fancy stimulating your circulation with a good thrashing. Built in the early 1980s in a modernistic Soviet style, this is the finest bathhouse in Central Asia.

**Rakhat Fitness** (☎ 255 58 88; www.rakhat-fitness.kz; Abay 48; ⌚ 7am-11pm), near the Central Stadium, has the best **public swimming pool** (per day 4000T, 12 visits 13,000T) in the city, 50m long and open year-round (it's covered in winter). No medical certificate is required.

Two shopping malls, **Ramstor** (Furmanov 226) and **Mega Center Alma-Ata** (Rozybakiev 247A), have small **skating rinks** (Mega Center has a climbing centre too), and in January and February you can skate on the iced-over football field at the

**Dinamo Stadium** (☎ 261 48 67; Nauryzbay Batyr 89). But Central Asia's top skating experience is out in the hills at Medeu (p130).

**Fantasy World** (cnr Abay & Musrepov; admission 1200T; 🕑 1-9pm) is an up-to-the-minute amusement park with rides that will thrill anyone – 200T extra for the vertiginous Cobra loop or the ultra-popular dodgems.

## ALMATY WALKING TOUR

**Respublika alanghy** (**1**; opposite) is the best place to start an Almaty walk; not only is it all downhill from here, but on a clear morning the square provides a panoramic view of the snowcapped mountains. Head east along Satpaev and turn down Dostyq. Behind the large **statue (2)** of the iconic writer Abay Kunanbaev, is the **Palace of the Republic** (**3**; p126), a concert hall. Here you could detour for a ride on the **Kök-Töbe cable car** (**4**; opposite) for great views across the city.

A block north of the **Hotel Kazakhstan** (**5**; p122), turn west along Shevchenko to the magnificent **Academy of Sciences** (**6**; cnr Shevchenko & Qonaev) building, one of the true gems of Soviet monumental architecture. Fountains and parks around the building make this a cool spot to linger in summer. Check out the 'Eastern Calendar' fountain with Chinese zodiac creatures on the east side of the academy.

Head downhill on tree-lined Tölebaev as far as Qabanbay Batyr, where you can drop into the city's best coffee shop, **Coffeedelia** (**7**; p123), for a pause and refreshments. Head west to the fine neoclassical **Abay State Opera & Ballet Theatre** (**8**; p126). Two blocks north of here is a small park in front of another imposing Soviet pile, the old parliament, now the **Kazakh-British Technical University** (**9**; Töle Bi btwn Abylay Khan & Panfilov). In the park you'll find a **statue (10)** to local war heroes Manshuk Mametova and Alie Moldagulova, which replaced the one of Lenin, removed after independence.

Head east along Töle Bi then north on Qonaev to **Panfilov Park** (**11**; p118). Strike west along Gogol, lined with some of the city's fanciest shops, then a block north on Abylay Khan and then east along Zhibek Zholy. This pedestrianised street, with cafés, a few buskers and artists, is Almaty's (sort of) version of Moscow's Arbat. A few blocks east is the **Zelyony Bazar** (**12**; p125), the city's most colourful market, with a true flavour of Central Asia. Just north of the market along Pushkin you can (except on Friday) visit Almaty's blue-domed, white-marble **central mosque (13)**, built

**WALK FACTS**

**Start** Respublika alanghy
**Finish** Central mosque
**Distance** 8km
**Duration** Four hours

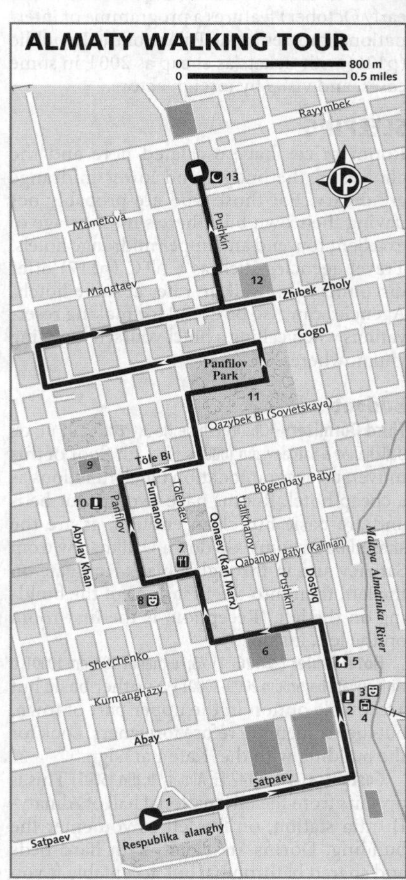


in 1999 and the largest in the country, with space for 3000 worshippers (women must cover their heads, arms and legs here).

## FESTIVALS & EVENTS

**Nauryz** (22 March) sees colourful parades in the city, and horse-racing and even the occasional game of *kökpar* at the Hippodrome (p127).

There's an international **jazz festival** at the State Philharmonia (p126) in early April, and in early August, the **Voice of Asia** pop contest/festival, a kind of Asian Eurovision, is held either in variable venues in Almaty or out at Medeu (p130).

The **Eurasia Film Festival** (late September and early October) features a programme of international movies at the Palace of the Republic (p126) with tickets as cheap as 200T in some cases, and visits by foreign actors.

## SLEEPING

Room prices have escalated here and the choices in the budget and lower midrange are dreary. For those who are probably not paying their own bills there's no shortage of excellent top-end and upper midrange hotels. Travel agencies such as CATC (p117) offer discounts from walk-in rates at some hotels. Agencies can also be useful for making reservations when calling a hotel yourself is getting you nowhere.

### Budget

**Third Dormitory** (Obshchezhitie No 3; ☎ 262 01 61; cnr Ualikhanov & Satpaev; dm 1000T) The 4th floor of this university accommodation block functions as a cheap hotel. Rooms have two or four beds and are basic but clean enough, as are the shared bathrooms. Go down Ualikhanov from Satpaev and in through a black iron gate on the left, then into the first door of the building on the left. 'Reception' is the first room on the left, inside.

**Hotel Saulet** (☎ 267 11 75; Furmanov 187; dm 1000T, d with private bathroom 2000-5000T) Another basic but acceptable option in the upper part of town, but they sometimes refuse foreigners. Look for the building with the 'Kafe Bar' sign.

**Gostinitsa** (☎ 260 42 13; Almaty-II; dm 1500T) This is upstairs from the international hall of Almaty-II train station, on the left as you enter the building. Dorms are small, with hard beds and shared bathrooms, but acceptable if you arrive late. You can have a bed for one hour for 500T, or from morning to evening for 1000T.

**Hotel Dan** (☎ 273 75 22; fax 274 76 15; Zhandosov 1; r with shared bathroom 3000-3750T, with private bathroom 4000-6000T) Dilapidated but habitable and reasonably friendly, the Dan is in an OK area about 200m west of the Russian consulate. Most rooms have TV, some have a phone. Bus 66 and trolleybus 12 run past here; the entrance is back from the street, at the west end of the building.

**Hotel Turkistan** (☎/fax 266 41 36; Maqataeva 49; s/d 3000/5000T) This modernised hotel opposite the Zelyony Bazar, used by many traders from China and other Central Asian countries, is decent value but security may not be the tightest. Standard rooms have TV, phone and bathroom with small bathtub.

**Hotel Tranzit** (☎ 233 04 38, 233 04 16; Zheltoqsan 12; s/d 3800/5500T, midnight-noon 3000/4000T, 2hrs per person 1500T) Just outside Almaty-II station, the Tranzit has clean if weary rooms with private bathroom, TV and phone.

#### APARTMENTS

Stantours (p117) can provide apartments for US$60 to US$80 per night, with a two-night minimum and an obligatory airport or station transfer (US$30). Karlygash Makatova (p118) also provides apartments starting at US$40.

### Midrange

**Hotel Zhetisu** (☎ 250 04 07; fax 250 04 16; Abylay Khan 55; s/d with shared bathroom 4200/6300T, with private bathroom s 5400-9800T, d 7800-20,900T; 💻) This is not a place that lifts the spirits: reception may pretend the rooms with shared bathroom don't exist and it's a good idea to unplug the phone to avoid middle-of-the-night calls from prostitutes. But the location is pretty central and the rooms are clean, reasonably big and equipped with satellite TV. Rates include breakfast. In-house services include a one-computer 'business centre' and a travel agency. Trolleybuses 5 and 6 from Almaty-II station along Abylay Khan go past the door.

**Hotel Kazakhstan** (☎ 291 91 01; www.ceebd.co.uk/hotelkazakhstan; Dostyq 52; s/d unrenovated 6400/11,600T, renovated 14,800/19,800T; 💻) This 26-floor hotel was built in 1977 and its rooms are typical of upper-range Soviet tourist hotels – comfy enough but uninspiring. The renovated ones have more modern décor and thicker carpets, but similarly small bathrooms. All include breakfast, satellite TV and modem connections. Unfortunately the top-floor Cosmos Café, where the buffet breakfast used to be served, was closed for renovations at last check.

**Saya Hotel** (☎ 272 32 65; fax 261 16 10; Furmanov 135; s/d with shared bathroom 8000/12,000T, d with private bathroom 15,000-30,000T) Helpful staff and just 12 pretty, well-equipped rooms with breakfast included.

**Hotel Uyut** (☎ 279 55 11; fax 279 89 79; Gogol 127/1; s/d from 8850/12,500T; ) Next door to the Kazzhol, this hotel has similar standards but lacks the same welcoming touch. Breakfast is included.

**our pick Hotel Kazzhol** (☎ 250 89 41; www.kazju.kz; Gogol 127/1; s/d from 9900/11,900T; ) This friendly, sparkling-clean hotel on a quiet lane between Gogol and Zhibek Zholy is the best value at this sort of price. Desk staff speak English, the smart rooms all have writing desks, satellite TV and minibars, and there's an excellent little European and Kazakh restaurant downstairs. Rates include breakfast.

**Hotel Almaty** (☎ 272 00 70/47; www.hotel-almaty.kz; Qabanbay Batyr 85; s 10,000-15,000T, d 17,000-30,000T; ) This large concrete pile opposite the Abay State Opera & Ballet Theatre was recently upgraded and provides pleasing pine-furnished rooms with gleaming bathrooms. Reception speaks some English and there's a 24-hour pharmacy in the building. All rooms are equipped with phone, TV and minibar. Breakfast is included.

**Hotel Tyan-Shan** (☎ 291 91 60/1; Qonaev 151; s/d 12,800/16,000T; ) Three-star branch of the Tien Shan Grand Hotel (below), with very big, comfortable, carpeted rooms, plus sauna and fitness room – good value.

**Hotel Otrar** (☎ 250 68 48; www.group.kz; Gogol 73; s/d from 14,288/17,328T; ) Well situated facing Panfilov Park, the Otrar dates from Soviet times but stands up very well. It has spick-and-span rooms with air-con and satellite TV, a fitness room, sauna and a good help-yourself breakfast (included in rates).

### Top End

**Hotel Ambassador** (☎ 250 89 89; www.ambassadorhotel.kz; Zheltoqsan 121; s/d US$177/234; ) Very good smaller hotel in the heart of the city, in a modernised 1930s building with classical décor. Free airport pickups offered. Breakfast is included.

**Tien Shan Grand Hotel** (☎ 244 96 99; ghts_reservation@mail.ru; Bögenbay Batyr 115; s/d from 38,000/46,000T; ) Elegant new medium-sized hotel in the handsome former Geology Ministry building, facing a small park. Has an excellent spa with saunas, massage and a good pool. Rates include breakfast.

**Hyatt Regency Almaty** (☎ 250 12 34; www.almaty.hyatt.com; Satpaev 29/6; s/d from 52,900/59,800T; ) One of Almaty's two luxury international hotels, built around a huge glass-domed atrium. It's a little further from the centre than the InterContinental.

**InterContinental Almaty** (☎ 250 50 00; www.ichotelsgroup.com; Zheltoqsan 181; r from 53,000T; ) Just southwest of Respublika alanghy, this glitzy high-rise hotel is widely known by a former name, the Ankara. It has plenty of five-star amenities including seven restaurants, cafés and bars, and a costly business centre. Glass lifts glide up and down the 12-storey atrium. Rooms are very comfy with broadband internet access, and breakfast is included.

## EATING

You won't find a better range of good restaurants anywhere else in Central Asia, so make the most of them. A large range of international cuisines is represented and some places have great design and ambience too.

### Cafés

**Coffeedelia** (☎ 272 64 09; Qabanbay Batyr 79; coffees, juices, cakes & pastries 280-800T; 8am-midnight Mon-Thu, 8am-1am Fri, 9am-1am Sat, 9am-midnight Sun) Almaty's best and trendiest coffee house, with a relaxed atmosphere; fabulous cakes and pastries, a range of good coffees, teas and juices; and free wi-fi internet. On weekend evenings it morphs into a preparty gathering spot, with DJs providing the sound on Friday.

**Biskvit** (☎ 291 66 92; coffees, cakes & pastries from 300T; Shevchenko 18; 8am-midnight) Another great coffee house, marginally smarter than Coffeedelia, with arguably the best coffee in town. Good for breakfast too.

### Restaurants

**Yubileyny** (cnr Gogol & Abylay Khan; dishes 100-300T; 24hr) Hats off to the bloke who introduced tortilla-wrapped doner kebabs to Almaty. Long lines form all day for these tasty creations, stuffed with meat, sour cream, sliced carrot and French fries, served out front of the large supermarket here. There's *plov* too, to take away or eat in the cafeteria areas either side, which also do good coffee, great doughnuts and self-serve meals. The perfect zone for easy food on the go.

**Qorqyt Ata** (☎ 273 50 07; Zhibek Zholy 68; dishes 200-600T; 9am-10pm) A good-value budget place beside the Silk Way Mall on pedestrianised Zhibek Zholy. Offerings include *plov*, *manty*, shashlyk and pizzas.

**Shi Bon Kha** (☎ 273 56 76; Qonaev 64; dishes 300-600T; noon-midnight) This cottage-like restaurant, in a courtyard, specialises in inexpensive Dungan (Chinese Muslim) food, including terrific spicy *laghman* (noodle, meat and vegetable soup). No alcohol here.

**Kafe Keruen** (☎ 273 98 50; Zhibek Zholy 77A; mains 400-800T; ⌚ noon-midnight) The covered outdoor area here is a nice place to watch the passing parade on pedestrianised Zhibek Zholy, though the food doesn't quite live up to the promise of the exotic menu which includes Galician molluscs and fajitas El Paso as well as a huge variety of shashlyk.

**Dastarkhan** (☎ 272 54 27; Shevchenko 75; dishes 400-2000T; ⌚ 24 hr) A good place for Kazakh as well as Russian food, with several modern rooms on two floors (one of them even nonsmoking), plus sidewalk tables. You can have *beshbarmak* or Balkhash *sudak* (pike) here as well as basics such as *plov*, *laghman* and *manty* and a big choice of lamb dishes.

**Inara** (☎ 291 78 06; Kaldayakov 58; dishes 500-750T; ⌚ 11am-11pm) Opposite the State Philharmonia, arboretum-style Inara has friendly service, a buzzy atmosphere and big, cheap plates of barbecued meat with onion and cucumber trimmings – an authentic Kazakh experience.

**Kishlak** (☎ 261 56 01; Seyfullin 540A; meat dishes 500-800T; ⌚ noon-2am) This atmospheric Uzbek restaurant near Respublika alanghy is decked with vines and bamboo and offers some low *chaikhana*-type tables with cushions and optional hookahs. The salads, shashlyk and fish dishes are all great. There's a dance show on Friday and Saturday nights.

**Printsessa Turandot** (☎ 292 38 32; Abay 103; dishes 500-1200T; ⌚ noon-midnight) A reasonably priced Chinese restaurant at the side of the Auezov Theatre, popular with locals and a few foreigners. Vegetarians will like the clay-pot-baked tofu and eggplant dishes. If it's too cold on the large terrace, the red-and-gold wallpaper inside will help warm you up.

**Traktir Zhili-Byli** (☎ 250 75 13; Kurmanghazy 43; mains 600-950T, salad bar 1200T; ⌚ noon-midnight) Good-value Russian food in a rustic, log-walled setting.

**Restoran Printsessa** (Princess; ☎ 261 06 27; Tölebaev 53; dishes 600-1000T; ⌚ noon-midnight) Come to this large, bustling restaurant just off Gogol for a filling Chinese meal. The menu offers a big choice including a good chicken, chilli and peanuts dish.

**Mama Mia** (☎ 273 38 73; Gogol 87; dishes 600-1300T; ⌚ noon-midnight) Bright, relaxed, little pizza/pasta/salad house with efficient service and a good choice of tasty food.

**Namaste** (☎ 292 24 84; cnr Satpaev & Baytursynuly; mains 700-2000T; ⌚ 11am-last guest) This small, tranquil restaurant does excellent Indian, Thai and Chinese food – great for vegetarians.

**American Bar & Grill** (☎ 250 50 13; www.rosinter.ru; Töle Bi 41; dishes 790-3000T; ⌚ 24hr) The burgers (790T) are the best in Almaty and there's a big American, Tex-Mex and Italian choice, in a ranch-style interior with good rock, jazz or swing music. The wooden outdoor annex is packed in summer.

**Shvabsky Domik** (☎ 261 05 14; www.shvabskiy-domik.kz; Abylay Khan 121; mains 800-2000T, set lunch 650-900T; ⌚ 24 hr) This spacious, German-cottage-style establishment serves reliably good international food with a strong German emphasis – lots of sausage and meat.

**our pick Safran** (☎ 293 83 83; Dostyq 36; mains 800-1800T, set lunch 900-1200T; ⌚ noon-midnight) Flavoursome Middle Eastern food in a beautiful, spacious Middle Eastern setting makes Safran a great place to head when you have 4000T to 5000T to spend on dinner. Tasty dishes range from hummus and falafel to carrot-and-cumin soup, sea-bass ceviche and Moroccan chicken with pumpkin-and-ginger sauce.

**Zheti Qazyna** (☎ 273 25 87; Abylay Khan 58A; mains 800-8000T; ⌚ noon-midnight) This Uzbek-themed restaurant is the place for Central Asian cooking at its finest. Old favourites such as *manty*, *laghman* and *samsa* (samosas) are styled for the Western palate, and there are Kazakh specialities including *beshbarmak* too. It's at least worth patronising for the colourful ambience and welcoming staff. On the same premises are Caramel, an equally popular European restaurant, and the Japanese-Chinese Tsi, and you can order from all three menus in any part. Two courses will cost a minimum of 1400T, and you can easily spend a whole lot more. The entrance is actually on Maqataev.

**Pomodoro Caffé** (☎ 261 83 26; Panfilov 108; pasta 1000-1600T, other dishes up to 4000T; ⌚ noon-midnight Mon-Sat) Gourmet little Italian spot with an Italian owner-chef preparing delicious salmon-and-cheese ravioli, spaghetti with courgettes and shrimps in cream sauce, and much more. He makes some of his own pasta.

**Mad Murphy's** (☎ 291 28 56; Töle Bi 12; dishes 1100-1700T; ⌚ food noon-10pm) This evergreen Irish pub (opposite) has plenty of good pub food in big portions.

**Thai** (☎ 291 01 90; Dostyq 50; mains 2000-7000T; ⏰ 11am-11pm) This very swish restaurant with a pleasant outdoor summer terrace specialises in Thai and Japanese dishes. The quality is high and the fish in most dishes is flown in direct from Muscat, Oman.

### Self-Catering

There are plenty of large, well-stocked supermarkets with many Western imports on their shelves.

**Yubileyny** (☎ 250 75 50; cnr Gogol & Abylay Khan; ⏰ 24hr) One of the biggest supermarkets in Almaty, with a deli and all manner of Western food and toiletries.

**Stolichny** (☎ 266 25 55; cnr Abylay Khan & Qabanbay Batyr; ⏰ 24 hr) Best-quality goods of any downtown supermarket, huge wine section and good deli counter.

**Zelyony Bazar** (Green Market, Kök Bazar; Zhibek Zholy 53; ⏰ 8am-5pm Tue-Sun) Stalls at this large central market are piled with nuts, fresh and dried fruit, smoked fish, vegetables and enormous hunks of fresh meat. You can get *kumys* (fermented mare's milk) and *shubat* (fermented camel's milk) here too. Cafés overlooking the action will serve you a bowl of *laghman*, tea and bread for less than 300T.

Further good supermarkets are **SM Market** (Maqataeva; ⏰ 24hr), **Silk Way City Gipermarket** (☎ 267 74 74; Töle Bi 71; ⏰ 24hr) and **Ramstor** (☎ 258 75 75; Furmanov 226; ⏰ 9am-11pm).

## DRINKING

Finding a drink for any budget isn't difficult in Almaty as many daytime cafés and restaurants become bars by night. Beer gardens under sunshades sprout around the city in summer.

**Soho** (☎ 267 03 67; Qazybek Bi 65; ⏰ 9pm-3am) Expats and local friends and colleagues pack Soho every night for tankards of beer, international food and crowded dancing to the excellent resident rock-blues band. It's got a sort of urban-global theme, with lots of pictures of New York mixed in with flags for every nationality – one place that never lacks atmosphere.

**Mad Murphy's** (☎ 291 28 56; Töle Bi 12; ⏰ 11.30am-1am) This Irish pub is the most consistently popular expat haunt for a stout, pub grub (opposite), darts, pool and football on big screens.

**Shtab** (Zheltoqsan; beer from 150T; ⏰ 10am-midnight) Tiny local beer bar opposite Hotel Ambassador, with half-a-dozen tables and a big selection of local and foreign draft beers including Kazakhstan's best, Shymkentskoe.

**Tinkoff** (☎ 292 49 00; Satpaev 27A; beer 0.5/1/1.5L 500/900/1400T; ⏰ noon-2am) This trendy, modern, three-floor bar-restaurant brews its own draught beer in six varieties, and the open roof terrace is great in summer. The 2nd-floor, with ceiling-to-floor windows, serves sausages, shashlyk and pizzas (800T to 1600T) and has occasional live music.

**San Siro** (☎ 272 05 94; Bögenbay Batyr 117; ⏰ 24hr) Almaty's temple of TV football – it has different soccer matches on different screens and can even show you a programme of upcoming games. It serves a good range of food too.

**Vogue** (☎ 264 16 99; Satpaev 11) Fashionable preclub bar with décor inspired by *Vogue* magazine – old-gold drapes, grapefruit-toned couches.

**Guinness Pub** (☎ 291 55 85; Dostyq 71; ⏰ 11am-2am) Popular pub near the Hotel Kazakhstan, with the famous Irish stout on tap, as well as pool tables, food and live music most nights.

**Dublin Pub** (☎ 272 14 75; Bayseyitova 45; ⏰ 11am-1am) A smaller, wood-panelled Irish pub on a quiet street near Respublika alanghy. It has assorted international food and the terrace is nice in summer.

## ENTERTAINMENT

If you can make some sense of Russian, *Time Out Almaty* (www.timeout.kz) is a great source of listings, reviews and contact details.

### Cinema

English-language films dubbed into Russian, including top recent releases, form a high proportion of the programming at Almaty's many cinemas. Admission costs 400T to 900T. For programmes see www.kino.kz or www.timeout.kz.

The **Kinoteatr Tsezar** (☎ 273 63 93; Furmanov 50; 500T; ⏰ 8pm Mon) shows arthouse movies for much of the year.

### Concerts, Ballet, Opera & Theatre

Almaty is blessed with a good theatre scene and it's well worth catching at least one performance while you're here. Keep an eye open for concerts by the renowned **State Kurmangazy Orchestra of Folk Instruments** (www.orchestra.kz) or the Otrar Sazy Kazakh Folk Orchestra.

**Abay State Opera & Ballet Theatre** (☎ 272 79 34; Qabanbay Batyr 110; ticket office 10am-6pm) Almaty's top cultural venue; three or four performances a week at 6.30pm. Classics such as *Swan Lake*, *La Bohème*, *Aida* and *Carmen* are a few of the regular shows. Also look out for Kazakh operas such as *Abay* and *Abylay Khan*.

**Auezov Kazakh Drama Theatre** (☎ 292 33 07; Abay 103) Elegant example of Soviet architecture with almost nightly drama performances.

**Kazkontsert Hall** (☎ 279 14 26; Abylay Khan 83) Classical, jazz and other concerts.

**State Philharmonia** (☎ 291 80 48, 291 75 21; www.philharmonic.kz; Kaldayakov 35) A range of performances including symphony, chamber, jazz, organ and traditional music.

**Palace of the Republic** (Dvorets Respubliki; ☎ 291 55 23; Dostyq 102) Stages assorted musical events including pop concerts.

## Gay & Lesbian Venues

There's a small underground scene in Almaty and the gay bars tend to come and go, so you might need to ask around to find out what is new. For some club info (in Russian) see www.gay.kz or www.timeout.kz.

**Real Club** (☎ 233 57 26; Rayymbek 152; Sun-Thu men free, Fri & Sat 600T, women Sun-Thu 500T, Fri & Sat 1000T; 11pm-6am) This is consistently the most popular gay club but it changes locations a lot. Has shows at 2am Friday and Saturday nights.

**XXX** (☎ 276 58 02, 705-1483837; Zhubanov 18V; women 300-500T, men 500-700T; from 11pm Tue-Sun) Friendly, mostly lesbian club out in the west of the city, 6km beyond the Central Stadium.

Da Freak (right) is gay-friendly.

## Live Music

**Cuba** (☎ 291 29 32; Bögenbay Batyr 102; admission 1500T; from noon) This Mexican-Russian restaurant is Almaty's Latin music hotspot with live bands whipping up a great atmosphere from 10pm to 1am Thursday and midnight to 3am Friday and Saturday. For Friday and Saturday you need to book a table by about 6pm. Dinner with drinks costs 2000T to 4000T.

**Members Bar** (☎ 250 50 00; Mezzanine, InterContinental Almaty, Zheltoqsan 181; 7pm-2am Mon-Sat) Cocktail-lounge-style jazz music. Resident artist at the time of writing, Geraldine Hunt, puts on a fine show from 11pm Tuesday to Saturday.

Soho (p125) has a polished rock and blues band nightly from 10pm.

## Nightclubs

Almaty's educated and aware students and 20-somethings have spawned a pretty good, ever-developing club scene. Flyers will get you in cheap to some clubs. *Time Out Almaty* has up-to-date listings in Russian. There are lots of special events and parties: www.night.kz (in a mix of English and Russian) has a calendar. Full-moon raves happen in summer out at Lake Kapshagay, with DJs flown in from Europe.

our pick **Da Freak** (☎ 273 13 37; Gogol 40; admission 1500T; 11pm-6am Fri & Sat) The best electronic club in town, Freak has two dance floors, the country's top DJs and sometimes guests from Moscow or Western Europe. The clientele is mostly a cool, 20ish, local crowd but there's a smattering of international 20s-to-35s in there too. The entrance is round the back of the Zhuldyz restaurant in Panfilov Park.

**Stereo** (☎ 293 04 93; Dosmukhamedov 115; admission 1000T; 10pm-4am Tue-Thu, 11pm-6am Sat & Sun) Successful new club on a lane between Abay and Kurmanghazy: There's house or chill-out in one room with Soviet-style décor and soul, funk and R&B in the other.

**Mostafterpartyclub** (☎ 233 04 57; www.most-club.kz; Kommunalnaya 12; admission 1000-1500T; 11pm-5am Sun-Thu, 11pm-9am Fri & Sat) This late club is big with a nouveau-riche and expat crowd. There's deep tech and tribal on the big dance floor, plus an oriental-style hookah room and a lounge-bar also with DJs. On Fridays and Saturdays retro '80s sessions start at 11pm; the afterparty begins at 3am.

**Gas** (☎ 272 74 74; Shevchenko 100; admission free-500T; 10pm-6am Wed-Mon) Another popular electronic haunt with DJs; no sportswear in this shiny glass-and-steel environment.

**Petroleum** (☎ 261 35 35; Shevchenko 100; men/women 2000/1500T; 10pm-6am) Upstairs from Gas, this flashy DJ dance club pumps out hip-hop and techno to an older crowd including foreign business chaps and local working girls. This is a place where you may want to dress up.

**Crystal** (☎ 292 52 95; Timiryazev btwn Baytursynuly & Markova; admission 2000T; 11pm-6am Fri & Sat) An 'elite' New York–style club popular with the Range Rover crowd, Crystal has DJs playing mostly European and American house and R&B (in separate rooms). The entrance is on Timiryazev. Downstairs is **Nice Bar** (☎ 292 38 25; Volodarskogo 29), with sink-into sofas and velvet-curtained private alcoves.

### Sport

**Hippodrome** (☎ 294 86 00; Zhansugirov) Horse races and occasionally *kökpar* (see Buzkashi, p59), take place several kilometres north of the centre. Get someone to call ahead and see what's on. Take a taxi, or bus 8 northbound on Qonaev from Töle Bi.

**Central Stadium** (☎ 292 47 10; Abay 48) Club and international soccer matches are played here.

## SHOPPING

**TsUM** (☎ 273 29 51; Zhibek Zholy 85; 10am-9pm Mon-Sat, 10am-8pm Sun) Visit this large central department store, composed of dozens of small shops, for the experience as well as to buy. It deals mainly in electronic goods, clothes, cosmetics, glass, china and gifts, and prices are reasonable. On the ground floor you'll find a bigger variety of mobile phones than you've ever seen in one place, and the top floor has the best range of kitsch souvenirs and gifts in the country – ornamental swords and horse whips, fur and felt hats, traditional jewellery and miniature yurts, camels and Golden Men.

**Republican Palace of Schoolchildren** (☎ 264 25 93; Dostyq 114) The Central Asian Crafts Fairs held here from 10am to 5pm a couple of Sundays a month from December to early March, offer a good range of artisanry at good prices. The craft and carpet stalls in the Central State Museum and Kazakhstan Museum of Arts (p120) are worth a look too. A 2m by 3m Kazakh carpet typically costs around US$400.

**Tengri Umai** (☎ 258 11 52; Panfilov 103) This gallery has the country's best selection of modern art, by artists from Kazakhstan and other former Soviet republics. Bright colours predominate and there's some very appealing work here.

**Meloman** (☎ 273 10 24; Gogol 58; 10am-midnight) A good place for recorded music, plus DVDs and videos in Russian and Kazakh. It's a national chain and there are several other branches in Almaty.

For sports gear, including trainers and winter sports equipment, head to **Sport Land** (☎ 272 06 06; Tole Bi 78; 10am-8pm) or **Megasport** (☎ 273 09 02; Maqataev 84; 10am-8pm).

Almaty's burgeoning middle class shops at supermarkets and glitzy malls stocked with expensive, often imported, goods and at international stores such as Zara, Yves Rocher and Benetton, which you'll find dotted all around the city centre. The main malls include **Silk Way City** (☎ 267 74 70; Töle Bi 71; 24hr), **Ramstor** (☎ 258 75 75; Furmanov 226; 9am-11pm) and the biggest and newest, **Mega Center Alma-Ata** (Rozybakiev 247A).

### Markets

Watch out for pickpockets in these places.

**Zelyony Bazar** (Green Market; Zhibek Zholy 53; 8am-5pm Tue-Sun) A sprawling place with a big indoor hall and vendors spread outside too. Much of it is devoted to food (see p125) but there are stalls with clothing and other goods.

**Barakholka** (Tue-Sun) This huge, crowded flea market is on the ring road in the northwestern outskirts. Uzbeks, Chinese, Uyghurs and others converge here to sell everything from animals, fridges and cars to fur hats, jeans and shoes, at very good prices. Weekends, especially early Sunday morning, are the busiest times. Take any 'Barakholka' bus westbound on Rayymbek.

## GETTING THERE & AWAY

Almaty is Kazakhstan's main air hub and is linked to most major Kazakhstan cities by daily trains. Long-distance buses reach many cities in southern, northern and eastern Kazakhstan, but a long haul is usually more comfortable by train.

For further information on international travel to/from Almaty, see Transport in Kazakhstan (p183) and Transport in Central Asia (p461).

### Air

Flights, nearly all by Air Astana or SCAT, go once or more daily to Aktau (22,500T to 27,000T), Aqtöbe (28,200T), Astana (20,000T), Atyrau (35,000T), Karaganda (19,000T), Kyzylorda (16,500T to 18,400T), Pavlodar (27,400T), Shymkent (16,000T) and Ust-Kamenogorsk (18,500T to 25,000T); five times a week to Semey (16,500T); four times to Kokshetau (24,500T) and Petropavlovsk (24,500T); three times to Uralsk (32,500T); and twice to Taraz (12,500T). For international flights see below.

Tickets can be bought at many agencies around town including the **Gorodskoy Aerovokzal** (City Air Terminal; cnr Zhibek Zholy & Zheltoqsan; 8am-10pm).

#### AIRLINE OFFICES

Not all airlines have offices in Almaty, but agencies such as CATC (p117), which sells tickets for all airlines, should be able to help if you can't contact an airline. Airlines flying from Almaty to international destinations include the following (subject to change, of course):

**Air Astana** (☎ 250 68 50; www.airastana.com; Hotel Otrar, Gogol 73) Moscow twice daily, Amsterdam, Beijing and Dubai four times weekly, Frankfurt and Istanbul three times weekly, Delhi and London twice weekly, Hanover and Seoul once weekly.

**Asiana Airlines** (☎ 257 25 25; www.flyasiana.com; Office 511, Hotel Kazakhstan 67, Dostyq 52) Seoul weekly, with connections to Asia, Australia and the US.

**British Airways** (☎ 272 40 40; www.britishairways.com; Dostyq 43) London three times weekly.

**China Southern Airlines** (www.cs-air.com) Ürümqi (US$300) five times weekly.

**Georgian National Airlines** (☎ 279 52 25; www.national-avia.com; Zhibek Zholy 125) Tbilisi twice weekly.

**Imair** (☎ 279 38 84; www.imair.com; Zhibek Zholy 125) Baku twice weekly.

**Kam Air** (www.flykamair.com) Kabul once weekly.

**KLM** (☎ 250 77 47; www.klm.com; Hotel Otrar, Gogol 73) Amsterdam five times weekly.

**Kras Air** (☎ 261 04 14; www.krasair.ru; Dostyq 85) Novosibirsk and Krasnoyarsk once weekly.

**Lufthansa** (☎ 250 50 52; www.lufthansa.com; Hyatt Regency Almaty, Satpaev 29/6) Frankfurt daily.

**Pulkovo** (☎ 273 26 11; www.pulkovo.ru; Furmanov 65) St Petersburg three times weekly.

**SCAT** (www.scat.kz) Dushanbe twice weekly; once weekly to Moscow, Yerevan and Bayan-Ölgii (Ulgit), Mongolia (US$250).

**Tajik Air** (☎ 257 21 55; www.tajikistan-airlines.com) Dushanbe three times weekly.

**Transaero** (☎ 273 93 90; www.transaero.ru; Furmanov 53) Moscow daily.

**Turkish Airlines** (☎ 250 10 67; www.turkishairlines.com; Furmanov 100) Istanbul daily.

**UM Air** (☎ 257 19 49; www.umairlines.com; Akhmetov 6) Kiev twice weekly.

**Ural Airlines** (☎ 223 98 48; www.uralairlines.com; Pobeda 52) Yekaterinburg twice weekly.

**Uzbekistan Airlines** (☎ 261 19 62; www.uzairways.com; Office 125/126, Qazybek Bi 50) Tashkent daily (US$185).

## Bus, Minibus & Taxi

Long-distance buses currently use the **Sayran bus station** (Novy avtovokzal; ☎ 276 26 44; cnr Töle Bi & Utegen Batyr), 5km west of the centre, but there are plans to replace Sayram with a new terminal even further out west, so check before you go there. Destinations include Karaganda (2800T, 20 hours, 2pm and 10pm), Shymkent (1400T, 12 hours, 8pm and 9.30pm), Taldyqorghan (650T, four hours, 17 daily), Taraz (1100T, nine hours, six daily), Turkistan (1200T, 15 hours, 11pm), Ust-Kamenogorsk (3100T, 22 hours, 7.30am and 5.30pm) and Zharkent (800T, six hours, five daily). For road transport to Bishkek (Kyrgyzstan) and Ürümqi (China), see p184 and p183 respectively.

Quicker minibuses to some of the nearer destinations wait at the front of the Sayran bus station building and even quicker shared taxis wait on Utegen Batyr (at the side of the bus station). To Taldyqorghan it's 700T (four hours) by minibus and 2000T (three hours) by taxi; to Taraz it's 1200T (eight hours) by minibus and 3000T (six hours) by taxi.

Most nearer destinations are served by the **Sayakhat bus station** (Stary Avtovokzal; ☎ 230 25 29; Rayymbek). Buses go every 15 minutes to Talgar (60T, 30 minutes) and Issik (Yesik; 60T, 45 minutes), and there are several minibuses to Kegen (800T, three to four hours). Services to Taldyqorghan may be added here.

## Car

One of the very few car rental companies operating here is **Europcar** (☎ 258 16 81; www.europcar.com; Bayseyitova 33). Small and medium-sized cars cost around US$125 to US$160 per day with unlimited kilometres. A driver can be provided for an extra fee.

## Train

Nearly all main long-distance trains stop at **Almaty-I station** (☎ 296 33 92), 8km north of the centre at the end of Seyfullin, but fortunately most terminate at the more convenient **Almaty-II station** (☎ 296 55 44), at the end of Abylay Khan on the northern edge of the central area. There are train ticket offices in the centre, including in the Gorodskoy Aerovokzal (p127), as well as inside the stations and on Abylay Khan just south of Almaty-II, where tickets are available 24 hours. You need to show your passport when buying tickets.

Destinations served at least daily (in some cases several times daily), with typical 2nd-class *(kupeynyy)* fares, include Astana (5300T, 19 to 21 hours), Aqtöbe (5500T, 40 to 46 hours), Kokshetau (6500T, 25 hours), Kyzylorda (3600T, 22 hours), Pavlodar (6700T, 28 to 33 hours, from Almaty-I only), Petropavlovsk (8000T, 31 hours), Semey (3500T, 20 to 22 hours), Shymkent (3000T, 12 to 15 hours), Taraz (2765T, 10½ hours), Turkistan (3200T, 16 hours) and Uralsk (6500T, 54 hours). Trains for Atyrau (6000T, 52 hours) and Mangyshlak (Aktau; 7000T, 67 hours) depart every second day.

For Karaganda and Astana you can take advantage of the Talgo: a sleek, Spanish-built, fast overnight train with lovely clean bathrooms. Unfortunately it can't travel at full speed because the Kazakh track isn't up to that. Train 1 departs Almaty-II just after 7pm (it doesn't stop at Almaty-I), reaching Astana at 8.20am. The one-way fare in 3rd/2nd/1st class to Astana is 9400/15,800/17,300T (2nd class is a two-person compartment).

The only direct train to Moscow (23,000T) is train 7, leaving at 6am on even dates and taking a cool 81 hours via Shymkent, Aqtöbe, Uralsk and Saratov. You can get there half a day quicker by changing trains two or three times en route. There are also direct daily trains to Novosibirsk.

## GETTING AROUND

### To/From the Airport

Several buses from the airport run through the city centre (a 30- to 40-minute ride). Check the map to decide which is best. At research time, the nearest bus stop to the airport was 250m along the street outside the parking area. Bus 492 runs to Sayakhat bus station, west on Rayymbek, south on Nauryzbay Batyr then west on Abay. Going to the airport it heads north on Zheltoqsan instead of Nauryzbay Batyr. Bus 79 goes to Sayakhat bus station, south on Pushkin, west on Gogol, south on Furmanov, west on Abay and south on Baytursynuly, and vice-versa. Marshrutka 526 goes to Sayakhat bus station, south on Pushkin, west on Maqataev, south on Furmanov and southwest on Al-Farabi, and vice-versa. All cost 100T.

A taxi from the airport to the centre shouldn't cost more than 2000T, though drivers may try to get 4000T or 5000T. Going out to the airport you may be able to get a taxi for 1000T. For 1500T, you can call one on ☎ 255 53 33 (24 hours; no English spoken).

### Public Transport

Almaty has a vast network of bus, trolleybus, tram and marshrutka (small buses) routes. Fares are usually 40T. They can get very crowded, so if you have much baggage or are short of time, it's simpler to take a taxi.

All services mentioned here follow the same routes in both directions unless stated.

#### THE BUS STATIONS

From Sayran bus station, buses 37, 94 and 166 run east along Töle Bi to the centre. Buses 94 and 166 turn north on Qonaev, then east on Gogol to Gorky Park. The 37 turns north on Zheltoqsan then east on Rayymbek to Sayakhat bus station; going out to Sayran it heads south on Nauryzbay Batyr instead of Zheltoqsan. Tram 4 heads east from Sayran along Töle Bi, then south on Baytursynuly, east on Shevchenko, north on Qonaev and east on Maqataev.

Many routes including buses 29, 32, 37, 79 and 492 and marshrutkas 526 and 537 pass Sayakhat bus station: just look for one saying 'Sayakhat' and heading in the right direction.

#### THE TRAIN STATIONS

From Almaty-II, trolleybuses 5 and 6 head south on Abylay Khan, then west on Abay to the Central Stadium, Fantasy World and beyond. Marshrutka 537 goes east to Sayakhat bus station, south to the Zelyony Bazar (Pushkin), west on Gogol, south on Furmanov then southwest on Al-Farabi.

From Almaty-I, bus 2 and marshrutka 528 run to Sayakhat, the Zelyony Bazar (Pushkin) and Gogol then south on Furmanov as far as Ramstor.

#### OTHER USEFUL ROUTES

In the central area, Furmanov is the main artery for north–south routes, used by buses 2, 63 and 79 and marshrutkas 526, 528 and 537, among others; Gogol and Abay are the principal east–west routes. Tram 4, along Qonaev and Shevchenko, is another useful service.

**Bus 29** Sayakhat bus station, Pushkin, Kaldayakov, Bögenbay Batyr (Qabanbay Batyr northbound), Dostyq, Butakovka.

**Bus 32** Sayakhat bus station, Rayymbek, Nauryzbay Batyr (Zheltoqsan northbound), Timiryazev.

**Bus 35** Abay from Dostyq to Central Stadium, Fantasy World and beyond.

**Bus 63** Zelyony Bazar (Pushkin), Gogol, Furmanov, Al-Farabi to Saina.

**Bus 66** Gogol (north side of Panfilov Park), Kaldayakov, Dostyq, Abay, Zhandosov.

**Bus 139** Zelyony Bazar, Maqataev, Nauryzbay Batyr (Zheltoqsan northbound), Abay to Central Stadium.

**Marshrutka 500** Zelyony Bazar, Pushkin, Gogol, Kaldayakov, Bögenbay Batyr, Dostyq, Abay, Zhandosov.

**Marshrutka 520** Ramstor, Furmanov, Satpaev, southwest on Zhandosov.

**Trolleybus 1** Gorky Park, Gogol, south on Auezov to Timiryazev.
**Trolleybus 2** Zelyony Bazar (Zhibek Zholy), Pushkin, Gogol, Auezov, west on Abay.
**Trolleybus 11** Zelyony Bazar (Zhibek Zholy), Gogol, Kaldayakov, Dostyq, Abay, south on Baytursynuly.
**Trolleybus 12** Gorky Park, Gogol, Auezov, southwest on Zhandosov.
**Trolleybus 19** Zelyony Bazar (Zhibek Zholy), Gogol, Kaldayakov, Dostyq, Abay to Central Stadium, Fantasy World and beyond.

### Taxi

There are some official taxis – marked with chequerboard logos or other obvious signs – but many private cars also act as taxis. Just stand at the roadside with your arm out and you'll rarely have to wait more than six or eight cars before one stops. Say where you're going and how much you're offering. If you can't agree a price, let the car go and wait for another. A ride in the centre of Almaty should cost 200T to 400T, depending on distance (a bit more at night). You can call a cab on ☎ 255 53 33 (24 hours; no English spoken): minimum fare is 500T.

## AROUND ALMATY

There are many great excursions to be made from Almaty, notably into the Zailiysky Alatau range climbing south to the Kyrgyzstan border. Easy day trips include Medeu, Chimbulak and Bolshoe Almatinskoe lake. The two main access routes into the Zailiysky Alatau foothills south of the city are the valleys of the Malaya (Little) Almatinka and Bolshaya (Big) Almatinka rivers. See the Almaty to Lake Issyk-Köl map (p132) for an overview of this region. If you're heading high into the mountains, make sure you have a good map and/or a guide. In winter and spring, watch out for avalanches. See the Trekking Warning p134.

Akademkitap No 1 bookshop in Almaty sells a good range of trekking maps covering this area, while GEO sells topographical maps (p116). If you can find it, *The Hiker's Guide to Almaty* by Arkady Pozdeyev outlines 40-odd day hikes and longer around Almaty. See Travel Agencies (p117) and Tourist Information (p117) for some providers of guided trips.

Given the deteriorating state of the roads as you travel east from Almaty, it's better to consider destinations such as the Charyn Canyon and the Karkara Valley as overnight trips. These are covered in the Southeast Kazakhstan section (p134).

### Medeu & Chimbulak

These are Almaty's playgrounds in the Malaya Almatinka valley, both easily visited on a day trip from the city. If you want to avoid crowds come on a weekday.

The winter sports facilities here are good enough for Almaty to have made an (unsuccessful) bid to hold the 2014 Winter Olympics. The settlement of Medeu, at 1700m, is a scattering of buildings around the huge Medeu ice rink, about 15km southeast of central Almaty. Chimbulak at 2300m is Central Asia's top skiing centre. Both are starting points for good day hikes and for treks in the Zailiysky Alatau: see Medeu to Butakovka Hike (opposite) and Trekking to Lake Issyk-Köl (p136) for routes.

Medeu is always several degrees cooler than Almaty, and Chimbulak is cooler still. Except in summer, rain in Almaty means snow and zero visibility at the higher elevations.

The 10,500-sq-metre **Medeu ice rink** (☎ 327-271 62 15; admission adult/under 13yr 600/300T; 🕑 noon-4pm & 6-11pm Mon-Fri, 11am-4pm & 5-11pm Sat, 10am-4pm & 5-11pm Sun approx Nov-Apr), built in 1972, is made for speed skating and many champion skaters have trained here. Even when the rink is closed people come to relax at the shashlyk and drink stands, and to take a walk in the surrounding valleys and hills. You can rent skates for 600T per two hours, though you need to leave your passport or 10,000T as deposit.

What looks like a dam in the main valley above the ice rink (about 3km by road or 800-odd steps on foot) is actually there to stop avalanches and mudslides. The road climbs a further 4.5km from this barrier to the surprisingly swish **Chimbulak ski resort** (☎ 327-258 19 99; www.chimbulak.com), with a vertical drop of 900m and a variety of ski runs for all levels. The ski season runs from about November to April. A new quad lift was added in 2003 and the ski-rental equipment, including snowboards, is also in good condition, costing 2000T to 5000T per day depending on quality. Day/half-day lift passes are 4000/2500T Monday to Friday, 5000/3000T Saturday and Sunday, with individual lift tickets at 400T. Since it takes three lifts to reach the Talgar Pass at around 3200m, a day pass makes sense if you're going to ski the whole mountain. Ski

### MEDEU TO BUTAKOVKA HIKE

The further from Medeu you hike, the prettier the scenery becomes. This trek through the wooded Komissarov (Kim-Asar) Valley and over the 2060m Komissarov Pass can be completed in half a day, or extended to a full day if you continue on the 2870m Butakovka Pass. From Medeu take the paved road heading up the east side of the valley 100m below the ice rink, towards the Qazaq Aul restaurant. Continue up the road until you reach the track that heads past some buildings belonging to the forest service. The trail rises steeply to the Komissarov Pass. From here you can either hike along the north ridge of the Komissarov spur back to Medeu, or head east through a forest leading to a narrow ravine. The trail forks in several places but all routes will eventually bring you to the Butakovka valley. From here you can head up the valley to the Butakovka Pass or down to Butakovka village, where bus 29 returns to Almaty.

**Stage One** Medeu to Komissarov Pass (two hours).
**Stage Two** Komissarov Pass to Butakovka valley (two to three hours).
**Stage Three** Butakovka valley to Butakovka Pass (four hours).
**Stage Four** Butakovka Pass to Butakovka (two to three hours).

lessons are US$15 per hour (US$20 at weekends) in groups of three, or US$22 (weekends US$28) for individual lessons. Some instructors speak English.

You can take walks from Chimbulak itself. A track continues 8km up the Malaya Almatinka valley and, in summer, it's a 3km hike up to the Talgar Pass. Warning: there is year-round avalanche danger wherever you see snow. Pik Komsomola (4330m) rises 3km south of the Talgar Pass, the nearest of a ring of glacier-flanked peaks around the top of the Malaya Almatinka valley, which are favourites with Almaty climbers.

If you are staying at Chimbulak, you can entertain yourself in the evening at the modern **bowling alley** (per hr 2000T; ☉ noon-3am).

#### SLEEPING & EATING

**Hotel Chimbulak** (☎ 327-258 19 99; www.chimbulak.com; r/pol-lux/lux 9000/13,000/30,000T) This lodge at the Chimbulak resort has a great location at the foot of the chairlift, but you'll pay for it through the nose. Most of the rooms are unrenovated and not very exciting, but the *lux* units do have a Jacuzzi. The standard and *pol-lux* rooms go for 5000 and 9000T respectively from about April to November.

**Hotel Vorota Tuyuk Su** (☎ 327-260 72 15; r with shared bathroom 5200-8700T, with private bathroom from 8700T) Two kilometers up the road past Chimbulak, this handsome stone lodge has 26 comfortable rooms in attractive wooden cottages, plus a restaurant with mainly Russian food, a bathhouse and billiards room – somewhat cosier than Hotel Chimbulak.

**Qazaq Aul** (Kazakh Village; ☎ 327-271 64 17; dishes 350-650T; ☉ 11am-midnight) This restaurant inside several traditionally decorated yurts is a treat. Squatting around low tables, you can enjoy local specialities such as *beshbarmak* and *manty*. Take the road up to the left (east) about 100m below the ice rink: the restaurant is 700m up here.

Elsewhere the main food option is shashlyk but there are also a couple of **cafés** (dishes 300-700T) with *plov, manty,* soups and salads up at Chimbulak. If you're planning a hike or intend to camp, bring food with you.

#### GETTING THERE & AWAY

From Almaty, buses 6 (40T) and 6A (65T) go to Medeu (30 minutes) every few minutes from Dostyq, opposite the Hotel Kazakhstan. The last buses back leave Medeu about 10pm. Taxis from Medeu to Chimbulak cost 1000T to 1500T, or 500T per person on a shared basis.

### Bolshoe Almatinskoe Lake Area

West of the Malaya Almatinka valley lies its 'big sister', the Bolshaya Almatinka valley.

Coming from the city the first thing you will encounter is a gate where a guard collects 200T per person for entry to the Ile-Alatau National Park. The nearby **Sunkar eagle farm** (☎ 327-255 30 76; admission 150T; ☉ daylight hr), which also keeps hunting dogs, is worth a look. At 4pm except Monday, an entertaining display of several species of trained raptors in flight is staged (1000T). A couple of kilometres further is the bus stop at the GES-2 hydroelectric station, also called Kokshoky. The road forks here, with the right branch heading to the settlement of Alma-Arasan (4km), and the left branch following the Bolshaya Almatinka River.

The track up the Bolshaya Almatinka valley passes another small hydroelectric station, GES-1, after about 8km, and brings you after a further 7km or so to the picturesque 1.6km-long **Bolshoe Almatinskoe lake** (2500m), resting in a rocky bowl in the Zailiysky Alatau foothills. The lake is a hike of four or five hours from GES-2, with a rise of nearly 1100m. This is a starting point for many trekking routes in the mountains and across to Lake Issyk-Köl in Kyrgyzstan (p136). The lake is frozen

## TREKS FROM THE BOLSHAYA ALMATINKA VALLEY

The GES-2–Kosmostantsia–Alma-Arasan loop is a fine, day-long trek of about 31km. It can be extended to a two- or three-day circuit if you head south from Bolshoe Almatinskoe lake and over the Almaty-Alagir Pass (3660m).

More challenging routes link the Bolshaya Almatinka and Malaya Almatinka valleys. To go from GES-2 to Chimbulak via the Lokomotiv Glacier and Lokomotiv Pass (4050m, Grade 1B), the Tuyuksu Glacier and the Malaya Almatinka River, takes two or three days. See the Trekking Warning, p134.

### GES-2–Kosmostantsia–Alma-Arasan Trek

You can start from where the bus stops at GES-2 hydroelectric station, but time and effort will be saved by taking a taxi further to GES-1 (see p134). Here climb the metal steps beside the broad water pipe rising sharply up the gorge, then walk up the pipe for the most direct route to Bolshoe Almatinskoe lake. The road is a more serpentine route to the same place. From the lake, follow the road uphill to the right, past the observatory and up to Kosmostantsia at the head of the Zhusalykezen Pass (3336m). From here a trail runs north to the summit of Pik Bolshoy Almatinsky (3681m), or you can descend to the Prokhodnaya River valley, which runs north to the Alma-Arasan Resort. From here, bus No 93 runs back to the city or you can continue walking back to GES-2.

**Stage One** GES-2 (Kokshoky) to GES-1 (two hours).
**Stage Two** GES-1 to Bolshoe Almatinskoe lake (two hours).
**Stage Three** Bolshoe Almatinskoe lake to Kosmostantsia (three hours).
**Stage Four** Kosmostantsia to Alma-Arasan (four to five hours).

from November to June and only takes on its famous turquoise tinge once the silt of summer meltwater has drained away. It's a good bird-watching spot, especially during the May migration. A supposed 4WD track heads south from the lake and over the Ozyorny Pass (3507m) and eventually to Lake Issyk-Köl in Kazakhstan, but at the time of writing this was in impossibly bad condition for motor vehicles, though OK for mountain bikers.

Two kilometres up the track to the west from the lake (about a 40-minute walk), at 2750m, is the outlandish **Tian Shan Astronomical Observatory**, sometimes still referred to by its Soviet-era acronym, Gaish. The observatory has the second-biggest telescope in the former USSR, with magnification of around 600 times, installed in 1991. The telescope only operates at part-capacity due to lack of funding but is still used for research into the active nuclei of galaxies. A former radar dish is now used as a satellite TV receiver. It's possible to stay here (see right) and take tours of the working sections (in Russian) for 500T.

At the head of the Zhusalykezen Pass (3336m), 6km southwest from the observatory, is the **Kosmostantsia**, a group of wrecked buildings belonging to various scientific research institutes. Some research into solar radiation is still carried out here.

### SLEEPING & EATING

If you're not camping by the lake, there are a couple of places to stay.

**Tian Shan Astronomical Observatory** (☎ 327-221 1144, 327-276 21 67; r per person 3000T) This unique lodging has prime lake and mountain views, though it can be full on weekends from May to September. The rooms have electric heaters for warmth, but if you are looking for a bargain, ask if you can stay in one of the basic wooden cottages *(domick)*. There is food here (meals 2500T) and you can ask for a packed lunch if you're hiking.

**Alpine Rose** (☎ 327-264 03 25; r with shared bathroom 7000T, with private bathroom from 8700T) This mock Swiss chalet–style hotel is halfway between GES-1 and the lake. Rooms are clean and comfortable and the atmospheric bar has house-brewed beer. They also have a *banya* (bathhouse) and billiards room. You can rent snowmobiles here in winter (13,000T per hour).

**Tau Dastarkhan** (☎ 327-258 35 43) Several places to eat, from roadside shashlyk stands up, are dotted along the road from Almaty to GES-2.

The Tau Dastarkhan group of restaurants, 500m before GES-2, includes Kazakh, Georgian and German eateries, plus pastry and deli cafés, open-air grills and even a pool. Prices are midrange.

### GETTING THERE & AWAY

From central Almaty, take bus 63 or marshrutka 526 south on Furmanov and along Al-Farabi to the big roundabout on the southern edge of the city where Al-Farabi meets Navoi and Saina. Here switch to bus No 28 or 93 heading up the hill to the south. Both go to GES-2 (Kokshoky) and bus 93 continues to Alma-Arasan. The last bus back from GES-2 is at about 9.45pm.

The Bolshoe Almatinskoe lake road is normally passable in a 4WD all the way to Kosmostantsia, and in non-4WDs as far as GES-1. An Almaty city taxi will bring you this far for about 1500T.

> **TREKKING WARNING**
>
> It's feasible to trek unguided if you have suitable experience and equipment, but take extreme care with the weather. You *must* be equipped for sudden bad conditions. The trekking season lasts from about mid-May to mid- to late September; July and August have the most reliable weather, but at any time it can often rain or even snow in the mountains, even when it's warm in Almaty. If you're caught unprepared by a sudden storm, it could be fatal.
>
> Check what lies in store before embarking on any trek – some routes cross glaciers and tricky passes over 4000m high. When in doubt, go with a guide.

# SOUTHEAST KAZAKHSTAN

The region from Almaty to Lake Balkhash is known as Zhetisu (Russian: Semirechie) meaning Land of Seven Rivers. There are actually more than 800 rivers, many fed by glaciers in the Zailiysky and Zhungar Alatau ranges, making it a rich area for agriculture. There's plenty to see and do in Zhetisu and the mountains along Kazakhstan's borders with Kyrgyzstan and China – a blessing for anyone based in Almaty or whose Kazakhstan travels are restricted to this corner of the country.

## ZAILIYSKY ALATAU & KÜNGEY ALATAU ЗАИЛИЙСКИЙ АЛАТАУ И КУНГЕЙ АЛАТАУ

The Zailiysky Alatau, and the Küngey Alatau further south of Almaty, are spurs of the Tian Shan running east–west between Almaty and Kyrgyzstan's Lake Issyk-Köl.

The mountains are high and beautiful, with many peaks over 4000m, lots of glaciers and Tian Shan firs on the steep valley sides. In summer the valleys are used as summer pasture and herders set up yurt camps. These mountains make for excellent trekking and there are dozens of trails of varying length, many starting from Medeu, Chimbulak, GES-2 or Bolshoe Almatinskoe lake, which are easily reached from Almaty (see Around Almaty, p130). Some of the best-used trails go right across to Lake Issyk-Köl. See p117 for recommended Almaty travel agencies offering guided treks.

Passes marked on maps as Unclassified (N/K) or 1A are simple, with slopes no steeper than 30 degrees; glaciers, where they exist, are flat and without open crevasses. Grade 1B passes may have ice patches or glaciers with hidden crevasses and may require ropes. Passes of grade 2A and above may require special equipment and technical climbing skills.

### Maps

Good Russian-language maps are available in Almaty from Akademkitap and GEO (p116). The *Marshrutnaya Turistskaya Karta* (Tourist Route Map) series (Moscow, 1990–91) covers specific routes in an unusual but workable section-strip format, mostly at 1:50,000. The *Turistskie Marshruty g. Almaty-oz. Issyk-Kul* map (Astana, 2000) covers the whole area between Almaty and Lake Issyk-Köl at 1:200,000 and grades all the passes in the region.

## KOLSAY LAKES ОЗЁРА КОЛЬСАЙ

These three pretty lakes lie amid the steep, forested foothills of the Küngey Alatau, 110km southeast of Almaty as the crow flies, but over 300km by road via Chilik (Shelek) and Zhalanash. This is the start of a popular trekking route over to Lake Issyk-Köl in Kyrgyzstan.

The lakes are strung along the Kolsay River, about 1800m to 2850m high, southwest of the village of Saty. A minibus to Saty (1200T,

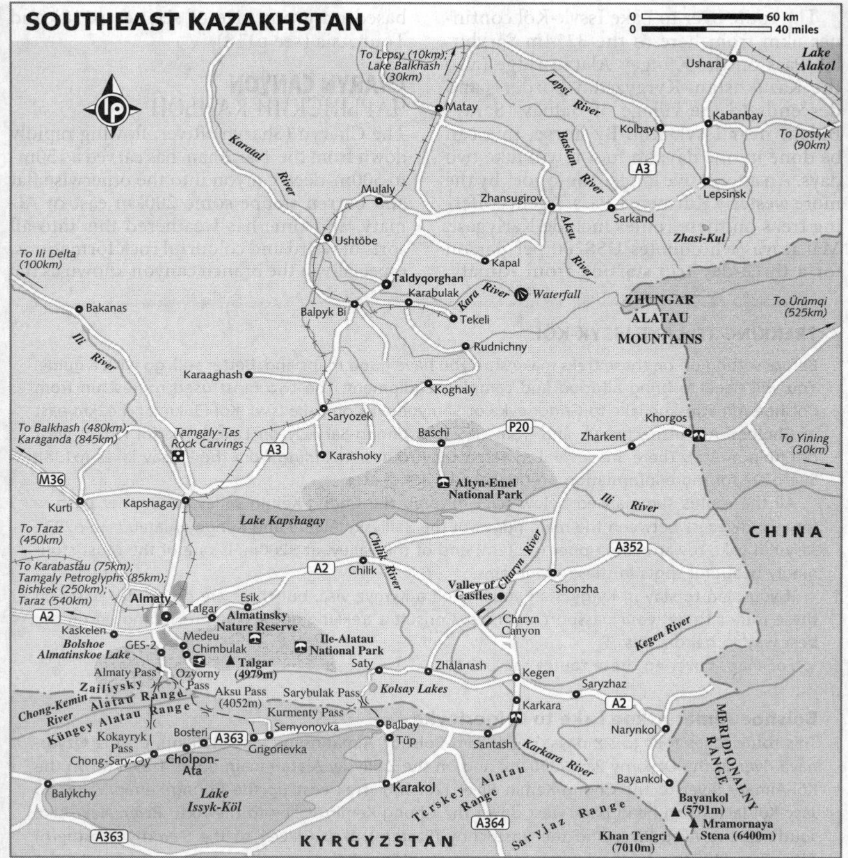


six hours) leaves Almaty's Sayakhat bus station about 8am. Alternatively get a bus to Zhalanash and find a ride for the last 40km to Saty. From Saty it's about 15km by road to the 1km-long Nizhny (Lower) Kolsay lake at 1800m. Midway between Saty and the lake there is a checkpoint where you'll pay a park entrance fee of 1000T per person.

In Saty, **Yelshibay Umbetaliev** (☎ 327-772 77 18; Beregovaya 8; dm incl meals 2500T) has homestay accommodation and can offer walking and horse-riding trips – the EIRC in Almaty (p117) can put you in contact with him. You should be able to hire a horse and/or guide in Saty for around US$30 per day.

Jibek Joly (p117) has a spartan, six-room wooden guesthouse overlooking Nizhny Kolsay lake, for which it quotes US$25 per person full board, though travellers who arrived here independently reported being asked US$35 without meals. Cheaper cottages lower down cost 1000T to 1500T per person (though the same travellers also reported being charged extortionate prices for food by an irascible village administrator while staying here). Camping by the lake is 750T per tent.

The Sredny (Middle) Kolsay lake is the biggest and most beautiful, 5km from the lower lake via a hike of about three hours rising to 2250m. The surrounding meadows are used as pasture and are a good camping spot. From the Sredny lake to the smaller Verkhny (Upper) Kolsay lake at 2850m is about 4km and takes about three hours.

The route over to Lake Issyk-Köl continues 6km from here to the 3274m Sarybulak Pass on the Küngey Alatau ridge (also the Kazakhstan–Kyrgyzstan border), and descends to the village of Balbay (Saray-Bulak) near Issyk-Köl. By horse, this can be done in one day; on foot it will take two days. An alternative longer route goes by the more westerly Kurmenty Pass. Agents offering treks on these routes include Karlygash Makatova (who quotes US$200 per person for a three-day trip starting from Almaty, based on group size of six; see p118) and Tour Asia (see p118).

## CHARYN CANYON
## ЧАРЫНСКИЙ КАНЬОН

The Charyn (Sharyn) River, flowing rapidly down from the Tian Shan, has carved a 150m- to 300m-deep canyon into the otherwise flat and barren steppe some 200km east of Almaty, and time has weathered this into all sorts of weird and colourful rock formations, especially in the branch canyon known as the

### TREKKING TO LAKE ISSYK-KÖL

Before setting off on these treks make sure you have good maps and, better still, go with a guide. You will need to bring all food and camping equipment. The two most used routes run from Bolshoe Almatinskoe lake to Grigorievka or Semyonovka on Lake Issyk-Köl (35km and 42km east of Cholpon-Ata respectively); and from GES-2 to Chong-Sary-Oy on Lake Issyk-Köl (15km west of Cholpon-Ata). There are several more easterly routes, including from the Kolsay lakes (p134). See p294 for more information on the Lake Issyk-Köl area.

All the routes summarised below pass through the Chong-Kemin valley, a summer pasture for yurt-dwellers between the main ridges of the Zailiysky Alatau and Küngey Alatau (see p293). Jasy-Kül Lake towards the upper (eastern) end of the valley, at 3200m, is one of the most stunningly beautiful spots in these mountains.

If you plan to stay in Kyrgyzstan you'll need a Kyrgyz visa, but there are no border posts on these routes to get your passport stamped. Consult a trekking agency before setting off on the best way to handle this.

For maps covering these routes see p134.

#### Bolshoe Almatinskoe Lake to Grigorievka

This route takes four to six days. Head from Bolshoe Almatinskoe lake (2500m), up the Ozyornaya river to the Ozyorny Pass (3507m) and on the Zailiysky Alatau main ridge. Travel down the Köl-Almaty River to the Chong-Kemin River (2800m). Trek east up the Chong-Kemin Valley to Jasy-Kül lake. Then head back west down the Chong-Kemin Valley to the Aksu River. Next hike south up the Aksu River and the Vostochny (Eastern) Aksu Glacier to the Severny (Northern) Aksu Pass (4052m, on the Küngey Alatau main ridge) before heading eastward down to the Chong Aksu River, to the foot of 4330m Mt Autor Bashi. Finally follow the river eastward, then southward to Grigorievka.

#### Variation from Chimbulak

Three days can be added to the preceding route by going from Chimbulak, across the Talgar (Bolshoe Talgarsky) Pass (3160m) and down to the Levy Talgar River (2300m). Follow the Levy Talgar River south then head west up the Turistov River to Turistov Pass (3930m). Next trek southwest down the Kyzylsay River to the Ozyornaya river. From here travel up the Ozyornaya river to Ozyorny Pass then continue as on the preceding route.

#### GES-2 to Chong-Sary-Oy

This is a more westerly route of about six days. From GES-2, head south through Alma-Arasan and up the Prokhodnaya valley to the Almaty (Prokhodnoy) Pass (3600m) on the Zailiysky Alatau main ridge. Trek south past Primul Lake below the pass and down the Almaty River to the Chong-Kemin River (2700m). From here, go west down the Chong-Kemin River then south up the Severnaya (Northern) Orto-Koy-Su River to the Kokayryk Pass (3889m), on the Küngey Alatau main ridge. Finally head south down the Yuzhnaya (Southern) Orto-Koy-Su River to Chong-Sary-Oy.

Valley of Castles. This is no Grand Canyon, but it's worth a visit. Although the canyon can be visited in a long day trip from Almaty, overnight camping (free) offers a more relaxed pace. April, May, June, September and October are the best months to come: it's too hot in summer. It costs 208T per person to enter the canyon area.

To get here, take a bus from Almaty's Sayakhat bus station heading to Kegen or Narynkol. The buses cross the Charyn River just upstream from the canyon, which is as close as you can get by road; ask to be let out as close as possible to the canyon. From here it's 12km by dirt road to the Valley of Castles, which is around 5km long and up to 50m deep. If you're lucky you might get a taxi or lift there; if not, it's a walk!

Don't try to swim in the river, which is deceptively fast.

Many Almaty travel agencies offer trips to Charyn Canyon. The EIRC (p117) offers weekend day-trips by bus for 1500T per person; CATC charges around 45,000T for up to 20 people; a taxi goes for around US$200.

## KARKARA VALLEY
## КАРКАРАНСКАЯ ДОЛИНА

The beautiful, broad valley of the Karkara River, 200km east of Almaty, is an age-old summer pasture for herds from both sides of what's now the Kazakhstan–Kyrgyzstan border. The river forms the border for some 40km before heading north to join the Kegen River, beyond which it becomes the Charyn.

From Kegen, 250km by road across the steppe from Almaty, a scenic road heads south to Karkara, then to the border post about 28km from Kegen. The road, normally open from about April to October, then veers west towards Tüp and Lake Issyk-Köl in Kyrgyzstan. No public transport reaches the border, but several daily minibuses run to Kegen (800T, three to four hours) from Almaty's Sayakhat bus station, and from Kegen you can get up the valley and into Kyrgyzstan by hitching or taxi. At Santash, 19km into Kyrgyzstan, you can find a bus or shared jeep to Tüp or Karakol.

A *chabana* (cowboy) festival, with a market, traditional foods and sports such as *kökpar* (see Buzkashi, p59) and *kyz kuu* (where a man chases a woman on horseback), is held on the Kazakh side of the border for two or three days around 10–15 August each year. It brings together Kazakh and Kyrgyz herders in a reminder of the valley's historic role as a meeting place of nomads and Silk Road traders.

Mountain-tourism company Kan Tengri (p118) maintains a summer base camp at about 2200m on the Kazakh side of the international border. Primarily a staging post for treks and climbing expeditions to the central Tian Shan, the camp also offers accommodation to all comers. Accommodation is in tents, with hot showers, a café and bar; full board costs US$45. It's open from late June to late August. It's possible to join helicopter flights to the central Tian Shan from here, but you may need a border-zone permit for this, so ask ahead.

For information on the Kyrgyz side of the Karkara Valley, see left.

## CENTRAL TIAN SHAN
## ЦЕНТРАЛЬНЫЙ ТЯНЬ ШАНЬ

Kazakhstan's highest and most magnificent mountains rise in the country's far southeastern corner where it meets Kyrgyzstan and China. Mt Khan Tengri (7010m) on the Kyrgyz border is widely considered the most beautiful and demanding peak in the Tian Shan, and there are many more 5000m-plus peaks around it in all three countries, including Mramornaya Stena (Marble Wall, 6400m) on the Kazakh–Chinese border, and Pik Pobedy (7439m) south of Khan Tengri on the Kyrgyz–Chinese border.

Khan Tengri is flanked by two long, west-running glaciers, the North Inylchek Glacier on its Kazakh side and the South Inylchek glacier on its Kyrgyzstan side.

The Almaty-based mountain-tourism firms Kan Tengri and Tour Asia (p118) offer a variety of exciting one- to five-week treks and full-scale mountaineering expeditions in and around this area in July and August, using tent base camps on the two Inylchek glaciers and at Bayankol (Ak-Kol) to the north, all at altitudes of around 4000m. Access is often by helicopter, using the Karkara Valley base camp as a staging and acclimatisation post. With Kan Tengri, a typical two-week trek costs around €1000, while a three-week trek with a bit of 'easy' climbing should be around €1400. Check the companies' websites for current offerings. Many treks include helicopter flights around the main peaks and glacier hikes to the foot of Khan Tengri and/or Pik Pobedy. Kan Tengri (p118) even offers heli-skiing trips with descents from peaks as high as 5800m. Karlygash Makatova (p118) can arrange two-day flying visits with a night at one of the Inylchek camps and a Khan Tengri fly-past.

See p312 for information on the Kyrgyz part of the Central Tian Shan.

## LAKE KAPSHAGAY & THE ILI RIVER ОЗЕРО КАПЧАГАЙ И РЕКА ИЛИ

Lake Kapshagay is a 100km-long reservoir formed by a hydroelectric dam on the Ili River near the town of Kapshagay, 70km north of Almaty. Many Almaty residents have *dacha* (country or holiday houses) here and the lake has cold, fresh water. Its best beaches are on the north shore, past the dam. Kapshagay is about to become the Kazakh Las Vegas, if government plans announced in 2006 go ahead: all the country's casinos are to be relocated here or to Burabay, north of Astana.

The **Ili River** flows west out of China into the lake, then northwest to Lake Balkhash. The river is navigable by kayak all the way from lake to lake (around 460km), and by raft at least some of the way, and is warm enough for swimming in summer. Around 25km downstream from Kapshagay are the **Tamgaly-Tas rock carvings**, a group of six striking Buddha or Shiva figures with Sanskrit-like inscriptions carved into the rock in about the 8th century AD – rare evidence of early Buddhist or Hindu influence in Kazakhstan. A set of runic-type inscriptions on other rocks nearby are not nearly so old – they were carved for the making of a Kazakh film, *Kyz-Zhibek* (Silk Girl), in the 1950s. Almaty agencies will bring you to the carvings by road or a road-kayak combination. Karlygash Makatova (p118) does day trips starting at US$55 per person with kayaking.

As it approaches Lake Balkhash, the Ili enters a delta wetland region of many lakes, marshes and thick, junglelike vegetation – with great fishing for catfish, carp, zander, bream and other species. Kan Tengri (p118) has a fishing camp with comfortable bungalows in the Ili delta. For an enthusiastic account of fishing here visit www.thisistravel.co.uk and type 'Kazakhstan' in the search box.

Buses run to Kapshagay town (200T, 1¼ hours) every half-hour, 7.30am to 9pm, from Almaty's Sayran bus station.

## TAMGALY PETROGLYPHS ПЕТРОГЛИФЫ ТАМГАЛЫ

Not to be confused with the Tamgaly-Tas rock carvings (above), the Tamgaly petroglyphs are the most impressive of many petroglyph groups in southeastern Kazakhstan and one of only two Kazakhstan sites on the Unesco World Heritage List. Situated in a lushly vegetated canyon in an otherwise arid region near Karabastau, 170km northwest of Almaty, they number 5000 separate carvings from the Bronze Age and later, in several groups. The varied images include sun-headed idols, women in childbirth, bull sacrifice, hunting scenes and a big variety of animals, and are best seen in the afternoon when most sunlight reaches them. The Tamgaly canyon has been a ritual site for nomadic peoples since at least the second half of the 2nd millennium BC and there are also ancient burial mounds here. Many Almaty agencies run day trips here: bus trips offered by the EIRC (p117) are 1300T per person.

## ZHARKENT ЖАРКЕНТ

**pop 34,000**

Zharkent (formerly Panfilov), on the northern fringe of the Ili valley, is the last real town in Kazakhstan on the bus route to China (see p183 for border information). The area has a high Uyghur population.

There is little to see here except the **Yuldashev Mosque**, named for the Uyghur migrant who initiated it. Like Almaty's Zenkov Cathedral, the mosque is built without metal nails, but the curious design incorporates a minaret in the form of a Chinese pagoda beside a more conventional Central Asian dome, with gates in the style of the Timurid epoch. And adding to the cross-cultural symbolism, the mosque's ground-floor windows look Russian.

## TALDYQORGHAN ТАЛДЫКОРГАН

**☎ 3282 / pop 110,000**

The surprise transfer in 2001 of the *oblys* (regional or provincial) capital from Almaty to smaller Taldyqorghan (Russian: Taldy-Kurgan) breathed new life into this previously declining town. It's now quite a bustling place with attractive, wide, central streets and a leafy central park on Abay. Situated 265km northeast of Almaty, Taldyqorghan is chiefly of interest to visitors as a staging post to Lepsinsk and the Zhungar Alatau mountains, as well as the southern shore of Lake Balkhash.

### Orientation & Information

The Almaty–Semey highway runs roughly west–east through town under the name Zhansugirov. Birzhan Sal, Aqyn Sara and Abay head north off this into the centre, crossing partly pedestrianised Tauelsizdik, the main street, after 400m, and Kabanbay Batyr one block further north. The regional government building and the palace of culture flank the central square on Tauelsizdik, between Abay and Aqyn Sara. The bus station is 1km south of Zhansugirov, along Shevchenko.

**Halyk Bank** (Abay) Has an ATM.

**Kazkommertsbank** (cnr Tauelsizdik & Aqyn Sara) Has an ATM.

**Qazaqtelekom** (Aqyn Sara 137; 8am-11pm, internet 9am-6pm Mon-Fri, 9am-2pm Sat) You can phone and use the internet here.

## Sights

If you have time to kill, check out the busy daily **market** (cnr Abay & Gaukhar-Ana), a block north of Kabanbay Batyr, and have a look at the **Regional Museum** (Abay 245; 9am-1pm & 2-6pm Tue-Sun). The leafy **Central Park** on Abay is pleasant.

## Sleeping & Eating

**Hotel Kus-Zholy** (22 14 32; Zhansugirov; r 4500-6000T) Lovely big rooms with bathroom, big beds, ornate furnishings, multichannel TV and phone. It's not central though, 2.3km west of the corner of Abay.

**Hotel Sulu Tör** (27 24 19; fax 27 22 28; Kabanbay Batyr; r 5000-13,000T) Excellent new central hotel with Chinese-inspired décor, just south of Abay. All rooms have good bathrooms with glassed-in showers, heating/aircon and big TVs. Has a restaurant and internet (per hour 300T) too.

**Café Dos** (24 30 35; Tauelsizdik 85A; dishes 150-300T; lunch & dinner) Shashlyk, steaks, *manty*, chicken, salads and drinks are served to the accompaniment of music videos in this unmissable brick castle. The interior is decorated with reproduction medieval weapons, sets of antlers and a full suit of armour.

**Restoran Parliament** (dishes 200-400T; breakfast, lunch & dinner) Next door to Hotel Kus-Zholy this has mainly Russian dishes and turns into a disco on weekend evenings.

**Hessen Pub** (27 22 17; Aqyn Sara 137; dishes 200-600T; noon-2am) This German-style beer hall is the best place to eat in the centre, with an extensive menu of salads, soups and meat dishes. An unobtrusive rock/pop band plays in the evenings.

## Getting There & Around

Buses run about hourly round the clock to Almaty (700T, six hours), and two or three times daily to Zharkent (900T, six hours), Semey (2160T, 17 hours) and Ust-Kamenogorsk (2060T, 16 hours). Shared taxis and minibuses leave from outside the stations when they have a load: to Almaty, shared taxis take about three hours for 2000T per passenger. There's a train station next to the bus station but Taldyqorghan is off the main Turksib railway line.

Marshrutka 13 (30T) runs up and down Zhansugirov and into centre along Aqyn Sara. Marshrutka and bus 7 go along Shevchenko from Zhansugirov to the bus station.

# LEPSINSK ЛЕПСИНСК

**pop 2000**

This quaint and tranquil farming village lies 1020m high at the foot of the Zhungar Alatau mountains which lie along the Chinese border. Lepsinsk's homestay programme, operating from May to September, makes it an ideal base for exploring this beautiful and little-visited range with its thick forests, mountain lakes, abundant wildlife (including bears, wolves, maral deer and many raptors), glaciers and several snowy peaks over 4000m. The wildflowers in the Lepsinsk valley in June and July are spectacular. This is a border zone so you need a border-zone permit (5000T), which takes 20 to 30 days to obtain (or 25,000T for one-week processing), so be sure to plan ahead. Contact the EIRC in Almaty (p117) to organise the permit and also to make arrangements for your visit.

Though no longer a Soviet-style collective, Lepsinsk farmers still tend their many cattle on a cooperative basis, with groups of two or three horsemen taking daily turns to watch over the animals as they graze the steppe outside the village.

## Activities

Good one-day outings by foot or horse include to Lepsinsk Canyon, with a rushing river and a beach for relaxing, swimming and fishing, and Muslim's Honey Farm, where you can taste fresh honey and explore the surrounding countryside. A longer trek or ride of two to three days, camping overnight, goes up to Zhasi-Kul, a mountain lake with a magical green colour 24km from the village. Treks of five to 10 days high into the Zhungar Alatau are also possible. Guides keep their eyes and ears open for wildlife as you go. Prices per day are: guide, 2000T; horse, 1500T; camping equipment, 600T; trekking provisions, 600T.

### Sleeping & Eating

Homestay accommodation with three meals is a very reasonable 2000T per person: you'll probably be housed in the cosy and welcoming home of the homestay coordinator, Sabir Mikhalyov, and enjoy excellent meals made almost entirely with local ingredients.

### Getting There & Away

The jumping-off point for Lepsinsk is Kabanbay (also known by its former name Andreevka), 250km northeast of Taldyqorghan on the road to Usharal and Semey. Buses to Kabanbay (1440T, 11 hours) leave Almaty's Sayran bus station seven times daily. It's a good idea to get an overnight service such as the 9.15pm departure. There are also nine daily buses (740T, five hours) from Taldyqorghan to Kabanbay, plus faster minibuses (1000T) and shared taxis (1200T). If you're coming from the north, Almaty-bound buses from Semey and Ust-Kamenogorsk will stop at Kabanbay (around 1700T and 11 hours from either place).

Buses leave Kabanbay for the 45km ride up to Lepsinsk (200T, one hour) at 6.15am and 3.45pm Monday, Wednesday, Friday and Sunday, returning at 8am and 5pm the same days. A taxi should be 1500T, or 500T per person if shared.

## LAKE BALKHASH ОЗЕРО БАЛХАШ

You'll get glimpses of the western end of central Asia's fourth-largest lake if you travel by road or train from Almaty to Astana, but if you want to visit the lake, nicer places are found on its southern shore, accessible from Taldyqorghan. The Karatal River has excellent fishing, especially in the remote region where it flows into Lake Balkhash. You can get there from Ushtöbe by taxi. Some of the best beaches are at the salty eastern end of the lake, 20km north of the train depot of **Lepsy**. There are about 10 summer guesthouses here charging 500T to 1000T per night including meals, although locals bring their own food and cook. The season lasts from mid-June to the end of August; at other times it's likely to be completely boarded up. Lepsy can be reached by train, or by bus from Taldyqorghan (550T, three hours).

Balkhash covers 17,400 sq km, but is only 26m at its deepest point. There are fears that it may be suffering an Aral Sea–type shrinkage because of interference with the flow of the Ili River, its main water source, upstream from the lake. By some accounts Balkhash's water level has fallen by as much as 2m in 30 years. Critics blame the Kapshagay hydroelectric dam and diversion of the Ili's waters in China.

# SOUTHERN KAZAKHSTAN

This is the most Kazakh part of Kazakhstan: Kazakhs are generally the great majority in the population, having been settled here in large numbers during Soviet collectivisation. It's a fascinatingly varied region whose chief attractions begin in the Aksu-Dzhabagly Nature Reserve with its pristine mountain country, great hiking and horse riding and good-value homestays. Shymkent is the region's atmospheric main city. At Turkistan the Mausoleum of Kozha Akhmed Yasaui is Kazakhstan's most sacred Muslim shrine and a magnificent piece of Timurid architecture.

## TARAZ ТАРАЗ

☎ 3262 / pop 360,000

Ask any Kazakh what they know about Taraz and they'll probably say 'vodka' as this is where the country's favourite brand is produced. It's a quiet, Soviet-style place with leafy boulevards and one excellent museum.

Medieval Taraz reached its peak in the 11th and 12th centuries as a wealthy Silk Road stop and capital of the Turkic Karakhanid state which also ruled Bukhara for a while. Levelled by Jenghiz Khan, it didn't resurface until the 19th century when the Kokand khanate refounded it as a northern frontier town.

The Soviet regime settled many internal exiles here, renamed the town Dzhambul after the locally-born Kazakh bard Zhambyl Zhabaev and added phosphate factories to pump up the economy. Since independence, the name has changed again and the factories have closed, which has at least cleaned up the air.

### Orientation & Information

The meeting of east–west Töle Bi with north–south Abay is the centre of town. West from here a government square, Dostyq alanghy, stretches along Töle Bi.

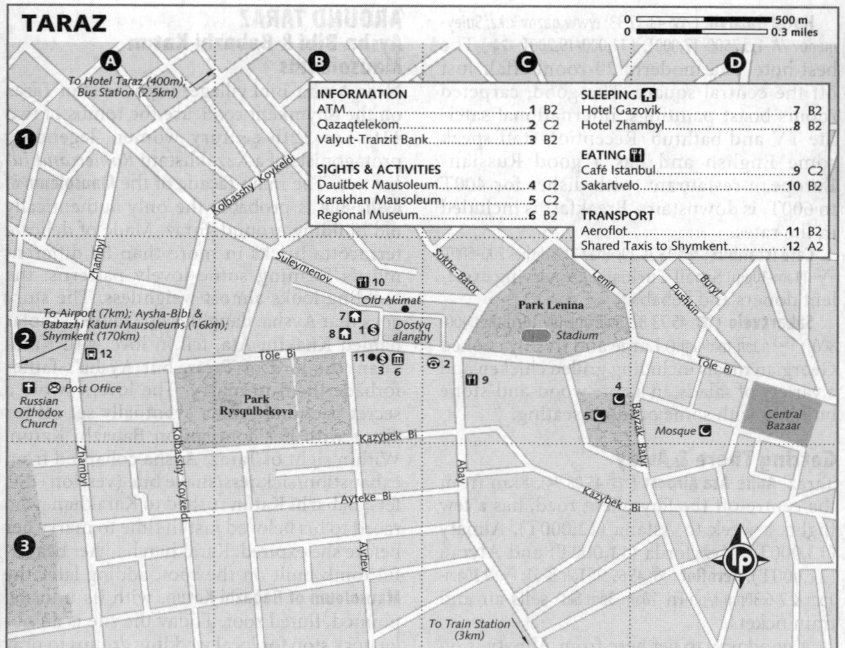


**ATM** (Qarzhy Ministrligi, Dostyq alangi) In lobby of Finance Ministry building.

**Qazaqtelekom** (☎ 45 38 54; Abay 124; internet per hr 150T; ⌚ 8am-10pm Mon-Fri, 10am-10pm Sat & Sun) You can also phone from here (24 hours).

**Valyut-Tranzit Bank** (☎ 45 66 11; Töle Bi 59; ⌚ 24hr) Has an exchange office.

## Sights

Taraz' **Regional Museum** (☎ 23 25 85; Töle Bi 55; admission 150T; ⌚ 9am-1pm & 2-6pm Mon-Sat) was completely renovated for the city's 2000th anniversary celebrations in 2002 and is one of the best local museums in the country. Its pride and joy is the domed rear building housing an impressive collection of *balbals,* totemlike stones bearing the carved faces of honoured warriors or chieftains, dating from the 6th to 9th centuries AD. Nomadic early Turks left these monuments at many sacred sites in southern Kazakhstan.

Two small mausoleums in a wooded park near the town centre, both 20th-century reconstructions, are worth a look. The 12th-century **Karakhan Mausoleum** marks the grave of a revered Karakhanid potentate known as Karakhan or Aulie-Ata (Holy Father). The **Dauitbek Mausoleum**, for a 13th-century Mongol viceroy, is said to have been built lopsided in revenge for the man's infamous cruelty. Both buildings are Islamic shrines today.

Look in the sprawling **Central Bazaar** (Töle Bi) for inexpensive Chinese silk and some Central Asian crafts. Buses 2 and 16 run along Töle Bi from Park Lenina.

## Sleeping & Eating

**Hotel Taraz** (☎ 43 34 91; Zhambyl 75A; s 2000-4500T, d 2800-7000T) The cheap option, though inconveniently placed halfway between the bus station and city centre (about 2km from each), Hotel Taraz has simple but adequate rooms, friendly staff and a bar and restaurant. From the bus station, buses 10 and 26 pass by; from the train station you can take marshrutka 077.

**Hotel Zhambyl** (☎ 45 25 52; fax 45 17 50; Töle Bi 42; s 4690-7860T, d 8640-10,910T) Rather stern desk staff but comfortable rooms with bathroom, phone, TV and fridge, and you get the room for 24 hours.

**Hotel Gazovik** (☎ 43 32 33; www.gazovik.kz; Suleymenov 7A-1; s 7500-17,000T, d 11,000/19,200T; ❄) The best hotel is a modern, 20-room affair just off the central square. The good, carpeted rooms boast paintings, international satellite TV and bathtub. Reception staff speak some English and has a good Russian-European restaurant, with dishes for 400T to 600T, is downstairs. Breakfast is included in the rates.

**Café Istanbul** (☎ 45 25 29; Abay 117; dishes 200-500T; ⏰ 11am-10pm) Small Turkish café serving excellent doners and kebabs.

**Sakartvelo** (☎ 45 73 82; Suleymenov 16; dishes 400-800T; ⏰ noon-midnight) Large and freshly cooked Georgian meals including grilled chicken and a variety of salads, in a cute wood-and-stone building with some outdoor seating.

## Getting There & Away

Taraz' **Aulie-Ata Airport** (☎ 45 08 94), 8km from the centre off the Shymkent road, has a few flights a week to Astana (12,000T), Almaty (13,000T), Kyzylorda (11,000T) and Atyrau (21,000T). **Aeroflot** (☎ 45 69 50; Töle Bi 61; ⏰ 9.30am-1pm & 2-6.30pm Mon-Fri, 10am-3pm Sat) sells air and train tickets.

A good way to get here from Almaty is on the daily 6.15pm train 11 (2765T). It arrives in Taraz at 4.45am and continues to Shymkent (700T). Train 12 to Almaty leaves at 10.58pm. The station is on Baluan Shcholak about 4km south of the centre.

Numerous buses leave around 10pm for Almaty (1100T, nine hours) from the bus station on Zhambyl, 4km northeast of the centre, and from the train station. Marshrutkas (1200T, eight or nine hours) and shared taxis (3000T, six hours) to Almaty leave from the bus station during daytime. Marshrutkas to Shymkent (500T, three hours) and Bishkek (500T, five hours) also leave from the bus station. Shared taxis to Shymkent (1200T, 2½ hours) wait on Zhambyl just north of Töle Bi.

## Getting Around

From the train station, bus and marshrutka 040 run to Abay, Kazybek Bi and Töle Bi in the centre, and bus 47 heads up Abay to the corner of Töle Bi. From the bus station marshrutkas 46 and 032 head to the same intersection, while bus 26 and marshrutka 029 run along Zhambyl to the intersection with Töle Bi.

# AROUND TARAZ

## Aysha-Bibi & Babazhi Katun Mausoleums

Near Aysha-Bibi village, 16km west of Taraz on the Shymkent road, are the tombs of two 11th- or 12th-century women, legendary protagonists of a Kazakhstani *Romeo and Juliet* tale. The main façade of the **Mausoleum of Aysha-Bibi** is probably the only authentically old building around Taraz. Made of delicate terracotta bricks in more than 50 different motifs forming some lovely patterns, the building looks almost weightless. The story goes that Aysha, daughter of a famed scholar named Khakim-Ata, fell in love with Karakhan, the lord of Taraz, but Aysha's father forbade them to marry. The lovers swore a secret pact and Aysha eventually set off for Taraz with her companion Babazhi Katun. Within sight of Taraz, Aysha collapsed from exhaustion/sickness/snake bite (versions differ); Babazhi Katun rushed to Karakhan, who raced to his beloved just in time to marry her before she expired. Karakhan had her beautiful tomb built on the spot, adding later the **Mausoleum of Babazhi Katun**, with its unusual pointed, fluted roof. Today the site is an obligatory stop for local wedding groups to pray and take photos.

A sign points to the mausoleums about 300m south from the main road in the village. Shymkent-bound marshrutkas will take you to Aysha-Bibi or you can hire a taxi in Taraz.

# SHYMKENT ШЫМКЕНТ

**☎ 3252 / pop 500,000**

South Kazakhstan's most vibrant city, with a booming bazaar and lively downtown, Shymkent has more of a Central Asian buzz on its leafy streets than anywhere else in the country. Stop here to soak up the atmosphere, eat well and cheaply, and head out to nearby places of interest including Turkistan, Sayram, Otrar and the Aksu-Dzhabagly Reserve.

The Mongols razed a minor Silk Road stop here; the Kokand khanate built a frontier fort in the 19th century; Russia took it in 1864; and the whole place was rebuilt in Soviet times. Shymkent smelts lead, makes cigarettes and refines oil, but it's best known for Kazakhstan's best beer, Shymkentskoe Pivo. The population today is about half Kazakh, a quarter Russian and 15% Uzbek.

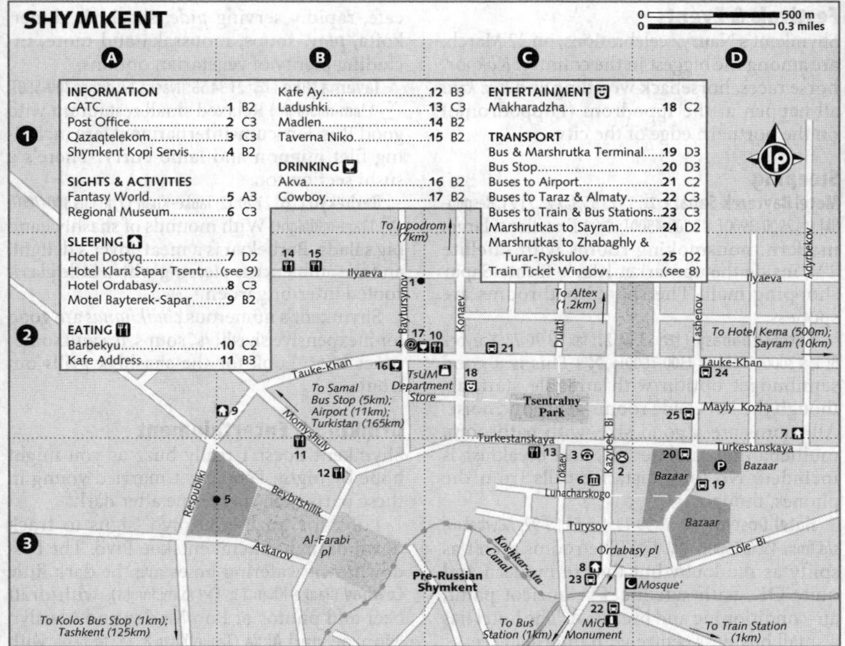


Mosquitoes are an irritant from late June to late July.

## Orientation

Shymkent's main central streets are north–south Kazybek Bi and east–west Tauke-Khan and Turkestanskaya. The bus and train stations are both about 1km south of Ordabasy ploshchad, a busy intersection at the south end of Kazybek Bi.

## Information

You'll find ATMs at TsUM department store and the Qazaqtelekom office.

**Altex** (☎ 53 54 93; Kazybek Bi 119) Trips to Aksu-Dzhabagly Nature Reserve, Turkistan and Otrar, by Shamil Rafikov, who speaks some English.

**CATC** (☎ 21 14 36; cat-chimkent@alarnet.com; Ilyaeva 18/217) Local branch of one of Kazakhstan's best travel and air-ticket agencies.

**Qazaqtelekom** (Turkestanskaya 18; internet per hr 150T; 🕒 10am-8pm) You can also phone and use ATMs here, 24 hours.

**Shymkent Kopi Servis** (☎ 21 21 75; Baytursynov 8; internet per hr 150T; 🕒 8.30am-10pm) Public internet facility – the sign says 'Copy X Grand'.

## Sights

The **Regional Museum** (☎ 53 02 22; Kazybek Bi 13; admission 100T; 🕒 9am-6pm Tue-Sun) has excellent exhibits on Shymkent's history as a caravan town, plus material on old Otrar and Aksu-Dzhabagly Nature Reserve, and, on the newly renovated upper-floor, displays on the Russian and Soviet eras.

The **bazaar** (Tashenov; 🕒 8am-8pm Tue-Sun) is Shymkent's biggest show, a bustling market spilling over with fresh produce, spices, bread, cheap clothes, mechanical spare parts and kitchen utensils as well as some gaudy traditional costumes and less-portable wooden chests with colourful stamped-tin decoration.

**Fantasy World** (Tekhnopark; Respubliki; rides 50-300T; 🕒 3-11pm Mon-Fri, 11am-11pm Sat & Sun), opposite the Hotel Shymkent, is a popular amusement park and evening hang-out. To its southeast is the ceremonial square **Al-Farabi ploshchad** with landmark clock tower and giant TV screen. Southeast from Al-Farabi, across the small Koshkar-Ata canal, you will find the few remaining streets of **pre-Russian Shymkent**.

## Festivals & Events

Shymkent's Nauryz celebrations, on 22 March, are among the biggest in the country. *Kökpar*, horse races, horseback wrestling and *kyz kuu* all happen at the Ippodrom (Hippodrome) on the northern edge of the city.

## Sleeping

**Motel Bayterek-Sapar** (☎ 33 75 55; fax 23 21 21; Respubliki 4; s 2900-3900T, d 3500-4500T; ⊠) Excellent, large, modern, nonsmoking rooms with satellite TV, inside the upmarket Klara-Tsentr-Sapar shopping mall. The shared bathrooms are spotless.

**Hotel Ordabasy** (☎ 53 64 21; fax 53 70 78; Kazybek Bi 1; s 3000-5700T, d 4300-7000T; ❄) This is a good semibudget option with amiable staff, although the streetside rooms get traffic noise. All rooms are a good size, with bathroom, multichannel satellite TV, and breakfast is included. No long-distance calls from the phones, though.

**Hotel Dostyq** (☎ 53 99 73; fax 54 59 92; Adyrbekov; s/d from 4500/5500T; ❄ 💻) The rooms aren't as spiffy as the lobby but they're modern and quite OK, with satellite TV, apricot paint, air-conditioning and breakfast. The hotel has a small business centre with internet access.

**Hotel Klara Sapar Tsentr** (☎ 23 23 33; saparhtl@mail.ru; Respubliki 4; s 5900-8900T, d 7400-10,400T; ❄) Bright new hotel with good, English-speaking service. Rooms boast satellite TV and paintings of local scenes, and rates include an hour in the sauna. The hotel has a small business centre with internet access.

**Hotel Kema** (☎ 54 03 44; fax 54 05 97; Tauke-Khan 93A; s/d from 8320/8840T; ❄) Though a little out of the centre, this is a good upmarket option with well-furnished rooms.

## Eating

**Kafe Ay** (☎ 53 43 05; Momyshuly 1; dishes 60-100T; 🕑 11am-7pm) A great place if you want to stuff yourself with excellent, inexpensive shashlyk, *plov* and *laghman*.

**Madlen** (Ilyaeva 17; coffees & desserts 90-250T; 🕑 10am-midnight) Great coffee house with delicious cakes and desserts, and pavement tables too.

**Ladushki** (Turkestanskaya 12; main dishes around 100T; 🕑 9am-9.15pm) With décor like a kids' restaurant, Ladushki is actually a highly popular cafeteria where you can get a serve of *manty* for 30T or three pastries and a coffee for under 100T.

**Kafe Address** (☎ 53 43 00; Momyshuly 3; dishes 120-450T; 🕑 10am-midnight) Terrific, bright, Turkish café, rapidly serving *pide*, shashlyk, doner, kofta, *plov*, soups, moussaka and more, including plenty of vegetarian options.

**Taverna Niko** (☎ 21 34 58; Ilyaeva 17; dishes 300-550T; 🕑 11am-midnight) Relaxed small restaurant with good Russian-cum-international fare including filet mignon and lamb curry. There's a sushi section too.

**Barbekyu** (☎ 21 20 12; Tauke-Khan 11; mains 300-700T; 🕑 11am-midnight) With mounds of shashlyk and big salads, Barbekyu is a meat-lover's delight, and the ambience is pleasing with a little glass-roofed interior garden.

Shymkent's numerous *chaikhanas* are good for inexpensive shashlyk, soups, tea and sometimes beer. Look for the shashlyk grills out front.

## Drinking & Entertainment

Shymkent doesn't really buzz as you might hope by night. People get married young in these parts then stay home after dark.

Look for 'razlivnoe pivo' signs to track down draught Shymkentskoe Pivo. The best downtown watering holes are the dark little **Cowboy** (Tauke-Khan 11; 🕑 to midnight), with draft beer and photos of Bob Marley and Marilyn Monroe, and **Akva** (Tauke-Khan 8; 🕑 to 3am), with a quirky maritime theme.

The newest hot spot is **Makharadzha** (Maharajah; ☎ 53 52 91; Konaev), with eye-catching neon out front. Here you'll find bowling, billiards (both open 11am to 2.30am) and a glitzy nightclub (men 1500T to 2000T, women 500T to 1000T; open 10pm to 4am) playing a complete mix of Western, Russian, Kazakh and Turkish pop and hip-hop.

## Getting There & Away

### AIR

Flights from the **airport** (☎ 53 52 95), 12km northwest of the centre, go daily to Almaty (20,000T) and Astana (18,000T), and twice weekly to Aktau (21,000T), Kyzylorda (11,000T), Atyrau (17,000T) and Moscow (47,000T).

### BUS, MARSHRUTKA & TAXI

Fleets of large, comfortable buses leave for Taraz and Almaty at 7pm from outside the train station and from beneath the MiG fighter plane monument opposite Ordabasy ploshchad. You can book seats earlier in the day: to Almaty they cost between 800T and 1500T depending on the bus and whether you sit near the front (more expensive) or back.

From the **bus station** (☎ 54 01 66), buses leave for Turkistan (250T, three hours, about hourly 9am to 6pm), Almaty (900T to 1000T, 12 hours, at 4pm, 6pm and 7pm), Karaganda (2760T, 20 hours, 11am), Astana (3000T, 24 hours, 2pm), Taraz (400T, four hours, five times daily) and Kyzylorda (800T, seven hours, at 11am and 3pm). Marshrutkas depart when full to Turkistan (350T, two hours), Taraz (500T, three hours) and Kyzylorda (1000T, six hours). Shared taxis to Taraz (1200T, 2½ hours) go from the street outside the bus station to the west. More buses for Karaganda and Astana leave from outside the train station at 6pm.

For Chernyaevka on the Uzbekistan border, shared taxis and marshrutkas (500T, one to 1¼ hours) depart from the Kolos stop on Respubliki in southwestern Shymkent. Some may continue into Tashkent (around 1500T from Shymkent), where they will usually drop you at a metro station; otherwise it is a 10-minute taxi ride from the border to the nearest metro station (Buyuk Ipak Yuli), or 25 minutes (US$5) to the city centre.

#### TRAIN

The **train station** (☎ 95 21 20) is at the end of Kabanbay Batyr. At least four trains a day go to Taraz (700T, four to five hours) and Almaty (2500T to 3500T, 12 to 15 hours), and three or more to Turkistan (four hours) and Kyzylorda (nine hours). There are also trains to Aqtöbe (27 hours) daily, to Moscow (50 hours) most days, and to Mangyshlak (Aktau, 53 hours), Atyrau (37 hours) and Astana (24 hours) every two days. The best Almaty service is train 12, leaving at 5.40pm. The Hotel Ordabasy has a **train ticket window** (☎ 53 46 05; 🕓 8am-1pm & 2-8pm).

### Getting Around

From the airport, marshrutka 12 runs to Tauke-Khan in the centre. To get to the airport, you can catch it heading west on Tauke-Khan between Dulati and Konaev. A taxi costs 500T to 1000T.

From the train station buses 5 and 21 and marshrutkas 5, 9, 12 and 21 run to Ordabasy ploshchad, then along Kazybek Bi and west along Tauke-Khan (No 5 continues round to Respubliki).

From the bus station, walk north along the street on the west side of the station (Ayteke-Bi) and pick up bus 2, 8, 17, 65 or 75, or marshrutka 2, 50 or 65 to Ordabasy ploshchad. Both 65s continue up Kazybek Bi and west on Tauke-Khan.

Getting to the train and bus stations you can take (among others) bus or marshrutka 9 east on Tauke-Khan or from Ordabasy ploshchad.

## AROUND SHYMKENT

### Sayram

**pop 40,000**

About 10km east of Shymkent, the busy little town of Sayram was a Silk Road stop long before Shymkent existed: in fact it's one of the oldest settlements in Kazakhstan, dating back possibly 3000 years. Kozha Akhmed Yasaui (see p148) was born here and Sayram is a stop for many pilgrims en route to his mausoleum at Turkistan. Sayram's population today is almost entirely Uzbek.

Most of the main monuments can be seen in a walk of about 1½ hours starting from Sayram's central traffic lights (ask marshrutka conductors for the Tsentr stop). Walk up Amir Temur, away from two mosque domes, and take the first street (unpaved) on the right. About 100m along, in a small fenced field on your right, is the circular, brick-built **Kydyra Minaret**, about 15m high and probably dating from the 10th century. You can climb up inside to view the Aksu-Dzhabagly mountains away to the east. Return to the central crossroads and continue straight ahead, passing the bazaar on your left. Just after the bazaar, on the right, is the 13th-century **Karashash-Ana Mausoleum**, where Akhmed Yasaui's mother lies buried beneath the central tombstone. Continue 200m, passing the modern **Friday Mosque** on your right, to the large **Mirali Bobo Mausoleum**, where a leading 10th-century Islamic scholar lies buried. Now turn back and take the street to the left, Botbay Ata, before the Friday Mosque. This street follows the line of the old city walls, curving round to the right after 150m. Botbay Ata ends at a larger street, Yusuf Sayrami, where you'll see Sayram's modern **city gates** on your right. Head left along Yusuf Sayrami and you'll reach a green-and-yellow sign marking the spot where (according to legend) Kozha Akhmed Yasaui's mentor Aristan Bab handed him a sacred persimmon stone, which had been given to Aristan Bab by the Prophet Mohammed (never mind that Aristan Bab lived five centuries after Mohammed's death).

About 200m past this spot, turn left into a cemetery to the three-domed **Abd al Aziz-Baba Mausoleum**. Its occupant is believed to have been a leader of the Arabic forces that brought Islam to the Sayram area way back in AD 766. Pilgrims come here for help in averting misfortune and the 'evil eye'.

For Sayram's two other main monuments it's easiest to get a taxi from the central crossroads. It shouldn't cost more than 200T to see both sites and return. The **Maryam Ana Mausoleum** is about 1km up Amir Temur from the crossroads, while the small 14th-century **Ibragim Ata Mausoleum**, where Akhmed Yasaui's father lies, is on the northern edge of town, with a modern mosque and medressa attached.

Several chaikhanas around the central crossroads serve inexpensive shashlyk, tea, soups, bread and *plov*. Frequent marshrutkas to Sayram (50T, 30 minutes) leave from Shymkent bazaar – the corner of Tauke-Khan and Tashenov is one place to catch them.

## Aksu-Dzhabagly Nature Reserve

This beautiful 1319-sq-km patch of valleys and mountains climbing to the Kyrgyz and Uzbek borders east of Shymkent is the longest established (1926) and one of the easiest visited of Kazakhstan's nature reserves. The reserve, at the west end of the Talassky Alatau range (the most northwesterly spur of the Tian Shan), stretches from the edge of the steppe at about 1200m up to 4239m at Pik Sayram. The main access point is the village of Zhabaghly, 70km east of Shymkent as the crow flies and the base of one of Kazakhstan's longest-running and best-organised ecotourism programmes.

Aksu-Dzhabagly is promoted as the home of the tulip, and in April and May its alpine meadows are dotted with the wild bright-red Greig's tulip. Wildlife you stand a chance of spotting includes bears, ibex, argali sheep, paradise flycatchers and golden eagles. The scenery, a mix of green valleys with rushing rivers, snow-capped peaks and high-level glaciers, is gorgeous. You can visit any time of year, but the best months to come are April to September.

From Zhabaghly village it's 6km southeast to the reserve entrance, then 6km (about 1½ hours' walk) to Kshi-Kaindy, a mountain refuge near a waterfall at 1700m, then a further 6km to Ulken-Kaindy, a second refuge. From Ulken-Kaindy it's 10km to a group of some 2000 stones with petroglyphs up to 900 years old, below a glacier descending from the 3800m peak Kaskabulak. A good way to visit these sites is by horse, spending two nights at Ulken-Kaindy. More demanding treks will take you over 3500m passes with nights in caves. Another great spot is the 300m-deep Aksu Canyon at the reserve's western extremity, a 25km drive from Zhabaghly village. In September and early October the canyon is a busy raptor migration route.

The community ecotourism and homestay programme here is run by the NGO **Wild Nature** (Dikaya Priroda; ☎/fax 325-385 56 86, 701-4387086, baskakova2008@mail.ru; Taldybulak 14, Zhabaghly). Director Svetlana Baskakova, a knowledgeable biologist and great guide, speaks excellent English. Wild Nature charges per day include: guide, 3750T; horse, 1500T; camping in the reserve including meals, 4200T to 5000T per person; vehicle to Aksu Gorge, 6000T return. Obligatory fees for entering the reserve are 1050T per person per day, plus 1300T per group per day for an accompanying ranger. Zhenia & Lyuda's (below) also offers well-run excursions in the reserve with English-speaking guides, and both outfits offer interesting trips outside the reserve, including to the Chokpak bird-ringing station, 20km north, and to the little-visited Karatau mountains further north.

Shymkent-based travel firm, Altex (p143), maintains a camp of surprisingly comfortable metal-box cabins in a pretty location in a canyon beside the Sayram River on the west side of the reserve. A three-day/two-night trip runs about US$150 to US$200, including food, guide and transfers from Shymkent. From the camp it's possible to take a long day hike to two small lakes at 2000m, or tackle the more demanding Pik Sayram, a two-day climb requiring equipment.

### SLEEPING

**Wild Nature** (Dikaya Priroda; ☎/fax 325-385 56 86, 701-4387086; baskakova2008@mail.ru; Taldybulak 14, Zhabaghly) Offers comfortable homestays with hot showers in Zhabaghly village for 3800T per person per night (full board with local meals). Contact Wild Nature in advance: either direct, or through the EIRC in Almaty (p117), which can also help with travel arrangements.

**Zhenia & Lyuda's Boarding House** (☎ 325-385 56 96, 701-7175851; www.innaksu.com; Abay 36, Zhabaghly; per person full board 5000T) This friendly English-speaking biologist couple have transformed their home on Zhabaghly's main street into a cosy small hotel. All rooms have two single beds and private bathroom. They also offer a wide range of outings. They have been in the business since 1990 and know their job.

#### GETTING THERE & AWAY

Marshrutkas to Zhabaghly village (250T, two hours) leave the corner of Malyly Kozha and Tashenov in Shymkent (see map p143) about 11am and 2pm. Alternatively, there are marshrutkas about every half-hour, 7.30am to 3pm, from the same stop to Turar-Ryskulov (also called Vanovka, 200T), where you can get a taxi (500T) for the final 25km to Zhabaghly. Taxis from around the same stop in Shymkent charge about 2000T to Zhabaghly.

The Shymkent-bound train No 11 departing Almaty-II station at 6.15pm daily arrives about 7am at Tulkibas (3000T), a 15-minute taxi ride (1200T) from Zhabaghly village, best booked in advance through your accommodation.

### Sayram-Ugam National Park

This park abutting the Uzbek border immediately southwest of the Aksu-Dzhabagly Reserve offers similar attractions and biodiversity to Aksu-Dzhabaghy. A recently established community ecotourism programme provides homestays in the villages of Kaskasu and Dikhankol and the town of Lenger, outside the park's northern boundary. This is a less visited and cheaper alternative to Aksu-Dzhabagly, and you can even combine the two areas via a 60km, two- or three-day foot or horse trek between Zhabaghly and Kaskasu villages.

Good outings into the hills by foot or horse are to Kaskasu Canyon and Ak-Mechet Gorge (day trips), and Susingen Lake (two or three days, camping). Community-ecotourism prices per day are 2000T per guide (English speakers available) or horse, 3000T for homestays or camping including meals. There's a 200T per person park entrance fee.

Homestays are slightly more basic than at Zhabaghly, with outside toilets (except at Lenger). At Kaskasu and Lenger you can stay in yurts (2900T).

Make arrangements through the Ecotourism Information Resource Centre (p117) in Almaty, or contact the local coordinator, **Abdeshev Alikhan** (☎ 300-222 03 28; a3@ok.kz), at Kafe Kara-Kia in Lenger. He speaks little English, though.

Lenger is 40km southeast of Shymkent; Dikhankol is 75km and Kaskasu 100km. The ecotourism people offer taxis from Shymkent to Lenger (1200T, 30 minutes), Dikhankol (2300T, 1¼ hours) and Kaskasu (2800T, 1½ hours). From Shymkent bazaar there are frequent marshrutkas (100T, 40 minutes) and shared taxis (150T, 40 minutes) to Lenger, plus one afternoon bus to Dikhankol (200T, two hours) and Kaskasu (200T, 2½ hours).

### Otrar

About 150km northwest of Shymkent lie the ruins of Otrar, the town that brought Jenghiz Khan to Central Asia. Much of the rest of Asia and Europe might have been spared the Mongols if Otrar's governor had not murdered the great khan's merchant-envoys here in 1218. A thriving Silk Road town where the scientist Al-Farabi (AD 870–950) was born, Otrar was mercilessly trashed by Jenghiz' forces after a six-month siege in reprisal for the envoy outrage. It was rebuilt afterwards but eventually abandoned around 1700 after being trashed again by the Zhungars (Oyrats). Today it's just a large dusty mound, known locally as Otyrar-Töbe, 11km north of the small town of Shauildir, but recent excavation and conservation work with Unesco help has revealed some interesting bits of what lies below the surface.

En route from Shymkent, stop at the **Otrar Museum** (☎ 325-442 17 22; Zhibek Zholy 1; admission 100T; ⌚ 9am-6pm) in Shauildir. Worthwhile tours in English cost only 100T. At **Otyrar-Töbe** (admission 100T; ⌚ 8am-dusk), you can inspect low walls and pillar-stumps of the 14th-century Palace of Berdibek (where Timur died in 1405), the palace mosque and a bathhouse – all post-Jenghiz – and a small residential area and a section of city wall from the 10th to 12th centuries.

Two kilometres from the ruins is the **Aristan-Bab Mausoleum**, the tomb of an early mentor of Kozha Akhmed Yasaui. The existing handsome, domed, brick building here dates from 1907 and is a stop for pilgrims heading to Turkistan (p148).

Marshrutkas to Shauildir (500T, two hours) leave up to 15 times daily from the Samal bus stop in Shymkent's northwestern suburbs (reachable by city buses 9 and 58 from Ordabasy ploshchad). Alternatively, get a Turkistan-bound marshrutka from Shymkent's main bus station to Törtköl (350T, 1¼ hours), then pick up a Shauildir-bound marshrutka (200T, 45 minutes), or taxi, there. From Turkistan, Shymkent-bound marshrutkas can drop you at Törtköl. A taxi from Shauildir to Otyrar-Töbe and Aristan-Bab shouldn't cost more than 1000T round-trip.

## TURKISTAN ТУРКЕСТАН

**☎ 32533 / pop 100,000**

At Turkistan, 165km northwest of Shymkent in the Syr-Darya valley, stands Kazakhstan's greatest architectural monument and its most important site of pilgrimage. The mausoleum of the first great Turkic Muslim holy man, Kozha Akhmed Yasaui, was built by Timur in the late 14th century on a grand scale comparable with his magnificent creations in Samarkand. Turkistan has no rivals in Kazakhstan for manmade beauty. It's an easy day trip from Shymkent, though staying overnight is enjoyable.

Turkistan was already an important trade and religious centre by the time the revered Sufi teacher and mystical poet Kozha Akhmed Yasaui was born at Sayram, probably in 1103. Yasaui underwent ascetic Sufi training in Bukhara, but lived much of the rest of his life in Turkistan, dying here, it's thought, about 1166. He had the gift of communicating his understanding to ordinary people through poems and sermons in a Turkic vernacular, a major reason for his enduring popularity. He founded the Yasauia Sufi order and is said to have retired to an underground cell at the age of 63 for the rest of his life, in mourning for the Prophet Mohammed who had died at the same age. Local lore today has it that three pilgrimages to Turkistan are equivalent to one to Mecca.

Yasaui's original small tomb was already a place of pilgrimage before Timur ordered a far grander mausoleum built here in the 1390s. Timur died before it was completed and the main façade was left unfinished – it remains today bare of the beautiful tilework that adorns the rest of the building, with scaffolding poles still protruding from the brickwork. From the 16th to 18th centuries Turkistan was the capital of the Kazakh khans.

### Orientation & Information

Coming by road from Shymkent, you'll enter Turkistan from the southeast along Tauke Khan and the mausoleum will loom into view on your left. Sultanbek Qozhanov, two blocks

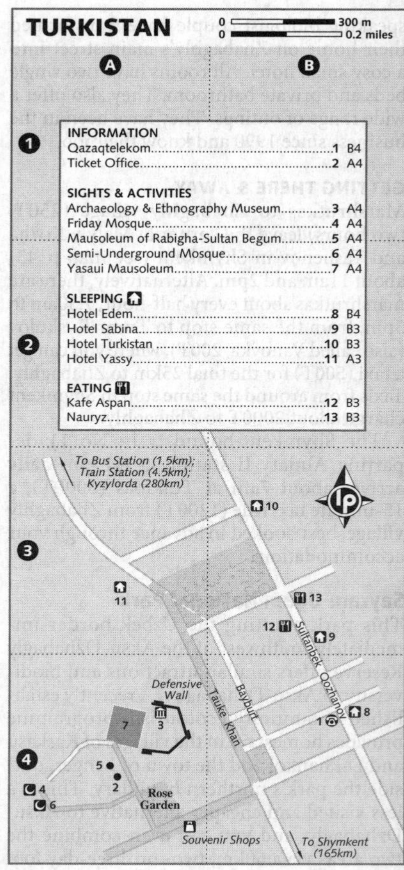


east of Tauke Khan, is the main street, with several hotels and restaurants. The bus station is about 2km northwest of the centre, and the train station is 5km west.

You can phone from **Qazaqtelekom** (Sultanbek Qozhanov; ⏰ 8am-midnight).

### Sights

Approaching the Yasaui Mausoleum through a lovely **rose garden**, you'll see on the left, just past the ticket office, a good replica of the small 15th-century **Mausoleum of Rabigha-Sultan Begum** (the original was torn down for tsarist building material in 1898). Rabigha-Sultan Begum was Timur's great-granddaughter and wife of Abylqayyr Khan, a 15th-century leader of the then-nomadic Uzbeks. Abylqayyr put the finishing touches to the structure of the Yasaui mausoleum's façade (note the distinct brickwork at the top of the arch) but was killed in the 1468 feud which split the Uzbeks and effectively gave birth to the Kazakh people.

The **Yasaui Mausoleum** (admission 200T; 9am-6pm) itself has a slightly museum-like feel despite being a place of pilgrimage. Visitors don't usually remove shoes though women normally wear headscarves. The main chamber is cupped with an 18m-wide dome, above a vast, 2000kg, metal *kazan* (cauldron) for holy water, given by Timur. Around this central hall are 34 smaller rooms on two floors: Yasaui's tomb lies beyond an ornate wooden door at the end of the chamber: you can view it through a grille from a room on its right-hand side. Don't miss the mausoleum's mosque, with its beautifully tiled mihrab.

The glorious blue, turquoise and white tiling on the outside of the building merits close inspection. Note the particularly lovely fluted rear dome, above Akhmed Yasaui's tomb chamber.

A number of other monuments, all included in the ticket, stand nearby. To the west, on a small hill, are the wood-pillared, 19th-century **Friday Mosque** (Zhuma Meshiti) and, next door, the 12th-to-15th-century **semi-underground mosque** with the cell Yasaui to which is said to have withdrawn. Just east of the mausoleum, built into its defensive wall, the **Archaeology & Ethnography Museum** has material on old Turkistan and many other ancient settlements in the Syr-Darya valley.

## Sleeping & Eating

**Hotel Sabina** (3 14 05; Sultanbek Qozhanov 16; s/d 900/1500T) Turkistan's budget option was being remodelled at research time, which will probably make it more expensive. But the rooms are still smallish, sharing bathrooms, so it should remain in the budget bracket.

**Hotel Yassy** (4 01 83/4; Tauke Khan 1; s 3000-3750T, d/tr 4500/6000T; ) The best place in town, with comfortable rooms sporting satellite TV and balconies, some with splendid views of the mausoleum. There's also an efficient restaurant here (dishes 200T to 400T). Breakfast is included in room rates. No intercity phone calls though.

**Hotel Turkistan** (4 21 97; fax 4 14 26; Sultanbek Qozhanov; r 4500) East of Hotel Yassy, this is just as good, with thick red carpets, but you gotta pay for breakfast.

**Nauryz** (3 22 78; Sultanbek Qozhanov; dishes 100-250T; 9am-3am) This colourful restaurant, built in a mock old-Turkistan style complete with duck pond, serves up excellent Turkish food (plus shashlyk, salads and pizzas) and is quite a late-night hang-out, with music echoing around the town.

**Kafe Aspan** (Sultanbek Qozhanov; dishes 130-300T; noon-midnight) Across the street, this is neater and quieter, with good salads, soups and meat dishes.

## Getting There & Around

From the bus station, buses run to Shymkent (250T, three hours) about hourly from 9am to 6pm, while marshrutkas head to Kyzylorda (700T, four hours) when full. Marshrutkas for Shymkent (350T, two hours) go from a yard about 200m south of the bus station.

The train station has at least two daily trains west to Kyzylorda (five hours), Aralsk (14 hours) and Aqtöbe (27 hours), and east to Shymkent (four hours), Taraz (eight hours) and Almaty (19 hours).

'Avtovokzal' buses and marshrutkas (all 20T) run between Sultanbek Qozhanov and the bus station.

# SAURAN

Northwest of Turkistan stands probably the best preserved and most atmospheric of all the many ruined Silk Road cities in the Syr-Darya valley. Sauran was inhabited until the 18th century and its circuit of limestone walls, plus the remains of some bastions and gates, still stand despite conquerors and the elements. It's visible about 1.5km west of the Turkistan–Kyzylorda highway, some 40km out of Turkistan – looming on a low hill like something out of *The Lord of the Rings* (but remember: it's Sauran, not Sauron). The site is normally unsupervised. A taxi from Turkistan should cost around 2500T to 3000T round-trip.

# KYZYLORDA КЫЗЫЛОРДА

**32422 / pop 200,000**

On the Syr-Darya river, 280km northwest of Turkistan, Kyzylorda (meaning Red Capital) was the capital of Soviet Kazakhstan from 1925 to 1929 but was dropped in favour of cooler Almaty when the Turksib railway reached there. Evidence of this former glory can be seen in the ornate train station. Today nearby oil and gas operations are restoring

### BAYKONUR COSMODROME

The Baykonur Cosmodrome, in amid semidesert about 250km northwest of Kyzylorda, has been the launch site for all Soviet- and Russian-crewed space flights since Yury Gagarin, the first human in space, was lobbed up in 1961. In fact the launch site wasn't really in Baykonur, which is actually a town 300km to the northeast, but the USSR told the International Aeronautical Federation that Gagarin's launch point was Baykonur, and that name has stuck. The Russian military town of Baykonur (formerly Leninsk), built to guard and service the cosmodrome, is on the Syr-Darya river south of the cosmodrome itself. The train station between town and cosmodrome is called Töretam. The launch site is about 30km north of here.

After the collapse of the USSR, the cosmodrome became a useful card in Kazakhstan's dealings with Russia, which inherited the Soviet space programme. In 1994 Kazakhstan agreed to lease Baykonur to Russia for 20 years for US$115 million a year (the lease has since been extended to 2050). A few months later the Kazakh cosmonaut Talgat Musabaev and the Russian Yury Malenchenko took off on a symbolic joint visit to the Mir space station. Launches are periodically halted when things go amiss. Visit the Karaganda Ecological Museum (p168) if you're interested in seeing some of the debris that has fallen to earth from Baykonur-launched rockets.

Today Kazakhstan is developing its own space programme. Its first communications satellite was launched from Baykonur in 2006. Kazakhstan and Russia are working together on a launch complex for the new Russian Angara rocket, which is more powerful and supposedly more eco-friendly (because of its kerosene-and-oxygen fuel) than existing systems.

This area is not open to casual travellers. Trying to talk or bribe your way in from Töretam won't get you anywhere near the cosmodrome and could get you into a lot of trouble. Some travel agencies in Kazakhstan, however, can arrange group visits on which you may or may not see a launch, depending on the schedule, weather etc. These include **Sayakhat** (☎/fax 324-227 21 85, 6 26 76; sayahat1973@mail.ru; Hotel Kyzylorda, Tokmaganbetova 22) in Kyzylorda, which quotes 15,000T per person (up to 10 people); the Karaganda Ecological Museum (p168); and Asia Discovery (p118).

some prosperity to the city, which is enjoying a colourful facelift. Mosquitoes are a pest here.

The **Historical Museum** (☎7 61 52; Auezova 20; admission 80T; 9am-5pm), spreading over 14 halls on archaeology, natural history and ethnography, has an English-language interpreter and is translating all explanatory material into English. The **Syr-Darya Promenade** is a popular evening hang-out (and make-out point) from late spring to early autumn. The **Old Bazaar** (Ayteke Bi; 9am-7pm) still has a hectic Central Asian atmosphere.

## Sleeping & Eating

**Hotel Kyzylorda** (☎7 11 21; fax 26 12 54; Tokmaganbetova 19; r from 6000T; ) This recently remodelled central hotel, located opposite the Historical Museum, also boasts a café and internet café.

**Hotel Asetan** (☎6 25 43; Ayteke Bi 28; r from 6000T) Not far from Hotel Kyzylorda, the Asetan, also recently remodelled, has large, comfortably furnished rooms.

**Restoran Baron** (☎7 62 60; Konaev; mains 350-500T; 10am-2am) This friendly place located near the train station does some of the best shashlyk in town, including fish varieties.

**Remet** (☎6 21 41; Auezova 7; dishes 350-1500T; 10am-2am) Another friendly place with decent pizza; the nonsmoking upstairs section is the coolest place in town.

## Getting There & Away

The airport, 17km south of the city, has flights to Almaty (14,000T to 17,000T) daily, and to Aktau (19,000T), Astana (17,000T), Atyrau (14,000T to 19,000T), Shymkent (11,000T), Taraz (11,000T), and Moscow (40,000T) up to four times weekly. Train services are the same as for Turkistan. A few buses and marshrutkas run daily to Turkistan (600T to 700T, four to five hours), Shymkent (800T to 1000T, six to seven hours) and Aralsk (900T, seven hours).

# ARALSK АРАЛЬСК

☎32433 / pop 36,000

Aralsk, 475km northwest of Kyzylorda on the same road and railway, used to be an important fishing port on the shores of the Aral Sea. A large mosaic in its train station depicts how in 1921 Aralsk's comrades provided fish for people starving in Russia. Today a large part of the Aral Sea is gone, victim of Soviet irrigation schemes that took water from its lifelines, the Syr-Darya and Amu-Darya rivers, and pushed the shoreline 60km out from Aralsk (see p77). If you want to witness the notorious Aral Sea environmental disaster first-hand, Aralsk is easier to visit, and more interesting, than similarly defunct ports in Uzbekistan. Nor is everything quite so gloomy here: efforts to save part of the sea seem to be succeeding (see the boxed text, below) and a small-scale fishing industry has started up again.

## Sights & Activities

A few rusting **boats** lie in the former harbour, just outside the hotel. In 2003, in honour of Aralsk's 100th birthday, some were put on platforms and painted as a tribute to fallen heroes. In the centre of town, the local **history museum** (admission 150T; 🕓 9am-noon & 2-6pm Tue-Sun) has some old photos of the fishermen in action, along with contemporary local paintings of the disaster itself.

Close to the harbour is the ruined fish processing plant, Aralrybprom, which finally went bankrupt in the late 1990s, having stayed alive 20 years after the Aral departed by canning fish from the Baltic and Vladivostok. A new plant on the edge of the city, **Kambala Balyk** (Nurzhaubaeva), now employs 60 people processing fish from the Aral's revived fishing industry, sending produce as far as Russia, Ukraine and northern Kazakhstan.

At **Zhalanash**, a former fishing village 63km west of Aralsk, you can still see a **ship cemetery**, where several abandoned hulks rust in the open desert.

The NGO **Aral Tenizi** (☎ 2 22 56, 2 36 51, 701-2608923; www.aralsk.net; Makhataeva 10) can arrange English-speaking guides and drivers to visit the sites. Ask for English-speaking Akmaral Utemisova. A day trip to the ship cemetery and the sea costs US$92 per 4WD (up to four passengers); to the dike (220km one-way) it's US$115. Trips on fishing boats are also possible. Aral Tenizi charges all clients a US$20-per-group membership fee including a visit to the Kambala Balyk fish factory. Try to contact staff ahead, to allow time to make your arrangements.

Readers have recommended **Ismalaev Almatbek** (☎ 2 35 75) as a reliable driver with good local connections.

### THE ARAL SEA: A (SMALL) ENVIRONMENTAL SUCCESS STORY

The piles of dried flounder are stacked ever higher the closer you get to Aralsk, and the women who sell them ever pushier. Where do these fish come from? Some come from the surviving puddles around the Aral, but more and more are being hauled out of the Aral itself – that is, the Little Aral.

With the help of international aid agencies and lenders like the World Bank, Kazakhstan has revived the northeast corner of the Aral, now severed from its southern body.

A mud dike was built across the last channel connecting the northern and southern portions in the 1990s. With no outlet to the south, the Little Aral started to fill up again with water from the Syr-Darya. The sea crept back to within 27km of Aralsk, only to recede again after the dike collapsed in 2002. Between the 1960s and 2003 the Aral Sea lost about three-quarters of its 68,000-sq-km area and some 80% of its water.

From 2003 to 2005, a new, US$85-million, 13km-long, 10m-high concrete dike was built between the two parts of the sea. Within a few months of its completion, water levels in the Little Aral had already risen by several metres, faster than expected. Rehabilitation of waterworks along the Syr-Darya also helped, by increasing the flow of water into the sea. By mid-2006, water was within 23km of Aralsk, and fishing boats were operating from the new Kök-Aral dike and even some outlying villages. Flounder is the main catch: introduced to the Aral from the Sea of Azov in 1979, this proved the only species able to survive the Aral's extreme salinity in the 1990s. Since then pike, pike-perch, bream and carp have found their way back into the Little Aral. Locals also say the noxious dust storms that plagued communities such as Aralsk have stopped.

The dike probably condemns the larger southern lake to accelerated evaporation, but proponents argue that the southern Aral is a lost cause anyway, with no hope of an increase in water from the Amu-Darya, which flows through Turkmenistan and Uzbekistan.

### Sleeping & Eating

**Aral Tenizi** (☎ 2 22 56, 2 36 51, 701-2608923; www.aralsk.net; Makhataeva 10; per person US$15) The NGO Aral Tenizi offers accommodation with host families – with reliable running water, it says. Breakfast is included.

**Aibek B&B** (☎ 2 32 56; Makhataeva 19; d with shared bathroom 3500T) Near the old port, this basic homestay has clean rooms with home-cooked meals.

**Yaksart Hotel** (☎ 2 14 79; Makhataeva 14; d 3500T, ste per person US$38; ) Aralsk's hotel is opposite Aibek B&B. It doesn't always have running water.

For meals, the two best central bets are **Rakhat** (Gorkogo; dishes 100-300T; 11am-midnight), a modern place serving Russian and Kazakh standards and a few European variations, and **Chin-Son** (Portovaya; dishes 100-300T; 11am-midnight), with spicy Korean dishes.

### Getting There & Around

Aralsk's train station, called Aralskoe More, is a 10-minute walk northeast of the central square. The Almaty–Aqtöbe train 23 arrives at 10.30pm, and the Aqtöbe–Almaty train 24 arrives at 4.29am. In July and August, departure train tickets can be brutally hard to come by. Buy them for the next night's train when you arrive. Even better, buy onward or return tickets before arriving.

Buses depart to Kyzylorda (900T, seven hours) between 8pm and 11pm from the train station. It's advisable to go and reserve a place around 6pm. Aral Tenizi (p151) can arrange taxis to or from Kyzylorda (15,000T, four to five hours).

# WESTERN KAZAKHSTAN

Most Westerners who come to Kazakhstan's far west – so far west that the part beyond the Ural River is in Europe – are involved in exploiting Kazakhstan's biggest oil and gas fields: Tenghiz (oil), Karachaganak (gas) and the offshore oil of Kashagan beneath the Caspian Sea. Oil has brought boom times to the region's four main cities, though elsewhere the human population is pretty sparse and the landscape is chiefly desert, apart from marshy areas around the northeast Caspian coastline.

For those with a taste for adventurous exploring, the deserts east of Aktau, dotted with underground mosques, ancient necropolises, abandoned caravanserais and spectacular rock formations, are just the ticket.

Western Kazakhstan is a gateway to Central Asia from Azerbaijan or Russia, and there are even flights from Europe to Atyrau and Uralsk.

The region is one hour behind Astana, Almaty and the rest of the country.

## AQTÖBE АҚТӨБЕ

☎ 3132 / pop 300,000

Aqtöbe (formerly Aktyubinsk), on the main railway to Moscow about 100km from the Russian border, is a developing commercial hub that has experienced an influx of multinational oil and gas companies and an accompanying facelift.

Near the lively market is the local **museum** (☎ 21 13 67; Altynsarin 14; admission 50T; 9am-1pm & 2-6pm) where Rosa, an English-speaking curator, might be available to give you a tour.

### Sleeping & Eating

**Hotel Aktyubinsk** (☎ 56 28 29; hotel@aktobe.kz; Abylkhair Khan 44; s/d 3600/4200T) Central hotel with clean Soviet-style rooms equipped with TV and fridge. From the station take bus 1 or 15, or a taxi (300T).

**Hotel Albion** (☎ 21 00 18; albion_hotel@rambler.ru; Ayteke Bi 13; r US$184-219; ) The best in town, with spacious, modern rooms, within walking distance of the train station.

**Kofeynya Espresso** (☎ 57 27 55; Abylkhair Khan 85; 9am-9pm) A nice coffee shop where you can rent a laptop with wi-fi (300T per hour), on the 2nd-floor of a blue-domed business centre.

**Stanbul Café** (Abylkhair Khan 57A), near the main mosque which has the distinction of doubling as a shopping mall, is an economical Turkish haunt with decent kebabs, soups and salads.

Next door to Stanbul Café is **Chindale** (Abylkhair Khan), an upscale Japanese-Korean restaurant.

### Getting There & Away

Flights go to Almaty (28,000T) and Astana (21,000T to 24,000T) daily, and Atyrau (14,300T) and Aktau (15,250T) most days. There are two weekly flights to Moscow.

Trains from the **station** (☎ 21 17 77) run to Uralsk (1500T, 10 to 12 hours) and Almaty (5500T, 40 to 46 hours) twice daily; to Aktau (3100T, 24 hours), Atyrau (2050T, 14 hours), Moscow (37 hours) and Tashkent (29 to 32 hours) at least once daily; and to Astana (27 hours) and Bishkek (38 hours) every two days. Russian officials have started checking for Russian transit visas on trains between Aqtöbe and Uralsk, which duck into Russia for about 100km en route.

## URALSK УРАЛЬСК

☎ 3112 / pop 250,000

Closer to Vienna than Almaty and straddling the dividing line between Asia and Europe, Uralsk (Kazakh: Oral) is the first or last city for some Central Asian overlanders. It's also a base for many expat oilmen hauling themselves out to the pumping stations at Karachaganak, 150km east of the city.

Uralsk, founded by Cossacks in the 17th century, has its roots in Russia, as is clear from the beautiful, brightly painted, traditional Russian architecture throughout the centre. Lenin saw to it that Uralsk was included in the Kazakh SSR in order to make Russian migrants feel happier.

Teatralnaya, the main pedestrian street, is Uralsk's mini version of Moscow's Arbat. Kazakhstan's first **drama theatre**, a handsome brick affair, has stood here for 150 years. The main boulevard, Dostyk, has some of the finest architecture in town, including two Russian Orthodox churches, brilliantly lit at night.

A famous Russian serf rebellion was launched in 1773 at what's now the **Pugachev Museum** (☎ 50 65 86; Dostyk 35; 🕓 closed Mon & Tue). Yemelyan Pugachev led a group of Cossacks and hundreds of thousands of serfs in a rebellion against the autocratic Catherine the Great that spread to the Ural Mountains and along the Volga. The museum is in Pugachev's original log house in Uralsk's oldest district, Kuriny, with plenty of replica and original furniture and artefacts – best reached by taxi.

### Sleeping & Eating

The **Hotel Oral** (☎ 50 60 17; Kurmangazy 80; r 2000-6000T) and **Sayakhat Hotel** (☎ 51 30 03; Temir Masina 38; r 4000-11,000; 💻) are remodelled Soviet hotels offering a clean place to sleep. There are two Western-style hotels where at least some English is spoken: **Hotel Chagala** (☎ 50 60 17; www.chagalagroup.com; Temir Masina; r 11,000-24,000T) and the excellent **Pushkin Hotel** (☎ 51 35 60; www.pushkinhotel.com; Dostyk 148B; s/d US$130/208) with friendly staff, great new furniture and a Venetian feel.

Dozens of restaurants line Dostyk from the train station to the Ural River. **Camelot** (☎ 50 39 01; Dostyk 185; mains 700-2500T), right in the centre, is the classiest place in town, great for varieties of the local red fish and the imaginative names of its dishes (English menu available). The Western-style **Dixie Pub** (Atrium Mall, Teatralnaya 17; mains 700-1800T) serves everything from fried calamari to a good burrito, in absolutely American-sized portions.

### Getting There & Away

Uralsk has direct flights to Astana (22,000T), Atyrau, and Aktau five or six times weekly; to Almaty (24,500T) three times; to Moscow twice; and to London (by Astraeus, www.flyastraeus.com) and Baku once.

There are daily trains to Moscow (29 hours) and Almaty (54 hours). Trains to Almaty go via Aqtöbe, passing through part of Russia en route – check visa requirements.

Minibuses to Atyrau (2200T, six hours) leave Uralsk's train station at 6am, 7am and 9am. Shared taxis to Atyrau (4000T to 5000T, five hours) also go from the station.

## ATYRAU АТЫРАУ

☎ 3122 / pop 147,000

Atyrau, 30km up the Ural River from its mouth on the Caspian Sea, began as a Russian fort in the 16th century and today acts as command station for the huge Tenghiz oilfield 200km south. Tengizchevroil, the multibillion-dollar joint venture exploiting the field, has its headquarters in this predominantly Kazakh town.

With direct flights from Amsterdam and Istanbul, Atyrau is a possible entry point into Kazakhstan, but unless you're here to work there's not very much reason to linger.

### Orientation

The Ural River meanders through the town, flowing roughly north–south beneath the central bridge on Abay and marking the border between Asia and Europe. West of the bridge, on the European side, Abay becomes Satpaev. The train station is on the northeastern edge of town, 5km from the centre. The airport is 8km west of the centre.

### Information

**CATC** (☎ 35 40 75/6/7; cat-atyrau@alarnet.com; Azattyq 25; 🕓 9am-1pm & 2-6.30pm Mon-Fri, 9am-1pm Sat)

Ticketing and travel agency; offers discounts on rooms at some hotels.

**Halyk Bank** (☎ 25 15 37; Satpaev 4; 🕑 8.30am-12.45pm & 2.15-4pm Mon-Fri, 9am-1pm Sat) Currency exchange.

**Qazaqtelekom** (Abay btwn Azattyq & Makhambet; 🕑 8am-11pm) Phone from here.

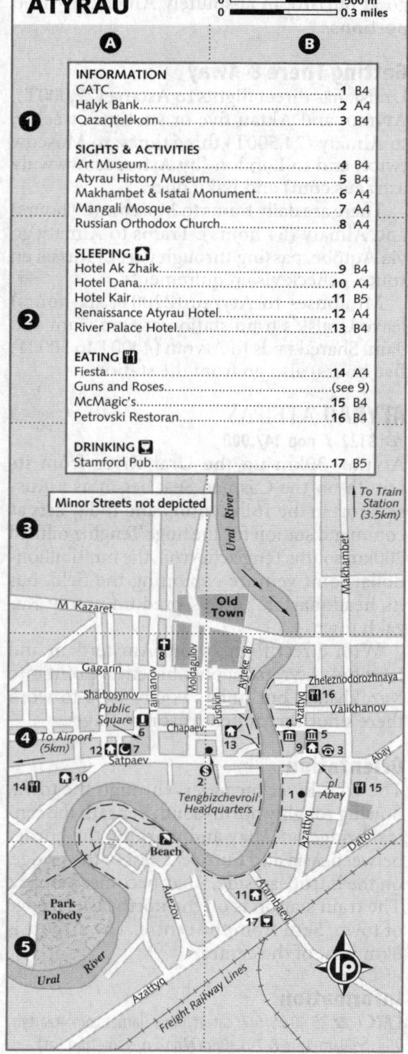


## Dangers & Annoyances

There have been occasional attacks and muggings on foreigners in Atyrau, chiefly in and around nightclubs and bars. Avoid confrontations and travel by official taxi after dark.

Mud coats the streets after wet spells from autumn to spring. If you visit during this time, bring appropriate footwear.

## Sights & Activities

The modernised **Atyrau History Museum** (☎ 22 29 12; Azattyq 9B; admission 200T; 🕑 9am-1pm & 2-6pm Tue-Sun) has some interesting displays including a replica of the local 'Golden Man' – a 2nd-century-BC Sarmatian chief with gold-plated tunic, found in 1999 – and a room on recently excavated Saraychik, an old trading centre 55km north of Atyrau, where several khans of the Golden Horde were buried.

Opposite the History Museum is the **Art Museum** (☎ 25 48 03; Azattyq 11; admission 200T; 🕑 10am-1pm & 2-7pm Tue-Sun), worth a look for its collection of paintings on Atyrau life.

On Satpaev 800m west of the bridge is a newish **public square** fitted with fountains, a monument to 19th-century Kazakh freedom fighters Makhambet and Isatai, and an annoying jumbo TV. The modern, blue-domed **Mangali Mosque** (Satpaev) is nearby. In the crumbling 'old town' north of here, a well-maintained **Russian Orthodox church** (Taimanov), dating from 1888, emerges like a jewelled finger from the surrounding shacks.

## Sleeping

There's no shortage of good hotels – at a price.

**Hotel Kair** (☎ 25 07 65; Atambaev 19A; s/d from 4600/6200T) A relatively inexpensive, well-kept place south of the river; no food or bar though.

**Hotel Ak Zhaik** (☎ 32 78 81/2; fax 32 20 11; www.akzhaikhotel.com; Azattyq; s/d 10,000/18,000T; ❄ 💻) Recently renovated, this very central hotel has comfy rooms and a slew of useful facilities including ATM, train ticket office, pub with wi-fi internet and a good lobby café. Breakfast is included.

**Hotel Dana** (☎ 21 08 75/63; danahotel@mail.ru; Tolebaev 40; s/d from 12,800/18,000T; ❄) About 1.5km west of the bridge, the Dana is a medium-sized hotel in vaguely alpine style with excellent, large, carpeted rooms and good service. Breakfast included in rates.

**River Palace Hotel** (☎ 25 52 36, 35 52 41; www.hotelriverpalace.com; Ayteke Bi 55; d/ste US$162/324; ) The luxurious, Italian-owned River Palace shares a modernistic riverfront building with apartments and offices. The rooftop pool (2000T for nonguests in summer) is a welcome and popular feature.

**Renaissance Atyrau Hotel** (☎ 90 96 00; www.renaissancehotels.com/guwbr; Satpaev 15B; r from 28,000T; ) Elegant new international-class luxury Marriott hotel with all the facilities.

## Eating & Drinking

**McMagic's** (☎ 25 54 45; Makhambet 116A; dishes 200-700T; 10am-midnight) In the big Daria store building, this is a reasonable Western-style burger and pizza bar.

**Guns & Roses** (☎ 32 78 78; Hotel Ak Zhaik, Azattyq; dishes 600-2500T; 8am-1am) Cosy English pub serving meals from English breakfast and salads to steaks and pasta. Also offers free wi-fi, live rock from 8pm Thursday to Saturday, and three big screens for sport.

**Petrovski Restoran** (☎ 32 10 99; Azattyq 2; mains 800-2500T; 8am-1am) Good European dishes and breakfasts are served at this stylish, pop-art-decked little place.

**Fiesta** (☎ 97 03 76; Satpaev 5B; mains 800-2500T; noon-midnight) Excellent oriental and Tex-Mex restaurant with relaxed ambience, in a residential area off the main road.

**Stamford Pub** (☎ 25 29 32; Azattyq 78A; beer 300-600T; 5pm-2am Sun-Thu, 5pm-5am Fri & Sat) Lively pub with a good rock/jazz band playing Thursday to Sunday nights. Packed with an international after-work crowd on Friday night.

## Getting There & Away

From the **airport** (☎ 20 92 51/2) there are daily flights to Aktau (12,000T), Astana (from 23,500T) and Almaty (26,500T to 32,000T); to Aqtöbe (14,300T) and Uralsk (13,000T) most days; and to Kyzylorda (19,000T), Taraz (21,000T), Baku (23,000T), Moscow, Amsterdam and Istanbul a few times weekly.

From the **train station** (☎ 36 06 95; Vokzalnaya 1) trains go daily to Mangyshlak (Aktau; 2700T, 21 hours), Aqtöbe (2050T, 15 hours) and Astrakhan (3700T, 14 hours); and to Almaty (6000T, 52 hours) and Astana (5000T, 46 hours) every two days. There's a ticket office in the Hotel Ak Zhaik.

A bus to Uralsk (3000T, seven hours) leaves the train station at 3am or 4am. Later, there are minibuses and shared taxis (5000T per person, five hours), also from the train station.

## Getting Around

Taxis to or from the airport should cost 500T but you may have to pay more coming into town. Buses and marshrutkas 3, 10, 14, 15 and 21 run between the train station and the centre and along Satpaev.

# AKTAU АКТАУ

☎ 3292 / pop 166,000

Stuck between the desert and the Caspian, hundreds of kilometres from anywhere else of any size, with all its water derived from desalination, Aktau is perhaps the most oddly situated of all the weirdly located places scattered across the former USSR.

Local uranium and oil finds were the reason Soviet architects began to lay out a model town of wide, straight streets here in 1958. Thanks to the sandy beaches on the blue Caspian and temperate climate (several degrees above zero in January), the place was also developed as an elite Soviet holiday resort.

Now uranium and tourism are in decline, but the oil industry is picking up the slack. With its broad streets, benign climate, seaside location and reasonable standard of living, Aktau is a pleasant town to spend a day or two. More of a reason to come here, though, are the natural and manmade wonders of the surrounding region, Mangistau – see p157.

## Orientation

The only significant street with a name is Kazakhstan Respublikasy Prezidentininy dangghyly (not surprisingly, many people still call it Lenina), a broad avenue sloping down from northwest to southeast, parallel to the coast. Aktau addresses are based on *mikrorayon* (microdistrict) and *dom* (building) numbers: 4-17-29 means Mikrorayon 4, Dom 17, Apartment 29.

## Information

**Caspian Tour** (☎ 42 66 54; menzhan@rambler.ru; Dvorets Brakosochetania, Mikrorayon 14) Travel agency offering tours in and outside the city; the office is inside Aktau's wedding-ceremony palace.

**CATC** (☎ 50 75 04; cat-aktau@alarnet.com; West Wing, Hotel Aktau, Mikrorayon 2; 9am-6.30pm Mon-Fri, 9am-1pm Sat) English-speaking travel agency offering flight and hotel bookings, visa support and cars with drivers.

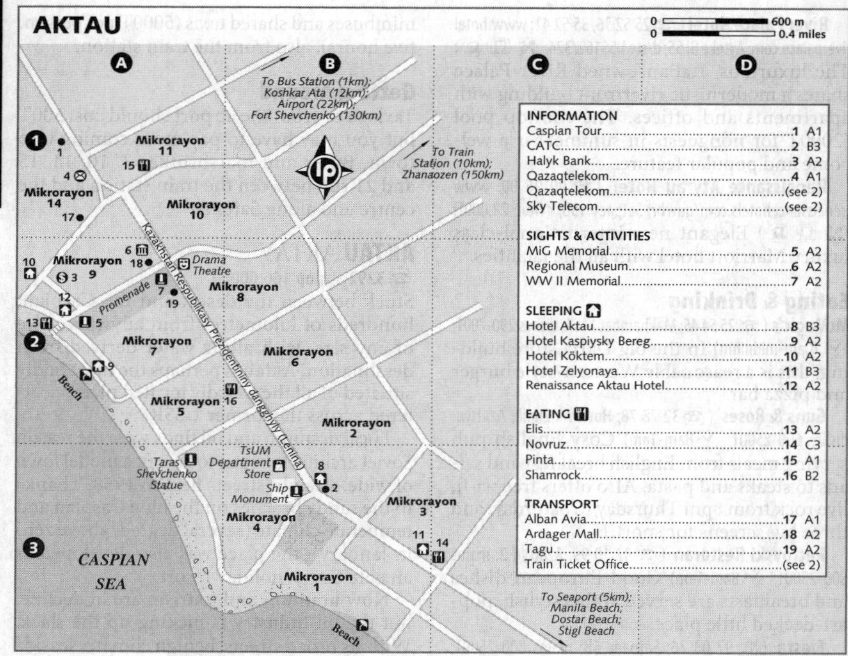


**Halyk Bank** (Mikrorayon 9, Dom 6; 8.30am-3pm Mon-Fri) Currency-exchange office.

**Qazaqtelekom** Hotel Aktau (West Wing, Hotel Aktau, Mikrorayon 2; 9am-9pm Mon-Fri, 10am-7pm Sat & Sun); Main Office (Kazakhstan Respublikasy Prezidentininy dangghyly, Mikrorayon 14; 8am-8pm Mon-Sat) You can phone from these offices.

**Sky Telecom** (West Wing, Hotel Aktau, Mikrorayon 2; internet per hr 300T; 9am-6pm) Public internet on two computers.

**Turist** (☎ 43 00 00; pbalatov@nursat.kz; Mikrorayon 9, Dom 4, Office 110; 10am-7pm) Experienced travel agency offering tours in and outside the city.

## Dangers & Annoyances

As in Atyrau, foreigners have been the target of some attacks and muggings in Aktau, chiefly in and around bars and nightspots. Avoid confrontations and travel by official taxi after dark.

## Sights

To best savour Aktau's atmosphere, stroll along the pedestrian walk from the large **WWII Memorial** beside Kazakhstan Respublikasy Prezidentininy dangghyly to the **MiG fighter plane memorial** at the seaward end of the street. From the MiG you can descend flights of steps to the breezy **seafront**, a mixture of low cliffs, rocks and thin sandy strips. There are better, sandier beaches, costing 100T to 200T to access, south of town: **Manila**, about a 15-minute taxi ride (200T); the longer, less crowded **Dostar** (300T by taxi, 20 minutes); and **Stigl** (400T to 500T by taxi, 30 minutes).

Interesting displays about the Caspian and the Mangistau archaeological heritage make the **Regional Museum** (Mikrorayon 9, Dom 23A; 10am-5pm Tue-Sat) worth a visit.

## Sleeping

**Hotel Aktau** (☎ 50 47 07, 50 47 50; laura1@pochta.ru; Kazakhstan Respublikasy Prezidentininy dangghyly, Mikrorayon 2, Dom 66; r 4680-12,450T; ) Despite renovations a few years ago, the Aktau already feels haggard again. Still, it's one of the less expensive places and rooms do have multichannel satellite TV. Some have sea views too. Breakfast is included.

**Hotel Kaspiysky Bereg** (Caspian Shore Hotel; ☎ 50 16 41; fax 50 62 09; Mikrorayon 7; r 5000-13,000T) This homy small hotel near the seashore has good-sized rooms sporting glassed-in showers and attractive Chinese silk 'paintings'. Breakfast is included.

**Hotel Köktem** (☎ 43 44 79; koktem_aktau@mail.online.kz; Mikrorayon 14, Dom 10; r 9800-14,000T; ) Well-run, welcoming hotel with sizeable, well-equipped, comfy rooms and English-speaking receptionists. Rates include breakfast.

**Hotel Zelyonaya** (Green Hotel; ☎ 50 73 04; Mikrorayon 3, Dom 100; r US$110-165) This impeccably managed hotel is about 1km east of the Hotel Aktau. It only has suites and apartments, all large and well-furnished; and breakfast is included.

**Renaissance Aktau Hotel** (☎ 30 06 00; fax 30 06 01; www.renaissancehotels.com/scobr; Mikrorayon 9; s/d from US$270/282; ) Aktau's Marriott hotel provides superstylish modern rooms and suites boasting wi-fi internet, satellite TV and in most cases sea views. The hotel has a heated pool and two elegant eateries. Breakfast is included.

## Eating & Drinking

**Novruz** (☎ 51 66 66; Mikrorayon 3; mains 600-900T; admission after 8pm 400T; noon-2am) Enclosed in a courtyard and enlivened with plants and a fountain, this pleasant restaurant near Hotel Zelyonaya serves up European, Middle Eastern, Russian and Kazakh dishes. The Salman beer (brewed next door) is a nice local touch.

**Pinta** (☎ 31 17 40; Mikrorayon 11, Dom 8A; mains 800-1800T; noon-3pm & 6pm-1am) A cosy, relaxed, small restaurant with excellent service and a Russian-international menu specialising in pork, chicken and fish. A great coffee-and-cakes café (open 10am to 11pm) adjoins the restaurant.

**Elis** (☎ 43 85 02; Mikrorayon 7; dishes 800-1800T; noon-2am) The publike upper bar at this multipurpose leisure centre on the coastal embankment serves a range of good international food, and a solid rock and pop band plays from 9pm except Wednesday.

**Shamrock** (☎ 52 18 38; Mikrorayon 5, Dom 5; dishes 900-2000T, draught beer 0.5L from 600T; noon-2am) An authentic and popular Irish pub, Shamrock serves large helpings of Italian, Mexican, English, Russian and *even* Irish food. A good rock and jazz band plays Wednesday, Friday and Saturday from 10pm.

## Getting There & Around

Aktau's **airport** (☎ 46 85 73) is 23km north of the centre (around 1000T by taxi). There are flights six or seven days a week to Almaty (from 23,250T), Astana (18,000T to 25,000T), Aqtöbe (15,250T), Atyrau (12,000T to 14,500T) and Uralsk (17,250T). SCAT also flies to Kyzylorda (19,250T), Shymkent (21,250T), Astrakhan (Russia; 16,000T), Baku (Azerbaijan; 13,550T), Yerevan (Armenia; 21,550T) and Tbilisi (Georgia; 24,350T). There are five flights a week to Baku by Azerbaijan Airlines (14,000T to 27,000T) and three flights a week to Moscow by Transaero (32,000T to 62,000T). You'll find air ticket offices at the **airport** (☎ 46 82 25; 24hr) and **Ardager shopping mall** (☎ 42 71 71; 9am-1pm & 2-9pm). **Alban Avia** (☎ 42 74 00; Mikrorayon 14, Dom 59) specialises in Baku flights and onward connections.

Aktau's **train station** (☎ 46 52 50), called Mangyshlak, is 12km east of the centre. Trains leave daily for Atyrau (2700T, 20 hours), Aqtöbe (3100T, 26 hours), Astana (5500T, 50 hours) and on odd dates for Almaty (7000T, 67 hours) via Aralsk and Shymkent. There's a **train ticket office** (Mikrorayon 2; 8am-1pm & 2-6.30pm) outside the Hotel Aktau. A taxi from station to city centre costs around 600T.

The **bus station** (Mikrorayon 28), in the north of town, has no bus services but marshrutkas leave when full to Zhanaozen and Shetpe (both 300T, two hours). There are also taxis to Zhanaozen and Fort Shevchenko (both 500/2000T for one place/whole cab, two hours).

A sea ferry to Baku, Azerbaijan leaves about every seven to 10 days from the seaport in the southeast of town. Cabin fares for the scheduled 18-hour crossing run from 7800T to 10,000T. Information and tickets are available from **Tagu** (☎ 51 39 89; cs-kz.narod.ru; Mikrorayon 7, Dom 12; 9am-1pm & 2-6pm Mon-Sat, 10am-3pm Sun). Take some food.

Bus and marshrutka 3 run from Hotel Aktau up Kazakhstan Respublikasy Prezidentininy dangghyly as far as the main Qazaqtelekom office, then east to the bus station, and vice-versa.

# AROUND AKTAU

The stony deserts of the Mangistau region, of which Aktau is capital, stretch 400km east to the border of Uzbekistan. Dotted with dramatic canyons and rock outcrops, surprising lakes, strange underground mosques, ancient necropolises and abandoned caravanserais, this fascinating region has barely begun to be explored even by archaeologists. A branch of the Silk Road once ran across these wastes, and sacred sites, some with strong Sufic associations, are located where people buried their dead or where holy men dwelt. The underground mosques may have originated as cave-hermitages for ascetics who retreated to the deserts.

A few sites, including Beket-Ata and Fort Shevchenko, can be reached by public transport of sorts, but for most places you need a knowledgeable driver with a 4WD vehicle. Getting to these places along rough tracks across the surreal desert, with only the occasional herd of camels or sheep for company, is part of the fun. Stantours in Almaty (p117) and local firms Caspian Tour and Turist (p155) are all experienced operators offering trips here. Day trips from Aktau in a 4WD for up to four passengers generally cost US$200 to US$250; itineraries of several days for small or large groups are also available.

### Koshkar Ata

All Kazakhstan is dotted with picturesque cemeteries or necropolises set outside villages and towns and Mangistau has a notable concentration of them: locals boast the figure 362, many of them very ancient. One of the most interesting is **Koshkar Ata**, at Akshukur, 12km north of Aktau on the Fort Shevchenko road. Its skyline of miniature domes and towers resembles some Arabian fairytale-fantasy, and just inside the entrance is an old tomb adorned with an unusually realistic ram carving, in contrast to the highly stylised rams known as *koita* found elsewhere.

### Fort Shevchenko & Around

The dusty little town of Fort Shevchenko stands 130km north of Aktau near the tip of the Mangyshlak Peninsula. The **Local Museum** (admission 100T; 9am-noon & 2-6pm), in a yurt-shaped building near the taxi stand, includes material on the region's necropolises and underground mosques, but the best reason to come here is the **Shevchenko Museum** (admission 100T; 9am-noon & 2-6pm), behind the Local Museum. The great Ukrainian poet and artist Taras Shevchenko (1814–61) spent seven years in exile here in the 1850s, and the museum, housed in the former Russian military commandant's house (dating from 1850), exhibits many of his penetrating landscapes, local scenes, portraits and self-portraits. Beside the house is the cellarlike **zemlyanka** (admission 100T; 9am-noon & 2-6pm), where the sympathetic commandant permitted Shevchenko to live and work. **Kafe Aybi** (Abdikhalykov; dishes around 250T; 10am-12.30am), by Fort Shevchenko's taxi stand, serves salads, *manty* and other local standards.

#### THE PILGRIMAGE TO BEKET-ATA

Beket-Ata, 285km southeast of Aktau, is an underground mosque to which the revered clairvoyant, healer and teacher Beket-Ata (1750–1813) retreated in the later part of his life, ultimately dying and being buried here. A Mangistau native, Beket-Ata studied in Bukhara and on his return he is believed to have set up four or five mosques, including this one where he founded a Sufi school. Every day dozens of pilgrims – and on holidays, hundreds – make the bumpy journey across the deserts to pray and receive Beket-Ata's inspiration. The underground mosque (three caves) is set in a rocky outcrop, overlooking a desert canyon. You won't quickly forget the journey here across otherworldly desertscapes and the pilgrimage atmosphere that touches all visitors.

Aktau tour firms run two-day trips to Beket-Ata costing US$400 to US$500 for up to four people. To do it independently, start by taking a marshrutka from Aktau bus station to the oil town of Zhanaozen (300T, two hours), 150km by paved road. From Zhanaozen bus station get a taxi to the bazaar (100T), where four-passenger 4WD vehicles leave every morning for Beket-Ata, charging 2000T per person or 6000T for the vehicle, round-trip. You'll spend most of the 135km to Beket-Ata lurching and bumping along steppe and desert tracks. En route, vehicles stop at Shopan-Ata, 55km from Zhanaozen, an ancient underground mosque and large necropolis dating back to at least the 10th century, where Shopan-Ata, a mentor of Beket-Ata, dwelt. The Zhanaozen–Beket-Ata trip takes five to six hours, and most groups sleep (free) in the pilgrim-hostel-cum-mosque-cum-dining-hall at Beket-Ata, before leaving early the next morning.

On arrival at Shopan-Ata and Beket-Ata all visitors are expected to purify themselves by using the squat toilets. If you're travelling with pilgrims, be ready to join in prayers and ritual walks round sacred trees too. You may be invited to join meals of the Kazakh national dish *beshbarmak* at both places, sitting round big bowls of food, eating with the right hand only.

About 5km beyond Fort Shevchenko, the coastal village of **Bautino**, with some pretty 19th-century Russian-style cottages, is developing as a service base for offshore oil and gas operations.

Shared taxis to Fort Shevchenko (500T, two hours) leave when full from Aktau's bus station. The last ones head back to Aktau around 5pm.

### Other Destinations

**Shakpak-Ata**, though now deserted, is perhaps the most intriguing of all the area's underground mosques – a unique cross-shaped affair with three entrances, four chambers and a central hall supported by sculpted columns, cut behind a cliff some 125km north of Aktau, within view of the Caspian coast. Shakpak-Ata probably dates back to the 10th century, and its walls are adorned with Arabic inscriptions and drawings of plants and hands. The cliff is peppered with burial niches, and there's a necropolis of similar age below it, with more than 2000 tombs. The easiest approach is via Tauchik, with the last 25km on unpaved steppe roads.

Near the coast some 30km west of Shakpak-Ata (or 90km east from Fort Shevchenko), is **Sultan-Epe**. This is another underground mosque and necropolis pairing, on the edge of a deep, thickly vegetated canyon. Holy man Sultan-Epe, buried here, is considered the protector of sailors.

Around 90km southeast from Shakpak-Ata, in the vicinity of Shetpe, is **Sherkala** (Lion Rock), a 332m-high chalk outcrop rising mysteriously from the steppe. At its foot are the remains of a medieval caravanserai-fort. Between Shakpak-Ata and Sherkala is Torysh or the **Valley of Balls**, scattered with hundreds of giant stone balls, some over 2m wide. Within 20km of Sherkala is **Kyzylkala**, a ruined Silk Road town.

Each of these sites can be reached in day trips from Aktau and in some cases you can combine more than one in the same day.

# NORTHERN KAZAKHSTAN

This is the most Russified part of Kazakhstan but it's also the location of the new capital Astana, chief crucible of the prosperous, multiethnic Kazakhstan of the future, an extravagant exercise in capital-city creation and the pole around which the north of the country is being revived.

Though known for their bitter winters and Soviet-created industrial cities, the northern steppes also harbour surprising areas of natural beauty: the flamingo-filled lakes of Korgalzhyn; the rocky hills, forests and lakes near Burabay; and the verdant countryside and tranquil villages southwest of Kokshetau.

Until the 19th century, this region was largely untouched except by Kazakh nomads and their herds. As Russia's hand stretched southwards, Russian and Ukrainian settlers came in growing numbers to farm the steppe – a million or more by 1900. Kazakh resistance was largely futile. In Soviet times, the Kazakhs were forced into collective farms and industrial cities such as Karaganda and Kostanay, which sprouted to exploit coal, iron ore and other minerals. Then in the 1950s huge areas of steppe were turned over to wheat in Khrushchev's Virgin Lands scheme (p111). A new influx of settlers, deportees and prisoners arrived from other parts of the USSR to work all the new projects.

In the 1950s most of the labour camps were closed, but a lot of the survivors stayed. Since the collapse of the Soviet Union many ethnic Germans, Russian and Ukrainians have left, but Kazakhs still number less than one-third in several areas.

Astana apart, northern Kazakhstan sees more Westerners here to adopt children than Western tourists. Weatherwise, the best months to come are May, June, August and September. Winters are severe, with howling blizzards and temperatures down to -30°C in January.

## ASTANA АСТАНА

☎ **3172 / pop 550,000**

Love it or hate it, Astana is here to stay as Kazakhstan's capital. Just a medium-sized provincial city known for its bitter winters when President Nazarbaev named it out of the blue in 1994 as the country's future capital, Astana replaced Almaty in 1997. Since then its skyline has grown more fantastical by the year as a reported 8% of the national budget is lavished on transforming vast acreage south of the Ishim River into a new governmental-administrative zone, with daring buildings combining Islamic, Soviet, Western and wacky futuristic influences.

Ministries and functionaries were obliged to make an early move to Astana and are now in the process of shifting again to their permanent quarters from temporary ones in the old

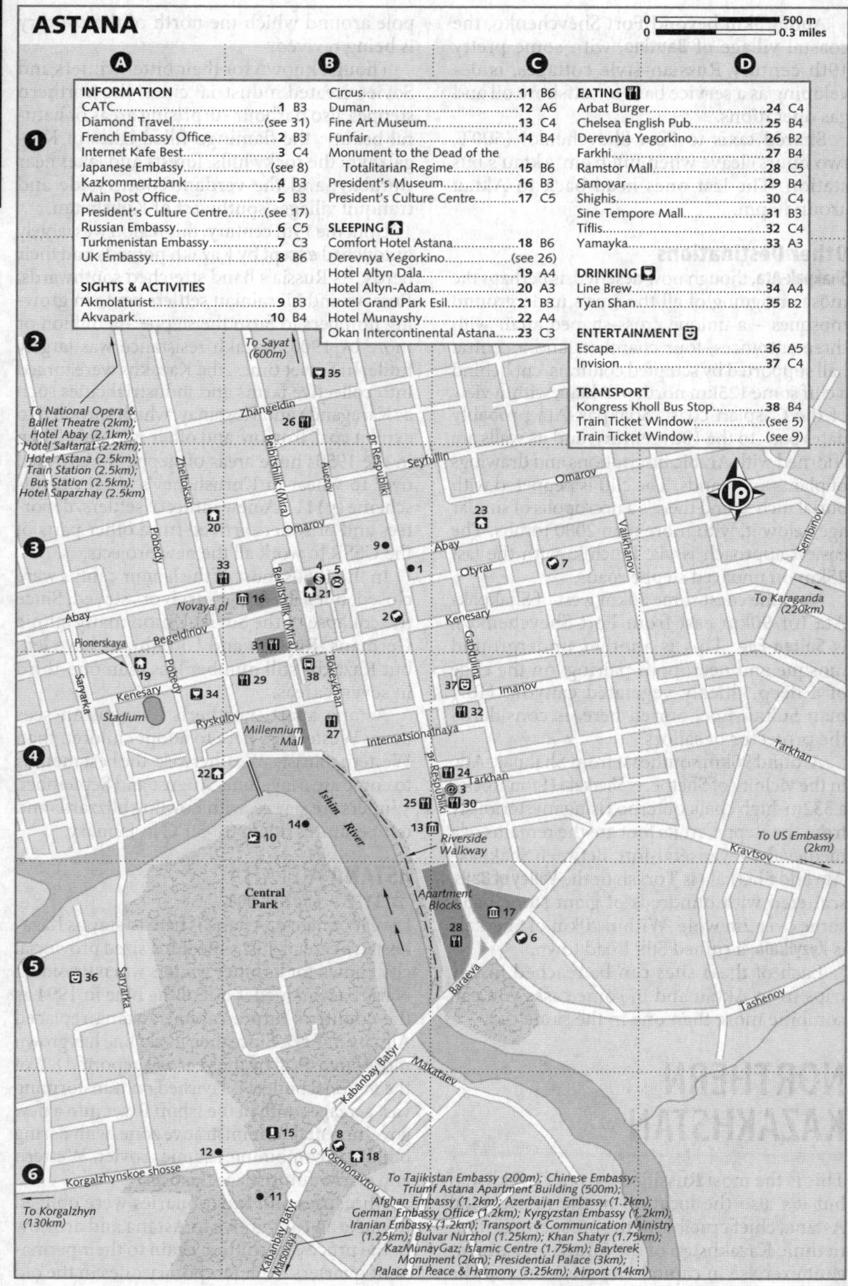
ASTANA
0 500 m
0 0.3 miles
INFORMATION
CATC 1 B3
Diamond Travel (see 31)
French Embassy Office 2 B3
Internet Kafe Best 3 C4
Japanese Embassy (see 8)
Kazkommertzbank 4 B3
Main Post Office 5 B3
President's Culture Centre (see 17)
Russian Embassy 6 C5
Turkmenistan Embassy 7 C3
UK Embassy 8 B6
SIGHTS & ACTIVITIES
Akmolaturist 9 B3
Akvapark 10 B4
Circus 11 B6
Duman 12 A6
Fine Art Museum 13 C4
Funfair 14 B4
Monument to the Dead of the Totalitarian Regime 15 B6
President's Museum 16 B3
President's Culture Centre 17 C5
SLEEPING
Comfort Hotel Astana 18 B6
Derevnya Yegorkino (see 26)
Hotel Altyn Dala 19 A4
Hotel Altyn-Adam 20 A3
Hotel Grand Park Esil 21 B3
Hotel Munayshy 22 A4
Okan Intercontinental Astana 23 C3
EATING
Arbat Burger 24 C4
Chelsea English Pub 25 B4
Derevnya Yegorkino 26 B2
Farkhi 27 B4
Ramstor Mall 28 C5
Samovar 29 B4
Shighis 30 C4
Sine Tempore Mall 31 B3
Tiflis 32 C4
Yamayka 33 A3
DRINKING
Line Brew 34 A4
Tyan Shan 35 B2
ENTERTAINMENT
Escape 36 A5
Invision 37 C4
TRANSPORT
Kongress Kholl Bus Stop 38 B4
Train Ticket Window (see 5)
Train Ticket Window (see 9)
To Sayat (600m)
To National Opera & Ballet Theatre (2km); Hotel Abay (2.1km); Hotel Saltanat (2.2km); Hotel Astana (2.5km); Train Station (2.5km); Bus Station (2.5km); Hotel Saparzhay (2.5km)
Zhangeldin
Seyfullin
Omarov
Abay
Otyrar
Kenesary
Imanov
Internatsionalnaya
Tarkhan
Kravtsov
Tashenov
Sembinov
Valikhanov
Gabdulina
pr Respubliki
Auezov
Beibitshilik (Mira)
Zheltoksan
Pobedy
Begeldinov
Pionerskaya
Saryarka
Ryskulov
Bokeykhan
Novaya pl
Stadium
Millennium Mall
Ishim River
Riverside Walkway
Central Park
Apartment Blocks
Baraeva
Kabanbay Batyr
Makataev
Kosmonavtov
Korgalzhynskoe shosse
Masovaya
To Karaganda (220km)
To US Embassy (2km)
To Korgalzhyn (130km)
To Tajikistan Embassy (200m); Chinese Embassy; Triumf Astana Apartment Building (500m); Afghan Embassy (1.2km); Azerbaijan Embassy (1.2km); German Embassy Office (1.2km); Kyrgyzstan Embassy (1.2km); Iranian Embassy (1.2km); Transport & Communication Ministry (1.25km); Bulvar Nurzhol (1.25km); Khan Shatyr (1.75km); KazMunayGaz; Islamic Centre (1.75km); Bayterek Monument (2km); Presidential Palace (3km); Palace of Peace & Harmony (3.25km); Airport (14km)

centre north of the river. Foreign embassies are still trickling in. The old centre, which retains a feel of the provincial city that it was, is due to live on as Astana's commercial and cultural centre when the new government complex is fully operational: the target date is 2030, by which time Astana will boast a population of over a million.

Astana has undergone several identity changes since it was founded in 1830 as a Russian fortress called Akmola (a Kazakh name meaning either 'white tomb' or 'white plenty'). When Nikita Khrushchev announced his Virgin Lands scheme, Akmola became the project's headquarters and was renamed Tselinograd (Virgin Lands City) in 1961. After the USSR collapsed, Akmola got back its old name, and would have kept it if Nazarbaev's plan to shift the capital here hadn't attracted such unfavourable comments. Cynics jibed that Akmola would be the president's own political 'white tomb'. Thus the place became simply Astana – Kazakh for 'capital'. Reasons cited by Nazarbaev for the change were Astana's more central and less earthquake-prone location than Almaty, and better transport links with Russia.

Some people find Astana impersonal, and compare the poverty in which some Kazakhs still live with the billions spent on fantasy architecture. But many Kazakhstanis are clearly proud of their new capital, and as an exercise in nation building its merits are obvious. It's a fascinating process to witness.

## Orientation

The old part of the city, north of the Ishim River (Yesil in Kazakh), is centred on the square at the south end of Beibitshilik (Mira). Most of the city's hotels, restaurants, shops and life are still north of the river, with Respubliki, running south to the main bridge over the Ishim, the liveliest zone. The new governmental hub of Kazakhstan is growing up south of the river (known portentously as the Levy Bereg or Left Bank).

The train and bus stations are side-by-side 3km north of the centre; the airport is 17km to the south.

## Information

### INTERNET ACCESS

**Internet Kafe Best** (☎ 21 11 67; Respubliki 8; internet per hr 300T; ⏲ 9am-2am) Lives up to its name with plenty of normally speedy computers, webcams and CD burning (200T).

**President's Culture Centre** (☎ 22 33 38; Respubliki 2; internet per her 200T; ⏲ 10am-7pm Mon-Sat) There's internet in the library here; bring your passport.

### MONEY

ATMs are available at banks, shopping malls and elsewhere. Foreign-exchange booths are dotted around the city, including at **Kazkommertzbank** (☎ 32 35 18; Abay 66; ⏲ 9.30am-5pm Mon-Fri), which changes travellers cheques. There's a Western Union window in the main post office.

### POST

**Main post office** (Auezov 71; ⏲ 8am-7pm Mon-Fri, 9am-6pm Sat, 10am-3pm Sun)

### TELEPHONE

Look for 'Peregovorny Punkt' signs to locate public phone offices. **Internet Kafe Best** (left) offers international calls for 30T to 50T per minute.

### TRAVEL AGENCIES

**CATC** (☎ 32 78 44; cat-astana@alarnet.com; Respubliki 30; ⏲ 9am-6pm Mon-Fri, 9am-1pm Sat) Air and train tickets, hotel bookings.

**Diamond Travel** (☎ 15 38 77; Sine Tempore Mall, Beibitshilik 9; ⏲ 10am-9pm) Airline-booking and travel agent.

## Sights & Activities

### NORTH OF THE RIVER

The gleaming, blue-domed **President's Culture Centre** (☎ 22 33 00; Baraeva 1; admission 90T; ⏲ 10am-6pm Tue-Sun) houses the high-quality main museum. The ground floor holds traditional Kazakh items – a brightly decked yurt, carpets, costumes, elaborate horse tackle. Upstairs you'll find the archaeological section, including models of some of the country's most important old buildings, and the Hall of Gold and Precious Stones, with the obligatory Golden Man replica. The 3rd-floor covers Kazakhstan's history from the 14th century on. Explanatory material is in English, Kazakh and Russian. Photos are not allowed.

The **Fine Art Museum** (☎ 21 54 30; Respubliki 3; admission 100T; ⏲ 10am-6pm Tue-Sun) is a little further up Respubliki. The small permanent collection includes some striking works and there are regularly changing temporary exhibitions.

The **President's Museum** (☎ 75 12 92; Beibitshilik 11, entrance on Abay; admission free; ⏲ tours 10.30am, noon, 2.30pm & 4pm Tue-Sun) is a fascinating peep into the pomp and circumstance surrounding the country's leader. Housed in the former presidential palace, it's a succession of supremely lavish galleries and halls decked with beautiful gifts to President Nazarbaev from foreign governments and grateful citizens. Check out the bank of Cold War–style direct-line phones in the antechamber to the presidential office itself. Tours are given in Russian but it's normally OK to stray from the group.

### SOUTH OF THE RIVER

The central park on the south side of the river (reachable by a footbridge from the south end of Zheltoksan) is home to an antiquated **funfair** and the gleaming modern **Akvapark** (☎ 39 12 20; admission before/after 4pm 400/500T; ⏲ 11am-8pm), with a good indoor pool with slides, and outdoor slides and pools open from around May to September. At the south end of the park, near Kabanbay Batyr, is the **Monument to the Dead of the Totalitarian Regime**, a mound with stark sculptures commemorating victims of Soviet repression. Close by is **Duman** (☎ 24 22 22; www.duman.kz; Kabanbay Batyr 4; admission 200T, oceanarium 1400T; ⏲ 10am-8pm Tue-Sun), Astana's noisy modern leisure centre, with a collection of unappealing cafés and bars, Rodeo, Gladiator and Sumo rides, a 3D cinema and – what makes it worth visiting – a state-of-the-art Oceanarium with 2500 marine creatures from around the globe and a 70m shark tunnel.

The UFO-shaped building opposite Duman is Astana's **Circus**. About 1.5km further along Kabanbay Batyr, the huge curved headquarters of the state energy company, **KazMunayGaz**, appears on the right (west), looking across a flyover and along the main showpiece axis of the new capital, 2km-long **Nurzhol bulvar**. The most daring of all Astana's architectural fantasies, the **Khan Shatyr** (see below), is going up behind KazMunayGaz.

First up on the north side of Nurzhol is the tall **Transport & Communications Ministry** – dubbed the 'Lighter' for its form by irreverent locals. Detour a block south here to the new **Islamic Centre** (⏲ 9am-8pm) with a beautiful four-minaret mosque. The mosque's interior is an exquisite multidomed space with inscriptions and geometrical patterning in blue, green, gold and red.

Many of the imposing and fanciful buildings along Nurzhol bulvar are still works in progress. But a line of central gardens and plazas leads inexorably to the 97m **Bayterek monument** (☎ 24 08 35; admission 500T; ⏲ 10am-10pm), a white latticed tower crowned by a large golden orb. The Bayterek embodies a Kazakh legend in which the mythical bird Samruk lays a golden egg containing the secrets of human desires and happiness in a tall poplar tree, beyond human reach. A lift glides visitors up to the inside of the golden egg, where you can ponder the symbolism, enjoy expansive views

### ASTANA, CAPITAL OF FANTASY

First, sharks hatch out 3000km from the nearest ocean (in Astana's Oceanarium). Now, winter is turned to summer. Any Kazakhstanis still unconvinced that their country was a miracle in the making had to think again at the announcement in 2006 of Astana's most fantastical project, the Khan Shatyr.

Astana already had a President's Culture Centre that is stylistically part-yurt, part-mosque; it has egg-shaped domes and green conical towers along Nurzhol bulvar; it has a throwback to pure Stalin-Gothic in the Triumf Astana apartment building on Kabanbay Batyr; it has the Bayterek monument resembling a giant soccer World Cup trophy; and it has a 61m glass-and-steel pyramid called the Palace of Peace & Harmony. Now it's getting the nearest thing to a real Xanadu-style 'pleasure dome' that humanity has ever created.

The **Khan Shatyr** (www.khanshatyr.com) will be an enormous, transparent, leaning, tentlike structure, 150m high, made of a special heat-absorbing material that will produce summer temperatures inside even when it's -30° outside. Due to open in 2008, this is to be a minicity with squares, streets, beaches, canals, shopping mall, gardens, cinemas, restaurants, pavement cafés, swimming and wave pools, beach volleyball, a concert hall and even a small golf course. Like the Palace of Peace & Harmony, the Khan Shatyr is designed by celebrated British architect Norman Foster.

This is not likely to be the last Astana surprise Nazarbaev has up his sleeve. Also planned are a 'Harvard of the Steppes' university for 35,000 students, a 390m bullet-shaped centrepiece tower of blue glass, and 740 sq km of parks and forests on previously empty steppe.

and place your hand in a print of President Nazarbaev's palm looking eastward to the giant new **presidential palace**. The tall pyramid behind the palace is the glass-and-steel **Palace of Peace & Harmony**, home for the triennial Congress of World and Traditional Religions, hosted by Kazakhstan.

Bus 18 comes to Nurzhol bulvar from the Kongress Kholl stop in the city centre, and bus 28 come from Respubliki.

## Tours

Travel agency **Sayat** (☎ 39 51 13; Druzhby 13) has a kiosk (open supposedly 9am to 7pm) outside the train station where you can join daily two-hour city tours in Russian costing 500T. **Akmolaturist** (☎ 33 08 12; tourist.astanainfo.kz; Office 22, Hotel Abay, Respubliki 33) offers a range of city tours lasting two to three hours with English-speaking guides for 24,000T to 31,000T per minibus, or 9260T to 11,100T for guide if you provide the transport.

## Sleeping

Hotel prices in Astana are high. The more economical lodgings cluster near the train and bus stations. The information desk in the train station ticket hall has a list of private apartments *(kvartiri)* available from around 4000T per day. Some are within a few blocks of the station and you can look at them before deciding.

**Hotel Astana** (☎ 93 28 97; Gvardeyskoy Divizii 310; dm 1200-1500T, s/d 5200/6000T) Inside the west end of train station building, the Astana is charmless but clean. The dorms have up to six beds and shared bathrooms.

**Hotel Saparzhay** (☎ 38 11 36; Gvardeyskoy Divizii; s 2000T, d 2000-6000T) Dreary digs upstairs in the bus station, though the receptionists are friendly enough. Rooms have toilets but showers cost 200T.

**Hotel Abay** (☎ 93 32 96; Birzhan-Sala 3A; s 5000T, d 4600-10,000T; ❄) Decent lodgings 1½ blocks out the front of the train station, just inside a small sidestreet. The rooms are a little worn but good-sized, with phone, bathroom and TV. For under 12 hours, you pay half-price.

**Hotel Saltanat** (☎ 38 31 21; Akzhayyk 17; s/d 5000/6000T) The Saltanat, 500m from the train station (turn left at the intersection with the large Opera & Ballet Theatre), has neat, decent-sized rooms, recently decorated in pastel shades – half-price for under 12 hours.

**Hotel Altyn-Adam** (☎ 32 71 34; fax 32 23 54; Seyfullin 26; r 7000-12,000T) A good modern hotel where the rooms have nice touches such as oil paintings, shoe-cleaning gear and glassed-in showers. The beds in the cheaper rooms are a bit of a squeeze for two. Almost 50% off for stays under 12 hours. Breakfast is included.

**Hotel Munayshy** (☎ 32 53 43; fax 32 51 81; Irchenko 14; r 10,000-15,000T; ❄) Little Munayshy has a great location overlooking the river. The dozen rooms are comfy, with satellite TV, breakfast and there's a billiard room for your idle moments. This is another half-day/half-price establishment.

**Hotel Altyn Dala** (☎ 32 33 11; altyn_dala@mail.kz; Pionerskaya 19A; s 11,000-14,000T, d 14,000-25,000T) This excellent hotel, tucked down a short street a block west of Novaya ploshchad, has cosy rooms with solid wood furniture, and a courteous reception desk. Rates include both breakfast and lunch. It's advisable to ring ahead as its 70 places can be full.

**Derevnya Yegorkino** (Yegorkino Village; ☎ 32 35 54; Auezov 93; r 13,000-21,000T; ❄) A charming boutique inn straight out of an old Russian fairytale, Yegorkino is upstairs from the restaurant of the same name. The colourful quilts, sink-into armchairs and carved wooden furnishings are quite unlike Astana's standard business hotels. Includes breakfast.

**Comfort Hotel Astana** (☎ 22 10 22; www.comforthotel.kz; Kosmonavtov 60; s/d 20,160/30,240T; ❄ 💻) South of the river, the cosy, two-storey Comfort lives right up to its name. With quiet lobby lounge, international restaurant, gym and attentive, professional service it's a tasteful retreat from the city hustle. Rates include breakfast.

**Hotel Grand Park Esil** (☎ 59 19 01; www.grandparkesil.kz; Beibitshilik 8; s/d 21,850/24,955T; ❄ 💻 🏊) This recently-upgraded, classically elegant hotel is right in the centre. Breakfast is included.

**Okan Intercontinental Astana** (☎ 39 10 00; www.ichotelsgroup.com; Abay 113; s/d from US$309/367; ❄ 💻 🏊) Astana's most prestigious and biggest hotel, with plush rooms, several restaurants and health club with indoor pool. Breakfast included.

## Eating

**Arbat Burger** (Respubliki 10A; dishes 300-700T; 🕑 10am-2am) Great Turkish café doling out doners, chicken fingers, burgers, *pides* and tempting sweets.

**Shighis** (Respubliki 8; dishes 300-800T; 🕑 9am-4am) A popular evening hangout for 20s and teens, Shighis also serves fast food slowly all day.

**Samovar** (☎ 32 43 16; Kenesary 24; mains 500-900T; 24hr) Cheerful Russian restaurant-café where helpful, red-silk-shirted waiters serve a good range of fare from breakfasts, *bliny* (pancakes) and soups to lunch and dinner mains.

**Yamayka** (Jamaica; ☎ 32 35 69; Abay 51; mains 500-900T; noon-4am) The unlikely prospect of Jamaican food in Astana is a reality here, along with Russian, Mexican and Southeast Asian dishes, eaten under grass huts and on colourful plates. Or choose the more mod second room with nightly live music.

**Chelsea English Pub** (☎ 21 77 27; Respubliki 7; mains 900-2700T; noon-2am) Less a pub than a restaurant with pub décor. Nor does it have English beer or much footy on the TVs. But it does serve international edibles from pasta and salads to fish and steaks, in a congenial ambience.

**Tiflis** (☎ 22 12 26; Imanov 14; mains 1000-2500T; noon-2am) This upscale Georgian restaurant has gone all out with its décor, right down to the mock wood porches, hay carts and waitresses decked out in traditional robes. The Georgian food is pretty good too.

**Farkhi** (☎ 32 18 99; Bökeykhan 3; mains 1000-2500T; noon-1am) Excellent Kazakh and Uzbek food and good service, in a beautifully decorated yurt-shaped building, with a nice garden for summer.

**our pick** **Derevnya Yegorkino** (☎ 32 38 78; Auezov 93; mains 1000-3000T; noon-midnight) Astana's most inviting restaurant has two floors and a garden area in authentic Russian-village style with heavy carved doors and ivy-covered timber shacks. It serves lovely Russian salads, fried field mushrooms, sturgeon sautéed in wine, and sweet pancake desserts. The cigars and Moldovan wine are a plus. It's the best place in town and an experience in itself.

**Sine Tempore Mall** (Beibitshilik 9; 10am-9pm) and **Ramstor Mall** (Respubliki 1; 9am-11pm) carry quality foods, including pricey Western imports, and have Western-style cafés good for snacks and drinks (600T to 1330T for good pizzas at Sine Tempore).

## Drinking

**Tyan Shan** (☎ 31 44 95; Auezov 28; 24hr) From 5pm to 8pm Wednesday the matrons serve all-you-can-drink beer at this expat hang-out, as long as you buy 1000T worth of food (and can put up with the ear-battering live music).

**Line Brew** (☎ 23 63 73; Kenesary 20; 0.5L beer 800T; noon-2am) You can't miss Line Brew's extraordinary, red-brick castle building. And the interior is, well, like the inside of a castle, with a tavern atmosphere. The beers are Belgian, and there's good food too.

Local teens and 20s hang out in the evening in several cafés and bars in the 'Arbat' area on Respubliki, including Arbat Burger and Shighis (p163).

## Entertainment

**Escape** (☎ 24 37 91; Saryarka 3; women/men 1000/1500T; 11pm-5am) The hippest club in Astana, with House and fast techno on the main stage, R&B, rap and hip-hop on the second. Situated in the Kaspy sports complex.

**Invision** (☎ 51 64 07; City Cinema, Imanov 13; admission 500-1500T; 10pm-4am) Another two-hall club, more popular with a teenage crowd.

**National Opera & Ballet Theatre** (☎ 39 27 60; Akzhayyk 10) This theatre stages plenty of world classics.

## Getting There & Away

From the **airport** (☎ 77 77 77), Air Astana flies daily to Almaty (20,300T), Aktau (24,300T) and Atyrau (29,200T), and twice or more weekly to Aqtöbe (24,200T), Kyzylorda (13,000T), Pavlodar (6500T), Ust-Kamenogorsk (12,000T), Petropavlovsk (5500T), Semey (9000T), Uralsk (22,000T) and Taraz (13,000T). SCAT flies daily to Shymkent (18,000T) and has further flights to Aqtöbe and Atyrau. International flights go to Amsterdam (Air Astana), Frankfurt (Air Astana and Lufthansa), Hanover (Air Astana), Istanbul (Turkish Airlines), St Petersburg (Pulkovo Airline), Tashkent (Uzbekistan Airlines), Kiev (Um Air) and Moscow (Air Astana and Transaero). There are air ticket offices at window No 10 in the **train station** (9am-6pm) and at the **Hotel Abay** (Respubliki 33; 8am-8pm).

From the **train station** (☎ 93 21 00; Gvardeyskoy Divizii), trains go to Karaganda (1500T, four hours) at least 10 times daily, Almaty (5300T, 13 to 21 hours) at least six times, Kokshetau (600T to 1700T, five hours) at least three times and Pavlodar (1400T, 8½ hours) at least twice. There are also services to Semey, Shymkent, Aqtöbe, Atyrau, Aktau, Petropavlovsk, Omsk and Moscow. The speedy, comfortable, overnight Talgo train to Almaty (13 hours), train 2, leaves at 7.15pm, costing 9400/15,800T in 3rd/2nd class. There are train ticket windows in the **main post office** (Auezov 71; 9am-1pm & 2-

6pm Mon-Sat, 9am-3pm Sun) and at **Hotel Abay** (Respubliki 33; 8am-8pm).

From the **bus station** (☎ 38 11 35; Gvardeyskoy Divizii), buses and marshrutkas run to many destinations in northern, eastern and southern Kazakhstan, including Karaganda (630T, 4½ hours, 12 or more daily), Kokshetau (1000T, five hours, 10 daily), Pavlodar (1350T, seven to eight hours, six daily), Semey (2200T, 15 hours, five daily) and Ust-Kamenogorsk (3100T, 19 hours, three daily). Shared taxis to Kokshetau and Karaganda wait outside the bus station.

### Getting Around

Bus 10 (30T) runs every 15 to 30 minutes between the bus station and the airport (a one-hour trip), via Akzhayyk, Beibitshilik, Seyfullin, Respubliki and Kabanbay Batyr. A taxi between the airport and the centre is about 1500T. Buses 21, 25 and 31 run from the train station to the Kongress Kholl (Congress Hall) stop in the city centre, then south on Respubliki at least as far as Ramstor. Buses stop running about 11pm. Taxis around the central area cost 200T to 300T (400T or 500T at night).

## AROUND ASTANA

About 150km southwest of the capital, **Korgalzhyn Nature Reserve** includes both virgin feather-grass steppe and numerous lakes which make it a water-bird habitat of major importance, with more than 300 species recorded. It lies at the crossroads of two major migration routes. Between April and September, salty Lake Tenghiz supports a large breeding colony of pink flamingos – the world's most northerly habitat of these graceful birds, which migrate to the Caspian Sea during winter.

The small town of Korgalzhyn, just east of the reserve, has a community ecotourism programme with comfortable **homestays** (per person room-only 800T, incl 3 meals 2125-2500T) in local homes, and guided bird-watching trips outside the reserve itself but still with plenty of lakes and interesting birdlife (guides cost around 400T per hour). Contact the EIRC in Almaty (p117) or the NGO **Rodnik** (☎/fax 316-372 10 43; oorodnik@mail.ru; Madina 20, Office 5; 9am-6pm Mon-Fri) in Korgalzhyn. Akmolaturist (p163) has cabins in the reserve and offers three-day guided visits for 148,000T for groups of five (206,000T for groups of 10), including accommodation, meals and transport from Astana.

Four buses or minibuses run daily from Astana bus station to Korgalzhyn (350T, 2½ hours). A taxi is 4000T (you might find one going on a shared basis for 1000T per person).

## LAKE BURABAY ОЗЕРО БУРАБАЙ

☎ **31630**

Situated 250km north of Astana, the Burabay area has been termed the 'Kazakh Switzerland', although the mountains qualify only as steep hills. The dense pine woods, strange rock formations and scattered lakes, however, are in stark contrast to the surrounding flat steppe. Apart from being a nice place to relax, Burabay is good for hiking, rock climbing or cross-country skiing in winter. Things might change, however: under government plans announced in 2006, Burabay is due to become one of two towns where all Kazakhstan's casinos are to be concentrated (the other is Kapshagay).

The gateway to the lake district is the tongue-twister town of Shchuchinsk. Lake Burabay is 20km north, with the village of **Burabay** (Russian: Borovoe) on its eastern shore. Here you'll find a rustic **Nature Museum** (Kenesary; admission 120T; 10am-6.30pm Tue-Sun), 1km south of the central taxi stand, with a small zoo housing two Przewalski's horses, a pair of huge maral deer, and a few bears and wolves in pitifully small cages. At the north end of the village the Burabay National Park begins at a road barrier marked Sanatori Borovoe. From here it's a pleasant 3.6km walk along the north-shore road to **Okzhetpes**, a striking 380m-tall rock pile between the lake and the tallest peak hereabouts, the 947m Kokshe.

The formation of Okzhetpes is explained by a legend that also covers **Zhumbaktas**, the Sphinx-like rock that pokes out of the water in front of it. While Abylay Khan's army was fighting the Zhungars, a beautiful princess was captured and brought to Burabay. It was decreed that she should marry a Kazakh. The princess agreed, saying whoever could shoot an arrow to the top of Okzhetpes could have her hand. All her potential suitors failed the first time, hence the name Okzhetpes which means 'Unreachable-by-Arrows'. But on a second attempt her true love hit the target. His rivals were so angry that they killed him. The distraught princess flung herself into the lake, thus creating Zhumbaktas (Mysterious Stone).

A short footpath heading north from Okzhetpes leads to a point where both Lake Burabay and the neighbouring, larger Lake Bolshoe Chebachye can be seen.

### Sleeping & Eating

Several good new hotels have popped up recently. It's also fairly easy to find private apartments or rooms (around 1000T per person): in summer *babushkas* (old women) hang around the taxi stand offering these.

**Baza Otdykha Akmolaturist No 1** (☎ 317-233 02 07; Kenesary; s 2000-2500T, d 3500-4000T) By the roundabout at the entrance to Burabay from Shchuchinsk, 2km south of the central taxi stand, this little place provides cosy rooms for up to six people, with a kitchen and clean shared bathrooms. Meals are available for an extra 1500T per person. It's best to book through Akmolaturist in Astana (p163).

**Baza Otdykha Akmolaturist No 2** (☎ 317-233 02 07; Shorsa 7; s/d wooden chalet 3300/5300T, ste full board 13,500/15,500T) Choose between very comfy big rooms or neat wooden cabins. All rates include breakfast. Again, best to book through Akmolaturist (p163).

**Hotel Aq Bulaq** (☎ 7 27 39; Kenesary 6; r without/with meals 6000/7500T) A good small hotel, with billiards and sauna, located two blocks east of the main street, towards the north end of town. In the summer season full board is obligatory (11,000T for two).

**Hotel Nursat** (☎ 7 13 01; bereke2030@mail.ru; Kenesary 26; r 7000-12,000T) This excellent red-brick hotel, almost opposite the Nature Museum, has bright, comfy rooms with quirkily stylish bathroom fittings, plus one of Burabay's better restaurants (mains 400T to 700T).

**Kafe Alina** (☎ 7 20 20; Kenesary 23; mains 300-550T; 🕑 9am-1am) The most inviting little eatery in town, done out in pinks and purples and serving a decent range of salads and meat dishes.

You'll find several cafés and beer-and-shashlyk places – some open-air and summer-only – around the taxi stand.

### Getting There & Away

Marshrutkas to Burabay village go from Astana bus station (900T, four hours, 9am and 11am) and from Kokshetau bus station (300T, 1½ hours, three times daily). Otherwise, go to Shchuchinsk and get a taxi (shared 150T to 200T, whole cab 500T to 1000T) or marshrutka (70T) from there to Burabay. From both Astana (800T, 3½ hours) and Kokshetau (250T, one hour) at least 15 daily buses and marshrutkas go to Shchuchinsk; quicker shared taxis are 2000T and 600T respectively. There are also about six daily trains from both places: Shchuchinsk's station is officially called Kurort-Borovoe.

## KOKSHETAU КОКШЕТАУ

**☎ 3162 / pop 125,000**

Though one of the country's least affluent cities, Kokshetau, 290km north of Astana, is a friendly and pleasant enough jumping-off point for the community-ecotourism homestays located in a pretty rural area to its southwest, or for Lake Burabay. Have a stroll around the central area between Abay and Auezov, where you'll find the main governmental buildings and several green park areas.

Contact the NGO **Ekos** (☎/fax 26 64 60; akmol-ekos@mail.ru; Chapaeva 37) at the west end of town to set up a trip to the **ecotourism villages** of Ayyrtau, Imantau or Sandyktau, about 80km to 100km southwest of Kokshetau. The main attraction here is the experience of village life amid unspoiled countryside with lakes, woodlands, rocky hills and walking and riding routes, green from spring to autumn. The **homestays** (per person with 0/1/2 meals 2060/2600/3000T) are mostly in modernised village homes, with friendly families. Guides cost 360T per hour, horses 1500T to 2000T per day, and local taxis 40T per kilometre. A 48-hour visit normally adds up to between 9000T and 18,000T per person in total. Buses from Kokshetau bus station run about five times daily to Imantau, 10 times to Sandyktau and 10 times to Saumalkol, 20km northwest of Ayyrtau (there are no buses to Ayyrtau itself). It's a ride of about two hours, costing 300T, to any of the three places.

### Sleeping & Eating

**Hotel Kokshetau** (☎ 25 64 92; Abay 106; s 2300-4300T, d 4800-6800T; 💻) This Soviet-era hotel has dowdy rooms and a smoky smell throughout, but some of the most helpful and friendly staff in the country – plus an internet café.

**Hotel Zhekebatyr** (☎ 26 61 19; zhekebatyr@mail.ru; Auezov 184; s/d from 6500/8800T; 🍴) The best hotel, with comfy modern rooms sporting satellite TV, a restaurant, and a sauna with spring-fed pool. Breakfast is included.

**Novinka Fast Food** (Kuybysheva; dishes 165-550T; 🕑 10am-11pm) Bright Turkish café with the best pizzas in town, good pastries and no alcohol.

**Kafe Classic** (☎ 25 87 27; Abay 89; mains 500-800T; ⌚ 11am-2am) Neat central restaurant with art on the walls and an outdoor terrace, serving good salads and meat dishes.

### Getting There & Away

Kokshetau has four weekly flights to/from Almaty (24,500T). The train and bus stations are at the end of Abay, 2km east of the centre. At least three daily trains go to Astana (600T to 1700T, five to six hours) and Petropavlovsk (1500T, four hours). Cheaper but equally dawdly buses go at least 10 times daily to both places. There's also a daily bus service to Pavlodar (14 hours) and Omsk, Russia (10 hours). Bus 1 (25T) runs between the stations and town centre; a taxi is 250T.

## PETROPAVLOVSK ПЕТРОПАВЛОВСК

☎ 3152 / pop 200,000

Just 60km from the Russian border, Petropavlovsk is as much a part of Siberia as of Kazakhstan and has a high Russian population. It's older and architecturally more diverse than many places in Kazakhstan.

### Orientation & Information

The train and bus stations are west of the centre on Ruzaeva, at the west end of Internatsionalnaya which is the city's central axis. Konstitutsia (formerly Lenina), tree-lined and pedestrianised for much of its length, parallels Internatsionalnaya two blocks north. The main north–south streets are Mira and Zhambyl Zhabaev (not to be confused with Zhumabaev, two blocks further east).

**Main post office** (Pushkina) Opposite the Drama Theatre; has good high-speed internet.

### Sights & Activities

The city **art museum** (Auezov; ⌚ 10am-5pm), located between Internatsionalnaya and Universitetskaya, is housed in an attractive wooden villa that once belonged to a rich timber merchant. The collection includes modern and traditional paintings, and collections of *netsuke* (small wooden carvings), household objects and icons.

The **local museum** (☎ 46 20 97; Konstitutsia 48; admission 50T; ⌚ 10am-5.30pm Wed-Sun), in a sturdy red-brick building near the corner of Auezov, traces Petropavlovsk's growth from its origins as a Cossack fort.

The Ishim River flows 2km east of the centre. Take trolleybus No 2 along Internatsionalnaya. On the way you'll pass the handsome, onion-domed **Russian Orthodox church**, surrounded by pretty gingerbread-style Russian cottages.

### Sleeping & Eating

**Hotel Kyzyl Zhar** (☎ 46 11 84; cnr Auezov & Konstitutsia; s/d from 2500/4500T) A central location, clean rooms and friendly staff make this the best option in town.

**Hotel Kolos** (☎ 33 69 00; Internatsionalnaya 82; r from 3000T) A five-minute walk west of the Domino Theatre, this hotel has plain but clean rooms with TV and phone.

**Doner Restaurant** (Internatsionalnaya 27; dishes 200-400T; ⌚ 9am-11.30pm) Near the corner with Zhumabaev, this Turkish café serves good kebabs, burgers and pizzas, and excellent desserts.

**Slavyansky Dvor** (Konstitutsia 52; mains 500-1000T; ⌚ noon-midnight) Set in a period brick building opposite the central park, this charming bistro serves excellent fish, salads and French wine amid heavy wood tables and iron fixtures.

### Getting There & Around

There are flights to Almaty (24,500T) via Kokshetau four times weekly, and to Astana (5500T) twice a week. The airport is a 15-minute taxi ride (800T) from the centre.

Trains go at least three times daily to Kokshetau (1500T, four hours), at least twice to Astana (3200T, 9½ hours) and once or more to Almaty (8000T, 31 hours). For Russia there are daily trains to Omsk (4½ hours), Yekaterinburg (Sverdlovsk; 10 to 13 hours) and Moscow (41 to 46 hours). Rail schedules here are on Moscow time (two hours behind Astana time in summer, three hours in winter).

There are around 10 daily buses to Kokshetau (800T, three hours) and five to Astana (2100T, eight hours) from the **bus station** (☎ 33 03 69), and plenty of taxi drivers willing to do a deal on rides to Kokshetau.

It's about a 20-minute walk from the stations to the centre, or take trolleybus 2 or 4 (27T) along Internatsionalnaya.

## KARAGANDA КАРАГАНДА

☎ 3212 / pop 410,000

Smack in the steppe heartland, 220km southeast of Astana and 1000km northwest of Almaty, Karaganda (Kazakh: Qaraghandy) is famous for two things: coal and labour camps. The two are intimately connected, as the big 'KarLag' network of Stalin-era camps around Karaganda was set up to provide slave labour for the mines. At its peak the KarLag system extended over an area larger than France. Prison labour also built much of Karaganda itself, which was founded in 1926.

Mining in the area continues today, with the remaining mines owned by the Indian-owned, Europe-based Mittal Steel, to feed its steelworks at Temirtau, 25km north of Karaganda.

Karaganda's population has shrunk by 100,000 since the Soviet collapse, with many ethnic-German residents (descendants of Stalin-era deportees) departing for Germany. But it's a pleasant city, with avenues of trees and a large central park providing greenery, and the downtown revived with shopping malls, cafés and restaurants.

## Orientation

The train and bus stations are beside each other at the south end of the city centre. Bukhar Zhirau (formerly Sovietsky), the main street, heads north through the centre from here, flanked by several shopping malls, with the spacious central park to its west. Parallel to Bukhar Zhirau are Voynov-Internatsionalistov (one block west), and Yerubaev and Gogol, one and two blocks east.

## Information

**CATC** (☎ 41 28 26; cat-karaganda@alarnet.com; Office 29, Bukhar Zhirau 55) Good agency for flight tickets. The entrance is from the Qaynar shopping centre on Voynov-Internatsionalistov.

**Gogol Library** (☎ 56 76 55; Yerubaev 44; 9am-6pm) The 'American corner' upstairs has internet and English-speakers. Also internet on the ground floor.

**Internet Kafe Traffik** (Bukhar Zhirau 46; internet per hr 210-270T; 9am-9pm) Efficient, comfortable place with a fax service too.

## Sights & Activities

The **Karaganda Ecological Museum** (☎ 41 33 44; www.ecomuseum.freenet.kz; Bukhar Zhirau 47; admission unguided/guided 100/300T; 9am-7pm Mon-Sat), run by a dedicated environmental NGO, has to be the most imaginative museum in the country. Everything can be touched and this includes large rocket parts that have fallen on the Kazakh steppe after Baykonur space launches, and debris collected from the Semey Polygon (p175). The guided tours, available in English, are well worth it. The entrance is beneath an 'Ortalyqkazzherqoynany' sign at the side of the building. The museum can also arrange tours to sites of ecological interest/problems in Kazakhstan, including Lake Balkhash, the Semey Polygon and Baykonur Cosmodrome, with English-speaking guides. Typical price: US$60 to US$90 per person per day.

The renovated **Karaganda Oblast Museum** (☎ 56 31 21; Yerubaev 38; admission 200T; 9am-6pm) includes a Russian-language video of the town's history, plus a section on Gulags. Guided tours (300T) in English or Russian add significantly to the interest.

In winter you can ice-skate at the **Shakhter Stadium** (northern Bukhar Zhirau; per 2hr 200T; noon-10pm Fri-Sun) – real local fun!

## Sleeping & Eating

**Lyux-Otel Gratsia** (☎ 41 24 59; fax 41 24 43; Voynov-Internatsionalistov; s/d with shared shower 1600/3200T, r with bathroom 4400-6000T) Good-value budget place with comfy, quite bright rooms. It's a blue-painted building behind the City Mall shopping centre.

**Hotel Karaganda** (☎ 42 52 04; Bukhar Zhirau 66; r 2200-9000T) With a convenient central location and a range of rooms at different prices, this suits many people. It's nothing fancy but adequate. Rooms have hot water, telephone and TV.

**Hotel Chayka** (☎/fax 41 53 26; Krivoguza; s 4300-6700T, d 6500-8000T, VIP r 14,000-16,500T) Plush hotel built in 1982 for the Soviet-era elite including cosmonauts and rock stars, and still in fine nick. Rooms have balconies, satellite TV, soft furnishings and include breakfast. It's just north of the central park.

**Bon Appetit** (Abzal shopping centre, mid-Bukhar Zhirau; mains 120-450T; 10am-9pm) Bright, spacious eatery in the back of the Abzal. Offerings range from *manty* and strogonoff to pizza and spaghetti. Try the tasty Korean soup *kuksi*.

**Johnnie Walker Pub** (☎ 41 19 08; Bukhar Zhirau 36; dishes 750-2200T; noon-1am) Haggis in Karaganda? This Scottish pub serves burgers, steaks, fish and chips and of course the Scottish national dish.

## Entertainment

**Fabrick** (☎ 56 11 21; Loboda) and **Klondayk** (cnr Mira & Gogol) are stylish clubs playing a mix of Russian and Western dance music. Entry ranges from 1000T to 2000T.

**Dvorets Kultury** (Bukhar Zhirau 32) This ornate blue theatre is the top venue for ballet, opera and concerts.

### Getting There & Around

Karaganda has daily flights to/from Almaty (19,000T), plus flights to Moscow four times weekly, and weekly flights to Frankfurt and Hanover by Air Astana.

The **train station** (☎ 43 36 36) has services to Almaty (4100T, nine to 17 hours) at least seven times daily; Astana (1500T, four hours) at least nine times; and to Pavlodar, Kokshetau, Petropavlovsk, Taraz and Shymkent at least daily. The Talgo Astana–Almaty fast train (p164) stops here but tickets don't go on sale until two hours before departure.

Destinations served from the **bus station** (☎ 43 18 18) include Astana (630T, 4½ hours, hourly, 7am to 7pm), Pavlodar (1600T, eight hours, six daily), Almaty (2800T, 20 hours, one daily) and Semey, Shymkent and Ust-Kamenogorsk (all daily). Minivans (1000T) and shared taxis (1500T) outside the bus station will whisk you to Astana in 2½ hours.

Trolleybus 1 and bus 26 run north along Bukhar Zhirau from the stations.

## AROUND KARAGANDA

At **Spassk**, the site of a KarLag camp 35km south of Karaganda, is a huge mass prisoners' grave beside the Almaty highway, with eerie groups of three crosses scattered around the site and monuments installed in the 1990s by countries whose nationals died here (including France, Japan, Poland, Latvia and Lithuania). A taxi there and back should cost around 1500T from Karaganda.

**Dolinka** village, 35km southwest of Karaganda, was the administrative headquarters for the whole KarLag system. The old officers' club is now the village's main shop and a modest **KarLag Museum** (☎ 321-565 82 22; admission free; ⏲ 9am-6pm Mon-Fri) is housed in the old KarLag hospital. Marina Ivanovna, the museum's director, should be able to show you round the now-empty headquarters building, with its basement holding cells. Get to Dolinka by Shakhtinsk-bound bus 121, leaving Karaganda bus station about every 10 minutes. Get off at the Vtoroy Shakht stop after about 45 minutes (130T), take a taxi into Dolinka (200T, 1.5km) and ask for the *muzey* (museum).

# EASTERN KAZAKHSTAN

Ust-Kamenogorsk, a relatively prosperous regional capital, is the gateway to the Altay Mountains – one of the most beautiful corners of Kazakhstan but one for which you need to plan ahead because a border-zone permit is required (see p172).

The region's other main city, Semey, is one of Kazakhstan's most historically interesting places but suffers from the effects of Soviet nuclear testing in the nearby Semipalatinsk Polygon.

## UST-KAMENOGORSK (ÖSKEMEN) УСТЬ-КАМЕНОГОРСК (ӨСКЕМЕН)

☎ 3232 / pop 320,000

Ust-Kamenogorsk (Kazakh: Öskemen), 800km north of Almaty, is a fairly lively city with generally low-key Soviet architecture, at the confluence of the Irtysh and Ulba Rivers. Founded as a Russian fort in 1720, Ust-Kamenogorsk has grown from a small town since the 1940s when Russians and Ukrainians began arriving to mine and process local copper, lead, silver and zinc. These industries still keep the city out of the economic doldrums, but are bad news for air quality: Ust has a high rate of respiratory infection.

### Orientation

Central Ust-Kamenogorsk is focused on pretty Park Kirova. The main streets are Ushanova, running north from the Irtysh bridge to the bustling bazaar; Kirova, two blocks west; and Ordzhonikidze, which crosses them both leading to the main bridge across the Ulba. Across the Ulba, Ordzhonikidze splits into Abaya and Lenina. The bus station is a short distance along Abaya, while the main train station, Zashchita, is 5km northwest along Lenina, and the airport 4km further in the same direction.

### Information

**Altai Expeditions** (☎ /fax 24 57 09; altai_expeditions@dvn.kz; Office 115, Gorkogo 46) Run by experienced, enthusiastic, English-speaking Andrey Yurchenkov, Altai Expeditions offers a big range of active trips and nature tours in the Altay, plus day trips to a Bronze Age astronomical complex and other intriguing sites outside Ust-Kamenogorsk. Email for the current trip list: a wide-ranging two-week Altay tour, for example, starts at around US$700 per person.

**Pushkin Library** (☎ 26 13 33; www.pushkinlibrary.kz; Ushanova 102; internet per hr 180T; 🕑 9am-6pm Tue-Sun) You can access the internet on the ground floor or in the American Culture Center or German information centre upstairs.

**Rakhmanovskie Klyuchi** (☎ 55 21 00; www.altaytravel.ru; Tikhaya 11) This travel firm owns the Rakhmanovskie Klyuchi health resort (p172) near Mt Belukha, and offers foot and horse treks in the Altay, plus rafting, skiing and snowboarding elsewhere in the region.

## Sights

Clustered around pretty **Park Kirova** (🕑 7am-7pm) are some of Ust-Kamenogorsk's oldest buildings and several worthwhile museums. The **Ethnography Museum** (admission per branch 100T); Korpus No 1 ☎ 26 85 29; Uritskogo 67; 🕑 10am-5pm Tue-Sun); Korpus No 2 ☎ 26 31 59; Gorkogo 59; 🕑 9am-6pm), with traditional costumes, carpets, musical instruments, yurts and icons, is in two buildings facing corners of the park. The good **History Museum** (☎ 25 54 60; admission 150T; Uritskogo 40; 🕑 9am-5pm) has a ground-floor natural history section with stuffed regional wildlife including a snow leopard and a giant Maral deer (the antlers of which are considered an aphrodisiac in Korea), and interesting history exhibits upstairs that reveal a huge number of old burial mounds in the region. In the northern part of the park itself is a replica **Russian pioneer village** (admission 50T; 🕑 variable) of log cabins, furnished and decorated in period style.

It's nice to take a walk beside the Irtysh or Ulba to the **Strelka**, where they meet, marked by a large Heroes of the Soviet Union memorial.

## Sleeping

**Hotel Irtysh** (☎ 25 29 12; fax 25 09 85; Auezova 22; r 2500-12,000T; ) With its range of rooms at different prices, this place fits the bill for most travellers. All rooms are adequately comfortable and have at least shower, phone and cable TV. Rates include breakfast. The receptionists are amiable, and the hotel also offers currency exchange, ATM, business centre, restaurant, 24-hour café and air ticket office.

**Hotel Ust-Kamenogorsk** (☎ 26 18 01; fax 26 16 03; Proletarskaya 158; s/d 4500/7000T) This is similar to Irtysh, but less welcoming.

**Shiny River Hotel** (☎ 27 25 25; fax 27 14 18; Solnechnaya 8/1; s 9500-23,000T, d 12,500-27,000T; ) New in 2006, this excellent hotel overlooks the Ulba with tasteful, modern rooms, and a classy, expensive restaurant (main dishes around 2000T). English is spoken, and breakfast is included.

**Hotel De Luxe** (☎ 24 09 93; alex2000@ukg.kz; Uritskogo 28A; s/d 16,500/20,500T; ) This brand-new, 17-room hotel was on the verge of opening at the time of research and is sure to be a good-quality option.

## Eating

**Maslenitsa** (☎ 25 09 00; Uritskogo 117A; dishes 100-400T; 9am-11pm) The house speciality, meat-and-cheese-stuffed *bliny* are unique in this neck of the woods. It's a trendy place under the same ownership as the equally popular Pizza Blues, and does a big choice of soups, salads and main dishes.

**Doner** (dishes 200-400T) Kirova (☎ 26 87 04; Kirova 49; 9am-10pm); Ushanova (Ushanova; 10am-10pm) Colourful and busy Turkish café serving doners, burgers, shish kebabs and good Middle Eastern sweets: you may have trouble finding a lunchtime seat at the downtown branch.

**Pitstsa Blyuz** (Pizza Blues; pizzas 300-700T; 11am-11pm) Gorkogo (☎ 24 81 67; Gorkogo 56); Lenina (☎ 27 11 01; Lenina 1); Ushanova (☎ 25 23 66; Ushanova 64) Highly popular local chain serving pretty good pizza and salads, and great cakes, in clean, bright surroundings. Upstairs at the Ushanova branch is Kofe Blyuz, a coffee lounge with free wi-fi.

**Stary Tbilisi** (☎ 25 63 92; Krasnykh Orlov naberezhnaya 117A; dishes 800-1000T; 11.30am-1am) Pretty Georgian restaurant decorated with grapevines over stone and brick walls. Especially nice in summer when you can sit outside facing the Ulba.

The two best supermarkets, both well stocked, are **Supermarket Daniel** (Abaya 1/1; 24hr) and **Kolos** (Auezova 15; 24hr).

## Entertainment

### SPORT

**Olympik Bouling** (Krylova 93; per game 500T; 3pm-4am Mon-Fri, 1pm-4am Sat & Sun) A fun hang-out with 10 lanes, this claims to be the biggest bowling centre in Kazakhstan.

From September to April, don't miss **Kazzinc Torpedo** (www.kazzinc-torpedo.kz) at the **Dvorets Sporta** (☎ 27 22 50; Abaya 2; admission 250-300T). One of the top ice hockey teams in the former Soviet Union, Torpedo have produced a number of NHL players. They play in both the Russian and Kazakhstan championships. Look for posters outside the stadium: face-off is usually at 6.30pm.

### NIGHTCLUBS

**Mega** (☎ 57 00 00; Kirova 31; admission 1000T; 8pm-5am) This popular club plays Russian pop in between the techno, and they spray foam to dance in every once in a while. The floor has a raised platform in the centre and bars at the sides.

**Takhami** (Auezova 47; from 7pm) With lots of chrome and an illuminated red dance floor, Takhami attracts singles as well as couples and is good for meeting people. Mainstream pop and dance music starts around 11pm.

**Staver** (☎ 25 29 27; Hotel Irtysh, Auezova 22; women/men 300/500T, Fri & Sat 1000T; from 10pm) Disco-bar with a reasonably mature crowd including couples, playing mainly Russian and Western pop. Some nights there are dance shows.

## Getting There & Away

From the **airport** (☎ 42 84 84) there are daily flights to Almaty (18,500T to 25,000T), four a week to Astana (12,000T) and two to Moscow. SCAT flies to Bayan-Ölgii, Mongolia (14,000T), on Wednesday. Buses 2 and 39 run to the airport from Auezova in the centre. A taxi costs around 1000T. A good ticket agency is **CATC** (☎ 25 28 50; cat-oskemen@alarnet.com; Uritskogo 123).

From the **bus station** (☎ 27 26 26; Abaya) buses and marshrutkas run several times daily to Semey (900T, four hours), and a few times to Astana (3100T, 19 hours), Almaty (3100T, 22 hours), Katon-Karagay (900T, nine hours), Pavlodar (2100T, 13 hours), Barnaul (2400T, 12 hours) and Novosibirsk (3600T, 17 hours). Shared taxis to Semey from the bus station cost 2000T – most leave in the morning.

Buses to China also go from the bus station. At the time of research there was a daily service to Ürümqi (3500T, 15 hours) crossing the border at Bakhty east of Makanchi, and a bus at 6pm Wednesday and Sunday to Altay, China (4725T, 24 hours) via the border at Maykapshagay. Ticket office staff say these buses are open to third nationalities, but you should double-check, and make sure you have all necessary paperwork.

Ust-Kamenogorsk's main train station is **Zashchita** (☎ 40 87 37). The main line heads north into Russia to meet the Semey–Novosibirsk line, with trains every two days to Barnaul and Novosibirsk. It takes at least 11 hours to reach Semey this way and you need a Russian visa and possibly a double-entry Kazakh visa to do so, so it's much better to go by road. For trains heading south, get a bus (400T, three hours) or shared taxi (1200T) from Ust-Kamenogorsk bus station to the train station at Zhangyztobe, 150km southwest. From here trains leave for Almaty (16 to 18 hours) at noon and 7.45pm (subject to change). You can buy tickets for these at Ust-Kamenogorsk's **train ticket offices** (Uritskogo 80 ☎ 25 70 96; 8am-6pm Mon-Sat, 8am-4pm Sun; Lenina 4 ☎ 27 28 77; 8am-7pm). Coming from the south by train, get off at Zhangyztobe and you'll find Ust-Kamenogorsk–bound taxis and maybe buses waiting there.

### Getting Around

From outside the bus station, trams 1, 2, 3 and 4 (20T) run to Ordzhonikidze and Ushanova on the east side of the Ulba; buses 6, 8 and 35 (40T) will take you to Auezova for the Hotel Irtysh.

## ALTAY MOUNTAINS АЛТАЙ

In the far eastern corner of Kazakhstan the magnificent Altay Mountains spread across the borders to Russia, China and, only 50km away, Mongolia. At the time of research you still needed a border-zone permit (see opposite) to go beyond the village of Uryl in the Bukhtarma Valley, or to visit the Markakol Nature Reserve to the south.

The hassle of getting to this sparsely-populated region is well worth it. Rolling meadows, snow-covered peaks, forested hillsides, glaciers, pristine lakes and rivers, an array of archaeological sites and rustic villages with Kazakh horsemen riding by make for scenery of epic proportions. Asian legends refer to 4506m Mt Belukha, a twin-headed peak on the Kazakh–Russian border, as Shambhala, 'a paradisal realm that will be revealed after humanity destroys itself'.

Due to the permit requirements and scarcity of public transport, it makes sense to visit the area with the help of a good travel company such as Altai Expeditions or Rakhmanovskie Klyuchi (p169). These firms can obtain the border-zone permit for you in 30 to 45 days for around US$15 to US$20. Speedier processing (10 to 12 days) may be possible for around US$50.

### Rakhmanovskie Klyuchi

The charming health resort of Rakhmanov's Springs is 30km up a mountain track from the village of Berel and 450km from Ust-Kamenogorsk (a 10- to 12-hour drive). It was built in the 1960s by a mining company, but is now privately owned by the Rakhmanovskie Klyuchi company (p169). You'll find wooden cottages, some with kitchen, linked by boardwalks through pine forests, nestling in a mountain valley. This is the perfect base for exploring the Altay valleys, mountains, rivers, lakes and passes. Mt Belukha can be seen from the Radostny Pass, a one-hour walk up from the resort. From July to September the resort offers a variety of one- to two-week group horse and foot treks, and ascents of Belukha, costing from €160 to €360 per person. Check with the company about shorter trips. In winter there's cross-country skiing.

Accommodation per person per day, including meals, runs from 5200T to 19,500T depending on the room, plus around 7500T for bus or minibus transport there and back. There are packages for 12-day stays.

Near Berel you can visit the Scythian burial mounds where in 1997 archaeologists discovered the amazingly preserved body of a 4th-century BC prince, buried with several horses and carriages.

### Lake Markakol

This beautiful 38km-long lake is at the heart of the Markakol Nature Reserve, south of Katon-Karagay village. The lake, 1500m above sea level and surrounded by forests and 3000m-plus mountains, is noted for its pure waters and is a great winter ice-fishing spot. Altai Expeditions (p169) specialises in trips here, with fishing and horse trekking among the possibilities. In summer the lake can be

**ABAY, CULTURAL GURU**

Writer, translator and educator Abay (Ibrahim) Kunanbaev (1845–1904) was born on the northern fringe of the Shyngghystau hills south of Semey. Son of a prosperous Kazakh noble, he studied both at a medressa in Semey and later in a Russian school there. This education opened him to ideas far beyond the traditional Kazakh compass. His later translations of Russian and other foreign literature into Kazakh, and his public readings of them, as well as his own work such as the philosophical *Forty-one Black Words,* were the beginning of Kazakh as a literary language and helped broaden Kazakhs' horizons.

Abay valued Kazakh traditions but was also decidedly pro-Russian. 'Study Russian culture and art – it is the key to life,' he wrote. In Soviet times, Abay's reputation was 'officially licensed' by Moscow, and his Russophile writings were enshrined. Today he is the number one Kazakh cultural guru.

reached by the 'Austrian Rd', a hairy 4WD mountain track from Katon-Karagay, built by Austrian POWs during WWI. At other times access is by a much longer southern route via Kurchum, crossing the Bukhtarminsky Reservoir by ferry.

## SEMEY (SEMIPALATINSK) СЕМЕЙ (СЕМИПАЛАТИНСК)

**☎ 3222 / pop 292,000**

Semey, 200km down the Irtysh from Ust-Kamenogorsk, is sadly better known to the world by its Russian name Semipalatinsk. Between 1949 and 1989 the Soviet military exploded some 460 nuclear bombs in the Polygon, an area of steppe west of the city. Locals say they knew when tests were taking place because the ground would shake – often on Sunday morning. An unprecedented wave of popular protest, the Nevada-Semipalatinsk Movement, was largely instrumental in halting the tests in 1989. Short-term visitors are not considered to be at any risk, however the bomb effects live on: radiation has taken a severe toll on the health of many thousands of people in Semey and beyond (see p111).

Despite its Soviet-generated sufferings, Semey is one of Kazakhstan's more interesting cities. Set in the territory of the Middle Horde, noted for their eloquence and intellect, the city and area have produced several major Kazakh writers and teachers, notably the national poet Abay Kunanbaev (1845–1904). In 1917 Semey was the capital of the short-lived Alash Orda independent Kazakhstan government.

Like Ust-Kamenogorsk, Semey was founded, in 1718, as a Russian fortification against the Zhungarians. In the 19th century, writer Fyodor Dostoevsky was among several democracy-minded Russian intellectuals who spent years of exile here. Their presence spurred a flowering of arts and learning among educated local Kazakhs.

Semey today is one of Kazakhstan's more economically depressed cities, but the centre is steadily brightening up with new stores and restaurants. A multimillion-dollar suspension bridge across the Irtysh, funded with Japanese loans, gives the place a modern skyline.

### Orientation

The Irtysh flows northwestward across the city, with nearly everything of use or interest on its northeastern side. The main streets, slicing across town from southwest to northeast, are Shakarima and Internatsionalnaya ulitsa. The bus station is on Valikhanov three blocks northwest of Shakarima, next to the busy bazaar; the train station is just off the north end of Shakarima, 2km from the centre.

### Information

**Internet Tsentr** (Momyshuly 4; internet per hr 120T; 9am-10pm) Central internet access.

**Istok** (☎ 52 48 99, 333-3685554; istok@semsk.kz; Office 108, Lenin 4) Local environmental NGO; can organise tours of the area. English-speakers may be available.

**Shara** (☎ 52 48 71; shara@relcom.kz; Office 203, Shugaeva 4) Travel agency offering tours of the city and area with English-speaking guides for US$10 per hour plus transport.

### Sights

#### MUSEUMS

The big, domed **Abay Museum** (☎ 52 24 22; Lenin; admission 125T; 10am-12.30pm & 2-5pm) is dedicated to the 19th-century humanist poet Abay Kunanbaev (see boxed text, above). Along with displays about Abay's life, the museum has

sections on the Alash Orda government and his literary successors, including Mukhtar Auezov (1897–1968), author of the epic Kazakh novel *Abay Zholy* (The Path of Abay). Free guided tours are available, but in Russian or Kazakh only.

The well laid-out **Dostoevsky Museum** (☎ 52 79 42; Dostoevskogo 118; admission 100T; 9am-6pm Mon-Sat) is on a leafy street a block east of Abay ploshchad, built beside the wooden house where the exiled writer lived from 1857 to 1859 with his wife and baby. The museum displays Dostoevsky's life and works, covering his childhood in Moscow, residence in St Petersburg, five years in jail at Omsk, five years of enforced military service at Semey, and his creative life from 1860 to 1881. The rooms where he lived have been maintained in the style of his day, and the vast amount of images of Dostoevsky alone makes it worth a visit, even if you can't understand the mainly Russian text. Tours, in Russian or Kazakh, cost 150T.

The **History & Local Studies Museum** (☎ 52 07 32; Lenin 5; admission 100T; 9am-5pm Mon-Sat) has a small display on nuclear testing and the Nevada-Semipalatinsk Movement, material on regional history, and a collection of traditional Kazakh artefacts. Founded by Russian exiles in 1883, this claims to be the oldest museum in Kazakhstan.

The large **Fine Arts Museum** (Pushkin 108; admission 100T; 10am-5.30pm Tue-Sat) has some good works by Kazakh, Russian and Western European painters from the 16th century onwards, including a not-to-be-missed Rembrandt etching.

## OLD SEMEY

Looking somewhat forlorn on a concrete island beside Abay is one of the **fort gates** built in 1776, flanked by a couple of cannons. The blue-and-gold-domed Russian Orthodox **Voskresensky Sobor** (Resurrection Cathedral) stands 300m further along the street. This is the oldest part of Semey and the streets northeast of here have many old one-storey wooden houses.

The **Anet Baba Kishikuly Mosque** (Abay 48), 400m beyond the Fine Arts Museum, was built by Tatar merchants in the 19th century in distinctly Russian-influenced style. It boasts twin minarets and a pillared interior with a big chandelier. Bus 35 runs along here.

**IRTYSH RIVER**

There's a curious collection of **Communist statues** – a kind of graveyard of Lenin and Marx busts, presided over by the giant Lenin from the nearby square, northwest of the Hotel Ertis and past the Dastar cinema.

**Polkovnichy Island** is reached by the bridge next to Arlan Bowling on Abay. Just over 1km from the bridge on the left is a sombre yet grandiose **nuclear memorial** erected in 2002 for victims of the nuclear tests. The marble centrepiece of *Stronger than Death* is a mother covering her child; above billows a Polygon mushroom cloud etched into a 30m-high black tombstone.

## Sleeping

**Hotel Semey** (☎ 56 36 04; hotsemey@relcom.kz; Kabanbay Batyr 26; s/d with shared bathroom 1000/1600T, with private bathroom 3500/4800T or 5400/6000T) Hotel Semey has old-fashioned Soviet-style rooms but is well enough kept, even if hot water is only available a few hours a day. Reception staff may tell you that only the largest *'lyux'* rooms are available, but persistence will probably uncover a cheaper vacancy. There are two cafés and a restaurant.

**Hotel Ertis** (Hotel Irtysh; ☎ 56 64 77; Abay 97; s/d with shared bathroom 1500/2000T, s with private bathroom 3000T, d with private bathroom 4000-10,000T) A gloomy, 11-storey second choice if the Semey is full. No hot water for the cheap rooms.

**Hotel Binar** (☎ 52 39 34; fax 56 15 58; Lenin 6; s 4500-20,000T, d 6500-13,000T; ) This low-key, two-storey place is the cream of Semey's hotel crop, just a block from Abay ploshchad. The rooms are cosy, carpeted and well-furnished, and breakfast and use of the sauna is included in the price.

## Eating

**Istanbul Picnic** (☎ 56 08 89; Momyshuly 3; dishes 100-400T; 9am-11pm) This bright, popular, downtown Turkish café serves reasonably good doners, *plov*, shashlyk and vegetarian lentil soup.

**Kofeman** (☎ 56 55 38; Internatsionalnaya; dishes 150-600T; 10am-1pm) Semey's fashionable coffee lounge, also doing English and Mexican breakfasts, souvlaki, pasta and *bliny*. The latte is a true work of art!

**Traktir Yolki-Palki** (☎ 52 57 47; Ibraev 147; mains 400-850T; 9am-1am) Behind the heavy wooden street door are two relaxed, tavernlike rooms where you can enjoy traditional Russian cooking (including breakfasts) as well as a big variety of drinks.

**Restoran Eldorado** (☎ 52 58 42; Shakarima; mains 500-1000T; 10am-midnight) With a calm ambience and tasteful landscape paintings, this is one of the nicest places to eat. You can choose Chinese as an alternative to the mainly Russo-European fish and meat dishes.

## Entertainment

**Kafe Solyanka** (☎ 56 31 35; Baysetov 48; admission after 6pm 200-300T; 24hr) Vivacious café with a warm atmosphere and live pop musicians from 6pm. It's in the side of the larger Rahat Palace restaurant.

**Vostok** (Momyshuly; 11am-midnight) There's more live pop nightly at this popular teens-and-20s hang-out. Downstairs is an informal café; upstairs is a restaurant with 200T admission in the evenings.

## Getting There & Away

From the **airport** (☎ 44 36 77), 17km south of the city, there are five weekly flights to Almaty (16,000T) and three to Astana (9000T). **Avia Agentstvo** (☎ 56 57 69; Shakarima; 9am-6pm) sells air and train tickets.

From the **bus station** (☎ 52 09 25; Valikhanov), 12 daily buses and marshrutkas run to Ust-Kamenogorsk (800T to 1100T, five hours), four to Pavlodar (1200T, five to six hours), three to Astana (2200T to 2430T, 15 hours) and one to Taldyqorghan (1790T, 14 hours). Others go at least daily to Karaganda, Zaysan, Barnaul and Omsk. Quicker shared taxis to Ust-Kamenogorsk or Pavlodar gather here too.

The **train station** (☎ 98 32 32) has three or four daily departures to Almaty (3500T, 20 to 22 hours), and trains every two days to Pavlodar (1400T, eight hours) and Astana (2800T, 17 hours) and most days to Barnaul (4300T, 12 to 16 hours) and Novosibirsk (5600T, 16 hours).

## Getting Around

Buses 11 and 13 run from the train station to the centre along Shakarima. From the theatre on Abay ploshchad, bus 35 runs to the bazaar and bus 50 to the bus station.

# AROUND SEMEY

## Kurchatov

Kurchatov, 120km west of Semey and known locally just as Konechnaya (The End), was the command centre for the Semipalatinsk

Polygon. The nuclear testing zone itself stretched some 100km to 120km south and west from Kurchatov. Today, the semideserted town is home to Kazakhstan's **National Nuclear Centre** (Natsionalny Yaderny Tsentr; ☎ 322-512 33 33; www.nnc.kz; Lenina 6), which, among other things, works on the development of nuclear power in Kazakhstan.

Trains and buses go to Kurchatov from Semey, but unless you have organised it in advance you may have trouble getting into the gruesome **museum** (admission free; 9am-6pm Mon-Fri), the only real reason to visit the place. The museum has a model of the first test site, where aircraft, buildings, metro tunnels and live animals were placed close to 'ground zero' to test the explosion's effects. Animal parts are pickled in formaldehyde.

It would be very dangerous to enter the Polygon itself without special equipment including radiation suits and a Geiger counter, despite the fact that it is frighteningly unsupervised. Explosion sites and radiation hotspots are not marked and local people even wander over the area grazing livestock and collecting firewood.

Ask about the travel info for Kurchatov from the **Semey Akimat** (City Hall; ☎ 322-2526230, 52 30 04; Rm 436, Government House, Kozbagarov, Semey), Karaganda Ecological Museum (p168), the Ust-Kamenogorsk travel firm Altai Expeditions (p169) or the National Nuclear Centre (see above).

## PAVLODAR ПАВЛОДАР

**☎ 3182 / pop 330,000**

A further 320km down the Irtysh valley from Semey, on the road to Omsk in Russia, Pavlodar was developed as an industrial town in Soviet times. Its skyline is dominated by massive, rabbit-hole-style Soviet-era apartment blocks, but quiet Lenina on the western edge of town has pre-Soviet character and a few good museums.

The Irtysh forms the western boundary of the city, with the main street, Satpaeva, running parallel a couple of blocks east. Kutuzova, 1.5km further east, is another north–south axis. Toraygyrova runs across the north ends of both streets, continuing 300m east past Kutuzova to the bus and train stations.

### Sights

Pavlodar's not-to-be-missed sight is the **Mashhur Zhusip Mosque** (cnr Kutuzova & Krivenko), the biggest mosque in Kazakhstan, built in 2001. Looking like an intergalactic space station from a 1950s sci-fi film, it rises out of the city with rocketlike 68m-high minarets and a green dome shaped like Darth Vader's helmet. The attendants are welcoming and will show you the expansive main prayer hall (women must view this from the upper gallery).

The beguiling **Bogaev Museum** (☎ 32 12 10; Lenina 200; admission 50T; 9am-1pm & 2-6pm Mon-Fri), set in the one-storey wooden home of a local photographer and humanitarian, shows off early-20th-century photographs of life around Pavlodar. Bogaev (1884–1958) had a keen eye for traditional Kazakh culture, often hiding in bushes to capture his subjects. He won local fame for creating the city's first museum, and taking photos of young soldiers before they went off to war. Nearby, the **History Museum** (☎ 32 37 06; Lenina 147; admission 50T; 10am-6pm Tue-Sun) takes the Pavlodar story right through from sabre-tooth tigers to the latest religious architecture.

### Sleeping & Eating

**Hotel Sariarka** (☎ 56 18 27; Toraygirova 1; s 2200-7900T, d 4400-8300T) This 12-storey block overlooking the Irtysh has been modernised but it still has that old Soviet feel even though the staff are friendly enough and some speak some English. Still, all rooms have bathrooms with hot showers, and breakfast is included. There are four places to eat and an air-ticket office, too.

**Hotel Kazakhstan** (☎ 32 05 20; Satpaeva 71; r 4300-7800T) Has just 20 or so excellent, good-sized, renovated rooms with satellite TV, modern bathrooms and breakfast included. Two imposing black lions flanking the entrance enhance that secure feeling.

**Dilizhans** (☎ 32 12 73; cnr Yestaya & Frunze; pizza 250-700T; 24hr) Fast-food joint near the Hotel Kazakhstan with a fetish for road signs. You can chart your progress from Astana on the giant ceiling map.

**Café Africa** (☎ 32 45 11; Satpaeva 75; dishes 300-800T; 11am-1am) The ochre-painted walls and tribal art are tasteful, less so the caveman-style outfits worn by the waitresses. Still, this trendy locale between the Kazakhstan and Nurtau hotels is a pleasant oddity in Pavlodar, with platters full of spicy meat or fish. The hookahs are a bonus.

### Getting There & Around

There are daily flights to Almaty (23,200T) and a weekly flight to Moscow (37,000T).

Eight daily buses run to Semey (1200T, five to six hours), three continuing to Ust-

Kamenogorsk (2160T, 10 to 11 hours). Five go to Astana (1350T, seven to eight hours). Minibuses outside the train station offer quicker rides to Astana for 1500T.

Trains run at least twice daily to Astana (1400T, eight to nine hours), once or more to Almaty (6700T, 28 to 33 hours) and every two days to Semey (1400T, eight hours). There are also services to Omsk, Novosibirsk and Moscow (57 hours) in Russia.

City buses 10 and 22 run from the train and bus stations to Satpaeva.

# KAZAKHSTAN DIRECTORY

## ACCOMMODATION

The improving economy and large business-travel sector have brought the opening of many luxurious new hotels and the upgrading of many old ones, especially in cities touched by the oil boom. If you have US$50 to US$200 per night to spend on a room, you can enjoy comfortable, well-equipped, tasteful accommodation and good service. For budget travellers, unrenovated Soviet-built hotels are the main option. They're generally adequate but down-at-heel. Some cities have cheap dorms (*komnaty otdykha*, literally rest rooms) in their train stations.

One blessing is that some hotels, often better-class ones, offer discounts of up to 50% if you occupy the room for not more than 12 hours, a period known as a *pol-sutki*.

## ACTIVITIES

Southeast and East Kazakhstan, with their high mountains along the Kyrgyz, Chinese and Russian borders, offer the greatest outdoor excitement. There's good hiking, horse riding and even mountain biking in the Zailiysky Alatau south of Almaty (p130 and p134), in the central Tian Shan (p137 and further east, and in Aksu-Dzhabagly Nature Reserve (p146). From Lepsinsk (p139) you can hike in the Zhungar Alatau mountains, and further north are the gorgeously beautiful Altay Mountains (p172) on the Kazakh–Russian border. Ascents of Belukha in the Altay, and Khan Tengri and other peaks in the central Tian Shan, are superb challenges for climbers in July and August.

Skiers and snowboarders enjoy Central Asia's best facilities at the modern Chimbulak resort (p130) south of Almaty, from approximately November to April, with the famous giant outdoor ice-skating rink at Medeu nearby. Amazing summer heli-skiing is possible on the glaciers of the central Tian Shan.

Rafters can tackle the Ili River below Kapshagay (p138) and the Uba and Ulba Rivers near Ust-Kamenogorsk (p169). The delta where the Ili enters Lake Balkhash is the country's best and most varied fishing area, while Lake Markakol (p172) offers great winter ice-fishing.

Bird-watchers should make for Aksu-Dzhabagly Nature Reserve, the Zailiysky Alatau and the Korgalzhyn Nature Reserve (p165) – the world's most northerly flamingo habitat.

Some local agencies specialising in active tourism are listed on p117 and p169. The EIRC in Almaty (p117) is another good source of assistance.

### PRACTICALITIES

- Local broadcasting and press are in Russian and Kazakh, but TVs in better hotels often receive international satellite channels such as CNN and BBC World. Caspionet is a local channel with some (very dry) news in English.
- Local English-language papers such as the *Almaty Herald* and *Kazakhstan Monitor* are pretty thin on news.

## CUSTOMS

On arrival or departure you must fill in a customs declaration if you are carrying cash worth more than US$3000.

## EMBASSIES & CONSULATES

### Kazakhstan Embassies in Central Asia

Kazakhstan has embassies in Tashkent (Uzbekistan; p262), Bishkek (Kyrgyzstan; p345), Ashgabat (Turkmenistan; p436) and Dushanbe (Tajikistan; p392).

### Kazakhstan Embassies & Consulates in Other Countries

Kazakhstan's diplomatic missions abroad include the following (see www.mfa.kz for an updated list of all Kazakh embassies):

**Afghanistan** ( ☎ 020-70284296; sher@ceretechs.com; House 10, 10th St, Wazir Akbar Kham, Kabul)
**Azerbaijan** ( ☎ 12-465 6521; embassyk@azdata.net; 889-82 Hassan Aiev, Baku)
**Canada** ( ☎ 416-593 4043; www.kazconsul.ca; Suite 600, 347 Bay St, Toronto M5H 2R7)
**China** Beijing ( ☎ 10-6532 6182; www.kazembchina.org; 9 Dong 6 Jie, San Li Tun,100600); Visa & Passport office in Ürümqi ( ☎ 991-381 5796; kazpass@mail.xj.cninfo.net; Kunming Lu 31) Consulate in Shanghai ( ☎ 21-6275 2838; www.kazembchina.org; Room 1005/1006, Orient International Plaza, 85 Loushanguan Rd 200336)
**France** ( ☎ 1-4561 5200/06; www.amb-kazahstan.fr; 59 rue Pierre Charron, 75008 Paris)
**Germany** ( ☎ 030-4700 7111; www.botschaft-kasachstan.de; Nordendstrasse 14-17, 13156 Berlin) Consulates in Bonn, Frankfurt, Hanover and Munich.
**Hong Kong** ( ☎ 2548 3841; www.consul-kazakhstan.org.hk; Unit 3106, 31-fl, West Tower, Shun Tak Centre, 200 Connaught Rd Central, Sheung Wan)
**Iran** ( ☎ 21-256 5933; www.kazembassy-iran.org; 4 North Hedayat St, Corner of Masjed Alley, Darrus, Tehran)
**Japan** ( ☎ 03-3791 5273; embkazjp@gol.com; 9-8, Himonya 5-chome, Meguro-ku, Tokyo 152-0003)
**Mongolia** ( ☎ 97611-31 22 40; kzemby@mbox.mn; Dom Diplomatov 95-11 Mongol Uls, Ulaan Baatar)
**Netherlands** ( ☎ 070-361 6990; kazachstan-consul@planet.nl; Mauritskade 37, 2514 HE Den Haag)
**Pakistan** ( ☎ 51-226 29 25; embkaz@isb.comsats.net.pk; House 10, Street 19, F-8/2, Islamabad)
**Russia** Moscow ( ☎ 495-927 17 10; www.kazembassy.ru; Chistoprudny bulvar 3A, 101000) Consulate in Astrakhan ☎ 8512-25 18 85; www.kazembassy.ru; ulitsa Akvarelnaya 2B, Astrakhan; 414056) Consulate in Omsk ( ☎ 3812-32 52 13; kzconsul@omskcity.com; ulitsa Valikhanova 9); Consulate in St Petersburg ☎ 812-312 09 87; kazconsulspb@mail.ru; ulitsa Galernaya 11)
**Singapore** ( ☎ 65366100, 65361407; www.kazakhstan.org.sg; 10 Collyer Quay, 13-10/11 Ocean Building, Singapore 049315)
**UK** ( ☎ 020-7581 4646; www.kazakhstanembassy.org.uk; 33Thurloe Sq, London SW7 2SD) Consulate in Aberdeen ( ☎ 01224-622465; kazcon@btconnect.com; 10 N Silver St, Aberdeen AB10 1RL.
**USA** ( ☎ 202-232 5488; www.kazakhembus.com; 1401 16th St NW, Washington DC 20036)

## Embassies & Consulates in Kazakhstan

Many embassies have moved to Astana or are in the process of moving, and many of the others have representative offices there. Many countries are also maintaining consulates or offices in Almaty. In the following listings main missions are given first.

**Afghanistan** Astana (Map p160; ☎ 317-2242946; Diplomatichesky Gorodok C-10); Almaty office ( ☎ 327-292 79 42; af_embassyalmaty@yahoo.com; Rimskogo-Korsakova 8/1)
**Australia** (Map p114; ☎ 327-277 7879; gaslink@bigpond.com; 9th-fl, Al-Farabi 5/2A, Almaty)
**Azerbaijan** (Map p160; ☎ 317-224 15 81; www.azembassy.kz; Diplomatichesky Gorodok C-14, Astana)
**Canada** (Map p114; ☎ 327-250 11 51/52; geo.international.gc.ca/canada-europa/kazakhstan; Karasay Batyr 34, Almaty)
**China** Astana (Map p160; ☎ 317-224 13 90; fax 24 13 81; Diplomatichesky Gorodok 2); Almaty office (Map p114; ☎ 327-2700223; Baytasov 12)
**France** Almaty (Map p114; ☎ 327-258 25 04/08; www.ambafrance-kz.kz; Furmanov 173); Astana office (Map p160; ☎ 317-2580884; Respubliki 25)
**Germany** Almaty (Map p114; ☎ 327-250 61 55/57; www.almaty.diplo.de; Furmanov 173); Astana office (Map p160; ☎ 317-2241482; Diplomatichesky Gorodok C-12)
**Iran** Almaty (Map p114; ☎ 327-254 19 74; iranembassy@itte.kz; Lugansky 31-33); Astana office (Map p160; ☎ 317-224 25 11; Diplomatichesky Gorodok B-7)
**Japan** Astana (Map p160; ☎ 317-297 78 43; www.kz.emb-japan.go.jp/jp; 5th fl, Presidential Plaza Bldg, Kosmonavtov 62); Almaty office (Map p114; ☎ 327-298 06 00; Qazybek Bi 41)
**Kyrgyzstan** Astana (Map p160; ☎ 317-224 20 24; kr@mail.online.kz; Diplomatichesky Gorodok V-5); Almaty consulate (Map p114; ☎ 327-291 66 10; gen.consul.kz@mail.ru; Lugansky 30A)
**Mongolia** (Map p114; ☎ 327-220 08 65; monkaze@kazmail.asdc.kz; Aubakirov 1, Almaty) Near Kargalinka sanatorium.
**Netherlands** (Map p114; ☎ 327-250 37 73; www.nlembassy-almaty.org; Nauryzbay Batyr 103, Almaty)
**Pakistan** (Map p114; ☎ 327-273 35 48; parepalmaty@yahoo.com; Tölebaev 25, Almaty)
**Russia** Astana (Map p160; ☎ 317-222 2 483; www.rfembassy.kz; Baraeva 4); Almaty consulate (Map p114; ☎ 327-274 61 22; cons.rf@nursat.kz; Zhandosov 4) Uralsk consulate ( ☎ 311-2511626; rusconsul@nursat.kz; Oktyabrskaya 78)
**Tajikistan** Astana (Map p160; ☎ /fax 317-224 13 15; Marsovaya 15, Mikrorayon Chubary); Almaty office (Map p114; ☎ /fax 327-269 70 59; Sanatornaya 16, Mikrorayon Baganashyl) The Almaty office is in the south of the city: take bus 63 or marshrutka 526 or 537 south from Furmanov as far as the Vodozabornaya stop on Al-Farabi (the second stop after Kazgu, the state university). Walk west along Al-Farabi and turn left (south) at the traffic light after 100m. The consular section is 100m up this road, on the left-hand side.
**Turkmenistan** Astana (Map p160; ☎ 317-228 08 82; tm_emb@at.kz; Otyrar 64); Almaty consulate (Map p114; ☎ /fax 327-2509604; cnr Abay 76/109 & Auezov)

**POST-SOVIET NAME CHANGES**

Most Kazakh cities now have Kazakh names instead of their Soviet-era Russian names. In many cases these are close to the Russian (eg Almaty instead of Alma-Ata). Less obvious changes include Astana for Tselinograd, Aktau for Shevchenko, Taraz for Dzhambul and Atyrau for Guriev. In some cases, mostly in the north, Russian names have beaten off the Kazakh challenge: most people still talk of Uralsk, not Oral, and Ust-Kamenogorsk is more common than Öskemen. Semey is still routinely called Semipalatinsk by Russian-speakers.

Most city streets also have new Kazakh names. These may just be a Kazakhisation of a Russian name (eg Lenin köshesi instead of Lenina ulitsa) or they may be something completely different. Sometimes Kazakh and Russian appear side-by-side on street signs. To confuse things further, Russified spellings of new Kazakh names (eg Kabanbay for Qabanbay) are quite common too. Meanwhile, many local people continue to use the old Soviet names in any case.

In this chapter we use the names that are most commonly used.

**UK** Astana (Map p160; ☎ 317-255 62 06; www.britishembassy.gov.uk/kazakhstan; 6th fl, Renco Bldg, Kosmonavtov 62); Almaty Office (Map p114; ☎ 327-2506191; Furmanov 173)

**USA** Astana (Map p160; ☎ 317-2702100; www.usembassy.kz; Bldg 3, 23-22 ulitsa, Mikrorayon Ak Bulak 4) Almaty office (Map p114; ☎ 327-2507612; Zholdasbekov 97)

**Uzbekistan** (Map p114; ☎ 327-291 78 86, 291 02 35; fax 91 10 55; Baribaev 36, Almaty)

## FESTIVALS & EVENTS

The biggest festivities around the country are for Nauryz, the Muslim spring/equinox festival on 22 March, with traditional sports, music festivals and family get-togethers. Shymkent is a particularly good place to be for Nauryz (see p144). Around 10 to 15 August, a festival of traditional sports and foods is staged by Kazakh and Kyrgyz livestock herders in the remote Karkara valley east of Almaty.

## HOLIDAYS

**1 & 2 January** New Year.
**7 January** Russian Orthodox Christmas.
**8 March** International Women's Day.
**22 March** Nauryz (see p450).
**1 May** Unity Day.
**9 May** Victory Day.
**30 August** Constitution Day.
**25 October** Republic Day.
**16 December** Independence Day.
**Variable** Qurban Ait (Islamic Feast of Sacrifice; the last day of the Haj pilgrimage to Mecca).

## INTERNET ACCESS

All medium-sized and bigger cities have public internet facilities, charging generally 150T to 300T per hour. Just here and there you'll find a café or bar with wi-fi access.

## INTERNET RESOURCES

**Caspian Information Centre** (www.caspianinfo.org) News and research on Kazakhstan.

**Kazakhstan Embassy in London** (www.kazakhstanembassy.org.uk) Has a range of information on the country and some helpful links.

**UNDP** (www.undp.kz) Good resource on varied topics.

**Unesco** (www.unesco.kz) Unesco's Almaty office is its Central Asia headquarters and this site has many useful links.

## MAPS

The best source of topographical maps of Kazakhstan's regions is GEO in Almaty p116).

## MONEY

Prices in this chapter are given in the currency they are normally quoted in – usually tenge (T) but occasionally US dollars or euros.

You will find changing, extracting and wiring money easier in Kazakhstan than anywhere else in the region. ATM cards are definitely the way to go. There are machines in every city and most small towns – at banks, shopping centres, supermarkets, hotels and some train stations. Look for 'Bankomat' signs. Most accept Maestro, Plus, Cirrus, Visa and MasterCard, with instructions in English. Kazkommertsbank, Halyk Bank and Turan Alem Bank all have widespread ATMs.

You can make purchases with credit cards (Visa and MasterCard preferred) at a fair number of shops, restaurants, hotels and travel agencies. There is often a surcharge for doing so.

Bring a little cash (euros or US dollars) to start out and as a fallback if you run out of tenge. Exchange offices (marked 'Obmen Valyuty') are common on city streets.

You can change travellers cheques (denominated in US dollars or euros; Amex is the most widely accepted brand) for a 2% fee (usually with a US$2 minimum) at some banks. Kazkommertzbank and Halyk Bank are most dependable.

Tenge notes and coins are 10,000, 5000, 2000, 1000, 500, 200, 100, 50, 20, 10, five, two and one.

At the time of research, exchange rates were as follows:

| Country | Unit | | Tenge |
|---|---|---|---|
| Australia | A$1 | = | 105T |
| Canada | C$1 | = | 116T |
| China | Y1 | = | 17T |
| euro zone | €1 | = | 177T |
| Japan | ¥10 | = | 11T |
| Kyrgyzstan | 1som | = | 3T |
| New Zealand | NZ$1 | = | 92T |
| Pakistan | Rs 10 | = | 22T |
| Russia | R10 | = | 51T |
| UK | UK£1 | = | 262T |
| USA | US$1 | = | 128T |
| Uzbekistan | 100S | = | 10T |

## POST

Airmail letters under 20g to anywhere outside the CIS cost 150T. A 2kg parcel of books by surface/airmail costs around 2600/4500T (depending on the destination).

If you have anything of importance to post it's generally safer and quicker to use an international courier firm. **DHL** (www.dhl.com) has a particularly wide network of drop-off centres around the country.

## REGISTRATION

The aggravating requirement to register your passport with the migration police (OVIR) has been effectively done away with for most travellers in Kazakhstan. For the 28 nationalities on the 'economically developed and politically stable' list (see opposite), registration may be carried out when visas are issued at a Kazakhstan embassy or consulate, and *all* nationalities should have their passports automatically registered at the country's international airports, at Aktau port, and at land borders (although you may have to insist at smaller border points). Two entry stamps (one is not enough) on your migration card are the indication that registration has taken place and is valid for 90 days. If for some reason you don't get registered on arrival and you are staying more than five days, you need to register within five calendar days of entering. Many hotels and travel agencies can do this for you for a fee of US$20 to US$30, or you can spend time going to the local office of OVIR where registration is free.

Unfortunately the rules are open to different interpretations and while very few travellers experience any problems, the only 100% watertight way of avoiding them is to register, which is easy in most main cities except Almaty, where OVIR has even refused to register passports, saying it is not necessary.

Check the latest situation when you get your visa and again when you reach Kazakhstan.

## TELEPHONE & FAX

You can make phone calls for cash from some Qazaqtelekom offices, from call offices signed 'Peregovorny Punkt', and from some shops and kiosks with phones for public use. From a Qazaqtelekom office or *peregovorny punkt*, local calls are generally free, while other calls within Kazakhstan cost 10T to 25T per minute, calls to Kazakhstan mobile numbers and other ex-Soviet states around 50T per minute, and other international calls are 200T to 300T per minute.

To use a street phone *(taksofon)*, you need a *taksofon* card *(taksofonaya karta)*, sold at some newsstands, kiosks and Qazaqtelekom offices. These cost around 130/250/350T for 25/75/125 units. On local calls you get about one minute per unit. Slot the card into the phone, wait till the display stops changing, then dial your number. Important: when the number answers, press the button next to the lips symbol so that they can hear you.

For long-distance calls, dial the long-distance prefix ☎ 8 before the country code (if it's an international call), city code and local number. If you're calling another town in the same *oblys* (14 administrative regions), replace the first three digits of the city code with a ☎ 2.

You can cut costs for long-distance and international calls by using a Nursat i-Card or a Luxtelecom card, mostly sold at shops and kiosks selling mobile-phone cards (of which there are many). With these cards you scratch clear a PIN on the back, then dial a local access number given on the card. Instructions are then available in English.

You can't use these cards on street phones; you *can* use them from private phones, some hotel rooms, mobile (cell) phones and usually call offices and kiosks. Nursat i-cards cost 700T, 1400T or 2100T: calls cost about 20T per minute to Kazakhstan mobile phones, 30T to other Kazakhstan and ex-Soviet numbers, 35T per minute to the UK, US, Canada or Germany and 125T per minute to most other places.

Almost everyone in Kazakhstan has a mobile phone. Mobile numbers have 10 digits and to call them you must dial the long-distance access code, ☎ 8, first. To use your own mobile in Kazakhstan, get it unlocked for international use before you leave home, then it will cost 1000T to 2000T to get a new SIM card activated by a Kazakhstan mobile-phone network such as Beeline, Kmobile or KCell. Mobile-phone offices and shops are everywhere. You add credit by buying cards with PINs or through some ATMs.

Calls from hotel rooms are typically double the call-office rate.

Fax services are available from some Qazaqtelekom offices and internet cafés, and many hotels. Sending a one-page fax typically costs 50T to 100T within Kazakhstan and around 250T to Europe or North America.

## TRAVEL PERMITS

Special permits (sometimes called a *propusk*) are needed for sensitive border areas in eastern Kazakhstan, notably the Altay Mountains, Lepsinsk and Khan Tengri. Tour agents should be able to arrange such permits, if their services are used to visit the restricted areas, but processing can take up to 45 days.

Entry to some national parks and nature reserves also requires a permit, usually arranged quickly through the local park office, for a fee of 200T to 300T.

## VISAS

One-month, single-entry tourist and business visas can usually be obtained at Kazakhstan consulates or embassies *without* a letter of invitation (LOI) if you are from any of 28 'economically developed and politically stable' countries: the EU pre-enlargement 15 plus Australia, Canada, Iceland, Japan, Liechtenstein, Malaysia, Monaco, New Zealand, Norway, Singapore, South Korea, Switzerland and the USA. Required documentation usually includes your passport (not a photocopy), a letter from you explaining the purpose of your visit, a photo and an application form available from the Kazakhstan Foreign Ministry website (www.mfa.kz – go to 'Consular Information') and often on embassy websites. A few consulates, such as Shanghai, still insist on genuine hotel bookings, in which case it will be easier to obtain an LOI.

For visas of more than one month or more than one entry, or if you are not from one of the 28 countries mentioned above, you must obtain 'visa support' in the form of a LOI. This is available through many travel agencies in Kazakhstan (see p117), Central Asia specialist travel agencies in other countries or Kazakh businesses that are organising your visit. In your application to the embassy or consulate you need to submit your invitation's official reference number, and often a copy of the invitation itself (fax or email copies are fine). Allow two to three weeks to obtain the LOI before you apply for the visa itself. Agents' fees for obtaining LOIs normally range from around US$30 to US$70 depending on the visa required (more for urgent processing).

Fees for the visa itself vary from one consulate to another. A single-entry, one-month tourist visa, for example, costs UK£23 in London, €27 in Madrid and US$105 in Washington. Urgent processing is usually available at extra cost.

Single-entry, one-month visas are also available with an LOI on arrival at Almaty, Astana, Atyrau, Uralsk and Ust-Kamenogorsk airports. Fees, payable in cash (US dollars), are US$40 to US$70 for a tourist/business visa. A photograph will be required and a form has to be filled in on the spot. When you request an LOI from a travel agency for this purpose, tell them why: not all agencies can provide LOIs suitable for visas on arrival.

Transit visas for up to five days in the country are available for US$25 on arrival at Almaty airport if you can show an original onward air ticket (no LOI needed). It's best to verify this regulation before departure. At Kazakh embassies and consulates, transit visas may be issued based on air or train tickets into and out of the country and an onward visa: fees range from UK£13 in London to US$95 in Washington.

Some consulates, including those in London and Washington, will deal with visa applications by mail; others may require you to apply for and collect your visa in person. Processing time at consulates in the West is normally three to five working days.

Kazakhstan's visa rules are modified from time to time. Recommended travel agents and websites of Kazakhstan embassies and its Foreign Ministry usually have up-to-date information.

If you are in a country without a Kazakhstan embassy or consulate (such as Australia, Ireland, New Zealand or Sweden), you can apply to Kazakh missions in other countries – London and Washington are usually the best bets. Visa agents will do the legwork for fees of around US$50 to US$70 per visa plus courier charges and the visa-processing costs. To save money, consider getting visas in countries en route to Central Asia.

See 'Visas for Onward Travel' in other countries' Directory sections in this book for information on obtaining Kazakhstan visas in other Central Asian countries. In Baku (Azerbaijan), one-month, single-entry tourist visas are issued the same day for US$40. The Kazakh embassy in Ulaan Baatar, Mongolia, is best avoided as it charges particularly high fees. Travellers report that one-month Kazakh tourist visas cost around US$30 in China. Most recent information is that the embassy in Beijing is open for applications from 9am to noon on Monday, Wednesday and Friday. Go just before 9am with your passport, a photocopy and one photo, and you should be able to pick up the visa at 4.30pm the same day. In Ürümqi it may be possible to get visas the same day, or you may have to go back next time the office opens (normally only for a few hours twice a week). The Ürümqi office also has a habit of moving.

## Copies

You are supposed to carry your passport with your visa in it, and your migration card, at all times to show to police or military on demand. To avoid the security problems of always carrying these valuable documents on your person, your embassy or consulate will usually be able to provide free certified copies to carry around instead. These will be acceptable in most cases.

## Extensions

Extending a Kazakh tourist visa is only possible with a medical certificate saying you are unable to travel. Business visas can be extended through many travel agencies: fees start around US$50.

## Visas for Onward Travel

For contact details of embassies and consulates in Kazakhstan, see p178.

**Afghanistan** Thirty-day tourist visas (US$30) processed in three days in Almaty. Agents will charge double.

**China** In Almaty one-month, single-entry visas cost US$30 to US$40 and take five working days. An LOI may be required. The office opens for visa applications and issuance from 9am to noon Monday, Wednesday and Friday: be prepared for long queues. For costlier rapid service apply on Monday: your visa will be ready on Wednesday. Using an agent is much easier: Stantours (p117) can get your visa in five working days for US$90.

**Kyrgyzstan** Almaty is the best place in Central Asia to get a Kyrgyz visa. The consulate accepts applications from 10am to 1pm Monday to Thursday (get there at 9.30am to minimise queuing time). Take your passport and one photo. A one-month tourist visa takes three working days for US$45; urgent service (picking up between 3pm and 5pm the same day) is US$90.

**Pakistan** Three-month visas issued in two days.

**Russia** Get your Russian visa before you leave home. Like most Russian missions in Central Asia, the Almaty consulate is a headache. You have to supply originals of all documents, including an invitation, which may or may not be accepted. Transit visas may only be available to drivers of cars (not even their passengers). Things are slightly better at the embassy in Astana and the consulate at Uralsk, where processing is normally three working days, but you still need to provide original documents, possibly requiring courier fees to have them sent by a sponsor in Russia.

**Tajikistan** Tourist visas are issued the same day in Almaty but an LOI from a Tajik travel agency (available from many agencies in Almaty) is usually required. One/two/four weeks costs US$80/100/120. The office is open 10am to 6pm Monday to Friday: apply in the morning. Normal processing is half-price but takes 12 working days.

**Turkmenistan** To get a Turkmen visa here you either need to book a tour through a travel agency, or have an onward visa enabling you to get a transit visa. You'll have to go in person with your passport to the embassy or consulate. Procedures are easier in Astana, Tashkent and Dushanbe, where the embassies are more used to transit travellers, than in Almaty.

**Uzbekistan** Some Almaty travel agents can provide Uzbek LOIs hassle-free if given enough time (US$35 for about two weeks at Stantours). The embassy accepts applications from 2pm to 4.30pm Monday to Thursday. Go at 1pm, put your name on a list and you'll probably get in before the door closes around 4pm. Visas are issued on the spot if you apply with an LOI. Uzbekistan's no-LOI option for some Continental European nationalities and Japan is not always respected here: if an application without LOI is accepted, you will usually have to come and queue again after three working days. Tourist visas cost US$55/65/75 for seven/15/30 days, US$95 for three months: for more than one entry, add US$10 per entry. US citizens pay US$100 for any visa. Transit visas, available without LOI if you have an onward visa to any neighbouring country, are US$35 for 72 hours, and normally take three working days.

# TRANSPORT IN KAZAKHSTAN

## GETTING THERE & AWAY

### Entering Kazakhstan

Once a bureaucratic nightmare, the entry procedures into Kazakhstan are streamlined these days. Bribery is no longer common, although the road border between Tashkent and Shymkent can be problematic (see p184). On arrival you fill in a migration card, which should be stamped to show that your passport has been registered (see p180). Keep this card in your passport: you must hand it in when you leave the country.

### Air

#### AIRLINES & AIRPORTS

Kazakhstan has steadily improved air connections with the outside world. The two biggest and busiest airports are at **Almaty** (☎ 327-270 33 33; www.alaport.com) and **Astana** (☎ 317-277 77 77; www.astanaairport.kz). Almaty has direct international flights to at least 25 cities in Europe and Asia, on airlines including KLM, British Airways, Lufthansa, Turkish Airlines, China Southern, Transaero and the Kazakh-and-British-owned Air Astana. Astana has direct flights to Amsterdam, Frankfurt, Hanover, Istanbul, Kiev, Moscow and St Petersburg. Uralsk, Atyrau and Karaganda also have direct flights to Western Europe. Aktau is the main hub for trans-Caspian flights; Ust-Kamenogorsk has flights to Bayan-Ölgii (Mongolia). All these cities, plus Shymkent and Kyzylorda, have flights to Moscow and often other CIS cities too.

For other Central Asian cities, Almaty has flights to Tashkent (US$185) daily by Uzbekistan Airlines, and Dushanbe five times weekly by Tajikair or SCAT. From Astana, Uzbekistan Airlines flies weekly to Tashkent (US$230).

**DEPARTURE TAX**

There is no departure tax when leaving Kazakhstan.

For regularly updated schedules, visit www.centralasiatourism.com. See p127 for airline contact details in Almaty.

### Land

#### BORDER CROSSINGS

##### To/From China

Few hassles from officialdom are reported these days at either Khorgos (the main road crossing) or Dostyk (the rail crossing), though waits can be long.

From Almaty's Sayran bus station, sleeper buses are scheduled to Ürümqi (5900T, 24 hours) at 7am daily except Sunday, and buses to Yining (3900T, 12 hours), about 100km from the border, at 7am Wednesday and Saturday. Departures are not always reliable, however. An alternative is to take a bus or minibus to Zharkent, 40km before Khorgos, then a taxi (about 600T) or minibus to the border, and a taxi from there to Ürümqi. The crossing is usually crammed with Kazakh and Uyghur families and traders with vast amounts of baggage. If you're coming from Ürümqi, note that the bus tickets are not sold at the bus station there but in the Bian Jiang Bing Guan hotel in the southern part of Ürümqi.

The Zhibek Zholy (Silk Road) train departs Almaty-II station for Ürümqi at 10.59pm Saturday (a Kazakh train) and Monday (a Chinese train). It's scheduled to take 30 hours, crossing the border at Dostyk (Druzhba). Kupeyny (2nd-class couchette) tickets cost 8500T. The return train gets into Almaty-II at 5.58am Monday and Wednesday. The trains have restaurant cars but it makes sense to bring some of your own food and drink too. At Dostyk, you have to wait several hours while the train bogies are changed and customs checks take place. The train toilets are locked during this time except for the 20-minute dash between the Kazakhstan and China border posts: get in line early for this!

The trains can get fully booked two weeks in advance. From Almaty the Monday train is particularly popular and tickets on free sale are rare. You can save trouble by booking through an agent: Stantours (p117) charges US$10 to

US$15 for the service, plus any late-ticket surcharges (typically US$20). The international ticket office at Almaty-II opens from 8am to 1pm and 2pm to 7pm. You may have to show a Chinese visa when buying a ticket.

From Ust-Kamenogorsk in eastern Kazakhstan, there are buses to Ürümqi and the Chinese town of Altay. See p171 for details.

#### To/From Kyrgyzstan

Official Kazakh–Kyrgyz border crossings are largely hassle-free.

Seven daily buses and a similar number of minibuses (600T to 700T), as well as shared taxis (2000T to 2500T), make the four- to five-hour run to Bishkek from Almaty's Sayran bus station, crossing the border at Korday. There are also overnight buses all the way to Cholpon-Ata and Karakol from Sayran, and minibuses to Bishkek from Taraz (500T, five hours).

No public transport makes the Karkara valley crossing, south of Kegen, Kazakhstan, and east of Tüp and Ken-Suu, Kyrgyzstan, but from about April to October you can get through by a combination of hitching, taxi and patience (see p137).

Trekkers and mountain bikers making the haul across the mountains between Almaty and Lake Issyk-Köl should note that there is no official crossing point so it's impossible to get a passport stamp. Consult a trekking agency before setting off.

#### To/From Russia

There are many road crossings between Kazakhstan and Russia. For train and bus connections, see p468 and city sections in this chapter.

#### To/From Turkmenistan

There is a remote border point 200km south of Zhanaozen, which is a two-hour marshrutka ride east of Aktau. From the border it's 50km south to the Turkmen town of Bekdash and a further 200km to Turkmenbashi. The roads are very rough for about 50km each side of the border. There's no public transport from either side – expect to pay about 6000T for a taxi from Zhanaozen to the border, and US$40 from the border to Turkmenbashi. Vehicle queues at the border can be long.

#### To/From Uzbekistan

The main road crossing is at Chernyaevka between Shymkent and Tashkent. This is an unpredictable border: some travellers breeze through, others have taken five hours. There are reports of corruption on both sides, especially the Kazakh side. If it looks bad, consider paying 1000T to 1500T to one of the 'facilitators' hanging around the border. The border is open 8am to 10pm (Astana/Almaty time).

Shared taxis and marshrutkas to the border (500T, one to 1¼ hours) depart from Shymkent's Kolos bus stop – see p144.

Daily trains run from Aqtöbe, Aralsk, Kyzylorda and Turkistan to Tashkent via the border point at Saryagash. Coming from Almaty you can meet these trains at Arys, 60km west of Shymkent.

Another road and rail crossing exists between Beyneu, western Kazakhstan, and Kungrad, Uzbekistan. Self-driving readers have reported that the road is poor and little used but the crossing is hassle-free. Uzbek customs is in Kungrad. Daily trains run from Beyneu to Kungrad (10 hours; customs are done on the train), and on Saturday and Wednesday (from Beyneu) train 332, coming from Saratov (Russia) via Atyrau (Kazakhstan), continues to Tashkent via Nukus and Samarkand.

### Sea

#### BORDER CROSSINGS

#### To/From Azerbaijan

A sea ferry between Aktau and Baku, Azerbaijan, leaves about every seven to 10 days (cabin berth 7800T to 10,000T, about 18 hours) – see p157 for more details. This service is reportedly less comfortable and less regular than the Baku–Turkmenbashi ferry.

## GETTING AROUND

### Air

A good network of domestic flights links cities all round Kazakhstan and fares are reasonable. The main airlines are **Air Astana** (4L; www.airastana.com), a Western-style, Kazakh-British joint venture; and **SCAT** (DV; www.scat.kz in Russian), a Kazakh airline flying prop-driven Russian planes. SCAT is significantly cheaper on many routes. For flight schedules see www.centralasiatourism.com.

### Buses

Bus services are fairly good except in western Kazakhstan. Most intercity buses are modern, and generally a little cheaper and faster, and often more frequent, than a 2nd-class train ride. A typical bus trip costs 125T per hour (50km to 60km). Quality of intercity roads generally isn't bad, but for trips of more than five or six hours trains are usually more comfortable.

### Marshrutkas, Minibuses & Taxis

For many trips up to four or five hours, assorted marshrutkas, minibuses and shared taxis offer an alternative. They're generally found waiting outside bus and train stations. Marshrutkas and minibuses usually cost a little more than buses; shared taxis are double or triple.

### Train

Train travel is a good way to meet people and get a feel for the country's terrain and vast size. Ticket queues can be slow and it's best to buy your ticket in advance. All cities have downtown train booking offices, identified by the words Zheleznodorozhnaya Kassa (Russian) or Temir Zhol Kassasy (Kazakh), where you can buy tickets at a small commission without having to schlep to the station. Take your passport when buying tickets.

A few train lines between Kazakhstan cities – such as Semey–Ust-Kamenogorsk, Aqtöbe–Uralsk and Aqtöbe–Kostanay – pass through Russian territory and you may be asked for a Russian transit visa on these legs. Ask beforehand about the latest situation.

# Uzbekistan
# Узбекистан

No country in Central Asia seems to have it so good, yet at the same time have it so bad, as Uzbekistan. The region's cradle of culture for more than two millennia, it is the proud home to a spellbinding arsenal of architecture and artefacts, all deeply infused with the raw, fascinating history of the country. But as students of that history know, it's also sprung a few bad apples over the years. Tyrants enamoured by the country's physical bounty have run the territory we now call Uzbekistan since time immemorial.

Concentrating on the good, if there was a Hall of Fame for Central Asian cities, Uzbekistan would own the top-three entries: Samarkand, Bukhara, Khiva. The names practically epitomise the region, conjuring up images of knife-twirling dervishes, serpentine desert caravans and architecture that blends with the sand.

Seen in person, the Big Three do not disappoint (the occasional overzealous restorative effort notwithstanding). Alas, they sometimes overshadow the country's other attractions, which include dazzling bazaars, ancient desert fortresses and an impressive array of largely unsung natural attractions.

All of that is enough to eclipse the bad memories evoked by names such as Jenghiz Khan, Timur, Nasrullah Khan and Stalin. The country's long-serving current leader, Islam Karimov, is no saint either. Despite it all, the Uzbek people remain good-spirited and genuinely hospitable – yet another prime attraction in this oddly endearing country.

**FAST FACTS**

- **Area** 447,400 sq km
- **Capital** Tashkent
- **Country Code** ☎ 998
- **Famous For** *Plov,* tasty pomegranates, Samarkand, Timur (Tamerlane), being Borat's neighbour
- **Languages** Uzbek, Russian, Tajik, Karakalpak
- **Money** Uzbek sum; US$1 = 1238S; €1 = 1628S
- **Phrases** *Salom aleikum* (Hello); *Rakhmat* (Thank you)
- **Population** 25.2 million

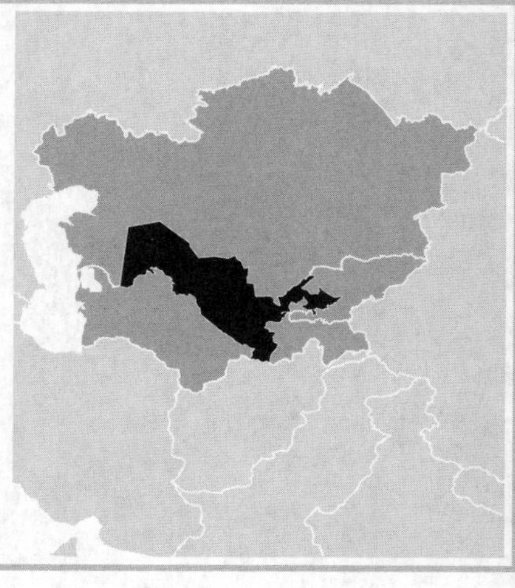

## HIGHLIGHTS

- **Samarkand** (p223) The breathtaking Registan leads a formidable cast of larger-than-life Timurid architectural gems.
- **Bukhara** (p236) Exquisitely preserved holy city boasting stunning 15th-century medressas, awesome B&Bs and fascinating history.
- **Quirky Cultural Gems** Carmen for a dollar at Tashkent's Alisher Navoi Opera & Ballet Theatre (p207) and Central Asia's greatest art collection in Nukus' Savitsky Museum (p259).
- **Khiva** (p252) The last independent khanate frozen in time amid the desert.
- **Crafty Uzbekistan** Silk in Margilon (p220), ceramics in Rishton (p221), *suzani* (silk and cotton coverlets) in Shakhrisabz (p232) and everything under the sun in Bukhara (p246).

## ITINERARIES

- **Three days** Start in Bukhara, either with a domestic flight from Tashkent or overland from Turkmenistan. Wander around Lyabi-Hauz, tour the Ark, and gape at the 47m Kalon Minaret and the stunning medressa ensembles. Pamper yourself in a bodacious B&B, then zip to Samarkand the next morning to explore the four pearls of Timurid-era architecture: the Registan, Bibi Khanym Mosque, Shah-i-Zinda and Guri Amir Mausoleum. On day three exit to Tajikistan, taking a detour on the way to Shakhrisabz or the Urgut bazaar (Sunday and Thursday only).
- **One week** Fly to Urgench from where it's a short shared-taxi ride to the 'museum city' of Khiva. Spend a day wandering around the walled old city, Ichon-Qala. The next day travel by shared taxi to Bukhara and Samarkand, giving each place an extra day. On your last day in Tashkent catch an opera and a museum or two.
- **Two weeks** Fly west to Nukus and spend a half-day appreciating Central Asia's greatest art collection in the Savitsky Museum. Head south to Khiva via the ancient ruined fortresses of Elliq Qala. Around Bukhara, take a time-out from architecture with a yurtstay near Lake Aidarkul. After three days covering Samarkand and vicinity, history buffs should head south to the archaeological oasis of Termiz before flying back to Tashkent for some museum hopping, good food and a night or two on the town. Bazaar lovers should consider the Fergana Valley instead of Termiz.
- **One month** All the above sights can be seen in a month at a more relaxed pace. You can hit both Termiz and the Fergana Valley and devote more time to exploring Uzbekistan's natural wonders: including hiking, rafting or skiing in Ugam-Chatkal National Park, and camel trekking, hiking and community-based tourism near Lake Aidarkul and the Nurata Mountains.

### HOW MUCH?

- Snickers bar US$0.40
- 100km bus ride US$1
- One-minute phone call to the US/UK US$1.05/0.95
- Internet per hour US$0.50-0.80
- Uzbek skull cap US$2-4
- 1L of bottled water US$0.40
- Domestic beer (bar) US$0.75-1
- Domestic beer (store) US$0.50
- Shashlyk US$0.30-0.50
- 1L of petrol US$0.50

## CLIMATE & WHEN TO GO

Large areas of Uzbekistan are desert. Summer is long, hot and dry; spring is mild and rainy; autumn has light frosts and rains; and winter, although short, is unstable with snow and temperatures below freezing.

From June to August average afternoon temperatures hit 32°C or higher. The average annual maximum temperature is 40°C in June. Most rain falls in March and April.

The summer furnace of 35°C days lasts 40 days from mid-July to the end of August. The worst of winter lasts 40 days from Christmas to the first week of February; see also the Climate Charts, p446.

In this chapter, the high season is spring (mid-March to the end of May) and autumn (September to the beginning of November). Summer is from June to August, and winter is from December to February.

 



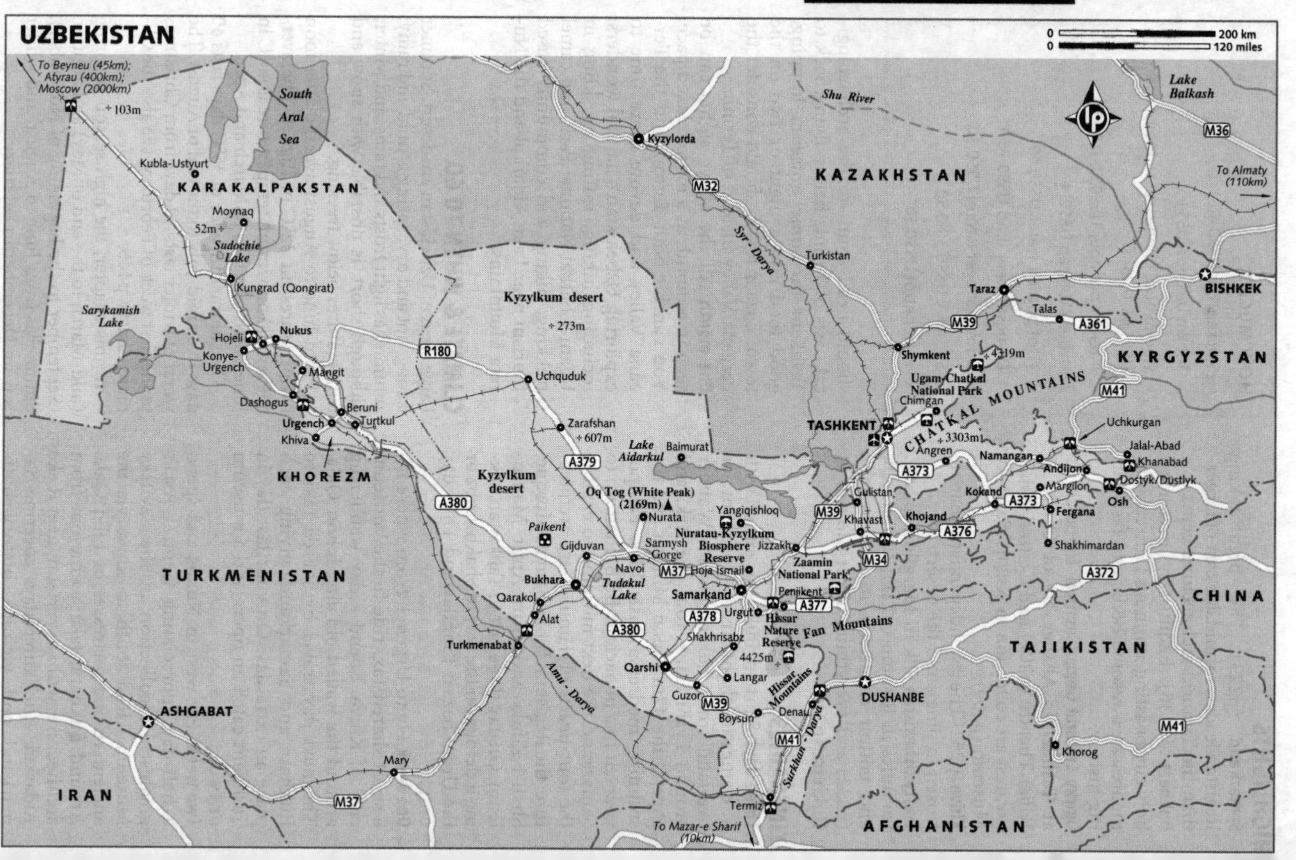
UZBEKISTAN
0 200 km
0 120 miles
To Beyneu (45km); Atyrau (400km); Moscow (2000km)
103m
South Aral Sea
Kubla-Ustyurt
KARAKALPAKSTAN
Moynaq
52m
Sudochie Lake
Kungrad (Qongirat)
Sarykamish Lake
Hojeli
Nukus
Konye-Urgench
Mangit
Dashogus
Beruni
Urgench
Turtkul
Khiva
KHOREZM
Kyzylkum desert
273m
R180
Uchquduk
Zarafshan
607m
A379
Lake Aidarkul
Baimurat
Kyzylkum desert
A380
Oq Tog (White Peak) (2169m)
Nurata
Paikent
Gijduvan
Navoi
Sarmysh Gorge
Yangiqishloq
Nuratau-Kyzylkum Biosphere Reserve
Jizzakh
M37
Hoja Ismail
Zaamin National Park
TURKMENISTAN
Bukhara
Tudakul Lake
Samarkand
Penjikent
Qarakol
Alat
A378
Urgut
A377
Hissar Nature Reserve
Fan Mountains
Turkmenabat
Amu - Darya
A380
Shakhrisabz
4425m
Qarshi
Langar
Hissar Mountains
Guzor
M39
Boysun
Denau
Surkhan - Darya
M41
ASHGABAT
Mary
M37
IRAN
Termiz
To Mazar-e Sharif (10km)
AFGHANISTAN
Shu River
Kyzylorda
M32
KAZAKHSTAN
Syr - Darya
Turkistan
Lake Balkash
M36
To Almaty (110km)
Taraz
BISHKEK
Talas
A361
M39
Shymkent
4319m
KYRGYZSTAN
Ugam-Chatkal National Park
Chimgan
CHATKAL MOUNTAINS
M41
TASHKENT
3303m
Angren
Uchkurgan
Namangan
Jalal-Abad
Khanabad
A373
Andijon
Dostyk/Dustlyk
Margilon
Osh
Gulistan
Kokand
A373
Fergana
M39
Khavast
Khojand
A376
Shakhimardan
M34
A372
CHINA
TAJIKISTAN
DUSHANBE
M41
Khorog

**TRAVELLING SAFELY IN UZBEKISTAN**

As in many police states, the main danger is the overzealous police. Proceed with extreme caution in all border areas, which are heavily patrolled and generally off-limits to foreigners without special permits. Also note that much of the Uzbek–Tajik border, and parts of the Uzbek–Kyrgyz border, have been mined. Uzbekistan Airways has a generally clean track record, although a Termiz–Tashkent flight crashed in 2004, killing 37.

## HISTORY

The land along the upper Amu-Darya, Syr-Darya and their tributaries has always been different from the rest of Central Asia – more settled than nomadic, with patterns of land use and communality that has changed little from the time of the Achaemenids (6th century BC) to present day. An attitude of permanence and proprietorship still sets the people of this region apart.

### Ancient Empires

The region was part of some very old Persian states, including Bactria, Khorezm and Sogdiana. In the 4th century BC Alexander the Great entered Cyrus the Great's Achaemenid empire. He stopped near Marakanda (Samarkand) and then, having conquered the Sogdians in their homeland mountains, married Roxana, the daughter of a local chieftain (see p37).

Out of the northern steppes in the 6th century AD came the Western Turks – the western branch of the empire of the so-called Kök (Blue) Turks. They soon grew attached to life here and abandoned their wandering ways, eventually taking on a significant role in maintaining the existence of the Silk Road (see p53). The Arabs brought Islam and a written alphabet to Central Asia in the 8th century but found the region too big and restless to govern.

A return to the Persian fold came with the Samanid dynasty in the 9th and 10th centuries. Its capital, Bukhara, became the centre of an intellectual, religious and commercial renaissance. In the 11th century the Ghaznavids moved into the southern regions. For some time the Turkic Khorezmshahs dominated Central Asia from present-day Konye-Urgench in Turkmenistan, but their reign was cut short and the region's elegant oases ravaged by Jenghiz Khan in the early 13th century.

Central Asia again became truly 'central' with the rise of Timur (also known as Tamerlane), the ruthless warrior and patron of the arts who fashioned a glittering Islamic capital at Samarkand.

### The Uzbeks

Little is known of early Uzbek history. At the time the Golden Horde was founded, Shibaqan (Shayban), a grandson of Jenghiz Khan, inherited what is today northern Kazakhstan and adjacent parts of Russia. The greatest khan of these Mongol Shaybani tribes (and probably the one under whom they swapped paganism for Islam) was Özbeg (Uzbek, ruled 1313–40). By the end of the 14th century these tribes had begun to name themselves after him.

The Uzbeks began to move southeast, mixing with sedentary Turkic tribes and adopting the Turkic language; they reached the Syr-Darya in the mid-15th century. Following an internal schism (which gave birth to the proto-Kazakhs; see p42), the Uzbeks rallied under Mohammed Shaybani and thundered down upon the remnants of Timur's empire. By the early 1500s, all of Transoxiana ('the land beyond the Oxus') from the Amu-Darya (Oxus River) to the Syr-Darya (Jaxartes River) belonged to the Uzbeks, as it has since.

The greatest (and last) of the Shaybanid khans, responsible for some of Bukhara's finest architecture, was Abdullah II, who ruled from 1538 until his death in 1598. After this, as the Silk Road fell into disuse, the empire unravelled under the Shaybanids' distant cousins, the Astrakhanids. By the start of the 19th century the entire region was dominated by three weak, feuding Uzbek city-states – Khiva, Bukhara and Kokand.

### The Russians Arrive

In the early 18th century the khan of Khiva made an offer to Peter the Great of Russia (to become his vassal in return for help against marauding Turkmen and Kazakh tribes), stirring the first Russian interest in Central Asia. But by the time the Russians got around to marching on Khiva in 1717, the khan no longer wanted Russian protection, and after a show of hospitality he had almost the entire 4000-strong force slaughtered.

The slave market in Bukhara and Khiva was an excuse for further Russian visits to free a few Russian settlers and travellers. In 1801 the insane Tsar Paul sent 22,000 Cossacks on a madcap mission to drive the British out of India, with orders to free the slaves en route. Fortunately for all but the slaves, the tsar was assassinated and the army recalled while struggling across the Kazakh steppes.

The next attempt, by Tsar Nicholas I in 1839, was really a bid to pre-empt expansion into Central Asia by Britain, which had just taken Afghanistan, although Khiva's Russian slaves were the pretext on which General Perovsky's 5200 men and 10,000 camels set out from Orenburg. In January 1840, a British officer, Captain James Abbott, arrived in Khiva (having travelled from Herat in Afghan disguise) offering to negotiate the slaves' release on the khan's behalf, thus nullifying the Russians' excuse for coming.

Unknown to the khan, the Russian force had already turned back, in the face of a devastating winter on the steppes. He agreed to send Abbott to the tsar with an offer to release the slaves in return for an end to Russian military expeditions against Khiva. Incredibly, Abbott made it to St Petersburg.

In search of news of Abbott, Lieutenant Richmond Shakespear reached Khiva the following June and convinced the khan to unilaterally release all Russian slaves in Khiva and even give them an armed escort to the nearest Russian outpost, on the eastern Caspian Sea. Russian gratitude was doubtlessly mingled with fury over one of the Great Game's boldest propaganda coups.

When the Russians finally rallied 25 years later, the khanates' towns fell like dominoes – Tashkent in 1865 to General Mikhail Chernyaev, Samarkand and Bukhara in 1868, Khiva in 1873, and Kokand in 1875 to General Konstantin Kaufman.

## Soviet Daze

Even into the 20th century, most Central Asians identified themselves ethnically as Turks or Persians. The connection between 'Uzbek' and 'Uzbekistan' is very much a Soviet matter. Following the outbreak of the Russian Revolution in 1917 and the infamous sacking of Kokand in 1918, the Bolsheviks proclaimed the Autonomous Soviet Socialist Republic of Turkestan. Temporarily forced out by counter-revolutionary troops and *basmachi* (Muslim guerrilla fighters), they returned two years later and the Khiva and Bukhara khanates were forcibly replaced with 'People's Republics'.

Then in October 1924 the whole map was redrawn on ethnic grounds, and the Uzbeks suddenly had a 'homeland', an official identity and a literary language. The Uzbek Soviet Socialist Republic (SSR) changed shape and composition over the years as it suited Moscow, hiving off Tajikistan in 1929, acquiring Karakalpakstan from Russia in 1936, taking parts of the Hungry Steppe (the Russian nickname for the dry landscape between Tashkent and Jizzakh) from Kazakhstan in 1956 and 1963, then losing some in 1971.

For rural Uzbeks, the main impacts of Soviet rule were the forced and often bloody collectivisation of the republic's mainstay (agriculture) and the massive shift to cotton cultivation. The Uzbek intelligentsia and much of the republic's political leadership was decimated by Stalin's purges. This and the traditional Central Asian respect for authority meant that by the 1980s *glasnost* (openness) and *perestroika* (restructuring) would hardly trickle down here; few significant reforms took place.

## Independence

Uzbekistan's first serious noncommunist popular movement, Birlik (Unity), was formed by Tashkent intellectuals in 1989 over issues that included Uzbek as an official language and the effects of the cotton monoculture. Despite popular support, it was barred from contesting the election in February 1990 for the Uzbek Supreme Soviet (legislature) by the Communist Party. The resulting communist-dominated body elected Islam Karimov, the first secretary of the Communist Party of Uzbekistan (CPUz), to the new post of executive president.

Following the abortive coup in Moscow in August 1991, Karimov declared Uzbekistan independent. Soon afterward the CPUz reinvented itself as the People's Democratic Party of Uzbekistan (PDPU), inheriting all of its predecessor's property and control apparatus, most of its ideology, and of course its leader, Karimov.

In December 1991, Uzbekistan held its first direct presidential elections, which Karimov won with 86% of the vote. His only rival was a poet named Mohammed Solih, running for the small, figurehead opposition party Erk (Will or Freedom), who got 12% and was soon driven into exile (where he remains to this day). The real opposition groups, Birlik and the Islamic Renaissance Party (IRP), and all other parties with a religious platform, had been forbidden to take part.

A new constitution unveiled in 1992 declared Uzbekistan 'a secular, democratic presidential republic'. Under Karimov, Uzbekistan would remain secular almost to a fault. But it would remain far from 'democratic'.

### Onward to Andijon

The years after independence saw Karimov consolidate his grip on power. He remained firmly in charge of everything from municipal gardeners' salaries to gold production quotas – as he was, under a different title, even before independence. Dissent shrivelled thanks to control of the media, police harassment and imprisonment of activists. Through it all, the economy stagnated and the devastating cotton monoculture continued.

A new threat emerged in February 1999 when a series of devastating bomb attacks hit Tashkent. This led to a crackdown on radical Islamic fundamentalists – *wahabis* in the local parlance – that extended to a broad spectrum of opponents. Hundreds of alleged Islamic extremists were arrested on trumped-up charges. The IRP, with support in the Fergana Valley, was forced underground and Erk was declared illegal.

Karimov won a third consecutive term in January 2000, garnering 92% of the votes. Foreign observers deemed the election a farce and international condemnation was widespread. But the 9/11 attacks on the United States gave Karimov a reprieve. The Uzbek president opened up bases to the US and NATO for use in the war in Afghanistan, then sat back and watched the US aid money – US$500 million in 2002 alone – start flowing in.

As an added bonus for Karimov, solidarity with the US in the 'War on Terror' effectively gave him a licence to ratchet up his brutal campaign against the *wahabis*. Once again Karimov used this licence to brand anyone he wanted to silence a 'terrorist'. Another rigged election in 2004, this one parliamentary, drew only modest international criticism.

Such was the situation on 13 May 2005 when events in the eastern city of Andijon rocked the country and instantly demolished Uzbekistan's cosy relationship with the United States. The Andijon Massacre, as it was later dubbed, was touched off when two dozen powerful local businessmen were jailed for being members of Akramiya, a local extremist Islamic movement. A group of their allies stormed the prison where they were being held, touching off a massive but largely peaceful demonstration in Andjion's main square. The authorities overreacted, and somewhere between 200 and 1000 civilians were killed by government troops in the ensuing melee.

International condemnation of Andijon was swift in coming. After Uzbekistan refused to allow an independent international investigation, the US withdrew most of its aid and the EU hit the country with sanctions. The post-9/11 thaw in Uzbekistan's relations with the West was over.

## CURRENT EVENTS

Indignant in the face of Western criticism over Andijon, Karimov's response has been to kick most US-funded NGOs out of the country. The US Peace Corps and high-profile NGOs such as Freedom House, the Open Society Institute and Internews have all been forced to leave in the face of registration problems or similar technicalities.

Domestically, Karimov has used the Andijon events to launch what Human Rights Watch has called an 'unprecedented' crackdown against opposition political activists and independent journalists. Nor have international journalists been immune to the onslaught. The BBC, which had been among the last Western news organisations still operating in the country, was harassed out of Tashkent in October 2005. It remains next to impossible for a foreign journalist to get a visa into Uzbekistan.

Yet a thaw in relations with the West by late 2007 or 2008 is not out of the question. The EU extended its sanctions in late 2006 but there were strong signs that the sanctions would be lifted by late 2007. The US was at least starting to talk about a *rapprochement*. Just as tellingly, Tashkent's relations with Russia, which had not, coincidentally, improved in the wake of Andijon, were showing signs of becoming chillier.

**UZBEK SURVIVAL TIPS**

1. Private cars for intercity trips are much cheaper if hired at the shared-taxi stand for your destination, rather than through your hotel.
2. The winter low season is wonderful in Uzbekistan – cool, dry and you'll have the place to yourself.
3. Negotiate for everything, but especially at state-owned hotels – both fancy Tashkent versions and the grubby regional variety, all of which give steep discounts.
4. Always have your documents ready in the Uzbek metro, the one place you will almost always get stopped by police.



Karimov, for his part, seemed finally willing to make concessions of his own. In late 2006 he fired the governor of Andijon province – an admission, some say, that the government bore at least some responsibility for the events of May 2005. Also in late 2006, two Western NGOs successfully defended themselves in an Uzbek court against accusations of financial improprieties.

Will Karimov finally meet Western governments' main demand – an independent probe of Andijon? That remains to be seen. But neither Karimov nor the West, it appears, want their break-up to last for ever.

Meanwhile, Karimov's second term as president is scheduled to end in December 2007. While the constitution limits Uzbek presidents to two terms, few believe the president will allow himself to be disempowered by something as feeble as the constitution. In all likelihood, Karimov will extend his term through a rigged referendum or a constitutional amendment, and will remain in power indefinitely.

## PEOPLE

Centuries of tradition as settled people left the Uzbeks in a better position than their nomadic neighbours to fend off Soviet attempts to modify their culture. Traditions of the Silk Road still linger as Uzbeks consider themselves good traders, hospitable hosts and tied to the land.

The focal point of society is still the network of urban (mahallas) districts, where neighbours attend one another's weddings, celebrations and funerals. Advice on all matters is sought from an *aksakal* (revered elder, literally 'white beard'), whose authority is conferred by the community. In sinister, Soviet fashion, Karimov has usurped these structures by employing *aksakals* as district custodians and informants.

While Uzbek men toil to make ends meet, women struggle for equality. Considered second-class citizens in the workplace and in the home, women are not given the same rights as their Western counterparts, or even their Kyrgyz and Kazakh neighbours. Although the Soviets did much to bring women into the mainstream of society, no amount of propaganda could entirely defeat sexist attitudes. There are some signs of change – dress codes continue to liberalise, for example, but old habits die hard and women in conservative families are expected to be subservient to their husbands.

Domestic violence occurs in 40% of Uzbek homes, yet overall household control lies in the hands of the husband's mother. Abuse, however, rarely leads to divorce, and there are occasional reports of suicide by self-immolation, a cultural trait that dates back to pre-Islamic Zoroastrianism.

### Population

Tashkent is Uzbekistan's biggest city and the Fergana Valley is home to Uzbekistan's largest concentration of people, a third of the population. Samarkand, the second city, is Tajik-speaking, as are many of the communities surrounding it, including Bukhara and Qarshi. The further west you travel the more sparsely populated the land becomes. Karakalpakstan, home to Kazakhs, Karakalpaks and Khorezmians, has seen its population dwindle as a result of the Aral Sea disaster (p77). Around 40% of Uzbeks live in cities, with the rest in rural farming towns and villages.

The national population growth rate has fallen since independence (although it's still high at 2.5% per year) with tens of thousands of Slavs emigrating each year and with the sudden disappearance of subsidies for large families. Over half the population is under 15 years of age. A number of minority groups make up a tiny portion of the population, most notably Koreans and Russians in Tashkent. There is still a miniscule Jewish population in Bukhara (p237) and an even smaller one in Samarkand.

## RELIGION

Around 85% of Uzbeks claim to be Muslim (nearly all are the Hanafi Sunni variety), although only around 5% to 15% are practising. Around 5% of the population are Christian. The Fergana Valley maintains the greatest Islamic conservative base, with Bukhara ranking number two. In the wake of the 1999 bomb attacks in Tashkent, mosques are no longer permitted to broadcast the azan (call to prayer), and mullahs have been pressured to praise the government in their sermons. Attendance at mosques has fallen for fear of practising Muslims being observed and harassed by government agents.

Although Uzbeks are tolerant of other religions, Western Christian missionaries have failed to gain a foothold, many having been harassed out of the country.

## ARTS

Traditional art, music and architecture – evolving over centuries – were placed in a neat little box for preservation following the Soviet creation of the Uzbek SSR. But somehow, in the years to follow, two major centres of progressive art were still allowed to develop: Igor Savitsky's collection of lost art from the 1930s, stashed away in Nukus (p258), and the life-stories told inside Tashkent's notorious Ilkhom Theatre (p207) both survived as puddles of liberalism in a sea of communist doctrine.

Nowadays, Uzbekistan's art, music, film and literary figures are divided into those that are approved by the government and those that are not. Patriotic odes and art – those that glorify the young nation and its leadership – are welcomed and financed by the central budget.

The Amir Timur Museum in Tashkent is one of the best examples of state-supported art, with its mock Timurid dome and interior murals filled with scenes of epic nation building.

Local pop and rap stars also sing to Uzbekistan's greatness. Yulduz Usmanova, a parliamentarian from Margilon, resurrected a scandal-filled career with ballads that urged dedication to the *yurtbashi* (national leader). Dado's classical Uzbek pop sounds vaguely Latin American. The ever-changing girl band Sitora is another one to look out for. Grizzled rockers Bolalar date back to the *perestroika*-era.

Many other forms of art, particularly those offering a philosophy and expression deeper than nationalism, aren't officially banned, but with scant means of private finance, their creators are left with little outlet for creativity.

The most notable 'dissident group' is the Fergana School, made up of a dozen or so artists and writers whose works were published in the early 1990s literary magazine *Zuizda Vastaka* (Star of the East). The government ordered the publication closed in 1994 and the Fergana School has since gone underground.

### RECOMMENDED READING

*Chasing the Sea: Lost Among the Ghosts of Empire in Central Asia,* by Tom Bissell, is a sort of travelogue-cum–history lesson about Uzbekistan written by an ex–Peace Corps volunteer on an assignment to investigate the disappearing Aral Sea. It is quick-witted and insightful.

*Journey to Khiva,* by Philip Glazebrook, is a relentlessly downbeat review of Uzbekistan as it transitioned to independence in the early 1990s. Glazebrook mixes in the history of Uzbekistan as he travels through it, but is sorely disappointed at every turn, due largely to what he sees as cultural robbery by the Soviets. It serves as an interesting chronicle and reference point of Uzbek life in 1990.

*Uzbekistan – the Golden Road to Samarkand,* by Calum Macleod and Bradley Mayhew, is an elegant Odyssey guide that offers detailed historical and practical coverage of Uzbekistan's Silk Road cities, plus the main historical sites in the neighbouring republics, with literary excerpts and fine photography.

*Murder in Samarkand,* by Craig Murray, is a damning account of atrocities committed by the Karimov administration, penned by a maverick former British ambassador to Uzbekistan. Equally damning is Murray's account of his own government's efforts to discredit him in the context of the 'War on Terror'. At the time of research Michael Winterbottom was directing a movie based on the book.

 



## ENVIRONMENT

Uzbekistan spans several ecosystems, and topographic and geographic shifts. Its eastern fringes tilt upwards in a knot of rugged mountains – Tashkent's Chatkal and Pskem Mountains run into the western Tian Shan range, and Samarkand's Zarafshon Mountains and a mass of ranges in the southeast flow into the Pamir Alay. This isolated, rocky and forested terrain makes up an important habitat for the bear, lynx, bustard, mountain goat and even the elusive snow leopard. Flowing down from these mountains are the life-giving rivers, the Amu-Darya and the Syr-Darya.

To the west of the well-watered mountains are vast plains of desert or steppe: the Ustyurt Plateau (p261) and the vast, barren Kyzylkum (Red Sands) desert. Despite its bleakness, this land is far from dead; the desert is home to the gazelle, various raptors and other critters you'd expect to find – monitors, scorpions and venomous snakes.

There are some 15 *zapovednik* (nature reserves) in Uzbekistan, the largest of which is the Hissar Reserve (750 sq km), located in the Kashkadarya region due east of Shakhrisabz. This remote region of pine and juniper forests includes the country's largest glacier, Severtsov, and its highest peaks – 4425m Khojapiryokh and an unnamed 4643m peak east of that on the Tajik border.

### Environmental Issues

Much, if not all, of this territory is threatened by Uzbekistan's lacklustre environmental protection laws and the deterioration of its national park system, which does not have the funds to prevent illegal logging and poaching.

The faltering of the reserves, however, pales in comparison to the Aral Sea disaster (p77). In addition to the existing tragedy of the Aral, there's the issue of notorious Vozrozhdenia Ostrov (Rebirth Island, or 'Voz Island'), which the Soviets once used to test chemical weapons. In 2002 the island became a peninsula, sparking fears that contamination would migrate southward to the mainland. United States government contractors were brought in to destroy the toxic elements, and today the island is safe to visit.

## FOOD & DRINK

*Plov* (p204), a Central Asian pilaf consisting of rice and fried vegetables, and shashlyk (meat roasted on skewers over hot coals) are the national staples. Every region has its own variation of *non* bread, commonly known by its Russian name, *lepyoshka;* the raised rim of Kokand's speciality makes it a particularly fine shashlyk plate. Samarkand's *non* resembles a giant bagel without the hole.

*Buglama kovoq* (steamed pumpkin) is a light treat. *Moshkichiri* and *moshhurda* are meat and mung bean gruels. *Dimlama* (also called *bosma*) is meat, potatoes, onions and vegetables braised slowly in a little fat and their own juices; the meatless version is *sabzavotli dimlama*. *Hunon* or *honum* is a noodle roll, usually with a meat and potato filling. Uzbeks are fond of *dulma (*stuffed cabbage and grape leaves, tomatoes, peppers and quinces).

Apricot pits are a local favourite; they're cooked in ash and the shells are cracked by the vendor before they reach the market.

Besides green tea, nonalcoholic drinks include *katyk,* a thin yogurt that comes plain but can be sweetened if you have some sugar or jam handy. See the Central Asia Food & Drink chapter for more information (p82).

# TASHKENT ТАШКЕНТ

☎ (3) 71 / pop 2.1 million / elev 478m

Gritty Tashkent, Central Asia's hub, is an eccentric kind of place. In one part of the city Russian-speaking cabbies scream down broad Soviet-built avenues. Across town, old men wearing long, open-fronted *chapan* (quilted coats) cart nuts through a maze of mud-walled houses towards a crackling bazaar. In a third part of town hundreds gather amid steaming cauldrons for their daily repast of *plov*.

In the middle of it all roosts the president, his puppet Senate nearby in a freshly built hulk of white glory on Mustaqillik maydoni (Independence Sq). This is meant to be the new centre of the formerly centreless capital. The behaviour of the centre, of course, dictates the mood in the outskirts – a mood that actually seems pretty good considering you're in a supposed police state.

Like most places that travellers use mainly to get somewhere else, Tashkent is no instant charmer. But peel under its skin and suddenly you're thinking, hey, maybe it's not all that bad. Many expats truly love living in Tashkent, and many visa-foraging travellers find themselves wishing they could stay a few more days.

**TASHKENT MUST-SEES**

**Chorsu Bazaar** Haggle till you drop in this vast goods emporium (p200).

**History Museum of the People of Uzbekistan** The great repository of Uzbek history (p201).

**Central Asian Plov Centre** Worlds' best place to sample the Central Asian ambrosia (p204).

**Khast Imom** An ancient Quran lies hidden in Old Town's alleys (p200).

**Ilkhom Theatre** Progressive theatre with English subtitles (p207).

And it's not just Tashkent's Jekyl-and-Hyde, Muslim-and-Soviet oddness that gets people's attention. There's a cosmopolitan populace enjoying real, live culture, a rapidly improving restaurant scene and the best nightlife in the Muslim world east of Beirut (or at least Baku). There's also plenty of green space, a clutch of interesting museums and, within a 1½-hour drive, great hiking, rafting and skiing in remarkably accessible Ugam-Chatkal National Park.

## HISTORY

Tashkent's earliest incarnation might have been as the settlement of Ming-Uruk (Thousand Apricot Trees) in the 2nd or 1st century BC. By the time the Arabs took it in AD 751 it was a major caravan crossroads. It was given the name Toshkent (Tashkent, 'City of Stone' in Turkic) in about the 11th century.

The Khorezmshahs and Jenghiz Khan stubbed out Tashkent in the early 13th century, although it slowly recovered under the Mongols and then under Timur and grew more prosperous under the Shaybanids in the late 15th and 16th centuries.

The khan of Kokand annexed Tashkent in 1809. In 1865, as the Emir of Bukhara was preparing to snatch it away, the Russians under General Mikhail Grigorevich Chernyayev beat him to it, against the orders of the tsar and despite being outnumbered 15 to one. They found a proud town, enclosed by a 25km-long wall with 11 gates (of which not a trace remains today).

The newly installed Governor General Konstantin Kaufman was to gradually widen the imperial net around the other Central Asian khanates. Tashkent also became the tsarists' (and later the Soviets') main centre for espionage in Asia, during the protracted imperial rivalry with Britain known as the Great Game (p45).

Tashkent became the capital of the Turkestan Autonomous SSR, declared in 1918. When this was further split, the capital of the new Uzbek Autonomous SSR became Samarkand. In 1930, this status was restored to Tashkent.

Physically, Tashkent was changed forever on 25 April 1966, when a massive earthquake levelled vast areas of the town and left 300,000 people homeless (see the Earthquake Memorial, p202). Soviet historians made much of the battalions of 'fraternal peoples' and eager urban planners who came from around the Soviet Union to help with reconstruction.

But when Moscow later announced it would give 20% of the newly built apartments to these (mainly Russian) volunteers and invite them to stay, local resentment boiled over in street brawls between Uzbeks and Russians in the so-called Pakhtakor Incident of May 1969.

Security in the city, particularly in the metro stations, has been high since February 1999 when six car bombs killed 16 and injured more than 120. The blasts were attributed by the government to Islamic extremists, but it will probably never be known who was responsible.

## ORIENTATION

Before the 1966 earthquake, the Ankhor canal separated old (Uzbek) and new (Russian) Tashkent, the former a tangle of alleys around the **Chorsu Bazaar**, the latter with shady avenues radiating from what is now Amir Timur maydoni (Public sq). The city has since grown out of all proportions and sprawls over a vast plain. Covering it on foot requires long walks and it's best to use public transport.

Uzbeks perhaps still consider Chorsu their 'centre'. The Soviet centre was Mustaqillik maydoni, which has attained prominence anew thanks to its huge new Senate building. Amir Timur maydoni is a useful reference point, with Broadway (p200) leading off to the west.

Tashkent's *vokzal* (train station) is 2.5km south of Amir Timur maydoni; the airport is 6km south of Amir Timur maydoni; and the public bus station is about 14km southwest of Amir Timur maydoni, at Sobir Rahimov metro.

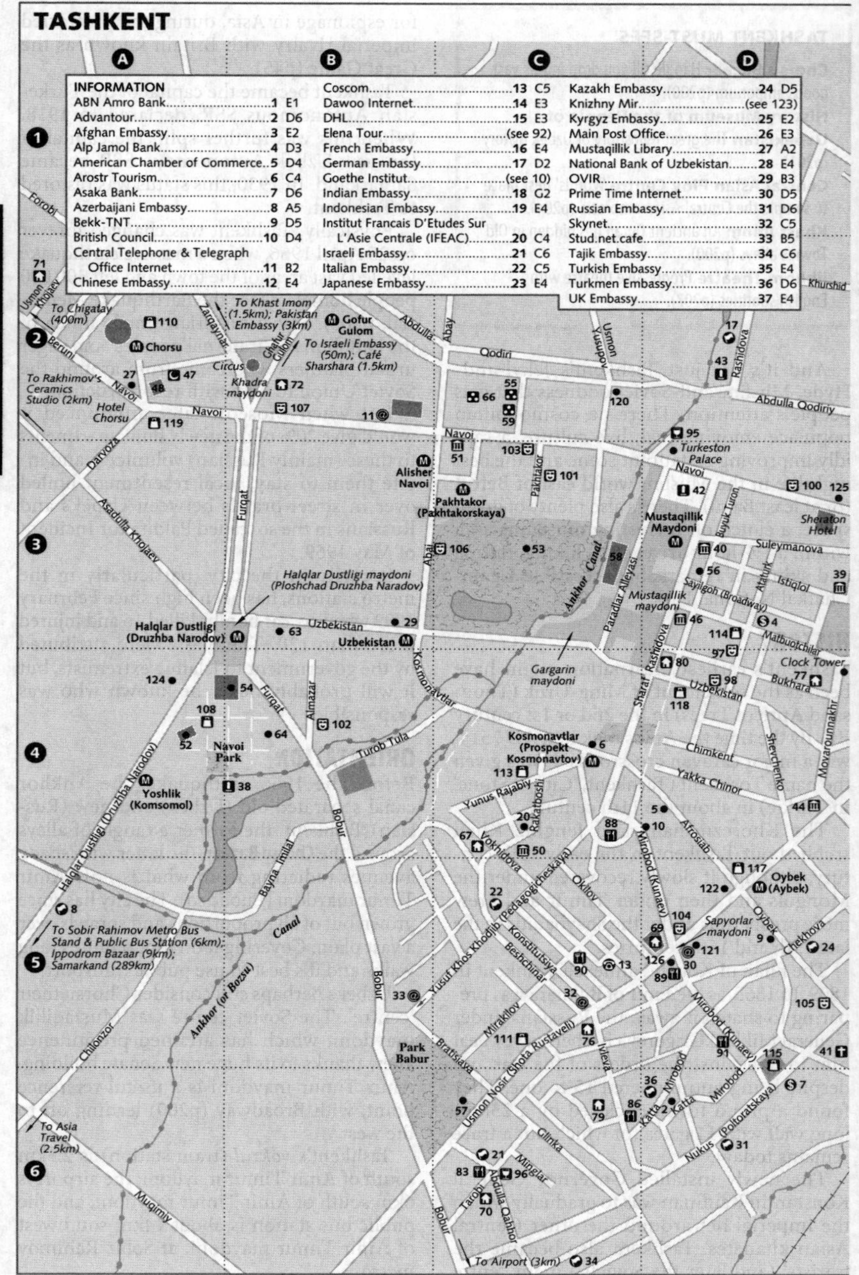
TASHKENT
A
B
C
D
1
2
3
4
5
6
INFORMATION
ABN Amro Bank......1 E1
Advantour......2 D6
Afghan Embassy......3 E2
Alp Jamol Bank......4 D3
American Chamber of Commerce..5 D4
Arostr Tourism......6 C4
Asaka Bank......7 D6
Azerbaijani Embassy......8 A5
Bekk-TNT......9 D5
British Council......10 D4
Central Telephone & Telegraph Office Internet......11 B2
Chinese Embassy......12 E4
Coscom......13 C5
Dawoo Internet......14 E3
DHL......15 E3
Elena Tour......(see 92)
French Embassy......16 E4
German Embassy......17 D2
Goethe Institut......(see 10)
Indian Embassy......18 G2
Indonesian Embassy......19 E4
Institut Francais D'Etudes Sur L'Asie Centrale (IFEAC)......20 C4
Israeli Embassy......21 C6
Italian Embassy......22 C5
Japanese Embassy......23 E4
Kazakh Embassy......24 D5
Knizhny Mir......(see 123)
Kyrgyz Embassy......25 E2
Main Post Office......26 E3
Mustaqillik Library......27 A2
National Bank of Uzbekistan......28 E4
OVIR......29 B3
Prime Time Internet......30 D5
Russian Embassy......31 D6
Skynet......32 C5
Stud.net.cafe......33 B5
Tajik Embassy......34 C6
Turkish Embassy......35 E4
Turkmen Embassy......36 D6
UK Embassy......37 E4
Forobi
Usmon Khojaev
To Chigatay (400m)
Beruni
Chorsu
To Rakhimov's Ceramics Studio (2km)
Hotel Chorsu
Navoi
Zarqaynar
To Khast Imom (1.5km); Pakistan Embassy (3km)
Gofur Gulom
Ghafur Gulom
To Israeli Embassy (50m); Café Sharshara (1.5km)
Circus
Khadra maydoni
Abdulla Qodiriy
Abay
Qodiri
Usmon Yusupov
Rashidova
Darvoza
Asadulla Khojaev
Furqat
Alisher Navoi
Pakhtakor (Pakhtakorskaya)
Pakhtakor
Turkeston Palace
Buyuk Turon
Sheraton Hotel
Khurshid
Mustaqillik Maydoni
Suleymanova
Istiqlol
Atatürk
Sayilgoh (Broadway)
Mustaqillik maydoni
Paradlar Alleyasi
Ankhor Canal
Halqlar Dustligi maydoni (Ploshchad Druzhba Naradov)
Halqlar Dustligi (Druzhba Narodov)
Uzbekistan
Kosmonavtlar
Gargarin maydoni
Sharaf Rashidova
Matbuotchilar
Clock Tower
Bukhara
Almazar
Navoi Park
Turob Tula
Kosmonavtlar (Prospekt Kosmonavtov)
Chimkent
Yakka Chinor
Shevchenko
Movarounnakhr
Yoshlik (Komsomol)
Halqlar Dustligi (Druzhba Narodov)
Yunus Rajabiy
Rakatboshi
Vokhidova
Mirobod (Kunaev)
Afrosiab
Oybek (Aybek)
Oybek
Chekhova
Bayna Imilal
Bobur
Canal
Oktov
Yusuf Khos Khodjib (Pedagogicheskaya)
Konstitutsiya
Beshchinar
Sapyorlar maydoni
To Sobir Rahimov Metro Bus Stand & Public Bus Station (6km); Ippodrom Bazaar (9km); Samarkand (289km)
Ankhor (or Bozsu)
Chilonzor
Miraklov
Park Babur
Bratislava
Usmon Nosir (Shota Rustaveli)
Ivleva
Mirobod
Katta Mirobod
Mirobod (Kunaev)
Nukus (Poltoratskaya)
Glinka
Minglar
Tarobi
Abdulla Qahhor
To Asia Travel (2.5km)
Muqimiy
To Airport (3km)

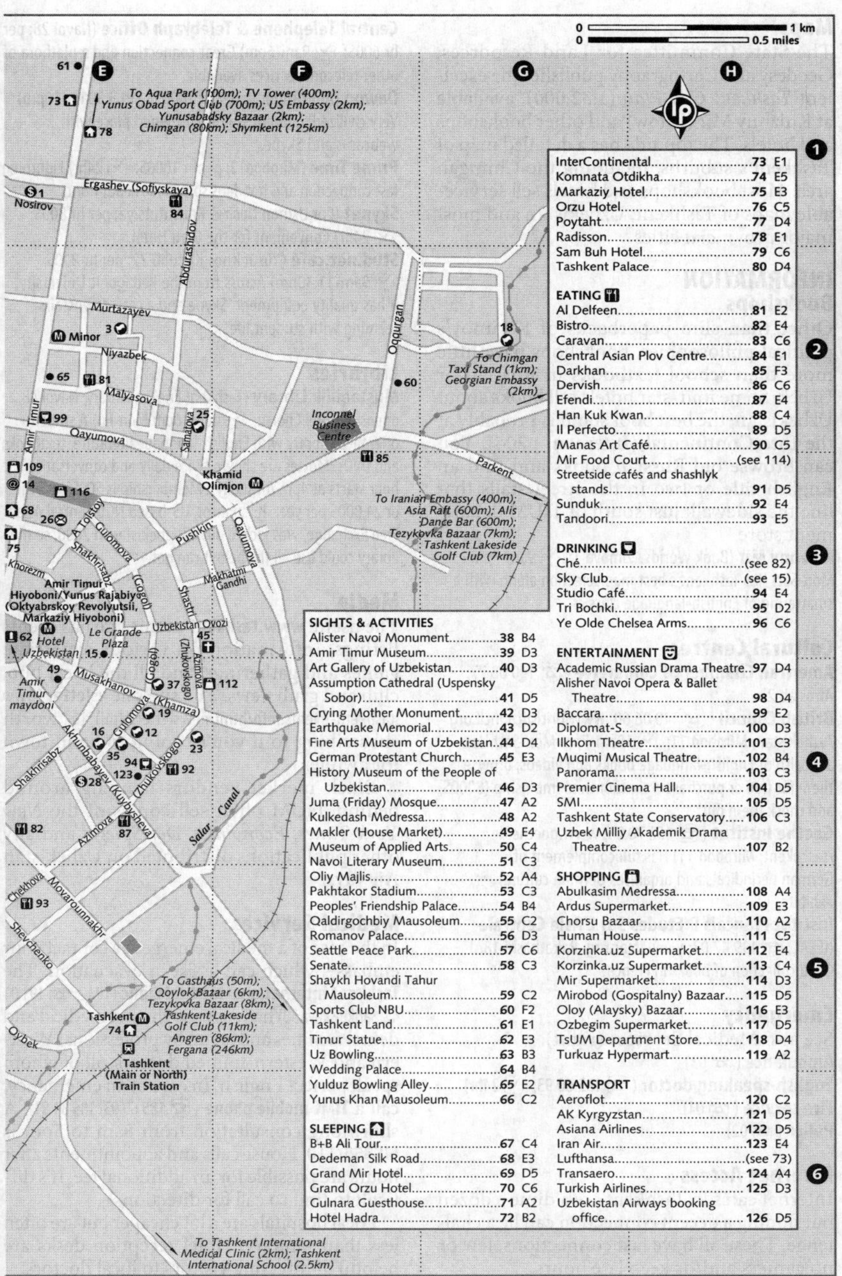
0 1 km
0 0.5 miles
E F G H
1 2 3 4 5 6
To Aqua Park (100m); TV Tower (400m); Yunus Obad Sport Club (700m); US Embassy (2km); Yunusabadsky Bazaar (2km); Chimgan (80km); Shymkent (125km)
Ergashev (Sofiyskaya)
Nosirov
Abdurashidov
Murtazayev
Minor
Niyazbek
Malyasova
Oqqurgan
To Chimgan Taxi Stand (1km); Georgian Embassy (2km)
Amir Timur
Qayumova
Samatova
Inconnel Business Centre
Parkent
Khamid Olimjon
To Iranian Embassy (400m); Asia Raft (600m); Alis Dance Bar (600m); Tezykovka Bazaar (7km); Tashkent Lakeside Golf Club (7km)
A Tolstoy
Gulomova
Pushkin
Qayumova
Shakhrisabz
Khorezm
(Gogol)
Makhatmi Gandhi
Shastri
Amir Timur Hiyoboni/Yunus Rajabiy (Oktyabrskoy Revolyutsii, Markaziy Hiyoboni)
Le Grande Plaza
Hotel Uzbekistan
Uzbekistan Ovozi
Azimova (Zhukovskogo)
Amir Timur maydoni
Musakhanov (Khamza)
(Gogol)
Gulomova
Akhunbabayev (Kuybysheva)
(Zhukovskogo)
Salar Canal
Azimova
Chekhova
Movarounnakhr
Shevchenko
To Gasthaus (50m); Qoylok Bazaar (6km); Tezykovka Bazaar (8km); Tashkent Lakeside Golf Club (11km); Angren (86km); Fergana (246km)
Tashkent
Oybek
Tashkent (Main or North) Train Station
To Tashkent International Medical Clinic (2km); Tashkent International School (2.5km)
SIGHTS & ACTIVITIES
Alister Navoi Monument....38 B4
Amir Timur Museum....39 D3
Art Gallery of Uzbekistan....40 D3
Assumption Cathedral (Uspensky Sobor)....41 D5
Crying Mother Monument....42 D3
Earthquake Memorial....43 D2
Fine Arts Museum of Uzbekistan....44 D4
German Protestant Church....45 E3
History Museum of the People of Uzbekistan....46 D3
Juma (Friday) Mosque....47 A2
Kulkedash Medressa....48 A2
Makler (House Market)....49 E4
Museum of Applied Arts....50 C4
Navoi Literary Museum....51 C3
Oliy Majlis....52 A4
Pakhtakor Stadium....53 C3
Peoples' Friendship Palace....54 B4
Qaldirgochbiy Mausoleum....55 C2
Romanov Palace....56 D3
Seattle Peace Park....57 C6
Senate....58 C3
Shaykh Hovandi Tahur Mausoleum....59 C2
Sports Club NBU....60 F2
Tashkent Land....61 E1
Timur Statue....62 E3
Uz Bowling....63 B3
Wedding Palace....64 B4
Yulduz Bowling Alley....65 E2
Yunus Khan Mausoleum....66 C2
SLEEPING
B+B Ali Tour....67 C4
Dedeman Silk Road....68 E3
Grand Mir Hotel....69 D5
Grand Orzu Hotel....70 C6
Gulnara Guesthouse....71 A2
Hotel Hadra....72 B2
InterContinental....73 E1
Komnata Otdikha....74 E5
Markaziy Hotel....75 E3
Orzu Hotel....76 C5
Poytaht....77 D4
Radisson....78 E1
Sam Buh Hotel....79 C6
Tashkent Palace....80 D4
EATING
Al Delfeen....81 E2
Bistro....82 E4
Caravan....83 C6
Central Asian Plov Centre....84 E1
Darkhan....85 F3
Dervish....86 C6
Efendi....87 E4
Han Kuk Kwan....88 C4
Il Perfecto....89 D5
Manas Art Café....90 C5
Mir Food Court....(see 114)
Streetside cafés and shashlyk stands....91 D5
Sunduk....92 E4
Tandoori....93 E5
DRINKING
Ché....(see 82)
Sky Club....(see 15)
Studio Café....94 E4
Tri Bochki....95 D2
Ye Olde Chelsea Arms....96 C6
ENTERTAINMENT
Academic Russian Drama Theatre....97 D4
Alisher Navoi Opera & Ballet Theatre....98 D4
Baccara....99 E2
Diplomat-S....100 D3
Ilkhom Theatre....101 C3
Muqimi Musical Theatre....102 B4
Panorama....103 C3
Premier Cinema Hall....104 D5
SMI....105 D5
Tashkent State Conservatory....106 C3
Uzbek Milliy Akademik Drama Theatre....107 B2
SHOPPING
Abulkasim Medressa....108 A4
Ardus Supermarket....109 E3
Chorsu Bazaar....110 A2
Human House....111 C5
Korzinka.uz Supermarket....112 E4
Korzinka.uz Supermarket....113 C4
Mir Supermarket....114 D3
Mirobod (Gospitalny) Bazaar....115 D5
Oloy (Alaysky) Bazaar....116 E3
Ozbegim Supermarket....117 D5
TsUM Department Store....118 D4
Turkuaz Hypermart....119 A2
TRANSPORT
Aeroflot....120 C2
AK Kyrgyzstan....121 D5
Asiana Airlines....122 D5
Iran Air....123 E4
Lufthansa....(see 73)
Transaero....124 A4
Turkish Airlines....125 D3
Uzbekistan Airways booking office....126 D5

## Maps

The State Committee for Land Resources, Geodesy and Cartography publishes the excellent *Tashkent City Plan* (1:32,000), available at Knizhny Mir (below) and other bookshops and hotels. The flip side has a detailed map of Tashkent's suburbs, including the Chimgan area. Most bookshops and hotels sell serviceable maps of Tashkent, Uzbekistan and most major provincial cities.



# INFORMATION

## Bookshops

Other than slim paperbacks of Karimov's political philosophies, bookshops have little more than school textbooks in Russian or Uzbek. Some four-star hotels sell books about Uzbekistan; the best bookstand is probably at the InterContinental (Intercon; p204). You can browse old Russian books and find an English title or two in the street stalls that line the sidewalk just south of TsUM department store.

**Knizhny Mir** (Book World; Azimova 1; 9am-7pm Mon-Sat) Has Tashkent's best map selection along with a smattering of English-language classics.

## Cultural Centres

**American Chamber of Commerce** (☎ 140 08 77; Afrosiab 2)

**British Council** (☎ 140 06 60; www.britishcouncil.org/uzbekistan; Mirobod 11; 10am-7pm Mon-Sat) Has a wealth of English-language books and videos; browse them for free or purchase a six-month membership (8000S) and check them out.

**Goethe Institut** (☎ 152 70 23; www.goethe.de/taschkent; Mirobod 11) Has full complement of German periodicals and organises German cultural exhibits.

**Institut Francais D'Etudes Sur L'Asie Centrale** (IFEAC; ☎ 139 47 03; www.ifeac.org; Rakatboshi 18A) Good collection of books in French.

## Emergency

See also Medical Services (right).

**Ambulance** (☎ 03)

**English-speaking doctor** (☎ 185 60 93; 24hr)

**Fire service** (☎ 01)

**Police** (☎ 02)

## Internet Access

Internet cafés in Tashkent are a dime a dozen but finding a decent connection can be a challenge. These all have fast connections, few or no gamers and/or keep late hours.

**Central Telephone & Telegraph Office** (Navoi 28; per hr 600S; 9am-6pm) Great connection and a plethora of other telecom services available.

**Dawoo** (Amir Timur 4; per hr 1000S; 8.30am-10pm) Very civilized, gamerless Korean-owned place with webcams and Skype.

**Prime Time** (Mirobod12; per hr 1000S; 24hr) Lightning fast connection and hot dogs sold in kiosk out front.

**Skynet** (Cnr Usmon Nosir & Konstitutsiya; per hr 800S; 24hr) Convenient for the Orzu Hotel.

**Stud.net.café** (Yusuf Khos Khodjib 72; per hr 800S; 9am-11.30pm) Across from the Pedagogic University, it has quality equipment, Skype and a café downstairs teeming with student life.

## Libraries

**Mustaqillik Library** (Tashkent English Library; Navoi 48, opposite Hotel Chorsu; noon-6pm Mon-Fri) A student-orientated library with English-language literature, textbooks and DVDs. Movies are shown twice daily and conversation hour starts at 4pm most days. Membership is 500S per visit or 24,000S per year. Its sponsor, US-based NGO Central Asian Free Exchange, was kicked out of Uzbekistan in 2006, so the library could use all the help it can get.

## Media

The useful **www.tashkent-events.info** has events listings, information on various expatriate games and gatherings, and all the latest pub, club and grub news. The site's **newsletter** (www.tashkent-events.info/html/newsletter.html) is worth subscribing to if you're going to be in town for awhile.

Black market vendors hanging around behind TsUM often sell copies of the *New York Times, Economist, Der Spiegel* and any other publications distributed on Uzbekistan Airways.

## Medical Services

In the case of a medical emergency contact your embassy, which can assist in evacuation. The **Tashkent International Medical Clinic** (TIMC; ☎ 191 01 42; Sarikulskaya 38) has state-of-the-art medical and dental facilities and is run by professional Western and Western-trained doctors, all of whom speak perfect English. In case of an emergency, call a **TIMC mobile phone** (☎ 185 60 93, 185 84 81). A short/long consultation from 8am to 5pm is US$55/110. House calls and appointments after hours are possible for an additional fee. It's difficult to find so call for directions.

Local hospitals are a lot cheaper but are often less than sanitary. Hotel reception desks are helpful in directing visitors to local doctors.

### Money

Exchange facilities are everywhere. Try the Markaziy, InterContinental, Poytaht and Tashkent Palace hotels for 24-hour service. Black market moneychangers (see p263) still work the bazaars and can also be found at TsUM and other points (ask any taxi driver).

The ATMs in town are often cashless, with the notable exception of those of **Asaka Bank** (Nukus 67), which issue unlimited wads of crisp US$50 and US$100 bills to MasterCard holders at – get this – 0% commission. Other Asaka ATMs are at the InterContinental and Grand Mir hotels. More prevalent but less reliable are the Visa-card ATMs located in most four-star hotels. When working, these dispense Uzbek sum.

**ABN Amro** (Nosirov 77) Charges 4% for cash advances against MasterCard, Maestro and Visa cards.
**Alp Jamol Bank** (Ataturk 21) Charges 4% to change travellers cheques and gives cash advances against Visa.
**National Bank of Uzbekistan** (NBU; Gulomova 95; 8am-4pm Mon-Fri) Charges a 2% fee for cashing travellers cheques, and gives cash advances against Visa (3.5%) and MasterCard (4%).

### Post

The **main post office** (pochta bulimi; 133 42 02; Shakhrisabz 7; 8am-6pm) has unreliable general delivery.

**DHL** (120 66 00; Uzbekistan 2) has an office in Le Grande Plaza hotel. A cheaper option is **Bekk-TNT** (152 17-87; Oybek 20). All four-star hotels offer express mail services, usually using one of the above.

### Registration

See p264 for information on registering with the Office of Visas & Registration (OVIR) in Tashkent.

### Telephone

**Central Telephone & Telegraph Office** (144 65 35; Navoi 28; 8am-11pm).

### Travel Agencies

Contrary to what the government would have you believe, it's easy to go it alone in Uzbekistan. Still, if you can afford them, travel agencies are useful for planning hassle-free excursions, prearranging domestic air tickets and securing qualified guides for outdoor activities such as trekking, rafting and heli-skiing. And unless you have friends in Uzbekistan they are essential for visa support.

**Advantour** (120 00 50; www.advantour.com, mnazarov@advantour.com; Katta Mirobod 116) The reliable outfit located in the Rovshan Hotel can customise tours for both groups and individuals. The personable and knowledgeable husband-and-wife owners speak perfect English. They were relocating at research time.
**Arostr Tourism** (137 17 64; www.arostrtour.com; arostr@mail.ru; Afrosiab 13-45) Operated by the attentive and personable Airat Yuldashev, Arostr is a good choice for individual travellers. Airat arranges obligation-free visas plus homestays and self-contained apartments in Tashkent.
**Asia Travel** (173 51 07; www.asia-travel.uz; Chilonzor 97) Has outgrown its usefulness for individual travellers, but maintains stranglehold on heli-skiing and certain other outdoor activities (see p101). Also sells topographical maps.
**Elena Tour** (132 02 99; www.elenatour.uz; trekking@elenatour.uz; Azimova 63, Apt No 1) Few people know the local mountains like agency head Boris Karpov, who also leads the twice-per-month excursions of the Tashkent Hiking Club (p202). It also runs the full gamut of standard tours. See also p101.
**Stantours** (www.stantours.com) Based in Kazakhstan, it is nonetheless the best source of advice on procuring Central Asian visas in Tashkent.

## DANGERS & ANNOYANCES

The *militsia* (police) have become much less of a nuisance to travellers in recent years. Worried about Uzbekistan's international image, President Karimov has curbed the police habit of shaking down travellers for bribes, although this still occurs, particularly at metro stations. See Crooked Officials (p448) for tips on dealing with police.

### Scams

Upon arrival at Tashkent International Airport, you might be approached at customs by a man offering to help you fill out your customs declaration form; although a friendly enough gesture, travellers have been asked for money (usually US$5) for this unofficial service. Avoid this by asking for two customs forms in English and fill them out on your own. A similar annoyance occurs at the luggage carousel. Your bags might be taken off before they reach daylight and delivered on a cart by an attendant who will ask for a US$5 tip.

## SIGHTS

Modern Tashkent is a big, sprawling city that's best appreciated for its whole rather than its parts. If you're short on time, pick your spots and hone in on them by car. At

**LIGHTS GO DOWN ON BROADWAY**

For years Sayilgoh, otherwise known as Broadway, was the centre of tourist life in Tashkent. While the rows of Soviet kitsch vendors, souvenir hawkers and open-air arts and craft galleries were on the tacky side, it was nonetheless a great place to grab a beer, people watch, meet other travellers and kill time while waiting for visas to come through.

But that all changed abruptly in September 2006 after President Karimov took a stroll down Broadway. Not surprisingly, the haphazard nature of the street ran anathema to his vision of an orderly police state. A couple of days later several dozen *militsia* (police) unceremoniously broke down the street stalls and evicted the vendors.

As of this writing, Broadway continues to languish in its new guise of world's most boring pedestrian avenue. It could yet make a comeback, but for now it remains yet another symbol of Karimov's heavy hand.



minimum check out Khast Imom, Chorsu Bazaar and a few museums. If you have a few more days cover as much as you can on foot – you'll catch random glimpses of city life that are often more rewarding than the sights themselves. Old Town makes for the best wandering.

## Old Town

The Old Town (Uzbek: *eski shakhar*, Russian: *stary gorod*) starts beside Chorsu Bazaar and the Chorsu Hotel. A maze of narrow dirt streets is lined with low mud-brick houses and dotted with mosques and old medressas. These few handsome religious buildings date from the 15th and 16th centuries.

Taxi drivers get lost easily here. On foot, you could easily get lost too, but that's part of the fun. Wandering around you'll often be invited into someone's home, where you'll discover that the blank outer walls of traditional homes conceal cool, peaceful garden courtyards.

### CHORSU BAZAAR & AROUND

Tashkent's most famous farmers market, topped by a giant green dome, is a delightful slice of city life spilling into the streets off Old Town's southern edge. If it grows and it's edible, it's here. There are acres of spices arranged in brightly coloured mountains; Volkswagen-sized sacks of grain; entire sheds dedicated to candy, dairy products and bread; interminable rows of freshly slaughtered livestock; and – of course – scores of the pomegranates, melons, persimmons, huge mutant tomatoes and whatever fruits are in season. Souvenir hunters will find *kurpacha* (colourful sitting mattresses), skull caps, *chapan* and knives here.

The grand 16th-century **Kulkedash medressa** (admission 1000S) sits beside Tashkent's principal **Juma (Friday) mosque** on a hill overlooking Chorsu Bazaar. The 15th-century mosque was once a place of execution for unfaithful wives. The mosque was a sheet-metal workshop and the medressa a storage space during Soviet times. Both were renovated in the mid-'90s, and on warm Friday mornings the plaza in front overflows with worshippers.

### KHAST IMOM

The official religious centre of the republic is located 2km north of the Circus, on Zarqaynar. Here you'll find the newly restored **Moyie Mubarek Library Museum** (☎ 160 03 02; Zarqaynar 114; admission 1200S; 🕑 9am-4pm), which houses the 7th-century Osman Quran (Uthman Quran), said to be the world's oldest. This enormous deerskin tome was brought to Samarkand by Timur, then taken to Moscow by the Russians in 1868 before bring returned to Tashkent by Lenin in 1924 as an act of goodwill towards Turkestan's Muslims. It is Tashkent's most impressive and important sight. The museum also contains 20,000 additional books and 3000 rare manuscripts. The library is next to the spartan **Telyashayakh Mosque**.

Across the street is the 16th-century **Barakhon Medressa**, which houses the Muslim Board of Uzbekistan, whose grand mufti is roughly the Islamic equivalent of an archbishop. Northwest of here is the **Imam Ismail al-Bukhari Islamic Institute**, a two-year post-medressa academy with about 200 students. It was one of two medressas in Central Asia left open in Soviet times (the other was in Bukhara). Nearby is the little 16th-century **mausoleum of Abu Bakr Kaffal Shoshi**, an Islamic scholar of the Shaybanid period. Enter through the back to view his large tomb and five smaller ones.

### Yunus Khan Mausoleum

Across Navoi from the Navoi Literary Museum are three 15th-century mausoleums. The biggest, on the grounds of the Tashkent Islamic University, bears the name of Yunus Khan, grandfather of the Mughal emperor Babur. The mausoleum itself sits locked and idle, but you can check out its attractive Timurid-style *pishtak* (entrance portal). Access is from Abdulla Qodiri. Two smaller mausoleums are east of the university grounds, accessible via a small side street running north from Navoi – the pointy-roofed **Qaldirgochbiy** and the twin-domed **Shaykh Hovandi Tahur**. Next to the latter is a mosque with beautifully carved wooden doors and attractive tilework.

### Museums & Galleries

The **History Museum of the People of Uzbekistan** (☎ 139 17 79; Sharaf Rashidova 30; admission 3000S, guided tour in English 2000S, 🕒 10am-5pm Tue-Sun) is a must-stop for anyone looking for a primer on the history of Turkestan from ancient times to the present. The 1st floor has ancient Zoroastrian and Buddhist artefacts, including a small Buddha from a Kushan temple excavated at Fayoz-Tepe near Termiz. On the 2nd floor English placards walk you through the Russian conquests of the khanates and emirates, and there are some foreboding newspaper clippings of revolts in Andijon and elsewhere being brutally suppressed by the Russians around the turn of the 20th century. The 3rd floor, naturally, is dedicated to Karimov. A placard contains what is surely one of Karimov's more ironic quotes. About the Soviet Union, he says: 'Socialist transformation lead to the creation of the totalitarian state, coercive nationalisation of the economy, elimination of political pluralism and greatly damaged national originality.'

The four floors of the **Fine Arts Museum of Uzbekistan** (☎ 136 74 36; Movarounnakhr 16; admission 3000S; 🕒 10am-5pm Wed-Sun, 10am-2pm Mon) walk you through 1500 years of art in Uzbekistan, from 7th-century Buddhist relics, to the art of pre-Russian Turkestan, to Soviet realism, to contemporary works. There are displays of east Asian and south Asian art and even a few c-19th century paintings of second-tier Russian and European artists hanging about. Nineteenth- and 20th-century Central Asian masters are well represented, and there's an impressive section on Uzbek applied art – notably some brilliant old plaster carvings *(ghanch)* and the silk-on-cotton embroidered hangings called *suzani*.

The **Museum of Applied Arts** (☎ 153 39 43; Rakatboshi 15; admission 1200S, guide 2000S; 🕒 9am-6pm) occupies an exquisite house full of bright *ghanch* and carved wood. It was built in the 1930s, at the height of the Soviet period, but nonetheless serves as a good sneak preview of the older architectural lurking in Bukhara and Samarkand. The ceramic and textile displays here, with English descriptions, are a fine way to bone up the regional decorative styles of Uzbekistan, and there's a pricey gift shop to trap impulse buyers.

The richly decorated **Amir Timur Museum** (☎ 133 62 28; Amir Timur 1; admission 3000S; 🕒 10am-5pm Tue-Sun) is a must for aficionados of kitsch and cult-making. Murals show Timur commissioning public projects and praising his labourers, yet conspicuously overlooking his bloody, skull-stacking military campaigns.

The recently opened **Art Gallery of Uzbekistan** (☎ 133 56 74; Buyuk Turon 2; admission 400S, guided tour 2000S; 🕒 11am-5pm Tue-Sat) rolls out rotating exhibits of Uzbekistan's top contemporary artists in its circular, Guggenheim-like interior.

Besides memorabilia of 15th-century poet Alisher Navoi and other Central Asian literati, the **Navoi Literary Museum** (☎ 144 12 68; Navoi 69; admission 3000S; 🕒 10am-5pm Mon-Fri, 10am-1pm Sat) has replica manuscripts, Persian calligraphy, and old miniatures that offer a glimpse of life in the 15th and 16th centuries.

### Navoi Park

Downtown Tashkent's largest park, sprawling southward from Halqlar Dustligi metro, is a haven for joggers, Sunday strollers, and appreciators of Uzbek eccentricity. Soviet architects had a field day here, erecting a pod of spectacularly hideous concrete monstrosities, the most eye-catching of which is the **Peoples' Friendship Palace**, which appears like a moon-landing station from a 1950s film set. Looming inside is an enormous concert hall with 4200 seats.

Southeast of the Friendship Palace is the equally appalling **Wedding Palace**, a vulgar, crooked chunk of Khrushchev-era concrete. The tightly guarded building southwest of the Friendship Palace is the **Oliy Majlis** (parliament). It currently functions as a giant rubber stamp in its infrequent sessions. Nearby is a vast promenade and a post-Soviet **monument to Alisher Navoi**, Uzbekistan's newly chosen cultural hero.

Continuing south you'll find some amusement park rides and a large manmade lake, which you can traverse in hired peddle boats in the warm months.

## Other Sights

Tashkent's main streets radiate from **Amir Timur maydoni**, where a glowering bust of Marx has been replaced by a suitably patriotic **statue of Timur** on horseback. A glance under the statue reveals that the stallion has been divested of a certain reproductive appendage. Just who stole it is one of Tashkent's great mysteries. Fortunately the horse's formidable family jewels remain intact – for now.

Further west, good-luck pelicans guard the gates to the newly refurbished **Mustaqillik maydoni** (Independence Sq), where crowds gather to watch parades on Independence day and whenever else Karimov feels the need to stir up a bit of nationalistic spirit. The shiny white edifice on the west side of the square is the brand new **Senate** building. Its ample size and appearance suggest that it was built to outdo the United State's Senate building. The president's office and most ministries take up the southern portion around Gagarin maydoni. East of the square across Rashidova, the animal-festooned façade of the Tsarist-era **Romanov Palace** faces the Art Gallery of Uzbekistan, and is now closed to the public.

North of Mustaqillik maydoni is the **Crying Mother Monument**. Fronted by an eternal flame, it was constructed in 1999 to honour the 400,000 Uzbek soldiers who died in WWII. The niches along its two corridors house their names. Karimov has built a nearly identical monument near the centre of most major Uzbek cities. Hey, at least he's not building Turkmenbashi-style monuments to himself.

The New Soviet men and women who rebuilt Tashkent after the 1966 earthquake are remembered in stone at the **Earthquake Memorial**. Newlyweds flock here to have their photos taken on weekends.

The **TV Tower** (Amir Timur; admission 400S; ⌚ 10am-9pm Tue-Sun), a 375m three-legged monster, the epitome of Soviet design, stands north of the InterContinental. The price of admission gets you up to the 100m viewing platform. You'll need your passport to buy a ticket. To go up to the next level (about 220m) you'll have to grease the guard's palm – 2000S should do the trick. At 110m there's a revolving restaurant that serves a decidedly mediocre set Russian meal (3100S).

At the other end of town, Babur Park is home to the poignant **Seattle Peace Park**, a collection of small tiles designed by Tashkent- and Seattle-based schoolchildren in the 1980s. The tiles, many of which are cracked or missing, recall the Cold War era with messages such as 'You can't hug your child with nuclear arms', in Russian or English.

Near Mirobod Bazaar is one of Tashkent's four Orthodox churches, the **Assumption Cathedral** (Uspensky Sobor), which is bright blue with copper domes. A **German Protestant Church**, once used as a recital hall and now holding Lutheran services again, is on Azimova.

It's worth taking the metro to reach some of these sites, if only to visit some of the lavishly decorated stations. A must is the Kosmonavtlar station with its unearthly images of Amir Timur's astronomer grandson, Ulugbek, and Soviet cosmonaut Yuri Gagarin, among others.

# ACTIVITIES

Thanks to President Karimov's personal affinity for the game, tennis courts have sprung up across the country. You can rent equipment and play at one of the eight courts of the **Yunus Obad Sport Club** (☎ 134 77 60; Amir Timur; per hr 5000-7000S) in the shadow of the TV Tower. The club also boasts an ocean-sized Olympic **pool** (per hr 5000S). Another option for tennis, swimming and gym is **Sports Club NBU** (☎ 268 44 59/69; Oqqurgan 16; ⌚ 6am-9pm), located about 600m east of Khamid Olimjon metro.

There are a couple of places to go bowling, including **Yulduz Bowling Alley** (☎ 132 20 02; Amir Timur 60; 3000S per game; ⌚ 10am-midnight) and **Uz Bowling** (☎ 132 17 84; Uzbekistan 8/1).

Runners and walkers can join the local branch of the **Hash House Harriers** as they cruise the streets of Tashkent every Sunday before repairing to the nearest watering hole. Hashers meet at the Hotel Uzbekistan (5pm summer, 4pm spring and fall, and 3pm winter). Call or email organiser **Charles Rudd** (☎ 139 13 02; ruddcl@interconcepts.com) to confirm times.

The **Tashkent Hiking Club** (tashkenthikingclub@yahoo.com) goes hiking around Chimgan every other Sunday and takes occasional weekend excursions further afield.

The Korean-designed **Tashkent Lakeside Golf Club** (☎ 195 09 91/2/3; tashgolf@dostlink.net; Bektemir District 1; 1 round US$62) is at Lake Rokhat, on the southeast edge of the city.

Just north of the InterContinental, Uzbekistan's largest amusement park, **Tashkent Land** (Amir Timur; adult/child 5000/2500S; 10am-7pm Tue-Sun), has a handful of creaky Soviet rides. It's an amusing diversion, just don't expect Walt Disney World. More worthwhile in the warm months is the **Aqua Park** (Amir Timur; adult/child 3000/1500S; 9am-8pm May-Sep) just north of Tashkent Land.

## TOURS

There aren't any organised city tours per se, but most fancier hotels and travel agencies can whip up a guide for no more than US$5 per hour, or US$30 per day.

## FESTIVALS & EVENTS

Tashkent hosts the 14-day international music festival **Il Khom 20** (Inspiration 20) annually in March or April. It features avant-garde and New Age music, and is held in the new Tashkent State Conservatory (p207). During even-numbered years Tashkent hosts a **film festival** in September featuring Asian, African and Latin American films.

## SLEEPING

The foreign operators of several of Tashkent's fancier hotels pulled out of Uzbekistan in the wake of the 2005 Andijon incident, turning management over to the state. These hotels, including the Markaziy (formerly the Sheraton) and Tashkent Palace (formerly Le Meridien), have gone downhill in terms of service and maintenance, but the flipside is that they have become fantastically cheap. Simply ask and you shall receive at least a 50% discount off the rack rate – not bad considering that their four-star facilities remain basically intact.

Alas, there's no such buyer's market at the budget end. The Tara Hotel, once Tashkent's main backpacker ghetto, no longer accepts foreigners. Homestays are technically illegal and thus operate in the shadows. You can try asking about them at the Makler (p204) or at any taxi stand.

### Budget

**Hotel Hadra** (☎ 244 28 08; Ghafur Ghulom 53A; 2-bed dm 4000S) The darkest hole in all of Central Asia is a bit brighter thanks to an application of paint to the walls of at least one room. But it's still pretty dark, and it still doubles as a decidedly low-class brothel. It's in an dank apartment block next to the Circus.

**Komnata Otdikha** (☎ 199 76 49; Vokzal; 3-bed dm 7000S, r/ste US$20/25) It's a spectacular deal and, for now at least, it's brand new. The rooms are bright, white, clean and huge, and the dorm rooms ideal for three people. Its location inside the train station makes it a top draw, so get there early or try calling ahead if you know some Russian or Uzbek.

**Gulnara Guesthouse** (☎ 160 28 16; gulnara@globalnet.uz; Usmon Khojaev 40; per person US$15) Cheap prices, filling breakfasts and an Old Town location make this friendly, family-run B&B a hit with backpackers. The rooms are nothing to write home about but the Soviet-style single beds are comfortable enough. It's hard to find; from Chorsu Bazaar head west on Beruni and take a right after 400m on the first real street, Usmon Khojaev (Azad). It's about 150m to the guesthouse on the left.

our pick **B+B Ali Tour** (☎ 153 71 62; ali_tour@tkt.uz; Vokhidova 26/2; s/d/tr US$15/30/39, 4-person apt US$60) The Soviet charms of owner Alisher Khabibullaev and the convivial, slapdash nature of his guesthouse are just the tonic to ease you into the chaotic embrace of travel in post-Soviet Uzbekistan. English and French is spoken, and assistance with travel arrangements offered – along with plenty of free vodka and a free dinner or two if you stick around long enough.

### Midrange

**Sam Buh Hotel** (☎ 120 88 26; Tsekhovaya 1; www.traveluz.com; s/d US$25/30) Sam Buh's rooms trump those of the nearby Orzu Hotel in terms of space, although couples will have to make do with twin beds. It is a bit hard to find, so call for a pick-up.

**Orzu Hotel** (☎ 120 88 22; www.orzu-hotels.com; Ivleva 14; s/d US$25/35) Friendly English-speaking service is the high-point here. The 36 rooms are small but smart and include satellite TV and a large buffet breakfast of crepes, eggs, cereal and juice. Request a room off the busy street.

our pick **Poytaht** (☎ 120 86 76; www.poytaht.uz; Movarounnakhr 4; s/d US$40/60) Of all the great deals to be had at the mid- to top end in Tashkent, the Poytaht is the best. It's no Intercon service-wise, but you won't be complaining about the comfy king-sized beds, tidy and spacious Scandinavian-style rooms, sumptuous buffet breakfast and pond-sized swimming pool – all within a pomegranate throw of central Amir Timur maydoni. Try negotiating a further US$5 to US$10 discount.

**Markaziy Hotel** (☎ 138 30 00; markaziy.hotel@mail.ru; Amir Timur 15; s/d US$70/90; ) The Markaziy has suffered less than others from its transition from private to state ownership. Most of the glorious vestiges of its four-star past remain, including two pools, inviting king-sized beds with fine linens, smart art and, most importantly, rooms with space to swing a giraffe. Negotiate hard here. Prices listed are before discounts.

Also recommended:

**Grand Orzu Hotel** (☎ 120 88 77; www.orzu-hotels.com; 27 Tarobi; s/d US$33/38; ) Highlight is the pleasant poolside patio; pay the extra US$10 extra for the huge suite.

**Tashkent Palace** (☎ 120 5800; www.tashkent-palace.com; Buyuk Turon 56; s/d US$120/130; ) Can't beat the location near Opera House. Negotiate hard. Prices listed are before discounts.

## Top End

**Dedeman Silk Road** (☎ 120 37 00; Amir Timur 7/8; www.dedemanhotels.com; s/d US$160/180; ) This Turkish-run high-rise delivers spiffy business-standard rooms, free high-speed internet access and nearly flawless service in the centre of the city. In the wake of Tashkent's great hotel ownership shuffle, the Dedeman has emerged, along with the Intercon, as the favourite among foreign businessmen. Unlike the Intercon, staff are open to negotiations here – expect to pay about US$90 for a double.

**Hotel InterContinental** (Intercon; ☎ 120 70 00; www.ichotelsgroup.com, tashkent@interconti.com; Amir Timur 107A; s/d/ste US$235/255/400; ) Just north of the city centre, this is the city's best hotel, with unmatched service and a full range of business and leisure facilities: indoor swimming pool, business centre, a bookshop, boutiques, free wi-fi in the lobby and several excellent restaurants. The rooms lack character but have every amenity you could want.

Also recommended:

**Grand Mir** (☎ 140 20 00; www.grandmirhotel.com; Mirobod 2; s/d US$120/160; ) This Turkish-owned outfit is a behemoth, but a fine behemoth.

**Radisson** (☎ 120 49 00; www.radisson.com; Amir Timur 88; s/d US$125/140; ) Small discounts available at this cozy four-star stand-by.

## Rental Accommodation

A short walk east down Musakhanov from Amir Timur maydoni is a bus depot where a dozen or so apartment brokers gather informally at a spot called **Makler** (house market; Khorezm). Weekly rental prices start at about US$100 for a basic studio apartment, but hard negotiations should bring that down substantially. You'll need to visit in person to negotiate.

Arostr (p199) has two self-contained apartments for US$25 in the city centre.

# EATING

National, European, Middle Eastern and of course Russian cuisine are all well represented in Tashkent, although good Southeast Asian food is hard to come by. For lunch on Tuesday and Friday try the 4000S Indonesian smor-

### PLOV GLORIOUS PLOV

Few things excite the Uzbek palate like *plov*, that wonderful conglomeration of rice, vegetables and meat bits swimming in lamb fat and oil. This Central Asian staple has been elevated to the status of religion in Uzbekistan, the country with which it is most closely associated. Each province has its own style, which locals loudly and proudly proclaim is the best in Uzbekistan – and by default the world. That *plov* is an aphrodisiac goes without saying. Uzbeks joke that the word for 'foreplay' in Uzbek is *'plov'*. Men put the best cuts of meat in the *plov* on Thursday; not coincidentally, Thursday's when most Uzbek babies are conceived. Drinking the oil at the bottom of the *kazan* (large *plov* cauldron) is said to add particular spark to a man's libido.

To sample *plov* styles from various regions of the country – and drink the oil if you dare – head to the celebration of *plov* that is the **Central Asian Plov Centre** (Cnr Ergashev & Abdurashidov; meals 2000S; lunch). Get there before noon for the best selection. Walk past the mob of people crowding around steaming *kazans* and take a seat inside, where a waitress will eventually come and serve you. Your group's order will arrive Uzbek-style on a single plate from which everybody will eat. The best day to come? Why Thursday, of course!

UZBEKISTAN

gasbord served up from noon to 2pm at the Indonesian Embassy (p262).

### Cafés, Chaikhanas & Fast Food

For cheap eats and cheap beer there are hundreds of street-side cafés, Korean noodle outfits and shashlyk stands to choose from; one cluster is on Mirobod, 500m south of the Uzbekistan Airways booking office. The many chaikhanas (teahouses) around Chorsu Bazaar are both cheap and colourful. Hygiene is variable; look for high turnover and service right off the fire.

**Darkhan** (Pushkin; kebabs 500-1000S, 0.5L beer 400S) Cheap and fast outdoor food court with big wooden tables shaded by trees. There are several stalls here serving *laghman* (noodles), *samsa* (samosas), kebabs, salads and some of the cheapest beer in town.

**Mir Food Court** (Ataturk 1; meals 1000-3000S) This is where well-heeled teenagers gather to preen in the city's best approximation of a Western fast-food court, with pasta, burgers, sandwiches and kebabs on offer. A coffee shop on the top floor of the mall serves a decent cup of coffee.

**Café Sharshara** (☎ 144 58 35; Bobojonova 10; mains 3000S) Chaikhana real estate comes no riper than the canalside patch occupied by this popular Old Town stand-by. The sprawling patio is cooled by gentle mist from the rumbling manmade waterfall on premises, making it an almost perfect warm-weather spot for a shashlyk and a cold Shimkent (1500S). There's live evening entertainment in the warm months.

**Il Perfecto** (☎ 153 28 52; Mirobod 9A; mains 3000-5000S; lunch & dinner) The impressive coffee menu and reliable free wi-fi access here are a godsend for guidebook writers and other laptop-addicted souls, but unconscionably they don't open until 11am. Also serves OK Italian food.

### Home Restaurants

One place to taste true Uzbek cooking is in an Old Town home restaurant. These establishments have no signs or shop fronts – just tables in a courtyard, where you're served one or two simple dishes, plus tea or beer.

One such neighbourhood, called Chigatay, contains dozens of these establishments. Boys practically drag you off the street for the midday and evening (after 7pm) meals. From Tinchlik metro, walk to the closest traffic signal on the main street, Beruni prospekti, and turn right into Akademik Sadikov. Most of the home restaurants are between five and 10 minutes, walk along (or just off) this street. Look to pay about 3000S per dish.

### Restaurants

our pick **Al Delfeen** (☎ 133 19 85; Malyasova 3; appetizers 1500, mains 3000-5000S) There are simply not enough superlatives in the English language to describe the cuisine at this Syrian restaurant. Load up on appetizers such as *baba ganush* (eggplant purée), hummus, falafel, *samsa* and tabbouleh, all redolent with ancient spices and bathing in exotic oils. If you still have room, dive right into the equally scrumptious mains – try the *mosakan* (chicken cooked with sumac and olive oil). Once you're finished, lie back on your outdoor *tapchan* (bedlike sitting platform) and send wisps of heavenly *shisha* (hookah) smoke skyward whilst marvelling at your luck for finding such a place.

**Sunduk** (☎ 132 11 46; Azimova 63; mains 2500-4000S; lunch & dinner) The designers of this diminutive eatery, kitted out like a French country kitchen, were just begging for it to be called 'cute'. We'll not only oblige them, but also point out that their European cuisine is excellent, as is the handwriting on their menus – on homemade paper, no less. Its 5000S business lunch is popular with the diplomatic set, many of whom work nearby.

**Dervish** (mains 2500-4500S) It's mud-walled dining at its best in this caravanserai-style restaurant known for its homemade wine and reasonable prices. Beautiful trinkets, Rishton ceramics, and *suzani* line the walls of the vaguely cave-like interior. There's a patio for claustrophobic types. The eclectic dishes ooze local flavours and have cheeky names such as 'Egyptian Nights', and 'Arabian Fairly Tales' (chicken fillet with honey, nuts and butter).

**Efendi** (☎ 133 15 02; Azimova 79A; kebabs 3000-4000S) There's a menu here but don't bother – just saunter inside and choose from among the hundreds of kebabs and mouth-watering Turkish salads on display in glass refrigerators. In no time you'll be back outside enjoying your booty on the pleasant if somewhat noisy – and nonalcoholic – streetside patio.

**Manas Art Café** (☎ 152 38 11; Miralikov; mains 3000-5000S; lunch & dinner) To dine in a yurt without schlepping over the desert on a camel, head here. There's a large yurt tastefully done up in traditional style and a smaller 'modern yurt' with *shisha* pipes and chill-out tunes. The Uzbek–Euro fusion food is excellent and priced right, but if you're planning on having 12 beers go elsewhere – the cheapest here is 4000S! Reservations recommended.

**Caravan** (☎ 255 62 96; Abdulla Qahhor 22; mains from 4000S; ⏰ lunch & dinner) Tashkent's quintessential theme restaurant is tarted up like a made-for-Hollywood Uzbek home. Its Westernised Uzbek cuisine is tasty, but comes saddled with bill-inflating service and 'entertainment' charges. The attached store is filled with crafts from all over the country and is open late, making Caravan a great place for both a nibble and a last-minute gift-buying spree.

**Bistro** (☎ 152 11 12; Movarounnakhr 33; mains 4000-8000S; ⏰ lunch & dinner) This scrumptious Italian eatery serves up large portions of pasta, pizza and grilled meats along with bottles of Uzbek or Georgian wines. The Roquefort salad is to die for. It's in a candle-lit, courtyard setting, with live music. Next door are three sister restaurants – Omar Khayyam (Lebanese), Shintaco (Japanese) and La Casa (Mexican). The latter morphs into the Ché nightclub in the evening (opposite).

**Han Kuk Kwan** (☎ 152 33 22; Yusuf Khos Khodjib; mains 5000-7000S; ⏰ lunch & dinner) Tashkent's large population of ethnic Koreans is what drives demand for all those Korean restaurants around town. Han Kuk Kwan is one of the nicer places, serving up platters full of small salads and main dishes such as *bi-bim-bab,* made with rice, egg and chopped meat. Large portions partially offset the high prices.

**Tandoori** (☎ 133 53 92; Chekhova 5; mains 6000-8000S; ⏰ lunch & dinner) Formerly Taj, this long-time favourite continues to churn out Tashkent's best Indian food – including a plethora of veg options. It was never long on character, but that may change thanks to renovations being done at the time of research. If not, you can always escape to the rooftop dining area.

### Self-Catering

Western-style supermarkets and minimarkets (p208) are now abundant but for fresh produce you are much better off at a farmers market (p208).

## DRINKING

**Ye Olde Chelsea Arms** (Abdulla Qahhor 25; mains 5000-12,000S) It's grossly overpriced and the gaudy décor will hardly make real Londoners feel at home, but it fills up every night and outdraws Tashkent's two Irish pubs. It's also the only place in Tashkent where you can recline in a streetside 'throne booth' and nibble on Welsh rabbit (12,000S).

**Studio Café** (Toi-Tepa 1, cnr Azimova; ⏰ 11am-midnight) The nouveau riche Uzbek crowd and hip, Hollywood-themed interior belie that you can actually get a reasonably priced beer here – a pint of Shimkent costs 1500S. The streetside patio is sweet, while inside bartenders adeptly shake up a dizzying array of cocktails to the beat of crisp-sounding Russian and Western pop.

**Tri Bochki** (Three Barrels; Navoi 2; mains 3000-5000S, 0.3/0.5L beer 594/990S, evening entertainment charge 594S) Occupying a prime, shady nook right on Ankhor Canal, this brewpub-restaurant has some of the best – and best-priced – homebrew in town. The house recipe was supposedly invented by German monks in 1514. There's live jazz by night and an equally cacophonic chorus of birdsong by day. From the bridge near Turkeston Palace on Navoi walk 50m north, passing two other restaurants on the way.

**Gasthaus** (Fargona Yuli 7; 0.5L beer 1000-1500S) Spry waitresses in German country outfits serve up foaming litre steins of homemade brew to the strains of oompah music in this *biergarten* by a busy *autobahn*. The unfiltered brew is particularly endearing and goes well with the real Bavarian sausages (6000S). The summer patio is popular despite the street noise and the 20% service charge.

## ENTERTAINMENT

Opera, theatre and ballet options are readily available, most catering to an older crowd with the exception of the Ilkhom Theatre. To get their groove on, Uzbeks gravitate to 'dance bars'. These quintessential Central Asian nightclubs are basically restaurants that morph into rollicking dance parties once dinner's over. Lengthy floor shows are *de rigueur* at such places, and the shenanigans can last until 2am or later. Regular nightclubs stay open until 4am but may close earlier on weekdays.

### Cinemas

**Panorama** (☎ 144 51 60; Navoi 15; 1200S) Tashkent's biggest movie theatre, although films are dubbed into Russian.

**Premier Cinema Hall** (☎ 152 16 25; www.premier.uz; cnr Usmon Nosir & Mirobod) Occasionally shows movies in English on request.

## Nightclubs

**Ché** (☎ 132 21 51; Movarounnakhr 33; ) Mexican restaurant by day, Ché turns into a cosy, loungey club by night that plays good chillout music and draws an alternative crowd. It might be dead or it might be really, really happening.

**Sky Club** (☎ 120 66 00; Uzbekistan 2; cover 3000S, women admitted free except Sat) As other clubs have come and gone like so many Tashkent NGOs, Sky Club, on the 14th floor of Le Grande Plaza hotel, remains popular year-in, year-out. Its giant, flashing Twister board of a dance floor will either serve as a cheap thrill or make you want to jump out the window, depending on how much alcohol you've consumed.

**SMI** (☎ 152 57 53; Oybek 32) More bar than nightclub, this is where people gravitate after an evening of club hopping. The flow of so many inebriated people to one place can have a creative effect on the environment. As one British expat put it, 'SMI morphs into whatever you want it to be at six in the morning'. SMI is the Russian acronym for 'mass media', and the walls pay due homage to the honourable craft of the scribbler.

**Diplomat-S** (Navoi) The place has a nutty, slutty streak that belies its serious name. One of the few clubs where you can still be making poor lifestyle decisions at 3am on a Tuesday night.

Check out Uzbeks in their element at two of the best dance bars in town, **Alis** (☎ 300 96 69; Mashkhadiy 21; admission weekends 2000S, weekdays free) and **Baccara** (☎ 137 63 58; cnr Amir Timur & Qayumova; admission weekends 2000S, weekdays free). Reserve a table ahead of time on weekends because you need a seat to get in.

## Sport

Soccer matches are held at the **Pakhtakor (Cotton Picker stadium)**, in the central park between Uzbekistan and Navoi. Tickets (local matches 500S to 1500S, international matches 8000S) can be bought directly from the stadium box office.

## Theatres & Concert Halls

Tashkent has a full cultural life, some of it, such as drama, of interest mainly to Uzbek and Russian speakers.

**Alisher Navoi Opera & Ballet Theatre** (☎ 133 90 81; Ataturk 28; admission 1500S; box office 10am-7pm show days, performances 6pm Mon-Fri, 5pm & noon matinees some weekends), where you can enjoy quality classical Western opera almost any night (except during the months June to August) at Alisher Navoi, one of Central Asia's best cultural bargains and a highlight for all visitors to Tashkent. Shows change daily – in just a week you can see *Swan Lake, Carmen, Rigoletto* and the Uzbek opera *Timur the Great*. The interior harbours various regional artistic styles – a different one in each room – executed by the best artisans of the day, and under the direction of the architect of Lenin's tomb in Moscow. Japanese prisoner of wars constructed the building itself in 1947. For 3000S you can take a self-guided tour (book at the box office), but it's cheaper to see a show!

**Ilkhom Theatre** (☎ 142 2241; www.ilkhom.com; Pakhtakor 5; tickets 2500-5500S; box office 11am-6.30pm, shows 6.30pm Tue-Sun) Tashkent's other main cultural highlight is this progressive theatre, which stages productions in Russian but occasionally has English subtitles. Known for bucking trends, its productions often touch on gay themes and racial subjects, putting off some locals but thrilling Tashkent's expat community, many of whom are big supporters of the theatre. You'll see such oddities as Shakespeare plays entwined with Beatles music. The theatre also stages occasional jazz concerts as well as art exhibitions in its lobby.

Other theatres of interest:

**Academic Russian Drama Theatre** (☎ 133 81 65; Ataturk 24; 1000-3000S; shows 6.30pm Mon-Fri, 7pm Sat & Sun) Classical Western drama in Russian.

**Muqimi Musical Theatre** (☎ 395 36 55, Almazar 187; tickets 1500S; shows 6pm) Best bet for traditional Uzbek folk singing, dancing and operettas such as *Brothers, Matchmakers* and *Bridegroom's Contest*.

**Peoples' Friendship Palace** (☎ 395 92 51; Halqlar Dustligi maydoni) Big events are staged here, including pop concerts.

**Tashkent State Conservatory** (☎ 241 29 91; Abai 1) Chamber concerts, Uzbek and Western vocal and instrumental recitals in an impressive new edifice. Entrance is around the back.

**Uzbek Milliy Akademik Drama Theatre** (☎ 144 17 51; Navoi 34; tickets 2000S; shows 6.30pm) Uzbek and classical Western drama in Uzbek language.

# SHOPPING

## Handicrafts & Art

**Abulkasim Medressa** (Navoi Park; 9am-6pm) Close to the Oliy Majlis in Navoi Park, this medressa has been turned into an artisans' school and workshop where local painters, lacquer workers and potters ply and teach their craft. It's a great place to buy the fruits of their labour, plus souvenirs such as rugs, *suzani* and ceramics brought in from the regions. Up on the 2nd floor, Andijon native Madraimov Abdumalik Abduraimovich fashions fine traditional Uzbek musical instruments and can wax eloquent in English about the nuances of the *dutar* (two-stringed guitar), *tambur* (long-necked string instruments) and *rabab* (six-stringed mandolin).

**Human House** (☎ 361 38 38; www.humanhuman.net; Usmon Nosir 30/9; ⏰ 10am-7pm Mon-Sat) Thus shop not only has a good selection of carpets, skull caps, *suzani* and other textiles from various Uzbek provinces, but also doubles as one of Tashkent's most fashionable boutiques, featuring modern clothing infused with Uzbek styles and designs. It also stages quarterly fashion shows to exhibit the work of its hand-picked designers. Human House's Unesco-supported latest project, dubbed Human Made, is a silk-making and weaving school/factory on the outskirts of town. 'We are going to build our own generation of weavers to help revive the craft of textiles in Tashkent', says commercial director Dina Malkova. The factory will offer tours similar to those given by the Yodgorlik Silk Factory in Margilon (p220) and should be open by the time you read this.

**Caravan** (☎ 255 62 96; Abdulla Qahhor 22) A gallery, studio and café all rolled into one. The prices are competitive with shops across the country, so it makes a reasonable place to stock up on items you might have missed while travelling. The ceramics of Rustam Usmanov and other Rishton masters are sold here (p221).

**Rakhimov Ceramics Studio** (☎ 149 04 35; www.rakhimovceramic.org; Kukcha Darbaza 15; ⏰ by appointment) As much museum as a ceramics shop (p232).

Most museums and top-end hotels have overpriced souvenir shops, including the Museum of Applied Arts (p201) and the Fine Arts Museum (see p201).

### Open-Air Bazaars

**Tezykovka** (Tolarik 1; ⏰ Sun) The local, vast 'flea market'. Also known as Yangiobod Market, this sombre sea of junk – 'anything from nails to nukes' as one resident put it – is located in the Khamza district, and reached by bus 30 from the Mustaqillik metro. Keep a close watch on your purse or wallet in this or any bazaar.

In warm weather, a big goods bazaar sprawls by the **Ippodrom** (Halqlar Dustligi prospekti; ⏰ Tue-Sun). The biggest day by far is on Sunday. The Ippodrom is 2km southwest from Sobir Rahimov metro.

#### FARMERS MARKETS

Tashkent has at least 16 open-air farmers markets or bazaars (Uzbek: *dekhqon bozori*, Russian: *rynok*). The following are the most interesting to visit:

**Chorsu Bazaar** See p200.

**Mirobod Bazaar** (Gospitalny) A fiesta of fruit bathing in the teal-green glow of its giant, octagonal flying saucer of a roof.

**Oloy Bazaar** (Alaysky; Amir Timur) This heavily policed market lacks the character of Chorsu, but will serve you well if your hotel is in the Amir Timur maydoni area.

### Supermarkets

The biggest supermarket in downtown Tashkent is on the ground floor of **Turkuaz Hypermart** (formerly GUM; Akhunbabaev Sq; ⏰ 9am-8.30pm), at the west end of Navoi across the street from the mothballed Hotel Chorsu. This is also probably your best bet for Western brand-name clothing and travel accessories such as money belts and rucksacks.

Around Broadway, you can get Western-brand food and toiletries at the large and modern **Mir supermarket** (Ataturk 1; ⏰ 9am-9pm). The best choice along busy Amir Timur is **Ardus** (Amir Timur 3; ⏰ 9am-8pm). **Korzinka.uz supermarket** (Azimova; ⏰ 8am-10pm) is smaller; there is another branch on Yunus Rajabiy, south of Kosmonavtlar metro. **Ozbegim supermarket** (Afrosiab 41; ⏰ 8.30am-9pm) is near Oybek metro. All have imported Western foods, though the selection tends to vary from week to week.

### Silk

They don't have the atmosphere of the bazaars, but for the best prices and a surprisingly good selection of silk by the metre, try the big department stores *(univermag)* – **TsUM** (cnr Uzbekistan, near Sharaf Rashidova) in the centre and Turkuaz Hypermart (see above).

## GETTING THERE & AWAY

### Air

Domestic flights leave from the domestic terminal, about 150m from the international terminal, 6km south of the centre.

From Tashkent, Uzbekistan Airways flies to Andijon (one way US$31, 1½ hours, five weekly), Bukhara (US$36, 1½ hours, at least daily except Saturday), Fergana (US$30, one hour, daily except Sunday), Nukus (US$51, 1½ hours, twice daily), Termiz (US$40, 1½ hours, three daily), Samarkand (US$22, one hour, five weekly) and Urgench (US$55, one hour, three daily).

Most of the above routes are serviced by a mix of Boeings and Russian planes such as Tupolevs and Yaks. If you are leery of the latter, pick up a timetable at the Uzbekistan Airways office to see what is flying where.

#### AIRLINE OFFICES

British Airways pulled out of Uzbekistan in early 2007 on the heels of exits by Air France and KLM. These airlines might return if Uzbek–EU relations improve. The airlines listed below can still be found in Tashkent.

**Aeroflot** (☎ 220 05 55 Abdulla Qodiri 1A; ⏰ 9am-6pm Mon-Fri, 10am-3pm Sat) Daily flights to Moscow (US$425 return).

**AK Kyrgyzstan** (formerly Altyn Air; ☎ 152 16 45; Mirobod 27) Daily to Bishkek (one way US$140).

**Asiana Airlines** (☎ 40 09 01; Afrosiab 16) Office was relocating at the time of research. Round-trip to Seoul for US$1000.

**Iran Air** (☎ 133 81 63; Azimova 1) Flies to Tehran (one way/return US$346/543) on Monday.

**Lufthansa** (☎ 137 60 65; tasgulh@dlh.de; Hotel InterContinental, Amir Timur 107A) Services most major world cities via Uzbekistan Airways planes to Frankfurt; final destination cannot be Frankfurt.

**Transaero** (☎ 139 99 35; Halqlar Dustligi 6A) Moscow (one way US$256) three times a week.

**Turkish Airlines** (☎ 136 79 89; Navoi 11A) İstanbul (one way/return US$423/510) four times a week.

#### BUYING TICKETS

Outbound tickets are best bought at the **Uzbekistan Airways booking office** (☎ 066, 140 02 00; www.uzairways.com; Usmon Nosir 9; ⏰ 8am-7pm). An information desk in the centre of the booking office will direct you towards an English-speaking agent. There is a money exchange office in the same building. Most private travel agencies can book international flights only. You can buy last-minute tickets on domestic flights from a little booth inside the domestic terminal. For more tips, see p266.

### Bus & Shared Taxi

Private buses, marshrutkas and shared taxis to Samarkand, Bukhara and Urgench leave from a lot on Halqlar Dustigli kocahsi, about 7km southwest of Navoi Park near Sobir Rahimov metro. The main lot for buses and other vehicles to Termiz and Qarshi is in the huge private bus yard behind the Ippodrom Bazaar, 3km beyond Sobir Rahimov metro on Halqlar Dustigli. Tashkent's **public bus station** (Halqlar Dustligi), across the street from Sobir Rahimov metro, serves mainly regions around Tashkent and is of little use to travellers.

There are two main departure points for shared taxis and marshrutkas to the Fergana Valley: the parking lot of the train station; and Qoylok Bazaar, about 10 minutes east of Tashkent on the Fergana Hwy. The former is harder to get to but you'll be rewarded with cheaper shared taxis.

For Chimgan you'll find shared taxis around Buyuk Ipak Yoli metro (per seat 5000S, 1½ hours). For information on getting to the Tajikistan and Kazakhstan borders, see p266.

There aren't any schedules, but there are dozens of vehicles heading to all of the above destinations throughout the day. There are fewer vehicles to distant Urgench. As long as you don't arrive too late, you'll have no problem finding a ride and should be on your way within an hour. For more land travel hints, see p268.

Sample routes and fares for shared taxis, marshrutkas and buses are below.

#### BUS, SHARED TAXI & MARSHRUTKA TIMETABLE

| Destination | Shared taxi (cost/duration) | Marshrutka (cost/duration) | Bus (cost/duration) |
|---|---|---|---|
| Andijon | 12,000S/5hr | 8000S/7hr | – |
| Bukhara | 20,000S/7hr | 11,000S/8hr | 7000S/11 hr |
| Fergana | 12,000S/4hr | 7000S/5½hr | – |
| Kokand | 12,000S/3hr | 6000S/4hr | – |
| Samarkand | 9000S/3½hr | 6000S/4½ hr | 3500S/6hr |
| Termiz | 25,000S/9½hr | 12,000S/14 hr | |
| Urgench/Khiva | 35,000S/14hr | – | 12,000S/20 hr |

### Train

The most comfortable if not the most flexible way to travel westward from Tashkent is via train out of Tashkent's newly renovated **train station** (vokzal; ☎ 005), next to the Tashkent metro.

There are new 'high-speed' trains with airplane-style seating running to both Samarkand (2nd class/1st class 6500/12,000S, four hours, five times per week at 7am) and Bukhara (2nd class/1st class 11,000/15,000S, eight hours, daily at 8.10am). The Bukhara train, known as the 'Sharq', stops in Samarkand.

Slower but cheaper Soviet-style passenger night trains still trundle to those and other cities. The following prices are for *platskartnyy* (hard sleeper) carriages: Bukhara (11,000S, 12½ hours, daily), Kungrad (via Nukus; 20,000S, 22 hours, twice weekly), Qarshi (14,000S, nine hours, odd days), Samarkand (7500S, six hours, twice daily), and Urgench (17,000S, 20 hours, twice weekly).

Public transport serving the train station includes tram 8 (from Chorsu via Navoi kuchasi), tram 9 (via Usman Nosir; Shota Rustaveli), bus 60 (from Amir Timur kuchasi) and bus 3 (via Nukus kuchasi). Look for the '*vokzal*' sign.

#### BUYING TICKETS

The main ticket booth is in a separate building around the back and to the right as you face the main lobby of the train station. But foreigners often get directed to a special ticket booth to the left as you enter the lobby. To buy tickets from the 'locals' booth you first must register with the Office of Visas & Registration (OVIR) in an office toward the back of the main lobby.

## GETTING AROUND

### To/From the Airport

Buses are the cheapest way to/from the airport. Coming from the airport, they're also an alternative to the greedy, sometimes crooked, taxi drivers. Unfortunately they stop running at 10.30pm despite the fact that many flights arrive in the middle of the night.

Bus 67 travels up Usmon Nosir to the centre of town, and continues up Amir Timur to the Intercon, a 35-minute journey. Marshrutka 62 follows the same route. Bus 77 goes up Babur to/from Halqlar Dustligi maydoni. Bus 11 runs to/from the Hotel Chorsu via Navoi and Amir Timur maydoni.

The 7km, 20-minute taxi ride to/from the Hotel Uzbekistan should cost no more than 2000S, but an unofficial airport cartel won't accept less than about US$10 from foreigners for the trip from the airport. They might even tack on a 'luggage fee' equal to double the agreed fare once you reach your destination.

To avoid this, simply walk three minutes out to the main road to hail a cab, or take a bus to the centre and flag down a cheaper taxi there.

If you do end up taking an airport taxi, just make sure to agree on a firm price beforehand.

#### TAXI TIPS

Every car is a potential taxi in Tashkent, but essentially there are two forms: licensed cabs and 'independent' cabs. The former have little roof-mounted 'taxi' signs. The latter are just average cars driven by average dudes.

Independent taxis generally leave it up to you to pick the price, which is fine. As long as you don't insult them with your offer, they almost always accept it. Give 500S for short trips (less than 2km), 1000S for midrange, 1500S for cross-town, and 2000S to the city's outskirts (ie Ippodrom Bazaar). If they complain, hand over another 200S and shut the door. (Of course these prices could go up slightly in the event of inflation or a petrol price spike.)

Licensed cabs – especially those waiting outside bars and hotels – are a different beast. Do not go anywhere in a licensed cab without agreeing to a price first. Use the same rate guidelines as above, but be ready to pay slightly more – these are professionals after all (professionals who will demand quadruple the going rate if you don't agree on a price up front).

If you don't care for nickel-and-dime haggling and just want to book a damn taxi, you'll pay only slightly higher rates by dialling ☎ 062, ☎ 144 88 11 or ☎ 139 99 99.

Cab drivers tend not to know street names, so use landmarks – big hotels and metro stations work best – to direct your driver to your destination.

## Car

Any hotel or travel agency can arrange a comfortable private car and driver from about 8000S per hour and up. You'll pay much less – 4000S to 6000S per hour, depending on your negotiating skills – on the street (see opposite for more tips). Murad Tashpulatov speaks good English, knows the streets and charges reasonable rates. Email him at mtashpulatov@rambler.ru.

## Public Transport

Buses, trolleybuses and trams cost 160S to 200S, payable on board to the conductor or driver. Most of them are marked in Latinised Uzbek and given a number (older buses are still marked in Cyrillic).

The destination of public buses, trams, trolleybuses and marshrutkas is written clearly in the window. One useful bus is the 91, which goes between Chorsu Bazaar and Hotel InterContinental via Navoi. Another is bus 67, which travels from the airport to the Intercon via Usmon Nosir, Shakhrisabz and Amir Timur. Your hotel can always help direct you to where you want to go via public transport.

## Metro

Tashkent's **metro** (per trip 140S; 🕔 5am-midnight) is the easiest way to get around. During the day you'll never wait more than five minutes for a train, and the stations are clean and safe. You'll need to buy a token *(zhyton)* for each trip. The metro was designed as a nuclear shelter and taking photos inside is strictly forbidden – a pity given their often times striking design.

Despite the use of Uzbek for signs and announcements, the system is easy to use, and well enough signposted that you hardly need a map. If you listen as the train doors are about to close, you'll hear the name of the next station at the end of the announcement: *'Ekhtiyot buling, eshiklar yopiladi; keyingi bekat…'* ('Be careful, the doors are closing; the next station is…').



# AROUND TASHKENT

## Chimgan & Around

Just over an hour northeast of Tashkent by car lies **Ugam-Chatkal National Park**, an outdoor haven loaded with of hiking and adventure-sport opportunities as well as more relaxing pursuits. The mountains here are not quite as extreme or scenic as the higher peaks around Almaty and Bishkek, but certain activities – rafting, kayaking and heli-skiing come to mind – are more accessible and at least as challenging.

This entire area is known locally as Chimgan, a reference to both its biggest town and its central peak (3309m). For an overview of outdoor activities here, see p213.

You don't have to be an X-gamer to enjoy Chimgan. A major sanatoria centre in Soviet times, today it has hatched a few modern resorts and retreats to complement the usual diet of decrepit yet still-functioning concrete Soviet hulks. And the Chorvoq Reservoir offers

TASHKENT METRO

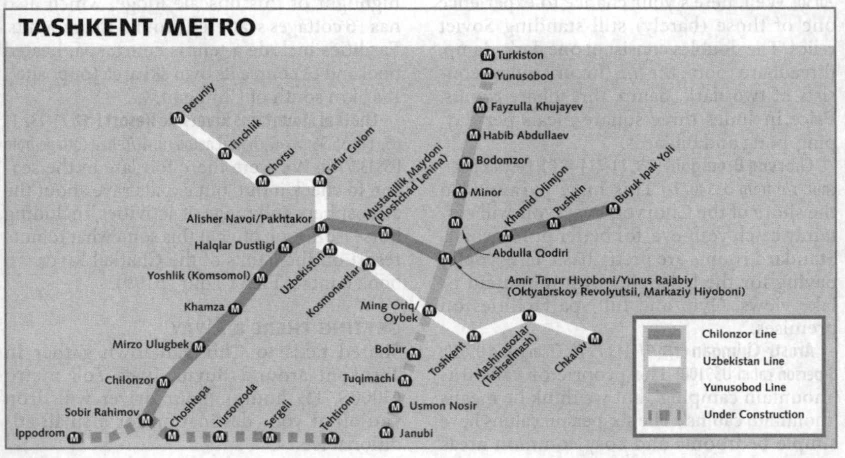

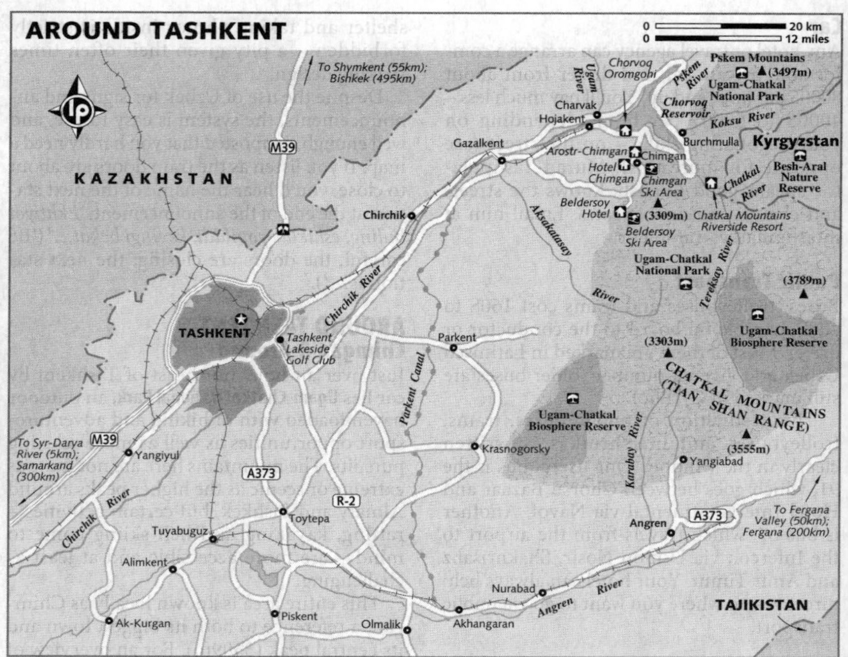


more mellow outdoor pursuits such as fishing, swimming and canoeing – ask about these at the Chorvoq Oromgohi hotel.

### SLEEPING

**Hotel Chimgan** (☎ 27-153 49 86; Chimgan; s/d/lux US$10/20/30) Well, here's your chance to experience one of those (barely) still-standing Soviet relics. The doubles consist of one dark, damp, threadbare room; the *lux* (luxury room) consists of two dark, damp, threadbare rooms. Price includes three square meals per day, ping-pong and billiards.

**Chorvoq Oromgohi** (☎ 71-714 48 81; Poselok Bokachul; s/d from US$40/52) This huge pyramid on the shore of the Chorvoq Reservoir will certainly catch your eye, for better or for worse. Standard rooms are pretty basic fare; you're paying for the balconies with mountain or lake views. Gym and full spa facilities on premises.

**Arostr-Chimgan** (☎ 97-443 75 75; Chimgan; d US$50, 6-person cabin US$100) The proprietor calls this 'mountain camping', but we think he means 'mountain cabins'. The six-person cabins have simple bedrooms and cosy common areas with fireplaces and satellite TV. *The* place to ride out a blizzard with good company and a few handles of vodka.

**Beldersoy Hotel** (☎ 90-176 38 26, in Tashkent 71-132 17 90; r US$110, 4-person cottage from US$140; ☒ ☒) The balconies with views of the valley are the highlight of this upscale lodge, which also has 16 cottages scattered around the grounds. Facilities include a tennis court, spa, heated pool and of course its own ski area (opposite). It's 5km south of Chimgan.

**Chatkal Mountains Riverside Resort** (☎ 71-132 11 66, 119 35 95; www.chatcal.narod.ru; 4-/6-bed cottage from US$130/180) We were there too late in the season to check it out, but expats rave about the atmosphere and range of activities, including horse riding, on offer at this somewhat remote resort on the banks of the Chatkal River. To book contact Elena Tour (p199).

### GETTING THERE & AWAY

Shared taxis to Chimgan town gather in Tashkent around Buyuk Ipak Yoli metro (5000S, 1½ hours). Your driver will drop you off at your destination for a small additional fee.

## OUTDOOR ACTIVITIES IN THE CHIMGAN AREA

Ugam-Chatkal National Park and the Chimgan area are developing a growing reputation for adventure sports. This national park covers the mountainous area east and southeast of the Kyrgyzstan border, from the city of Angren in the south all the way up to the Pskem Mountains in the fingerlike, glacier-infested wedge of land jutting into Kyrgyzstan northeast of Chimgan town. The Pskem top out at 4319m but are off-limits because of their location in a sensitive border zone. Should the situation change, this will become prime virgin trekking territory.

### Trekking

For now, all of the national park's accessible terrain lies in the Chatkal Mountains, which stretch into Kyrgyzstan. Lacking the stratospheric height of the big Kyrgyz and Tajik peaks, the appeal of the Chatkals is their accessibility. Escaping civilization involves walking just a short way out of Chimgan town or the Beldersoy ski area.

The best long hike here is the six- to eight-day trek from Chimgan town to Angren (can also be done in reverse). It takes you past Chimgan mountain and on through the Chatkal State Biosphere Reserve, staying well east of the nettlesome Kyrgyzstan border. Another day hike is the six- to eight-hour return trip from Beldersoy Hotel to some ancient petroglyphs near Chimgan mountain.

The problem with independently setting out on these or any other hikes in the Chatkals is that the routes are not marked and good topographical maps are about as common as Caspian Tigers (which died out from these parts in the 1970s). You might check to see if Asia Travel (p199) is selling any old Soviet topographical maps. Barring that, you're left with your compass and the stars. Unless you are skilled in backcountry navigation you should hire a local guide. The best is Boris of Elena Tour (p199), although he doesn't speak much English.

Before entering the park you're supposed to get a permit from the national park office in Gazalkent, but you can probably get by without one for short day hikes. Keep in mind that many of the trails around here lead into Kyrgyzstan, which creates a whole new set of complications. Simply put, there is plenty of grey area about what you need and what you don't need, and about where you can go and where you can't go – so hire a guide skilled at navigating red tape as well the backcountry.

### Rafting & Kayaking

The raging gazpacho of the Pskem, Ugam and Chatkal Rivers offer prime white water for experienced kayakers and rafters, although the season for each is fairly short.

The Chatkal is difficult to access but its Class-V rapids, which originate in Kyrgyzstan, are said to be absolutely world class. The rafting season is September to October. One- to two-day trips are possible on the Ugam River (best in June–July), but most of its length is in Kazakhstan so you'll need a Kazakh visa as well as special permits from both Kazakhstan and Uzbekistan. Or you can just run the last 10km in Uzbekistan. You'll need a Kyrgyz visa and similar permissions to run the Chatkal. The experts-only Pskem is exclusively in Uzbekistan but is off-limits for now.

**Asia Raft** (Map pp196-7; ☎ in Tashkent 71-360 09 18; http://asiaraft.netfirms.com/eng; Mavlono Rieziy 77) swears it can secure the necessary permits to make these trips happen. If not, it offers alternative rafting trips throughout Uzbekistan and Central Asia, most of them lasting several days.

Elena Tour runs a rafting trip for less extreme sorts south of Tashkent on the Syr-Darya, starting near Bekobad on the Tajikistan border. More of a drifting trip than a rafting trip, you can sign up for one to three days.

### Skiing & Heli-skiing

The Beldersoy and Chimgan areas encompass both the best and the worst of Soviet-style ski resorts. The best: limited grooming, some unexpectedly steep terrain, rock bottom prices and plenty of hot wine and shashlyk. The worst: crummy lifts, limited total acreage and no snow-making to speak of.

While the resorts are not worth a special trip to Uzbekistan, the helicopter skiing most definitely is. While the Chatkals aren't huge, they are blanketed in some of the driest, fluffiest powder you'll find anywhere. And the winter weather is relatively stable, lessening the chances of getting grounded for days on end. But the best part is the price – US$355 per day for about 6000 vertical metres. That's a little more than half of what you'll pay in North America. Book heli-skiing through Asia Travel (most other agencies go through them).

# FERGANA VALLEY
# ФЕРГАНСКАЯ ДОЛИНА

The first thought many visitors have on arrival in the Fergana Valley is, 'Where's the valley?' From this broad (22,000 sq km), flat bowl, the surrounding mountain ranges (Tian Shan to the north and the Pamir Alay to the south) seem to stand back at enormous distances – when you can see them, that is. More often these spectacular peaks are shrouded in a layer of smog, produced by what is both Uzbekistan's most populous and its most industrial region.

It's also the country's fruit and cotton basket. Drained by the upper Syr-Darya, the Fergana Valley is one big oasis, with some of the finest soil and climate in Central Asia. Already by the 2nd century BC the Greeks, Persians and Chinese found a prosperous kingdom based on farming, with some 70 towns and villages. The Russians were quick to realise the valley's fecundity, and Soviet rulers enslaved it to an obsessive raw-cotton monoculture that still exists today.

The valley's eight million people are thoroughly Uzbek – 90% overall and higher in the smaller towns. Despite this, on the whole its towns are architecturally uninspiring. But the province has always wielded a large share of Uzbekistan's political, economic and religious influence. Fergana was at the centre of numerous revolts against the tsar and later the Bolsheviks. In the 1990s the valley gave birth to Islamic extremism in Central Asia. President Karimov's brutal crackdown on alleged extremists eventually came to a head in the form of the Andijon Massacre in 2005 (p191).

The post-Andijon crackdown has increased the police presence in the valley, but it's not something that's likely to affect most tourists as long as they keep a low profile. The valley's people remain the most hospitable and friendly in the country. Other attractions are exceptional crafts, several kaleidoscopic bazaars and the proximity of the mountains, most of which lie in Kyrgyzstan.

## Dangers & Annoyances

Standards of dress are a potential source of misunderstanding in the valley. Except per-

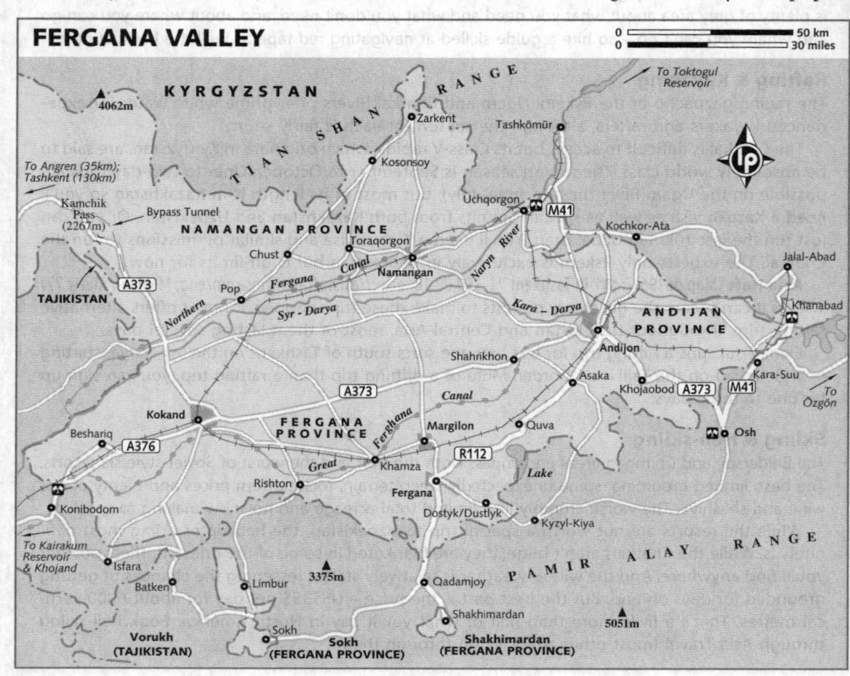

haps in the centre of Russified Fergana town, too much tourist flesh will be frowned upon, so dress modestly (ie no shorts or tight-fitting clothes). Women travellers have reported being harassed when walking alone in cities such as Andijon, especially at night.

Security is tight in the valley compared with other parts of the country and police road blocks are common. The police are friendly enough, just keep your passport at the ready and be agreeable when being questioned.

### Getting There & Around

There is no public bus service between Tashkent and the Fergana Valley – only chartered buses are allowed on the scenic, winding road through the mountains, which is best negotiated by shared taxi as opposed to wobbly looking Daewoo Damas marshrutkas. See the individual city entries for specific details on land and air transport to/from Tashkent.

The few slow trains that lumber between Tashkent and the Fergana Valley go through Tajikistan. Do not board these without a Tajik transit visa and a double-entry Uzbek visa. Details on these trains, which are generally more trouble than they are worth, are not included in this chapter.

Travel within the valley is almost always by shared taxi or marshrutka, and rarely by bus.

## KOKAND КОКАНД

**☎ (3) 73 / pop 200,000**

As the valley's first significant town on the road from Tashkent, Kokand is a gateway to the region and stopping point for many travellers. With an architecturally interesting palace and several medressas and mosques, it makes for a worthwhile half-day visit before heading in or out of the region.

This was the capital of the Kokand khanate in the 18th and 19th centuries and the valley's true 'hotbed' in those days – second only to Bukhara as a religious centre in Central Asia, with at least 35 medressas and hundreds of mosques. But if you walk the streets today, you will find only a polite, subdued Uzbek town, its old centre hedged by colonial avenues, bearing little resemblance to Bukhara.

Nationalists fed up with empty revolutionary promises met here in January 1918 and declared a rival administration, the 'Muslim Provincial Government of Autonomous Turkestan' led by Mustafa Chokayev. Jenghiz Khan would have admired the response by the Tashkent Soviet, who immediately had the town sacked, most of its holy buildings desecrated or destroyed and 14,000 Kokandis slaughtered. What little physical evidence of Kokand's former stature was either left to decay, or mummified as 'architectural monuments'. A handful of these wonders have been brought back to life as working mosques and medressas.

### Orientation

The Khan's Palace stands in the central Muqimi Park. Most restaurants and shops of interest are on or just off the 1km stretch of Istiqlol running east–west between Muqimi Park and Abdulla Nabiev maydoni. The mosque-sprinkled old-town lanes squeezed between Khamza, Akbar Islamov and Furquat make for good wandering.

### Information

**Asaka Bank** (Istoqol) Exchanges money and advances cash on MasterCard.

**Internet Centre** (Istanbul 8; per hr 900S; ⏰ 7am-11pm) Also offers phone calls abroad for 1000S per minute.

**Internet Club** (Navoi 1; per megabyte 200S, ⏰ 8am-midnight)

**OVIR** (☎ 553 68 78; cnr Turkiston & Istiqlol; ⏰ 2-4pm Tue & 9am-noon Sat)

**Post & telephone office** (Potelyakhov House, cnr Istiqlol & Istanbul; ⏰ 7am-7pm Mon-Fri, 7am-5.30pm Sat & Sun)

**Uzbektourism** (☎ 552 38 92; Kamal-Kazi Medressa, Khamza 83; ⏰ 9am-6pm Mon-Sat) Offers English-speaking guided tours of all Kokand and other Fergana Valley sights.

### Sights

#### KHAN'S PALACE

The **Khan's Palace** (☎ 553 60 46, http://museum.dinosoft.uz; Istiqlol 2; admission 1200S, guided tour 3000S; ⏰ 9am-5pm), with seven courtyards and 114 rooms, was completed in 1873 –just three years before the tsar's troops arrived, blew up its fortifications and abolished Khudoyar Khan's job. He fled – not from the Russians but from his own subjects. Indeed he fled *to* the Russians at Orenburg and a comfortable exile (he was later killed by bandits as he returned through Afghanistan from a pilgrimage to Mecca).

Roughly half of the palace used to be taken up by the now-demolished harem, where Khudoyar's 43 concubines would wait to be chosen as wife for the night – Islam allows

UZBEKISTAN

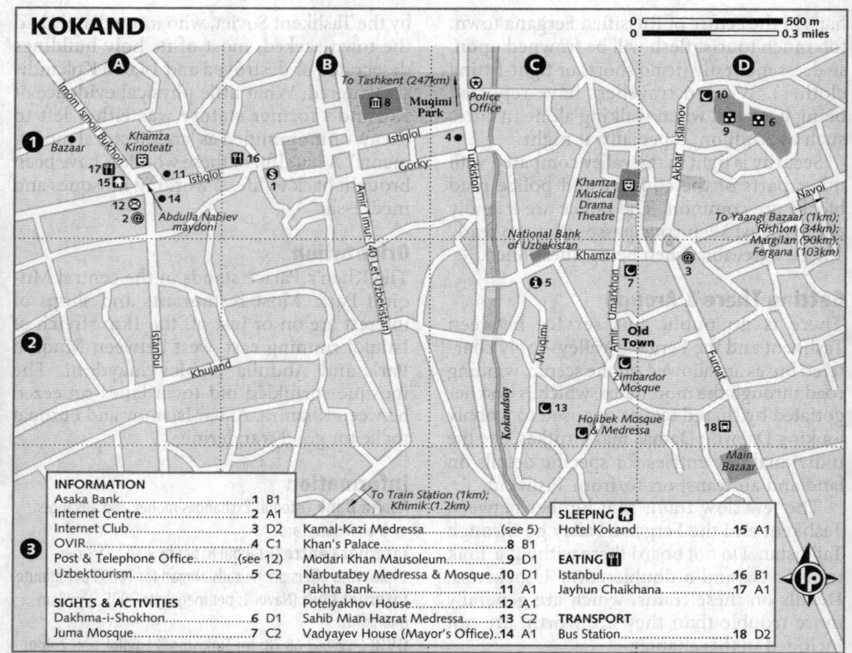


only four wives so the khan kept a mullah at hand for a quick marriage ceremony (the marriage set up to last just one night).

Six courtyards remain and their 27 rooms collectively house the Kokand Regional Studies Museum, with displays of varying degrees of interest. The princes' courtyard, occupied by the khan's sons when they moved out of the harem in early adolescence, now houses a folk museum and Soviet-style souvenir shop where you can buy old coins and other communist trinkets. There's an art museum in the khan's bedroom, while the throne room near the entrance features a model of the palace in its heyday. In the guest room, now a history museum, you'll find fascinating photos of the khan's army in front of the unfinished palace in 1871.

Guided tours are given by the museum's English-speaking director, who is also a good source of information on the region.

### NARBUTABEY MEDRESSA

The Bolsheviks closed the 1799 Narbutabey Medressa but it's now open again and currently has about 20 students. To win wartime support from Muslim subjects, Stalin had the adjacent **mosque** reopened. When you step inside this complex you will be surrounded by an eager mob of young students, who are more than happy to give you a free tour of the premises and the neighbouring graveyard. Both men and women are welcome.

The **graveyard**, accessible from the medressa courtyard or from the street, has several prominent mausoleums associated with another khan, Umar. Inside the graveyard, to the right, is the bright sky-blue cupola of the unrestored **Modari Khan Mausoleum**, built in 1825 for the khan's mother. To the left is the 1830s **Dakhma-i-Shokhon** (Grave of Kings), the tomb of the Umar Khan and other family members, with an elegant wooden portal carved with Quranic verses and/or Umar's poetry.

Nasrullah Khan, the emir of Bukhara, is said to have kidnapped Umar's wife, an independent-minded poetess named Nodira, and demanded that she marry him. When she refused, Nasrullah had her beheaded, along with her children and her brothers-in-law. Originally buried behind Modari Khan, she was adopted by the Soviets as a model

Uzbek woman and moved to a prominent place beneath a white **stone tablet**, beyond Dakhma-i-Shokhon.

#### RUSSIAN BUILDINGS

Around Abdulla Nabiev maydoni (named for a prominent Kokand Bolshevik) is a knot of sturdy brick buildings, built by the Russians in turn-of-the-20th-century 'mixed style', with sculptured façades and copper cupolas. They include the former headquarters of the German-Turkestan Bank (now the **Pakhta Bank**), **Potelyakhov House** (1907; now the main post and telegraph office) and **Vadyayev House** (1911; now the mayor's office).

#### SAHIB MIAN HAZRAT MEDRESSA

From the Uzbektourism office on Khamza, walk five minutes down Muqimi to the truncated remnants of the large 19th-century Sahib Mian Hazrat Medressa, where the great Uzbek poet and 'democrat' Mohammedamin Muqimi (1850–1903) lived and studied for the last 33 years of his life. There is a small **museum** (admission 500S) in Muqimi's old room, which contains a few of his personal belongings, plus Arabic calligraphy by Muqimi himself.

#### JUMA MOSQUE

Kokand's most impressive mosque, built in the early 19th century, is centred on a 22m minaret and includes a huge, colourful *aivan* (arched portico) supported by 98 red-wood columns brought from India. Ten more columns are in the mosque itself. The entire complex has reverted to its former Soviet guise as a **museum** (Khamza 5; admission 1200S; ⌚ 9am-5pm), with one room housing a collection of *suzani* and ceramics from the region. Admission includes a free tour in Russian.

### Sleeping & Eating

A fancy new hotel was scheduled to open east of town near Yaangi Bazaar sometime in 2007. Until that happens, you may be better off continuing on to Fergana. Backpackers, on the other hand, might want to avoid more expensive Fergana and roost at bargain-basement Hotel Kokand.

**Hotel Kokand** (☎ 533 64 03; Imom Ismoil Bukhori 1; s/d 4000/8000S) This central, Soviet-style hotel has electricity, running water and a friendly staff. We wouldn't call it clean, but the beds are OK and at least the rooms don't reek as bad as some hotels of this ilk.

**Khimik** (☎ 553 46 86; Akhmad Yesavi; s/d 8000/10,000) Located near the train station, this hotel is a virtual clone of Hotel Kokand, only with slightly cleaner rooms, much cleaner bathrooms and a much worse location.

**Istanbul** (Istiqlol 16; ⌚ 6am-10pm) This quasi-fast-food eatery is the only option in town after about 7pm. Its sausage-and-egg breakfast is a godsend for those staying at the Hotel Kokand.

**Jayhun Chaikhana** (Imom Ismoil Bukhori; shashlyk 500S) This popular chaikhana next to the Hotel Kokand tends to close early along with the small bazaar nearby, but during daylight hours it's the best option in town.

Vegetarians and self-caterers can go to the main bazaar by the bus station, or a small one near the hotel.

### Getting There & Around

All transport options leave from the bus station by the main bazaar on Furqat. Marshrutkas and shared taxis leave every 15 minutes throughout the day to Rishton (marshrutka/taxi per person 800/3000S, 45 minutes), Fergana (1200/4000S, 1½ hours) and other points in the valley. Cheaper, slower buses leave every 45 minutes to Fergana and Andijon (1300S, three hours). There are plenty of shared taxis to Tashkent (12,000S, three hours).

There are two daily trains to Andijon (1200S, five hours, 5am and 2pm) from the **train station** (Amir Timur 40).

Useful public transport options include marshrutka 2 or 4 from the main bazaar to the Hotel Kokand area, or number 15, 28 or 40 north from the bazaar to the Juma Mosque.

## FERGANA ФЕРГАНА

☎ (3) 73 / pop 216,000

Tree-lined avenues and pastel-plastered tsarist buildings give Fergana the feel of a mini-Tashkent. Throw in the best services and accommodation in the region, plus a central location, and you have the most obvious base from which to explore the rest of the valley.

Fergana is the valley's least ancient and least Uzbek city. It began in 1877 as Novy Margelan (New Margilon), a colonial annexe to nearby Margilon. It was briefly known as Skobelov, named after the city's first military governor, and then assumed Fergana in the 1920s. It's a nice enough place to hang out, and somewhat cosmopolitan with its relatively high proportion of Russian and Korean citizens.

## Orientation

The streets radiate out from what's left of the old tsarist fort, 10m of mud-brick wall within an army compound (off-limits to visitors) behind the city and provincial administration buildings. The centre of the city is around the Hotel Ziyorat, within walking distance of central Al-Farghoni Park and the bazaar. The airport is 6km south of town.

## Information

The Asia Hotel has a 24-hour currency exchange.

**Asaka Bank** (cnr Navoi & Kuvasoy) You can get cash out on your MasterCard here.

**Infinity Internet Café** (Navoi 18-23; per megabyte 150S; ⌚ 9am-10pm) Convenient for Hotel Asia and Valentina's Guesthouse.

**National Bank of Uzbekistan** (Al-Farghoni 35) Cash-advance office for Visa cardholders is on the 3rd floor (commission 4%). Also changes travellers cheques.

**OVIR** (Ahunbabayev 35)

**Post office** (Mustaqillik 35; ⌚ 8am-6pm)

**Simus** (Marifat 45; per hr 800S; ⌚ 8am-8pm) Internet café near the taxi stand.

**Uzbektourism** (☎ 224 77 40; Hotel Ziyorat; guides per day US$20 plus transport; ⌚ 8am-5pm Mon-Fri) Helpful staffer Nargiza speaks English and can arrange multilingual tours to just about anything worth seeing in the Fergana Valley. If it's closed try the hotel concierge.

## Sights

Fergana's most appealing attraction is the **bazaar**, filled with good-natured Uzbek traders, leavened with Korean and Russian vendors selling homemade specialities. It sprawls over several blocks north of the centre, posing a considerable obstacle to the flow of traffic.

The **Regional Museum of Fergana** (☎ 224 31 91; Usman Khojayev 26; admission 1000S; ⌚ 9am-5pm Wed-Sun, 9am-1pm Mon) is sparse. Visitors can inspect satellite photos showing where all that cotton grows and some items on the valley's ancient Buddhist and shamanist sites. Other displays include a Stone Age diorama with some excessively hairy Cro-Magnons, and a few photos of pre-Soviet life.

## Sleeping

**Hotel Ziyorat** (☎ 224 77 42; Dekhon 2A; s/d US$12/20) By the standard of barely renovated Soviet hotels,

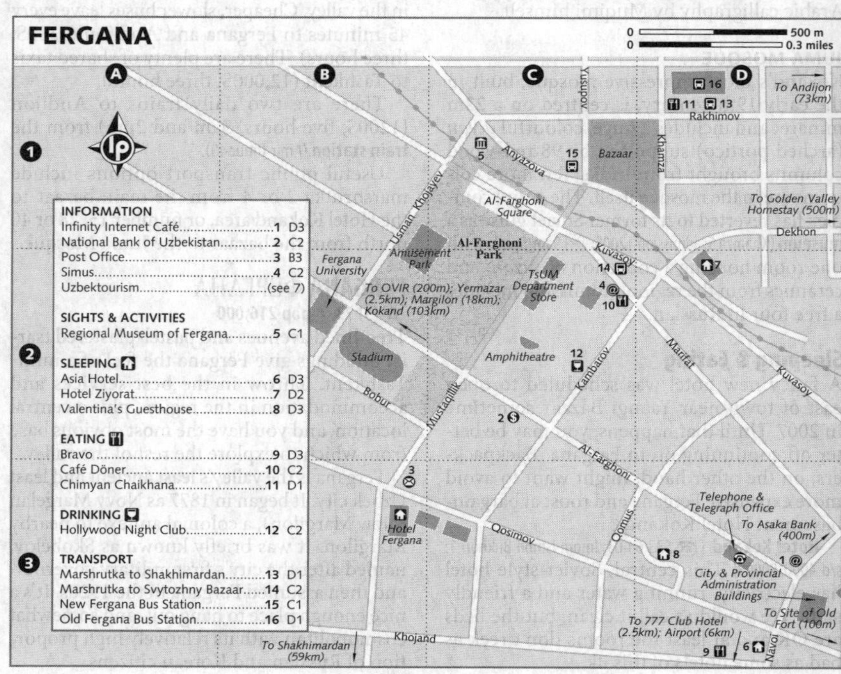

this one ranks right up there with the best of 'em (ie once you get past the filthy, 1960s-era flooring and peeling wallpaper, it starts to run out of glaring flaws). Satellite TV and minibars are why the supposedly non-negotiable prices are a bit high.

**Valentina's Guesthouse** (☎ 224 89 05, 8-590 272 4072; daniol26@yahoo.com; r per person US$15; ) Hidden in an ugly apartment block between Qosimov, Al-Farghoni and Qomus is this deluxe homestay, with four big rooms kitted out with DVD players, minibars and king-sized beds. The apartment block, topped by a huge antenna, sticks out like a sore thumb; take the left-hand entrance. Valentina speaks Russian.

**Golden Valley Homestay** (☎ 223 21 00, 562 13 49; lola_2004@simus.uz; Shakirovoy 10; r per person US$15; ) This one's a bit out of the way, but gets props from travellers. Call for a pick-up and negotiate hard. You can also stay in Golden Valley's *dacha* (holiday bungalow) outside the city.

**777 Club Hotel** (☎ 224 37 77; www.hotel777.uz; Pushkin 7A; s/d US$25/40; ) A hotel with a built-in chicken-and-egg conundrum: What came first, the phone number or the name? The receptionist didn't have an answer to that one, but she cheerfully showed us tasteful rooms scattered about the most attractive hotel grounds in the Fergana Valley. With a few bungalows and a festive poolside bar, it's as close as you're liable to come to Club Med in double-land-locked Uzbekistan.

**Asia Hotel** (☎ 224 52 21; http://asiahotels.marcopolo.uz; Navoi 26; s/d/lux US$22/28/40; ) This smart hotel associated with überpowerful Marco Polo travel agency caters mainly to tour groups. Facing competition from the likes of 777, it's furiously adding swanked-out rooms and facilities like a new indoor pool and business centre. Beds here are rock hard. Complain vigorously about the US$3 pool fee.

## Eating & Drinking

**Café Döner** (Marifat 45; mains 1000-1500S) If you confuse this fast-food eatery with Döner Kebab next door, don't despair: it has virtually identical menus of kebabs, pizzas and mushy doner burgers.

our pick **Bravo** (Khojand 12; meals 2000-3000S) Nowhere is Fergana's liberal bent more evident than in this bohemian little café. The cosy interior, shabby-chic to the core, is plastered with the products of local artists and awash with the strains of live jazz. There's no menu, just ask what's available and pick. In the warm months the action moves outside to the patio, redolent of shashlyk. Expect a fair share of artists, musicians and drunks enjoying life until well into the evening. The next morning they'll be back for espresso. Hell, this place would be hip in Paris.

**Hollywood Night Club** (Kambarov; entry 1000S) This cavernous club, behind the department store, tolerates vodka-shooting Ferganans and their late-night antics.

There are also several decent restaurants along the canal across the street from the Ziyorat Hotel. Self-caterers will enjoy the bazaar area, where there are several Uzbek chaikhanas, including **Chimyan** (cnr Rakhimov & Khamza; laghman 1000S). Shashlyk stands occupy Al-Farghoni Park in the warm months; a cluster of them are across the street from TsUM department store.

## Getting There & Away

### AIR

**Uzbekistan Airways** (Fergana Airport; 8am-5pm) has flights to/from Tashkent (one way small/big plane US$30/21, one hour, daily except Sunday). Two of the six weekly flights are on the bigger plane.

### BUS & SHARED TAXI

Shared taxis, marshrutkas and a few buses depart to Andijon throughout the day from the old Fergana bus station, north of the bazaar (marshrutka/taxi per seat 1200/3000S, one hour; bus 700S, two hours). This is also the spot to find rides to Margilon (marshrutka/taxi per seat 200/500S, 20 minutes) and Shakhimardan (see p221).

The main transport hub for westbound traffic is the Yermazar long-distance bus station, 3km northwest of the centre on the road to Margilon. Here you'll find shared taxis to Tashkent (13,000S, four hours) and shared taxis and marshrutkas to Kokand (marshrutka/taxi per seat 1200/4000S, 1½ hours) and Namangan (1500/5000S, 1¾ hours).

For Rishton (marshrutka/shared taxi per seat 800/3000S, 45 minutes), use the new Fergana bus station on the western edge of the bazaar.

## Getting Around

The airport is a 25-minute trip on marshrutka 6 or bus 21 to/from the Svytozhny Bazaar stop across from Halq Bank in the centre of town. Going to the airport you can flag down

UZBEKISTAN

**SILK PRODUCTION IN UZBEKISTAN**

Although silk-thread production and clothmaking have been largely automated, the raising of silkworms is still almost entirely a 'cottage industry', with most worms raised in individual farmers' homes, as they have been since perhaps the 4th century AD.

Out of its stock from previous years' husbandry, the Uzbekistan government distributes an average of 20g of young silkworm grubs to any farmer willing to 'raise' them in late April and early May. Each farmer prepares special rooms with large bedding boxes. The worms' diet consists of chopped up mulberry leaves culled from trees along lowland roads and canals. The farmers use the leftover branches as fuel, and the stripped mulberry trees regrow their branches the following year.

The initial 20g of grubs takes up about a square metre of space and consumes about 3kg of leaves a day. At the end of just a month, each of those originally microscopic creatures has grown to the size of a little finger, and together they occupy two or three rooms and devour some 300kg of leaves each day! Then abruptly they stop eating altogether and spend a week or so rolling themselves up into a cocoon of silk fibres. The farmers sell the cocoons back to government silk factories – typically 80kg to 120kg of cocoons at about US$1 to US$2 per kilogram.

Some worms, called 'seed-worms', are set aside and allowed to hatch as moths, which will lay eggs and produce the next generation of grubs. The rest are killed inside their cocoons by steaming (otherwise they would break out and ruin the silk filaments), and each cocoon is boiled and carefully unwound. A typical tiny cocoon yields about 1200m of filament! Twelve or 13 filaments are twisted together to make industrial thread, which is used to make clothing.

Uzbekistan produces about 20,000 metric tonnes of cocoons a year, making it the third-largest silk producer in the world. The centre of the industry is in Margilon.

either in front of Hotel Asia, but check with the driver to make sure he's going all the way to the *aeroport*.

Marshrutka 14 is useful for getting from the Svytozhny Bazaar stop to Yermazar bus station.

## AROUND FERGANA

### Margilon Маргилан

☎ (3) 73 / pop 145,000

If you've been travelling along the Silk Road seeking answers to where in fact this highly touted fabric comes from, Margilon, and its Yodgorlik Silk Factory, should be your ground zero.

Although there is little to show for it, Margilon has been around for a long time, probably since the 1st century BC. For centuries its merchant clans, key players in Central Asia's commerce and silk trade, were said to be a law unto themselves; even in the closing decades of Soviet rule, this was the heart of Uzbekistan's black-market economy.

#### SIGHTS

Margilon has two truly worthwhile attractions: its Sunday bazaar and the **Yodgorlik (Souvenir) Silk Factory** (☎ 233 88 24; silk@mail.ru; Imam Zakhriddin; 8am-5pm). There's a wonderful (and free) tour here where you'll witness traditional methods of silk production (unlike those used at the city's increasingly moribund mass-production factories). The entire process is on display, from steaming and unravelling the cocoons to the weaving of the dazzling *khanatlas* (hand-woven silk patterned on one side) fabrics for which Margilon is famous. Amazingly, it's almost all done sans electricity, just as it was 1500 years ago. After the tour (available in English, French, Russian or German), you can buy silk by the metre: US$4 for *khanatlas*, US$8 for *adras* (half-cotton, half-silk) and US$10 for *shoyi* (pure silk). There is also premade clothing, carpets and embroidered items for sale.

A much less sanitized experience is Margilon's fantastic Sunday **Kuntepa Bazaar**, 5km west of the centre. It's a time capsule full of weathered Uzbek men in traditional clothing exchanging solemn greetings and gossiping over endless pots of tea, with hardly a Russian or a tourist in sight. Margilon's conservative streak, extreme even by Fergana Valley standards, is on full display here, with Uzbek matrons dressed almost exclusively in the locally produced *khanatlas* dresses and head scarves and men in skull caps and *chapan*. On Sunday mornings it's difficult to move among the throngs of people. Some travellers say it's the most interesting bazaar in the country.

Kuntepa Bazaar also happens on Thursdays; other days it's pretty dead. When it's not happening you might check out Margilon's large central farmers market, which was undergoing full reconstruction in early 2007.

Half a kilometre east of the farmers market is the reconstructed **Khonakhah Mosque**, a Juma (Friday) mosque that gets packed with thousands of worshippers every Friday. On other days the mosque's courtyard is one of the city's more peaceful places. Foreign visitors are welcome to enter and check out an unrestored section of the mosque's prayer room dating to the 15th century. It was hidden behind a bakery in Soviet times and spared destruction. It's on the right when you enter the courtyard.

#### GETTING THERE & AWAY

See p215 for transport from Fergana. Marshrutkas and taxis drop you off near the town's main intersection, kitty-corner from the central bazaar.

### Rishton Риштан

☎ (3) 73

This town just north of the Kyrgyzstan border is famous for the ubiquitous cobalt and green pottery fashioned from its fine clay. About 90% of the ceramics you see in souvenir stores across Uzbekistan originates here – most of it handmade.

Some 1000 potters make a living from the legendary local loam, which is so pure that it requires no additives (besides water) before being chucked on the wheel. Among the most accomplished masters of the Rishton school is **Rustam Usmanov** (☎ 453 73 45, 452 15 85; Ar-Roshidony 230; ⏲ by appointment), erstwhile art director of the defunct local collectivised ceramics factory. Of Tatar stock, Usmanov now has a workshop in his home on the main road through town and offers tours, lunch and vodka shots to travellers who call ahead (as many tour groups do).

Usmanov says that Rishton potters are facing a potential crisis, as the purest clay is becoming scarce. Usmanov's taking no chances: a week before we visited he had bought 120 tonnes. Enough to last five or six years, we wondered? 'Enough to last 20 years', he said.

Usmanov has a small museum on premises and is a leading member of an independent potters' association dedicated to preserving traditional techniques. You can visit other masters as well and buy beautiful platters, jugs and vases fresh out of the oven. **Alisher Nazirov**

#### SHAKHIMARDAN, THAT WHACKY ENCLAVE

One of the odder results of Stalin's diabolical gerrymandering around the Fergana Valley is the existence of an archipelago of tiny 'islands' of one republic entirely surrounded by another. One of these is the Uzbek enclave of Shakhimardan, 55km south of Fergana (another, equally scenic but off-limits to foreigners because it's home to a major dam, is Sokh, 50km south of Kokand).

Shakhimardan's main appeal for visitors is that it's nestled in a 1500m-high alpine valley, a fine place to clear your lungs and take an easy look at the Pamir Alay mountains in surrounding Kyrgyzstan. Kyrgyzstan has been trying to reclaim Shakhimardan for years, but as of this writing it remained stubbornly in Uzbek hands, making it nearly impossible for foreigners to visit legally. While locals shuttle freely over the border crossings between Fergana and Shakhimardan, this path is off-limits to foreigners – even to foreigners with multiple-entry Kyrgyz and Uzbek visas. The only legal way to get to Shakhimardan is thus to cross the border near Osh and proceed to Shakhimardan from there. For that you'll need multiple-entry Kyrgyz and Uzbek visas.

Touts at the old Fergana bus station say that they can sneak foreigners across the border in marshrutkas. The asking price starts at 17,000S for the 1¼-hour trip. As this can cause big-time headaches if you encounter a border guard in a bad mood, we cannot recommend it.

If you manage to enter Shakhimardan legally, there is a legendary trek amid glaciers and 5000m peaks to **Daroot-Korgon** in southwestern Kyrgyzstan. However, given the tenuous border situation, this trek is better launched from hard-to-reach Khaidakan, Kyrgyzstan, nearby.

With any luck the situation will change and Shakhimardan, which also offers up some good day hiking in sight of Ak-Suu peak (5359m), will once again become a trekking hotbed. The main attraction is the half-day hike and cable-car ride from town to the icy lake of **Kuli Kulon**, nestled in the Pamir Alays at 1740m. Check with Elena Tour in Tashkent (p199) for updates on the situation.

UZBEKISTAN

 

(☎ 452 33 43; Ferganskaya 152) is another master who gives tours.

Of course there is so much affordable Rishton in Uzbekistan that you needn't trek all the way here to buy it, but it's interesting to see where it all came from.

Rishton is best visited as a stop on the way to Fergana from Kokand (or vice-versa). It's about a 45-minute shared taxi or marshrutka ride from either (marshrutka/taxi per seat 800/3000S).



## ANDIJON АНДИЖАН

**☎ (3) 74 / pop 350,000**

Andijon – the Fergana Valley's largest city and its spiritual mecca – will forever be linked with the bloodshed of 13 May 2005 (p191). The very word 'Andijon' is a hot potato in Uzbekistan; just mentioning it is enough to stop any conversation in its tracks.

That's a shame because both culturally and linguistically Andijon is probably the country's purest Uzbek city, and the best place to observe Uzbeks in their element. Architecturally there's not much to see here – an earthquake in 1902 took care of that. Rather, its Andijon's bazaars and chaikhanas, brimming with colour and life, that make a trip out here worthwhile. Andijonians are warm and friendly by nature, and whatever concerns they have about their paranoid government appear not to have negatively affected their demeanour.

Most travellers who pass through Andijon are on their way to or from Kyrgyzstan and don't linger long because of security concerns. Make no mistake: the local police are on their guard here and do routinely stop foreigners. Have your papers in order and take the normal precautions, but don't let all the hype that Andijon is 'dangerous' prevent you from coming.

### Orientation & Information

Museums, medressa, bank, shops and the post office are clustered in the old town around central Kolkhozny Bazaar (farmers market). The neighbouring bus and train stations are 3km to the south. Roughly in between is Babur Sq, where the violence took place in 2005.

Change money on the black market at Kolkhozny Bazaar.

### Sights

Andijon's Sunday **Jahon Bazaar** is the biggest bazaar on the Uzbek side of the Fergana Valley. On Sunday and Thursday it is teeming with people, most of whom are involved in the shuttle trade with Kyrgyzstan. From Kolkhozny Bazaar, it's 4km northeast on marshrutka 6, 10 or any saying Жахон базар.

Jahon Bazaar is rather quiet on other days, but bazaar lovers will find no shortage of markets here. **Kolkhozny Bazaar** spills into the streets of the old town, making it a fine place for people-watching. **Yaangi Bazaar** is another big market located just south of the bus station.

Across from Kolkhozny Bazaar on Oltinkul is the handsome 19th-century **Juma Mosque & Medressa** (admission 1200S; 9am-4pm Tue-Sun), said to be the only building to survive the 1902 earthquake. It reopened as a working medressa in the 1990s but was turned into a museum of local ethnography after a police crackdown on suspected Islamic militants. The museum has a quirky souvenir shop loaded with Soviet trinkets. Next door is a dusty **regional museum** (admission 500S; 9am-5pm Tue-Sun), with the usual historical exhibits and stuffed animals.

The marginally more interesting **Babur Literary Museum** (9am-4pm Tue-Sun) occupies the site of the royal apartments where Babur lived and studied as a boy within Ark-Ichy, the town's long-gone citadel. It's on a small lane west of Kolkhozny Bazaar.

### Sleeping & Eating

**Hotel Andijon** (Fitrat 241; s/d US$12/24, with shared bathroom US$4/8) This no-frills hotel across from Babur Sq sports small but clean rooms, basic bathrooms and impossibly small TVs. There are a couple of very nice, renovated *lux* rooms (US$50). The chaikhana behind the hotel is the best place to eat in town.

There are two fairly decrepit old Intourist cinderblocks right next to each other in a huge park 2km south of the bus station. **Sport Hotel** (☎ 226 10 78; Mashrab 21; s/d US$18/35) is perhaps a slight step up from **Oltyn Vody** (☎ 226 79 90; Mashrab 19; s/d US$12/24).

Chaikhanas abound near the bazaars and just about everywhere else. For nonchaikhana fare try **Golden Chicken Restaurant** (Fitrat; meals 2000S), 200m west of Hotel Andijon, with quick Uzbek, Turkish and Western meals.

### Getting There & Around

**Uzbekistan Airways** (☎ 224 42 23; airport) has five weekly flights to/from Tashkent (one way US$31, 1½ hours). The airport is about 3km southwest of Yaangi Bazaar.

All vehicular transport roosts near the bus station. There are plenty of rides to Fergana (marshrutka/shared taxi per seat 1200/3000S, 1¼ hour; bus 700S, two hours) and Tashkent (shared taxi per seat 14,000S, five hours).

Two daily trains trundle to Kokand (1200S, four hours).

Marshrutka 33 races around a fixed route as if taxi driving was a freestyle sport. It travels from Juma Medressa, past Babur Sq, Yaangi Bazaar and Hotel Oltyn Vody before coming within 1km of the airport. To get closer to the airport, transfer to marshrutka 4 at Oltyn Vody.

For information on transport to Kyrgyzstan, see p267.

# CENTRAL UZBEKISTAN

## SAMARKAND САМАРКАНД

☎ (3) 66 / pop 405,000 / elev 710m

We travel not for trafficking alone,
By hotter winds our fiery hearts are fanned.
For lust of knowing what should not be known
We take the Golden Road to Samarkand.

These final lines of James Elroy Flecker's 1913 poem *The Golden Journey to Samarkand* evoke the romance of Uzbekistan's most glorious city. No name is so evocative of the Silk Road as Samarkand. For most people it has the mythical resonance of Atlantis, fixed in the Western popular imagination by poets and playwrights of bygone eras, few of whom saw the city in the flesh.

From the air your eye locks onto the domes and minarets, and on the ground the sublime, larger-than-life monuments of Timur, the technicolour bazaar and the city's long, rich history, indeed work some kind of magic. Surrounding these islands of majesty, modern Samarkand sprawls across acres of Soviet-built buildings, parks and broad avenues used by buzzing Daewoo taxis.

You can visit most of Samarkand's high-profile attractions in two or three days. If you're short on time, at least see the Registan, Guri Amir, Bibi-Khanym Mosque and Shah-i-Zinda.

Note that the people of Samarkand, Bukhara and southeastern Uzbekistan don't speak Uzbek but an Uzbek-laced Tajik (Farsi). Some members of the ethnic Tajik minority wish Stalin had made the area part of Tajikistan, but the issue is complicated by ethnic Uzbek city folk who speak Tajik.

### History

Samarkand (Marakanda to the Greeks), one of Central Asia's oldest settlements, was probably founded in the 5th century BC. It was already the cosmopolitan, walled capital of the Sogdian empire when it was taken in 329 BC by Alexander the Great, who said, 'Everything I have heard about Marakanda is true, except that it's more beautiful than I ever imagined.'

A key Silk Road city, it sat on the crossroads leading to China, India and Persia, bringing in trade and artisans. From the 6th to the 13th century it grew into a city more populous than it is today, changing hands every couple of centuries – Western Turks, Arabs, Persian Samanids, Karakhanids, Seljuq Turks, Mongolian Karakitay and Khorezmshah have all ruled here – before being obliterated by Jenghiz Khan in 1220.

This might have been the end of the story, but in 1370 Timur decided to make Samarkand his capital, and over the next 35 years forged a new, almost-mythical city – Central Asia's economic and cultural epicentre. His grandson Ulugbek ruled until 1449 and made it an intellectual centre as well.

When the Uzbek Shaybanids came in the 16th century and moved their capital to Bukhara, Samarkand went into decline. For several decades in the 18th century, after a series of earthquakes, it was essentially uninhabited. The emir of Bukhara forcibly repopulated the town towards the end of the century, but it was only truly resuscitated by the Russians, who forced its surrender in May 1868 and linked it to the Russian empire by the Trans-Caspian railway 20 years later.

Samarkand was declared capital of the new Uzbek SSR in 1924, but lost the honour to Tashkent six years later.

### Orientation

A map of Samarkand's centre shows the city's Russian-Asian schizophrenia. Eastward are the tangled alleys of the old town, whose axis is pedestrian Tashkent kochasi. Across town, shady 19th-century Russian avenues radiate westward from Mustaqillik maydoni,

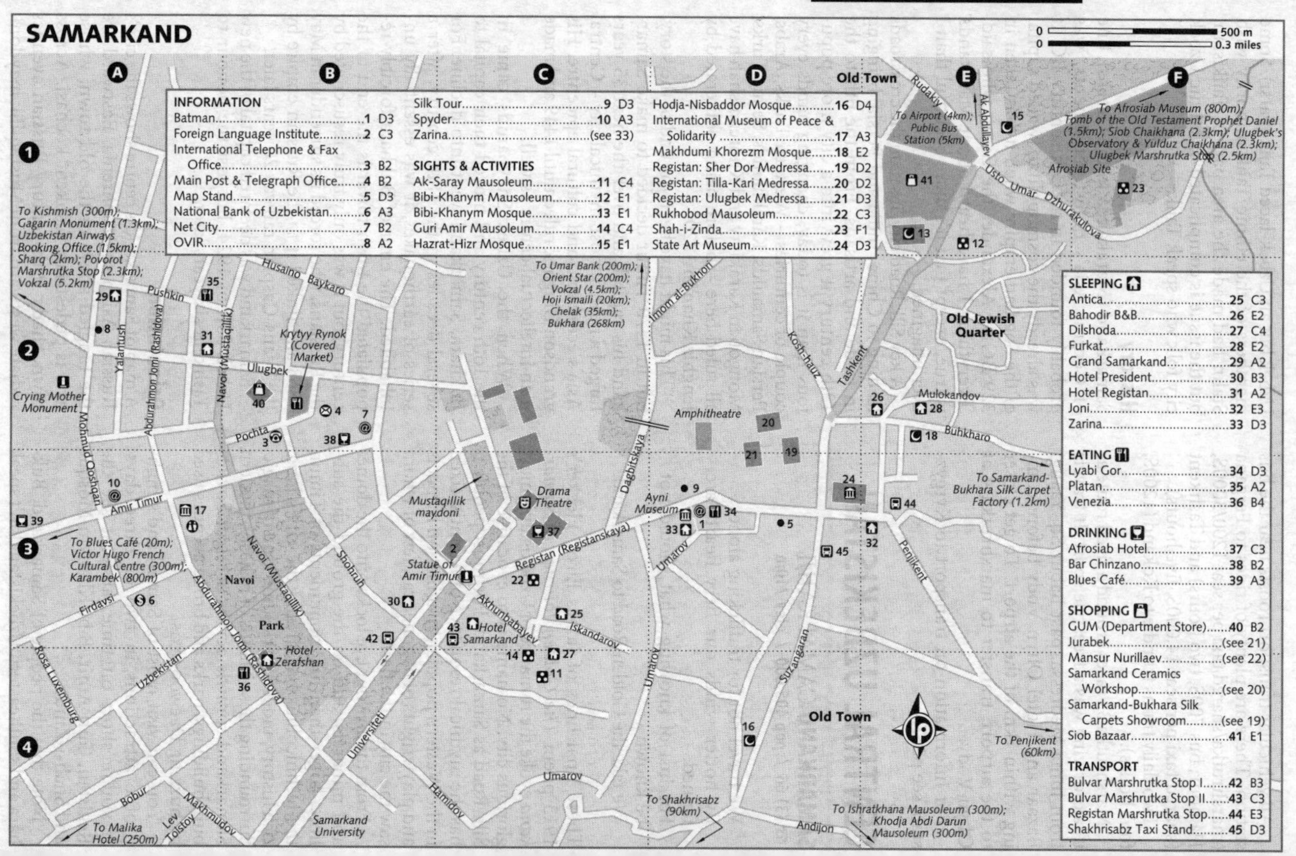
SAMARKAND
0 500 m
0 0.3 miles
INFORMATION
Batman....1 D3
Foreign Language Institute....2 C3
International Telephone & Fax Office....3 B2
Main Post & Telegraph Office....4 B2
Map Stand....5 D3
National Bank of Uzbekistan....6 A3
Net City....7 B2
OVIR....8 A2
Silk Tour....9 D3
Spyder....10 A3
Zarina....(see 33)
SIGHTS & ACTIVITIES
Ak-Saray Mausoleum....11 C4
Bibi-Khanym Mausoleum....12 E1
Bibi-Khanym Mosque....13 E1
Guri Amir Mausoleum....14 C4
Hazrat-Hizr Mosque....15 E1
Hodja-Nisbaddor Mosque....16 D4
International Museum of Peace & Solidarity....17 A3
Makhdumi Khorezm Mosque....18 E2
Registan: Sher Dor Medressa....19 D2
Registan: Tilla-Kari Medressa....20 D2
Registan: Ulugbek Medressa....21 D3
Rukhobod Mausoleum....22 C3
Shah-i-Zinda....23 F1
State Art Museum....24 D3
SLEEPING
Antica....25 C3
Bahodir B&B....26 E2
Dilshoda....27 C4
Furkat....28 E2
Grand Samarkand....29 A2
Hotel President....30 B3
Hotel Registan....31 A2
Joni....32 E3
Zarina....33 D3
EATING
Lyabi Gor....34 D3
Platan....35 A2
Venezia....36 B4
DRINKING
Afrosiab Hotel....37 C3
Bar Chinzano....38 B2
Blues Café....39 A3
SHOPPING
GUM (Department Store)....40 B2
Jurabek....(see 21)
Mansur Nurillaev....(see 22)
Samarkand Ceramics Workshop....(see 20)
Samarkand-Bukhara Silk Carpets Showroom....(see 19)
Siob Bazaar....41 E1
TRANSPORT
Bulvar Marshrutka Stop I....42 B3
Bulvar Marshrutka Stop II....43 C3
Registan Marshrutka Stop....44 E3
Shakhrisabz Taxi Stand....45 D3
To Kishmish (300m); Gagarin Monument (1.3km); Uzbekistan Airways Booking Office (1.5km); Sharq (2km); Povorot Marshrutka Stop (2.3km); Vokzal (5.2km)
To Umar Bank (200m); Orient Star (200m); Vokzal (4.5km); Hoji Ismaili (20km); Chelak (35km); Bukhara (268km)
To Airport (4km); Public Bus Station (5km)
To Afrosiab Museum (800m); Tomb of the Old Testament Prophet Daniel (1.5km); Siob Chaikhana (2.3km); Ulugbek's Observatory & Yulduz Chaikhana (2.3km); Ulugbek Marshrutka Stop (2.5km)
Afrosiab Site
Old Town
Old Jewish Quarter
Krytyy Rynok (Covered Market)
Crying Mother Monument
Amphitheatre
Drama Theatre
Mustaqillik maydoni
Ayni Museum
Statue of Amir Timur
Hotel Samarkand
Hotel Zerafshan
Navoi Park
Samarkand University
To Blues Café (20m); Victor Hugo French Cultural Centre (300m); Karambek (800m)
To Samarkand-Bukhara Silk Carpet Factory (1.2km)
To Penjikent (60km)
To Shakhrisabz (90km)
To Ishratkhana Mausoleum (300m); Khodja Abdi Darun Mausoleum (300m)
To Malika Hotel (250m)
Rudakiy
Ak Abdullayev
Usto Umar Dzhurakulova
Husaino Baykaro
Pushkin
Yalantush
Abdurahmon Jomi (Rashidova)
Navoi (Mustaqillik)
Ulugbek
Pochta
Mohmud Qoshqari
Amir Timur
Firdavsi
Shohruh
Registan (Registanskaya)
Dagbitskaya
Imom al-Bukhori
Kosh-hauz
Tashkent
Mulokandov
Buhkharo
Penjikent
Suzangaran
Umarov
Akhunbabayev
Iskandarov
Universiteti
Hamidov
Rosa Luxemburg
Uzbekistan
Bobur
Makhmudov
Lev Tolstoy
Andijon

the administrative centre of the modern city and province.

Most sights are within a couple of kilometres west and north of the Registan. The newer downtown area is also centred around a pedestrian thoroughfare, Navoi. A useful tourist landmark, roughly betwixt the city's two halves, is mothballed Hotel Samarkand on the parklike boulevard called Universiteti.

### MAPS

A detailed, accurate 2004 map called *Guide of Samarkand* (scale 1:13,000) includes a full list of sights and facilities. Buy it at the small map stand opposite the Registan for 2000S.

## Information

### CULTURAL CENTRES

**Victor Hugo French Cultural Centre** (☎ 233 66 27; dilallia@yahoo.fr; Baraka 26; 🕑 2-6pm) French papers and magazines, plus 24 French TV channels. Manager Dila has great travel tips and may be able to arrange a homestay in a pinch.

### INTERNET ACCESS

**Batman** (Registan 3; per hr 600S; 🕑 8am-10pm) Snail-slow café near Registan.

**Net City** (Akhunbabayev 68; per hr 500S; 🕑 8am-midnight) Fast connection (usually), Skype, webcams, and range of computing services.

**Spyder** (Amir Timur 44; per hr 600S; 🕑 8am-midnight) Net City's only serious competition, with even better computers.

### MONEY

The exchange offices at the Hotel Afrosiab and Hotel President work until early evening.

**National Bank of Uzbekistan** (Firdavsi 7; 🕑 9am-4pm Mon-Sat) Cashes travellers cheques and charges Visa card holders 4% for cash advances.

### POST & COMMUNICATIONS

**International telephone & fax office** (Pochta 9; 🕑 8am-8pm) Standard Uztelekom rates here (p264).

**Main post & telegraph office** (Pochta 5)

### REGISTRATION

**OVIR** (☎ 233 69 34; cnr Mohmud Qoshqari & Ulugbek) Look for large metal gate.

### TRAVEL AGENCIES

Local travel agencies can organise cars, guides and the standard camel trekking and yurtstays (p262). Of these, Silk Tours is the most experienced. Ask about the annual *kupkari* (Tajik: *buzkashi)* match, a traditional pololike game played with a headless sheep/goat/calf carcass, around Navruz (Navrus; 21 March).

**Orient Star** (☎ 235 93 67; www.tour-orient.com; Dagbitskaya 33) Large agency claims to be the authority on trekking in the Zerafshan and Hissar Mountains, and in Tajikistan.

**Silk Tour** (☎ 233 17 35; www.silktour.uz; sogda@intal.uz; Registan 38) Also known as Sogda Tour, it has refreshing ideas for touring the region. Saad from the Tashkent office is an authority on just about everything Uzbek.

**Zarina** (esprit@rol.uz) The French-speaking manager of this hotel p229 also runs a travel agency that can arrange the standard yurtstays and camel trekking, plus an overnight trek into the Amankutan gorge in the Zerafshan Mountains.

## Sights

You can enter the courtyards of some of the main sights outside working hours for free or by 'tipping' the guard on duty; the Registan and Bibi-Khanym are spectacular in the early morning light; Guri Amir is sublime by night.

### THE REGISTAN

This ensemble of majestic, tilting medressas – a near-overload of majolica, azure mosaics and vast, well-proportioned spaces – is the centrepiece of the city, and one of the most awesome single sights in Central Asia. The **Registan** (cnr Registan & Tashkent; admission 3700S; 🕑 8am-7pm Apr-Oct, 9am-5pm Nov-Mar), which translates to 'Sandy Place' in Tajik, was medieval Samarkand's commercial centre and the plaza was probably a wall-to-wall bazaar.

The three grand edifices here are among the world's oldest preserved medressas, anything older having been destroyed by Jenghiz Khan. They have taken their knocks over the years courtesy of the frequent earthquakes that buffet the region; that they are still standing is a testament to the incredible craftsmanship of their builders. One look at the already crumbling blue dome of the recently rebuilt Bibi-Khanym Mosque nearby demonstrates clearly the inferiority of modern methods. The Soviets, to their credit, worked feverishly to protect and restore these beleaguered treasures, but they also took some questionable liberties, such as the capricious addition of a blue outer dome to the Tilla-Kari Medressa.

**Ulugbek Medressa** on the west side is the original medressa, finished in 1420 under Ulugbek (who is said to have taught mathematics here; other subjects included theology, astronomy and philosophy). Beneath the little corner domes were lecture halls, and at the rear a large mosque. About 100 students lived in the two storeys of dormitory cells here.

The other buildings are rough imitations by the Shaybanid Emir Yalangtush. The entrance portal of the **Sher Dor (Lion) Medressa**, opposite Ulugbek's and finished in 1636, is decorated with roaring felines that look like tigers but are meant to be lions, flouting Islamic prohibitions against the depiction of live animals. It took 17 years to build but still hasn't held up as well as the Ulugbek Medressa, built in just three years.

In between is the **Tilla-Kari (Gold-Covered) Medressa**, completed in 1660, with a pleasant, gardenlike courtyard. The highlight here is the mosque, intricately decorated with gold to symbolize Samarkand's wealth at the time it was built. The mosque's delicate ceiling, oozing gold leaf, is flat but its tapered design makes it look domed from the inside.

Many of the medressas' former dormitory rooms are now art and souvenir shops. In the high season a variety of traditional shows are put on for tourists in the Sher Dor courtyard, including mock Uzbek weddings and *kurash,* a form of Uzbek wrestling. There are also tacky evening sound-and-light shows put on for tour groups in the square, which can usually be watched for free from afar.

For optimal views, police guards eagerly offer to escort visitors to the top of a minaret for 3000S. Don't pay more than 2000S.

### BIBI-KHANYM MOSQUE

The enormous congregational **Bibi-Khanym Mosque** (Tashkent kochasi; admission 2400S; ⌚ 8am-7pm Apr-Oct, 9am-5pm Nov-Mar), northeast of the Registan, was finished shortly before Timur's death and must have been the jewel of his empire. Once one of the Islamic world's biggest mosques (the main gate alone was 35m high), it pushed construction techniques to the limit. Slowly crumbling over the years, it finally collapsed in an earthquake in 1897.

Legend says that Bibi-Khanym, Timur's Chinese wife, ordered the mosque built as a surprise while he was away. The architect fell madly in love with her and refused to finish the job unless he could give her a kiss. The smooch left a mark and Timur, on seeing it, executed the architect and decreed that women should henceforth wear veils so as not to tempt other men.

Recent restoration, though shoddy in places (notice the tiles falling off the cupolas), has reinstated the main gateway and several domes. The interior courtyard contains an enormous marble Quran stand that lends some scale to the place. Local lore has it that any woman who crawls under the stand will have lots of children.

Across Tashkent kochasi is Bibi-Khanym's own compact 14th-century **mausoleum** (admission 1200S; ⌚ 8am-6pm).

### SHAH-I-ZINDA

Its shiny restoration in 2005 has been called an abomination by some, but this **avenue of mausoleums** (admission 2400S; ⌚ 8am-7pm Apr-Oct, 9am-5pm Nov-Mar) remains Samarkand's most moving sight. The name, which means 'Tomb of the Living King', refers to its original, innermost and holiest shrine – a complex of cool, quiet rooms around what is probably the grave of Qusam ibn-Abbas, a cousin of the Prophet Mohammed who is said to have brought Islam to this area in the 7th century.

A shrine to Qusam existed here on the edge of Afrosiab long before the Mongols ransacked it in the 13th century. Shah-i-Zinda began to assume its current form in the 14th century as Timur and later Ulugbek buried their family and favourites near the Living King.

These tombs featured the finest unrenovated glazed tilework in Central Asia until they were controversially restored as part of the Karimov administration's drive to 'beautify' Uzbekistan's architectural monuments. While still stunning, the tombs have undeniably lost some of their power.

The most beautiful tomb remains the Shadi Mulk Aka Mausoleum (1372), resting place of one of Timur's wives, second on the left after the entry stairs. The exquisite tilework here was of such exceptional quality that it merited little restoration.

Shah-i-Zinda is an important place of pilgrimage, so enter with respect and dress conservatively.

### GURI AMIR MAUSOLEUM & AROUND

Timur, two sons and two grandsons, including Ulugbek, lie beneath the surprisingly modest **Guri Amir Mausoleum** (Akhunbabayev; admission 2400S; ⌚ 8am-7pm Apr-Oct, 9am-5pm Nov-Mar) and its trademark fluted azure dome.

Timur had built a simple crypt for himself at Shakhrisabz, and had this one built in 1404 for his grandson and proposed heir, Mohammed Sultan, who had died the previous year. But the story goes that when Timur died unexpectedly of pneumonia in Kazakhstan (in the course of planning an expedition against the Chinese) in the winter of 1405, the passes back to Shakhrisabz were snowed in and he was interred here instead.

As with other Muslim mausoleums, the stones are just markers; the actual crypts are in a chamber beneath. In the centre is Timur's stone, once a single block of dark-green jade. In 1740 the warlord Nadir Shah carried it off to Persia, where it was accidentally broken in two – from which time Nadir Shah is said to have had a run of very bad luck, including the near-death of his son. At the urging of his religious advisers he returned the stone to Samarkand, and of course his son recovered.

The plain marble marker to the left of Timur's is that of Ulugbek, and to the right is that of Mersaid Baraka, one of Timur's teachers. In front lies Mohammed Sultan. The stones behind Timur's mark the graves of his sons Shah Rukh (the father of Ulugbek) and Miran Shah. Behind these lies Sheikh Seyid Umar, the most revered of Timur's teachers, said to be a descendent of the Prophet Mohammad. Timur ordered Guri Amir built around Umar's tomb.

The Soviet anthropologist Mikhail Gerasimov opened the crypts in 1941 and, among other things, confirmed that Timur was tall (1.7m) and lame in the right leg and right arm (from injuries suffered when he was 25) – and that Ulugbek died from being beheaded. According to every tour guide's favourite anecdote, he found on Timur's grave an inscription to the effect that 'whoever opens this will be defeated by an enemy more fearsome than I'. The next day, 22 June, Hitler attacked the Soviet Union.

Outside the mausoleum you'll find the remains of what stood here before Guri Amir was built: a 14th-century complex consisting of a *khanaka* (Uzbek: *hanako;* a Sufi contemplation hall and hostel for wandering mendicants), mosque and mausoleum.

Down a lane behind the Guri Amir is the derelict little **Ak-Saray Mausoleum** (1470), with some unrestored, barely visible interior frescoes and majolica tilework inside. It's usually locked but there may be a guy hanging around to open up – for a fee, of course.

Between Guri Amir and the main road is **Rukhobod Mausoleum**, dated 1380 and possibly the city's oldest surviving monument. It now serves as a souvenir and craft shop.

### ANCIENT SAMARKAND (AFROSIAB)

At a 2.2-sq-km site called Afrosiab, northeast of the bazaar, are excavations of Marakanda (early Samarkand) more or less abandoned to the elements. The **Afrosiab Museum** (☎ 235 53 36; Tashkent kochasi; admission 2300S; 🕑 9am-6pm) leads the visitor through the 11 layers of civilisation that is Afrosiab. From the museum, walk 1km north to the current excavation site where you may find weather-beaten archaeologists picking coins out of the dust.

The restored **Tomb of the Old Testament Prophet Daniel** (admission 1200S; 🕑 8am-6pm) is 400m northeast of the museum, on the banks of the Siob River (turn left off Tashkent kochasi just before the bridge). The building is a long, low structure topped with five domes, containing an 18m sarcophagus – legend has it that Daniel's body grows by half an inch a year and thus the sarcophagus has to be enlarged. His remains, which date to at least the 5th century BC, were brought here for good luck by Timur from Susa, Iran (suspiciously, an alleged tomb of Daniel can also be found in Susa).

Continuing north you'll encounter the remains of **Ulugbek's Observatory**, one of the great archaeological finds of the 20th century. Ulugbek was probably more famous as an astronomer than as a ruler. His 30m astrolab, designed to observe star positions, was part of a three-storey observatory he built in the 1420s. All that remains is the instrument's curved track, unearthed in 1908. The small on-site **museum** (admission 2400; 🕑 9am-6pm) has some miniatures depicting Ulugbek and a few old ceramics and other artefacts unearthed in Afrosiab.

The best way to reach Afrosiab is on foot. Cross the intersection north of Bibi-Khanym and follow pedestrian Tashkent kochasi for about 1km to the Afrosiab Museum; Ulugbek's observatory is 1.5km beyond that. If it's too hot to walk, marshrutka 17 from the Registan takes an 8km detour via the bazaar and Samarkand's northern suburbs; marshrutka 45 follows the same roundabout route from Hotel Samarkand. At the time of writing the city was building a new road east of Shah-i-Zinda that should make driving to Afrosiab easier.

#### STATE ART MUSEUM

Samarkand's largest **museum** (☎ 235 37 80; cnr Registan & Tashkent; admission 2400S; ⏰ 9am-6pm) walks you through the history of art in the region, starting with archaeological finds from Afrosiab and the Timurid era. The highlight is probably the decorative and applied arts exhibits upstairs, which include an impressive collection of old carpets – including some splendid 200-year-old Afghan and Persian specimens – prayer rugs, nuptial sheets and *suzani*. Downstairs are some photos of Samarkand 100 years ago and a quirky collection of Qurans that includes one of the world's largest (1m by 1.5m).

#### NAVOI KOCHASI & PARK

Samarkand's Russified downtown area tends to escape tourists' radar, which is unfortunate because it's quite un-Sovietised and charming. Gussied-up locals stroll along Navoi (formerly Leninskaya), a sight that would have Lenin rolling in his coffin.

The quirky **International Museum of Peace & Solidarity** (☎ 223 17 53; http://peace.museum.com; ⏰ by appointment only) used to occupy a building in central **Navoi Park**, but the building was demolished in 2006 to pave the way for park renovations. The museum should have a new home by the time you read this. Curator Anatoly Ionesov has a remarkable collection of disarmament and environmental memorabilia and has collected thousands of signatures, including some very famous ones, in the name of peace.

#### OTHER SIGHTS

Across the intersection from the bazaar, the **Hazrat-Hizr Mosque** (Tashkent kochasi; admission 1200S, minaret 1000S; ⏰ 8am-6pm) occupies a hill on the fringes of Afrosiab. The 8th-century mosque that once stood here was burnt to the ground by Jenghiz Khan in the 13th century and was not rebuilt until 1854. In the 1990s it was lovingly restored by a wealthy Bukharan and today is Samarkand's most beautiful mosque, with a fine domed interior and views of Bibi-Khanym, Shah-i-Zinda and Afrosiab from the minaret. The ribbed *aivan* ceiling drips colour.

If you prefer your ruins really ruined, it's worth the slog out to the Tomb Raider–style, 15th-century **Ishratkhana Mausoleum** (Sadriddin Ayniy). With a preponderance of pigeons and an eerie crypt in the basement, this is the place to film your horror movie. Across the street is the **Khodja Abdi Darun Mausoleum** (Sadriddin Ayniy), which shares a tranquil, shady courtyard with a mosque and a *hauz* (artificial stone pool). To get here take marshrutka 22 or 32.

South of the Registan on Suzangaran is the fine **Hodja-Nisbaddor Mosque**, a small 19th-century summer mosque with an open porch, tall carved columns and brightly restored ceiling. Another recently restored gem is the **Makhdumi Khorezm Mosque** (Bukhoro), 100m east of the Registan. If it's locked ask the caretaker to let you in for a glimpse at the lush ceiling tilework.

Out by the Uzbekistan Airways office, the **Gagarin Monument** (cnr Gagarin & Ulugbek) will thrill lovers of Soviet iconography. It looks like it was plucked out of a giant cereal box.

## Tours

For guides, go through your hotel or a travel agency. Recommended guides are listed below.

**Denis Vikulov** (⏰ 270 73 28; scootter@rambler.ru speaks English) Caters to budget travellers.
**Farruh Bahronov** (☎ 241 01 02 speaks English and French.) Also runs a shop at the Registan's Ulugbek Medressa.
**Firuza Fazilova** (☎ 260 14 25 speaks German.)
**Natalya Tyan** (☎ 222 58 42 speaks French.)
**Svetlana Li** (☎ 222 74 64; svetlana5de@yahoo.de speaks German.)

The going rate for trained guides is US$5 per hour. Students often cost less, and can be found through Dila at the Victor Hugo Centre (p225), or try the **Foreign Language Institute** (☎ 233 61 74; Akhunbabayev 93).

## Festivals & Events

Most of the action during Samarkand's **Navruz Festival** (see p263) takes place at the Registan and in Navoi Park. The city is also home to the **Sharq Taronalari** (Melodies of the East) international music festival, held every other year (next in 2007 and 2009) in August at Registan Sq. Every 18 October is **Samarkand Day**, with various cultural events and exhibitions.

## Sleeping

You'll find little reason to stray from Samarkand's B&Bs, which aren't quite up to Bukhara's lofty standards but are far preferable to the tour group–laden hotels.

#### BUDGET

Cheap private homestay options are limited. Email the Victor Hugo Centre before you arrive and see if its staff have any ideas.

**Bahodir B&B** (☎ 220 30 93; Mulokandov 132; dm from US$6, s/d US$10/16) Bahodir's hammerlock on the backpacker constituency speaks volumes about the power of low prices. OK, so it does have tasty vegetarian dinners (US$1) and a friendly communal atmosphere. But it also has barely functional plumbing, 'towels' that began their careers as dishrags 30 years ago and mattresses that would be no saggier had they spent the previous five years in an elephant pen. If you can't sleep, read the notebook filled with backpacker advice and war stories.

**Hotel Registan** (☎ 233 55 90; Ulugbek 36; s/d US$7/10) We hardly recommend this musty Soviet relic in the new part of town, but if everything else is full it's not *that* bad and it certainly won't break the bank.

**our pick** **Antica** (☎ 235 20 92; Iskandarov 58; antica 2006@rambler.ru; s/d with shared bathroom from US$10/20, s/d/tr from US$20/30/45; ) This boutique B&B is the only place in Samarkand where you can really capture the vibe of living in a traditional home. The rooms vary in design but all are generously furnished with antique carpets, *suzani* and trinkets; those in the 19th-century annexe have hand-carved walnut-wood doors and mosquelike ribbed, brightly painted ceilings. The main house, with two towering, vaulted windows, is set around a lush garden courtyard shaded by pomegranate, persimmon and fig trees. Dinners (US$7) are hearty and at least one family member can wax philosophical in English, German, French or Spanish.

**Furkat** (☎ 235 62 99; hotelfurkat@mail.ru; Mulokandov 105; s with shared bathroom US$10, s/d US$20/30; ) Samarkand's original B&B still gives the competition much to imitate, including richly decorated rooms, carved wood doors and flexible pricing. Its three floors may be out of place in old town, but you can't argue with the result: splendid views of the Registan and the snow-capped Fan Mountains. Staff bolt the front door shut annoyingly early here; night owls should consider Furkat's two annexes.

**Joni** (☎ 235 69 41; hotel_joni@yahoo.com; Penjikent 9; s/d US$18/36) There's a variety of rooms on offer at this well-located B&B. Ten of them are set around a courtyard with an odd, stringed sculpture as its centrepiece. Check out a few rooms and test the beds – some sag to the coils.

### MIDRANGE

**Dilshoda** (☎ 235 03 87; www.dilshoda.by.ru; Ak Saray 150; s/d US$20/30; ) Set in the shadow of Guri Amir, this B&B serves up warm if basic rooms with nice carpets, narrow beds and small bathrooms. The chipper host family serves up mouthwatering three-course dinners (US$4) upon request. Discounts are not beyond the realm of possibility if you're staying a while.

**Zarina** (☎ 235 07 61; www.hotel-zarina.com; Umarov 4; s/d from US$20/35; ) Located on an alley behind the Ayni Museum, this B&B has a alluring courtyard with three *tapchan* and a small pool. Alas, the smallish regular rooms do not quite match the standard of the courtyard and are a bit overpriced. More spacious deluxe doubles with satellite TV cost US$45.

**Malika** (☎ 233 01 97; www.malika-samarkand.com; s/d US$35/45; ) The Malika chain's signature hotel doesn't disappoint, with 26 spacious, tastefully understated rooms, fine food and a few traditional touches thrown in. Its mix of style and service makes it far and away the best true hotel in Samarkand, although its location is somewhat tragic.

### TOP END

**Grand Samarkand** (☎ 233 28 80; Yalantush 38; grand-samarkand@mail.ru; s/d US$50/70; ) This midsized offering is ugly on the outside but swanky on the inside, with extra-wide twin beds, fancy TVs and new everything. It was just getting its wings at the time of research, but you can expect a nice range of amenities.

**Hotel President** (☎ 233 24 75; www.uzhotelpresident.com; Shohruh 53; s/d/ste US$105/165/300; ) Beyond the luxurious, airplane hangar–like lobby, this new high-rise doesn't show much creativity. The rooms have the expected bells and whistles and those facing east have views of the Registan.

## Eating

Contrary to popular belief there are plenty of good eateries in Samarkand. Most are in the newer Russian part of town, far removed from the touristy Registan area.

### CHAIKHANAS & HOME RESTAURANTS

**Lyabi Gor** (Registan 6; mains 1000-2000S) One of the most popular chaikhanas in the country because of its prime location opposite the Registan, it pleases the tourist masses with generous helpings of *manty* (steamed dumplings), *laghman*, *shorpa* (meat and vegetable soup), shashlyk and cheap beer. Get there early or it may run out of shashlyk or close.

**Yulduz Chaikhana** (Tashkent kochasi; mains 1000-2000S) Another popular chaikhana, this one is near the Ulugbek Observatory. The menu is the same as at Lyabi Gor or any other chaikhana.

**Siob** (mains 1000-2000S; ⌚ lunch & dinner May-Sep) This dreamy chaikhana lays out *tapchan* on the banks of the babbling Siab (Siob) River. Turn right off Tashkent kochasi down a dirt road near the river and follow for 1km.

You can wash *plov* down with vodka at one of several decent home restaurants behind the Ulugbek Observatory. Ask to be pointed in the right direction. There's another strip of home restaurants in the old town between the bazaar and Imom al-Bukhori. These tend to work sporadically so ask around.



#### RESTAURANTS

**Karambek** (☎ 221 27 56; Gagarina 194; mains 1500-2500S) This traditional restaurant trounces touristy Oasis restaurant in Navoi Park. The national- and Russian-influenced cuisine is surprisingly good, and can be enjoyed in a variety of settings, from private country hut to airy streetside patio.

**Platan** (☎ 233 80 49; Pushkin 2; mains 2000-3000S; ⌚ lunch & dinner) The main dining facility – a sort of tropical-style, thatched-roof yurt – counts as one of Samarkand's stranger structures. The menu, which includes Arabian-, Thai- and Egyptian-style meat dishes, is no less charismatic, but all dishes are cooked-to-order and tasty.

**Kishmish** (☎ 231 03 82; Baraka 7; mains 2000-3000S) Another traditional-style place, this one has outdoor seating for 200 people. It was in the middle of a management change when we visited, but word is that new management will maintain the elaborate nightly floor shows that are its main draw.

At the time of research a promising Italian restaurant called **Venezia** (Abdurahmon) was getting set to open its doors across from the Hotel Zerafshan.

### Drinking & Entertainment

**Bar Chinzano** (Amir Timur 10; ⌚ 9am-midnight) This smoky bar draws a friendly, Russian-speaking crowd of regulars and is one of the few options in town for late-night eats – try the pizza.

**Blues Café** (Amir Timur 66; ⌚ noon-11.30pm) Dizzy, Louie, BB and company adorn the walls and set the bluesy vibe at this snug cocktail lounge. The nightly live jazz usually takes the form of Eddie the solo piano player, but occasionally a larger ensemble materializes. The creative snack menu includes *khachapuri* (cheese-filled Georgian *samsa*).

**Sharq** (Ulugbek 91; admission women/men Fri & Sat 1500/2500S, Sun-Thu free; ⌚ 9pm-2am) The Registan area shuts down around 9pm, but there's action downtown if you look hard enough. This is a pool bar weeknights but turns into a pretty good club on weekends, albeit one catering mainly to a younger set.

Your only late-night options are the two nightclubs at the **Afrosiab Hotel** (☎ 231 11 95; Registan 2) which are usually moribund but have their occasional moments at weekends.

### Shopping

There are souvenir shops and craft workshops of varying quality at all the big sights, in particular at the Rukhobod Mausoleum and the Registan. At the Registan look out for the **Samarkand Ceramics Workshop** (Tilla-Kari Medressa), one of the few places still practising the Samarkand school of ceramicmaking. **Jurabek** (Ulugbek Medressa) sells beautiful old textiles. Samarkand-Bukhara Silk Carpets (see p232) also has a Registan-based **showroom** (Sher Dor Medressa). Accomplished miniaturist Mansur Nurillaev is at the Rukhobod Mausoleum.

Around and behind Bibi-Khanym, the frenetic, colourful main farmers market, called **Siob Bazaar**, is great for vegetarians and photographers, and may reward silk and souvenir hunters as well. You can also find silk at **GUM** (Ulugbek), but silk buffs are better off going to Urgut (p232).

### Getting There & Away

#### AIR

**Uzbekistan Airways** (☎ booking office 334 10 89; Gagarin 84) flies between Samarkand and Tashkent daily except Friday for US$36. To get to the airport take any marshrutka to the Povorot (Поворот) stop and get out at Gagarin. Tickets for all domestic flights must be bought here.

#### LAND

Tashkent is four hours away by car across a flat, dry landscape that tsarist Russians nicknamed the Hungry Steppe, now a monotonous stretch of factories and cotton fields. The main departure point to Tashkent for private buses and shared taxis is the Ulugbek marshrutka stop, about 300m east of the observatory (bus/shared taxi per seat 3500/9000S, six/3½ hours). Marshrutkas to/

from Tashkent congregate at the train station (5000S).

Shared taxis to Termiz (per seat 16,000S, five hours) gather at 'Grebnoy Kanal' on the city's outskirts about 10km east of the Ulugbek stop. Infrequent Tashkent–Termiz buses pass by Grebnoy Kanal, but don't count on them having seats. One early morning bus departs to Termiz (4500S, 8½ hours) from the dying public bus station, 500m past the airport turnoff.

Buses to Bukhara via Navoi depart from opposite the Ulugbek stop on Tashkent kochasi (3500S, five hours). They run all night, but more frequently (at least two per hour) up until 7pm. Some go on to Urgench (7500S, 13 hours). You'll find a few shared taxis to Bukhara (per seat 11,000S, three hours) around this bus stop, but the main departure point is the Povorot marshrutka stop about 1km west of the Gagarin Monument on Ulugbek kochasi.

For Shakhrisabz, shared taxis congregate on Suzangaran, about 100m south of the 'Registan' marshrutka stop (per seat 2500S, 1½ hours). Most go only as far as Kitab, where you pick up a marshrutka for the last 10km. For Penjikent, see p267.

#### Train

The speedy *Registan* train, with airplane-style seating, departs five times a week to Tashkent at 5pm (2nd class/1st class 6500/12,000S, four hours). The equally priced and equally speedy Bukhara–Tashkent express *Sharq* train rolls through Samarkand daily at 11am. There are also two slower regular passenger trains daily to Tashkent (*platskartny* 7500S, six hours); one originates in Bukhara.

For Bukhara you can pick up the *Sharq* heading west at about 1.10pm (2nd class/1st class 5700/9200S, 3½ hours). The daily Tashkent–Bukhara passenger train rumbles through Samarkand at 1.45am (*platskartny* 7500S, six hours). The cheapest option to Bukhara is the daily 'suburban' train (1200S, six hours). There is also a daily suburban train to Qarshi (850S, four hours).

The trains from Tashkent to Urgench and to Kungrad via Nukus go via Samarkand (see p210).

The **train station** (☎ 229 15 32; Rudakiy) is 5km northwest of Navoi Park. Take any marshrutka that says 'Вокзал', such as 73 or 17 from the Registan.

### Getting Around

#### TO/FROM THE AIRPORT

Marshrutka 73 goes from the airport to the Registan area, while 20 goes to the Bulvar (Бульвар) stop near the mothballed Hotel Samarkand. Walk 500m out to main road for more options, such as 53 to the Registan. A taxi from the airport to the Registan will cost about 4000S, or walk out to the main road and pay 1500S.

#### PUBLIC TRANSPORT

Marshrutkas (200S to 300S) and the city's few remaining buses (150S) run from about 6am until 8pm or 9pm. To get between the Registan area and Navoi in the heart of the downtown area use Marshrutka 3, 21, 22 or 41 and get off at the GUM (ГУМ) stop. Plenty of buses go from the Registan to the Bulvar stop, which is also close to downtown. Marshrutkas from the Hotel Samarkand to the Siob Bazaar say 'Сиёб базар', but remind the driver to drop you off or he may bypass it.

## AROUND SAMARKAND

### Hoja Ismail

In Hoja Ismail, a village 20km north of Samarkand, is one of Islam's holier spots, the modest **Mausoleum of Ismail al-Bukhari** (admission 2000S, guided tour in English 1000S; 7am-8pm). Al-Bukhari (AD 810–887) was one of the greatest Muslim scholars of the *Hadith* – the collected acts and sayings of the Prophet Mohammed. His work is regarded by Sunni Muslims as second only to the Quran as a source of religious law. Following his refusal to give special tutoring to Bukhara's governor and his children, he was forced into exile here.

This peaceful place of pilgrimage contains a mosque, a small museum and two courtyards, the main one containing Ismail al-Bukhari's gorgeous tomb, made of yellow marble and inlaid with majolica. It's surrounded by an *aivan*, under which an imam usually sits, chanting prayers. The *aivan's* brightly painted ceiling uncharacteristically lacks red – supposedly on the orders of President Karimov, who wanted to avoid communist associations.

It's essential to dress conservatively here, respect the calm and reverent atmosphere, and ask before you take photos.

Hoja Ismail village is 4km off the road to Chelek. Marshrutkas from Samarkand leave from outside Umar Bank on Dagbitskaya in Samarkand (500S, 30 minutes). Marshrutka

### SOCIALLY RESPONSIBLE SHOPPING

Besides being blessed with former Soviet Central Asia's most splendid architecture, Uzbekistan boasts the region's richest textile industry – as evidenced by the sometimes baffling array of fabrics spilling out of tourist attractions from Tashkent to Khiva.

If you're the sort who can't tell the difference between an 18th-century Nuratinsky *suzani* (silk and cotton coverlets) or some farmer's dirty old handkerchief, the least you can do is buy responsibly. Uzbekistan is hardly known for being small-business friendly, but across the country a growing number of individual artisans and merchants have set up small-scale, tourist-focused enterprises that are turning profits while also contributing to the cultural and economic revival of local communities.

A pioneer of 'socially responsible' shopping is **Yulduz Mamadiyorova** (☎ 529 39 67; yulduz 1967@mail.ru), who runs a weaving project in Shakhrisabz that employs more than 100 local women. Hand-weaving is an ancient tradition in Shakhrisabz, and according to Yulduz every woman in the city knows how to stitch in the local style. However, they have traditionally lacked capital for raw materials and lacked markets for their products.

Yulduz' idea was simple – she would supply her women with raw materials on credit and promise to buy their finished *suzani*, handbags, clothing and other products. 'This is so they don't have to waste time selling at the bazaar', she explains. 'Instead, they get money immediately to feed their families.'

With seed money from foreign friends and international donors, Yulduz launched the project with 10 women in 2005. Within three months she was employing 60 women, within a year 150. 'If it were possible, I'd work with all the women in Shakhrisabz', she says.

But to make that a reality she'll need more money. Yulduz no longer stitches herself. Instead, much of her efforts go towards marketing and 'studying European tastes' to make sure her products, which mix traditional and modern styles, will be in demand.

Unfortunately, Yulduz has had problems finding a reliable retail outlet in Uzbekistan. Most items are custom ordered or sold at semimonthly expositions in Tashkent. Yulduz hopes to have

11 passes the Umar Bank taxi stand from the Hotel Samakand.

## Urgut

This town makes a popular day trip from Samarkand because of its vast **Sunday Bazaar**, one of the best places to buy silk and old textiles in the country. Some readers report being disappointed by this market, but that may be because they showed up on the wrong day! This market is only happening on Sunday, and to a lesser extent on Thursday. Arrive at the crack of dawn for best results. Serious collectors will be mainly interested in the section devoted to textiles and jewellery, but the entire bazaar is fantastic. To get here take a marshrutka from the Registan stop (1000S, 45 minutes).

## Zerafshan & Hissar Mountains

If you have a few days to explore, the road south to Termiz offers up some scenic, rarely explored detours, most notably to the paradisiacal mountain retreat of Langar and its famous mausoleum on a hill.

Several Samarkand travel agencies (p225) lead one- to three-day hikes in the Zerafshan Mountains between Samarkand and Shakhrisabz. South of Shakhrisabz, the Hissar Nature Reserve is home to Uzbekistan's highest peaks (about 4500m) and offers some of Central Asia's least-explored trekking routes.

Keep in mind that both the Hissar and Zerafshan Mountains are in sensitive border zones. Before planning a trek here, first check to ensure that the region is open; at the time of research it was. Trekking in the Hissars requires a special permit and you should proceed only with an experienced guide. Talk to Orient Star travel agency in Samarkand about obtaining permits and trekking in the Hissars.

# SHAKHRISABZ ШАХРИСАБЗ

☎ (3) 75 / pop 75,000

Shakhrisabz is a small, un-Russified town south of Samarkand, across the hills in the Kashka-Darya province. The town is a pleasant Uzbek backwater and seems to be nothing special – until you start bumping into the ruins dotted around its backstreets, and the a showroom up and running by 2007 next to Ak-Saray in Shakhrisabz (below). Until then you'll find a few bags and articles of clothing on sale at Human House (p208) in Tashkent.

In nearby Samarkand, 400 more women – plus a few men – are gainfully employed at **Samarkand-Bukhara Silk Carpet Factory** (Map p224; ☎ 231 07 26; Hojom 12; www.silkcarpets.net; 🕑 by appointment). Let's be frank: Uzbekistan is not the place to buy carpets in Central Asia, and almost anything of quality comes from Turkmenistan. But the owners here, besides being Turkmen, use only natural dyes to churn out hand-woven silk carpets of truly exceptional quality.

Just as important in a country where child-labour runs rampant and most private companies offer only three-month contracts to avoid paying benefits, the factory works according to strict Western employment standards.

'Our people work eight hours a day, five days a week, 11 months a year with a month off at full pay', says owner Abdullahad Badghisi, whose family has been making carpets for six generations in Turkmenistan, Afghanistan and Uzbekistan. He adds that all workers must take a break every half-hour, 'because happy employees make beautiful carpets'.

The factory's magnificent carpets, which exhibit a range of Turkmen, Caucasian, Afghan and other styles, are proof of that theory. In business here since 1992, the factory is now a well-worn stop on the tour-bus trail. Abdullahad walks visitors through a tour of all stages of the silk- and carpet-making process, from unwinding the silk cocoons to washing the finished carpets.

These carpets can take months to make and are consequently expensive – expect to pay upwards of US$1200 for a 6-sq-metre silk carpet. But, as Abdullahad notes, 'A good carpet is an investment'.

Other socially responsible shopping options in Uzbekistan are Human House, the 'Unesco' carpet workshops in Bukhara and Khiva, and Tashkent-based **Rakhimov Ceramics Studio** (p208). The latter has started a small potters' workshop to revive several ancient schools of ceramics making. This is a great place for serious ceramics aficionados to witness some fine pieces of pottery and learn about Uzbekistan's myriad ceramic styles. Among the five students here are two Shakhrisabz brothers who, it is hoped, will resuscitate the waning Shakhrisabz school that their grandfather once practised.

megalomaniac ghosts of a wholly different place materialise. This is Timur's hometown, and once upon a time it probably put Samarkand itself in the shade. It's worth a visit just to check out the great man's roots.

Timur was born on 9 April 1336 into the Barlas clan of local aristocrats, at the village of Hoja Ilghar, 13km to the south. Ancient even then, Shakhrisabz (called Kesh at the time) was a kind of family seat. As he rose to power, Timur gave it its present name (Tajik for 'Green Town') and turned it into an extended family monument. Most of its current attractions were built here by Timur (including a tomb intended for himself) or his grandson Ulugbek.

You can easily see all of Shakhrisabz as a day trip from Samarkand. There are a couple of sleeping options for those who want to linger and absorb the city's easy-going provincial vibe.

## Orientation

Almost everything of interest in Shakhrisabz happens along a 2km stretch of the town's main road, Ipak Yoli (Uzbek for 'Silk Road'). The long-distance bus station is south of town, about 5km beyond the Kok-Gumbaz Mosque.

## Information

**Internet Café** (Ipak Yoli; internet per hr 600S, international calls per min 850S; 🕑 7am-6pm) Internet, fax and phone.

**National Bank of Uzbekistan** (Firdavsi)

**Uzbektourism** (Ipak Yoli 26; 3-hr city tour US$15) The Orient Star hotel hosts the local Uzbektourism office, which can promptly summon English, German and French-speaking guides for city tours.

## Sights

### AK-SARAY PALACE

Just north of the centre, **Timur's summer palace** (White Palace; admission free, access to staircase 1000S; 🕑 9am-6pm) has as much grandeur per square centimetre as anything in Samarkand. There's actually nothing left of it except bits of the gigantic, 40m-high *pishtak*, covered with gorgeous, unrestored filigree-like mosaics. This crumbling relic blending seamlessly with everyday life will thrill critics of the country's over-sanitized restoration efforts elsewhere.

Ak-Saray was probably Timur's most ambitious project, 24 years in the making, following a successful campaign in Khorezm and the 'import' of many of its finest artisans. It's well worth climbing the 116 steps to the top of the *pishtak* to truly appreciate its height. It's staggering to try to imagine what the rest of the palace was like, in size and glory. In what was the palace centre stands a new **statue of Amir Timur**. It's not uncommon to see 15 weddings at a time posing here for photos at weekends, creating quite a mob scene.

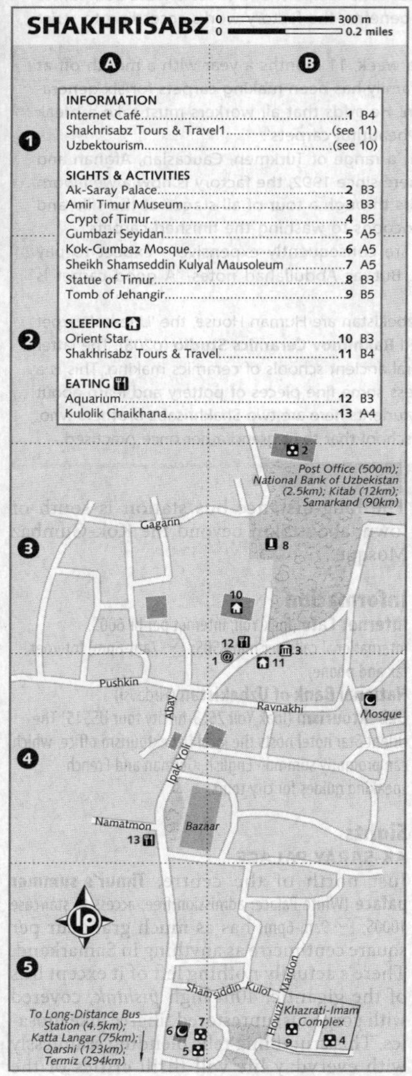


### KOK-GUMBAZ MOSQUE & DORUT TILYOVAT

This large **Friday mosque** (Ipak Yoli; admission 2400S; ⌚ 8.30am-6pm) was completed by Ulugbek in 1437 in honour of his father Shah Rukh (who was Timur's son). The name, appropriately, means 'blue dome'. It has been in an almost constant state of renovation for years. The palm trees painted on the interior walls are calling cards of its original Indian and Iranian designers.

Behind Kok-Gumbaz was the original burial complex of Timur's forebears. On the left as you enter the complex is the **Mausoleum of Sheikh Shamseddin Kulyal**, spiritual tutor to Timur and his father, Amir Taragay (who might also be buried here). The mausoleum was completed by Timur in 1374.

On the right is the **Gumbazi Seyidan** (Dome of the Seyyids), which Ulugbek finished in 1438 as a mausoleum for his own descendants (although it's not clear whether any are buried in it).

### KHAZRATI-IMAM COMPLEX

A walkway leads east from Kok-Gumbaz to a few melancholy remnants of a 3500-sq-metre mausoleum complex called Dorussiadat or Dorussaodat (Seat of Power and Might), which Timur finished in 1392 and which may have overshadowed even the Ak-Saray Palace. The main survivor is the tall, crumbling **Tomb of Jehangir**, Timur's eldest and favourite son, who died at 22. It's also the resting place for another son, Umar Sheikh (Timur's other sons are with him at Guri Amir in Samarkand).

In an alley behind the mausoleum (and within the perimeter of the long-gone Dorussiadat) is a bunker with a wooden door leading to an underground room, the **Crypt of Timur**. The room, plain except for Quranic quotations on the arches, is nearly filled by a single stone casket. On the casket are biographical inscriptions about Timur, from which it was inferred (when the room was discovered in 1963) that this crypt was intended for him. Inside are two unidentified corpses.

**AMIR TIMUR MUSEUM**

Housed inside the renovated Chubin Medressa is this simple **museum** (Ipak Yoli; admission 2000S; 9am-5pm). Its highlight is a model depicting Timur's entire kingdom, from Egypt to Kashgar. Beyond the boundaries of the kingdom, a yellow line illustrates his 'protectorates', including Kiev and Moscow. If that doesn't interest you, the museum is probably not worth the price of admission, although there are some old Buddhist and Zoroastrian artefacts here that predate Timur by many centuries. The museum was planning to add an art gallery.

### Sleeping & Eating

Sleeping options are limited. If all else fails, ask about a homestay from the staff of the Aquarium café.

**Shakhrisabz Tours & Travel** (☎ 522 05 82; Ipak Yoli; r per person 10,000S) There are a few rooms here but they are positively unique – basically open spaces with mosque-style patchwork carpeting, two basic beds and not much else. Staff will throw a couple *kurpacha* on the floor to accommodate bigger groups. *The* place to go local. Staff can also take you hiking in the Zerafshon or Hissar Mountains.

**Orient Star** (☎ 522 06 38; www.tour-orient.com; Ipak Yoli 26; s/d US$25/44; ) This is about the only deal in town and it's often occupied by tour groups, so book ahead in the high season. The Orient Star chain had just taken it over from the government when we visited and was planning an ambitious expansion and renovation of the simple but serviceable rooms.

**Aquarium** (☎ 522 39 72; Ipak Yoli 22) This bustling café has a good view of Ak-Saray and serves up the usual shashlyk, *laghman* and vodka shots.

**Kulolik Chaikhana** (Ipak Yoli; breakfast, lunch & dinner) This former mosque houses a massive *tapchan* under its octagonal roof. It's the most popular place in town –usually a sign that it's the best.

In the bazaar you'll find vendors hawking *samsa*, shashlyk, yummy soups and the usual mountains of delicious fruit.

### Getting There & Around

Shakhrisabz is about 90km from Samarkand, over the 1788m Takhtakaracha (Amankutan) Pass. The pass is intermittently closed by snow from January to March, forcing a three-hour detour around the mountains. For details on getting here from Samarkand, see p230.

Buses and shared taxis to a handful of other destinations leave from the long-distance bus station, south of town. To Tashkent's Ippodrom station there are about six daily buses (4000S, eight hours) and regular shared taxis (per seat 12000S, five hours). To get to Bukhara take a shared taxi to Qarshi (per seat 2000S, 1½ hours) and change there.

## NURATA

☎ 436 / pop 40,000

To the north of the featureless Samarkand–Bukhara 'Royal Rd', the Tian Shan Mountains produce one final blip on the map before fading unceremoniously into desertified insignificance. The Nurata Mountains top out at just over 2000m, but are rapidly becoming, along with manmade Lake Aidarkul further north, the centre of Uzbekistan's growing ecotourism movement. Most tour agencies launch trips into this area from Samarkand, Bukhara or even Tashkent, but individual travellers on a budget are advised to take public transport to Nurata and start their explorations there.

Modest Nurata is most famous for its old, circle-patterned *suzani*, which can sell for thousands of dollars at international auctions, but it also has a few quirky tourist attractions, most notably an old **fortress of Alexander the Great**. You can make like Alexander – go ahead, even throw on your suit of armour – and clamber all over the fortress, which looms over the town like a giant sandcastle. Behind the fortress, a path leads 4km to the **Zukarnay Petroglyphs**, which date to the Bronze Age. Ask the curator at the museum (see p236) how to find the trail. If it's too hot to walk, there are sometimes guys with motorcycles hanging out near the museum who will whisk you out there for a couple of thousand sum. (If you miss these, there are many more petroglyphs at Sarmysh Gorge, accessible by car 40km northeast of Navoi.)

More experienced trekkers can get a ride 10km east and launch an assault on camel-humped **Oq Tog** (White Peak; 2169m). Plan on at least a full day if you want to go the whole way.

Beneath Alexander's fortress you'll encounter the anomaly of several hundred trout occupying a pool and well next to a 10th-century mosque and caravanserai. This is the

### GOING LOCAL IN THE NURATA MOUNTAINS

South of Lake Aidarkul, there is great hiking and bird-watching in the mountains of the **Nuratau-Kyzylkum Biosphere Reserve** (www.nuratau.com), which is also the site of an exciting new **community based tourism project** – the only one of its kind in Uzbekistan. As of this writing three families had converted their homes into rustic guesthouses under this UN Development Programme–sponsored 'cultural tourism' project. Expect that number to climb. The families offer hiking, horse riding, traditional cooking lessons and the opportunity to breathe in mountain air and sleep on *tapchan* (tea beds) under the stars.

This is a great opportunity to interact with the local ethnic Tajiks in their element – and a great way to ward off architecture burnout if you've seen one too many medressas. For booking information and details on getting there, contact Elena Tours (p199) or the project **field office** (☎ 72-452 17 68/7, Russian only) in Yangiqishloq, a small town 80km west of Jizzakh and 160km east of Nurata. Yangiqishloq makes a good jumping-off point for both the reserve and the guesthouses.

UZBEKISTAN

**Chashma Spring**, formed, it is said, where the Prophet Mohammed's son-in-law Hazrat Ali drove his staff into the ground. These 'holy' fish live off the mineral-laden waters of the spring and canals that feed it. Also on the grounds here is a small **museum** (admission 500S; 9am-5pm) with some old ceramics and other trinkets. The curator is Nurata's best source of regional information, although he does not speak English.

Spend the night in Nurata only if you're desperate. The appalling but cheap **Hotel Bahkri** (s/d with shared bathroom 1300/2500S), 500m from Chashma Spring on the road to the centre, is the only gig in town. Water and electricity are sporadic. Eating options are limited to what you can buy at the small market near the Navoi taxi stand. Navoi has better lodging options, such as the **Yoshlik Hotel** (☎ 436-224 40 21; Halqlar Dustligi 138; s/d US$17/34; ).

#### LAKE AIDARKUL

After briefly taking in Nurata's sights, you'll want to hightail it to this manmade lake formed from the diverted waters of the Syr-Darya in 1969. On the west and north banks of the lake, there are four or five yurt camps, most of which offer fishing and, more intriguingly, **camel trekking**.

The best-known and easiest to access is the **Yangikazgan Yurt Camp** (☎ in Navoi 436-661 43 59; murat2005@bk.ru; yurt per person US$25-30) about 75km north of Nurata. You won't be roughing it: there are eight comfortable camel-hair yurts here and you'll be fed well. Showing up unannounced may work, but you're best off calling ahead to reserve (ask for Murat). Other yurt camps include one in Baimurat and another in Saphoz Nurata. The best time for camel trekking is from March to May when the spring rains turn the floor of the Kyzylkum desert green. Most camel treks are just a few hours, although Yangikazgan Yurt Camp can organise multiple-day treks. Prices for multiple-day treks are negotiable and depend on the amount of people in your group.

#### GETTING THERE & AWAY

To get to Nurata, take a shared taxi (per seat 3000S, one hour) or bus (1000S) from Bukhara to Navoi, from where shared taxis go to Nurata (2000S, one hour). In Nurata it's easy to hire an ordinary taxi at the Navoi taxi stand to Lake Aidarkul. Negotiations start at 15,000S for Yangikazgan (70km), and 25,000S for Baimurat (110km) and Saphoz Nurata (100km).

## BUKHARA БУХАРА

**☎ (3) 65 / pop 255,000**

Central Asia's holiest city, Bukhara has buildings spanning a thousand years of history, and a thoroughly lived-in old centre that probably hasn't changed much in two centuries. It is one of the best places in Central Asia for a glimpse of pre-Russian Turkestan.

Most of the centre is an architectural preserve, full of medressas, a massive royal fortress and the remnants of a once-vast market complex. The government has pumped a lot of money into restoration, even redigging several *hauz* filled in by the Soviets. Although the centre has become a bit too clean and quiet ('Ye Olde Bukhara' as one traveller put it), the 21st century has still been kept more or less at bay, and the city's accommodation options go from strength to strength.

Until a century ago Bukhara was watered by a network of canals and some 200 stone pools where people gathered and gossiped, drank and washed. As the water wasn't changed often, Bukhara was famous for plagues; the average 19th-century Bukharan is said to have died by the age of 32. The Bolsheviks modernised the system and drained the pools.

You'll need at least two days to look around. Try to allow time to lose yourself in the old town; it's easy to overdose on the 140-odd protected buildings and miss the whole for its many parts.

## History

It was as capital of the Samanid state in the 9th and 10th centuries that Bukhara – Bukhoro-i-sharif (Noble Bukhara), the 'Pillar of Islam' – blossomed as Central Asia's religious and cultural heart, and simultaneously brightened with the Persian love of the arts. Among those nurtured here were the philosopher-scientist Ibn Sina and the poets Firdausi and Rudaki – figures with stature in the Persian Islamic world that, for example, Newton or Shakespeare enjoyed in the West.

After two centuries under the smaller Karakhanid and Karakitay dynasties, Bukhara succumbed in 1220 to Jenghiz Khan, and in 1370 fell under the shadow of Timur's Samarkand.

A second lease on life came in the 16th century when the Uzbek Shaybanids made it the capital of what came to be known as the Bukhara khanate. The centre of Shaybanid Bukhara was a vast marketplace with dozens of specialist bazaars and caravanserais, more than 100 medressas (with 10,000 students) and more than 300 mosques.

Under the Astrakhanid dynasty, the Silk Road's decline slowly pushed Bukhara out of the mainstream. Then in 1753 Mohammed Rahim, the local deputy of a Persian ruler, proclaimed himself emir, founding the Mangit dynasty that was to rule until the Bolsheviks came.

Several depraved rulers filled Rahim's shoes; the worst was probably Nasrullah Khan (also called 'the Butcher' behind his back), who ascended the throne in 1826 by killing off his brothers and 28 other relatives. He made himself a household name in Victorian England after he executed two British officers (see p242).

In 1868, Russian troops under General Kaufman occupied Samarkand (which at the time was within Emir Muzaffar Khan's domains). Soon afterward Bukhara surrendered, and was made a protectorate of the tsar, with the emirs still nominally in charge.

In 1918 a party of emissaries arrived from Tashkent (by then under Bolshevik control) to persuade Emir Alim Khan to surrender peacefully. The wily despot stalled long enough to allow his agents to stir up an anti-Russian mob that slaughtered nearly the whole delegation, and the emir's own army sent a larger Russian detachment packing, back towards Tashkent.

But the humiliated Bolsheviks had their revenge. Following an orchestrated 'uprising' in Charjou (now Turkmenabat) by local revolutionaries calling themselves the Young Bukharans, and an equally premeditated request for help, Red Army troops from Khiva and Tashkent under General Mikhail Frunze stormed the Ark (citadel) and captured Bukhara.

Bukhara won a short 'independence' as the Bukhara People's Republic, but after showing rather too much interest in Pan-Turkism it

### BUKHARA'S JEWS

South of Lyabi-Hauz is what's left of the old town's unique **Jewish Quarter**. There have been Jews in Bukhara since perhaps the 12th or 13th century, evolving into a unique culture with its own language – Bukhori, which is related to Persian but uses the Hebrew alphabet. Bukhara's Jews still speak it as do about 10,000 Bukhara Jews who now live elsewhere (mainly Israel).

They managed to become major players in Bukharan commerce in spite of deep-rooted, institutionalised discrimination. Jews made up 7% of Bukhara's population at the time of the Soviet Union's collapse, but today only about 800 remain.

The Jewish community centre and **synagogue** (☎ 365-224 23 80; Sarrafon 20), is roughly across from Salom Inn, holds regular services and also sponsors a functioning Jewish school just around the corner. A century ago there were at least seven synagogues here, reduced after 1920 to two. The second synagogue is located 300m south of Kukluk Bazaar.

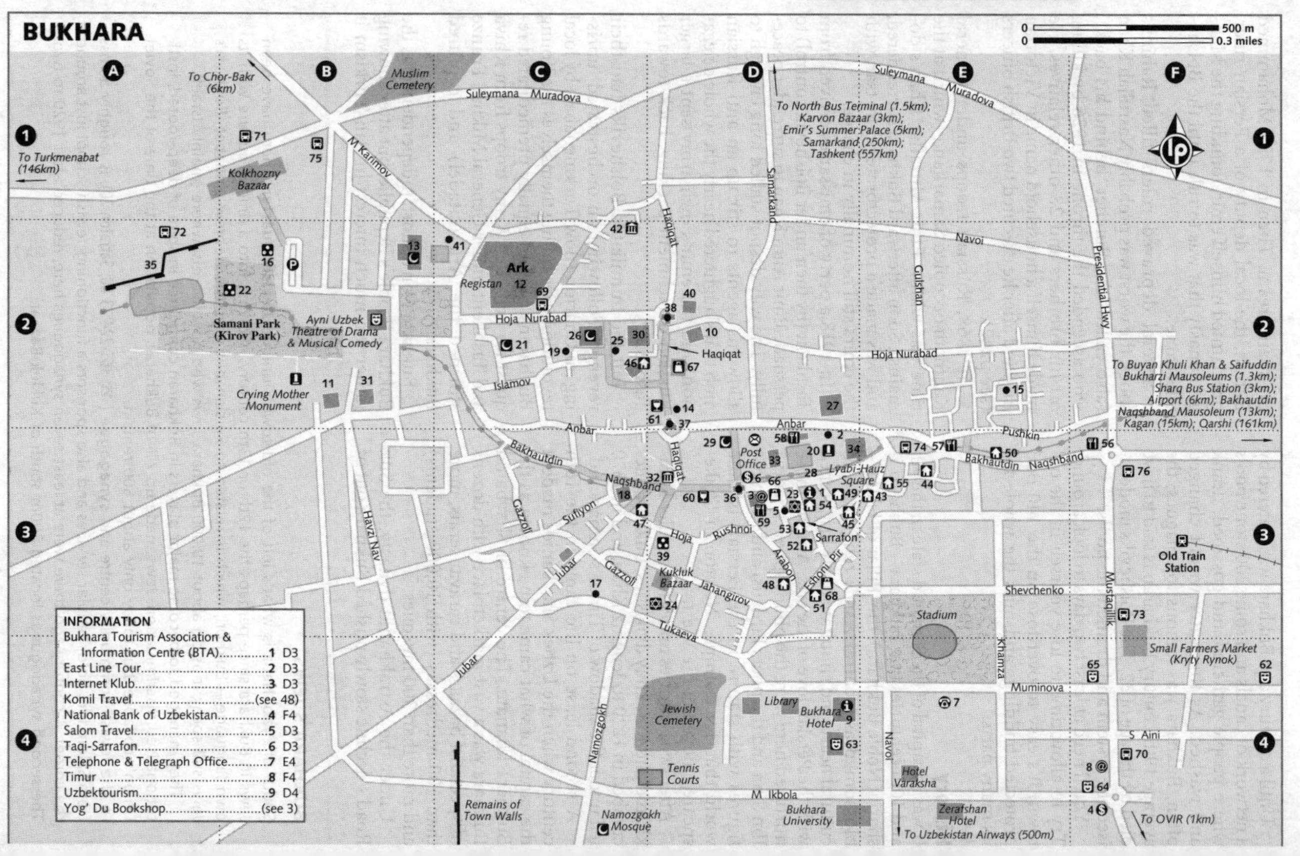
BUKHARA
0 500 m
0 0.3 miles
To Chor-Bakr (6km)
To Turkmenabat (146km)
Muslim Cemetery
Suleymana Muradova
M Karimov
Kolkhozny Bazaar
Ark
Registan
Hoja Nurabad
Samani Park (Kirov Park)
Ayni Uzbek Theatre of Drama & Musical Comedy
Crying Mother Monument
Islamov
Haqiqat
Samarkand
Navoi
Gulshan
Presidential Hwy
To North Bus Terminal (1.5km); Karvon Bazaar (3km); Emir's Summer Palace (5km); Samarkand (250km); Tashkent (557km)
To Buyan Khuli Khan & Saifuddin Bukharzi Mausoleums (1.3km); Sharq Bus Station (3km); Airport (6km); Bakhautdin Naqshband Mausoleum (13km); Kagan (15km); Qarshi (161km)
Anbar
Pushkin
Bakhautdin
Naqshband
Post Office
Lyabi-Hauz Square
Sarrafon
Rushnoi
Hoja
Arabon
Eshoni Pir
Sufiyon
Gazzoli
Havzi Nav
Jubar
Kukluk Bazaar
Jahangirov
Tukaeva
Old Train Station
Shevchenko
Mustaqillik
Stadium
Khamza
Muminova
Small Farmers Market (Kryty Rynok)
Library
Bukhara Hotel
Jewish Cemetery
Tennis Courts
Namozgokh
Namozgokh Mosque
Remains of Town Walls
M Ikbola
Navoi
Hotel Varaksha
Bukhara University
Zerafshan Hotel
S Aini
To Uzbekistan Airways (500m)
To OVIR (1km)
INFORMATION
Bukhara Tourism Association & Information Centre (BTA)....1 D3
East Line Tour....2 D3
Internet Klub....3 D3
Komil Travel....(see 48)
National Bank of Uzbekistan....4 F4
Salom Travel....5 D3
Taqi-Sarrafon....6 D3
Telephone & Telegraph Office....7 E4
Timur....8 F4
Uzbektourism....9 D4
Yog' Du Bookshop....(see 3)

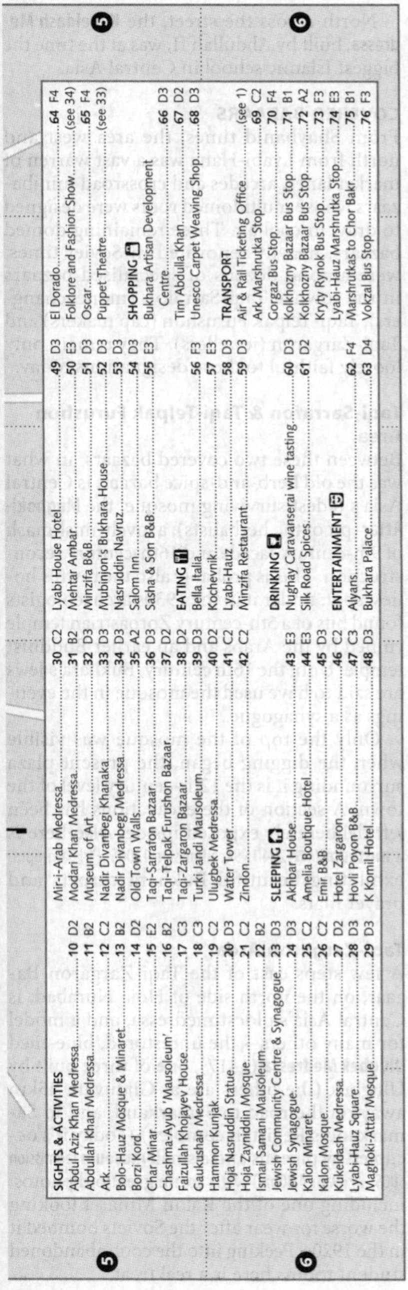

was absorbed in 1924 into the newly created Uzbek SSR.

## Orientation

An oasis in the enveloping Kyzylkum desert, Bukhara sits 250km downstream of Samarkand on the Zerafshan River. The heart of the *shahristan* (old town), is the pool and square called Lyabi-Hauz; the landmark Kalon Minaret is five minutes further, the Ark five more. Further west are Samani Park and the main farmers market, Kolkhozny Bazaar.

The bulk of the modern town lies southeast of the historical centre. The long-distance North Bus Terminal is 2km north of the centre. The airport is 6km southeast of town, the train station 9km beyond that in Kagan.

## Information

### BOOKSHOPS

**Yog' Du Bookshop** (Bakhautdin Naqshband 88) Sells picture books and maps of Bukhara and Uzbekistan.

### INTERNET ACCESS

**Internet Klub** (Bakhautdin Naqshband 88; per hr 800S; 9am-11pm) Slow but central.

**Timur** (Mustaqillik; per hr 800S; 10am-11pm) This is the best of several internet cafés located between S Aini and M Ikbola.

### MONEY

Changing more than US$50 at a time can be a problem in the high season so stack up on wads of sum before you arrive. If you buy souvenirs in dollars do your vendor a favour and be discreet.

**National Bank of Uzbekistan** (223 69 73; M Ikbola 3; 9am-4pm Mon-Fri) Changes travellers cheques and gives cash advances on Visa cards.

**Taqi-Sarrafon** (Bakhautin Naqshband; 8.30-6pm Mon-Sat) Exchange booth next to 'moneychangers' bazaar.

### REGISTRATION

**OVIR** (223 88 68; Murtazaeva 10/3) Located roughly behind Uzbekistan Airways; register here if you are not staying in an official hotel.

### TELEPHONE & FAX

**Bukhara Tourism Association & Information Centre** (see p240) Will help you dial internationally with Uzbek discount calling cards.

**Telephone & telegraph office** (Muminova 8) International calls for standard Uztelekom rates (p264).

UZBEKISTAN

**SIGHTS & ACTIVITIES**

Abdul Aziz Khan Medressa 10 D2
Abdullah Khan Medressa 11 B2
Ark 12 C2
Bolo-Hauz Mosque & Minaret 13 B2
Borzi Kord 14 D2
Char Minar 15 E2
Chashma-Ayub 'Mausoleum' 16 B2
Faizullah Khojayev House 17 C3
Gaukushan Medressa 18 C3
Hammon Kunjak 19 C2
Hoja Nasruddin Statue 20 D3
Hoja Zayniddin Mosque 21 C2
Ismail Samani Mausoleum 22 B2
Jewish Community Centre & Synagogue 23 D3
Jewish Synagogue 24 D3
Kalon Minaret 25 C2
Kalon Mosque 26 C2
Kukeldash Medressa 27 D2
Lyabi-Hauz Square 28 D3
Maghoki-Attar Mosque 29 D3
Mir-i-Arab Medressa 30 C2
Modari Khan Medressa 31 B2
Museum of Art 32 D3
Nadir Divanbegi Khanaka 33 D3
Nadir Divanbegi Medressa 34 D3
Old Town Walls 35 A2
Taqi-Sarrafon Bazaar 36 D3
Taqi-Telpak Furushon Bazaar 37 D2
Taqi-Zargaron Bazaar 38 D2
Turki Jandi Mausoleum 39 D3
Ulugbek Medressa 40 D2
Water Tower 41 C2
Zindon 42 C2

**SLEEPING**

Akhbar House 43 E3
Amelia Boutique Hotel 44 E3
Emir B&B 45 D3
Hotel Zargaron 46 C2
Hovli Poyon B&B 47 C3
K Komil Hotel 48 D3
Lyabi House Hotel 49 D3
Mehtar Ambar 50 E3
Minzifa B&B 51 D3
Mubinjon's Bukhara House 52 D3
Nasruddin Navruz 53 D3
Salom Inn 54 D3
Sasha & Son B&B 55 E3

**EATING**

Bella Italia 56 F3
Kochevnik 57 E3
Lyabi-Hauz 58 D3
Minzifa Restaurant 59 D3

**DRINKING**

Nughay Caravanserai wine tasting 60 D3
Silk Road Spices 61 D2

**ENTERTAINMENT**

Alyans 62 F4
Bukhara Palace 63 D4
El Dorado 64 F4
Folklore and Fashion Show (see 34)
Oscar 65 F4
Puppet Theatre (see 33)

**SHOPPING**

Bukhara Artisan Development Centre 66 D3
Tim Abdulla Khan 67 D2
Unesco Carpet Weaving Shop 68 D3

**TRANSPORT**

Air & Rail Ticketing Office (see 1)
Ark Marshrutka Stop 69 C2
Gorgaz Bus Stop 70 F4
Kolkhozny Bazaar Bus Stop 71 B1
Kolkhozny Bazaar Bus Stop 72 A2
Kryty Rynok Bus Stop 73 F3
Lyabi-Hauz Marshrutka Stop 74 E3
Marshrutkas to Chor Bakr 75 B1
Vokzal Bus Stop 76 F3

#### TOURIST INFORMATION

**Bukhara Tourism Association & Information Centre** The best and only genuine tourist office in the country, this German-funded NGO was abruptly shut down by the state in early 2007. While the fate of the Bukhara Tourism Association (www.dreambukhara.org) remained up in the air at press time, travel magazine Discovery Central Asia was getting ready to reopen the excellent Tourism Information Centre, which will double as a bookshop. The Centre's new address was undetermined when we went to press.

**Uzbektourism** (☎ 223 12 36; bukhtour@bcc.com.uz; Bukhara Hotel, Muminova 8) Useful mainly for its stable of multilingual guides (per hour US$5).

#### TRAVEL AGENCIES

**East Line Tour** (☎ 224 22 69; www.eastlinetour.com; Mekhtar Ambar 91) In a town that's perfect for exploring on bike, this is the only agency that rents them (per day US$5). Also runs full gamut of tours, but specialises in bird-watching tours around Tudakul Lake and further afield.

**Komil Travel** (p244)

**Salom Travel** (☎ 224 41 48, 224 37 33; www.salomtravel.com; Sarrafon 9) Owner Raisa Gareyeva was one of the first private travel agents and is one of the best. Among Salom's unique excursions: endangered Persian gazelles north of Karaul Bazar; swimming in Tudakul Lake; and the excavated remains of the pre-Islamic era city of Paikent, 60km northwest of Bukhara.

## Sights & Activities

#### LYABI-HAUZ

Lyabi-Hauz, a plaza built around a pool in 1620 (the name is Tajik for 'around the pool'), is the most peaceful and interesting spot in town – shaded by mulberry trees as old as the pool. The old tea-sipping, chessboard-clutching Uzbek men who once inhabited this corner of town have been moved on by local entrepreneurs bent on cashing in on the tourist trade. Still, the plaza maintains its old-world style and has managed to fend off the glitz to which Samarkand's Registan has succumbed.

On the east side is a statue of **Hoja Nasruddin**, a semimythical 'wise fool' who appears in Sufi teaching-tales around the world.

Further east, the **Nadir Divanbegi Medressa** was built as a caravanserai, but the khan thought it was a medressa and it became one in 1622. On the west side of the square, and built at the same time, is the **Nadir Divanbegi Khanaka**. Both are named for Abdul Aziz Khan's treasury minister, who financed them in the 17th century.

North across the street, the **Kukeldash Medressa**, built by Abdullah II, was at the time the biggest Islamic school in Central Asia.

#### COVERED BAZAARS

From Shaybanid times, the area west and north from Lyabi-Hauz was a vast warren of market lanes, arcades and crossroad minibazaars whose multidomed roofs were designed to draw in cool air. Three remaining domed bazaars, heavily renovated in Soviet times, were among dozens of specialised bazaars in the town – Taqi-Sarrafon (moneychangers), Taqi-Telpak Furushon (cap makers) and Taqi-Zargaron (jewellers). They remain only loosely faithful to those designations today.

##### Taqi-Sarrafon & Taqi-Telpak Furushon Area

Between these two covered bazaars, in what was the old herb-and-spice bazaar, is Central Asia's oldest surviving mosque, the **Maghoki-Attar** (pit of the herbalists), a lovely mishmash of 9th-century façade and 16th-century reconstruction. This is probably also the town's holiest spot: under it in the 1930s archaeologists found bits of a 5th-century Zoroastrian temple ruined by the Arabs and an earlier Buddhist temple. Until the 16th century, Bukhara's Jews are said to have used the mosque in the evenings as a synagogue.

Only the top of the mosque was visible when the digging began; the present plaza surrounding it is the 12th-century level of the town. A section of the excavations has been left deliberately exposed inside. Also here is a **museum** (☎ 224 15 91; admission 1200S; 9am-6pm) exhibiting beautiful Bukhara carpets and prayer mats.

##### Taqi-Zargaron Area

A few steps east of the Taqi-Zargaron Bazaar, on the north side of Hoja Nurabad, is Central Asia's oldest medressa, and a model for many others – the unrestored, blue-tiled **Ulugbek Medressa** (1417), one of three built by Ulugbek (the others are at Gijduvan, 45km away on the road to Samarkand, and in Samarkand's Registan complex). Today it's occupied by pigeons and a small **museum** (admission 500S; 9am-4.30pm) with some great old photos, including one of the Kalon Minaret looking the worse for wear after the Soviets bombed it in the 1920s. Peeking into the cool, abandoned student rooms here is a real treat.

By contrast, the student rooms across the way at the 16th-century **Abdul Aziz Khan Medressa** are occupied, rather typically, by souvenir shops. This is another unrestored gem, built by its namesake to outdo the Ulugbek Medressa in size and splendour. The highlight is the prayer room, now a **museum of wood carvings** (admission 1200S; 9am-5pm), with spectacular original *ghanch*-work. It is said that Abdul Aziz had the image of his face covertly embedded in the prayer room's mihrab (Mecca-facing niche) to get around the Sunni Muslim prohibition against depicting living beings (Adul Aziz Khan was a Shiite). Also flouting that prohibition was the stork who used to live in the nest on the tower to the left of the medressa's *pishtak*. The only other medressa in town that depicts living beings is the Nadir Divanbegi Medressa.

### KALON MINARET & AROUND

When it was built by the Karakhanid ruler Arslan Khan in 1127, the **Kalon Minaret** (admission 3000S) was probably the tallest building in Central Asia – *kalon* means 'great' in Tajik. It's an incredible piece of work, 47m tall with 10m-deep foundations (including reeds stacked underneath in an early form of earthquake-proofing), which in 850 years has never needed any but cosmetic repairs. Jenghiz Khan was so dumbfounded by it that he ordered it spared.

Its 14 ornamental bands, all different, include the first use of the glazed blue tiles that were to saturate Central Asia under Timur. Up and down the south and east sides are faintly lighter patches, marking the restoration of damage caused by Frunze's artillery in 1920. Its 105 inner stairs are accessible from the Kalon Mosque.

A legend says that Arslan Khan killed an imam after a quarrel. That night in a dream the imam told him, 'You have killed me; now oblige me by laying my head on a spot where nobody can tread', and the tower was built over his grave.

At the foot of the minaret, on the site of an earlier mosque destroyed by Jenghiz Khan, is the 16th-century congregational **Kalon Mosque** (admission 1000S), big enough for 10,000 people. Used in Soviet times as a warehouse, it was reopened as a place of worship in 1991.

Opposite the mosque, its luminous blue domes in sharp contrast to the surrounding brown, is the working **Mir-i-Arab Medressa**. Especially at sunset, it's among Uzbekistan's most striking medressas, but tourists can only go as far as the foyer. From there you may peer through a grated door into the courtyard, where you might see students playing ping-pong.

The medressa is named for a 16th-century Naqshbandi sheikh from Yemen who had a strong influence on the Shaybanid ruler Ubaidullah Khan and financed the original complex. Both khan and sheikh are buried beneath the northern dome.

### THE ARK & AROUND

The **Ark** ( 224 13 49; Registan Sq; admission 2400S, guide 3600S; 9am-6pm), a royal town-within-a-town, is Bukhara's oldest structure, occupied from the 5th century right up until 1920, when it was bombed by the Red Army. It's about 80% ruins inside now, except for some remaining royal quarters, now housing several **museums**.

At the top of the entrance ramp is the 17th-century **Juma (Friday) Mosque**. Turn right into a corridor with courtyards off both sides. First on the left are the former living quarters of the emir's *kushbegi* (prime minister), now housing an exhibit on archaeological finds around Bukhara.

Second on the left is the oldest surviving part of the Ark, the vast **Reception & Coronation Court**, whose roof fell in during the 1920 bombardment. The last coronation to take place here was Alim Khan's in 1910. The submerged chamber on the right wall was the treasury, and behind this room was the harem.

To the right of the corridor were the open-air royal stables and the *noghorahona* (a room for drums and musical instruments used during public spectacles). Now there are shops and a natural-history exhibit.

Around the Salamhona (Protocol Court) at the end of the corridor are what remain of the royal apartments. These apparently fell into such disrepair that the last two emirs preferred full-time residence at the summer palace (see p247). Now there are several museums here, the most interesting of which covers Bukhara's history from the Shaybanids to the tsars. Displays include items imported to Bukhara, including an enormous *samovar* (urn used for heating water) made in Tula, Russia. Another room contains the emir's throne. Enhanced colour photographs, donated by the now-departed Dutch Embassy in Tashkent, add a spark of life to the otherwise musty exhibits.

### STODDART & CONOLLY

On 24 June 1842 Colonel Charles Stoddart and Captain Arthur Conolly were marched out from a dungeon cell before a huge crowd in front of the Ark, the emir's fortified citadel, made to dig their own graves and, to the sound of drums and reed pipes from atop the fortress walls, were beheaded.

Colonel Stoddart had arrived three years earlier on a mission to reassure Emir Nasrullah Khan about Britain's invasion of Afghanistan. But his superiors, underestimating the emir's vanity and megalomania, had sent him with no gifts, and with a letter not from Queen Victoria (whom Nasrullah regarded as an equal sovereign), but from the governor-general of India. To compound matters Stoddart violated local protocol by riding, rather than walking, up to the Ark. The piqued Nasrullah had him thrown into jail, where he was to spend much of his time at the bottom of the so-called 'bug pit', in the company of assorted rodents and scaly creatures.

Captain Conolly arrived in 1841 to try to secure Stoddart's release. But the emir, believing him to be part of a British plot with the khans of Khiva and Kokand, tossed Conolly in jail too. After the disastrous British retreat from Kabul, the emir, convinced that Britain was a second-rate power and having received no reply to an earlier letter to Queen Victoria, had both men executed.

Despite public outrage back in England, the British government chose to let the matter drop. Furious friends and relatives raised enough money to send their own emissary, an oddball clergyman named Joseph Wolff, to Bukhara to verify the news. According to Peter Hopkirk in *The Great Game,* Wolff himself only escaped death because the emir thought him hilarious, dressed up in his full clerical regalia.

Outside, in front of the fortress, is medieval Bukhara's main square, the **Registan**, a favourite venue for executions, including those of the British officers Stoddart and Conolly (above).

Behind the Ark is **Zindon** (☎ 224 95 02; admission 1200S; ⌚ 9am-4.30pm), the jail, now a museum. Cheerful attractions include a torture chamber and several dungeons, including the gruesome 'bug pit' where Stoddart and Conolly languished in a dark chamber filled with lice, scorpions and other vermin.

Beside a pool opposite the Ark's gate is the **Bolo-Hauz Mosque**, the emirs' official place of worship, built in 1718. Beside it is a now-disused 33m **water tower**, built by the Russians in 1927. If you are going to climb this (as the author did), you best not be afraid of heights (as the author is) or rickety-looking Soviet structures. The views of the Ark and beyond are worth the 1000S demanded by the local shepherd or whoever else is around.

### ISMAIL SAMANI MAUSOLEUM & AROUND

This **mausoleum** in Samani Park, completed in 905, is the town's oldest Muslim monument and probably its sturdiest architecturally. Built for Ismail Samani (the Samanid dynasty's founder), his father and grandson, its intricate baked-terracotta brickwork – which gradually changes 'personality' through the day as the shadows shift – disguises walls almost 2m thick, helping it survive without restoration (except of the spiked dome) for 11 centuries.

Behind the park is one of the few remaining, eroded sections (a total of 2km out of an original 12km) of the Shaybanid **town walls**; another big section is about 500m west of the Namozgokh Mosque.

Nearby is the peculiar **Chashma Ayub 'mausoleum'** (admission 500S; ⌚ 9am-4.30pm), built from the 12th to 16th centuries over a spring. The name means 'Spring of Job'; legend says Job struck his staff on the ground here and a spring appeared. Inside you can drink from the spring. It is now, sadly, overshadowed by a glistening new glass-walled memorial to Imam Ismail al-Bukhari next door.

### FAIZULLAH KHOJAEV HOUSE

The **Faizullah Khojaev House** (Tukaeva; ☎ 224 41 88; admission 2000S, Russian-/English-speaking guide 800/12,000S; ⌚ 9am-5pm Mon-Sat) was once home to one of Bukhara's many infamous personalities, the man who plotted with the Bolsheviks to dump Emir Alim Khan. Faizullah Khojaev was rewarded with the presidency of the Bukhara People's Republic, chairmanship of the Council of People's Commissars of the Uzbek SSR, and finally liquidation by Stalin.

The house was built in 1891 by his father, Ubaidullah, a wealthy merchant. Faizullah

Khojaev lived here until 1925, when the Soviets converted it into a school. Slow restoration of the elegant frescoes, *ghanch*, latticework and Bukhara-style ceiling beams (carved, unpainted elm) has been going on for years; the newly restored bedroom opened to the public in 2007. Call ahead to book an English guide. Tours include a small fashion show.

#### OTHER SIGHTS

Deep in the old town is the tiny, decrepit **Turki Jandi mausoleum** (Namozgokh) favoured for getting one's prayers answered. It's the resting place of a holy man known as Turki Jandi, his two sons, several grandsons and numerous other relations. Its importance is signalled by the hundreds of other graves around it – allegedly in stacks 30m deep! It's under slow, devoted restoration and was closed when we visited.

Photogenic little **Char Minar**, in a maze of alleys between Pushkin and Hoja Nurabad, bears more relation to Indian styles than to anything Bukharan. This was the gatehouse of a long-gone medressa built in 1807. The name means 'Four Minarets' in Tajik, although they aren't strictly minarets but simply decorative towers. Unesco restored one collapsed tower and fixed another in 1998.

West of Taqi-Sarrafon is the interesting 16th-century **Gaukushan Medressa** with chipped majolica on its unrestored façade. Across the canal is a little brother of the Kalon Minaret. Nearby, the **Museum of Art** (☎ 224 58 53; admission 600S; ⏲ 9am-4.30pm Thu-Tue) has mostly 20th-century paintings by Bukharan artists, some of which can be purchased in a gallery on the ground floor. It's in the former headquarters of the Russian Central Asian Bank (1912).

Across from the Ark on Hoja Nurabad, the interior of the 16th-century **Hoja Zayniddin Mosque** has some of the best very old, original mosaic and *ghanch*-work you're going to see anywhere.

Southeast of Samani Park are two massive medressas, one named for the great Shaybanid ruler **Abdulla Khan**, and one for his mother called **Modari Khan** (mother of the khan). The latter is locked, the former contains yet more crafts shops.

Two kilometres east of the centre on Bakhautdin Naqshband, the mammary-like twin domes of the **Saifuddin Bukharzi Mausoleum** tower over the delicate little **Buyan Khuli Khan Mausoleum**. With sheep grazing in the foreground and a massive cooking-oil factory looming in the background, this spot might as well be a metaphor for Central Asia. Taxi drivers know this place as 'Rayon Fatobod Bogi'. The architectural highlight here is the 14th-century majolica on the smaller mausoleum, resting place of a Mongol khan. The larger mausoleum was built over the grave of Saifuddin Bukharzi (1190–1261), poet founder of an influential Sufi order.

### Activities

Readers rave about Bukhara's famed *hammomi* (baths), most notably the **Borzi Kord** (Taqi-Telpak Furushon; admission 3000S, massage 7000S; ⏲ 6am-7pm Wed-Mon). It's technically a men's bathhouse, but groups of tourists can reserve it after hours for mixed use.

**Hammom Kunjak** (Ibodov 4; admission 3000S, massage 5000S; ⏲ 7am-6pm) Is the women's bathhouse behind Kalon Minaret.

### Tours

Guides can be booked directly or through the Tourist Information Centre or Uzbektourism. Our recommendations include the following.

**Aka Ilkhom** (☎ 224 49 65) From Emir Travel; German.
**Gulya Khamidova** (☎ 223 01 24) English.
**Nellia** (☎ 224 41 48) From Salom Travel; French.
**Noila Kazidzanova** (☎ 228 20 12) English.
**Zinnat Ashurova** (☎ 522 20 37) English.

Maksuma, a guide at the Ark (p241), is an archaeological specialist who can recommend excursions to excavations and petroglyphs in the desert north of Bukhara.

### Festivals

The four-day **Silk & Spices Festival** in early May is a celebration of local folk art as well as silk and spices, with lots of music and dancing in the streets.

### Sleeping

Bukhara's wonderful, largely traditional-style B&Bs set the standard for accommodation in Central Asia. Unfortunately, cheap accommodation is becoming scarce as budget places upgrade to accommodate tour groups.

#### BUDGET

**Mubinjon's Bukhara House** (☎ 224 20 05; Sarrafon 4; r US$5-15 per person) Bukhara's pioneer B&B is housed in a home dating from 1766. Traditional *kurpacha* are spread on the floor and the bathrooms are basic but the legendary Mubinjon – a true Bukharan eccentric – can direct you to traditional baths. Mubinjon doesn't speak much English but makes himself understood. Other than the mosquitoes, which are unbearable in summer, it's backpacker bliss. The house is about 100m south of Salom Inn; look for the Olympic symbols painted on the garage door.

**Nasruddin Navruz** (☎ 224 34 57; umka_83@mail.ru; Babahanova 37; s/d/tr US$15/20/30; ) This simple but effective guesthouse has 10 rooms set around a courtyard. The beds don't look like much but they are comfortable and there's enough space in most rooms for a few spare pieces of furniture. Negotiable prices makes this attractive for the backpacker set.

Locals, including **Madina Tordieva** (☎ 224 61 62, 718 61 63), hang out around Lyabi-Hauz and sometimes the North Bus Station offering homestays for US$5 to US$10.

### MIDRANGE

**Mehtar Ambar** (☎ 224 41 68; www.mehtarambar.ws; Bakhautdin Naqshband 91; s/d/tr US$20/40/50; ) If you're looking for something a little different from all those old classic Bukhara homes, consider this even older caravanserai. Rooms are a bit small but it is, afterall, it's a caravanserai. The 2nd-floor rooms are spiffier and better equipped, with minibar and TV. Low season is negotiating season.

**Salom Inn** (☎ 224 41 48, www.salomtravel.com; Sarrafon 3; r US$25-40; ) This long-running establishment has small but classy wood-furnished rooms with traditional interior decorations, including antiques and colourful wall hangings. It's run by the highly regarded Salom Travel (p240), which has an office around the corner.

**K Komil Hotel** (☎ 223 87 80; www.komiltravel.com; Barakiyon 40; s/d/tr US$25/40/45; ) This friendly B&B has stunning *ghanch*-work and a young, laid-back proprietor who speaks good English and runs an adventure-oriented travel agency. Komil recently opened an annexe with modern rooms to complement pre-existing digs in an authentic 19th-century rich person's home. Good vegetarian food is an added bonus.

**Hovli Poyon B&B** (☎ 224 18 65; hovli-poyon@mail.ru; Usmon Hodjaev 13; s/d/tr/q US$25/40/45/60; ) Few Bukhara B&Bs are more memorable than this one, set in a 19th-century house dripping with both character and history. It was a gift for Emir Ahad Khan, and the grand *aivan* and huge courtyard festooned with fruit trees are certainly emir-worthy. If it were not a hotel it could easily be a museum. The rooms, of various sizes, are simple with traditional touches but need new beds.

**Amelia Boutique Hotel** (☎ 224 12 63; www.hotelamelia.com; Bozor Hoja 1; s/d US$30/40; ) All hairs are in place at this cosy, casual boutique. Pinewood furniture gives it a foresty feel, but traditional elements such as niched walls and a 19th-century *aivan* bring you back to Bukhara. The mud-walled suite downstairs is a pearl.

our pick **Akhbar House** (☎ 224 21 12; akhbarhouseantiques@yahoo.com; Eshoni Pir 22; s/d US$30/50; ) Yet another 19th-century beauty, this one could also be a museum, especially considering the quality of owner Akhbar's collection of *suzani* and other antiques. The interior of the dining room, restored but not repainted, is just right. Dinners, if pre-ordered, are cooked in a mud oven in the middle of the courtyard; guests are encouraged to don old-style Uzbek outfits for their repast. The rooms, naturally, are exquisitely adorned. It's hard to find – walk 50m past Sasha & Son B&B, turn right, and it's the mud-walled building on your left.

**Emir B&B** (☎ 224 49 65; www.emirtravel.com; Husainov 17; s/d/tr US$30/50/65; ) This place consists of two buildings set around twin courtyards in the heart of the old Jewish Quarter, run by the friendly and knowledgeable Milla, who also runs a travel agency. One has traditional-style rooms filled with *ghanch* and trinket-laden niches, the other is all modern and shiny. All rooms are spacious and a couple are massive. Request a room with a TV if you can't survive without the BBC.

**Sasha & Son B&B** (☎ 224 49 66; www.sacholga.narod.ru; Eshoni Pir 3; s/d US$35/50; ) Behind a beautifully carved wooden front door is a maze connecting several small edifices with large, tastefully restored rooms done up in classic Bukhara style. Comfortable sitting tables with colourful cushions dot the courtyards. All rooms have satellite TV and modern bathrooms with fine tilework. The staff is more professional than friendly here.

**Minzifa** (☎ 224 56 28; www.minzifa.com; Eshoni Pir 63; s/d US$35/50; ) The ubiquitous local style is faithfully on display here, although the style is toned down a bit by softer than usual colour schemes. A true boutique, it has some of the friendliest service in town, ultracomfy oversized twin beds and eight uniquely decorated rooms. It also has a cosy house bar, a 180-year-old front door and even a small 'gym'.

**Hotel Zaragon** (☎ 224 58 21; zaragon@mail.ru; Haqiqat 3; s/d US$35/50; ❄) Its location amid Bukhara's holiest architectural monuments won't make preservationists happy, but it's hard to ignore such prime views of Kalon Minaret and Mir-i-Arab's sparkling domes. Rooms lack character but some are so big you can hardly see the TV across the room. Even if you don't stay here, consider a drink in the shadow of the minaret on its 2nd-floor porch.

**Lyabi House Hotel** (☎ 224 24 84; www.lyabihouse.com; Husainov 7; s/d US$40/60; ❄ 💻) No place in town better combines authentic old-Bukhara design with modern amenities and professional service. Highlights are the stunning rooms and a dignified *aivan* with carved wooden columns where breakfast is served. If money's no object, look no further. Request a room away from the noisy reception area.

## Eating

Many visitors go no further than Lyabi-Hauz for sustenance, but if you tire of chaikhana fare, Bukhara has a growing number of alternatives.

**Lyabi-Hauz** (Lyabi-Hauz; mains 1200S) Dining alfresco around the venerable pool with greybeards, local families and plenty of other tourists is the quintessential Bukhara experience. There are two chaikhanas here, both serving shashlyk, *plov, kovurma laghman* (with meat and tomato sauce) and cold Azia beer.

**Kochevnik** (Bakhautdin Naqshband; mains 2000-3000S) This Korean eatery is ideally situated near Lyabi-Hauz and complements its Asian fare with Russian food. Lest you be sceptical about its authenticity, it's co-owned by an ethnic Korean.

**Bella Italia** (☎ 224 33 46; Bakhautdin Naqshband; mains 3000-5000S) It's not the world's best Italian food, but nor is it the worst and by this point in your trip you're undoubtedly ready for some pasta.

**Minzifa** (☎ 224 61 75; set meals US$7) This cosy eatery with rooftop seating is a welcome addition to Bukhara's dining scene, serving up excellent European food in the heart of the touristy Jewish Quarter. Advanced booking required.

There's another good chaikhana in the park across the street from the Ark. Both Alyans and El Dorado double as restaurants and have OK food (right).

For self-caterers there are farmers markets, including Kolkhozny Bazaar and the Sunday and Thursday Kukluk Bazaar, buried deep in the Jewish Quarter.

## Drinking

**Silk Road Spices** (Halim Ibodov 5; unlimited tea & sweets 2500S) This boutique teahouse offers a delightful diversion from all that sightseeing. It has exactly six spicy varieties of tea and coffee, served with rich local sweets such as halvan and *qandalat*.

**Nughay Caravanserai wine tasting** (Bakhautdin Naqshband 78; per 8 large samples 4000S; 🕒 11am-9pm) Djamal Akhrarov has an informal wine shop and tasting room in this 18th-century caravanserai. The local wines are surprisingly good, in particular the Cabernets.

## Entertainment

Bukhara's old town is eerily silent by night, which is part of its charm, but there are several early-evening entertainment options.

**Puppet performance** (admission US$5; 🕒 6pm & 7pm late Mar-May & Sep-early Nov, by appointment Jun-Aug) Held at a theatre on the western end of Lyabi-Hauz, this is the consensus reader favourite entertainment option. The three-part amateur performance, with a traditional wedding ceremony as the usual theme, is held in Tajik, Uzbek and English.

**Folklore & fashion show** (admission US$5, optional dinner 5000S; 🕒 6.30pm Apr-May & Sep-Oct, 7.30pm Jun-Aug, by appointment Nov-Mar) Across Lyabi-Hauz in the Nadir Divanbegi Medressa, this is a nightly show with traditional musical performances and dancing. Do not book this through Uzbektourism or you may be forced to buy the dinner at a premium; book at the gate or through the Tourist Information Centre instead.

Both of the above shows are staged mainly for the tour-bus crowd but individuals can piggyback. Shows are often cancelled if there are no tour groups in town.

For anything rowdier than puppets you must head southeast of the centre into the newer part of town.

**Oscar** (Muminova; 🕒 8pm-2am) This small club draws a young, very local crowd. Foreigners are welcome but will most definitely be exotic.

**Bukhara Palace Hotel** (☎ 223 00 24; Navoi 8; 🕒 till 3am) The basement nightclub here gets going on weekends.

As in much of the country, locals tend to gravitate towards 'dance bars', basically restaurants that devolve into bacchanalian dance parties after dinner, often with floor shows. Two to sample are **Alyans** (Muminova 33) and **El Dorado** (M Ikbola).

## Shopping

With many tourist sights overflowing with vendors, it's not hard to find a souvenir in Bukhara. They are, of course, of varying quality.

For carpets, you couldn't ask for a better shopping atmosphere than at the silk-weaving and carpet centre in the late 16th-century **Tim Abdulla Khan** (Haqiqat; 9am-6pm), near Taqi-Telpaq Furushon Bazaar (a *tim* was a general market). Vendors are not pushy and will openly inform you on what's handmade and what's machine-made. You can watch silk-carpet weavers in action here, as well at the **Unesco Carpet Weaving Shop** (☎ 223 66 13; Eshoni Pir 57; 9am-5pm Mon-Sat). It no longer has anything to do with Unesco (which helped them launch in 2001), but uniquely produces only Bukhara designs. Call ahead to book a tour in English.

At the **Bukhara Artisan Development Centre** (Bakhautdin Naqshband) you can watch artisans at work on a variety of handicrafts including silk-embroidered tapestries, miniature paintings, jewellery boxes and chess sets.

Serious *suzani* and textile collectors should head to Akhbar House (p244) for a glimpse of owner Akhbar's fantastic collection. Much of it isn't for sale but he may be willing to part with gems from his personal collection for the right price.

## Getting There & Away

### AIR

**Uzbekistan Airways** (☎ 233 50 60; Navoi 15), about 1km southeast of the town centre, has flights from Bukhara to Tashkent (US$36, 1½ hours, at least daily except Saturday).

### LAND

All vehicular transport to Tashkent and Samarkand leaves from the North Bus Station, about 3km north of the centre. Here you'll find plenty of private buses (Samarkand 3500S, five hours; Tashkent 7000S, 11 hours) and shared Nexias (Samarkand per seat 11,000S, three hours; Tashkent 20,000S, seven hours), plus a few marshrutkas. There are plenty of departures and everything leaves when full. Shared taxis to Navoi also depart from here (per seat 2500S, 45 minutes), or take a slower bus for 800S.

About 1.5km north of here is Karvon Bazaar, departure point for Urgench/Khiva. Shared taxis congregate in a lot on the less-crowded south end of the market. The going rate is 20,000S per seat for Urgench (4½ hours). Drivers demand up to 5000S extra for Khiva; you're better off transferring in Urgench. A few marshrutkas allegedly head to Urgench from this lot before noon (12,000S). For buses to Urgench (5000S, eight hours), you have to wait out on the main road in front of the taxi stand and flag buses originating in Tashkent, which come through sporadically.

To get to the North Bus Station or Karvon Bazaar take public bus 2 or 21, or marshrutka 67 or 73, from the train station stop (site of the old train station, 2km east of the Lyabi-Hauz marshrutka stop).

The 'Sharq' bus station east of the centre has no useful buses. However, shared taxis depart from across the street to Qarshi (per seat 6000S, 1½ hours), Shakhrisabz (12,000S, four hours), Termiz (20,000S, six hours) and Denau on the Tajik border (25,000S, six hours).

See p268 for information on getting to Turkmenabat.

### Train

The *Sharq* high-speed train zips from Kagan to Tashkent every morning at 7.20am (2nd class/1st class 11,000/15,000S, 7½ hours) via Samarkand (5700/9200S, 3½ hours). Unless you have a desire to watch Russian action movies and videos on a blaring TV, opt for 2nd class, where the nuisance is limited to blaring Russian pop.

A slower passenger train rumbles to Tashkent nightly at 6.40pm (*platskartny* 11,000S, 12½ hours). It also goes through Samarkand (*platskartny* 7500S, six hours). A final option to Samarkand is the daily 'suburban' train (1200S, six hours). The trains from Tashkent to Nukus, Kungrad and Urgench go via Navoi, not Bukhara (p210). Lastly, there's a daily suburban train to Qarshi (850S, 3½ hours).

A thrice weekly overnight Kagan–Urgench train (12 hours) was due to launch in the second half of 2007.

To get to Kagan take marshrutka 68 from the Lyabi-Hauz stop (300S, 25 minutes). There is an **Air & Rail Ticketing Office** (☎ 224 64 86; Naqshband) right across from Lyabi-Hauz.

## Getting Around

### TO/FROM AIRPORT

The airport is 6km east of town. Figure on 1500S for a 10-minute taxi trip between the centre and the airport. Marshrutka 100 or bus

10 to/from the train station, Kryty Rynok or Gorgaz stops takes 15 to 20 minutes.

**PUBLIC TRANSPORT & TAXI**
From the Lyabi-Hauz stop, marshrutka 52 goes to the new part of town via Mustaqillik, while both 52 and 68 get you to the useful train station stop, where you can pick up transport going just about anywhere. Useful destinations are Kolkhozny Bazaar (Колхозный базар), the Ark stop (Арк) and Karvon Bazaar (Карвон базар).

You should be able to get anywhere in town in a taxi for less than 1500S, as long as you avoid the cheats who hang out at the Lyabi-Hauz stop. From the centre a one-way taxi should cost about 3000S to Bakhautdin Naqshband Mausoleum and Kagan; less to Emir's Palace and Chor-Bakr.

## AROUND BUKHARA

### Emir's Summer Palace

For a look at the kitsch lifestyle of the last emir, Alim Khan, go out to his summer palace, Sitorai Mohi Hosa (Star-and-Moon Garden), now a **museum** (admission 3600S, guide 3600S; 9am-5pm Wed-Mon, 9am-2.30pm Tue), 6km north of Bukhara.

The three-building compound was a joint effort for Alim Khan by Russian architects (outside) and local artisans (inside), and no punches were pulled in showing off both the finest and the gaudiest aspects of both styles. A 50-watt Russian generator provided the first electricity the emirate had ever seen. In front of the harem is a pool where the women frolicked, overlooked by a wooden pavilion from which – says every tour guide – the emir tossed an apple to his chosen bedmate.

To get here take bus 7 or 21 or marshrutka 70 from the train station stop. The palace is at the end of the line.

### Bakhautdin Naqshband Mausoleum

East of Bukhara in the village of Kasri Orifon is one of Sufism's more important **shrines** (admission free; 8am-7pm), the birthplace and the tomb of Bakhautdin (or Bakha ud-Din) Naqshband (1318–89), the founder of the most influential of many ancient Sufi orders in Central Asia, and Bukhara's unofficial 'patron saint'. For more on Sufism, see p65.

The huge main dome of the complex covers a 16th-century *khanaka*, now a Juma (Friday) mosque. In front of it is a precariously leaning minaret. Two more mosques surround Bakhautdin's tomb in the courtyard to the left. The lovingly restored *aivan* here is one of the country's most beautiful. The tomb itself is a simple 2m-high block, protected by a horse-mane talisman hanging from a post. Tradition says that it is auspicious to complete three anticlockwise circumambulations of the tomb.

Back in the main courtyard you'll spot more locals walking anticlockwise around a petrified tree. Legend has it that this tree sprouted where Bakhautdin stuck his staff, upon returning from a pilgrimage to Mecca. He then added drops of holy water from Mecca to a nearby well. Faucets near the minaret continue to supply this well's allegedly holy water to pilgrims, who splash their faces with it and bring it home by the jug-full for good luck. The legend of the well may hold water, but there's a problem with the tree story – it's only 350 years old!

Marshrutkas 125 and 60 go straight to the compound from the train station and Ark stops in Bukhara (300S, 25 minutes).

### Chor-Bakr

This 16th-century **necropolis** (admission 1000S, 8.30am-8pm) or 'town' of mausoleums 6km west of Bukhara, is yet another sight that has fallen victim to overambitious restoration.

It was built in Shaybanid times near the graves of Abu-Bakr, devoted friend of the Prophet Mohammed and later first caliph, and his family. A large Juma mosque on the left and a former *khanaka* on the right dominate the complex, much of which lay hauntingly in ruin before the recent restoration made it look like so many other neat-and-tidy sights in Uzbekistan.

From the stop on the east side of Kolkhozny Bazaar, just off M Karimov, take marshrutka 107 labelled 'Чорбакр' (300S, 10 minutes).

## TERMIZ ТЕРМЕЗ

☎ (3) 76 / pop 120,000 / elev 380m

Modern-day Termiz bears few traces of its colourful cosmopolitan history. However, set in attractive landscapes on the fringes of town are some ancient monuments and sites attesting to more glorious times.

Termiz today has an edgy, Wild West border-town feel. The expat crowd is a mix of aid workers, archaeologists, oil prospectors and German soldiers from the Luftwaffe base at

UZBEKISTAN

**FEAR & LOATHING IN TERMIZ** *Greg Bloom*

Officially, registration laws in Termiz are no different than in any other Uzbek city. You need a registration docket from your hotel, but separate special permits are no longer required.

Apparently somebody forgot to tell that to the police in Termiz, where this author spent two hours in a white interrogation room at OVIR exchanging courtesies with three plainclothes cops. What was I doing in Termiz? How long was I here? Why had I been to Russia? And Cambodia, China, Tajikistan, Kyrgyzstan, the Philippines, Ukraine? Was I a journalist?

Being a journalist in Uzbekistan, of course, means instant expulsion. No, I was just a humble tourist.

Shockingly, they didn't search my belongings. Had they done so they would have discovered two pads filled with a month's worth of notes – instant proof that I was lying. Instead they just checked my photos, mostly of touristy sights.

They let me go eventually, but why had they grabbed me? They had insisted that I was required to have a special permit, but I knew this to be untrue. It's certainly possible that I was a suspected journalist. It's also possible that my hotel, the Osiyo, was not registered to take foreigners, and that somebody had blown the whistle on me for staying there.

Whatever the reason, there are lessons to be learned from my Termiz experience. First of all, Termiz has some of the most paranoid and most unpredictable police in Uzbekistan. While you don't technically need a permit, you are subject to their whims. If they say you need a permit, well then you need a permit. To minimize problems, stay in a registered hotel and don't be a journalist.

Another lesson is that it's always a good idea for solo tourists to keep a low profile in sensitive areas such as Termiz and the Fergana Valley.

Termiz airport. A steady flow of contraband from Afghanistan crosses the Amu-Darya here on its way to Europe. Throw in Uzbekistan's most paranoid cops (see above) and you have all the makings of a spy novel.

## Orientation & Information

The main road is Al-Termizi, with the train station at its northern end. The clock tower on the corner of Al-Termizi and Navoi marks the central axis of town. The bus station is 2km west of this. Most hotels and the archaeological museum are south of here.

**Asaka Bank** (Navoi 45) Currency exchange and cash advance for MasterCard holders.

**Internet Café** (Al-Termizi; per hr 600S; ⌚ 8am-1am) Located across from the clock tower.

## Sights

The **Termiz Archaeological Museum** (☎ 227 58 29; http://archaeomuseum.freenet.uz; Al-Hakim Termizi 29; admission 2000S; ⌚ 9am-6pm), 1km south of the train station, is reason enough to visit Termiz. Unveiled in 2001, the museum is a treasure trove of artefacts collected from the many ravaged civilisations that pepper the Surkhandarya province of which Termiz is the main city. 'Surkhandarya is the only region in Central Asia where you'll find archaeological sites from all the major eras of Central Asian history', the museum curator truthfully proclaims. 'The museum was opened by our president, Islam Karimov. Look, there's his photo!'

Whatever, the museum makes a great first stop to determine what sites you might want to visit, thanks to an excellent model of Surkhandarya which depicts the most important sights. Serious archaeological buffs will want to spend a few days in the region, heading up to the mountainous, cave-strewn area around Boysun, where Neanderthal bones, petroglyphs and a wealth of Stone Age relics have been discovered.

There are several sights around Termiz that can be visited in a half-day. You should hire a car to see them all or it could take a half-week. Figure on paying a driver 3000S to 4000S per hour. The main sights lurk northwest of the city on the road to Qarshi. Driving out here you'll notice various piles of rubble in the cotton fields of what used to be Termiz (and is now known as Old Termiz). These are Buddhist ruins, levelled by Jenghiz Khan along with the rest of Old Termiz in 1220.

Today archaeologists are busy trying to reverse some of the damage at **Fayoz-Tepe**, a 3rd-century AD Buddhist monastery complex 9km west of the bus station. Discovered only in 1968, in recent years it's been restored and partially rebuilt with support from Unesco. The modern-looking teapot dome protects the monastery's original stupa, visible through a glass window. Looking southwest from here, the remains of **Kara-Tepe**, a Buddhist cave monastery, are visible on the banks of the Amu-Darya. Like the river, the monastery is off-limits because it's right on the Afghan border, although tour groups sometimes visit with the help of well-connected travel agencies.

Closer to town is a slightly younger but still quite sacred edifice, the **Mausoleum of Al-Hakim al-Termizi**. Its namesake was a 9th-century Sufi philosopher, known locally as Al-Hakim, the city's patron saint. In a triumph for preservationists, the interior's cheap plaster *ghanch*-work, spuriously installed as part of the government's general monument 'beautification' drive, is being gradually removed to expose the original 15th-century brick. The mausoleum gets packed to the gills on Wednesday when the faithful are served lunch. The Amu-Darya is once again in sight here; photographing it is forbidden so be discreet.

Termiz' other main sites are clustered northeast of town off the airport road. The restored Timurid-style **Sultan Saodat Ensemble** of mausoleums probably won't impress you if you've been to Samarkand. Buried here are members of the dynasty that ruled Termiz from the 11th to 15th centuries, the Sayyids. About 5km closer to town is a real ruin, the mud-walled **Kyr Kyz** (Forty Girls) fortress. Legend has it that 40 young women lived here in the 11th century after their nobleman-husband was slain, successfully fighting off sex-crazed nomads before eventually succumbing to their own ambition to avenge their husband's murder.

## Tours

**Gulya** (☎ 222 71 25; gul_1992@rambler.ru) is a very friendly guide who works part time at the archaeological museum. **Alisher Choriev** (☎ 222 88 14, 227 53 24) is another capable English-speaking guide.

## Sleeping & Eating

Entire wings of some hotels are booked out indefinitely by German soldiers, including the Dostlyk Hotel and the recently renovated Surkhon Hotel. That leaves the following as the best options:

**Osiyo** (☎ 222 89 09; r per person 4500S) This is your bargain-basement choice, although as we found out there is some question as to whether they can accept foreigners (see opposite). It's a steal at these prices though, with spacious rooms and comfortable linens, although the leaky windows could create mosquito problems in the summer. It's a five-minute walk from Hotel Meridien.

**Hotel Tennis Court** (☎ 222 79 33; Al-Termizi 29B; s/d US$6/10) It was closed for renovations when we visited but is a budget-traveller favourite. It's opposite the archaeology museum.

**Hotel Meridien** (☎ 227 26 74; Alpomysh 23; s/d US$60/80; ❄) This newly opened high-rise has huge rooms in pastel colours and a decent restaurant that's open to all well into the evening. The cigarette-puffing receptionist is indicative of service that is a tad informal for a 'four-star' hotel, but it certainly leads the pack as far as facilities and amenities go.

**Boysun** (Dostlyk Park, Fifth Rayon; mains 1000-2000S) Reputed to have some of the best Surkhandarya food in town, as well a cheap, greasy breakfast of sausages and eggs that's useful if you're staying at the nearby Osiyo or Tennis Court hotels.

**Jasmin** (Navoi, Fifth Rayon; 1000-2000S) A vintage local eatery, this is the place to sample *chopancha,* a Surkhandarya meat-and-potatoes dish. It's on the outskirts of town about 1.5km beyond the Hotel Meridien.

On Friday and Saturday nights the Surkhon Disco Bar attracts stein-banging German soldiers and working girls after their euros.

## Getting There & Around

**Uzbekistan Airways** (☎ 223 79 29; Gagarin 36) has three flights a day to/from Tashkent (US$40, 1½ hours). The airport is 15km north of town. Take marshrutka 11 from Yubileny Bazaar.

Shared taxi is the way to go to/from Samarkand (per seat 16,000S, five hours) and Bukhara (20,000S, six hours). There's also a daily bus to Samarkand (4500S, 8½ hours). For Bukhara, you may have to transfer in Qarshi. There are a couple of evening buses to Tashkent (12,000S, 14 hours) via Samarkand or take a shared taxi (25,000S, 9½ hours).

All of the above leave from the bus station, reachable via marshrutka 6 from Yubileny Bazaar.

 

Do not board the Tashkent–Termiz or Samarkand–Termiz trains unless you have a Turkmen transit visa and a double-entry Uzbek visa. New lines to Termiz from Kitab and Guzar will open in late 2007 at the earliest.

For information on getting to Tajikistan see p267.



# KHOREZM ХОРЕЗМ

## URGENCH УРГЕНЧ

☎ (3) 62 / pop 140,000

Urgench, the capital of Khorezm province, is a standard-issue Soviet grid of broad streets and empty squares, 450km northwest of Bukhara across the Kyzylkum desert. When the Amu-Darya changed course in the 16th century, the people of Konye-Urgench (then called Urgench), 150km downriver in present-day Turkmenistan, were left without water and started a new town here. Today travellers use Urgench mainly as a transport hub for Khiva, 35km southwest. It's also a good launch point for the 'Golden Ring' of ancient fortresses in southern Karakalpakstan.

### Orientation

The town's axis is Al-Khorezmi, with the clock tower at its intersection with Al-Beruni marking the centre of things. The train station is 600m south of the centre down Al-Khorezmi, the airport is 3km north, and most hotels and the main bazaar are near the clock tower.

### Information

**Bahadir & Bakhtiyar Rakhamov** (☎ Bahadir 352 41 06, 512 12 41, Bakhtiyar 517 51 33) English-speaking father-and-son driving tandem offer all-day excursions to the *qalas* (fortresses; US$50 per carload), and Moynaq (US$100).

**Delia Madrashimova** (☎ 226 88 34; per day US$30) Good English-speaking guide is your best bet for excursions to the *qalas* or Khiva if you're staying in Urgench.

**Internet Café** (cnr Al-Khorezmi & Al-Beruni; per hr 1200S; 🕑 9am-11pm)

**Post, telephone & telegraph office** (Clock tower, cnr Al-Khorezmi & Al-Beruni)

**Uzbekistan Airways** (☎ 226 88 60; Al-Khorezmi 1; 🕑 8am-6pm) There's a currency-exchange kiosk here.

### Sleeping & Eating

**Hotel Urgench** (☎ 226 20 22; Al-Khorezmi & Pakhlavan Mahmud; s/d US$20/40) This formerly notorious hotel has been renovated and now displays perfectly acceptable, clean Soviet-style rooms.

**Khorezm Palace** (☎ 224 99 99; www.khorezmpalace.uz; Al-Beruni 2; s/d/ste US$80/110/300; ❄ 💻 🏊) If you can't go a minute without your creature comforts, you may wish to consider staying here and day-tripping to Khiva. It's certainly the flashest place west of Bukhara, with all the amenities you would expect at these prices.

**Chaikhana Urgench** (Al-Khorezmi 35/1; mains 100-1500S) Located right next to the Hotel Urgench, this café serving a variety of shashlyk, *laghman* and *plov* is the best deal in town.

### Getting There & Away

#### AIR

Uzbekistan Airways (left) has two or three flights daily to Tashkent (one way US$55).

#### LAND

Shared taxi is the favoured way across the Kyzylkum desert to Bukhara and beyond. Regular shared taxis and a few morning marshrutkas leave from a stand near the bus station (marshrutka/taxi per seat 12,000/20,000S, 4½ hours). Less frequent are shared taxis to Tashkent (per seat 35,000S, 12 hours), but you can always transfer in Bukhara – also the preferred method for getting to Samarkand.

The **bus station** (☎ 227 57 25; Al-Khorezmi), just north of the train station, has an afternoon bus to Bukhara (5000S, eight hours), an evening bus to Samarkand (7500S, 13 hours) and a morning bus to Tashkent (12,000S, 19 hours) via Bukhara and Samarkand. There are usually a few private buses heading east as well. There are a few buses per day to Nukus (2500S, 2¼ hours), as well as shared taxis that are more frequent in the morning (per seat 8000S, 1½ hours). If nothing's going to Nukus, go to Beruni and change there.

Shared taxis and marshrutkas to Khiva leave from a lot just south of the bazaar (marshrutka/taxi per seat 500/800S).

For instructions on getting to Dashogus, Turkmenistan, see p268.

#### Train

From the **train station** (Al-Khorezmi), there's a twice-weekly passenger train to Tashkent (*platskartnyy* 17,000S, 20 hours) via Zarafshan, Navoi and Samarkand. This train no longer goes through Turkmenistan.

## Getting Around

Marshrutka 3 runs along Al-Khorezmi between the train station and the airport, stopping near the hotels, bazaar and bus station en route.

# AROUND URGENCH

## Ancient Khorezm

The Amu-Darya delta, stretching from southeast of Urgench to the Aral Sea, has been inhabited for millennia and was an important oasis long before Urgench or even Khiva were important. The historical name of the delta area, which includes parts of modern-day northern Turkmenistan, was Khorezm (see also p432).

The ruins of many Khorezmian towns and forts, some well over 2000 years old, still stand east and north of Urgench in southern Karakalpakstan. With help from Unesco, local tourism officials recently dubbed this area of Khorezm the 'Golden Ring of Ancient Khorezm' and put out a snazzy brochure designed to lure more Khiva-bound tourists to the *qalas*. The area's traditional name is Elliq Qala (Fifty Fortresses).

For fans of old castles in the sand, this is an area not to be missed. Outdoor and nature enthusiasts will also find plenty to do here, from scrambling among the *qala* ruins, to camel trekking near Ayaz-Qala, to hiking in Badai Tugai Nature Reserve. The Unesco brochure is well worth picking up if you're considering an excursion here; look for it in the Bukhara or Khiva tourist information centres.

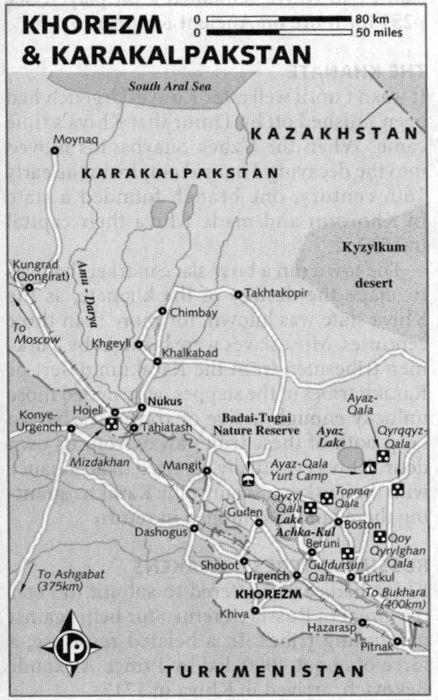


Place names in this section are given in Karakalpak, the official language of the region in which they lie.

### ELLIQ-QALA

There are about 20 forts that you can explore here today, and who knows how many that have yet to be discovered (the 'Fifty Fortresses' moniker is an approximation). Archaeologists are active in this area; in 2006 an Australian team digging near Lake Achka-Kul discovered a large town thought to date from the 4th-century BC. That and newer discoveries might be accessible by the time your read this.

The most well-known *qala* is impressive, mud-walled **Ayaz-Qala**, which is actually a complex of three forts about 25km north of Boston. Its heyday was the 6th and 7th centuries. In its shadow is **Ayaz-Qala Yurt Camp** (☎ 361-350 59 09, 361-532 43 61; ayazkala_tur@mail.ru; per person US$30), with several yurts big enough to hold five to eight people. One of the main attractions out here is **camel trekking** (per hr/day US$5/30). You can also go swimming or fishing in nearby Ayaz *qol* (lake), desert hiking or just relax. A good chef and a solar panel generator installed by Unesco ensures that you won't really be roughing it out here. Call ahead to reserve yurts and camels, and to discuss transport options.

The oldest, most unique, and most difficult-to-pronounce fort is circular **Qoy Qyrylghan Qala**, which archaeologists believe doubled as a pagan temple and an observatory complex. It was in use as early as the 4th century BC. Drivers will be reluctant to take you here via the poor road from Beruni; instead, drive south towards Turtkul and turn north on a paved road towards the mammoth **Guldursun Qala**, built as early as the 1st century but in use until the Middle Ages. Qoy Qyrylghan Qala is 18km west of Guldursun Qala.

Two other not-to-be-missed *qalas* are **Toprak Qala** and **Qyzyl Qala**, on opposite sides of the road about 10km west of Boston. The former is a temple complex of the rulers of the Khorezm borders in the 3rd and 4th centuries.

Near the latter you'll see students working the cotton fields in the autumn.

#### BADAI-TUGAI NATURE RESERVE

This **reserve** (admission per person US$7) is a strip of *tugai* forest on the east bank of the Amu-Darya, around 60km north of Urgench. In the 1960s and '70s the Soviet cotton-growing schemes cleared out most forest area, and this is one of the few areas preserved. *Tugai* is a very dense, junglelike forest of trees, shrubs and prickly salt-resistant plants and creepers, unique to Central Asia's desert river valleys. Only about a fifth of the Amu-Darya's and Syr-Darya's *tugai* has survived. Fauna includes Karakal desert cats, jackals, wild boar, foxes and badgers, although you are unlikely to see any animals besides Bukhara deer hanging out in the resident breeding station.

### Getting There & Away

The only way to explore Elliq Qala is with private transport. See p250 for a recommended guide and driver. If they aren't available, try your luck with taxi drivers in Urgench. Make absolutely sure they know this area, arm yourself with the Unesco brochure (which has a map of the area) and negotiate hard. Look to pay about US$50 for an all-day excursion to visit unlimited forts and, if you desire, the Badai-Tugai Nature Reserve. The best strategy is to visit Guldursun Qala first and go anticlockwise, but few drivers will do this unless you insist on it!

## KHIVA ХИВА

☎ **(3) 62 / pop 50,000**

Khiva's name, redolent of slave caravans, barbaric cruelty and terrible journeys across deserts and steppes infested with wild tribesmen, struck fear into all but the boldest 19th-century hearts. Nowadays it's a mere 35km southwest of Urgench, past cotton bushes and fruit trees.

The historic heart of Khiva (Uzbek: Xiva), unlike that of other Central Asian cities, is preserved in its entirety – but so well preserved that the life has almost been squeezed out of it. As a result of a Soviet conservation programme in the 1970s and '80s, it's now a squeaky-clean official 'city-museum'. Even among its densely packed mosques, tombs, palaces, alleys and at least 16 medressas, you need imagination to get a sense of its mystique, bustle and squalor.

A few of the historic buildings in Ichon-Qala are functioning mosques or shrines, but most are museums. You can see it all in a day trip from Urgench, but you'll take it in better by staying longer. Khiva is at its best by night when the moonlit silhouettes of the tilting columns and medressas, viewed from twisting alleyways, work their magic.

### History

Agriculture and human settlement go back four, perhaps six, millennia in Khorezm, the large, fertile Amu-Darya river delta isolated in the midst of broad deserts. So Khiva, on the southern fringe of the delta, may be very old but its exact age is not known. Legend has that it was founded when Shem, son of Noah, discovered a well here; his people called it Kheivak, from which the name Khiva is said to be derived.

Khiva certainly existed by the 8th century as a minor fort and trading post on a side branch of the Silk Road, but while Khorezm prospered on and off from the 10th to the 14th centuries, its capital was at Old Urgench (present-day Konye-Urgench in Turkmenistan), and Khiva remained a bit player. See p251 for more on Ancient Khorezm.

#### THE KHANATE

It wasn't until well after Konye-Urgench had been finished off by Timur that Khiva's time came. When the Uzbek Shaybanids moved into the decaying Timurid empire in the early 16th century, one branch founded a state in Khorezm and made Khiva their capital in 1592.

The town ran a busy slave market that was to shape the destiny of the khanate, as the Khiva state was known, for more than three centuries. Most slaves were brought by Turkmen tribesmen from the Karakum desert or Kazakh tribes of the steppes, who raided those unlucky enough to live or travel nearby. To keep both of these tribes away from its own door, Khiva eventually resorted to an alliance with the Turkmen against the Kazakhs, granting them land and money in return.

#### RUSSIAN INTEREST AWAKENS

Khiva had earlier offered to submit to Peter the Great of Russia in return for help against marauding tribes. In a belated response, a force of about 4000, led by Prince Alexandr Bekovich, arrived in Khiva in 1717.

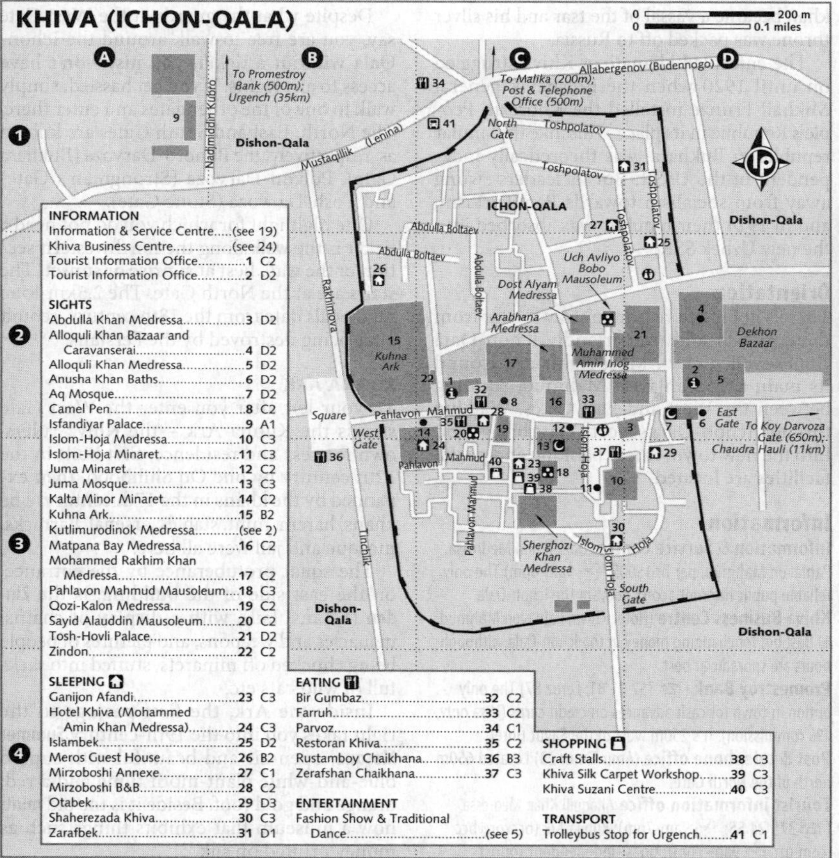


Unfortunately, the khan had by that time lost interest in being a vassal of the tsar. He came out to meet them, suggesting they disperse to outlying villages where they could be more comfortably accommodated. This done, the Khivans annihilated the invaders, leaving just a handful to make their way back with the news. The khan sent Bekovich's head to his Central Asian rival, the Emir of Bukhara, and kept the rest of him on display.

In 1740, Khiva was wrecked by a less gullible invader, Nadir Shah of Persia, and Khorezm became for a while a northern outpost of the Persian empire. By the end of the 18th century it was rebuilt and began taking a small share in the growing trade between Russia and the Bukhara and Kokand khanates. Its slave market, the biggest in Central Asia, continued unabated, augmented by Russians captured as they pushed their borders southwards and eastwards.

See p189 for details on Khiva's role in the Great Game.

### RUSSIAN CONQUEST

When the Russians finally sent a properly organised expedition against Khiva, it was no contest. In 1873 General Konstantin Kaufman's 13,000-strong forces advanced on Khiva from the north, west and east. After some initial guerrilla resistance, mainly by Yomud Turkmen tribesmen, Mohammed Rakhim II Khan surrendered unconditionally. Kaufman then indulged in a massacre of the Yomud. The khan became a vassal of the tsar and his silver throne was packed off to Russia.

The enfeebled khanate of Khiva struggled on until 1920 when the Bolshevik general Mikhail Frunze installed the Khorezm People's Republic in its place. This, like the similar republic in Bukhara, was theoretically independent of the USSR. But its leaders swung away from socialism towards Pan-Turkism, and in 1924 their republic was absorbed into the new Uzbek SSR.

## Orientation

There's not much reason to stray too far from the compact and user-friendly Ichon-Qala (inner-walled city). Most sights are around its main axis, Pahlavon Mahmud, running between the West and East Gates. Walking through Ichon-Qala's North Gate brings you into the new town, where banking and postal facilities are located.

## Information

**Information & Service Centre** (Qozi-Kalon Medressa, Pahlavon Mahmud; per hr 1500S; 9am-6pm) The only reliable public internet access point in the Ichon-Qala.

**Khiva Business Centre** (Hotel Khiva, Pahlavon Mahmud 1) Best bet for changing money in the Ichon-Qala, although hours are sporadic at best.

**Promestroy Bank** (☎ 357 31 81; Feruz 87) The only option in town for cash advances on credit cards (Visa only, 1% commission). It's 250m west of the Sayut Hotel.

**Post & telephone office** (Amir Timur 23) Located 650m north of the North Gate.

**Tourist information office** Alloquili Khan Medressa (☎ 375 24 55; 9am-7pm); Kuhna Ark (bccxor@bcc.com.uz; 9am-7pm); Quasi-independent tourist centre has its main branch in front of the Kuhna Ark, and another branch at Alloquli Khan Medressa manned by a Japanese consultant. It arranges guides (US$5 per hour) and sell maps and information booklets. When the consultant leaves town, opening hours miraculously shrink.

## Sights

### ICHON-QALA GATES & WALLS

The main entrance to the **Ichon-Qala** (2-day admission 7200S, camera 5000S, video 7000S; ticket booth & sights 9am-6pm) is the twin-turreted brick West Gate (Ota-Darvoza, literally 'Father Gate'), a 1970s reconstruction – the original was wrecked in 1920. The two-day ticket gives you access to all the sights and museums in the Ichon-Qala besides the Islom-Hoja Minaret, the Pahlavon Mahmud Mausoleum and the Akshaikh Baba Complex in Kuhna Ark.

Despite what the guards at the West Gate say, you are free to walk around the Ichon-Qala without a ticket, you just won't have access to any sights. If you get hassled, simply walk to one of the other gates and enter there. The North, East and South Gates are known as, respectively, the Buhoro-Darvoza (Bukhara Gate), Polvon-Darvoza (Strongman's Gate) and Tosh-Darvoza (Stone Gate).

One highlight for which you do not need a ticket is the **walk** along the northwestern section of the wall, best at sunrise or sunset. The stairs are at the North Gate. The 2.5km-long mud walls date from the 18th century, rebuilt after being destroyed by the Persians.

### KUHNA ARK

To your left after you enter the West Gate stands the Kuhna Ark – the Khiva rulers' own fortress and residence, first built in the 12th century by one Oq Shihbobo, then expanded by the khans in the 17th century. The khans' harem, mint, stables, arsenal, barracks, mosque and jail were all here.

The squat protuberance by the entrance, on the east side of the building, is the **Zindon** (Khans' Jail), with a display of chains, manacles and weapons, and pictures of people being chucked off minarets, stuffed into sacks full of wild cats etc.

Inside the Ark, the first passage to the right takes you into the 19th-century **Summer Mosque**, open-air and beautiful with superb blue-and-white plant-motif tiling and a red, orange and gold roof. Beside it is the old **mint**, now a museum that exhibits things such as money printed on silk.

Straight ahead from the Ark entrance is the restored **throne room**, where khans dispensed judgement (if not justice). The circular area on the ground was for the royal yurt, which the no-longer-nomadic khans still liked to use.

To the right of the throne room, a door in the wall leads to a flight of steps up to the **Oq Shihbobo bastion**, the original part of the Kuhna Ark, set right against the Ichon-Qala's massive west wall. At the top is an open-air pavilion with good views over the Ark and Ichon-Qala.

### MOHAMMED RAKHIM KHAN MEDRESSA

East of the Kuhna Ark, across an open space that was once a busy palace square (and place of execution), the 19th-century Mohammed Rakhim Khan Medressa is named after the khan who surrendered to Russia in 1873 (although he had, at least, kept Khiva independent a few years longer than Bukhara). A hotchpotch of a museum within is partly dedicated to this khan, who was also a poet under the pen name Feruz.

Khiva's token camel, Katya, waits for tourists to ride or pose with her outside the medressa's south wall.

#### KALTA MINOR MINARET

Just south of the Kuhna Ark stands the fat, turquoise-tiled **Kalta Minor Minaret**. This unfinished minaret was begun in 1851 by Mohammed Amin Khan, who according to legend wanted to build a minaret so high he could see all the way to Bukhara. Had it been completed it surely would have been the world's tallest building, but the Khan dropped dead in 1855 and it was never finished.

East of the minaret, beside the medressa housing Restoran Khiva, is the small, plain **Sayid Alauddin Mausoleum**, dating to 1310 when Khiva was under the Golden Horde of the Mongol empire. You might find people praying in front of the 19th-century tiled sarcophagus. To the east is a **Music Museum** in the 1905 **Qozi-Kalon Medressa**.

#### JUMA MOSQUE & AROUND

East of the Music Museum, the large Juma Mosque is interesting for the 218 wooden columns supporting its roof – a concept thought to be derived from ancient Arabian mosques. The few finely decorated columns are from the original 10th-century mosque, though the present building dates from the 18th century. From inside, you can climb the 81 very dark steps of the 47m **Juma Minaret** (1000S).

Opposite the Juma Mosque is the 1905 **Matpana Bay Medressa**, containing a museum devoted to nature, history, religion and the medressa itself. East of the Juma Mosque, the 1855 **Abdulla Khan Medressa** holds a tiny nature museum. The little **Aq Mosque** dates from 1657, the same year as the **Anusha Khan Baths** (Anushahon Hammomi; admission 3000S) and is located by the entrance to the long tunnel of the East Gate.

#### ALLOQULI KHAN MEDRESSA, BAZAAR & CARAVANSERAI

The street leading north opposite the Aq Mosque contains some of Khiva's most interesting buildings, most of them created by Alloquli Khan – known as the 'builder khan' – in the 1830s and '40s. First come the tall **Alloquli Khan Medressa** (1835) and the earlier **Kutlimurodinok Medressa** (1809), facing each other across the street, with matching tiled façades.

North of the Alloquli Khan Medressa are the **Alloquli Khan Bazaar & Caravanserai**. The entrance to both is through tall wooden gates beside the medressa. The bazaar is a domed market arcade, still catering to traders, which opens onto Khiva's modern **Dekhon Bazaar** at its east end.

#### TOSH-HOVLI PALACE

This palace, which means 'Stone House', contains Khiva's most sumptuous interior decoration, including ceramic tiles, carved stone and wood, and *ghanch*. Built by Alloquli Khan between 1832 and 1841 as a more splendid alternative to the Kuhna Ark, it's said to have more than 150 rooms off nine courtyards, with high ceilings designed to catch any breeze. Alloquli was a man in a hurry – the Tosh-Hovli's first architect was executed for failing to complete the job in two years.

#### ISLOM-HOJA MEDRESSA

From the East Gate, where the slave market was held, go back to the Abdulla Khan Medressa and take the lane to the south beside it to the Islom-Hoja Medressa and minaret – Khiva's newest Islamic monuments, both built in 1910. The **minaret**, with bands of turquoise and red tiling, looks rather like an uncommonly lovely lighthouse. At 57m tall, it's Uzbekistan's highest. A host of vendors, street cleaners or random scallywags will try to collect money from you for the privilege of climbing the 118 steps to the top; you'll probably end up paying one of them 500S to 1000S.

The medressa holds Khiva's best museum, exhibiting Khorezm handicrafts through the ages – fine woodcarving; metalwork; jewellery; Uzbek and Turkmen carpets; stone carved with Arabic script (which was in use in Khorezm from the 8th to the 20th centuries); and large pots called *hum* for storing food underground.

Islom Hoja himself was an early-20th-century grand vizier and a liberal (by Khivan standards): he founded a European-style school, brought long-distance telegraph to the city, and built a hospital. For his popularity, the khan and clergy had him assassinated.

#### PAHLAVON MAHMUD MAUSOLEUM

This revered **mausoleum** (Islom Hoja; admission 500S), with its lovely courtyard and stately tilework, is one of the town's most beautiful spots. Pahlavon Mahmud was a poet, philosopher and legendary wrestler who became Khiva's patron saint. His 1326 tomb was rebuilt in the 19th century and then requisitioned in 1913 by the khan of the day as the family mausoleum.

The beautiful Persian-style chamber under the turquoise dome at the north end of the courtyard holds the tomb of Khan Mohammed Rakhim II who ruled from 1865 to 1910. Leave your shoes at the entrance. Pahlavon Mahmud's tomb, to the left off the first chamber, has some of Khiva's loveliest tiling on the sarcophagus and the walls. Pilgrims press coins and notes through the grille that shields the tomb. Tombs of other khans stand unmarked east and west of the main building, outside the courtyard.

### DISHON-QALA

The Dishon-Qala was old Khiva's outer town, yet another creation of the 'builder khan' Alloquli, and surrounded by its own 6km wall. Most of it is buried beneath the modern town now, but part of the Dishon-Qala's wall remains, 300m south of the South Gate.

The **Isfandiyar Palace** (Mustaqillik; admission 1000S; 9am-6pm) on Mustaqillik was built between 1906 and 1912, and like the emir's Summer Palace in Bukhara displays some fascinatingly overdone decorations in a messy collision of East and West. The rooms are largely bare, allowing one to fully appreciate the gold-embroidered ceilings and lavish touches such as 4m-high mirrors and a 50kg chandelier. The harem, in case you're wondering, was behind the huge wall to the west of the palace. It's undergoing renovation and may open some day.

Beyond Dishon-Qala, surrounded by a low mud wall 11km east of central Khiva you'll find **Chaudra Hauli**, the summer residence of a 19th-century Khivan nobleman. You can climb up the slender four-storey tower for views of the surrounding flatness and then enjoy a drink at the little café nearby.

## Tours

Our recommended guides are listed below.

**Amon** (☎ 225 42 45, 719 42 45) French.

**Elena Alayarova** (☎ 229 46 22, 517 78 32) German.

**Khojamuratova Gulimkhan** (☎ 375 95 96, 513 40 76) English.

**Marina Alayarova** (☎ 226 53 06; marina_allayarova@yahoo.com) German & English.

## Sleeping

### BUDGET

**Otabek** (☎ 375 61 77; Islom Hoja 68; r with shared bathroom per person US$7) Backpackers will have few complaints at this small family-run B&B. The two triples and one quad have cosy beds and warm carpeting, and perky daughter Barno speaks good English. You can self-cater and store your stuff in the owners' fridge, or pay US$3 for dinner – often *plov* and salad. Owners were planning to expand the place by 2008.

**Meros Guest House** (☎ 375 76 42; Abdulla Boltaev 57; s/d US$10/20) The six simple rooms here are a steal considering they all have private bathrooms. There aren't many amenities, but what's here – nice twin beds with bedside tables – is beyond what you'd expect for this price.

**Islambek** (☎ 375 30 23; www.islambekhotel.nm.ru; Toshpolatov 60; s/d US$15/20; ) The 20 bright rooms here are a bit overdone but represent an indisputably good value, with nice linens and enough space and furniture for an afternoon tea session in your room. Then again you're probably better off taking tea on the roof, where the view's much better.

Also recommended:

**Ganijon Afandi** (☎ 211 40 69; Pahlavon Mahmud; dm US$6-7) Was repeatedly closed when we visited but gets good reports from readers.

**Zafarbek** (☎ 375 71 85; zafar22@intal.uz; Toshpolatov 28; s/d US$15/30 ) Not thrilling but the pink rooms get the job done.

**Mirzoboshi** (☎ 375 27 53; mirzaboshi@inbox.ru; Pahlavon Mahmud 1; 2-bed & 4-bed dm US$10) Is a mud- and brick-walled B&B located right in the heart of the Ichon-Qala across from Katya the camel's lair; the entrance is around the back. You essentially move in with the family by occupying one of the two dorm rooms. Budget travellers are welcome to roll out a mattress and sleeping bag on the floor of the *aivan* over the courtyard, which has a magical view of the Juma Minaret. For more privacy opt for their clean new **annexe** (☎ 375 91 88; Toshpolatov 24; s/d from US$15/30; ).

#### MIDRANGE

**our pick** **Shaherezada Khiva** (☎ 375 95 65; www.khivashaherezada.com; Islom Hoja 35; s/d US$25/40; ) Finally, a classy, midrange B&B that truly distinguishes itself from the unimaginative Khivan pack. With beautiful wooden beds and furniture, *tapchan* dining in a remarkable dining room, and large rooms strewn with beautiful carpets and porcelain, the Shaherezada would stand out in B&B-rich Bukhara. The kicker is that every exquisite piece of wood here – including the truly memorable front door – was hand-carved in the workshop of the owner. Where do the superlatives end? Not with this review, we assure you.

**Hotel Khiva** (☎ 375 49 45; Pahlavon Mahmud 1; per person US$26; ) This state-run oddity, which is in fact the 19th-century Mohammed Amin Khan Medressa, is begging for a private owner to take it over and tap its immense potential. OK, so the cramped rooms, former *hujra* (study cells), are supposed to be part of the fun. Less fun are the saggy beds and the complete lack of amenities. Expect poor or no service.

**Malika** (☎ 375 26 65; www.malika-khiva.com; Kadriyakovov 19A; s/d US$35/50) This is Khiva's best true hotel, located just a three-minute walk north of the North Gate. The rooms, set around an interior courtyard, are clean and include twin beds that can be shoved together. It also runs a yurt camp on a lake 20km from Khiva for the same price.

### Eating

The choices are limited, frankly. The chaikhanas in the Ichon-Qala are OK but gouge you a bit on food and especially beer. Leave the Ichon-Qala and prices suddenly halve.

#### ICHON-QALA

**Zerafshan Chaikhana** (Islom Hoja; mains 1500S) This chaikhana in the old stone Tolib Maksum Medressa is blessed with superb atmosphere and a half-decent *plov*.

**Bir Gumbaz** (Pahlavon Mahmud; mains 2000S) A diminutive chaikhana, it's known for tasty soups and its artist's view of Kalta Minor.

**Farruh** (Pahlavon Mahmud; mains 2000S) It's expensive for a chaikhana but you're paying for the atmosphere, which consists of colourfully decorated yurts.

**Restoran Khiva** (Pahlavon Mahmud; meals US$7-8) Located next to the Hotel Khiva in the spacious Matniyaz Divanbeg Medressa, this is probably the pick of the bunch. But it's not cheap and it's often booked out to tour groups.

#### DISHON-QALA

**Parvoz** (Mustaqillik 5; chicken shashlyk 1000S) It's well-worth escaping the hallowed walls of the Ichon-Qala to attend this upscale chaikhana overlooking a *hauz*. It serves filling meals of *manty*, shashlyk, soup and other staples, along with Azia beer at half the price you'll pay inside the North Gate, a few metres away.

**Rustamboy Chaikhana** (A Kariy; mains 1000S) Exit the West Gate, cross the street and you'll bump into a *hauz* flanked by this large chaikhana, serving national dishes.

### Entertainment

**Fashion & traditional dance show** (admission to both shows without/with dinner 7000/10,000S, to 1 show 5000S; dusk) This show takes place in the Alloquli Khan Medressa nightly in the high season, by request at other times. Book tickets through the tourist information office or at the gate, and be sure to ask for a discount, which is often granted to tourists.

### Shopping

**Khiva Silk Carpet Workshop** (☎ 375 72 64; www.khiva.info/khivasilk; Pahlavon Mahmud; 9am-6pm Mon-Sat) Apprentice carpet makers hand-weave silk rugs patterned after Khiva-style majolica tiles, doors and miniature paintings. At this workshop there's lots of natural-dyed silk hanging around and you can watch women work the looms. Unesco sponsored its launch in 2001 and it's now operating on its own. Ask the personable English-speaking manager Jalol for a tour. There is a second workshop in the Kutlimurodinok Medressa, where there are other handicraft workshops as well.

**Khiva Suzani Centre** (Islom Hoja) The British Council and Operation Mercy helped this centre get its wings in 2004. The now-independent centre churns out wonderful handmade silk and *adras* creations.

Other souvenir and craft shops are wedged into many Ichon-Qala attractions. The main drag for craft stalls is the narrow alley that runs west from Islom-Hoja Minaret.

### Getting There & Away

The easiest way to travel between Urgench and Khiva is by marshrutka or shared taxi from the stand by the trolleybus stop, just outside the North Gate (marshrutka/taxi per seat 500/800S, 45 minutes). Keep off the interminable trolleybus (250S, two hours), which terminates inconveniently short of Urgench.

A couple of late-morning to early-afternoon private buses per day depart when full to Tashkent (13,000S, 19 hours) via Samarkand and Bukhara from the Koy-Darvoza Gate, east of the city. If you are heading east your best bet is to go to Urgench and pick up a shared taxi there (see p250).



# KARAKALPAKSTAN

If you're attracted to desolation, you'll love the Republic of Karakalpakstan. The Karakalpaks, who today number only about 400,000 of the republic's 1.2 million population (it's also home to about 400,000 Uzbeks and 300,000 Kazakhs), are a formerly nomadic and fishing people, first recorded in the 16th century. Today they are struggling to recapture a national identity after being collectivised or urbanised in Soviet times. Karakalpak, the official language of the republic, is Turkic, close to Kazakh and less so to Uzbek.

Karakalpakstan was probably at its most prosperous in the 1960s and '70s when the fruits of expanded irrigation from the Amu-Darya were being felt. But today the destruction of the Aral Sea has rendered Karakalpakstan one of Uzbekistan's most depressed regions. The capital, Nukus, gains Tashkent subsidies to keep itself a model city for the region, but a drive into outlying areas reveals a region of dying towns and blighted landscapes.

In a cruel irony, Karakalpaks have been forced to embrace the devil in the sense that cotton – the very crop that devastated the Aral Sea in the first place – is now one of the region's main industries. The government practice of sending children into the cotton fields is alive and well here, as any autumn jaunt into the Karakalpak countryside will prove.

## NUKUS НУКУС

**☎ (3) 61 / pop 230,000**

The isolated Karakalpak capital lies 166km northwest of Urgench, well beyond the reach of most tourist buses. Nukus (Karakalpak: Nökis), a quiet city of tree-lined avenues and nondescript Soviet architecture, is the gateway to the fast-disappearing Aral Sea and home to a remarkable art museum that for some travellers is worth the hardship of getting here.

**NUKUS**

0 — 500 m
0 — 0.3 miles

**INFORMATION**
Jupiter ... 1 A4
National Bank of Uzbekistan ... 2 B3
Post & Telephone Office ... 3 B4
Savitsky Museum ... (see 5)

**SIGHTS & ACTIVITIES**
Natural History Museum ... 4 B3
Savitsky Karakalpakstan Art Museum ... 5 B3

**SLEEPING**
Hotel Nukus ... 6 B3
Hotel Tashkent ... 7 A4

**EATING**
Mona Lisa ... 8 A4
Sheraton Café ... 9 B3

**TRANSPORT**
Airline Booking Office ... 10 B3
Buses to Airport and Train Station ... 11 A3
Shared Taxi Stand ... 12 A3

To Bes Qala Nukus (500m)
Park
To Airport (5km)
Rzaev
Rashidova (Lenina)
Dosnazarov
Dosliq
Tatibayev
Bazaar
Yernazar Alakoz
Pushkin
Gharezsizlik
Lumumba
Karakalpakstan
Government Buildings
To Train Station (3km)
Amir Timur
Berdakha
To Amu Darya (3km); Hojeli (15km); Mizdakhan (19km); Moynaq (210km)
To Long-Distance Bus Station (5km); Urgench (166km)

### Orientation

The main central streets (Karakalpak: *köshesi*) are Karakalpakstan and Gharezsizlik, both ending east at a square surrounded by government buildings. The airport is 6km north of the centre on Dosnazarov, the train station about 3km from the centre at Dosnazarov's south end and the long-distance bus station is 6km south of the centre on Berdakha.

### Information

**Bes Qala Nukus** (☎ 224 51 69; www.kr.uz/besqala, bqntravel2006@rambler.ru; U Yusupov 16) This new travel agency, run by the helpful Tazabay Uteuliev, is your best bet for trips to the Ustyurt Plateau and the Aral Sea, and also visits Moynaq and the *qalas*.

**Jupiter** (Karakalpakstan; per hr 400S; 8am-11pm) Internet. Located next to Tsentr Bank.

**National Bank of Uzbekistan** (Gharezsizlik 52) Cash advances for Visa and American Express cardholders (3% to 4%).

**Post & telephone office** (Karakalpakstan 7; 7am-7pm)

**Savitsky Museum** (☎ 222 88 83; Rzaev 127) Not only is this the best art museum in Central Asia, but it's also effectively one of the best tourist information centres. The multilingual staff here knows the region well and can arrange tours to Midakhan, Moynaq and the Elliq Qala region. The museum also can arranges homestays.

## Sights

### SAVITSKY KARAKALPAKSTAN ART MUSEUM

The **Savitsky Museum** (☎ 222 25 56; www.museum.set global.net; Rzaev 127; admission 7000S, guide 3000S, photos 18,000S; 9am-5pm Mon-Fri, 10am-4pm Sat & Sun) opened in 2002 in a new, marble-fronted building on the north part of town, and houses one of the most remarkable art collections in the former Soviet Union. The museum owns some 90,000 pieces of art, only a fraction of which are actually on display. About half of them were brought here in Soviet times by renegade artist and ethnographer Igor Savitsky. Many of the early-20th-century Russian paintings, which did not conform to Soviet Realism, were banned by Moscow, but found protection in these isolated backwaters.

The museum rotates its huge collection every few months, so you could visit many times and continue to see new works. The 2nd floor contains ethnographic exhibits and the 3rd floor is reserved for the 'lost art'. The museum gift shop sells books on the museum as well as locally made handicrafts.

If you crave more – or if don't have the time or money to see the main collection – the Savitsky Museum has an **extension** (admission 2000S, guide 2000S; 9am-5pm Mon-Fr, 10am-4pm Sat & Sun) on the 2nd floor of the History Museum (see below). Same idea here – the paintings rotate so you never quite know what you're going to see, but you'll rarely be disappointed.

### NATURAL HISTORY MUSEUM

This **museum** (Karakalpakstan; admission US$2, guide US$1; 9am-5pm Mon-Fri & 10am-4pm Sat) is minor league compared to the Savitsky, but still contains a strong exhibition of fauna and flora of the Karakalpakstan region. The very last Turan (Caspian) tiger, killed in 1972, stands stuffed and mounted in a corner. Traditional jewellery, costumes, musical instruments, yurt decorations and local archaeological finds are also on display.

## Festivals & Events

The annual **Pakhta-Bairam** festival takes place on the first Sunday after Karakalpakstan meets its cotton-picking quota, usually in late November or early December. Competitions are held in traditional sports such as wrestling, ram-fighting and cock-fighting. You might also witness those sports on **Navruz** (21 March) or on Day of Memory & Honour (9 May; formerly Victory Day).

## Sleeping & Eating

**Hotel Nukus** (☎ 222 88 38; Lumumba 4; s/d from US$10/20; ) Conveniently located in the heart of town, this old hotel has been spruced up. The renovated 1st-floor rooms, at US$20 per person, are reserved for 'tourists'. The cheaper upstairs rooms with cable TV are a better value. Breakfast is included. The manager, Zerafshon, is a great source of regional transport tips.

**Hotel Tashkent** (☎ 224 18 28; Berdakha 59; per person US$15) This decrepit high-rise at the western end of Karakalpakstan offers spacious, if rundown, rooms that are poor value at the asking price, but you can probably bargain them down. Most rooms have balconies – ask for a room with a 'view' of Nukus.

**Sheraton Café** (☎ 222 87 81; Gharezsizlik 53; mains 2000-3000S) It may not live up to its international hotel namesake, but the Sheraton still serves up an exciting array of European dishes with Russian and Uzbek influences. It has a lively evening atmosphere that can get clouded with smoke and full of wavering, bloodshot Karakalpaks unable to hold their liquor.

**Mona Lisa** (☎ 224 0632; Gharezsizlik 107; mains 3000-5000S) This Georgian home restaurant was popular with NGO staff when there were still NGOs in Uzbekistan. Now it resorts to overcharging tourists. Insist on ordering from the Russian menu, where the prices are half those on the English menu.

The Savitsky Museum has a café serving sandwiches and salads. There is also a handful of good, cheap cafés between the Hotel Tashkent and the central bazaar, 500m north along Yernazar Alaköz.

## Getting There & Away

**AIR**

There are Uzbekistan Airways flights twice daily to/from Tashkent (US$51, 1½ hours). Book tickets at the airport or the **airline booking office** (☎ 222 79 95; Pushkin 43; ⏰ 9am-5pm).

**LAND**

Shared taxis depart for Urgench from the long-distance bus station (6km south of town) and from opposite the bazaar (per seat 8000S, 1½ hours). All go via Beruni in southern Karakalpakstan. There are also several buses per day to Urgench from the bus station (2500S, 2¼ hours). For information on getting to Moynaq, see opposite. For the Turkmen border, see p268.

For buses to Tashkent, your best bet is the private-bus lot in front of the Hotel Nukus. There are two buses to Tashkent per day from there (12,000S, 20 hours), plus one bus to Samarkand (10,000S, 15 hours). Additional buses to Tashkent leave from the long-distance bus station. All go via Bukhara. There are also several weekend buses to Almaty from the Hotel Nukus lot (US$50, two days).

**Train**

A twice-weekly train from Kungrad (100km northwest of Nukus) to Tashkent comes through Nukus (*platskartny* 20,000S, 22 hours), with stops in Urgench, Navoi and Samarkand on the way. There is also a Monday train to Almaty (two days).

## Getting Around

Bus 3 runs between the airport and the bazaar. For the bus station and train station, take marshrutka 20 from opposite the bazaar. A taxi from the airport, train or bus station to the centre is under 2000S.

# AROUND NUKUS

## Mizdakhan

On a hill near Hojeli, 19km west of Nukus are the remains of ancient Mizdakhan, once the second-largest city in Khorezm. Inhabited from the 4th century BC until the 14th century AD, Mizdakhan remained a sacred place even after Timur destroyed it; tombs and mosques continued to be built here right up to the 20th century.

Today the main attraction is a hill littered with those mosques and mausoleums, some ruined, some intact. The most impressive is the restored **Mausoleum of Mazlum Khan Slu**, dating from the 12th to 14th centuries. On the neighbouring hill towards Konye-Urgench are the remains of a 4th- to 3rd-century BC fortress called Gyaur-Qala, which is worth checking out if you missed the forts of Elliq-Qala (p251) to the south.

To get here from Nukus, take a shared taxi from the bazaar (per seat 1000S, 20 minutes), or go to the stadium bus stop (marshrutka 19 goes there) and hop on a marshrutka to Hojeli (300S, 30 minutes). From Hojeli, take the road to Konye-Urgench (Turkmenistan). About 2km along you'll pass a honey-coloured cemetery on your left; another 2km further is Mizdakhan – look for the turquoise dome on the hilltop. The entrance is 500m past the main gate. An ordinary taxi to/from Nukus is 3500S each way.

# MOYNAQ МУЙНАК

**☎ (3) 61 / pop 8000**

Moynaq, 210km north of Nukus, encapsulates more visibly than anywhere the absurd tragedy of the Aral Sea. Once one of the sea's two major fishing ports, it now stands more than 150km from the water. What remains of Moynaq's fishing fleet lies rusting on the sand, beside depressions marking the town's last futile efforts in the early 1980s to keep channels open to the shore.

Moynaq used to be on an isthmus connecting the Ush Say (Tiger's Tail) peninsula to the shore. You can appreciate this on the approach to the town, where the road is raised above the surrounding land. The former shore is about 3km north.

Moynaq's shrinking populace suffers the full force of the Aral Sea disaster, with hotter summers, colder winters, debilitating sand-salt-dust storms, and a gamut of health problems (see p77). Not surprisingly, the mostly Kazakh residents are deserting the town.

## Sights

Poignant reminders of Moynaq's tragedy are everywhere: the sign at the entrance to the town has a fish on it; a fishing boat stands as a kind of monument on a makeshift pedestal near Government House. The local museum in the city hall has some interesting photos of the area prospering before the disaster.

The **beached ships** are hard to find and you may need to ask around. They are a five-minute walk south of the Oybek Hotel, across

**VISITING THE ARAL SEA**

Catching a glimpse of the notorious Aral Sea's new southern shoreline holds no small amount of appeal for adventurous travellers. It's possible, but the least rigourous route is not from Moynaq! It's easier and more scenic to drive northwest along navigable dirt tracks from Kungrad via bird-laden Sudochie Lake, to the desert backwater of Kubla Ustyurt. From there, head north along the tawny, treeless moonscape of the Ustyurt Plateau to the Aral's extreme southwestern shore, about 40km north of Kubla Ustyurt.

Your reward will be superb, clifftop views of the desertified former seabed and the thin blue line of the Aral's new shoreline in the distance. A few kilometres east, rough tracks lead down from the plateau and on to the new shoreline, where you can swim and camp. This descent is tricky to find so your driver best know what he's doing. You can return the way you came or, from the top of the descent, loop southeast along the Ustyurt Plateau to Moynaq.

It's also possible to do this loop in reverse, starting from Moynaq. But most drivers in Moynaq – including, we have heard, some guys who make the trip on Russian Ural motorcycles – will try to take you due north to the southern shoreline of the sea's eastern half. This route involves a tough, 185km slog along the Aral's former seabed just to reach the first traces of murky, shallow water. And the seabed is impassable if it rains.

No matter how you go, it's essential that your driver have a 4WD vehicle and intimate knowledge of the tracks heading north from Moynaq and Kungrad. Of course you are much less likely to get lost if you hire a travel agency, such as Bes Qala Nukus (p258).



the main road and beyond the collection of homes. To see more ships, take a right turn up the road that is 250m before the hotel. Before you reach the war memorial, peer out over the former sea and you'll spot some ships about 1km away, across the grassy steppe.

If you can't make it out to Moynaq to see the ships yourself, the satellite images on **Google Earth** (www.earth.google.com) are almost as eerie.

From the **war memorial**, which once had great views of the Aral Sea, you can spot a lake southeast of town, created in an attempt to restore the formerly mild local climate. It didn't quite work, but it's at least given the locals a source of recreation.

## Sleeping

**Oybek** (☎ 222 18 68; r with shared bathroom 6000S) There's no electricity, no running water, and it looks like a giant poo volcano erupted in the shared bathroom. But the champagne brunch is just divine. Not really. Fortunately they keep the large rooms much cleaner than the bathroom. Ask for directions because it has no address and no sign.

Readers recommend **Aitjanov Sagitjan** (☎ 351 72 12; aitsagit@rambler.rup; Amir Timur 2; per person US$25) for homestays. He is based in Nukus so contact him a few days in advance to make arrangements.

Eating can be a problem. See what the Hotel Oybek can whip up, or try to finagle an invite into a local's home. It's not a bad idea to bring some snacks along.

## Getting There & Away

The bus station is at the south end of the long main street. Two decrepit and over-crowded buses run daily between Moynaq and Nukus (2000S, 3¾ hours). They depart Nukus from the long-distance bus station at 9am and 3pm, passing by the Hotel Tashkent about 10 minutes later. The return buses from Moynaq are also at 9am and 3pm. You can also take an even more crowded bus to Kungrad (Qongirat) and change there.

It's swifter to take a shared taxi to Kungrad from opposite the bazaar in Nukus, and transfer in Kungrad to another shared taxi. This will cost 8000S to 10,000S in total and save you two hours of driving time.

A day trip from Nukus in an ordinary taxi costs about US$60, US$100 from Urgench.

# UZBEKISTAN DIRECTORY

## ACCOMMODATION

All accommodation rates are for rooms with private bathroom unless otherwise stated. The B&B scene in Uzbekistan has taken off more than in any other Central Asian republic. The best are in Bukhara where European consultants have been called in to promote

**STREET NAME CHANGES**

In trying to erase the Soviet period, streets everywhere were given new, suitably Uzbek names shortly after independence (the exceptions were streets named after revered Russian writers and cosmonauts, such as Chekhov, Pushkin, Tolstoy and of course Gagarin). A decade-and-a-half later all the maps have been changed, but the new names still haven't really stuck, at least in big cities such as Tashkent and Samarkand.

We use the new street names throughout this chapter, but where relevant we have included the old names next to the new names on maps. If your taxi driver doesn't know the new street name, try the old name.



the expansion and improvement of B&Bs. Uzbekistan's first community-based tourism programme opened in the Nuratinsky Mountains in 2006 (p236). Yurtstays are possible too (below).

Another organisation that advertises community-based tourism programs across Uzbekistan on its website is Orexca.com.

## ACTIVITIES

**Camel trekking**, usually combined with a yurtstay, is the most intriguing activity, though most trips are relatively short jaunts around one of the yurt camps in Lake Aidarkul (p236) or Ayaz-Qala (p251). There are nomads lurking in that there desert, and they can be found. Whether they'll invite you in for a homestay is another matter, but you might ask. Talk to East Line Tours in Bukhara for ideas (p240). It is also the authority on **bird-watching** (www.birdwatching-uzbekistan.com), of which Uzbekistan is meant to offer the best in Central Asia.

Other popular outdoor activities are **trekking**, **rafting** and **skiing**, all remarkably accessible from Tashkent (see p91 and p213).

## EMBASSIES & CONSULATES

### Uzbek Embassies in Central Asia

Uzbekistan has embassies in Kazakhstan (p178), Kyrgyzstan (p345), Tajikistan (p392) and Turkmenistan (p436). A complete list of Uzbek missions abroad is on the website of the **Ministry of Foreign Affairs** (www.mfa.uz).

### Uzbek Embassies & Consulates

**Afghanistan** (☎ 93-20-230 01 24; Kabul, Vazir Akbar Khan, 13th St, 3rd Row, House 14)
**Azerbaijan** (☎ 99-412-97 25 49; fax 97 25 48; 1st Hwy, 9th Alley 437, Batamdart, 370021, Baku)
**China** (☎ 86-10-6532 6304/5; fax 6532 6304; Beijing 100600, Sanlitun, Beixiao gie 11)
**France** (☎ 331-5330 0353; fax 5330 0354; 22 rue d'Aguesseau, 75008, Paris)
**Germany** (☎ 49-30-394 09 80; www.uzbekistan.de; Perleberger Strasse 62, Berlin 10559) Consulate in Frankfurt.
**Malaysia** (☎ 603-42-53 24 06; N. 2, Jalan 12, Taman Tun Abdul Razak, 68000 Ampang, Selangor Darul Ehsan, Malaysia)
**Pakistan** (☎ 92-51-226 47 46; fax 226 17 37; House 2, 21st St, F8/3, Kohistan Rd, Islamabad) Consulate in Karachi.
**Russia** (☎ 7-095-230 00 76; fax 238 8 18; Pogorelskiy pereulok 12, Moscow, 109017)
**Turkey** (☎ 90-312-441 38 71; fax 442 70 58; Sancak mahallesi 211, Sokak 3, 06550 Yildiz-Cankaya, Ankara) Consulate in İstanbul.
**UK** (☎ 44-020-7229 7679; www.uzbekembassy.org; consular section, 41 Holland Park W11 3RP, London; ⏲ 10am-1pm Mon, Wed & Fri)
**USA** (☎ 1-202-887 5300; www.uzbekistan.org; consular section, 1746 Massachusetts Ave NW, Washington DC 20036; ⏲ 10am-noon Mon-Fri) Consulate-General in New York.

### Embassies & Consulates in Uzbekistan

The following are all located in Tashkent (☎ 371 or 71; see Map pp196–7). Hours of operation listed below are for visa applications only. For information on visas for onward travel see p265.

**Afghanistan** (☎ 134 84 32; Murtazayev 6/84; ⏲ 9am-2pm Mon-Fri)
**Azerbaijan** (☎ 173 94 65; Halqlar Dustligi 25)
**China** (☎ 133 80 88, consul 133 47 18; Gulomova 79; ⏲ 9am-noon Mon, Wed & Fri)
**France** (☎ main 133 53 84, citizens' services 133 0583; Akhunbabayev 25)
**Georgia** (☎ 162 62 43; Mukhitdinova 6)
**Germany** (☎ 120 84 40; www.taschkent.diplo.de; Rashidova 15)
**India** (☎ 140 09 83; www.indembassy.uz; Kara-Bulak 15-16; ⏲ 9.30am-noon Mon-Fri)
**Indonesia** (☎ 132 02 36; Gulomova 73)
**Iran** (☎ 68 69 68; Parkent 20; ⏲ 9am-noon Mon-Thu)
**Israel** (☎ 120 58 08; www.tashkent.mfa.gov.il; Abdulla Qahhor 4)
**Italy** (☎ 152 11 19; Yusuf Khos Khodjib 40)
**Japan** (☎ 120 80 60; 1-28 Azimova)
**Kazakhstan** (☎ 152 15 54; kazembassy@kaz.uz; Chekhov 23; ⏲ 9am-noon Mon-Fri)
**Kyrgyzstan** (☎ 133 89 41; krembas@globalnet.uz; Samatova 30; ⏲ 9-11.30am & 3-4pm Mon-Fri)

**Pakistan** (☎ 398 21 73; www.geocities.com/pakembtash; Abdur Rakhmonov [Sofiyskaya] 15; applications Tue 10-11am, pickup Wed 11am) Take trolleybus 2 from Chorsu Market.
**Russia** (☎ 120 35 19; Nukus 83; 9.30am-1pm Mon, Wed & Fri)
**Tajikistan** (☎ 54 99 66; Abdulla Qahhor katta VI 61; 10am-noon Mon-Fri)
**Turkey** (☎ 113 03 00; Gulomova 87)
**Turkmenistan** (☎ 120 52 78; Katta Mirobod 10; 11am-1pm Mon-Fri)
**UK** (☎ 120 78 52; www.britishembassy.gov/uzbekistan; Gulomova 67)
**USA** (☎ 120 54 50; www.usembassy.uz; Moyqorghon katta V 3) Bus 95 goes near its new location north of the TV Tower.

## FESTIVALS & EVENTS

There are colourful celebrations throughout the country during the vernal equinox festival of **Navrus**; (celebrated on 21 March). Festivities typically involve parades, fairs, music, dancing in the streets, plenty of food and in some places a rogue game of *kupkari*. Samarkand has a good one (p228), but the most famous is probably the Unesco-supported festival in Boysun, between Termiz and Samarkand (not covered in this book).

## HOLIDAYS

**January 1** New Year's Day.
**March 8** International Women's Day.
**March 21** Navruz.
**May 9** Day of Memory and Honour (formerly Victory Day).
**September 1** Independence Day.
**October 1** Teachers' Day.
**December 8** Constitution Day.

For information on Islamic holidays observed in Central Asia, see p449.

## INTERNET ACCESS

Internet cafés are found in most places travellers go, although access is annoyingly slow outside a handful of spots in Tashkent. A recent government initiative brought free wi-fi access to about a dozen restaurants in Tashkent. Wi-fi is rare outside of Tashkent.

## INTERNET RESOURCES

For tourist information the best sites are those of travel agencies **Advantour** (www.advantour.com), p199 and **Silk/Sogda Tour** (www.silktour.uz), p225. Another good site with lots of travel articles is www.sairamtour.com. For news, see below.

## MEDIA

No level of independent media exists in Uzbekistan, where all newspaper, TV and radio coverage is government sanctioned before going public. Anything independent dealing with Uzbekistan is online and offshore.

The government blocks politically sensitive Uzbek-language websites, but you can access most English-language sites, regardless of political bent, from within the country. You should be able to access all of the following except neweurasia from Uzbek internet cafés.

**http://uzbekistan.neweurasia.net** Excellent blog discussing hot topics of the day, with extensive links to other useful sites.
**www.crisisgroup.org** Analysis and lengthy reports on the latest Uzbek political developments.
**www.enews.fergana.ru** Watchdog website that focuses primarily on politics.
**www.eurasianet.org/resource/uzbekistan** Volume of articles plummeted after site sponsor Open Society Institute was kicked out of Uzbekistan.
**www.rferl.org** Probably the best source of objective hard news on Uzbekistan.

## MONEY

Few currencies burn a hole in your pocket like the Uzbek sum. The highest Uzbek note (1000S) is worth only about US$0.80. One US$100 bill turns into a satchel full of ragged bills, usually tied together with a rubber band.

Reform policies have brought the black market and bank rates to similar levels, so there is no longer any desperate need to change on the black market, although this may be the quickest (or only) way of getting sum for US dollars, especially in the provinces. You can usually find black-market money swappers working the bazaars. If you have to go this route, be wary of corrupt police, who may demand 'fines'.

Credit cards are accepted at an increasing number of midrange and top-end hotels. A select few ATMs can be found in Tashkent (p199).

In the provinces, MasterCard users should look for Asaka Bank for cash advances, while Visa and Amex holders will usually (but not always) be able to get cash advanced at **National Bank of Uzbekistan** (NBU; full branch list at http://eng.nbu.com/branches). The NBU is also usually the best bet for cashing travellers cheques. Be sure to list your travellers cheques on your customs declaration form or you won't be able to cash them.

The US dollar is king in Uzbekistan; bring plenty. Euros and pounds warrant poorer rates and are more difficult to exchange outside of Tashkent. At the time of research, the exchange rates were as follows:

| Country | Unit | | Sum |
|---|---|---|---|
| Afghanistan | 1Afg | = | 24.76 |
| Australia | A$1 | = | 967 |
| euro zone | €1 | = | 1629 |
| Kazakhstan | 1T | = | 9.67 |
| Kyrgyzstan | 1som | = | 31.93 |
| Tajikistan | 1TJS | = | 360.93 |
| Turkmenistan | 100M | = | 28.81 |
| UK | UK£1 | = | 2412 |
| USA | US$1 | = | 1238 |

Hotels, guides and other businesses catering to tourists often list prices in US dollars, but (in theory) it is illegal to pay for goods and services in anything besides Uzbek sum. This book follows local convention in listing most prices besides hotels in Uzbek sum.

## POST

An airmail postcard costs 350S, a 20g airmail letter costs 450S and a 1kg package costs 7810S. The postal service is not renowned for speed or reliability in delivering letters or parcels; send your friends two postcards and hope they will receive at least one. International couriers are listed under Post in the Tashkent section (p199).

## REGISTRATION

Checking into a hotel means automatic registration. Make sure you get a registration slip (staff sometimes need reminding) as these are often asked for when departing the country.

If you spend a night in a private home you are supposed to be registered with the local Office of Visas & Registration (OVIR), but as this can create more problems than it solves for you and your hosts, it's probably best not to. Instead, ask the next hotel you stay at to fill in those missing days on your docket. Keep in mind that there are fines – or more likely bribes – to be paid if you get caught unregistered.

For more questions or details, contact your embassy or the Tashkent central **OVIR office** (☎ 132 65 70; Uzbekistan 49A).

## TELEPHONE

Mobile phone operators issue local SIM cards free-of-charge with the purchase of minimum US$5 prepaid cards. Contrary to popular belief it is legitimate for foreigners to buy these. The main office of **Coscom** (Map pp196-7; ☎ 120 72 65; www.coscom.uz; Vokhidova 38, Tashkent; ⏰ 8am-7pm) has English-speaking staff that will change your phone settings to English. Domestic calls with mobile operators Coscom, Beeline or MTS cost US$0.04 to US$0.05 per minute. International text messages only cost about US$0.03 per message.

Uzbekistan's antiquated telephone system is creaky but functional. Per-minute calls from the central telephone offices in Tashkent and most other major cities are: to the UK 1150S, to the USA 1250S and to Australia 1750S. Post offices and various stores and kiosks sell a range of cards good for discounted long-distance calls out of Uzbekistan. Most internet cafés listed in this book (at least those in the big cities) offer Skype.

A better option is to buy a Verizon/MCI prepaid calling card, which can be used outside Uzbekistan as well. A 100-unit card costs US$30 and is good for about 73 minutes to the USA or Europe (US$0.41 per minute). A better-value 600-unit card is also available. They are distributed by InterConcepts Incorporated – contact **Charles Rudd** (☎ 139 13 02; ruddcl@interconcepts.com).

Within Uzbekistan, dialling local is easy – just dial the seven-digit number or, if that fails, the last six or five digits of the number.

Dialling another city is harder. From mobile phones, dial the full Uzbek country and city (or mobile phone) code (☎ +998-XX) followed by a *seven-digit* number (if the number you're dialling lists only six digits, simply add a ☎ 2); if that doesn't work dial ☎ 8 instead of ☎ +998; if that still doesn't work try dialling the number with no code – you may unknowingly be within the limits of the city you are dialling.

From landlines, dial ☎ 83 followed by the regional code. If that doesn't work, drop the ☎ 3, which may have been phased out by the time your read this.

Calling Uzbek mobile phones is trickier and depends on the carrier. The code for Unitel is

> **INCOMING AREA CODES**
>
> When calling from outside Uzbekistan dial ☎ +998, the area code marked in the individual sections (without the ☎ 3), and the seven-digit number.

☎ 90, for MTS ☎ 98 and for Coscom ☎ 93. To dial, for instance, a Coscom phone from outside Uzbekistan or from another mobile carrier, you'd dial ☎ +998-93-XXX XXXX; to dial it from a landline within Uzbekistan you'd dial ☎ 8-593-XXX XXXX; and to dial it locally or from another Coscom phone you'd just dial ☎ XXX XXXX.

To call out of Uzbekistan dial ☎ 8, wait for a tone, then dial ☎ 10.

## TRAVEL PERMITS

Border permits are required for all mountain areas near the Tajik and Kyrgyz borders, including most of Ugam-Chatkal National Park (p213), the Zarafshan and Hissar Mountains (p232), and Zaamin National Park (not covered in this book). Secure these with the help of a travel agency before setting out.

## VISAS

Uzbek visa rules change frequently and depend entirely on the state of the country's relations with the US and EU. At the time of writing, citizens of the following countries were technically exempt from letters of invitation (LOIs): Austria, Belgium, France, Germany, Italy, Japan, Latvia, Malaysia, Spain, Switzerland and the UK. Everybody else needs LOIs, as do citizens of the above countries who are applying for visas outside their country of citizenship. No matter what your citizenship, it will always be much easier and quicker to obtain an Uzbek visa with an LOI. See the website of the travel agency **Advantour** (www.advantour.com) for updated LOI requirements.

Any Uzbek travel agency can arrange LOI support, but most demand that you also purchase a minimum level of services – usually hotel bookings for at least three nights. A few agencies provide LOI support for a fee with no strings attached, including Arostr and Stantours (p199). Allow two weeks for LOI processing or pay double for four- to five-day processing.

The standard tourist visa is a 30-day, single-entry visa. They cost a flat US$100 for US citizens, slightly less for most other nationalities. Multiple entry costs an additional US$10 per entry. Tourist visas lasting more than 30 days are almost impossible to obtain. Three-day transit visas cost US$30 and require a visa for an onward country (eg Tajikistan).

Visa processing time depends upon the embassy. London, Dushanbe, Bishkek and Almaty can issue on-the-spot visas with an LOI. It may be possible to pick up your visa upon arrival at Tashkent International Airport if there is no Uzbek embassy in your country of residence, but you'll need full visa support for this from a travel agent.

### Visa Extensions

A one-week visa extension costing about US$75 is available from the Ministry of Foreign affairs booth at Tashkent International Airport. Travel agents will be reluctant to perform this service so go there on your own. Longer extensions are time-consuming, expensive and involve much red tape. Many frustrated travellers give up and go to neighbouring Kazakhstan or Kyrgyzstan and buy a new visa. If you insist on trying, seek support from a Tashkent-based travel agency.

### Visas for Onward Travel

For contact details of embassies and consulates in Tashkent, see p262. Contact David at Stantours (p199) for updated information and honest advice. If you can avoid purchasing LOI support, Stantours will tell you.

**Afghanistan** A 30-day visa costing US$40 is issued on the spot.

**Azerbaijan** A 30-day visa costing US$40 is issued in maximum three days. No rush service available. An LOI is technically needed but it's possible to get one without.

**China** A 60-day visa costs US$30 for five-day processing time, double that for same-day processing. An LOI helps here.

**Georgia** No visas required for US, EU, Canadian or Japanese citizens staying 90 days or fewer. A 90-day visa for Australians, Kiwis and South Africans costs about US$40.

**India** A six-month multiple-entry visa costs US$60 for US citizens, US$40 for UK, EU, Australian citizens; seven-day minimum processing time.

**Iran** This embassy can be difficult but travellers report recent service improvements. First you must apply for an authorisation through an Iranian agent such as www.iranianvisa.com. From Uzbekistan this costs $US39/72 for regular/rush service. When this finally arrives (check to make sure it has), you can apply for a 30-day tourist visa (valid for three months), which costs $US45 for seven- to 10-day processing, or $US72 for three- to seven-day processing. Women must have hair covered in application photos.

**Kazakhstan** A 30-day visa (US$35) takes two days to process. An LOI is needed for multiple entry or for visas longer than 30 days.

**Kyrgyzstan** A 30-day visa costs US$40 for same-day processing. No LOI needed for US, Commonwealth, and most EU citizens.

**Pakistan** A 30- or 60-day visa costs about US$72 for EU citizens, US$120 for Americans and US$42 for Australians. An LOI is recommended but not mandatory. Two-day processing.
**Russia** Present original travel voucher and booking confirmation to apply for a 30-day tourist visa. Prices for 10-day processing are about US$70 for US citizens and about US$30 to US$50 for EU and Australian citizens. Pay $25 extra for five-day processing and US$85 extra for same-day rush. Be prepared for long queues.
**Tajikistan** If at all possible get your Tajik visa elsewhere because this embassy is a nightmare. One-week/two-week/one-month visa costs US$30/40/50. Allow 12 days to process or pay double for a rush, which takes two to five days. All nationalities require an LOI. Surly staff will direct you towards their favoured travel agent – do not listen to them!
**Turkmenistan** Five-day transit visas issued without LOI for US$46; allow 10 days to process. Arrive two hours early to put your name on a waiting list. You can keep your passport during processing, but when you pick up the visa you must show a visa for an onward country (eg Azerbaijan). Tourist visas require difficult-to-obtain LOIs and cost US$45 to US$90, with one- to three-day processing (see p439). You'll also need to present a complete itinerary.

## VOLUNTEERING

The expulsion of most Western NGOs in 2005–2006 put a damper on volunteering opportunities in Uzbekistan. That said, the few do-good groups that remain in Uzbekistan will always have a need for self-starters with language skills. Mike Humphrey (scout_pmh@yahoo.com) works with the local branch of Sisters of Mother Teresa, and may have ideas for travellers who are serious about helping the poor or local schools.

The volunteer situation is bound to change depending on the state of Uzbekistan's relations with the West. A good person to contact for the latest news on the comings and goings of charities and volunteer groups is Kevin Glass (director@tashschool.org), director of the **Tashkent International School** (Map pp196-7; ☎ 37-191 96 67; www.tashschool.org; Sarikulskaya 38).

# TRANSPORT IN UZBEKISTAN

## GETTING THERE & AWAY

### Entering Uzbekistan

As long as your papers are in order, entering Uzbekistan should be no sweat. You will be asked to fill out two identical customs declarations forms, one to turn in and one to keep (which will be handed in upon departure). The customs form is necessary for changing travellers cheques and will smooth your departure, so don't lose it. Be sure to declare every cent of every type of money you bring in; travellers have reported being hassled for the most minor discrepancies, especially at land border crossings. See Scams in the Tashkent section (p199) for airport concerns.

### Air

If arriving by air, your grand entrance into Uzbekistan will most likely occur at **Tashkent International Airport** (☎ 37-40 28 01, VIP 37-54 86 48). A few flights from Russia arrive in regional hubs such as Samarkand, Bukhara and Urgench.

The numerous *aviakassa* (private ticket kiosks) scattered around major cities can help book international tickets on Uzbekistan Airways and other airlines. For a full list of airlines flying to/from Uzbekistan, see p209.

Uzbekistan Airways has convenient booking offices in Tashkent (p208) and all regional hubs. A second international booking office in Tashkent is located on the ground floor of the international terminal.

Sample fares on Uzbekistan Airways to/from Tashkent at the time of research were (one way/return) Almaty US$185/330; Ashgabat US$170/279; Astana US$230/396; Baku US$324/375; Bangkok US$540/622; Bishkek US$145/259; Delhi US$345/460; Frankfurt US$560/755; London US$560/780; Moscow US$270/429; Paris US$560/760. It's not a bad idea to reconfirm international tickets with Uzbekistan Airways a week or two before your departure in high season.

There is no departure tax for domestic or international flights from Uzbekistan.

### Land

#### BORDER CROSSINGS

#### To/From Afghanistan

The Friendship Bridge linking Termiz with northern Afghanistan was finally opened to tourist traffic in 2005. While Afghan officials seem happy with this arrangement, the Uzbeks frequently close their side of the border for security or other concerns. Contact OVIR (p199) or a reliable travel agency in Tashkent before attempting this border crossing, which may require – and in any case will be easier with – official (written) permission from the Uzbek government.

To get to the border from Termiz, take marshrutka 21 from Yubileny Bazaar (200S, 20 minutes). The bridge is 10km south of town. From the Afghan side you're looking at about a US$10 taxi ride to Mazar-e-Sharif.

#### To/From Kazakhstan

Despite their very long common border there are just two main places to cross. The more common is the Chernyaevka crossing between Tashkent and Shymkent. By all accounts this is a chaotic, unpredictable border; some travellers report breezing through, others report waits of up to six hours. If it looks bad it may be worth paying a US$10 to US$15 fast-track fee to one of the 'facilitators' hanging about on both sides of the border. There are reports of corruption on both sides, but especially on the Kazakh side.

It's a 6000S cab ride to the border from central Tashkent, or you can take a cheaper shared taxi or marshrutka from Yunusabadsky Bazaar. You'll have to walk the final 200m through a series of check posts. The border is open 7am to 9pm (Tashkent time). On the Kazakh side, pick up a shared taxi or marshrutka to Turkistan or Shymkent (US$4). There is also a Tuesday Tashkent–Almaty train (55,000S, 25 hours) that originates in Nukus.

The other crossing is by train or road between Karakalpakstan and Beyneu in western Kazakhstan. For full details on this crossing and more information on crossing into Uzbekistan from Kazakhstan, see p184. Uzbek customs is in Kungrad, a good 225km southeast of the border crossing. The daily trains from Kungrad to Beyneu leave at 7.40am (10 hours).

#### To/From Kyrgyzstan

The only border crossings into Kyrgyzstan that are open to foreigners are at Uchkurgan (northeast of Namangan); Dustlyk (Dostyk), between Andijon and Osh; and Khanabad (between Andijon and Jalal-Abad). These crossings are generally hassle-free, although they have become more strict since the Andijon incident in May 2005. Shared taxis and minibuses are plentiful on the Kyrgyz side of any crossing you take. Most travellers use the Osh crossing. Take a marshrutka from Andijon to Dustlyk (see p222), walk across the border and pick up public transport on the other side for the short trip to Osh.

Thrice-daily Tashkent–Bishkek buses (US$8, 12 hours) pass through a long section of Kazakhstan and you will need a transit visa. You must catch this bus on the Kazakh side of the Chernyaevka border crossing north of Tashkent. For more information see 'To/From Kazakhstan', left.

#### To/From Russia

From Moscow, a thrice-weekly train departs at 7.35pm, arriving in Tashkent about 66 hours later (hard sleeper/soft sleeper US$130/200). The return train leaves Tashkent at 11.35pm.

There are also daily trains between Tashkent and southern Russia (Saratov or Ufa) that go via Kazakhstan.

#### To/From Tajikistan

Most travellers making a beeline from Tashkent to Dushanbe drive to Khojand via the pain-free Oybek border crossing and then take a Tajik domestic flight. To get to this border from Tashkent take a marshrutka or shared taxi from Qoylok Bazaar to Bekobod and get off at Oybek (marshrutka/taxi per seat 2500/5000S, 1½ hours), about 35km shy of Bekobod, near Chanak village. The border post is visible from the road. Once across the border take a taxi to Khojand (US$10) or a taxi to nearby Bostan (5TJS) and then a minibus to Khojand. An ordinary taxi between Tashkent and Oybek costs about US$30.

The other main border crossings are Samarkand–Penjikent and Denau–Tursanzade. Marshrutkas to the Penjikent border depart regularly from the Registan stop in Samarkand (1500S, 45 minutes). Walk across the border and pick up a shared or ordinary taxi (per seat US$2) for the 22km ride to Penjikent. You may have to remind the Tajik border guards to stamp your passport.

Denau is a two-hour drive from Termiz, a five-hour drive from Samarkand, or a six-hour drive from Bukhara, with regular shared taxis making the trip from each city. Shared taxis from Samarkand (per seat 20,000S) and Bukhara (25,000S) do not go through Termiz. From Termiz, there are regular marshrutkas to Denau (departing from Yubileney Bazaar) and a morning train to the border town of Sariosiyo (5000S, four hours). In Tajikistan, a taxi from Tursanzade to Dushanbe takes 45 minutes and costs US$10.

For info on getting to Khojand via Konibodom, see p396.

### To/From Turkmenistan

The three main border points are reached from Bukhara, Khiva/Urgench and Nukus. You have to pay US$12 to enter Turkmenistan (US$10 entrance fee, US$2 bank charge) and you need dollars for this. Each crossing requires a potentially sweltering walk of 10 to 20 minutes across no-man's-land.

From Bukhara, regular shared taxis (per seat 2000S, 40 minutes) and marshrutkas (1000S) make the trip from the Kolkhozny Bazaar to Olot (or Qarakol), about 7km short of the border, from where you'll have to hire your own car for about 2000S. A shared taxi from there to Turkmenabat should cost you around US$0.50 for the 40-minute drive. Readers report that this border crossing closes for lunch between 1pm and 2pm.

From Khiva or Urgench it costs about 15,000S to hire a car to the border, from where it's a short, US$1 taxi ride to Dashogus. Alternatively, you can take a cheaper shared taxi or marshrutka to Shovot and catch a taxi there for about 3000S. In Khiva, shared taxis to Shovot leave from a stand about 100m east of the East Gate; in Urgench they leave from the bazaar.

From Nukus it's about a 10,000S, 30km ride to the Konye-Urgench border crossing. Alternatively, take public transport to Hojeli (see p260) and take a shared taxi from Hojeli to the border (per seat 1000S). Once you've walked across the border you can pick up a shared taxi to Konye-Urgench (US$0.75).

For information on exiting Turkmenistan, see p396).

## GETTING AROUND

### Air

Most routes along the tourist trail are well-served by domestic flights to/from Tashkent, if not to each other (see p208). If you book fewer than three days in advance, Uzbekistan Airways will usually say the plane is full. In that case, paying a 'finder's fee' (to the ticket agent or touts on the street) of US$5 to US$20 should free up a blocked seat. Buying a ticket for a later date and flying stand-by often works too.

### Bus & Marshrutka

Clapped-out state buses are fast disappearing from Uzbek roads, undercut by a boom in private buses that do not keep schedules and leave when full. They are newer and more comfortable, but can be slow as drivers and touts are preoccupied with over-selling seats and transporting cargo and contraband.

Marshrutkas take the form of 11- to 14-seat vans, or seven-seat Daewoo Damas minvans. For simplicity's sake, we do not distinguish between the two types in this chapter.

### Car

Driving your own car is possible, provided you have insurance from your home country and a valid international driving licence. Be prepared for the same kind of hassles you'll experience anywhere in the former Soviet Union: lots of random stops and traffic cops fishing for bribes. There are no car-rental agencies. In Uzbekistan, motorists drive on the right and seat belts are not at all required.

### Shared & Ordinary Taxi

Shared taxis save tons of time but are of course more costly than buses. They ply all the main intercity routes and also congregate at most border points. They leave when full from set locations – usually from near bus stations – and run all day and often through the night. Prices fluctuate throughout the day/week/month/year, increasing towards the evening, on weekends and on holidays. See p472 for more shared-taxi tips. Ordinary taxis give you the freedom to stop and explore but obviously cost more money.

### Trains

Trains are perhaps the most comfortable and safest, if hardly the fastest, method of intercity transport. That said, the new 'high-speed' commuter trains between Tashkent, Samarkand and Bukhara, with airplane-style seating, are not much slower than a shared taxi and a *lot* more comfortable. Book them a couple days in advance, as they are popular.

Other long-haul trains are of the deliberate but comfortable Soviet variety, with *platskartny* (hard sleeper), *kupeyny* (soft sleeper) and sometimes dirt-cheap *obshy* (general) compartments available.

# Kyrgyzstan Кыргызстан

Kyrgyzstan is tucked into Central Asia's geographical vortex amid a massive knot of colliding mountain ranges. Monster mountains and their associated scraggy valleys, glaciers, gorges and ice-blue lakes dominate over 90% of the country.

Keen on trekking or horse riding? Just pick a range – there's plenty to choose from – and head to the *jailoos,* high-altitude summer pastures of glorious, untrammelled alpine scenery. In true nomadic style, spend the nights camped under a star-crowded sky or bed down in a yurt. Be warned though, the Kyrgyz are renowned for their hospitably and guests are often treated to fermented mare's milk and bowls of fresh yogurt.

Indeed, nomadic traditions are alive and kicking in Kyrgyzstan. You can take to the hills around Lake Issyk-Köl, the earth's second-largest alpine lake, with a trained eagle to hunt rabbit or cheer wildly alongside the locals during a game of *kok boru,* a ferocious battle in which mounted riders wrestle one another for the corpse of a headless goat.

Cash-strapped locals, struggling to eek out a living in postcommunist Asia, have turned to tourism for help. The creation of sustainable projects are revolutionising budget travel, pushing Kyrgyzstan to the forefront of community tourism and bringing in a little extra money for families. By contrast, now that the long, unyielding arm of Russian law is no longer on the scene, corruption by officials and political turmoil are part of daily life.

Kyrgyzstan may be small, it may be often overlooked but, just like the players in a game of *kok boru,* this tenacious nation packs a powerful wallop and may yet run off with the prize as Central Asia's most appealing and accessible republic.

**FAST FACTS**

- **Area** 198,500 sq km
- **Capital** Bishkek
- **Country Code** ☎ 996
- **Famous For** Towering mountains, eagle hunting, nomadic yurts
- **Languages** Kyrgyz, Russian
- **Money** Kyrgyz som: US$1 = 38.77som, €1 = 50.7
- **Phrases** *Salam.* (Hello.); *Rahmat.* (Thank you); *Jaqshi.* (Good.)
- **Population** 5.2 million (2006 estimate)

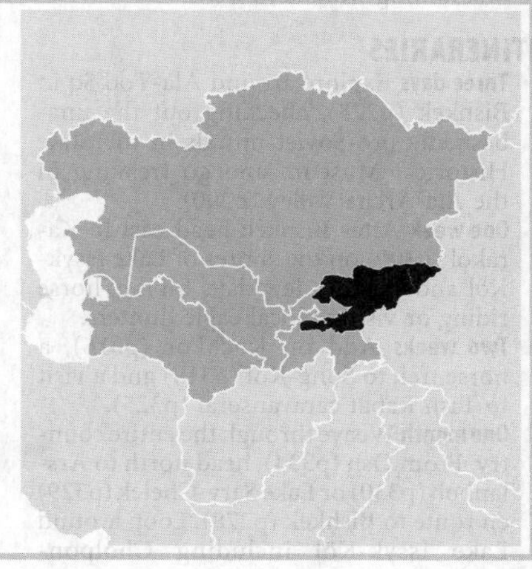

KYRGYZSTAN

**HOW MUCH?**

- Snickers bar US$0.40
- 100km bus ride US$1.70
- One-minute phone call to the USA US$0.63
- Internet per hour US$0.75-1
- Kyrgyz hat US$3-6
- 1L of bottled water US$0.40
- Bottle of beer US$1
- Shashlyk US$0.80
- 1L of petrol US$0.60

## HIGHLIGHTS

- **Horse treks** (p343) See the Kyrgyz countryside at its best by riding high into the mountains and galloping across summer pastures.
- **Lake Issyk-Köl** (p294) Hemmed in by mountains this bizarrely un-freezeable lake is the country's premier attraction.
- **Altyn Arashan** (p306) Breath-taking scenery, steaming hot pools and the first glimpse of the secret Ala-Köl lake makes for great trekking.
- **Osh** (p334) For centuries Silk Road traders have haggled their way from one stall to the next in a bazaar that locals claim is older than Rome – join them.
- **Arslanbob** (p330) Go nuts in the world's largest walnut forest on a network of blossoming woodland treks.

## ITINERARIES

- **Three days** Explore around Ala-Too Sq in Bishkek (p278), checking out the unabashedly pro-Soviet murals in the State Historical Museum and go trekking in the Ala-Archa Valley (p290).
- **One week** After Bishkek head east to Karakol (p300) on the shores of Lake Issyk-Köl and spend a few days hiking, horse riding or visiting local eagle hunters.
- **Two weeks** Add on Kochkor (p316), a horse trek to Song-Köl (p318) and a visit to Tash Rabat caravanserai (p325).
- **One month** Weave through the entire country. From Osh (p334), head north to Arslanbob (p330) or Lake Sary-Chelek (p329) en route to Bishkek (p278). Loop around Lake Issyk-Köl including Cholpon-Ata (p296) before continuing to Kochkor and Naryn (p319). Exit to China via the Torugart Pass (p325).

## CLIMATE & WHEN TO GO

Siberian winds bring freezing temperatures and snow from November to February, with ferocious cold in the mountains. The average winter minimum is –24°C.

Throughout the country springtime buds appear in April and May, though nights can still be below freezing. Mid-May to mid-June is pleasant, though many mountain passes will still be snowed in. From the end of June through to mid-August most afternoons will reach 32°C or higher, with a maximum of 40°C in Fergana Valley towns such as Jalal-Abad; mountain valleys are considerably cooler. Like most of the region, Bishkek gets most of its rainfall in spring and early summer.

Of course in the mountains the 'warm' season is shorter. The best time to visit is July to September, although camping and trekking are pleasant from early June through mid-October. Avalanche danger is greatest during March and April and from September to mid-October.

Overall, the republic is best for scenery and weather in September, with occasional freezing nights in October. See the climate charts, p446, for more details.

## HISTORY

### Early Civilizations

The earliest notable residents of what is now Kyrgyzstan were warrior clans of Saka (also known as Scythians), from about the 6th century BC to the 5th century AD. Rich bronze and gold relics have been recovered from Scythian burial mounds at Lake Issyk-Köl and in southern Kazakhstan.

The region was under the control of various Turkic alliances from the 6th to 10th centuries. A sizeable population lived on the shores of Lake Issyk-Köl. The Talas Valley in southern Kazakhstan and northwest Kyrgyzstan was the scene of a pivotal battle in 751, when the Turks and their Arab and Tibetan allies drove a large Tang Chinese army out of Central Asia.

The cultured Turkic Karakhanids (who finally brought Islam to Central Asia for good) ruled here in the 10th to 12th centuries. One of their multiple capitals was at Balasagun

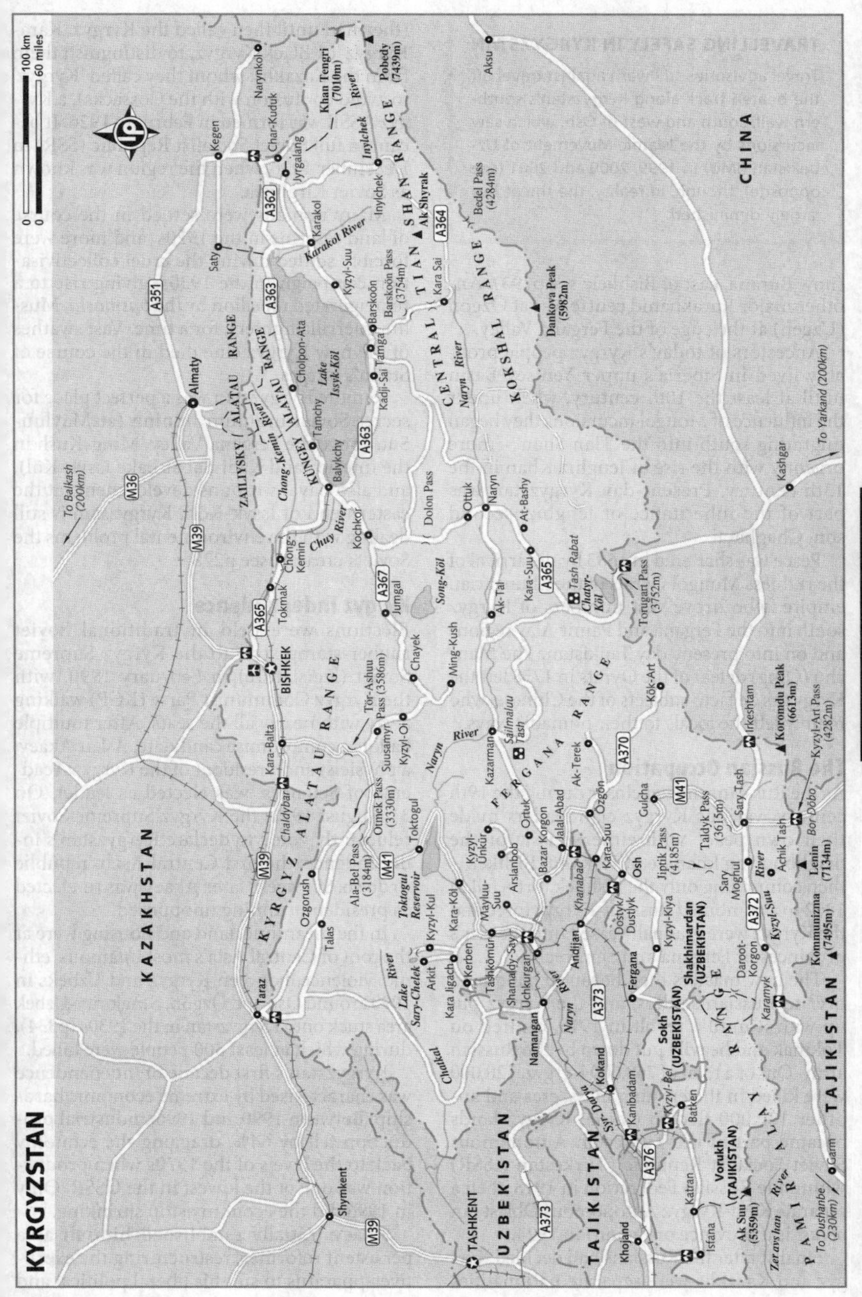
KYRGYZSTAN
0 100 km
0 60 miles
KAZAKHSTAN
UZBEKISTAN
TAJIKISTAN
CHINA
TASHKENT
BISHKEK
Almaty
Shymkent
Taraz
Talas
Ozgorush
Kara-Balta
Chaldybar
Tokmak
Chong-Kemin
Kochkor
Balykchy
Tamchy
Cholpon-Ata
Kadji-Sai
Tamga
Barskoön
Kyzyl-Suu
Karakol
Jyrgalang
Char-Kuduk
Narynkol
Kegen
Saty
Inylchek
Khan Tengri (7010m)
Pobedy (7439m)
Ak Shyrak
Aksu
Bedel Pass (4284m)
Barskoön Pass (3754m)
Kara Sai
Dankova Peak (5982m)
Naryn
At-Bashy
Ottuk
Dolon Pass
Kara-Suu
Tash Rabat
Chatyr-Köl
Torugart Pass (3752m)
Kashgar
To Yarkand (200km)
Ak-Tal
Song-Köl
Jumgal
Chayek
Ming-Kush
Tör-Ashuu Pass (3586m)
Suusamyr
Kyzyl-Oi
Otmek Pass (3330m)
Ala-Bel Pass (3184m)
Toktogul
Toktogul Reservoir
Kazarman
Saimaluu Tash
Kök-Art
Ak-Terek
Irkeshtam
Koromdu Peak (6613m)
Kyzyl-Art Pass (4282m)
Bor Döbö
Achik Tash
Lenin (7134m)
Kommunizma (7495m)
Sary Tash
Taldyk Pass (3615m)
Gulcha
Özgön
Jalal-Abad
Ortuk
Bazar Korgon
Arslanbob
Kyzyl-Ünkür
Kara-Suu
Osh
Khanabad
Jiptik Pass (4185m)
Sary Moghul
Daroot-Korgon
Kyzyl-Suu
Karamyk
Dostyk
Dustlyk
Kyzyl-Kiya
Shakhimardan (UZBEKISTAN)
Sokh (UZBEKISTAN)
Andijan
Fergana
Mayluu-Suu
Kara-Köl
Kyzyl-Kul
Arkit
Kerben
Kara Jigach
Tashkömür
Shamaldy-Say
Uchkurgan
Namangan
Kokand
Kanibadam
Kyzyl-Bel
Batken
Vorukh (TAJIKISTAN)
Ak Suu (5359m)
Katran
Isfana
Khojand
Garm
To Dushanbe (230km)
To Balkash (200km)
Lake Sary-Chelek
Chatkal
Lake Issyk-Köl
Karakol River
Inylchek River
Chong-Kemin River
Chuy River
Naryn River
Syr Darya
Zer avs han River
ZAILIYSKY ALATAU RANGE
KÜNGEY ALATAU RANGE
KYRGYZ ALATAU RANGE
TIAN SHAN RANGE
CENTRAL RANGE
KOKSHAL RANGE
FERGANA RANGE
PAMIR
ALAY RANGE
A351
A362
A363
A364
A365
A367
A370
A372
A373
A376
M36
M39
M41

KYRGYZSTAN

**TRAVELLING SAFELY IN KYRGYZSTAN**

Travel advisories still warn against travel off the beaten track along Kyrgyzstan's southern wall, south and west of Osh, which saw incursions by the Islamic Movement of Uzbekistan (IMU) in 1999, 2000 and 2001 (see opposite), though, in reality, the threat has largely diminished.

(now Burana, east of Bishkek; see p293). Another major Karakhanid centre was at Özgön (Uzgen) at the edge of the Fergana Valley.

Ancestors of today's Kyrgyz people probably lived in Siberia's upper Yenisey Basin until at least the 10th century, when under the influence of Mongol incursions they began migrating south into the Tian Shan – more urgently with the rise of Jenghiz Khan in the 13th century. Present-day Kyrgyzstan was part of the inheritance of Jenghiz' second son, Chaghatai.

Peace was shattered in 1685 by the arrival of the ruthless Mongol Oyrats of the Zhungarian empire, who drove vast numbers of Kyrgyz south into the Fergana and Pamir Alay regions and on into present-day Tajikistan. The Manchu (Qing) defeat of the Oyrats in 1758 left the Kyrgyz as de facto subjects of the Chinese, who mainly left the locals to their nomadic ways.



## The Russian Occupation

As the Russians moved closer during the 19th century, various Kyrgyz clan leaders made their own peace with either Russia or the neighbouring khanate of Kokand. Bishkek – then comprising only the Pishpek fort – fell in 1862 to a combined Russian-Kyrgyz force and the Kyrgyz were gradually eased into the tsar's provinces of Fergana and Semireche.

The new masters then began to hand land over to Russian settlers, and the Kyrgyz put up with it until a revolt in 1916, centred on Tokmak and heavily put down by the Russian army. Out of a total of 768,000 Kyrgyz, 120,000 were killed in the ensuing massacres and another 120,000 fled to China. Kyrgyz lands became part of the Turkestan Autonomous Soviet Socialist Republic (Turkestan ASSR) within the Russian Federation in 1918, then a separate Kara-Kyrgyz Autonomous Oblast (an *oblast* is a province or region) in 1924.

Finally, after the Russians had decided Kyrgyz and Kazakhs were separate nationalities (they had until then called the Kyrgyz 'Kara-Kyrgyz' or Black Kyrgyz, to distinguish them from the Kazakhs, whom they called 'Kyrgyz' to avoid confusion with the Cossacks), a Kyrgyz ASSR was formed in February 1926. It became a full Soviet Socialist Republic (SSR) in December 1936, when the region was known as Soviet Kirghizia.

Many nomads were settled in the course of land reforms in the 1920s, and more were forcibly settled during the cruel collectivisation campaign in the 1930s, giving rise to a reinvigorated rebellion by the *basmachi*, Muslim guerrilla fighters, for a time. Vast swathes of the new Kyrgyz elite died in the course of Stalin's purges.

Remote Kyrgyzstan was a perfect place for secret Soviet uranium mining (at Mayluu-Suu above the Fergana Valley, Ming-Kush in the interior and Kadj-Sai at Lake Issyk-Köl), and also naval weapons development (at the eastern end of Issyk-Köl). Kyrgyzstan is still dealing with the environmental problems the Soviets created, see p278.

## Kyrgyz Independence

Elections were held in traditional Soviet rubber-stamp style to the Kyrgyz Supreme Soviet (legislature) in February 1990, with the Kyrgyz Communist Party (KCP) walking away with nearly all the seats. After multiple ballots a compromise candidate, Askar Akaev, a physicist and president of the Kyrgyz Academy of Sciences, was elected as leader. On 31 August 1991, the Kyrgyz Supreme Soviet reluctantly voted to declare Kyrgyzstan's independence, the first Central Asian republic to do so. Six weeks later Akaev was re-elected as president, running unopposed.

In the meantime, land and housing were at the root of Central Asia's most infamous 'ethnic' violence, between Kyrgyz and Uzbeks in 1990 around Osh and Özgön, a majority-Uzbek area stuck onto Kyrgyzstan in the 1930s (p334), during which at least 300 people were killed.

Kyrgyzstan's first decade of independence was characterised by extreme economic hardship. Between 1990 and 1996, industrial production fell by 64%, dragging the economy back to the levels of the 1970s when production was one of the lowest in the USSR. Only in 1996 did the economy stop shrinking.

Akaev initially established himself as a persistent reformer, restructuring the executive apparatus to suit his liberal political and economic attitudes, and instituting reforms considered the most radical in the Central Asian republics.

## The Tulip Revolution

By the early 2000s, Kyrgyzstan's democratic credentials were once again backsliding in the face of growing corruption, nepotism and civil unrest. The 2005 parliamentary elections were plagued by accusations of harassment and government censure. Demonstrators stormed governmental buildings in Jalal-Abad and civil unrest soon spread to Osh and Bishkek. On 24 March the relatively peaceful Tulip Revolution effectively overthrew the government amid bouts of looting and vandalism. President Akayev fled by helicopter to Kazakhstan and on to Moscow – subsequently resigning and becoming a university lecturer.

New presidential elections were held in July 2005 and the opposition leader and former prime minister, Kurmanbek Bakiyev, swept to victory, appointing Felix Kulov his prime minister.

## Kyrgyzstan Today

Despite the fastest privatisation programme and the most liberal attitudes in Central Asia, the economy is still in bad shape. Unemployment (and particularly underemployment) is rife and the average monthly wage is currently about US$55 in Bishkek, and less than half this in the countryside.

The Kyrgyz-Canadian gold-mining company Kumtor single-handedly produces 18% of the republic's GDP, making the republic very vulnerable to drops in the world price of gold. Still, the economy is getting better; growing by 7% in 2003 and 2004. Kyrgyzstan is still the only Central Asian member of the World Trade Organization (WTO).

Kyrgyzstan's mountains effectively isolate the country's northern and southern population centres from one another, especially in winter. The geographically isolated southern provinces of Osh and Jalal-Abad have more in common with the conservative, Islamised Fergana Valley than with the industrialised, Russified north. Ancient but still-important clan affiliations reinforce these regional differences and in a recent survey, 63.5% of Kyrgyz people thought that north-south cultural divisions were the main destabilising factor within society.

Kyrgyzstan's southern Batken district remains at risk in terms of potential Islamic fundamentalist insurgence. In 1999 militants from the Islamic Movement of Uzbekistan

### GER TODAY, GONE TOMORROW

If your idea of 'roughing-it' is sleeping with the window open then visiting Kyrgyzstan may be a mistake. If, on the other hand, you don't mind sleeping in a sheep, you'll have a blast. Of course you don't actually sleep *in* a sheep, but it's pretty close. Yurts (*bosuy* in Kyrgyz, *kiiz-uy* in Kazakh and also known as gers in English) are made of wool, smell like mutton and can be found peppered all over grassy fields like giant mushrooms. They are also practical – warm in winter, cool in summer and relatively light and portable.

Yurts are made of multilayered felt *(kiyiz* or *kiiz)* stretched around a collapsible wooden frame *(kerege)*. The outer felt layer is coated in waterproof sheep fat, the innermost layer is lined with woven mats from the tall grass called *chiy* to block the wind. Looking up, you'll see the *tyndyk*, a wheel that supports the roof (and which is depicted on Kyrgyzstan's national flag). Long woven woollen strips of varying widths, called *tizgych* and *chalgych,* secure the walls and poles. Start to finish, a yurt requires around three hours to set up or pull down if you are Kyrgyz and about three days for everyone else.

The interior is richly decorated with textiles, wall coverings, quilts, cushions, camel and horse bags, and ornately worked caskets. Floors are lined with thick felt *(koshma)* and covered with bright carpets *(shyrdaks or ala-kiyiz),* and sometimes yak (like cows but with bad hair) skin. The more elaborate the decoration, the higher the social standing of the yurt's owners.

Spending a night in a yurt is easy – Community Based Tourism (CBT; p277) can arrange authentic yurtstays, particularly in central Kyrgyzstan, from Suusamyr to Naryn. Nothing gets the nomadic blood racing through your veins like lying awake at night under a heavy pile of blankets, staring at the stars through the *shanrak* (the hole in the roof that allows air and light to enter and smoke from the fire to escape), wondering if wolves will come and eat your horse.

(IMU; based in Tajikistan) took four Japanese geologists hostage. Kyrgyzstan's Minister for Interior Security flew down to oversee the rescue operation and was himself promptly kidnapped. The Japanese were eventually freed but several locals were killed in the ensuing fighting.

Then, one year later, an Islamic group captured four American climbers. The Americans reportedly escaped with a well-timed tug of a rope that sent the terrorist leader plummeting to his death.

Although those conflicts set nerves jangling in Bishkek, Islamic fundamentalism is not officially seen as a serious threat. The US bombings in Afghanistan have largely pulled the rug from under the militants' feet, killing most of the IMU leadership and its Al-Qaeda–supplied support network.

## CURRENT EVENTS

In the wake of the Tulip Revolution, little seems to have changed. President Bakiyev now finds himself faced with the same criticisms that he levelled at his predecessor – corruption, a refusal to initiate promised constitutional reform and a reluctance to curb his own presidential powers.

In November 2006, under growing pressure from thousands of demonstrators shouting for his resignation, Mr Bakiyev finally backed down, agreeing to a number of concessions that opposition leaders say will help fight corruption.

Bishkek's Manas Airport remains another contentious issue. The airport doubles as the country's main international hub and the United States Ganci Air Base. The opening of a US military base at Manas Airport and the Russian airbase just down the road at Kant, highlights the strategic realignment of the republic and the heightened rivalries between the region's former and current superpowers in a post-9/11 Central Asia.

Certainly the lines of KC-135 tanker transport planes, C-130 cargo planes and the presence of a military base in a civilian airport creates a sobering impression on arrival. The base is used to aid aerial operations in Afghanistan and at the time of research the government was negotiating a hundredfold increase in rent to US$200 million.

## PEOPLE

There are about 80 ethnic groups in Kyrgyzstan; the principle ethnicities being Kyrgyz (66%), Uzbek (14%) and Russian (10%). Notable minorities include the Dungan, Ukrainian and Uyghur peoples. The Kyrgyz are outnumbered almost two to one by their livestock and about two-thirds of the population lives in rural areas.

Since 1989 there has been a major exodus of Slavs and Germans – more than 200,000 Russians and at least 75% of all Germans. At its peak in 1993, 130,000 people left Kyrgyzstan, of whom 90,000 were Russians. The emigration trend has slowed in recent years until the 2005 revolution, which triggered a 'second wave' of those seeking Russian citizenship. Most cite the dearth of job prospects and continued economic hardship as the main reason for leaving. Many fear that the steady stream of departing skilled workers and educated professionals will have dire effects on the economy.

### THE KIDNAPPED BRIDE

Kyrgyz men have a way of sweeping a woman off her feet – off her feet and into a waiting car or even a taxi. Kidnapping is the traditional way young men find themselves a wife. Although the practice has been illegal since 1991 the custom is once again on the upswing. Some say it's a reassertion of national identity although many point to the rising cost of wedding celebrations and brides (Kyrgyz women command a 'bride price') and a well-executed abduction can dramatically slash wedding costs.

An old Kyrgyz adage foretells that tears on the wedding day bode for a happy marriage, and it is true, many marriages that begin this way turn out to be some of the most successful in rural Kyrgyzstan. Perhaps this explains why parents of kidnapped daughters consent to the forced marriage when consulted as part of the kidnapping process. If the girl is to escape, and some do, it takes a lot of determination and courage to withstand the tremendous amount of pressure that is brought to bear. For further information and video interviews, check out journalist Petr Lom's excellent report at www.pbs.org/frontlineworld/stories/kyrgyzstan.

**BLAZING SADDLES, FLYING FEATHERS**

Nomadic sports are very popular in Kyrgyzstan and have seen a revival in recent years. The most spectacular of these, an all-out mounted brawl over a headless goat, is *kok boru,* also known as *ulak-tartysh* or *buzkashi* (p59). The Kyrgyz name means 'grey wolf', which reveals the sport's origins as a hunting exercise.

*Kyz-kumay* (kiss-the-girl) involves a man who furiously chases a woman on horseback in an attempt to kiss her. The woman gets the faster horse and a head start and, if she wins, gets to chase and whip her shamed suitor. Ah, young love. This allegedly began as a formalised alternative to abduction, the traditional nomadic way to take a bride.

Other equestrian activities in Kyrgyzstan include *at chabysh* (p310), a horse race over a distance of 20km to 30km; *jumby atmai,* horseback archery; *tiyin enmei,* where contestants pick up coins off the ground while galloping past; and *udarysh,* horseback wrestling.

*Kok boru* is often incorporated into Independence Day celebrations and other festivals and CBT (p277) arrange demonstrations upon request (5500som) if you give them a few days notice.

When not wrestling over dead livestock or being whipped by young girls the traditional nomad might take to the hills for a spot of eagle-hunting. Hunting with golden eagles is not to be confused with falconry, which in these parts is looked down upon as a pastime for children and delinquents.

A skilled hunter *(berkutchi)* and his bird typically go after foxes, badgers, rabbits and occasionally wolves. The capture and training of eagles takes three to four years and is a highly ritualised activity. The best time to see eagles in action is after their summer moult between October and February. Community-Based Tourism arrange demonstrations, particularly around Lake Issyk-Köl (Bokonbayevo, p312 or Kadji-Sai, p311) although be warned, things end badly for the bunny.

Kyrgyz (with Kazakhs) in general, while probably the most Russified of Central Asian people, were never as deeply 'Leninised', judging by the ease with which they have turned away from the Soviet era. There has been none of the wholesale, hypocritical race to cleanse all Soviet terminology that afflicts Uzbekistan.

For more on the Kyrgyz people refer to p59.

## RELIGION

Like the Kazakhs, the Kyrgyz adopted Islam relatively late and limited it to what could fit in their saddlebags. Northern Kyrgyz are more Russified and less observant of Muslim doctrine than their cousins in the south (in Jalal-Abad and Osh provinces). One consequence of this is the high number of young women boasting hip-hugging jeans on the streets of Bishkek with nary a head scarf between them.

Dwindling communities of Russian Orthodox Christians are still visible, particularly in Bishkek and Karakol, both of which have Orthodox cathedrals.

## ARTS

### Literature

Central Asian literature has traditionally been popularised in the form of songs, poems and stories by itinerant minstrels or bards, called *akyn* in Kyrgyz (p276). Among better-known 20th-century Kyrgyz *akyns* are Togolok Moldo (real name Bayymbet Abdyrakhmanov), Sayakbay Karalayev and Sagymbay Orozbakov.

Kyrgyzstan's best-known living author is Chinghiz Aitmatov (born 1928), whose works have been translated into English, German and French. Among his novels, which are also revealing looks at Kyrgyz life and culture, are *Djamila* (1967), *The White Steamship* (1970), *Early Cranes* (1975) and *Piebald Dog Running Along the Shore* (1978), the latter was made into a prize-winning Russian film in 1990.

In *The Day Lasts Longer Than a Century* (1980) two boys witness the arrest by the NKVD (*Narodny Komissariat Vnutrennih Del;* Interior Ministry) of their father, who never returns (Aitmatov lost his father in Stalin's purges and the loss of a father is a recurring theme in his work). *The Place of the Skull* (1986) confronted previously taboo subjects such as drugs and religion and was an early attack on bureaucracy and environmental destruction. *Djamila* and *The Day Lasts Longer Than a Century* are fairly easy to find in English.

#### MANAS

The *Manas* epic is a cycle of oral legends, 20 times longer than the *Odyssey,* which tells of the formation of the Kyrgyz people through

KYRGYZSTAN

### CRAFTY CARPETS

No craft smacks more of Kyrgyzstan than the quintessential nomadic felt rug called a *shyrdak*. *Shyrdaks* are pieced together from cut pieces of sheep's wool after weeks of washing, drying, dyeing and treatment against woodworm. The appliqué patterns are usually of a *kochkor mujuz* (plant motif), *teke mujuz* (ibex horn motif) or *kyal* (fancy scrollwork) bordered in a style particular to the region. Brightly coloured designs were introduced after synthetic dye became readily available in the 1960s, although natural dyes (made from pear and raspberry leaves, dahlia and birch root, among others) are making a comeback. Neutral-coloured *shyrdaks* are also easy to find and resist fading. In summer Kyrgyz women work together to hand stitch each felt piece into place eventually knocking out a beautiful carpet that will last for more than three decades.

The 'blurred' design of the *ala-kiyiz* (rug with coloured panels pressed on) is made from dyed fleece, which is laid out in the desired pattern on a *chiy* (reed) mat. The felt is made by sprinkling hot water over the wool, which is then rolled up and rolled around until the wool compacts.

Before you purchase a *shyrdak*, ensure that it's hand-made by checking for irregular stitching on the back and tight, even stitching around the panels. Also check the colour will not run (lick your finger and run lightly over the colours to see that they do not bleed). The best *shyrdaks* are said to be made around Naryn. There are women's *shyrdak* cooperatives in Bishkek and Kochkor and CBT coordinators can often put you in touch with *shyrdak* makers.



the exploits of a hero-of-heroes called Manas. Acclaimed as one of the finest epic traditions, this '*Iliad* of the steppes' is the highpoint of a widespread Central Asian oral culture.

The *Manas* narrative revolves around Manas, the khan, or *batyr* (heroic warrior), and his exploits in carving out a homeland for his people in the face of hostile hordes. Subsequent stories deal with the exploits of his son Semety and grandson Seitek. Manas is of course strong, brave and a born leader; he is also, to an important extent, the embodiment of the Kyrgyz' self-image.

*Manas* in fact predates the Kyrgyz, in the same sense that Achilles or Agamemnon predate the Greeks. The stories are part of a wider, older tradition that have come to be associated with the Kyrgyz people and culture. The epic was first written down in the mid-19th century by the Kazakh ethnographer Shoqan Ualikhanov.

*Akyns* who can recite or improvise from the epics are in a class by themselves, called *manaschi*. Latter-day bards wear sequined costumes and recite short, memorised snippets of the great songs in auditoriums. Traditionally the illiterate bards would belt out their 24-hour long epics in yurts, to enthralled audiences for whom the shifting, artful improvisations on time-worn themes were radio, TV, rap music, performance poetry and myth rolled into one, but that tradition is now dead.

The end of the oral tradition was inevitable with the advent of literacy (though the Soviets tried to pack it off early in the 1950s when there was a movement to criticise the epic as 'feudal'). Yet interest in *Manas* is on the rise. Books, operas, movies, comic books, and TV serials based on *Manas* are thriving.

*Manas* mania received an exponential boost when the Kyrgyz government and Unesco declared 1995 the 'International Year of *Manas*' and the '1000th Anniversary of the *Manas* Epos'. When a small, poor country spends US$8 million (by some estimates) on celebrating an oral epic, one can be pretty sure it's not just because the government really digs rhyming verse. Manas has become, once again, a figure for the Kyrgyz to hang their dreams on. Legend has even assigned Manas a tomb, located near Talas and supposedly built by his wife Kanykey, where Muslim pilgrims come to pray.

## Other Arts

Kyrgyzstan's Aktan Abdykalykov is a rising star of Central Asia cinema. His 1998 bittersweet coming-of-age *Beshkempir* (The Adopted Son) was released to critical acclaim and *Maimil* (The Chimp) received an honourable mention in Cannes in 2001. Both are well worth viewing.

*Yak Born in Snow* is a fascinating Soviet documentary of Kyrgyz yak herders, available for viewing at Yak Tours (p302) in Karakol.

Kyrgyz traditional music is played on a mixture of *komuz* guitars, a vertical violin known as a *kyl kyayk*, flutes, drums, mouth harps (*temir komuz,* or *jygach ooz* with a string) and long horns.

## ENVIRONMENT

### The Land

Kyrgyzstan is a bit larger than Austria plus Hungary; 94% of the country is mountainous. The country's average elevation is 2750m with 40% over 3000m high and three-quarters of that under permanent snow and glaciers.

The dominant feature is the Tian Shan range in the southeast. Its crest, the dramatic Kokshal-Tau, forms a stunning natural border with China, culminating at Pik Pobedy (7439m), Kyrgyzstan's highest point and the second-highest peak in the former USSR. The Fergana range across the middle of the country and the Pamir Alay in the south hold the Fergana Valley in a scissor-grip.

In a vast indentation on the fringes of the Tian Shan, Lake Issyk-Köl, almost 700m deep, never freezes due to its high salinity. Kyrgyzstan's only significant lowland features are the Chuy and Talas Valleys, adjacent to Kazakhstan. Its main rivers are the Naryn, flowing almost the full length of the country into the Syr-Darya in the Fergana Valley, and the Chuy along the Kazakhstan border.

### Wildlife

Kyrgyzstan offers an annual refuge for thousands of migrating birds, including rare cranes and geese. The country is believed to have had the world's second-largest snow leopard population, although numbers are declining rapidly. Issyk-Köl and Sary-Chelek lakes are Unesco-affiliated biosphere reserves.

### Environmental Issues

At the end of the Soviet era there were an estimated 14 million sheep in Kyrgyzstan. Since then flock numbers have been privatised and

**COMMUNITY-BASED TOURISM**

Thanks to several innovative Kyrgyz grass-root organisations, it is ridiculously easy for travellers to scramble over the cultural divide and rub shoulders with the locals.

Shepherd's Life and Community Based Tourism (CBT) are the two programmes you'll hear being bandied about most often and there is considerable overlap in the services they provide. In a nutshell, both connect tourists with a wider network of guides, drivers and families willing to take in guests, either in villages or *jailoos* (summer meadows), across the country. You can use the network of information offices to organise anything from a comfortable homestay to a fully supported horse trek. Because each office is independently run the level of service varies but standout CBT offices include the following:

**Arslanbob** (p331)
**Bishkek** (p282)
**Jalal-Abad** (p332)
**Karakol** (p302)
**Kochkor** (p316)
**Naryn** (p320)

Other CBT offices include Tamchy (p296), Bokonbayevo (p312), Kazarman (p322), Osh (p336), Talas (p328), Sary Moghul (p341), and Lake Sary-Chelek (p329) – see those entries for more details. Contact CBT Bishkek for details for their planned offices in Gulcha, Kerben and Batken.

Homestays are ranked from one to three edelweiss and generally cost around 250som to 350som per day for bed and breakfast and 100som per additional meal. Depending on the quality and availability of local restaurants, it is often cheaper to eat out. Horse hire is 400som to 500som per day and guides range from 400som to 1000som per day. A car and driver costs 9som to 10som per kilometre, though this is dependent on the price of fuel. It's worth picking up a copy of the *CBT Guidebook* (170som, or download it for free from www.cbtkyrgyzstan.kg) that lists each office's services, a description of local trips and useful town maps.

Shepherd's Life is cheaper than CBT, slightly less organised and has five coordinators, in Kochkor (p316), Jumgal (p318), Naryn (p320), At-Bashy (p324) and Jangy Talap (near Ak-Tal; p322).

For an overview of these organisations' aims and objectives, see p92.

KYRGYZSTAN

divided. Economic hardship, a loss of effective management and a lack of governmental infrastructure have seen flocks numbers dwindle to about six million.

Individuals lack the means for covering shepherds' wages, meeting transport costs or maintaining infrastructure (eg bridges) that would allow these small flocks to travel to traditional summer *jailoos*. This in turn has resulted in serious undergrazing of mountain pastures leading to a succession of foreign plant invasions. Meanwhile pastures near villages are ironically overgrazed, leading to degraded fields prone to soil erosion.

Uranium for the Soviet nuclear military machine was mined in Kyrgyzstan (the Kyrgyz SSR's uranium sector earned the sobriquet 'Atomic Fortress of the Tian Shan'), and as many as 50 abandoned mine sites in Kyrgyzstan alone might now leak unstabilised radioactive tailings or contaminated groundwater into their surroundings. Independent Kyrgyzstan has closed most of the mines and institutes and begun to grapple with the environmental problems they created.

In 1998 almost 2 tonnes of cyanide and sodium hydrochloride destined for the Kumtor gold mine spilled into the Barskoön River and thence Issyk-Köl, reportedly leaving several people dead, hundreds seeking medical treatment, and thousands evacuated.

Kyrgyzstan's rivers offer vast hydropower potential, though so far this only fulfils about 25% of the requirements, and expanded development will inevitably collide with environmental considerations. The country's reserves of fresh water, locked up in the form of glaciers, remain its greatest natural resource although as these are shrinking providing plenty of water in the short term it's a double-edged sword with seemingly disastrous long-term effects.

## FOOD & DRINK

Spicy *laghman* (noodle) dishes reign supreme, partly the result of Dungan (Muslim Chinese) influence. Apart from standard Central Asian dishes (p82), *beshbarmak* (literally 'five fingers', since it is traditionally eaten by hand) is a special holiday dish consisting of large flat noodles topped with lamb and/or horsemeat cooked in vegetable broth. *Kesme* is a thick noodle soup with small bits of potato, vegetable and meat. *Jarkop* is a braised meat and vegetable dish with noodles.

*Hoshan* are fried and steamed dumplings, similar to *manty* (stuffed dumplings), best right off the fire from markets. Horsemeat sausages known as *kazy, karta* or *chuchuk* are a popular vodka chaser, as in Kazakhstan.

In Dungan areas (eg Karakol or certain suburbs of Bishkek), ask for *ashlyanfu*, made with cold noodles, jelly, vinegar and eggs. Also try their steamed buns made with *jusai*, a mountain grass of the onion family, and *fyntyozi*, spicy cold rice noodles. *Gyanfan* is rice with a meat and vegetable sauce.

*Kymys* (fermented mare's milk), available in spring and early summer, is the national drink. *Bozo* is a thick fizzy drink made from boiled fermented millet or other grains. *Jarma* and *maksym* are fermented barley drinks, made with yeast and yogurt. Shoro is the brand name of a similar drink, available at most street corners in Bishkek. All four, and tea, are washed down with *boorsok* (fried bits of dough). *Kurut* (small balls of tart, dried yogurt) are a favourite snack.

Issyk-Köl honey is said to be the best in Central Asia, and locally made blackcurrant jam is a treat. Kids and elderly people in Cholpon-Ata sell strings of dried fish and you can buy larger smoked fish in the bazaars.

Tea is traditionally made very strong in a pot and mixed with boiling water and milk in a bowl before serving.

# BISHKEK БИШКЕК

**☎ 312 / pop 900,000 / elev 800m**

Bishkek feels green – but not just because of the trees. Green because it's young, wet-behind-the-ears, racing to grow up and unsure of want it wants to become.

A cosmopolitan capital? It needs a heap more money for that. A dignified Silk Road legacy? Bishkek needs a tad more history. Little exists that predates WWII although Lenin is still here in his concrete overcoat (albeit recently demoted to a smaller square) and a larger-than-life Frunze still sits on a bronze horse facing the train station (though his name has been removed).

What's more, Bishkek seems small and bony like a teenager. There's not that much to it. It's yet to fill out. You can race around the museums and be back hanging at the bar, debating politics with the large contingent of American expats before your bar stool has cooled. Yes, nothing gets the heart racing like a few vodka shots and a well-timed reference to the US military base at a civilian airport.

But it's not only high-octane alcohol that fuels debate and there is more than mountains that separate the capital from the more conservative south. Yearly street demonstrations (2004, 2005 and 2006), the spasmodic dosing of demonstrators with tear gas and a coup (2005) paints a troubling picture of this upstart capital but the reality is far more congenial. The only serious trouble you're likely to encounter is the Kyrgyz proclivity for Chinese food and karaoke. Dangerous stuff.

## HISTORY

In 1825, by a Silk Road settlement on a tributary of the Chuy River, the Uzbek khan of Kokand built a little clay fort, one of several along caravan routes through the Tian Shan mountains. In 1862 the Russians captured and wrecked it, and set up a garrison of their own. The town of Pishpek was founded 16 years later, swelled by Russian peasants lured by land grants and the Chuy Valley's fertile black earth.

In 1926 the town, rebaptised Frunze, became capital of the new Kyrgyz ASSR. The name never sat well; Mikhail Frunze (who was born here) was the Russian Civil War commander who helped keep tsarist Central Asia in Bolshevik hands and hounded the *basmachi* rebellion into the mountains.

In 1991 the city became Bishkek, the Kyrgyz form of its old Kazakh name. A *pishpek* or *bishkek* is a churn for *kumys*. Numerous legends (some quaint, some rude) explain how it came to be named for a wooden plunger. Others conclude disappointingly that this was simply the closest familiar sound to its old Sogdian name, Peshagakh, meaning 'place below the mountains'. With the 4800m, permanently snowcapped rampart of the Kyrgyz Alatau range looming over it, the Sogdian name still fits.

## ORIENTATION

Bishkek sits on the northern hem of the Kyrgyz Alatau mountains, an arm of the Tian Shan. Nineteenth-century military planners laid out an orderly, compass-oriented town and getting around is quite easy.

East–west Jibek Jolu prospektisi (Silk Road Ave), just north of the centre, was old Pishpek's main street. Now the municipal axes are Chuy and parklike north–south Erkindik. The busiest commercial streets are Kiev and Soviet. At the centre yawns Ala-Too Sq, flanked by Panfilov and Dubovy (Oak) Parks. Street numbers increase as you head north or west.

### Maps

**Geoid** (☎ 21 22 02; Room 4, 3rd fl, Kiev 107; ⏰ 8am-noon & 1-5pm Mon-Fri) sells Bishkek city maps in Cyrillic, as well as trekking and 1:200,000 topo maps (from 150som). For more on maps see p346. The building is accessed through an unmarked door just west of DHL.

## INFORMATION

### Bookshops

**Fatboys** (Chuy 104) Maintains a library where books can be borrowed for two weeks free of charge. If you are into bodice-ripping romance novels, you'll think you have died and gone to heaven.

**Metro** (☎ 21 76 64; Chuy 168A) Has a small, but fantastically eclectic selection of titles. Ask for the cabinets to be unlocked for unfettered browsing. Books cost the US jacket price plus US$5.

The bookshop in the Dom Druzhby centre has the *Manas* epic in English along with a city walking map and the Hyatt Regency (p286) will flog you a *Herald Tribune* or *Time* for US$7.

### Emergency

**Ambulance** (☎ 103)
**Fire service** (☎ 101)
**Police** (☎ 102)

### Internet Access

**In-tel Internet** (☎ 66 05 56; Kiev 92; per hr 30som; ⏰ 8am-midnight) Also offers cheap internet phone calls.

### Medical Services

Pharmacies are marked *darykhana* (Kyrgyz) or *apteka* (Russian) and there is a 24-hour one on the north side of the Hyatt; the **Metro-pol** (☎ 68 10 05; Soviet 340; ⏰ 24hr).

**Kyrgyz Republic Hospital** (☎ outpatients 22 89 60, 24hr emergencies & hospital ambulance ☎ 26 69 16; Kiev 110) Probably the best bet for medical attention is also known as State Clinic No 2. Bring an interpreter.

**Tsentr Semeinoi Meditsiny** (Centre of Family Medicine; ☎ 66 06 44, 66 06 91; Bokonbayevo 144A) Some readers have recommended it. By Logvinenko

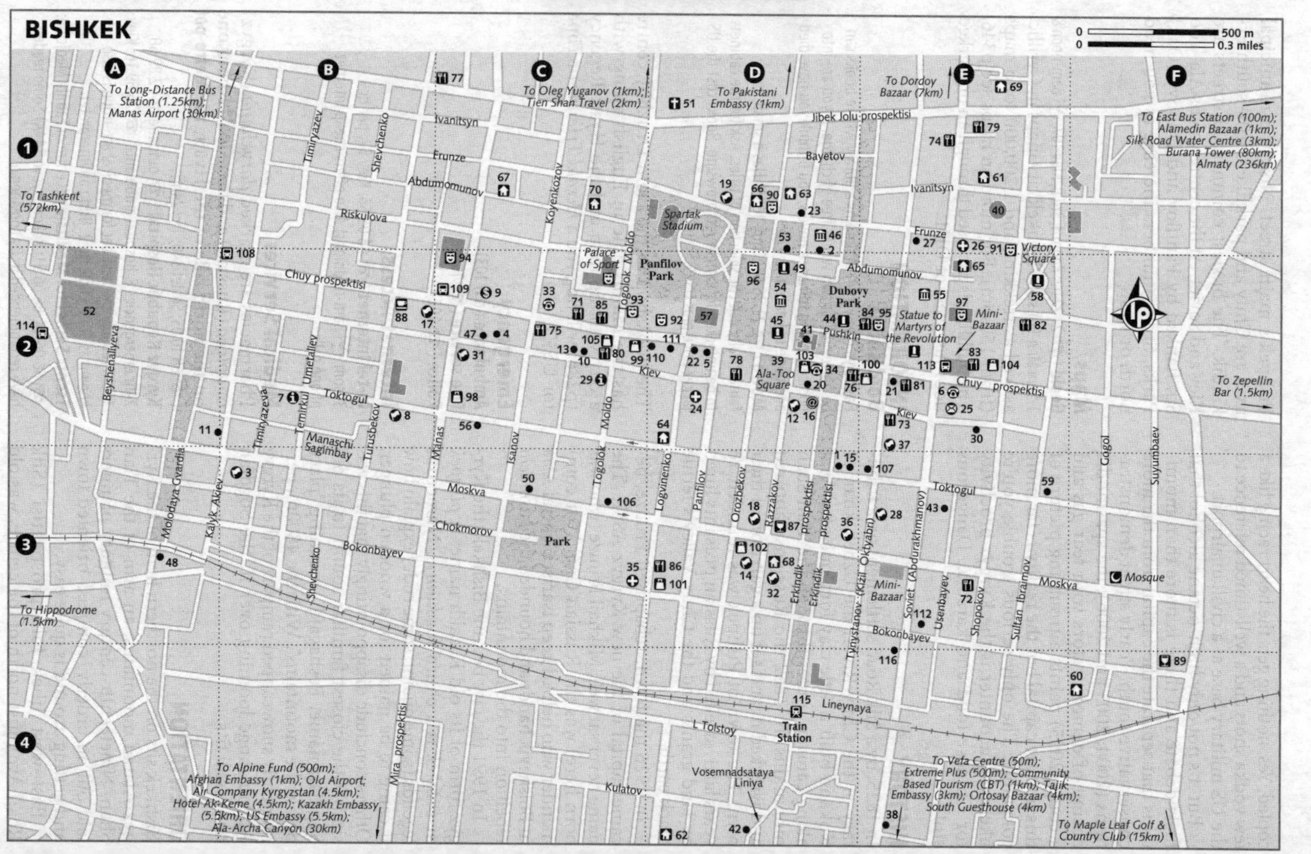
BISHKEK
A
B
C
D
E
F
1
2
3
4
0 500 m
0 0.3 miles
To Long-Distance Bus Station (1.25km); Manas Airport (30km)
To Oleg Yuganov (1km); Tien Shan Travel (2km)
To Pakistani Embassy (1km)
To Dordoy Bazaar (7km)
To East Bus Station (100m); Alamedin Bazaar (1km); Silk Road Water Centre (3km); Burana Tower (80km); Almaty (236km)
To Zepellin Bar (1.5km)
To Tashkent (572km)
To Hippodrome (1.5km)
To Alpine Fund (500m); Afghan Embassy (1km); Old Airport; Air Company Kyrgyzstan (4.5km); Hotel Ak-Keme (4.5km); Kazakh Embassy (5.5km); US Embassy (5.5km); Ala-Archa Canyon (30km)
To Vefa Centre (50m); Extreme Plus (500m); Community Based Tourism (CBT) (1km); Tajik Embassy (3km); Ortosay Bazaar (4km); South Guesthouse (4km)
To Maple Leaf Golf & Country Club (15km)
Jibek Jolu prospektisi
Bayetov
Ivanitsyn
Frunze
Abdumomunov
Riskulova
Shevchenko
Timiryazev
Chuy prospektisi
Toktogul
Moskva
Bokonbayev
Chokmorov
Kalyk Akiev
Molodaya Gvardia
Beyshenaliyeva
Manas
Turusbekov
Temirkul Umetaliev
Manaschi Sagimbay
Timiryazeva
Mira prospektisi
Isanov
Koyenkozov
Togolok Moldo
Logvinenko
Panfilov
Orozbekov
Razzakov
Erkindik prospektisi
Tynystanov (Kizil Oktyabr)
Kiev
Soviet (Abdurakhmanov)
Usenbayev
Shopokov
Sultan Ibraimov
Gogol
Suyumbaev
Pushkin
Lineynaya
L Tolstoy
Vosemnadsataya Liniya
Kulatov
Spartak Stadium
Panfilov Park
Palace of Sport
Dubovy Park
Ala-Too Square
Statue to Martyrs of the Revolution
Mini-Bazaar
Victory Square
Park
Mosque
Train Station

## Money

There are exchange desks all over Bishkek, including most hotels.

**Demir Kyrgyz Bank** (☎ 61 06 10; Chuy 245; ⏰ 9am-noon & 1-4pm Mon-Thu, til 2.30pm Fri) Changes Amex travellers cheques for 3% and gives Visa and Maestro credit card advances for 2.5%.

**Kazkommertsbank** (Soviet 136; ⏰ 9am-1pm, 2-6pm Mon-Fri, 9am-4pm Sat) Has two ATMs outside and another by the left (west) exit of TsUM department store and outside Central Asian Travel. All accept foreign cards with a 2% commission. This bank handles the payments for the Kazakh visa in US dollars.

## Post

**American Resources International** (ARI; ☎/fax 66 00 77; bishkek@aricargo.com; Erkindik 35) Ships larger items if you are moving to/from Bishkek.

**DHL** (☎ 61 11 11; fax 61 11 13; Kiev 107)

**FedEx** (☎ 65 00 12; fax 65 01 28; Moskva 217)

**Main post office** (Soviet; ⏰ 7am-8pm Mon-Sat,

**INFORMATION**

American Resources International (ARI)........1 D3
American University in Central Asia........2 D1
ATM........(see 5)
ATM........(see 104)
British Consulate........3 B3
Celestial Mountains........4 C2
Central Asia Tourism Corporation (CAT)........5 D2
Central Telecom Office........6 E2
Centre of Tourism Development of Silk Road........7 B2
Chinese Embassy........8 B2
Demir Kyrgyz Bank........9 C2
DHL........10 C2
Ecotour........(see 50)
Fatboys........(see 81)
FedEx........11 A2
French Consulate........12 D2
Geoid........13 C2
German Embassy........14 D3
Glavtour........15 D3
In-tel Internet........16 D2
Indian Embassy........17 B2
Iranian Embassy........18 D3
Japanese Embassy........19 D1
Kazkommertsbank........(see 116)
Kyrgyz Concept (Air Tickets)........20 D2
Kyrgyz Concept (Branch)........21 E2
Kyrgyz Concept (Information)........22 D2
Kyrgyz Concept (Main Office)........23 D1
Kyrgyz Republic Hospital........24 D2
Main Post Office........25 E2
Maison du Voyageurs........(see 102)
Metro Bookshop........(see 88)
Metro-pol........26 E1
Ministry of Education, Science & Culture........27 E1
Netherlands Consulate........28 E3
Novinomad........29 C2
Office of Visas & Registration (OVIR)........30 E2
Russian Consulate........31 C2
Russian Embassy........32 D3
Telephone Office........33 C2
Telephone Office........34 D2
Tsentr Semeinoi Meditsiny........35 C3
Turkish Embassy........36 D3
Uzbek Embassy........37 E2

**SIGHTS & ACTIVITIES**

Ak Sai........38 E4
Ala-Too Square........39 D2
Asia Mountains........(see 60)
Circus........40 E1
Dom Druzhby........41 D2
Dostuck Trekking........42 D4
Edelweiss........43 E3
Erkindik (Freedom) Statue........44 D2
Erkindik Statue........45 D2
Frunze House-Museum........46 D1
International Mountaineering Camp (IMC) Pamir........47 C2
ITMC Tien-Shan........48 A3
Lenin Statue........49 D2
Log House........50 C3
Orthodox Church........51 D1
Osh Bazaar........52 A2
Parliament Buildings........53 D1
State Historical Museum........54 D2
State Museum of Fine Arts........55 E2
Top Asia........56 C2
White House........57 D2
WWII Monument........58 E2
Zhirgal Banya........59 E3

**SLEEPING**

Asia Mountains Guest House........60 F4
Hotel Ak-Say........61 E1
Hotel Alpinist........62 D4
Hotel Sary Chelek........63 D1
Hotel Semetei........64 D2
Hyatt Regency........65 E2
International School of Management & Business........66 D1
Radison Guesthouse........67 C1
Sabyrbek's B&B........68 D3
Sakura Guesthouse........69 E1
Silk Road Lodge........70 C1

**EATING**

Adriatico Paradise........71 C2
Ak Emir Bazaar........72 E3
Astana Café........73 E2
Bakit Restaurant........74 E1
Beta Stores........75 C2
Bombay Restaurant........76 D2
Café Faisa........77 C1
Café Lusfu........78 D2
Café Mazai........79 E1
Chaykana Jalal-Abad........80 C2
Fatboys........81 E2
Khuadali........82 E2
Kontinental........(see 82)
Labyrinth Café........83 E2
Nayuz Café........(see 73)
Old Edgar........84 E2
Santa Maria........85 C2
Shanghai........(see 82)
Tekco Supermarket........86 D3

**DRINKING**

2x2........(see 75)
Bar Navigator........87 D3
Metro........88 B2
Steinbrau........89 F4

**ENTERTAINMENT**

Billiards Club........90 D1
Galaxia........91 E1
Golden Bull........92 D2
Moscow Disco........93 C2
Philharmonia........94 C2
Russian Drama Theatre........95 E2
State Academic Drama Theatre........96 D2
State Opera & Ballet Theatre........97 E2
XO........(see 91)

**SHOPPING**

Antique Shop........98 C2
Asahi Ecological Art and Handicraft........99 C2
Asia Gallery........100 E2
Kyrgyz Style........101 D3
Maison du Voyageurs........102 D3
North Face........(see 75)
Pro Photo........103 D2
Red Fox........(see 38)
Saimaluu Tash Art Gallery........(see 41)
TsUM........104 E2
Tumar Art Salon........105 C2

**TRANSPORT**

Aeroflot........106 C3
British Airways........107 E3
Bus from Airport drop off........108 B2
Bus to Manas Airport........109 C2
China Southern........(see 111)
Esen Air........110 D2
Itek Air........111 D2
KLM........(see 107)
Kyrgyzstan Airlines........112 E3
Lufthansa........(see 65)
Minibuses to Dordoy Bazaar........113 E2
Osh Bazaar Bus Stand........114 A2
Train Station........115 D4
Turkish Airlines........116 E4
Uzbekistan Airlines........(see 10)

### BIZARRE BISHKEK

There's plenty to do in Bishkek besides preparing for the next trek. After the must-see nearby sights of **Burana Tower** (p293) and **Ala-Archa Canyon** (p290) mix it up with locals down in **Osh Bazaar** (p284). A Barbie in a burka for your niece? An *ak kalpak* (a felt, occasionally tasselled, hat) for dad? They'll love it. Stuff your modesty and a towel in a day-pack and head to the **Zhirgal Banya** (p284) to give yourself a sound thrashing with a birch branch – you naughty little nomad! Later that night stun the locals with your Mick Jagger 'unleashed' impersonation at one of the street-side karaoke stalls along Chuy prospektisi.

8am-7pm Sun) There is a separate mailroom for EMS (Express Mail Service), between the post and telecom offices.

## Registration & Visas

**Office of Visas & Registrations** (OVIR; Kiev 58; ⏲ 9.30am-12.30pm & 2-5pm Mon-Fri) If required, this is the place to register (see p346) and apply for visa extensions (400som).

## Telephone & Fax

**Central telecom office** (cnr Soviet & Chuy; ⏲ 7am-8.30pm) Also provides international fax service. There are smaller telephone offices on the corners of Chuy and Erkindik, and Chuy and Isanov.

## Tourist Information

**Centre of Tourism Development of Silk Road** (☎ 62 72 96; Toktogul 216, Apt 1) Sponsored by the Norwegian Government, it helps promote tourism. Trekking gear and tents are available to rent.

**Community Based Tourism** (CBT; ☎ 55 93 31; www.cbt kyrgyzstan.kg; Gorky 58; ⏲ 9am-6pm Mon-Fri, 9am-2pm Sat, closed Sat in winter) Gives information on CBT groups across the country (see p277) and sells the *CBT Guidebook* (170som), which outlines services available at each office. Take minibus 180 that runs up Soviet and then turns east onto Gorky. The office is well signed, 1km along Gorky on the right.

**Novinomad** (☎ 62 23 81; www.novinomad.com; Togolok Moldo 28) Has a noticeboard for contacting other travellers and is an invaluable source of regional information. Recommended.

## Travel Agencies

The following agencies are starting to figure out what budget-minded individual travellers want.

**Alpine Fund** (☎ 54 24 99; www.alpinefund.org; apt 16, Mira 74) This nonprofit organisation, established to assist Kyrgyz youth, runs weekend hikes and climbs in Ala-Archa National Park, including overnight summit attempts on Peak Uchitel (4572m). It also rents trekking gear.

**Celestial Mountains** (☎ 21 25 62; www.celestial.com.kg; Kiev 131-4) British-run agency that specialises in the Torugart Pass but can also offer visa support and cultural tours. Runs a hotel in Naryn. Contact Ian Claytor.

**Central Asia Tourism Corporation** (CAT; www.cat.kg; Chuy 124); air tickets (☎ 66 36 65); tourism (☎ 66 36 64) Visa support, rental cars, air tickets, accommodation and inclusive tours.

**Ecotour** (☎ /fax 21 34 70; www.ecotour.kg; Moskva 145/1) Ecofriendly and flexible with budget demands. Stay in traditional yurts with solar-heated water, and small hydroelectric turbines at Temir Kanat, Ak-Sai, Tuura-Su, Kara-Talaa, Jeti-Öghuz and Bosteri for €20 per night (includes three meals and horse riding). Contact English-speaking Elmira or German-speaking Zamira.

**Glavtour** (☎ 66 32 32; www.glavtour.kg; Toktogul 93) Books flights; the website lists airfares from Bishkek. Visa cards accepted.

**Kyrgyz Concept** (www.concept.kg); main office (☎ 66 13 31, fax 66 02 20; office@concept.kg; Razzakov 100); branch (☎ 90 08 66; Tynystanov 231); information (☎ 66 60 06; Chuy 126); air tickets (☎ 90 04 04; aero3@concept.kg; Kiev 69) Offers cultural programmes at the higher end of the travel spectrum. Can arrange visa support (US$145 Uzbek visa, three weeks), Bishkek homestays (US$36 to US$48), horse trekking, cultural shows and can even put you in touch with a Kyrgyz costume designer. It is also a reliable international ticket agency. Credit cards accepted.

**Novinomad** (☎ 62 23 81; www.novinomad.com; Togolok Moldo 28) An excellent operator for cultural tours, Torugart trips and trekking and translating services. Can book CBT and yurt-camp accommodation across the country.

**Maison du Voyageurs** (☎ 66 63 30; Moskva 122, cnr with Orozbekov) Organises flexible, general-interest trips throughout Kyrgyzstan and neighbouring countries for small groups. French-speaking guides available.

**Silk Road Water Centre** (☎ /fax 28 41 42; www.rafting.com.kg; Musa Jalil 104, Bishkek 720051, contact Alexander Kandaurov) Specialists in white-water rafting, kayaking and fishing trips on the Chuy, Chong-Kemin, Kekemeren and Naryn rivers.

Local guides include **Amanbayev Zakir** (☎ 502 55 36 53; www.guide.mail333.com) and Nurdan of the South Guesthouse (see p285). Both lead personal tours, arrange transport and book accommodation nationwide. Nurdan also has extensive regional knowledge and will happily arrange local excursions and treks to the more obscure of the canyons around Bishkek (p291).

## DANGERS & ANNOYANCES

Bishkek smiles during the day but is neither safe nor well lit after dark. At this time, all the normal Central Asian security rules apply (p447). If you're out after dark, stick to main streets, avoid the parks and steer clear of the area around the train station.

Crooked plain-clothed policemen are a problem in Bishkek, particularly at Osh Bazaar and at the corner of Soviet and Moskva. They will demand your passport and try to look in your bag and search your money (palming some). Legally you are required to carry your passport at all times but it's always worth trying to give them only a copy. If your passport is at an embassy, then get the embassy to write this on a photocopy of your passport.

## SIGHTS

### Ala-Too Square

This sea of concrete ceased to be called Lenin Sq in 1991. Lenin enjoyed centre stage on his plinth until August 2003, when he was relegated to the square behind the museum and replaced by (yet) another statue of Erkindik (Freedom). The Kyrgyz flag in the square is lowered every day at dusk.

Sure, there are yurts, a mummy, carpets, embroidery and even open-air *balbals* (Turkic totemlike gravestones) in the **State Historical Museum** (adult/student 45/20som, camera 100som; 9am-1pm & 2-6pm Tue-Sun), but the highlight is the mural-cum-shrine to Lenin and the Revolution upstairs. Former US president Ronald Reagan is immortalised wearing a skull, astride a missile and grinning wildly. Nazi Germany is depicted as a rampaging bear while (surprise, surprise) Mother Russia as a beautiful woman clutching a white dove. English and lighting is minimal.

The grand façades across Chuy prospektisi from Lenin are just that – façades, about 10m deep, erected in Soviet times in front of the venerable but unsuitably drab Ilbirs knitwear factory.

The unmarked marble palace full of chandeliered offices just west of the square, the **'White House'**, is the seat of the Kyrgyzstan government, including the president's office and the republic's parliament. Behind this is **Panfilov Park**, full of rusting rides and arcades.

The conspicuously older structure northeast of Ala-Too Sq at Pushkin 68 was the headquarters of the Central Committee of the Kyrgyz ASSR, declared in 1926. It's now home to the **Dom Druzhby** community centre for advocacy and self-help groups, as well as a drab zoology museum.

Beyond this is **Dubovy (Oak) Park**, full of strollers on warm Sundays, a few open-air cafés and some neglected modern sculpture, and funnily enough, century-old oaks. Where **Erkindik prospektisi** (Freedom Ave) enters the park, there is an open-air art gallery. Nearby is the Erkindik (Freedom) Statue, formerly a statue of Felix Dzerzhinsky, founder of the Soviet secret police.

### State Museum of Fine Arts

This decaying **museum** (☎ 66 15 44; Soviet 196; adult/student 130/20som; 10am-1pm & 2-6pm), also called the Gapar Aitiev Museum of Applied Art, features Kyrgyz embroidery, jewellery, utensils, eye-popping felt rugs, works by local artists, and a startling collection of reproduction Egyptian and classical statues.

### Frunze House-Museum

Is this thatched cottage really where the little Frunze played with his toy soldiers, or

#### MIKHAIL VASILIEVICH FRUNZE

Frunze was born in what was then Pishpek in 1885. After an early adulthood full of revolutionary excitement in Moscow, and numerous arrests, he eventually commanded the Red Guards who occupied the Moscow Kremlin in October 1917. He was a major player in the Russian Civil War, directing the defeat of the White forces of Admiral Kolchak in Siberia and the rout of General Wrangel in the Caucasus. It was Frunze who led the Bolshevik forces that seized Khiva and Bukhara in 1920, and pushed the *basmachi* (Muslim guerrila fighters) out of the Fergana Valley.

Replacing Trotsky as War Commissar, Frunze introduced compulsory peacetime military service, and moulded the Red Army into a potent tool of the Revolution. After Lenin's death, he survived several mysterious auto accidents, but died a victim of Stalin's paranoia in 1925, during an officially ordered stomach operation.

just the Soviet way with history? In any case the meticulous two-storey **museum** (☎ 66 06 07; Frunze 364; admission 40som; ⏰ 10am-5.30pm Wed-Mon) engulfing it – showcasing Frunze as a military and family man, plus the requisite posters, weapons, flags and statues – has itself become a piece of history.

### Victory Square

This weedy plaza with an immense yurt-shaped **WWII monument**, erected on the 40th anniversary of the end of the war, sprawls across an entire city block. On cold evenings you might see a knot of young men passing the bottle and warming themselves at its eternal flame. On weekends it's the destination for an endless stream of wedding parties posing for photographs.

The nearby Circus, on Frunze, that once played to packed houses in Soviet times looks like a 1950s UFO that crash landed and never had the impetus to move again.

### Russian Remnants

Among poignant reminders that there is still a Russian community here are the pretty, blue-steepled **Orthodox church** (Jibek Jolu), and an incongruous, well-preserved Russian-style **log house** (Moskva), west of Togolok Moldo (now the Ecotour office).

### Markets

The city has three daily farmers markets, all fairly distant from the centre. **Osh bazaar**, 3km to the west on Chuy, though not very colourful, offers a glimpse of Kyrgyz and Uzbeks from the more conservative south of the republic. Produce is sold inside the main bazaar and all around the outside of the complex. There is a separate clothes market south of the main produce bazaar. To get there take trolleybus 14 on Chuy, bus 20 or 24 on Kiev, or 42 from Soviet.

Smaller markets include the **Alamedin bazaar**, 2.5km to the northeast (trolleybus 7 or 9 from TsUM, return by bus 20 or 38), and **Ortosay Bazaar**, 6km to the south (trolleybus 12 on Soviet). All are open daily but are biggest on weekends.

**Dordoy Bazaar** (nicknamed Tolchok, which means 'jostling crowd') is a huge weekend flea market of imported consumer goods and junk about 7km north of the centre. You might strike gold with the occasional North Face jacket here. Buses 185, 132, 25 and 200 run to Dordoy from the northern corner of Soviet and Chuy.

### Baths

Buy tickets for the **Zhirgal Banya** (cnr Sultan Ibraimov & Toktogul; bath 55som, Russian/Finnish sauna 55/60som; ⏰ 8am-9pm) from the *kassa* (ticket office) around the side. Old ladies sell birch twigs outside the baths for those into a bit of self-flogging.

## ACTIVITIES

A number of agencies in Bishkek organise a range of activities in the region.

### Trekking & Mountaineering

Apart from the companies listed below, many of the travel agencies (p282 also offer trekking. For information on likely trekking routes near Bishkek, see p290.

**Ak-Sai** (☎ 54 42 77; www.ak-sai.com, www.basecampkg.com; Soviet 65) Provides trekking, mountaineering, biking, heli-skiing and visa support. It operates base camps at Inylchek and Pik Lenin, and the Red Fox camping store (p289).

**Asia Mountains** (☎ 69 40 73; www.asiamountains.co.uk; Lineynaya 1A) A well-organised agency charging US$25 to US$55 per person per day, depending on the programme. Can get border permits for the central Tian Shan, even if you aren't trekking with them. Runs a base camp at Achik Tash and a guesthouse in Bishkek (opposite).

**Dostuck Trekking Ltd** (☎ 42 74 71, ☎/fax 54 54 55; www.dostuck.com.kg; Vosemnadsataya Liniya 42-1) Offers ascents to peaks, including base camps near Khan Tengri, Pobedy and Lenin as well as less specialised, fixed-date treks including yurt camps in the Suusamyr Valley and Tash Rabat. Can arrange helicopter transport and border permits.

**Edelweiss** (☎ 28 07 88; www.edelweiss.elcat.kg; Usenbayev 68/9) Trekking, mountaineering, heli-skiing, horse tours, ski trips and visa support. Contact Slava Alexandrov.

**International Mountaineering Camp Pamir** (IMC Pamir; ☎ 66 04 69; www.imcpamir.netfirms.com; Apt 30, Kiev 133) Trekking and mountaineering programmes and operates the Achik Tash base camp at the foot of Peak Lenin. Contact Bekbolot Koshoev.

**ITMC Tien-Shan** (☎ 65 12 21; www.itmc.centralasia.kg; Molodaya Gvardia 1A) Competent adventure-travel operator offering package and piecemeal help, including visa support; mountaineering, with base camps at Khan Tengri, Achik Tash (Pik Lenin) and Koh-i-Samani (Kommunizma); trekking; heli-skiing; mountain biking; and crossing the Torugart. Not to be confused with its former partner at Tien-Shan Travel.

**Tien-Shan Travel** (☎/fax 27 05 76; www.tien-shan.com; Sherbakov 127) Ex-cartographers with expedition gear and a menu of set group tours into the mountains, but unaccustomed to walk-in clients. Contact Vladimir Birukov.

**Top Asia** (☎ /fax 21 16 44; www.topasia.kg; Toktogul 175) Offers trekking, mountaineering and horse riding.

### Other Activities

Nor does the fun stop with just walking amid the mountains. It is also possible to ride through, raft down, climb over, ski on or even just picnic at these mountains. Most Bishkek travel agencies (p282) and CBT (p277) can arrange horses, local yurtstays and guides.

For the low down on skiing see p292 or for white-water rafting options see p293. Contact the travel agencies (p282, for more information on the other activities. Some of the trekking companies listed (opposite and p282 also organise these activities.

## FESTIVALS & EVENTS

Once upon a time, on summer Sundays, you might have seen traditional Kyrgyz horseback games at the Hippodrome, southwest of the centre. Lately the best you can expect around Bishkek are exhibition games during the **Nooruz festival** (Navrus; 21 March; p345) and on **Kyrgyz Independence Day** (31 August).

## SLEEPING

### Budget

**South Guesthouse** (☎ 57 26 23, 95 87 30; www.geocities.com/south_gh; 4th fl Aaly Tokombaev 31B; dm US$2) This backpacker crash pad is waaaay down in the extreme southern suburbs (8th *microrayon*); you should most definitely call in advance, as it does fill up. It's essentially a two-person apartment converted into a dorm room for 10, so it may be too commune-like for some. The travellers' book is full of useful tips. Take minibus 232, 252 or 150, or trolleybus 6 or 3 and get off when the bus turns off Soviet. From the bus stop, cross the road, go into the first gap between apartment blocks, turn left and go in the second door on the left. To gain access, press 135 simultaneously and pull the door. A taxi to/from the centre costs 80som. Nurdan, the owner, offers an airport pickup (330som) and is a knowledgeable guide for off-the-beaten-track destinations.

**Hotel Ak-Say** (☎ 68 19 06; Ivanitsyn 117; s/d 187/374som) Slowly decaying but a cheap, bearable alternative to staying in a dorm if you don't mind common squat toilets and cold-water basins (a hot shower is 15som). The neighbourhood behind the Circus is a bad one so be careful at night.

**Sabyrbek's B&B** (☎ 62 13 98; sabyrbek@mail.ru; Razzakov 21; dm/s 200/300som) Sabyrbek offers beds and meals (100som; these are social events) in his ramshackle house. It's a friendly place – it needs to be – there's only one shower. The cat's called Nicole Kidman and the dog bites. Unfortunately Sabyrbek's brothers like a drink – and they don't do it alone. The location is great; look for an unmarked gate opposite the German embassy, next to a kiosk.

**Sakura Guesthouse** (☎ 66 63 26; kobuhe-hikita@hotmail.om; Michurina 38; dm/d 200/500som) This new cheapie is already proving popular with its reasonably convenient location and crash-pad atmosphere. Beds are in six-bed dorms – one with an attached shower and sauna. Bathroom facilities are either shared with the family inside their home or by way of an outdoor pit toilet. Look for the small signs pointing the way from Soviet, past the Jibek Jolu intersection.

**Hotel Sary-Chelek** (☎ 66 26 27; Orozbekov 87; d 600som) Reports vary but some complain of flooded bathrooms and Soviet-era beds. Check that the door locks, and ignore the gurgling loo.

**International School of Management & Business** (☎ 62 31 07; fax 66 36 14; Panfilov 237; d 800som, pol-lux 1260som) Double rooms share a toilet and shower (hot water most of the time) with one other double and are clean, comfortable and soulless. The hotel is also known as the Salima.

Rental apartments and private homestays can be arranged through NoviNomad (p282), Dostuck Trekking (opposite) and Kyrgyz Concept's main office (p282) for around US$10 to US$25 per person per night.

### Midrange

**Radison Guesthouse** (☎ 66 37 85; Abdumomunov; d US$25; ⊠) This unsigned guesthouse (behind pink walls and a green gate) is run by a motherly manager and her son. The twin rooms are spotlessly clean with a small en suite and prices includes breakfast.

**Hotel Semetei** (☎ 21 83 24; Toktogul 125; d 1200-1500som, q 1760som) Rickity lifts take you to large, sunny rooms, each with fridge, TV and small hot-water bathroom. The two-roomed quad is excellent value.

our pick **Asia Mountains Guest House** (☎ 69 02 35; www.asiamountains.co.uk; Lineinaja 1A; s/d/tw US$36/42/48; ⊠) Trekking groups love this clean, fresh lodge, and with good reason. Guests have access to a

KYRGYZSTAN

kitchen and a nice communal seating area ideal for swapping climbing stories. The travel agency of the same name is in the basement. The guesthouse is on the outskirts, tucked down an alley by the railway line. Breakfast is included.

**Hotel Alpinist** (☎ 44 15 22; Paniflov 113; s/d US$36/48) Looking like a misplaced prop from *The Sound of Music* this altitudinous-themed hotel is about 30 minutes by foot from the city centre. Facilities include a restaurant, climbing wall, conference room and transport to local ski fields.

### Top End

**Hotel Ak-Keme** (☎ 63 25 49; Mira 93; s/d US$90/120; ) Formally known as the Pinara, this Turkish-built, four-star hotel saw the original Turkish owners retake their investment by force after loans were defaulted on during the 2005 revolution. Exciting stuff. There is a Turkish sauna, outdoor pool (nonguests 500som), casino, 11th-floor open-air terrace restaurant and tennis court but poorly trained staff. Ask for a balcony with a mountain (southern) view. Breakfast is included.

**Silk Road Lodge** (☎ 66 11 29; www.silkroad.com.kg; Abdumamunova 229; s/d €74/85, deluxe €90, ste €102; ) Run by the Celestial Mountains travel agency, rooms are equipped with everything (iron, fridge, hairdryer, kettle and satellite TV) but style. None the less it's a good option. There's a small heated plunge pool and live music on the weekends. Travellers cheques and credit cards accepted.

**Hyatt Regency** (☎ 66 12 34; www.bishkek.regency.hyatt.com; Soviet 191; s/d US$275, lux d US$320, ste US$560; lux ste $1060, plus 20% tax, discounts available; ) Five stars make this the plushest pad in town although the décor is somewhat schizophrenic with the calming, natural colours at odds with the peacock-bright *shyrdaks* (felt carpets). Facilities include the Crostini Restaurant, Opera Lounge, the @191 bar, an outdoor pool (nonguests 900som), fitness club and the obligatory casino. Breakfast is a cheeky US$25 extra.

## EATING

Most restaurants add a 10% service charge and a few cheeky blighters even exhort extra for background music.

### Cafés & Chaikhanas

**Astana Café** (Kiev; mains 30som; lunch & dinner) Has a great atmosphere and cheap Uyghur food, including chicken shashlyk (20som) and tasty salads. At night the place is jumping and there's a small cover charge for the (for once) decent live music.

**Nayuz Café** (Kiev; lunch & dinner) Is next door and similar to the Astana, with a large selection of vodka.

**Chaikhana Jalal-Abad** (☎ 61 00 83; cnr Kiev & Togolok Moldo; mains 35-85som; lunch & dinner) Has pleasant bamboo huts, cordial staff and, as the name suggests, serves up southern specialities such as *larzuro* (fried beef and vegetables), salads and shashlyk.

our pick **Café Faiza** (☎ 66 47 37; Jibek Jolu; mains 30-100som; lunch & dinner) It's a wildly popular Kyrgyz restaurant in the north of town that offers high-quality local dishes at reasonable prices. You won't get near the place at lunch.

**Labyrinth Café** (Chuy; mains 30-180som; lunch & dinner) Cheap eats and cheap beer can be found next door to TsUM at this open-air café serving Central Asian dishes such as Kazakh-style ribs and *beshbarmak* (flat noodles with a meat broth). Find a spot under the willows or umbrellas and settle in for some serious people-watching.

**Café Lusfu** (☎ 62 27 88; Kiev 77; mains 80som; lunch & dinner) Has filling and delicious Chinese meals served with a dubious disco, passionate dancing and heart-felt karaoke.

Bishkek has Central Asia's best *samsas* (samosas), sold hot out of miniovens all around town for around 10som each. The chicken or cheese ones are generally the best.

Several fast-food stands around town sell dangerous-looking doner kebabs *(gamburgers)* for around 15som.

### Restaurants

**Fatboys** (☎ 28 73 50; Chuy 104; 8am-10pm Mon-Sat, 9am-10pm Sun; breakfast, lunch & dinner; mains 50-120som, minimum charge 50som) A prime foreigners' hang-out – especially at breakfast with fresh juices, fruit teas, hash browns, bacon, eggs, yogurt, muesli and pancakes. If only the staff weren't so morose.

**Bakit Restaurant** (☎ 29 64 04; Soviet 214; meat mains 120som, veg mains 50som; lunch & dinner) The place to go if you have a hunger – it has decent-sized servings. The menu has been incorrectly translated so you don't always get what you think you ordered. It's worth the gamble.

**Café Mazai** (☎ 66 50 81; Soviet 199; salads 50som, mains 100-130som; lunch & dinner) Hop down the stairs into a faux cave, an indubitable burrow of rabbit specialities. The English menu details

KYRGYZSTAN

such dishes as 'fillet of rabbit' and the 'rabbit juicy' along with more conventional fare.

**Old Edgar** (☎ 66 44 08; mains 85-160som; ⌚ lunch & dinner) Choose from a good selection of Russian salads, fish (perch with mushrooms) and pizza in what feels like an underground, intimate Bavarian lodge. The aprés-ski vibe is reinforced by live music and a good bar. It's on the west side of the Russian Drama Theatre.

**Bombay Restaurant** (☎ 62 51 15; Chuy 110; meat mains 170-225som, veg mains 110-150som; ⌚ breakfast, lunch & dinner) Serves everything subcontinental, from vegetable *thalis* to *masala* curries with a sizeable side-order of cheesy décor.

**Santa Maria** (☎ 21 24 84; Chuy 217; mains 110-250som; ⌚ lunch & dinner) Anyone who has ever tried ordering Korean dishes in Russian will appreciate the picture menu at this upscale place. There are also a few European and Japanese dishes thrown in for good measure. Our eyes were on the *nis ratatoly* (lamb chops with shredded eggplant, potato and rice). Visa cards accepted.

**Adriatico Paradise** (☎ 21 76 32; Chuy 219; mains 200-300som; ⌚ lunch & dinner) The excellent Italian food here is prepared by a genuine Italian chef, with imported ingredients and Chianti wines. A 30cm pizza costs 200som and pasta dishes run at around 225som. Lunch deals (pasta and salad) cost 140som.

Side by side on the south side of Victory Sq, are three decent Chinese restaurants: the friendly **Khuadali** (☎ 0512-280418; Ogonbayev; mains 120som; ⌚ lunch & dinner), the popular **Shanghai** (☎ 68 14 12; Ogonbayev; mains 120som; ⌚ lunch & dinner) and the slightly cheaper **Kontinental** (☎ 28 04 11; Ogonbayev; mains 100som; ⌚ lunch & dinner).

## Self-Catering

**Ak Emir Bazaar** (cnr Moskva & Shopokov) A great place for do-it-yourselfers, with samosas, roast chicken, pickled Korean salads, honey, buckets of blackcurrants and *piroshki* (Russian-style pies) – plus fruit and vegetables.

**Beta Stores** (Chuy 150) You can get everything from baklava to bottled *kymyz* (24som) in the most popular supermarket in town. Trekkers will find the soup mixes useful.

**Tekco Supermarket** (Logvinenko 21; ⌚ 24hr) A small, but well-stocked store. There is a bakery and Western-style meat and dairy chillers.

# DRINKING

Remember, in Bishkek you are never far from a shot of vodka. For those too busy to actually go inside a bar, most street stalls sell 'kiosk shots' (also known as juice grams) of vodka or cognac for 5som a nip.

The following places also serve excellent food.

**Steinbräu** (☎ 29 38 81; Gertse 5; 0.4L draught beer 40-52som) The German-style pilsner and recommended dark beer (Salvator) is brewed on-site here and is the main draw. The round tables and kids' play area are great for groups and families. Georgian wines and a full menu of German food (mains 175som), from sausages to pretzels, adds to the Munich beer-hall vibe. For added punch try the beer cocktails (Cologne lager and Flagman vodka).

**Metro** (☎ 21 76 64; Chuy 168A; beer 50-70som; ⌚ 1-9pm) With international sports parading across a large-screen TV and American rock and pop belting from the speakers, the Metro provides expats with a slice of American and pizza in one handy package. Add this to the on-site bookshop (p279) and the Bar and Grill restaurant (mains 100som to 150som) and it is easy to see why this is one of the most popular Westerner hang-outs in town.

**2X2** (☎ 21 24 97; cnr Isanova & Chuy; beer 60som, cocktails 70-400som) Imported grappa and coffee draw the faithful to this chic Italian-run pastel-and-chrome bar. Visa cards accepted.

**Bar Navigator** (☎ 66 51 51; Moskva 103; 1L beer 60-70som) A stylish spot where embassy workers shell out 100som for a gin and tonic or 60som for a cappuccino. The good live music makes it a classy place for a date. It also serves great appetisers and vegetarian meals.

# ENTERTAINMENT

## Theatres & Concert Halls

**Philharmonia** (☎ 21 92 92; Chuy 210, by Belinsky) Features Western and Kyrgyz orchestral works and the occasional Kyrgyz song-and-dance troupe, but you may need a local person to identify these from the playbills. In front of the Philharmonia is a statue of the legendary hero Manas slaying a dragon, flanked by his wife, Kanykey, and his old adviser, Bakayn. The *kassa* is on the west side.

**State Opera & Ballet Theatre** (☎ 66 18 41; Soviet 167) Opposite the State Museum of Fine Arts, classical Western as well as local productions play in this elegant building to half-empty halls. Check the billboards outside for current productions.

**State Academic Drama Theatre** (☎ 21 69 58; Panfilov 273) On the east side of Panfilov Park, this is the place for popular Kyrgyz-language works, more often than not written by Chinghiz Aitmatov, Kyrgyzstan's premier man of words.

**Russian Drama Theatre** (☎ 22 86 30; Tynystanov, Dubovy Park) For classics in Russian.

The Jetigen and Samaa ensembles and Ordo Sakhna folk troupe are also good to see. Ask NoviNomad (p282) about upcoming concerts.

### Other Entertainment

Bishkek nightclubs seem to attract a middle-aged, mainly male clientele who are in town for *'biznez'* and a good time. There's also bowling, billiards and golf.

**Zepellin Bar** (☎ 28 34 92; Chuy 43; cover 50som; 🕒 10pm-5am) The best of the lot with Russian rock bands playing to a young crowd most nights. It's 2km east from TsUM; a taxi costs 70som.

**Golden Bull** (☎ 62 01 31; Chuy 209; foreigners/Kyrgyz men free/200som, beer 60som; 🕒 10pm-5am) The place attempts to please everyone with its blend of American, Russian, Kyrgyz and Turkish mix of pop and R&B. The floorshow (Thursday to Saturday) features skimpily clad male and female dancers (read: strippers).

**Moscow Disco** (☎ 21 39 05; Togolok Moldo 7, women/men 150/200som; 🕒 10pm-5am) Consists of an outside marquee-covered bar and windowless rooms behind fluorescent orange doors. Play Station games on a large plasma TV cost 40som per hour.

**Galaxia** (☎ 29 75 13; cnr Frunze & Shopokov) Offers ground floor bowling (per game before/after 6pm 140/190som, for children 90/140som) and an upstairs disco, **XO** (🕒 noon-3am; women/men 300/400som).

You can play pool for 80som an hour in the **billiards club** (☎ 22 83 42; cnr Orozbekov & Frunze), underneath the Consul Restaurant.

Maple Leaf Golf & Country Club is Kyrgyzstan's first nine-hole golf course, southeast of Bishkek near the village of Kara Jigach.

## SHOPPING

Bishkek has the country's best collection of souvenirs and handicrafts, though you can often find individual items cheaper at their source (eg *shyrdaks* in Naryn, hats in Osh). For details on markets, see p284.

**TsUM** (☎ 29 27 94; Chuy 155) This state-run department store is surprisingly well stocked with a photo shop (digital!) and a large selection of made-for-tourist postcards and souvenirs on the 2nd floor. It sells pirated CDs and DVDs on the 3rd floor.

There is also a cluster of camera shops on Chuy prospektisi around Ala-Too Sq including **Pro Photo** (Chuy) that develops digital photos (7som per print).

The **Vefa Centre** (cnr Soviet & Gorky) will transport you to an American-style, air-conditioned mall, stocking Western brands at Western prices. The cinema on the 3rd floor screens Hollywood blockbusters dubbed in Russian (180som).

### Artwork

**Asia Gallery** (☎ 62 45 05; Chuy 108; 🕒 11am-6pm Mon-Fri, 11am-4pm Sat) Features modern Kyrgyz art, with some artists' workshops in the yard out the back.

**Sailmaluu Tash Art Gallery** (Pushkin 78; 🕒 11am-5pm Tue-Sat) On the north side of Dom Druzhby, this place sells interesting but pricey pottery.

Stroll along the covered gallery in Dubovy Park to see local artists selling woodcarvings, oil paintings and charcoal portraits most afternoons.

### Carpets

**Kyrgyz Style** (Kyrgyz Korku; ☎ 62 12 67; www.kyrgyzstyle.kg; Apt 12, Bokonbayev 133) A nonprofit organisation that sells high-quality *shyrdaks, ala kiyiz* (felt rugs featuring coloured panels), hats, bags and slippers to support social development in Kyrgyzstan. It's on the ground floor, accessed from the back of the apartment block.

**Asahi Ecological Art & Handicraft** (☎ 66 57 10; info@asahikyrgyz.com; Chuy 136; credit cards 10% surcharge) Not necessarily the cheapest store in town but the carpets, kilims and *shyrdaks* here are beautiful, top-quality pieces. Those nomads sure do know how to cut a rug.

Another place to look for *shyrdaks* is in the souvenir shops in the State Historical Museum.

### Handicrafts

You can find Kyrgyz men's hats – the familiar white felt *ak kalpak* or the fur-trimmed *tebbetey* – for sale in TsUM or, much cheaper, in the north building at Osh Bazaar.

There are some gimmicky souvenirs in the cabins in front of Beta Stores, also near Ala-Too Sq and opposite Panfilov Park on Chuy. All sell jewellery, wooden soldiers (Manas and company), Kyrgyz handicrafts and the odd *shyrdak*.

**Antique Shop** (☎ 62 19 10; http://alwian.host.net.kg; Manas 47; 🕒 10am-1pm & 2-5.30pm Mon-Fri, until 3.30pm

Sat) An Aladdin's cave of Soviet, Kyrgyz and Russian antiques, strong on coins and memorabilia. Visa cards accepted.

**Maison du Voyageurs** (☎ 66 63 30; Moskva 122, cnr Orozbekov) A wide selection of crafts from all over Kyrgyzstan, all marked with prices, the artist and the region they come from. The entrance is around the back and marked 'CATIA'.

**Tumar Art Salon** (☎ 21 26 53; Togolok Moldo 36) Sells high-quality, high-priced embroidery. Credit cards accepted.

### Outdoor Supplies & Cycle Parts

**Extreme Plus** (☎ 97 51 07; Gorki 41) Has a good selection of outdoor equipment including bicycle components, trekking supplies, skis, tents and gas stoves. It's open all weekend in winter for ski and snowboard rental (US$15 per day).

**Red Fox** (☎ 54 42 33; Soviet 65) Sells and rents mountain bikes (600som per day), camping supplies, mountaineering equipment, and cycle parts.

Do you have a sloppy head or need your bearings greased? Contact local cycle specialist **Oleg Yuganov** (☎ 67 09 74; Serova 149), who has helped many stranded cyclists get back in the saddle. He works irregular hours from his home, north of the centre. Phone first.

Outdoor clothing can be bought at the North Face store on the 2nd and 3rd floors of the Beta Stores (p287).

## GETTING THERE & AWAY

### Air

For spectacular trips by Yak-40, between the mountain tops and the clouds to Fergana Valley try one of the following national carriers.

**Air Company Kyrgyzstan** (AC Kyrgyzstan, formerly Altyn Air; ☎ 54 58 15; www.altynair.kg; Mira 95) flies several times a day to Osh (US$40 to US$50), twice weekly to Batken (US$48) and thrice weekly to Jalal-Abad (US$40 to US$50). **Esen Air** (☎ 66 34 82; esenair@yandex.ru; Chuy 130) flies every Thursday and Sunday to Ürümqi, China (US$182) via Osh (US$50).

**Kyrgyzstan Airlines** (☎ 62 21 23; Soviet 129) flies to Jalal-Abad and Osh daily. Both cost between US$40 and US$50.

#### AIRLINE OFFICES

The following international airline offices in Bishkek are useful for reconfirming or changing dates of an existing flight but are not the cheapest places to book international tickets:

**Aeroflot** (☎ 62 09 76; Moskva 121)

**British Airways** (☎ 66 09 00; fax 66 08 68; Toktogul 93)

**China Southern** (formerly Xinjiang Airlines; ☎ 66 46 68; Chuy128/3) Can book Ürümqi–Kashgar tickets.

**KLM – Royal Dutch Airlines** (☎ 66 15 00; fax 66 34 50; Toktogul 93)

**Lufthansa** (☎ 66 56 00; Hyatt Regency, Soviet 19)

**Turkish Airlines** (☎ 66 00 08; thyfru@elcat.kg; Soviet 136, cnr Bokonbayevo)

**Uzbekistan Airways** (☎ 21 48 63; uzb-air@elcat.kg; Kiev 107)

For details of international flights and fares see p348. For booking airline tickets see Kyrgyz Concept, Central Asia Tourism or Galvtour (p282).

### Bus & Shared Taxi

The west *(zapadny)* or long-distance bus station is the place for catching long-distance buses and shared taxis; get there via bus 7 on Kiev, bus 35 or 48 or minibus 113 or 114 from Jibek Jolu, or trolleybus 5 on Manas.

Prowling around the periphery of the bus station are the shared-taxi and private-car drivers, poised to pounce the moment they spy you. Battle past the drivers to the cheaper, but less comfortable, long-distance minibuses. Further still is the near-empty terminal and what remains of the country's bus network.

On the bus station's upper floor are 21 ticket booths, all closed bar one and the station's only English sign – 'The disables [sic] soldiers and participants in the Great Patriotic War are served in the first place'. There's an information office next to counter 21 and a 24-hour exchange here too. Don't trust the schedule board.

Morning buses depart to Karakol (195som, 8½ hours) stopping at Cholpon-Ata (130som) and most places in between. There is sometimes a single daily bus to Naryn (175som) and At-Bashy (195som) at 7am. Other infrequent destinations include Kochkor (125som), Bokonbayevo (130som) and Almaty in Kazakhstan (250som). The bus to Tashkent in Uzbekistan (285som) requires a Kazakh transit visa.

The private minivans offer better value or, to ride in comfort, wedge yourself into a shared taxi. To hire the whole car, offer to pay for all four seats.

Minivans and shared taxis leave when full throughout the day. Prices fluctuate with petrol costs and seasonal variations. The per seat fares for minibuses/shared taxis include: Karakol (250/400som), Cholpon-Ata (150/300som), Kochkor (200/250som to 300som), Naryn (250/350som to 450som), At-Bashy (300/450som), Bokonbayevo (200/250 som to 300som), Tamchy (150/250som to 300som), Balykchy (120/200som) and a seat to Almaty in a minivan is 250som.

For Osh, ramshackle minibuses (600som) and private cars (600som to 1200som) leave from here and at the Osh Bazaar bus stand. The trip takes around 15 hours depending on the road and vehicle.

The Osh Bazaar bus stand also has local buses to destinations west such as Sokuluk, Tash-Bulak, Kashka-Suu and Chong-Tash. Buses 160, 169 and 177 go several times a day to Kashka-Suu, for Ala-Archa National Park; inquire at the ticket office at the entrance to the bus stand.

The east *(vastotshny avtovaksal)* bus station is for regional points east such as Kant, Tokmak, Chong-Kemin, Kemin, Kegeti and Issyk-Ata.



### Train

Trains 17 and 27 run four times a week from Bishkek to Moscow (from 3900som) via Almaty. It is also possible to travel to Tashkent by rail but all trains pass through Kazakhstan.

## GETTING AROUND

### To/From the Airport

**Manas airport** (☎ 60 31 09), 30km northwest of the centre, doesn't quite live up to its poetic namesake and now doubles as an American air-force base. Bus 153 (15som, one hour) runs from the old airport by the Pinara Hotel, but the closest it gets to the centre is a stop in front of the Philharmonia. Marshrutka 325 runs from Osh Bazaar to the airport and marshrutnoe 380 will drop you at the corner of Chuy and Molodiya Guardia (20som).

A taxi between the airport and the centre costs around 350som. Ekspress Taxis at the airport can arrange a reliable taxi. Most flights arrive in the middle of the night playing nicely into the hands of the taxi touts. Haggle.

### Bus

Municipal trolleybuses cost 3som, payable as you disembark at the front or to the conductor. At rush hour these are so crammed that you must plan your escape several stops ahead. Ford Transit minibuses (5som) are generally better, as they are faster and less crowded.

Some useful minibus routes:

**No 110** From Osh bazaar, along Moskva to Soviet and then south.

**Nos 113, 114** From the west (long-distance) bus station, down Jibek Jolu to Alamedin Bazaar.

**Nos 125, 126** From Soviet (opposite the Orient International restaurant) south down Mira prospektisi to the old airport, US embassy and Hotel Issyk-Köl.

**Trolleybus 4** From Osh bazaar, along Moskva, left on Soviet and then north to Jibek Jolu.

### Car & Taxi

Most travel agencies (p282) can arrange a car and driver but you are better off just hiring a taxi for the day at a fraction of the price.

Essentially anyone with a car is a taxi. Official taxis, marked by the checkerboard symbol, are most reliable. The best-quality taxis are **Super Taxi** (☎ 152) or **Salam Taxi** (☎ 188). A short ride in the city costs around 70som, more at night.

You can book a taxi 24 hours a day on ☎ 182 for a small surcharge.

## AROUND BISHKEK

Rolling out of the Kyrgyz Alatau, the Ala-Archa, Alamedin and dozens of parallel streams have created a phalanx of high canyons, good for everything from picnics to trekking and skiing to mountaineering.

### Trekking & Spas

There are many possible do-it-yourself summer treks, but bring your own food and gear and be prepared for cold weather and storms even in summer. There is limited public transport and you are best off hiring a taxi to drop you at the trailheads, though Bishkek travel agencies (p282) and trekking companies (p284) can provide transport and arrange guided trips.

#### ALA-ARCHA CANYON

In this very grand, rugged but accessible gorge south of Bishkek, you can sit by a waterfall all day, hike to a glacier (and ski on it, even in summer) or trek on to the region's highest peaks. Most of the canyon is part of a state nature park, and foreigners must pay an entrance fee of 30som. For some hiking routes, see p292.

The park gate is 30km from Bishkek. Some 12km beyond the gate, at 2150m, the sealed

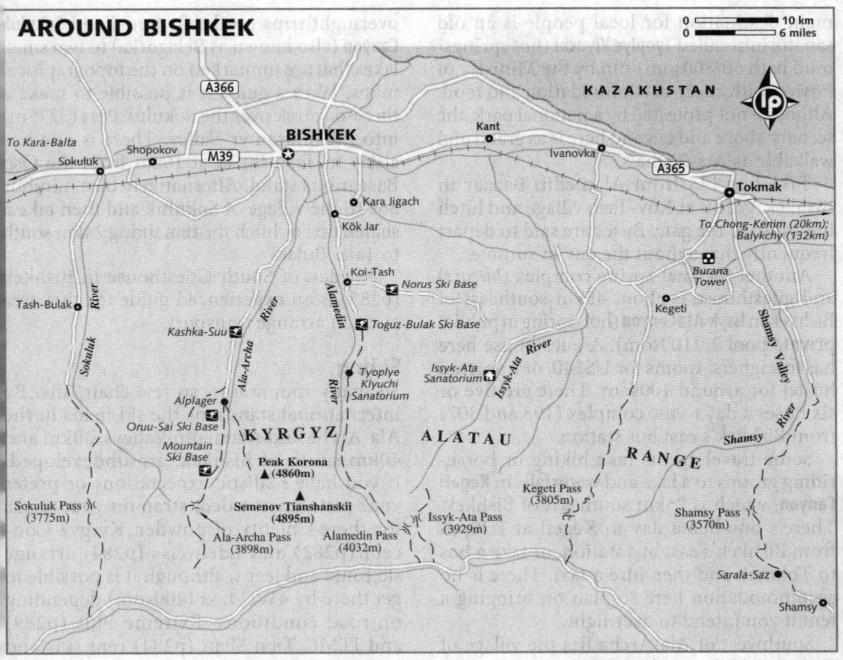


road ends at the *alplager* (base camp), home to a weather station, an A-frame lodge and a shabby hotel. In summer it has recreational facilities, baths and a sauna. Beyond this point the only transport is by foot or 4WD.

### Sleeping & Eating

The best way to enjoy Ala-Archa is by bringing your own tent and sleeping bag. The only year-round accommodation is a wooden **hotel** (d 200som) in the *alplager*, with a dozen spartan doubles, a common toilet and no running water, or the nearby A-frame, alpine-style **lodge** (☎ 0543-91 60 48; s/d/tr US$40/50/70, lux US$80). Try to avoid visiting on Saturday or Sunday, when '*biznezmen*' turn up by the BMW-load to drink vodka and eat salami.

### Getting There & Away

Bishkek travel agencies can arrange pricey day and longer trips including guides and gear. The best budget alternative would be to hire a taxi or hitch (though you'll still end up paying for the ride).

From Osh Bazaar bus stand in Bishkek, bus 365 runs five times a day to the gate (30som). Ask *vorota zapovednika*? (nature park gate?) when you board. You may even find minibuses running as far as the *alplager*. If these aren't running (likely outside of summer weekends), take a minibus from the Osh Bazaar bus stand as far as Kashka-Suu village, 7km from the park gate (itself 12km from the *alplager*), and hitch or hike from there.

Also from Bishkek, on Moskva, west-bound bus 11, and on Soviet, west-bound bus 26, go about 12km south to the end of the line near the city limits, from where you can hire a taxi or hitch (ask for *alplager*, not just 'Ala-Archa').

A taxi from Osh Bazaar costs around 150som one way to the gate, or 200som to the *alplager*. If you are planning to return the same day negotiate a rate for the day, otherwise you face a long hike back to the gate or leave yourself to the mercy of the taxi sharks at the *alplager*.

## OTHER CANYONS

Several valleys east of Ala-Archa have good walks and fewer visitors. In next-door **Alamedin Canyon**, 40km south of Bishkek, the main destination for local people is an old sanatorium called **Tyoplye Klyuchi** (hot springs/mud bath 60/800som) run by the Ministry of Power, with cheap accommodation and food. Although not protected by a national park, the scenery above and beyond here is as grand and walkable as Ala-Archa's.

Take bus 145 from Alamedin Bazaar in Bishkek, get off at Koy-Tash village and hitch the 14km to the gate. Buses are said to depart frequently throughout the day in summer.

Another thermal-spring complex *(kurort)* and guesthouse is about 45km southeast of Bishkek in **Issyk-Ata Canyon** (hot-spring in public/private pool 25/100som). A guesthouse here has foreigners' rooms for US$40, or a spartan hostel for around 100som. There are five or six buses a day to the complex (193 and 307) from Bishkek's east bus station.

Some travel agents take hiking or horse-riding groups to a lake and waterfalls in **Kegeti Canyon**, which is 75km southeast of Bishkek. There's one bus a day to Kegeti at 1.30pm from Bishkek's east bus station, or take a bus to Tokmak and then hire a taxi. There is no accommodation here so plan on bringing a tent if you intend to overnight.

Southwest of Ala-Archa lies the village of Tash-Bulak, from where you can make nice overnight trips up the fir tree–lined **Sokuluk Canyon** (also known as Belagorka) to two small lakes that are unmarked on the topographical maps. With a guide it is possible to make a three-day trek over the Sokuluk Pass (3775m) into the Suusamyr Valley. There is one bus a day to Tash-Bulak at 10am from the Osh Bazaar bus stand. Alternatively take minibus 369 to the village of Sokuluk and then take a shared taxi or hitch the remaining 24km south to Tash-Bulak.

Nurdan of South Guesthouse in Bishkek (p285) is an experienced guide for this area and can arrange transport.

### Skiing

So many mountains, so few chair lifts. By international standards the ski fields in the Ala-Archa and Alamedin Valleys, 30km and 40km south of Bishkek, are undeveloped. If you have realistic expectations or prefer your piste uncrowded, strap on your sticks for there's plenty of powder. Kyrgyz Concept (p282) and Edelweiss (p284) arrange ski tours and jeeps, although it is possible to get there by 4WD taxi (400som) depending on road conditions. Extreme Plus (p289) and ITMC Tien Shan (p284) rent skis and boards.

### TREKKING IN ALA-ARCHA

There are dozens of trekking and climbing possibilities here, but three main options. The gentlest walk runs 300m down-valley from the *alplager* (base camp), then across a footbridge and southwest up the **Adygene Valley**. Along this way is a climbers' cemetery in a larch grove, a pretty and poignant scene. The track continues for about 7km to 3300m, below Adygene Glacier.

The most popular trek goes straight up the main canyon on a disused 4WD track about 22km, to the abandoned **Upper Ala-Archa Mountain Ski Base**. There's a run-down ski chalet here, where trekkers can stay if it's not full. This is a long and tiring walk so start early in order to reach the ski chalet before nightfall.

Most demanding and dramatic is **Ak-Say Canyon**, with access via Ak-Say Glacier to the area's highest peaks. A trail climbs steeply to the east immediately above the *alplager,* continuing high above the stream. A strenuous three hours brings you to a camping area at the base of the icefall at 3350m (with a backpackers' tent city in summer). Another hour's or two's graft brings you to the beautiful glacial valley. Beyond here, climbers use a steel hut beside the glacier at 4150m (accessible only with some glacier walking). Serious climbing routes continue up to the peaks of Korona (4860m) and Uchityel (4572m). Semenov Tianshanskii (4895m), the highest peak in the Kyrgyz Alatau, is nearby.

You should be particularly careful about altitude sickness on this route. Try to do at least one day hike before tackling this route and don't sleep any higher than the icefall on the first night. See p479 for more info.

The trekking season around Ala-Archa is May to September or October, though the trail to the Ak-Say Glacier can be covered in snow even in August. Geoid in Bishkek (p279) sells a good 1:50,000 topographic map of the entire park, called *Prirodnyy Park Ala-Archa*.

### HELI-SKIING

Despite mountains of snow, the Terskey Alatau range has little in the way of ski-field development and many side valleys, ridges and glaciers are seldom, if ever, skied. Several companies such as Bishkek's Ak Sai Travel (p284) and Karakol's Turkestan (p302) can arrange heli-skiing – Kyrgyzstan's answer to the chairlift shortage.

MI-8-MTB helicopters ferry groups of up to 15 skiers and boarders plus guides and pilots to terrain within a zone selected according to snowfall, the weather, and your group's ability. It is possible to get as many as six different adrenaline-inducing descents within a day's skiing. It's worth checking that the guides carry an emergency radio to contact either the helicopter or mountain rescue in case of emergency.

**Tourist Center Kashka-Suu** (☎ 43 48 35; Kashka-Suu; d/tr/q 760/1050/1400som; lift pass adult/child 250/90som, ski rental 250som) operates a rope tow and the country's only chairlift (provided there is electricity) in a picturesque gorge on the northern slope of Kyrgyz Ridge in the Ala-Archa Valley. The hotel sleeps 65, is rather pleasant and includes a sauna, restaurant and ice-skating.

**Oruu-Sai Ski Base** (☎ 47 37 79; d/q US$25/45 lux US$70; rope tow pass 200som, ski rental 250-400som) has three temperamental rope tows and an instructor.

**Norus Ski Base** (☎ 66 11 11) in the Alamedin Valley has one old and one new rope tow. Accommodation is in an A-frame hotel.

**Toguz-Bulak Ski Base** (r 500som, cottage US$80-$100; 3 meals 300som; rope tow pass 300som, ski/snowboard rental 400-600som) is at a small field with only one platter (600m long) in the Alamedin Valley.

For information on heli-skiing see above.

### White-Water Rafting

It is also possible to raft some of the rivers spilling from the mountains. The most commonly rafted river is a 25km stretch of the Chuy between Tokmak and Balykchy (Class II to IV, group of four to seven US$35 per person, two hours) although some people extend this by continuing on the calm section of the river for a further two hours. See the Silk Road Water Centre (p282) to arrange trips.

## BURANA TOWER

East of Kegeti at the mouth of the Shamsy Valley, 80km from Bishkek, is a 1950s Soviet restoration of the so-called Burana Tower, an 11th-century monument that looks like the stump of a huge minaret. A mound to the northwest is all that's left of the ancient citadel of Balasagun, founded by the Sogdians and later, in the 11th century, a capital of the Karakhanids, which was excavated in the 1970s by Russian archaeologists. The Shamsy Valley itself has yielded a rich hoard of Scythian treasure, including a heavy gold burial mask, all either spirited away to St Petersburg or in storage in Bishkek's State Historical Museum.

You can climb the octagonal minaret (30som) to get an overview of the old city walls. On the other side of the citadel mound is an interesting collection of 6th- to 10th-century *balbals* (Turkic totem-like stone markers). The small **museum** (admission 60som; 🕓 8am-5pm) has 11th-century Christian carvings, Buddhist remains and Chinese coins, as well as info on local literary hero Haji Balasagun and his masterwork, the *Kutudhu Bilik*. Next door are the foundations of several mausoleums.

To get to Burana on your own, take the frequent 353 minibus from Bishkek's east bus station to Tokmak (40som, 45 minutes), from where it's about a 24km (250som) round trip by taxi. Buses run to Burana from Tokmak at 7am, 12.10pm and 3.30pm, returning 90 minutes later. The minaret could easily be visited en route to or from Issyk-Köl.

To the north, **Tokmak** has a large Sunday animal bazaar on the outskirts of town. Buses run frequently from the east bus station.

## CHONG-KEMIN VALLEY

The 80km-long Chong-Kemin Valley and National Park lies about 140km east of Bishkek, along the Kazakh border. The valley is famous locally as the birthplace of deposed president Akaev, but more importantly for travellers, it provides another great opportunity to roll up your sleeping bag and trek into the hills.

Trekking routes lead up the valley to Jasy-Köl (Green Lake) and either the Ozyorny Pass (3609m) to Kazakhstan's Bolshoe Almatinskoe region or the Ak-Suu Pass (4062m) to Grigorievka on the northern shores of Issyk-Köl.

**SOVIET SECRETS**

The town of Chong-Tash, 10km from Kashka-Suu village, holds a dark secret. On one night in 1937, the entire Soviet Kyrgyz government – nearly 140 people in all – were rounded up, brought here and shot dead, and their bodies dumped in a disused brick kiln on the site. Apparently almost no-one alive by the 1980s knew of this, by which time the site had been converted to a ski resort. But a watchman at the time of the murders, sworn to secrecy, told his daughter on his deathbed, and she waited until *perestroika* to tell police.

In 1991 the bodies were moved to a mass grave across the road, with a simple memorial, apparently paid for by the Kyrgyz author Chinghiz Aitmatov (whose father may have been one of the victims). The remains of the kiln are inside a fence nearby.

Minibuses 365 runs daily to Chong-Tash from the Osh Bazaar bus stands in Bishkek.

For trekking information see the boxed text, p136.

There's no formal accommodation in the valley but travellers recommend contacting Temirlan Daniyarov in Kaindy, the last hamlet in the valley, who can arrange a place to stay and horse treks. There are two buses a day to Chong-Kemin (70som, 2½ hours) from Bishkek's east bus station, at 10am and 1pm. Otherwise take a more frequent 352 bus to Kemin (45som, one hour) and then take a shared taxi the remaining 50km to Chong-Kemin (40som) or to Kaindy (80som).

KYRGYZSTAN

# LAKE ISSYK-KÖL & THE CENTRAL TIAN SHAN

# ОЗЕРО ИССЫК-КУЛЬ И ЦЕНТРАЛЬНЫЙ ТЯНЬ ШАНЬ

Lake Issyk-Köl (also Ysyk-Köl) is basically a huge dent, filled with water, between the Küngey (Sunny) Alatau to the north and the Terskey (Dark) Alatau to the south, which together form the northern arm of the Tian Shan. The name means 'warm lake'. A combination of extreme depth, thermal activity and mild salinity ensures the lake never freezes; its moderating effect on the climate, plus abundant rainfall, have made it something of an oasis through the centuries.

The Kyrgyz are proud of their lake and like a beautiful women on the arm of a Bishkek *biznezman,* she is trotted out, tarted up and paraded around whenever international guests needs to be impressed. And why not? For beautiful she is – in all her querulous moods. Even as storms rage across her northern sandy shores, the steep and stony south lies calm and still.

Scores of streams pour into the lake but none escape her. Over 170km long, 70km across and the second-largest alpine lake in the world (after Lake Titicaca in South America), Issyk-Köl is a force of nature and she knows it.

Some people say the lake level has periodically risen and fallen over the centuries, inundating ancient shoreline settlements. Artefacts have been recovered from what is called the submerged city of Chigu, dating from the 2nd century BC, at the east end. Mikhaylovka inlet, created by an earthquake near Karakol, reveals the remains of a partly submerged village. Despite recent fluctuations, geological evidence points to a long-term drop – some 2m in the last 500 years.

After tsarist military officers and explorers put the lake on Russian maps, immigrants flooded in to found low-rise, laid-back, rough-and-ready towns. Health spas lined its shores in Soviet days, with guests from all over the USSR, but spa tourism crashed along with the Soviet Union, only reviving in the last few years thanks to an influx of moneyed Kazakh tourists. Choplan-Ata (p296) is the safest bet for those keen for a Russian-style rub down but for a surreal experience head to the Jet-Öghüz Sanatorium (p309), once a favoured holiday-spot for Soviet dignitaries and cosmonauts and now Centrals Asia's leading contender as the most likely place to be haunted. Close your eyes and listen to the place fall apart.

The part of the central Tian Shan range accessible from the lake comprises perhaps the finest trekking territory in Central Asia. The

**ISSYK-KÖL BIOSPHERE RESERVE**

The Issyk-Köl region has an astonishing array of ecosystems, from desert and semi-desert in the southwest to steppe, meadow, forest, and subalpine and glacial to the north and southeast. Local fauna includes Marco Polo sheep, ibex, wild boar, snow leopards, ibisbill, manul, Himalayan snowcocks, wild geese, egrets and other waders.

Plans are therefore afoot to create a reserve the size of Switzerland around the lake. This would consist of a mountainous core area, a buffer zone that would allow seasonal land use, and a transition and rehabilitation zone. The proposals will link up several existing reserves.

most popular treks hop between valleys south of Karakol or lead from Almaty to the lake.

## History

The Kyrgyz people migrated in the 10th to 15th centuries from the Yenisey river basin in Siberia, and in all probability arrived by way of Issyk-Köl. This high basin would be a natural stopover for any caravan or conquering army as well. It appears to have been a centre of Saka (Scythian) civilisation and legend has it that Timur (Tamerlane) used it for a summer headquarters (p299). There are at least 10 documented settlements currently under the waters of the lake and treasure hunters have long scoured the lake for flooded trinkets attributed to everyone from Christian monks to Jenghiz Khan.

The first Russian, Ukrainian and Belarussian settlers came to the east end of the lake in 1868. Karakol town was founded the next year, followed in the 1870s by Tüp, Teploklyuchenka (Ak-Suu), Ananyevo, Pokrovka (now Kyzyl-Suu) and a string of others, many of whose Cossack names have stuck. Large numbers of Dungans and Uyghurs arrived in the 1870s and '80s following the suppression of Muslim uprisings in China's Shaanxi, Gansu and Xinjiang provinces. Local Kyrgyz and Kazakhs were still at that time mostly nomadic.

The Issyk-Köl region (and in fact most of Kyrgyzstan beyond Bishkek) was off limits to foreigners in Soviet times. Locals mention vast, officially sanctioned plantations of opium poppies and cannabis around the lake, though most of these had disappeared under international pressure by the early 1970s.

More importantly, Issyk-Köl was used by the Soviet navy to test high-precision torpedoes, far from prying Western eyes. An entire polygon or military-research complex grew around Koy-Sary, on the Mikhaylovka inlet near Karakol. In 1991 Russian President Boris Yeltsin asked that it be continued but Kyrgyz President Askar Akaev shut down the whole thing, ordering it to be converted to peaceful pursuits. These days the most secretive thing in the lake is the mysterious *jekai*, a Kyrgyz version of the Loch Ness monster.

Jokes about the 'Kyrgyz navy' refer to a fleet of some 40 ageing naval cutters, now mothballed at Koy-Sary or decommissioned and hauling goods and tourists up and down the lake.

## Getting There & Away

The western road access to Issyk-Köl is a 40km-long, landslide-prone, slightly sinister canyon called Shoestring Gorge (Boömskoe ushchelie), which climbs into the Alatau east of Tokmak, with a howling wind funnelling up it most of the time.

There's a police checkpoint just west of Balykchy, where cars are searched for drugs and an 'ecotax' is collected from each inbound vehicle from outside Issyk-Köl and Naryn provinces.

From the north, a rough jeep road (4WD only) from Almaty's Bolshoe Almatinskoe lake leads over the Ozerny Pass, through the Chong-Kemin Valley and then the Kok Ayryk Pass to Chong-Sary-Oy near Cholpon-Ata. There's no public transport along the route, the bridges often get washed out and there's no immigration post, making it a particularly tricky option for foreigners. It might make an interesting mountain-bike trip if you can sort out the visa situation.

# TAMCHY ТАМЧЫ

☎ 3943

This small lakeshore village, 35km from Cholpon-Ata, has a decent beach and offers a quieter alternative to larger, bustling Cholpon-Ata. Out of season, you'll likely see more donkeys than tourists on the beach. The town boasts one small supermarket, near the mosque on the main road (Manas), which is big on vodka and light on everything else. By the end of September you'll find more life in a morgue.

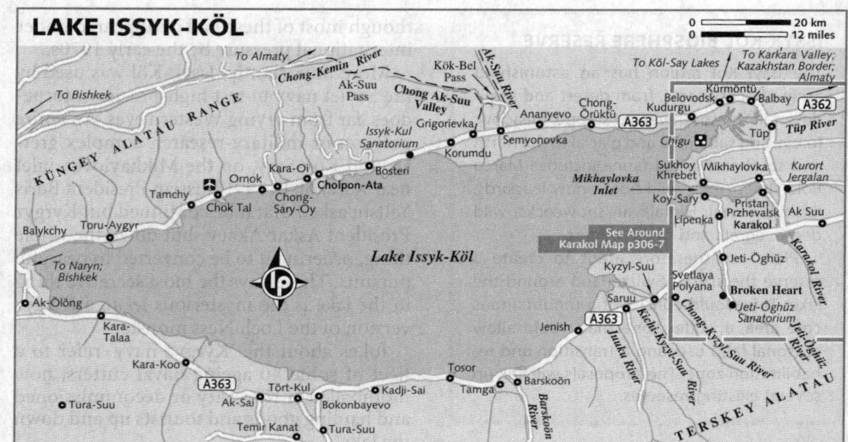




**Tamchy Guesthouse** (cnr Batikov & Chyngyshbaeva; s/d 100/200som) In a town where you get what you pay for, these green-and-white beach sheds are the cheapest option around. Because of the decrepit state of the rooms and lack of shower facilities, they are sometimes reluctant to check in foreigners.

**CBT** (☎ 2 13 39; cnr Batikov & Isabekov; dm 250-300som) Right on the beach and a five-minute walk from the main road. Offers decent rooms (price includes breakfast) and can put you in touch with other homestays in the area. It also arranges donkey rental, day trips and overnight yurtstays in the hills north of town. Contact Kudaibergen Kurenov.

During the summer months many locals rent rooms to Kazakh holidaymakers and, once over their disbelief that a foreigner wants to stay, are happy to take in guests. Ask around.

There's lots of minibus traffic through to Bishkek (90som) and Cholpon-Ata (50som). Flag down anything with wheels going your way on the main road. The Issyk-Köl airport, 3km outside Tamchy near the village of Chok Tal, is currently closed for renovation thanks to a Russian grant.

## CHOLPON-ATA ЧОЛПОН АТА

☎ 3943

Cholpon-Ata hums during high season (mid-July to August) when the town is besieged by Russian, Kazakh and local holidaymakers, all of whom head for the beach, which is about as far away from the ocean as you can get. The number of cafés jump from about five to around 30 in the height of summer if you include all the 'Mum and Dad' operations selling borscht, shashlyk and beer.

Sports teams from other Central Asian republics and Russia compete here in early September in track and field events and soccer tournaments. Besides the beach, the ancient rock inscriptions on the outskirts of town are the village's main attraction. The sanatorium, formerly a retreat for the Communist Party elite, has fallen into disrepair, although it's still operational.

### Orientation & Information

The town has two reference points: the bazaar and, 1km west, the cluster of shops around the post office. Both are on the main road.

There's internet access at the **post office** (per hr 20som plus 8som megabyte) and lots of exchange booths around town.

**Investbank** (🕑 8am-5pm Mon-Fri, 9am-3pm Sat) gives advances on Visa and MasterCard for 3% commission and has an ATM. The bank is set off the road, within the newly revamped children's park.

**Ecocentre** (☎ 4 22 76; Soviet 61; 🕑 9am-5pm Mon-Fri) is a Kyrgyz-German cooperative opened in 2004 to help formulate sustainable tourism initiatives within the local community. Currently there is little information in English and the small exhibit of flora and fauna from within the Issyk-Köl Biosphere is in Russian. This could change with the opening of a Tourist Information Centre on the right side of the building in 2007. The Ecocentre also offers accommodation within the same building in a series of clean, functional, although pricey, rooms.

## Sights & Activities

### BEACHES & BOATS

A pleasant public beach lies 1km south of the west bus station. Walk south from the bus station to the chalets of the Gost Residenza and then head east, across a bridge over a lagoon to the beach. In true Soviet style, the Speedo-sporting, pot-bellied men here like to sunbathe standing up. The presidential beach house is nearby; when the president is in town the police are out in force. Keep your passport at the ready and an eye out for his luxury yacht. There is another larger beach called Alytn-Köl, 4km east of Cholpon-Ata.

The Manas Cultural Park on the lakeshore has a small sculpture garden.

The **Kruiz Yacht Club** (☎ 4 43 73) has a handful of sailboats (US$25 per hour for up to six people) and even an overpriced scuba-diving centre.

### PETROGLYPHS

Above the town is a huge field of glacial boulders, many with pictures scratched or picked into their surfaces. Some of these **petroglyphs** (adult/student 30/5som, guides per person 40som; daylight) date from the later Bronze Age (about 1500 BC) but most are Saka-Usun (8th century BC to 1st century AD), predating the arrival of the Kyrgyz in the area. The Saka priests used the sacred site for sacrifices and other rites to the sun god and lived in settlements that are currently underwater in the Cholpon-Ata bay. Later engravings date from the Turkic era (5th to 10th century). Most are of long-horned ibex, along with some wolves, deer and hunters, and some rocks appear to be arranged in sacred circles. Late afternoon is a good time to view the stones, which all face south.

Take the signed road opposite the boatyard turn-off north for 2.2km, bearing left to a section of black iron fence. The stones are behind this. There's a nice view of Issyk-Köl below. Guided tours of the petroglyphs can be arranged at the regional museum and help pinpoint the field's more impressive inscriptions.

There are more petroglyphs in the region, at Kara-Oi, a 2km walk from the site, and near Ornok (4km up the new jeep road to Kazakhstan).

### REGIONAL MUSEUM

This small **Issyk-Köl museum** (☎ 4 21 48; Soviet 69; adult/camera 35/250som; 9am-6pm) is worth a quick visit. The emphasis is on archaeology, with displays of local Scythian (Saka) gold jewellery, *balbal* gravestones and a fine set of mouth harps. Other rooms are devoted to ethnography, Kyrgyz bards, music and costume.

### TREKKING & HORSE RIDING

Ornok forest, north of the petroglyph park, is popular with locals who collect mushrooms here during August. Follow the old logging



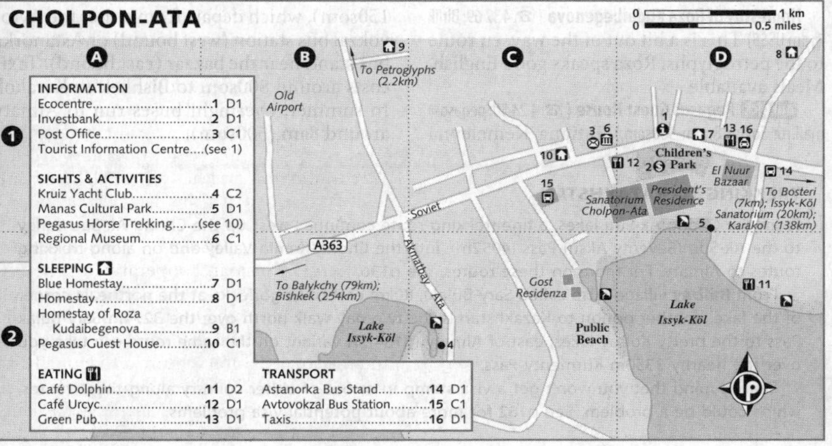

road on the left side of the valley, keep the river on the right.

**Pegasus Horse Trekking** (☎ 4 24 50; pegaso@mail.ru; Soviet 81) is run by the same lady who operates the B&B of the same name. She organises horse treks to Ornok Valley and along the lakeshore, offers expert instruction for less-confident riders and can arrange multiday excursions to Grigorievka (opposite) and beyond. With a few days notice she will also organise a display of nomadic equestrian games (17,000som to 20,000som) at the local hippodrome. During July these can be seen for free as part of the Unesco-supported horse games.

## Sleeping

Plenty of families rent out rooms (*komnat* in Russian) in Cholpon-Ata. The best people to ask are the elderly ladies at the bus station, although someone may approach you directly if you have a backpack and look lost.

**Blue Homestay** (☎ 4 23 02; Soviet 39; d/tr 200/300som) Unsigned but unmistakably painted dark blue, this is a good option with a communal kitchen and dining area, large garden and shared bathroom. The houses nearby are also homestays and also unsigned. Ask for '*Gastinochnyi Dom*' when you ring the doorbell, or just look lost.

**Homestay** (☎ 4 39 51; cholponalim@maril.ru; Osmanova 4; dm 200som) A five-minute walk north of the El Nuur Bazaar, this is a friendly place, but a bit out of the way. Look for the tatty basketball hoop hanging off the garage. Meals are available.

**Homestay of Roza Kudaibegenova** (☎ 4 32 69; Birlik 1; dm US$5) This is a bit out of the way, en route to the petroglyphs. Roza speaks good English. Meals available.

**our pick** **Pegasus Guest House** (☎ 4 24 50; pegaso@mail.ru; Soviet 8; dm 300som;) Tatiana Kemelevna and her irrepressible son, Bukit, have a good handle on budget backpacker requirements and can offer advice on local activities and all things equine. The price includes breakfast and the house is clean and comfortable and centrally located near the post office.

## Eating & Drinking

Most cafés close between October and May.

**Café Urcyc** (Soviet 68; mains 50-85som; ⌚ lunch & dinner) Nestled among a string of cafés, it serves decent food at reasonable prices.

**Green Pub** (☎ 4 29 76; Soviet 11; mains 80-150som, tap beer 35som; ⌚ summer only, lunch & dinner) This Russian-operated restaurant gives *shashlik* (80som) a new twist by threading vegetables between the meat chucks. The barbecue fish (150som) is also recommended.

**Café Dolphin** (mains 40-60som; ⌚ summer only) Serves the best *plov* (45som) in Cholpon-Ata and doles out ice cold beers to thirsty sunbathers.

## Getting There & Away

Cholpon-Ata, being the premier resort town for nearby and comparatively wealthy Kazakhs, is particularly prone to fluctuating transport costs. During summer, shared-taxi prices are doubled for tourists and locals alike. Prices here are low-season rates.

Buses run every hour from 7am to 7pm to/from Bishkek (100som) and continue to Grigorievka (35som), Ananyevo (50som), and Karakol (80som). There are also minibuses (Bishkek 150som; Karakol 100som) and shared taxis (Bishkek 200som; Karakol 150som), which depart from either the Avtovokzal bus station (west bound) or Astanorka bus stand near the bazaar (east bound). Taxis costs around 800som to Bishkek or Karakol. In summer, overnight buses run to Almaty around 8am (500som).

### TREKKING TO KAZAKHSTAN

From the Chong Ak-Suu lakes, a fine trekking route continues west up the Chong Ak-Suu Valley to the Ak-Suu (Severny Aksu) Pass (4052m), into the Chong-Kemin Valley and on along trekking routes to Almaty. For more on these routes, see p136.

From **Balbay** village (also called Sary-Bulak), 80km east of Grigorievka at the northeast corner of the lake, another option to Kazakhstan is the two-day walk north over the 3274m Sary-Bulak Pass to the pretty Kolsay lakes, east of Almaty (p134). A variant on the same route can take you over the nearby 3350m Kurmenty Pass.

Bear in mind that you won't get a visa stamp in or out of either country along these routes, which could be a problem. See p182 for more about potential visa problems.

## GRIGORIEVKA & THE AK-SUU VALLEY

It's possible to take a detour from Grigorievka village up the Chong Ak-Suu Valley to a trio of alpine lakes. The Helvetas-supported **Rural Advisory Service (RADS) coordinator** (contact Nazgul Namazbaeva, Russian only; Likholetova 6) in Grigorievka, a couple of kilometres off the main road, can theoretically arrange transport, horses and yurtstays up in the valley, though the programme hasn't yet had much experience. Pegasus Horse Trekking (p298) organises horse treks between Grigorievka and Semenovka gorges overnighting in either tents or yurts. Alternatively, you could hitch and hike up the valley 22km or so to the sea-green lakes. There are two yurts, a sanatorium and a yurt café along the valley, with a yurtstay (check first) by the first lake.

The nearby village of Semenovka offers access to the Kichi (Little) Ak-Suu Valley, which has the Kyrchyn Gorge and a winter sports centre.

## KARKARA VALLEY КАРКАРАНСКАЯ ДОЛИНА

The eastern gateway to the Issyk-Köl Basin is an immense, silent valley called Karkara, straddling the Kyrgyzstan–Kazakhstan border. On the Kyrgyzstan side it begins about 60km northeast of Karakol and widens out to 40km or more, shoulder-deep in good pasture during summer. Every herder in the Karakol region (and in the Kegen region on the Kazakhstan side) brings animals up here in summer to fatten, and the warm-weather population is an easy-going mix of Kyrgyz and Kazakh *chabana* (cowboys), their families and their yurts.

The name Karkara means Black Crane, after the graceful migratory birds that stop here in June and again in August to September, en route between South Africa and Siberia.

Summer's end brings the **Shepherds' Festival**, an annual gathering of cowboys and herders at the end of August. Horseback games and eagle hunting are held at the yurt camps near Char-Kuduk village.

In his *A Day Lasts Longer Than a Century* the Kyrgyz writer Chinghiz Aitmatov has the ancient Kyrgyz peoples arriving here from the Yenisey region of Siberia.

Some people suggest that Timur (Tamerlane) made Karkara his summer headquarters for several years, and point to a house-size pile of round stones in the southwest part of the valley. These, they say, were Timur's way of estimating his losses in eastern campaigns – each departing soldier put a rock on the pile, each returnee removed one, and the stones that remained represented the dead. The name of the site, **San-Tash**, means 'Counting Stones'.

Sceptics and amateur historians point to an adjacent, stone-lined pit that appears to be the remnant of a burial chamber, and suggest that the football-size stones were just used to cover the chamber, and were removed by archaeologists or grave-robbers. Either way, the site has a dreamy, magical feel.

### Sleeping

**Ethnotour Santash** (☎ in Karakol 3922-2 32 36; per person €12) the TIC in Karakol can put you in touch with a fledgling yurt camp, near the Kyrgyz village of Char-Kuduk and close to the Alpinist's and the Kazakh company Kan Tengri's base camps, just across the river in Kazakhstan (p136). Breakfast is included, or three meals cost €18.

Another **yurt camp** (0502-21 70 79; B&B 400som) near Karkara village can also arrange trekking within the area. Contact Tolon Jumanaliv.

Shaidelda, who runs **Shaidylada's B&B** (☎ 3945-2 14 11; Belinskaya 1) in Tüp village once ran a yurt camp in the valley and may still be a useful source of information. Breakfast is included and other meals are 120som.

### Getting There & Away

The Karkara Valley is about 50km east of Tüp or 70 much prettier but rougher kilometres from Karakol (p183) via Novovoznesenovka. On the Tüp route a round trip by taxi from Karakol is about 1800som one-way. Ask for *pamyatnik San-Tash* (San-Tash Monument), just opposite a small collective farm settlement, 19km from the Kazakhstan border.

Derelict buses run from Karakol's Ak Tilek Bazaar to San-Tash (60som) via Tüp at 12.30pm. There's also a slow daily bus to Char-Kuduk via San-Tash. There are daily buses to Kyzyl Jar (former Sovietskoe) or on to the mining town of Jyrgalang (Russians call it Jergalan *shakhta*, which means 'mine'); you might try hitching from Kyzyl Jar.

The Karkara (Karkyra) River forms the modern Kyrgyzstan–Kazakhstan border through part of the valley and this makes an interesting route to or from Kazakhstan. If you are headed to Kazakhstan make sure you get a border stamp, even if it means waiting some time. You will of course need valid visas for both republics. There's no cross-border public transport.

**HIDDEN TREASURES**

Large mounds on both sides of the road just west of the village of **Belovodsk** (50km east of Ananyevo or 15km west of Tüp) are said to be unexcavated Scythian (Saka) burial chambers. Other mounds excavated near Barskoön, across the lake, yielded bronze vessels and jewellery (now in museums in St Petersburg). There are more in the Karkara Valley just across the Kazakh border. One near the town of Yessik in Kazakhstan yielded a fabulous golden warrior's costume, now Kazakhstan's greatest archaeological treasure (p119).

At Belovodsk is a turn-off south to the hamlet of Svetyy Mys, which at least one Soviet archaeologist insisted was the site of a 4th- or 5th-century Armenian Christian monastery. The story goes that its inhabitants were driven out by surrounding tribes, but not before hiding a huge cache of gold (and, some say, the bones of St Matthew) that has never been found. From the hills above, the village roads can be seen to trace something approximating an Orthodox cross.

Coming from the Kazakhstan side, you can get a Kegen, Saryzhaz or Narynkol bus from Almaty and get off at Kegen, from where it's a difficult 28km hitch south to the border itself. A taxi from Karakol to Almaty via Kegen takes about seven hours and costs around US$120, including car customs fees.

## KARAKOL КАРАКОЛ

☎ 3922 / pop 66,000

Karakol is a peaceful, low-rise town with backstreets full of Russian gingerbread cottages, shaded by rows of huge white poplars. Around the town are apple orchards, for which the area is famous. This is the administrative centre of Issyk-Köl province, and the best base for exploring the lakeshore, the Terskey Alatau and the central Tian Shan. It also has a very good Sunday market. In fact, try to time your visit to include a Sunday, when the animal bazaar and Russian Cathedral are at their most active.

It's not quite paradise for those who live here – the economic stresses since independence and the decline in spa tourism have led to considerable hardship, thinned out available goods and services, and returned a kind of frontier atmosphere to this old boundary post.

The town name means something like 'black hand/wrist', possibly a reference to the hands of immigrant Russian peasants, black from the valley's rich soil.

### History

After a military garrison was established at nearby Teploklyuchenka (Ak-Suu) in 1864, and it dawned on everybody what a fine spot the area near the lake was – mild climate, rich soil, a lake full of fish, and mountains full of hot springs – the garrison commander was told to scout out a place for a full-sized town. Karakol was founded on 1 July 1869, with streets laid out in a European-style checkerboard, and the garrison was relocated here. The town's early population had a high proportion of military officers, merchants, professionals and explorers.

It was called Przewalski in Soviet times, after the explorer Nikolai Przewalski, whose last expedition ended here, and who is buried on the lakeshore nearby (p305). The town didn't escape a trashing by the Bolsheviks. Its elegant Orthodox church lost its domes and became a club; only one small church on the outskirts was allowed to remain open. Of nine mosques (founded by Tatars, Dungans and various Kyrgyz clans), all bar the Dungan's were wrecked.

### Orientation

Karakol has a central square, but the real commercial hubs are the Jakshilik Bazaar (nicknamed *gostinny dvor* – the Russian equivalent of a caravanserai or merchants' inn, after its namesake in St Petersburg) and also Ak Tilek Bazaar (good wishes). The long-distance bus station is about 2km to the north and the 'better' part of the town is considered to be west of the river.

### Information

#### INTERNET ACCESS

**Art Gallery Dali** (☎ 2 39 33; Lenina 152; per hr 30som; 🕒 8am-8pm summer, 8.30am-6.30pm winter) Also has internet phone and Skype.

**Post office** (Gebze; per hr 30som; 🕒 8am-noon & 1-5pm Mon-Fri)

#### LAUNDRY

**Red Crescent Laundry** (☎ 2 43 55; Dupen Lerbishev 188; per item 5-20som; 🕒 8am-7pm) You can clean more than clothes here – there is a small public *banya* (bath; 35som).

KYRGYZSTAN

## MEDICAL SERVICES

**Karakol Medical Clinic** (☎ 5 13 23; Jusup Abdrakhmanov; ⏰ 8am-5pm) Large and pink, this building is directly opposite the Tourist Information Centre (TIC) whose staff are happy to help translate in an emergency. Doctors keep individual hours and there is a pharmacy on the ground floor.

## MONEY

Moneychangers everywhere will change crisp, near-new US dollars into som.

**AKB Bank** (☎ 5 37 45; Toktogul; ⏰ 8.30am-noon & 1-3pm Mon-Fri) Changes US-dollar travellers cheques into som for a 3% commission (minimum US$5) and gives cash advances on Visa and MasterCard for 2.5% commission.

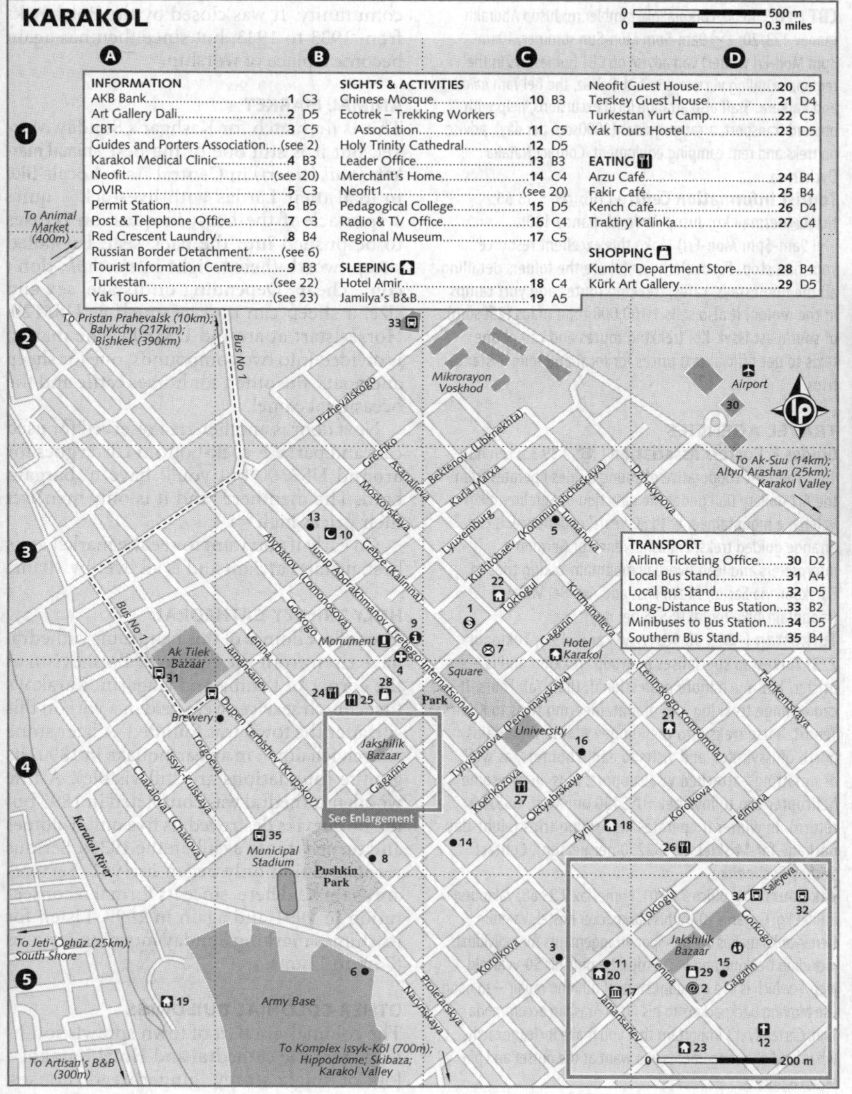

Go in the main building, turn left and head upstairs; look for the Western Union sign.

### REGISTRATION & VISAS

**OVIR** (Room 114, Kushtobaev) A 30-day visa extension costs 600som. To register it's 70som.

### TOURIST INFORMATION

**CBT** (☎ 5 50 00; cbtkarakol@rambler.ru; Jusup Abdrakhmanov 123/20; 🕑 9am-5pm Mon-Sun summer, 10am-3pm Mon-Fri winter) Can advise on CBT homestays in the region, including yurtstays in Jeti-Öghüz, the Bel Tam *jailoo* and Karkara. Staff also arrange local excursions, help with onward transport, arrange guides (1000som per day), advise on treks and rent camping equipment. Contact Natalia Ovcharova.

**Tourist Information Centre** (TIC; ☎ 5 13 56; ticigu@netmail.kg; Jusup Abdrakhmanov 130; 🕑 9am-5pm Mon-Fri) Make this excellent resource your first stop. Particularly useful are the folders detailing all the homestays, cafés, trekking routes and yurt camps in the region. It also sells 1:100,000 topo maps (250som) of southeast Issyk-Köl trekking routes and can phone taxis to get official taxi prices for local and long-distance trips.

KYRGYZSTAN

### TRAVEL AGENCIES

**Guides & Porters Association** (☎ 2 39 33; Lenina 152) This new cooperative of young guides operates from the Art Gallery Dali under the direction of Serebrennikov Valeriy, a mountaineer with 30 years' experience. It can arrange guided treks, English, French or German interpreters and lead five-day mountain-biking trips to Barskoön via Saruu, Juuku Pass and Ara-Bel Valley (mountain-bike rental US$25 per day).

**Turkestan** (☎ 5 98 96; www.karakol.kg; Toktogul 273) Turkestan specialises in group trekking and is pricier, but much more professional, than Yak Tours. It can arrange trekking and mountaineering trips to Khan Tengri, horse treks into the Küngey Alatau mountains north of Issyk-Köl, and visits to eagle hunters, as well as no-strings-attached visa support, plus an awesome helicopter trip to Inylchek (US$150 one way, US$250 return). In winter it operates heli-skiing trips (eight-day package for 14 skiers, US$2250 per person). Contact Sergey Pyshnenko.

**Yak Tours** (☎ office 5 69 01, home/fax 2 23 68; yaktours@infotel.kg; Gagarin 10) At his backpacker hostel, Valentin Derevyanko makes on-the-spot arrangements for individuals, including trekking and horse trips. He puts his 50-year-old jeep – which is in a constant state of running repair – to good use ferrying backpackers to his Altyn Arashan accommodation. Certainly it's important that you make it clear exactly what kind of arrangements you want at the outset and pin down a price.

## Sights

### CHINESE MOSQUE

What looks for all the world like a Mongolian Buddhist temple on the corner of Bektenov and Jusup Abdrakhmanov is in fact a mosque, built without nails, completed in 1910 after three years' work by a Chinese architect and 20 Chinese artisans, for the local Dungan community. It was closed by the Bolsheviks from 1933 to 1943, but since then has again become a place of worship.

### ANIMAL MARKET

This is no match for Kashgar's Sunday Market, but it is still one of the best **animal markets** *(mal bazari)* in Central Asia. Locals like to load their Lardas with livestock – quite a spectacle if the beast in question refuses to be pushed into the back seat. Fat-tailed sheep, worth their weight in *shashlik*, don't come cheap. Depending on its age, sex and size, a sheep can cost as much as US$120. Horses start at around US$300. The market is divided into two compounds, one for sheep and goats; the other, for horses cattle and the occasional camel.

Next door is another area reserved for used cars and parts. A rock-bottom Larda goes for around US$300 but you'll have to bargain hard. The men here (and it is only men) set their prices high.

Go early if you want to see the market at its best: it starts at 5am and is all over by 10am.

### HOLY TRINITY CATHEDRAL

The yellow domes of this handsome cathedral have risen from the rubble of Bolshevism at the corner of Lenina and Gagarin. Karakol's first church services were held in a yurt on this site after the town was founded. A later stone church fell down in an earthquake in 1890 (its granite foundations are still visible). A fine wooden cathedral was completed in 1895 but the Bolsheviks destroyed its five onion-domes and turned it into a club in the 1930s. Serious reconstruction only began in 1961. Services are again held here, since its formal reconsecration in 1991 and again in 1997. Listen for its chimes marking Sunday morning services (7am to 11am).

### OTHER COLONIAL BUILDINGS

The colonial-era part of town sprawls southwest from the cathedral and Hotel Karakol – lots of single-storey 'gingerbread' houses, mostly plain but some (eg those built by wealthier officers and scientists) are quite pretty, and a few (those of Russian merchants and industrialists) have two storeys. Among decaying former merchants' houses are the **Pedagogical College** on Gagarin opposite the cathedral, the **radio & TV office** on Gebze (Kalinina), a block south of Hotel Karakol, and another old **merchant's home** at the corner of Koenközova and Lenina.

#### REGIONAL MUSEUM

Karakol's modest **regional museum** (Jamansariev 164; admission 50som, camera 10som; 9am-5pm Mon-Fri, 10am-4pm Sat & Sun summer) is in a sturdy colonial brick building, once the home of a wealthy landowner. It's of limited interest with exhibits on the petroglyphs around Issyk-Köl, a few Scythian bronze artefacts, a Soviet history of the Kyrgyz union with Russia, some Kyrgyz applied art and photographs of old Karakol – all of it better with a guide.

#### OTHER SIGHTS & ACTIVITIES

The leafy **Pushkin Park** by the stadium, four blocks south of the centre, includes the collective grave of a squad of Red Army soldiers killed in the pursuit of *basmachi*.

About 3km south of the centre (take bus 1) is Central Asia's very first **hippodrome**. Headless goats are still passionately fought over by mounted horsemen during **Independence Day (31 August)** celebrations. If you are in town at this time, the games are well worth checking out.

### Activities

Karakol's travel agencies (opposite) organise activities such as horse riding, skiing, mountaineering and mountain biking.

#### TREKKING

At the height of summer it seems that every other traveller has just descended down a mountain and immediately bandies around superlative-studded sentences that cause the other half to rush out, rent a sleeping bag and take to the hills. With so many trekking opportunities and a concentration of well-informed travel agencies (opposite) there is no good reason not to. See the boxed text, p308 for a sample of the possible routes. The **TIC** (opposite) also rents tents (US$5), sleeping bags (US$4), backpacks (US$2) and sleeping mats (US$1).

**Alp Tour Issyk Köl** (☎ 2 05 48; khanin@infotel.kg) This professional company offers a range of treks around Karakol and further afield, including Kazakhstan and Khan Tengri base camp. They can arrange border permits in a day (US$25), supply guide/cooks (US$25/35 per day), porters (US$18) and climbing guides for Khan Tengri (US$40 to US$50). The staff will also resupply your own long-distance treks and arrange daily transport on request to the Karakol ski base in winter. Contact Stas & Igor.

**Ecotrek – Trekking Workers Association** (☎ 5 11 15; karakol@rambler.ru; Toktogula 112A) Rents trekking equipment including sleeping bags (100som), two-/three-person tents (160som), primus stoves (40soms) and sells gas canisters. The staff can also arrange guided treks (guides, cooks and porters) and guided horse treks in the surrounding valleys including a five-day trek from their yurt camp in the Valley of the Flowers, and Jeti-Öghuz to Altyn Arashan.

**Leader** (☎ 5 41 84; root@lider.cango.net.kg; Bldg 142, Apt 6, Jusup Abdrakhmanov 142) This NGO rents out trekking equipment to fund its youth development programmes. Equipment includes backpacks (50som per day), tents (100som to 150som), sleeping bags (50soms), sleeping mats and stoves (20som each) and mountaineering equipment (not rope). You can find Leader on the corner of Gorkogo, just north of the mosque, hidden on the 2nd floor of an apartment block and accessed from the east.

**Neofit** (☎ 2 06 50; www.neofit.kg/Kyrgyzstan.htm; Jamansariev 166) All kinds of trekking support including outfitting and border permits; based in the Neofit guesthouse.

## Sleeping

Karakol has more homestays than you can shake a sleeping bag at and both CBT and TIC (opposite) can put you in touch with the local homestays. Generally prices range from 250som to 450som per person including breakfast and most can provide dinner for an additional 100som to 120som, although (depending what you are served) this is not always the best value; local restaurants are often cheaper.

**Turkestan Yurt Camp** (☎ 5 64 89; Toktogul 273; tent site & shower usage €2, yurt dm & shower usage €5, r per person €10) The slightly muttony-smelling yurt dorms here have a base-camp feel as trekking expeditions bustle in and out in the Russian Zil trucks. The meals (3 meals €15) are served up in a cosy wooden bar.

**Yak Tours Hostel** (☎ 5 69 01, ☎ /fax 2 23 68; yaktours@infotel.kg; Gagarin 10; dm 200som) This was the first backpacker-style hostel in Central Asia. Facilities include left luggage, equipment rental, an info board, a communal kitchen and a small collection of videos on Central Asia. There is an eclectic array of rooms, some comfortable private and secure, others less so with beds in corridors (separated by a curtain). You can pitch a tent in the yard for 50som. Chef Babalina makes tasty food (meals from 100som). The downside is there's only one bathroom.

**Gala's Group** (r per person 200-350som) Runs four apartments around town that make for a cheap alternative to midrange hotels. Options range from single rooms to apartments with two double rooms, an equipped kitchen, hot showers and phone. Book at the TIC.

**Artisan's B&B** (☎ 5 01 71; Murmanskaya 114; dm 350som) This appropriately named B&B is run by a family of artisans who built everything by hand themselves; from the house itself to the painted Chinese horoscope on the ceiling.

**Terskey Guesthouse** (☎ 2 62 68; www.teskey.narod.ru; Asanalieva 44; dm 400som) It has Western-style bathrooms, a Russian-style sauna, excellent food and a laundry service. The son, Taalai, speaks good English; his mother is a wonderful host and his father owns a terminally ill taxi.

**Neofit Guesthouse** (☎ 2 06 50; neofit@issyk-kul.kg; Jamansariev 166; s 400som) A central, clean option, popular with trekkers who swap stories over a beer in the sociable courtyard. There's a wide range of old-fashioned but comfortable rooms with a private bathroom (but common shower), plus parking and a bizarre dungeon (summer only) restaurant.

**Jamilya's B&B** (☎ 4 30 19; kemelov@hotmail.com; Shopokova 34B; dm 450som) The mother-and-son team both speak excellent English and offer rooms with a hue – lime, purple, yellow or blue. The bathrooms are spotless, the balcony pleasant and there is a yurt (400som) in the front garden. The son is also a capable guide.

**Hotel Amir** (☎ 5 13 15; info@hotelamir.kg; Ayni 78; s/d US$39/56, baby's cot/child's bed US$15; 💻) Opened in 2006 this hotel fills a void in the midpriced market, offering simple but bright and cheerful rooms with *ala-kiyiz* wall hangings and queen-sized beds. It has its own power generator and a rather plain café. Breakfast is included.

## Eating

**Traktiry Kalinka** (☎ 2 77 77; Jusup Abdrakhmanov 99; dishes 30som; 🕒 lunch & dinner, closed Sun) The grumpy service here doesn't mar the cosy décor, good selection of salads and cold draught beer. Look for the pretty Russian façade.

**Arzu Café** (☎ 2 39 99; Kushtobaev 17; mains 30-80som; 🕒 lunch & dinner) Has good vegetarian options that are very filling and popular with locals at lunchtime. Nonvegetarians might try the *breizol* (55som) – battered meat rolled around tomatoes and other vegetables.

**Fakir Café** (☎ 2 06 56; cnr Gorkogo & Kushtobaev; mains 60som; 🕒 lunch & dinner) Offers a wide selection of dishes from Uyghur to Georgian, inside and outside seating, English menus, friendly staff and decent portions.

**Kench Café** (☎ 2 07 07; cnr Telmona & Gebze; meal 120som; 🕒 lunch & dinner) One of the better restaurants in town, in the southern outskirts and with an English menu. The chicken with mushroom sauce is recommended.

You'll also find Dungan snacks such as *ashlyanfu* (meatless, cold, gelatine noodles in a vinegary sauce) in the Al-Tilek Bazaar for only a few som. It can be quite spicy so watch the red stuff. The best Dungan food is of course in Dungan homes, where a slap-up meal may have eight to 10 courses (Dungan weddings can have up to 30 courses). Yak Tours (p302) can arrange a good **Dungan feast** (per person US$6-10) if you can get a group together.

## Shopping

**Kürk Art Gallery** (Jakshilik Bazaar) Has some nice, neutral-coloured *shyrdaks* and an interesting collection of *voilochnaya shapka* – felt hats worn in *banyas* to bring the sweat out.

The **Kumtor Department Store** (TsUM; Toktogul) has some made-for-tourist items.

Jamilya's B&B sells and custom orders *shyrdaks* and is affiliated to Kyrgyz Style (p288) in Bishkek. Place an order, travel around central Kyrgyzstan for a week or two, and then pick up the finished product.

## Getting There & Away

Karakol's **long-distance bus station** (Przhevalskogo) has a mix of comfortable modern buses and tired Soviet-era buses to Bishkek (190som, eight hours) hourly between 7am and 3pm, and at night between 8pm and 11pm. These stop in Cholpon-Ata (80som) and Balykchy (110som) following the northern shore route.

Out in front of the long-distance bus station are faster *arenda* (buses that leave when full; 200som) and shared taxis (450som) to Bishkek. There is one bus a day in summer to Almaty (450som) but note that this runs via Bishkek not the Karkara Valley.

Buses also run via the southern shore from the **southern bus stand** (Toktogul) to Bishkek four times daily and will drop you at Barskoön (55som), Tamga (60som), Bokonbayevo (80som) and Balykchy (120som). The first scheduled departure is at 9.30am, the last at 3.30pm. For Naryn and Kochkor, change at Balykchy.

Minibuses and shared taxis also depart from here for all southern-shore destinations when full.

Most local buses (eg to Pristan Prahevalsk, Ak-Suu, Jeti-Ögüz and Barskoön) go from the local bus stand in the centre of town, at the Ak Tilek Bazaar. You will also find taxis here for local hire around the region, but agree on a price and waiting time beforehand.

Flights to Bishkek and Osh remain suspended although the airline ticketing office at the airport can sell tickets departing from Bishkek or Osh airports.

### Getting Around

Marshrutka minibuses trundle back and forth between the bus station and the centre. Taxis are fairly plentiful and cost around 50som in town, 60som at night. You can book a taxi at **Salam Taxis** (☎ 2 22 22) or **Issyk-Kul Taxis** (☎ 161).

Minibus 103 runs a loop through the centre and around town.

## AROUND KARAKOL

### Przewalski Memorial & Pristan Prahevalsk

Thanks perhaps to the efforts of Soviet historiographers, and to the fact that he died here, the Russian explorer Nikolai Przewalski (below) is something of a local icon, an increasingly poignant reminder of what the Russians accomplished in this part of the world. His grave and memorial museum are 7km north of Karakol on the Mikhaylovka Inlet. A visit with a Russian guide still has the flavour of a pilgrimage.

The **museum** (Muzey Prezhezhwalskovo; admission 50som) features a huge map of Przewalski's explorations in Central Asia and a gallery of exhibits on his life and travels, plus a roll call of other Russian explorers. Captions are in

#### PRZEWALSKI

The golden age of Central Asian exploration was presided over by Nikolai Mikhailovich Przewalski. Born in Smolensk on 12 April 1839, his passion from an early age was travel. His father was an army officer and young Nikolai, under heavy pressure to be one too, apparently decided that an army career would give him the best chance to hit the road, although he never enjoyed the military life.

To prove to both the Russian Geographical Society and his senior officers that he would be a good explorer, he persuaded the Society to sponsor his first expedition, to the Ussuri River region in the Russian Far East from 1867 to 1869. The results impressed everyone, the Society agreed to help finance future trips, and the army gave him the time he needed, insisting only that on his return from each trip he be debriefed first before saying anything to the Society.

Przewalski's Faustian bargain got him his freedom to travel in return for being, in effect, an army agent. He never married, going on instead to become a major general and the most honoured of all the tsarist explorers. He focused on Central Asia, launching four major expeditions in 15 years:

- Mongolia, China and Tibet (1870–73)
- Tian Shan, Lop Nor, Taklamakan Desert and northern Xinjiang (1876–77)
- Mongolia, China and Tibet (1879–80)
- Mongolia, China, Tibet, Taklamakan Desert and Tian Shan (1883–85)

Those starting in Mongolia were devoted to finding a route into Tibet. On the one non-Tibet trip, he discovered the tiny steppe-land horse that now bears his name – Przewalski's horse (p76).

On the last of these trips he arrived via the Bedel Pass at Karakol. In 1888 he was at Bishkek (then Pishpek) outfitting for his next, grandest, expedition. While hunting tiger by the Chuy River he unwisely drank the water, came down with typhus and was bundled off to Lake Issyk-Köl for rest and treatment. From here he wrote to the tsar asking to be buried beside the lake, dressed in his explorer's clothes. He died at the military hospital on 20 October 1888.

Russian. There is usually an English-speaking guide on duty, delightful in her earnest explanations. Look out for the murals that change perspective from different angles.

The grave and monument overlook the Mikhaylovka Inlet and a clutter of cranes, docks and warehouses – all once part of the old Soviet top-secret 'polygon' for torpedo research. **Pristan** (Russian for pier) is a nearby strip of lakeshore several kilometres long that includes a sea of *dachas* (holiday bungalows) to the northeast and a popular beach to the west. The old military zone villages of Mikhaylovka, Lipenka and certain parts of Pristan Prahevalsk are off limits to foreigners.

To get here on your own, take a public bus (8som to 10som) or a shared taxi (15som) marked Дачи (Dachi) or Пляж Plaj (Beach) from Karakol just north of the local bus stand, departing every hour or so. A taxi to the museum costs 100som one way.

## Altyn Arashan

Probably the most popular destination from Karakol is a spartan hot spring development called Altyn Arashan (Golden Spa), set in a postcard-perfect alpine valley at 3000m, with 4260m Pik Palatka looming at its southern end.

Much of the area is a botanical research area called the Arashan State Nature Reserve and is home to about 20 snow leopards and a handful of bears, although the only animals you're likely to see are the horses and sheep belonging to local families.

## AROUND KARAKOL

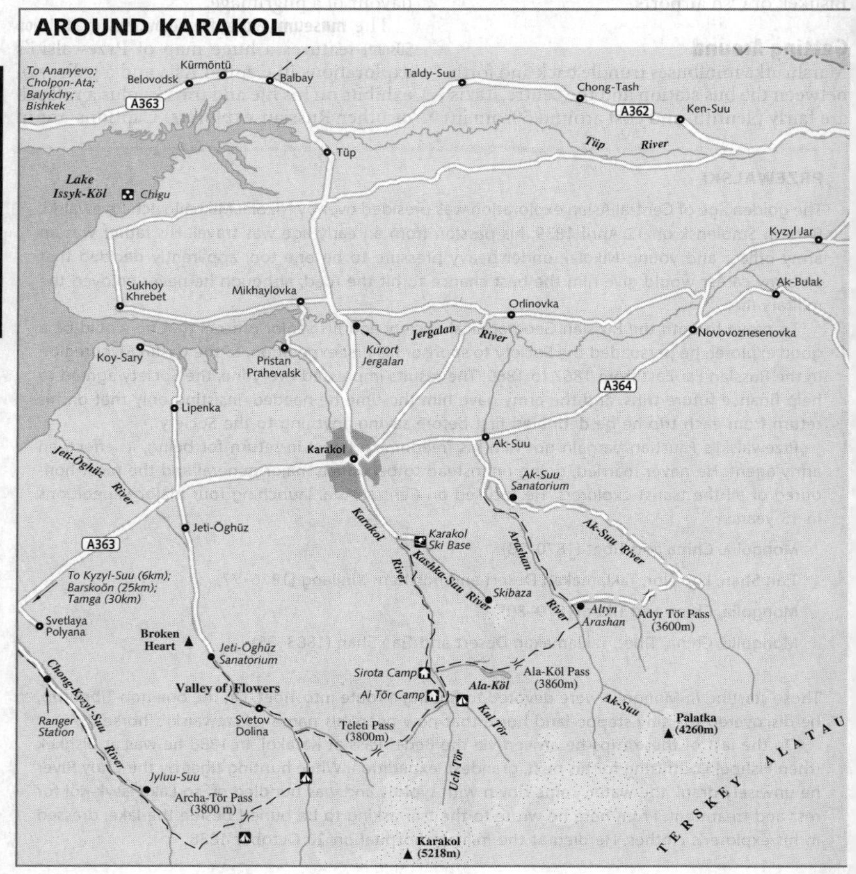

During Soviet times it is rumoured that 25 snow leopards were trapped here and shipped to zoos around the world until Moscow cancelled all collecting and hunting permits in 1975.

Altyn Arashan has several small **hot-spring developments** (US$1-$2). Natural hot water flows into a series of concrete pools enclosed by wooden sheds. The pools reek of sulphur but there is a translated certificate pinned to the door extolling the curative properties of these waters and listing, in exhaustive detail, the diseases they will cure.

Each shed is lockable and you can get the key from the house closest to whichever shed you select. It is a great way to relax and it's almost mandatory to run, screaming, into the icy river afterwards.

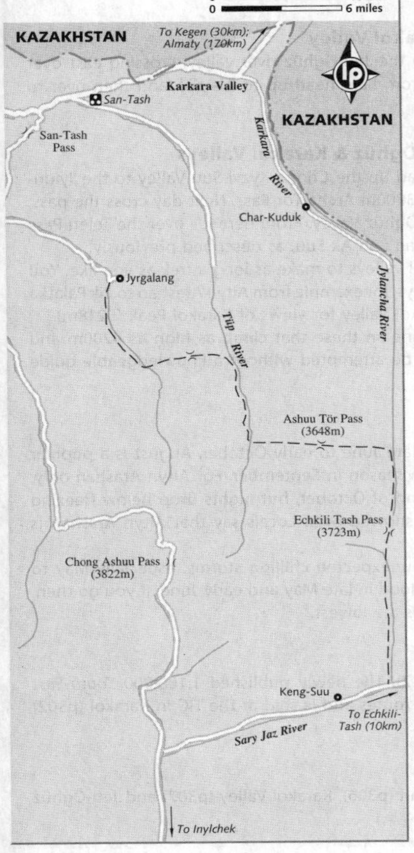


Across the stream is a little log house and museum with stuffed animals of the region. From the springs it's about a five hour walk on foot to the snout of the Palatka Glacier, wrapped around Pik Palatka.

### SLEEPING & EATING

**Yak Tours Camp** (dm 400som, with 3 meals 600som) The first place you come to is run by Karakol's Yak Tours. The communal lounge has an atmospheric open fire but the bedding upstairs is usually dirty. On nights when the guide, Valentin, stays the food is excellent, at other times, less so and occasionally meals are dispensed with altogether. There are no hot springs here.

**Arashan Travel Hotel** (incl hot pool usage dm 250som, yurt 400som) The next along from Yak Tours and a small step up in cleanliness; the beds are however, in large dorms. Staff can also organise guides and horses and run a small shop selling essentials (Snicker bars, Coke and toilet paper). Meals are 80som to 200som and the hot pools cost 50som.

There are six families that take guests, but none of the six have phones in the valley. If one place is full, they will refer you to the next.

By far your best option is to take a tent and camp somewhere undisturbed. You can buy a few things here in summer but it's better to bring your own food (and purifying tablets for the water), plus a bit of tea, salt, sugar or coffee for the caretaker.

### GETTING THERE & AWAY

An avalanche-prone road, strewn with rocks and winter debris, makes for a slow crawl up to the springs by 4WD. A taxi (200som) or minibus 358 (10som) can drop you at the turn-off to Ak-Suu Sanatorium. From here it's a steep, five- to six-hour (14km) climb south on the 4WD track beside the Arashan River, through a piney canyon full of hidden hot and cold springs.

Valentin of Yak Tours will bring you up to Altyn Arashan from Karakol in his jeep for about US$25 per 4WD. The TIC or CBT in Karakol can arrange transport for a similar fee. There's little traffic so hitching is hit and miss. You can hike in as the climax of several possible treks to/from the Karakol Valley (see p308).

## Karakol Valley

Due south of Karakol lies the beautiful Karakol Valley. The valley is a national park, which means there's a 250som entry fee collected at the gate.

## TREKKING AROUND KARAKOL

The Terskey Alatau range that rises behind Karakol offers a fine taste of the Tian Shan. Of numerous possible routes that climb to passes below 4000m, the best of them take in the alpine lake Ala-Köl above Karakol and the Altyn Arashan (p306) hot springs above Ak-Suu (Teploklyuchenka).

### Ak-Suu to Altyn Arashan & Back

Minimum one or two nights. Five hours up the Arashan Valley, climbing from 1800m to 3000m. A day-hike extension could take you 4½ hours further up the valley, branching east and then south for views of Palatka (4260m).

### Karakol Valley to Arashan Valley, via Ala-Köl

Minimum three nights. Hike up from the end of the bus 1 route for about four hours to where the Ala-Köl Valley branches to the left. Two hours up takes you to the carved wooden Sirota camp; another five hours takes you past waterfalls to the high-altitude and barren Ala-Köl lake. A 30-minute walk along the north shore offers camping at the base of the pass. The trail to the 3860m Ala-Köl Pass is indistinct and the crossing can be tricky at the end of the season, so consider a guide from September onwards. Five hours downhill from the pass brings you to Altyn Arashan, from where you can hike down to Ak-Suu the next day.

### Jeti-Öghüz to Altyn Arashan, via the Karakol Valley

Minimum four or five nights. The trail heads up the Jeti-Öghüz river valley, crossing east over the 3800m Teleti Pass into the Karakol Valley. From here head up to Ala-Köl, and then over to Altyn Arashan and Ak-Suu (see above).

### Kyzyl-Suu to Altyn Arashan, via the Jeti-Öghüz & Karakol Valleys

Minimum six to eight nights. From Kyzyl-Suu head up the Chong-Kyzyl-Suu Valley to the Jyluu-Suu hot springs or on to a camp site below the 3800m Archa-Tör Pass. Next day cross the pass, head down the Asan Tukum Gorge into the Jeti-Öghüz Valley. From here it's over the Teleti Pass to the Karakol Valley and to Ala-Köl, Altyn Arashan and Ak-Suu, as described previously.

You can combine any number of these parallel valleys to make as long a trek as you like. You can also add on wonderful radial hikes up the valleys, for example from Altyn Arashan to Pik Palatka or up the Kul Tör Valley at the head of the Karakol Valley for views of Karakol Peak (5218m).

There are also longer, more technical variations on these that climb as high as 4200m and cross some small glaciers, but these should not be attempted without a knowledgeable guide and some experience with glacier walking.

### When to Go

The season for the treks noted here is normally late June to early October. August is a popular time for picking mushrooms; blackcurrants are in season in September. For Altyn Arashan only, you could go as early as May or as late as the end of October, but nights drop below freezing then and the surrounding mountain passes are snowed over. Locals say that Altyn Arashan is loveliest in June and in September.

Weather is the region's biggest danger, with unexpected chilling storms, especially May to June, and September to October. Streams are in flood in late May and early June; if you go then, plan your crossings for early morning when levels are lowest.

### Maps

These routes are indicated on the map (pp306–7). The newly published 1:100,000 *South-East Issyk-Köl Lake Coast Trekking Map* shows all these routes and is sold at the TIC in Karakol (p302) and Geoid in Bishkek (p279) for 250som.

### Getting to the Trail Heads

For access to trail heads, refer to the Altyn Arashan (p306), Karakol Valley (p307) and Jeti-Öghüz (opposite) sections of this chapter.

**TREKKING**

The valley offers some fine hikes (see opposite), although you really need to invest in a tent, stove and a day's hiking before the valley reveals its charm. Further up the main valley, at the junction of several valleys and trekking routes is the Ai Tör camp, run by Alp Tour Issyk Köl (p303), with shower, *banya* (US$3), tent sites (100som), mountain rescue, radio service and park permit check.

From May to mid-October you can make a strenuous day hike (or better an overnight camping trip) to a crystal-clear lake called Ala-Köl (3530m). You can also reach this lake in four hours over the ridge from Altyn Arashan; in fact this is on several alternative trek routes to/from Altyn Arashan (see opposite).

A taxi from Karakol to the park gate is 50som. Bus 1 will take you part of the way, from where you can start hiking or hitching.

**SKIING**

About 17km south of Karakol, the Kashka-Suu valley becomes the area's winter playland of snow and ice. The season kicks off at the end of November and runs to March although canny locals sometimes get an additional two weeks worth of skiing in May when avalanches create temporary ski fields.

In 2005 a Russian-Kyrgyz construction company revamped the tiny resort, modernising the facilities and injecting new life into the tired complex. It still has a way to go though.

**Karakol Ski Base** (☎ Bishkek 312-53 18 70, Karakol 3922-5 14 54; www.karakol-ski.com; lift pass adult/child US$8/4, ski kit/snowboard rental US$10/12, guided ski tour US$12) operates five T-bar tows (only one was operational in the 2006 season) to a height of 3040m and one sledge drag. Together they access over 20km of trails. Most trails run through coniferous fir woodlands and the guided, winter forest ski tours are a magical experience. Thanks to the recent cash injection, the rental equipment has gone from the stuff Scott might have used to cross the Antarctic to brand-spanking-new Rossignols.

**Karakol Ski Resort** (d/tw/apt US$40/40/60, chalet US$150) operates the Karakol Ski Base and the only accommodation on the mountain itself. There are a total of six doubles, four triples and two apartments (each with two bedrooms) within the hotel and two A-frame chalets that each sleeps eight to 10 people. The rooms are basic but comfortable, all with TV and en suite. There is also an attached restaurant (three meals US$10).

The other option is to stay in Karakol town, and hire a 4WD to take you up to the ski base. The TIC (p302) and many of the trekking companies (p303) can arrange this, but be sure to negotiate waiting time if you want a lift down. For heli-skiing see p293.

## Jeti-Öghüz

About 25km west of Karakol, at the mouth of the Jeti-Öghüz Canyon, is an extraordinary formation of red sandstone cliffs that has become a kind of tourism trademark for Lake Issyk-Köl.

Jeti-Öghüz village is just off the main around-the-lake road. South of the village the earth erupts in red patches, and soon there appears a great splintered hill called Razbitoye Serdtse or **Broken Heart**. Legend says two suitors spilled their blood in a fight for a beautiful woman; both died, and this rock is her broken heart.

The other side of the hill forms the massive wall of Jeti-Öghüz. The name means **Seven Bulls** (named after the seven main bluffs), and of course there is a story here too – of seven calves growing big and strong in the valley's rich pastures. Erosion has meant that the bulls have multiplied. They are best viewed from a ridge to the east above the road. From that same ridge you can look east into Ushchelie Drakonov, the Valley of Dragons.

Below the wall of Seven Bulls is one of Issyk-Köl's surviving spas, the ageing **Jeti-Öghüz Sanatorium** (☎ 9 37 19; s 170som, massage 200som; ⏲ summer only), built in 1932 with a complex of several plain hotels, a half-empty, semiheated pool, a restaurant (meals 100som) and some woodland walks. Former Russian president Boris Yeltsin and former Kyrgyzstan president Askar Akaev had their first meeting here in 1991 – and it has been downhill ever since. Russian cosmonaut Yuri Gagarin also decompressed here. It's the kind of place that's full of history and makes you want to jam the chair under the doorknob when you sleep.

From here you can walk up the parklike lower canyon of the Jeti-Öghüz River to popular summer picnic spots. Some 5km up, the valley opens out almost flat at **Svetov Dolina**, the Valley of Flowers (Kok Jayik in Kyrgyz); it's a kaleidoscope of colours in May when the poppies bloom. There are also said to be pre-Islamic petroglyphs up here, similar to those at Cholpon-Ata.

The **Festival of National Cuisine & Folklore** is held in the yurt camp in the Jeti-Öghüz gorge on the last Sunday in July. It is a good opportunity to sample Kyrgyz, Tartar, Russian and Dungan specialities.

Yurt camps include the pleasant **Jenish Gol** (per person US$10) on the left of the road, Ecotrek (p303) on the right and finally the pricier **Saidahmat** (bed & full board €20). All are normally accessible by car and offer a nice taste of the mountains if you are short of time, and a good base for day hikes if you have a couple of days. Karakol TIC (p312) and CBT (p302) can advise on prices and help with bookings. The upper valley is accessed by five bridges that sometimes get washed out so check the best route with locals before setting off.

Jeti-Öghüz canyon is one of several alternatives for treks to/from Altyn Arashan and Ala-Köl (p308).



#### GETTING THERE & AWAY

Buses run from Karakol's local bus stand at 10am to Jeti-Öghüz village and at 4pm to the sanatorium (25som), 6km further away. Shared taxis (50som) and a noon minibus (40som) also run between Karakol's Ak Tilek Bazaar and the sanatorium. To return from the sanatorium, stand by the main road and wave down the first car heading back to town; most drivers happily act as impromptu shared taxis.

A taxi from Karakol costs 280som to the spa, 350som to the Valley of Flowers and around 500som to the yurt camps at the top of the valley.

## BARSKOÖN & TAMGA
## БАРСКООН & ТАМГА

☎ 3926

Barskoön village was an army staging point in the days of Soviet–Chinese border skirmishes, and the small adjacent settlement of Tamga is built around a former military sanatorium, now open year-round to all. Today Barskoön is all Kyrgyz, with more horses than cars; Tamga is mainly Russian.

The area's most illustrious resident was the 11th-century Mahmud al-Kashgari, the author of the first-ever comparative dictionary of Turkic languages, *Divan Lughat at-Turk* (A Glossary of Turkish Dialects), written in Baghdad during 1072–74.

### Sights & Activities

**Shepherds Way Trekking** (☎ 29 74 06, Bishkek 312-29 74 06, Barskoön 2 61 33; www.kyrgyztrek.com) is a very professional local company that runs horse treks into the mountains behind Barskoön. It's run by local brothers Ishen and Raiymbek Obelbekov and Ishen's wife, Gulmira.

Shepherds Way Trekking also helped host the 2005 inaugural **At Chabysh (Horse Racing) Festival** (Kyrgyz Ate Foundation; ☎ 502-518315; www.atchabysh.com) held in early November. By hosting a series of horse games and races the festival aims to promote the breeding of the Kyrgyz horse, which along with its associated nomadic traditions is now faced with extinction. The feature event is raced over a gruelling 47km course between Barskoön and Tosor villages.

In Barskoön you can see yurts in production at the **Ak Orgo yurt workshop** (☎ 9 67 54; Lenin 93; mekenbek@hotmail.kg;), including machines that make felt and devices that bend the wood and reeds for the curved yurts. It takes the 27 employees two months to make a yurt, which retail here at around US$4500. The workshop is on the right as you drive into Barskoön from the east. Contact Mekenbek Osmonaliev.

Locals pack picnics and head 20km up the huge Barskoön Valley to the **Barskoön Waterfall**, where *kymyz* is sold from summertime yurts near a defaced inscription by Russian cosmonaut Yuri Gagarin. It's possible to climb 1½ hours up to closer views of the falls. Shared taxis (160som return) run from Barskoön sanatorium to the falls along the well-maintained road that leads to the Kumtor gold mine.

The Canadian gold-mining company Centarra Gold operates the **Kumtor Gold Mine**, the eighth-largest gold field in the world in the mountains behind Barskoön. There are no tours of the operations, presumably as result of environmental concerns (p278) and you'll need a special invitation to get past the various checkpoints. The gold mine is at 4200m and even in summer it snows regularly.

Tamga has a nice beach and locals recommend a beach 5km west. Also, 6km up the valley there is a Tibetan inscription known as **Tamga Tash** but you'll need local help to find it.

The Tamga Guesthouse arranges one- to three-day treks or horse trips up to the Tamga Gorges or Ochincheck Lake, or a four-day trip to Chakury Köl at a lofty 3800m.

### Sleeping

**Tamga Guesthouse** (☎ 9 53 33; Ozyornaya 3; per person €8, full board €15) In Tamga village, this is run by a friendly Russian couple, and has a lovely fruit garden and sauna (US$2 per person). It's used mostly by trekkers from the affiliated Kyrgyz Travel but anyone can stay and use it as a trekking base. It's the first road on the right as you pull into town. Contact Denikin Alexandr.

Dostuck Trekking (p284) has a **yurt camp** (full board US$18) by the lakeshore near Tosor village.

### Getting There & Away

Barskoön is about 90km west of Karakol, with daily buses to/from Karakol (55som) and Balykchy. Buses from Karakol to Barskoön leave at 9.30am, noon, 4pm and 5pm from the southern bus stand and there are more frequent minibuses (70som), which leave when full. A private taxi to Karakol costs 1000som and to Kadji-Sai 350som.

## KADJI-SAI КАДЖИ-САИ

☎ **3941 / pop 4500**

Surrounded by low, wind-and-water–carved canyons, Kadji-Sai makes for a convenient midway point between Bishkek and Karakol. In 1947 Kadji-Sai became somewhat of a 'Soviet secret' when uranium was mined here by Soviet Russia; at that time the town had no official name but was simply referred to as Frunze (after the capital) 10. The uranium, however, was of poor quality and the mine closed three years later.

The town is set 3km back from the main road that runs the length of Issyk-Köl. Minibuses will drop you near the petrol station, cafés and TIC on the main road; from here it is a 10som taxi ride up to the village.

The second **TIC** (☎ 9 25 61; asan-77@mail.ru; Ozernaya 1; 9am-5pm Mon-Sat, closed Jan) to open in Kyrgyzstan does an excellent job putting travellers in touch with yurt camps, homestays, eagle hunters and local guides to local sights. It also sells a 1:200,000 Russian topographical map (300som) of the region.

### Sights

There are no must-sees in Kadji-Sai although the TIC can recommend a number of short treks to local geological formations including the **Kydyrmadjar Gorge** and **Skazka Rocks** – pillars of rock sculptured by the elements. The 14km taxi ride here will cost 600som including waiting time and swimming stops along the way.

The local **eagle hunter** (☎ 9 21 37; Sportivnaya 6), Ishenbek, in additional to running Zina's B&B, guides horseback hunting trips (5000som per group; plus horse hire, 400som per person) into the surrounding hillside in search of wild rabbits and foxes. Ishenbek will also put on hunting demonstrations using domesticated rabbits reared for food (2000som per group) but be warned, it's not pretty for the bunny.

### Sleeping

**B&B Valeria** (☎ 9 22 54; Gagarina 29; dm 300som) Run by the local apiculturist who will show you his 80 or so hives when they are in town – every autumn the bees are brought down from the *jailoos*. Besides delicious honey (served with the included breakfast) you can expect fresh fruits and vegetables from the garden. Additional meals cost 150som.

**Zina's B&B** (☎ 9 21 37; Sportivnaya 6; dm without/with meals 200/400som) The star attraction here is Kydyrov, a five-year-old hunting eagle and his handler, Ishenbek, who is happy to explain the rearing and training of eagles. The eagle is fully trained and will not attack children or domesticated pets. Three meals cost an additional 200som.

### Getting There & Away

Minibuses, buses and shared taxis will stop at the intersection of the main road between Balykchy (minibus 90som) and Karakol (minibus 70som) and the road that leads to town. Taxis also wait here to ferry passengers the 3km to town.

## BOKONBAYEVO БОКОНБАЕВО

☎ **3947 / pop 12,500**

There doesn't seem to be much going on in sleepy Bokonbayevo. Community-Based Tourism's promotional booklet describes it as 'much overlooked' and at first it's easy to see why but scratch below the surface and you'll find a bustling Kyrgyz community worthy of closer inspection. Ditch this guide in your hotel room and spend an afternoon wandering the streets and meeting the locals – we were invited to take alarmingly graphic photos of a sheep being slaughtered then butchered with a kitchen knife; it wasn't pretty.

Most of the town's activity is centred along Bolot Mambetov where the local minibuses and shared taxis arrive and depart from. There is a string of shops, a small bazaar, a smaller police office, CBT and a mosque all within this block. If you are not eating at your homestay, the café 100m from CBT serves up a fine *laghman* (40som) along with other Kyrgyz staples.

### Information

**CBT** (☎ office 9 31 66, home 9 13 12; reservation@cbtkyrgyzstan.kg; Bolot Mambetov; 🕐 10am-5pm Mon-Fri summer) In addition to homestays this office operates three yurtstays around town and can arrange treks, horse treks and eagle hunting demonstrations. Contact Bakyt Choitonbaev.

### Sights & Activities

There are several trekking opportunities in the nearby Terskey Alatau mountains and Konur Ölön Valley. Community-Based Tourism can advise on trails and arrange yurtstays. For the adventurous it is possible to trek to Naryn from here.

The local **eagle hunter** (1-3 people 1100som, group 1500som), Talgar, and his eagle, Tumara, put on a deadly demonstration in a field on the outskirts of town. If you wish, insist that you want the whole shebang with the sacrificial rabbit as opposed to a piece of meat tied to a string. On all accounts Tumara isn't too excited by the meat-on-a-string routine. Organise demonstrations through CBT.

The **Birds of Prey Festival** is worth a visit if you are in the area in early August when falconers from around Issyk-Köl compete here with their eagles, hawks and falcons. Although this festival is still in its infancy there are plans to include Kyrgyz hunting-dog demonstrations soon. Contact CBT for exact dates.

### Sleeping

**Asanakunova Jyldyz Homestay** (☎ 9 14 12; Osmoev 35; dm 350) It's a five-minute walk from the town centre and run by a large but quiet extended family who will mainly leave you to your own devices. Breakfast is included, additional meals are 100som.

**Hotel Paxat** (☎ 9 16 31; cnr Turusbekov & Atakan) The owners of the only hotel in Bokonbayevo were out of town at time of research but neighbours assured us that it does open regularly.

### Getting There & Away

Minibuses run to Tamga (40som), Balykchy (80som) and Karakol (90som) from opposite (east bound) and to the left (west bound) of the CBT. Shared taxis charge 180som to Karakol and 280som to Bishkek.

## AROUND BOKONBAYEVO & KADJI-SAI

Both the CBT in Bokonbayevo and the TIC in Kadji-Sai arrange trips to the local sights.

For a Dead Sea–like swimming experience try the buoyant but eye-stinging salty waters of **Shor-Köl**, 40km west of Bokonbayevo. It's best reached by taxi (1500som return from Kadji-Sai).

If you find yourself still lacking in spirit and health, locals suggest climbing to the sacred summit of Tastar-Ata, to drink from the large **Stone Pot** you'll find there. According to local folklore the pot was used by Manas himself while in residence and the stone pillars found in the area are referred to as the **Forty Soldiers of Manas**. The grassy south side makes an easier accent than the forested north side.

### Yurtstays

Community-Based Tourism Bokonbayevo (left) operates a yurtstay at Bel Tam, 17km from Bokonbayevo, beyond Tuura-Su.

During the summer, Kadji-Sai TIC (p311) can arrange stays in, and treks from, several fledgling yurt camps (full board 350som) in the mountain *jailoos* and along the shores of Issyk-Köl.

Ecotour (p282) has full-service yurts at neighbouring Temir Kanat and at Tuura-Su village at the west end of the Kongur Ölön Valley.

## THE CENTRAL TIAN SHAN
## ЦЕНТРАЛЬНЫЙ ТЯНЬ ШАНЬ

This highest and mightiest part of the Tian Shan system – the name means Celestial Mountains in Chinese – is at the eastern end of Kyrgyzstan, along its borders with China and the very southeast tip of Kazakhstan. It's an immense knot of ranges, with dozens of summits over 5000m, culminating in Pik Pobedy (Victory Peak, 7439m, second-highest in the former USSR) on the Kyrgyzstan–China border, and Khan Tengri (Prince of Spirits or Ruler of the Sky, 7010m), possibly the most beautiful and demanding peak in the Tian Shan, on the Kazakhstan–Kyrgyzstan border. Locals call the latter peak 'Blood Mountain', as the pyramid-shaped peak glows crimson at sunset.

The first foreigner to bring back information about the central Tian Shan was the

Chinese explorer Xuan Zang (602–64), who crossed the Bedel Pass in the 7th century, early in his 16-year odyssey to India and back. His journey nearly ended here; in the seven days it took to cross the pass, half of his 14-person party froze to death.

The first European to penetrate this high region was the Russian explorer Pyotr Semenov in 1856 (for his efforts the tsar awarded him the honorary name Tian-Shansky). In 1902–03 the Austrian explorer Gottfried Merzbacher first approached the foot of the elegant, Matterhorn-like Khan Tengri, but it was only climbed in 1931, by an Ukrainian team.

Of the Tian Shan's thousands of glaciers, the grandest is 60km-long Inylchek (Engilchek), rumbling westward from both sides of Khan Tengri, embracing an entire rampart of giant peaks and tributary glaciers. Across the glacier's northern arm, where it joins the southern arm, a huge, iceberg-filled lake – Merzbacher Lake – forms at 3300m every summer. Some time in early August, the lake bursts its ice-banks and explodes into the Inylchek River below.

Along with the eastern Pamir, the central Tian Shan is Central Asia's premier territory for serious trekking and mountaineering. Several Central Asian adventure-travel firms will bring you here by helicopter, 4WD and/or foot right up to these peaks. Even intrepid, fit, do-it-yourselfers can get a look at Inylchek Glacier (below).

## Information

Mid-July to August is the only feasible season to visit as at these elevations winter temperatures around the glacier are –15°C during the day and –25°C at night.

The best book to take along is Frith Maier's comprehensive *Trekking in Russia & Central Asia,* which has several maps and basic route descriptions for this region.

### TREKKING TO THE INYLCHEK GLACIER

The most common trekking route to the Inylchek Glacier is the remote and wild five- or six-day trek from Jyrgalang, 70km east of Karakol. Most trekkers will need support for this trek, not least because you will need a military permit from Karakol to head up the Sary Jaz Valley. There's one daily bus from Karakol to Jyrgalang.

**Stage one** From Jyrgalang the trail heads south up the valley, before cutting east over a 2800m pass into the Tüp Valley (seven to eight hours).

**Stage two** Over the 3648m Ashuu Tör Pass into the Janalach Valley (six hours).

**Stage three** Head south over the 3723m Echkili-Tash Pass into the Sary Jaz Valley.

**Stage four** Seven hours hike up the Tüz Valley to camp at the junction of the Achik Tash River.

**Stage five** Cross the river and head up four hours to the tricky Tüz Pass (4001m), from where there are stunning views of the Inylchek Glacier and Nansen Peak. From here it's a long descent to the Chong-Tash site at the snout of the Inylchek Glacier.

It's possible to hire a 4WD (5000som from the CBT in Karakol) to the yak farm in Echkili-Tash and join the trek there, leaving only two or three days to reach Chong-Tash. From Chong-Tash you face a one- or two-day hike back west to Ak-Jailoo or Maida Adyr camp and Inylchek town.

To continue from Chong-Tash on to the Inylchek Glacier you definitely need the support of a trekking agency to guide you over the glacier, keep you in supplies and let you stay in its base camps. With an experienced guide it's possible to continue from Chong-Tash over the glacier for one long day to Merzbacher Lake and to continue the next day to the camps. A popular excursion for trekking groups based here is to make a trekking ascent of Mt Diky (4832m) or Pesni Abaji (4901m), or to hike up the Zvozdochka Glacier to the foot of Pik Pobedy (7439m). Most groups take in a stunning helicopter route around the valley and out to Inylchek town and you might be able to buy a ride back up to Inylchek for US$150.

The best time for trekking in this region is July and August. See p314 for information on permits, maps and agencies.

KYRGYZSTAN

**PERMITS**

To go into the sensitive border zone past Inylchek town or anywhere in the upper Sary Jaz Valley you need a military border permit *(propusk)* from the permit station of the Russian border detachment stationed at the army base of Karakol's original garrison. Trekking agencies normally need a week to 20 days (US$15) to arrange this but can do it in a day (US$25).

You must have a letter with the stamp of a recognised travel agency in Karakol, Bishkek or Almaty, a list of everyone in your party and your itinerary. To climb in the region you'll need a mountaineering permit, which trekking companies can get you for US$105.

### Dangers & Annoyances

This is not a place to pop into for a few days with your summer sleeping bag – be properly equipped against the cold, which is severe at night, even in summer, and give yourself plenty of time to acclimatise to the altitude.



### Sleeping & Eating

There are several base camps in the Inylchek Valley: en route at scruffy Maida Adyr and the newer, nicer Gribkov Camp at Ak-Jailoo, 20km nearer the glacier; as well as at several locations up on the glacier in tent-towns owned and run by ITMC Tien-Shan, Ak-Sai Travel and Dostuck Trekking (see p284) in Bishkek and Kan Tengri in Almaty, among others. The Ak-Jailoo camp is run by **Tour Khan Tengri** (☎ in Karakol 3922-2 72 69; www.travelkg.narod.ru/company.htm) and has wooden buildings (per person US$20), yurts (US$12) and camp space (US$2 to US$10), plus meals (US$4 to US$7). ITMC's camp costs around US$3 per night in a tent, or US$8 in huts and there's a sauna and bar. You can camp here and just pay for meals, although food is pricey.

Kan Tengri maintains the only camp on the north side of the glacier and also a yurt camp at 2200m at the edge of the Karkara Valley. All these are intended for trekkers and climbers, but anybody with the urge to see this cathedral of peaks can make arrangements with those firms, and pay a visit.

### Getting There & Away

Bishkek trekking agencies (p284) organising climbs and treks in the central Tian Shan include Dostuck Trekking, Edelweiss, ITMC Tien-Shan, Ak-Sai and Tien-Shan Travel in Bishkek; Turkestan (p302) and Alp Tour Issyk-Kul (p303) in Karakol; and Kan Tengri and Tour Asia in Almaty (p118).

Access to the region surrounding Khan Tengri is by road, air or on foot. It's a four-hour (150km) trip on a roller-coaster, all-weather road from Karakol via Inylchek town, a mining centre at about 2500m and 50km west of the snout of the Inylchek Glacier. Do-it-yourselfers could hire a UAZ Jeep from CBT Karakol, for around 5000som or a 4WD 15-seater from Alp Tour Issyk-Kul for US$200. Even though maps show a road between Ak Shyrak and Inylchek, the last part of this road is no longer passable and access via this approach is by foot only. The new road to Ak-Jailoo has a US$10 toll for jeeps, or US$20 for trucks.

If you've got the cash, take a mind-boggling helicopter flight over the Tian Shan to Khan Tengri base camp with Kan Tengri from its Karkara Valley base camp, or with other agencies from Gribov Camp. It's possible to hitch a lift on a helicopter from Maida Adyr to the base camps for US$100 (plus US$1 per kilo if you have more than 30kg of luggage). These run every two days in August.

You can trek to Khan Tengri's north face from Narynkol (Kazakhstan), Jyrgalang (Kyrgyzstan) or, less interestingly, from the Ak-Jailoo road head.

# CENTRAL KYRGYZSTAN

The mountainous heart of Kyrgyzstan offers travellers unrivalled opportunities to explore *jailoos* on foot, horseback or by 4WD. At every turn you will find a family offering to put you up for the night or a group of herdsmen who will eagerly invite you into their yurt for a cup of tea and a bowl of fresh yogurt. Add this to some of the world's most glorious alpine lakes and it is easy to see why central Kyrgyzstan now rivals Lake Issyk-Köl in the hearts and minds of travellers.

Until the opening of the Irkeshtam Pass (p339) in 2002 the only way eastward to China was via the problematic Torugart Pass (p325). The Torugart still remains a hit-and-miss undertaking; frequent border closures, unpredictable weather and the Chinese requirement for expensive prearranged transport deters many overlanders from tackling this stunning route.

## BISHKEK TO NARYN

The route begins as you would for Lake Issyk-Köl, winding up the **Shoestring Gorge** towards Balykchy before a short cut (by taxi) heads over a small pass and past the azure **Orto-Tokoy Reservoir**, effectively nipping off the Balykchy corner.

Three hours (185km) from Bishkek is the town of Kochkor (p316) and 38km past that, tiny **Sary-Bulak**, where you can buy *laghman* and snacks by the roadside. It's another 11km on to the 3038m summit of the **Dolon Pass**, the highest point on the Bishkek–Naryn road, and a further 16km to **Ottuk**, a tidy Kyrgyz settlement. A further 24km brings you to a fork in the road – both branches of which take you the 10km into Naryn.

## KARAKOL TO NARYN

This route follows the southern shores of Lake Issyk-Köl to Balykchy, winding between the barren, low rock escarpments that characterise this side of the lake.

From Bokonbayevo the road heads inland passing the picturesque village of **Ak-Sai** with its haystacks, apple orchards and cemetery, whose graves sprout a multitude of Islamic stars and crescents, to **Balykchy**. Here you'll almost certainly need to switch minibuses to head south towards Kochkor. Ask to be dropped off at the southern bus stand on

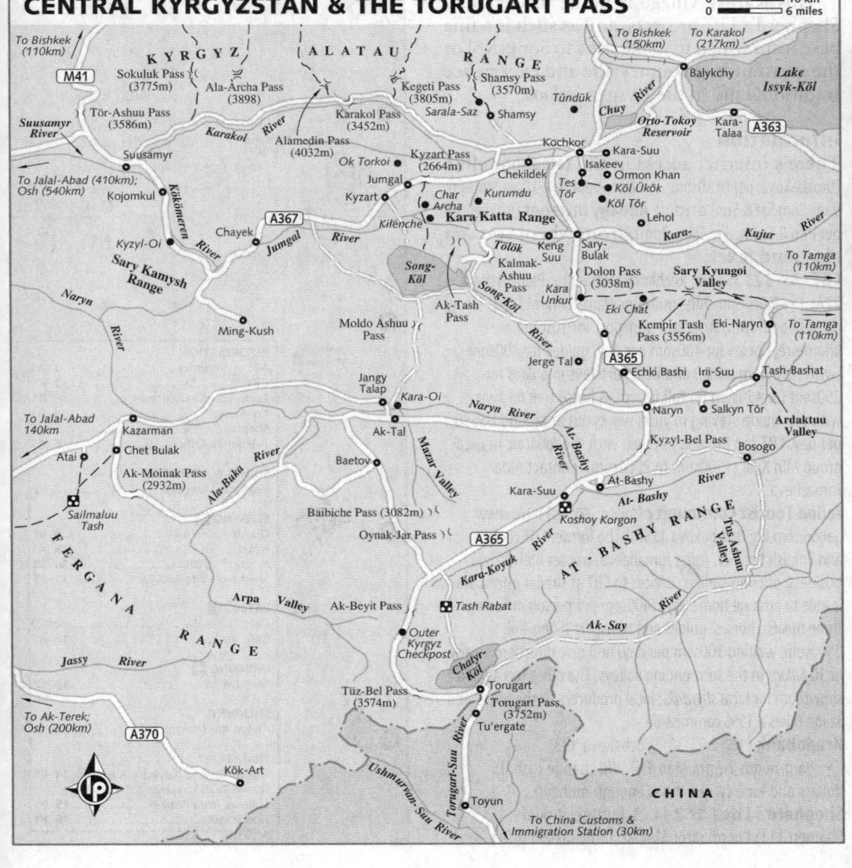

the outskirts of Balykchy to catch a waiting south-bound shared taxi (50som to 70som) to Kochkor.

An alternative road that cuts between Tamga and Naryn is seldom used, requiring your own 4WD transport.

## KOCHKOR КОЧКОР

**☎ 3535 / pop 16,000 / elev 1800m**

The little alpine, tree-lined, town of Kochkor (Kochkorka in Russian) is the kind of place where everyone seems to know everyone else. People and vehicles congregate around the roadside bazaar on Orozbakova. One side of the road has colourful vegetable stalls, the other side a clothes market. Taxi drivers whisper their destinations as you stroll pass as if surreptitiously selling drugs.

This Kyrgyz village is home to CBT and Shepherd's Life projects, and as such is a fine base from which to make trips to Song-Köl or the surrounding countryside and experience traditional life in the Kyrgyz *jailoos*.



### Information

There's internet access in the **telephone office** (Orozbakova; per hr 30som; 8am-noon & 1-10pm Mon-Fri, 9am-2pm Sat & Sun) and at **Aildagy Internet** (Isakeev 31; per min 0.5som; 9am-7pm), from where you can also send faxes.

**CBT** (☎ 2 23 55; cbt_kochkor@rambler.ru; Pioneerskaya 22A; 9am-8pm Jun–mid-Sep, 9am-5pm mid-Sep–May, closed noon-1pm) Arranges transport for 10som per kilometre, horses for 400som per day, guides for 800som (with their own horse) and B&B yurtstays in *jailoos* for 250som (or 450som for full board). A horse trek for two with one guide staying in yurts works out at around US$30 per day. CBT can put you in touch with the folkloric musical group Min Kyal (1500som to 2000som). Contact Aida Jumasheva.

**Jailoo Tourist Community** (Jailoo; ☎ 2 11 16; www.jailoo.com.kg; Orozbakova 125/3) The former CBT coordinator and English teacher, Asipa Jumabaeva, has set up her own business, offering similar services to CBT at similar prices. She is able to arrange homestays (400som per person including three meals), horses, guides and transport (Song-Köl 1800som, waiting 100som per day) and give directions to any of 10 *jailoos* in the surrounding valleys. The office has a good showroom for local *shyrdaks;* local producers fix the prices and Jailoo takes a 15% commission.

**Kredobank** (☎ 2 21 38; Orozbakova 133; 8am-noon, 1-5pm Mon-Fri) Will change cash US dollars and euro (when it has enough money!).

**Shepherd's Life** (☎ 2 14 23, Kuttuseyit uulu Shamen 111) Coordinator Mairam Ömürsakova offers

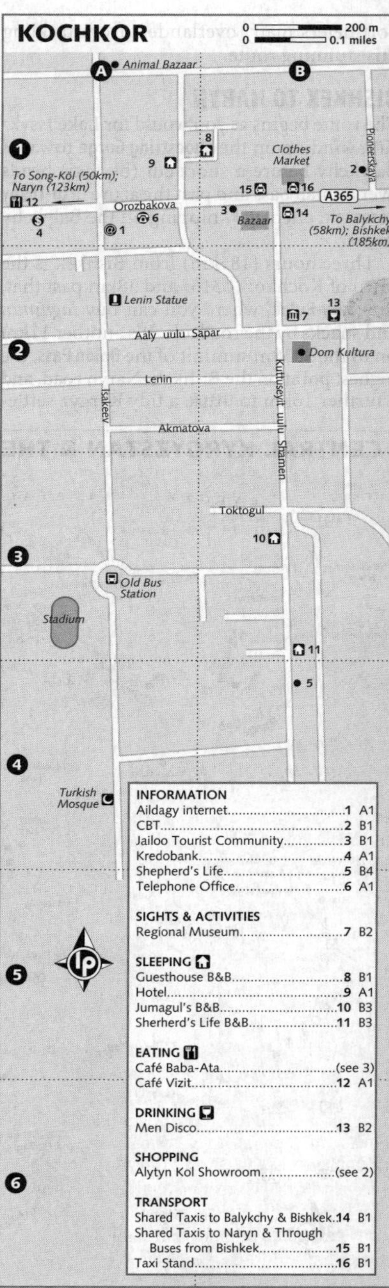

similar services to CBT at similar prices but with slightly ropier arrangements. Cars rent for 9som per kilometre and a yurt B&B is 250som with meals an additional 100som. Mairam speaks Russian and Kyrgyz only but her son Urmat speaks excellent English. Like the other agencies, horse riding, luggage storage and guiding services can all be arranged here. She can also be found at Altyn Kol woman's collective behind CBT where she works.

## Sights & Activities

There's not much to do in the town except visit the small **regional museum** (admission 50som; 9am-noon & 1-5pm Sun-Fri). A fine yurt is on display along with a collection of local Kyrgyz crafts, plus all the usual Soviet-era local heroes such as the local scientist Bayaly Isakeev. More Soviet heroes are celebrated in the busts to the east of the museum.

There is also a good **livestock market** in town on Saturday morning.

Kochkor makes a good base for horse treks and yurtstays in the region.

## Sleeping

There are more than 20 homestays in Kochkor, most costing 300som to 350som with breakfast, and CBT can put you in contact with all of them. The B&Bs listed here are mentioned in case the CBT office is closed. All include breakfast and serve home-cooked meals for an additional 100som.

**Hotel** (☎ 2 13 21; s/d 110/220som) This no-frills outfit offers simple rooms with two beds and old mattresses. There is only one duvet per bed so in cold weather you'll need to rug up before sleeping. There is an outside toilet but no showers. Unless you are desperately trying to save money the B&Bs are better options.

**Guesthouse B&B** (☎ 2 19 97; Shamen 14; dm 300som) It's a CBT-affiliated guesthouse with a central location and beds for five people. The grandmother here makes an apricot jam to die for and one of the daughters, Nargiz, speaks English.

**Jumagul's B&B** (☎ 2 24 53; Kuttuseyit uulu Shamen 58; dm 300som) Hosts Jumagul Akhmadova and her husband do a good job here, offering two large twin rooms. The B&B has a Russian sauna for guests and a clean squat toilet in the garden.

**Shepherd's Life B&B** (☎ 2 24 81, Kuttuseyit uulu Shamen 91; dm 300som) Considering that this is run by Shepherd's Life, the farmyard vibe is entirely appropriate. An orchard and stable separate the two main buildings – each have a selection of rooms; some with beds, others with *shyrdaks*.

## Eating & Drinking

**Café Vizit** (☎ 2 17 60; Orozbakova; mains 50-90som; lunch & dinner) The Vizit is the best value in town, dishing up delicious, no-fuss meals with no-fuss names. The unappealingly christened 'Chinese meat' (65som) is a delicious, diced-beef stir-fry.

**Café Baba-Ata** (☎ 2 25 05; Orozbakova 125; mains 50-90som; lunch & dinner) Thanks to its central location, outside summer seating and DJ this café is popular with travellers although the menu is limited and the food only passable.

**Men Disco** (☎ 0502-948444; Park Seyil) Locals and travellers alike can get their freak on at this unfortunately named disco. The karaoke machine has Western and Russian pop so here's your chance to bring Guns n Roses to the Central Asian masses. Friday is dead as locals opt for the mosque instead.

## Shopping

Kochkor is one of the best places to buy *shyrdaks*.

**Altyn Kol** (Golden Hands; Pioneerskaya) This local women's collective has a *shyrdak* showroom next to the CBT office. A good-quality 1.6m by 2.25m rug will set you back 5000som. It can arrange airmail postage (8000som for this size) or delivery to either Osh or Bishkek.

Good-quality *shyrdaks* are also for sale at Jumagul's B&B and at Jailoo, which has a large selection of naturally dyed felt products using barberry, walnut, juniper, immortal and wormwood. A *shyrdak* here costs about US$30 (natural colours), US$35 (artificial dye) and US$40 (natural colours using natural dyes) per square metre. The highly decorative, 10m-long *örmöks* (woven belts) that are wrapped around the insides of yurts (US$30 per metre) are also sold here.

## Getting There & Away

Most people take a seat in a shared taxi from opposite the bazaar to Bishkek (200som), Balykchy (60som, one hour) and Naryn (150som to 200som). Infrequent afternoon buses and minibuses pass through to Chayek (150som) and Ming Kush via Jumgal, picking up passengers by the bazaar at Orozbakov.

# AROUND KOCHKOR

The following trips can all be arranged by CBT, Jailoo or Shepherd's Life. By yourself, you'll have difficulties finding yurtstay accommodation.

One of the most popular trips is to **Sarala-Saz** (53km northwest), a wide open *jailoo* with fine views, from where you can take day trips on horseback to petroglyphs. Community-Based Tourism organises **horse games** here in August. For dates ask at the CBT in Kochkor or Bishkek. An adventurous two- or three-day horse trek leads from Sarala-Saz over the 3570m Shamsy Pass and down the Shamsy River valley to Tokmak.

**Köl Ükök** (Treasure Chest) is a beautiful mountain lake above Tes Tör *jailoo,* south of Kochkor and is a recommended overnight or three-day trip. Take a taxi 6km to Isakeev and then trek by horse or on foot half a day to the *jailoos*. Before June it's better to stay at Tes Tör (four hours from Isakeev by horse); after June you can stay up by the lake (six hours from Isakeev). Day excursions from the lake include the **Köl Tör** glacial lake, a couple of hours further up into the mountains. For a slightly longer alternative trip take a taxi 15km to Kara-Suu village and then go first to Kashang Bel or Bel Tepshay (Bel means pass), for views of Issyk-Köl, and then ride or hike the next day to Köl Ükök (seven hours).

If you really want to get off the beaten track, the **Shepherd's Life coordinator** (☎ 3522-4 14 57; Lenin 22) in **Jumgal**, history teacher Stalbek Kaparbekov, can arrange horses to, and accommodation at, the nearby *jailoos* of Ok Torkoi and Kilenche. Jumgal is the first village after the Kyzart Pass, and is sometimes referred to as Dos Kulu. There are also Shepherd's Life coordinators further west in **Chayek** (☎ 3536-2 2879; Moldaliev 4; contact Guljan Mykyeva) and **Kyzart** (contact Abdykazar Talgar); contact the Kochkor office for details.

## LAKE SONG-KÖL
## ОЗЕРО СОН-КОЛ

Alpine lake Song-Köl (Son-Kul), at 3016m, is one of the loveliest spots in central Kyrgyzstan. All around it are lush pastures favoured by herders from the Kochkor Valley and beyond, who spend June to August here with their animals. Visitors are welcome, and this is a sublime place to camp and watch the sun come up. The cold, crystal-clear air, far away from light pollution and smog, guarantees a starry night sky so grand it is able to dwarf even this open landscape. You can make any number of day hikes into the surrounding hills for excellent views. The lake is jumping with fish, and you might be able to trade tea, salt, sugar, cigarettes or vodka with the herders for milk, *kurut* (dried yogurt balls) or full-bodied *kymys*. In any case bring plenty of food and water.

Naryn and Kochkor CBT and Shepherd's Life projects offer more than a dozen **yurt-stays** (per person full board 450som) around the lake, where you can also ride horses. There is no real need to arrange horses prior to arrival unless you are planning an extensive excursion as horses are easily rented directly from the locals. Bishkek-based travel companies such as NoviNomad (north shore) and ITMC Tien-Shan (south shore) operate tourist yurt camps in summer, where you can stay if there are no groups.

The lake and shore are part of the Song-Köl Zoological Reserve. Among animals under its protection are a diminishing number of wolves and lots of waterfowl, including the Indian mountain goose. The weather is unpredictable and snow can fall at any time so dress and plan accordingly. July to mid-September is the best season. Tourist organisations arrange **horse games** at the lake on the last Saturday in July and August (check with CBT in Kochkor). The lake is frozen from November to May.

It is possible to trek to Ak-Tal (see p322), a tiny village south of Song-Köl on the Naryn–Kazarman road.

### Getting There & Away

It's 50km from the Bishkek–Naryn road to the lake: 6km to Keng-Suu (Tölök) village, 21km to the end of the narrow valley of the Tölök River, and then a slow 23km (1½ hours) up and over the Kalmak-Ashuu Pass into the basin. This upper road is normally open only from late May to late October. The valley has little traffic and no regular buses.

A car hired from Kochkor through CBT or Shepherd's Life is the easiest option to get here. Prices depend upon the price of petrol; rates are currently 9som to 10som per kilometre. Generally a car costs around 1800som to 2000som for the return trip. You may find something cheaper in the bazaar.

There are at least three other unpaved 4WD tracks to the lake: from west of the lake at Chayek, to the south from Jangy Talap (p322) just off the Naryn–Kazarman road, and a winter road from the southeast corner of the lake to the Bishkek–Naryn road. It's therefore possible to drive in from Kochkor and out to

Naryn or Chayek, making a nice, although expensive (as you will have to pay the return price of both cars) loop route. Hitching is possible but only if you have lots of time and your own supplies.

It's also possible to trek in to the lake on foot or horseback from Kyzart, near Jumgal, in one or two days, staying in shepherds' yurts in the Char Archa and Kilenche *jailoos* although check with Kochkor travel agencies to ensure the current location of yurts en route. This approach has the merit of avoiding the expensive transport to Song-Köl as the 11am minibus from Bishkek continues to Kyzart from Kochkor.

A second approach on horseback or foot lies to the east, from Chekildek, just west of Kochkor, over the Kara Katta range, into the Tölök Valley and then over the Ak-Tash Pass, taking around three days. The CBT and Shepherd's Life representatives in Kochkor or Shepherd's Life in Jumgal (opposite) can arrange accommodation, horses and a guide for around 1400som per day, plus food. Without a tent you really need a guide as it's impossible to find the yurtstays by yourself.

## NARYN НАРЫН

**☎ 3522 / pop 38,000 / elev 2030m**

Naryn makes a convenient base for visits to both Song-Köl and the Tash Rabat caravanserai and from here it is possible to strike westward to Jalal-Abad via Kazarman. Naryn is derived from the Mongolian for 'sunny' – a rare moment of Mongol irony. The region's one real claim to fame is that the best quality *shyrdaks* are said to be made here.

### Orientation

Dusty brown Naryn is strung along the milky-blue Naryn River for 15km. The town fails to fatten into anything decent, barely 2km at its widest point. The road from Bishkek forks north of the town, each branch of the fork leading to one end of town. A trolleybus (3som) and minibuses (5som) run along the main street, Lenina.

If there's a centre it's probably the *hakimyat* (municipal administration) on Lenina although the most visible sign on this street is the English graffiti ('Melanie you are the best girl in the world') across the roof of the bus shelter 500m to the east. Other travellers'



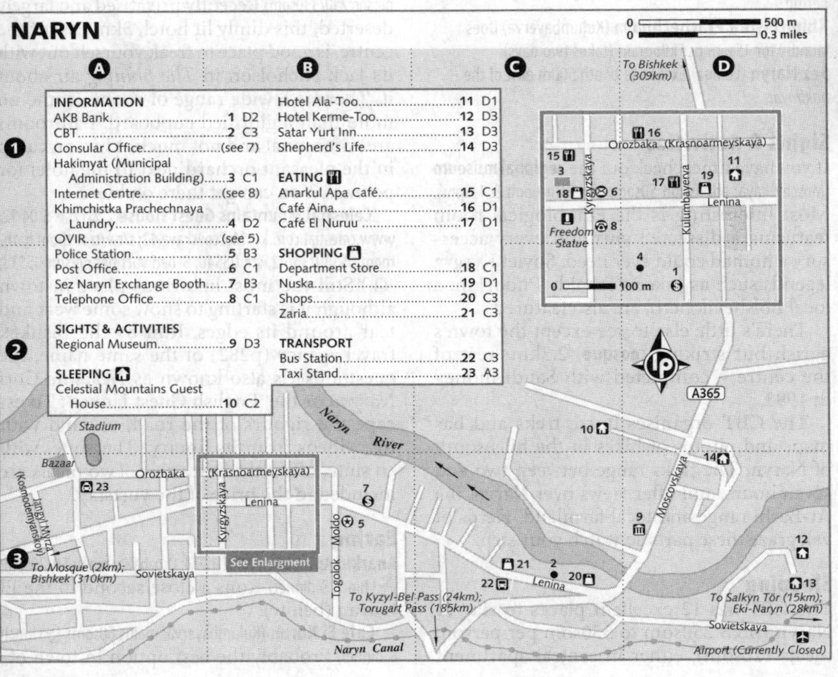

landmarks are the small bazaar on Orozbaka, and the bus station, 800m east of the *hakimyat* on Lenina.

## Information

In an emergency it's possible to extend your visa at the Consular Office of the Ministry of Foreign Affairs in the Special Economic Zone building, or at the **OVIR office** (Togolok Moldo 11).

The **Internet Centre** (Kyrgyzskaya; per hr 30som) on the south side of the **telephone office** (Kyrgyzskaya) has decent connections. The **post office** (Lenina) is across the road.

Naryn is the last place to change money before the Chinese border.

**AKB Bank** (1st fl, Kulumbayerva; 8.30am-noon & 1-5pm) Can change clean US dollars (and occasionally euros) as can CBT.

**CBT** (5 08 95, 5 08 65; naryn_tourism@rambler.ru; Lenina 8) Contact Kubat Abdyldaev, a fount of information and can arrange regional yurtstays (250som), transport and horse treks. In addition to arranging trips to Song-Köl and Tash Rabat it has internet (per hour 30som), rents bicycles (150som per hour) and burns digital photos to CD (50som). A car to Kashgar via the Torugart Pass costs US$300 and it takes one day to organise the Chinese permit.

**Khimchistka Prachechnaya** (Kulumbayerva) Does laundry for 15som per kilogram (takes two days).

**Sez Naryn** (Lenina) Exchange booth 500m east of the *hakimyat.*

KYRGYZSTAN

## Sights & Activities

If you have time, check out the **regional museum** (Moscovskaya; admission 50som; 9am-noon & 1-5pm). Most interesting is the ethnological room featuring a dissected yurt and every accessory a nomad could ever need. Soviet Kyrgyz legends such as Jukeev Tabaldy Pudovkin, a local Bolshevik hero, are also featured.

There's little else to see except the town's garish but striking **mosque**, 2.5km west of the centre – completed with Saudi money in 1993.

The CBT organises horse treks and has maps and photos of hikes in the hills south of Naryn. The treks range between two and seven hours, and offer views over Naryn, the At-Bashi range and local farmland. Herds of yak graze these parts so watch your step.

## Sleeping

The CBT has 12 excellent places to stay in Naryn (B&B 250som to 350som per person, meals 120som), either in central apartment blocks or suburban houses; many in the eastern Moscovskaya suburb. Try the CBT first to see what's available.

**Hotel Ala-Too** (2 18 72; Lenina; s/d 100/120som, tw/tr 300/450som, tw semi lux 800som) The standard rooms are pretty dilapidated but they are the cheapest in town and come with a stinky toilet. The renovated *lux* rooms are clean, spacious and surprisingly pleasant, with hot water and a balcony (for some rooms).

**Shepherd's Life** (4 14 57, 5 08 65; shepherds-life@rambler.ru; Kalykova 14; dm 200som) The coordinator Marima Amankulova's house and homestay (meals 100som) are one and the same in the eastern Moscovskaya suburb and one of the cheapest in town (because there is no shower). A 20som taxi or 5som minibus ride will save you the 15-minute walk from the bus station.

**Satar Yurt Inn** (5 03 22; Checkeybaeva; yurtstay 200som, dm 300som) This is a collection of seven or eight tourist yurts, each of which contains five beds. Facilities include Western toilets, a shower that was under repair and a small restaurant (meals 60 to 100som). The twin and double rooms are modest but clean.

**Hotel Kerme-Too** (2 26 21; Checkeybaeva; r/ste per person 250/330som) Recently privatised and largely deserted, this dimly lit hotel, 3km east of the centre, is good place to freak yourself out with its Jack Nicholson in *The Shining* air about it. There is a wide range of rooms, some no more than a glorified cupboard. Bathrooms are communal and not much. You can camp in the pleasant orchard next to the hotel for pennies. You can get there on bus 2.

**Celestial Mountains Guest House** (/fax 5 04 12; www.celestial.com.kg; Moscovskaya 42; s/tw/tr without bathroom US$30/36/42, ste US$40, 3-bed yurt per person US$13; ) Still the most luxurious place in town although it is starting to show some wear and tear around its edges. Run by the Bishkek travel agency (p282) of the same name, the guesthouse is also known as *Nebesnie Gori Naryna* or the 'English Guest House'. To escape the rigours of the road, unwind with free videos from its library. The suite, with en suite, offers the best value. Two meals are included in the price of the yurtstay.

## Eating

**Anarkul Apa Café** (2 12 74; Orozbaka; mains 50-70som; lunch & dinner) Runs a close second to the El Nuruu (below).

**Café El Nuruu** (Kulumbayerva; mains 60som; lunch & dinner) Probably the best option in town offering more than the usual standards. The *zharenie* chicken stir-fry is recommended (55som).

**Café Aina** (☎ 2 47 78; Orozbaka; mains 60-150som; ⏰ lunch & dinner) Tries its hand at most things, from pizza to Chinese, touching on some European favourites (pancakes 15som) along the way. It has an English menu and unlike most others, stay open on Sunday.

The bazaar has a usual line-up of dairy products for self-caterers. You can also get good-quality canned goods, sausage and cheese in the private shops at the eastern crossroads.

### Shopping

**Zaria** (Lenina) This NGO produces export-quality *shyrdaks* but keeps erratic hours so it is worth asking CBT to phone ahead. The entrance is difficult to spot; it's opposite the bus stop and displays a small paper sign in its window.

**Nuska** (Lenina) Again, difficult to find and often closed. This local designer produces high-quality *shyrdaks* that have been exhibited abroad. Look for the sandwich board on the street. The store is set back off the road behind the friendly ladies selling bread and vegetables from street stalls.

### Getting There & Away

Minibuses depart between 8am and 10am from the bus station on Lenina for Bishkek (200som, six hours). Buses to Kazarman (180som, seven hours) depart at 8.30am on Tuesday and Friday. From June to August the daily bus to Jangy Talap leaves between 2pm and 3pm (80som, 2½ hours) and in winter at 1pm. Buses also go to At-Bashy (25som) to the south.

Shared taxis are a good alternative but the sharklike taxi drivers outside the bus station go into a feeding frenzy at the sight of a foreigner. Beware of the friendly guy who grabs your bag and takes you to a car that conveniently happens to be going your way and then charges you a finder's fee. A seat in a shared taxi costs 45som to At-Bashy, 100som to Jangy Talap, 200som to Kochkor and 300som to 350som to Bishkek. To hire your own taxi costs 1200som to 1300som to Bishkek, 2250som to Tash Rabat, 900som to Eki-Naryn.

## AROUND NARYN

### Activities

CBT (opposite) can give the lowdown on a range of trips around Naryn, including yurtstays in the Ardaktuu Valley and Tyor Jailoo in the Eki Naryn Valley. Given a few days' warning, it can organise the following multiday horse treks. Most horse trips start from Echki-Bashy, 25km north of Naryn. Ask CBT about visits to the Tian Shan deer nursery at Irii-Suu (great for kids) and day trips up the Ak-Tam valley to see petroglyphs.

**Echki-Bashy to Bokonbayevo** (seven days by horse) Via Tuura-Suu.

**Echki-Bashy to Song-Köl** (four days by horse, five days by foot) Treks to the east side of the lake overnighting in tents and yurts. From Song-Köl it is possible to continue by car to Kochkor.

**Jangy Talap to Song-Köl** (two days by horse, three days by foot) Starting from Jangy Talap (Kurta) village, west of Naryn to Song-Köl's southern shore, overnighting in yurts (July and August) or tents.

**Naryn State Reserve** (2½ days by horse, 4½ days by foot) Transport by car to the state reserve then you follow the Big Naryn River to Karakalka village overnighting with the ranger or staying in tents. It is possible to arrange transport or trek independently to Barskoön from Kararalka.

### Eki-Naryn Area

The scenic Kichi (Little) Naryn Valley stretches to the northeast of Naryn and offers plenty of opportunities for exploration. The main settlement is at Eki-Naryn, 30km northeast of Salkyn Tör, close to where the Kichi Naryn River meets the Naryn.

Around 10km north of Tash-Bashat is a fascinating swastika-shaped forest, said to have been planted by German prisoners of war under the noses of their Soviet captors.

Buses leave Naryn for Eki-Naryn at 8am on Monday, Wednesday and Friday (40som), or you could take a taxi for around 700som. With your own transport it's possible to continue northeast and then swing west to follow the Kara-Kujur Valley back to Sary-Bulak and the main Naryn–Kochkor road.

If you don't wish to camp in the valley, check with CBT and Shepherd's Life in Naryn for service providers in the area. Community-Based Toursim arranges homestays at Lehol, and Shepherd's Life have a summer yurtstay at Ardakty Jailoo.

## NARYN TO JALAL-ABAD

If you're planning to travel directly between the Fergana Valley and the Bishkek–Torugart road, it's possible to cut right across central Kyrgyzstan between Jalal-Abad and Naryn instead of going around via Bishkek. This route goes via Kazarman (220km from Naryn), a rough-and-ready gold-mining town in the middle of nowhere. The mountain pass to the Fergana Valley is closed from November to late May or early June.

## Naryn to Kazarman

From Naryn there are two ways to reach Kazarman and the one you'll end up taking largely depends on the transport you end up catching. The shorter route (five to six hours, excluding running repairs) favoured by shared taxis starts with a fairly monotonous drive along straight roads as far as Ak-Tal (or Ak-Talaa – White Fields), 75km west of Naryn. Things dramatically improve after the road turns right here, crosses the Naryn River and starts to wind through a higgledy-piggledy landscape of desert bluffs and badlands along a road blasted in 1903 by the Russian military. As you climb higher, the road gets dustier and all car windows are wound tightly shut; sit on the right to avoid dehydration in the baking sun. Statues of camels that look more like llamas on the left-hand side signal the top of the pass, after which there is another series of hair-pin bends and jaw-dropping views as the road winds down to Kazarman.

The second route, favoured by buses (eight hours), is the same as far as Ak-Tal but, instead of turning off towards Song-Köl, continues to Baetov, a forgotten rayon capital 40km southwest of Ak-Tal. The road eventually crosses the Ala-Buka River before climbing the 2932m Ak-Moinak Pass that leads to Kazarman.

At the Ak-Tal junction there is also a lonely 4WD track that leads up to the southern shore of Song-Köl (65km) via 33 switchbacks and the Moldo Ashuu Pass.

In **Ak-Tal** travellers report there is accommodation at **Konurchok Hotel** (☎ 03537-9 15 50; Zina Oshyrbaeva; r 100-150som; contact Busara Sagyndykova) or at Jangy Talap (also known as Kurtka), about 4km from Ak-Tal, with a **Shepherd's Life coordinator** (☎ 051-776 35 97; Yntymak 45; B&B 200som, sauna 20som; contact Sveta Jusupjanova) which can arrange accommodation and transport. There's one bus daily to Jangy Talap from Naryn at 4pm and there are irregular shared taxis (70som per seat). If you have time, try to track down the photogenic **Taylik Batyr Mausoleum**, near Kara-Oi village, around 8km from Jangy Talap.

## Kazarman

**☎ 3738 / pop 15,000 / elev 1230m**

Kazarman is the kind of town that begs to be bypassed. Even the main road (Kadykulov) from Naryn to Jalal-Abad sweeps by on the southern outskirts of town. However it's not all bad; raw, untamed Kazarman's redemption lies in the nearby petroglyphs of Sailmaluu Tash.

The town exists to serve the open-cast Makhmal gold mine about an hour to the east, and the nearby ore-processing plant, but not much of the wealth has trickled down into local hands.

Buses and taxis turn off the Naryn–Jalal-Abad through road and drop you five blocks north on the town's main drag, Jeenaliev (also called Mira). From west to east on Jeenaliev you'll find the Sailmaluu Tash park office, the Dom Kultura building, bus station, cafés and CBT office. One block north of the cafés is a tiny bazaar.

### INFORMATION

**CBT** (☎ 4 17 36; Apt 3, Jeenaliev 20) If the office is locked, knock on the door of coordinator Janara Tuiteeva's house opposite the office behind light blue gates. There's not much in the way of service here, but staff should be able to sort out a B&B and guided tours to Sailmaluu Tash and the nearby Tuz and the Kargalyk mountains.

**Sailmaluu Tash park office** (☎ 4 16 76; Jeenaliev) About 200m west of CBT is the only other place in town that can help arrange a visit to the petroglyphs. It is both cheaper and staff more informed than the CBT.

### SLEEPING & EATING

Now that the sole hotel in Kazarman has closed, homestays are the only accommodation option. There are also a half-dozen CBT **homestays** (B&B 300som, meals 90som), including the difficult to find homestay of English-speaking **Bakhtygul Chorobaeva** (☎ 2 19 16, 4 13 77; Kadyrkulova 35), five blocks south of the centre.

**Ulan Tuiteev** (Kadyrkulova 6) The local CBT guide provides a homestay and with help arrange treks to Sailmaluu Tash. As you arrive in town look for the small B&B sign on Kadyrkulova pointing down a side lane. Follow this for 75m to an even smaller lane on the right. Look for the large silver gate at the end of this lane. Knock loudly.

For privacy and a central location try the CBT **apartment** (Apt 6, Jeenaliev 20), behind the CBT office, which sleeps four in two rooms. There are two more homestays on Bekten (18 and 36), two blocks south of Jeenaliev.

KYRGYZSTAN

We must have caught Kazarman on a bad day; of the three cafés along the main drag, two were open but had no food and the third, **Café Aimrza** (Jeenaliev), was only serving *laghman* (35som).

### GETTING THERE & AWAY

Buses depart Kazarman for Naryn (180som) on Wednesday and Saturday at around 8am (eight hours). At other times shared taxis and 4WDs congregate next to the bus parking lot on Jeenaliev, 50m west of CBT, and leave if and when they fill up. A seat in a shared taxi to Naryn costs 400som (5½ hours), Bishkek 800som, and 400som per seat in 4WDs bound for Jalal-Abad (four to six hours). Occasional minibuses also depart from here to Bishkek (600som).

Because of the very real possibility that there will be no-one to share your shared taxi, budget for the worst-case scenario – having to fork out for all four seats.

## Sailmaluu Tash

The several thousand 'embroidered stones' of Sailmaluu Tash are Central Asia's most dramatic petroglyphs. Over the millennia Aryan, Scythian and Turkic peoples have added to the earliest Bronze Age carvings. The carvings are spread over two slopes and depict hunting, shamanistic rites and battle scenes, some dating back more than 4000 years.

The petroglyphs are difficult to reach and are for the committed and adventurous. From Kazarman there are two route options, via Atai, 20km west along the road to Jalal-Abad, and the second via Chet Bulak south of Kazarman (so you can take one up and another one back). Both trips involve a car trip of about 45 minutes, followed by a half-day hike or horse trip. The petroglyph gallery is only accessible from June to mid-September. It's best to spend the night at yurts near the site and explore the stones for a few hours early the next morning, although a rushed day trip is also possible.

CBT can arrange an overnight horse trip for around 7500som for two people. This includes 4WD hire, guide (for two days), horses for two people and admission tickets (450som per person, per day). Food is extra, as is accommodation in yurts if available. Otherwise bring your own tent.

You can get a better deal at the park office *(monpekettik zharalypish parky)* on Kazarman's main street. Staff can organise guides and accommodation in a yurt (1000som) for as many as you can squeeze in.

It is also possible to approach Sailmaluu Tash on a longer route from the Fergana Valley, from Kalmak-Kyrchyn up the Kök Art Valley. The CBT in Jalal-Abad (p332) can arrange transport and horses from the western approach, from where you can descend to Kazarman.

## Kazarman to Jalal-Abad

There are no scheduled buses to Jalal-Abad, only when and if they fill up will Nivas and Russian 4WDs depart (400som per person).

The road begins benignly enough, but the asphalt soon splutters out leaving a degraded dirt road, long overdue for some serious attention. Parts have been gouged away by rainwater run-off and the views down into the ravines from the crumbling track will have you reaching for your nonexistent seat belt. The road finally crests a 3100m summit at a spot commemorated by a statue of an eagle and a row of ugly pylons. From the scenery on the Fergana side you can see why the area is referred to as Central Asia's breadbasket. All going well the trip finishes sometime between four and six hours later at Jalal-Abad bazaar. The previous author's Niva broke down 27 times along this route.

# NARYN TO TORUGART

## At-Bashy

At-Bashy is off the Naryn–Torugart road, 6km by an easterly access road, 4km by a westerly one, and truly the far end of populated Kyrgyzstan. Sandwiched between the At-Bashy and Naryn Tau ranges, the town has a great location and can be used as a springboard for visits to Tash Rabat, Koshoy Korgon and the Torugart Pass. Through the Shepherd's Life programme you could also arrange visits to the surrounding villages of Tus Bogoshtu (6km), Kök Köl (40km), or further afield to Bosogo Jailoo – a forested region ideal for trekking and, during September, blackcurrant picking.

### ORIENTATION

From the bus station at the east end of town head 1.5km west past the new mosque to the cinema and city administration building. Turn right at this building and head north on Atty Suleimanov towards the low hill that marks the canal 1km in the distance. Continue

 

### HEADING TOWARDS THE TORUGART PASS

It's about 130km from Naryn to the outer border checkpoint and a further 60km to the main customs station at Torugart, a total of about 4½ hours' driving if you make no stops.

From Naryn it's 24km to the low **Kyzyl-Bel Pass**, with a stupendous view right down the crest of the At-Bashy range (highest point 4786m). The road runs along the foot of this range and around the far (west) end of it to Torugart. About 13km and 20km from the pass are two turn-offs to the village of **At-Bashy**, the closest point to the border accessible by regular bus, and an hour's drive from Naryn.

West of At-Bashy is a yawning, red-walled notch on the north side of the valley; the road crosses a stream that drains everything through this notch and down to the Naryn River. Low bluffs west of the stream partly conceal a bizarre landscape of perfectly rounded, sandy hills. By the roadside is a splendid Kyrgyz graveyard.

About 14km west of the second At-Bashy access road is a turn-off to Kara-Suu village and the ruins of **Koshoy Korgon**.

Some 40km west of At-Bashy the road turns to gravel, but for a startling 3km before it does so, it becomes as wide and smooth as a four-lane superhighway: a military airstrip, apparently never used. About 21km from the end of the airstrip is the turn-off south to **Tash Rabat**.

Approximately 28km west of this turn-off is the low **Ak-Beyit Pass** at the end of the At-Bashy range. Then it's 4km to the **outer checkpoint**, an hour's drive from At-Bashy, and another fine view – to the crest line, on the border itself.

South from the outer checkpoint the road rapidly degenerates as views of the Fergana range rise to the west. Some 26km on, at the 3574m **Tüz-Bel Pass**, it swings east and skirts **Chatyr-Köl**. Black cranes and Indian mountain geese pause at the lake during their transcontinental migrations – one reason why the lake and its marshy shoreline are protected as the Chatyr-Köl Zoological Reserve. An old Soviet-era double electrified fence (no longer live) runs near the road. As the road climbs, the surrounding mountains seem to just melt away.

Fifty kilometres from the outer checkpoint and 7km from the Kyrgyzstan customs and immigration station, a big red-and-yellow sign says 'Narzan'; 50m off the road in a field of bubbling mud is a gushing cold spring, fizzy and tasty.



four blocks and turn left down a dirt road, Arpa, for 250m to get to Tursan's homestay. A taxi will cost 30som.

#### SLEEPING & EATING

**Homestay of Tursan Akieva** (☎ 3534-219 44; Arpa 25; dm 200som) Tursan is the local coordinator of Shepherd's Life and offers a family atmosphere (breakfast included, meals 90som) in a home resplendent with *shyrdaks* and carpets. Tursan also arranges transport to Tash Rabat and Torugart, dispenses info on local *shyrdak* cooperatives and puts travellers in touch with several yurtstays in surrounding mountains.

There are a couple of grotty cafés at the bus station and on Lenin, plus a small bazaar about 600m west of the bus station.

#### GETTING THERE & AWAY

There are scheduled daily buses in the morning to Naryn (25som, 1½ hours), a 6.30pm night bus to Bishkek (189som, eight hours) and Kara-Suu (25som, 30 minutes). A seat in a shared taxi to Bishkek costs 450som, or 50som to 60som to Naryn.

Taxis ask 1200som (negotiate waiting time) return to Tash Rabat, though you could get one cheaper through Tursan at the Shepherd's Life programme. Taxis also scout for passengers at the bazaar on Lenin.

### Koshoy Korgon

In a field behind the village of Kara-Suu are the eroded ruins of a large citadel, occupied during the 10th to 12th (or early 13th centuries), and probably Karakhanid. An appealing local legend tells that the Kyrgyz hero Manas built the citadel and a mausoleum here for his fallen friend Koshoy.

A private taxi (four seats) from At-Bashy to the site costs about 400som for a return visit. About 14.5km west of the western access road to At-Bashy, by a petrol station on the Naryn–Torugart road, turn south (signposted) to Kara-Suu village. Take the first left turn in the village after the mosque and silver war memorial, continue past all the houses and then take a right and then another right to the ruins, 3km from the main road.

Next to the ruins, Shepherd's Life has a **homestay** (200som), which could be a good base for hikes in the At-Bashy range.

### Tash Rabat

About 60km from At-Bashy a dirt track heads into a hidden, surprisingly level valley, surrounded by lush corduroy hillsides that has been offering shelter to well-to-do travellers for centuries in a fortified **caravanserai** (adult/child 50/25som; 9am-5pm mid-May–mid-Oct) that looks like a mausoleum, sunk into the hillside.

Local sources say it dates from the 15th century, although some sources say the site dates from the 10th century, when it was a Christian monastery. Either way historians agree that at one time Tash Rabat (Kyrgyz for stone fortress) must have had significant Silk Road political and trade importance to justify the investment of the labour required for its construction.

It's irregular shape and improbable location has fuelled a number of local legends. One relates how a ruling khan devised a test for his two sons to see whom was worthy to inherit his throne. One son determined to prove that he could provide for his people pursued the development of education, agriculture and industry. The other son amassed armies and built fortresses. Tash Rabat stands as a silent reminder of a warmongering man who lost a khanate to his philanthropic brother.

A clumsy Soviet restoration was completed in 1984. A few fragments of the original central mosque are visible in the main chamber; leading off this are many other chambers, including a well (some say a treasury, in the far left corner) and a dungeon (in the central right chamber). An opening in the far right corner leads to what the caretakers say is a tunnel, explored generations ago for as far as about 200m, and perhaps once leading to a lookout point to the south.

Community-Based Tourism Naryn (p320) sells a photocopied pamphlet, *A Self-Guided Tour of Tash Rabat*, which helps fill in some of the gaps.

From Tash Rabat a six-hour horse ride or hike will take you to a broad ridge overlooking **Chatyr-Köl**; if you continue for a couple of hours, you can stay the night in a yurt at Chatyr-Köl before returning to Tash Rabat the next day. Remember that you are about 3500m high here, so even a short walk could set your head pounding. Neither Tash Rabat nor Chatyr-Köl are in a restricted border zone. The caretakers at Tash Rabat can arrange the trip and rent horses for 70som per hour or 420som per day and a trekking guide for 420som per day or a mounted guide for 620som per day, making this a great place to spend a day or two exploring.

You can stay at the **yurts** (250som) of Shepherd's Life (meals 90som) or the caretaker's yurts across from the caravanserai. There are two more yurtstays located 1km back downstream.

There's no public transport here and because of snow the road is closed between mid-Octover to mid-May. A day trip by taxi from Naryn to Tash Rabat (two hours) costs around 2250som; otherwise drivers charge an additional 550som per day for food and lodging. For a further 70som you can visit Koshoy Korgon (opposite) on the same day. Alternatively, it is also possible (and recommended) to include Tash Rabat as a side trip en route to the Torugart Pass although this involves setting out an hour and a half earlier and an additional US$10 to cover the extra kilometres.

## TORUGART PASS
## ПЕРЕВАЛ ТОРУГАРТ

Torugart is one of Asia's most unpredictable border posts. Even the most painstaking arrangements can be thwarted by logistical gridlock on the Chinese side or by unpredictable border closures (eg for holidays, snow or heaven knows what else).

Most of the traffic through the pass is trucks carrying scrap metal and animal hides from Kyrgyzstan, or porcelain, thermoses, beer and clothing from China. The trucks accumulate in huge tailbacks at both sides, for 500m or more in the mornings.

From the Kyrgyzstan customs and immigration station it is 6.8km to the summit. Below this, about 5km away, is a checkpoint, though the main Chinese customs and immigration post is another 70km away.

The Torugart Pass is normally snow-free from late May through to September. The crossing is theoretically kept open all year, but is icy and dangerous in winter. The **customs & immigration facilities** are open from 10am to 5pm Monday to Friday, but in reality you must cross between 9am and noon. Besides the various customs sheds, inspection pits and immigration offices, there is a spartan state 'hotel', though most people who stay do so in basic caravans 1km before the customs area.

### Red Tape

Essentially many of the difficulties crossing the pass boil down to Torugart being classified by the Chinese as a 'Class 2' border crossing, for local traffic only, and so special regulations are in force for foreigners, many of which seem deliberately set up to milk foreigners of some hard currency. For example, foreigners aren't allowed to take the weekly bus that runs between Kashgar and Kyrgyzstan. The bottom line is that you must have onward Chinese transport arranged and waiting for you on the Chinese side to be allowed past the Kyrgyz border post.

Kyrgyz border officials are insistent on written confirmation of this onward transport into China, and detain visitors until their transport arrives at the summit from Kashgar. The best thing to have is a fax from an accredited Chinese tour agency, who will come and meet you. No special endorsement is required on your Chinese visa.

The three-point border – two border controls 12km apart and a security station in between makes for further confusion. You are not allowed to walk or cycle on the Chinese side of the border in no-man's-land. It is therefore *essential* that your Kyrgyz transport continues past the custom post to the actual border to meet your prearranged Chinese onward transport. Only drivers with a Kyrgyz Foreign Ministry special permit can go this far. Normally the Chinese guards at the arch radio to Kyrgyz immigration when your transport arrives and only then are you allowed to leave the Kyrgyz border post. See right for further advice and p349 for general advice.

### Travel Agencies

Arranging the whole trip from Bishkek to Kashgar currently costs from around US$100 to US$200 per person in a group of four, depending on the agent and the vehicle.

Of Bishkek's travel agencies (p282), NoviNomad was the cheapest we found, charging US$285 for a car from Bishkek to Kashgar seating three (excluding driver's food and accommodation). Celestial Mountains, Kyrgyz Concept and ITMC Tien Shan (p284) were also competitively priced and worth checking.

Community-Based Tourism Naryn (p320) also arranges reliable transport to Kashgar from Naryn for US$300 per vehicle (US$120 for Kyrgyz transport, US$180 for Chinese transport) in a car capable of seating four. Allow one full day to organise.

Most agents can make arrangements with a cooperating Chinese agency for onward transport. The charge for this is set by the Chinese agency and normally paid in US dollars to the Chinese driver once in China. If this is the case, get a printed confirmation of the price from your Kyrgyz agent to avoid any dispute later. You could deal directly with a Chinese travel agency from abroad but it's generally easier to let the agency make the arrangements.

If you do wish to contact Chinese agencies, you could try **John's Information Café** (☎ 86-998-255 1186; johncafé@hotmail.com) or **Caravan Café** (☎ 86-998-298 1864; www.caravancafé.com, www.asianexplorations.com; 120 Seman Lu) in Kashgar, though neither are that easy to contact in advance and we have received complaints about both.

### Cycling

It is possible to cycle the Torugart – but not the whole way. From Naryn it is a 2½-day ride to Tash Rabat and from there it is possible to ride past the Kyrgyz customs as far as the borderline from where you will also need prearranged Chinese transport (two cyclists per car).

Community-Based Tourism Naryn (p320) can arrange the Chinese transport (US$180 per car) and provide a covering letter (US$50) that states a Chinese representative is waiting on the Chinese side for you and your bike. The covering letter will also explain that you have been informed not to leave the main road past the Korgon Tash checkpoint, and will only camp by the roadside.

### Crossing the Pass

#### KYRGYZSTAN

When both sides of the border finally open, you and your driver show confirmation of onward transport and then, cold and frustrated, wait until the radio call comes from the Chinese side that your onward transport has arrived. After this you march into customs, bags in tow, where officials collect the customs form you filled out when you entered the Commonwealth of Independent States (CIS) and try (and probably succeed) to sell you a customs form for 30som. You then proceed through immigration. Meanwhile, your vehicle is being strip-searched in a garage next door.

After inspection you jump back into your vehicle and continue 7km to the border. If you don't have transport for this section, this is where your headache begins, as you'll have to negotiate with a driver to give you a lift and with the officials to let you pass.

#### SUMMIT

In the border zone, roughly halfway between the two customs and immigration stations, permitted vehicles are allowed, but apparently no pedestrians. At the summit, your new driver and some Chinese soldiers will be waiting for the transfer. Big handshakes all around. Don't forget to take a look at the beautiful pass, which you just fought so hard to cross.

#### CHINA

Another 5km later you will arrive at the original Chinese border post, where the Bishkek–Kashgar bus passengers will be patiently unrolling every carpet and draining every thermos for the customs patrol. Just to keep up appearances, the guards will have you line up all your baggage and then choose one at random to dig through.

It's surprising how the climate and landscape change when you cross the pass. The Chinese side is abruptly drier, more desolate and treeless, with little physical development other than adobe Kyrgyz settlements. The road runs through Kyzylsu Kyrgyz Autonomous County.

The 100km of road closest to the border is a miserable washboard surface, spine-shattering to travel along and choked with dust. At the junction of the Torugart and Irkeshtam roads is the spanking new Chinese customs and immigration station.

Chinese immigration is open 1pm to 5pm Beijing time but officers will wait for you if you are late. Here you fill out entry forms and get your passport stamped, both relatively painless. The post has a Bank of China branch, a couple of simple noodle shops and a small guesthouse, though travellers in either direction are discouraged from staying. From here to Kashgar it's 60km of paved road.

The whole Torugart–Kashgar trip is 160km, a 3½- to four-hour 4WD trip.

# BISHKEK TO OSH & THE KYRGYZ FERGANA VALLEY

From the standpoint of landscape, the Bishkek–Osh road is a sequence of superlatives, taking the traveller over two 3000m-plus passes, through the yawning Suusamyr Valley, around the immense Toktogul reservoir, down the deep Naryn River gorge and into the broad Fergana Valley.

The road has improved dramatically recently as the government tries to solder the two halves of the country together using better transport and communication links. The Bishkek to Toktogul stretch is still blocked occasionally by rock falls and avalanches. Snow fills the passes from late October until March; the road is kept open but is dangerous. Scheduled transport thins out by October, although cars continue to push through.

## BISHKEK TO TASHKÖMÜR

### Bishkek to Suusamyr Valley

Even before you climb out of the Chuy Valley from Kara-Balta, the craggy Kyrgyz Alatau range rises like a wall. The road climbs through a crumbling canyon towards the highest point of the journey, the 3586m **Tör-Ashuu Pass** at the suture between the Talas Alatau and Kyrgyz Alatau ranges. Instead of climbing over, the road burrows through, in a series of dripping tunnels (built by the same team that constructed the metros in Leningrad and Moscow) that open to a grand, eagle's-eye view of the Suusamyr Basin.

There is a 45som toll collected (or checked) at each end of the Tör-Ashuu Pass.

In 2001 the longest tunnel (2.6km) was the scene of a freak accident when a car broke down midway through causing a traffic-jam. By the time the truck drivers turned off their engines four people had died from carbon monoxide poisoning.

About 4½ hours out of Bishkek a road shoots off, straight as an arrow, across the basin towards Suusamyr, Chayek and eventually the Bishkek–Naryn road (p315). This is classic Kyrgyz yurt country, with plenty of summer roadside stands, offering fresh *kymys* (1L 30som) and other dairy products.

After another 1¼ hours another road branches right, over the 3330m Otmek Pass 106km towards Talas, and Taraz in Kazakhstan.

### Suusamyr Valley

This rarely visited valley combines a backdoor route to the Kochkor area (see p317) with classic central Kyrgyzstan mountain landscapes. No buses go all the way to Kochkor so you'd have to hitch from Kyzyl-Oi as far as Chayek, probably with one of the many coal trucks headed to a mine near Song-Köl. Adventurous trekkers can visit the valley as part of a trek to/from Bishkek over the Kyrgyz Alatau via the Sokuluk (3775m), Ala-Archa (3898m) or Alamedin (4032m) passes.

In **Suusamyr** town it's possible to arrange homestay accommodation with Kubanychbek Amankulov (look for the tourist info sign on the main road). He can also arrange transport and yurtstays in *jailoo*s east at Joo Jurok (30km from Suusamyr; contact Negizbek Imankulov), 20km north at Boirok (contact Eshbolot Cheinekeev) and 13km southeast at Sandyk (contact Kubat Amankulov). Little English is spoken at any of these.

**Kyzyl-Oi** (ask for Artyk Kulubaev at the shop 'Aksar') has a fledgling homestay programme, which also offers horse and foot treks to the Köl Tör lakes (five hours on horse; up the Char Valley, staying at the yurt of Bayish Toltoev, and then over the Kumbel Pass) and also to *jailoos* in the Sary Kamysh range to the south of town. Artyk can arrange horse hire, guides and food. Homestays include those of Tungatar Konushbaev, Katya Kulmursaeva, and Kanat Soltonkulov, the latter with a *banya,* and *shyrdaks* for sale. The programme hasn't had many tourists and is less polished than CBT.

**Dostuck Trekking** (p284) operates a yurt camp in the Suusamyr Valley; book a spot in advance.

Transport from Kyzyl-Oi runs almost daily to Suusamyr, from where there are daily buses to Bishkek's Osh Bazaar.

From Kyzyl-Oi it's 40km or so to Shepherd's Life coordinators at Chayek (p318) and Jangy Talap (p322), from where you can arrange horse trips to Song-Köl (p318).

### Talas

☎ 3422

The town of Talas itself has little of interest except the **Manas Ordu**, claimed to be the 14th-century tomb of Manas (actually the tomb of Kenizek Khatum, the daughter of a regional governor, buried in 1334), east of town in the village of Tash Aryk. The Talas Valley was the scene of a pivotal battle between Arab and Chinese armies in the 8th century. Today, there are a couple of cafés, a medical clinic and some fledgling sustainable-tourism projects.

**CBT Talas** (☎ 5 29 19; cbt_talas@list.ru; Kayimov Yuzhnaya 76) offers accommodation (250 to 420som) around town and at Ozgorush, 50km northeast of town, and a yurtstay in Besh-Tash (Five Stones) National Park. It can also arrange guides and horses. The park is 15km from town and the first yurt is 38km from town. Contact Turdubek Aiyilchiev.

Minibuses run over the Otmek Pass between Talas and Bishkek's Osh Bazaar at least once a day. The road through the Talas Valley goes as far as Taraz in Kazakhstan and makes an interesting alternative route to Kazakhstan.

### Suusamyr Valley to Tashkömür

A further 30 minutes' drive after the turn-off to Talas the road climbs again, up to the 3184m summit of the **Ala-Bel Pass** over the Suusamyr-Tau mountains. Lower, broader and longer than the Tör-Ashuu Pass, it is nevertheless colder, and said to be the bigger wintertime spoiler. The beautiful valley down the south side of the pass is part of the **Chychkan state zoological reserve** (*chychkan* means mouse).

The flash **Ak Ilbirs Hotel** (s/d 850/1650som, lux s/d 1600/3200som), by the roadside, is recognisable by a line of flags and its suitably alpine architecture. The standard rooms have more reliable hot water than the *lux*. Meals are 40som to 100som.

The town of **Toktogul** (population 70,000) and the reservoir it sits next to are named after a well-known Kyrgyz *akyn,* Toktogul Satilganov (1884–1933), who was born here. It takes over an hour to detour around the vast Toktogul Reservoir. Some tour groups camp on the far side of the reservoir. Several roadside stalls on the south side of the lake serve delicious fried *farel* (trout).

The town of **Kara-Köl** (population 22,000) is of note only for its dam, part of the Nizhnenarynskiy Kaskad, a series of five dams down the lower gorge of the Naryn River. This *kaskad* (dam), topmost in the series, was completed in 1976 after 14 years' work and is a pretty awesome feat of Soviet engineering:

KYRGYZSTAN

210m high, 150m wide at the top, and holding back a 19-billion-cubic-metre lake. Just about everybody in town works for the hydroelectric station Toktogulsky Gidroelektrostantsia (GES). Kara-Köl is not to be confused with the much pleasanter town of Karakol on Lake Issyk-Köl. The dam isn't visible from the road and a visit needs special permission.

South of Kara-Köl the gorge of the **lower Naryn River** is an impressive passage, with sheer walls and towering pillars of red sandstone, and a little road clinging to the side – but keep your gaze upwards. Looking down you will see that there is no longer any river at all, just a depressing series of narrow, utterly still lakes behind the dams of the Nizhnenarynskiy Kaskad. At lower elevations the gorge bristles with pylons. Sit on the 'west' side of the bus for the best views of the ruination.

## Tashkömür

☎ 3745

About 5½ hours, drive from Toktogul is the coal-mining town of Tashkömür, strung for miles along the west side of the river below one of the dams. The deserted slag heaps outside the town are silent testament to the collapse of Kyrgyzstan's coal industry since independence. The town itself is one of the lowlights of Kyrgyzstan, but it is one of the main starting points to beautiful Lake Sary-Chelek, 70km west.

The town **gostinitsa** (hotel; r per person 70som) next to the bus station has ratty rooms without bathrooms. A better bet is to follow the train tracks 500m from the bus station to a blue-tiled **gostinitsa** (☎ 2 06 33; Lenina, r per person 200som), which is better than the smashed windows and deserted foyer might suggest.

There are a few cheap cafés serving luke-warm *laghman* at lunchtime near the bus station, along with what may well be Central Asia's most pitiful bazaar.

From the bus station in the centre of town a minibus leaves at 5.30am for Osh (170som); 6.20am, 7.20am and 12.20pm for Jalal-Abad (90som); 9am for Bishkek (350som); 9.45am for Kerben (49som); and at 10am and 1.30pm for Kara Jigach (55som). To get a shared taxi, head 3km from town to the Naryn River bridge, where there is a collection of kiosks and food stalls and a telephone office. A seat in a shared taxi costs 250som to Osh, 150som to Jalal-Abad and 650som to Bishkek.

## LAKE SARY-CHELEK ОЗЕРО САРЫ-ЧЕЛЕК

☎ 3742 / elev 1878m

This beautiful 7km-long alpine lake, nature reserve and biosphere lies hidden in the northern flanks of the Fergana Valley amid groves of wild pistachios, walnuts and fruit trees. The lake is thought to have been created by an earthquake that caused a giant landslide about 800 years ago and reaches a depth of 234m.

There is a park entry fee of US$10 (50som for locals), plus 60som per car. The park is part of Unesco's Western Tian Shan Biodiversity project and lynx, bears and maral deer live in the surroundings. Sadly, there is little sign of even the most basic level of environmental protection.

The base for visits to the lake is the small village of Arkit, actually inside the park, where you'll find the **park office** (zapovednik; ☎ 2 22 84), a nearby **nature museum** (zapovednik; 🕑 8am-noon & 1-5pm) and a couple of homestays. The lake is 15km from here, accessible by car. An lookout has just been built halfway along the road.

**CBT** (☎ 3125 5 93 31; reservation@cbtkyrgyzstan.kg) has a coordinator (Bazarkul Zhooshbaev) in Kyzyl-Kul village in the Kara-Suu Valley, who can arrange accommodation in homes or yurts (250 to 300som), plus arrange horses and guides for treks up the valley to Kara-Suu Lake and beyond over the Kemerty Pass to Lake Sary-Chelek. Four sleeping bags and three tents are available to rent.

### Trekking

Once you get to the lake there's not much else to do except go for a walk. A good three- to four-hour loop hike offers views of four other lakes. Follow the faint path east uphill behind the lakeshore caretaker's house for fine views of Sary-Chelek. The path then drops down into a meadow and follows the base of the ridge to swing around to Iyri Köl lake, which makes a good lunch stop. At the far end of the small lake take a right turn to a smaller reedy lake, then climb and take another right. After you drop down to the fourth lake it's easier to follow the left branch and join the road. The right path is scenic but involves a tricky river crossing at the far end.

It's possible to make a six-day trek in to Sary-Chelek from Leninopol (catch a daily bus from Talas). An easier trek starts from Kyzyl-Kul in the next-door valley. From here it's a long day's walk up the valley to Kara-Suu Lake, where you can stay in a CBT-arranged yurt. The next day is a hard slog over the 2446m Kemerty Pass and then down to Sary-Chelek, either directly or via Iyri Köl lake.

Both routes are marked on the 1:120,000 *Cherez Talasskii Khrebet k Ozeru Sary-Chelek*, available at Geoid in Bishkek (p279).

## Sleeping & Eating

Arkit's homestays are generally more basic than those of CBT or Shepherd's Life and all include breakfast.

**Attakur Omurbekov's Guesthouse** (☎ 9 21 41; dm 100som) Another 250m up the main road from the Saberia (below) on the opposite of the street is another friendly option. All the household action takes place around the kitchen (meals 50som) in a garden shed. Omurbekov will take you up to Sary-Chelek in his car for 400som.

**Saberia Guesthouse** (dm 150som) About 1km from the first gates, and recognisable by its sign, the Saberia is run by the town's eccentric but charming English teacher and her husband, a vodka-drinking ornithologist. Guests wash in the river although water can be heated. The hosts can also help arrange horses for trekking.

**Sultan Chukotaev** (☎ 9 21 36; dm 200som) Arguably the most professional homestay in town with a detached house converted into three guest rooms, one with Western-style beds.

There is also a government hotel with fairly decent rooms and Café Millenium (which doubles as the post office and bus stop) can rustle up food given some warning.

At the lake itself it is possible to camp but you need to get written permission (no fee) from the park office in Arkit. Otherwise try **Toskool-Ata Kumbozu** (cabin per person US$15) where each cabin has an en suite toilet (no shower) or stay in its nearby yurtstay. Meals are extra.

## Getting There & Away

The lake's remote location makes it a real pain to reach by public transport; consider hiring a taxi here if nowhere else in the country.

By public transport you need to catch the 10am or, better, the 1.30pm bus from Tashkömür to Kara Jigach (55som, three hours) and then hitch or wait for the afternoon buses from Kerben (Karavan) to pass through en route to Arkit (20som) between 6pm and 7pm. The route to Kara Jigach passes neglected coal mines and weird eroded *hoodoos* (rock columns). The decrepit local snub-nosed buses are packed, hot, uncomfortable and mind-numbingly slow. From Arkit you'll need to hire a car (400som return) or hike (four hours, but little traffic) to the lake.

Heading back, there is a bus from Arkit to Kara Jigach at 7.30am (the bus continues on to Kerben), from where you can catch a bus to Tashkömür at 9.30am or 3pm.

If you are headed for the CBT coordinator, the 4.20pm bus from Kerben to Kyzyl-Suu also passes through Kara Jigach between 6pm and 7pm, returning the next day at 7am.

A taxi from Tashkömür will cost around 2000som to Arkit or 500som per seat if you are lucky enough to find a shared one. A taxi from Osh costs US$150 but you will need to leave by 6am to pass the first gate by 2pm when it closes.

# ARSLANBOB АРСЛАНБОБ

☎ 3722 / elev 1600m

Arslanbob is an elevated oasis, a vast tract of blossoming woodland and home to the largest walnut grove on earth (11,000 hectares) and part of the even larger (60,000 hectare) walnut forest that extends between the spurs of the Fergana and Chatkal ranges.

Buses often drop passengers 200m uphill from the bus station at the main square by a stone lion, a taxi stand and the CBT office. From here the road continues uphill, branching left to the *turbaza* (former Soviet holiday camp) and right to the upper waterfall. Behind the town are the wall-like Babash-Ata Mountains and a raft of trekking opportunities.

On the other side of the square is a rickety wooden bridge spanning a rocky stream. Over the bridge are the town's cafés, a (summer only) bazaar and the local mosque. This is a fairly conservative village; so don't walk around in shorts and singlets.

From mid-September the town undergoes a mass exodus when locals move into the forest and go nuts. Each year 1500 tonnes of walnuts (and 5000 tonnes of apples, pistachios and cherry plums) are harvested in the Arslanbob valley and by all accounts gathering nuts is fun. Tradition dictates that during the harvest each family kill a sheep and share the meat with their neighbours. The fire-lit autumn nights are a time to sing songs, retell stories and eat way too much greasy mutton.

KYRGYZSTAN

## History

The nuts of Arslanbob are somewhat of a misnomer. While native to Central Asia they originated in Malaysia and somehow, many thousands of years ago, spread to this isolated valley. Locals will tell you this was the work of a modest gardener, charged by the Prophet Mohammed with finding paradise on earth. He travelled through many lands until he stumbled upon a picturesque valley, framed by mountains, watered by mountain rivers but lacking in trees. Delighted with this discovery, the Prophet sent him a bag of fruit and nut seeds which the hero scattered from a mountaintop.

By the time Alexander the Great led his troops to these parts the forests were already locally famous as hunting grounds. On his return to Greece he took with him the humble Kyrgyz walnut from which European plantations were founded; hence the walnut is commonly, but mistakenly, referred to as the 'Greek nut'.

## Information

**CBT** (☎ 5 47 98, 0503-34 24 76; arslanbob_2003@rambler.ru) Has an excellent branch, which can help with everything from homestays and transport to horse treks. Contact Hayat Tarikov.

## Sights & Activities

There are several day-hike options, though the most popular is the three-hour return hike to a holy 80m-high **waterfall**. The last half hour is an uphill grind over a slippery scree slope – wear good shoes as the return leg is like walking down a slope of marbles. Horses are available but aren't all that useful as you still have to slog up the last hill yourself. The fence in front of the falls is covered in votive rags, harking back to a pre-Islamic animism. An easier walk leads about 45 minutes to a smaller **twin waterfall** (23m) to the east, from where you can continue to a **walnut forest** and the **shrine of Ibn Abbas**. It is also possible to walk to the **Dashman walnut forest** via Gumhana village and Jaradar in a long day.

Back at the village square, check out the riverside **mazar** (tomb) of Arslan Bab-Ata, after whom the town and mountains are named.

### TREKKING

Community-Based Tourism can arrange a couple of trekking options to the holy lakes of Köl Kupan (marked Kulan on maps), Paino Köl, Kabyr Köl and Ainek Köl (Mirror Lake), collectively referred to as the Köl Mazar. This makes for a fine three- or four-day trek or horse trek, stopping at a cube-shaped holy rock en route. Community-Based Tourism has a couple of ratty tents for rent but it's best to bring your own equipment.

Instead of retracing your steps you can continue over the Kerets Pass and east along the Kerets Valley, with the Nurbuu-Tau Mountains to the north, until you swing south down the Kara-Unkor Valley. You can then continue down to Kyzyl Ünkür or head back to Arslanbob via the Kara-Bulak Valley for an excellent five- or six-day trek.

A CBT-organised trek with a guide, cook and three meals costs around US$18 per person per day on foot or US$27 per day on horseback, assuming there are two people. A horse costs 400som per day; donkeys are cheaper.

The adjacent **Kyzyl Ünkür** (Red Cavern) Valley has a network of hiking and fishing routes equal to, if not grander than, those around Arslanbob. Community-Based Tourism plans to set up some homestays here but until then you'll need a tent and supplies (the *turbaza* is currently closed). Travellers recommend the trek north from Kyzyl Ünkür, up the Kara Ünkür Valley to tiny Kön-Köl (you can do this section by car) and then northeast over the Kymysh Bel Pass (3754m) to the fish-stocked Kara-Suu and Kalka-Tash Lakes. From here you can head down the Kara-Suu Valley to join the main Bishkek–Osh road at Kök Bel, between Kara-Köl and Toktogul, or return on a loop back to Kyzyl Ünkür via Kön-Köl Pass, either way making an intrepid six-day trek.

### SKIING

Community-Based Tourism is developing the mountain *jailoos* surrounding Arslanbob for cross-country skiing. The idea has a lot of merit but is still in its infancy with only five pairs of old skis and boots available for hire. Proposed transport to the *jailoos* would be via 4WD and on foot with the aid of snowshoes.

## Sleeping & Eating

**Turbaza Arslanbob** (☎ 5 28 40; s 50som, pol-lux 100som, lux/superlux 200/300som) Run-down but rustic, this scruffy former Soviet holiday camp has dozens of bungalows scattered around 29 hectares of grounds. Only the best rooms have hot water and en suite toilets but even these are quite basic. There's an open-air swimming pool

KYRGYZSTAN

popular with locals as is the disco that keeps most people awake half the night.

**Zinaida Mamajanova** (Aral 13; dm 250som) From the main square, walk 30m west and turn left onto a small dirt track that follows a stream downhill. Keep heading downhill after you leave the stream for another 100m until you spot the CBT sign on the right.

**CBT** (☎ after hour 2 19 62, 2 56 43; cbt_ja@rambler.rudm; 250-300som) The best digs in town are the 15 or so CBT-affiliated homestays scattered around the village. These aren't always easy to find or centrally located, so call into the office to check out your options.

our pick **Maksudov Mirzarahim** (Rodopad 58; dm 300som) To get here, take the road running along the left side of the bazaar. It's a 10-minute, uphill walk on a windy dirt road. Take the fifth road on the right and look out for the CBT sign. Muksudov is a local walnut gatherer and a fine host. Delicious food is served on a fantastic deck with views over the 'small waterfall' river. Recommended.

The traditional **Chaikhana Chinar** (mains 20som), just across the river from the village square in front of the mosque has been serving green tea for centuries and is still a popular haunt of the silver-bearded elders who gather here.

The *manty* served in the chaikhana next to the bazaar also comes recommended by local NGO volunteers.

### Getting There & Away

From Bazaar Korgon take an hourly (until 4.30pm) Arslanbob bus to the end of the line (35som to 45som, 2½ hours) or grab a seat in a shared taxi (50som to 60som). There are also three absurdly full buses a day from Bazaar Korgon to Kyzyl Ünkür (65km) via Arslanbob. To go to Sary-Chelek, head from Bazaar Korgon to Tashkömür.

From Jalal-Abad, take an hourly bus (40 minutes) or shared taxi (25som to 35som per seat) to Arslanbob. A taxi from Arslanbob to Jalal-Abad costs around 400som.

## JALAL-ABAD ДЖАЛАЛ-АБАД

☎ 3722 / pop 74,000

Jalal-Abad (the City of Jalal, after a 13th century warrior) may be Kyrgyzstan's third-largest city but you wouldn't know it from its laid-back, easy-going feel. In its Soviet heyday the town boasted an upmarket health resort, still alive today but none-too-healthy. Most everything of use to travellers can be found on Lenina between the bazaar in the northwest and Hotel Mölmöl (a 10-minute walk) in the southeast.

### Information

**CBT** (☎ after hr 2 19 62, 2 56 43; cbt_ja@rambler.ru; Toktogul 3-20; 🕒 9am-5pm Mon-Fri) Contact Ruhsora Abdullaeva in Russian or Shakhnauza in English. This helpful branch has photocopy maps, arranges local accommodation and transport, and offers horse treks to Sailmaluu Tash from its western approach. From the bazaar head along Lenina to tree-lined Toktogul, turn right and it's near the second crossroad on the left.

**Kazkommerts Bank** (☎ 58 52 57; Lenina 14; 🕒 9am-1pm & 2-6pm Mon-Fri) Has an ATM, cashes travellers cheques (3% commission) and exchanges US dollars and euros.

**Sputnik Agency** (☎ 5 07 06; Lenina 17) Opposite Hotel Mölmöl, it sells airline tickets.

**Titan Internet** (☎ 2 10 00; Lenina 26A; per hr 20som) Also downloads flash cards and burns CDs.

### Sights

**Jalal-Abad thermal springs** (🕒 6.30-9am, noon-2pm & 5-8pm) have been attracting pilgrims from as far away as India and Afghanistan since the 10th century and are still the city's chief attraction. Locals clutching empty bottles wait at the wooden circular building for the doors to be unlocked thrice daily in order to get a dose of the curative, sulphuric waters.

In the same park you will also find the ratty-around-the-edges, Soviet era **Jalal-Abad Sanatorium**. The complex is a confusing labyrinth of several buildings; ask for the administration office past the **Lenin statue**. Here you can arrange to be kneaded like a piece of dough. A neck-twisting massage costs a mere 50som but it's worth shelling out an extra 50som for the full spine-cracking, shoulder-slapping, back massage. Acupuncture (50som) is also available; the masseuse however does not use disposable needles and therefore, not recommended.

Shared taxis depart regularly from the intersection of Lenina and Toktogul (10som) for the park gates. Ask for the 'sanatorium'.

### Sleeping

**Hotel Mölmöl** (☎ 5 50 59; Lenina 17; s without/with private shower 211/250som, d 460/500som, tr 538/598som, lux 915som) This spartan, but essentially clean, ex-Soviet survivor offers standard rooms with either communal or attached bathrooms. If the blood splatters on the Brezhnev-era wallpaper are anything to go by, the mosquitoes here can get vicious.

**Matlyba's homestay** (☎ 2 33 70; Toktogul 33; dm 350som) If the CBT office is closed, try the house behind mint-green walls, on the opposite side of the street. Run enthusiastically by a motherly Uzbek woman, the garden has a *takhta* (bed-like sitting platform), which is a fine spot to have a beer.

**Nigora Homestay** (☎ 2 56 43; Chutskaya 33; dm 450som) This delightful homestay has three guest rooms and a staggering amount of bedding – the work of the three daughters who, as is the Uzbek custom, make the mattresses *(korpa)* and blankets *(aykandoz)* for their wedding day. It's a 15-minute walk north from Lenina up Erkindik; at the fork in the road take the right branch, it's just around the bend.

The CBT offers 14 comfortable **homestays** (350-450som), all of which are good, although some are a little way from the centre. Meals are 100som.

### Eating

**Café Alymbekdatka** (☎ 0502-26 25 83; cnr Lenina & Erkindik; mains 50som; lunch & dinner) Located on the same intersection as Hotel Mölmöl this seasonal café has pleasant tea-beds shaded by colourful awnings. There's no menu but it's a great spot to try *kymys* and *kurdoch* (mutton and potato) – eat it quickly, before the fat congeals.

**Café Navruz** (☎ 2 10 90; Toktogul park; mains 60-150som; breakfast, lunch & dinner) It's the newie in town. If Jalal-Abad had much hustle and bustle, this would be the place to escape it. It has a great parkside location; just off Lenina, inside a grand, blue building with a huge wrap-around balcony.

There are a number of cafés around the small square on Lenina between Toktogul and Erkindik. All are cheap, serving decent soups, Russian standards and Central Asian favourites. In the evening the place takes on a beer-garden vibe.

### Getting There & Around

#### AIR

Kyrgyzstan Airlines and AC Kyrgyzstan fly six times a week to/from Bishkek (US$40 to US$50). Buy tickets at the airport or Sputnik Agency. Marshrutkas 1 and 5 from the centre go to the airport via the bus station. A taxi to the airport costs 50som to 80som.

#### BUS

Scheduled buses depart for Bazaar Korgon (for Arslanbob) every 20 minutes (20som, 30 minutes); Tashkömür at 8am, 12.50pm and 3.15pm (90som, three hours); and Kerben at 8.40am, 1pm and 2.50pm (125som, four to five hours). Minibuses to Osh leave every half-hour or so until 5pm (70som).

Also departing from the bus station, shared taxis run frequently to Osh (150som) and Özgön (70som), Bazaar Korgon (40som) and less frequently to Tashkömür (120som).

For villages neighbouring Jalal-Abad you'll need to head for the local bus stand in the far northern corner of the bazaar past the fresh produce. Here you'll also find private cars (1200som in a Volga) and minibuses (700som a seat) going to Bishkek. Shared Nivas and 4WDs for the mountain route to Kazarman (400som per seat) also depart from near here.

Minibus 10 runs along Lenina from the Hotel Mölmöl to the bazaar and bus station 3km to the west (5som). A private taxi to the bus station costs 50som to 80som.

## AROUND JALAL-ABAD

### Ortuk

About 60km north of Jalal-Abad is the village of **Ortuk**, a CBT-supported destination set in walnut and cherry forests. Community-Based Tourism has four **homestays** (B&B 300-350som) in the village, from where you can make day horse trips to local *jailoos* and a cave complex. Contact CBT in Jalal-Abad (opposite) for details. The local bus stand, north of the bazaar in Jalal-Abad has daily buses to Ortuk and nearby Kara-Alma. Otherwise hire a car through CBT for around 1440som for an overnight return trip.

## ÖZGÖN УЗГУН

☎ 3233

Özgön (Uzgen), 55km northeast of Osh, is today best known as the centre of three nights of ferocious Kyrgyz-Uzbek fighting in 1990 (p334). Few outward scars are evident today. The town is nominally 85% Uzbek; locals say it was about two-thirds Uyghur in pre-Soviet days.

Özgön is claimed to be the site of a series of citadels dating back to the 1st century BC; there is also a story that the town began as an encampment for some of Alexander the Great's troops. It was one of the multiple Karakhanid capitals in the 10th and 11th centuries.

All that remains of this history is a quartet of Karakhanid buildings – three joined 12th-century **mausoleums** and a stubby 11th-century **minaret** (whose top apparently fell down in an earthquake in the 17th century), faced with very fine ornamental brickwork, carved terracotta and inlays of stone. Each mausoleum is unlike the others, though all are in shades of red-brown clay (there were no glazed tiles at this point in Central Asian history). In the corner of the right-hand-side mausoleum, a small section has been deliberately left off to reveal older layers of the middle one (the Mausoleum of Nasr ibn Ali, founder of the Karakhanids). You can climb the minaret for 5som.

Apart from the architectural attractions Özgön's bazaar is an interesting place to wander around, particularly if you haven't seen much of Uzbekistan.

To get to the mausoleums turn right out of the main (new) bus station on Manas. The road curves to the right past the entrance to the bazaar, which is where shared taxis and minibuses will probably drop you off. From the bazaar it's a 10-minute walk to the statue of Lenin (opposite the post office), from where you can see the minaret in the square behind.



### Sleeping & Eating

**Kurmanjau Datka** (☎ 0502-76 24 80; Manas 74/1; d 500som) It's about 400m from the bazaar, on the left, behind a fence of blue-and-yellow latticework. This hotel and café has four rooms, all decorated with wallpaper that belongs in a museum and run by a lady with an extremely loud voice.

**Restaurant Almaz** (☎ 2 61 20; Manas; mains 50-60som) Probably the best in town, with dishes such as trout in champagne (65som) and lots of good salads.

The best atmosphere comes free with the *shashlyk* in the bazaar chaikhanas.

### Getting There & Away

Shared taxis to Jalal-Abad lurk down a side street, a block east of the bazaar, near Restaurant Almaz, and cost 60som a seat. Shared taxis to Osh cost 50som and run all day.

## AROUND ÖZGÖN

The village of **Ak-Terek**, about 60km east of Özgön, has five **homestays** (B&B 250som), which can be arranged through village head Jengish Akmataliev. Daily buses run every afternoon to Ak-Terek (40som) from Özgön's old bus station.

From Ak-Terek you can take a horse 35km further to Kara Shoro National Park, where there are yurtstays. An adventurous option is the seven-day horse trek along the Jassy River and over the Fergana range to the Arpa Valley, and from there to Naryn.

## OSH ОШ

☎ 3222 / pop 300,000

Osh is Kyrgyzstan's second-biggest city and the administrative centre of the huge, populous province that engulfs the Fergana Valley on the Kyrgyzstan side. It is one of the region's genuinely ancient towns (with a history dating back to at least the 5th century BC) but few souvenirs remain. In many ways it's still quite a Soviet place: whereas other cities scrubbed Lenin's name from their street maps, Osh merely shifted it politely one block away. A huge Lenin statue still stands opposite the city administration building.

Osh suffers a kind of demographic schizophrenia, being a major centre of Kyrgyzstan but with a strong (40%) Uzbek population more in tune with Uzbekistan and the rest of the Fergana Valley, but isolated from it by one of the world's more absurd international borders.

### History

The standard refrain from anyone you ask is 'Osh is older than Rome'. Legends credit all sorts of people with its founding, from King Solomon (Suleyman) to Alexander the Great. Certainly it must have been a major hub on the Silk Road from its earliest days. The Mongols smashed it in the 13th century but in the following centuries it bounced back, more prosperous than ever.

More recently, 'Osh' has become a byword for ethnic conflict in the festering, gerrymandered closeness of the Fergana Valley. In fact the worst of 'Osh' took place 55km away in Özgön, during three nights of savage Uzbek-Kyrgyz violence in June and July 1990, during which at least 300 people (some unofficial estimates run to 1000) died from a variety of ugly causes while Soviet military and police authorities stood oddly by.

Although the largest group, the Uzbeks, dominate local business, Kyrgyzstan has forced upon them an almost totally Kyrgyz (and apparently widely corrupt) municipal administration, by which they feel constantly 'plundered'.

Rumours abound of weapons stockpiled for future conflicts. But considering the likelihood

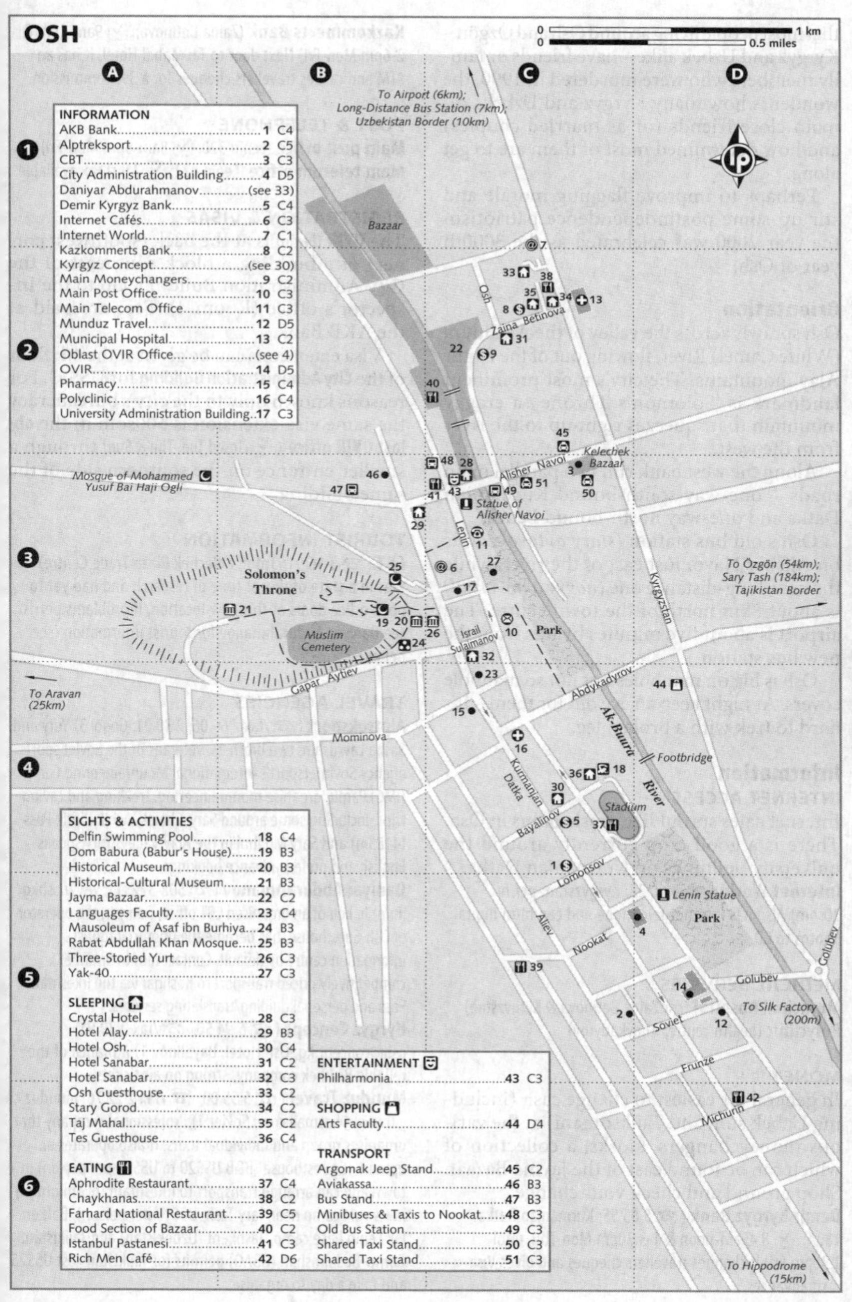
OSH
0 1 km
0 0.5 miles
A
B
C
D
1
2
3
4
5
6
INFORMATION
AKB Bank.....1 C4
Alptreksport.....2 C5
CBT.....3 C3
City Administration Building.....4 D5
Daniyar Abdurahmanov.....(see 33)
Demir Kyrgyz Bank.....5 C4
Internet Cafés.....6 C3
Internet World.....7 C1
Kazkommerts Bank.....8 C2
Kyrgyz Concept.....(see 30)
Main Moneychangers.....9 C2
Main Post Office.....10 C3
Main Telecom Office.....11 C3
Munduz Travel.....12 D5
Municipal Hospital.....13 C2
Oblast OVIR Office.....(see 4)
OVIR.....14 D5
Pharmacy.....15 C4
Polyclinic.....16 C4
University Administration Building.....17 C3
SIGHTS & ACTIVITIES
Delfin Swimming Pool.....18 C4
Dom Babura (Babur's House).....19 B3
Historical Museum.....20 B3
Historical-Cultural Museum.....21 B3
Jayma Bazaar.....22 C2
Languages Faculty.....23 C4
Mausoleum of Asaf ibn Burhiya.....24 B3
Rabat Abdullah Khan Mosque.....25 B3
Three-Storied Yurt.....26 C3
Yak-40.....27 C3
SLEEPING
Crystal Hotel.....28 C3
Hotel Alay.....29 B3
Hotel Osh.....30 C4
Hotel Sanabar.....31 C2
Hotel Sanabar.....32 C3
Osh Guesthouse.....33 C2
Stary Gorod.....34 C2
Taj Mahal.....35 C2
Tes Guesthouse.....36 C4
EATING
Aphrodite Restaurant.....37 C4
Chaykhanas.....38 C2
Farhard National Restaurant.....39 C5
Food Section of Bazaar.....40 C2
Istanbul Pastanesi.....41 C3
Rich Men Café.....42 D6
ENTERTAINMENT
Philharmonia.....43 C3
SHOPPING
Arts Faculty.....44 D4
TRANSPORT
Argomak Jeep Stand.....45 C2
Aviakassa.....46 B3
Bus Stand.....47 B3
Minibuses & Taxis to Nookat.....48 C3
Old Bus Station.....49 C3
Shared Taxi Stand.....50 C3
Shared Taxi Stand.....51 C3
To Airport (6km); Long-Distance Bus Station (7km); Uzbekistan Border (10km)
Bazaar
Osh
Zaina Betinova
Kelechek Bazaar
Alisher Navoi
Statue of Alisher Navoi
Lenin
Mosque of Mohammed Yusuf Bai Haji Ogli
Solomon's Throne
Muslim Cemetery
Israil Sulaimanov
Park
Gapar Aytiev
Abdykadyrov
To Aravan (25km)
Mominova
Kyrgyzstan
To Özgön (54km); Sary Tash (184km); Tajikistan Border
Ak-Buura River
Footbridge
Kurmanjan Datka
Stadium
Bayalinov
Lomonsov
Lenin Statue
Park
Aliev
Nookat
Golubev
Golubev
To Silk Factory (200m)
Soviet
Frunze
Michurin
To Hippodrome (15km)
KYRGYZSTAN

that most people living around Osh and Özgön – Kyrgyz and Uzbek alike – have friends or family members who were murdered in 1990, the wonder is how many Kyrgyz and Uzbeks remain close friends (or as married couples) and how determined most of them are to get along.

Perhaps to improve flagging morale and stir up some postindependence patriotism the year 2000 was celebrated as the 3000th year of Osh.

## Orientation

Osh sprawls across the valley of the Ak-Buura (White Camel) River, flowing out of the Pamir Alay mountains. The city's most prominent landmark is 'Solomon's Throne', a craggy mountain that squeezes right up to the river from the west.

Along the west bank run two parallel main roads – one-way south-bound Kurmanjan Datka and one-way north-bound Lenin.

Osh's old bus station *(stary avtovokzal)* is on Alisher Navoi just east of the river, while the new, long-distance one *(novyy avtovokzal)* is about 8km north of the town centre. The airport is about five minutes by bus from the new bus station.

Osh is big on manholes but not so manhole covers. At night keep an eye out for them – it's hard to trek with a broken leg.

KYRGYZSTAN

## Information

### INTERNET ACCESS

Internet cafés sprout like mushrooms in Osh. There is a good crop currently around the university buildings on Kurmanjan Datka.

**Internet World** (☎ 5 60 38; Kyrgyzstan; per hr 30som) Also has internet telephone and can burn digital photos to CD.

### MEDICAL SERVICES

**Municipal hospital** (cnr Zaina Betinova & Kyrgyzstan)

**Polyclinic** (health centre; Abdykadyrov)

### MONEY

In general it's easiest to change cash (including Uzbek sum and Tajiksomani) at the various moneychangers' kiosks, a collection of which can be found east of the Jayma Bazaar. Shop around and check your change.

**Demir Kyrgyz Bank** (☎ 5 65 55; Kurmanjan Datka 180A; 🕑 8.45am-noon & 1-3.30pm Mon-Thu, until 1.30pm Fri) It changes travellers cheques and gives Visa cash advances.

**Kazkommerts Bank** (Zaina Betinova; 🕑 9am-1pm & 2-6pm Mon-Fri) Next door to Taj Mahal Hotel, it has an ATM and cashes travellers cheques for a 3% commission.

### POST & TELEPHONE

**Main post office** (Lenin 320; 🕑 8am-5pm Mon-Fri)

**Main telecom office** (Lenin 422; 🕑 24hr) Fax available.

### REGISTRATION & VISAS

The **OVIR** (Lenin) is at the back (southwest corner) of a building a block southeast of the City Administration Building. Go to the Inspector's office (Room 4). Fees are paid at the AKB Bank.

Visa extensions can be given at the 4th floor of the **City Administration Building** for US$53. For reasons known only to the city's bureaucracy the same visa extension is 600som in the **oblast OVIR office** (🕑 closed Tue, Thu & Sun) through a smaller entrance on the southern side of the same building.

### TOURIST INFORMATION

**CBT** (☎ 3 16 91; 3rd fl, Kelechek Plaza Trade Centre) Was in a state of flux at time of research and had yet to open office doors at this new location. If problems persist, see Daniyar Abdurahmanov for tourist information (see below).

### TRAVEL AGENCIES

**Alptreksport** (☎ /fax 7 69 06, 2 30 01; Gogol 3) Yury and Sasha Lavrushin, two brothers, veterans of the Soviet sports agency Sovintersport's International Mountaineering Camp (IMC) Pamir, organise mountaineering, trekking and caving trips, including some around Sary-Chelek, Achik, Jiptik Pass (4185m) and Sary Moghul in the Alay Valley. Yury speaks English and prefers advance bookings.

**Daniyar Abdurahmanov** (☎ 502-372311; www.oshkg.info) In lieu of an organised CBT office, Daniyar, the operator of Osh Guesthouse, has become the unofficial tourist information centre by default. Contact him to arrange competitively priced transport to Kashgar via the Irkeshtam Pass and personal guiding/translating services.

**Kyrgyz Concept** (☎ 5 94 50, ☎ /fax 2 79 91; osh@concept.kg; Osh Hotel, Bayalinov 1) A branch of the reliable Bishkek company, strong on air tickets.

**Munduz Travel** (☎ 5 55 00, ☎ /fax 2 22 76; munduz_tourist@hotmail.com; Soviet 1) Professional company that organises group and individual tours. It also operates an upmarket guesthouse (B&B US$20 to US$35 per person) in town and can arrange transport to Irkeshtam (overnighting in its yurt camp near Sary Tash, US$10 per person), Batken, Pik Lenin base camp, Tashkent (Uzbekistan) and Tajikistan. Gorno-Badakhshan (GBAO) permits for Tajikistan cost US$25 and take a day to organise.

## Sights

You might find keen students of English or other languages to act as unofficial guides to the city at Osh University's **Languages Faculty** (Infac; Kurmanjan Datka 250).

### BAZAAR

The thunderous daily **Jayma Bazaar** is one of Central Asia's best markets, teeming with Uzbeks, Kyrgyz and Tajiks dealing in everything from traditional hats and knives to pirated cassettes, horseshoes (forged at smithies in the bazaar), Chinese tea sets and abundant seasonal fruit and vegetables. It stretches for about 1km along the west side of the river, and crosses it in several places. It's most dynamic on Sunday morning, and almost deserted on Monday.

### SOLOMON'S THRONE & AROUND

A jagged, barren rock that seems to loom above the city wherever you go, **Solomon's Throne** has been a Muslim place of pilgrimage of some importance for centuries, supposedly because the Prophet Mohammed once prayed here. From certain perspectives it's said to resemble a reclining pregnant woman, and is especially favoured by hopeful mothers.

In 1497, 14-year-old Zahiruddin Babur, newly crowned king of Fergana built himself a little shelter and private mosque on the rock's high eastern promontory. In later years this came to be something of an attraction in its own right. It collapsed in an earthquake in 1853 and was rebuilt. Then in the 1960s it was destroyed by a mysterious explosion; most local people are convinced it was a Soviet attempt to halt the persistent pilgrim traffic and put a chill on 'superstition' (ie Islam). After independence it was rebuilt.

Local people call it **Dom Babura**, Babur's House. If you speak Russian, the friendly Uzbek caretaker will tell you more, and offer you a prayer for a few som. The steep 25-minute climb begins at a little gateway behind a futuristic silver dome on Kurmanjan Datka. The promontory offers long views but little to see except for a vast **Muslim cemetery** at the foot of the hill. Dusk is a good time to visit.

Nearby are three museums collectively referred to as the **Historical Archaeological Museum Complex** (🕓 9am-noon & 1-6pm), although don't expect the locals to recognise such a mouthful of English. All three museums keep the same hours.

The **Historical Museum** (admission 50som, photos 10som each, guides 15som), built during the Osh 3000-year celebrations, is the best of the three. It's strong on local archaeology and ethnography but has little info in English. There are some great weapons, displayed as if caught up in a mad whirlwind.

Outside the giant **three-storied yurt** (admission 25som) has a collection of national clothing, traditional textiles and *shyrdaks*.

Up the hill is the last of the trio, the **Historical-Cultural Museum** (admission 50som). With typical Soviet subtlety, a hole was blasted in the side of this sacred mountain into one of its many caves, and a grotesque sheet-metal front stuck on – a carbuncle now visible from great distances. Inside is a series of badly lit exhibits of potsherds, old masonry, rocks, bugs and mangy stuffed animals.

Back down at the bottom of the hill is the small **Rabat Abdullah Khan Mosque**, dating from the 17th or 18th century but rebuilt in the 1980s. It's a working mosque (ie male visitors only, and by permission only; shoes off at the entrance). The small **Mausoleum of Asaf Ibn Burhiya** to the south along the base of the hill is of little historical or architectural interest.

### OTHER SIGHTS

There isn't much, other than a long riverbank **park** stretching from Alisher Navoi to Abdykadyrov. A central feature is an old **Yak-40** plane, a one-time video salon, looking poised to leap over the river. There's a *palvankhana* (wrestling hall) here but wrestling bouts are infrequent.

Locals swim in the **Ak-Buura River** during summer or head to the **Delfin swimming pool** (adult/child per session 30/10som; 🕓 sessions 9am-2pm & 2-6pm), a stone's throw away. Neither are particularly clean.

Osh **hippodrome**, 16km south of town at Tolüken village (minibus 24), puts on Kyrgyz national sports and eagle-hunting competitions during national holidays.

## Sleeping

### BUDGET

Couples and small groups should consider taking advantage of the per room rate of some midpriced hotels, which effectively reduces prices to about 200som per person with private bathroom. Community-Based Toursim (opposite) will undoubtedly offer homestays when its new office is open.

**Osh Guesthouse** (☎ 3 06 29; www.oshguesthouse.hotbox.ru; Flat 48, Apt 8, Kyrgyzstan; dm/d US$4/6.50) A popular backpacker crash pad with the only dorms in town. It can get very cramped when full; you'll either love it or hate it. Pluses include a hot shower, laundry service, meals (40som to 60som) and internet access. The owner, Daniyar Abdurahmanov, is a fount of knowledge. Solo travellers with the view of sharing transport to the Irkeshtam Pass often meet here. The apartment can be hard to find. Take the alley by a row of kiosks, take a diagonal right by the rubbish dump and turn left at the second apartment building; it's the third entrance on the left, top floor.

**Hotel Alay** (☎ 5 77 33; palvan@yandex.ru; Alisher Navoi; s 252-400som, d 308-504som, tr 308som, lux 1000som) This is an ex-Soviet dinosaur in a prime location with cheap but tired and dated rooms. Quality runs the gauntlet from rooms that share the common toilets (no seat or light bulb, so expect to squat in the dark) to those with en suites and hot-water showers.

**Hotel Sanabar** (☎ 2 54 37; cnr Kurmanjan Datka & Israil Sulaimanov; d 400som) It has tiny rooms with even tinier bathrooms. The staff is surly, preferring to snarl than smile, but the rooms are essentially clean and the showers have occasional hot water.

**Hotel Sanabar** (☎ 3 45 27; Zaina Betinova; d 400som) Same name, different deal. The bare rooms here share a clean communal shower. Keep in mind this place is opposite a lively bazaar, which is either an exciting plus or a noisy intrusion, depending on how you feel about lively bazaars.

**Stary Gorod** (☎ 2 49 24; Zaina Betinova 18A; 4-person apt 1500som; ❄) These self-contained apartments are a good deal with air-con, 40-channel TVs, twin bedrooms, separate bathrooms and fully equipped kitchens.

### MIDRANGE

**Taj Mahal** (☎ 3 96 52; Zaina Betinova; d 600, lux 800som) Small and bright, this Indian-built hotel has clean and pleasant doubles with hot water and towels. There are only five rooms so try to book ahead.

**Crystal Hotel** (☎ 2 04 47; Alisher Navoi 50A; tw with shared bathroom US$20, s/d US$50/70, lux ste US$100; ❄) Has a central location with small, clean rooms equipped with minifridge, TV and air-con. Rooms overlooking the main room are a little noisy.

**Tes Guesthouse** (☎ 2 15 48; guesthouse@oshmail.kg; Say Boyu 5; s/d from €20/30; 💻) Tourists are welcome although this guesthouse is used mostly by NGO consultants. The pleasant piney rooms come with spotless bathrooms and are decorated with national handicrafts from local artisans. There's a coffee machine, TV room, internet access and a washing machine. Prices include breakfast. Recommended.

**Hotel Osh** (☎ 7 56 14; Bayalinov; s/d US$44/48, lux US$150) Still reliving its Soviet glory days and now the biggest rip-off in town. It's ridiculously over priced; the rooms are old and the toilets leak. On the plus side, the hotel makes for a great landmark; taxi drivers sometimes refer to it as the Intourist hotel or Osh Nuru and there is the casino…

## Eating

The chaikhanas along Kyrgyzstan near the intersection with Zaina Betinova are everything good teahouses should be; kebab masters lovingly fanning *shashlik*, tea beds, beer on tap and a lively evening atmosphere. Be careful not to be dragged into a round (or two) of vodka shots! Self caterers will appreciate the abundance of groceries and fresh vegies available in the food section of Jayma Bazaar. Good natured haggling may go down well but most produce has a fixed price and remember that lean meat is considerably cheaper than fatty cuts.

**Aphrodite Restaurant** (☎ 0502-743577; Lenin; salad 35-70som, mains 65-80som; 🕑 lunch & dinner) A good restaurant by the entrance to the stadium with indoor and outdoor seating and beer on tap.

**Rich Men Café** (☎ 2 43 03; Kurmanjan Datka; salads 35-50som, mains 75-120som; 🕑 lunch & dinner) South of town and recognisable by the blue awning, the Rich Men Café is top-notch. Good meat and fish dishes are complemented by specialities such as eggs stuffed with red or black caviar (80som) and excellent service. Wine and Soviet champagne are served, as are excellent beer snacks.

**Istanbul Pastanesi** (☎ 2 24 51; Alisher Navoi; meals 45som; 🕑 breakfast, lunch & dinner) Bypass the burgers and head straight for the delicious honey-drenched baklava, a guaranteed taste sensation.

our pick **Farhad National Restaurant** (Nookat 83; group serves only; 🕑 dinner) Join the celebrating locals in one of the 20 private rooms surrounding an open courtyard. Specialising in traditional Kyrgyz cuisine, mains are ordered by weight and 1kg of *plov* (400som) feeds six adults. The minimum order is 500g and orders need to be placed by midafternoon to allow the chefs time to prepare (Munduz Travel can help). Order *ysyryk* (burning grass), take a deep breath and kick back on your *topchan* (tea bed). Recommended.

## Shopping

By the entrance to the Jayma Bazaar is one of the best and cheapest places in Kyrgyzstan to buy an *ak kalpak* (from 60som); for an exceptional statement go the full nine yards and get a towering monstrosity with scrollwork (250som). Pottery and clay Central Asian figurines can be bought cheaply in the **Arts Faculty** (Kyrgyzstan 80).

## Getting There & Away

### AIR

There's an **aviakassa** (booking office; ☎ 2 22 11; Kurmanjan Datka 287; 🕑 9am-noon & 1-6pm Mon-Fri), just northwest of Hotel Alay.

From Osh there is a daily flight to Bishkek (US$40 to US$50), and twice-weekly flights to both Ürümqi, China (US$220) and Moscow (US$225 to US$300).

### BUS & CAR

The old bus station and the shared taxis near Jayma Bazaar are Osh's transport hub.

From the old bus station, minibuses leave for Özgön (40som, every 40 minutes), Jalal-Abad (70som, every 20 minutes), Daroot-Korgon (400som, 10am) and all points in Kyrgyzstan's southern arm (Sary Tash, Kyzyl-Kiya, Aravan, Gulcha and others), though departures for these latter destinations are a little unreliable. Buses to Batken (250som) via Kyzyl-Kiya also leave from the old bus station although, as they run via Sokh, an Uzbek visa is required.

Shared taxis for all of the above run from here or near here, the locals will soon point you in the right direction (often a stand behind Kelechek Bazaar). Typically a seat in a shared taxi is about 50som more expensive than a minibus fare. Shared taxis also run to Toktogul, Tashkömür and Kerben when full.

Shared-taxi prices to Bishkek fluctuate dramatically as seasonal labour travels to and from Moscow for work. When demand is high (April to July) you can expect to pay as much as 1200som per seat to Bishkek and only 600som for the same journey in reverse. This trend is reversed when the labour force returns to Osh in winter.

If you want to hire transport to Irkeshtam or Tajikistan and the Pamir Hwy, you could ask around here or try a travel agency that will charge around US$150 for a trip to Achik Tash in the Alay Valley. Private cars organised through a travel agency cost 2500som to Arslanbob and US$130 to Batken (avoiding the enclaves).

The Argomak 4WD stand just uphill from the old bus station has early morning 4WDs and minibuses to Sary Moghul (450som) and a Daroot-Korgon bus (300som, 10 hours), both via Sary Tash.

Another stand west of Hotel Alay has buses to Aravan and Nookat. Minibuses and taxis to Nookat run from just behind the Philharmonia.

Minibuses 107 and 113 run from opposite the old bus station to the Uzbek border (5som, 10km) via the long-distance bus station. Minibuses 136 and 137 travel north on Lenin from Hotel Alay to the Uzbek border.

## Getting Around

Marshrutnoe 102 runs southbound on Kurmanjan Datka from the old bus station to Hotel Osh and Turbaza Ak-Buura; it returns northbound down Lenin. Other southbound minibuses on Kurmanjan Datka include 101A, 134, 135, 125, 138 and 114. Virtually all minibuses pass by Jayma Bazaar at some stage.

Minibus 102A and 107A shuttle between the airport and the Jayma Bazaar in the centre of town (5som).

A taxi around the centre costs between 30som and 50som, 80som to 100som to the airport and 50som to the new bus station.

# OSH TO IRKESHTAM PASS

The Irkeshtam Pass opened to international traffic in May 2002 and quickly superseded the Torugart as the most popular route into western China from Central Asia. It reconnects the Fergana Valley with Kashgar along an ancient branch of the Silk Road.

## Sary Tash

☎ 3243

Sary Tash is conveniently situated at the convergence of three roads and makes a good place to break the Murgab (Tajikistan) to Osh or Kashgar (China) to Osh trip. Local rumours abound that the town is also a major stopover for smugglers trafficking opium and hashish from Afghanistan via Tajikistan. Because of the bleak climatic conditions there is little agriculture and most men work at the border

KYRGYZSTAN

### TRAVELLING TO THE IRKESHTAM PASS

The east-bound road that leaves Osh for China climbs gently into the Alay Range via the Jiptik Pass (4185m) and the village of Gulcha. There is a roadside café and a CBT homestay in Gulcha but little reason (other than some hot springs) to overnight. The road, that had initially followed the Taldyk River, now follows the Gülchö as it climbs – this time in earnest – the steeper but lower Taldyk Pass (3615m) to the surprisingly open Alay Valley and Sary Tash.

While it is possible to leave Osh at 1am to arrive at Irkeshtam Pass by 9am you'll end up travelling in the dark and miss much of the stunning scenery. Instead consider starting later and overnighting in Sary Tash and then continuing at 6am the following day to the border controls at Irkeshtam.

From Sary Tash the road rapidly deteriorates into a corrugated dirt track that guarantees to rattle your teeth from your skull. To travel the 90km takes between two and three hours depending on how recently it has rained. This road, which was due to be upgraded in 2004, hasn't seen the business end of a bulldozer for some time. The hamlet of Nura is 7km before the border.

#### Getting There & Away

Arranging the whole trip with a travel agency from Osh to Irkeshtam (275km) currently costs from around US$135 to US$150 per car, which can seat four. Most travel agencies in Osh can organise a car although people generally use either Osh Guesthouse (p338) or Munduz Travel (p336). Either way it is important to explain exactly what is expected, where you will spend the night and agree on a price beforehand. The Osh Guesthouse car aims to depart every Tuesday and Thursday in summer.

On the Chinese side it is possible to catch a shared taxi (from US$9 per person) to Kashgar although you'll have to bargain hard. Be ruthless. Most shocking of all – the road is not only sealed, it even has kerbs.

There is a direct bus between Osh and Kashgar (US$50 plus 100som) that leaves the Osh long-distance bus station twice weekly (Wednesday and Sunday). Be warned that you may have to overnight on the bus or at the border so be sure to bring enough food and water.

The other option is to take the Daroot-Korgon bus (300som) from Osh's old bus station as far as Sary Tash and hitch to the border the next day. It is also worth asking around at the back far corner of the Argomak 4WD stand in Osh for cars bound for Sary Tash. In the morning locals often look for passengers here to help cover their fuel costs and the trip to Sary Tash can cost as little as 350som.

Hitching from Sary Tash to the border is fairly straight-forward as long as you start early enough to catch the Chinese Kamaz trucks as they pass. Expect the driver to ask for anything between 50som to 200som for the lift.

Travelling in reverse is just as simple. For a pack of cigarettes the Kyrgyz custom officials are happy to pop you on a Chinese truck for a mind-numbingly slow trip downhill to Sary Tash. From there you can catch the daily bus from Daroot-Korgon to Osh or hang around the town's main intersection from where impromptu shared taxis depart.

or are involved in animal husbandry. There is a small market on Wednesday.

Since the opening of the Irkeshtam Pass, locals have been quick to open their homes to tourists. The cafés and shops at the intersection can point the way.

The ladies at **Ieda Café & Hotel** (dm 100som) are super friendly and can help arrange transport to the border if you are hitching. In all there are three large lockable rooms and a smaller, less appealing room. Meals are 30som to 50som.

There's also a **homestay** (dm 200som). From the intersection take the road towards Sary Moghul but turn hard right taking the right fork in the road. The homestay is 50m up a dirt road in a house with blue doors and window frames. The price includes meals.

See above for travel info.

### Crossing the Irkeshtam Pass

Crossing the **Irkeshtam Pass** (9am-noon & 2pm-3.30pm Mon-Fri) can be a time-consuming affair.

KYRGYZSTAN

Ten kilometres before the border is the first of two checkpoints. Here everyone is required to show their passport so names can be matched to a master list of bus passengers. Assuming nobody had a last-minute name change the bus is allowed to continue to the second checkpoint and luggage inspection. Finally, you can expect to spend between 1½ to 2½ hours at the border itself depending on how many trucks are waiting before you.

If you are hitching, ask the border-post army officers to put you on a truck to cross the 7km of no-man's-land to the Chinese immigration (closed 11am to 2pm Kyrgyz time).

Unlike the Torugart, no permits are required to get to, or over, the pass.

See p349 for general advice.

## ALAY VALLEY АЛАЙСКАЯ ДОЛИНА

The far southern arm of Kyrgyzstan is the exclusive turf of trekkers and mountaineers, consisting as it does mostly of the heavily glaciated Pamir Alay range, a jagged, 500km-long seam running from Samarkand to Xinjiang. The range is threaded right up the middle by the muddy Kyzyl-Suu River (known as the Surkhob further downstream in Tajikistan – the two names mean Red Water in Kyrgyz and Tajik respectively) to form the 60km-long Alay Valley, the heart of the Kyrgyz Pamir.

Today it is hard to believe that at one time two of Central Asia's earliest and busiest Silk Road branches crossed the Pamir Alay from Kashgar, at Kök-Art and at Irkeshtam. In the 19th century adventurers, explorers and spies roamed the area trying to curry favour with the Uzbek Khanate of Kokand and out do each other in a series of double-dealings and high-altitude espionage known in English as the Great Game and in Russian as the Tournament of Shadows (p45).

The Alay Valley is the main access point for mountaineering expeditions into Tajikistan's High Pamir – to 7495m Koh-i-Samani (formerly Pik Kommunizma, the highest point in the former USSR), 7134m Koh-i-Garmo (Pik Lenin) or 7105m Pik Korzhenevskaya.

Access from Kyrgyzstan is along the A372 from Osh, via Sary Tash and the 3615m Taldyk Pass. This is also the main route into Tajikistan's Gorno-Badakhshan region. It's possible to access the valley from Dushanbe in Tajikistan via the Garm Valley as well.

A trip into the Alay region is not a lightweight jaunt. There is little traffic on the main roads and food supplies are limited, even in summer. From October to May the A372 is often closed by snow, and even in summer snow and rainstorms can appear without warning. The best trekking months are July and August.

For information on taking the M41 Pamir Hwy to Gorno-Badakhshan, see p386.

### PERMITS

In theory you need a border zone permit to go within 50km of the CIS–Chinese border and the Alay Valley. However, the removal of the check-post at Sary Tash means that you will not be asked for this permit en route to the Alay Valley, only perhaps at Achik Tash base camp. This can change, so check with a trekking agency before setting off.

Trekking agencies (see below) can arrange a permit (US$10) with a minimum of one week's notice if you need one. Make sure that the permit clearly mentions the Chong-Alay and Alay rayons of Osh *oblast*.

To travel the Pamir Hwy requires a Tajik GBAO permit, which travel agencies in Bishkek or Osh can arrange.

### TREKKING

The Pamir Alay is one of the most remote and rugged parts of Central Asia – this is one place where you can't just head off with a 1970s Soviet map and a handful of Snickers bars. ITMC Tien-Shan, IMC Pamir, Dostuck Trekking, Ak-Sai Travel and Top Asia (p284) all organise trekking and mountaineering trips in both the Kyrgyz and Tajik sides of the valley. Munduz Travel and Alptreksport in Osh (p336) can also arrange trekking support; the latter has a lot of experience in the region.

### Sary Moghul

☎ 3243

The dusty village of Sary Moghul, 30km west of Sary Tash, offers the valley's best views of Pik Lenin. Up until 2004 the entire village and surrounding 37,000 hectares of arable land was rented by Tajikistan. The newly established CBT (contact Umar Tashbekov) in the village centre near the village administration office *(ail okmotu)* can arrange home-/yurtstays and horse treks to the Pik Lenin base camps.

The daily Daroot-Korgon bus passes through town (10am) on its way to/from Sary Tash (50som) and Osh (300som). The other option is to flag down a car as it leaves town to Sary

Tash (50som, one hour) or, if you are lucky, all the way to Osh (400som, six hours).

### Pik Lenin & Achik Tash

Trekking possibilities in the Alay Valley are legion, but serious trekkers head for Pik Lenin (now officially called Koh-i-Garmo). The peak is known as one of the most accessible 7000-ers in the world. It is the highest summit of the Pamir Alay and lies right on the Kyrgyz–Tajik border. The snow-covered ridges and slopes are not technically difficult to climb with many ascents passing **Lipkin Rocks**, named after a pilot who crashed here and then calmly walked out.

Altitude sickness and avalanches are a serious problem; in 1991 an earthquake-triggered avalanche obliterated Camp II on the Razdelnaya approach, killing 43 climbers in the process. It remains the world's worse mountaineering disaster.

For details on trekking around Pik Lenin, see Frith Maier's *Trekking in Russia & Central Asia*.

At Achik Tash meadows (3600m), 30km south of Sary Moghul, IMC Pamir and most of the trekking agencies mentioned, p341, operate Pik Lenin base camps and programmes in summer. To get there you'll have to fix arrangements in advance.

There are weekly farmers markets in Daroot-Korgon (on Monday), Kashka-Suu (Tuesday) and Sary Moghul (Sunday) where you can buy basic foodstuffs. Several trailer shops offer the usual kiosk fare in Sary Tash. Beyond this bring all your own food.

#### GETTING THERE & AWAY

You should be able to hire a 4WD from Sary Moghul to Achik Tash (17km) for US$20 return. A hired 4WD from Osh to Achik Tash can be negotiated down to US$150 if you ask around the Argomak 4WD stand. Trekking-agency vehicles come at about US$175 one way. Daniyar Abdurahmanov, Kyrgyz Concept and Munduz Travel (p336) all organise transport to Achik Tash; you may be able to work in with one of their trips to Irkeshtam Pass to help reduce the cost.

## SOUTHWESTERN KYRGYZSTAN

The southern wall of the Fergana Valley forms a curious claw of Kyrgyz territory, although access to most of the mountain villages here comes from the Fergana Valley territory of Tajikistan or Uzbekistan. The beautiful valleys of the Turkestan ridge in particular offer superb trekking territory and the beautiful pyramid-shaped **Ak-Suu** peak (5359m), with its sheer 2km-high wall, is one of the world's best extreme rock-climbing destinations.

This mountain idyll was shattered, however, when Islamic militants from Tajikistan kidnapped Japanese geologists and then four American climbers here in 1999 and 2000 (p273). The valleys are now thought to be safe once again but you should check before heading off to the Karavshin, Leilek and Ak-Suu Valleys.

Even without the threat of political insurgency, this is not a particularly easy place to make your first Central Asian trek. Access can prove tricky (inter-republic buses have ground to a halt), and you'll need an Uzbek, Kyrgyz and Tajik visa to transit hassle-free through these republics, as well as a spurious trekking permit. Moreover, some of the passes with Tajikistan are said to be mined. For the time being you are better off planning any trek in the region with an established trekking operator in Bishkek (p284) or Tashkent (p199).

### Batken

Because of the difficulty and added expense of crossing the Tadjik and Uzbek enclaves Batken remains largely unexplored and consequently has little tourist development. At the time of writing CBT were taking their first tentative steps in recruiting and training families to host homestays and it is best to contact the Bishkek office (p282) for details on homestays within this region.

The city has many cafés but only two hotels constructed for Soviet administrators a number of years ago that have seen little maintenance or custom since. Travellers have recommended the **B&B of Dalmira Checheeva** (14 Shestdyesat Let Oktyabria ulitsa).

Shared taxis to Osh and to Isfara (Uzbekistan) depart every morning from the post office. Buses from Batken to Osh and Isfana leave from the bus station early in the morning. Public transport to Batken passes through the enclaves. Even with multi-entry visas travellers have reported hassles at the borders. The best option is to use minor roads that scoot around the enclaves but, in doing so, you'll be forced to hire a taxi or arrange your own transport. Osh Guesthouse (p338) and Munduz Travel (p336) will arrange a car from Osh for US$130 to US$150.

# KYRGYZSTAN DIRECTORY

## ACCOMMODATION

Homestays are the bedrock of accommodation in rural Kyrgyzstan, particularly those of the CBT programme (p277), and always include breakfast. Even though the prices are listed as dorms you will usually not be expected to share rooms with strangers; however, friends travelling together will be expected to share a room. Most homestays are comfortable but not luxurious; a *shyrdak* rug and a snugly pile of duvets and pillows as bedding and an *umuvalnik* – a portable washbasin that stores water in a top compartment – for washing. The bathroom will often be a pit toilet (with a seat) and some homestays have Russian-style *banyas*. Yurtstays offer similar bedding, less privacy and (if your're lucky) basic outhouses. Non-CBT homestays are generally much less comfortable.

Different from yurtstays are private tourist yurt camps, mostly used by groups but open to anyone if there's space. Costs here are around US$25 per person with three meals, and often include some horse riding or other activities.

The unravelling of the Soviet Union has left the once swanky sanatoria high and dry, devoid of customers but choc-bloc full of nostalgia.

The main cities (Bishkek, Osh, Jalal-Abad and Karakol) all boast midrange hotels which are comfortable and clean but invariably come with peeling paint, pre-independence wallpaper and gurgling plumbing. Recent confidence in the tourist sector has seen improvements and this trend is expected to continue. Hotel accommodation seldom includes breakfast and since most rooms contain two beds the tariff for a single and a double are often the same, effectively doubling the cost for solo travelers.

Top-end accommodation is limited to Bishkek where you can expect a far higher standard (and price) equal to that of their international counterparts. Former Soviet flagship hotels have found privatisation difficult and while their flags may still be flying high they are ridiculously overpriced and under resourced.

### PRACTICALITIES

- The *Times of Central Asia* (www.timesca-europe.com) is the local English-language newspaper, based in Bishkek.
- Popular radio stations include *Kyrgyz Radio* and *Kyrgyzstan Obondoru* (Kyrgyzstan Melodies).
- The two major Kyrgyz TV stations are KTR – *Kyrgyz State Television and Radio Corporation* and KORT – *Kyrgyz Public Radio and Television.*
- The Secam system is used for videos.
- The electrical supply is 220V, 50 Hz
- Kyrgyzstan uses the metric system

## ACTIVITIES

### Four-Wheel-Drive Trips

There are several opportunities for 4WD safaris. One possible road leads from Talas over the Kara Bura Pass into the Chatkal river valley and then loops around to Sary-Chelek. Other tracks lead from Naryn to Barskoön, and Barskoön to Inylchek, through the high Tian Shan.

### Horse Riding

Kyrgyzstan is the best place in Central Asia to saddle up and join the other nomads on the high pastures. Community-Based Tourism offices throughout the country can organise horse hire for around 70som per hour or 400som per day.

The horses often give the impression they're only a hoof-beat away from reverting to their wild roots and galloping off to a distant mountain pasture but novice riders are seldom given unruly horses if they make their concerns known.

With so many horse-trekking possibilities it is difficult to recommend one over another and it is worth asking other travelers for any new or outstanding routes. Community-Based Tourism is opening and closing routes continuously based on the location and availability of its guides in the summer *jailoos* however the following are outstanding:

- Horse trek over the 3570m Shamsy Pass from Salaral-Saz Jailoo to Tokmak (p317)
- Two- or three-day horse trips to/from Kyzart or Jumgal to Song-Köl (p318)
- Horse trek from Echki-Bashy to Bokonbayevo or Song-Köl (five to six days; p321)

For organised trips, the following companies are recommended:

**AsiaRando** (☎ 3132-47710/47711, 517-73 97 78; www.asiarando.com; Padgornaya 67, Rot Front, Chuy Oblast)

KYRGYZSTAN

**POST-SOVIET NAME CHANGES**

The Kyrgyz language has not been as bluntly imposed on nonspeakers in Kyrgyzstan as has Uzbek in Uzbekistan. In larger towns in the north at least, streets and squares are labelled in both Kyrgyz and Russian. In some smaller towns, the old Russian signs are still in place and Russian forms persist (in Osh and other towns in the south you'll hear Uzbek terms as well). Many Soviet-era names have been retained.

We try to use the most current names, but in each town we use the grammatical forms (Kyrgyz, Russian or Uzbek) that seem to be in common use. The government prefers to close hyphenated place names (such as Cholponata), which is yet to catch on with its citizenry (who prefer Cholpon-Ata).

A Kyrgyz street is *köchösü* (Russian: *ulitsa*), an avenue is *prospektisi* (Russian: *prospekt*), a boulevard *bulvary* (Russian: *bulvar*), a square *ayanty* (Russian: *ploshchad*).

Horse-riding trips to Song-Köl from its base in Rotfront village. Contact Gérard and Dominique Guillerm.

**Shepherd's Way** See p310 for details of trips around Lake Issyk-Köl.

### Mountaineering

Kyrgyzstan is the major base for climbing expeditions to Khan Tengri (p312) and Pik Lenin (in Tajikistan but accessed from Kyrgyzstan; p342). There are many unclimbed peaks in the Kokshal range bordering China. Most of the Bishkek trekking agencies (p284) arrange mountaineering expeditions.

The Kyrgyz Alpine Club has a useful website (www.kac.centralasia.kg).

### Rafting

Rafting is possible on the Kokomoron, Chuy, Naryn and Chong-Kemin Rivers (Grades II to V). The season runs from 25 June until 15 September and wetsuits are essential in the glacial melt water. Contact **Silk Road Water Centre** (p282) to take the plunge.

### Skiing

Despite the fact that 94% of the country averages over 2700m, skiing is still in it's infancy. Currently the only 'ski fields' are around Bishkek (p292) and Karakol (p309). The season runs mid-November until mid-March. With the advent of heli-skiing (p293) Russian-built MI-8 helicopters are ferrying adrenaline junkies to altitudes of over 4500m for descents of up to 5km.

### Trekking

Covered in mountains and lakes, Kyrgyzstan offers unrivalled opportunities to take to the hills. Around Bishkek (p290), Karakol (p309), Kochkor (p318), Naryn (p320), Arslanbob (p331) and Sary-Chelek (p329) are the major trekking regions although any CBT office will suggest countless alternatives.

#### TREKKING PERMITS

Trekking and mountaineering permits were abolished by the Kyrgyz government in 2002 but at least one local authority has tried to keep them in an effort to raise funds. Batken (for the Ak-Suu and Karavshin regions) charges US$30 for a permit.

## CUSTOMS

If you've bought anything that looks remotely antique and didn't get a certificate saying it's not, you can get one from the 1st floor of the Foreign Department of the **Ministry of Education, Science & Culture** (☎ 62 68 17; Room 210, cnr Tynystanov & Frunze).

## EMBASSIES & CONSULATES

### Kyrgyz Embassies in Central Asia

There are Kyrgyz embassies in the Central Asian capitals of Almaty (p178), Ashgabat (p437), Dushanbe (p392) and Tashkent (p262).

### Kyrgyz Embassies & Consulates

If there is no Kyrgyz embassy in your country, inquire at the Kazakh embassy if there is one. There are additional embassies in Belarus, Ukraine, India, Malaysia, Switzerland and the UAE.

If you intend to cross into Kyrgyzstan from China over the Torugart Pass, you will need to secure your Kyrgyz visa in either Beijing or Ürümqi.

**Austria** (☎ 01-535 0378; fax 535 0379; kyrbot@mail.austria.eu.net; Naglergasse 25/5, 1010, Vienna)

**Belgium** (☎ 02-640 1868; aitmatov@photohall.skynet.be; 47 Rue de L'Abbaye, 1050, Brussels) Issues visas on the spot for US$50.

**China** (☎ 010-6532 6458; kyrgyz@public3.bta.net.cn; 2-7-1 Ta Yuan Diplomatic Office Bldg, Liangmahe Naniu 14 hao, Chaoyang District, Beijing; 3-6pm Mon, Wed & Fri) Walk down San Li Tun Da Jie until it meets the river and turn left. It's a further five minutes along in an imposing building flying many flags. The embassy is on the 7th floor behind a small, unmarked white door next to the stairwell. A one-month tourist visa costs US$55/110 and is issued in seven/three days. The Central Asia Hotel in Ürümqi issues visas for US$56/112 in three/five days.

**Germany** Berlin (☎ 030-3478 1338; www.botschaft-kirgisien.de; Otto-Suhr-Allee 146, 10585); Bonn (☎ 0228-36 52 30; kirgistan.bonn@t-online.de; 194A Friesdorferstrasse, 53175); Frankfurt (☎ 069-9540 3926; Bronnerstrasse 20) A 30-day visa costs €50. Only German and Russian are spoken at the Berlin branch.

**Iran** Mashhad (☎ 051-818444); Tehran (☎ 021-229 8323, 283 0354, krembiri@kanoon.net; Bldg 12, 5th Naranjastan Alley, Pasdaran St)

**Russia** (☎ 095-237 4601/4882/4571; fax 237 4452; Bolshaya Ordynka ulitsa 64, 109017, Moscow) Also in Ekaterinburg.

**Switzerland** (☎ 022-707 9220; http://missions.itu.int/kyrgyzstan; 26 Rue Maunoir, 1207, Geneva)

**Turkey** Ankara (☎ 312-446 84 08; kirgiz-o@tr-net.net.tr; Boyabat Sokak 11, Gaziosmanpasa, 06700); İstanbul (☎ 212-235 6767; genkon@tr.net; 7 Lamartin Caddesi, Taksim)

**UK** (☎ 020-7935 1462; www.kyrgyz-embassy.org.uk; Ascot House, 119 Crawford St, W1U 6BJ, London; 9.30am-12.30pm) A one-/two-month tourist visa costs UK£45/60.

**USA** (☎ 202-338 5141; www.kyrgyzembassy.org; 1732 Wisconsin Ave, NW, Washington DC 20007) A one-month tourist visa costs US$50 and is ready in 10 days. Also a consulate in New York.

## Embassies & Consulates in Kyrgyzstan

Some of the smaller embassies listed below are little more than a rented room in an obscure apartment block and can be hard to find. All the following are in Bishkek (area code ☎ 312; see Map p280). For information on visas for onward travel see p347.

For letters of support try travel agencies (p282) such as Kyrgyz Concept and CAT. The nearest Turkmen embassy is in Almaty.

**Afghanistan** (☎ 42 63 72; cnr Ayni & Toktonalieva) Run by a relative of General Dostum, the Uzbek warlord based in Mazar-e Sharif.

**China** (☎ 22 24 23; fax 6630 14; Toktogul 196; 9.15am-noon Mon, Wed & Fri)

**France** (☎ 66 00 53; ag-consul@elcat.kg; cnr Razzakov & Kiev) Look for the model Eiffel Tower outside.

**Germany** (☎ 66 66 12; fax 66 66 30; gerembi@elcat.kg; Razzakov 28) Rumoured to be moving near the American embassy soon.

**India** (☎ 21 08 62; fax 62 07 08; 3rd fl, Chuy 164-A; 9am-1pm & 2-5.30pm Mon-Fri)

**Iran** (☎ 22 69 64; fax 62 00 09; Razzakov 36; 9am-5pm Mon-Fri)

**Japan** (☎ 61 18 75; fax 61 18 82; Frunze 503)

**Kazakhstan** (☎ 66 04 15; Mira 95A; 10am-noon Mon-Thu)

**Netherlands** (☎ 66 02 22; fax 66 02 88; Suite 1, Tynystanov 199) Honorary consulate.

**Pakistan** (☎ 62 17 02; pakemb@asiainfo.kg; Serov 37; 9-11am Mon-Fri) May well refer you to a travel agency.

**Russia** (☎ 22 17 75; rusemb@imfiko.bishkek.su; Manas 55) This consular office is the one to get visas.

**Tajikistan** (☎ 51 23 43; fax 51 14 64; Kara-Dar'inskaya 36, Kök-Jar microrayon; 9-11am Mon-Fri) The embassy is lost in suburbia. Take trolleybus 17 to the Kök-Jar *mikrorayon* (region). The trolley will turn twice, first left, then right. After the second turn watch for Pizza Inn on the left and get off. Walk down the road alongside Pizza Inn until a T-intersection. In front of you is the Tajik Embassy.

**Turkey** (☎ 22 78 82; fax 66 05 20; Moskva 89; 9am-noon Mon-Fri)

**UK** (☎ 65 28 55; Kalik Akiyeva 11/24) This is an Honorary Consulate; behind the World Bank.

**USA** (☎ 55 12 41; pao@usis.gov.kg; Mira 171)

**Uzbekistan** (☎ 66 30 78, 66 20 65; fax 66 44 03; Tynystanov 104/38; Tue-Fri)

# FESTIVALS & EVENTS

Kyrgyzstan isn't exactly full of festivals. The most exciting are the **horse games** at the end of July and August (notably Independence Day, 31 August) at Bishkek, Cholpon-Ata, Karakol and the *jailoos* around Song-Köl and Kochkor. Gruelling horse races are also held during the At **Chabysh festival** (p310) in Barskoön in early November. NoviNomad in Bishkek (p282) and the nearest CBT can offer details.

During the recently revived **Nooruz** (21 March) celebrations expect to see sporting events, traditional games, music festivals and street fairs particularly around Osh and Jalal-Abad.

The **Birds of Prey Festival** (p312), held early August in Bokonbayevo, offers an excellent opportunity to see eagle hunters and falconers compete.

# HOLIDAYS

See p449 for information on the Muslim public holidays of Ramadan and Eid festivals.

**1 January** New Year's Day.
**7 January** Russian Orthodox Christmas.
**23 February** Army Day.
**8 March** International Women's Day.
**21 March** Nooruz.

KYRGYZSTAN

**24 March** Anniversary of the March Revolution.
**1 May** International Labour Day.
**5 May** Constitution Day.
**9 May** WWII Victory Day.
**31 August** Independence Day.
**7 November** Anniversary of the October Revolution.

## INTERNET RESOURCES

**Celestial Mountains Tour Company** (www.celestial.com.kg) An exhaustive resource on all things Kyrgyz.
**Community Based Tourism** (www.cbtkyrgyzstan.kg) Contact details and prices for its services.
**Helvetas** (www.helvetas.kg) General info, Altyn Kol handicrafts and Shepherd's Life.
**Kyrgyzstan Info** (www.kirgistan.info) Travel info to off-the-beaten-track places in northern Kyrgyzstan.
**Kyrgyzstan.Org** (www.kyrgyzstan.org) Current events, travel advice, visa regulations, events links.
**Times of Central Asia** (www.timesca-europe.com) Current events.

## MAPS

Geoid in Bishkek (p279) has a Kyrgyzstan country map (Cyrillic and English), an interesting Silk Road of Kyrgyzstan map, trekking route maps and 1:200,000 Soviet topographic maps of various parts of Kyrgyzstan. Most maps are in Russian.

Trekking maps available at the agency:
**Ala-Archa** (1:50,000) Routes up to Ak-Say Glacier and the ski base, in English.
**Cherez Talasskii Khrebet k Ozeru Sary-Chelek** (1:200,000) From Leninopol to Sary-Chelek over the Talas mountains.
**Kirgizskii Khrebet** (1:200,000) Topographical map, covering the Kyrgyzsky Mountains south of Bishkek. There's also a separate 1:150,000 schematic map showing peaks in the same region.
**Ozero Issyk-Kul** (1:200,000) Topographical map, covering trekking routes to Kazakhstan via the Chong-Kemin Valley.
**Sokh** (1:200,000) Alay Mountains.
**South-East Issyk-Köl Lake Coast** (1:100,000) Trekking routes around Karakol, including the Jeti-Öghüz Valley, Altyn Arashan and Ala-Köl.
**Tsentralniy Tyan-Shan** (1:150,000) Schematic map of Inylchek Glacier and around.

## MONEY

The Kyrgyz som is divided into 100 tiyin. Notes come in 1000, 500, 200, 100, 50, 20, 10, five and one som denominations. Banks and licensed moneychanger booths (marked *obmen balyot*) exchange US dollars provided the notes are unblemished in near-mint condition and, if possible, post 2001. There are ATMs in Bishkek, Jalal-Abad and Osh that dispense both US dollars and som. Travellers cheques can be cashed in these places and in Karakol (3% commission). Most prices in this chapter are listed in som apart from higher-priced items which, as is the custom in Kyrgyzstan, are listed in US dollars although a few businesses in the hospitality industry fix their prices in euros. There is no black market for currency transactions and exchange rates at the time of research were as follows:

| Country | Unit | | Som |
|---|---|---|---|
| Australia | A$1 | = | 30.17 |
| Canada | C$ | = | 34.20 |
| China | Y1 | = | 4.94 |
| euro zone | €1 | = | 50.73 |
| Kazakhstan | 10T | = | 3.03 |
| New Zealand | NZ$1 | = | 26.13 |
| Russia | R1 | = | 1.47 |
| Switzerland | 1Sfr | = | 32.08 |
| Tajikistan | 1TJS | = | 12.07 |
| UK | £1 | = | 74.90 |
| USA | US$1 | = | 38.77 |
| Uzbekistan | 100S | = | 3.14 |

If you need to wire money, MoneyGram has services at main post offices and Western Union works through most banks.

## POST

An airmail postcard costs 25som and a 20g letter costs 30som to all countries. Parcels are shipped at US$11 per kilogram and airmail is often less expensive than sea freight.

**DHL** (www.dhl.kg) has offices in Bishkek and Osh and charges US$92 to send 1kg to North America. **FedEx** (www.fedex.com) has an office in Bishkek. A 1kg box to North America costs US$75.

## REGISTRATION

Foreigners from 28 countries, including the US, UK, Australia, Canada, Israel and most European countries no longer need to register with OVIR (Office of Visas and Registrations; UPVR in Kyrgyzstan). Other countries (one notable example is Dutch citizens) need to register within three days of arriving in Kyrgyzstan.

## SHOPPING

Small pottery figurines shaped as bread sellers, musicians, and 'white beards' are for sale everywhere but most are made at the Arts Faculty n Osh. Hats are also for sale everywhere but nost are factory-made in Toktogul. The most popular buys are *shyrdaks* (p276).

Other souvenirs include miniature yurts and embroidered bags, chess sets featuring Manas and company, horse whips, *kymys* shakers, eather boxes, felt slippers and musical instruments such as the Kyrgyz mouth harp.

## TELEPHONE

International telephone rates are 15som per minute to Central Asia and 25som per minute to other countries. Domestic calls cost about 7som per minute and local calls 1som per minute. Some older telephones require you to dial 3 after the person picks up.

To make an international call, dial ☎ 00 plus the international code of the country you wish to call.

To make an intercity call, dial ☎ 0 plus the city code.

To call a mobile (either Bitel or Katel) dial ☎ 0 first plus the number, except for Bitel 312 mobile numbers from a land line in which case you do not dial ☎ 0.

Internet phone calls cost as little as 5som per minute to the USA.

To send a fax, Telecom offices charge around US$5 a page. You are better off scanning it at an internet café and sending an email.

If you have a GSM mobile phone, you can buy a SIM card from **MobiCard** (☎ 312-60 02 22) and scratchcards in units of 200, 400 and 1000.

Sim cards are available from Bitel and Mega Com for 120som. No registration is required. Bitel has the better coverage.

## VISAS

Kyrgyzstan is the easiest of the Central Asian republics for which to get a visa. Kyrgyz embassies issue 30-day tourist visas, with fixed dates, to 28 nationalities (see Registration, opposite, or visit www.kyrgyzembassy.org) without letters of support. These nationalities can also obtain a visa on arrival at Bishkek's Manas International Airport (US$35) although not at land borders.

Most nationalities from the former Soviet bloc, as well as Japanese, Turks and Kazakhs do not need visas.

If there is no Kyrgyz embassy in your country, go through a Kazakh embassy instead, although a letter of invitation regardless of nationality is then required. Central Asian travel agencies (p457) can provide these for US$20 to US$30.

It's illegal to enter Kyrgyzstan except at a designated border crossing, which makes cross-border treks (eg Almaty to Issyk-Köl) technically illegal. You'll need a travel agency to help smooth over these problems if you intend to take these treks.

### Travel Permits

Certain sensitive border areas such as the Khan Tengri region and Alay Valley require a military border permit (*propusk pa granzona;* US$10), which trekking agencies can arrange in about 10 days.

### Visa Extensions

A 30-day visa extension is easy to get from OVIR offices in Bishkek (p282), Karakol (p302), Osh (p336) and Naryn. These cost 400som to 600som and are processed the same day.

### Visas for Onward Travel

For contact details of embassies and consulates in Kyrgyzstan, see p345.

**China** This embassy hasn't realised the Cultural Revolution is over and won't issue tourist visas without an invitation from a Xinjiang tourist agency. ITMC Tian Shan (p284) and Celestial Mountains (p282) can get an invitation in a week (US$50). Thirty-day visas cost US$50 for Americans, US$30 for others and take a week to issue (urgent service: three days, twice the price).

**India** Accepts visa applications 2pm to 4pm Mon to Fri. A standard six-month tourist visas cost 1835som for US citizens, 1105som for other nationalities. Two photos are necessary. Visas take three to five days to issue.

**Iran** Transit visas of 10 days' duration are issued in one week. You need a letter of invitation for a tourist visa.

**Kazakhstan** Get to the embassy early and put your name on the list to get inside. Fees need to be paid at the Kazkommertsbank (p281). For a transit visa bring your ticket out of Kazakhstan (and copy), the visa for the country being visited next (and copy), one photo, a photocopy of your passport and Kyrgyz visa; takes five/three days (US$20/35).

**Russia** Visas are only available from the consular office (55 Manas; open 9am till noon and 2.30 till 3.30pm Monday, Tuesday & Thursday), not the embassy. You'll need a letter of invitation and four passport photos. Transit visas cost US$16/32 in a week/day and you'll need tickets in and out of Russia. Fees are paid at the Kairat bank, four blocks north.

**Tajikistan** Thirty-day visas were available in four working days (US$50 plus 50som). Bring photo, passport, a photocopy of passport and a letter of invitation, although at the time of research this was not always required. The friendly Tajik ambassador often helps with the application form.

**Uzbekistan** You need to get a Russian speaker to phone the embassy and put your name on the list. Arrive by 10am; take along one photo, passport, a photocopy of passport, the letter of invitation and a Russian translator. Bishkek tour agencies (such as NoviNomad and Kyrgyz Concept) provide translators (US$20), although it may be worth negotiating a price with a student from the American University. Tourist visas (US$102 for US citizens, US$72 for other nationalities) issued on the same day at 3pm; pay when you get it.

# TRANSPORT IN KYRGYZSTAN

## GETTING THERE & AWAY

### Entering Kyrgyzstan

Remote border posts, for example at Karkara and along the Pamir Hwy, from Tajikistan may not stamp your visa with an entry stamp but you should insist that this is done, otherwise you'll have problems. Generally, entering the country presents no difficulties.

### Air

Bishkek's Manas airport is the main international hub although there are also flights to Moscow, Ürümqi and Dushanbe from Osh. The national carrier, Air Company Kyrgyzstan (AC Kyrgyzstan) was formerly Altyn Air.

From Bishkek, Central Asian destinations include Tashkent (US$100, with Uzbekistan Airways, AC Kyrgyzstan), Ürümqi (US$210, Kyrgyzstan Air, China Southern, Esen Air) and Dushanbe (US$150, Tajik Air, AC Kyrgyzstan).

One-way/return airfares for Russia include Yekaterinburg (US$230/460, AC Kyrgyzstan, twice weekly), Novosibirsk (US$200/400, AC Kyrgyzstan, thrice weekly) and Moscow (US$250/400, Aeroflot, AC Kyrgyzstan, Itek Air, daily).

Other international destinations reached directly from Bishkek are limited to Dubai (US$300/600, AC Kyrgyzstan, once weekly), İstanbul (US$428/560, Turkish Airlines, once weekly) and London (US$675/852, British Airways, four times weekly).

Between June and September AC Kyrgyzstan also has a weekly flight to Hanover and Frankfurt for US$450/900 one way/return.

Because flight choice is limited, many choose to fly to Tashkent (p266), Almaty (p183) or Ürümqi (China) and connect from there. A transit visa will be required if you plan to leave these airports. Note that it's only three hours by road between Almaty and Kyrgyzstan and KLM runs a free Bishkek–Almaty ground shuttle service for their customers, leaving Bishkek in front of the Dostuk Hotel on the day of flights at 6pm (transit visa required).

A similar Lufthansa bus departs at 7pm from Grand Hyatt. It's free if you buy your ticket in Bishkek, otherwise it costs US$25. The bus leaves Almaty airport at 12.30am, arriving in Bishkek at 3.30am.

For more details on airline offices in Bishkek, see p289. The US$10 international departure tax and 4% government tax is included in the ticket price.

### Land

#### BORDER CROSSINGS

For more on the complicated jigsaw borders of the Fergana Valley, see p471. One thing to note is that transport along Kyrgyzstan's southern arm from Osh to Batken passes through the Uzbek enclave of Sokh so you'll need to get an Uzbek visa or hire a taxi to take you on a dirt road detour around the enclave.

#### To/From China

Of the two land crossings from China the 3752m **Torugart Pass** (p325) is the more complicated and expensive, requiring pricey, prearranged Chinese transport.

The newer and easier border crossing is the **Irkeshtam Pass** (p340) linking Kashgar to Osh and the Fergana Valley. It has none of the restrictions of the Torugart and you can take taxis, hitch on trucks or even cycle.

See Passing the Pass (opposite) for general tips on these borders.

#### To/From Kazakhstan

Minibuses go directly from Bishkek to Almaty (250som, 4½ hours) every hour or two, as do private cars (350som per seat). There is a passport check at the border by the Chuy River and you will need a Kazakh visa.

A back-door route into Kazakhstan is possible through the Karkara Valley. There's no through transport so you'll have to hire a taxi or hitch part of the way. See p299 for details.

**TAKING THE HIGH ROAD**

The mountain borders of Kyrgyzstan, Tajikistan and China have become destinations within themselves. A cathedral of peaks, head-spinning altitudes and mythically remote roads guarantee that these are not your usual ho-hum, forgettable border posts. To ensure a hassle free crossing there are some things worth bearing in mind.

- Avoid crossing a pass on any day that might even conceivably be construed as a holiday on either side, or in Russia, as the border will probably be closed.
- Attempting to cross on a Friday is tricky, as if the border is temporarily closed for snow or some other reason you won't be able to re-try for another three days. Try to arrive at the border as early as possible as things tend to grind to a halt at lunchtime.
- Be aware of time-zone differences. In summer (roughly April to September) China (ie Beijing) time is two hours later than Kyrgyzstan time, and in winter three hours later.
- Check the weather. Have your paperwork right.
- For high-altitude passes be aware that at the beginning and end of the season you really need a 4WD not a little Toyota minivan. Also remember that there is little reliable petrol, oil or parts along the way.

There is a new 96km 4WD road from near Cholpon-Ata over to Chong-Kemin Valley and beyond to Almaty but you need a 4WD for this rough route and as there's no border control, you'll have headaches getting a visa stamp.

Trains run four times a week from Bishkek to Almaty and on to Moscow (train 17, 4021som, Monday and Thursday ; train 27, 3900som, Wednesday and Saturday).

### To/From Tajikistan

The main crossing for travellers is at the Bor Döbo checkpoint on the Pamir Hwy, between Murgab district and Sary Tash. To travel on the Pamir Hwy a GBAO permit that says 'Murgab district' is required. Another remote crossing leads southwest from the Pamir Alay Valley into the Garm Valley and on to Dushanbe, although this is currently closed to foreigners.

From the Fergana Valley it's possible to cross from Batken to Isfara (not Isfana) in Tajikistan.

### To/From Uzbekistan

From Bishkek buses go from the west bus station to Tashkent three times a day between 6pm and 9pm for about 285som; however, at the time of research these were only going as far as the Kazakh–Uzbek border at Chernyaevka, from where you had to take a minibus a few kilometres into Tashkent. These buses run through Kazakhstan and require a Kazakh transit visa, which makes flying a competitive option.

From Jalal-Abad take a taxi or minibus (20som) to Khanabad (formerly Sovietabad) and cross by foot. Note that the Kara-Suu border crossing is not open.

From Osh take a taxi (50som) or minibus (Nos 107, 113, 136, 137 or 138, 5som) to Dustlyk/Dostyk and then get a seat in a shared taxi to Andijon. Osh Guesthouse in Osh (p338) can help arrange a car direct to Tashkent or Andijon.

It is also possible to travel to/from Tashkent by rail but all pass through Kazakhstan necessitating a Kazakh visa.

See p468 for more on travelling around the region.

## GETTING AROUND

Travelling around Kyrgyzstan is generally quite straightforward. The bus system is slowly unravelling and so for most trips your best bet is the shared taxis or marshrutka (minibuses), which wait for passengers at most bus stations.

Shared taxis also act as private taxis if you are willing to pay for all four seats and most travel agencies also arrange private cars.

For airlines flying domestic routes between Bishkek, Osh and Jalal-Abad, see p289.

# Tajikistan Таджикистан/Точикистон

A Persian-speaking outpost in a predominantly Turkic region, Tajikistan is in many ways the odd one out in Central Asia. With its roots in ancient Sogdiana and Bactria, the modern country is a fragile patchwork of clans, languages and identities, forged together by little more than Soviet nation-building and the shared hopes for a peaceful future.

That peace was shattered in the 1990s, when a brutal civil war claimed over 50,000 lives, turning the remote mountainous republic into the bloodiest corner of the former Soviet empire. Though the wounds are still raw, a decade after the war most Tajiks are moving forward with their lives, as if awakening from a bad dream, and a mood of guarded optimism has returned.

The good news is that today Tajikistan is safe, stable and scenically spectacular. The Pamir region – 'the Roof of the World' – is easily the country's highlight, offering breathtaking high-altitude scenery, excellent ecotourism options, humbling mountain hospitality and the Pamir Highway – one of Asia's greatest road trips.

Once the playing fields of 'Great Game' spies and explorers, Tajikistan is now the playground for cutting-edge adventure travel, from walks through the Wakhan Valley to 4WD trips out to remote valleys and nights in remote Kyrgyz yurt camps. For fans of remote mountain scenery, or anyone who ranks places like northern Pakistan or western Tibet as their favourite destinations, Tajikistan will glimmer as the most exciting republic in Central Asia.

Anyone following this road has the added thrill of knowing that few 'foreign devils' have passed this way since Francis Younghusband, the consummate 'Great Game' player, was expelled from the Pamirs by the Russians in 1891, marking the region's closure to the outside world for the next 100 years.



**FAST FACTS**

- **Area** 143,100 sq km
- **Capital** Dushanbe
- **Country Code** ☎ 992
- **Famous for** Civil war, Pamir Highway, mountains, hospitality, drug trafficking
- **Languages** Tajik, Russian, Uzbek and half a dozen Pamiri languages
- **Money** Tajik somani (TJS); US$1=3.4TJS, €1=4.3TJS
- **Phrases in Tajik** *khob.* (OK.); *mebakhshed.* (sorry.); *khair.* (goodbye.)
- **Population** 7.32 million (2006 estimate)

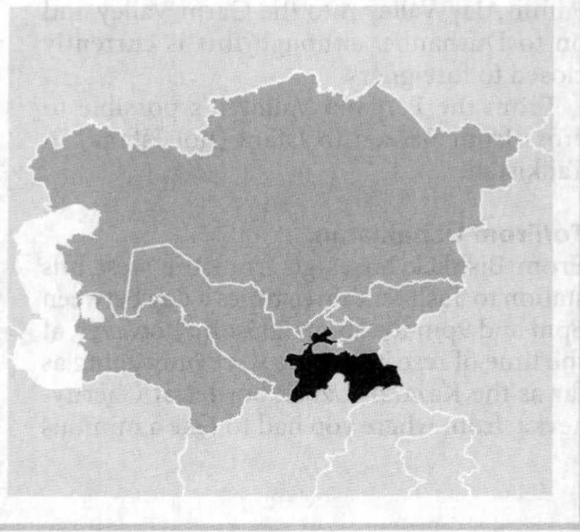

**HOW MUCH?**

- Snickers bar US$0.40
- 100km shared taxi ride US$8
- Internet connection per hour US$1.20
- Tajik skullcap US$2
- Homestay US$5-6
- Litre of bottled water US$0.40
- Litre of petrol US$1

## HIGHLIGHTS

- **Pamir Highway** (p386) One of the world's great road trips, offering jaw-dropping high-altitude lakes and fine community-based homestays.
- **Wakhan Valley** (p384) Remote and beautiful valley, shared with Afghanistan, and peppered with Silk Rd forts, Buddhist ruins and spectacular views of the snowbound Hindu Kush.
- **Yurt stays** (p388) Breakfast on fresh yogurt and cream while overnighting with a Kyrgyz family on the high pastures of the Pamir plateau.
- **Fan Mountains** (p373) Austere but beautiful trekking destination of turquoise lakes and Tajik shepherds, easily accessible from Samarkand.
- **M34** (p368) The mountain drive between Dushanbe and Khojand or Penjikent takes you over high passes and into towering mountain scenery.
- **Iskander-Kul** (p373) Lovely lake at the eastern end of the Fan Mountains and a great place to relax or go hiking.
- **Istaravshan** (p371) Exotic bazaar and lazy backstreets full of forgotten mosques and domed tombs.

## ITINERARIES

- **Three days** Drive from Samarkand or Khojand to Dushanbe (with an overnight stop in Iskander-Kul if you hire your own taxi) and then fly out of Dushanbe to Bishkek or Almaty. Alternatively, visit Penjikent from Samarkand, continue to Khojand via Istaravshan and then dip back into Uzbekistan.
- **One week** Khojand to Dushanbe with stops in Istaravshan, Iskander-Kul and Hissar. Or perhaps a short trek in the Fan Mountains. You could just about travel the Pamir Hwy from Dushanbe to Osh in a week, but only with your own transport.
- **Two weeks** Ten days is really the minimum amount of time required to travel the Pamir Hwy if you plan to arrange things as you go. Try to budget an overnight in the Wakhan Valley and at least one yurtstay in the eastern Pamirs, as the area has so much to offer.
- **Three weeks** This will be enough time to get you from Khojand in the north, over the mountains to Dushanbe via Istaravshan and then along the Pamir Hwy to Osh, with maybe a short trek in the Fan Mountains. Try to add on an overnight trip from Murgab to somewhere like Jalang, Pshart or Bulunkul.

## CLIMATE & WHEN TO GO

Northern, central and southern Tajikistan sizzle in summer (June to September), with temperatures over 40°C (105°F). Unfortunately this is the best time to visit the mountains. Spring (March to May) brings mild temperatures but frequent heavy showers. April is the best time to visit southern Tajikistan in bloom.

In winter (November to February) temperatures in Dushanbe hover near freezing, while temperatures in the Pamirs plummet to between -20°C and -45°C. The Anzob and Shakhristan passes between Khojand and Dushanbe are generally closed from late November to late May, though the new tunnel under the Anzob pass should keep the road to Penjikent open year-round.

March, April, September and October are probably the best times to visit. The best time of year for trekking is September. The Pamir region is best visited in July to late September, though the Pamir Hwy technically remains open year-round. During early summer (June and July), meltwater can make river crossings dangerous in mountainous areas.



## HISTORY

### Tajik Ancestry

Tajik ancestry is a murky area, with roots reaching back to the Bactrians and Sogdians. Tombs from the eastern Pamir show that Saka-Usun tribes were grazing their flocks here from the 5th century BC, when the climate was considerably lusher than today.

In the 1st century BC the Bactrian empire covered most of what is now northern

TAJIKISTAN

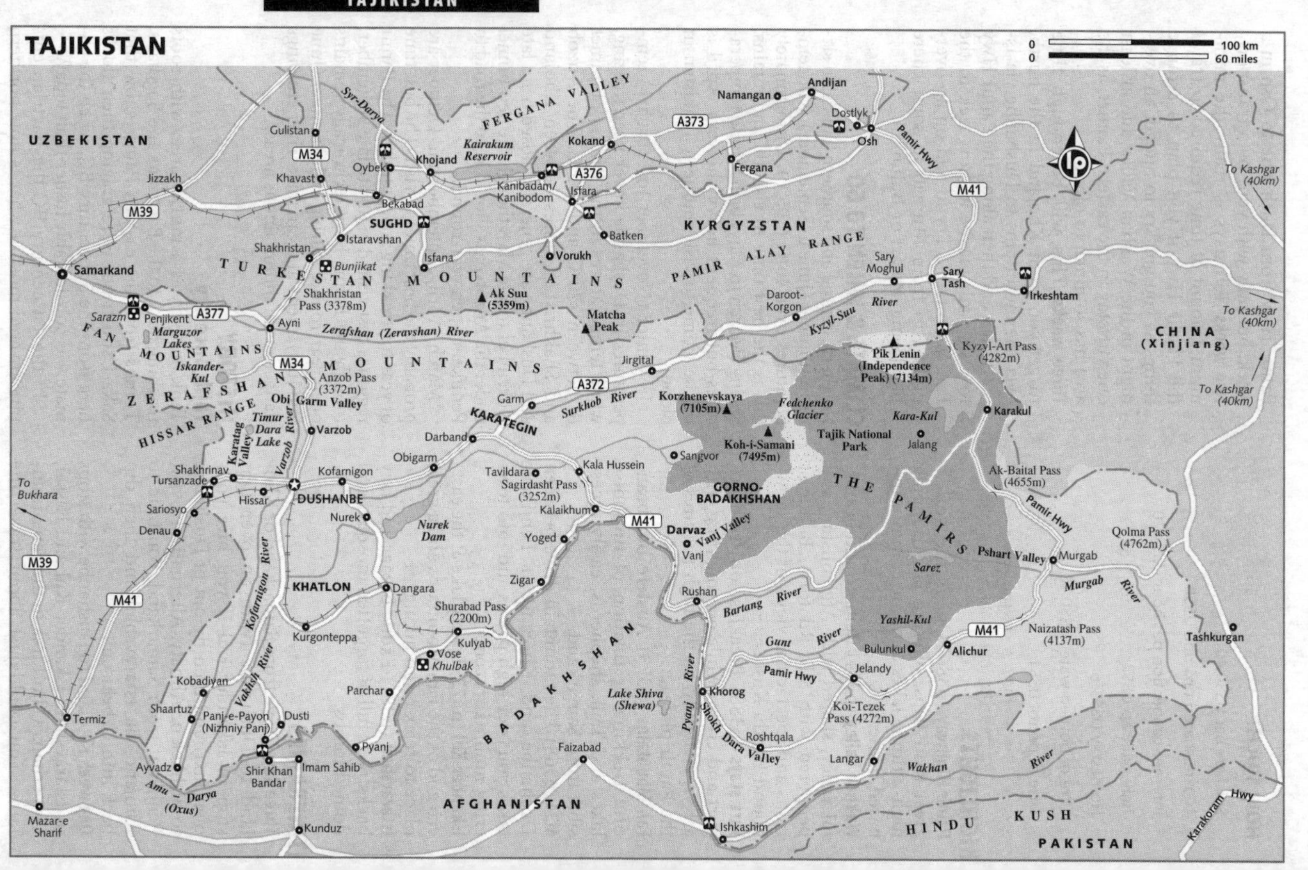
TAJIKISTAN
0 100 km
0 60 miles
UZBEKISTAN
KYRGYZSTAN
CHINA (Xinjiang)
AFGHANISTAN
PAKISTAN
HINDU KUSH
FERGANA VALLEY
TURKESTAN MOUNTAINS
PAMIR ALAY RANGE
ZERAFSHAN MOUNTAINS
FAN MOUNTAINS
HISSAR RANGE
KARATEGIN
THE PAMIRS
BADAKHSHAN
GORNO-BADAKHSHAN
SUGHD
KHATLON
DUSHANBE
Samarkand
Jizzakh
M39
Gulistan
M34
Khavast
Oybek
Khojand
Bekabad
Syr-Darya
Kairakum Reservoir
Kanibadam/Kanibodom
Isfara
A376
Kokand
A373
Fergana
Namangan
Andijan
Dostlyk
Osh
Pamir Hwy
M41
To Kashgar (40km)
Batken
Vorukh
Istaravshan
Shakhristan
Bunjikat
Isfana
Shakhristan Pass (3378m)
Ak Suu (5359m)
Matcha Peak
Sary Moghul
Sary Tash
Irkeshtam
Daroot-Korgon
Kyzyl-Suu River
Sarazm
Penjikent
A377
Ayni
Zerafshan (Zeravshan) River
Marguzor Lakes
Iskander-Kul
Anzob Pass (3372m)
Obi Garm Valley
Timur Dara Lake
Varzob River
Varzob
Karatag Valley
Jirgital
A372
Garm
Surkhob River
Pik Lenin (Independence Peak) (7134m)
Kyzyl-Art Pass (4282m)
Korzhenevskaya (7105m)
Fedchenko Glacier
Kara-Kul
Karakul
Koh-i-Samani (7495m)
Tajik National Park
Jalang
Darband
Obigarm
Sangvor
Shakhrinav
Tursanzade
Hissar
Kofarnigon
Tavildara
Sagirdasht Pass (3252m)
Kala Hussein
Ak-Baital Pass (4655m)
To Bukhara
Sariosyo
Denau
Nurek
Nurek Dam
Kalaikhum
Darvaz
Vanj Valley
Vanj
Yoged
Pshart Valley
Murgab
Qolma Pass (4762m)
Sarez
Murgab River
Kofarnigon River
Dangara
Zigar
Rushan
Bartang River
Shurabad Pass (2200m)
Kurgonteppa
Kulyab
Vose
Khulbak
Yashil-Kul
Naizatash Pass (4137m)
Tashkurgan
Gunt River
Bulunkul
Alichur
Pamir Hwy
Jelandy
Kobadiyan
Vakhsh River
Parchar
Lake Shiva (Shewa)
Khorog
Pyanj River
Shaartuz
Panj-e-Payon (Nizhniy Panj)
Dusti
Termiz
Koi-Tezek Pass (4272m)
Shokh Dara Valley
Roshtqala
Pyanj
Faizabad
Langar
Wakhan River
Ayvadz
Shir Khan Bandar
Imam Sahib
Amu - Darya (Oxus)
Mazar-e Sharif
Kunduz
Ishkashim
Karakoram Hwy

**TRAVELLING SAFELY IN TAJIKISTAN**

There are few specific risks in Tajikistan. The mountain passes between Tajikistan and Uzbekistan have been land-mined, as have parts of the Pyanj River banks that form the border with Afghanistan, so don't go for a stroll in these areas.

If you're going to be travelling the Pamir Hwy, particularly if you are headed from Osh to Karakul or Murgab in one day, there are serious risks associated with altitude sickness (see p479) for more information).

Southern Tajikistan has a malaria risk along the Afghan border and along the lower Vakhsh Valley as far north as Kurgonteppa. See p477.

Don't drink the tap water in Dushanbe, as there are occasional water-spread typhoid outbreaks.

Afghanistan. Their contemporaries, the Sogdians, inhabited the Zerafshan (Zeravshan) Valley in present-day western Tajikistan (where a few traces of this civilisation remain near Penjikent). Alexander the Great battled the Sogdians and besieged Cyropol (Istaravshan), before founding modern-day Khojand. The Sogdians were displaced in the Arab conquest of Central Asia during the 7th century AD. The Sogdian hero Devastich made a last stand against the Arabs at Mount Mug in the Zerafshan (Zeravshan) Mountains, before he was finally beheaded by the Muslim vanquishers.

Modern Tajikistan traces itself back to the glory days of the Persian Samanid dynasty (AD 819–992), a period of frenzied creative activity which hit its peak during the rule of Ismail Samani (AD 849–907), known in Tajikistan as Ismoili Somoni. Bukhara, the dynastic capital, became the Islamic world's centre of learning – nurturing great talents such as the philosopher-scientist Abu Ali ibn-Sina (known in the West as Avicenna) and the poet Rudaki – both now claimed as sons of Iran, Afghanistan and Tajikistan.

## A Blurring of Identity

Under the Samanids, the great towns of Central Asia were Persian (the basis of Tajikistan's modern-day claims on Samarkand and Bukhara), but at the end of the 10th century a succession of Turkic invaders followed up their battlefield successes with cultural conquest. Despite contrasting cultures, the two peoples cohabited peacefully, unified by religion. The Persian-speaking Tajiks adopted Turkic culture and the numerically superior Turks absorbed the Tajik people. Both were subject to the vicissitudes of Central Asia and weathered conquests by the Mongols and, later, Timur (Tamerlane). Most of the territory of modern Tajikistan remained on the fringes of the Timurid empire.

From the 15th century onwards, the Tajiks were subjects of the emirate of Bukhara, who received 50% of Badakhshan's ruby production as a tax. In the mid-18th century the Afghans moved up to engulf all lands south of the Amu-Darya (Oxus River), along with their resident Tajik population, and later seized parts of Badakhshan (including temporarily the Rushan and Shughnan regions). The Amu-Darya still delineates much of the Afghan–Tajik border today.

## The 'Great Game' & the Basmachi

As part of the Russian empire's thrust southwards, St Petersburg made the emirate of Bukhara a vassal state in 1868, which gave Russia effective control over what now passes for northern and western Tajikistan. But the Pamirs, which account for the whole of modern-day eastern Tajikistan, remained a no-man's-land, literally, falling outside the established borders of the Bukhara emirate and unclaimed by neighbouring Afghanistan and China. Russia was eager to exploit this anomaly in its push to open up possible routes into British India.

The Pamirs became the arena for the strategic duel between Britain and Russia that British poet and author Rudyard Kipling was to immortalise as the 'Great Game', a game in which Russia's players eventually prevailed, securing the region for the tsar (p45). It was in the eastern Pamirs, after visiting Murgab, Alichur and Rang-Kul, that Francis Younghusband was thrown out of the upper Wakhan by his Tsarist counterpart, sparking an international crisis between Britain and Russia. Russia backed up its claims by building a string of forts across the Pamirs. The Anglo-Russian border treaty of 1895 finally defined Tajikistan's current borders with Afghanistan and China.

Following the Russian revolution of 1917, new provisional governments were established in Central Asia and the Tajiks found themselves part of first the Turkestan (1918–24), then the Uzbekistan (1924–29) Soviet Socialist Republics (SSRs), despite pushing for an autonomous Islamic-oriented republic. The next year Muslim *basmachi* guerrillas began a campaign to free the region from Bolshevik rule (see the boxed text p367). It took four years for the Bolsheviks to crush this resistance, and in the process entire villages were razed. The surviving guerrillas disappeared into Afghanistan, from where they continued for years to make sporadic raids over the border.

## Soviet Statehood

In 1924, when the Soviet Border Commission set about redefining Central Asia, the Tajiks got their own Autonomous SSR (ASSR). Although only a satellite of the Uzbek SSR, this was the first official Tajik state. In 1929 it was upgraded to a full union republic, although (possibly in reprisal for the *basmachi* revolt) Samarkand and Bukhara – where over 700,000 Tajiks still lived – remained in Uzbekistan. As recently as 1989 the government of Tajikistan was still trying to persuade the Soviet leadership to 'return' the area lost in this cultural amputation. Territorial tensions with the modern government of Uzbekistan over the two cultural centres remain .

The Bolsheviks never fully trusted the Tajikistan SSR and during the 1930s almost all Tajiks in positions of influence within the government were replaced by stooges from Moscow. The industrialisation of Tajikistan was only undertaken following WWII, after the loss of much of European Russia's manufacturing capacity. But living standards remained low and in the late 1980s Tajikistan endured 25% unemployment, plus the lowest level of education and the highest infant-mortality rate in the Soviet Union.

For most of the Soviet era Tajikistan was heavily reliant on imports from the rest of the Union – not just food, but fuel and many other standard commodities. When the Soviet trading system started to disintegrate, Tajikistan was left badly equipped to fend for itself, and dangerously unbalanced.

## From Civil Unrest...

In the mid-1970s, Tajikistan began to feel the impact of the rise of Islamic forces in neighbouring Afghanistan, particularly in the south around Kurgan-Tyube (Kurgonteppa). This region had been neglected by Dushanbe's ruling communist elite, who were mainly drawn from the prosperous northern city of Leninabad (now Khojand). In 1976 the underground Islamic Renaissance Party (IRP) was founded, gathering popular support as a rallying point for Tajik nationalism. Although in 1979 there had been demonstrations in opposition to the

### DIGGING UP THE PAST

Southern and Central Tajikistan is amazingly rich in archaeological sites. There's little to actually see today but finds from the region are displayed in museums across the world.

The site of **Sarazm**, west of Penjikent, ranks as one of the oldest cities in Central Asia. Finds include a fire temple and the grave of a wealthy woman dubbed the 'Queen of Sarazm', dating from the 4th-century BC.

The Sogdian site of **Bunjikat**, further north near Shakhristan, was the 8th-century capital of the kingdom of Ushrushana, and is noteworthy for a famous Sogdian mural depicting a wolf suckling twins, in a clear echo of the Roman legend of Romulus and Remus.

The ancient site of **Kobadiyan** (7th- to 2nd-centuries BC) in southern Tajikistan is famed as the location for the discovery of the Oxus Treasure, a stunning 2500-year-old Archaemenid treasure-trove that is now in the British Museum (www.thebritishmuseum.ac.uk/compass/, search for 'Oxus Treasure').

Nearby is the ruined Greco-Bactrian temple of **Takht-i-Sangin**, where a famous ivory portrait of Alexander the Great (see p362) was discovered. It was close to here that Alexander crossed the Oxus in 329 BC.

South of Kurgonteppa is the 7th to 8th-century **Adjina Tepe** (Witches Hill), where in 1966 archaeologists unearthed Central Asia's largest surviving Buddha statue (see p362).

Other nearby archaeological sites include the 9th- to 11th-century citadel and palace of Khulbak at Khurbanshaid, 7km from Vose, not far from Kulyab.

Explore the website www.afc.ryukoku.ac.jp/tj for more on these and other sites.

### THE OPIUM HIGHWAY

Central Asia is a major transit route for the global trade in heroin, most of which comes from Afghanistan, the world's largest producer of opium and supplier of 90% of Europe's heroin habit. Most of the illicit trade crosses the porous border between Tajik and Afghan Badakhshan. In fact, Tajikistan seizes roughly 80% of all drugs captured in Central Asia and stands third worldwide in seizures of opiates (heroin and raw opium).

Not all of the drugs leave the region; addiction in Central Asia has mushroomed in recent years and in its wake has come one of the world's fastest growing rates of HIV infection.

Warlords and criminal gangs control most of the business, although the army, police and border guards all have fingers in the opium bowl. Drugs have even turned up in Kazakh diplomatic bags and on Russian military flights. In 2005 a homemade aircraft (a parachute with a motor attached!) was shot down flying above the border with Tajikistan with 18kg of heroin. Drug money has financed everything from arms for Tajikistan's civil war to the new villas you see lining the Varzob valley north of Dushanbe.

In modern Central Asia, camel caravans of silks and spices have been replaced, it seems, by Ladas packed with heroin. The Silk Road has become an opium highway.

Soviet invasion of Afghanistan, the first serious disturbances were in early 1990 when it was rumoured that Armenian refugees were to be settled in Dushanbe, which was already short on housing. This piece of Soviet social engineering sparked riots, deaths and the imposition of a state of emergency. Further opposition parties emerged as a result of the crackdown.

On 9 September 1991, following the failed coup in Moscow and declarations of independence by other Central Asian states, Tajikistan proclaimed itself an independent republic. Elections were held 10 weeks later and the Socialist Party (formerly the Communist Party of Tajikistan or CPT) candidate, Rakhmon Nabiev, was voted into power. There were charges of election rigging but what really riled the opposition was Nabiev's apparent consolidation of an old-guard, Leninabad-oriented power base that refused to accommodate any other of the various clan-factions that make up the Tajik nation.

Sit-in demonstrations on Dushanbe's central square escalated to violent clashes and, in August 1992, anti-government demonstrators stormed the presidential palace and took hostages. A coalition government was formed, but sharing power between regional clans, religious leaders and former communists proved impossible and Tajikistan descended into civil war.

## ...To Civil War

During the Soviet era, Moscow managed to hold the lid on a pressure-cooker of clan-based tensions that had existed long before Russian intervention. Tajikistan's various factions – Leninabadis from the north, Kulyabis from the south and their hostile neighbours from Kurgan-Tyube, Garmis from the east, and Pamiris from the mountainous province of Gorno-Badakhshan (GBAO) – had all been kept in line under Soviet rule. When independence came, the lid blew off. Civil war ensued and the clan struggles claimed around 60,000 lives and made refugees of over half a million.

As a way out of the internecine conflict Imomali Rakhmanov was chosen from the Kulyab district to front the government. The Kulyabis simply fought their way to power with a scorched-earth policy against their Islamic-leaning rivals from the Garm Valley and Kurgan-Tyube.

Rakhmanov was sworn in as president after a disputed election and an all-out assault from Kulyabi and Leninabad forces to get him into office. Kulyabi forces, led by Sanjak Safarov (who had previously spent 23 years in prison for murder), then embarked on an orgy of ethnic cleansing. Anyone found in Dushanbe with a Badakhshan or Khatlon ID card was shot on the spot.

The November 1992 elections did nothing to resolve the conflict (the opposition in exile refused to take part in the voting) and the Islamic opposition continued the war from bases in the Karategin region and Afghanistan, echoing the *basmachi* campaigns of 70 years earlier. An economic blockade of Badakhshan led to famine in the Pamirs during 1992–93.

Rakhmanov was propped up by Russian forces, which had been drawn into the conflict as de facto protectors of the Kulyab regime. Russian troops controlled some 50 military posts along the Afghan border. 'Everyone must realise', Boris Yeltsin said in a 1993 pronouncement, 'that this is effectively Russia's border, not Tajikistan's.' Russia (and later Uzbekistan) feared that if Tajikistan fell to Islamic rebels, Uzbekistan would be next.

In late 1994 a second presidential election was held, in which Rakhmanov romped to victory. This surprised no-one, as he was the only candidate. Opposition parties had been outlawed.

### Precarious Peace

A bad peace is better than a good war.

*Khatlon villager*

Pressure on Rakhmanov from Russia (and the faltering loyalty of his own commanders) forced the government to negotiate with the opposition, which was then in exile in Iran. Finally, in December 1996 a ceasefire was declared, followed up by a peace agreement on 27 June 1997. The agreement set up a power-sharing organisation, the National Reconciliation Commission (CNR), headed by the opposition leader Sayid Abdullo Nuri, which guaranteed the United Tajik Opposition (UTO) 30% of the seats in a coalition government in return for a laying down of arms.

When the dust settled, it was clear that independence and civil war had proven catastrophic for Tajikistan, which had always been the poorest of the Soviet republics. During the civil war Tajikistan's gross domestic product (GDP) per capita shrank 70% to US$330, plunging it from part of a global superpower to one of the 30 poorest countries in the world within a decade. Two complete harvests were missed and the region suffered major subsequent droughts. Standards of living in the country had gone back 20 years or more.

Spirits were lifted in September 1998 when the Aga Khan, spiritual leader of the Islamic Ismaili sect, visited GBAO. The Aga Khan Foundation had effectively fed the Pamir region since the start of the civil war and some 80,000 Pamiris came out to hear their spiritual leader tell them to lay down their arms, while another 10,000 Afghan Tajiks strained their ears across the river in Afghanistan.

## CURRENT EVENTS

Though the Tajik economy remains on life support, health and education standards remain low and life in the region remains hard, Tajiks are savouring the stability and prospects for the near future are improving.

The million or so Tajiks who work abroad, mostly in Russia, send back around US$200 million a year in remittances, the equivalent of the Tajik national budget. Largely thanks to this injection of cash, the economy is finally picking up, with annual growth rates hovering between 6% and 10%.

That said, the annual national budget of Tajikistan remains less than the budget of a major Hollywood movie, and 40% of that is required for the upkeep of the military presence on the Afghan border. Over 70% of Tajikistan's people live on less than US$2 per day. The legal minimum wage was only recently doubled to just over US$4 per month.

### POST-SOVIET NAME CHANGES

Few cartographical changes accompanied the transformation of the Tajikistan Soviet Socialist Republic to the independent Republic of Tajikistan. Dushanbe was once Stalinabad but shed that unfashionable name in the 1950s. Only with the demise of communism did Tajikistan's second city, Leninabad, revert to its ancient name of Khojand, and the *oblast* (administrative division) of which it is the capital became Sughd. Ordjonikdzeabad (25km east of Dushanbe), named for the Georgian who imposed Bolshevism in the Caucasus, reverted to Kofarnikhon. Ura-Tyube became Istaravshan. Komsomolbad reverted to Darband.

Up in the mountains, Tajikistan's Pik Kommunizma became Koh-i-Samani, Pik Lenin became Koh-i-Istiqlal (Independence Peak, though it's still widely referred to as Pik Lenin) and Revolution Peak became Koh-i-Abu Ali Ibn Sino (Avicenna).

Tajik was made the state language in 1989, though Russian was reintroduced as the second state language in 1995. Street signs in Dushanbe now sport the Tajik forms *kuchai* (street), *khiyeboni* (avenue) and *maydoni* (square).

**RECOMMENDED READING**

The new *Odyssey Guide to Tajikistan* (2007), by Robert Middleton and Huw Thomas, is a literate and detailed guide to Tajikistan.

*Travel through Tajikistan* (2006), by Fozilov Nurullo, is a locally produced guidebook with some useful background information on Tajikistan. It's only available in Dushanbe.

For something more old school, George Curzon's *The Pamirs and the Source of the Oxus* is a classic text delivered to the Royal Geographical Society in 1896 and recently reprinted in paperback by Elibron Classics. It's full of lovely detail on the Pamir region.

Elibron have also republished TE Gordon's 1876 *The Roof of the World* and John Wood's 1872 *A Journey to the Source of the River Oxus*.

Fans of antique travel literature will also like Anna Louise Strong's *The Road to the Grey Pamir*, detailing a journey on horseback in 1930 from Osh to Murgab, but it's hard to find.

More up-to-date (2006), *Tajikistan in the New Central Asia: Geopolitics, Great Power Rivalry and Radical Islam* by Lena Jonson (IB Tauris), is a scholarly, and modern look at Tajikistan.

Frank Bliss' *Social and Economic Change in the Pamirs* is a encyclopedic but fascinating examination of Badakhshan: from its history, culture and complex ethnography to the effect on the region of the collapse of the USSR and the civil war. It's a pricey tome, so try to track it down through a library.

Presently, the country exists on a drip-feed of credits and loans. Tajikistan has been forced to mortgage its future to the Kremlin, giving Russia half of the shares in the Nurek hydroelectric plant, as well as controlling interests in other national industries.

Thanks to the very passable 1300km border with Afghanistan, Tajikistan is one of the world's major drug conduits. Tajik customs officials make 80% of all drug seizures in Central Asia and the country is the world's third-largest seizer of heroin and opium, seizing literally tonnes of the stuff every year. Up to 50% of Tajikistan's economic activity is thought to be somehow linked to the drug trade.

Since 1992 Tajikistan has been a parliamentary republic with legislative power vested in an elected 230-member parliament, or *oli majlis*. The political landscape remains heavily clan-based. The parliament is fronted by the president, Imomali Rakhmanov, who won a third term in 2006 in an election that international observers described as 'neither free nor fair'. A referendum in 2003 gave him the green light to run for another two terms, until 2020.

## PEOPLE

It's only last century that 'Tajik' came to denote a distinct nationality. Despite their predominantly Persian ancestry, there has been so much intermarrying that it's often hard to distinguish Tajiks from their Turkic neighbours (Tajik skullcaps closely resemble Uzbeks, adding to the confusion). Pure-blooded Tajiks tend to have thin European-looking faces, with wide eyes and a Roman nose.

There are some recognisable ethnic subdivisions among the Tajiks. As well as the Pamiris (p375), there are dwindling numbers of Yaghnabis (or Jagnobis), direct descendants of the ancient Sogdians, in the mountain villages of the Zerafshan (Zeravshan) Valley. Sogdian, the lingua franca of the Silk Road and last widely spoken in the 8th century, is still spoken there.

About 65% of Tajikistanis are Tajik, 25% are Uzbek, 3.5% are Russian and 6.5% are other groups. Much of the population of the eastern Pamirs are Kyrgyz, who arrived here from the Alay valley in the 18th and 19th centuries.

For more information on the people of Tajikistan, see p60.

### Population

Population figures are only approximate because the demographics of Tajikistan have been fluctuating wildly since the civil war of the 1990s. In addition to the 60,000 or so killed, more than half a million Tajiks were displaced from their homes during the war, while the majority of the country's 600,000 Russians headed north. Another 60,000 Tajiks fled to Afghanistan, joining the 4.4 million Tajiks who have lived there since the southern region of Badakhshan was annexed by Kabul in the 18th century. One in four families now has a family member working abroad.

Tajikistan exemplifies the demographic complexity of the Central Asian republics. Its 4.4 million Tajiks constitute only 65% of the country's population, and fewer than half of the world's Tajiks (there are more Tajiks in Afghanistan than Tajikistan, and large groups also live in Uzbekistan, Kazakhstan and China's Xinjiang province). Some 25% of Tajikistan's population are Uzbeks, with whom there is considerable ethnic rivalry. Average family sizes remain high, with seven or eight kids the norm. Over 40% of Tajikistan's population is under the age of 14.

## RELIGION

About 80% of Tajikistan's people are Sunni Muslim, though most Pamiris are Ismailis and follow the Aga Khan (p377). Between 1990 and 1992, over 1000 new mosques were built in Tajikistan.

In the late 1990s radical Islamist organisations such as the Islamic Movement of Uzbekistan (IMU) used Tajikistan (particularly the Sangvor and Tavildara Valleys) as a base for armed incursions into Kyrgyzstan and Uzbekistan, with the implicit support of the Tajik government and Russian military. These organisations have largely lost relevance with the removal of support from the Taliban and Al-Qaeda in Afghanistan, though the recent arrests of members of the largely peaceful Hizb-ut-Tahir movement show the continued support for Islam as a political force.

## ARTS

When Tajikistan was hived off from Uzbekistan in 1929, the new nation-state was forced to leave behind all its cultural baggage. The new Soviet order set about providing a replacement pantheon of arts, introducing modern drama, opera and ballet, and sending stage-struck Tajik aspirants to study in Moscow and Leningrad. The policy paid early dividends and the 1940s are considered a golden era of Tajik theatre. A kind of Soviet fame came to some Tajik novelists and poets, such as Mirzo Tursunzade and Sadruddin Ayni, the latter now remembered more as a deconstructor of national culture because of his campaign to eliminate all Arabic expressions and references to Islam from the Tajik tongue.

Since independence, ancient figures from the region's Persian past have been revived in an attempt to foster a sense of national identity. The most famous of these figures is the 10th-century philosopher-scientist Abu Ali ibn-Sina, author of two of the most important books in the history of medicine. He was born in Bukhara when it was the seat of the Persian Samanids, to whom Rudaki, now celebrated as the father of Persian verse (and with a tomb outside Penjikent in Tajikistan), served as court poet. Tajiks also venerate Firdausi, a poet and composer of the *Shah Nama (Book of Kings)*, the Persian national epic, and Omar Khayyam, of *Rubaiyat* fame, both born in present-day Iran but at a time when it was part of an empire that also included the territory now known as Tajikistan. Similar veneration goes out to Kamalddin Bekzod (1455–1535), a brilliant miniaturist painter from Herat.

Pamiris have a particular veneration for Nasir Khusraw (1004–1088), an Ismaili philosopher, poet and preacher who worked in Merv and was exiled to Badakhshan, where he wrote his *Safarname,* the account of his extensive seven-year travels throughout the Muslim world.

Tajik Persian poetry is fused with music by *hafiz* (bard musicians). *Falak* is a popular form of melancholic folk music, often sung a cappella. Music and dance is particularly popular among the Pamiri and Kulyabi.

## ENVIRONMENT

### The Land

At 143,100 sq km, landlocked Tajikistan is Central Asia's smallest republic. More than half of it lies 3000m or more above sea level. The central part encompasses the southern spurs of the Tian Shan and Pamir Alay ranges, while the southeast comprises the Pamir plateau. Within these ranges are some of Central Asia's highest peaks, including Koh-i-Somoni (former Pik Kommunizma) at 7495m. The Fedchenko Glacier, a 72km-long glacial highway frozen to the side of Koh-i-Somani, is one of the longest glaciers in the world outside of the polar region and, at 800m thick, allegedly contains more water than the Aral Sea.

The western third of the country is lowland plain, bisected to the north by the Hissar, Zerafshan (Zeravshan) and Turkestan ranges – western extensions of the Tian Shan that continue into Uzbekistan. The mountain peaks with their sun-melted icecaps are the source of a fibrous network of fast-flowing streams, many of which empty into Tajikistan's two major rivers – the Syr-Darya (Jaxartes River), rising in the Fergana Valley and flowing through Khojand, and the Amu-Darya, formed from the confluence of two Pamir rivers, the Vakhsh and the Pyanj.

Together, the Amu-Darya and the Pyanj mark most of the country's 1200km border with Afghanistan. Tajikistan's other borders are much less defined: in the east, 430km of border with China meanders through Pamir valleys, while to the north and west are the seemingly random jigsaw borders with Kyrgyzstan and Uzbekistan.

For administrative purposes the country is divided into three *viloyat* (provinces): Sughd (Khojand), Khatlon (Kurgonteppa) and the 60,000-sq-km autonomous mountain region of Kohistani Badakhshan (Gorno Badakhshan Autonomous Oblast, or GBAO), with much of the central region (including the Garm Valley) ruled directly from Dushanbe.

Tajikistan's territory also includes the strange northern enclave of Vorukh, stranded inside Kyrgyzstan.

### Wildlife

Tajikistan's impressive megafauna includes snow leopards (perhaps 200 or so), a dozen brown bears, between 5000 and 10,000 Marco Polo sheep and around 12,000 ibex. The best place to see Marco Polo sheep *(arkhar* in Kyrgyz) and ibex *(echki* or *kyzyl kyik)* is around Jarty-Gumbaz in the eastern Pamir, particularly after December, when they come to lower altitudes for the rut.

Poaching (largely by border guards) is a major problem. Marco Polo sheep numbers have fallen 300% since independence and down 800% from the 1960s. Marco Polo sheep meat is sold openly in Murgab bazaar, for less per kilo than mutton.

### Environmental Issues

The 2.6 million hectare Tajik (Pamir) National Park was founded in 1992 as the largest in Central Asia, covering a whopping 18% of Tajikistan. That's the good news. The bad news is that the park exists only on paper, with only four employees to police and administer it (and none stationed inside the park).

The lack of burnable fuel in the eastern Pamir has led to the disappearance of the slow-growing (and fast-burning) *tersken* bush within a radius of 100km from Murgab, adding to desertification in the treeless region. The population of Murgab is still considered environmentally unsustainable. Several organisations are trying to introduce solar ovens but progress has been slow.

Recent reports indicate that Tajikistan's glaciers have started to retreat as a result of global warming. The area of Fedchenko Glacier has shrunk by 10% in recent years.

## FOOD & DRINK

For a general rundown of common Central Asian dishes, see p82.

Tajik dishes include *nahud sambusa* (chickpea samosas) or *nahud shavla* (chickpea porridge). Tajiks also prepare many bean and milk soups, while *oshi siyo halav* is a unique herb soup. *Tuhum barak* is a tasty egg-filled ravioli coated with sesame-seed oil. *Chakka* (*yakka* to Tajik speakers around Samarkand and Bukhara) is curd mixed with herbs, and delicious with flat-bread. *Kurtob* is a wonderful rural dish of bread, yogurt, onion and *cilantro* (coriander) in a creamy sauce. In Badakhshan you might try *borj* – a meat and grain mix that resembles savoury porridge.

In Kyrgyz yurts, expect lots of tea, yogurt, *barsook* (fried bits of dough) and *kaimak* (cream). If you're lucky you might get *beshbarmak* (noodles and mutton) or *oromo,* a rolled-up steamed pastry flavoured with meat and butter.

*Shir chai* is a salty, soupy brew of tea with goats' milk, salt and butter that makes a popular breakfast in the Pamirs. It sits somewhere between milk tea and Tibetan yak butter tea and is guaranteed to put hairs on your chest. Rice pudding *(shir gurch* in Kyrgyz; *shir brench* in Tajik) is another popular Pamiri breakfast choice.

Both Hissar and Dushanbe brew their own beer, though bottled Russian imports like the Baltika range are the most common. Obi Zulol and Pamir are the best brands of fizzy mineral water, bottled in Istaravshan and Khorog. Dushanbe and even Khorog manufacture their own sickly sweet colas and luminous lemonades; the best of these is RC (Royal Crown) Cola.

# DUSHANBE ДУШАНБЕ

☎ 37 / pop 600,000 / elev 800m

With a cool backdrop of mountains, lazy tree-lined avenues and pastel-hued neoclassical buildings, Dushanbe is Central Asia's best-looking capital – especially now that the bullet holes have been plastered over. Once scary and

 

**DUSHANBE MUST-SEES**

**Museum of National Antiquities** (p362) Stand face to face with Central Asia's largest surviving Buddha and the ivory portrait of Alexander the Great.

**Hissar** (p367) Get out of the city on a half-day excursion to the fort, museum and medressas here.

**Restaurants** (p364) Savour the big-city comforts of the city's Turkish, Georgian, Iranian and even Ecuadorian restaurants before heading to the survival cuisine of the mountains.

**Rudaki** Stroll leisurely past the pastel-coloured buildings and tree-lined cafés of Dushanbe's main drag.

more than a little dangerous a decade ago, the Tajik capital is currently blossoming and is now one of Central Asia's most pleasant cities, if just a little dull.

## HISTORY

Although the remains of a settlement dating to the 5th century BC have been found here, modern-day Dushanbe has little history beyond last century. As recently as 80 years ago, Dushanbe (then spelled Dushyambe) was a small, poor village known chiefly for its weekly bazaar (Dushanbe means Monday in Tajik).

In 1920 the last emir of Bukhara took refuge in Dushanbe, fleeing from the advancing Bolsheviks. He was forced to continue his flight early the next year as the Red Army added the Tajik settlement to the expanding Bolshevik empire. The Russian hold was shaken off for a spell when in 1922 Enver Pasha and his *basmachi* fighters liberated Dushanbe as part of their crusade to carve out a pan-Islamic empire (see the boxed text, p367), but following his death in a gun battle in southern Tajikistan, Bolshevik authority was quickly reasserted.

With the arrival of the railroad in 1929, Dushanbe was made capital of the new Soviet Tajik republic and renamed Stalinabad – a name it bore until the historical reinvention of the Khrushchev era. The region was developed as a cotton- and silk-processing centre and tens of thousands of people were relocated here, turning the rural village into a large, urban administrative and industrial centre. The city's numbers were further swollen by Tajik émigrés from Bukhara and Samarkand, which had been given over to Uzbek rule.

After almost 70 uneventful years of relative peace, if not prosperity, 1990 saw festering nationalistic sentiments explode into rioting, triggered by rumoured plans to house Armenian refugees in Dushanbe. Twenty-two people died in clashes with the militia.

There were further demonstrations in the autumn of 1991, organised by opposition factions dissatisfied with the absence of political change in Tajikistan. The statue of Lenin that stood opposite the parliament building disappeared overnight, and young bearded men and veiled women took to the streets of Dushanbe, calling for an Islamic state.

During the civil war the city remained a capital of chaos. It was kept under a dusk-to-dawn curfew, with armed gangs controlling the roads in and out, and lawless brigands patrolling the streets. Shoot-outs between rival clans were common and most Russians fled the country. Random acts of violence continued through the 1990s (such as the storming of the Presidential Palace in 1997), but by 2002 the situation had stabilised enough to lift the citywide curfew. These days Dushanbe is savouring its peace and on the upswing.

## ORIENTATION

The focus of Dushanbe is the wide, tree-lined prospekt (avenue) Rudaki, which runs north from the train station on Maydoni Ayni (*maydoni* means square). Roughly central on Rudaki is Maydoni Azadi, surrounded by government buildings and now under the stern gaze of a sorcererlike Shah Ismail Samani, the founder of the Samanid dynasty. His statue ousted Lenin's from the top spot in 1999 on the 1100th anniversary of the Samanid dynasty.

Almost everything useful or interesting is within a 15-minute walk of here. The exception is the main bus station, which is some 3km away on kuchai Ibn Sina in the western part of town. The airport is in the southeastern suburbs of the city, 5km from the centre, along Ahmad Donish.

## INFORMATION

### Cultural Centres

**Bactria Centre** (☎ 227 02 57; dushanbe.ecotourism@acted.org; Mirzo Rizo 22; 🕑 8am-5pm Mon-Sun) The 3rd-floor of this language and cultural centre houses an ecotourism centre which offers information on community-based tourism projects in the Pamirs and homestays in Dushanbe. Contact Ruhafzo. It also houses the Handicraft Centre (see p365). If you fancy chatting to Tajik students, come along for English hour every Wednesday at 4.30pm.

TAJIKISTAN

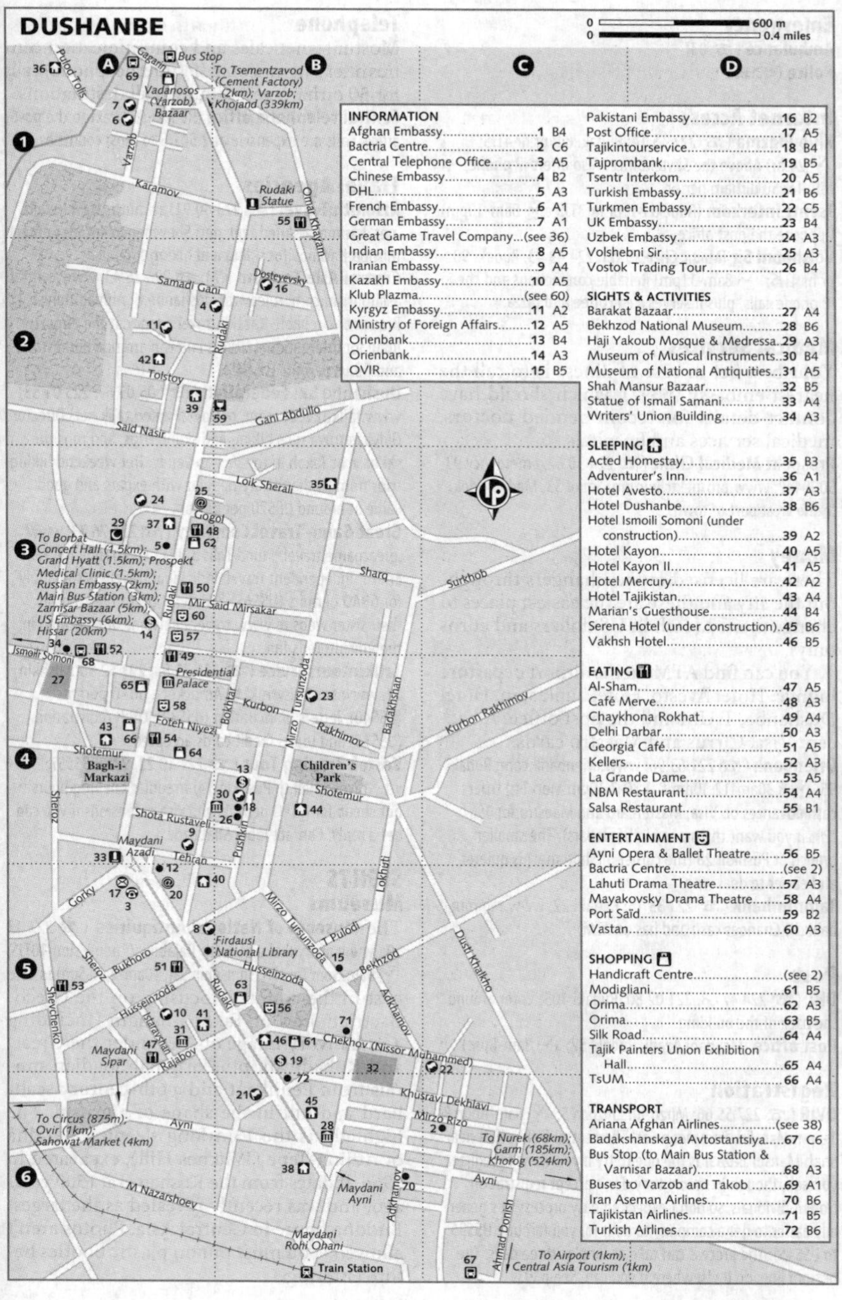
DUSHANBE
0 600 m
0 0.4 miles
A
B
C
D
1
2
3
4
5
6
INFORMATION
Afghan Embassy....1 B4
Bactria Centre....2 C6
Central Telephone Office....3 A5
Chinese Embassy....4 B2
DHL....5 A3
French Embassy....6 A1
German Embassy....7 A1
Great Game Travel Company....(see 36)
Indian Embassy....8 A5
Iranian Embassy....9 A4
Kazakh Embassy....10 A5
Klub Plazma....(see 60)
Kyrgyz Embassy....11 A2
Ministry of Foreign Affairs....12 A5
Orienbank....13 B4
Orienbank....14 A3
OVIR....15 B5
Pakistani Embassy....16 B2
Post Office....17 A5
Tajikintourservice....18 B4
Tajprombank....19 B5
Tsentr Interkom....20 A5
Turkish Embassy....21 B6
Turkmen Embassy....22 C5
UK Embassy....23 B4
Uzbek Embassy....24 A3
Volshebni Sir....25 A3
Vostok Trading Tour....26 B4
SIGHTS & ACTIVITIES
Barakat Bazaar....27 A4
Bekhzod National Museum....28 B6
Haji Yakoub Mosque & Medressa....29 A3
Museum of Musical Instruments....30 B4
Museum of National Antiquities....31 A5
Shah Mansur Bazaar....32 B5
Statue of Ismail Samani....33 A4
Writers' Union Building....34 A3
SLEEPING
Acted Homestay....35 B3
Adventurer's Inn....36 A1
Hotel Avesto....37 A3
Hotel Dushanbe....38 B6
Hotel Ismoili Somoni (under construction)....39 A2
Hotel Kayon....40 A5
Hotel Kayon II....41 A5
Hotel Mercury....42 A2
Hotel Tajikistan....43 A4
Marian's Guesthouse....44 B4
Serena Hotel (under construction)....45 B6
Vakhsh Hotel....46 B5
EATING
Al-Sham....47 A5
Café Merve....48 A3
Chaykhona Rokhat....49 A4
Delhi Darbar....50 A3
Georgia Café....51 A5
Kellers....52 A3
La Grande Dame....53 A5
NBM Restaurant....54 A4
Salsa Restaurant....55 B1
ENTERTAINMENT
Ayni Opera & Ballet Theatre....56 B5
Bactria Centre....(see 2)
Lahuti Drama Theatre....57 A3
Mayakovsky Drama Theatre....58 A4
Port Saïd....59 B2
Vastan....60 A3
SHOPPING
Handicraft Centre....(see 2)
Modigliani....61 B5
Orima....62 A3
Orima....63 B5
Silk Road....64 A4
Tajik Painters Union Exhibition Hall....65 A4
TsUM....66 A4
TRANSPORT
Ariana Afghan Airlines....(see 38)
Badakshanskaya Avtostantsiya....67 C6
Bus Stop (to Main Bus Station & Varnisar Bazaar)....68 A3
Buses to Varzob and Takob....69 A1
Iran Aseman Airlines....70 B6
Tajikistan Airlines....71 B5
Turkish Airlines....72 B6
Bus Stop
To Tsementzavod (Cement Factory) (2km); Varzob; Khojand (339km)
Vadanosos (Varzob) Bazaar
Pulod Tolis
Gagarin
Varzob
Karamov
Rudaki Statue
Omar Khayam
Samadi Gani
Dosteyevsky
Rudaki
Tolstoy
Gani Abdullo
Said Nasir
Loik Sherali
Gogol
To Borbat Concert Hall (1.5km); Grand Hyatt (1.5km); Prospekt Medical Clinic (1.5km); Russian Embassy (2km); Main Bus Station (3km); Zarnisar Bazaar (5km); US Embassy (6km); Hissar (20km)
Sharq
Surkhob
Mir Said Mirsakar
Ismoil Somoni
Presidential Palace
Tursunzoda
Badakhshan
Kurbon
Kurbon Rakhimov
Bokhtar
Foteh Niyezi
Rakhimov
Shotemur
Bagh-i-Markazi
Children's Park
Sheroz
Shota Rustaveli
Pushkin
Maydani Azadi
Tehran
Lokhuti
Gorky
Mirzo Tursunzoda
T Pulodi
Firdausi National Library
Husseinzoda
Bekhzod
Bukhoro
Dusti Khalkho
Adkhamov
Shevchenko
Istaravshan
Rajabov
Maydani Sipar
Chekhov (Nissor Muhammed)
Khusravi Dekhlavi
Mirzo Rizo
To Circus (875m); Ovir (1km); Sahowat Market (4km)
Ayni
To Nurek (68km); Garm (185km); Khorog (524km)
M Nazarshoev
Maydani Ayni
Maydani Rohi Ohani
Train Station
Ahmad Donish
To Airport (1km); Central Asia Tourism (1km)

TAJIKISTAN

### Emergency

**Ambulance** (☎ 03)
**Police** (☎ 02)

### Internet Access

**Klub Plazma** (☎ 227 15 14; Rudaki 84; pr hr 4TJS; 24 hr) Above the Skytel office. Also offers IP phone calls for 50 dirham per hr.
**Tsentr Interkom** (Rudaki 81; pr hr 3TJS; 8am-10pm) Opposite the post office.
**Volshebni Sir** (Magic Cheese; ☎ 224 43 43; Rudaki 98; pr hr 4TJS; 8am-11pm) Reliable connections and cheap IP phone calls, plus it serves iced coffee and pizza.

### Medical Services

Your best bet in case of illness is to call the nearest embassy (p392), which should have contact details for recommended doctors, medical services and hospitals.
**Prospekt Medical Clinic** (☎ 224 30 62, emergency 93-5000447; www.prospektclinic.org; Sanoi 33, Medgorodok) In the west part of town.

### Money

There are licensed moneychangers throughout the city and these are the easiest places to change money (cash in US dollars and euros only).

You can find ATMs at the airport departure lounge, Hotel Avesto, Hotel Tajikistan, Hotel Dushanbe, TsUM and the post office. All accept Visa, Cirrus and Maestro cards.
**Orienbank** (☎ 221 63 96; www.orienbank.com; Rudaki 95; 8.30am-12.30pm & 1.30-3.30pm Mon-Fri) Offers cash advances on Visa, MasterCard and Maestro for 1% (2% if you want the money in US dollars). The smaller branch at Pushkin 28 (the corner of Shotemur) is quieter and easier to deal with.
**Tajprombank** (☎ 221 33 15; Rudaki 22; www.tajprombank.tj) Changes cash and has an ATM.

### Post

**DHL** (☎ 224 47 68, 221 02 80; Rudaki 105) Enter around the back of the building.
**Post office** (Maydani Azadi, Rudaki 57; 8am-8pm)

### Registration

**OVIR** (☎ 227 55 66; Mirzo Tursunzoda 5; 8am-noon & 1-5pm Mon-Fri, 8am-noon Sat) The central OVIR office near Shah Mansur Bazaar is the one to try if you want to register yourself, though in theory they don't accept registration from individuals, so don't expect an easy process. It's generally easier to get a company to do it for you (around US$35 to US$45). The process can take as long as three days. The bottom line; do it elsewhere if you can. See p393.

### Telephone

Most internet cafés and communication centres offer international IP (internet phone) calls for 50 dirham per minute to all destinations.
**Central telephone office** (Rudaki 55) Next to the post office. Calls are expensive at 2.50TJS to most countries.

### Travel Agencies

**Azimuth Travel** (☎ 223 40 91; azimuth_travel@tajik.net, karimov@skifed.tajik.net; Shevchenko 46/58) Contact Dilshod Karimov for skiing and hiking trips.
**Central Asia Tourism** (CAT; ☎ 226 25 43; www.centralasiatourism.com, rules@cat-dushanbe.tj; Ahmad Donish 1) Branch of a reliable Kazakh travel agency at the airport; good for international tickets and can arrange homestays and GBAO permits (US$45).
**Dushanbe Ski Federation** (☎ 505 05 67, 223 01 33; www.tajiktraveller.com, petrova@skifed.tajik.net) Director Gulya Petrova runs hiking and skiing trips, and runs the ski base at Takob in the Varzob Valley. Her weekend hiking trips from Dushanbe are popular with expats and good value at around US$20 per person.
**Great Game Travel Company** (☎ 224 76 73; www.greatgame.travel; Pulod Tolis 5/11) Can arrange full tours and/or independent travel. Individual travellers can apply for GBAO permits (US$65) and flight ticket bookings at their sister website www.traveltajikistan.com. Located in the Adventurer's Inn.
**Tajikintourservice** (☎ 221 71 84, 223 52 80; Pushkin 22; www.tis.tj, tis@mkf.tj) Air tickets, GBAO permits (US$40), letters of invitation (US$30), OVIR registration (US$35) and tours. Credit cards accepted.
**Vostok Trading Tour** (☎ 221 10 22, 93-5555557; vtt_travel@mail.tj; Pushkin 14) Irregular opening hours but cheap for GBAO permits and visa extensions if you can get a reply. Contact Iqbol Shabozov.

## SIGHTS

### Museums

The **Museum of National Antiquities** (☎ 227 13 50; www.afc.ryukoku.ac.jp/tj; Rajabov 7; admission 10TJS; 9am-5pm Tue-Fri, 9am-4pm Sat, 10am-2pm Sun) is the best in the country, focusing on the Greco-Bactrian sites of Takht-i-Sangin (including a small ivory image of Alexander the Great) and Kobadiyan, plus original Sogdian murals from Penjikent and a 6th-century scabbard and hilt in the shape of a griffin. The highlight is the 13m-long sleeping Buddha of Adjina-Tepe (Witches Hill), excavated in 1966. It dates from the Kushan era, 1500 years ago, and was recently revealed as the largest Buddha figure in Central Asia. Photos aren't allowed. You must put on plastic booties before entering.

The **Bekhzod National Museum** (☎ 221 60 36; Rudaki 31; admission 6TJS; 9am-4pm Tue-Sat, 9am-3pm Sun), on a commanding site on Maydani Ayni, includes standard exhibits on natural history, art, ethnography and archaeology, but little English text. There are a few gems among the filler, including a lovely *minbar* (mosque pulpit) and *mihrab* (niche marking the direction of Mecca) from Istaravshan and a fine painting of Lenin meeting oppressed women of the world in Moscow's Red Square. There's a chilling reconstruction of a *zindan* (jail) on the 2nd floor. The top floor is given over to a Soviet/presidential collection – look for the alabaster carvings in the stairwell.

The **Museum of Musical Instruments** (☎ 223 32 10; Bokhtar 23; admission 5TJS, student 1TJS; 11am-6pm) is also known as the Gurminj Museum after the owner, Badakhshani actor Gurminj Zavkybekov. There are lots of antique instruments, including a *gijak* (fiddle), *doira* (tambourine/drum) and *rubab* (six-stringed mandolin), plus old photos and memorabilia. Ask about upcoming musical concerts. The museum is hidden across from the mosaic of justice and next to a district court.

### Mosques & Monuments

With its crescent-topped minaret and burnished golden dome, the **Haji Yakoub mosque** and **medressa**, just west of the Hotel Avesto, is one of the few visible manifestations of Islam in Dushanbe. The mosque is named after Haji Yakoub, a Tajik religious leader who fled to Afghanistan. Women are only allowed in the courtyard.

Tajikistan's Persian past is invoked in the façade of the **Writers' Union Building** (Ismoili Somoni). It's adorned like a medieval cathedral with saintly, sculpted-stone figures of Sadruddin Ayni, Omar Khayam, Firdausi and other writers from the Persian pantheon.

Dushanbe's most visible monument to nation-building is the rather kitsch **statue of Ismail Samani (Ismoili Somoni)**, the 10th-century Samanid ruler, occupying prime place on Maydani Azadi (Freedom Square). The monument replaced a much smaller statue of Lenin, which now stands in the Bagh-i-Markazi (Central Park).

### Markets

While not particularly exotic or Eastern in flavour, the large, covered **Barakat Bazaar** (Ismoili Somoni) is the centre of commercial activity in Dushanbe. It's north of the Hotel Tajikistan. The more interesting **Shah Mansur Bazaar** is a block north of Maydoni Ayni.

## SLEEPING

Dushanbe's accommodation options aren't fantastic. Homestays exist but are hard to track down. The main midrange and top-end choices are either ageing Soviet-era hotels or private modern mansions that cater mostly to local businessmen and visiting consultants.

### Budget

**Hotel Dushanbe** (☎ 221 96 55; Rudaki 7; dm US$10) The 4th- and 5th-floor rooms here are the cheapest in town, but are stiflingly hot in summer and the shared bathrooms are grotty. You may have to share a room.

**Acted Homestay** (☎ 918-689925; 178 Mirzo Tursunzoda; dm US$10) This simple local home has a pit toilet. Try also the Bactria Centre (see p360) for other possible homestays.

**Vakhsh Hotel** (☎ 227 81 88; Rudaki 24; s/d 38/75TJS, lux 140TJS) During the civil war this hotel was occupied by bands of bearded mujaheddin rebels and peppered with bullet holes, but don't worry it has since been renovated! Rooms are simple but clean and there's hot water. Try for a room with a balcony view of the Ayni Opera & Ballet Theatre. The *lux* suites aren't really worth the extra money.

our pick **Adventurer's Inn** (☎ 224 76 73; www.greatgame.travel, guesthouse@greatgame.travel; Pulod Tolis 5/11; s/d US$20/30) Despite a temperamental shower and the occasional grubby sheet, this is still our pick for the best sleeping spot in town. Major pluses are the shared bathroom (bigger than many hotel rooms), the excellent breakfasts (included in the price) and the relaxed vibe. There are only four rooms (named after Pamiri explorers), so book in advance, especially in July and August. The guesthouse is run by the Great Game Travel Company (see opposite), who can also arrange homestays (US$15 to US$20 per person), OVIR registration (US$45) and airport pickup (US$30). The guesthouse is hidden in the backstreets behind the Vadanosos (Varzob) Bazaar, across a bridge over the sewer pipe behind the German embassy (!), so can be tricky to find the first time.

### Midrange & Top End

**Hotel Dushanbe** (☎ 221 96 55; Rudaki 7; d US$25, lux US$50-80; ) The rooms capture the dubious charms of a 1970s Soviet apartment block but have nice leafy views of Maydani Ayni, at the southern end of Rudaki, and the bathrooms are surprisingly clean. The multiple arms of this peaceful monster are kept in check by a crack army of floor ladies in dressing gowns. There's an ATM and a bowling alley.

**Hotel Tajikistan** (☎ 221 62 62; Shotemur 22; s/d US$50/70, pol-lux $90, lux $130) English may be spoken in the reassuring lobby but everything else here is 100% Soviet and horribly overpriced. Rooms are small and come with hot water, a kettle and fridge. Only some rooms have air-con. South-facing rooms benefit from park views. A newly renovated wing should soon offer four-star rooms. Credit cards are accepted.

**Hotel Kayon** (☎ 221 62 29; kayon@tajnet.com; Bokhtar 7; s/d US$50/60, lux US$100/120; ) Live the nouveau riche life in comfortable modern rooms with breakfast, satellite TV and very clean bathrooms. There are two half-*lux* rooms and six *lux*. Not much English is spoken.

**Hotel Kayon II** (☎ 223 07 61; Kuybeshov 1; d US$80; ) Connected to Hotel Kayon, is much the same, but bigger and harder to find.

**Hotel Mercury** (☎ 224 44 91; www.hotel-mercury.tj; Tolstoy 9; r US$60-80, lux US$100-130; ) This privately-run hotel is probably the best value top-end place in town. The 20 spacious modern rooms come with satellite TV, computer and a kettle, and the reception can order in food from a variety of local restaurants. Credit cards aren't accepted but the hotel has its own ATM. There's even a kitschy garden waterfall.

**Hotel Avesto** (☎ 221 12 80; fax 224 62 84; Rudaki 105; s/d US$55/70, pol-lux US$90, lux US$100; ) Old-fashioned and chronically overpriced monster with a dreary Soviet feel, though some rooms have a fine view of the mosque and the suites are big enough to get lost in. The management must be waiting for the Brezhnev-era wallpaper to come back into style. The US and Russian embassies used to be here, so expect some rooms to be bugged. The 4th-floor business centre offers broadband internet.

**Marian's Guesthouse** (☎ 223 01 91, 93-5050089; marians@tajnet.com; Shotemur 67/1; per person US$80-100; ) Visiting consultants love this comfortable refuge, so reserve a room in advance (there are only eight) or you won't even get past the paranoid security guards. There's laundry, satellite TV, wi-fi internet, breakfast included and evening driver service. One room has its bathroom down the hall. The guesthouse is hard to find; head down the little alley just after the TV-station building (with its satellite dish) across from the Children's Park and look for the black-and-white gates. Contact Gulnura Razukova.

Three five-star hotels are under construction: the **Serena Hotel** (www.serenahotels.com) at the southern end of Rudaki; the Turkish-built **Hotel Ismoili Somoni** (Rudaki), further north on Rudaki; and a **Grand Hyatt** (Ismoili Somoni), located beside Komsomol Lake. All are due to open in 2008.

## EATING

### Cafés & Chaikhanas

The cheapest eats are to be found at the *chaikhanas* (teahouses) in the markets and in Bagh-i-Markazi (Central Park).

**Georgia Café** (☎ 227 13 26; Rudaki 29; mains 4-8TJS; lunch & dinner) Expand your culinary horizons with dishes like *khachapuri* (like a pizza with no toppings), *solyanka* (beef in tomato sauce) and *sacsivi* (cold chicken with nuts in cream sauce) in this intimate little café, washed down with a glass of imported Georgian wine.

**NBM Restaurant** (☎ 227 37 72; Rudaki 74; mains 5-11TJS; breakfast, lunch & dinner) Rivalling the Merve is this equally excellent Turkish café, with pleasant open-air seating overlooking Rudaki. The food is great, from *pide*s (Turkish-style pizzas) to excellent Iskender kebabs, and don't overlook the salad counter inside for some great aubergine dishes. Top it off with a sweet pastry rather than the unjustifiably popular homemade ice cream.

our pick **Café Merve** (☎ 221 94 09; Rudaki 92; mains 7-10TJS, snacks 2-4TJS; 7am-midnight) Our favourite eatery in town is this excellent bustling cafeteria, churning out Turkish kebabs, Turkish *börek* (little pies), pizza, salads, cakes and coffee, plus the best breakfast bets in town (feta cheese and olives). It can be hard to get a seat at lunchtime.

**Chaykhona Rokhat** (☎ 221 76 54; Rudaki 84; mains 7-10TJS; lunch & dinner) This unusual, Soviet-era attempt at a grand Persian-style *chaikhana* is great for people-watching but is perhaps better for a drink or snack than a meal. Lose yourself in the ceiling paintings while you wait for your waiter, as the service borders on neglect.

### Restaurants

**Kellers** (☎ 224 79 21; Ismoili Somoni 6; mains 6-14TJS; lunch & dinner) A mix of expats and local business people come for the house-brewed

German-style beer (2TJS for 0.5L), pleasant outdoor seating, and authentic Chinese and European food.

**Delhi Darbar** (☎ 224 66 11; delhi@tajik.net; Rudaki 88; mains 9-11TJS, Fri buffet 22TJS; 🕑 lunch & dinner) The self-proclaimed 'gateway of Indo-Fusion cuisine' offers popular Friday-night buffets. The food is more 'fusion' than Indian but it's not bad. Offers takeaway.

**Salsa Restaurant** (☎ 224 88 57; cnr Karamov & Omar Khayam; starters 4-9TJS, mains 10-14TJS) Just what you didn't expect in Dushanbe; an Ecuadorian restaurant serving everything from carrot cake and cocktails to Mexican and Italian dishes, complemented by a decent selection of wines and real coffee. This is definitely your only chance in Central Asia to try Ecuadorian *llapingachos* (fried potato and mozzarella cheese with peanut sauce).

**Al-Sham** (☎ 227 12 00; Rajabov 11; starters 6-10TJS, mains 12-15TJS; 🕑 lunch & dinner) This Lebanese and Syrian restaurant (Al-Sham is the Arabic name for Damascus) has sophisticated décor, with carved wooden grills and outdoor seating and there's an authentic range of *meze* (starters), plus all your main-dish grills and kebabs. There's no English menu, so take a knowledgeable friend if you don't know your *kubba* (croquettes of lamb and cracked wheat) from your *baba ganoush* (smoky eggplant dip).

**La Grande Dame** (☎ 935-010089; www.lagrandedamecafé.com; cnr Bukhoro & Shevchenko; mains 20-37TJS; 🕑 10am-10pm) If you need a slice of Western familiarity to go with your Lavazza coffee, try this cool French-style brasserie. The menu (available online) offers everything from lunchtime baguettes to salmon blinis with sour cream and caviar (19TJS) and a Sunday brunch with treats like French toast and eggs benedict.

## ENTERTAINMENT

Nightlife is a bit hit and miss in Dushanbe. You'll have to try to decipher the Cyrillic notice boards outside the following theatres to find out what's on.

**Ayni Opera & Ballet Theatre** (☎ 221 44 22; Rudaki 28) There's still life left in this classy theatre, with the odd opera and classical music concert, plus it has possibly the finest interior in Dushanbe. Tickets cost from 10TJS.

**Bactria Centre** (☎ 227 02 57; dushanbe.ecotourism@acted.org; Mirzo Rizo 22; 🕑 8am-5pm Mon-Sun) Screens foreign (and occasional Tajik) films every Tuesday and Thursday evenings at 6pm as well as occasional exhibitions and music concerts, and is a good place to tap into Dushanbe's cultural life. See also p360.

**Borbat Concert Hall** (☎ 221 59 58; Ismoili Somoni 26) Hosts occasional Tajik music concerts.

There are Tajik plays at the **Lahuti Drama Theatre** (☎ 221 37 51; Rudaki 86) and the nearby **Mayakovsky Drama Theatre** (☎ 221 31 32; Rudaki 76), the latter with a Russian emphasis.

There are several nightclubs, including **Port Saïd** (☎ 224 88 02; Rudaki 114; 🕑 Mon, Wed, Fri 9pm-4am; cover 10TJS) and the flashier **Vastan** (☎ 224 09 36; Rudaki 88; closed Mon; cover 10TJS). Most women in these clubs are prostitutes so solo female travellers should think twice about going alone.

## SHOPPING

**Barakat market** (Ismoili Somoni) The place to pick up an embroidered *tupi* (skullcap) for US$3, or a *chapan* (cloak) for around US$8. You'll also find plenty of sequined, gold-stitched trousers and colourful dresses.

**TsUM** (☎ 221 51 11; Rudaki 83; 🕑 8.30am-5pm Mon-Sat) The central department store has some souvenirs among the shampoo and mobile phones. Items include *suzani* embroidery, stripey cloaks, hats, Pamiri socks, ceramic Central Asian figures, musical instruments and lots of *ikat* silks, plus practical items such as camera batteries, memory sticks and print film.

**Handicraft Centre** (☎ 227 02 57; Mirzo Rozo 22) Also called Tillya Teppe, this shop in the Bactria Centre (see p360) sells a good range of Pamiri handicrafts from both the Yak House (see p388) and De Pamiri (see p382), as well as maps of the Pamirs (US$12), music CDs and museum guidebooks.

**Modigliani** (☎ 227 04 74; art_modigliani@yahoo.com; 4a Chekhov/Nissor Muhammed) A small shop crammed with carpets, paintings, embroidery, pottery and especially jewellery.

**Silk Road** (☎ 227 43 05; Shotemur 32; 🕑 9am-6pm Mon-Fri) One of the best souvenir shops, and particularly good for Tajik robes, embroidery, carpets, scarves and those hard-to-find postcards.

**Orima** (Rudaki) This well-stocked Turkish supermarket is useful for imported Western food, cold beer and toiletries. There are branches next to Café Merve and across from Ayni Opera & Ballet Theatre.

**Tajik Painters Union Exhibition Hall** (cnr Rudaki & Ismoili Somoni; 🕑 10am-5pm Mon-Fri, 10am-3pm Sat) Worth a visit for three floors of modern Tajik art, much of which is for sale.

## GETTING THERE & AWAY

### Air

Tajikistan Airlines (see below) theoretically has flights to Garm, Penjikent, Ayni, Isfara, Vanj (Vanch) and Kulyab, most of them in winter only. In practice the only reliable regular services are to Khojand (three daily, US$55) and Khorog (daily, US$60).

Tickets for the 8am flight to Khorog (see p382) only go on sale at the airport at 7am the day before the flight and are grounded at the first sign of bad weather. Note that you can pay for tickets with a credit card at the main booking office, though if your flight is cancelled it's much easier to get a refund if you paid with cash.

For details of regional and international flights, see p395.

#### AIRLINE OFFICES

**Ariana Afghan Airlines** (☎ 227 27 09; ariana5duy@yahoo.com; Rudaki 7; 🕒 8am-3.30pm Mon-Sat) Located in the lobby of the Hotel Dushanbe. Confirm any booking as soon as you arrive in Dushanbe. Cash only.

**Iran Aseman Airlines** (☎ 221 97 03; cnr Ayni & Adkhamov; 🕒 8.30am-1pm, 2-5pm Mon & Wed-Fri, 8.30am-2pm Sat) Weekly to Mashhad and Tehran.

**Tajikistan Airlines** (☎ 229 82 06; cnr Chekhov & Lokhuti; 🕒 8am-7pm)

**Turkish Airlines** (☎ 227 78 05; thydushanbe@mkf.tj; Rudaki 18; 🕒 8.30am-5.30pm Mon-Sat) Popular weekly flight to Istanbul.

### Minibus & Shared Taxi

Frequent minibuses to Varzob (50 dirham) and Takob (3TJS), and irregular buses to Khoja Obi Garm (4TJS) depart from the bus stand west of the Vadonasos (Varzon) Bazaar in the north of town.

Shared taxis to Penjikent, Ayni, Istaravshan and Khojand leave mornings from the Tsementzavod (Cement Factory) stand in the north of town. A seat to Khojand costs anywhere from 70TJS to 100TJS, depending on the price of fuel, though many drivers ask for much more than this. Choose your car with care as the mountain roads are rough. Take minibus 24 here from along Rudaki or from near the Vadonasos (Varzon) Bazaar.

Minibuses and 4WDs to Khorog (556km, 21 hours, 100TJS) leave from the *Badakshanskaya avtostansiya* (Badakhshan bus stand) transport yard on Ahmad Donish (the road to the airport), near the railway bridge. Minibuses 1 and 8 pass here. Shop around and try to get a front seat and expect to hang around for hours for the vehicle to fill up. See p382 for more.

Transport to Garm (six hours, 25TJS) leaves mornings from a lot 8km east of the centre on the road to Kofarnikhon. Take a taxi or any minibus heading east from the Hotel Dushanbe and ask to be dropped at *devyati kilometr* (ninth kilometre).

Routes to southern Tajikistan (Kurgonteppa, Kulyab and as far down as Dusti and Pyanj) leave in the mornings from the main bus station in the western suburbs, 3km from the centre, though some services also leave from the Sahowat market in the 63rd *mikrorayon* in the southwestern suburbs. Bus Nos 29 and 18 run to the main bus station from Ismail Somani, or take a taxi (7TJS).

## GETTING AROUND

Buses and private minibuses buzz around town. Bus 3 (50 dirham) and trolleybus 1 (40 dirham) shuttle up and down Rudaki, stopping frequently; others such as trolleybus No 11 and minibus Nos 8 and 22 turn off at Ismoili Somoni.

The airport is a quick ride on buses 2, 8 or 12, all caught from Rudaki and marked фурудгох *(furudgoh)*. A taxi will cost from 10TJS to 15TJS, a little more in the middle of the night.

## AROUND DUSHANBE

The main M34 winds north through the valley of the Varzob River, past dozens of villas built in recent years by the city's nouveau riche. There's no one particular place to head for but there are plenty of picturesque locations, including the **Varzob Gorge**, 56km out of Dushanbe. Minibuses run to the village of Varzob and the ski resort at Takob (60km from Dushanbe), where there is some nice summer hiking.

Popular hiking destinations in Varzob Valley include the pretty 20m **Gusgarf Waterfall**, a 2½-hour walk up a side valley 7km south of Varzob (31km from Dushanbe), and further north, the Khoja Obi Garm valley (behind the sanatorium of the same name) and Siama Valley.

For a day or weekend hike, expatriates recommend the **Karatag Valley**, 80km east of Dushanbe (turn north from the main road to Tursanzade at Shakhrinav). From the village

### ENVER PASHA & THE BASMACHI

As the Bolsheviks were celebrating their victory in Central Asia, a dashing, courageous Ottoman Turkish soldier named Enver Pasha was making his way towards Central Asia. A Young Turk, Enver had served as the Ottoman Empire's minister of war during WWI but was forced to flee Turkey after the empire's defeat in 1918. He wound up in Moscow, where he convinced the Soviet leader that he was just the person to deliver Central Asia and British India on a platter. In exchange, Lenin would help him win control of what was left of the Turkish empire.

Enver left Moscow for Bukhara in November 1921, ostensibly to make ready an army for Lenin. In reality he had already decided to jilt his benefactors and follow his own dream: to conquer and rule a pan-Turkic state, with Central Asia as its core.

In Bukhara, Enver (known locally as Anwar Pasho) made secret contact with leaders of the *basmachi* (local bands of Turkic and Tajik freedom fighters), whose grassroots support and intimate knowledge of the mountain geography had already proven to be worthy foes of the infant Red Army. Enver gave his Bolshevik hosts the slip and rode east from Bukhara, gathering 20,000 recruits. Enver styled himself 'Commander in Chief of All the Armies of Islam' and people flocked to his campaign as to a holy war.

Initial successes were stunning. Enver's small army took Dushanbe in February 1922 and by the spring they had captured much of the former emirate of Bukhara. Enraged, the Bolsheviks sent 100,000 additional troops in to crush him. Moscow also played a political trump card: it permitted the Islamic courts to reconvene, gave residents of the Fergana Valley a massive tax cut and returned confiscated land. Support for the *basmachi* faltered.

With his rural support drying up, and with the Emir of Afghanistan turning a cold shoulder, Enver refused to surrender. He and a small band of his closest officers set out for the mountains east of Dushanbe, never to emerge again.

On 4 August 1922, less than nine months after his portentous arrival at Bukhara, Enver Pasha met his end in legendary fashion. Accounts of the final moments differ but the most popular holds that he galloped headlong with sabre drawn at the head of a suicidal charge against the machine-gun fire of a Bolshevik ambush. Even the location of his death is unknown, suppressed by the Soviets in case it became a nationalist rallying point (locals now say the location is near Badjuan, southeast of Dushanbe). Had he succeeded in his grandiose vision, Enver Pasha would have been the first Turkic conqueror of all Turkestan since Timur. The fact that he made the attempt is fuel enough for myth.

The *basmachi* (who today would be called *mujaheddin*) fought on, scattered and dwindling, until the early 1930s. They are now the subject of intensive research by post-Soviet historians, the first generation able to commemorate the *basmachi* without fear of repression.

of Hakimi it's a two- to three-hour (6km) hike to Timur Dara Lake. **Payron Lake** is about 8km further north, up the main Karatag valley and then northeast up a side valley.

In the same region, the **Shirkent Valley** has tricky-to-see, difficult-to-reach and hard-to-forget dinosaur footprints a 90-minute hike from the trailhead. You'll need a guide to find them (see p362).

Dramatic but no longer picturesque, the 330m-high **Nurek Dam**, the world's highest hydroelectric dam, used to be a big favourite with Intourist. The dam is 80km east of Dushanbe, near the new town of Nurek. If you are travelling on your own, take a Nurek or Dangara bus from Dushanbe's main bus station.

## Hissar

☎3139

On a wide mountain-fringed plain, 30km west of Dushanbe, are the remains of an 18th-century **fortress** (🕑 8am-6pm; admission 1TJS), that was occupied until 1924 by Ibrahim Beg, the local henchman of the Emir of Bukhara. Once a *basmachi* stronghold (see the boxed text above), the fortress was destroyed by the Red Army and all that remains is a reconstructed stone gateway (Darvaza-i-Ark) in the cleavage of two massive grassy hillocks. A scramble up the hill on the right (the former residence of the *beg*, or landlord) offers excellent views. The fort is depicted on the 20TJS note. The ticket office hawks postcards and Tajik skullcaps.

In front of the fortress are two plain medressas, the 16th-century **Medressa-i-Kuhna** and the **Medressa-i-Nau**, a later overspill (*nau* means 'new'). The older medressa (facing the fortress gate) contains a small **museum** (8am-5pm; admission 3TJS), which has displays of clothing, ceramics and jewellery with English captions. Next door are the foundations of a caravanserai built in 1808 and, in front of the medressa, the remains of the town *taharatkhana* (bathhouse). Behind the medressas is the **mausoleum** of 16th-century Islamic teacher Makhdum Azam.

At the foot of the slopes around the fortress is a **holy spring** and pleasant chaikhana.

#### GETTING THERE & AWAY

To get here from Dushanbe, take bus 8 west on Ismoili Somoni to Zarnisar Bazaar, then a minibus (1.50TJS) or shared taxi (3TJS per seat) to Hissar (30 minutes). In Hissar bazaar take a shared taxi (1TJS per seat) across from the bazaar to the fort, some 7km further past cotton fields. Ask for the *qala* (fortress; *krepast* in Russian).

# NORTHERN TAJIKISTAN

Tajikistan in the north squeezes between Uzbekistan and Kyrgyzstan before oozing across the mouth of the Fergana Valley, the Uzbek heartland.

South of Istaravshan, the twin Turkestan and Zerafshan (Zeravshan) ranges sever northern Tajikistan from Dushanbe and the bulk of the country's landmass. The M34 connects the two parts of the country, crossing the 3378m Shakhristan Pass (from Khojand) and the 3372m Anzob Pass en route, and offering superb views. An Iranian-financed tunnel has been built under the Anzob Pass but flooding means that it isn't yet fully operational; until then the route is closed from November to May.

Possible stops en route are Iskander-Kul lake (see p373) and the heavily eroded 13.5m-tall Varz-i-Minor minaret in Ayni village, dating from the 10th-century.

## KHOJAND ХОДЖАНД/ХУЧАНД

**3422 / pop 164,500**

Khojand (or Khojent) is the capital of northern Tajikistan (Sughd province) and the second-largest city in the country. It's also one of Tajikistan's oldest towns, founded on the banks of the Syr-Darya by Alexander the Great as his easternmost outpost, Alexandria-Eskhate. In 1986 Khojand – or Leninabad as it was then named – celebrated its 2500th anniversary. Commanding (and taxing) the entrance to the Fergana Valley, Khojand built palaces, grand mosques and a huge citadel before the Mongols steamrolled the city into oblivion in the early 13th century. Today the economically booming town is of marginal interest to visitors, useful mainly as a springboard to the spectacular overland route south to Dushanbe.

Khojand, made up mostly of Uzbeks, has remained aloof from Dushanbe, although it always provided Tajikistan's Soviet elite. When President Nabiev, a Khojand man, was unseated in 1992 and Tajikistan appeared to be becoming an Islamic republic, Khojand (Leninabad) province threatened to secede. Secure behind the Fan Mountains, it managed to escape the ravages of the civil war and remains the wealthiest part of the country, producing two-thirds of Tajikistan's GDP, with 75% of the country's arable land and only one-third of the population.

### Information

**Agroinvestbank** (Lenina; www.agroinvestbank.tj/eng; 8am-noon & 1-4pm Mon-Fri) The ATM on Lenina accepts foreign cards. The main office is on Kamoli Khojandi.

**Internet Klub Fortuna** (cnr Lenina & Kamoli Khojandi; 24 hr; per hr 2TJS)

**Orienbank** (Kamoli Khojandi; 8am-12.30pm & 1.30-5pm Mon-Fri) Cash advances on a Visa or MasterCard for 1% commission.

**OVIR** (Lenina; 8am-noon & 1-5pm Mon-Fri, 8am-noon Sat) For OVIR registration you'll need a photocopy of your passport, one photo, and the equivalent of US$15 plus 23TJS, paid into a nearby bank. If there are any problems (or if you are staying in a hotel outside of the centre) you may need to go to the main OVIR office on Kamoli Khojandi (same hours as Lenina office).

**Post Office** (Ordjonikdze; 8am-5.30pm Mon-Fri, 8am-3pm Sat, 8am-noon Sun)

### Sights

The city's oldest remains are the formless baked-earth walls of the 10th-century **citadel**, which once boasted seven gates and 6km of fortifications. This was also the site of Alexander's original settlement. The fort was the site of pitched battles in November 1998 between a rebel Uzbek warlord and government troops, during which 200 people were killed. The reconstructed eastern gate houses the **Museum of Archaeology and Fortifications** (Rakhmovlonbekova; admission 1TJS; 8am-5pm), which has some interesting 19th-century photos and plans of the original citadel. An English pamphlet explaining many of the exhibits is available for 7TJS. Be careful when photographing from the ramparts, as the citadel behind is occupied by the military.

At the other end of the reconstructed city walls, the new and strangely pointless **Historical Museum of Sughd Province** (admission 6TJS; Tue-Fri 8am-3pm, Sat & Sun 10am-3pm) has vaguely interesting displays on Timur Malik, the local hero who defended Khojand from the Mongol onslaught, and a mock-up of a traditional Tajik house, but for the moment at least, a real paucity of actual exhibits. A classic example of too much marble, too little substance. All in all, save your money.

At the south end of kuchai Lenina is **Panchshanbe Bazaar**, one of the best-stocked markets in Central Asia, especially on Thursdays (Panchshanbe in Tajik). The core of the bazaar is an elegant, purpose-built hall (1954) with arched entrance portals and a pink-and-lime-green neoclassical façade – think Stalin meets *1001 Nights*.

Opposite the bazaar, shielded from the hubbub by a calm white wall, are the **mosque**, **medressa** and **mausoleum of Sheikh Massal ad-Din**, a modest, relatively modern complex that is quietly busy with serious young men clutching Qurans and old white-bearded men reclining in the shade. Take a look at the carved wooden pillars lining the side *aiwans* (covered porticoes). The impressive khaki-coloured mausoleum was built in 1394. The 21m-tall minaret was added in 1895.

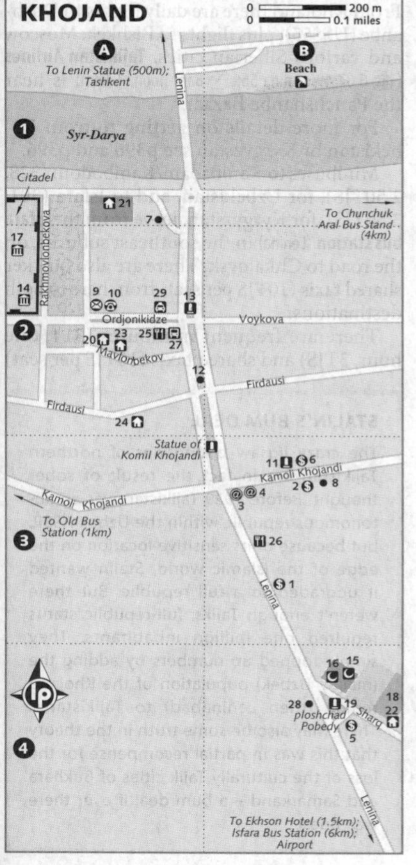


**INFORMATION**
Agroinvestbank....1 B3
Agroinvestbank (office)....2 B3
Internet Café....3 B3
Internet Klub Fortuna....4 B3
Moneychangers....5 B4
Orien Bank....6 B3
OVIR....7 A1
OVIR....8 B3
Post Office....9 A2
Telephone Office....10 A2

**SIGHTS & ACTIVITIES**
Bust of Marx and Lenin....11 B3
Eternal Flame....12 A2
Hammer & Sickle Monument....13 A2
Historical Museum of Sughd Province....14 A2
Mausoleum of Sheikh Massal ad-Din....15 B4
Mosque & Medressa of Sheikh Massal ad-Din....16 B4
Museum of Archaeology and Fortifications....17 A2
Panchshanbe Bazaar....18 B4
WWII Monument....19 B4

**SLEEPING**
Hotel Khuchand....20 A2
Hotel Leninabad....21 A1
Hotel Sharq....22 B4
Hotel Vahdat....23 A2
Tavkhid Hotel....24 A2

**EATING**
Café Ravshan....25 A2
Kavsar Café....26 B3
Orien Café....(see 6)

**TRANSPORT**
Bus Stop....27 A2
Bus stop....(see 13)
Tajikistan Airlines....28 B4
Taxi Stand....29 A2

TAJIKISTAN

Since the removal of its giant rival in Tashkent, Khojand's 22m-tall **statue of Lenin** is now the largest in Central Asia. It was moved here from Moscow in 1974. He's on the north side of the river, 300m beyond the bridge.

Other eye-catching Soviet memorabilia includes the bright red **hammer and sickle** in the centre of Lenina, a **bust of Marx and Lenin** on the side of an apartment block on Kamoli Khojandi and the **WWII monument** across from the Panchshanbe Bazaar. A statue of the poet **Komil (Kamoli) Khojandi** sits studiously in the middle of Lenina, not far from an eternal flame.

## Sleeping

**Hotel Sharq** (☎ 6 78 83; Sharq; d/tr/q 14/21/20TJS) Bunk down with Tajik traders on the top floor of this friendly but basic bazaar hotel. Rooms are spacious but there's only one toilet and no hot water (staff can direct you to a *banya* nearby).

**Ekhson Hotel** (☎ 6 69 84; Lenina; s/d 25/50TJS, lux 50/100TJS; ) The cheapest rooms offer the best value here, since the suites only add satellite TV and several bizarrely unfurnished rooms (the building was meant to be an apartment block). Bathrooms are fragrant but have hot water, as long as the electricity doesn't cut out. The hotel is about 1.5km south of the Panchshanbe Bazaar, at the fork in the road.

**Hotel Leninabad** (☎ 6 55 35; s/d 32/58TJS, lux 60/84TJS) This unfashionably-named state hotel is well placed on the corniche beside the Syr-Darya but is in a state of neglect. The rooms are Soviet hangovers, with stinky bathrooms, dim lighting and a broken lift, but are bearable. Communal showers (sometimes hot) are down the hall. The *lux* rooms are much more comfortable but for this money you are better off at the Ekhson Hotel (see above).

**Hotel Vahdat** (☎ 6 51 01; Mavlonbekov 3; pol-lux 160TJS, lux 200TJS; ) Next door to Hotel Khuchand, this place is similar, with slightly smaller rooms but satellite TV and English-speaking reception. Like the Khuchand and Tavkhid, rooms here only have one double bed.

**Tavkhid Hotel** (☎ 6 77 66; 117 Firdausi; pol-lux/lux 150/180TJS; ) A midrange option similar to Hotel Khuchand, with 12 rooms and foreign exchange facilities. Breakfast is included

**Hotel Khuchand** (☎ 6 59 97; Mavlonbekov 1; lux 170TJS; ) Probably the best hotel in this price range, with five absurdly large luxury rooms, a fridge, clean bathrooms and balconies overlooking the opera house fountain. No-one speaks English here.

## Eating

The bread is particularly good in Khojand; glazed and sprinkled with cardamom or sesame seeds. There are many *chaikhanas*, shashlyk grills and vats of *plov* around the bazaar.

**Café Ravshan** (Ordjonikidze 102; mains 5-7TJS; ⏰ 11am-8pm) The great chicken kebabs *(shashlyk akaroshka)* here make this our favourite place in town. There are also several *plov* stalls outside, which offer a cheap lunch.

**Kavsar Café** (Lenina; snacks 1-4TJS; ⏰ 11am-8pm) The wide range of salads and cakes are the draw here, plus the atmosphere is pleasant.

**Orien Café** (Kamoli Khojandi; mains 5TJS; ⏰ 10am-8pm) A bright and airy café next to Orienbank and a pleasant place to take a break or grab lunch.

## Getting There & Away

From Khojand there are daily flights to Dushanbe (US$55), plus flights to Bishkek, Moscow and various Siberian cities. **Tajikistan Airlines** (☎ 6 02 49; Lenina 56; ⏰ 8am-noon, 1-6pm) is near the Panchshanbe Bazaar.

For more details on getting to/from Uzbekistan or Kyrgyzstan see p396 and p396.

Minibuses to Kanibadam/Kanibodom (328, 2.50TJS), for Uzbekistan, and to Isfara (301, 3.50TJS), for Kyrgyzstan, leave from the **Isfara bus station** (Lenina) in the southeast suburbs, on the road to Chkalovsk. There are also quicker shared taxis (10TJS per seat) from here to both destinations.

There are frequent minibuses (314; one hour, 3TJS) and shared taxis (10TJS per seat)

### STALIN'S BUM DEAL

The crazy jigsaw boundaries of northern Tajikistan are in fact the result of sober thought. Before 1929 Tajikistan was an autonomous republic within the Uzbek ASSR, but because of its sensitive location on the edge of the Islamic world, Stalin wanted it upgraded to a full republic. But there weren't enough Tajiks; full-republic status required one million inhabitants. They simply topped up numbers by adding the (mainly Uzbek) population of the Khojand region (then Leninabad) to Tajikistan's. There may also be some truth in the theory that this was in partial recompense for the loss of the culturally Tajik cities of Bukhara and Samarkand – a bum deal if ever there was one.

south to Istaravshan from the **old bus station** (Kamoli Khojandi) in the west of town. Shared taxis to Penjikent (seven hours, 80TJS) also leave from here when full.

For shared taxis to Dushanbe (12 hours, 100TJS per seat) you need to take minibuses 18, 45 or 55 in the early morning from Lenina to the Chunchuk Aral bus stand in the north-eastern suburbs. Minibuses also run from here to Buston, from where you can take a taxi to the Oybek border crossing with Uzbekistan.

### Getting Around

Minibuses 2 and 80 run to the airport. For the Isfara bus station take minibus 35 or 55. To get to the old bus station on Kamoli Khojandi, take minibus 29. You can catch all these buses at the stand on the corner of Lenina and Ordjonikidze. To get off in the centre, alight at the bus stand by the hammer and sickle monument.

## ISTARAVSHAN ИСТАРАВШАН

**☎ 3454 / pop 50,000**

Called Kir by the Parthians, Cyropol by Alexander the Great and Ura-Tyube by the Russians, this small historic town has one of the best preserved old towns in Tajikistan, punctuated with some lovely traditional architecture. Bukhara it's not, but then there aren't any tourists either.

You can easily visit Istaravshan as either a day trip from Khojand or as an overnight stop en route to Dushanbe.

### Sights

The **Shahr-e-kuhna** (old town) is an interesting maze of alleys west of the main drag, Lenina. Buildings to track down include the working 15th-century **Abdullatif Sultan Medressa**, also known as the Kök Gumbaz (Blue Dome) after its eye-catching turquoise Timurid dome, and the nearby 19th-century **Hauz-i-Sangin Mosque**, with its fine ceiling paintings, dried *hauz* (pool) and tomb of Shah Fuzail ibn-Abbas. On the main road is the **Hazrat-i-Shah Mosque and Mausoleum** (Lenina 98), the town's main Friday mosque.

West of the old town, the four tin cupolas of the **Mazar-i-Chor Gumbaz** conceal Tajikistan's most impressive painted ceilings. To get here, walk west from the Abdullatif Sultan Medressa for five minutes to the main road and then take marshrutka 3 north to the tomb. If you're keen, you could also take a taxi from here for the short ride to the 17th-century **Sary Mazar** (Yellow Tomb), a complex of two tombs, a mosque and some 600-year-old chinar trees in the southwest of the old town.

The hill to the northeast of town is **Mug Tepe**, the site of the Sogdian fortress stormed by Alexander the Great in 329 BC (there are faint remains in the northwest corner). The imposing entry gate was actually built in 2002 during Istaravshan's 2500th anniversary celebrations. To get to the hill take the road just north of the Istaravshan Hotel. The Regional Museum across the road at the foot of the hill is always closed.

The colourful central **bazaar** is one of the biggest in the region and well worth a visit, especially on Tuesdays.

### Sleeping

**Istaravshan Hotel** (Lenina 80; s/d 10/20TJS) Rooms at the town's main hotel are spacious and quiet (you'll most likely be the only guests) but they've seen better days and the old lady in charge is quite batty. The ensuite bathrooms are just a tease – the hotel hasn't had water for years.

**Hotel Chashnobar** (☎ 2 49 61; s/d/q without bathroom 16/20/36TJS, d with bathroom 40TJS) The simple rooms here are a bit grubby but the pleasant courtyard seating area, hot showers and a good sauna/steam room make this the best place in town. It's 500m south of the bazaar, along the road to Dushanbe, and is sometimes referred to as the 'Muhib'.

**Isroil Hotel** (d 20-40TJS) Simple rooms with bathroom and satellite TV make this an OK bet but, just to the right of the main entrance to the bazaar, it can be noisy.

### Eating

Istaravshan is famed for its pears and sweet *kishmish* grapes. Invest in a kilo and retire to the **Aka Musa Chaykhana**, a nice Soviet-era *chaikhana* with fine tea beds but lacklustre service. It's next to the car-parts market, 200m north of the bazaar; the entrance is marked by a large mosaic.

There are lots of kebab places in front of and at the back of the bazaar. **Bar Tajikistan** across the main road from the bazaar serves up roast chicken and beer.

### Getting There & Around

Shared taxis to Dushanbe (276km, 10 hours, 50TJS to 100TJS per seat) leave from the southern end of the bazaar. Cars marked

'Tranzit' are generally often cheapest, since they are headed to Dushanbe for sale. Cars to Penjikent (seven hours) are a little further south. A taxi to Dushanbe via an overnight in Iskander-Kul starts at around US$100.

The easiest option to Khojand is one of the shared taxis (1½ hours, 10TJS per seat) across from the bazaar, otherwise minibuses (3TJS) run from the main bus stand, 3km north of the centre. Marshrutki 4 and 7 (25 dirham) shuttle up and down Lenina between the bazaar, the Hotel Istaravshan and the bus station.

## PENJIKENT ПЕНДЖИКЕНТ

**☎ 3475 / pop 50,000**

On a terrace above the banks of the Zerafshan (Zeravshan) River, 1.5km southeast of the modern, pleasant but somewhat dull modern town, are the ruins of **ancient Penjikent**, a major Sogdian town founded in the 5th century and abandoned in the 8th century. At its height the settlement town was one of the most cosmopolitan cities on the Silk Road and a rich trading centre, whose palace was decorated with ornate hunting scenes and pillars carved in the shape of dancing girls.

The ancient city has not been built upon since it was abandoned. You can make out the faint foundations of houses, two Zoroastrian temples and the shop-lined bazaar of the main *shakhristan* (town centre), as well as the obvious citadel to the west, but the best of the frescoes (some of them 15m long), sculptures, pottery and manuscripts were long ago carted off to Tashkent and St Petersburg. A small **museum** (admission 2TJS; ⌚ 10am-5pm) chronicles the excavations. Surrounding the site are scattered remains of a *rabad* (suburb) and necropolis. The ruins are an 800m walk from the end of marshrutka 5 (40 dirham) or a 15-minute walk from the bazaar. Visit in the early morning or afternoon to avoid the heat. For more on the excavations, including a map, see www.orientarch.uni-halle.de/ca/ca page.htm.

Some more finds and reproduction frescoes are on display at the **Rudaki Museum** (Rudaki; admission 3TJS; ⌚ 8am-5pm), 1.5km west of the bazaar in modern Penjikent. There are also tools from the nearby Neolithic site of Sarazm and a copy of documents found at Mt Mug, where the Sogdians made their last stand against the Arab invaders. A statue of Devastich, the last Sogdian leader, dominates the roundabout at the west end of town.

The museum's name arises from the claim that Penjikent was the birthplace of Abu Abdullah Rudaki, the Samanid court poet considered by many to be the father of Persian poetry. His modern **mausoleum**, a popular pilgrimage place, is located 58km west of Penjikent in the village of Panjrud, along with a small museum and guesthouse.

The best local excursion is to the picturesque **Marguzor lakes**, up in the Fan Mountains – see opposite for details.

### Sleeping & Eating

**our pick Homestay of Nematov Niyozkul** (☎ 5 31 34; niyozkul@mail.ru; Rudaki 22/16; dm US$10 full board) This comfortable traditional home is the best place to stay, hands down. There are plenty of duvets on the floor and the modern bathroom has hot water. Niyozkul can also arrange transport and treks in the Fan Mountains. His house is at the west end of town, about 700m from the Rudaki Museum, before the roundabout; ask for the '*ostanovka Samarkand*'.

**Hotel Penjikent** (☎ 5 22 30; Borbadi Marvazi 22; d/ste US$10/20) The former Intourist hotel is poor value, with run-down rooms and a chronic lack of water.

**Dusti Restaurant** (Rudaki; mains TJS2-4; ⌚ lunch & dinner) Canteen cuisine in grand style here, in an echoing dining hall opposite the post office on the main street. Otherwise, try the *chaikhanas* and canteens around the bazaar.

### Getting Around

Minibus 1 runs along Rudaki from Niyozkul's homestay, past the museum to the bazaar and then the bus station.

### Getting There & Away

Shared taxis run along the scenic mountain roads to Khojand (seven hours, 80TJS per seat) and Dushanbe (225km, eight hours, 100TJS per seat) from the bus station, 2km east of the central bazaar. Winter flights to Dushanbe (US$45) operate infrequently. The airport is 4km west of town.

Buses leave at around 9.30am, noon and 2.15pm for the Rudaki Mausoleum (5TJS, one hour), returning at 6am and 2.30pm. A third bus departing at 8.30am (and maybe 2.30pm) also makes a stop here before continuing 9km to Artush, for access to treks in the Fan Mountains.

For details of getting to Samarkand, in neighbouring Uzbekistan, see p396.

## FAN MOUNTAINS ФАНСКИЕ ГОРЫ

The Fannsky Gory (Russian for Fan Mountains) are one of Central Asia's most popular trekking and climbing destinations, being only a couple of hours from both Samarkand and Dushanbe. See the boxed text Trekking in the Fan Mountains (p374) for trekking route overviews.

If you don't have time for a trek, a great way to get a feel for the Fans is to make the day trip from Penjikent to the **Marguzor Lakes**, a 20km-long chain of seven turquoise lakes that is strung along the western end of the range. Try to make it to the last lake (Azor Chashma), 2km beyond Marguzor village and 63km from Penjikent, from where you can hike along the dramatic lakeshore (bring a picnic).

To hire a car for the day-trip costs around US$40 from Penjikent. Nematov Niyozkul (see opposite) is good at arranging reliable transport. Shoestringers could take the bus to Rashnar Poyon (just before the first lake), which departs Penjikent between noon and 2pm. Coming back, try to track down the impossibly cramped 4WD that runs daily between Marguzor village and Penjikent's Takhta Bazaar, just downhill from the main Penjikent bazaar.

One other gem accessible to nontrekkers is **Iskander-Kul**, a gorgeous mountain lake 24km off the main road, at the eastern end of the range. The lakeside **turbaza** (former Soviet holiday camp; per person 20TJS) enjoys a lovely spot, with 30 quiet chalets and a great lakeside restaurant. Bring warm clothes as the lake is at 2195m. There are pit toilets but no showers. You can get great overviews of the lake from the hill behind the *turbaza,* where a couple of Orthodox crosses mark climbers' graves. You can take a one-hour walk around the lake to the President's *dacha* (holiday bungalow), and there are plenty of longer overnight hikes further up into the Kaznok Valley behind Sarytag village. For a shorter hike the *turbaza* administrator can give directions to a 30m-high waterfall half-an-hour's walk downstream.

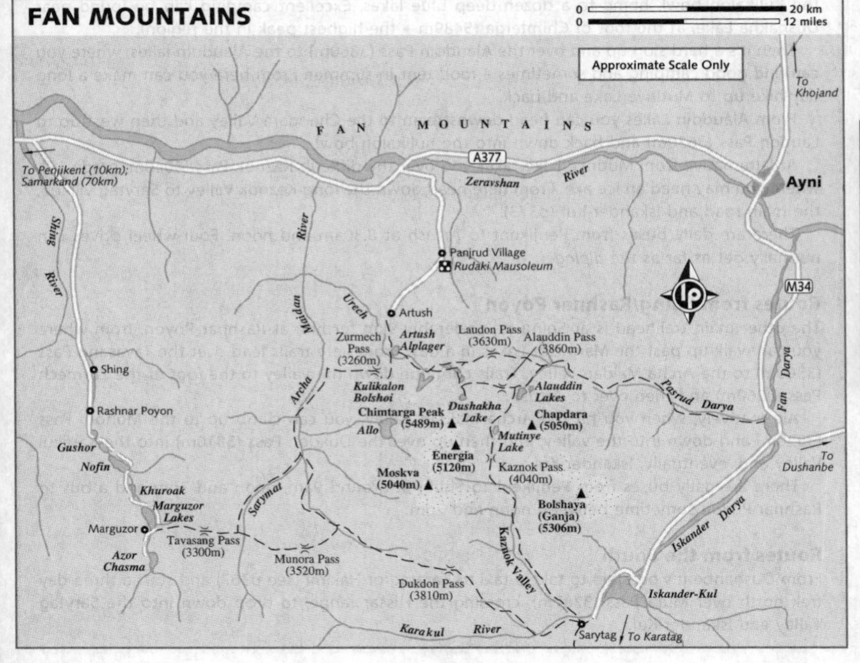

There's no public transport to the lake. It's just about possible to find a taxi at the mining settlement by the main M34 turn-off but it would be much easier to hire a car between Dushanbe and Penjikent/Khojand and visit en route. If you are hitching, weekends see the most traffic but are far less serene. Note that the road to Iskander-Kul branches off the larger road (to the mine) shortly after leaving the main M34 and crosses the river.

### TREKKING IN THE FAN MOUNTAINS

The Fannsky Gory – located in Tajikistan but most easily accessed from Samarkand – are one of Central Asia's premier trekking destinations. The rugged, glaciated mountains are studded with dozens of turquoise lakes, where Tajik shepherds graze their flocks.

Many Uzbek and Tajik travel agencies offer trekking programmes here, as do some overseas trekking companies (see p101), though it is a possible destination for experienced and fit do-it-yourselfers. To get to the Fans as an excursion from Uzbekistan you will need a Tajik visa and a double-entry Uzbek visa.

Daily buses run from Penjikent to Artush or Shing/Rashnar Poyon, the main trailheads. You might be asked to pay a trekking tax (see Travel Permits, p394) in Artush. You can get supplies in Penjikent, though it's better to bring your own lightweight foodstuffs. The region can be very hot and dry at the end of summer (August to early September). It's possible to hire pack donkeys at the trail heads for around US$10 per day.

The best maps are the hard-to-find 1:100,000 *Pamir Alay – Severno-Zapadnaya Chast* (1992 Tashkent) or the 1:100,000 *Fan Mountains Map and Guide* published abroad by EWP (www.ewpnet.com).

#### Routes from Artush

From Artush walk two hours (6km) up to the *alplager* (mountaineers' camp) where rooms and food are generally available (US$10 to US$15). From here it's a hard three-hour uphill hike into the Kulikalon bowl, home to a dozen deep blue lakes. Excellent camping can be found near Dushakha Lake, at the foot of Chimtarga (5489m – the highest peak in the region).

Then it's a hard slog up and over the Alauddin Pass (3860m) to the Alauddin lakes, where you can find good camping and sometimes a food tent in summer. From here you can make a long day-hike up to Mutinye Lake and back.

From Alauddin Lakes you can head downstream to the Chapdara Valley and then west up to Laudon Pass (3630m) and back down into the Kulikalon bowl.

An alternative from Mutinye Lake takes you over the difficult Kaznok Pass (4040m, grade 1B), where you may need an ice axe. From here head down the long Kaznok Valley to Sarytag village, the main road and Iskander-Kul (p373).

There are daily buses from Penjikent to Artush at 8.30am and noon. Four-wheel drives can normally get as far as the *alplager*.

#### Routes from Shing/Rashnar Poyon

The other main trailhead is at Shing or, preferably 9km further, at Rashnar Poyon, from where you can walk up past the Marguzor Lakes in a day. From here trails lead over the Tavasang Pass (3300m) to the Archa Maidan Valley. Trails continue down the valley to the foot of the Zurmech Pass (3260m) and then over to Artush.

Alternatively, when you hit the Archa Maidan Valley, you can climb up to the Munora Pass (3520m) and down into the valley, and then up over the Dukdon Pass (3810m) into the Karakul Valley and, eventually, Iskander-Kul.

There are daily buses from Penjikent to Shing at around 9am, noon and 3pm and a bus to Rashnar Poyon sometime between noon and 2pm.

#### Routes from the South

From Dushanbe it's possible to take a taxi to Karatag or Hakimi (see p367) and start a three-day trek north over Mura Pass (3787m), crossing the Hissar range, to drop down into the Sarytag Valley and Iskander-Kul.

TAJIKISTAN

# THE PAMIRS

> The plain is called Pamier, and you ride across it for twelve days together, finding nothing but a desert without habitations or any green thing, so that travellers are obliged to carry with them whatever they have need of. The region is so lofty and cold that you can not even see any birds flying. And I must notice also that because of this great cold, fire does not burn so bright, nor give out so much heat as usual.
>
> *Marco Polo,*
> Description of the World

They're known locally as Bam-i-Dunya (Roof of the World), and once you're up in the Pamirs it's not hard to see why. For centuries a knot of tiny valley emirates, the Pamirs feel like a land a little bit closer to heaven.

The word *pamir* means 'rolling pastureland' in ancient Persian, which is apt indeed, though some sources say the derivation is Paw-i-Mur or 'Legs of the Sun'. The Chinese called the mountains the Congling Shan, or 'Onion Mountains'. There is not one obvious Pamir range, rather a complex series of ranges separated by high-altitude valleys.

The western half of the region, Badakhshan, is characterised by deep irrigated valleys and sheer peaks reminiscent of the Wakhi areas of far northern Pakistan (which are also ethnically

Tajik). The eastern half of the region is the high, arid and sparsely inhabited Pamir plateau, home largely to Kyrgyz herders and their yurts. For the most part, the Pamirs are too high for human settlement.

The Pamirs contain three of the four highest mountains in the former Soviet Union, the apex of which is Koh-i-Samani (former Pik Kommunizm) at 7495m. Less than an Empire State Building shorter is Pik Lenin at 7134m. (There is much confusion over this peak's new name, which is either Koh-i-Istiqlal/Independence Peak or Abu Ali ibni Sino/Avicenna in Tajikistan, or Peak Sary Tash or even Achik Tash in Kyrgyzstan!). The Pamir is drained by the numerous tributaries of the Vakhsh and Pyanj Rivers which themselves feed into the Amu-Darya, Central Asia's greatest river.

Kohistani Badakhshan (still most commonly known as the Gorno-Badakhshan autonomous oblast, or GBAO) accounts for 45% of Tajikistan's territory but only 3% of its population. The 212,000 souls that do live here are divided between Pamiris and Kyrgyz. Culturally speaking, Badakhshan extends over the Pyanj River into Afghan Badakhshan, centred around Faizabad.

The slopes and high valleys are inhabited by hardier creatures, near-mythical animals such as the giant Marco Polo sheep, which sports curled horns that would measure almost 2m were they somehow unfurled, and the rarely seen snow leopard. During the Soviet era several scientific teams tried to track down the similarly elusive 'giant snowman', but in vain.

Chance encounters with yetis aside, the Pamirs region is generally safe to travel in, despite a healthy penchant for red tape. Tajik border guards assumed the unenviable task of keeping a lid on smuggling after the Russian troops departed the region in 2005.

## HISTORY

### The Legacy of Isolation

With no arable land to speak of and no industry, Gorno-Badakhshan has always relied heavily on Moscow and Dushanbe for its upkeep, with most of its processed goods and all of its fuel coming from outside the region.

The collapse of the USSR was a particularly hard blow for the region. As money and fuel supplies dried up, so the region's markets, state farms, irrigation channels and bus routes slowly ground to a halt. Suddenly local farmers and herders had to remember how to harvest their crops without machinery, skills that had been suppressed for decades. The largely Russian Soviet scientists packed up and left behind half-abandoned mines, research stations and observatories scattered across the Pamirs.

Frustrated by its marginal position and seeing no future in a collapsing Tajikistan, GBAO nominally declared its independence in 1992 and chose the rebel side in the civil war. Since then, the government hasn't been sending much in the way of aid or reconstruction.

Through most of the 1990s, humanitarian aid convoys kept the region from starvation, while establishing agricultural and hydroelectrical programmes in an attempt to create some degree of self-sufficiency. In 1993 the region grew 16% of its basic food needs; by 2006 that figure had risen to 80%.

#### PAMIRI HOUSES

If the chance arises it is worth accepting an offer to look inside a traditional *huneuni chid* (Pamiri house). Guests are received in the large five-pillared room with raised areas around four sides of a central pit, but there is also a smaller living space, a kitchen and a hallway. There are few, if any, windows; illumination comes through a skylight in the roof *(tsorkhona),* which consists of four concentric squares, representing the elements of earth, fire, air and water. Carpets and mattresses take the place of furniture and also serve as decoration along with panels of photographs – the most prominent of which is often a portrait of the Aga Khan.

The five vertical pillars symbolise the five main prophets (Fatima, Ali, Mohammed, Hassan and Hussein), as well as the five pillars (literally) of Islam and, some say, the five deities of Zoroastrianism (the structure of Pamiri houses goes back 2500 years). In a further act of symbolism, the number of roof beams relates to the seven imams and six prophets of Ismailism. The place of honour, next to the Hassan pillar (one of two pillars joined together), is reserved for the *khalifa* (village religious leader), so visitors should avoid sitting there. For some pointers on etiquette when visiting a Central Asian home, see p87 and p63.

The next stage is to create employment, much of which depends on education and tourism (see p388).

Despite this, 80% of the local population still earns less than US$200 per year. The region's largest employer, the Russian military, pulled out of the region in 2005, further worsening the situation. Over 15,000 Badakhshanis have left their homes in search of work outside the region.

It is hoped that the new highway between Murgab and Tashkurgan in China will help lift the region out of its isolation, though it's hard to see quite what the region currently has to export. Meanwhile the Aga Khan Foundation has been busy rebuilding bridges, literally, with Afghan Badakhshan on the other side of the Pyanj River, reuniting communities severed since the formation of the USSR.

## PAMIRI TAJIKS

Centuries of isolation in high-altitude valleys has meant that the Pamiris of Gorno-Badakhshan speak languages different not only from those of lowland Tajiks but from one another. Each mountain community has its own dialect of Pamiri, a language that, although sharing the same Persian roots as Tajik, is as different as English is from German. Shugnani (named after the emirate of Shugnan once based in the Gunt Valley) is the dialect spoken in Khorog, the Gunt Valley and among Badakhshani Tajiks in Murgab. Other languages in the mosaic include Wakhi, Ishkashimi and Rushani. *Khologh* is 'thank you' in Shugnani.

The mountain peoples of the eastern Pamirs are, however, solidly bound by their shared faith: Ismailism, a breakaway sect of Shiite Islam, introduced into Badakhshan in the 11th-century by Nasir Khusraw. Ismailism has no formal clerical structure, no weekly holy day and no mosques (rather multipurpose meeting halls called *jamoat khana,* which also double as meeting halls and community guesthouses). Ismailis greet each other with *yo-ali madat* (May Ali bless you), rather than the standard Islamic *asalam aleykum*. Each village has a religious leader known as a *khalifa,* who leads prayers and dispenses advice, assisted by a *rais* (community leader).

One of the few visible manifestations of the religion are the small roadside *oston* (shrines), covered in ibex horns, burnt offerings and round stones, at which passers-by stop to ask for a blessing. The horns are often the remnants of hunting trips and ensuing community meals known as *khudoi*. The shrines also act as charity stations; in return for a blessing, the Ismaili customarily leaves some money or bread for anyone in need.

The spiritual leader of the Ismailis is the Swiss-born Aga Khan, revered by Pamiris as a living god and the 49th imam. He's no remote, abstract deity – it's the Aga Khan's charity that has kept almost certain starvation at bay in GBAO; Pamiris venerate him as 'Our God who sends us food'.

Not having two potatoes to fry together has done nothing to lessen the legendary hospitality of the Pamiris.

## INFORMATION

### Permits & Registration

It is essential to have both a Tajik visa and a GBAO permit to travel in the Pamirs. To get the latter you'll need travel agency help; META in Murgab (see p388) charges US$24, Munduz Travel in Osh (see p336) charges US$25, Tour De Pamir (see p381) in Khorog charges US$30, Stantours (see p117) charges US$40 and the Great Game Travel Company (see p362) US$65. It's best to apply a couple of weeks in advance. There are rumours that the GBAO permit may be discontinued.

The permit is a separate piece of rather unofficial-looking paper and lists the districts to be visited, so make sure you get all the regions you want to visit (these are Ishkashim, Murgab, Vanj, Darvaz, Shugnan, Rushan and Roshtqala). Like registration, the GBAO permit is valid only for the duration of your visa.

If you can't pick up your permit in Dushanbe (ie if you want to travel from Osh) you'll have to ask the travel agency to email you a scan of the permit. You can then travel with a colour printout in its original size (around 6.5cm by 11cm) as far as Khorog and pick up the original there. Munduz Travel in Osh (see p336) claim to arrange GBAO permits in a day.

Permits are checked throughout the Pamirs, including at Kalaikhum, Khorog airport, Suchan (10km east of Khorog), outside Murgab, Karakul and Kyzyl-Art. Off the main highway, there are border checkposts at Tokhtamysh and Rang-Kul, and also at Ishkashim and Khargush, at either end of the Wakhan Valley.

You will also need additional permits if you want to visit Sarez or Zor-Kul lakes (see p394).

If you haven't registered previously in Tajikistan (see p393) you will have to register in Khorog. Coming from Osh, you should first register with OVIR in Murgab and then register again in Khorog (no fee for the second registration), where you'll get a passport stamp.

Moreover, travellers are supposed to register with the Kizmat-i-Amniyat-i-Milli (National Security Service, generally referred to as the KGB) in Murgab, even if you have registered elsewhere in Tajikistan. There is no fee and the Murgab Ecotourism Association (META; see p388) can help with this.

### What to Bring

Khorog has a fairly well-stocked bazaar but Murgab's is limited to bad Kyrgyz beer and expired Snickers bars so bring some snacks from home, especially if you're trekking or travelling off-the-beaten track. Gifts of photos of the Aga Khan go down well. Sunscreen, sunglasses and a torch (flashlight) are essential. Water purifying tablets are advisable.

It's essential to have warm clothing, though a fleece and windproof shell should generally suffice in midsummer. Amazingly strong winds can pick up very quickly in the Pamirs, something even Marco Polo moaned about. A sleeping bag is useful but not essential, as most homes and yurts can provide plenty of duvets. A tent is only really useful for wilderness treks.

Despite the high altitudes, mosquitoes can be voracious during early summer in the river valleys of Murgab and Ak-Suu and around Rang-Kul, so bring repellent if travelling in June, July or August (they are largely gone by September).

There's little electricity outside Khorog and reliable batteries are impossible to buy in the Pamirs so bring enough camera batteries to last until Osh or Dushanbe.

TAJIKISTAN

#### MAPS

Cartographer Marcus Hauser has produced an essential 1:500,000 colour tourist map to the Pamirs. It is for sale at the Bactria Cultural Centre (see p360) in Dushanbe and, less reliably, from META in Murgab, or directly from www.geckomaps.com.

### Money

Make sure you change enough money before arriving in the region. In Khorog it's possible to change cash (US dollars) and even get a cash advance off a credit card. In an emergency you might find someone willing to change dollars in Murgab (bring small denominations). Kyrgyz som are accepted between Murgab and the Kyrgyz–Tajik border.

## SLEEPING

Most of the tourist accommodation in the Pamirs is in homestays or yurtstays, which are simple but comfortable. Homestays generally have an outdoor toilet and a place to wash. Yurts don't supply toilets or bathrooms so you'll have to find a spare rock to squat behind (see p94). For a rundown on the structure of a yurt see p273. The ecotourism organisation META (see p388) offers accommodation throughout the eastern Pamirs.

If you are getting off-the-beaten track in the eastern Pamirs, check with MSDSP (See p380) about their guesthouses and homestays. Tourists can normally stay at **MSDSP guesthouses** (dm US$15) at Kalaikhum and Kala Hussein if they are not being used by MSDSP staff members. To find the local MSDSP office in any village ask for *Hazina* (treasure chest), the name by which the organisation is known locally.

## GETTING THERE & AROUND

The major transport options for the 728km Pamir Hwy between Khorog and Osh are hitching on trucks, renting a 4WD with driver or cramming in the occasional minivan.

### Minibus

There are dailyish minibuses between Murgab and Khorog and, less frequently, between Osh and Murgab. In Kyrgyzstan daily public buses run from Osh to Sary Tash (see p341). From Khorog, minibuses and shared 4WDs go to some surrounding valleys such as Jelandy, Ishkashim, Rushan, Langar and Roshtqala, though the timings generally require an overnight stay.

### Car Hire

Hiring a private vehicle (normally a Russian UAZ Jeep but possibly a Lada Niva) and a driver is relatively expensive, but gives you a flexibility that you will value on this scenic and fascinating trip. Please note that the transport rates listed in this section will doubtless change as the price of fuel rises.

At the time of research, META (see p388) in Murgab was offering 4WDs at between US$0.34 to US$0.38 per km, plus 15% commission, which worked out at US$315 from Murgab to Osh (420km), or US$330 from Murgab to Khorog via the Wakhan Corridor (you have to pay for the car's return trip to Murgab). To shave costs from Osh you could take a shared taxi to Sary Tash in Kyrgyzstan and arrange for a META 4WD to pick you up there.

Great Game Travel (see p362) charges US$0.70 per km for Land Cruiser hire. For other company's rates see p381. Independent car hire from Dushanbe to Khorog costs around US$200 for a Lada Niva.

The availability and cost of fuel is a significant factor in the cost of transport (prices generally rise in autumn, when supplies are scarcer), but what really counts is whether you have to pay for the vehicle's return trip; this essentially doubles the cost. META was considering introducing a one-way rate of between US$0.60 and US$0.70 at the time of research.

Hiring a 4WD independently costs less than going through an agency but you'll need to negotiate hard and speak decent Russian. Generally speaking, car hire is cheaper in Murgab than in Khorog. Make sure any rate includes petrol, vehicle maintenance and the driver's pay, food and accommodation. For every extra day that the driver waits for you (if you wish, for example, to do an excursion), add about US$10. Give the vehicle the once-over, check that the 4WD is operational and, if coming from Osh, check that the driver has a GBAO permit.

As a rough guide, a Russian UAZ Jeep needs around 16 litres of petrol per 100km, which works out at around US$0.16 per km for the petrol alone. Lada Nivas are generally cheaper than Jeeps, though the spiffier Chrysler Nivas cost more. The main problem with Russian Jeeps is the limited visibility from the back seat.

Finding petrol can be a problem in the Pamirs. A trip into remoter corners of the region generally involves at least one dash around town to find a obliging local with a jerry can of diluted fuel and a bucket.

### Hitching

Traffic is light along the Pamir Hwy and hitching is hard work. The main commercial traffic these days is the Chinese trucks which shuttle between the Qolma Pass, Murgab and a terminal 30km east of Khorog. It helps if you speak a few words of Chinese. If you break a journey you could end up waiting a long time for another ride, as trucks midroute are often full. Controls at checkpoints are particularly tedious for trucks.

Hitching from Osh is possible but finding a ride from Sary Tash to Murgab is problematic, as most vehicles are full by the time they get here.

## DUSHANBE TO KHOROG

If you are hiring a car between Dushanbe and Khorog, you have the choice of two routes; the main summer-only route via Tavildara and the Sagirdasht Pass to Kalaikhum, or the longer but year-round southern route via Kulyab and the Afghan border road. Minibuses take the Tavildara route

The condition of the Tavildara road is particularly bad and without prospect of improving any time soon. The southern route is longer but slowly being upgraded by Turkish road crews (there is a surreal three-lane stretch of highway at Zigar!), plus there are great views of the amazing cliffside footpaths and traditional villages on the Afghan side of the river, often less than 100m away. You pass several lovely Tajik villages en route, such as Yoged. Signs warn of mines along parts of this route so don't go wandering by the river bank.

The best place to break the trip is in Kalaikhum (also known as Kala-i-khum, Darvaz or Darwaz). The **homestay of Bakhrom Sangkakuf** (dm US$5), by the bridge, is a good bet, as is the **homestay of Katya Khudoyidodova** (☎ 2 14 44). There's also an **MSDSP guesthouse** (dm US$15) 1km down the road to Kulyab.

## KHOROG ХОРОГ

**☎ 35220 / pop 27,800 / elevation 2100m**

A small mountain-valley town, Khorog is the capital of the autonomous Gorno-Badakhshan (GBAO) region. It is strung out on either side of the dashing Gunt River and penned in by dry, vertical peaks. A few kilometres downstream, the Gunt merges with the Pyanj, marking the border with Afghanistan.

Until the late 19th century, present-day Khorog was a tiny settlement that loosely belonged to the domain of local chieftains, the Afghan Shah or the Emir of Bukhara. Russia installed a small garrison here following the Anglo–Russian–Afghan Border Treaty of 1896, which delineated the current northern border of Afghanistan on the Pyanj River.

Khorog was made the administrative centre of GBAO in 1925.

Khorog suffered badly in the wake of independence (at the depths of the economic crisis money disappeared altogether, replaced by barter) but things have picked up in recent years. In 2003 the Aga Khan pledged US$200 million to establish one of the three campuses of the University of Central Asia in Khorog's eastern suburbs. Khorog has one of the brightest and best educated populations of any town in Central Asia.

The town park, dug up to grow crops during the famine of the 1990s, is being renovated by the Aga Khan Trust for Culture.

Note that the town largely closes down on Sunday, when open restaurants and transport can be hard to find.

## Information

**Afghan consulate** (☎ 2 24 92; Gagarina) Visas are theoretically possible here, though you'll likely be referred to the embassy in Dushanbe. Phone ahead, as opening hours vary.

**Mountain Societies Development Support Project** (MSDSP; ☎ 2 26 99; msdspkhorog@msdsp.automail.com; Lenina 50) Can help with car hire for US$0.46 per km, plus US$20 per day, and can help with homestays in remote areas of the Pamirs (see opposite).

### INTERNET ACCESS

**Interkom Internet Café** (☎ 2 50 09; Khubonsho 1/1; per hr 3TJS; 🕑 7am-7pm)

**Uslugi Computer Photo Club** (Lenin 50; per hr 3TJS; 🕑 8am-8pm) At the post office.

### MONEY

**Agroinvestbank** (Garagina; 🕑 8am-noon & 1-3pm Mon-Fri) Offers cash advances on MasterCard, Maestro and Visa cards for a 2% commission. There's no sign, just look for the word 'Agrobank' scratched onto the side of a rusty tanker!

**Amonat Bank** (🕑 8am-12pm & 1-5pm Mon-Fri, 8am-noon Sat) Changes cash (US dollars and, at a pinch, euros) into somani.

### REGISTRATION

**OVIR** (Lenin; 🕑 8am-noon & 1-5pm Mon-Fri, 8am-noon Sat) If you haven't already registered in Tajikistan, do so here, next to the Amonat Bank. Enter through the blue door to the left of the main entrance. Registration costs US$20 and takes two minutes.

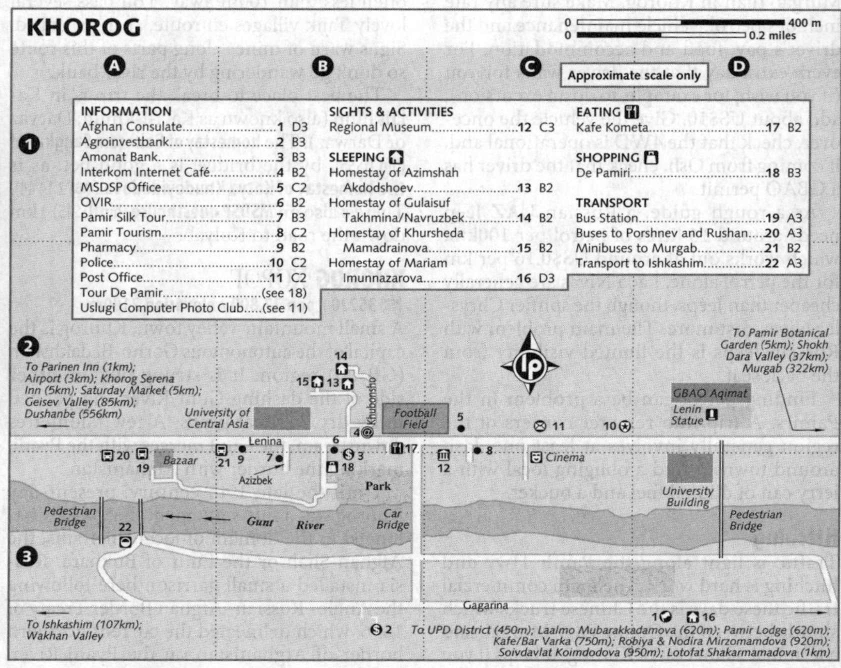

### TRAVEL AGENCIES

**Pamir Silk Tour** (☎ 505 23 61, 2 57 77; PST_pamirs@yahoo.com; Azizbek 1) Can arrange homestays, transport and GBAO permits. Contact Mullo Abdul Shagarf or Manzura Saidzoirova. Shagarf is also the local representative of the state tourism agency Sayoh, with an office at the GBAO *aqimat* (government building) on Lenina 26. Four-wheel drive hire costs US$0.70 per km.

**Pamir Tourism** (☎ 93-5009947, 2 52 99; pamirstourism@yahoo.com; www.pamirs-tourism.org; Lenina 55) Can arrange GBAO permits for US$35 and homestays throughout the eastern Pamirs. Four-wheel drive hire costs US$0.48 per km. Contact Ismoil Konunov.

**Tour De Pamir** (☎ 93-5007557, 2 37 96; tourdepamir@yahoo.com; Lenina 77) Contact Ergash or Abrigol, in the same building as De Pamiri. GBAO permits cost US$30 and 4WD hire costs US$0.50 per km.

## Sights

Khorog's surprisingly good **Regional Museum** (Lenina; admission 3TJS; 8am-noon & 1-5pm Mon-Sat) is well worth an hour of your time, if only to see the fabulous cross-bow mousetrap, as well as the first Russian piano to arrive in Badakhshan (10 Russian soldiers spent two months carrying it over the mountains from Osh!).

Tourists can visit the Saturday **market** by the bridge on the border with Afghanistan, by the Serena Inn, 5km west of town. It's not very exotic but you say *salaam* to local Afghan traders.

The **Pamir Botanical Garden**, 5km east of town, has a couple of hundred hectares of parkland and is the world's second highest botanical garden, reaching 3900m.

## Sleeping

The best places to stay are the town's homestays, though there are now a couple of midrange hotels for those requiring more comfort or privacy.

### HOMESTAYS

There are two main concentrations of homestays; in the centre of town east of the football pitch, and out in the pleasant UPD district, a half-hour walk (2km) southeast of town. Most homestays cost US$6 to US$8 per person without meals, unless otherwise noted. Khorog's travel agencies can arrange homestays in Khorog and throughout the Pamirs for US$10 to US$15 per person.

The following places are in the centre of town:

**Azimshah Akdodshoev** (☎ 2 27 45, 2 44 26; Khubonsho 1a; r US$10) One of the nicest traditional Pamiri homes but not overly friendly. Rates include two meals.

**Khursheda Mamadrainova** (☎ 2 47 54; Khubonsho 11; dm US$10) Good place with three comfortable rooms, an upper balcony and new indoor bathroom.

**Mariam Imunnazarova** (☎ 2 57 22, 2 30 62; Gagarina; US$10) Modern block with a Western toilet and hot shower. Next to the Afghan consulate.

**Gulaisuf Takhmina/Navruzbek** (☎ 2 45 54; Khubonsho 9) Lovely garden but basic toilet and very basic shower.

The following homestays are in the UPD district:

**Lotofat Shakarmamadova** (☎ 2 55 81; Bandalieva 506) Look for the black gate across from the Pamir Lodge.

**Soivdavlat Koimdodova** (☎ 2 39 70; Bandalieva 42) Traditional Pamiri home, with a bathroom planned; look for the black gate.

**Robiya & Nodira Mirzomamdova** (☎ 2 35 28; Bandalieva 47; dm US$10) One of the most comfortable, and able to take groups of eight, with a modern bathroom and garden tapchan (tea bed).

**Laalmo Mubarakkadamova** (☎ 2 69 99; Bandalieva 61/10)

### HOTELS

**our pick Pamir Lodge** (☎ 2 65 45; www.geocities.com/pamirlodge; Kuchai Gagarin 46; US$5 per person, breakfast & dinner US$3) The five rooms here are simple, with mattresses on the floor, but it's a lovely spot and Zubaida and Saidaziz Ilolov are delightful hosts. The shared Western bathroom and hot sauna are a luxury and the food is excellent (ask Zubaida to prepare her homemade *kurtob* – layered bread, yogurt, onion and coriander). The lodge was set up by Pakistani scholar Dr Ali Muhammed Rajput to fund the local *jamoat khana* (Ismali prayer and meeting hall), which is in the grounds. The lodge is just past the football pitch of the Gagarin School.

**Parinen Inn** (☎ 2 54 99; Lenina 69/50; s/d US$25/50) This private midrange hotel has seven clean modern rooms and Western bathrooms, plus a large lounge, riverside garden seating, satellite TV and parking. It's a little overpriced but is probably the best midrange option.

**Khorog Serena Inn** (☎ 2 32 28, satellite 00882216-89802194; serenainn@khorog.automail.com; s/d US$75/100 incl 20% tax) This is the best hotel in town, built in chic Badakhshani style (but with modern amenities) for the visit of Aga Khan. The six rooms are spacious and only used occasionally by consultants and the odd tour group. Credit cards are not accepted. It's by the bridge to Afghanistan, 5km northwest of Khorog bazaar.

A new 24-room Serena Inn is planned for the university district of upper Khorog in 2008.

## Eating

The best bet for dinner is your homestay or guesthouse.

**Kafe Kometa** (Lenina 6; mains 3TJS) This is the best place for a lunch in the centre, serving up decent Soviet food in pleasant surroundings.

**Kafe/Bar Varka** (Gagarin; mains 7TJS) Out in the UPD district, this slightly Mafiosi-looking place has spuriously dim lighting but a good range of salads and Russian dishes.

**Khorog Serena Inn** (☎ 2 32 28; mains 13-25TJS, beer 8-12TJS) This surprisingly reasonably priced hotel restaurant has the nicest setting in Khorog, with weekend barbecues and a riverside bar.

Look out in the bazaar for bottles of locally made sea-buckthorn juice and tart dog-rose juice *(shipovnik sok)*.

## Shopping

**De Pamiri** (☎ 2 37 96; yorali@rambler.ru; Lenina 77) This NGO initiative aims to revive traditional Pamiri crafts by offering a place for 45 artisans from across the Pamirs to market and sell their crafts. Products include excellent felt rugs and bags, musical instruments, Pamiri socks, embroidered skullcaps and Pamiri socks; view a selection of products at www.pamirs.org/handicrafts. Prices are marked and fixed, and 80% of earnings go to the artisans. Contact Yorali or Vatani.

## Getting There & Away

For an overview of transport along the Pamir Hwy see above.

### AIR

One of the main attractions of Khorog is the flight in from Dushanbe (US$60), which, depending on your confidence in the pilots of Tajikistan Airlines, will be one of the most exhilarating or terrifying experiences of your life. For the best views of Afghanistan sit on the right-hand side when flying from Dushanbe. Baggage allowance is 10kg; excess is 1% of the air ticket per 1kg.

Flights originate in Dushanbe and, in theory, run daily but they are grounded at the first sign of bad weather (which is frequent outside of the summer months). Passengers must then take their chances the next day, tussling for seats with those already booked on that flight. It can happen that, after a run of bad weather, hundreds turn up to fight for the first flight's 40 available seats. The bottom line is that you budget an extra day or two into your itinerary in case flights are cancelled and be prepared to travel overland if need be.

The airstrip is 3km west of town and taxis run to the centre.

> **FLYING TO KHOROG**
>
> In Soviet days the Dushanbe–Khorog flight was the only route on which Aeroflot paid its pilots danger money. For most of the 45-minute flight the aircraft scoots along mountain valleys, flying in the shadow of the rock face with its wingtips so close you could swear they kick up swirls of snow. It may be reassuring to know that only one flight has failed to make it safely in recent years, and that incident was apparently not as a result of pilot error or mechanical failure, but because the plane was brought down by rocket fire from Afghanistan.

### MINIBUS

Sturdy 4WD vans and Jeeps leave from the bazaar for Dushanbe (21 hours, 100TJS to 120TJS) when full. Get there in the morning and be prepared to hang around for hours before finally leaving. You might score a ride in a Land Cruiser for 150TJS per seat.

Minibuses to Murgab (eight hours, 50TJS) depart when full from 200m east of the bazaar, assuming there are enough passengers.

Four-wheel drives and minibuses to Ishkashim (three hours, 20TJS) leave in the late morning from a lot just across the river from the bazaar. You'll have to be lucky to find shared transport headed all the way to Langar, though they do exist. Drivers regularly squeeze eight passengers into the four seats!

There are also daily minibuses to Porshnev, Rushan, Roshtqala, Kalaikhum and, sometimes, Jelandy. The last three generally leave from the bazaar. Most transport leaves Khorog in the afternoon, taking villagers back home for the night. Note that very little transport runs on Sundays.

## Getting Around

Minibus 3 (1TJS) runs from the bazaar to the UPD district. The same trip by taxi costs around 5TJS.

# BARTANG VALLEY

The stark and elemental Bartang Valley is one of the wildest and most beautiful in the western Pamirs and offers a fine opportunity for an adventurous multiday 4WD adventure. At times the fragile road is only perilously inches between the raging river below and sheer cliffs above. Only the occasional fertile alluvial plain brings a flash of green to the barren rock walls.

The road into the Bartang branches off the main road to Dushanbe, just before the village of Rushan, 61km from Khorog. After the village of **Yemts**, famous for its musicians, look for the footbridge that marks the start of the wonderful hike up the **Geisev Valley** (see below). A further 9km up the main valley is the village of Khidjef, which offers more hiking routes (see below).

The lovely village of **Basid**, 50km further, boasts two shrines (tourists can't visit the upper one) and scenic forests 5km up a side valley. It's a good place to overnight.

About 9km from Basid, it's worth taking the very rough side road 9km up to **Bardara**, at the junction of two gorgeous valleys. The hospitable village has two ancient shrines and foot trails lead up to summer pastures and over high passes to Bachor. Ask to see the village *khalodelnik* (fridge).

The road to **Savnob** switches back high up the valley side and then down into a protected bowl. The ruined fort (used as a village toilet) and the hillside caves here served as protection against raids by Afghans, Kyrgyz or the neighbouring valley of Yazgulom. The village of **Roshorv**, high above the valley, is another possible detour. From Savnob the road continues to the start of trekking routes (see p391) near Ghudara.

Up a side valley are the villages of Nisar and **Barchadiev,** which is the trailhead for treks up to **Sarez** (see p384). You'll need a permit (see p394) to hike beyond Barchadiev.

## Sleeping

There are three homestays in the Geisev valley (see below). In Basid, tourists can stay at the **homestay** (dm US$5) of Niyazbek Niayazbekov, the head of the local *jamoat* (village committee).

In Savnob, stay at the homestays of Saodat Niyazova (with satellite TV!) or the garrulous English teacher Tobchibek Bekov. There are also homestays in Nisar (Niyazov Hosil) and Barchadiev (Mavlodaut Moscayev). Expect to pay around US$6 per person for a homestay, plus around US$4 for dinner and breakfast.

## Getting There & Away

Minibuses run between Savnob and Khorog but only every few days (35TJS), so the only practical way to visit the Bartang Valley is by hired car. A trip from Khorog to Savnob and back, via Bardara, eats up about 420km. Make sure your driver has a spare jerry can of fuel, as there is little, if any petrol available en route.

### TREKKING IN THE GEISEV VALLEY

The lovely traditional Pamiri villages and multicoloured lakes of the Geisev Valley offer the best short trekking destination from Khorog. Better still, a fledgling ecotourism project is supporting homestays in the valley's three villages, where travellers can buy food and hire donkeys and a guide if needed. This gives travellers the rare opportunity to hike amongst some of the loveliest scenery in the Pamirs without the need to carry a tent and food.

From the suspension bridge, 23km from the turn-off to the Bartang Valley, it's a 2½-hour walk uphill to the first village, by the second lake. From the first village it's an easy half-hour walk to the second village, and a further 30 minutes to the third village. From here it's an hour to the large third lake.

Beyond the third lake, you'll need tents to continue to the fourth and fifth lakes, summer pastures and glacier. For a demanding longer trek, it's possible to hike over the ridge to Ravmed in the Khidjef valley in two days, with the option of continuing up to the head of that valley for views of Patkhor Peak (6083m). A homestay is being established in Ravmed.

An overnight, or, better still, two-night excursion is the best way to soak up the gorgeous scenery. Car travel from Khorog to Geisev is 85km each way, which at current car-hire rates costs around US$40, plus a daily rate for the driver to wait for you. Cars should park 1.5km past the suspension bridge, up a small side road.

 

**AN ACCIDENT WAITING TO HAPPEN**

As if Tajikistan didn't have enough to worry about, geologists warn that the country faces a potential natural disaster of immense proportions. The watery 'Sword of Damocles' lies high in the Pamirs in the shape of Lake Sarez, a 60km-long body of disarmingly pretty turquoise water half the size of Lake Geneva. Lake Sarez was formed in 1911 when an earthquake dislodged an entire mountain side into the path of the Murgab River, obliterating the villages of Usoi and Sarez. Slowly but surely a 500m-deep lake formed behind the 770m-high natural dam of rocks and mud known as the Usoi Dam. If a regional earthquake were to break this plug or create a wave to breach the dam, as some experts think could happen, a huge wall of water would sweep down the mountain valleys, wiping away roads and villages deep into Uzbekistan, Turkmenistan and Afghanistan, with flood waters reaching as far as the Aral Sea. Experts warn that it would be the largest flood ever witnessed by human eyes.

High river flows often wash away sections of the road in early summer.

Past Savnob, a road of sorts continues on to Kök Jar (see p390) and Murgab but the road is in *very* bad condition and only worth contemplating at the end of summer and with a reliable 4WD. Check beforehand whether the road is open. As one local told us, 'The road to Kök Jar is fine but at the end of the trip both the car and driver will be destroyed.'

## SHOKH DARA VALLEY ШОХ ДАРА

A 4WD road winds up the Shokh Dara Valley southeast of Khorog, offering a fine overnight excursion from Khorog or, with your own transport, a loop route option, connecting with the Pamir Hwy and returning to Khorog via the Gunt Valley or the Wakhan.

About 34km from Khorog (7km before Roshtqala) you'll see an alluvial plain on the right that until 2002 was the village of **Dasht**. The huge mud slide killed 24 and diverted the river. Due to the lack of arable land, most Pamiris live on such volatile alluvial plains.

The main town in the valley is **Roshtqala** (Red Fort), named after the ruined fort above the town. The village has daily transport from Khorog and homestay accommodation.

One potential detour is the day-long walk from Vrang to scenic Durum-Kul. Alternatively, drive part of the way and make it a half-day hike (90 minutes each way). Further up the valley look out for **forts** at Shashbuvad and Deruj.

Just before **Javshanguz** are dramatic views of peaks **Engels** (6507m) and **Karla Marxa** (6723m). One enticing trekking route follows an old 4WD track over the 4432m Mats Pass into the Pamir Valley.

From Javshanguz the scenery blurs from the jagged valleys of the western Pamirs to the plateau scenery of the eastern Pamirs, as the rough 4WD road runs to **Turuntai-Kul**, 29km away and 6km off the main road. From here the main road winds down to the Pamir Hwy just beyond Jelandy, but there is a difficult river crossing en route for which you'll need a high-clearance 4WD. It's generally easier to cross near the lake; ask herders for the best route.

### Sleeping

There are homestays at Roshtqala and Javshanguz (with Arabshoev Mekhrabshoe and Mazabshoev Mazabsho).

### Getting There & Away

Minibuses to Roshtqala (5TJS) depart Khorog around noon, except on Sundays, returning to Khorog around 7am or 8am. Occasional transport continues further up the valley, or travellers can arrange to pay for the extra leg to Javshanghuz (around US$15 for the vehicle).

A day trip to Javshanghuz from Khorog costs around US$60 for the car.

## THE WAKHAN VALLEY

The Tajik half of the superbly remote Wakhan Valley, shared with Afghanistan, is a fantastic side trip from Khorog, either en route to Murgab or as a loop returning via the Gunt or Shokh Dara Valleys. The route's many side valleys reveal stunning views of the 7000m peaks of the Hindu Kush (Killer of Hindus), marking the border with Pakistan. Marco Polo travelled through the valley in AD 1274.

You will need to have Ishkashim marked on your GBAO permit to travel this road. There are military checkpoints at Khargush and near Namadguti.

Some 46km south of Khorog, and 7km from the junction at Anderob, the hot springs of **Garam Chashma** make for a nice soak and there are several homestays nearby.

Continuing south of Anderob towards Ishkashim, you'll see the **Koh-i-Lal ruby mine** from the road. The region's gem mines were mentioned by Marco Polo (who called the region Mt Shugnon) and Badakhshani rubies are still famed throughout the region. There are good views of Afghanistan from here, with its pyramid-shaped hay stacks and donkey caravans.

**Ishkashim** is the Wakhan's regional centre and largest village. Every other Saturday there is a transborder market at the bridge crossing to Afghanistan, 3km west of town.

Some 15km from Ishkashim, near the village of Namadguti, is the impressive Kushan-era **Khakha Fortress**, dating from the third century BC and rising from a platform of natural rock. The fort is currently occupied by Tajik border guards, so ask before taking pictures, though the lower parts of the fort are generally accessible. Just 300m further on is the interesting Ismaili *mazar* (tomb) of Shah-i-Mardan Hazrati Ali, one of many places in Central Asia that claim to be the final resting place of the Prophet's son-in-law.

Seven kilometres from Namadguti is the valley's major checkpost, across from a ruined fortress. A further 20km, is the village of **Darshai**, where trekking routes lead over the mountains to the Shokh Dara Valley.

A further 57km from Khakha, 3km past Ptup village, is the turn-off for the ruined 12th-century **Yamchun Fort** (also known as Zulkhomar Fort), the most impressive in the valley, complete with multiple walls and round watchtowers. The site is a 6km switch-backed drive from the main road and sits about 500m above the valley. Climb up the hillside west of the fort for the best views. About 1km further uphill from the fort are the **Bibi Fatima Springs** (8am-6pm; admission locals/foreigners 1/5TJS), probably the nicest in the region and named after the Prophet Mohammed's sister. Women believe they can boost their fertility by visiting the womblike calcite formations. Bring a towel and keep an eye on your valuables as there are no lockers. Men's and women's bath times alternate every half hour.

**Yamg** village is worth a brief stop for the **tomb** and **reconstructed house museum** of Sufi mystic, astronomer and musician Mubarak Kadam Wakhani (1843–1903). You can see the stone that he used as a solar calendar. If the museum is closed, ask around for Aydar Malikmadov.

**Vrang** is worth a stop for its fascinating 4th-century Buddhist stupas (some say fire-worshipping platforms). All around the ruins are the sulphurous remains of geothermal activity, as well as dozens of hermit caves. Walk through the village, cross the water channel and it's a steep scramble to the site. Locals can show you the village's water-driven mill. There's a small museum and shrine at the base of the hill.

Four kilometres further on, along the Wakhan plain, is Umbugh Qala, used by the Tajik military and so off-limits. Some 16km from Vrang you'll pass a colourful hot springs area, where locals stop for a hot bath. Four kilometres further, look across the river to the ruined Afghan fort of Qala-i-Panja, once the largest settlement in the Wakhan.

A further 29km (4km before Langar) is **Abrashim Qala** (Vishim Qala in Wakhi), the 'Silk Fortress' of Zong, built to guard this branch of the Silk Road from Chinese and Afghan invaders. The fort offers perhaps the most scenic views of all those in the valley. It's a steep 45-minute hike up the hillside, though 4WDs can drive part way via Dirj village.

**Langar** (population 1800) is strategically situated where the Pamir and Wakhan Rivers join to form the Pyanj, marking the start of Afghanistan's upper Wakhan, or Sarkhad region. It's an excellent base to visit surrounding sites. For a half-day hike, hire a local guide (US$5) for the hour-long walk uphill (500m vertical ascent) to a collection of over 6000 petroglyphs. The village *jamoat khana* is easily recognisable by its colourful wall murals. Across the road is the *mazar* of Shoh Kambari Oftab, the man who brought Ismailism to Langar.

**Ratm Fort** has a strategic location, surrounded on three sides by cliffs. It's 5.5km from Langar and a 15-minute walk off the main road through bushes. Its name means 'first' as it is the first fort in the valley.

From Langar the road continues 77km to a military check post at **Khargush**. En route keep your eyes peeled for Bactrian camels on the far (Afghan) side of the Pamir River. At Khargush the main road leads uphill over a pass (look behind for stunning views of the Koh-i-Pamir massif in Afghanistan) to the salt lake of **Chokur-Kul**, 25km from Khargush, which is normally teeming with bird life. From here it's 12km to the main Pamir Hwy.

The protected area of Zor-Kul, further up the Pamir Valley from the Khorgush checkpost, can only be visited with a permit from Dushanbe and permission from the border guards (though there are actually no checks if you approach the lake from its eastern end, via Jarty-Gumbaz – see p390). The lake was determined to be the source of the Oxus River during the 1842 expedition of Lieutenant Wood, when it was named Lake Victoria.

## Sleeping

In Ishkashim, the **Hanis Guesthouse** (☎ 2 13 55; per person US$10, or US$15 full board), run by Sanavbar Khonjonov, is a decent MSDSP-assisted homestay at the west end of town, next to the *militsia* (police) station. If Sanavbar is home, he can provide information about onward travel in Afghanistan.

To stay in Darshai ask for the friendly homestay of the Dilovar family.

At Yamchun, it's possible to stay the night at the nearby small **sanatorium** (dm 15TJS) or at the simple homestays of Otashbek Nazirov, Mirshakar Nazirov or Alifkhan Makonshoev in the village of Vitchkut, below the fort.

In Langar, it's possible to stay at the MSDSP-supported **jamoat khana** (dm US$10), also known as the House Museum, which boasts a Western-style toilet, and rates include breakfast and dinner. Other options here include the homestays of Nasab Talgunsho or Imomyor Baikaraev, both a five-minute drive away.

## Transport

Ishkashim has transport to Khorog (three hours, 20TJS) every morning (see p383). There are occasional minibuses from Langar to Ishkashim (20TJS) and Khorog (40TJS).

# THE PAMIR HIGHWAY
# ПАМИРСКОЕ ШОССЕ

The Pamir Hwy from Khorog to Osh (a section of the M41) was built by Soviet military engineers between 1931 and 1934, in order to facilitate troops, transport and provisioning to this very remote outpost of the Soviet empire. Off-limits to travellers until recently, the extremely remote high-altitude road takes you through Tibetan-style high plateau scenery populated by yurts and yaks and studded with deep-blue lakes.

Being a major drug-smuggling artery, the road has several border-guard checkpoints, where you will have to register. Most of the traffic these days is Chinese trucks and minivans travelling to/from Kashgar over the Qolma Pass.

Blue kilometre posts line the way with the distance from Khorog marked on one side and from Osh on the other.

## Khorog to Murgab

### THE GUNT VALLEY TO THE KOI-TEZEK PASS

The initial 120km stretch out of Khorog climbs the attractive and well-watered Gunt Valley. At the east end of town, by the campus of the new University of Central Asia, look for a monument to the Pamir Hwy in the form of the first car ever to make the trip from Osh to Khorog. Just past here, near a sign commemorating '70 years of the USSR', a large concrete overhang protects the road from landslides. At Suchan, 10km from Khorog, your passport and GBAO permit will be checked.

At Bogev village, 15km from centre of Khorog, it's possible to visit **Kafir-Qala** (Fortress of the Infidels), a faint ruined citadel with two circular Aryan temples. Further up the Gunt Valley, by the roadside before Shahzud, there's a pretty cascade created by a landslide. As the road continues to climb, there are spectacular views back to the dramatic vertical peaks of the Gunt Valley.

About 8km before Jelandy, just past a concrete ibex statue, a dirt road branches left to a **hot springs** complex, where you can soak in the curative hot water pool.

At **Jelandy**, at the 120km post, is a recently renovated **guesthouse** (dm 10-15TJS) with more hot springs and even a disco. This is a favourite stop for truck drivers out of Khorog, so don't expect much peace and quiet. It's a bit off the road; ask for the *kurort* (sanatorium).

A further 12km past Jelandy a rough dirt road branches right uphill to eventually join the Shokh Dara Valley (see p384). A side track on this road offers a challenging detour to the impressive high-altitude lake **Turuntai-Kul** (see p384).

The main road switchbacks to the 4272m **Koi-Tezek Pass**, after which the mountains pull back from the road to reveal the lunar-like high-altitude desert, framed by snowy peaks, that marks the start of the Pamir plateau. Some 16km on from the pass a statue of a Marco Polo sheep marks the entry to Murgab *rayon* (district).

TAJIKISTAN

### ADVENTURES AROUND YASHIL-KUL

Several good trekking routes start from the area north and west of Yashil-Kul, including to Sarez Lake or the loop route via Zarosh-Kul and Chapdar-Kul (see p391).

Alternatively, adventurers could spend a couple of days hiking and hitching down the Gunt Valley, along the northern shore of the lake, past Bachor to the Pamir Hwy near Shahzud. You'll need to navigate the cable crossing over the river where the Langor river joins the Gunt. It's possible to hire donkeys or horses (30TJS per day) at Bachor or Shahzud. Bachor, 18km from the Pamir Hwy, has three homestays, of the Sultanshah family, Shoidonboi Tursunbaev and Sangnanad Narodmamadov.

Another possible route, by foot or 4WD, follows the dirt track across the Sumantash plain, between Alichur and Bulunkul, passing the hot spring at Ak-Jar.

### BULUNKUL TO MURGAB

Just 36km after the pass a dirt road shoots off to the left for 16km, to the end-of-the-world Tajik settlement of **Bulunkul**, where it's possible to stay at the META-supported **homestay** (per person US$6) of Mahbuba Nabieva or at a nearby yurtstay. (For more on META see p388).

From the village it's a short drive or a one-hour walk to get views of **Yashil-Kul** (Green Lake, 3734m), a surreal turquoise lake framed by ochre desert. Look for the warm springs on the southern side. Archaeological sites by the lake include the 4000-year-old stone circles at the mouth of the Bolshoi Marjonai River and the **mausoleum of Bekbulat** on the north bank of the Alichur River. The area was once the major trade route between the eastern and western Pamirs.

Back on the highway, just past the turn-off to Bulunkul pause at the impressive viewpoint overlooking the salt lakes of the sweeping Alichur plain. The highway descends to the turn-off right to Khargush and the Wakhan (see p384), then passes Tuz-Kul (Salt Lake) and **Sassyk-Kul** (Stinking Lake), before reaching **Alichur** village. The plain around Alichur is one of the most fertile in the region and is dotted with Kyrgyz yurts in summer.

Just 14km past Alichur, stop at the remarkable holy **Ak-Balyk** (White Fish) spring by the side of the road. The nearby **fish restaurant** (fish 3-5TJS) is popular with Chinese truck drivers.

Just past Ak-Balyk a 4WD track branches north to the remote 11th-century ruins of a silver mine and caravanserai at **Bazar-Dara**, 40km from the highway in a side valley over the 4664m Bazar-Dara Pass. A visit to the site entails a five-hour 90km return drive along a very rough road. The site was once home to 1700 miners and you can just about make out raised dais and fireplaces and the remains of nearby baths, complete with underfloor heating. Climb above the site for the best overview. Just 5km further from the ruins are the Bronze-age **Ak-Jilga petroglyphs**, some of the world's highest at 3800m, which depict miniature chariots, archers, ibex and skeletons. META offers a yurtstay in the Shamurat Valley, on the south side of the pass, 12km from the Pamir Hwy.

About 20km further along the highway, 3km outside the village of **Bash Gumbaz** (itself 7km off the main highway) is a photogenic **Chinese tomb**, marking the high tide of Chinese influence on the Pamir. Five kilometres further down the main highway you'll pass **Chatyr Tash**, a large square stone that can be seen for miles.

A further 50km is another turn-off to the right, this time to the Jarty-Gumbaz region (p390). Around 25km down this track and well worth the detour is the wonderfully preserved Neolithic cave painting of **Shakhty** (see p390).

Back on the main road, there are two final police checks, 9km apart, just before you cross the Madiyan Valley and sweep into Murgab.

## Murgab

**☎ 3554 / pop 6500 / elevation 3576m**

The wild-east town of Murgab is a day's drive (310km) from Khorog. A former Tsarist garrison like Khorog, but rougher around the edges, Murgab isn't exactly charming but it is a good base from which to explore the eastern Pamirs. The town itself is half-Kyrgyz, half-Tajik (the surrounding communities are almost all Kyrgyz) and there is some tension between the two communities. On clear days, the 7546m-high Chinese peak of Muztagh Ata is visible to the northeast of town.

Electricity alternates daily between the two halves of town but is of such low voltage as to

 

### ECOTOURISM IN MURGAB

Created by the French NGO Acted as part of its Pamir High Mountain Integrated Project (http://phiproject.free.fr), the **Murgab Ecotourism Association (META)** has revolutionised independent travel in the Pamirs. Through a network of 60 community-based tourism providers, ranging from Jeep drivers to camel owners, the organisation essentially links together travellers and locals, helping to spread the economic benefits of tourism throughout the impoverished Murgab region. It's a really great place to organise a Pamir adventure, so try to budget a couple of extra days to take advantage of the programme.

The programme offers yurtstays in the Pshart and Madiyan Valleys, Bulunkul and Karakul and can arrange homestays in Karakul, Bulunkul, Rangkul and Alichur. There are more yurtstays further away at Rang-Kul, the Jalang Valley Kök Jar/Sheralu and in the Shamurat Valley (south of Bazar-Dara). Note that yurts start to move down from the higher mountain valleys in the middle of September.

Costs are US$5 to US$8 per person in a yurt, US$6 in a homestay, plus US$6 for three meals. Treks and English-speaking guides (US$15 per day) can also be arranged (ask them about the three-day trek from Elisu in the Madiyan Valley to Shamurat near Bazar-Dara, via herders' yurts in Chat and Koburgun), and they also organise 4WD hire and even camel trekking. Mountain-bike hire is planned. META collects a reasonable 15% commission on all services to cover its running costs. Feedback on the programme and its services is welcomed.

Acted has also protected several archaeological sties and helped set up the **Yak House** (see opposite), which trains around 250 local women in Tajik and Pamiri crafts to provide much-needed additional income to marginalised families.

be of marginal use, so don't expect to recharge batteries here.

Murgab operates on Badakhshani time, which is an hour after Dushanbe, and the same as neighbouring Kyrgyzstan.

Murgab House, a new ecocentre in the northern outskirts of town, houses META (see above), the Yak House (see opposite), a small museum and an internet café. The cleverly-designed building incorporates architectural elements from both a Kyrgyz yurt and a Pamiri house.



### INFORMATION

The one essential address is the our pick **Murgab Ecotourism Association** (META; ☎ 2 17 66; meta@acted.org; Murgab House; 9am-6pm); for details on META see the boxed text above. Apart from arranging trips, the office sells useful brochures on archaeological sites in the eastern Pamir, as well as Marcus Hauser's map of the Pamirs (US$11), plus you can browse its great Soviet-era maps of the region. Ask for Ubaidullah or Aimgul.

Travellers are required to register at the **KGB** (Kizmat-i-Amniyat-i-Milli) office across from the Lenin statue. META can help with this and will get the KGB to authorise any itinerary you book through them.

META can also help you with the required registration with OVIR (free if you have registered elsewhere in Tajikistan), which is also by the Lenin statue.

The *aqimat* (local government) requires visitors pay a US$1 per day 'ecological tax'. META collects this from people on its tours but you won't find anyone else asking for it.

### SLEEPING & EATING

META can arrange excellent **homestays** (dm US$6, meals US$5) in town, including those of Apal Doskulieva, Aizada Murzaeva, Yrys Toktobekova, Arzybai Matarozov and Gulnamo Nosirshoeva. Expect to get a bed on the floor, tasty homemade food, a clean outside squat toilet, an *umuvalnik* (hand basin), hot water in buckets and a warm welcome. META plans to grade the homestays and create a range of prices from US$6 to US$10. Several of the homestays are in the southern Jar-Bashy district of town.

**Surab's Guesthouse** (☎ 2 16 53; per person US$8, with full board US$15) This comfortable private guesthouse is run by English-speaking Surab and has comfortable rooms, with an outside toilet and sauna. Choose between beds or traditional mattresses on the floor. Look for the wooden house northwest of the centre.

**Ibrahim/Anara GH** (☎ 2 13 24; Frunze 30; dm US$10, hot bath US$3) The former Acted guest house has an indoor bathroom, generator, nice sitting area and a kitchen but lacks the family feel of the homestays. Breakfast and dinner included in the rates.

META driver Ergesh Tadjibaiev plans to offer a private **homestay** (☎ 2 15 47; Aksuu 7; dm US$4 or US$8 with dinner & breakfast) in the Koprö Bashy district south of town.

You can buy basic foodstuffs at the uninspiring bazaar in the north of town but your best bet for food is to eat in your homestay.

#### SHOPPING

The **Yak House** (Murgab House; 9am-6pm) is a showroom for Acted's crafts project, selling traditional Pamiri-style *chorapi* socks, plus table mats, pillow cases, felt wall-hangings and wool rugs, all decorated with traditional Kyrgyz motifs. Prices are marked, as are the names of the craftswomen.

#### GETTING THERE & AWAY

The easiest way to arrange transport is to band together a small group and hire a 4WD from META. The rate at the time of research was US$0.34 to US$0.38 per km, depending on the road quality, but this will doubtless rise over time with the price of fuel.

Minibuses to both Khorog (eight hours, 320km, 50TJS) and Osh (12 hours, 420km, 70TJS) depart every day or two when full. Expect to wait for hours for the vehicle to fill up. Private drivers also hang around the bazaar. One private driver recommended by some travellers is **Pamirbek** (☎ 2 13 38, 93-508 3973).

If you are thinking of hitching, most Chinese trucks headed to/from the Qolma Pass stop at a depot 2km northeast of town along the road to the Qolma Pass.

### Around Murgab

#### GUMBEZKUL VALLEY

One excellent short, but adventurous, trip is to hike up the **Gumbezkul Valley** from its junction with the Pshart Valley, 35km northwest of Murgab. The 9km hike takes you from a META yurtstay (see opposite) over the 4731m Gumbezkul Pass, steeply down the southern Gumbezkul Valley to another META yurtstay, from where a rough 4WD road leads 7km down to the Madiyan Valley, 22km from Murgab. The path is easy to follow and there are stunning views in both directions from the pass, though it's a steep scramble on either side. It's a half-day hike from yurt to yurt. A 4WD hire to drop you off at the northern yurts and pick you up the next morning on the other side of the pass costs around US$50 through META. META also offers yurtstays at Kyzyl Jilga and Jar Jilga (*jilga* means valley) further up the Pshart Valley. The turn-off to the Pshart Valley is 6km north of Murgab, by some Saka (Scythian) graves.

For a post-hike soak, the **Madiyan hot springs** (admission 1TJS), 35km from Murgab, are just up the Madiyan Valley from its junction with the southern Gumbezkul Valley – ask for the *issyk chashma* (hot spring in Kyrgyz).

#### RANG-KUL

The scenic **Rang-Kul** area, 65km from Murgab, is a potential detour en route to Karakul (see p391). Five kilometres after you turn off the Pamir Hwy are some Saka tombs. Further on are the lakes of Shor-Kul and Rang-Kul, with fine views of Muztagh Ata over the border in China.

META (see opposite) runs camel treks between herders' camps in the three valleys to the south of Rang-Kul. A three-day trek costs around US$135 per person for camel hire, food and accommodation, plus around US$100 per vehicle (not per person) to get you to Rang-Kul and back.

The nearby border with China was recently delimited, ceding a 10km strip to China, so you may have troubles getting beyond the border checkpost at Rangkul village, 15km past the lake.

#### SHAIMAK

To really get off-the-beaten track, take the road up the Ak-Suu Valley to Shaimak, 126km from Murgab, at the strategic junction of the borders of Tajikistan, Afghanistan, China and Pakistan. This is about as Great Game as it gets! You will need KGB approval to travel past the checkpoint before Tokhtamysh.

After crossing the lovely Subashi plain, the road passes the turn-off to the Qolma Pass (see p396), Tajikistan's only border crossing with China (currently closed to foreigners). You may be rewarded with views of Muztagh-Ata from here.

At the village of Tokhtamysh you could detour 1km across the river to a damaged bow-shaped geoglyph and the faint ruins of a 19th-century caravanserai. The scenery gets increasingly impressive, passing rolling Pamiri peaks, seasonal lakes and scenic yurts.

 

There's not much to **Shaimak** village (3852m), located below the impressive 5365m bluff of Ak Tash, except for its striking mosque and exciting views of the Little Pamir. The Chinese border is only 10km from here. You might get permission to continue to the geoglyphs and the 2500-year-old Saka *kurgans* (tombs) at Ak Beit, 3km south of Shaimak. Three days a year in June the border is opened to cross-border trade with Kyrgyz herders living in the very remote Little Wakhan region of Afghanistan, and is not open to foreigners.

If you have time on the way back, stop for a quick look at the beehive-shaped tombs at **Konye Kurgan** (Old Tomb), 7km from Murgab.

Return 4WD hire through META to Shaimak costs about US$100 for the 240km trip.

### SHAKHTY & ZOR-KUL

The impressive Neolithic cave paintings of **Shakhty** (4200m) are 50km southwest of Murgab, 25km off the Pamir Hwy, in the dramatic Kurteskei Valley. Soviet archaeologists apparently took shelter in the cave during a storm one night in 1958, only to awake the next morning open-mouthed in front of the perfectly preserved red-ink paintings of a bear hunt. Check out the strange birdman to the left. Don't get too close to the paintings to avoid damaging them. The cave is a five-minute scramble up the hillside; you'll never find it without a knowledgeable driver.

META offers a day tour that takes in Shakhty, the Shor-Bulak observatory (currently closed to foreigners) and Shor-Bulak pass, with fine views of Muztagh Ata, to the meteorite site of Ak-Bura in the Ak-Suu valley, and back to Murgab.

For a longer trip, continue south over two minor passes and past a seasonal lake rich in birdlife to the Istyk River and the remote Jarty-Gumbaz region. The slightly Mafiosi-feeling **hunting camp** (☎ 3554-2 16 39, 2 33 33; murgabhunt@mail.ru) here is marked by a hot water pool, a small Kyrgyz cemetery and a depressing stack of Marco Polo sheep horns. Contact Atobek Bekmuradov.

Basic accommodation is available at yurtstays in **Ak-Kalama**, 13km south of the hunting camp near the Afghan border, but it's better to continue 17km over a low pass to the impressive yurt camps at **Kara-Jilga**. The superb scenery here is classic Wakhan, with epic views over a string of glorious turquoise lakes (Kazan-Kul and Djigit-Kul) to the snow-capped Wakhan Range that borders Afghanistan. Continue east to the end of these lakes and you will be rewarded with rare views of **Zor-Kul** (elevation 4125m) stretching into distance. To continue on to Khargush you'll need hard-to-get permits (see p394) from Dushanbe to get past the border posts and watch towers.

From Jarty-Gumbaz it's possible to take an alternative route northwest to join the Pamir Hwy 3km east of Chatyr Tash. From Murgab to Jarty-Gumbaz and Zor-Kul and on to Chatyr Tash is about 225km.

Note that this region can be wet and boggy in early summer (June and July), making transport difficult.

### JALANG & KÖK JAR

North of Murgab and southwest of Karakul are several interesting sites, including the petroglyphs and pastures of **Jalang** (150km from Murgab), which make a great overnight trip from Murgab.

META has yurtstays at Jalang and also at Dangi, back at the junction with the main valley. Alternatively, stay at the yurt of Baba Nazar at Tora Bulak, 4km before Jalang. There are petroglyphs near the *aul* (yurt camp) at Jalang and in half a day it's possible to climb the 5129m peak to the southwest for fine views of the Pamirs.

The dirt road to Jalang branches off the Pamir Hwy near Muzkol and passes south of Mt Urtabuz (5047m). (Fit and acclimatised hikers can climb the peak for dramatic views of Kara-Kul, but you'll need a guide and most of the day to find the right route up.) The dirt road swings into the Kök Ubel Valley, past the small lake of Kurun-Kul, past fine views towards the impressive peaks of Muzkol (6128m) and Zartosh (6121m).

Fifty kilometres further, down the Kök Ubel valley takes you to the geometric stone symbols of **Kök Jar** (also known as Shurali), which are thought to have acted as a Stonehenge-like solar calendar as far back as 2500 years ago.

From here, the remote Tanymas Valley offers demanding trekking access to the **Fedchenko Glacier**, one of the world's longest. A very rough road continues southwest to meet the Bartang Valley (see p383) at Ghudara, but you should check that the road is passable before considering this very remote route.

If you are heading on to Karakul after Jalang, it's possible to take a short cut along the southern shores of the lake.

### Murgab to Sary Tash

North of Murgab, the road passes the turn-offs to the Pshart Valley (6km) and then Rang-Kul (24km), before swinging close to the Chinese border. In places the twin barbed-wire-topped fences run less than 20m from the road.

Soon the mountains close in as the road climbs towards the **Ak-Baital** (White Horse) Pass, at 4655m, the highest point of the journey. From here it's a long descent of some 70km to Kara-Kul, the highest lake in Central Asia. Just after the pass there are nice views back up a side valley leading to Muzkol Peak.

About 20km from the pass are the remains of a 19th-century Russian tsarist post, later used by the Red Army in battles with White Russians and *basmachi* rebels. A further 6km a dirt track to the left offers access to Jalang and Kök Jar (opposite).

Created by a meteor approximately 10 million years ago, **Kara-Kul** (3914m) has an eerie, twilight-zone air about it. The Chinese pilgrim Xuan Zang passed by the lake in AD 642, referring to it as the Dragon Lake. Marco Polo also passed by some six centuries later after transiting the Wakhan, and both Sven Hedin and Austrian traveller Gustav Krist later camped by the lake. Local Kyrgyz call the deep-blue, lifeless lake Chong Kara-Kul (Big Black Lake), compared to Kishi Kara-Kul (Lesser Black Lake) along the Karakoram Hwy in China. Although salty, the lake is frozen and covered in snow until the end of May.

The only settlement of any significance here is the lakeside village of **Karakul**, where META can arrange a homestay at the house of Saodat Kasymbekova or Tildakhan Kozubekova. Karakul lies right next to the CIS-Chinese border security zone and there's a passport check just before the village. Around 7km north of Karakul at Kara-Art, 500m off the road, there are some *kurgans* (burial mounds) and faint geoglyphs.

The border between Tajikistan and Kyrgyzstan is 63km from Karakul, just before the crest of the **Kyzyl-Art Pass** (4282m), but the Kyrgyz border post is a further 20km at **Bor Döbö**. Don't forget to look behind you here for a stunning panorama of the Pamir. Kyrgyzstan is one hour ahead of Tajikistan time (but the same as Murgab time). Kyrgyz border controls can take a long time, especially if you are travelling by truck.

At **Sary Tash**, 23km further, the A372 branches off southwest to the Pamir Alay Valley of Kyrgyzstan and the A371 heads northeast to the Kyrgyz–Chinese border post of Irkeshtam (p340). For more on the Alay Valley see p341.

# TAJIKISTAN DIRECTORY

## ACCOMMODATION

Lacking Uzbekistan's private B&Bs and Kyrgyzstan's comprehensive network of homestays, Tajikistan has patchy accommodation. Dushanbe is particularly short on good cheap accommodation. In fact, outside of the main towns, there is almost no formal hotel accommodation.

The Pamir region has an excellent network of homestays and yurtstays that offer easily the best accommodation and there are often informal homestays along many other mountain roads. If you hire a car, your driver will most likely know a family where you intend to stay. If you are invited to stay at someone's house a reasonable amount to offer is the equivalent of US$10 per person, including breakfast and dinner.

As with much of Central Asia, accommodation rates are often quoted in US dollars but you can pay in either US dollars or somani.

## ACTIVITIES

Trekking options are fantastic in Tajikistan, principally in the Fan Mountains and western Pamirs, though these are demanding, remote routes. Mountaineers will be in heaven and even a few hardcore kayakers are discovering Tajikistan's remote white water. See the Activities chapter on p91 for details.

The most obvious treks outside of the Fan Mountains include the following:

**Bazar-Dara** (four days) Loop trek to archaeological site and petroglyphs, heading in over the Bazar-Dara Pass and out via the 4918m Ak-Jilga Pass. See p387.

**Darshai Valley** (three to four days) Up the Darshai Valley to summer pastures and views of Mayokovskiy Peak. Back the same way or over a 4941m pass and down the Badom Valley to Roshtqala.

**Grum Grijimailoo Glacier** (four to five days) Two routes, from Kök Jar in the east up the Tanymas Valley, or north up the Khavraz Dara Valley from Pasor in the upper Bartang Valley.

**Gumbezkul Valley and Pass** (one day). See p389.

**Javshanguz to Langar** (two days) Following a former 4WD track over the 4432m Mats Pass into the Pamir Valley.

**Karatag Valley** (two to three days) To Timur Dara and Payron lakes, see p366.
**Yashil-Kul to Sarez Lake** (six to seven days) Via Bachor village, Andaravaj River, 4587m pass, Zarush-Kul, Vikhynch, Langar Valley, Irkhit dam, Murgab River to Barchadiev.

## EMBASSIES & CONSULATES

### Tajik Embassies in Central Asia

For Tajik embassies in Almaty (Kazakhstan), Ashgabat (Turkmenistan), Tashkent (Uzbekistan) and Bishkek (Kyrgyzstan) see the relevant country chapters. Bishkek and Almaty are good places to get a Tajik visa.

### Tajik Embassies & Consulates

**Afghanistan** (☎ 020 2301565; House 3, St 10, Wazir Akbar Khan) Tajik visas are reputedly difficult to get from here.
**Austria** (☎ 1-409 82 66 11; www.tajikembassy.org; Universitätesstrasse 8/1A, 1090 Vienna) Covering Austria and Switzerland.
**Belgium** (☎ 02-640 69 33; tajemb-belgium@skynet.be; 363-365 Ave Louise, 1050 Brussels)
**China** (☎ 10-6532 3039; 5-1-41 Dayuan Diplomatic Compound, 100 600 Beijing)
**Germany** (☎ 30-347 93 00; www.embassy-tajikistan.de; Otto-Sühr Allee 84, 10585 Berlin)
**Iran** (☎ 21-229 9584, 280 9249; tajemb-iran@mail.ru; Block 10, 3 Shahid Zinali, 610 Maidan-éKhiyobon, Tehran)
**Pakistan** (☎ 51-2294675; House 90, Main Double Rd, F-10/1 Islamabad)
**Russia** (☎ 095-290 38 46; www.tajikistan.ru; 13 Granatniy Pereulok, Moscow, 103001)
**Turkey** (☎ 312-446 1602; tajemb_turkey@hotmail.com; 36 M Ghandi Cad, Gaziosmanpasha, 06700 Ankara)
**USA** (☎ 202-223 6090; www.tjus.org; 1005 New Hampshire Ave NW, 20037 Washington DC)

#### VISAS FOR ONWARD TRAVEL

**Afghanistan** A 30-day visa (US$30) requires a letter of introduction from your embassy or a travel agency.
**China** Visas cost US$30 (one week to process) or US$50 (three days); one passport photo is required.
**Pakistan** Tourist visas require a letter from your embassy, two photos and a photocopy of your passport. You may need to wait for faxed visa approval from Islamabad. Prices are vague ('no more than US$100').
**Uzbekistan** Visas take three working days with a letter of invitation.

### Embassies & Consulates in Tajikistan

All of the following embassies are located in Dushanbe (map p361):
**Afghanistan** (☎ 221 64 18; fax 224 63 64; Pushkin 34; 9am-2pm Mon-Fri) Reeks of shashlyk and covered with photos of Ahmed Shah Masoud.
**China** (☎ 224 21 88; fax 224 41 22; Rudaki 143; 8.30am-11.30am Mon, Wed, Fri)
**France** (☎ 221 50 37; douchanbe.mission@netrt.org; Varzob 17)
**Germany** (☎ 221 21 89; www.duschanbe.diplo.de; Varzob 16; 8.30am-11.30am Mon-Fri) Represents those EU citizens without an embassy.
**India** (☎ 221 71 72; Bukhoro 45; 10am-noon, 2-4pm Mon-Fri)
**Iran** (☎ 221 00 72; fax 221 04 54; Tehran 18) Enter on the east side.
**Kazakhstan** (☎ 221 11 08; dipmiskz@tajnet.com; Husseinzoda 31/1; 9am-noon Mon, Wed, Fri) Look for the pastel-blue building set back from the main road.
**Kyrgyzstan** (☎ 221 63 84; kyremb@tajik.net; Studentcheskiy 67; 9am-noon Tue & Thu)
**Pakistan** (☎ 223 01 77; majeed@tojikiston.com; Dostoyevsky 1-3; 10am-1pm Mon-Fri)
**Russia** (☎ 221 10 15; www.rusembassy.tajnet.com; Abuali Ibn-Sino 29)
**Turkey** (☎ 221 22 08; turkdusa@tajnet.com; Rudaki 17/2)
**Turkmenistan** (☎ 21 73 87; fax 21 68 84; Chekhov 22; 9am-noon & 2-4pm Mon-Fri)
**UK** (☎ 224 22 21, emergency 917-708011; www.britishembassy.gov.uk/tajikistan; Mirzo Tursunzade 65)
**USA** (☎ 229 23 00; http://dushanbe.usembassy.gov; 109 Ismoili Somoni, Zarafshan district) Way out in the western suburbs.
**Uzbekistan** (☎ 224 15 86; 9am-noon Mon-Fri)

## FESTIVALS & EVENTS

Eid-e-Qurbon and Ramadan are celebrated in Tajikistan. See p449 for dates.

Ismaili communities in Badakhshan celebrate 24 March as Ruz-i-Nur, the Day of Lights, celebrating the first visit of the Aga Khan in 1995, as well as 11 July, the Day of the Imam.

With its links to a Persian past, Navrus (Nawroz) is the year's biggest festival and you are likely to see song and dance performances, and even *buzkashi* (a traditional pololike game), during this time (the latter most easily seen at Hissar).

## HOLIDAYS

**1 January** New Year's Day.
**8 March** International Women's Day.
**21–23 March** Eid e-Nawroz (Persian New Year), called Ba'at in Badakhshan.

**1 May** International Labour Day.
**9 May** Victory Day.
**27 June** Day of National Unity and Accord.
**9 September** Independence Day.
**6 November** Constitution Day.

## INTERNET ACCESS

Internet cafés are widespread in Dushanbe and Khojand, and cost around 4TJS per hour. Khorog has patchy internet access and connections are planned for Murgab.

## INTERNET RESOURCES

**Asia Plus** (www.asiaplus.tj/en) News service focusing on Tajikistan.
**National Museum of Antiquities** (www.afc.ryukoku.ac.jp/tj) Superb introduction to Tajikistan's history and the country's best museum.
**Pamirs.org** (www.pamirs.org) Excellent travel guide to the Pamirs, with virtual itineraries and good trekking information.
**Tajik Development Gateway** (www.tajik-gateway.org) News articles, weather forecasts and lots of links.
**Tajik Maps** (www.geocities.com/tajikmap/index.html) Collection of links to online maps of Tajikistan
**Travel Tajikistan** (www.traveltajikistan.com) Comprehensive travel site provided by the Great Game Travel Company.

Send an email to gulya@mariansguesthouse.com to subscribe to 'What's On in Dushanbe', a weekly mini-guide to Dushanbe, with classified ads from the expat community.

## MAPS

Marcus Hauser's 1:500,000 map of the Pamirs (see p378) is the best map of that region. It's available from www.geckomaps.com. A less detailed version is on view at www.pamirs.org/images/maps/pamir-gr.jpg.

Firma Geo in Almaty (see p116) is the best shot for 1:500,000 scale Russian maps covering Tajikistan (J-42 Dushanbe and J-43 Kashgar) from a series called *Generalnii Shtab*.

**Därr Expeditionsservice** (☎ 089-282032; Theresien Str 66, 80333 Munich; www.daerr.de) is one of the few places outside the region to sell these Russian topo maps. The website is in German only.

The University of Berne's Centre for Development and Environment has fascinating interactive topo and satellite maps of the Pamirs online at http://cdegis.unibe.ch/pamir/.

## MONEY

Tajikistan introduced the Tajik somani (TJS; divided into 100 dirham) in 2001. Somani notes come in one, five, 10, 20, 50 and 100 denominations. Dirham come in coins and notes.

Cash in US dollars, euros and Russian roubles are easily changed at numerous exchange booths. There is no black market for currency transactions.

You'll find a credit card and, more likely, cash the most practical ways to carry your money, especially if you are headed into the Pamirs. In Dushanbe, Khojand and Khorog you can access ATMs and/or get cash advances off a credit card, but at the time of research it was still impossible to cash travellers cheques. Both Uzbek sum and Kyrgyz som are accepted in border areas.

Exchange rates, current at the time of research, are listed below:

| Country | Unit | | Somani |
|---|---|---|---|
| Afghanistan | Afg1 | = | 0.069TJS |
| Australia | A$1 | = | 2.61TJS |
| China | Y1 | = | 0.43TJS |
| euro zone | €1 | = | 4.31TJS |
| Kazakhstan | 10 T | = | 0.26TJS |
| Kyrgyzstan | 10 som | = | 0.87TJS |
| Russian | R10 | = | 1.265TJS |
| UK | £1 | = | 6.45TJS |
| US | US$1 | = | 3.43TJS |
| Uzbekistan | 100 sum | = | 0.28TJS |

## POST

Tajikistan's postal service is a bit ropey and it's not uncommon for mail to take a month or more to reach its destination.

An international postcard/letter up to 20g costs around 0.75/1.35TJS to all countries except Russia. A package up to 1kg/2kg costs only around 13/20TJS. Rates to Russia are half this.

Couriers are the only reliable way to send important documents, though they charge up to US$70 for a 500g package. DHL has offices in **Dushanbe** (☎ 224 47 68) and **Khojand** (☎ 4 06 17).

## REGISTRATION

Foreigners staying in Tajikistan for longer than three days have to register with OVIR within 72 hours of arriving in Tajikistan. If entering from the north you'll probably have

TAJIKISTAN

to do this in Khojand. Coming from Osh you'll probably have to register with OVIR in Murgab and Khorog. Registering in Dushanbe is a real pain and is best avoided if you possibly can (see p362). You get a stamp in your passport when you register and this is generally checked when you exit the country, especially at Dushanbe airport. The fine for not registering is around US$100.

Registration costs US$15, plus 23TJS. The main hotels in Dushanbe can register you for a small fee, which makes their rates a better deal. Travel agencies will generally register you but you'll have to hang around for up to three or four days in the meantime.

If you are headed to the Pamirs, it makes sense to head to Khorog straight away and register there painlessly, or make a detour to Khojand and do it there.

Foreign travel companies and organisations are lobbying to get the OVIR registration scrapped.

## TELEPHONE

To call internationally (including to other Central Asian republics) dial ☎ 10, followed by the country code, the local code (without the 0) and the number.

International rates cost around US$1 per minute. Cheaper are the Internet Phone (IP) calls offered by many internet cafés, which cost as little as 50 dirham (see p362). Domestic local calls cost 20 dirham.

Dual-band GSM phones work in Tajikistan. Mobile network providers include **MLT** (www.mlt.tj), the Tajik-American joint venture **Indigo** (www.indigo.tj), **Beeline** (www.beeline.ru) and **Babilon-M** (www.babilon-m.com); websites are in Russian only. You may need a local to help you open an account. Indigo has roaming agreements with Cingular, O2 and Vodafone, and Babilon-M has similar arrangements with T-Mobile and Bell Wireless. For more details see www.gsmworld.com.

There are dozens of places in Dushanbe, with a concentration around TsUM, where you can buy a SIM card for your phone. Cards cost around 180TJS, which includes 150 minutes of local calls and free incoming calls for a month.

## TRAVEL PERMITS

Tajikistan has many internal checkpoints, particularly in Gorno-Badakhshan (GBAO), and the *militsia* in all towns are keen to check a foreigner's papers, so make sure you have impeccable documents.For information on the GBAO permit, see p377.

There is a theoretical trekking tax of US$50, or US$100 if over 6000m. Your tour company is supposed to collect this and if you are alone the only place you may encounter this is at Artush in the Fan Mountains. The only place you'll come across the highly spurious 'ecological fee' of US$1 per day is in the eastern Pamirs (around Murgab) or if booking a tour through a Tajik travel agent.

A permit from the **Ministry of Civil Defence and Emergency Situations** (☎ 224 30 33) in Dushanbe is currently required to visit Sarez Lake. You will need a travel agency to help to get this. The permit normally takes at least 10 days to issue.

To visit Zor-Kul (which is theoretically a nature reserve) you need a permit from the Ministry of Environment *(Vazorati Tabiyat)*. Even then you'll need permission from the local border guards. Great Game Travel and META can help with this.

## VISAS

These days most Tajik embassies abroad (see p392) will issue a 30-day tourist visa without a letter of invitation. There aren't that many Tajik embassies abroad so you may have to post your passport to an embassy in a neighbouring country and arrange return postage and a method of payment (often in a foreign currency). Budget plenty of time for this. Visas from the embassy in the USA are particularly expensive. The Tajikistan embassy in Tashkent (Uzbekistan) has a reputation for being more difficult than others.

A useful new regulation in 2006 entitles tourists from most countries (including the EU, Australia and USA) to obtain a 30-day visa on arrival at the airport without the need for a letter of invitation (LOI).

Even if you require a LOI, it's still possible to get the visa at the airport, as long as you have specified this with the travel agency issuing your LOI. Bring one photo and a photocopy of your passport. Visas at the airport costs US$30/40/50 for seven/14/30 days. Consular officials only reliably greet the Turkish Airlines flight from Istanbul; if you come on another flight you may have to leave your passport at the airport and return to get your visa the next day. Visas are not issued at land borders.

Tourist visas longer than a month are often available at embassies in Europe, though they may request a LOI and many travel companies are unable to provide a LOI for longer than one month. Visas longer than one month are generally not available at the airport.

The visa specifies exact dates (you have to travel within those dates but not on those dates), but not the towns to be visited.

Bear in mind that by the time you've paid for an LOI, visa, registration and the GBAO permit, red tape will have taken up a significant portion of your daily budget.

If for some reason you need a LOI, Tajikintourservice (see p362) charges US$30, Stan Tours (see p117) charges US$40 and Great Game Travel charges US$65. See p362 for contact details of these and other travel companies. LOIs are generally issued within two weeks (GBAO permits take a similar amount of time).

All Tajik visa issues are dealt with at the **Ministry of Foreign Affairs** (☎ 221 15 60; mfa@tajik.net, kumid@tojikistan.com, www.mid.tj; Rudaki 42) which is the big pink building on Maydoni Azadi in Dushanbe. As you face the building, you need to take the small door on the far right of the façade where you'll be given a pass to enter the building proper and told where to go.

### Visa Extensions

Visa extensions are a pain. If you need an extension, Tajikintourservice or Vostok Trading Tour in Dushanbe is your best bet. Extensions cost around US$40/50/60 for seven/14/30 days and take about a week to process. If you extend your visa, you'll also need to separately extend any existing registration (and possibly your GBAO permit).

# TRANSPORT IN TAJIKISTAN

## GETTING THERE & AWAY

With a limited number of flights and no international land transport, Tajikistan isn't the easiest republic to get to. This section deals with getting to Tajikistan from other Central Asian countries; for details on flying to Tajikistan from outside Central Asia see p464.

> **DEPARTURE TAX**
>
> Dushanbe has no international departure tax, whether by air or land.

### Entering Tajikistan

As long as your documents are in order you shouldn't have any major problems. Expect a certain amount of delay and chaos, even at the airport, where visa queues can easily take an hour.

Uzbek–Tajik border crossings are hostage to the current state of political relations between the two republics (which are often poor) and sudden unannounced closure by the Uzbeks.

### Air

#### AIRPORTS & AIRLINES

The most popular route into Tajikistan is the weekly flight between İstanbul and Dushanbe on Turkish Airlines (www.thy.com), though it arrives at an ungodly hour (plenty of taxis meet the flight).

Tajikistan Airlines (www.tajikistan-airlines.com) is the national airline – see p461 for flight connections. Other international connections include Pulkovo Airlines to St Petersburg and China Southern to Ürümqi.

Regional flight connections to/from Dushanbe include Bishkek (four weekly, US$155), Almaty (four weekly, US$175) and, less reliably, Osh (Air Company Kyrgyzstan, Friday, US$95). Ariana has a weekly flight to Kabul (US$106).

There are still no flights between Dushanbe and Tashkent; most people fly to Khojand and then travel overland to the Uzbek capital (five hours; see p396). Khojand has weekly flights to Bishkek (US$90) and Moscow (US$300).

### Land

There is almost no cross-border transport between Tajikistan and its neighbours, so you have to take a combination of minibuses and taxis to get to and from the borders.

#### BORDER CROSSINGS

**To/From Afghanistan**

It's possible to travel between Dushanbe and Kunduz (Afghanistan) in a day. The main and easiest crossing is at Panj-e-Payon (formerly Nizhniy Panj) in the south; don't confuse this with the town of Pyanj (or Pyanzh) 75km further east. To get to Panj-e-Payon take a shared taxi or, alternatively, a minibus to Dusti (12TJS; six hours) from Dushanbe or Kurgonteppa (Kurgan-Tyube) and then a taxi 27km to the border. A taxi between Dushanbe and the border costs around US$50, or US$15 per seat if sharing.

After Tajik immigration and customs checks, barges cross the Amu-Darya between 10am and noon (US$10 per person), from where you take a bus 1km (US$1) to the Afghan border controls at Shir Khan Bandar. The US-funded bridge should be finished by mid-2007. After another short transfer, you'll find transport (taxi 80Afg, one hour) running from here to Kunduz. Travellers report that the ferry and border is closed on Sundays.

The crossing at Ishkashim is easiest headed into Afghanistan; into Tajikistan you will need to show a GBAO permit (see p377) and those are technically only available inside Tajikistan (though you can print out an emailed scan of your permit). It's best to arrange someone from the agency to meet you at the crossing. The Afghan village of Ishkashim is 3km from the border crossing and you may have to walk this, as there's little transport at the border. From Afghan Ishkashim there's a daily minibus to Faizabad (600Afg, eight hours), or travel via Baharak.

A bridge over the Pyanj River at Khorog connects the Afghan and Tajik sides of Badakhshan but scant transport options mean this isn't a viable crossing point for most travellers.



#### To/From China

A road has been completed from Murgab to China over the 4362m Qolma Pass, to join the Karakoram Hwy in Xinjiang north of Tashkurgan. The border is open to Chinese and Tajiks but currently not open to foreigners, though this may well change in the future. If the pass does open, you'll have to find a way to get through the 7km of no-man's-land between customs posts. Reports of a Kashgar–Khorog bus have not yet materialised. The border is currently only open 15 days per month.

#### To/From Kyrgyzstan

From the Pamir Alay Valley you can cross into Tajikistan just north of the Kyzyl-Art Pass (south of Sary Tash). The Kyrgyz authorities generally don't stamp your passport when you enter Kyrgyzstan here at Bor Döbö, so try to keep some evidence that indicates when you arrived in Kyrgyzstan.

The border crossing into the Garm region at Karamyk between Doroot-Korgon and Jirgital is currently closed to foreigners.

From Khojand you need to get to Isfara (NB not Isfana) and then take a shared taxi or bus to Batken (see p342). Onward transport to Osh normally travels through the Uzbek enclave of Sokh and this creates visa headaches if you don't have multiple-entry Uzbek and Kyrgyz visas. (One way to avoid this is to pay a taxi driver extra to detour around the checkposts). If you are headed directly to Osh from Khojand and have an Uzbek visa it's easiest to just take taxis through the Uzbek Fergana Valley to Kokand, Andijon and the border at Dostyk (see below).

#### To/From Uzbekistan

Most travellers making a beeline between Tashkent and Dushanbe drive to Khojand and then take a domestic flight (US$55). It's also possible to drive via Samarkand and Penjikent, or even fly to Termiz and then drive to Dushanbe.

From Dushanbe the main border crossing is 55km west of the capital, near Tursanzade/Regar, crossing to Denau. Taxis from Dushanbe's Zarnisar Bazaar to the border cost 8TJS per seat (1½ hours), or take a bus to Tursanzade (3.50TJS) from the main bus station. En route you pass a huge aluminium factory, once one of the biggest in the USST. At the border, minibuses run to Denau town, where you may find a shared taxi direct to Samarkand.

From Khojand there are two main border crossings; Oybek in the northwest for Tashkent, and Kanibadam in the northeast for Kokand and the Fergana Valley. From Tashkent get a bus headed to Bekabad (note that foreigners cannot currently cross at Bekabad) and get off at Oybek (two hours), near Chanak village. The border post is visible from the road. Once across the border take a taxi to Khojand (US$15) or a taxi to nearby Bustan (5TJS) and then a minibus to Khojand. From Khojand to Tashkent it's easiest to take a taxi (US$15) to the Oybek border post, cross and then take an Uzbek taxi onwards. For a marshrutka (US$3) to Tashkent, walk a short way to the main crossroads.

For Kokand and the Fergana Valley take a bus to Kanibodom (2.50TJS), passing the massive Kairakum Reservoir en route, and then a minibus 9km to the border, cross the border by foot and then take multiple onward minibuses in Uzbekistan from Tamozhnaya to Besh Aryk (Beshariq) and then Kokand. You'll save a lot of time by taking a taxi direct from the border to Kokand.

It's easy to travel between Samarkand and Penjikent through a combination of minibuses and taxis. Shared taxis run from the Penjikent bazaar 22km to the border for 5TJS or 2000S (Uzbek sum) per seat, from where there are plenty of shared taxis on to Samarkand (a further 48km). The whole trip takes less than two hours. Change your Tajik somani into Uzbek sum in the Penjikent bazaar.

## GETTING AROUND

### Air

Tajikistan Airlines boasts domestic flights from Dushanbe throughout the country, but this is limited in reality to Khorog and Khojand. Flights out of Khorog are notoriously unreliable so if you are headed to Dushanbe to catch an international flight, budget an extra day or two in the capital in the event the flight is cancelled.

### Bus, Minibus & Shared Taxi

The bus/minibus network is limited to towns around Dushanbe and southern Tajikistan. Outside these areas you'll find shared taxis making the mountain run from Dushanbe to Penjikent and Khojand, as well as shared 4WDs and minibuses headed east to Khorog. Beyond this, you'll need a combination of hitching, luck and vehicle hire. NGOs are often a good source of information on local transportation.

Taxis are available in Khojand and Dushanbe for both local and long-distance runs and are the best option if you can afford them. See p378 for specific details of transport along the Pamir Hwy.

# Turkmenistan

Turkmenistan's dual persona is omnipresent. The lavish palaces in the capital, gold statues and marble monuments are as captivating as the deep mysticism and legend that hangs over pilgrimage sites and ancient ruins. This is a land that is at one time gripped by authority and yet overcome by spirituality.

Ancient cities like Merv, Dekhistan (also known as Misrian) and Konye-Urgench inspire visions of slow-moving caravans plodding along the ancient Silk Road. Remnants of their urban tissue are still there, slowly disintegrating under the weight of tribal warfare and time. Nature-lovers will also appreciate the haunting beauty of the Karakum (Black Sand) desert and the occasional quirks of coloured canyons, dinosaur footprints and burning gas craters.

The full Turkmen experience is ultimately about mingling with the Turkmen themselves, only a couple of generations removed from a nomadic lifestyle, they are a welcoming people whose hospitality is the stuff of legend. Proud of their heritage, women are seen decked out in colourful headscarves and ankle-length dresses decorated with Turkmen motifs. Everyone from young boys to *aksakals* (literally 'white beards', revered elders) will greet you warmly with a two-hand clasp and a slight bow.

Xenophobia runs deep in the upper echelons of Turkmen authority, a fact that constricts independent travel. Anyone with a tourist visa is required to hire a guide and despite hopes for change, the situation remains the same in this post-Niyazov era. While this may dampen your independent spirit, it is for now the only way to fully experience the country. Despite this inconvenience, Turkmenistan offers numerous off-beat experiences; you can overnight in a yurt, ride an Akhal-Teke horse or simply disappear for a few days into the desert wilderness.

**FAST FACTS**

- **Area** 488,100 sq km
- **Capital** Ashgabat (Aşgabat)
- **Country Code** ☎ 993
- **Famous For** Golden statues of Turkmenbashi, gas reserves, horses, carpets
- **Languages** Turkmen, Russian, Uzbek
- **Money** manat (M); black market US$1 = 24,500M
- **Phrases in Turkmen** Peace be with you./ Hello. *(salam aleykum)*; Thanks. *(sagh bol)*; How are you? *(siz nahili?)*
- **Population** approximately five million

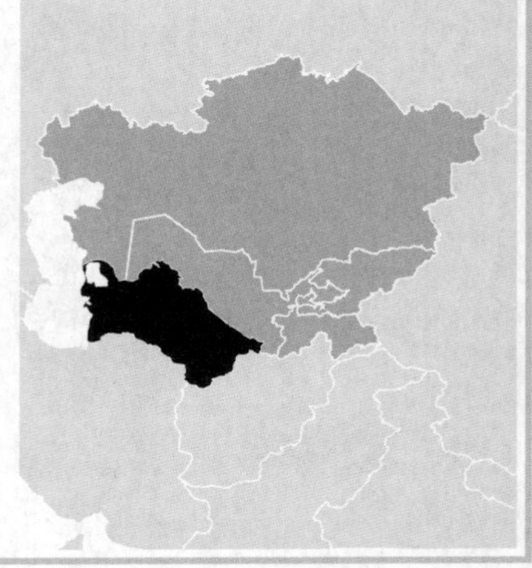

**HOW MUCH?**

- Snickers bar US$0.40
- 100km bus ride US$0.40
- Phone call to the US or UK (three-minute minimum) US$4
- Traditional hat US$8
- Good dinner in Ashgabat US$5
- Litre of bottled water US$0.25
- Litre of petrol US$0.02 (budget US$1.50 per litre to cover road tax)

## HIGHLIGHTS

- **Konye-Urgench** (p432) Ancient minarets, mausoleums and palaces that stand testament to the former glories of the Khorezmshah empire.
- **Karakum Desert** (p417) A formidable expanse of shifting sands and incredible lunar landscapes dotted with hardy Turkmen villages and bizarre gas craters.
- **Ashgabat** (p405) Former President Niyazov's self-congratulatory city, laden with gold statues, portraits and monuments of himself. It's also home to the wonderfully chaotic Tolkuchka Bazaar.
- **Yangykala Canyon** (p420) A painted desert that wouldn't look out of place in a John Ford film, and is great for camping and exploration.
- **Merv** (p426) History buffs will find joy at the extensive ruins of Merv, littered with ancient foundations and pottery shards. The largest archaeological excavation in the Near East, Gonur, is nearby.

## ITINERARIES

- **Three days** Arriving on a transit visa, see Ashgabat in a day, making sure to ride up the Monument to the Independence of Turkmenistan and wander Tolkuchka Bazaar. Cross the Karakum Desert and then wrap things up with a visit to historic Konye-Urgench.
- **Seven days** Spend at least three days around Ashgabat before heading east to visit the ancient sites of Merv and Gonur. From here, return to Ashgabat and travel north to Konye-Urgench, camping en route at the unforgettable Darvaza Gas Crater.
- **Two weeks** Along with the abovementioned sights, head west to Dekhistan, the Yangykala Canyon and Turkmenbashi. While in the Karakum Desert, scope out some remote villages for the chance to overnight in a yurt.
- **Three weeks** Explore the above sights at a slower pace and take the time for some activities, such as horseback riding in Geok-Dere, cave exploration in Kugitang Nature Reserve and hiking in Nokhur.

## CLIMATE & WHEN TO GO

Turkmenistan is the hottest country in Central Asia, although its dry desert climate means that it's not always uncomfortably warm. That said, only the insane or deeply unfortunate find themselves in Ashgabat in July and August, when the temperature can push 50°C. The best times to visit are between April and June, and September and early November. Winters are very cold in the north, although southern Turkmenistan almost never freezes.

## HISTORY

### From Conquerors to Communists

Stone Age sites have been identified in the Big Balkan Mountains but the first signs of agricultural settlements appeared in Kopet Dag in the 6th millennium BC. More Bronze Age sites have been located in the Margiana Oasis, where archaeologist Viktor Sarianidi has identified a sophisticated culture that encompassed several villages and an extensive capital. Rivers that shifted over the centuries caused the abandonment of these settlements, but paved the way for a great civilization around Merv. Alexander the Great established a city here on his way to India.

Around the time of Christ, the Parthians, Rome's main rivals for power in the West, set up a capital at Nissa, near present-day Ashgabat. In the 11th century the Seljuq Turks appropriated Merv, Alexander's old city and a Silk Road staging post, as a base from which to expand into Afghanistan.

Two centuries later Jenghiz Khan stormed down from the steppes and through Trans-Caspia (the region east of the Caspian Sea) to lay waste to Central Asia. Entire city-states, including Merv and Konye-Urgench, were razed and their populations slaughtered. Unlike Samarkand and Bukhara, the cities to the south failed to recover.

It's not known precisely when the first modern Turkmen appeared, but they are believed to have arrived in modern Turkmenistan in

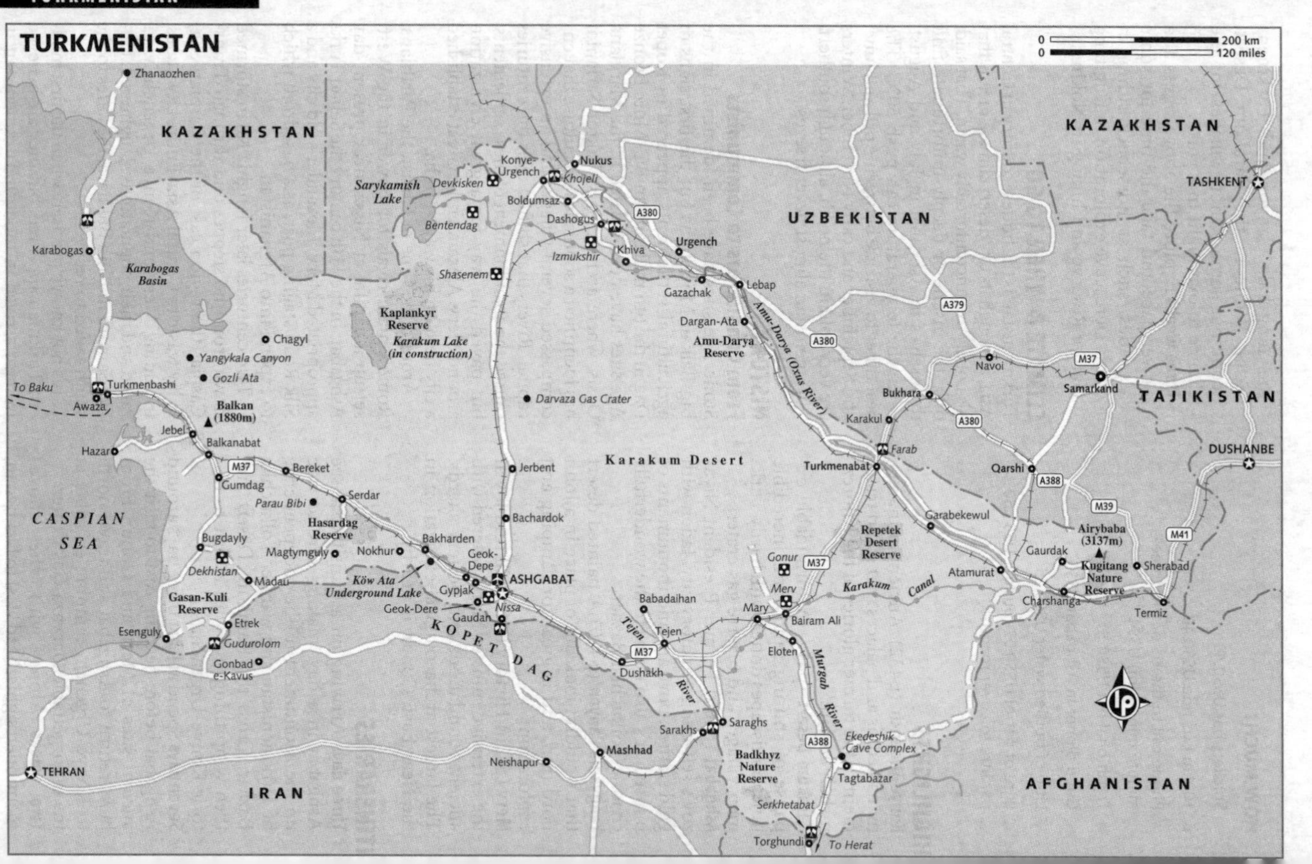
TURKMENISTAN
0 200 km
0 120 miles
KAZAKHSTAN
Zhanaozhen
Karabogas
Karabogas Basin
Sarykamish Lake
Devkisken
Bentendag
Konye-Urgench
Nukus
Khojeli
Boldumsaz
Dashogus
Izmukshir
Khiva
Urgench
A380
UZBEKISTAN
KAZAKHSTAN
TASHKENT
Shasenem
Gazachak
Lebap
Dargan-Ata
Amu-Darya Reserve
Amu-Darya (Oxus River)
A379
Kaplankyr Reserve
Karakum Lake (in construction)
Chagyl
Yangykala Canyon
Gozli Ata
To Baku
Turkmenbashi
Awaza
Balkan (1880m)
Darvaza Gas Crater
Navoi
M37
Samarkand
TAJIKISTAN
Bukhara
Karakul
A380
Farab
Turkmenabat
Qarshi
A388
DUSHANBE
Jebel
Balkanabat
Hazar
M37
Bereket
Gumdag
Serdar
Parau Bibi
Jerbent
Karakum Desert
Bachardok
Hasardag Reserve
CASPIAN SEA
Bugdayly
Magtymguly
Nokhur
Bakharden
Geok-Depe
ASHGABAT
Dekhistan
Madau
Köw Ata Underground Lake
Gypjak
Geok-Dere
Gaudan
Nissa
Gasan-Kuli Reserve
Etrek
Esenguly
Gudurolom
Gonbad e-Kavus
KOPET DAG
Garabekewul
Repetek Desert Reserve
M39
Airybaba (3137m)
M41
Gaurdak
Kugitang Nature Reserve
Sherabad
Gonur
M37
Merv
Karakum Canal
Atamurat
Charshanga
Termiz
Babadaihan
Mary
Bairam Ali
Tejen
Tejen River
M37
Dushakh
Eloten
Murgab River
Saraghs
Sarakhs
A388
Ekedeshik Cave Complex
Badkhyz Nature Reserve
Tagtabazar
Mashhad
Neishapur
TEHRAN
IRAN
AFGHANISTAN
Serkhetabat
Torghundi
To Herat

**TEN CRAZY THINGS YOU DIDN'T KNOW ABOUT TURKMENISTAN** *Bradley Mayhew*

- Turkmenistan plans to build Central Asia's largest artificial lake in the middle of the Karakum Desert at a cost of up to US$8 billion. Turkmenistan is already home to the world's longest irrigation canal, at 1370km.
- The Turkmen language has its own unique, copyrighted alphabet called 'Elipbi'.
- In 2003 the government confused everybody in Ashgabat by replacing all street names with a four-digit number code.
- The Turkmen Carpet Museum houses the world's largest hand-woven carpet, woven for the 10th anniversary of Independence.
- Central Asia's largest mosque is built on the site where former President Niyazov's mother and two brothers were killed by an earthquake in 1948.
- Turkmenosaurus is the name suggested by scientists for the dinosaur that left hundreds of footprints across the east of the country.
- The archaeological site of Anau has some of the world's earliest evidence of grain cultivation.
- Petrol in Turkmenistan costs US$0.02 per litre at the pumps.
- In Turkmenistan natural gas is free but matches aren't, with the result that many Turkmen keep their gas stoves burning 24 hours a day.
- The largest banknote in Turkmenistan is worth less than US$0.50.

the wake of the Seljuk Turks some time in the 11th century. A collection of displaced nomadic horse-breeding tribes, possibly from the foothills of the Altay Mountains, they found alternative pastures in the oases fringing the Karakum desert and in Persia, Syria and Anatolia (in present-day Turkey). Being nomads they had no concept of, or interest in, statehood and therefore existed in parallel to the constant dynastic shifts that so totally determined Central Asia's history.

Terrorising the Russians, who had come to 'civilise' the region in the early 19th century, Turkmen captured thousands of the tsar's troops, and sold them into slavery in Khiva and Bukhara. This invited the wrath of the Russian Empire, which finally quelled the wild nomads by massacring thousands of them at Geok-Depe in 1881.

After the Bolshevik revolution in 1917, the communists took Ashgabat in 1919. For a while the region existed as the Turkmen *oblast* (province) of the Turkestan Autonomous Soviet Socialist Republic, before becoming the Turkmen Soviet Socialist Republic (SSR) in 1924.

## The Turkmen SSR

Inflamed by Soviet attempts to settle the tribes and collectivise farming, Turkmen resistance continued and a guerrilla war raged until 1936. More than a million Turkmen fled into the Karakum desert or into northern Iran and Afghanistan rather than give up their nomadic ways. The Turkmen also fell foul of a Moscow-directed campaign against religion. Of the 441 mosques in Turkmenistan in 1911, only five remained standing by 1941.

Waves of Russian immigrants brought with them farming technology and blueprints for cotton fields. Turkmenistan's arid climate was hardly conducive to bumper harvests, and to supply the vast quantities of water required the authorities began work in the 1950s on a massive irrigation ditch – the Karakum Canal. The 1100km-long gully runs the length of the republic, bleeding the Amu-Darya (Oxus River) to create a fertile band across the south. Cotton production quadrupled, though the consequences for the Aral Sea have been catastrophic (see p77).

In 1985 the relatively unknown Saparmurat Niyazov was elected General Secretary of the Communist Party of Turkmenistan (CPT) and retained power until the collapse of the Soviet Union. Although totally unprepared for the event, Niyazov was forced to declare independence for Turkmenistan on 27 October 1991.

## Independence & The Golden Age

Determined to hold onto power, Niyazov renamed the CPT the Democratic Party of Turkmenistan for the sake of appearances before oxymoronically banning all other parties. His cult of personality began to flourish, starting with an order that everyone call him Turkmenbashi, which translates as 'leader of the Turkmen'. The president erected gold statues of himself and plastered buildings with his image. His Nazi-inspired slogan 'Halk, Watan, Turkmenbaşi' ('People, Nation, Me') was ubiquitous.

Tapping Turkmenistan's vast oil and gas reserves, Niyazov promised a Kuwait-style economy with enormous private wealth. Most of the profits, however, ended up funding Niyazov's ostentatious public-works projects. Public dissent was somewhat placated by enormous government subsidies for gas, water and electricity. The free ride was part of Niyazov's much touted 'Turkmen Golden Age' (Altyn Asyr).

Orwellian control of the media caused Reporters Without Borders to rank Turkmenistan second to last in its press freedom index (one spot ahead of North Korea). The repression was only highlighted after reporter Ogulsapar Muradova (Radio-Free Europe) was found dead in prison in 2006. She was jailed after she assisted a French filmmaker to produce a documentary on the president *(Turkmenistan: Welcome to Niyazovland)*.

Having drained the economy on his marble capital, Niyazov slashed pensions and funds for education. Libraries outside Ashgabat closed and university acceptances were limited to a privileged few. This paled in comparison to Niyazov's human-rights record, blackened by the jailing of thousands of political prisoners. The threat of sanctions by the EU had little effect.

## CURRENT EVENTS

An attack on the president's life occurred on the morning of 25 November 2002 when gunmen opened fire on his motorcade. The assassination attempt failed but provided grounds for an immense bloodletting of the remaining political opposition, including Niyazov's outspoken critic Boris Shikhmuradov. The one-time ambassador and dissident leader was tried, jailed and has not been heard from since.

Despite avoiding an assassin's bullet, President Niyazov proved mortal when he passed away on 21 December 2006, the result of a massive heart attack. Having groomed no heir, the death left a power vacuum that for a

### TURKMENBASHI – LEADER OF THE TURKMEN

Former President Saparmurat Niyazov may be dead, but his personality cult is alive and well. Born in 1940 in Gypjak, a village near Ashgabat, Niyazov knew tragedy from a young age – his father was killed in action during WWII, and his mother and brothers were killed in the 1948 earthquake that wiped out Ashgabat. Both his parents formed important parts of the personality cult – especially his mother Gurbansoltan Eje, after whom he renamed the month of April.

The young president grew up in an orphanage and went to study at St Petersburg's prestigious Technical Institute, returning to Ashgabat to work as an engineer at the Bezmein Power Plant just outside the Turkmen capital. Joining the Communist Party in 1962, Niyazov's first taste of real power came when he was appointed head of the party's Ashgabat City Committee. He was later selected by Mikhail Gorbachov to head the Communist Party of Turkmenistan – fingered for the position as he was seen as a deferent and obedient functionary.

The seamless transfer to president of an independent Turkmenistan after the USSR's collapse revealed, however, another side to Niyazov – one that loved nothing more than mass flattery, golden statues and lavish palaces.

Niyazov padded his legacy by penning poetry books and the *Ruhnama,* his version of Turkmen history and culture. Endearing himself to the public, he was frequently televised on national holidays passing out US$100 bills to children who sang to him. This was small change compared to the fortune he has amassed for himself; the NGO Global Witness claims Niyazov had around US$3 billion in slush funds at the time of his death.

Other publicity stunts included a weekly televised cabinet meeting in which Niyazov regularly sacked ministers and other high-ranking officials, usually on the basis of corruption. Under his rule, thousands of Turkmen were jailed, tortured, sent into internal exile or forced out of the country. Despite this, when he died in December 2006, delegates from 40 countries attended his funeral and hundreds of thousands of ordinary Turkmen arrived to pay their last respects.

brief moment opened the door for democratic reform and the return of exiled dissidents. Instead, a surprisingly smooth transfer of power occurred when Deputy Prime Minister Gurbanguly Berdymukhamedov grabbed the reins of power and won backing from Niyazov's inner circle. He was rubber stamped into power after elections in February 2007 (having won 90% of the popular vote). Berdymukhamedov had been Turkmenistan's health minister and according to reports from the exiled opposition, he is the former president's illegitimate son. While their relationship may never be known, the two men do bear an uncanny resemblance.

Berdymukhamedov began his presidency with positive reforms in the health and education sectors, lighting some fire under initiatives cut by Niyazov. However, state security remains as tight as ever, the media is still strictly controlled and democracy is alien terminology. Travellers wishing to visit the country continue to go through the same rigorous visa channels.

Turkmenistan's foreign policy is also unchanged; good news for Russia, which secured promises that its lucrative energy contracts would be honoured by the new regime. Niyazov's declaration of neutrality and his ability to keep out radical Islam in a volatile region allowed it to safely fend off harsh criticism from the West. Berdymukhamedov is expected to follow suit, so while the USA and EU continue to press Turkmenistan for democratic reforms, it's unlikely that anything more than carrot-dangling will be used to break the cycle of repression.

## PEOPLE

Turkmen remain nomadic at heart, if not still in practice, and carry themselves in a simple yet dignified manner that reflects their rural lifestyle. Nomadic rules, including the treatment of guests, still dominate home life. You can expect an embarrassing amount of attention when visiting a home; a younger member of the family may even be assigned to ensure that all your needs are catered to.

Turkmen are guided spiritually by a unique form of Central Asia animism. Holiday breaks are thus used for pilgrimage time. Women in particular use these pilgrimages as an opportunity to take a break from their home life, and you may see caravans of women on buses, headed to places like Parau Bibi (p419).

Despite Sovietisation, women who live outside Turkmenistan's towns are generally homemakers and mothers, and the men the breadwinners. The oldest woman in the household, however, wields the most authority in decision making.

### Population

If you believe the government's figures, the population of Turkmenistan is rising dramatically – over six million at present by the official count, although the UN and US government put that figure at five million in July 2006. Uzbeks, who make up about 5% of the population, live in the border cities of Konye-Urgench, Dashogus and Turkmenabat. Russians have left in huge numbers since independence, as it becomes increasingly hard to work without speaking Turkmen. Today they make up around 4% of the population. Turkmen ethnic groups make up 85% of the population, with other groups accounting for 6% of the population.

## RELIGION

Turkmen are deeply religious people; their traditional animist beliefs have been blended over centuries of time with Islam. Evidence of this is clear at mosques and mausoleums, which are often decorated with animist features such as snakes and rams' horns. Likewise, pilgrims arrive at these sites bearing tokens such as crib models, indicating a desire for children.

Sunni Islam is the state religion and each year 188 people (the number that can fit on a Turkmenistan Airlines plane) are hand-picked for a pilgrimage to Mecca. Turkmenistan's constitution guarantees freedom of religion, but Islam and Orthodox Christianity are the only freely practised religions. Other faiths, mainly Christian sects, have been forced to curtail their activities under government pressure, although the state-sponsored repression seen in the 1990s has eased somewhat.

## ARTS

Turkmen carpets are world famous and can be seen just about everywhere, although the best place to see them is in the bazaar. Silk, embroidery and jewellery are other crafts that have been perfected over the centuries. Museums often have fine displays of traditional silverwork used to decorate women's clothing.

### BOOK OF THE SOUL

Part of Niyazov's cult-building mission was the promotion of his book the *Ruhnama* (Book of the Soul), which was first published in 2001. This incredibly bizarre piece of writing sets out Niyazov's version of Turkmen history, culture and spirituality. At its heart, the *Ruhnama* is about traditional Turkmen values and advice on how each Turkmen should uphold them. There are discussions on Turkmenistan's neutrality and the exclusion of foreign influences. Much of the history section is revisionist and tends to favour mythology over historical fact.

Niyazov made *Ruhnama* compulsory reading for all Turkmen. Knowledge of the *Ruhnama* is needed to pass everything from college entrance exams to driving tests (Turkmen driving skills make it clear that the actual driving part is irrelevant in the test). Volume II was published in 2004.

Travellers will see the *Ruhnama* on display in all public buildings and on the shelves of bookshops. The book is also found in *Ruhnama* reading rooms, located in shopping malls and hospitals. A *Ruhnama* University is expected to open in 2010. The book has even been blasted into space and will orbit Earth for the next 150 years! Copies of *Ruhnama* (complete with glowing reviews) can be found on amazon.com, or you can read portions at www.rukhnama.com. There is some incentive to read the book – according to Niyazov, reading it 100 times guarantees you a place in heaven.

Certain forms of Western art were frowned upon by Niyazov, resulting in a ban on opera and ballet. Film making is likewise virtually nonexistent. Theatres do remain active, albeit with Turkmen-only song and dance acts, concerts and drama performances. The most impressive traditional singing, *bakhshi,* deals with folklore, battles and love, and is accompanied by a *dutar* (two stringed guitar). Shukur Bakhshi, singing competitions, can be heard at festivals.

Between the Soviets and Niyazov, contemporary Turkmen literature has been all but destroyed. Rahim Esenov was Turkmenistan's best literary hope until he was jailed following publication of his book *The Crowned Wanderer,* which portrays a history of Turkmenistan different from the *Ruhnama*. Esenov, in his late 70s, was arrested for attempting to smuggle copies of his book into the country. While in jail the books were burned although he did win an award from the PEN American Centre. Instead, Turkmen are encouraged to read the writings of poet Magtymguly Feraghy (1733–83) and, of course, former President Niyazov.

## BOOKS

*Unknown Sands: Journeys Around the World's Most Isolated Country* (Dusty Spark, 2006), by John W Kropf, is a travel memoir by an American who spent two years living in Ashgabat. Despite living within the confines of the diplomatic community (his wife is a US diplomat), Kropf manages to sneak away from the capital to give us a perspective of life on the ground for ordinary Turkmen.

*Tribal Nation: The Making of Soviet Turkmenistan* (2006), by Adrienne Lynn Edgar, is a scholarly account of the Soviet creation of Turkmenistan, with well-researched details on Soviet nation building of the 1920s and 1930s. The book also provides an understanding of Turkmen language and tribal law.

## ENVIRONMENT

The landscape in Turkmenistan is dramatic and more varied than you'd expect from a place where the Karakum desert takes up 90% of the country's area. To the east are the canyons and lush mountains of the Kugitang Nature Reserve, while to the south the Kopet Dag range rises up in a line towards the Caspian Sea. The territory littoral to the Caspian is particularly unusual – vast mud flats, coloured canyons and the enormous bulk of the Big Balkan massif make this one of the more bleakly beautiful places in the country.

### Wildlife

The most famous of Turkmenistan's many interesting species is the Akhal-Teke horse, a beautiful golden creature that is believed to be the ancestor of today's purebred. Dromedaries (Arabian camels) are everywhere, wandering scenically between villages and towns. Many of the Karakum's nastiest inhabitants are really exciting to see in real life – most importantly the grey *varan,* or *zemzen*, a large monitor lizard.

Despite its large size and particularly painful bite, Turkmen have traditionally welcomed the giant lizard as it devours or scares away snakes (such as cobras), eats mice and eradicates colonies of sandflies.

You are also likely to see desert foxes, owls and the very common desert squirrel.

Tarantulas and black widows are both indigenous to Turkmenistan, although you are unlikely to see them. Snake season is from April to May. Cobras, vipers and scorpions can all be found in the desert, so tread with caution. Turkmen folklore has it that once a snake has looked at you, you'll die shortly afterwards unless you kill it first.

### Environmental Issues

Turkmenistan has paid a heavy price for the irrigation of its southern belt using source water bound for the Aral Sea. While the Aral Sea is in Uzbekistan and Kazakhstan, its disappearance has led to desperate environmental problems in northern Turkmenistan, with the salination of the land taking its toll on the health of local people. Overfishing is another concern, as caviar-bearing sturgeon become rarer in the Caspian Sea. There is very little environmental consciousness in Turkmenistan, where no-one bothers to save gas, electricity or water because all are subsidised by the government. The result in Ashgabat is a thin layer of semipermanent smog.

### Nature Reserves

Turkmenistan's eight nature reserves are not designed for public use – they have been set aside for scientific research, as per the Soviet model. A permit is required to visit a reserve and these are available from the **Ministry of Nature** (☎ 39 60 02; 2035 köçesi 102, Ashgabat). It can take up to three weeks to process the application and these are usually only available in the low-season (October to May).

## FOOD & DRINK

Similar to other Central Asian countries, *plov* (rice, meat and carrots) and shashlyk are the staple dishes across Turkmenistan. *Plov* is produced with cottonseed oil, which provides its distinctive aroma, while shashlyk is considered at its best when cooked over the branches of a saxaul tree. Other favoured snacks include *samsa* (samosa, meat-filled pastries) and a variation on the meat pastry called *fitchi*, which is larger and round in shape.

*Dograma,* made from bread and pieces of boiled meat and onions, is a traditional Turkmen meal, although you will probably only see this during special occasions. A more common soup is *chorba* (soup of boiled mutton with potato, carrot and turnip, known elsewhere in the region as *shorpa). Manty* (steamed dumplings) served with sour cream is another popular dish.

Bread *(çörek)* is round, flat and delicious when it's fresh out of the oven, although it does harden quickly. *Çörek* holds a place of honour in Turkmenistan and it is surrounded by superstition; it must be handled with utmost respect and never served or left upside down, even crumbs are collected and left in a safe place. Never throw bread away and if you must discard it, don't leave it where it could be kicked or stepped on. *Çörek* is cooked in a *tamdyr,* a large earthen oven that is also considered holy. It's bad luck to destroy an old *tamdyr,* so these are simply left to disintegrate.

At breakfast you'll be served sour milk or *chal* (fermented camel's milk) in the desert. Mineral water is sold everywhere and is of good quality, while beer and vodka – a legacy of the Russians – are both popular alcoholic drinks. There are several decent Turkmen brands of both, although the most common beers are Berk and Zip.

# ASHGABAT

**☎ 12 / pop 650,000**

With its lavish marble palaces, gleaming gold domes and vast expanses of manicured parkland, Ashgabat ('the city of love' or Ashkabad in Arabic) has reinvented itself as a showcase city for the newly independent republic. Built almost entirely off the receipts of Turkmenistan's oil and gas sales, the city continues to boom, with whole neighbourhoods facing the wrecking ball in the name of progress.

Originally developed by the Russians in the late 19th century, Ashgabat became a prosperous, largely Russian frontier town on the Trans-Caspian railway. However, at 1am on 6 October 1948, the city vanished in less than a minute, levelled by an earthquake that measured nine on the Richter scale. Over 110,000 people died (two-thirds of the population), although the official figure was 14,000; this was the era of Stalin, when socialist countries didn't suffer disasters.

Ashgabat was rebuilt in the Soviet style, but its modern incarnation is somewhere between Las Vegas and Pyongyang, with a mixture of Bellagio fountains and Stalinist parade grounds. But at heart it's a fairly relaxed city, with good-value accommodation and a few quirky sights, making it a pleasant place to relax before a long haul across the desert.

## ORIENTATION

The main arteries of the city are Turkmenbashi şayoli (avenue), running all the way from the train station to the new suburb of Berzengi, and Magtymguly şayoli, running east to west. Many of the city's landmarks and institutions are on or near these streets.

In 2002 former President Niyazov renamed all the streets with numbers. Pushkin köçesi (street) is now 1984 köçesi, for example. This pointless exercise has only served to confuse, as nobody seemed to know the names of the streets anyway – some have changed as many as four times since the 1990s. For the most part, post-Soviet names have been used in this chapter, as they remain the most widely recognised.

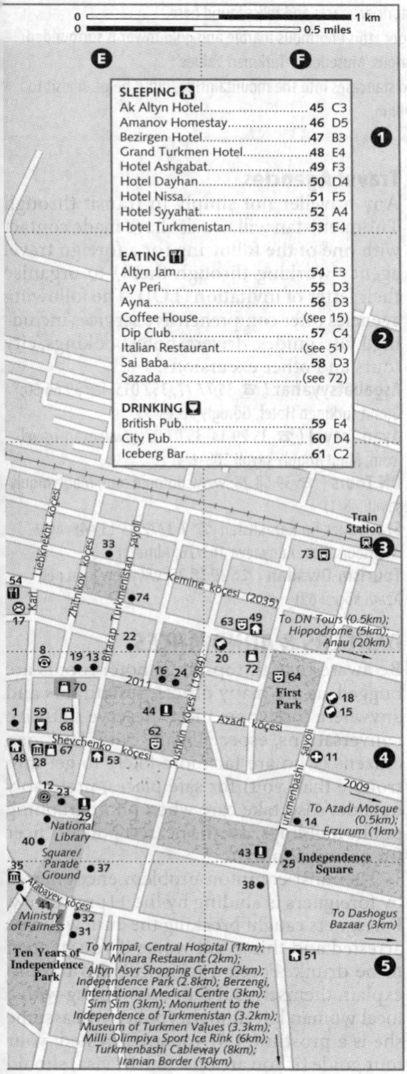

SLEEPING
Ak Altyn Hotel ........ 45 C3
Amanov Homestay ........ 46 D5
Bezirgen Hotel ........ 47 B3
Grand Turkmen Hotel ........ 48 E4
Hotel Ashgabat ........ 49 F3
Hotel Dayhan ........ 50 D4
Hotel Nissa ........ 51 F5
Hotel Syyahat ........ 52 A4
Hotel Turkmenistan ........ 53 E4

EATING
Altyn Jam ........ 54 E3
Ay Peri ........ 55 D3
Ayna ........ 56 D3
Coffee House ........ (see 15)
Dip Club ........ 57 C4
Italian Restaurant ........ (see 51)
Sai Baba ........ 58 D3
Sazada ........ (see 72)

DRINKING
British Pub ........ 59 E4
City Pub ........ 60 D4
Iceberg Bar ........ 61 C2

## INFORMATION

### Bookshops

Turkmen bookshops are little more than propaganda storefronts to promote national glory. Most central is **Miras Bookshop** (Turkmenbaşi şayoli 29; 10am-7pm), where over half the books are authored by Turkmenbashi.

### Emergency

Dial ☎ 01 for fire service, ☎ 02 for the police or ☎ 03 for an ambulance. The operators will speak Turkmen or Russian only.

### Internet Access

Your best chance to get online is at one of the top-end hotels. The President, Nissa and Grand Turkmen all have internet, but only the latter allows nonguests to use it. Bear in mind that the authorities monitor web traffic.

**Matrix** (☎ 35 54 59; World Trade Complex, 2005 köçesi 1; per hr US$2.20; 9am-7pm Mon-Sat) This is one of only a handful of internet cafés in the city. Expect a terribly slow connection and blocked websites.

### Laundry

Drycleaning can be done for reasonable rates at **Brilliant** (☎ 39 06 39; Magtymguly şayoli 99) and more expensively at the **Yimpaş** (Turkmenbashi şayoli 54; 9am-11pm) Turkish department store. Floor maids at most hotels will do a load of laundry for around US$5.

### Left Luggage

There is a left-luggage service *(kamera khraneniya)* at Ashgabat's main train station, where you can leave bags for about US$0.25 overnight.

### Medical Services

The main medical provision in Ashgabat is the vast **Central Hospital** (☎ 45 03 03, 45 03 31; Emre köçesi 1). Foreigners have to pay for their treatment, so insurance is essential. Among the staff is Dr Yahya, a Jordanian doctor who speaks English and is recommended by both the British and US embassies. The facility also includes a dental clinic. There is also the **International Medical Centre** (☎ 51 90 06, 51 90 08) in Berzengi. In the city centre is **Lechebnii Hospital** (☎ 39 08 77; Shevchenko şayoli), which is less well equipped.

**ASHGABAT MUST-SEES**

**Arch of Neutrality** (opposite) For the best views of the capital, ride the glass elevator to the top of this magnificently awful structure.
**Turkmenbashi Cableway** (p411) Survey the city with its desert backdrop from the top of this 3.5km long gondola.
**Tolkuchka Bazaar** (p411) As unlike modern Ashgabat as anywhere else on earth, and truly one of Central Asia's greatest and most colourful sights.
**National Museum** (p410) Enjoy the fine collection of historic artefacts and relics found here.
**Independence monument** (p410) Known as 'the plunger', this enormous marble and gold tower is surrounded by gushing fountains and bronze statues and contains the curious 'Museum of Turkmen Values'.
**Walk of Health** (p417) You don't have to be crazy to build staircases into the mountainside, but it helps. A visit to this spectacular waste of money and time is strangely compelling.

### Money

The best rates for black-market exchange can be found outside the **Turkmenistan Trade Centre** (Turkmenistan Söwda Merkazi; Magtymguly şayoli). The preferred currency is US dollars in cash.

There are several banks in the city centre, but they're not of much use to travellers as they don't have ATMs or change travellers cheques.

If you have a Visa card, use the **State Bank for Foreign Economic Affairs** (☎ 40 60 40; Garashyyzlyk şayoli 32; ⌚ 9.15am-4pm Mon-Fri), which is 4.5km south of downtown and 1.5km north of the Berzengi Hwy (Archabil şayoli). The bank charges a 4% commission on withdrawals.

If you use a MasterCard, go to **Senagat Bank** (☎ 45 44 21; Turkmenbaşi şayoli 42; ⌚ 9am-1pm & 2-5pm Mon-Fri) located next to the Yimpaş department store. It charges a 3% commission on withdrawals.

### Post

The main **post office** (☎ 35 15 55; Mopra köçesi 16; ⌚ 9am-5pm Mon-Fri, 9am-2pm Sat & 9am-1pm Sun) is very small. A letter to the USA is very reasonable at around US$0.08.

### Registration

**OVIR** (State Service for the Registration of Foreign Citizens; ☎ 39 13 37; 2011 köçesi 57; ⌚ 9am-noon & 2-5pm) For tourist registration see p438.

### Telephone & Fax

Most hotels offer international direct dialling (IDD) and fax facilities, although for better rates you can call from the **International Call Centre** (Karl Liebknekht köçesi 33; ⌚ 8am-7pm). Faxes can be sent from all top-end hotels and the International Call Centre.

### Travel Agencies

Any traveller not simply in transit through Turkmenistan will usually have made contact with one of the following (or a foreign travel agency working through them) to organise their letter of invitation (LOI). The following agencies offer comprehensive services including LOIs, guides, drivers, hotel bookings, city tours and other excursions.

**Aşgabatsyýahat** (☎ 35 77 77, 352 015; fax 39 66 60; Grand Turkmen Hotel, Görogly köçesi 7)
**Ayan Travel** (☎ 35 29 14, 35 07 97; www.ayan-travel.com; Magtymguly şayoli 108-2/4)
**DN Tours** (☎ 39 58 28; www.dntours.com; Magtymguly şayoli 48/1)
**Stantours** (in Kazakhstan ☎ 7 3272 63 13 44; www.stantours.com; Kunyaeva 163/76, Almaty)
**Tourism-Owadan** (☎ 39 18 25; www.owadan.net; Azadi köçesi 65)

## DANGERS & ANNOYANCES

Be aware that all top-range hotel rooms are bugged, as are many offices, restaurants and anywhere foreigners meet. Reserve sensitive conversations, especially any with Turkmen citizens (who are far more likely to get into trouble than you) for safe places, preferably outside. Also take care when photographing public buildings, ask the nearest police officer for permission first.

The most common problem encountered by foreigners is abiding by the 11pm curfew. Foreigners caught breaking the curfew can be arrested and things get worse if you happen to be drunk. Foreign men will also have to explain themselves if they are walking with a local woman late at night (police will assume she is a prostitute). If you are arrested, your tour guide (if you are on a tourist visa) should

**THE EVER-CHANGING FACE OF ASHGABAT**

Ashgabat's post-Soviet face-lift is a work in process. Niyazov spent the better part of his presidency transforming the capital into an all-marble 'White City', and still today whole neighbourhoods are being demolished to make way for palaces, apartments, fountains and enormous sculptures.

One of the most recent projects was a US$63 million artificial river that slices through the city for 11km. New buildings include the 'House of Free Creativity' with work space for more than 200 journalists. The US$17 million edifice was constructed in the shape of a book.

The demolitions have left hundreds of people homeless and the city authorities have no provision for rehousing or compensation. Turkmenbashi World of Fairytales, a new amusement park, was one of many projects that required the eviction of hundreds of families.

The destruction of old buildings is not limited to Ashgabat. During one trip to the Karakum desert, President Niyazov stopped at the town of Darvaza and, not pleased with its dilapidated state, had the village razed to the ground à la Jenghiz Khan. Apparently it was not living up to the lofty standards of the 'Golden Age'. The people living there were moved to other villages and the name 'Darvaza' was deleted from the maps.

Be aware that the Ashgabat map is particularly vulnerable to change during the lifetime of this book.

be able to help, but don't count on it. Take taxis after 11pm to avoid problems.

## SIGHTS

### Central Ashgabat

Being all but wiped from the earth in 1948, Ashgabat's sights can be divided neatly into two halves – the politicised, monolithic constructions of the Soviet government and the politicised, monolithic constructions of President Niyazov, with the latter increasing in number almost monthly while he was alive.

At the centre of Niyazov's monolithic Ashgabat is the embarrassingly large **Arch of Neutrality** (admission US$0.15; 8am-10pm), erected to celebrate the Turkmen people's unsurprisingly unanimous endorsement of Turkmenbashi's policy of neutrality in 1998. Above the arch itself is the real gem, a comic 12m-high polished-gold **statue of Niyazov**, which revolves to follow the sun throughout the day. Trips to the top give commanding views of the enormous **Independence Square**, on which sits the golden-domed **Palace of Turkmenbashi,** the **Ministry of Fairness**, the **Ministry of Defence** and the **Ruhyyet Palace**, all of which were built by the French corporation Bouygues Construction, the court builder to Niyazov. Behind this is the **Majlis** (parliament).

The Palace of Turkmenbashi is relatively restrained, but just walking towards the gates will cause soldiers to harass you, even though information about its construction is written in English, presumably for visitors to read.

Also in the vicinity is the **Museum of Fine Arts** (☎ 35 31 29; Alishera Navoi köçesi 88; admission US$10; 9am-5pm Wed-Mon), located in a beautiful new building with a big rotunda, two tiers and lots of gold ornament. The collection contains some great Soviet-Turkmen artwork: happy peasant scenes with a backdrop of yurts and smoke-belching factories. There is also a collection of Russian and Western European paintings, including one by Caravaggio, and a fine selection of Turkmen jewellery and traditional costumes.

Next to the Arch of Neutrality is the **Earthquake Memorial**, a bombastic bronze rendering of a bull and child (the baby Niyazov), under which lurks the **Earthquake Museum** (admission free; 9am-6pm). This is perhaps Ashgabat's most touching museum and the display includes once-banned photos of pre-1948 earthquakes as well as information about the five-year clean-up effort, the burying of 110,000 bodies and the building of a new city. Unfortunately the museum is usually locked (asking a guard nearby might get you inside).

Further down this long, manicured strip is the **Soviet war memorial**, a pleasingly subtle structure with an eternal flame at its centre. Off to the right is the **Presidential Administration** building, once the presidential residence and the Turkmen Communist Party Central Committee building in more austere times, and most recently the nerve centre of Turkmenbashi's private staff. The strip ends with **Ashgabat State University**.

The **statue of Lenin**, off Azadi köçesi, is a charmingly incongruous assembly of a tiny Lenin on an enormous and very Central Asian plinth. Right around the corner is the brand-new Magtymguly Theatre. Across the road, Lenin faces an austere concrete building that was once the **Archive of the Communist Party of Turkmenistan**. Its walls feature modernist concrete sculptures made by Ernst Neizvestny, the Russian artist who lived and worked in Ashgabat during the 1970s.

The **Carpet Museum** (Görogly köçesi 5; adult/student & child US$2/1; 10am-1pm & 2-6pm Mon-Fri, 10am-2pm Sat) is an excellent museum for anyone interested in the history of Turkmen carpet weaving. The 'expert commission' at the back of this new and well-curated space is the place to have your carpets valued and taxed, and the necessary documentation issued for export. While there's a limit to the number of rugs the average visitor can stand, the central exhibit, the world's largest hand-woven rug, really is something to see. Shutterbugs may want to restrain themselves as the camera fee is US$2 per shot.

## East of Downtown

More a statement of foreign-policy leanings than a sign of religious awakening, the **Azadi mosque** stands just south of Magtymguly şayoli, 600m east of the junction with Turkmenbashi. Similar in appearance to the Blue Mosque in İstanbul, the mosque sees few worshippers because of several accidental deaths during its construction.

The modern **mosque of Khezrety Omar**, off Atamurat Niyazov köçesi, is also worth visiting for its wonderfully garish painted ceilings. The angular, futuristic **Iranian mosque**, illuminated with green neon, is on Görogly köçesi on the western outskirts of the city on the way to Nissa.

The **Ashgabat Zoo** (2011 köçesi; admission US$0.20; 8am-7.30pm) is a curious diversion if you happen to be walking nearby, although animal-lovers may be appalled at the tiny living quarters set aside for the animals. The resident lion and bear in particular look severely downtrodden. At the time of writing, a new zoo was being planned, in which case this one will likely close.

Further west, the most famous graduate of **School No 20** was Saparmurat Niyazov, who attended classes here as a boy. There is a small museum inside and a classroom containing period desks. To find the school, walk north on 2060 köçesi, past the Azady World Languages Institute and take the next main left. Outside the school is a statue of the president lecturing a young girl.

## Berzengi

South of Moskovsky şayoli the surreal world of Berzengi begins – an entirely artificial brave new world of white-marble tower blocks, fountains, parks and general emptiness that culminates in the Berzengi Hwy (Archabil şayoli), which is home to a huge number of hotel complexes.

Altyn Asyr Shopping Centre, the curious pyramidical shopping centre at the northern end of **Independence Park** is reputedly the biggest fountain in the world. Inside it's rather less than impressive – an all but empty two-floor shopping centre, although there's a restaurant at the top (Minara, see p413), that's popular for weddings.

The **Monument to the Independence of Turkmenistan**, known universally to the foreign community as 'the plunger' (for reasons obvious as soon as you see it), is a typically ostentatious and tasteless monument that houses the **Museum of Turkmen Values** (☎ 45 19 54; admission US$10, camera US$1; 9am-5pm), a rather empty and overpriced look at traditional Turkmen clothing and jewellery. This is a popular spot for wedding groups to take photographs with a golden statue of the president, and the fountains are pleasant enough (a kind of totalitarian *Waterworld*, if you will).

Looking like a lost palace in the desert, the **National Museum** (☎ 48 90 20; Archabil şayoli 30; admission US$10; 10am-5pm) occupies a striking position in front of the Kopet Dag. The lavish Ancient History Hall includes Neolithic tools from western Turkmenistan and relics from the Bronze Age Margiana civilisation, including beautiful amulets, seals, cups and cult paraphernalia. There is also a model of the walled settlement uncovered at Gonur (see p428). The Antiquity Hall houses amazing rhytons – horn-shaped vessels of intricately carved ivory used for Zoroastrian rituals and official occasions.

Between the National Museum and downtown is **Turkmenbashi World of Fairytales** (Garashsyzlyk şayoli; admission US$0.04, each ride US$0.04; 9am-6pm). The US$50 million amusement park was unveiled with great fanfare in 2006, just in time for the nation's 15th anniversary celebrations. The park has 54 attractions, inluding a roller coaster that swoops over a giant map of the Caspian Sea.

### Tolkuchka Bazaar

The sight of withered men haggling for shaggy sheepskin hats, a braying camel suspended in midair by a crane or a sheep being driven away in a sidecar are a few of the oddities you can expect from the Tolkuchka Bazaar, one of Central Asia's most spectacular sights. The enormous market sprawls across acres of desert on the outskirts of Ashgabat, with corrals of camels and goats, avenues of red-clothed women squatting before silver jewellery, and villages of trucks from which Turkmen hawk everything from pistachios to car parts. Whatever you want, it's sold at Tolkuchka.

Expect to haggle. A *telpek* (sheepskin hat worn by Turkmen males) should go for around US$10, although the best *telpek* do go for US$15 or more. A fair price for a *khalat* (the attractive red-and-yellow striped robe worn by Turkmen men) is roughly US$15, while sequined skullcaps and embroidered scarves cost between US$2 and US$3.

Above all, Tolkuchka is the place for carpets. Predominantly deep red, most are the size of a double bed or a bit smaller, and the average price ranges from US$150 to US$250. Haggling might shave off US$50. Remember that you'll still need to get an export certificate for the carpet before taking it out of the country (see p435), these are available at the 'expert commission' behind the Carpet Museum (opposite).

Tolkuchka is in full swing every Saturday and Sunday from around 8am to 2pm and, on a slightly smaller scale, on Thursday morning. Watch out for pickpockets. The site is about 8km north Ashgabat, past the airport and just beyond the Karakum Canal. A taxi should cost around US$1.50. Buses go there from the corner of Magtymguly şayoli and 1958 köçesi (1958 is a block east of Turkmenbashi şayoli).

### Turkmenbashi Cableway

For some spectacular views of Ashgabat and the surrounding desert, take a ride up the **Turkmenbashi Cableway** (admission 1000M; 9am-10pm). The US$20 million cable car system, opened in 2006, starts from the base of the Kopet Dag (south of the National Museum) and climbs to a height of 1293m above sea level on a lower peak of the Kopet Dag. The upper terminal has souvenir shops, a restaurant, café, picnic spots, several high-powered telescopes for sightseeing and an 80m-high artificial waterfall. It takes 10 minutes to travel the 3.5km-long cableway.

## ACTIVITIES

Akhal-Teke horses are Turkmenistan's pride and joy, and many visitors come to Turkmenistan specifically to ride one. Highly recommended is the Alaja Farm, run by Katya Kolestnikova and located in Geok-Dere (also called Chuli). This is a professional stable, where the horses are well cared for and well fed (not always the case elsewhere). Riding here costs US$15 an hour or US$120 per day, worth the price for the beautiful golden stallions and some wonderful riding in the canyons around Geok-Dere. Contact Katya (☎ 800-66330362), or call her colleague Gulya Yangebaeva (☎ 42 63 58, 800-66340198), otherwise you can just turn up as the farm operates seven days a week. Take the Geok-Depe road out of Ashgabat and turn left at the sign for Geok-Dere. Continue through the village and Alaja is at the end on the right.

Another option for horse trips is the Shahmenguly stable operated by Hemra Gulmedov. You can do rides of a few hours or overnight pack trips into the desert. The stable is located 2km west of Geok-Depe village, which is northwest of Geok-Depe town. Hemra can be contacted through the travel agents in Ashgabat (see p408).

The only ice-skating rink in the country, **Milli Olimpiya Sport Ice Rink** (☎ 48 92 70; Berzengi; admission US$0.25; 9am-7pm) is hugely popular with locals so if you want to skate there you may need to call and make a reservation. It's on the Berzengi Hwy, a couple of hundred metres north of the Independence monument.

**Bowling** and **billiards** are both available on the 3rd floor of the Yimpaş department store (p415).

**Atlant** (☎ 36 26 16; per day US$2; 9am-10.30pm) is a modern gym located on the eastern side of the Kopet Dag stadium. Swimmers may want to check out the **Olympia Sport Water Palace**, a brand-new pool facility, located on Garashsyzlyk şayoli, opposite the puppet theatre.

## SLEEPING

Ashgabat has a range of affordable accommodation options, although it's thin in the midrange category. Niyazov's bizarre obsession with building hotels has left an enormous number of largely deserted and perfectly comfortable hotels in the suburb of Berzengi. Most tour companies suggest that their clients stay in these, although we've found them depressingly isolated.

## Budget

**Amanov Homestay** (☎ 39 36 72; 2028 köçesi 106; dm US$5) This eccentric homestay is located in a quiet neighbourhood a short taxi ride from downtown. The rooms are functional and clean, with constant hot water and decent shared toilets. The family also keeps pigeons. Not an option for people with tourist visas (see p435) as this is an unofficial hotel, but great for people who are transiting. Taxi drivers still know this street as Shaumyana. Ask for Murat when you arrive.

**Hotel Dayhan** (☎ 35 73 44, 35 73 72; Azadi köçesi 69; dm/s/d US$10/20/30; ❄) Among the budget hotels, this one has the best location, smack in the middle of downtown. Yet its quality leaves plenty to be desired as the rooms are pretty dingy and the bathrooms decrepit. It's also a busy place so a solo traveller might have to pay for all the beds in the room during high season.

**Bezirgen Hotel** (☎ 34 06 44; Mopra köçesi 45; s/d/lux US$10/20/30; ❄) This small hotel doesn't get much attention, but the rooms are surprisingly good value, especially for the solo traveller. The very large *lux* room has a sofa, TV and separate bedroom. The single room is likewise comfortable and well appointed. If you need to pass the time there is a billiards hall in the basement. It's located near the Azady World Languages Institute.

**Hotel Syyahat** (☎ 34 45 08, 34 42 20; Görogly köçesi 60a; s/d/tr US$15/30/33; ❄) Making a decent first impression, this hotel is on a leafy section of Görogly and sports a comfortable lobby with an enormous bronze profile of Turkmenbashi. Rooms come in varying states of decay and each seems to have its own wallpaper pattern. The bathrooms are not a highlight. For an extra US$5 you get a half-*lux* room that comes with TV. Hotel amenities include a bar and sauna. Breakfast is included in the rates. It's located a short taxi ride from downtown, or take trolleybus 6.

**Hotel Ashgabat** (☎ 35 74 05; Magtymguly şayoli 74; s/d US$20/30; ❄) Ashgabat's old Soviet standby recently gave its lobby a marble makeover, but the renovations have thus far failed to reach the guest rooms. Rooms are small and rundown, and the bathrooms lack sinks, but it's a decent choice because of the nice location, walking distance from most sights. For an extra US$5 per person, you can upgrade to a half-*lux* room with a TV, improved bathroom and a better view facing Magtymguly.

## Midrange

### CENTRAL ASHGABAT

**Hotel Turkmenistan** (☎ 35 05 44, 35 09 60; Bitrap Turkmenistan şayoli 19; s/d/ste US$40/50/60; ❄ 🅿) A little overpriced, but has an excellent location near the Arch of Neutrality. The rooms are unexciting and a little cramped, but the newly renovated bathrooms are good and the place is clean. Amenities include a Turkish bath in the basement.

### BERZENGI

This surreal, totally deserted strip of hotels nestles beneath the attractive Kopet Dag, a 10-minute drive from the city centre. The hotels are all government-run guesthouses and most are enormous, despite never having more than 20 rooms and looking more like private villas than hotels. There are some good bargains here if you don't mind the desolate location.

**Hotel Aziya** (☎ 48 01 80; Archabil şayoli 31; s/d US$25/30 ❄) Besides the mysterious dark blotches on the carpet, the rooms here seem OK. It attracts an interesting cast of characters in the evening but maybe they are just here for the food – there is an excellent Chinese restaurant downstairs. Breakfast is included.

**Hotel Ahal** (☎ 48 87 37; Archabil şayoli 35; s/d incl breakfast US$40/50; ❄ 🅿) Designed like a Timurid palace, the Ahal sports attractive, bright rooms and hardwood floors. It has a restaurant and an indoor pool, but no bar. Breakfast is included

**Hotel Independent** (☎ 48 87 00; Archabil şayoli 33; s/d US$40/45; ❄ 🅿) This huge hotel features an impressive vaulted ceiling and a spiral staircase at its entrance. Large rooms are en suite with a kitchenette and include breakfast. It's part of the Ahal Group, giving you access to the swimming pool next door and internet facilities at the President Hotel.

## Top End

**Hotel Nissa** (☎ 48 87 00/1/2/3/4; fax 48 81 55; Atabayev köçesi 18; s/d/ste US$50/60/90; ❄ 💻 🅿) This excellent hotel is one of the best in the city, and it is surprisingly cheap (perhaps as it is controlled by the president's son), with large, comfortable rooms and extras including an internet centre, breakfast buffet and 24-hour room service. Most travel agents can get discounts of up to 60% on the walk-in price.

**Ak Altyn Hotel** (☎ 36 37 00; akaltyn@online.tm; Magtymguly şayoli 141/1; s/d/ste US$60/65/120; ) Occupying a leafy location west of downtown, this 109-room hotel has well-appointed rooms and a fitness centre. The unusual name, which means 'White Gold', is a reference to cotton, and the exterior design is meant to look like a cotton ball. Sheraton had been managing the hotel for a time and has given the place a much needed upgrade. Breakfast is included.

our pick **Grand Turkmen Hotel** (☎ 51 05 55; fax 51 12 51; Görogly köçesi 7; s/d/ste US$75/80/140; ) Blessed with an unbeatable location, the Grand Turkmen is a great choice. The standard rooms are a bit cramped and the TV is small, but the rooms are in excellent shape. The suites are divided into a bedroom and cosy living room. It's a lively downtown place, walking distance to many restaurants and shops, and inhouse amenities include a fitness centre and sauna. Before checking in, make sure your room can be properly air-conditioned, as it's not terribly effective in all rooms.

**President Hotel** (☎ 40 00 00; presidenthotel@online.tm; Archabil şayoli 54; s/d/ste US$110/120/180; ) This 151-room behemoth is the newest, brashest hotel in Ashgabat. It has two swimming pools (one indoor, one outdoor), a gym, sauna, gift shop and grand marble hallway. Gaudy rooms come with little niceties like a bathrobe and a safe. The Italian restaurant on the top floor is one of the best in town. While the prices are reasonable (and groups get a 40% discount), its Berzengi location is fairly desolate. Breakfast is included in the rates.

## EATING

Ashgabat is not known for its cuisine and hygiene standards tend to be pretty low so have some GI-meds on hand to counteract the inevitable stomach bug. Still, meals are cheap and you can eat well on US$2 to US$3. Restaurants are mainly open for lunch and dinner. All shut at about 11pm, so it's best to get to a restaurant by 10pm at the latest.

### Restaurants

**Altyn Jam** (☎ 39 68 50; Magtymguly şayoli 101; 11am-11pm) Known as AJs to the foreign community, the 'Golden Bowl' is a pleasant place for lunch and has tasty and reliable European food. Desserts are especially good here, and it will deliver pizza to your hotel room.

**Erzurum** (☎ 27 53 71; Shevchenko köçesi 53; US$1.50-3; 10am-10.30pm) Smart and simple, the Ezurum serves up tasty Turkish fare including *pide* (Turkish pizza), and tasty cheese bread. The service is attentive and swift, although it can get very hot in the summer months due to the wood-fired oven.

**Minara Restaurant** (☎ 47 22 86; Altyn Asyr Shopping Centre, Independence Park; dishes US$2-4; 10am-11pm) This classy restaurant is located on the 5th floor of the enormous waterfall-mall in Independence Park. The views are great and the menu is varied, if not a little amusing – dishes include 'squirrel salad,' and 'English-style small cakes with brains'. The carp stewed in beer is recommended.

**Dip Club** (☎ 33 05 11; Görogly köçesi 117; dishes US$3-4; 11am-4pm & 6-11pm) Lebanese restaurant serving up tasty Middle Eastern favourites like hummus, *dolma* (vegetables stuffed in grape leaves), *moutabal* (grilled eggplant) and chicken *shawarma* (chicken cut from a spit and served in a pita). The atmosphere is a bit bland, but it does play Arabic music and has live music on weekends.

**Ay Peri** (☎ 39 50 69; Magtymguly şayoli 112; dishes US$3-5; 10am-11pm) This authentic Chinese joint specialises in spicy Sichuan dishes. The red lanterns add to the Asian décor, while the menu offers a few delicacies, including 'penis of maral Chinese vodka,' considered a health product. Whatever the health benefits, travellers should resist eating dishes that include endangered species such as the maral deer.

**Italian Restaurant** (☎ 22 11 35; Hotel Nissa, Atabayev köçesi 18; dishes US$6-7; 11am-11pm) Enjoys the reputation of being one of the best eateries in the city. The Parmesan is fresh, pepper is served from suitably enormous mills and there's a decent selection of Italian wine.

**Sim Sim** (☎ 45 33 43; Andaliba köçesi 50/1; 10am-11pm) Hidden among apartment blocks, Sim Sim serves an array of dishes you probably won't find anywhere else in the city, including shrimp shashlyk (US$7) and frogs legs in white wine (US$15). It attracts a young, hip crowd who eat and drink on the lively balcony and in the main dining room. To find this place take a taxi.

our pick **Ayna** (☎ 39 10 56; Kemine köçesi 156a; dishes US$8-15; 11am-11pm Mon-Sat, 5-11pm Sun) A seafood restaurant is no easy feat to pull off in Central

Asia, but this place manages by flying all its ingredients in from Moscow and Dubai. The tasteful interior is appropriately decorated with model ships and the service is friendly. Starters include an excellent seafood soup (US$5) and the tsar's salad (US$5), which includes red caviar, potato and sour cream. Baked scallops (US$15) and a pricey lobster (US$45) are among the mains.

### Quick Eats

**Şazada** (☎ 39 57 64; Turkmenistan Söwda Merkazi, Magtymguly şayoli; ⏲ 8am-11pm) A bizarre tribute to kitsch Americana, you'll find posters of Frank Sinatra, Marilyn Monroe and Elvis, rusting license plates and car fenders poking out from the walls. The food is a fairly lamentable attempt at hot dogs, burgers, sandwiches and pizza, but it's still a fun place for a drink or to see how young Ashgabatans spend their leisure time.

**Sai Baba** (☎ 39 57 64; Magtymguly şayoli 113; cake US$0.80; ⏲ 8am-11pm) Dessert-lovers will appreciate this cake, ice-cream and coffee shop.

**Coffee House** (☎ 39 60 06; Turkmenbashi 15A; dishes US$3; ⏲ 9am-11pm) The eclectic menu, excellent service and European-style atmosphere make this one of the more attractive restaurants in the city. As the name indicates, there is a nice selection of coffees imported from Indonesia, Africa and Latin America. Breakfast includes omelettes and pastries while afternoon appetisers might see you sampling the hummus or tabuleh. This place is very popular with Ashgabat's expats.

## DRINKING

There are few dedicated bars in Ashgabat and those that exist cater mainly to expats living in the city. For a cool drink on a hot summer day, check out one of the patio bars located in First Park. If you prefer to buy your own booze, make sure the bottle has a seal and try to spend more than US$1 (the super cheap stuff could blind you). One last reminder, pouring your own drink is bad form, wait for a friend to fill your cup.

**Iceberg Bar** (☎ 36 18 08; cnr Kemine köçesi & Revfov köçesi; ⏲ 10am-11pm) This tranquil beer garden, located behind the circus, serves up frothy pints of microbrewed beer and sizzling sticks of shashlyk.

**British Pub** (Florida; ☎ 39 33 36; Görogly köçesi 8; beer US$2; ⏲ 10am-4am) If it's pub grub, expats and large mugs of imported beer you're after then step into British Pub, which has been around for quite awhile, albeit under different names and management. The low-lit, dark-wood atmosphere is a bit sombre, but gets going at night with live music and free-flowing alcohol. The menu (dishes US$3) includes burgers, fish and chips, and steak; the fajitas are recommended. For something more ethnic, expats recommend trying Tandoori, located adjacent the British Pub.

**City Pub** (☎ 35 22 88; Alishera Navoi köçesi 54a; beer US$2.50; ⏲ 9am-11pm) In a worrying trend, City Pub is another real British pub that has found its way to Central Asia. Like a home away from home it contains scarves of every imaginable English football team, and is popular with both locals and expats.

## ENTERTAINMENT

### Cinemas

There are no cinemas in the city since Niyazov declared motion pictures 'un-Turkmen'. However, there is a **DVD Cinema** (☎ 45 42 66) in the Yimpaş department store. All the films are in Russian, but if you are the only customer you may be able to get them to put on the undubbed English version.

### Live Music

The best place to try for live music is the British Pub (see left), which hosts local rock bands a few nights a week. Fun, yet extremely tourist-oriented 'folk evenings' are organised by most travel agents for around US$20 per person, including dinner and a full programme of traditional dancing and singing.

### Nightclubs

There are a handful of nightspots operating in Ashgabat – anyone operating beyond 11pm needs a special licence, and so things are limited. Besides the following you could also check out the nightclubs inside the big hotels, such as the Nissa, Grand Turkmen and the Ak Altyn; these are all popular, but as they get lots of foreign businessmen they also attract large numbers of prostitutes.

**Kumush Ay** (Florida; ☎ 39 33 36, 39 33 51; Görogly köçesi 8; ⏲ 11pm-4am) The biggest, brashest nightclub in Ashgabat is this newly renovated venue, located above the British Pub and owned by the same people. The dance room is a flashing inferno of strobe lights and lasers, while a second room contains a huge bar and lots of padded nooks where you can sit and watch the action. Note that some taxi drivers may know this place by its alternative name, the Florida Nightclub.

**Mukan Club** (☎ 35 18 54; First Park; ⏰ 10am-11pm) Lively local bar that attracts an enthusiastic crowd of regulars.

### Sport

Ashgabat is a great place for horse-lovers. Every Sunday from the end of March until May, then again from the end of August until mid-November, the Hippodrome plays host to dramatic Turkmen horse races. It's 5km east of the city centre – either bus 4 down Magtymguly or a US$0.50 taxi ride.

The local football team is Kopet Dag, which plays at the Kopet Dag stadium. You should have no trouble picking up a ticket on match days.

### Theatre & Concert Halls

Ashgabat offers some excellent venues for watching musical and dramatic productions centred on Turkmen folklore and traditional music. The best place to watch Turkmen drama is at the **Mollanepes Drama Theatre** (☎ 35 74 63; Magtymguly şayoli 79; admission US$0.25). Performances are held Wednesday to Sunday at 7pm, although in summer (July to October) the theatre will probably be shut. For Turkmen musical performances, visit the **Magtymguly Theatre** (☎ 35 05 64; Shevchenko köçesi; admission US$0.25), which has shows Friday to Sunday at 7pm. It is also usually shut during the summer months.

While Turkmen productions flourish, the Russian Theatre is dying a slow death. No longer supported by the government, the once-proud **Pushkin Russian Drama Theatre** (☎ 36 41 93; Magtymguly şayoli 142; admission US$0.25) saw its original theatre demolished and was moved into a smaller facility near Gunesh Park. Performances are held at 7pm on Saturday and Sunday. Ballet and opera are not performed in Ashgabat, thanks to a presidential decree banning both.

## SHOPPING

The biggest and best supermarket in town is the **Yimpaş** (☎ 45 42 66; Turkmenbashi şayoli 54; ⏰ 7am-11pm), a huge Turkish shopping complex featuring, among other things, the only escalators in Turkmenistan. Here you can buy everything from frozen lobster to Doritos. If you want to buy inexpensive cotton clothing, visit the **Altyn Asyr Marketing Centre**, opposite the Grand Turkmen Hotel, which has outlet shops for the textile industry. For carpets, try the government-run **Carpet Shop** (☎ 35 25 50; Görogly köçesi 5), east of the Carpet Museum.

If you are looking to buy some locally produced art, try **Muhammed Art Gallery** (☎ 39 59 31; Görogly köçesi 12a), run by artist Allamurat Muhammedov. The unique collection has Muhammedov's own works set around his studio, plus a museum of ancient artefacts. The gallery is next to City Pub (look for the metal gate with the stained-glass horse design). Muhammedov, who speaks English, has displayed his art in galleries worldwide and welcomes foreign visitors in for tea.

The best shopping experiences are to be had at one of Ashgabat's many markets. While Tolkuchka Bazaar (see p411) is possibly the most fabulous in Central Asia, there are others in the town centre. The Russian Bazaar is great for CDs and clothing, while the **Tekke Bazaar** is recommended for foodstuffs, fruit and flowers. Niyazov books, calendars and lapel pins can be bought at the small **Ministry of Culture shop** (Asudaliq köçesi 33).

## GETTING THERE & AWAY

### Air

For information about flights from outside Central Asia see the Transport in Central Asia chapter (p461). Within Central Asia, Turkmenistan Airlines and Uzbekistan Airways both link Ashgabat and Tashkent (one way US$140).

Domestic Turkmenistan Airlines flights are heavily subsidised to make the ticket prices amazingly low. Consequently, demand is massive and flights need to be booked in advance as far ahead as possible. Timetables also change regularly but there are approximately five daily flights to Dashogus (US$11), three daily to Turkmenabat (US$12), two daily to Mary (US$11), two daily to Turkmenbashi (US$12), as well as regular flights to Kerki (Atamurat; US$10, via Turkmenabat) and three weekly to Balkanabat (US$11).

#### AIRLINE OFFICES

The following airlines fly to/from Turkmenistan (except where stated) and have offices in Ashgabat.

**Aeroflot** (☎ 39 87 92; Turkmenistan Söwda Merkazi; Magtymguly şayoli 73) No flights to Turkmenistan but this office can handle Aeroflot connections.

**Aerosvit Ukrainian Airlines** (☎ 35 01 64; www.aerosvit.com; Turkmenistan Söwda Merkazi, Magtymguly şayoli 73) Has twice weekly flights from Kiev via Baku for US$340 one way.
**Armavia** (☎ 39 05 48; Turkmenbaşi şayoli 15) Weekly flights to/from Yerevan.
**British Airways** (☎ 51 07 99; www.britishairways.com; Grand Turkmen Hotel, Görogly köçesi 7) British Airways doesn't fly to Ashgabat, but this office is useful as a travel agency.
**Lufthansa** (☎ 33 20 37, 33 20 56; www.lufthansa.com; Main concourse, Saparmurat Turkmenbashi Airport) Three flights per week from Frankfurt via Baku.
**Turkish Airlines** (☎ 39 29 19, 35 66 19; www.turkishairlines.com; Magtymguly şayoli 73) Four flights weekly from İstanbul to Ashgabat.
**Turkmenistan Airlines** (domestic ☎ 35 26 43, international 39 39 00; www.turkmenistanairlines.com; Magtymguly şayoli 82) From Ashgabat to Abu Dhabi, Amritsar, Bangkok, Birmingham, Delhi, Frankfurt, İstanbul, London and Moscow.
**Uzbekistan Airways** (☎ 37 82 03; www.uzairways.com; Main Concourse, Saparmurat Turkmenbashi Airport) Two flights a week connecting Tashkent.

### Bus, Marshrutka & Shared Taxi

Bus stands in Ashgabat are organised by destination, and are also used by shared taxis and marshrutki as much as buses. Fares for private cars fluctuate by demand and the make of the car.

Transport for Mary and Turkmenabat leaves from the hub to the left of the main train station, as you look at it. There are marshrutki to Mary (four hours, US$3) and Turkmenabat (6½ hours, US$5).

Transport for Balkanabat and Turkmenbashi leaves from the Old Airport *(stary aeroport)*. There are marshrutki and shared taxis to Balkanabat (4¼ hours, both US$4) and Turkmenbashi (six hours, both US$6.25). Near the private taxi lot is an official bus station, which runs three buses per day to Mary (4½ hours, US$1), four to Tejen (2½ hours, US$0.80), one to Serakhs (four hours, US$1) and one to Balkanabat (five hours, US$1.20). These buses depart early in the morning and by 2pm the bus station is locked up.

Transport for Dashogus and Konye-Urgench leaves from the Dashogus Bazaar (also called Azatlyk Bazaar). A marshrutka to Konye-Urgench costs US$4 (10 to 12 hours), while a seat in a shared taxi is US$6. Chartering a whole taxi will cost US$24. Prices to Dashogus are slightly higher: Lvov buses will take 18 hours for the trip (US$3.50) including a two-hour stop for lunch on the way. Ikarus buses (15 hours) are faster, while marshrutki (US$5) make the trip in 12 to 14 hours. A place in a taxi will cost US$9 and the trip takes 11 to 12 hours.

Short-distance destinations west of Ashgabat (eg Old Nissa) depart from the western side of Tekke Bazaar. A spot in a minibus to Bagyr (for Old Nissa) costs US$0.20.

### Train

The Ashgabat **train station** (☎ 39 38 04) is at the northern end of Turkmenbashi şayoli, a short taxi ride from downtown. There are two trains per day to Turkmenbashi (11 hours, US$2), three departures for Mary (8½ hours, US$1) and Turkmenabat (15 hours, US$1.50) and one incredibly slow train to Dashogus (24 hours, US$2). Trains are the slowest way to travel around the country and are not particularly comfortable either. Prices quoted above are for *kupe*/2nd-class.

## GETTING AROUND

### To/From the Airport

The best way to get into central Ashgabat from the airport is to take a taxi. They are both plentiful and cheap, especially if shared. Expect to pay US$1, but agree before getting in. Drivers are likely to try their luck asking for anything from US$5 to US$10 initially.

### Public Transport

Buses are crowded and slow, but dirt cheap and modern. With taxis being so cheap, there's little reason to use buses – unless you happen to be on a bus route and living out of the city centre. Ashgabat has no metro system or trams.

### Taxi

Official taxis are not particularly plentiful, but you can flag down cars with ease almost anywhere. Expect to pay US$0.15 to US$0.20 for a short trip within the city, and US$0.45 for a longer one. If in doubt, agree on a price beforehand, otherwise just hand the money over on arrival with extreme confidence. To order a taxi call ☎ 35 34 06.

## AROUND ASHGABAT

### Nissa & Around

Founded as the capital of the Parthians in the 3rd century BC, in its prime **Nissa** (admission US$1; ⏰ 8am-6pm) was reinforced with 43

**STAIRCASE TO...?**

One of Niyazov's more idiosyncratic projects, the **Walk of Health** is a concrete staircase built into the side of the Kopet Dag mountains. There are two walks – one 8km and one 37km. Once a year the Turkmen ministers and parliament members (along with thousands of other civil servants) head up the mountain in suits and ties. Niyazov used to see them off at the start then travel to the finish by helicopter so as to greet them as they come wheezing to the conclusion of the course. The president oft lamented that his heart was not good enough to do the walk himself, and so it was.

towers that sheltered the royal palace and a couple of temples. It was surrounded by a thriving commercial city. One ruling dynasty replaced another until the 13th century when the Mongols arrived, laid siege to the city and after 15 days razed it to the ground.

The ridges surrounding the plateau were the fortress walls; the steep, modern approach road follows the route of the original entrance. In the northern part of the city are the remains of a large house built around a courtyard, with wine cellars in nearby buildings.

The main complex on the western side includes a large circular chamber thought to have been a Zoroastrian temple. Adjoining it is the partly rebuilt 'tower' building. On the far side of the western wall are the ruins of a medieval town, today the village of Bagyr.

Coming by car from Ashgabat it is possible to take the road past Berzengi along the presidential highway. On the way you'll pass the **Palace of Orphans**, another bizarre Niyazov project with massive futuristic marble buildings, sporting facilities and its own mosque. The children in this village are educated to be government officials.

### Gypjak

The boyhood home of President Niyazov, Gypjak, is 11km west of Ashgabat. The major sight here is the gleaming **Turkmenbashi Ruhy Mosque**; the biggest structure of its kind in Central Asia, it can hold 10,000 worshippers. Four minarets soar above the gold-domed mosque, each 91m tall, representing the year of Turkmenistan's independence. The inscription over the main arch states '*Ruhnama* is a holy book; the Koran is Allah's book' and there are quotes from the *Ruhnama* etched into the minarets. Inside, you can contemplate the grandeur and extravagance of it all while sitting on enormous handwoven carpets. Next to the mosque is an elegant **mausoleum** containing the grave of former President Niyazov. Turkmenbashi was buried alongside his two brothers and his mother, the marker for his father is ceremonial.

The mosque and mausoleum are clearly visible from the main Ashgabat–Balkanabat road. Parking shouldn't be a problem – there is an enormous underground car park big enough for 400 vehicles.

### Geok-Depe

Midway on the main road between Ashgabat and Bakharden is the village of **Geok-Depe** (Green Hill), site of the Turkmen's last stand against the Russians. During the Soviet era the uncommemorated site of the breached earthen fortress, where 15,000 Turkmen died, was part of a collective farm. Today the large futuristic **Saparmurat Hajji Mosque**, and its sky-blue domes, stands beside the telltale ridges and burrows. The mosque's name refers to the president's pilgrimage to Mecca, from which he returned with US$10 billion in aid from the Saudi government. Niyazov's request that all Turkmen visit the mosque once a year is only loosely followed.

## KARAKUM DESERT

The Karakum desert is a sun-scorched expanse of dunes and sparse vegetation in the centre of Turkmenistan. It's Central Asia's hottest desert but manages to support a handful of settlements, including the oasis town of **Jerbent**, 160km north of Ashgabat. A ramshackle collection of homes, battered trucks, yurts and the occasional camel, Jerbent is being slowly consumed by the desert as sands continue to blow off the overgrazed dunes. While it doesn't look like much, the village does offer a glimpse of rural Turkmen life, and you can watch traditional cooking methods and sit down for tea inside a yurt.

If you have time, money and a sense of adventure, a travel agency can organise 4WD trips further into the desert towards ever more remote villages. As this requires much time, extra fuel and possibly a backup vehicle, you'll need to request that your guide lists agreed details of your trip on the itinerary.

Off-road trips usually require at least two vehicles, which costs around US$200 per day (depending on how many people are travelling, but this price is for groups of three to four people).

Although the village of **Darvaza** was recently demolished on the orders of the president, you'll still see it marked by the road on some maps. Darvaza is the halfway post between the capital and Konye-Urgench. It's also at the heart of the Karakum desert and has the added attraction of the **Darvaza Gas Craters**, one of Turkmenistan's most unusual sights. Apparently the result of Soviet-era gas exploration in the 1950s, the three craters are artificial. One has been set alight and blazes with an incredible strength that's visible from miles away. The other two craters contain bubbling mud and water.

The fire crater is best seen at night, when the blazing inferno can only be compared to the gates of hell. There is a naturally sheltered camping place behind the small hill, just south of the crater. Getting to the crater is a serious off-road ride and drivers frequently get lost or get stuck in the dunes. There is really no-one around to give directions, except perhaps at a kiosk near the railroad tracks. If you intend to walk from the road, just follow the light and bear in mind that it takes a good two hours to reach the crater.

All buses and marshrutki headed from Ashgabat to both Konye-Urgench and Dashogus go through Jerbent. There is irregular transport from Jerbent; it's a matter of asking around the village for a ride, and leaving when the vehicle is full. Let the driver know that you want to get off, although you'll probably have to pay the full price to Ashgabat, Konye-Urgench or Dashogus (p434). The gas crater is about four to five hours from Ashgabat and six to eight hours from Konye-Urgench.

# WESTERN TURKMENISTAN

Rather off-the-beaten path, even by Turkmenistan standards, the western part of the country is one of haunting moonscapes, ruined cities and minority tribes such as the mountain-dwelling Nokhurians. The region is economically crucial to Turkmenistan, being home to vast oil and gas reserves, as well as the fishing and caviar business centred on the Caspian Sea. Most people simply pass through here on the way to the port of Turkmenbashi, from where it's possible to continue on to Azerbaijan by ferry. But with a slower pace it's possible to see a handful of extraordinary sights, including some of the country's best natural phenomena, the Kopet Dag mountains and Yangykala Canyon, and the historically important Dekhistan (Misrian).

## KÖW ATA UNDERGROUND LAKE

Like entering Milton's underworld, only with changing rooms and a staircase, a visit to the **Köw Ata Underground Lake** (admission US$10; dawn-dusk) is a unique experience. You enter a cave at the base of a mountain and walk down a staircase, 65m underground, which takes you into a wonderfully sulphurous subterranean world. At the bottom awaits a superb lake of clear water naturally heated to about 36°C. Underground swimming is one of Central Asia's more unusual activities, and worth it if you don't mind the steep entry fee.

Follow the main road to Balkanabat from Ashgabat for the best part of an hour; the turn off to the lake is clearly marked to the left with a large sign for Köw Ata. By marshrutka or bus to Balkanabat or Turkmenbashi you could easily ask the driver to stop at the Köw Ata turn-off, although it's a good 90-minute walk from the road.

## NOKHUR

Wedged into the mountains just a few kilometres from Iran, this village offers a unique opportunity to hike in the hills and soak up some rural life. Nokhur was once a byword among Soviet Turkmen for everything rural and backwards. Thanks to their isolation, Nokhuris have retained unique traditions and a particular dialect of Turkmen. They claim ancestry from Alexander the Great's army and prefer to marry among themselves rather than introduce new genes to the tribe.

There are two sights in this fascinating village. One is the town's **cemetery**, where each grave is protected by the huge horns of the mountain goats that locals consider sacred – indeed many houses in the village have a goat's skull hanging on a stick outside to ward off evil spirits. You should not enter the cemetery, as it's for locals only, although photography is perfectly acceptable. A short walk beyond the cemetery is **Qyz Bibi**, a spiritualist-Muslim shrine, where people from all over the country come on pilgrimage. Qyz Bibi was the pre-Islamic patroness of women and the goddess of fertility. She is believed to dwell in the cave (the entrance of which is just 30cm to 40cm in diameter) at the end of a winding pathway that passes a huge, ancient tree where pilgrims tie colourful material in the hopes of conceiving a child.

There are four impressive waterfalls in the mountains beyond Nokhur, all of which can be visited by hiring a UAZ 4WD in Nokhur (ask your guide to ask around). The routes are fairly arduous, but great fun for day-tripping and taking in the impressive scenery.

For accommodation, it is possible to stay with a local family. The best homestay is with Gaib and Enebai, a local couple who welcome guests to their large mountain house (complete with satellite TV). They charge US$15 per person per night. Ask anywhere for Kinomekanik Gaib – he was the village's cinema projectionist before he retired.

There is a daily bus from Tekke Bazaar in Ashgabat to Nokhur (US$1, two hours) at 8am. The bus leaves from Nokhur at 8am the next day.

## PARAU BIBI

The **Mausoleum of Parau Bibi** has been an important place of pilgrimage since ancient times. According to lore, Parau Bibi was a virtuous young woman living in the area. During a time of enemy siege, Parau Bibi prayed that the mountain would open up and swallow her, lest she be carried off by the barbarian tribes. The mountain heard her pleas and accordingly engulfed her in the nick of time.

Locals later honoured her selfless act by creating a fertility shrine on the spot. The small white tomb, built from a cave in the cliffs, contains offerings such as model cribs, indicating the desire of the pilgrim. It is located at the top of a staircase 269 steps high, which you trudge up with other devotees. The mystical surrounds are enhanced by the steppe behind you, stretching endlessly into the distance.

Nearby, on the hillside, you can spot holes in the ground, delineating the underground *karyz* irrigation canals. A century ago there were more than 500 such canals in Turkmenistan, only 10 remain today.

The turn-off for Parau Bibi is 19km west of Serdar, follow the road another 8km to reach Parau Bibi. If it's late it's possible to spend the night under the pilgrim tents, although it does stay busy most of the night, so don't expect to get much sleep.

## BALKANABAT

☎ 222 / pop 110,000

Tucked below a range of imposing mountains and the only sign of civilisation as far as the eye can see, Balkanabat is the logical stopover on the long haul across western Turkmenistan. Oil was discovered in the vicinity in 1874 and a small refinery was built, only to be abandoned for 50 years after being bankrupted by competition from the Baku oil industry.

Originally called Nebit Dag, Balkanabat is a staging point for trips to Dekhistan and Yangykala Canyon. It may be necessary to overnight here between these destinations, bearing in mind that accommodation ranges between wretched and plush with nothing in between.

The main axis is Magtymguly şayoli, running east–west and parallel with the railway. At its midpoint is Niyazov Sq, watched over by a lonely statue of the former president. Note that Balkanabat uses both street names and block numbers *(kvartal)*.

**Balkansyyahat** (☎ 4 53 38; Kvartal 198) is a travel agency that can organise trips to Dekhistan or Big Balkan Mountain at somewhat inflated prices (a trip to Dekhistan costs around US$200). The office is located in the Hotel Nebitchi.

### Sights

The **Regional History Museum** (☎ 4 91 26; Gurtgeldi Annayew köçesi; admission US$1.20; 9am-1pm & 2-6pm Tue-Sun) contains an agglomeration of ethnography, archaeology and wildlife exhibits of the Balkan region. Note the display of local carpets, which contains anchor designs – symbols of the Caspian-dwelling Yomut Turkmens. There are also photos of Dekhistan to whet your appetite if you are headed that way. The museum is located opposite the Cultural Palace of Oil Workers.

A couple of blocks north of the museum, the **Balkanabat Carpet Factory** (Azady köçesi; 9am-6pm Mon-Fri) gives free tours of its facilities where you can watch young women painstakingly weave giant carpets by hand. There is a small museum featuring products churned out by the factory and a reasonably priced carpet shop.

On the west side of the city, you can take a look at the pretty **Russian Orthodox Church**, which stands just north of the defunct oil rig. Heading west, on the road to Turkmenbashi, is the **Monument to the Desert Explorers**, a handsome concrete statue of caravan men urging forward their obstinate camel in the midst of a fierce sandstorm.

### Sleeping & Eating

**Nebitdag Hotel** (☎ 6 71 92; Kyartel 115; dm US$1.30) This will appal even the most seasoned backpackers – prison-like rooms have four uncomfortable beds, crumbling walls and broken windows. Shower blocks are dysfunctional and the bathrooms down the hall are filthy. Mangy cats prowl the corridors to add a finishing touch. The only saving grace is the large balcony where you can escape for some fresh air. You have the option of paying for all the beds in a dorm if you want some semblance of privacy.

**Hotel Nebitchi** (☎ 4 53 35/6/7/8/9; Kvartal 198; s/d/ste US$70/100/150; ) The yurt-shaped Nebitchi offers surprisingly swank top-end accommodation, rivalling almost anything in Ashgabat. The 38 rooms are spacious and come with satellite TV and double beds. The restaurant in the lobby is perhaps the best in town and the hotel is the only place around with the internet. Note that the pool is only open in summer.

**Victoria** (☎ 4 03 06; Kvartal 197; dishes US$1.50; 10am-11pm) With its African masks and vines, Victoria attempts to create a jungle atmosphere, although the menu offers a fairly standard range of quasi-European dishes.

**Ruslan Restaurant** (☎ 4 07 40; Kvartal 200; dishes US$2; 11am-11pm) The disco ball and blaring Russian pop indicate this place is more bar than restaurant, and Ruslan has been known to host live music acts. But locals also claim it's the best restaurant in town, with a full European menu of meat, chicken, pork and fish dishes.

### Getting There & Away

The **train station** (☎ 7 09 35) is 1km west and 400m south of Niyazov Sq. There are two trains a day to Turkmenbashi (3½ hours), and two to Ashgabat (seven hours), one of which continues to Turkmenabat and Dashogus. The more convenient train to Turkmenbashi departs at 6.16am while the better train to Ashgabat departs at 7.50pm.

Marshrutkas and shared taxis gather in the lot in front of the train station. These travel to Ashgabat (US$2 to US$3, six hours) throughout the day. A taxi will do the trip for US$15.

Turkmenistan Airlines flies between Balkanabat and Ashgabat (US$11) on Tuesday, Thursday and Saturday. The airport is 2km east of the city. A **booking office** (☎ 3 35 25) is inside the railway station.

## DEKHISTAN

The ruined city of Dekhistan (also known as Misrian) lies deep in the barren wastelands south of Balkanabat, midway between the tumbledown villages of Bugdayly and Madau. The surrounding desolation begs the question: how did a city come to be here in the first place? Yet in the 11th century it was a Silk Road oasis city with a sophisticated irrigation system rivalling Merv and Konye-Urgench. It even managed to revive itself after destruction by the Mongols. It seems that some time in the 15th century the region suffered an ecological catastrophe. The forests of the Kopet Dag to the east had been exploited for centuries until the water supply failed and the well-watered slopes finally became a barren, deeply eroded lunar landscape.

Not much remains on the 200-hectare site, apart from two truncated 20m-high **minarets** from the 11th and 13th centuries, and the decorated remains of a portal that once stood before the Mosque of the Khorezmshah Mohammed. Excavations here have also revealed the remains of several caravanserais that once served the Silk Road traders.

The **cemetery**, 7km north of Dekhistan at Mashat, features five semiruined mausoleums, including the Shir-Kabir Mosque-Mausoleum, the earliest mosque in the country.

Unless you have your own vehicle, Dekhistan is difficult to get to. Public transport is nonexistent, although you should be able to get a taxi from Balkanabat. The round trip should cost US$50, including waiting time. Balkansyyahat (see p419) runs overpriced tours. In fair weather you can make good time over the flat *takyr* (clay) landscape, but after rain in the spring or autumn the *takyr* turns to mush, making Dekhistan all but unreachable.

## GOZLI ATA & YANGYKALA CANYON

A respected Sufi teacher in the early 14th century, Gozli Ata had a large following until his untimely death at the hands of Mongol invaders. His **mausoleum** (GPS: N40° 20.051′, E054° 29.249′), located in a natural depression of rocky desert, is now a popular place of pilgrimage. Gozli Ata's wife is buried in an adjacent mausoleum and according to custom visitors must first pray at her last resting place. A cemetery has sprung up nearby where gravestones contain a notch in the top where water can collect to 'feed' the soul of the deceased. Gozli Ata is 135km north of Balkanabat; an experienced driver is needed to find it.

From the turnoff to Gozli Ata (marked with a 9km sign), another road continues north to **Yangykala Canyon** (GPS: N40° 27.656′, E054° 42.816′). With bands of pink, red and yellow rock searing across the sides of steep canyon walls, Yangykala is a breathtaking sight and one of the most spectacular natural attractions in Turkmenistan. Just as alluring as the beautiful views is its solitary isolation in the desert; few Turkmen are aware of its existence.

The canyons and cliffs slash for 25km towards the Garagogazgol basin and lie approximately 165km north of Balkanabat and about 160km east of Turkmenbashi, making it easy to slot the canyon between the two cities. It's possible to camp on the plateau above the canyon, although it can get windy here. While most tour companies run trips here, not all include it on their standard itineraries, make inquiries when planning your trip.

## TURKMENBASHI

☎ 243 / pop 60,000

Turkmenbashi isn't quite the Mazatlan of the Caspian Sea but there is a certain relaxed air about the place, with a few nice beaches and some surprisingly good cafés. There is no reason to come all this way for the city itself, but it makes a useful base if you are catching the Caspian ferry to Baku or heading into Kazakhstan through the backdoor.

The first settlement here, Krasnovodsk, was established when a unit of Russian troops under Prince Alexander Bekovich set ashore in 1717 with the intention of marching on Khiva. They chose this spot because it was close to the place where the Oxus River (now the Amu-Darya) had once drained into the Caspian Sea, and the dry riverbed provided the best road across the desert. But the mission failed,

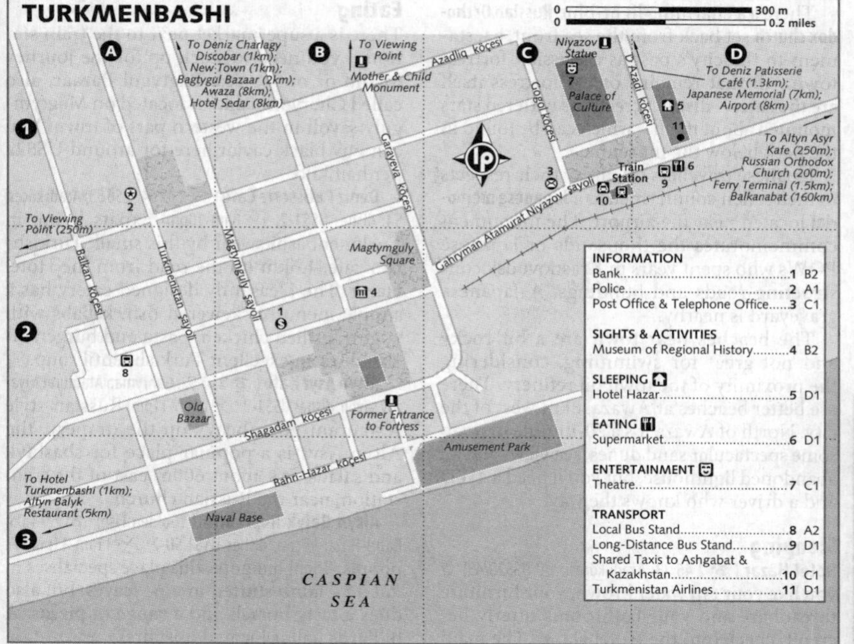

Bekovich lost his head and the Russians didn't come back for more than 150 years. In the late 1800s, Krasnovodsk grew in importance with the arrival of the Trans-Caspian railroad. Thousands of Japanese POWs were dumped here after WWII and ordered to construct roads and buildings. Since then the town has become somewhat cosmopolitan, with a mix of Russians, Turkmen, Azeris and a handful of Western oil workers.

## Sights

The **Museum of Regional History** (admission US$0.10, guided tour US$0.15; 9am-6pm Tue-Sun) is located in a quaint old structure west of Magtymguly Sq. The collections include disintegrating taxidermy, some interesting maps, models of the Caspian Sea, traditional Turkmen clothing and a yurt. In the last room a photo exhibition recalls an expedition made in 1936 by a group of fishermen from Krasnovodsk. Travelling in small boats, the fishermen made their way along the Caspian Sea shore and up the Volga river to Moscow, a 4650km journey that was completed in three months. One of their boats has become part of the exhibit.

There's a charming light-blue **Russian Orthodox church** set back from the sea front, a testament to the city's past as a Russian fortress town. All that remains of the fortress itself are the gates – distinct creations with red stars mounted about them – which can be found in the park below the museum.

Japanese travellers often pay their respects to their fallen countrymen at a **Japanese memorial** located near the airport. The monument commemorates the thousands of Japanese POWs who spent years in Krasnovodsk constructing roads and buildings. A Japanese graveyard is nearby.

The beaches near town are a bit rocky and not great for swimming, considering the proximity of the town oil refinery. There are better beaches at Awaza, 8km west of the city. North of Awaza it's a 20-minute drive to some spectacular sand dunes, sea views and an abandoned lighthouse, but you'll need a 4WD and a driver who knows the way.

## Sleeping

**Hotel Hazar** (2 46 33; Azadi köçesi; s/d US$28/43) If you like your tap water brown, your furniture threadbare and your bathrooms utterly decrepit, check into the Hotel Hazar. The main problem here, besides the miserable condition of the place, is that you are only allowed to pay in manat changed at the official state rate (you have to show a certificate from the bank), which makes the rooms terrible value for money.

**Hotel Turkmenbashi** (2 17 17, 2 13 14, 2 18 18; Bahri-Hazar köçesi; s/d US$100/120; ) Four-star-quality rooms with sea views and a range of facilities make this a great choice, especially from October to May when prices fall 50% out of peak season. The 90-room hotel includes a gym, bar, decent restaurant, laundry and the only internet access in the city. It's about 2km west of downtown, on the road to Awaza.

**Hotel Sedar** (2 15 81, 5 12 25; sedaroteli@online.tm; Awaza; s/d/ste US$100/120/200; ) With sweeping coastal views, luxurious rooms and total isolation, this is about as close as Turkmenistan gets to a holiday resort. Prices include breakfast and use of the sauna, indoor pool and fitness centre. Prices drop by 50% from October to May. Sedar is located 8km from town, with no eating or shopping facilities apart from what's at the hotel.

## Eating

There is a supermarket next to the train station if you need to stock up for the journey inland or out to sea. Bagtygul Bazaar, also called Cheryomushki, is located on Magtymguly şayoli in the western part of town. You can buy black caviar here for around US$22 per half kilo.

**Deniz Patisserie Café** (1 42 54, 2 56 53; Azadi köçesi 54; dishes US$1-2; 8am-10pm) Expats living in Turkmenbashi swear by this small, Turkish-run café, 1.5km up the road from the Hotel Hazar. The pleasantly designed eatery has a simple menu of skewered fish, kebabs with yogurt, grilled chicken, pasta and burgers. It also does an excellent Turkish lentil soup.

**Altyn Asyr Kafe** (2 07 52; Gahryman Atamurat Niyazov şayoli; dishes US$1-2; noon-11pm) Russian-style restaurant gone heavy on the drapery, the Altyn Asyr is a popular place for shashlyk and salads. It's about 600m east of the train station, near the Russian church.

**Altyn Balyk Restaurant** (Golden Fish; 7 74 05; Bahri-Hazar köçesi; dishes US$1.50-2; 11am-11pm) A popular local hangout, this place specialises in *dolma* – lamb stuffed in vine leaves, but also does a tasty borsch and a range of pizzas. A billiards hall is located upstairs.

### Entertainment

**Deniz Charlagy Discobar** (☎ 2 56 53; Magtymguly şayoli; ⏰ 11pm-4am) The lone nightclub in the city sports an oceanic theme and ship décor. It plays a mix of Russian and US pop. There is plenty of alcohol upstairs and a small restaurant downstairs.

### Getting There & Away

From the Turkmenbashi **ferry terminal** (☎ 2 44 91) there are several untimetabled ferries everyday to Baku in Azerbaijan (see p468).

Turkmenistan Airlines flies to and from Ashgabat (US$12) twice daily and to Dashogus (US$11). The **airline office** (☎ 2 54 74) is south of the Hotel Hazar in the same building. The airport is 8km east of the ferry terminal (located at the port).

Shared taxis leave outside the colourful train station on Atamurat Niyazov köçesi for Ashgabat (US$8 per seat or US$25 for the whole car, six hours). They also run north along the bad road to Kazakhstan (US$40 per car, seven hours), crossing the border and stopping at the town of Zhanaozen (Novy Uzen). Marshrutki also leave from here to Ashgabat via Balkanabat; they cost the same as a seat in a shared taxi and are far less comfortable.

An overnight train leaves daily from Turkmenbashi at 4.05pm for Ashgabat (arriving at 7.55am). A *kupe* (2nd-class seat) is US$1.20. Call ☎ 9 94 62 for information on train services.

### Getting Around

Turkmenbashi's local bus station is just off Balkan köçesi, about 500m west of the museum. From here you can catch infrequent transport to the airport, the seaport and Awaza at prices that are almost negligible. Taxis also hang around here, as well as near the train station, and charge around 3000M for most destinations around town, or 5000M for a ride to Awaza.

# EASTERN TURKMENISTAN

Squeezed between the inhospitable Karakum desert and the rugged Afghan frontier, the fertile plains of eastern Turkmenistan have long been an island of prosperity in Central Asia. The rise of civilisations began in the Bronze Age, reaching their climax with the wondrous city of Merv. The invading Mongols put paid to centuries of accumulated wealth but even today the region continues to outpace the rest of Turkmenistan, thanks mainly to a thriving cotton business. For visitors keen on history, eastern Turkmenistan offers some of the best sights in the country, including Merv, Gonur and the cave city at Ekedeshik. Nature-lovers may also want to throw Kugitang Nature Reserve into the itinerary, although getting there does take time and effort. The region is at its best in the autumn when harvest festivals add an element of colourful ambience to otherwise dreary Soviet-built cities.

## MARY

☎ 522 / pop 123,000

The capital of the Mary region is a somewhat spartan Soviet confection of administrative buildings and vast gardens disproportionate to the size of the city. Mary (pronounced mahrih) is also the centre of the major cotton-growing belt, which gives the city an air of prosperity; the markets bustle on weekends and commerce is surprisingly brisk.

Mary's history dates back to the 1820s when the Tekke Turkmens erected a fortress here, preferring the site to ancient Merv, 30km east. In 1884, a battalion of Russian troops, led by one Lieutenant Alikhanov, convinced the Turkmens to hand over control of the fort before things got bloody. Cotton production quickly picked up and the guarantee of continued wealth came in 1968 when huge natural gas reserves were found 20km west of the city.

Apart from the excellent regional museum there is nothing to hold the traveller down, although it makes for a handy base to explore the ancient cities of Gonur and Merv. The city has accommodation for all budgets, good transport links and some of the best shashlyk joints in the country.

### Orientation & Information

The town's main thoroughfare is Mollanepes şayoli, where you'll find the seven-storey Hotel Sanjar and the nearby Univermag department store. Further down Mollanepes is the Zelyony (Green) Bazaar and the Murgab River. Crossing the river en route to Merv you'll see the enormous Turkmenbashi Hajji Metcheti mosque. The central post and telegraph office is 1km east of the Sanjar on Mollanepes, while the central telephone office is

50m northwest of the post office. The Hotel Yrsgal Firmasay has public internet access for US$4 per hour.

**Yevgenia Golubeva** (☎ 3 14 85; evgeniagolubeva@yahoo.com) is an experienced, English-speaking tour guide, who used to be the deputy director of the Mary Museum. She can organise tours to nearby Merv and Gonur.

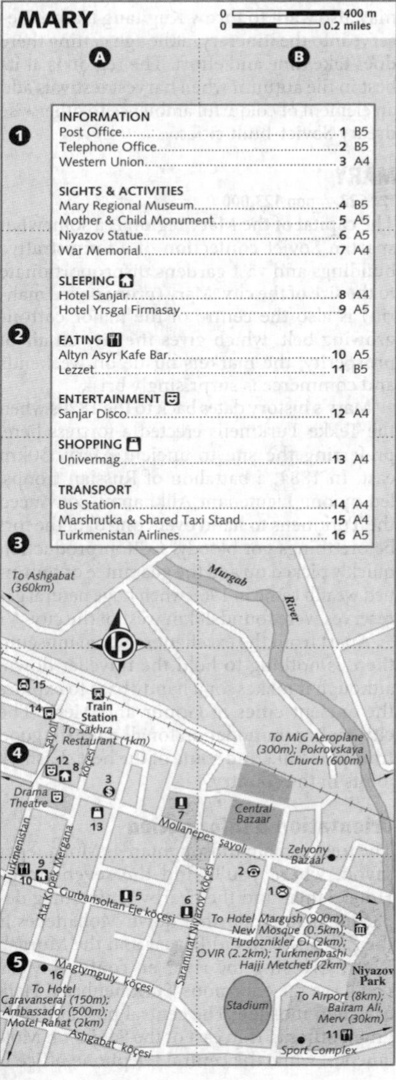


The **OVIR** (State Service for the Registration of Foreign Citizens; ☎ 4 50 40, 4 41 22; Turkmenbashi köçesi; 🕒 9am-6pm Mon-Fri, 9am-1pm Sat) handles registration.

## Sights

The highlight of the city is the **Mary Regional Museum** (admission US$1, camera US$5; 🕒 10am-5pm Tue-Sun), a 100-year-old mansion built by a Russian brick baron. The well-appointed collection hauls together artefacts from Merv and Margush, plus an extensive ethnography section. Room 1 contains a large, poorly proportioned model of Merv. Room 2 features the Bronze Age cities of Gonur and Togolok 21. The skeleton of a Margiana priestess is a replica – a series of deaths and misfortunes among museum staff persuaded them to have the original returned to where it was found. The fine quality and design of household items from Margiana is striking and rivals the collection of the National Museum in Ashgabat.

Other displays include an exhibition of Turkmen carpets from the museum's huge collection; a display of Turkmen household items; everyday, wedding and ceremonial clothing; and a fully decorated yurt. One room contains pottery created during the Mongol occupation; the use of blue evokes the Mongol predilection towards the sky, considered a heavenly being called *tenger*.

The other main sight in Mary is **Pokrovskaya Church**, a handsome red-brick affair built in 1900. The church is surrounded by pleasant parkland and its interior is crammed with religious icons. Walk a few hundred metres west and you'll spot a **MiG aeroplane** on display, a more ominous legacy of Russian occupation. To get to the church and aeroplane, head east on Mollanepes şayoli, cross the bridge over Murgab River, take the first left over railroad tracks, after two streets you'll see the MiG on your right.

In the town centre there are several new **statues** of former President Niyazov; the seated statue on the corner of Saparmurat Niyazov köçesi and Gurbansoltan Eje köçesis bears a striking resemblance to US President Kennedy. Behind the statue is a mosaic of a Turkmen carpet.

You can get your shopping done at the enormous **Central Bazaar** (Mollanepes şayoli). This is great place to stock up on fresh fruit. There are more shops in the Univermag, down the street. If you'd like to meet some local artists and buy their work, check out the **Hudoznikler Oi** (House of Artists; Turkmenbashi köçesi; 9am-6pm), a collection of artist studios. It is located 300m northwest of OVIR.

If you're still looking for something to do, you can walk around **Niyazov Park**, which contains some amusement rides, bumper cars and a handful of cafés. The park is a short walk east of the museum.

## Sleeping

**Motel Rahat** (6 42 04; Serkhetabat köçesi; s/d US$20/30; ) Despite the slightly out of the way location (2km from the town centre), the Rahat offers surprisingly nice budget digs. The spacious rooms are built around a courtyard of lemon trees and each comes with TV and a reasonably clean bathroom. The motel is built next to a truck stop on the road to the southern border and as such attracts plenty of Iranian truck drivers who can be found most nights in the bar downstairs. Thankfully it doesn't get too loud and the hotel section is safely separated from the bar.

**Hotel Sanjar** (7 10 76; Mollanepes şayoli 58; s/d US$25/30; ) This Soviet-era Intourist hotel is your standard pile of neglected concrete. The rooms have never been renovated and the bathrooms are simply miserable. The only reason to stay here is the location, smack in the middle of the city, but given that you're unlikely to linger too long the Rahat is a much better choice.

**Hotel Caravanserai** (3 93 50, 3 34 60; Nisimi köçesi 25; s/d/tr US$25/40/52) Pleasant and charming homestay with a local Turkmen family. The facilities are shared, but clean and have hot water, and there's a lovely garden.

**Hotel Yrsgal Firmasay** (7 21 27, 7 21 31; Ata Kopek Mergana köçesi 2; s/d US$40/50; ) Occupying a great location in the city centre, this midrange option has small but tidy rooms that include TV and a decent bathroom. The friendly, English-speaking staff is a bonus.

**Hotel Margush** (3 23 28, 3 46 01, 3 49 40; Gowshuthat köçesi 20; s/d/ste US$50/70/150; ) Mary's only top-end accommodation is located near the Murgab River, 1km north of the town centre. The 30 rooms are built around a pleasant lobby, each room contains a TV, fridge and small desk. The prices do not include breakfast, which is an option for an additional US$4.50. Other facilities, such as the sauna (US$1.50), fitness centre (US$1.20) and swimming pool (US$2), are also extra.

## Eating & Drinking

**Altyn Asyr Kafe Bar** (cnr Turkmenistan şayoli & Gurbansoltan Eje köçesi; noon-11pm) Locals will tell you that this place serves the best shashlyk in the country; a debatable claim indeed but the grilled meats are admittedly tasty. The patio is a nice place to enjoy your meal.

**Lezzet** (3 57 67; Ashgabat köçesi; 9am-9pm) Adding a little variety to the local restaurant scene, Lezzet serves up tasty pizzas and Turkish meals, including doner kebabs topped with yogurt.

**Sakhra Restaurant** (5 61 77; Magtymguly köçesi 40; 11am-11pm) This appears to be a vodka shop when you enter, but has two dining rooms which serve good Turkmen and Russian dishes. Service is a little fussy if you sit in the formal dining room (the bar dining room around the back is much nicer).

## Entertainment

**Ambassador** (5 61 77; Podeby köçesi; admission US$1; noon-3.30am) The flashiest bar in town has a small dance floor and even a bouncer at the door. It also seems to be the only strip club in the country, although the dance acts are infrequent and late at night (but still pretty racy for Mary).

Another option is the **Sanjar Disco** (Mollanepes şayoli; 7pm-1am), next to the eponymous hotel. It's extremely dark inside but entry is free.

## Getting There & Away

Mary is 3½ hours by car from Ashgabat and two hours from Turkmenabat. Marshrutki also run this route (US$3 , four hours and US$2, 2½ hours respectively). There are a couple of bus departures to both cities, but these leave early in the morning. There are also one or two morning buses to Serkhetabat, on the Afghan border (p441). The rest of the day you can use shared taxis and marshrutki, which leave from a lot next to the bus station.

Mary's revamped **train station** (9 22 45) has night trains to Ashgabat (*kupe,* US$1.50, eight hours). There's one night train to Turkmenabat (*kupe,* seven hours, US$1.50) and one that runs the whole way to Dashogus (*kupe,* US$2, 24 hours). There is no left-luggage facility, but the station does have an international phone office.

**Turkmenistan Airlines** (3 27 77; Magtymguly köçesi 11) has at least two flights per day to Ashgabat (US$11). If time is short, you could even take the morning flight, visit Merv and return on the same day to Ashgabat. The airport is 8km east of the city, on the road to Merv.

## MERV

In its heyday it was known as Marv-i-shahjahan, 'Merv – Queen of the World', and it stood alongside Damascus, Baghdad and Cairo as one of the great centres of Islam. A major centre of religious study and a lynchpin on the Silk Road, its importance to the commerce and sophistication of Central Asia cannot be underestimated. Today, almost nothing of the metropolis remains.

Before the sons of Jenghiz Khan laid waste to the great city and slaughtered its population, Merv had been a melting pot of religious faiths and ethnic groups. Its buildings of fired brick towered over the green oasis, and included palaces, mosques, caravanserais and thousands of private homes.

The scattered ruins left today include fortified walls, brick foundations and gazillions of shards of pottery. It became a Unesco World Heritage site in 1999 and is deservedly considered the most impressive historical site in the country. Merv can easily be visited on a day trip from Mary but it's essential to have your own transport, and preferably a guide to make sense of it all.

### History

Merv was known as Margiana or Margush in Alexander the Great's time. Under the Persian Sassanians, it was considered religiously liberal, with significant populations of Christians, Buddhists and Zoroastrians cohabiting peacefully. As a centre of power, culture and civilisation, Merv reached its greatest heights during the peak of the Silk Route in the 11th and 12th centuries, when the Seljuq Turks made it their capital. Legendary Merv may even have been the inspiration for the tales of Scheherazade's *The Thousand and One Nights*.

Merv suffered a number of attacks over the course of its history, but instead of being rebuilt on top of the older ruins, Merv slowly spread west. In total, five cities were constructed next to each other, largely because of the shifting rivers. The oldest section was the Erk Kala and in later centuries most people lived in the vast walled city called Sultan Kala.

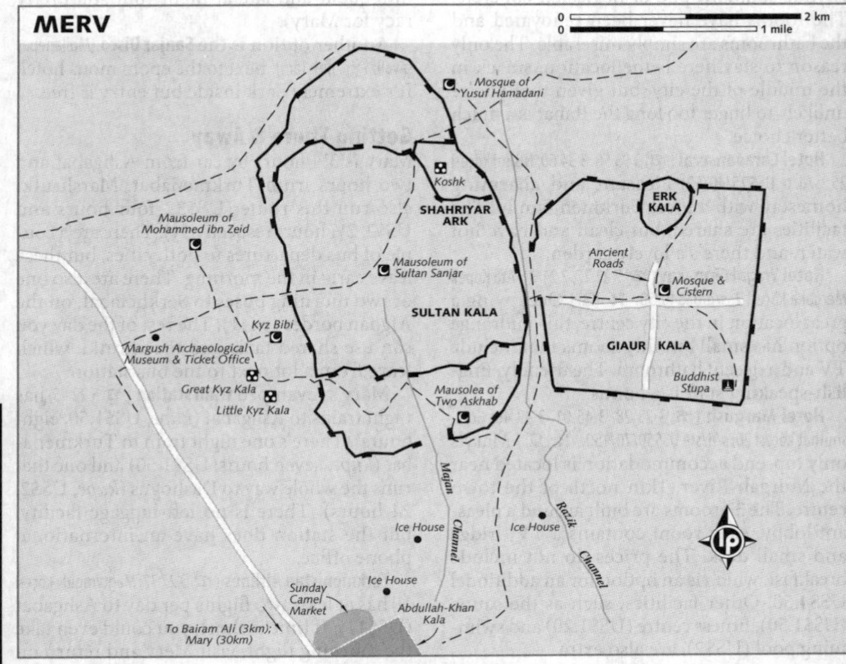

All of this was completely eradicated in 1221 under the onslaught of the Mongols. In 1218 Jenghiz Khan demanded a substantial tithe of grain from Merv, along with the pick of the city's most beautiful young women. The unwise Seljuq response was to slay the tax collectors. In retribution Tolui, the most brutal of Jenghiz Khan's sons, arrived three years later at the head of an army, accepted the peaceful surrender of the terrified citizens, and then proceeded to butcher every last one of the city's inhabitants, an estimated 300,000 people.

Merv made a small comeback in the 15th century and was soon at the centre of a territorial dispute between the rulers of Bukhara, Khiva and Persia. Persian influence eventually won out when a noble named Bairam Ali rebuilt the dam, which allowed the irrigated region to prosper and encouraged free trade. The Emir of Bukhara struck back with military force, captured the city, and utterly destroyed it in 1795.

Russia annexed Merv in 1884 and the Turkmen settlement became known as Bairam Ali. Russians monitored events from Mary, their newly built town 30km to the west.

## Sights

Coming from Mary you pass through the town of Bairam Ali, and turn left on a road heading north from the Central Bazaar. After 4km a sign points right towards the Merv complex. On the road towards ancient Merv is a small ticket office for the **Merv complex** (admission US$0.80, camera US$1.20, video US$2; 🕑 7am-dusk) and the **Margush Archaeological Museum** (admission free; 🕑 7am-dusk) which houses a tiny collection of artefacts and old photos.

### MOHAMMED IBN ZEID

From the ticket office, continue east and take your first left (north) to an early-Islamic monument, the 12th-century **Mausoleum of Mohammed ibn Zeid**. The small, unostentatious earthen-brick building, which was heavily restored early in the 20th century, benefits greatly from an attractive setting in a hollow that is ringed by spindly saxaul trees. Like the other Sufi shrines (Gozli-Ata and Kubra), this shrine is also an important site for Sufi pilgrims.

There's confusion as to who's actually buried under the black marble cenotaph in the centre of the cool, dark shrine. It's definitely not Ibn Zeid, a prominent Shiite teacher who died four centuries before this tomb was built and is known to be buried elsewhere.

### EARLIEST REMAINS

The oldest of the five Merv cities is **Erk Kala**, an Achaemenid city thought to date from the 6th century BC. Led by Alexander the Great, the Macedonians conquered it and renamed it Alexandria Margiana. Under Parthian control (250BC to AD226) Zoroastrianism was the state religion but Erk Kala was also home to Nestorian Christians, Jews and Buddhists.

Today Erk Kala is a big earthen doughnut about 600m across. There are deep trenches that have been dug into the ramparts by Soviet archaeologists. The ramparts are 50m high, and offer a bird's-eye view of the surrounding savannah-like landscape. On the ramparts it's easy to see small hills that were once towers.

From this vantage point you can see that Erk Kala forms part of the northern section of another fortress – **Giaur Kala**, constructed during the 3rd century BC by the Sassanians. The fortress walls are still solid, with three gaps where gates once were. The city was built on a Hellenistic grid pattern; near the crossroads in the middle of the site are the ruins of a 7th-century mosque. At the eastern end of the mosque is an 8m-deep water cistern that's been dug into the ground.

In the southeastern corner of Giaur Kala a distinct mound marks the site of a Buddhist stupa and monastery, which was still functioning in the early Islamic era. The head of a Buddha statue was found here making Merv the furthest western point to which Buddhism spread at its height.

### SULTAN KALA

The best remaining testimony to Seljuq power at Merv is the 38m-high **Mausoleum of Sultan Sanjar**, located in what was the centre of Sultan Kala. The building has been recently restored with Turkish aid and rises dramatically in the open plain.

Sanjar, grandson of Alp-Arslan, died in 1157, reputedly of a broken heart when, after escaping from captivity in Khiva, he came home to find that Jenghiz Khan's soldiers had laid waste to his beloved Merv.

The mausoleum is a simple cube with a barrel-mounted dome on top. Originally it had a magnificent turquoise-tiled outer dome, said to be visible from a day's ride away, but that is long gone. Interior decoration is sparse, though restoration has brought back the blue-and-red frieze in the upper gallery. Inside is Sanjar's simple stone 'tomb', although fearing grave robbers he was actually buried elsewhere in an unknown location! The name of the architect, Mohammed Ibn Aziz of Serakhs, is etched into the upper part of the east wall. According to lore, the sultan had his architect executed to prevent him from designing a building to rival this one.

The **Shahriyar Ark** (or Citadel of Sultan Kala) is one of the more interesting parts of Merv. Still visible are its walls, a well-preserved *koshk* (fort) with corrugated walls, and the odd grazing camel.

North of the Shahriyar Ark, outside the city walls, lies the **Mosque of Yusuf Hamadani**, built around the tomb of a 12th-century dervish. The complex has been largely rebuilt in the last 10 years and turned into an important pilgrimage site; it is not open to non-Muslims.

Archaeologists have been excavating a number of sites around Sultan Kala, revealing the foundations of homes. If you have an experienced guide they should know the location of recent digs.

#### KYZ KALA

These two crumbling 7th-century *koshks* outside the walls of Merv are interesting for their 'petrified stockade' walls, as writer Colin Thubron describes them, composed of 'vast clay logs up-ended side by side'. They were constructed by the Sassanians in the 7th century and were still in use by Seljuq sultans, 600 years later, as function rooms. These are some of the most symbolic and important structures in western Merv archaeology and they have no analogies anywhere else.

#### MAUSOLEUMS OF TWO ASKHAB

One of the most important pilgrimage sites in Turkmenistan are the mausoleums built for two Islamic *askhab* (companions of the prophet), Al-Hakim ibn Amr al-Jafari and Buraida ibn al-Huseib al-Islami. The two squat buildings sit in front of reconstructed Timurid *iwans* (*aiwans,* portals) that honour the prophets. In front of the mausoleums is a still-functioning water cistern.

#### ICE HOUSES

South of Sultan Kala and Giaur Kala are three ice houses built during the Timurid era. The giant freezers, made from brick and covered by a conical-shaped roof, were used to keep meat and other foods frozen during the summer. The ice house closest to Giaur Kala is perhaps the best-preserved structure. They now sit in a fairly neglected state, but are worth a quick look.

### Getting There & Away

The only way to see the site without an exhausting walk is by car. From Mary expect to pay US$7.50 for a car and driver for four hours (the minimum amount of time needed to see the main monuments). Buses go between Mary and Bairam Ali every half hour or so; the journey takes about 45 minutes. Guided tours are available from any travel agency and this is the way most people see Merv. Yevgenia Golubeva in Mary (see p423) includes Merv on her tour of the area.

## GONUR

Long before Merv raised its first tower, Bronze Age villages were assembling along the Murgab River in what is called the Margiana Oasis. The greatest of these ancient settlements, currently being excavated around **Gonur Depe** (Gonur Hill; admission US$1, camera US$1.20), has stunned the archaeological world for its vast area and complex layout.

The discoveries were first made in 1972 by Russian-Greek archaeologist Viktor Sarianidi, who still works at the site, continually uncovering new findings. Sarianidi considers Gonur to be one of the great civilisations of the ancient world and while this claim may be disputed, it certainly is a fascinating site. What is certain, however, is that Gonur is one of the oldest fire-worshipping civilisations, parallel to the Bactrian cultures in neighbouring Afghanistan. The first agricultural settlements appeared in the area around 7000 BC and developed a strong agriculture. It is believed the city was slowly abandoned during the Bronze Age as the Murgab River changed course, depriving the city of water. The current excavations have been dated back to 3000 BC.

Sarianidi believes that Gonur was the birthplace of the first monotheistic religion, Zoroastrianism, being at some point the home of the religion's founder, Zoroaster. The adjacent sites have revealed four fire temples, as well as evidence of a cult based around a drug potion prepared from poppy, hemp and ephedra plants. This potent brew is almost certainly the *haoma* (soma elixir) used by the magi whom Zoroaster began preaching against in Zoroastrian texts.

The excavations are ongoing and during your visit you may have a chance to speak with the archaeologists and inspect the most-recent findings. There is also significant effort being put into conservation, although the work being done (sealing the ruins with mud bricks) is covering up some of the most photogenic portions of the city. The Royal Palace and necropolis are the most fascinating sites to visit.

### Getting There & Away

Gonur is a two-hour drive from Mary and you'll need at least two hours there. A 4WD is required and the final 20km of road is little more than a rough track in the dirt. You can organise a trip through any travel agency or call Yevgenia Golubeva in Mary (see p423). Expect to pay US$40 to hire a driver, and a further US$30 for an indepth guided tour. There is nowhere in the area to buy food or water, so pack a lunch before setting off.

## TAGTABAZAR

The peaceful town of Tagtabazar lies 215km south of Mary on the road to Afghanistan. On the fringe of the former Russian Empire, it was here that the tsar locked horns with British-backed Afghanistan in one of the salvoes of the Great Game (see p45). A brief battle near the town (then called Pandjeh) left over 800 Afghans dead and Russia hanging onto victory by a thread. The battle ultimately forced Afghanistan and Russia into negotiations that delineated a border.

If you happen to be passing through Tagtabazar en route to Afghanistan, it's worth stopping to see the extraordinary **Ekedeshik cave complex** (admission US$2, tour US$1, camera US$3; 9am-5pm), located in the hills north of town. The main cavern is reached through a metal gate where a caretaker sells you a ticket. From here the cave stretches back 32m and includes 44 rooms on two levels. One room, containing a vaulted ceiling and a carved doorway, may have been used by a chief or priest. The curator will show you a staircase to more caverns below, but this section is off-limits.

The caves are sometimes locked, so before you go there inquire about the key-holder at the local governor's office. The caves are 3km north of town and accessible by private car or taxi.

## TURKMENABAT

☎ 422 / pop 203,000

Lying on the banks of the mighty Amu-Darya, between the Karakum desert and the fertile plains of Uzbekistan, Turkmenabat sits at a crossroads of cultures. On its streets you'll hear as much Uzbek as Turkmen and will likely be enjoying Uzbek produce, driven across the border a few kilometres to the north. Having only recently received a name change, most residents still refer to the town as Charjou, a title bequeathed during Russian occupation. Local history is in fact much older – the Silk Road city of Amul prospered here until its destruction by the Mongols in 1221.

Today Turkmenabat is the second-largest city in the country, but retains an anachronistic air with most of its commerce based on cross-border trade. There are few attractions to hold you down, but the city does have a reasonable collection of hotels and restaurants, making a logical stopover on the long journeys to Kugitang Nature Reserve, Mary or Dashogus.

### Sights

The **Lebap Regional Museum** (☎ 6 20 93; Shaidakov köçesi 35; admission US$0.20; 9am-1pm & 2-6pm Mon-Sat) is a unique brick structure with a rectangular tower and two brick minarets. It was originally built as a Shia mosque in the early 20th century but was turned into a museum by the Soviets in the 1960s. Downstairs, an ethnography section includes a fully furnished yurt, a diorama of a silversmith workshop and a requisite room of stuffed animals. The 2nd floor is given over to locally produced agricultural products and a *Ruhnama* display.

A couple of blocks northeast of the museum is the **Russian Orthodox Church** (Magtymguly şayoli), built to honour St Nicolas Maker of Miracles. Built in the late 19th century, the church is painted canary yellow and decorated on the interior with a rich collection of icons.

Turkmenabat has a couple of busting bazaars. The most convenient is **Zelyony (Green) Bazaar**, near the telephone office. A better choice if you are looking for carpets is the **Dunya Bazaar**, 8km south of downtown.

### Sleeping

At the time of writing the Hotel Amu Darya, opposite the train station, was undergoing renovation. Once a popular budget hotel, the Amu Darya should emerge solidly in the mid-range category.

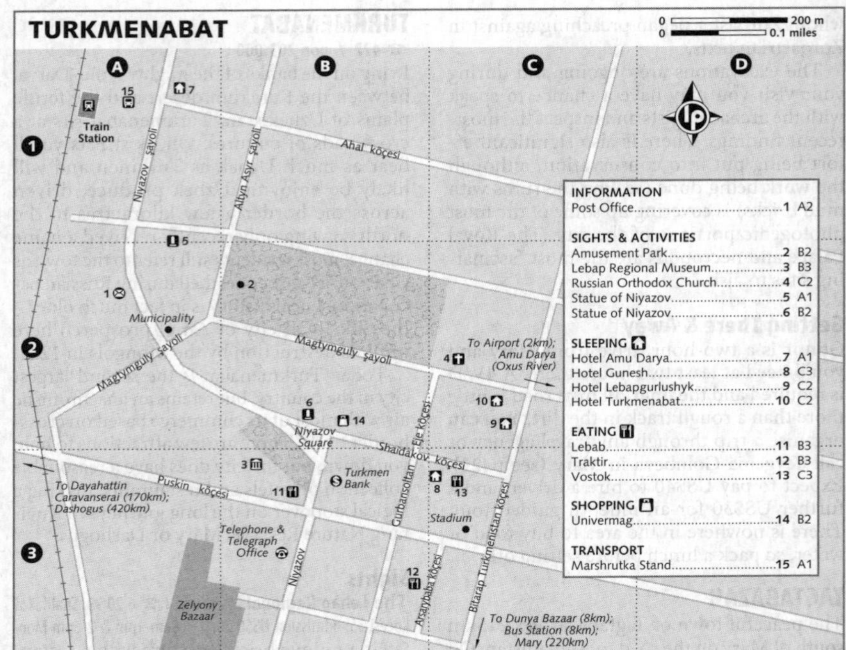


**Hotel Gunesh** (☎ 2 13 88; Shaidakov köçesi 36; per person US$6) Run-down and badly neglected, this downtown hotel has peeling walls and brusque staff. Rooms come with a sink but the communal toilets are down the hall.

**Hotel Lebapgurlushyk** (☎ 4 44 20, 4 41 04; Magtymguly şayoli 51A; per person US$6.50) This unpronounceable hotel is an old Soviet-era place, but friendly and decently looked after. The rooms are large apartments with a living room, a couple of bedrooms, a kitchen and collections of unmatched furniture. The hotel has hot water but the air-con fails to keep the large rooms cool in summer. It is located behind the Hotel Turkmenabat.

**Hotel Turkmenabat** (☎ 6 02 26; Magtymguly şayoli; s/d US$45/90; ❄) Although a little overpriced, the Turkmenabat offers the only rooms in town that approach the top-end category. Each of the 45 rooms has high ceilings and comfy beds, but the TV is tiny. There is a pleasant lobby and a bar, but unfortunately no restaurant.

## Eating

**Vostok** (☎ 4 94 18; Shaidakov köçesi 34; dishes US$1; ⏲ 9am-11pm) This basic eatery and bar, next to the Hotel Gunesh, attracts midday barflies for beer and tasty *samsa*. It also serves pizza, shashlyk and salads.

**Traktir** (☎ 6 14 38; Arsarybaba köçesi 14; meals US$2; ⏲ 11am-11pm) Although thousands of miles from the sea, the Traktir manages to recreate a maritime theme, with fishing nets, ropes and ship steering wheels tacked to the walls. The vast menu includes plenty of meat dishes; portions are big and the cuts rather fatty. The service is painfully slow but the menu forewarns you by giving the preparation time for each dish.

**Lebap** (☎ 6 35 21; Puşkin köçesi; meals US$2; ⏲ 9am-11pm) Popular local restaurant with bright yellow walls, paintings of Turkmen scenes and a general cheerfulness. The food is mainly Russian, with a wide selection of fish dishes and beers.

## Getting There & Away

There are around four flights a day between Turkmenabat and the capital (US$12, one hour). The airport is 2km east of the Hotel Turkmenabat. The **train station** (☎ 6 47 19), in the centre of town, has two daily trains to Ashgabat (US$2.50, 16 hours), Mary (US$1, seven hours) and Turkmenbashi (US$2.50, 23 hours). Outside the station you can catch marshrutki to Mary (US$2), Ashgabat (US$4) and other destinations. A ride to the Uzbek border will cost US$1 per seat, but you may need to bargain hard as starting prices can be much higher. There is another, more formal bus station 9km south of the centre of town, near Dunya Bazaar, but the transportation links from the lot outside the train station are just as good.

## DAYAHATTIN CARAVANSERAI

This Silk Road caravanserai stands on the ancient route between Amul of Khorezm and dates to around the 12th century (give or take a couple hundred years). Although abandoned around 500 years ago, most of the building stands intact, although in a fairly ruinous state. Pick your way through the enormous arched gateway into a central courtyard, surrounded by a vaulted arcade and small cells. Climbing up on the walls you can make out a second earthen wall that surrounded the compound. The caravanserai is around 170km northwest of Turkmenabat. It's located near a checkpoint and your guide will need to get permission to visit the site.

## KUGITANG NATURE RESERVE

Kugitang is the most impressive and pristine of Turkmenistan's nature reserves. Set up in 1986 to protect the Kugitang mountain range and its unique ecosystem, and in particular the rare markhor mountain goat (whose name comes from the Persian meaning 'almost impassable mountains'). Its extent includes the country's highest peak, Airybaba (3137m), several huge canyons, rich forests, mountain streams, caves and the unique **Dinosaur Plateau** (see the boxed text, below). Close to the plateau, outside the village of Hojapil, is the **Kyrk Gyz (Forty Girl) Cave**. The cave, located in a spectacular canyon, contains an unmarked tomb. On the ceiling of the cave you can see bits of mud from which dangle strips of cloth; according to local tradition, a wish is granted if the pilgrim can fling the mud pie and cloth to the ceiling and make it stick.

Visiting one of the **Karlyuk Caves** is also an incredible experience. The limestone caves are considered the most extensive network of caves in Central Asia. They have been known since ancient times, having been mentioned in Greek texts, but the Soviets were the first to fully explore and exploit the caves; it was during their rule that the onyx was harvested from the caves. The caves are also home to the blind cave loach, a sightless fish.

As the caves have not been readied for the tourist masses, only the Kapkytan Cave is accessible for visitors. Walking deep into the caves with one of the park rangers is both spooky and exciting, with some astonishing stalactites and stalagmites. Some of these natural wonders have been named by locals according to their form, including Medusa, a maiden and others of more phallic nature.

You'll need to organise a trip here through a travel agent who can get you a permit to visit and provide a driver. Accommodation is usually in a homestay with rangers or at a newly built hotel. Expect to pay US$40 per person per night for full board. It's possible

### TURKMENOSAURUS REX

Looking like someone took a giant stamp of a footprint and pounded it into the ground, the dinosaur footprints of Kugitang Nature Reserve seem almost too perfect to be real. But the tracks are indeed legit, and were left here by ambling dinosaurs some 155 million years ago.

According to local legend, the prints were left by elephants used by the armies of Alexander the Great. Scientists, however, will tell you that the prints were left during the Jurassic period by a species called Megalosauripus.

The location of the tracks is a plateau that is presumed to be the bottom of a shallow lake that dried up, leaving the dinosaur prints baking in the sun, after which a volcanic eruption sealed them in lava. There are more than 400 prints visible on a steep incline of limestone, the largest of which has a diameter of 80cm. Around Kugitang, more than 2500 prints have been found.

The giant dinosaurs were apparently joined by smaller dino creatures that left imprints resembling a human foot. In 1995 a Russian newspaper stirred up controversy when it reported that the prints were in fact human. Creationists have since lost no opportunity in taking advantage of the unlikely theory.

to fly from Ashgabat to Gaurdak (Magdanly) via Turkmenabat (US$13), far preferable than doing the arduous journey across the desert. Otherwise it's a five- to six-hour drive from Turkmenabat.

# NORTHERN TURKMENISTAN

Stalin's modus operandi in Central Asia sought the division of its people, thus resulting in the split of the Khorezm oasis – the northern bit with Khiva going to Uzbekistan and the southern portion, with Konye-Urgench, going to Turkmenistan. It remains this way today, with the Amu-Darya river wriggling its way in and out of the Uzbek and Turkmen borders. As part of historic Khorezm, the Turkmen portion still contains a sizable Uzbek minority and retains a culture apart from the rest of the country. Sadly, the region has not escaped the Aral Sea disaster and suffers from air, soil and water pollution. It's also the poorest part of the country, with little commerce apart from the smuggling of subsidised petrol to Uzbekistan. Still, it's worth visiting the area to explore some unique historical sights, especially if you are travelling to or from Uzbekistan.

## KONYE-URGENCH

**☎ 347 / pop 15,000**

The modern town of Konye-Urgench (from Persian 'Old Urgench') is a rural backwater with empty plazas, wandering livestock and back roads that end in agricultural fields. Yet centuries ago, this was the centre of the Islamic world, not the end of it.

The ancient state of Khorezm, located on a northerly Silk Road branch that leads to the Caspian Sea and Russia, was an important oasis of civilisation in the Central Asian deserts for thousands of years.

Khorezm fell to the all-conquering Seljuq Turks, but rose in the 12th century, under a Seljuq dynasty known as the Khorezmshahs, to shape its own far-reaching empire. With its mosques, medressa, libraries and flourishing bazaars, Gurganj became a centre of the Muslim world, until Khorezmshah Mohammed II moved his capital to Samarkand after capturing that city in 1210.

Jenghiz Khan arrived in 1221, seeking revenge for the murder of his envoys in Otrar as ordered by Mohammed II. Old Urgench withstood the siege for six months, and even after the Mongols broke through the city walls the residents fought them in the streets. The Mongols, unused to cities, burnt the houses but the residents still fought from the ruins. In the end, the Mongols diverted the waters of the Amu-Darya and flooded the city, drowning its defenders.

The Mongol generals went in pursuit of Mohammed II who eluded them for months until he finally died of exhaustion in 1221 on an island in the Caspian Sea. The tombs of his father, Tekesh, and grandfather, Il-Arslan, survive and are two of Old Urgench's monuments.

In the following period of peace, Khorezm was ruled as part of the Golden Horde, the huge, wealthy, westernmost of the khanates into which Jenghiz Khan's empire was divided after his death. Rebuilt, Urgench was again Khorezm's capital, and grew into what was probably one of Central Asia's most important trading cities – big, beautiful, crowded and with a new generation of monumental buildings.

Then came Timur. Considering Khorezm to be a rival to Samarkand, he comprehensively finished off old Urgench in 1388. The city was partly rebuilt in the 16th century, but it was abandoned when the Amu-Darya changed its course (modern Konye-Urgench dates from the construction of a new canal in the 19th century).

Today, most of Old Urgench lies underground, but there is enough urban tissue to get an idea of its former glories. Its uniqueness was acknowledged in 2005 when Unesco named it a World Heritage site. The modern town is somewhat short on tourist facilities and most travellers overnight in Dashogus.

### Sights

#### NEJAMEDDIN KUBRA MAUSOLEUM & AROUND

The sacred Nejameddin Kubra Mausoleum is the most important of a small cluster of sights near the middle of the town and is the holiest part of Konye-Urgench. The simple **Konye-Urgench Museum** (☎ 2 15 71; admission US$1; ⏰ 8am-1pm & 2-4pm Wed-Mon) is housed in the early-20th-century Dash Mosque, just before the main mausoleum complex. It includes some ancient Arabic texts and a few interestingly labelled artefacts from Old Urgench (eg 'blue polished eight-cornered thing'). Note the Christian symbols carved onto some of the stone pieces. Off the medressa courtyard are several rooms containing ethnographic displays of Turkmen culture, including a pottery workshop and carpet looms.

To one side of the mosque is the **Matkerim-Ishan Mausoleum**, which is also early 20th century.

The path past here leads to the **Nejameddin Kubra Mausoleum** on the left, and the **Sultan Ali Mausoleum** facing it across a shady little courtyard. Nejameddin Kubra (1145–1221) was a famous Khorezm Muslim teacher and poet, who founded the Sufic Kubra order, with followers throughout the Islamic world. His tomb is believed to have healing properties and you may find pilgrims praying here. The building has three domes and a tiled portal that appears on the brink of forward collapse. The tombs inside – one for his body and one for his head (which were kindly separated by the Mongols) are quite extraordinarily colourful with floral-pattern tiles.

### SOUTHERN MONUMENTS

The city's most striking **monuments** (admission US$1, camera US$0.70; 8am-6pm) are dotted like a constellation across an empty expanse straddling the Ashgabat road, 1km south of the main town.

**Turabeg Khanym Complex**, opposite the ticket office, is still the subject of some debate. Locals and some scholars consider this a mausoleum, though no-one is too sure who is buried here. Some archaeologists contend that it was a throne room built in the 12th century (it appears to have a heating system, which would not have been used in a mausoleum). Whatever its function, this is one of Central Asia's most perfect buildings. Its geometric patterns are in effect a giant calendar signifying humanity's insignificance in the march of time. There are 365 sections on the sparkling mosaic underside of the dome, representing the days of the year; 24 pointed arches immediately beneath the dome representing the hours of the day; 12 bigger arches below representing the months the year; and four big windows representing the weeks of the month. The cupola is unique in early Islamic architecture and has its equal only in Shiraz, Iran.

Crossing the road to the side of the minaret, the path through a modern cemetery and the 19th-century **Sayid Ahmed Mausoleum** leads to the **Gutlug Timur Minaret**, built in the 1320s. It's the only surviving part of Old Urgench's main mosque. Decorated with bands of brick and a few turquoise tiles, at 59m it's one of the highest minarets in Central Asia – though not as tall as it once was, and leaning noticeably. It's interesting to note that there is no entrance to the minaret – it was linked to the adjacent mosque by a bridge 7m above the ground. Since that mosque was destroyed, the only way into the minaret is by ladder. There are 144 steps to the top, although you can't climb it now.

Further along the track is the **Sultan Tekesh Mausoleum**. Tekesh was the 12th-century Khorezmshah who made Khorezm great with conquests as far south as Khorasan (present-day northern Iran and northern Afghanistan). It is believed that he built this mausoleum for himself, along with a big medressa and library (which did not survive) on the same spot. However, some scholars theorise that the building had earlier existed as a Zoroastrian temple. After his death in 1200 he was apparently buried here, although there is no tomb. There are recent excavations of several early Islamic graves near the entrance to the building.

Nearby is the mound of graves called the **Kyrk Molla** (Forty Mullahs Hill), a sacred place where Konye-Urgench's inhabitants held their last stand against the Mongols. Here you'll see young women rolling down the hill in a fertility rite – one of Konye-Urgench's more curious attractions.

Continue along the track to the **Il-Arslan Mausoleum**, Konye-Urgench's oldest standing monument. The conical dome, with a curious zigzag brick pattern, is the first of its kind and was exported to Samarkand by Timur. Il-Arslan, who died in 1172, was Tekesh's father. The building is small but well worth a close look. The conical dome with 12 faces is unique, and the collapsing floral terracotta moulding on the façade is also unusual. Further south lies the base of the **Mamun II Minaret**, which was built in 1011, reduced to a stump by the Mongols, rebuilt in the 14th century and finally toppled by an earthquake in 1895. At last you'll arrive at the so-called **portal of an unknown building**. The structure may have been either the gate to a caravanserai or a palace.

## Sleeping

**Chapayev Guesthouse** (per person US$2.50) This old farmhouse is basic but friendly and comfortable, and has a kitchen for self-caterers. It's also a great opportunity to meet a local family and you may be invited to tour the farm. Located on the road between the town and the border post with Uzbekistan, this place is only recommended if you have your own transport. The guesthouse has no phone. It is located 3km north of town, but it has no sign. If you are on a tour your guide should know the location.

**Gürgenç Hotel** (☎ 2 24 65; Dashogus köçesi; bed US$6) The only hotel in town appears to have been last renovated during the Mongol invasion. The old lady only speaks Turkmen, but seems used to backpackers. There's no running water, the floorboards seem to be growing vegetation and the finishing touch is bathrooms nailed shut. The outside pit toilets are less than luxurious.

## Eating

**Bedev Café** (☎ 2 10 44; Azadi köçesi; dishes US$3; 🕑 7am-9pm) While absolutely ordinary, this is probably the best place in town to grab a meal. It specialises in *samsa* and fresh *gatik* (yogurt). If you need to stock up on groceries, try the small shop next to this café.

## Getting There & Away

The town's bus station is a disorganised car park, a short distance from the Gürgenç Hotel and a taxi ride from the town centre, where taxis, marshrutki and buses meet and pick up passengers.

Frequent buses and marshrutki go to Ashgabat (US$4, 10 to 12 hours) and to Dashogus (US$0.50, two hours). Taxis leave for Ashgabat (seat/whole car US$6/US$24) and Dashogus (seat/whole car US$0.75/US$3.50) at all times of day.

A taxi to the border with Uzbekistan (20km away) should cost US$1 and can be picked up anywhere.

## Getting Around

The main sights of Konye-Urgench are spread out so it's best to use a car. There is no public transport as such, but you can flag down a taxi on the main roads or by the market. The trip to the southern monuments and back, with waiting time, is US$2.

# DASHOGUS

☎ 322 / pop 160,000

A Soviet model-town, Dashogus consists of an enormous boulevard lined with concrete buildings separated by vast acres of emptiness. Although there is little to attract the visitor, it does serve as a key transit point for travellers heading to or from Uzbekistan. Its most interesting features include the unusual **dinosaur sculptures** in the town centre and the excellent **Bai Bazaar**, a colourful market where you can buy pretty much anything.

## Sleeping

Given the dire state of accommodation in Konye-Urgench, most travellers prefer to overnight in Dashogus, two hours (94km) away by bus or train.

**Hotel Dashogus** (☎ 5 37 85; Turkmenbashi şayoli 5; s/d US$8/16; ❄) The requisite Soviet dinosaur still chugs along, accommodating budget travellers in rickety old rooms. The decrepit air is slightly relieved by nice balconies and friendly management. There is a bar and a small restaurant serving tasty bowls of *chuchvara (pelmeny* or *borek*, dumplings and broth).

**Hotel Uzboy** (☎ 2 60 15; Turkmenbashi şayoli 19/1; s/d/semi-lux US$30/50/75; ❄) Dashogus' newest hotel is a vast white-tile construction on the western side of town. Rooms are cramped, the carpets are worn down and beds are placed oddly on the floor. The best part of the place is the welcoming lobby, with its couches, bar and carpet shop. Breakfast is included in the price. If you've got money to burn, take the apartment, which sports a lounge, dining room and private sauna.

**Hotel Diyarbekir** (☎ 5 90 37; Turkmenbashi şayoli; s/d US$40/80; ❄) This Turkish-owned venture has 40 spacious rooms with TV and balcony. Other amenities include a sauna and restaurant. Despite its recent construction there is already plenty of wear, including dirty carpets, cracked mirrors and peeling walls. It's located opposite 'The Palace Named After Gurbansultan Eje', a cultural centre of sorts on the main drag.

## Eating

**Kafé Marat** (☎ 5 06 00; Turkmenbashi şayoli 15; dishes US$1; 🕑 10am-11pm) Decorated with faux torches, red curtains and Christmas lights year round, this festive restaurant is a lively downtown institution. The occasional live band adds to the atmosphere. The shashlyk isn't particularly good, but it makes some decent European dishes, pizza, pasta and *chuchvara*.

**Şatugi** (☎ 5 97 42; Al Khorezmi köçesi 6; 🕑 8am-11pm) Yellow curtains and flowery wallpaper abound in this ostentatious restaurant usually reserved for tour groups and weddings. The borsch and beef steak are good options here, as is the spaghetti. Find it on the edge of a park behind the Hotel Diyarbekir.

### Getting There & Away

The Dashogus airport is 14km south of the city. Flights from Ashgabat to Dashogus (US$11, five daily) last about 50 minutes, although demand far outstrips supply and you'd be hard-pressed to get a ticket. Turkmenistan Airlines also flies to Turkmenbashi (US$11, four weekly). You will only be able to board in Ashgabat if you have the required permits to visit the Dashogus region.

The bus station is near the Bai Bazaar, in the north of the city. Buses regularly go from here to Konye-Urgench (US$0.50, two hours) and Ashgabat (US$3.50 to US$5, 12 to 18 hours depending on the type of bus). Buses for Turkmenabat are less regular (US$3, 10 hours).

The **train station** (☎ 4 68 75) is on Woksal köçesi, about 600m east of Gurbansoltan köçesi. One train per day goes from here to Konye-Urgench (US$0.50, two hours) and Ashgabat (US$2.25, 24 hours). The rail line to Ashgabat was built on sand without foundation, forcing trains to crawl at agonisingly slow speeds. There is a rail line to Turkmenabat but a lack of demand has suspended services.

# TURKMENISTAN DIRECTORY

## ACCOMMODATION

Hotels throughout the country are generally dilapidated, and from the Soviet era, although bigger cities now boast foreign-managed three- and four-star ventures. Turkmen citizens can stay at a hotel at the local rate, which is usually 10 or 20 times lower than the price that foreigners are changed. So while you may have to pay for the lodging of your guide, this shouldn't cost more than a few dollars. Expect to pay for any extra services – breakfast is not usually included in the room rate and you'll be charged to use the gym or the pool.

There are only a handful of homestays and B&Bs in the country; the government has been reluctant to develop this industry and has recently shut down some fledgling operations. Note that it's illegal for tourists to sleep in a private home if a licensed hotel exists in the same city; some travellers have gotten in trouble for staying with a family or unlicensed guesthouse. This law does not apply for travellers on a transit visa.

Turkmenistan's wide open spaces make for good camping and there is nothing to stop you from pulling off the road and pitching a tent in the desert. Some of the best places for camping include Yangykala Canyon (p420) and the Darvaza Gas Crater (p418).

**PRACTICALITIES**

- The main daily newspapers are *Turkmenistan* and the Russian-language *Nevtralny Turkmenistan* (Neutral Turkmenistan). All papers are designed to glorify the president, as is obvious from the pictures on the front pages. There is no independent or privately owned press.
- The three state TV channels show scenes of Turkmen culture and nature. Satellite TV is widely available.

## ACTIVITIES

Horse-lovers from around the world flock to Turkmenistan to ride the unique Akhal-Teke thoroughbreds. Many travel agencies offer specialist horse-trekking tours with these beautiful creatures. For more information on riding these horses in Ashgabat, see p411.

Turkmenistan has wonderful potential for walking, although this pastime is still viewed with suspicion by the authorities. However, if you have permission to visit one of the nature reserves, hiking is usually no problem whatsoever. Some of the best places to explore are the Kugitang Nature Reserve (p431) and the mountains around Nokhur (p418).

## CUSTOMS

In Turkmenistan official regulations state that you need permission to export any carpet over 6 sq metres, though trying to export a smaller one without an export licence is also likely to be problematic. In all cases it's best to take your carpet to the Carpet Museum in Ashgabat (p410), where there is a bureau that will value and tax your purchase, and provide an export licence. This can take up to a few days. There are several fees to pay.

One to certify that the carpet is not antique, and this usually costs US$10 to US$30, and a second export fee that costs around US$50 per sq metre. When you buy a carpet at a state shop these fees should be included in the price, but definitely ask before forking over your money. Those in a hurry are best advised to buy from one of the many government shops in Ashgabat, where all carpets come complete with an export licence. Despite being more expensive than purchases made at Tolkuchka Bazaar, this still works out as very good value.

Antiques are difficult to impossible to export. If you are transiting through the country carrying antiques bought in Iran, Uzbekistan or elsewhere, make sure to list those items on your customs form when you enter the country. Anything that looks remotely old, used or scrubby could be considered an antique.

## DANGERS & ANNOYANCES

Health-wise it's best to be a cautious eater in Turkmenistan, which means avoiding salads and other cold foods – typhoid is not uncommon. Avoid drinking tap water, which contains traces of metal that can cause long-term health problems. Bring along Imodium for stomach bugs.

The biggest annoyance you'll experience is the officialdom, which mainly manifests itself in roadblocks every 50km to 100km, pointless document checks, army posts and registration each time you enter a new *welayat* (province). These usually take just a few minutes and your guide will probably do all the work. Take care when photographing public buildings, especially in Ashgabat. Local police take this very seriously and you may have your documents checked even if simply strolling near the Presidential Palace with a camera in your hand. There are no 'no photo' signs anywhere, so you'll need to ask the nearest policeman if it's OK to take a picture.

## EMBASSIES & CONSULATES

### Turkmen Embassies in Central Asia

Turkmenistan has embassies or consulates in Uzbekistan (p262), Tajikistan (p392) and Kazakhstan (p178).

### Turkmen Embassies & Consulates

Note that there is no Turkmen embassy in Baku (Azerbaijan) or Tbilisi (Georgia), but there is one in Yerevan (Armenia).

**Afghanistan** (☎ 020 2300541; House 280, Lane 3, St 13, Wazir Akbar Khan, Kabul); (☎ 040 223534; Walayat St, Herat); (☎ 050 5023; Darwaza-ye, Tashkurgan, Mazar-e Sharif)

**Armenia** (☎ 22 10 29; fax 22 21 72; 19 Kievyana, Yerevan)

**Belgium** (☎ 6481874, 6481929; fax 6481906; 106 Ave Franklin Roosevelt, Brussels)

**China** (☎ 65326975/6/7; fax 65326976; San Li Tun Diplomatic Office Bldg 1-15-2, 100600, Beijing)

**France** (☎ 0147550536; fax 0147550568; 13 rue Picot, 75016, Paris)

**Germany** (☎ 30 30102451/2; fax 30 30102453; Langobardenalle 14, D-14052, Berlin)

**India** (☎ 6118054; fax 11 6118332; C-17 Malcha Marg Chanakyapuri, New Delhi)

**Iran** (☎ 51 99940, 47660; fax 51 47660; Kucheye Konsulgari 34, Mashhad); (☎ 21 2542178, 2548686; fax 2540432; 39 Pardaran Ave, Golestan-5 St, Tehran)

**Pakistan** (☎ 2278699, 2214913; fax 278799; Nazim-ud-Din Rd, 22-a, F-7/1, Islamabad)

**Russia** (☎ 095 2916591, 2916636; fax 095 2910935; Filipovsky pereulok 22, 121019, Moscow)

**Turkey** (☎ 312 4416122/3/4; fax 312 4417125; Koza sokak 28, Chankaya 06700, Ankara); (☎ 212 6620221/2/3; fax 212 6620224; Gazi Evrenos Jadesi Baharistan sokak 13 Eshilkoy, İstanbul)

**UK** (☎ 020 7255 1071; fax 020 7323 9184; 14-17 Wells St, W1 3FP, London)

**Ukraine** (☎ 293449, 2286870; fax 2293034; Pushkin 6, Kiev)

**USA** (☎ 202 588 1500; fax 202 5880697; www.turkmenistanembassy.org; 2207 Massachusetts Ave, NW 20008, Washington DC)

**Uzbekistan** (☎ 71 120 52 78; fax 71 120 52 81; One Katta Mirabat 10, Tashkent)

### Embassies & Consulates in Turkmenistan

All the following legations are in Ashgabat (see Map pp406–7). The British embassy looks after the interests of Commonwealth nationals in Turkmenistan.

**Afghanistan** (☎ 48 07 57; Garashsyzlyk köçesi, Berzengi; 🕑 9am-5pm Mon-Fri)

**Armenia** (☎ 35 44 18, 39 55 42; Ingenernaya köçesi 37; 🕑 10am-12.30pm Mon-Fri)

**Azerbaijan** (☎ 36 46 08; fax 36 46 10; www.azembassy ashg.com; 2062 köçesi 44; 🕑 9am-1pm & 2-6pm Mon-Fri)

**China** (☎ 48 81 05; fax 48 18 13; Kuvvat Hotel, Berzengi; 🕑 3-6pm Tue & Fri)

**France** (☎ 36 35 50, 36 34 68; 3rd fl, Ak Altyn Hotel; 🕑 9am-1pm & 3-5pm Mon-Fri)

**Georgia** (☎ 33 08 28; fax 33 02 48; Azadi köçesi 139a; 🕑 9am-6pm Mon-Fri)

**Germany** (☎ 36 35 15/17-20; fax 36 35 22; 1st fl, Ak Altyn Hotel; 🕑 9am-noon Mon-Fri)
**Iran** (☎ 34 14 52; fax 35 05 65; Tehran köçesi 3; 🕑 8.30am-12.30pm Mon-Fri)
**Kazakhstan** (☎ 48 04 69, 48 04 72; fax 48 04 74 Garaşyzlik şayoli 11, 13, Berzengi; 🕑 9am-noon & 5-6pm Tue, Thu & Fri)
**Kyrgyzstan** (☎ 39 20 64; Görogly köçesi 14; 🕑 10am-noon & 4-6pm Mon-Fri)
**Netherlands** (☎ 34 67 00; fax 34 42 52; Tehran köçesi 17; 🕑 9am-6pm Mon-Fri)
**Pakistan** (☎ 48 21 28/9; fax 39 76 40; Garashsyzlyk köçesi 4/1, Berzengi; 🕑 9am-noon Mon-Fri)
**Russia** (☎ 35 39 57, 35 70 41; fax 39 84 66; Turkmenbashi şayoli 11; 🕑 9am-1pm & 3-6pm Mon-Fri)
**Tajikistan** (☎ 48 01 63; embtd@online.tm; Garashsyzlyk köçesi 4/2, Berzengi; 🕑 9am-1pm & 3-5pm Mon-Fri)
**UK** (☎ 36 34 62/3/4; www.britishembassy.gov.uk/turkmenistan; 3rd fl, Ak Altyn Hotel; 🕑 9am-5.30pm Mon-Fri)
**USA** (☎ 35 00 45, 39 87 64; http://turkmenistan.usembassy.gov; 1984 köçesi 9; 🕑 9am-6pm Mon-Fri)
**Uzbekistan** (☎ 33 10 62; fax 34 23 37; Görogly köçesi 50A; 🕑 10am-1pm Mon, Wed & Fri)

## GAY & LESBIAN TRAVELLERS

Homosexuality is illegal in Turkmenistan. There are no gay or lesbian bars in Ashgabat, but gay men sometimes meet in the park in front of the Lenin statue. Lesbianism remains an entirely alien concept in Turkmenistan.

## HOLIDAYS

Travel to Turkmenistan is restricted around the Independence Day celebrations, with letters of invitation usually issued only until mid-October and then again from November, and around Niyazov's birthday celebrations in mid-February. Transit travellers are unlikely to be affected by this. Note that most of the following holidays are on Sunday, which won't affect your travel plans much as most services will be closed anyway.

**1 January** New Year
**12 January** Remembrance Day (Battle of Geok-Depe)
**19 February** Flag Day (President's Birthday)
**March (first Sunday)** Dog Day
**11 March** Women's Day
**21 March** Navrus (spring festival); date varies
**April (first Sunday)** Drop of Water is a Grain of Gold Day
**27 April** Horse Day
**9 May** Victory Day
**18 May** Day of Revival & Unity
**19 May** Holiday of Poetry of Magtymguly
**25 May/last Sunday in May** Carpet Day
**21 June** Election of First President
**14 July** Turkmenbashi Holiday
**August (second Sunday)** Melon Holiday
**6 October** Remembrance Day (1948 Earthquake)
**27–28 October** Independence Day
**November (first Saturday)** Health Day
**17 November** Student Youth Day
**November (last Sunday)** Harvest Festival
**30 November** Bread Day
**7 December** Good Neighbourliness Day
**12 December** Neutrality Day

## INTERNET ACCESS

There's only one internet service provider in Turkmenistan: www.online.tm. The internet is almost unknown outside Ashgabat and even there access remains for the privileged few. Bear in mind that out-going emails may be monitored depending on the server you are using. The government also attempts to restrict some websites but there are loopholes (eg www.yahoo.com can be difficult, so try www.yahoo.co.uk and/or other yahoo servers).

## INTERNET RESOURCES

While most commentary on Turkmenistan has some sort of agenda, there are several interesting websites about the place.

**www.chaihana.com** For general information and archived articles.
**www.eurasianet.org/resource/turkmenistan/index.shtml** Another very strong news archive website.
**www.gundogar.org** The opposition website is invaluable for news and politics.
**www.stantours.com** For planning your trip.
**www.turkmenistaninfo.ru** News site with an English-language tab.
**www.turkmenistan.gov.tm** Turkmenistan's government sanctioned news and information page. It pops up in Russian but there is an English link.
**www.turkmens.com** A huge collection of Turkmenistan-related websites about culture, music, politics and history.

## MONEY

The currency in Turkmenistan is the manat (M). It's set at a fixed government exchange rate, but traded for far less on the black market. Notes come in denominations of 10,000, 5000 and 1000, with 1000 and 500 manat coins. The rate of exchange on the black market at the time of research was around 24,000M per US dollar. Check the rate daily however, as it does fluctuate. The following table gives an indication of official exchange rates.

| Country | Unit | Manat |
|---|---|---|
| Australia | A$1 | 4088 |
| Canada | C$1 | 4521 |
| China | Y1 | 664 |
| euro zone | €1 | 6858 |
| Iran | 100 rials | 56 |
| Japan | ¥1 | 44 |
| Kazakhstan | 1T | 42 |
| Kyrgyzstan | 1 som | 134 |
| New Zealand | NZ$1 | 3587 |
| Pakistan | Rs 1 | 85 |
| Russia | R1 | 197 |
| UK | UK£1 | 10,169 |
| USA | US$1 | 5200 |
| Uzbekistan | 10 sum | 41.77 |

The black market is easy and accessible to foreigners, and the only place you'll get a realistic exchange rate. Official bureaux de change and hotel exchange counters are best avoided, as they will exchange at the official rate, giving you 75% less for your money.

While it may seem a little dodgy to exchange money on the black market, everyone does it without fear of the police, in broad daylight no less. No one exchanges money at the official rate (except to buy airline tickets) so no exchange certificates are ever checked.

- Trade a round amount, for quick mental calculations.
- Fold it up in a pocket, to avoid fumbling in an open purse or wallet.
- Tell them what you have, but don't pull it out; some claim they want to check it for counterfeit, and may substitute smaller notes.

Cash advances on credit cards are only available in Ashgabat (p408) and ATMs are nonexistent. Outside Ashgabat emergency money can be wired through Western Union only. Credit cards are accepted by luxury hotels in Ashgabat, but by few other places; you'd be ill-advised to rely on them. Travellers cheques are not accepted anywhere so don't bother bringing any. It's best to bring US dollars in all sorts of denominations. Ones, fives and tens will prove handy when paying for just about anything; they are especially helpful around borders when you may need just a little cash for a taxi or a customs fees.

The only time you'll ever need to show an exchange receipt is for buying plane tickets. If you are not flying don't bother with the official rate and don't worry about collecting exchange receipts.

Finally, don't change too much money because if you have extra manat at the end of your trip you'll get a poor rate if you try to change back to dollars. Any rate, however, is better than what you'll get once you cross the border – it's hard to get rid of manat in neighbouring countries.

## POST

Like every other form of communication in Turkmenistan, all post is monitored and you can expect your postcards (if you can find any) to be scrutinised by government agents before being allowed through. Sending a postcard anywhere in the world costs US$0.10 and a 20g letter costs around US$0.20. A 3kg package costs around US$3.20.

## REGISTRATION

Anyone entering Turkmenistan on a tourist or business visa must be registered within three working days with State Service for the Registration of Foreign Citizens (aka OVIR) via the local bureau of the state tourism company. The tour company that invited you will undoubtedly organise this. Make sure to bring three passport photos and your entry card. You may also need a letter from your hotel proving that you are staying there. Transit visas do not need to be registered.

## TELEPHONE & FAX

Phone calls from hotels or anywhere else foreigners are likely to be may be listened in on, so keep conversations discreet. Fax provides one of the most secure means of communication. You can call internationally, nationally and send faxes from most big towns at the telegraph station, often referred to as *glavny telegraf*.

The major mobile phone provider is MTS. Pre-pay SIM cards are available from their offices, although visitors on a tourist visa may have a hard time getting one. Black market SIM cards may be available for US$100.

## TRAVEL PERMITS

Permits are needed to visit the border regions of Turkmenistan. Given that the centre of the country is largely uninhabited desert and the population lies on the periphery, you need permits for some of the most interesting areas. The cities of Ashgabat, Mary, Merv, Turkmenabat and Balkanabat are not restricted, but anywhere outside these areas should be listed on your visa, thus giving you permission to go there. Travellers on transit visas can usually transit the border zones along the relevant main road, if they correspond to the country they are supposed to exit to.

Nature reserves are likewise restricted to the public unless you have a special permit. If you think you might want to visit one, you'll need to put in a request to your travel agent well in advance, see p405.

The following areas are termed 'class one' border zones and entry without documentation is definitely not possible:

**Western Turkmenistan** Bekdash, Turkmenbashi, Hazar, Dekhistan, Yangykala, Gyzyletrek, Garrygala, Nokhur and surrounding villages.

**Northern Turkmenistan** Entire Dashogus region including Konye-Urgench, Dargan-Ata, Gazachak.

**Eastern Turkmenistan** Farab, Atamurat (Kerki) plus adjoining areas, Kugitang Nature Reserve, Tagtabazar, Serkhetabat.

## VISAS

All foreigners require a visa to enter Turkmenistan and transit visas are the only visas issued without a letter of invitation (LOI). Prices for visas vary enormously from embassy to embassy. As a general rule, plan on getting a visa at least six weeks ahead of entry to Turkmenistan, as the process (even for transit visas) is lengthy. Another good overall tip is to work through a Turkmen travel agent you trust. On entry every visa holder will need to pay an additional US$10 fee for an entry card that will list your exit point in Turkmenistan.

### Transit visas

The only visa that allows unaccompanied travel for tourists is the transit visa. Relatively easy to come by, they are normally valid for three days, although sometimes for five days and in extremely rare cases, seven and even 10 days. Turkmen embassies in Europe (opposed to Central Asia or Iran) are more likely to grant longer visas. Transit visas can be obtained at any Turkmen consulate, although if you apply without an LOI, the application will need to be forwarded to the Ministry of Foreign Affairs in Ashgabat, meaning a processing time of around 10 to 14 days.

No transit visa is extendable, save in the case of serious illness. The penalty for overstaying a transit visa is US$200, and you may be taken back to Ashgabat and deported on the next available flight at your expense.

Your route will normally not be indicated on the visa, but your entry and exit point (unchangeable) will be, and you will therefore run into trouble going anywhere not obviously between the two points (eg Nokhur or Kugitang). Transit visas are usually not valid if you are dealing with a Kazakh routing, a double-entry Uzbekistan visa or even an air ticket out of Ashgabat. Turkmen embassies regularly refuse transit visa applications, so don't count on getting one.

Note that the five day transit visa is not enough time to cycle across the country, (ie from Turkmenbashi to the Farab border point), as you're likely to lose one day at Turkmenbashi (the boat may be delayed).

### Tourist visas

Tourist visas are a mixed blessing in Turkmenistan. While they allow the visitor to spend a decent amount of time in the country (up to three weeks as a rule), they require accompaniment by an accredited tour guide, who will meet you at the border and remain with you throughout your trip. This obviously has cost implications, as you will have to pay your guide a daily rate (usually between US$30 and US$50), as well as sometimes pay for their meals and hotels. The latter cost is very small however, as Turkmen citizens pay a local rate, usually equivalent to US$1 or US$2 per night. Travel agents are key to getting you through checkpoints, but they will allow you to roam Ashgabat and the immediate environs unaccompanied. Most tour companies insist on travelling in private transport with the guide. But a few allow you to ride public transport with the guide, which drops the prices.

You can only get a tourist visa by going through a travel agency. Only travel agencies with a licence from the Turkmen government can issue LOIs. Many unaccredited agencies still offer LOI services, however, simply by going through an accredited agency themselves. The LOI will be issued with a list of all towns and regions you are planning to visit. In turn, these are the places that will be listed on your visa, and so therefore it's essential to decide what you want to see before applying. The LOI is approved by the State Service for the Registration of Foreign Citizens, which will decide whether or not you are an undesirable. The LOI can be processed in as little as 10 days, but usually takes three or four weeks. It is not unusual for it to be rejected for no apparent reason.

Once the LOI is issued (usually faxed or emailed to you by your travel agent), you can take it to any Turkmen embassy to get your visa. The original LOI is not needed, although it may be at consulates in Mashhad (Iran) and Herat (Afghanistan); see p436. The issuing of the visa itself is purely a bureaucratic formality, once the LOI has been issued. Normal processing time is three working days, but most Turkmen embassies offer a one-day express service for a surcharge. When you apply for the visa, you will be asked for exact dates of entry and exit, which will be put on the visa. While you may leave before the exit date, you cannot enter earlier or leave any later.

Armed with an LOI there is also the possibility of getting a visa on arrival at Ashgabat airport, Turkmenbashi and Farab by prior arrangement with your travel agent. In the case of Turkmenbashi and Farab the agent needs to arrange for the consul to be present. In any case the original LOI must be taken to the relevant border and the visa will be issued for a maximum of 10 days.

On arrival in Turkmenistan, you must be met by your guide *(geed)* who will bring you a small green travel document, the Entry Travel Pass. Without this document you will be denied entry to Turkmenistan. You should only exit the country at the point indicated on the travel permit, although if you alter your route there is the possibility of changing this in Ashgabat. To do this you will have to speak to your travel agent or guide and they can see what they can do. It is often possible to extend tourist visas in Ashgabat, again, only with the assistance of your travel agent.

### Visas for Onward Travel

The following countries have embassies and consulates in Turkmenistan that can provide information and visas for travel to them. For contact details, see p436

**Afghanistan** Can issue one-month visas for US$60, three-month visas for US$90. You need to show a letter from your employer.

**Armenia** Can issue a tourist visa in five days for US$57. It would be cheaper and faster to get a visa at the border.

**Azerbaijan** Issues tourist visas (US$40) and transit visas (US$20) in one week. They don't seem to mind making people wait so patience is required.

**China** Issues tourist visas in 15 days for US$50. The amount of time means this is not an option for most tourists.

**Georgia** Visas available for US$30. US citizens won't need one.

**Iran** Very friendly and helpful embassy – usually no problem to get transit visas within a week.

**Uzbekistan** Can issue a visa in 10 days, which is often not enough time for travellers on a short visit in Turkmenistan. LOI required for most Western nationals.

# TRANSPORT IN TURKMENISTAN

## GETTING THERE & AWAY

For information on getting to/from Central Asia see the Transport in Central Asia chapter (p461).

### Entering Turkmenistan

On entering the country, it's likely that your bags will be searched, although backpacks are rarely emptied – they prefer to use an X-ray machine. The numerous documents to be filled out are time consuming; pay close attention to the green Entry Travel Pass and the immigration card. There is also a customs declaration – list anything valuable you have with you and make sure it is stamped and that you keep a copy. On exit you'll need to fill out a second one, but be ready to show the original as well. Upon exiting some travellers have been asked to show the pictures on their digital camera – this is not the time to be caught with a flash card full of bridges, airports, government buildings and military bases.

### Air

The only international airport in Turkmenistan is **Saparmurat Turkmenbashi Airport** (☎ 37 84 11) in Ashgabat. For the contact details of

> **ENTRY & DEPARTURE TAX**
>
> For entry into Turkmenistan there is a US$10 fee per person. Bring cash in US dollars for this. There is an international departure tax of US$25, which is only included in the price of Turkmenistan Airlines tickets. If flying with any other airline, this is payable in cash at the airport. There is no domestic departure tax, nor by land or sea.

airlines that fly in and out of Turkmenistan, see p415.

## Land

Visitors with visas can enter Turkmenistan from all bordering countries, although the borders with Uzbekistan and Iran are the most frequently used. There are no international train or bus services to or from Turkmenistan at the present time. You should reckon at one to two hours for crossing the border at any point in the country (although three hours is not unheard of). All land borders are open from 9am to 6pm daily.

### BORDER CROSSINGS

#### To/From Afghanistan

Serkhetabat (formerly known as Gushgi) is the border town with Afghanistan. Crossing here is now a fairly hassle-free prospect, although be prepared to be thoroughly searched by both Turkmen and Afghan border guards. If you arrive late it's OK to overnight with a local family as there are no hotels in town.

The border post is 3km south of Serkhetabat town. Leaving Turkmenistan, there's a 1.5km walk to the first Afghan village of Torghundi and it's a two-hour taxi journey onwards to Herat. If you are coming to Turkmenistan, you'll need to catch a ride from Herat (US$20 in a shared vehicle) to Torghundi. Here you need to pay an US$11 customs fee at a bank in town (2km south of the border), or you might be able to pay an extra US$4 to the border guard to do this for you.

The Saparmurat border crossing near Kerki is used by UN staff, but was not recommended for independent travellers at the time of writing.

#### To/From Iran

The simplest exit point is Gaudan/Bajgiran, due south of Ashgabat and a corridor between the Kopet Dag into Iran. From Ashgabat, take a taxi (US$10 to US$15) for the 20km ride to Yablonovka checkpoint. Here you'll have your passport checked, after which you take a marshrutka shuttle to the border. Once through, it's a taxi (US$2.50) across some 20km of no-man's-land to Bajgiran where you can get buses or taxis (US$20, 4 hours) to Mashhad.

There are also borders with Iran at Saraghs (there is a Mashhad–Saraghs train, but no international trains into Turkmenistan) and Gudurolum (which is reachable by car or taxi only).

#### To/From Kazakhstan

From Turkmenbashi there is a good road to Karabogas (formerly Bekdash), with spectacular views of the Caspian Sea and the Karabogas Basin. En route you cross a bridge that spans the 5km long channel which connects the Caspian Sea and the inland gulf. The distance between the bridge and Karabogas town is around 60km.

Karabogas is a nearly abandoned Soviet industrial city, filled with vacant apartment blocks gutted for anything usable. The city is surrounded by surreal-looking salt lakes; the remnants of a once profitable sodium sulphate business gone belly up. From here is a 40-minute drive to the border on a rough dirt track.

Marshrutki (US$40 per car) go from Turkmenbashi to the Kazakh border and continue to Zhanaozen (Novy Uzen), where there is further transport to Aktau. Delays at the border can occur when caravans of traders appear together. Rather than wait for all the taxis to get through, it might be faster to get a lift to the border, walk across and then look for another ride on the Kazakh side. You should be able to get a ride from the Kazakh border to Zhanaozen (US$50, two hours), with a little patience.

#### To/From Uzbekistan

There are three crossings from Uzbekistan. Each crossing requires a walk of about 10 to 20 minutes across no-man's-land. Shared taxis are sometimes available to shuttle travellers across; the cost of which ranges from US$0.50 to US$1. Whether they are operating or not when you visit is a matter of luck.

The Farab crossing is closest to Bukhara (Uzbekistan) and Turkmenabat (Turkmenistan). The 45-km taxi ride to Farab from Turkmenabat should cost US$4 to US$6 for a taxi (or US$0.50 for a seat in a shared taxi). From the border, take a taxi (US$8) to Bukhara, or hire a taxi as far as Uzbek Olot (or Qarakul), where you can change to a shared taxi.

The Dashogus crossing is best if you are headed for Khiva or Urgench. A taxi from Dashogus to the Uzbek border is not more than US$1. From the border to Khiva expect to pay around US$10.

Less used is the Khojeli crossing, a 10-minute taxi ride (US$1) from Konye-Urgench. Once across the border it's a half-hour drive to Nukus in Karakalpakstan. A taxi from Konye-Urgench to the border is around US$1. From the border, take public transport to Khojeli (US$1) or a taxi all the way to Nukus (US$7). For more Uzbek border info, see p268.

### Sea

You can enter Turkmenistan by boat from Azerbaijan. See p468 for details.

## GETTING AROUND

### Air

Turkmenistan Airlines serves most main cities with a fleet of new Boeing 717s. As the main hub, all flights go in and out of Ashgabat, with the exception of a four times weekly flight between Dashogus and Turkmenbashi. For locals, ticket prices are absurdly cheap, around US$1 to US$2 to fly anywhere. These prices also apply to Peace Corps volunteers, diplomats and anyone else with local residency. Tourists and non-residents, however, must pay for tickets using the official rate of 5200M = US$1 (you'll have to show a bank receipt showing you changed money at the official rate).

Because seats are in high demand and sell out weeks in advance, you'll probably have to buy a ticket from a travel agent anyway. Agents will hold onto tickets until the last minute, knowing some foreigners will have no choice but to pay the inflated prices.

### Car & Motorcycle

Driving through Turkmenistan is perfectly possible, but expensive and full of hassles. A carnet is not needed, although you'll need to pay the following: US$30 transit fee; US$50 obligatory third-party liability insurance; US$2 bank fee; US$5 documentation fee; and US$10 for disinfection of your vehicle. Significantly, there's also a road tax calculated by the kilometre for your route through the country. Usually this totals around US$75 for cars and up to US$250 for larger vehicles. This effectively raises the cost of petrol (gas) from US$0.02 at the pumps to around US$1.50 in reality.

Driving in Turkmenistan is a veritable freestyle sport, with drivers weaving indiscriminately through traffic and drag racing off green lights – you can do nothing but adapt. The drivers of Mary are notoriously bad – even Ashgabat drivers avoid cars with Mary tags. One last warning: fines can be imposed if you enter a city with a dirty car; make sure your vehicle is spotless after hauling it across the desert.

# Central Asia Directory

CONTENTS



For country-specific information, refer to the individual country directories in each country chapter.

## ACCOMMODATION

Accommodation alternatives are springing up all over Central Asia, so thankfully the smoky Soviet-era leftovers need only be used as a last resort. Private places are almost always the best places to stay.

Options are uneven across the region. The excellent homestays of Kyrgyzstan and Tajikistan and the B&Bs of Uzbekistan offer the best alternatives to the Soviet-era fossils, but budget travellers will still find the latter a regular companion in Kazakhstan. Turkmenistan's visa regulations allow few alternatives to the state-run hotels. Central and northern Tajikistan are largely stuck in the Soviet era, though much of the Pamirs now has an informal network of homes and yurts that offer a fascinating and intimate look at the way local people live.

You can even sleep in a (admittedly run-down) medressa in Khiva (p257), a caravanserai in Bukhara (p244) or an astronomical observatory outside Almaty (p133).

### B&Bs

These are small private guesthouses, as opposed to homestays, though the distinction can be a fine one. The best are to be found in the Uzbek cities of Bukhara, Khiva and Samarkand. Rates tend to be around US$15 to US$25 per person and include breakfast.

**PRACTICALITIES**

- **Video Systems** Central Asia has the same video system as Russia, ie Secam, which is incompatible with Australia, most of Europe (apart from France and Greece) and the US.
- **Electricity** The entire former USSR is the same – nominal 220V at 50 cycles, using European two-pin plugs (round pins, with no earth connection) everywhere. Adaptors are available in department stores.
- **Newspapers and Magazines** *Steppe Magazine* (www.steppemagazine.com) is a glossy new twice-yearly magazine concentrating on Central Asia. It's for sale in Central Asia and the UK or by subscription. *Discovery Central Asia* (www.silkpress.com) is an interesting quarterly tourism magazine published in Uzbekistan. The *Times of Central Asia* (www.timesca-europe.com) is a subscription-only online newspaper covering the region.
- **Weights & Measures** Central Asia is metric. When you buy produce in markets make sure you know whether the price is per piece *(shtuk)* or by the kilo.

**BOOK ACCOMMODATION ONLINE**

For more accommodation reviews and recommendations by Lonely Planet authors, check out the online booking service at www.lonelyplanet.com. You'll find the true, insider lowdown on the best places to stay. Reviews are thorough and independent. Best of all, you can book online.

Meals are extra but can normally be provided for around US$5 each.

## Camping

In the wilds there's normally no problem with you camping, though there is always an inherent security risk with this. If you are obviously on someone's land then you should try to ensure that you have permission. Staying anywhere near habitation will result in an immediate audience. Popular trekking routes have established camping areas, frequented by Soviet alpinists during the Soviet era. You can normally camp at a *turbaza* (former Soviet holiday camp) or yurt camp for a minimal fee.

## Homestays

These are happily on the rise. For a bed of duvets on the floor and some type of breakfast you'll probably pay between US$6 (in rural Tajikistan and Kyrgyzstan) to US$15 per person (in Uzbekistan and cities) per night. Travel in Tajikistan and Kyrgyzstan in particular has been revolutionised by the homestay networks of the Murgab Ecotourism Association (META; p388), Community-Based Tourism (CBT; p277) and Shepherd's Life organisations (also on p277. Kazakhstan also has some homestays at between US$15 and US$30 per person with all meals.

Do not expect hotel-style comforts; rural toilets, for example, are likely to be squatters in the garden. Yurtstays often do not have any kind of toilet at all. Don't expect anything exotic either – you may well end up in a block of flats, in front of a television all evening. Levels of privacy vary. You might get access to a kitchen, especially if you are in a flat.

Potential hosts may accost you as you alight at a station or enter a tourist hotel; older people, generally women, tend to be the best to deal with. Sympathetic hotel reception staff may put you in touch with private homes in some cities. Many local private travel agencies can set you up with someone, though prices may be double local rates.

Friends you meet on the road may invite you home and ask nothing for it, but remember that most ordinary people have very limited resources so offer to pay anything from US$5 (rural Tajikistan and Kyrgyzstan) to US$10 in larger towns (add on around US$5 for dinner and breakfast in rural areas). In Turkmenistan and Uzbekistan in particular, staying with someone who hasn't gone through official channels with the Office of Visas & Registration (OVIR; in Russian *Otdel Vis i Registratsii)* could put them at risk, especially if your own papers aren't in order.

## Hotels

Though some are better than others, you almost never get what you pay for in Soviet-era tourist hotels, largely because tourists don't pay the same rates as locals. Many were in better shape before 1991, when the subsidies dried up. Doorknobs may come off in your hand; windows may not open or close. Electricity is usually dicey with dim or missing light bulbs. Toilets that leak but don't flush give bathrooms a permanent aroma and some bathrooms have long-term cockroach colonies. All beds are single, with pillows the size of suitcases. Guests themselves are essentially viewed as a dispensable inconvenience, ranking somewhere below room cleaners in the hotel pecking order.

**FLOOR-LADIES**

On every floor of a Soviet hotel a *dezhurnaya* (floor-lady; *dezhurnaya* is Russian for 'woman on duty') is in charge of handing out keys, getting hot water for washing, or *kipitok* (boiled water) for hot drinks, sometimes for a small fee. Even the most god-awful hotel can be redeemed by a big-hearted floor-lady who can find someone to do your laundry, find a light bulb or stash your bags while you're off on an excursion. Others can be a bit eccentric (one floor-lady in a hotel in Bishkek insisted on wiping the room clean with several old pairs of women's panties).

**LATE-NIGHT TELEPHONE CALLS**

Those late-night calls to your room aren't wrong numbers. All hotels with significant numbers of foreigners attract prostitutes, especially, it seems, in Kazakhstan (or was that just us?). Women guests rarely seem to get unexpected calls but several men have received calls from someone who knew their name, so somebody at the front desk knows what's going on. All you can do is work out how to temporarily disable your telephone and don't answer the door.

Uzbekistan leads the way in stylish private hotels, which are popping up all over the place. There are also a limited number of party or government guesthouses, *dachas* (holiday bungalows) and spas, which are now open to all. Most cities now have a choice of several modern and comfortable private hotels catering to local *biznezmen,* where nouveau riche is the dominant style.

If you're staying at a budget hotel that doesn't have hot water, ask about the local *banya* (public bath), which will.

Most hotels take your passport and visa for anywhere from half an hour to your entire stay, to do the required registration paperwork and to keep you from leaving without paying. Don't forget them when you leave – no-one is likely to remind you.

Budget-hotel room rates range from a few dollars in the countryside to around US$20 in the cities. We do not mention all of a hotel's price options in our reviews; even the worst hotels often have a few *lux* (deluxe) or *pol-lux* (semideluxe) suites for about twice the price of a basic room, sometimes with a bathtub and hot water.

Mid-range hotels and B&Bs will have air-con, satellite TV and a decent breakfast and range from US$30 to US$60 per night.

Top-end places in major cities are often foreign-managed and offer good restaurants and bars, a health club of sorts and travel services. You may get a better room rate by booking through a local travel agent, though most hotels offer their own discounts.

### Yurtstays

It's easy to arrange a yurtstay in central Kyrgyzstan and the eastern Pamirs region of Tajikistan. Yurts range from comfortable tourist camps with beds, electricity and a nearby toilet, to the real McCoy owned by shepherds who are happy to take in the occasional foreigner for the night. The CBT and Shepherd's Life organisations in Kyrgyzstan (see p277) and Murgab Ecotourism Association (META: see p388) in Tajikistan offer yurtstays in the mountain pastures of the Tian Shan and Pamirs. Don't expect a great deal of privacy and or much in the way of toilet facilities, but it's a fantastic way to get a taste of life on the high pastures. For upmarket yurtstays try Ecotour in Kyrgyzstan (see p282).

There are also yurts at Lepsinsk, near Taldy-Korghan, Aksu-Zhabaghly in Kazakhstan, and at a yurt camp in the Kyzylkum desert near Ayaz-Qala, Uzbekistan (see p251).

## BUSINESS HOURS

In general most government offices and banks are open from 9am to 5pm Mon to Friday, with an hour or two off for lunch, and possibly 9am to noon on Saturday. All offices and some shops are closed on Sundays. Exchange offices keep longer hours, including weekends. Post and telephone offices are sometimes open on weekends.

Museum hours change frequently, as do their days off, though Monday is the most common day of rest. Some just seem to close without reason and a few stay that way for years.

Public places in the former Soviet republics often display their business days visually, as a stack of seven horizontal bars with the top one representing Monday; blue means open, red means closed.

Restaurants are generally open for lunch and dinner. Many restaurants outside the capitals close quite early (around 9pm). In rural areas it is often worth telling a restaurant that you would like to eat there a couple of hours beforehand, to give them some time to prepare and to ensure that they are open.

## CHILDREN

Children can be a great icebreaker and a good avenue for cultural exchange, but travelling in Central Asia is difficult even for the healthy adult. Long bus and taxi rides over winding mountain passes are a sure route to motion sickness. Central Asian food is difficult to digest no matter what your age, and extreme temperatures – blistering hot in the city, freezing in the mountains – lead to many an uncomfortable moment. Islamic architecture and ruined Karakhanid cities may well leave your children comatose with boredom. A few places of added interest to children in summer include the amusement and aqua parks in Tashkent (p203 and Almaty (p119).

If you are bringing very young children into Central Asia, nappies are available at department stores, but bring bottles and medicines. Forget about car seats, high chairs, cribs or anything geared for children, though you'll always find a spare lap and helpful hands when boarding buses. It's possible to make a cot out of the duvets supplied in most homestays. *Lux* hotel rooms normally come with an extra connecting room, which can be ideal for children.

For more advice on travelling with children, pick up Lonely Planet's *Travel with Children*.

*We're Riding on a Caravan: An Adventure on the Silk Road* by Laurie Krebs is a childrens' picture book aimed at four to eight year olds that describes a trader's life on the Chinese section of the Silk Road.

*Stories From the Silk Road* by Cherry Gilchrist is story book aimed at a similar age group.

## CLIMATE CHARTS

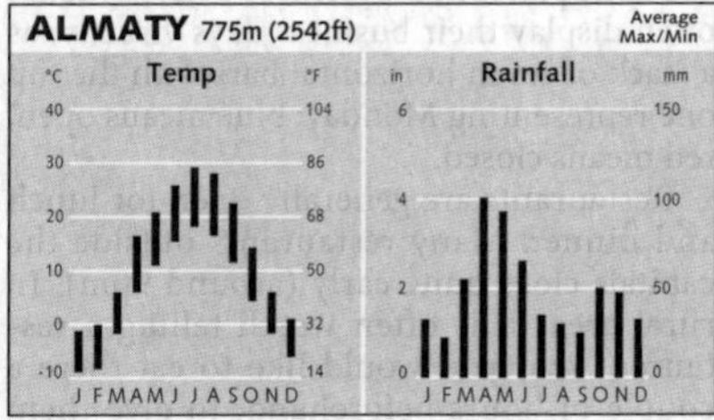


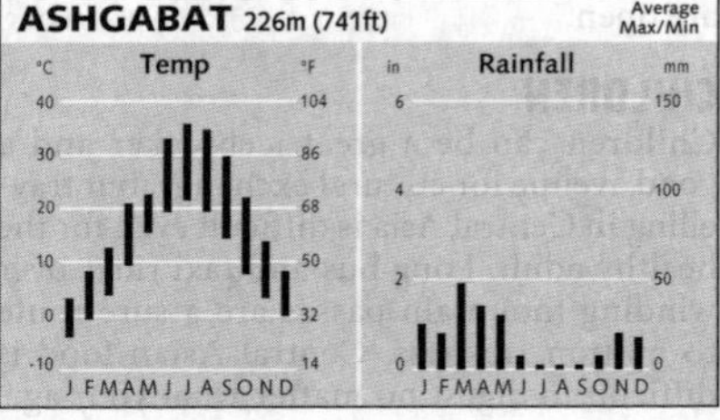


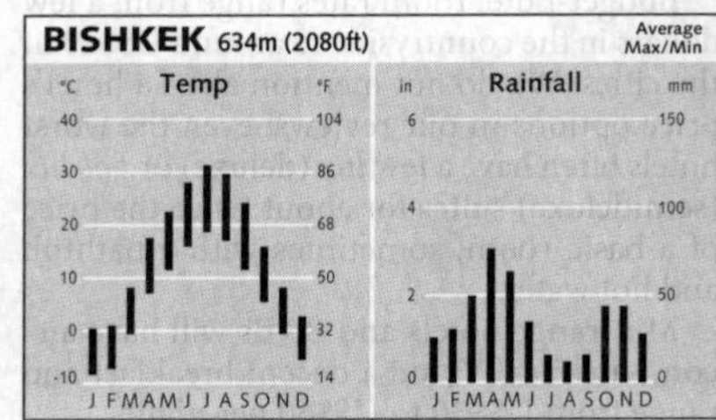


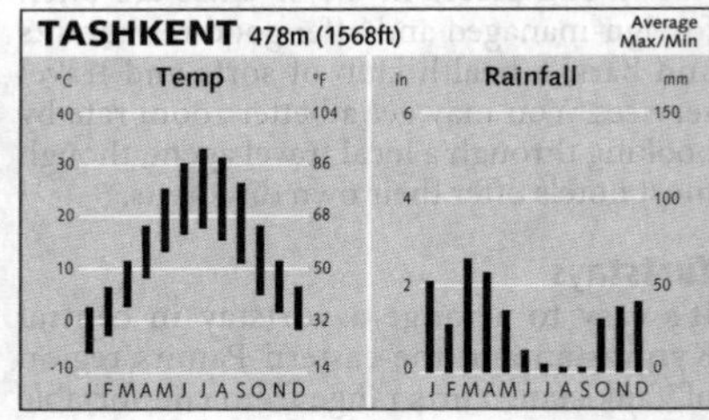


## CUSTOMS

Barring the occasional greedy official at a remote posting, few Western tourists have major customs problems in Central Asia. When they do, it's usually over the export of 'cultural artefacts'.

Declaring money on entry to a former Soviet republic is an awkward matter – total honesty reveals how much cash you're carrying to possibly dishonest officials, while fudging can create problems later. In general you are better off declaring everything (cash and travellers cheques) to the dollar. On arrival in Tashkent and Almaty officials may want you to pull out and display everything you've declared. Count up your money privately before you arrive. You won't have a problem unless you are trying to leave with more money than you arrived with (and if you work out how to do that, please let us know).

There are no significant limits on items brought into Central Asia for personal use, except on guns and drugs. Heading out, the main prohibitions are 'antiques' and local currency. Every country's regulations prohibit the export of endangered animals and plants, though few officials would recognise an endangered species if it bit them.

You may well be asked for the customs declaration you filled out when you first entered the country, so save all official-looking documents.

## Exporting Antiques

From the former Soviet republics, you cannot export antiques or anything of 'historical or cultural value' – including art, furnishings, manuscripts, musical instruments, coins, clothing and jewellery – without an export licence and payment of a stiff export duty.

Get a receipt for anything of value that you buy, showing where you got it and how much you paid. If your purchase looks like it has historical value, you should also have a letter saying that it has no such value or that you have permission to take it out anyway. Get this from the vendor, from the Ministry of Culture in the capital, or from a curator at one of the state art museums with enough clout to do it. Without it, your goodies could be seized on departure, possibly even on departure from another CIS state.

In Uzbekistan any book or artwork made before 1945 is considered antique. In Turkmenistan 'cultural artefacts' seems to embrace almost all handicrafts and traditional-style clothing, no matter how mundane, cheap or new.

To export a carpet from Turkmenistan you'll need to get the carpet certified (for a fee) at Ashgabat's Carpet Museum or buy it from one of the state carpet shops. See p435. for more on this.

# DANGERS & ANNOYANCES

Travel in Central Asia is a delight for those who are ready for it, but a potential nightmare for the unprepared. Don't expect anything to go smoothly, starting with the visa chase before you even go. Crime is minimal by Western urban standards, but it is slowly on the rise and visitors are tempting, high-profile targets. Local and regional transport can be unpredictable, uncomfortable and occasionally unsafe. Central Asian officials and police generally create more problems than they solve. For emergency phone numbers see the Quick Reference page on the inside front cover of this book. See boxes at the front of each country chapter for specific dangers to that country.

If you have an emergency or have your passport stolen you must immediately contact nearest embassy (which might be in a neighbouring republic if you are in Kyrgyzstan, Tajikistan or Turkmenistan). It will help if you have a photocopy of your passport to verify who you are. It's a good idea to register with your embassy upon arrival in Central Asia and to carry the telephone numbers of your embassies in the region.

This section, all about the headaches, is not meant to put you off. Rather, it is intended to prepare you for the worst. Here's hoping you don't run into any of these problems.

> **GOVERNMENT TRAVEL ADVICE**
>
> The following government websites offer travel advisories and information on current hot spots.
>
> **Australian Department of Foreign Affairs** (☎ 1300 139281; www.smartraveller.gov.au) Register online at www.orao.dfat.gov.au.
>
> **British Foreign Office** (☎ 0845-850 2829; www.fco.gov.uk/travel)
>
> **Canadian Department of Foreign Affairs** (☎ 1-800-267 6788; www.voyage.gc.ca)
>
> **US State Department** (☎ 1-888-407 4747; http://travel.state.gov) Register online at https://travelregistration.state.gov.

## Alcohol

Whether it's being poured down your throat by a zealous host, or driving others into states of pathological melancholy, brotherly love, anger or violence, alcohol can give you a headache in more ways than one. This is especially true in economically depressed areas, where violence hovers just below the surface and young men may grow abruptly violent, seemingly at random. The Islamic injunction against alcohol has had little obvious impact in ex-Soviet Central Asia.

## Crime

You can cut down on the potential for crime by following these tips:

- Be especially alert in crowded situations such as bazaars and bus station ticket scrums, where pockets and purses may be easily picked.
- Avoid parks at night, even if it means going a long way out of your way.
- Take officially licensed taxis in preference to private ones. At night don't get into any taxi with more than one person in it. See p473.
- Travellers who rent a flat are warned to be sure the doors and windows are secure, and never to open the door – day or night – to anyone they do not clearly know.

If you're the victim of a crime, contact the *militsia* (police), though you may get no help from them at all. Get a report from them if you hope to claim on insurance for anything that was stolen, and contact your closest embassy for a report in English. If your passport is stolen, the police should also provide a letter to OVIR, which is essential for replacing your visa. See p452 for some tips on how to minimise the danger of theft of credit cards or travellers cheques.

## Crooked Officials

The number of corrupt officials on the take has decreased dramatically since the 1st edition of this book and most travellers make their way through Central Asia without a single run-in with the local *militsia*. The strongest police presence is in Uzbekistan (particularly in the Tashkent Metro), followed by Turkmenistan and Tajikistan, where there are police checkpoints at most municipal and provincial borders. It's a near certainty that you'll meet a gendarme or two in bus and train stations in Uzbekistan, though most only want to see your papers and know where you're going. Uzbek police are particularly inquisitive in Termiz and the Fergana Valley.

If for whatever reason you didn't get an entry stamp when crossing a border, you may find yourself vulnerable to officials on the take. Keep as many hotel and bus receipts as you can that prove your movements.

If you are approached by the police, there are several rules of thumb to bear in mind:

- Your best bet is to be polite, firm and jovial. A forthright, friendly manner – starting right out with an *asalam aleykum* (peace be with you) and a handshake for whomever is in charge – may help to defuse a potential shakedown, whether you are male or female.
- If someone refers to a 'regulation', ask to see it in writing. If you are dealing with lower-level officers, ask to see their *nachalnik* (superior).
- Ask to see a policeman's ID and, if possible, get a written copy of the ID number. Do not hand over your passport unless you see this ID. Even better, only hand over a photocopy of your passport; claim that your passport is at your hotel or embassy.
- Try to avoid being taken somewhere out of the public eye, eg into an office or into the shadows; it should be just as easy to talk right where you are. The objective of most detentions of Westerners is simply to extort money, and by means of intimidation rather than violence. If your money is buried deeply, and you're prepared to pull out a paperback and wait them out, even if it means missing the next bus or train, most inquisitors will eventually give up.
- If you are taken to a police station, insist on calling the duty officer at your embassy or consulate. If your country has no diplomatic representative in the country you're in, call the embassy of a friendly country – for example the UK if you're from Australia or New Zealand.
- Make it harder for police on the take by speaking only in your own language.
- If officers show signs of force or violence, and provided they are not drunk, do not be afraid to make a scene – dishonest cops will dislike such exposure.
- Never sign anything, especially if it's in a language you don't understand. You have the right not to sign anything without consular assistance.
- Recent antinarcotics laws give the police powers to search passengers at bus and train stations. If you are searched, never let the police put their hands in your pockets – take everything out yourself and turn your pockets inside out.
- If police officers want to see your money (to check for counterfeit bills) try to take it out only in front of the highest-ranking officer. If any is taken insist on a written receipt for the sum. If you do have to pay a fine, insist that you do so at a bank and get a receipt for the full amount.

# DOCUMENTS

Besides your passport and visa, there are a number of other documents you may need to keep track of:

- Currency exchange and hard currency purchase receipts – you may need to show these when you sell back local money in a bank.
- Vouchers – if you prepaid accommodation, excursions or transport, these are the only proof that you did so.
- Hotel registration chits – in Uzbekistan you may need to show these little bits of paper (showing when you stayed at each hotel) to OVIR officials.

- Letters of invitation and any supporting documents/receipts for visa and permit support

It's wise to have at least one photocopy of your passport (front and visa pages), a copy of your OVIR registration, your travel insurance policy and your airline tickets on your person and another set of copies with a fellow traveller. It's also a good idea to leave a photocopy of your passport, travel insurance and airline ticket with someone you can contact at home.

Student and youth cards are of little use, though they can be helpful as a decoy if someone wants to keep your passport.

## EMBASSIES & CONSULATES

Listings of embassies and consulates can be found in the directories of each country chapter.

## GAY & LESBIAN TRAVELLERS

There is little obvious gay/lesbian community in Central Asia, though there are a couple of gay bars in Almaty. It's not unusual to see young women showing affection towards each other, nor is it uncommon to see men holding hands. However, this is a reflection of Asian culture rather than homosexuality.

In Uzbekistan, Turkmenistan and in Tajikistan, gay male sex is illegal, but lesbian sex does not seem to be illegal (it is seldom spoken about). Kazakhstan and Kyrgyzstan have lifted the Soviet-era ban on homosexuality. However, whether you're straight or gay, it's best to avoid public displays of affection.

The website www.gay.kz/eng/ has some information on gay life in Kazakhstan.

## HOLIDAYS

### Public Holidays

See the Holidays section of the relevant country Directory for details of each country's public holidays.

The following Islamic holidays are generally observed in Central Asia. Dates are fixed by the Islamic lunar calendar, which is shorter than the Western solar calendar, beginning 10 to 11 days earlier in each solar year. Religious officials have the formal authority to declare the beginning of each lunar month based on sightings of the moon's first crescent. Future holy days can be estimated, but are in doubt by a few days until the start of that month, so dates given here are only approximate. The holidays normally run from sunset to the next sunset.

Ramadan and Eid al-Azha are observed with little fanfare in most of Central Asia (where you shouldn't have major problems finding food during the daytime) but are becoming more popular.

**Eid al-Fitr** 13 October (2007), 2 October (2008), 21 September (2009), 10 September (2010) Also called Hayit in Uzbekistan and Orozo Ait in Kyrgyzstan. This involves two or three days of celebrations at the end of Ramadan, with family visits, gifts, banquets and donations to the poor.

**Eid al-Azha** 20 December (2007), 9 December (2008), 28 November (2009), 17 November (2010) Also called Qurban, Korban, Qurban Hayit or Qurban Ait in Central Asia. This is the Feast of Sacrifice, and is celebrated over several days. Those who can afford it buy and slaughter an animal, sharing the meat with relatives and with the poor. This is also the season for haj (pilgrimage to Mecca).

**Moulid an-Nabi** 31 March (2007), 20 March (2008), 9 March (2009), 26 February (2010) The birthday of the Prophet Mohammed. A minor celebration in Central Asia, though you might notice mosques are a little fuller.

### TOP CELEBRATIONS IN CENTRAL ASIA

- Independence Day in any ex-Soviet capital, but particularly in Tashkent (the only day of the year even the police don't demand bribes).
- Navrus (p450), the region's biggest festival, with celebrations ranging from wild games of *buzkashi* (a polo-like game played with a goat's carcass) outside Dushanbe, to lame funfairs.
- Summer horseback wrestling and other nomadic games organised by CBT on the *jailoos* (summer pastures) of Song-Köl (p318) and Sarala-Saz (p318), or Sunday horse races (March to May) in Ashgabat's hippodrome (p415).
- The At Chabysh horse festival (www.atchabysh.com) in early November at Barskoön in Kyrgyzstan (p310).
- Eagle hunting competitions (hunting with eagles) at the August Birds of Prey Festival, on the south side of Lake Issyk-Köl in Kyrgyzstan (p312).

**Ramadan** 13 September (2007), 2 September (2008), 22 August (2009), 11 August (2010) Also known as Ramazan, the month of sunrise-to-sunset fasting. Dates mark the beginning of Ramadan.

If you are crossing an international border it may be useful to know that Russian national holidays fall on 1 January, 7 January, 8 March, 1 May, 9 May, 12 June and 7 November. If heading to China don't cross the border on the Chinese national holidays of 1 January, 8 March, 1 July, 1 August, spring festival (some time in February) and the weeks following the major holidays of 1 May and 1 October.

### NAVRUS

By far the biggest Central Asian holiday is the spring festival of Navrus ('New Days' – Nauryz in Kazakh, Novruz in Turkmen, Nooruz in Kyrgyz). Navrus is an adaptation of pre-Islamic vernal equinox or renewal celebrations, celebrated approximately on the spring equinox, though now normally fixed on 21 March (22 March in Kazakhstan).

In Soviet times this was a private affair, even banned for a time. In 1989, in one of several attempts to deflect growing nationalism, Navrus was adopted by the then Soviet Central Asian republics as an official two-day festival, with traditional games, music and drama festivals, street art and colourful fairs, plus partying and visiting of family and friends. Families traditionally pay off debts before the start of the holiday.

## INSURANCE

Central Asia is an unpredictable place so insurance is a good idea. A minimum of US$1 million medical cover and a 'medevac' clause or policy covering the costs of being flown to another country for treatment is essential, as few reliable emergency services are available in the CIS. See p475 for more information on health insurance.

Some policies specifically exclude 'dangerous activities', which can include skiing, motorcycling, even trekking or horse riding. If these are on your agenda, ask about an amendment to permit some of them (at a higher premium).

Few medical services in Central Asia will accept your foreign insurance documents for payment; you'll have to pay on the spot and claim later. Get receipts for everything and save all the paperwork. Some policies ask you to call back (reverse charges) to a centre in your home country where an immediate assessment of your problem is made.

Insurance policies can normally be extended on the road by a simple phone call, though make sure you do this before it expires or you may have to buy a new policy, often at a higher premium.

## INTERNET ACCESS

Internet access is widely available throughout the region; just look for a roomful of teenagers playing games such as *Counterstrike*. The only place where you can't get reliable internet access is Turkmenistan.

## LEGAL MATTERS

It's unlikely that you will ever actually be arrested, unless there are supportable charges against you. If you are arrested, authorities in the former Soviet states are obliged to inform your embassy *(pasolstvah* in Russian) immediately and allow you to communicate with a consular official without delay. Always keep the contact details of your embassy on your person (see the Directory of the relevant country chapter for a list of these). Most embassies will provide a list of recommended lawyers.

Visitors are subject to the laws of the country they're visiting. All Central Asian republics carry the death sentence for drug-related offences, though Kyrgyzstan, Tajikistan and Turkmenistan currently have a moratorium on the death penalty.

## MAPS

Buy your general maps of Central Asia before you leave home. For a search of the available maps try www.stanfords.co.uk.

*Central Asia* (Gizimap, 1999) is a good 1:750,000 general elevation map of the Central Asian republics (plus Kashgar), though it excludes northern Kazakhstan and western Turkmenistan. It usefully marks many trekking routes.

*Central Asia – The Cultural Travel Map along the Silk Road* (Elephanti) is a similar (but not quite as good) 1:1.5 million Italian map, which concentrates on Uzbekistan and Tajikistan. Nelles' 1:750,000 *Central Asia* map is also good.

Reliable locally produced city and regional maps can be found in Kazakhstan and Kyrgyzstan, but are hard to find elsewhere. The

**DOLLARS & SOMS**

Prices in this book are sometimes given in US dollars, when that is the most reliable price denominator or if that's the currency you'll be quoted on the ground, although you normally actually pay in local currency. Prices quoted in the Turkmenistan chapter are in US dollars worked out at the black market rate.

You may need cash in US dollars when paying for visas, registration and some services with a private travel agency, though many of those now accept credit cards. Although officially you cannot spend foreign currency anywhere in Uzbekistan, private hotels and homestays normally accept US dollars and often give you change in local currency at the market rate. Most other homestays and drivers expect payment in local money.

Please note that you can expect prices to jump (or fall) every year; rates in this book, especially for transport, are therefore an indication more of relative than absolute values.

occasional Soviet-era city map, full of errors, languishes on the back shelf of some bookshops. Especially in Uzbekistan, where Soviet-era street names were jettisoned en masse, any map older than about 1994 will drive you crazy.

In Ashgabat's top-end hotels you can buy good Turkish-made maps of Ashgabat, Balkanabat, Dashogus, Mary and Turkmenbashi. A good map of Dushanbe is published in that city.

## MONEY

The 'stans banking systems have improved greatly in the last few years, with credit card transactions, wire transfers (particularly Western Union) and regulated foreign exchange available in most towns. In the countryside there are few facilities, so change enough cash to get you back to a main city.

If you plan to travel extensively in the region it's worth bringing a flexible combination of cash in US dollars or Euros, a few US- dollar or Euro travellers cheques and a credit card or two, to cover every eventuality.

### ATMs

Bishkek, Osh, Tashkent, Dushanbe and most cities in Kazakhstan have ATMs *(bankomats)* that accept Western credit cards, but these are not all that reliable and the last thing you need is to watch your card get eaten alive by an Uzbek ATM. Some ATMs charge a service fee of around 2%.

### Black Market

The existence of licensed moneychangers in every town has done away with the black market in all republics except Turkmenistan (see p437).

### Cash

Cash in US dollars is by far the easiest to exchange, followed by euros. Take a mixture of denominations – larger notes (US$100, US$50) are the most readily accepted and get a better rate, but a cache of small ones (US$10, US$5) is handy for when you're at borders, stuck with a lousy exchange rate or need to pay for services in US dollars. Cash is particularly useful in Turkmenistan, due to the black market (see p437).

Make sure notes are in good condition – no worn or torn bills – and that they are dated post-1994. Bills issued before 1990 are generally not accepted – if they are, the rate is often 30% less the normal US dollar rate. The newest US notes have an embedded thread running through them. In 2004 a new type of plastic-feeling US bill was introduced, though old bills remain legal tender.

Taxi drivers and market-sellers often fob off their own ragged foreign notes on tourists as change, so of course you should refuse to accept old notes too. At the time of research US$100 gave you a pile of Turkmen manat or Uzbek sum as thick as an airport paperback.

### Credit Cards

It's an excellent idea to bring a credit card as an emergency backup, though you shouldn't rely on it completely to finance your trip as there are still only a limited number of places where it can be used. Kazakhstan is the most useful place in Central Asia to have a credit card.

Major credit cards can be used for payment at top-end hotels and restaurants, central airline offices, major travel agencies and a few shops throughout the region. Visa is the most widely recognised brand, but others (American Express, JCB, MasterCard) are accepted in most places, as are the Cirrus and Maestro systems.

Cash advances against a Visa card and MasterCard are possible in the major capitals for commissions of 1% to 3%. You will need your PIN to access the ATMs but not for a cash advance. Asking for the '*terminal*' (the hand-held machine that processes the card transaction) indicates that you want a cash advance. Always get a receipt, in case you are asked for proof of changing money at customs or if there is any discrepancy when you get home.

Remember that by using credit cards in Turkmenistan you fail to make use of the black market (see p437).

## International Transfers

Bank-to-bank wire (telegraphic) transfers are possible through major banks in all capitals. Commissions of 1% to 4% are typical, and service takes one to five days. Western Union (www.westernunion.com) has partners in banks and post offices everywhere and remains the easiest way to send money.

## Moneychangers

Dealing with licensed moneychangers is the easiest way to change money in Kyrgyzstan, Kazakhstan and Tajikistan. They are readily found in small kiosks on nearly every block, and most will give a receipt if you ask them; rates may vary by 1% to 2% at most. Licensed changers are completely legal. Moneychangers are marked by signs such as ОБМЕН ВАЛЮТЫ (*obmen valyuty;* currency exchange) and ОБМЕННЫЙ ПУНКТ (*obmennyy punkt*; exchange point).

Nearly all tourist hotels have branch/bank-exchange desks where you can at least swap cash in US dollars for local money.

Swapping between currencies can be a pain, with most former Soviet republics uninterested in the others' money (an exception is Kazakhstan and Kyrgyzstan). In border areas you may need to deal with several currencies simultaneously; when trekking in the Khojand region it's necessary to carry a mixture of Tajik somani, Uzbek sum, US dollars and Kyrgyz som.

Try to avoid large notes in local currency (except to pay your hotel bills), since few people can spare much change.

### EXCHANGE RECEIPTS

Whenever you change money, ask for a receipt (*kvitantsiya* or *spravka* in Russian) showing your name, the date, the amounts in both currencies, the exchange rate and an official signature. Not everyone will give you one, but if you need to resell local currency through the banks (in Uzbekistan or Turkmenistan) you may need enough receipts to cover what you want to resell. You will not need a receipt to sell local currency into US dollars with moneychangers in other countries. Customs officials may want to see exchange receipts at crossings to non-CIS countries but it's unlikely.

At the time of research you had to sell Uzbek *sum* back at a main city office of the National Bank – not at the airport or the hotels, or the border. The easiest thing, of course, is to spend it up before you leave, change it to neighbouring currencies on the black market or swap it with travellers going the other way.

## Travellers Cheques

Travellers cheques can now be cashed in all the major Central Asian capitals, except Dushanbe. American Express and Thomas Cook are the most widely recognised types. Only Visa travellers cheques can be changed in Turkmenistan. US-dollar travellers cheques are the best currency to bring. Commissions run between 1% and 3%. It is possible to get your money in dollars instead of local currency, though the commission rate may be a little different.

Travellers cheques can also make good decoy money if pressed for a bribe, as most people don't know what to do with them. If visiting Uzbekistan you need to list your travellers cheques on your customs declaration form or you won't be able to cash them.

## Security

Thankfully, credit cards and travellers cheques are becoming more common in Central Asia, but you may still end up carrying large wads of cash.

Petty crime is a growing problem in all the former Soviet republics. Don't leave money in any form lying around your hotel room. Carry it securely zipped in one or more money belts or shoulder wallets buried deep in your clothing, with only what you'll immediately need (or would be willing to hand over to a thief or to an official on the take) accessible in an exterior pocket, wallet or purse.

When paying for anything substantial (eg a hotel bill or an expensive souvenir) or changing money on the street at an exchange kiosk, count out the money beforehand, out of public sight; don't go fumbling in your money belt in full view. There are tales of thieves targeting people coming out of banks with fat cash advances, so keep your eyes open.

Be careful when paying by credit card that you see how many slips are being made from your card, that you destroy all carbon copies, and that as few people as possible get hold of your card number and expiry date.

Make sure you note the numbers of your cards and travellers cheques, and the telephone numbers to call if they are lost or stolen – and keep all numbers separate from the cards and cheques.

### Tipping & Bargaining

Tipping is not common anywhere in Central Asia, though most cafés and restaurants in the capital cities add a 10% service charge to the bill, or expect you to round the total up.

Bribery, on the other hand, clearly can work in Central Asia but try to avoid it where possible – it feeds the already-widespread notion that travellers all just love throwing their money around, and makes it harder for future travellers. In fact a combination of smiles (even if over gritted teeth) and patient persistence can very often work better.

Shops have fixed prices but in markets (food, art or souvenirs) bargaining is usually expected. Press your luck further in places like art and craft markets, which are heavily patronised by tourists, and when negotiating transport hire. In Kyrgyzstan bargaining is usually reserved only for taxi drivers. In the markets asking prices tend to be in a sane proportion to the expected outcome. Sellers will be genuinely surprised if you reply to their '5000' with '1000'; they're more likely expecting 3500, 4000 or 4500 in the end.

## PHOTOGRAPHY & VIDEO

### Film & Equipment

Most department stores have Kodak franchise outlets that sell 35mm print film, but slide film is unheard of so it's wise to bring your own (more than you think you'll need – Central Asia is a photographer's dream). It's safest to get film developed at home, though most of the above franchises can develop print film for prices in line with their film prices.

Memory cards for digital cameras are quite prevalent in Central Asia these days. Most internet cafés can burn your photos onto a CD, as long as the burner works.

There are no significant customs limits on camera equipment and film for personal use. Declare video cameras on customs forms and carry by hand through customs, but don't leave the tape in it as it may be confiscated.

### Photographing & Videoing People

Most Central Asians are happy to have their picture taken, though you should always ask first. A lifetime with the KGB has made many older people uneasy about having their picture taken. Many people are also touchy about you photographing embarrassing subjects like drunks or run-down housing. You may find people sensitive about you photographing women, especially in rural areas. Women photographers may get away with it if they've established some rapport.

The Russian for 'may I take a photograph?' is *fotografirovat mozhno*? (fa-ta-gruh-**fee**-ra-vut **mozh**-na?).

## POST

The postal systems of Central Asia are definitely not for urgent items – due in part to the scarcity of regional flights. A letter or postcard will probably take two weeks or more to get outside the CIS. Kyrgyzstan and Kazakhstan are probably the most reliable places to send packages from.

Central post offices are the safest places to post things. Address mail as you would from any country, in your own language, though it will help to write the destination country in Cyrillic too. See the Post entries in the individual country directories for postal rates.

If you have something that absolutely must get there, use an international courier company. DHL (www.dhl.com) and FedEx (www.fedex.com) have offices in major cities. A document to a European country costs about US$40, a 500g package around US$42 to US$60, and it takes about four days.

Express Mail Service (EMS) is a priority mail service offered by post offices that ranks somewhere between normal post and courier post. Prices are considerably cheaper than courier services.

## REGISTRATION

This relic of the Soviet era allows officials to keep tabs on you once you've arrived. In Uzbekistan the hotel or homestay in which you stay the night is supposed to register you. Registration in Dushanbe is more involved and you are best to get a travel agency to do it for a fee (though there is some talk of scrapping this requirement). Kyrgyzstan has ended the need to register and in Kazakhstan tourists are generally registered automatically.

The place to register is an OVIR. There's one in every town, sometimes in each city district, functioning as the eyes and ears of the Ministry of the Interior's administration for policing foreigners. Though it has a local name in each republic (eg OPVR in Kazakhstan and Tajikistan, IIB in Uzbekistan, UPVR in Kyrgyzstan), everybody still calls it OVIR. In some remote areas where there is no OVIR office you may have to register at the *passportny stol* (passport office).

## SHOPPING

In general Uzbekistan offers Central Asia's best shopping; in fact most of central Bukhara and Samarkand's Registan are now one big souvenir stall.

Potential Central Asian buys include carpets, hats, musical instruments, felt rugs, wall hangings, silk, traditional clothing, ceramic figurines and even nomadic accessories such as horse whips and saddles.

Turkmenistan is the place for a 'Bukhara'-style carpet, though getting it out of the country can be a problem (see p435). The best places for a *shyrdak* (Kyrgyz felt carpet) are the women's cooperatives in Kochkor and elsewhere in Central Kyrgyzstan. CBT can often put you in touch with local *shyrdak* producers. You can find more Kyrgyz felt souvenirs at the Yak House (p388) and De Pamiri (p382), both in Tajikistan's Pamir region.

See p447 about exporting antiques or items that look antique.

Central Asian bazaars are enjoyable, even if you're just looking, with everything from Russian sparkling wine to car parts. Tolkuchka Bazaar, outside Ashgabat, has acres of carpets, handicrafts and silks. The best bargains are found in small-town bazaars. Another surprising souvenir source right under your nose is the local TsUM department store.

Turkmenistan's Ministry of Culture shop specialises in the region's most offbeat

### TOP PLACES FOR CRAFTS

For those interested in learning about local handicrafts, with an eye to purchasing, see the following in the main text. See also the boxed text 'Socially Responsible Shopping' on p232.

- **Ak Orgo Yurt Workshop, Barskoön** (p310) If you have a lots of cash and a generous baggage allowance, the ultimate Kyrgyz souvenir is your very own yurt
- **Altyn Kol, Kochkor** (p317) Local *shyrdak* (Kyrgyz felt carpet) cooperative.
- **Asahi Ecological Art and Handicraft** (p288) Beautiful, top-quality carpets, kilims and *shyrdaks*.
- **Bukhara Artisan Development Centre, Bukhara** (p246) Watch artisans at work here.
- **Caravan, Tashkent** (p208) Browse for stylish handicrafts over a cappuccino.
- **De Pamiri** (p382) Felt carpets, musical instruments and more from the western Pamirs
- **Kyrgyz Style, Bishkek** (p288) Cooperative showroom for high-quality *shyrdaks*.
- **Abulkasim Medressa, Tashkent** (p207) Local artisans work in an old medressa.
- **Tolkuchka Bazaar, Ashgabat** (p411) Turkmen crafts and 'Bokhara' carpets at this wonderful bazaar.
- **Unesco silk-carpet workshops, Khiva and Bukhara** (p257 and p246) Watch how carpets are made.
- **Yak House, Murgab** (p389) For Pamiri-style crafts, bags and socks.
- **Yodgorlik (Souvenir) factory, Margilon** (p220) Silk for US$4 per square metre, as well as *ikat* (brightly coloured cloth) dresses, carpets and embroidered items.

Stalinist souvenirs, including Niyazov busts, Niyazov vodka, Niyazov watches and even Niyazov baby food.

## SOLO TRAVELLERS

There are no real problems travelling alone in Central Asia. There isn't much of a traveller scene here but you'll meet other travellers in backpacker guesthouses in Bishkek, Osh and the main towns in Uzbekistan.

It's generally not too difficult to find travellers to share car hire costs for the Torugart, Irkeshtam or Pamir Highway trips. Local travel agents and community tourism providers can often help link you up with other travellers or try a post on the **Thorn Tree** (http://thorntree.lonelyplanet.com).

Travelling alone in Turkmenistan can be expensive. Hotel rooms are almost the same whether you have one of two people in your party and if you are on a tourist visa you'll have to bear the burden of hiring a guide for yourself.

## TELEPHONE & FAX

### International Calls

Private communications centres are the best place to make international calls. Many communications offices and Internet cafés in Kyrgyzstan and Tajikistan offer internet Phone (IP) calls, which route your call through low-cost Internet connections, which works out as a fraction of the cost of traditional calls (as low as US$0.15 per minute).

In smaller towns you can place international calls (as well as local and intercity ones) from the central telephone and telegraph offices. You tell a clerk the number and prepay in local currency. After a wait of anything from half a minute to several hours, you're called to a booth. Hotel operators also place calls, but for a hefty surcharge. International calls in the region generally cost between US$0.50 and US$2 per minute.

Calls between CIS countries are now treated as international calls, though they are figured at a different rate. Thus to call Uzbekistan from, say, Kyrgyzstan you would need to dial Kyrgyzstan's international access code, the Uzbek country code and then the Uzbek city code.

See the Quick Reference page (on the inside front cover) for individual republic codes, and the individual city entries in the country chapters for their telephone codes.

### Local Calls

Placing a local or trunk call on Central Asia's decomposing telephone systems is usually harder than placing an international one, especially as so many locals now use mobile phones. There are token-operated telephones on the streets of bigger cities, though many seem to be permanently out of order. At the ones that do work, you normally just pay cash to a small Uzbek boy seated by the phone. Some shops have a phone available for calls. Local calls are free from many hotels.

## TIME

The official time in most of Central Asia is Greenwich Mean Time (GMT) plus five hours, but transcontinental Kazakhstan straddles GMT plus five and six hours.

None of the Central Asian republics have Daylight Savings Time.

## TOILETS

Public toilets are as scarce as hen's teeth. Those that you can find – eg in parks and bus and train stations – charge the equivalent of US$0.10 or so to use their squatters (flush or pit). Someone may be out front selling sheets of toilet paper. Most are awful, the rest are worse. You are always better off sticking to top-end hotels and restaurants. Carry a small pencil-torch for restaurant toilets, which rarely have functioning lights, and for trips out to the pit toilet. *Always* carry an emergency stash of toilet paper.

Out in the *jailoos* (pastures) of Kyrgyzstan and Tajikistan there are often no toilets at all. You'll have to go for a hike, find a rock or use the cover of darkness. Always urinate at least 50m from a water source (and downstream!) and dig a hole and burn the paper after defecating (see p94).

Toilet paper appears sporadically for sale in markets and department stores, though tissues are a better bet than the industrial strength sandpaper that is ex-Soviet toilet paper. Flush systems and pit toilets don't like toilet paper; the wastepaper basket in the loo is for used paper and tampons (wrapped in toilet paper).

Before bursting in, check for the signs 'Ж' (Russian: *zhenski)* for women or 'M' *(muzhskoy)* for men.

## TOURIST INFORMATION

Intourist, the old Soviet travel bureau, gave birth to a litter of Central Asian successors –

Yassaui in Kazakhstan, Intourist Tojikistan in Tajikistan, Turkmensiyahat in Turkmenistan, and Uzbektourism in Uzbekistan. Few are of any interest to independent travellers. You are almost always better off with one of the growing number of private agencies or community-based-tourism projects.

Uzbektourism wins the booby prize – at best uninterested in individual travellers, at worst hostile to them, with few points for public interface beyond the service bureaus.

The best sources of information at home tend to be foreign travel firms specialising in Central Asia or the CIS.

## TRAVEL PERMITS

Uzbek, Kazakh, Tajik and Kyrgyz visas allow access to all places in the republics, save for a few strategic areas that need additional permits. Generally you should apply for these permits through a travel agency a few weeks before arrival.

In Kazakhstan some of the most interesting areas, such as Lepsinsk, the Altay region and Zhungar Alatau, require special permits that take from 10 days to three weeks to procure. The Baykonur Cosmodrome and the Polygon nuclear-testing site at Semey are firmly off limits.

In Kyrgyzstan any place within 50km of the Chinese border (such as the Inylchek Glacier, Alay Valley and Pik Lenin) requires a military border permit that is fairly easy to obtain through a trekking agency.

The Gorno-Badakhshan region of Tajikistan needs a separate permit, which takes a couple of weeks to arrange through a travel agency.

Turkmenistan presents a more complicated picture, as much of the country outside the main cities (restricted border zones) has to be listed on your visa for you to be able to visit it. You'll need the help of a travel agency to get the visa in the first place so your visa acts as your permit. For more information see Travel Permits in the individual country directories.

## VISAS

> To enter forbidden Turkistan without papers? I would sooner pay a call on the Devil and his mother-in-law in Hell.
>
> *Gustav Krist,* Alone in the Forbidden Land, 1939

### CHINESE VISAS

Chinese visas can be arranged in Tashkent and Dushanbe but are a real pain to organise elsewhere in Central Asia, since embassies often demand a letter of invitation from a Xinjiang tourist authority. These are available for around US$50 from travel agencies but can take a couple of weeks to arrange. It really helps to get a Chinese visa before you set off, though beware that you must normally enter China within 90 days of your visa being issued.

If you are travelling from China, bear in mind that the only consular agencies in Xinjiang are a Kazakh and Kyrgyz consulate in Ürümqi, where you can get visas within a couple of days. Beyond this, it's a long way back to Beijing.

Visas can be the single biggest headache associated with travel in ex-Soviet Central Asia, where the bureaucracy seems designed to actually hinder tourism and regulations mutate frequently. Collecting visas for a multicountry trip through Central Asia can take months and cost hundreds of US dollars.

Things are, however, getting easier. Visas for Kazakhstan, Tajikistan and Kyrgyzstan are now a formality for most nationalities and no letter of invitation is required. It's even possible to get a visa on arrival at Bishkek or Dushanbe airports. The difficulty involved in getting an Uzbekistan visa generally depends on how loudly your country criticises their human rights record, and has tightened up in the last year or two. Turkmenistan requires you to jump through the largest number of hoops.

The steps to obtain a visa and the attention it gets after you arrive differ for each republic, but their outlines are similar. The following information is general, with individual country variations detailed in the directories of the relevant country chapters.

### Letters of Invitation

The key to getting a visa for Turkmenistan and, for most nationalities, Uzbekistan, is 'visa support', which means an invitation, approved by the Ministries of Foreign Affairs and/or Interior, from a private individual, company or state organisation in the country you want to visit. After obtaining ministry approval, your sponsor sends the invitation (known as a letter of invitation or LOI, or visa support) to you, and when you apply at a consular office for your visa it's matched with a copy sent directly to them from the Ministry of Foreign Affairs.

The invitation should include your name, address, citizenship, sex, birth date, birthplace and passport details; the purpose, proposed itinerary and entry/exit dates of your visit; and the type of visa you will need and where you will apply for it. A business visa always requires a letter of invitation.

The cheapest way to get a visa invitation is directly, by fax or email, through a Central Asian travel agency. Many Central Asian agencies will just sell you a letter of visa support for between US$20 and US$40, which you pay when you arrive in the country. See the boxed text on below and also the Travel Agencies sections of capital cities for some trustworthy agencies in Central Asia. A few Western travel agencies can arrange visa invitation but charge up to five times the local fee.

Try to apply for letters of invitation a month, or preferably two in advance. Individual sponsors may need months to get their invitations approved before they can even be sent to you.

## Applying for a Visa

Visa applications can be made at some or all of the republics' overseas embassies or consulates, the addresses of which are listed in the Directories of individual country chapters. If your country doesn't have Central Asian representation you'll have to courier your passport to the nearest embassy, arrange a

### VISA WEB CONTACTS

#### Embassies

Useful embassy websites:

- www.kyrgyzembassy.org, www.kyrgyz-embassy.org.uk or www.botschaft-kirgisien.de
- www.kazakhembus.com, www.kazconsulny.org or www.kazakhstanembassy.org.uk
- www.tajikembassy.org or www.embassy-tajikistan.de
- www.uzbekconsulny.org, www.uzbekistan.org, www.uzbekistan.de or www.uzbekembassy.org
- www.turkmenistanembassy.org

#### Travel Agencies

The following travel agencies can arrange letters of invitation for their republic and in most cases the surrounding republics. Fees are around US$25 to US$35. Stantours is recommended by many travellers for impartial regional visa information.

- Central Asia Tourism, Almaty (www.centralasiatourism.com)
- Jibek Joly, Almaty (www.jibekjoly.kz)
- Stantours, Almaty (www.stantours.com)
- Turan-Asia, Almaty (www.turanasia.kz)
- Ayan Travel, Ashgabat (www.ayan-travel.com)
- DN Tours, Ashgabat (www.dntours.com)
- Celestial Mountains, Bishkek (www.celestial.com.kg)
- ITMC, Bishkek (www.itmc.centralasia.kg)
- Great Game Travel, Dushanbe (www.greatgame.travel or www.traveltajikistan.com)
- Advantour, Tashkent (www.advantour.com)
- Arostr Tourism, Tashkent (www.arostrtour.com)
- Dolores Tour, Tashkent (www.sambuh.com)
- Salom, Bukhara (www.salomtravel.com)

visa on arrival (see Visas on Arrival), or arrange your itinerary to get the visa in another Central Asian republic. Kazakh embassies will often issue visas for Kyrgyzstan if there is no Kyrgyz representation, though you need an LOI for this (whereas no invitation is required at a Kyrgyz embassy).

In addition to a letter of support, embassies may want a photocopy of the validity and personal information pages of your passport, two or three passport-size photos and a completed application form. Some may want more.

For Kyrgyzstan, Uzbekistan, Tajikistan and Kazakhstan visas do not list the towns to be visited and you are free to travel almost everywhere in these countries (see p456). The tourist-visa application for Turkmenistan requires you to list the name of every town you want to visit, and these will normally be printed on your visa. It's a good idea to ask for every place you might conceivably want to see, unless these are sensitive border towns or off limits to foreigners. There's no charge for listing extra destinations.

Bear in mind that many visas have either fixed-entry dates (Turkmenistan) or fixed-validity dates, so you may have to plan the dates of your itinerary closely in advance. If you are weaving in and out of republics, ie from Uzbekistan to Tajikistan's Pamir Hwy, Kyrgyzstan and then back to Uzbekistan, you'll need to ensure that the first visa is still valid for when you return to that republic (and that it's a double- or multiple-entry visa).

Even the most helpful Central Asian embassies in the West normally take a week or two to get you a visa. Most embassies will speed the process up for an express fee (often double the normal fee). Central Asian embassies within the CIS seem to be quicker, eg a day or less at Kyrgyz embassies in other Central Asian republics, a week or less at Kazakh embassies.

Visas can be more difficult to get in the run up to elections and national days (the latter in Turkmenistan only).

Try to allow time for delays and screw ups. Errors do happen – check the dates and other information on your visa carefully before you hit the road, and try to find out what the Cyrillic or other writing says.

### Visas on Arrival

If there's no convenient embassy in your country, you can get a visa on arrival at Bishkek and Dushanbe airports without an invitation, and at Almaty, Tashkent and Ashgabat airports as long as this has been arranged in advance with a travel agency in that country and you have a letter of invitation to prove it. It's possible to get a five-day transit visa on arrival at Almaty airport for US$25 without an LOI but you should have proof of an onward air ticket and an onward visa.

Responsible sponsors and agencies send representatives to meet their invitees at the airport and smooth their way through immigration. Even so, consular officials at the airport can be notoriously hard to find, especially if your flight arrives in the middle of the night, and may not be able to find your records scribbled in their big black book. You may also need to persuade the airline that you are guaranteed a visa as many are keen to avoid the costs and fines associated with bringing you back if your papers aren't in order. Try to get a visa in advance if possible.

Note that you cannot get a tourist visa at a land border of any Central Asian republic, though Kyrgyzstan plans to introduce this at some point.

### Getting Central Asian Visas in Central Asia

Some (not all) visas are simpler and cheaper to get after you arrive. It's relatively easy, for example, to get an Uzbek visa in Kazakhstan, or a Kazakh or Uzbek visa in Bishkek (Kyrgyzstan).

This could make your pretrip visa search much simpler, if you're willing to take some chances and have a week or so in a Central Asian republic to deal with the bureaucracy. Indeed, it might be possible (though we have not tried it) to leave home without any visas at all – eg fly to Bishkek and get a visa on arrival, then get a Kazakh or Uzbek visa in Bishkek and continue your trip there. This will work if you contact local travel agencies in advance to prepare any LOIs you might need. In general, though, you are better off getting at least one visa (Kyrgyz is the easiest, followed by Uzbekistan) before you board a plane to Central Asia.

### Transit & Multiple-Entry Visas

Even if you are just passing through a republic (eg flying into Almaty and transferring to Bishkek) you will need a transit visa. If you are also flying out this way you will need to apply for another transit visa (in this case in Bishkek). It is possible to get a five-day Kazakh transit visa for US$25 on arrival at Almaty airport (see 'Visas on Arrival' earlier).

You will need transit visas for some trips even if you are aren't stopping in the country. For example you will need a Kazakh transit visa to take the bus from Tashkent to Bishkek (which goes through Kazakhstan). You may also need a re-entry visa to get back into the first country; ie to travel from Fergana in Uzbekistan to Shakhimardan in Uzbekistan and back you should have a double-entry Kyrgyz visa and a double-entry Uzbek visa.

Train trips can be particularly tricky. New routings mean that you no longer need a Turkmen transit visa to take the Uzbek train between Tashkent and Urgench. Less convenient connections such as Tashkent to the Fergana Valley (requires a Tajik transit visa) and Bukhara to Termiz (requires a Turkmen transit visa) are worth avoiding.

Uzbekistan and Kazakhstan now even require other Central Asians to have a visa, in a move planned to boost security, which will only add to the visa queues at the respective embassies of those two countries.

### Getting Current Information

As with all official mumbo jumbo in Central Asia, the rules change all the time, so the information here may be out of date by the time you read it. Kyrgyzstan is even thinking of getting rid of visas entirely for some nationalities. Check Central Asian embassy websites (see the boxed text p457), the Lonely Planet Thorn Tree (www.lonelyplanet.com) and with one or more CIS-specialist travel or visa agencies.

### Visa Extensions

Extending an ordinary tourist visa after you get there is relatively easy in Kyrgyzstan, a bureaucratic tussle in Tajikistan and Uzbekistan (you can get a week's extension at Tashkent airport) and almost impossible in Kazakhstan and Turkmenistan. Travel agencies can normally help for a fee. You may find it easier to travel to a neighbouring republic and arrange another tourist visa.

## WOMEN TRAVELLERS

Despite the imposition of Soviet economic 'equality', attitudes in the Central Asian republics remain fairly male-dominated. Many local men cannot understand why women (in groups of any size, for that matter) would travel without men, and assume they have ulterior sexual motives. Although harassment is not so unrelenting as in some Middle Eastern countries, it tends to be more physical. Macho Uzbekistan tops the list, with Kyrgyzstan by far the least sexist.

Both men and women should seek permission before entering a mosque, particularly during prayer times when non-Muslims will feel uncomfortable. Women are generally not allowed in mosques in Tajikistan and the Fergana Valley. Most mosques in cities and the major tourist areas are open to all.

In bigger cities there is no taboo on unaccompanied local women talking to male visitors in public. Local men addressed by a woman in a couple direct their reply to the man, out of a sense of respect, and you should try to follow suit. Local women tend not to shake hands or lead in conversations. Because most local women don't drink in public, female visitors may not be offered a shot of the vodka or wine doing the rounds. But these are not taboos as such, and foreigners usually tend to be forgiven for what locals might consider gaffes.

Keen sensibilities and a few staunch rules of thumb can make a solo journey rewarding:

- Clothes do matter: a modest dress code is essential (even if local Russian women don't seem to have one).
- Walk confidently with your head up but avoid eye contact with men (smile at everybody else).
- Never follow any man – even an official – into a private area. If one insists on seeing your passport, hand over a photocopy as well as a photocopy of your OVIR registration (have quite a few of these); if he pushes you to follow him, walk away into a busy area.
- When riding in shared taxis choose one that already has other women passengers.
- Sit at the front of the bus, always between two women, if you can.
- When seeking information, always ask a local woman. Most matronly types will automatically take you under their wing if you show enough despair.
- If you feel as though you are being followed or harassed, seek the company of a group of women, or even children; big smiles will get you a welcome.

**THE INVISIBLE HUSBAND**

In some parts of Central Asia men are unused to seeing women travelling by themselves and you'll be continually asked where your husband is, but the system can often work in the lone woman's favour. So slip on a fake wedding ring and invent the invisible husband (In Russian: *'moy muzh'* means 'my husband'), who can then be used in uncomfortable situations. When being pressured to buy something in a shop, cast your eyes downward and murmur *'moy moosh'* (my husband doesn't give me any money). When a strange man tries to befriend you and you can't shake him, give a frantic glance at your watch and shout *'moy moosh'* (I am meeting my husband at any moment). When officials, guards or policemen demand a bribe, shrug your shoulders helplessly and cry *'moy moosh'* (my husband has left me here and there's nothing I can do!).

- If you are arranging a trek or car hire, ask the agency to include female travellers.
- Some local men will honestly want to befriend and help you; if you are unsure and have a difficult time shaking them, mention your husband (see the boxed text above).
- Wear a whistle around your neck in case you get into trouble. Blow on it relentlessly if you are absolutely in danger.

But it isn't all bad! The opportunities for genuine cross-cultural woman-to-woman interactions can generally be had during homestays, and usually outside the cities. Everyone loves to have their children cooed over and doing so will gain you friends as well as unique experiences. You may well see a side of Central Asia hidden to male travellers.

## WORK, STUDY & VOLUNTEERING

There are not many casual work opportunities in the region. What work is available is probably limited to English teaching and aid work, both of which are better arranged prior to your arrival in the region. The US Peace Corps and UK Voluntary Service Overseas (VSO) have a strong presence in the region, except in Uzbekistan.

You may find teaching positions in the region's universities, particularly the American University in Bishkek (www.auca.kg), the Samarkand State Institute of Foreign Languages (www.sifl.50megs.com) and the planned University of Central Asia (www.ucentralasia.org) in Khorog (Tajikistan), Naryn (Kyrgyzstan) and Tekeli (Kazakhstan).

The Alpine Fund (www.alpinefund.org) in Bishkek accepts six-month volunteers. You could also volunteer at Habitat Kyrgyzstan Foundation (www.habitat.elcat.kg). Some travellers have been able to help out at community-based tourism projects in Kyrgyzstan (see p277).

**American Councils** (☎ 202-833-7522; www.americancouncils.org; 1776 Massachusetts Ave., N.W., Suite 700, Washington, DC 20036) organises summer- and year-long academic exchanges and language study programmes in Central Asia.

# Transport in Central Asia

## CONTENTS



## GETTING THERE & AWAY

This chapter deals with travel into or out of Central Asia and includes general getting around advice for the region. For details of travel between and within Central Asian countries, see the transport sections of the individual country chapters.

### ENTERING CENTRAL ASIA

The region's main air links to the 'outside' are through the ex-Soviet republican capitals of Almaty (Kazakhstan), Bishkek (Kyrgyzstan), Tashkent (Uzbekistan), Ashgabat (Turkmenistan) and, to a lesser extent, Dushanbe (Tajikistan). A few smaller cities have further connections to Commonwealth of Independent States (CIS) countries outside of Central Asia, especially Russia.

The long-distance rail connections are mostly with Mother Russia – from Moscow to Tashkent and Almaty, and from the Trans-Siberian Railway to Almaty and Tashkent. The only other rail link is the Genghis Khan Express between Almaty and Ürümqi (and beyond) in China.

The other main overland links are three roads from China – one accessible year-round via Ürümqi to Almaty, and two warm-weather routes from Kashgar to Kyrgyzstan, over the Torugart or Irkeshtam Passes into Kyrgyzstan. Kashgar in turn can be reached by road over the Khunjerab Pass on Pakistan's amazing Karakoram Highway. A road link connects Mashhad in Iran to Ashgabat at two locations.

Finally there is the offbeat journey from Turkey through the Caucasus Mountains by bus to Baku (Azerbaijan), across the Caspian Sea by ferry to Turkmenbashi (Turkmenistan) and by train to Ashgabat, Bukhara and beyond. See 'From Turkey' (p465) for details.

> **THINGS CHANGE...**
>
> The information in this chapter is particularly vulnerable to change. Check directly with the airline or a travel agent to make sure you understand how a fare (and ticket you may buy) works and be aware of the security requirements for international travel. Shop carefully. The details given in this chapter should be regarded as pointers and are not a substitute for your own careful, up-to-date research.

### AIR

Many European and Asian cities now have direct flights to the Central Asian capitals. From North America and Australasia you will have to change planes at least once en route. Of the many routes in, two handy corridors are via Turkey (thanks to the geopolitics of the future) and via Russia (thanks to the geopolitics of the past). Turkish Airlines has the best connections and inflight service, while Russian and Central Asian carriers have the most connections. Turkey also has the advantage of a full house of Central Asian embassies and airline offices. Moscow has four airports and connections can be inconvenient.

#### Airports & Airlines

Tashkent – seven hours from London, 3½ hours from Moscow, Tel Aviv and Delhi, 4½ hours from İstanbul, 5½ hours from Beijing and 6½ hours from Bangkok – may have the most central airport in Eurasia. More flights go to Tashkent than to any other city in the region.

### CLIMATE CHANGE & TRAVEL

Climate change is a serious threat to the ecosystems that humans rely upon, and air travel is the fastest-growing contributor to the problem. Lonely Planet regards travel, overall, as a global benefit, but believes we all have a responsibility to limit our personal impact on global warming.

#### Flying & Climate Change

Pretty much every form of motor transport generates $CO_2$ (the main cause of human-induced climate change) but planes are far and away the worst offenders, not just because of the sheer distances they allow us to travel, but because they release greenhouse gases high into the atmosphere. The statistics are frightening: two people taking a return flight between Europe and the US will contribute as much to climate change as an average household's gas and electricity consumption over a whole year.

#### Carbon Offset Schemes

Climatecare.org and other websites use 'carbon calculators' that allow travellers to offset the greenhouse gases they are responsible for with contributions to energy-saving projects and other climate-friendly initiatives in the developing world – including projects in India, Honduras, Kazakhstan and Uganda.

Lonely Planet, together with Rough Guides and other concerned partners in the travel industry, supports the carbon offset scheme run by climatecare.org. Lonely Planet offsets all of its staff and author travel.

For more information check out our website: www.lonelyplanet.com.

Almaty is also a useful gateway to both Kazakhstan and Kyrgyzstan (Bishkek is just three hours by road). KLM and Lufthansa operate shuttles from Almaty airport to Bishkek for their clients (see p348).

Ashgabat is less well connected, most reliably by Lufthansa and Turkish Airlines, and Tajikistan is the least connected, with a popular weekly connection with Turkish Airlines. For Dushanbe it's possible to fly to Bishkek and take a regional flight, or fly to Tashkent and travel overland to Khojand and then take a domestic flight.

The following are the main Central Asian airlines, of which Uzbekistan Airways is probably the best:

**Air Astana** (www.airastana.com; airline code 4L; hub Almaty) Flies Almaty to Amsterdam, Bangkok, Beijing, Delhi, Dubai, Hanover, İstanbul, London, Moscow and Seoul; Astana to Frankfurt, Hanover and Moscow; Atyrau and Uralsk to Amsterdam.

**Air Company (AC) Kyrgyzstan** (www.altynair.kg; airline code QH; hub Bishkek) Moscow, Dubai, Dushanbe, Tashkent, Ürümqi, summer flights to Hanover and Frankfurt. Formerly known as Altyn Air.

**Tajikistan Airlines** (www.tajikistan-airlines.com; airline code 7J; hub Dushanbe) Flies to Munich (via İstanbul), Delhi, Moscow (Domodedovo), Sharjah, Tehran and Ürümqi, Bishkek, Almaty and various Siberian cities

**Turkmenistan Airlines** (www.turkmenistanairlines.com; airline code T5; hub Ashgabat) Flies to Abu Dhabi, Amritsar, Bangkok, Beijing, Birmingham, Delhi, Frankfurt, İstanbul, Kiev, London and Moscow.

**Uzbekistan Airways** (www.uzairways.com; airline code HY; hub Tashkent) Flies to Amsterdam, Athens, Baku, Bangkok, Beijing, Birmingham, Delhi, Dhaka, Frankfurt, İstanbul, Jeddah, Karachi, Kiev, Kuala Lumpur, London, Moscow, New York, Osaka, Paris, Seoul, Sharjah and Tel Aviv.

Other airlines that fly into Central Asia:

**Aeroflot** (www.aeroflot.ru; airline code SU; hub Sheremetyevo-2, Moscow) Flies to Tashkent and Bishkek.

**Aerosvit Ukrainian Airlines** (www.aerosvit.com; airline code VV; hub Kiev) Flies to Ashgabat weekly.

**Ariana Afghan Airlines** (www.flyariana.com; airline code FG; hub Kabul) Flies to Dushanbe weekly.

**Asiana Airlines** (www.flyasiana.com; airline code OZ; hub Kimpo Airport, Seoul) Flies to Tashkent and Almaty.

**Azerbaijan Airlines** (www.azal.az; airline code J2; hub Baku) Flies to Aktau.

**British Airways** (www.britishairways.com, www.flybmed.com; airline code BA; hub London Heathrow) Flies to Bishkek (four weekly via Tbilisi) and Almaty (three weekly via Ekaterinburg) under the name British Mediterrannean. Recently axed its four weekly flights to Tashkent.

**China Southern** (www.cs-air.com/en; airline code CZ;) Ürümqi to Almaty, Tashkent and Bishkek.

**Georgian National Airlines** (www.national-avia.com; airline code QB; hub Tbilisi) Weekly to Astana and twice-weekly to Almaty.

**Imair Airlines** (www.imair.com; airlines code IK; hub Baku) Flies to Almaty and Tashkent.
**Iran Air** (www.iranair.com; airline code IR; hub Tehran) Flies to Tashkent, Almaty and Ashgabat (via Mashhad).
**Iran Aseman** (www.iaa.ir; airline code EP; hub Tehran) Flies from Tehran and Mashhad to Ashgabat, Bishkek and Dushanbe.
**KLM** (www.klm.com; airline code KL; hub Schiphol Airport, Amsterdam) Flies to Almaty (twice weekly).
**Lufthansa** (www.lufthansa.com; airline code LH; hub Frankfurt) Flies to Almaty (five weekly), Astana (twice weekly) and Ashgabat (three weekly via Baku).
**Pulkovo Airlines** (www.pulkovo.ru; airline code FV; hub St Petersburg) Flies to Astana and Almaty (twice weekly), Dushanbe (weekly), Tashkent (weekly) and Bishkek (fortnightly).
**Transaero** (www.transaero.ru; airline code UN; hub Domodedovo Airport, Moscow) Flies to Almaty, Astana, Atyrau, Aktau, Shymkent, Karaganda, Tashkent and Bukhara.
**Turkish Airlines** (www.turkishairlines.com; airline code TK; hub İstanbul) Flies to Tashkent (four weekly), Ashgabat (three weekly), Almaty (five weekly), Astana (four weekly), Bishkek (three weekly) and Dushanbe (weekly) from İstanbul.
**Ukrainian Mediterranean** (UM Airlines; www.umairlines.com; airline code UF; hub Kiev) Flies to Almaty, Astana and Tashkent

## Tickets

Finding flights to Central Asia isn't always easy, as travel agents are generally unaware of the region (you'll have to help with the spelling of most cities and airlines) and many don't book flights on Russian or Central Asian airlines. You may need to contact the airlines directly for schedules and contact details of their consolidators, or sales agents, who often sell the airlines' tickets cheaper than the airlines themselves. For airline offices in Central Asia see Getting There & Away in the relevant capital city in each country chapter.

One thing to consider when arranging your itinerary is your visa situation. You may find it easier flying into, for example, Bishkek if that's the easiest place to arrange a visa from home.

> **DEPARTURE TAX**
>
> Departure taxes are figured into your air ticket so you won't face any extra charges when you fly out of Central Asia. The exception that proves the rule is Turkmenistan, where you'll pay a US$25 departure tax when flying out of Ashgabat airport on any airline other than Turkmenistan Airlines.

You might also consider that it's worth paying a little extra for a reliable airline such as KLM or Turkish Airlines, rather than a relatively inexperienced one, such as Kyrgyzstan Airlines.

Always check how many stopovers there are, how long these are and what time the flight arrives (many airlines arrive in the dead of night) as well as any restrictions on the ticket (ie on changing the return date, refunds etc).

Fares to the region tend to be 10% to 20% higher in peak travel season (roughly July to September and December in North America and Europe; December to January in Australia and New Zealand).

## Visa Checks

You can buy air tickets without a visa or a letter of invitation (LOI; see p456), but in most places outside Central Asia you may have trouble getting on a plane without one – even if embassies and travel agents tell you otherwise. Airlines are obliged to fly anyone rejected because of improper papers back home and are fined, so check-in staff tend to act like immigration officers. If you have made arrangements to get a visa on arrival, have your LOI handy at check-in and check with the airline beforehand.

## Airline Safety

Aeroflot, the former Soviet state airline, was decentralised into around 400 splinter airlines and many of these 'baby-flots' now have the worst regional safety record in the world, due to poor maintenance, ageing aircraft and gross overloading. In general though, the Central Asian carriers have lifted their international services towards international safety standards, at least on international routes.

In December 1997 a Tajikistan Airlines plane crashed in Sharjah, killing 85 passengers, and an Air Kazakhstan plane collided with a Saudi jet over Delhi killing 350 people. In January 2004 an Uzbekistan Airways Yak-42 crashed in Termiz killing 32 passengers. In 1993 a Tajikistan Airlines Yak-40 crashed on take-off from Khorog; it had 81 passengers in its 28 seats. Tajikistan Airlines is currently not allowed into British airspace, due to safety concerns.

See www.airsafe.com/events/airlines/fsu.htm for an overview of recent air accidents in the former Soviet Union.

**SAMPLE ONE-WAY AIR FARES FROM CENTRAL ASIA:**

These fares are a rough guide only.

- Tashkent–Bangkok US$540
- Tashkent–Baku US$324
- Tashkent–Delhi US$345
- Tashkent–Frankfurt/London/Paris US$560
- Bishkek/Dushanbe/Almaty–İstanbul US$428/400/405
- Bishkek–London US$675
- Bishkek–Dubai US$300
- Ashgabat–İstanbul US$340
- Dushanbe–Mashhad US$163
- Almaty–Frankfurt US$430
- Almaty–London US$645

### From Asia

From Beijing there are twice weekly flights to Tashkent on Uzbekistan Airways, and three weekly to Almaty on Air Astana and to Bishkek on Kyrgyzstan Airlines.

Ürümqi in China's Xinjiang province has weekly or twice weekly flights to/from Almaty (US$300; five weekly), Bishkek (US$180 to US$210), Osh (US$220) and Dushanbe (US$260).

Ariana Afghan Airlines flies once a week between Kabul and Dushanbe (US$108). Kam Air (www.flykamair.com) has slightly unreliable weekly flights from Almaty to Kabul (US$260).

Kazakhstan's Scat Air (www.scat.kz in Russian) runs a weekly flight between Almaty and Ölgii in western Mongolia (US$250) via Ust-Kamenogorsk (Öskomen; US$109 to Ölgii).

Uzbekistan Airways flies three times a week from Tashkent to Lahore in Pakistan.

### From Australia & New Zealand

Most flights to Central Asia go via Seoul (to pick up Asiana flights to Tashkent), Kuala Lumpur (Uzbekistan Airways to Tashkent), Bangkok (Uzbekistan Airways to Tashkent or Turkmenistan Airlines to Ashgabat) or İstanbul.

Sample routes include Sydney to Tashkent on Malaysia Airlines via Kuala Lumpur, or via Karachi on Qantas/British Airways/Pakistan International Airlines (PIA); and Sydney to Almaty via Seoul on Korean Airlines. For Dushanbe and Bishkek you'll probably have to go via İstanbul.

Online agencies include:

**Flight Centre** (Australia ☎ 133 133; New Zealand ☎ 0800 24 35 44; www.flightcentre.com)

**Gateway Travel** (☎ 02-9745 3333; www.russian-gateway.com.au; 48 The Boulevarde, Strathfield NSW 2135) Ex-USSR specialists with experience in booking flights to Central Asia.

**STA Travel** (Australia ☎ 134 STA; New Zealand ☎ 0800 474 400; www.statravel.com.au, www.statravel.co.nz)

**Trailfinders** (☎ 1300 780 212; www.trailfinders.com.au)

**www.travel.com.au** (www.travel.com.au)

### From Continental Europe

The best fares from Europe to Almaty are probably with Turkish Airlines, via İstanbul. Travellers on a tight budget may find it cheapest to fly from Germany to cities in northern Kazakhstan such as Uralsk, Kostanay or Astana, and then continuing by train to southern Central Asia.

**Tajikistan Airlines** (☎ 89-9759 4210; gartjk@i-dial.de) Located in Munich; operates Europe's only flights to Dushanbe (US$555 one-way from Dushanbe, weekly via İstanbul).

**Turkmenistan Airlines** (☎ 69-690 21968) Offices in Frankfurt (US$540 one way).

Discounted travel agencies include **Voyages Wasteels** (☎ 01-42 61 69 87; www.wasteels.fr) and **OTU Voyages** (☎ 01-55 82 32 32; www.otu.fr) in France and **STA Travel** (www.statravel.com; Frankfurt ☎ 69-7430 3292; www.statravel.de), which has dozens of offices across Europe. In Holland try **Airfair** (☎ 020-620 5121; www.airfair.nl).

### From Russia

There are flights from Moscow to most Central Asian cities, including Almaty (US$270), Tashkent (US$256 to US$270, daily), Dushanbe (US$280, daily), Khojand (US$270, weekly), Ashgabat (US$220), Bishkek (US$250), Osh (US$225 to US$300) and many Kazakh cities. There are slightly fewer connections from St Petersburg. Major Siberian cities such as Novosibirsk and Yekaterinburg also have connections to the capitals. You can often get seniors, student and under-30s discounts of 25% on Russian flights.

Uzbekistan Airways flies from Moscow to Samarkand, Urgench and Bukhara weekly for around US$230. Aeroflot fly from Moscow to Tashkent and Bishkek.

**Transaero** (☎ 495-788 8080; 2nd Smolensky Pereulok 3/4, Moscow) is an international-grade airline that flies from Moscow Domodedovo (see next paragraph) to Astana, Almaty, Tashkent, Bukhara and several other cities in Kazakhstan, and has connections to European destinations.

Note that Moscow has three airports: Sheremetyevo-1 (terminal one; www.sheremetyevo-airport.ru), the international Sheremetyevo (terminal two), and 'domestic' (ex-Soviet destinations) Domodedovo (www.domodedovo.ru) and Vnukovo. Aeroflot, Uzbekistan Airways and Air Astana now operate to/from Sheremetyevo-1. Transaero, Tajikistan Airlines, Turkmenistan Airways and Kyrgyzstan Airlines use Domodedovo airport. You will need to get a Russian transit visa in advance to transfer between airports and even between Sheremetyevo's two terminals. A bus service runs between Domodedovo and Sheremetyevo (terminal 1 and 2), costs around US$8 per person and takes at least two hours.

Travel agencies located in Moscow include **Infinity Travel** (☎ 495-234 6555; www.infinity.ru; Komsomolsky prospekt 13) for rail and air tickets and Central Asia packages, affiliated with the Travellers Guest House, and **G&R International** (☎ 495-378 0001; www.hostels.ru; 5th fl, Zelenodolskaya ul. 3/2).

### From Turkey

Turkish Airlines flies from İstanbul to Almaty (five weekly), Bishkek (two weekly), Dushanbe (weekly), Tashkent (three weekly) and Ashgabat (four weekly). The various republics' national airlines also fly once or twice a week. Alternatively you could fly from İstanbul or Trabzon to Baku, take the ferry to Turkmenbashi and a 12-hour train ride across the desert to Ashgabat.

One-way flights to İstanbul cost around US$400 from most Central Asian capitals.

### From the UK

The best summer fares to Almaty are about £450 return on KLM via Amsterdam and, possibly, Transaero. It's possible to buy an open-jaw return on KLM, eg into Almaty and out of, say, Karachi. Air Astana's direct flights from London to Almaty are sometimes good value at around £470 return.

The cheapest flights to Bishkek are probably with Aeroflot or Turkish Airlines and are somewhat more expensive than Almaty. British Mediterranean fly to Bishkek (via Tbilisi) and Almaty (via Yekaterinburg) but fares are generally higher.

To Tashkent the cheapest return fare is around £500 with Transaero, a reliable Russian airline. Other fares with Turkish Airlines or Lufthansa are £520 return. Uzbekistan Airways' London–Tashkent–Delhi run (four weekly, £500 return) is comfortable, with good service and decent food (but the return is no match, with exhausted Delhi passengers sprawled everywhere and poor food from Tashkent). The routing means that for not much extra you can continue on from Tashkent to Delhi or Bangkok, thus treating Tashkent as a stopover. Uzbekistan Airways also flies from Manchester. For details and prices contact **HY Travel** (☎ 020-7935 4775; 69 Wigmore St, London).

The cheapest flights to Ashgabat are with Turkish Airlines from London via İstanbul (overnight), four times a week for £550 return. **Turkmenistan Airlines** (☎ London 020-8577 2211; fax 8577 9900; Birmingham 0121-558 6363) flies three times a week from London to Ashgabat and four times a week from Birmingham to Ashgabat.

Easily the best way to Dushanbe is the weekly connection on Turkish Airlines via İstanbul but it isn't cheap at about £680 return. This flight often fills up several weeks in advance.

Online agencies include www.cheapflights.co.uk, www.ebookers.com, www.opodo.co.uk, www.expedia.co.uk and www.travelocity.co.uk.

Discounted travel agencies include:

**Flight Centre** (☎ 0870-499 0040; www.flightcentre.co.uk)
**STA Travel** (☎ 0870-1600 599; www.statravel.co.uk)
**Trailfinders** (☎ 0845-058 5858, 020-7938 3939; www.trailfinders.com)

### From the USA & Canada

From North America you generally have the choice of routing your trip via İstanbul (Turkish Airlines), Moscow (Aeroflot) or a major European city (KLM, British Airways, Lufthansa etc). Stopovers can be lengthy. From the west coast it's possible to fly to Tashkent via Seoul on Asiana.

From the USA, the best return fares to Central Asia at the time of writing were with Aeroflot from New York to Tashkent or Bishkek via Moscow for around US$1000 return.

 

Return fares from the east coast were around US$1080 to Almaty on American/Lufthansa and US$1400 with Northwest/KLM. To Ashgabat was US$1800 with Lufthansa.

**Uzbekistan Airways** (☎ 212-489 3954) flies from New York (JFK airport) to Tashkent (via Belgrade) three or four times a week, an 18-hour flight for almost the same fare, but you may have difficulties finding a travel agent to book it.

Online booking services include www.expedia.com, www.orbitz.com and www.travelocity.com.

Discounted agencies include:

**Gateway Travel** (☎ 800-441 1183)
**STA Travel** (☎ 800-781 4040; www.statravel.com)
**Travel CUTS** (☎ 416-979 2406; www.travelcuts.com) Canadian travel discounter.



# LAND

## Border Crossings

Cross-border roads that are open to foreigners (by bus, taxi or hired car) are listed in the table on below) and covered in the Transport sections of the relevant country chapters. There are literally dozens of crossings between Russia and Kazakhstan.

## Bus

From China, there are twice-weekly buses (Monday and Tuesday) from Kashgar to Osh (US$50) via the Irkeshtam Pass (p348 and p340), and also direct buses from Ürümqi (daily except Sunday) and Yining (twice weekly) to Almaty (p183). Foreigners are currently not allowed to take the twice-weekly bus between Kashgar and Bishkek (US$50), via Naryn (US$25).

**MAJOR BORDER CROSSINGS INTO CENTRAL ASIA**

| Border | Crossing | Means of Transport | Page | Comments |
|---|---|---|---|---|
| Iran-Turkmenistan | Gaudan/Bajgiran | car | p441 | From Mashhad to Ashgabat; change transport at the border |
| Iran-Turkmenistan | Saraghs | car/rail | p441 | The best bet if you want to head straight for Mary/Merv |
| Azerbaijan-Turkmenistan | Turkmenbashi | Boat | p468 | Upgrade to a cabin when on board |
| Afghanistan-Turkmenistan | Gushgi/Torghundi | car | p441 | You'll need to arrange this with a Turkmen travel agent |
| Afghanistan-Uzbekistan | Termiz | car | p266 | Across the Friendship Bridge from Mazar-i-Sharif |
| Afghanistan-Tajikistan | Panj-e-Payon (Nizhniy Panj) | boat | p395 | From Kunduz, involves a ferry crossing until the new bridge opens in 2007 |
| Afghanistan-Tajikistan | Ishkashim | car/foot | p395 | Getting a GBAO permit can be a problem entering Tajikistan |
| China-Tajikistan | Qolma (Kulma) Pass | car | p396 | Currently closed to tourists but might open soon |
| China-Kazakhstan | Khorgos | bus | p183 | Direct buses run from Yining and Ürümqi to Almaty, or change buses at the border |
| China-Kazakhstan | Dustlyk/Ālāshānkou | rail | p183 | Twice-weekly direct trains between Almaty and Ürümqi take 30 hours and cost US$60 |
| China-Kazakhstan | Bakhty/Tachéng | bus | p171 | Little-used crossing from Ürümqi |
| China-Kazakhstan | Maykapshagay/Jeminay (Jímunai) | bus | p171 | Little-used crossing but direct buses to buses to/from Altai in China |
| China-Kyrgyzstan | Torugart Pass | car | p348 and p327 | Relatively expensive as you must hire your own transport in advance on both sides |
| China-Kyrgyzstan | Irkeshtam Pass | car/bus | p348 and p340 | Weekly bus between Kashgar and Osh (US$50) or take a taxi, closed weekends |

**SILK ROAD BY RAIL**

Silk Road romantics, train buffs and nervous fliers can cross continents without once having to fasten their seatbelt or turn off their cell phones. From Moscow (or even St Petersburg) you can take in the transition to Central Asia on the three-day train trip to Tashkent or Almaty. From here you can add on any number of side trips to Samarkand, Bukhara or even Urgench (Khiva), all of which are on the railway line. Then from Almaty it's possible to continue on the train to Ürümqi in China and even to Kashgar. From Ürümqi you can continue along the Silk Road by train east as far as Beijing, Hong Kong or even Lhasa or Saigon, making for an epic transcontinental ride. It's not always comfortable and it will take some time, so why do it? Because like Everest, it's there.

There are also direct buses between Ust-Kamenogorsk in eastern Kazakhstan and the towns of Ürümqi (daily) and Altay (twice weekly) in Xinjiang province (see p171 for details), though few foreigners take these buses.

## Car & Motorcycle

Although car or motorbike is an excellent way of getting around Central Asia, bringing your own vehicle is fraught with practical problems. Fuel supply is uneven, though modern petrol stations are springing up throughout the region. Prices per litre swing wildly depending on supply. Petrol comes in four grades – 76, 93, 95 and 98 octane. In the countryside you'll see petrol cowboys selling plastic bottles of fuel from the side of the road, often of very poor quality.

The biggest problem is the traffic police (Russian, GAI). Tajikistan's roads have almost as many checkpoints as potholes. In Uzbekistan there are police skulking at every corner, most looking for excuses to wave their orange baton and hit drivers (local or otherwise) with a 'fine' (*straf*). There are no motoring associations of any kind.

The state insurance offices, splinters of the old Soviet agency Ingosstrakh, have no overseas offices that we know of, and your own insurance is most unlikely to be valid in Central Asia. You would probably have to arrange insurance anew at each border. See Getting Around (p471) for more information on hiring a car within Central Asia.

## Train

There are three main rail routes into Central Asia from Russia. One comes from Moscow via Samara or Saratov, straight across Kazakhstan via Kyzylorda to Tashkent (3369km), with branch lines to Bishkek and Almaty (4057km). Another, the Turkestan-Siberian railway or 'Turksib' (see www.turksib.com for timetables) links the Trans-Siberian railway at Novosibirsk with Almaty. A third route goes around the other side of the Aral Sea via Urgench, Bukhara and Samarkand to Tashkent, with a branch line to Dushanbe.

These 'iron roads' don't have quite the romance or the laid-back feel of the Trans-Siberian railway, but they are usually cheaper than flying, and allow Central Asia to unfold gradually, as you clank through endless plains, steppe and desert.

Another line crosses Kazakhstan via Karaganda. From the Caspian Sea yet another line crosses Turkmenistan – the Trans-Caspian route. No international trains run to or from Turkmenistan. A line connects Mashhad in Iran with Ashgabat in Turkmenistan, but no passenger trains run along this line at present.

Completed in 1992, after being delayed almost half a century by Russian-Chinese geopolitics, is a line from China via Ürümqi into Kazakhstan, joining the Turksib for connections to Almaty or to Siberia.

### CLASSES

A deluxe sleeping carriage is called *spets-vagon* (SV, Russian for 'special carriage', abbreviated to CB in Cyrillic; some call this *spalny vagon* or 'sleeping carriage'), *myagkiy* (soft) or 1st class. Closed compartments have carpets and upholstered seats, and convert to comfortable sleeping compartments for two.

An ordinary sleeping carriage is called *kupeyney* or *kupe* (which is the Russian for compartmentalised), *zhyosky* (hard) or 2nd class. Closed compartments are usually four-person couchettes and are comfortable.

A *platskartny* (reserved-place) or 3rd-class carriage has open-bunk accommodation. *Obshchiy* (general) or 4th class is unreserved bench-type seating.

With a reservation, your ticket normally shows the numbers of your carriage *(vagon)* and seat *(mesto)*. Class may be shown by what looks like a fraction: eg 1/2 is 1st class two berth, 2/4 is 2nd class four berth.

### FROM CHINA

The 1359km Silk Road Express between Ürümqi and Almaty leaves twice a week and takes about 33 hours, which includes several hours at the border for customs checks and to change bogies. Sleeper tickets cost around US$66 and are easily booked in either Ürümqi or Almaty. See p183.

### FROM RUSSIA

Most trains bound for Central Asia depart from Moscow's Kazan(sky) station. Europe dissolves into Asia as you sleep, and morning brings a vast panorama of the Kazakh steppe.

Train connections between Russia and Central Asia have thinned out in recent years. At the time of writing, fast trains left three times a week to/from Tashkent (No 5/6, 66 hours), every other day to/from Almaty (No 7/8), three or four times a week to/from Bishkek (Nos 17/18 and 27) and three times a week to/from Dushanbe (No 319/320). Trips take about three days. There are other, slower connections but you could grow old and die on them. Trains out of Moscow have even numbers; those returning have odd numbers.

Typical fares for a 2nd-class *(kupeyney)* berth are US$200 Moscow–Tashkent and US$180 Moscow–Almaty (via Astana).

Other offbeat connections include the Astrakan–Dushanbe (twice weekly), the St Petersburg–Astana(everyotherday)andSaratov–Nukus–Andijon (weekly) lines.

For a useful overview of international trains to/from Central Asia see www.seat61.com/silkroute.htm. For an online timetable see www.poezda.net.

### SEA

The Baku (Azerbaijan) to Turkmenbashi ferry route (seat US$47, 12 to 18 hours) across the Caspian is a possible way to enter and leave Central Asia. Buy the cheapest seat: once on board you'll doubtless be offered a cabin by a crewmember, for which you should realistically pay US$10 to US$20. The best cabins have private bathrooms and are comfortable, although all are cockroach infested.

Boats usually leave several times a day in both directions, but there is no timetable. You'll simply have to arrive and wait until the ship is full of cargo. You should leave with a couple of days left on your visa in case the boats are delayed, which is very possible. Stock up on food and water beforehand, as there is little food available on board. Crossings can end up taking 32 hours.

There are irregular boats every week or 10 days between Baku and Aktau (18 to 24 hours, US$61 to US$78) in Kazakhstan. One of these ferries sunk in October 2002, killing all 51 people aboard.

Boats also sail occasionally from Turkmenbashi to Astrakan in Russia.

# GETTING AROUND

Flying is the least interesting and arguably the least safe mode of transport in Central Asia, but to some destinations and in some seasons it's the only sensible alternative. Trains are slow but crowded and generally not very convenient outside Kazakhstan. Buses are the most frequent and convenient way to get between towns cheaply, though trips can be cramped and vehicles are prone to breakdowns. The best option in many areas is a car: shared taxis or private drivers are often willing to take you between cities for little more than a bus fare (see p472).

The biggest headache for travellers crossing the region is that most inter-republic bus services have been cut. Travellers generally have to get a shared taxi or minibus to and from both sides of the border (see the boxed text p471). Crossings into Uzbekistan are the most tightly controlled, particularly coming from Tajikistan.

## AIR

Flying saves time and takes the tedium out of Central Asia's long distances. It's also the only sensible way to reach some places, particularly in winter. But the Central Asian airlines have some way to go before meeting international safety standards on their domestic routes. Flights are particularly good value in Turkmenistan, where a domestic flight costs around US$10!

You generally have to pay for air tickets in local currency (there's often an exchange booth nearby), though you can pay in US ollars in Kyrgyzstan. Some airline offices and avel agencies accept credit cards

Apart from the national Central Asian irlines (see p461), there are a couple of omestic airlines, such as Kyrgyzstan's Itek ir and Altyn Air (www.altynair.kg/en), hich are pretty good. Domestic and inter-epublic services are no-frills; you might get warm glass of Coke if lucky. For long flights onsider packing lunch.

At the time of writing there were no Almaty–ishkek or Dushanbe–Tashkent services. lajor internal connections still run daily.

Flights between the biggest cities generlly stick to their schedules, but those serving smaller towns are often delayed without xplanation and cancellations are common, sually a result of fuel shortages (big-city ights get priority). Printed schedules are nreliable; routes and individual flights are onstantly being cancelled or reintroduced. he only sure way to find out what's flying is to ask at an air booking office. In any case, confirm any flight 24 hours prior to departure.

Tickets for Central Asian airlines are most easily purchased from private travel agents *(aviakassa)*. You'll often need your passport and visa. Many booking offices have a special window for foreigners and/or for international flights. It is rarely possible to book a return flight.

The airfare diagram (see p470) shows approximate one-way foreigners' fares in US-dollar equivalents, for the major regional connections. Expect these fares to change over time.

Seating is a bit of a free-for-all (there are often no assigned seats), especially if the flight is overbooked. To minimise the risk of loss or theft, consider carrying everything on board.

Helicopter flights were once popular in the Tian Shan and Pamir Ranges but rising fuel costs have made most services prohibitively expensive (around US$1300 per hour).



## TRAVEL AGENCIES & ORGANISED TOURS

Throughout this book, in the relevant city sections, we list reliable Central Asian travel agencies abroad who can help with the logistics of travel in Central Asia – whether it be visas, a few excursions or an entire tailored trip.

The following agencies outside the region can arrange individual itineraries and/or accommodation, tickets and visa support.

### Australia

**Passport Travel** (☎ 03-9867 3888; www.travelcentre.com.au, www.russia-rail.com; Suite 11A, 401 St Kilda Rd, Melbourne, Victoria 3004) Accommodation and rail tickets.

**Russian Gateway Tours** (☎ 02-9745 3333; www.russian-gateway.com.au; 48 The Boulevarde, Strathfield NSW 2135) Airfares to Central Asia, hotel bookings, homestays, visa invitations and airport transfers.

**Sundowners** (☎ 03-9672 5300; www.sundowners.com.au; Suite 15, Lonsdale Court, 600 Lonsdale St, Melbourne, Victoria 3000) Small-group and independent tours into Central Asia.

### The UK

**Regent Holidays** (☎ 0870-499 0911; www.regent-holidays.co.uk; 15 John St, Bristol BS1 2HR) Offer short tours, and can cobble together an individual itinerary.

**Scott's Tours** (☎ 020-7383 5353; www.scottstours.co.uk; 141 Whitfield St London W1T 5EW) Hotel bookings, visas and more.

**Silk Road and Beyond** (020-7371 3131; www.silkroadandbeyond.co.uk; 371 Kensington High Street, London, W14 8QZ)

**Steppes East** (☎ 01285-651 010; www.steppeseast.co.uk; 51 Castle St, Cirencester GL7 1QD)

### The USA

**Mir Corporation** (☎ 800-424 7289; www.mircorp.com; Suite 210, 85 South Washington St, Seattle, WA 98104) Independent tours, homestays and visa support with accommodation.

**Red Star Travel** (☎ 800-215 4378, 206-522 5995; www.travel2russia.com; Suite 102, 123 Queen Anne Ave N, Seattle, WA 98109) Organises tours, individual itineraries, accommodation, train tickets, visa support with booking.

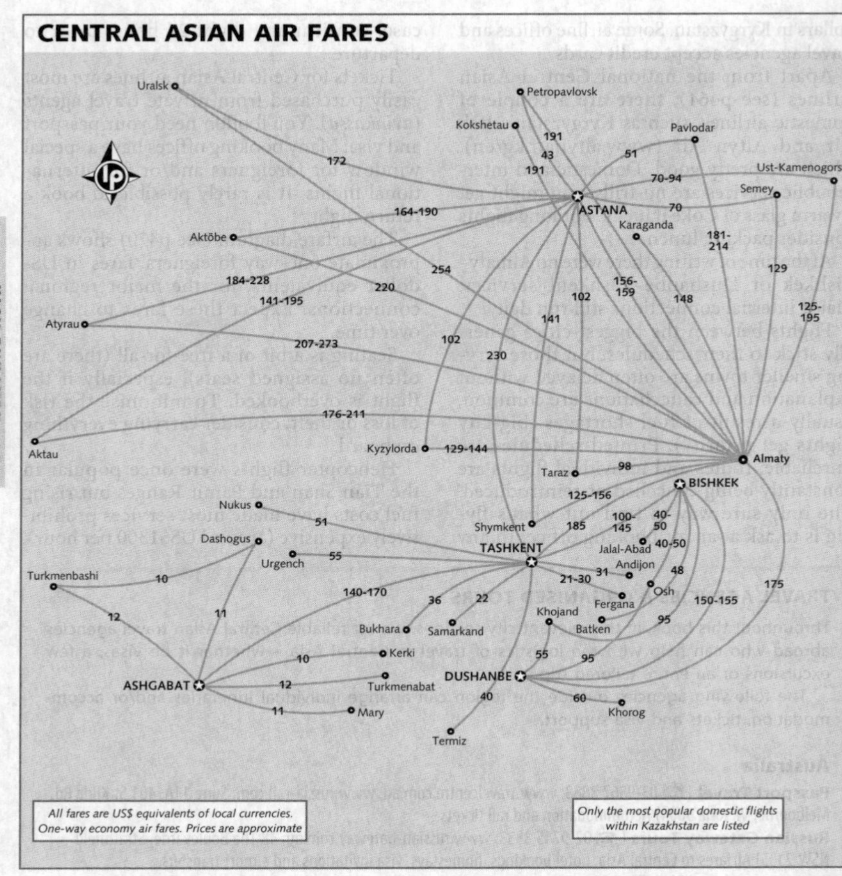


Maintenance is also patchy; avoid them except in summer and go only if the weather is absolutely clear.

## BUS

This is generally the best bet for getting between towns cheaply. The major transport corridors are served by big long-distance coaches (often reconditioned German or Turkish vehicles), which run on fixed routes and schedules, with fixed stops. They're relatively problem-free and moderately comfortable, with windows that open and sometimes with reclining seats. Luggage is locked safely away below. Journey times depend on road conditions but are somewhat longer than a fast train.

Regional buses are a lot less comfortabl and a bit more…interesting. Breakdowns ar common. They are also used extensively b small-time traders to shift their goods aroun the region, and you could gradually becom surrounded by boxes, bags, and both live an dead animals.

Private minibuses, generally calle marshrutka (Russian for 'fixed route'), ar a bit more expensive, sometimes faster, an usually more hair-raising. They generall have fixed fares and routes but no fixed time table (or no departure at all if there aren' enough passengers to satisfy the driver), an will stop anywhere along the route. The can be clapped-out heaps or spiffy nev Toyota vans.

Keep in mind that you're at the mercy of the driver as he picks up cargo here and there, loading it all around the passengers, picks up a few friends, gets petrol, fixes a leaky petrol tank, runs some errands, repairs the engine, loads more crates right up to the ceiling – and then stops every half-hour to fill the radiator with water.

### Tickets

Most cities have a main intercity bus station (Russian: *avtovokzal,* Kyrgyz and Uzbek: *avtobekat)* and may also have regional bus stations (sometimes several) serving local towns.

Try to pick buses originating from where you are, enabling you to buy tickets as much as a day in advance. Tickets for through buses originating in a different city may not be sold until they arrive, amid anxious scrambles. At a pinch you could try paying the driver directly for a place.

Most large bus stations have police who sometimes create headaches for foreigners by demanding documents. Be wary of any policeman who approaches you at a bus station. Long-distance bus stations are, in general, low-life magnets, rarely pleasant after dark. Disregard most bus-station timetables.

## CAR

Car is an excellent way to get around Central Asia and it needn't be expensive. Main highways between capitals and big cities (eg Almaty–Bishkek–Tashkent–Samarkand–Bukhara) are fast and fairly well maintained. Mountain roads (ie most roads in Kyrgyzstan and Tajikistan) can be blocked with snow in winter and plagued by landslides in spring.

See Car & Motorcycle (p467) for advice about driving your own vehicle through Central Asia.

### Hire

Almaty and Bishkek have a Hertz/Avis franchise and travel agencies can hire you out a Mercedes or 4WD, but you are almost always better off hiring a taxi for the day.

Community-based tourism organisations and travel agencies hire 4WDs for remoter areas of Kyrgyzstan and Tajikistan. Hiring a car unlocks some of Central Asia's best mountain scenery and is well worth it, despite the cost. CBT in Kyrgyzstan (see p277) charges around US$0.25 per km, META (p388) in Tajikistan's eastern Pamirs charges US$0.34 to US$0.38 per kilometre. Travel agencies are more expensive.



### JIGSAW BORDERS

When Stalin drew the borders between the different republics in 1924 no-one really expected them to become international boundaries. Areas were portioned off on the map according to the whims of Party leaders, without much regard to the reality on the ground. As these crazy jigsaw borders solidify throughout post-Soviet Central Asia, many towns and enclaves are finding themselves isolated, as the once complex web of regional ties shrinks behind new borderlines.

The Fergana Valley has been particularly affected. Travellers (and locals) may find it tricky to get to more remote areas or trekking bases by public transport. Borders sometimes close, especially between Uzbekistan and Tajikistan. Cars with Tajik number plates can no longer cross into Uzbekistan, and Uzbek border guards often give locals the third degree.

Buses no longer run from central Uzbekistan into the Fergana Valley along the natural route via Khojand but rather take the mountain road from Tashkent over the Kamchik Pass. Only train connections exit the Fergana Valley through its mouth.

Trains are not immune to these border shenanigans, as lines occasionally veer into other republics. Trains from Astrakan and Khojand to Termiz and Dushanbe dip into Turkmenistan and Turkmen guards sometimes board the train to fine travellers without a Turkmen visa.

The bottom line is that there are now border checks at many hitherto disregarded borders and you need a visa any time you cross into another republic. If you are just transiting in another republic before heading back into the first you should invest in a double- or multiple-entry visa. There are exceptions, eg the Tajikistan–Kyrgyzstan border.

These problems may be short-lived, as new transport connections are springing up everywhere. Uzbekistan has built a railway line to bypass Turkmenistan and roads have sprung up in Kyrgyz parts of the Fergana Valley to avoid Uzbek border guards. But these are just a few of the thousands of ties that bind the ex-Soviet republics to one another and to Russia, and disentangling them will take decades.

Long-distance taxi hire in Turkmenistan is around US$0.10 per km.

### Taxi

There are two main ways of travelling by car in Central Asia if you don't have your own vehicle: ordinary taxi or shared taxi.

#### ORDINARY TAXI

This form of travel is to hire an entire taxi for a special route. This is handy for reaching off-the-beaten-track places, where bus connections are hit-and-miss or nonexistent, such as Song-Köl in Kyrgyzstan. Select your driver with care, look over his car (we took one in Kyrgyzstan whose exhaust fumes were funnelled through the back windows) and assess his sobriety before you set off. See opposite)for more on Central Asian taxis.

You'll have to negotiate a price before you set off. Along routes where there are also shared taxis, ordinary taxis are four times the shared taxi per-person fare. Make sure everyone is clear which route you will be taking, how long you want the driver to wait at a site and if there are any toll or entry fees to be paid. You will need to haggle hard.

You can work out approximate costs by working out the return kilometre distance; assume the average consumption of cars is around 12 litres per 100km and then multiply the number of litres needed by the per litre petrol cost (constantly in flux). Add to this a daily fee (anything from US$5 up to the cost of the petrol) and a waiting fee of around US$1 per hour and away you go.

#### SHARED TAXI

Shared taxi is the other main form of car travel around Central Asia, whereby a taxi or private car does a regular run between two cities and charges a set rate for each of the four seats in a car. These cars often wait for passengers outside bus or train stations and some have a sign in the window indicating where they are headed. Cars are quicker and just as comfortable as a bus or train, and can work out to be just a little more expensive than a bus. In Kyrgyzstan per-person fares are so cheap that two or three of you can buy all four seats and stretch out. Otherwise smaller cars can be a little cramped. The most common car is the Russian Zhiguli, fast being replaced by modern Daewoo models such as the Nexia (the most comfortable) and the smaller and cheaper Tico, both made in Central Asia. The front seat is always the one to aim for.

These services are particularly useful in Kyrgyzstan along certain major routes such as Bishkek–Almaty, Bishkek–Osh, and Naryn–Bishkek. Other useful shared taxi routes are Bukhara–Urgench/Khiva, Samarkand–Termiz, Dushanbe–Khojand and Ashgabat-Mary.

## HITCHING

In Central Asia there is generally little distinction between hitching and taking a taxi. Anyone with a car will stop if you flag them down (with a low up-and-down wave, not an upturned thumb) and most drivers will expect you to pay for the ride. If you can negotiate a reasonable fare (it helps to know the equivalent bus or shared taxi fare) this can be a much quicker mode of transport than the bus. There's also a good chance you'll be invited to someone's house for tea.

Hitching to parks and scenic spots is generally much easier on the weekends but you'll lose some of the solitude at these times.

Normal security rules apply when trying to arrange a lift; don't hitch alone, avoid flagging down cars at night and try to size up your driver (and his sobriety) before getting in.

## LOCAL TRANSPORT

Most sizable towns have public buses, and sometimes electric trolleybuses. Bigger cities also have trams, and Tashkent has a metro system. Transport is still ridiculously cheap by Western standards, but usually packed because there's never enough money to keep an adequate fleet on the road; at peak hours it can take several stops for those caught by surprise to even work their way to an exit.

Public transport in smaller towns tends to melt away soon after dark.

### Bus, Trolleybus & Tram

Payment methods vary, but the most common method is to pay the driver cash on exit. Manoeuvre your way out by asking anyone in the way, *vykhodite?* (getting off?).

### Marshrutka

A marshrutka taxi, or marshrutnoe (marsh-*root*-na-yuh tahk-*see*), is a minibus running along a fixed route. You can get on at fixed stops but can get off anywhere by saying '*zdyes pazhalsta*' (zd-*yes* pa-*zhal*-stuh; here please). Routes are hard to figure out and schedules

**TAXI PRECAUTIONS**

Avoid taxis lurking outside tourist hotels – drivers charge far too much and get uppity when you try to talk them down. Never get into a taxi with more than one person in it, especially after dark; check the back seat of the car for hidden friends too. Keep your fare money in a separate pocket to avoid flashing large wads of cash. Have a map to make it look like you know your route. If you're staying at a private residence, have the taxi stop at the corner nearest your destination, not the specific address.

erratic, and it's usually easier to stick to other transport. Fares are just a little higher than bus fares.

### Taxi

There are two kinds of taxis: officially licensed ones and every other car on the road. Official taxis are more trustworthy, and sometimes cheaper – if you can find one. They rarely have meters and you'll have to negotiate a fare in advance. Or let a local friend negotiate for you – they'll do better than you will.

Unofficial taxis are often private cars driven by people trying to cover their huge petrol costs. Anything with a chequerboard logo in the window is a taxi. Stand at the side of the road, extend your arm and wait – as scores of others around you will probably be doing. When someone stops, negotiate destination and fare through the passenger-side window or through a partially open door. The driver may say '*sadytse*' (sit down) or beckon you in, but sort the fare out first. It helps a lot if you can negotiate the price in Russian, even more so in the local language.

A typical fare across Dushanbe at the time of research was around US$3; less in Tashkent and Bishkek, and less than half that in Ashgabat. Fares go up at night and extra charges are incurred for bookings.

## TRAIN

Lower-class train travel is the cheapest but most crowded way to get around Central Asia. Travel in the summertime is best done at night. Kazakhstan is probably the only country where you'll find yourself using the train system much.

### Connections

Trains can be useful to cover the vast distances in Kazakhstan. Certain corridors, such as the Turksib (Semey–Almaty) are well served by fast trains every day or two. The morning commuter trains from Tashkent to Samarkand and Bukhara are faster than the buses and feature airplane-style seats. There's also a useful overnight Tashkent–Bukhara run. As an indication of journey times, Urgench–Tashkent is 20 hours and Tashkent–Almaty is 25 hours on a fast train.

Elsewhere, connections are drying up as fast as the Aral Sea; few trains run to Dushanbe any more (those that do take a very roundabout route and may require a Turkmen transit visa) and there are no direct lines, for example, between Ashgabat and any other Central Asian capitals.

Many trains to and from Russia can be used for getting around Central Asia, and may be faster and in better condition. But any train originating far from where you are is likely to be filthy, crowded and late by the time you board it.

### Tickets

Book at least two days ahead for CIS connections, if you can. You will probably need to show your passport and visa. A few stations have separate windows for advance bookings and for departures within 24 hours; the latter is generally the one with the heaving mob around it (beware of pickpockets). Many tourist hotels have rail-booking desks (including their own mark-up). Few travel agencies are interested in booking trains.

If you can't get a ticket for a particular train, it's worth turning up anyway. No matter how full ticket clerks insist a train is, there always seem to be spare *kupeyny* (2nd-class or sleeping carriage) berths. Ask an attendant.

A few sample *kupeyny* fares (one-way) from Tashkent are US$18 to Urgench and US$12 to Bukhara. Fares from Almaty include Semey (US$27), Taraz (US$22) and Astana (US$41 or US$73 to US$135 express). A seat on the daytime commuter train costs US$9.70/12 to Samarkand/Bukhara.

# Health

Dr Trish Batchelor

## CONTENTS



Stomach and digestive problems are by far the most common problem faced by visitors to Central Asia. A diet of mutton, bread and *plov* seems to induce diarrhoea and constipation in equal measure!

Since independence, health rates across the region have dropped and many diseases formerly eradicated or controlled in the time of the USSR, such as tuberculosis (TB) and diphtheria, have returned.

Minor risks such as malaria, rabies and encephalitis depend largely upon the location and/or months of travel. More common during the searing summer months is heat exhaustion, so make sure you keep cool and hydrated in the 35°C heat. Most short-term travels to the main tourist areas remain problem-free.

## BEFORE YOU GO

Pack medications in their original, clearly labelled containers. A signed and dated letter from your physician describing your medical conditions and medications (using generic names) is also a good idea. If carrying syringes or needles, be sure to have a physician's letter documenting their medical necessity. If you have a heart condition, bring a copy of your ECG taken just prior to travelling.

If you take any regular medication, bring double your needs in case of loss or theft. In most Central Asian countries you can buy many medications over the counter without a doctor's prescription, but it can be difficult to find some of the newer drugs, particularly the latest antidepressant drugs, blood pressure medications and contraceptive methods.

Make sure you get your teeth checked before you travel – there are few good dentists in

### INTERNET RESOURCES

There is a wealth of travel-health advice on the internet. It's also a good idea to consult your government's travel-health website before departure, if one is available.

- Australia (www.dfat.gov.au/travel/)
- Canada (www.travelhealth.gc.ca)
- New Zealand (www.mfat.govt.nz/travel)
- South Africa (www.dfa.gov.za/consular/travel_advice.htm)
- UK (www.doh.gov.uk/traveladvice/)
- USA (www.cdc.gov/travel/)
- Lonely Planet (www.lonelyplanet.com) – good basic health information
- World Health Organization (WHO; www.who.int/country) – a superb book called *International Travel & Health* is revised annually and available online
- MD Travel Health (www.mdtravelhealth.com) – provides complete travel-health recommendations for every country and is updated daily

Central Asia. If you wear glasses take a spare pair and your prescription.

## INSURANCE

Even if you are fit and healthy, don't travel without health insurance – accidents do happen. Declare any existing medical conditions you have – the insurance company *will* check if your problem is pre-existing and will not cover you if it is undeclared. You may require extra cover for adventure activities such as rock climbing. If you're uninsured, emergency evacuation is expensive – bills of over US$100,000 are not uncommon.

Make sure you keep all documentation related to any medical expenses you incur.

## RECOMMENDED VACCINATIONS

Specialised travel-medicine clinics are your best source of information; they stock all available vaccines and will be able to give specific recommendations for you and your trip. Most vaccines don't produce immunity until at least two weeks after they're given, so visit a doctor four to eight weeks before departure. Ask your doctor for an International Certificate of Vaccination (otherwise known as the yellow booklet), which will list all the vaccinations you've received.

The only vaccine required by international regulations is yellow fever. Proof of vaccination will be required only if you have visited a country in the yellow-fever zone within the six days prior to entering Kazakhstan.

Uzbekistan, Kazakhstan and Kyrgyzstan all require HIV testing if staying more than three months (two months for Uzbekistan). Foreign tests are accepted under certain conditions, but make sure to check with the embassy of your destination before travelling.

### MEDICAL CHECKLIST

Recommended items for a personal medical kit:

- Antifungal cream (eg clotrimazole)
- Antibacterial cream (eg muciprocin)
- Antibiotics for skin infections (eg amoxicillin/clavulanate or cephalexin)
- Antibiotics for diarrhoea (eg norfloxacin, ciprofloxacin or azithromycin for bacterial diarrhoea; tinidazole for giardiasis or amoebic dysentery)
- Antihistamine – there are many options (eg cetrizine for day and promethazine for night)
- Antiseptic (eg Betadine)
- Antispasmodic for stomach cramps (eg Buscopan)
- Decongestant (eg pseudoephedrine)
- DEET-based insect repellent
- Diamox if going to high altitude
- Elastoplasts, bandages, gauze, thermometer (but not mercury), sterile needles and syringes, safety pins and tweezers
- Ibuprofen or another anti-inflammatory
- Indigestion tablets (eg Quick Eze or Mylanta)
- Laxative (eg Coloxyl)
- Oral rehydration solution for diarrhoea (eg Gastrolyte), diarrhoea 'stopper' (eg loperamide) and antinausea medication (eg prochlorperazine)
- Paracetamol
- Permethrin to impregnate clothing and mosquito nets, for some regions, see p477
- Steroid cream for allergic/itchy rashes (eg 1% to 2% hydrocortisone)
- Thrush (vaginal yeast infection) treatment (eg clotrimazole pessaries or Diflucan tablets)
- Ural or equivalent if prone to urine infections

The World Health Organization recommends the following vaccinations for travellers to Central Asia:

**Adult Diphtheria & Tetanus** Single booster recommended if none in the previous 10 years. Side effects include sore arm and fever.

**Hepatitis A** Provides almost 100% protection for up to a year; a booster after 12 months provides at least another 20 years' protection. Mild side-effects such as headache and sore arm occur in 5% to 10% of people.

**Hepatitis B** Now considered routine for most travellers. Given as three shots over six months. A rapid schedule is also available, as is a combined vaccination with hepatitis A. Side effects are mild and uncommon, usually headache and sore arm. In 95% of people lifetime protection results.

**Measles, Mumps and Rubella** Two doses required unless you have had the diseases. Occasionally a rash and flulike illness can develop a week after receiving the vaccine. Many young adults require a booster.

**Polio** In 2002 only Uzbekistan reported cases of polio. Only one booster is required as an adult for lifetime protection.

**Typhoid** Recommended unless your trip is for less than a week. The vaccine offers around 70% protection, lasts for two to three years and comes as a single shot. Tablets are also available; however, the injection is usually recommended as it has fewer side-effects. Sore arm and fever may occur.

**Varicella** If you haven't had chickenpox discuss this vaccination with your doctor.

These immunisations are recommended for long-term travellers (more than one month) or those at special risk:

**Meningitis** Recommended for long-term backpackers aged under 25.

**Rabies** Side effects are rare – occasionally headache and sore arm.

**Tick-borne Encephalitis** (Kyrgyzstan, Uzbekistan) Sore arm and headache are the most common side effects.

**Tuberculosis** Adult long-term travellers are usually recommended to have a TB skin test before and after travel, rather than vaccination.

## FURTHER READING

Lonely Planet's *Healthy Travel – Asia & India* is a handy pocket size and packed with useful information, including pretrip planning, emergency first aid, immunisation and disease information, and what to do if you get sick on the road. Other recommended references include *Traveller's Health* by Dr Richard Dawood and *Travelling Well* by Dr Deborah Mills – check out the website (www.travellingwell.com.au).

# IN TRANSIT

## DEEP VEIN THROMBOSIS (DVT)

Deep vein thrombosis (DVT) occurs when blood clots form in the legs during plane flights, chiefly because of prolonged immobility. Though most blood clots are reabsorbed uneventfully, some may break off and travel through the blood vessels to the lungs, where they can cause life-threatening complications.

The chief symptom of DVT is swelling or pain of the foot, ankle or calf, usually but not always on just one side. When a blood clot travels to the lungs, it may cause chest pain and difficulty in breathing. Travellers with any of these symptoms should immediately seek medical attention.

To prevent the development of DVT on long flights, you should walk about the cabin, perform isometric compressions of the leg muscles (ie contract the leg muscles while sitting), drink plenty of fluids, and avoid alcohol and tobacco.

## JET LAG & MOTION SICKNESS

Jet lag is common when crossing more than five time zones; it results in insomnia, fatigue, malaise or nausea. To avoid jet lag try drinking plenty of fluids (nonalcoholic) and eating light meals. Upon arrival, seek exposure to natural sunlight and readjust your schedule (for meals, sleep etc) as soon as possible.

Antihistamines such as dimenhydrinate (Dramamine), promethazine (Phenergan) and meclizine (Antivert, Bonine) are usually the first choice for treating motion sickness. Their main side effect is drowsiness. A herbal alternative is ginger, which works like a charm for some people.

# IN CENTRAL ASIA

## AVAILABILITY OF HEALTH CARE

Health care throughout Central Asia is basic at best. Any serious problems will require evacuation. The clinics listed in the relevant country chapters can provide basic care and may be able to organise evacuation if necessary. In Central Asia a pharmacist is known as an *apoteka* in Russian or *dorikhana* in Turkic. Clinics are widely known as *polikliniks*.

Self-treatment may be appropriate if your problem is minor (eg travellers' diarrhoea), you are carrying the relevant medication and you cannot attend a recommended clinic. If you think you may have a serious disease, especially malaria, travel to the nearest quality facility immediately to receive attention. It is always better to be assessed by a doctor than to rely on self-treatment.

Buying medication over the counter is not recommended, as fake medications and poorly stored or out-of-date drugs are common.

To find the nearest reliable medical facility, contact your insurance company, your embassy or a top-end hotel.

## INFECTIOUS DISEASES

### Brucellosis

Risk: Kazakhstan, Kyrgyzstan, Tajikistan, Uzbekistan, Turkmenistan. It is rare in travellers but common in the local population, it's transmitted via unpasteurised dairy products. Common symptoms include fever, chills, headache, loss of appetite and joint pains.

### Hepatitis A

Risk: all countries. A problem throughout the region, this food- and waterborne virus infects the liver, causing jaundice (yellow skin and eyes), nausea and lethargy. There is no specific treatment for hepatitis A, you just need to allow time for the liver to heal. All travellers to Central Asia should be vaccinated.

### Hepatitis B

Risk: all countries. The only sexually transmitted disease that can be prevented by vaccination, hepatitis B is spread by contact with infected body fluids, including via sexual contact. The long-term consequences can include liver cancer and cirrhosis.

### HIV

Risk: all countries. HIV is transmitted via contaminated body fluids. Avoid unprotected sex, blood transfusions and injections (unless you can see a clean needle being used) in Central Asia.

### Influenza

Risk: all countries. Present particularly in the winter months, symptoms of the flu include high fever, muscle aches, runny nose, cough and sore throat. Vaccination is recommended for those over the age of 65 or with underlying medical conditions such as heart disease or diabetes. There is no specific treatment, just rest and painkillers.

### Leishmaniasis

Risk: Kazakhstan, Turkmenistan, Uzbekistan. This sandfly-borne parasite is very rare in travellers but common in the local population. There are two forms of the disease – one which only affects the skin (causing a chronic ulcer) and one affecting the internal organs. Avoid sandfly bites by following insect avoidance guidelines.

### Malaria

Risk: southern Tajikistan, southeastern Turkmenistan and far southern Uzbekistan; only present in the extreme south in the warmer summer months (June to October). Malaria is caused by a parasite transmitted by the bite of an infected mosquito. The most important symptom of malaria is fever, but general symptoms such as headache, diarrhoea, cough or chills may also occur. Diagnosis can be made only by taking a blood sample.

Two strategies should be combined to prevent malaria – general mosquito/insect avoidance and antimalaria medications. Before you travel, it is essential you seek medical advice on the right medication and dosage. In general, Chloroquine is recommended for Turkmenistan and southern Uzbekistan. Some resistance to Chloroquine is reported in southern Tajikistan (mainly Khatlon province), so get your doctor's advice on whether to take Chloroquine, Larium (Mefloquine), Doxycycline or Malarone. See the World Malaria Risk Chart (www.iamat.org/pdf/worldmalariarisk.pdf) for detailed information.

To prevent mosquito bites, travellers are advised to take the following steps:

- Use a DEET-containing insect repellent on exposed skin. Natural repellents such as citronella can be effective, but must be applied more frequently than products containing DEET.
- Sleep under a mosquito net impregnated with permethrin.
- Choose accommodation with screens and fans (if not air-conditioned).
- Impregnate clothing with permethrin in high-risk areas.
- Wear long sleeves and trousers in light colours.
- Use mosquito coils.
- Spray your room with insect repellent before going out for your evening meal.

HEALTH

### Rabies

Risk: all countries. Still a common problem in most parts of Central Asia, this uniformly fatal disease is spread by the bite or lick of an infected animal – most commonly a dog. Having a pretravel vaccination means the postbite treatment is greatly simplified. If an animal bites you, gently wash the wound with soap and water, and apply iodine-based antiseptic. If you are not vaccinated you will need to receive rabies immunoglobulin as soon as possible and seek medical advice.

### STDs

Risk: all countries. Sexually transmitted diseases most common in Central Asia include herpes, genital warts, syphilis, gonorrhoea and chlamydia. People carrying these diseases often have no signs of infection. Condoms will prevent gonorrhoea and chlamydia but not warts or herpes. If after a sexual encounter you develop any rash, lumps, discharge or pain when passing urine seek immediate medical attention. If you have been sexually active during your travels, have an STD check upon your return.

### Tuberculosis (TB)

Risk: all countries. Medical and aid workers, and long-term travellers who have significant contact with the local population should take precautions against TB. Vaccination is usually given only to children under the age of five, but adults at risk are recommended pre- and post-travel TB testing. The main symptoms are fever, cough, weight loss, night sweats and tiredness.

### Typhoid

Risk: all countries. This serious bacterial infection is spread via food and water. It gives a high and slowly progressive fever and headache, and may be accompanied by a dry cough and stomach pain. Be aware that vaccination is not 100% effective so you must still be careful what you eat and drink. Dushanbe had typhoid outbreaks in 2003 and 2004.

### Travellers' Diarrhoea

Travellers' diarrhoea is defined as the passage of more than three watery bowel actions within 24 hours, plus at least one other symptom, such as fever, cramps, nausea, vomiting or feeling generally unwell. It is by far the most common problem affecting travellers – between 30% and 50% of people will suffer from it within two weeks of starting their trip.

Travellers' diarrhoea is caused by a bacterium and, in most cases, treatment consists of staying well hydrated; rehydration solutions such as Gastrolyte are the best for this. It responds promptly to treatment with antibiotics such as norfloxacin, ciprofloxacin or azithromycin. Loperamide is just a 'stopper' and doesn't get to the cause of the problem. It can be helpful, for example, if you have to go on a long bus ride. Don't take loperamide if you have a fever, or blood in your stools. Seek medical attention quickly if you do not respond to an appropriate antibiotic.

### Amoebic Dysentery

Amoebic dysentery is actually rare in travellers but is often misdiagnosed. Symptoms are similar to bacterial diarrhoea, ie fever, bloody diarrhoea and generally feeling unwell. You should always seek reliable medical care if you have blood in your diarrhoea. Treatment involves two drugs: Tinidazole or Metroniadzole to kill the parasite in your gut, and a second drug to kill the cysts. If left untreated, complications such as liver or gut abscesses can occur.

### Giardiasis

Giardia is a parasite that is relatively common in travellers. Symptoms include nausea, bloating, excess gas, fatigue and intermittent diarrhoea. 'Eggy' burps are often attributed solely to giardia, but research in Nepal has shown that they are not specific to giardia. The parasite will eventually go away if left untreated, but this can take months. The treatment of choice is tinidazole; metronidazole is a second option.

### Other Diseases

Kazakhstan occasionally reports outbreaks of human plague in the far west. Outbreaks are often caused by eating diseased meat but are also transmitted by the bites of rodent and marmot fleas. There were also isolated outbreaks of anthrax in south Kazakhstan in 2000.

Crimean-Congo Haemorragic Fever is a severe viral illness characterised by the sudden onset of intense fever, headache, aching limbs, bleeding gums and sometimes a rash of red dots on the skin, a week or two after being bitten by an infected tick. Though not all ticks are infected, it's a minor risk for trekkers and campers in Central Asia during the summer months. Insect repellent will help keep the blighters off you.

## ENVIRONMENTAL HAZARDS

### Altitude Sickness

This is a particular problem in high-altitude regions of Kazakhstan, Kyrgyzstan and Tajikistan. With motorable roads (such as the Pamir Hwy) climbing passes of over 4000m, it's a problem not just restricted to trekkers.

Altitude sickness may develop in those who ascend rapidly to altitudes greater than 2500m. Being physically fit offers no protection. Risk increases with faster ascents, higher altitudes and greater exertion. Symptoms may include headaches, nausea, vomiting, dizziness, malaise, insomnia and loss of appetite. Severe cases may be complicated by fluid in the lungs or swelling of the brain.

To protect yourself against altitude sickness, take 125mg or 250mg of acetazolamide (Diamox) twice or three times daily, starting 24 hours before ascent and continuing for 48 hours after arrival at altitude. Possible side effects include increased urinary volume, numbness, tingling, drowsiness, nausea, myopia and temporary impotence. Acetazolamide should not be given to pregnant women or anyone with a history of sulfa allergy. For those who cannot tolerate acetazolamide, the next best option is 4mg of dexamethasone taken four times daily. Unlike acetazolamide, dexamethasone must be tapered gradually upon arrival at altitude. Dexamethasone is a steroid, so it should not be given to diabetics or anyone for whom steroids are contraindicated. A natural alternative is gingko.

When travelling to high altitudes, avoid overexertion, eat light meals, drink lots of fluids and abstain from alcohol. If your symptoms are more than mild or don't resolve promptly, see a doctor.

The Murgab Ecotourism Association (META; see p388) in Tajikistan's eastern Pamirs has a hyperbaric chamber in case of altitude-related emergencies.

### Food

Eating in restaurants is the biggest risk factor for contracting travellers' diarrhoea. Ways to avoid it include eating only freshly cooked food, avoiding food that has been sitting around in buffets, and eating in busy restaurants with a high turnover of customers. Peel all fruit, cook vegetables and soak salads in iodine water for at least 20 minutes.

### Insect Bites & Stings

Bedbugs don't carry disease but their bites are very itchy. They live in the cracks of furniture and walls, and then migrate to the bed at night to feed on you. You can treat the itch with an antihistamine.

Lice inhabit various parts of your body but most commonly your head and pubic area. Transmission is via close contact with an infected person. They can be difficult to treat and you may need numerous applications of an anti-lice shampoo such as permethrin. Pubic lice are usually contracted from sexual contact.

Ticks (*kleshch* in Russian) are contracted after walking in rural areas. They are commonly found behind the ears, on the belly and in the armpits. If you have had a tick bite and experience symptoms such as a rash at the site of the bite or elsewhere, fever or muscle aches, you should see a doctor. Doxycycline prevents tick-borne diseases.

Anyone with a serious bee or wasp allergy should carry an injection of adrenaline (eg an Epipen) for emergency treatment. For others, apply ice to the sting and take painkillers.

#### DRINKING WATER

- Never drink tap water, especially in Karakalpakstan, Khorezm, Dushanbe and remoter Kazakhstan
- Bottled water is generally safe – check the seal is intact at purchase.
- Avoid ice.
- Avoid fresh juices – they may have been watered down.
- Boiling water is the most efficient method of purifying it.
- The best chemical purifier is iodine. It should not be used by pregnant women or those with thyroid problems.
- Water filters should also filter out viruses. Ensure your filter has a chemical barrier such as iodine and a small pore size, eg less than four microns.

### Skin Problems

Take meticulous care of any cuts and scratches to prevent complications such as abscesses. Immediately wash all wounds in clean water and apply antiseptic. If you develop signs of infection (increasing pain and redness) see a doctor.

### Sunburn

Even on a cloudy day sunburn can occur rapidly, especially at high altitudes. Always use a strong sunscreen (at least factor 30), and always wear a wide-brimmed hat and sunglasses outdoors. If you become sunburnt stay out of the sun until you have recovered, apply cool compresses and take painkillers for the discomfort. One percent hydrocortisone cream applied twice daily is also helpful.

## WOMEN'S HEALTH

Supplies of sanitary products may not be readily available in rural areas. Birth control options may be limited so bring adequate supplies of your own form of contraception.

Heat, humidity and antibiotics can all contribute to thrush. Treatment is with anti-fungal creams and pessaries such as clotrimazole. A practical alternative is a single tablet of fluconazole (Diflucan). Urinary tract infections can be precipitated by dehydration or long bus journeys without toilet stops; bring suitable antibiotics.

# Language

## CONTENTS



Central Asia is a multilingual area, and so this chapter includes words and phrases from six different languages that you may find useful. The official languages of the former Soviet Central Asian countries are Kazakh, Kyrgyz, Tajik, Turkmen and Uzbek, but Russian is still the language of government and academia (rather like English in India). Therefore the one language most useful for a visitor is still Russian; you'll find that it's the second language for most adults, who were taught it in school. A few words of the local language will nonetheless give a disproportionate return in goodwill. At home, educated people normally speak a mishmash of Russian and their native tongue.

Learning the Russian Cyrillic alphabet is a very good idea, as most of the Cyrillic-based alphabets of Central Asia will then be familiar as well (see The Russian Cyrillic Alphabet on p482 and Non-Russian Cyrillic Letters on p484).

Learning to count in local languages will allow you to listen in on discussions of prices in the markets. In public it's now often worthwhile letting non-Russians know in advance that you're not Russian, either by saying so or by starting out in English.

For a comprehensive guide to Russian, get a copy of Lonely Planet's *Russian Phrasebook*. For an excellent guide to the other languages of Central Asia, get a copy of Lonely Planet's *Central Asia Phrasebook*.

## RUSSIAN

Two words you're sure to use during your travels are здравствуйте *(zdrastvuyte)*, the universal 'hello' (but if you say it a second time in one day to the same person, they'll think you forgot you already saw them!), and пожалуйста *(pazhalsta)*, the multipurpose word for 'please' (commonly used with all polite requests), 'you're welcome', 'pardon me', 'after you' and more.

The easiest way to turn a statement into a question is just to use a rising tone and a questioning look, or follow it with *da?*, eg 'Is this Moscow?', Это Москва, да? *(eta maskva da?)*. A sentence is made negative by putting не *(ni)* before its main word, eg 'This is not Moscow', Это не Москва? *(eta ni maskva)*.

Two letters have no sound, but modify others. A consonant followed by the 'soft sign' **ь** is spoken with the tongue flat against the palate, as if followed by the faint beginnings of a 'y'. The rare 'hard sign' **ъ** after a consonant inserts a slight pause before the next vowel.

### Greetings & Civilities

**Hello.**
*zdrast*·vuy·te — Здравствуйте.

**Goodbye.**
da svi·*da*·ni·ya — До свидания.

**How are you?**
kak di·*la*? — Как дела?

**I'm well.**
kha·ra·*sho* — Хорошо.

**Yes/No.**
da/net — Да/Нет.

**good/OK**
kha·ra·*sho* — хорошо

**bad**
*plo*·kha — плохо

**Thank you (very much).**
(bal'*sho*·ye) spa·*si*·ba — (Большое) Спасибо.

**What's your name?**
kak vas za·*vut*? — Как вас зовут?

**My name is ...**
mi·*nya za*·vut ... — Меня зовут ...

**Where are you from?**
at·*ku*·da vy? — Откуда вы?

**Australia**
af·*stra*·li·ya — Австралия

**Canada**
ka·*na*·da — Канада

| | |
|---|---|
| **France** | |
| *fran*·tsi·ya | Франция |
| **Germany** | |
| ger·*ma*·ni·ya | Германия |
| **Ireland** | |
| ir·*lan*·di·ya | Ирландия |
| **New Zealand** | |
| *no*·va·ya ze·*lan*·di·ya | Новая Зеландия |
| **the UK (Great Britain)** | |
| ve·li·ka·bri·*ta*·ni·ya | Великобритания |
| **the USA** | |
| se she a/a·*me*·ri·ka | США/Америка |

## Language Difficulties

| | |
|---|---|
| **I don't speak Russian.** | |
| ya ni ga·va·*ryu* pa *ru*·ski | Я не говорю по-русски. |
| **I don't understand.** | |
| ya ni pa·ni·*ma*·yu | Я не понимаю. |
| **Do you speak English?** | |
| vy ga·va·*ri*·te pa ang·*liy*·ski? | Вы говорите по-английски? |
| **Could you write it down, please?** | |
| za·pi·*shi*·te pa·*zhal*·sta | Запишите пожалуйста. |

## Transport & Travel

To get off a *marshutnoe* minibus say *astanavitye pazhalsta.*

| | |
|---|---|
| **Where is ...?** | |
| gde ...? | Где ...? |
| **When does it leave?** | |
| kag·da at·prav·*lya*·et·sya? | Когда отправляется? |
| **What town is this?** | |
| ka·*koy* e·ta *go*·rat? | Какой это город? |
| **How much is a room?** | |
| *skol'*·ka *sto*·it *no*·mer? | Сколько стоит номер? |

| | |
|---|---|
| **airport** | |
| ae·ra·*port* | аэропорт |
| **bus** | |
| af·*to*·bus | автобус |
| **hotel** | |
| gas·*ti*·ni·tsa | гостиница |
| **railway station** | |
| zhi·lez·na da·*rozh*·nyy vag·*zal* | железно дорожный вокзал (abbr. ж. д.) |
| **square/plaza** | |
| *plo*·shchat' | площадь (abbr. пл.) |
| **street** | |
| *u*·li·tsa | улица (abbr. ул.) |
| **toilet** | |
| tua·*let* | туалет |
| **train** | |
| *poy*·ezt | поезд |



**THE RUSSIAN CYRILLIC ALPHABET**

| Cyrillic | Roman | Pronunciation |
|---|---|---|
| А, а | a | as the 'a' in 'father' (in stressed syllable); as the 'a' in 'ago' (in unstressed syllable) |
| Б, б | b | as the 'b' in 'but' |
| В, в | v | as the 'v' in 'van' |
| Г, г | g | as the 'g' in 'god' |
| Д, д | d | as the 'd' in 'dog' |
| Е, е * | e | as the 'ye' in 'yet' (in stressed syllable); as the 'yi' in 'yin' (in unstressed syllable) |
| Ё, ё ** | yo | as the 'yo' in 'yore' |
| Ж, ж | zh | as the 's' in 'measure' |
| З, з | z | as the 'z' in 'zoo' |
| И, и | i | as the 'ee' in 'meet' |
| Й, й | y | as the 'y' in 'boy' |
| К, к | k | as the 'k' in 'kind' |
| Л, л | l | as the 'l' in 'lamp' |
| М, м | m | as the 'm' in 'mad' |
| Н, н | n | as the 'n' in 'not' |
| О, о | o | as the 'o' in 'more' (in stessed syllable); as the 'a' in 'hard' (in unstressed syllable) |
| П, п | p | as the 'p' in 'pig' |
| Р, р | r | as the 'r' in 'rub' (rolled) |
| С, с | s | as the 's' in 'sing' |
| Т, т | t | as the 't' in 'ten' |
| У, у | u | as the 'oo' in 'fool' |
| Ф, ф | f | as the 'f' in 'fan' |
| Х, х | kh | as the 'ch' in 'Bach' |
| Ц, ц | ts | as the 'ts' in 'bits' |
| Ч, ч | ch | as the 'ch' in 'chin' |
| Ш, ш | sh | as the 'sh' in 'shop' |
| Щ, щ | shch | as 'sh-ch' in 'fresh chips' |
| Ъ, ъ | | 'hard sign' (see p481) |
| Ы, ы | y | as the 'i' in 'ill' |
| Ь, ь | ' | 'soft sign'; (see p481) |
| Э, э | e | as the 'e' in 'end' |
| Ю, ю | yu | as the 'u' in 'use' |
| Я, я | ya | as the 'ya' in 'yard' (in stressed syllable); as the 'ye' in 'yearn' (in unstressed syllable) |

*** Е, е** are transliterated *ye* when at the beginning of a word

**** Ё, ё** are often printed without dots

## Money & Shopping

| | |
|---|---|
| **How much is it?** | |
| *skol'*ka *sto*·it? | Сколько стоит? |
| **Do you have ...?** | |
| u vas est' ...? | У вас есть ...? |
| **bookshop** | |
| *knizh*·nyy ma·ga·*zin* | книжный магазин |
| **currency exchange** | |
| ab·*men* val·*yu*·ty | обмен валюты |

### Emergencies – Russian

**I need a doctor.**
mne *nu*·zhin vrach — Мне нужен врач.
**hospital**
bal'*ni*·tsa — больница
**police**
mi·*li*·tsi·ya — милиция
**Fire!**
pa·*zhar*! — Пожар!
**Help!**
na *po*·mashch'!/ pa·ma·*gi*·ti! — На помощь!/ Помогите!
**Thief!**
vor! — Вор!

**market**
*ry*·nak — рынок
**money**
*den'*gi — деньги
**pharmacy**
ap·*te*·ka — аптека
**shop**
ma·ga·*zin* — магазин

### Time & Days

Dates are given as day-month-year, with the month usually in Roman numerals. Days of the week are often represented by numbers in timetables; Monday is 1.

| | | |
|---|---|---|
| **When?** | kag·*da*? | Когда? |
| **today** | si·*vod*·nya | сегодня |
| **yesterday** | vchi·*ra* | вчера |
| **tomorrow** | *zaf*·tra | завтра |

| | | |
|---|---|---|
| **Monday** | pa·ni·*del'*nik | понедельник |
| **Tuesday** | *ftor*·nik | вторник |
| **Wednesday** | sri·*da* | среда |
| **Thursday** | chit·*verk* | четверг |
| **Friday** | *pyat*·ni·tsa | пятница |
| **Saturday** | su·*bo*·ta | суббота |
| **Sunday** | vas·kri·*sen'*e | воскресенье |

### Numbers

**How many?** *skol'*ka? — Сколько?

| | | |
|---|---|---|
| **0** | nol' | ноль |
| **1** | a·*din* | один |
| **2** | dva | два |
| **3** | tri | три |
| **4** | chi·*ty*·ri | четыре |
| **5** | pyat' | пять |
| **6** | shest' | шесть |
| **7** | sem' | семь |
| **8** | *vo*·sim' | восемь |
| **9** | *de*·vit' | девять |
| **10** | *de*·sit' | десять |
| **20** | *dva*·tsat' | двадцать |
| **30** | *tri*·tsat' | тридцать |
| **40** | *so*·rak | сорок |
| **50** | pyat'di·*syat* | пятьдесят |
| **60** | shest'di·*syat* | шестьдесят |
| **70** | sem'di·*syat* | семьдесят |
| **80** | vo·sim·di·*syat* | восемьдесят |
| **90** | di·vya·*no*·sta | девяносто |
| **100** | sto | сто |
| **1000** | *ty*·sya·cha | тысяча |

## KAZAKH

Kazakh is a Turkic language. Since 1940 it has been written in a 42-letter version of the Cyrillic alphabet (see p482 and p484). At least as many people in Kazakhstan speak Russian as Kazakh. Any political tension over language issues has been rather neatly sidestepped by making Kazakh the official state language, but permitting the predominant language in local regions to be used in written government business, and giving Russian national language status as 'language of interethnic communication'.

Russian is the first language for some urban Kazakhs as well as the large Russian minority who form about 35% of the population. Few people speak English or other Western languages, but many of those who do tend to work in the tourist industry or with foreigners.

Street signs are sometimes in Kazakh, sometimes in Russian, sometimes in both. In this book we use the language you're most likely to come across in each town.

### Kazakh Basics

| | |
|---|---|
| **Peace be with you.** | *assalamu aleykum* |
| **And peace with you.** (response) | *waghaleykum ussalam* |
| **Hello.** | *salamatsyz be* |
| **Goodbye.** | *qosh-sau bolyngdar* |
| **Thank you.** | *rakhmet* |
| **Yes/No.** | *ia/zhoq* |
| **How are you?** | *khal zhagh dayyngyz qalay?* |
| **I'm well.** | *zhaqsy* |
| **Do you speak English?** | *aghylshynsa bilesiz be?* |
| **I don't understand.** | *tusinbeymin* |
| **Where is...?** | *... qayda?* |
| **How much?** | *qansha?* |

LANGUAGE

**NON-RUSSIAN CYRILLIC LETTERS**

| Cyrillic | Roman | Pronunciation |
|---|---|---|
| **Kazakh** | | |
| Ә, ә | a | as the 'a' in 'man' |
| Ғ, ғ | gh | as the 'gh' in 'ugh' |
| Қ, қ | q | a guttural 'k' |
| Ң, ң | n | as the 'ng' in 'sing' |
| Ө, ө | ö | as the 'u' in 'fur' |
| Ұ, ұ | u | as the 'u' in 'full' |
| Ү, ү | ü | as the 'oo' in 'fool' |
| Һ, һ | h | as the 'h' in 'hat' |
| І, і | i | as the 'i' in 'ill' |
| **Tajik** | | |
| Ғ, ғ | gh | as the 'gh' in 'ugh' |
| Ӣ, ӣ | ee | as the 'ee' in 'fee' |
| Қ, қ | q | as the 'k' in 'keen' |
| Ӯ, ӯ | ö | as the 'u' in 'fur' |
| Ҳ, ҳ | kh | as the 'h' in 'hat' |
| Ҷ, ҷ | j | as 'j' in 'jig' |
| **Uzbek** | | |
| Ғ, ғ | gh | as the 'gh' in 'ugh' |
| Қ, қ | q | a guttural 'k' |
| Ў, ў | u | as the 'oo' in 'book' |
| Ҳ, ҳ | kh | as the 'ch' in 'Bach' |
| **Kyrgyz** | | |
| Ң, ң | ng | as the 'ng' in 'sing' |
| Ө, ө | ö | as the 'u' in 'fur' |
| Ү, ү | ü | as the 'ew' in 'few' |



**airport** *aeroport*
**bus station** *avtobus vokzal*
**doctor** *dariger*
**friend** *dos*
**hospital** *aurukhana*
**hotel** *qonaq uy/meymankhana*
**police** *militsia*
**restaurant** *restoran*
**toilet** *azhetkhana*
**train station** *temir zhol vokzal*

**bad** *zhaman*
**boiled water** *qaynaghan su*
**bread** *nan*
**expensive** *qymbat*
**good** *zhaqsy*
**meat** *yet*
**rice** *kurish*
**tea** *shay*

**Monday** *duysenbi*
**Tuesday** *seysenbi*
**Wednesday** *sarsenbi*
**Thursday** *beysenbi*
**Friday** *zhuma*
**Saturday** *senbi*
**Sunday** *zheksenbi*

**1** *bir*
**2** *yeki*
**3** *ush*
**4** *tört*
**5** *bes*
**6** *alty*
**7** *etti*
**8** *sakkiz*
**9** *toghyz*
**10** *on*
**100** *zhus*
**1000** *myng*

## KYRGYZ

Kyrgyz is a Turkic language that has been written using a Cyrillic script since the early 1940s (see p482 and the boxed text opposite). Along with neighbouring countries Uzbekistan and Turkmenistan, Kyrgyzstan is in the process of changing over to a modified Roman alphabet. While international Roman letters have already been adopted for vehicle number plates, Kyrgyzstan is the slowest of these three countries in implementing the change from a Cyrillic to a Roman alphabet.

In 2000 the government afforded Russian official-language status, but there is currently also a strong push to promote Kyrgyz as the predominant language of government, media and education. It's a move not without its detractors, who see it as a politically motivated means of discriminating against non-Kyrgyz–speaking minorities.

### Kyrgyz Basics

**Peace be with you.** *asalamu aleykom*
**And peace with you.** (response) *wa aleykum assalam*
**Hello.** *salam*
**Goodbye.** *jakshy kalyngydzar*
**Thank you.** *rakhmat*
**Yes/No.** *ooba/jok*
**How are you?** *jakshysüzbü?*
**I'm well.** *jakshy*
**Do you speak English?** *siz angliyscha süylöy süzbü?*
**I don't understand.** *men tüshümböy jatamyn*
**Where is ...?** *... kayda?*
**How much?** *kancha?*

| | |
|---|---|
| **airport** | *aeroport* |
| **bus station** | *avtobiket* |
| **doctor** | *doktur* |
| **friend** | *dos* |
| **hospital** | *oruukana* |
| **hotel** | *meymankana* |
| **police** | *militsia* |
| **restaurant** | *restoran* |
| **toilet** | *darakana* |
| **train station** | *temir jol vokzal* |

| | |
|---|---|
| **bad** | *jaman* |
| **boiled water** | *kaynatilgan suu* |
| **bread** | *nan* |
| **expensive** | *kymbat* |
| **good** | *jakshy* |
| **meat** | *et* |
| **rice** | *kürüch* |
| **tea** | *chay* |

| | |
|---|---|
| **Monday** | *düshömbü* |
| **Tuesday** | *seyshembi* |
| **Wednesday** | *sharshembi* |
| **Thursday** | *beishembi* |
| **Friday** | *juma* |
| **Saturday** | *ishembi* |
| **Sunday** | *jekshembi* |

| | |
|---|---|
| **1** | *bir* |
| **2** | *eki* |
| **3** | *üch* |
| **4** | *tört* |
| **5** | *besh* |
| **6** | *alty* |
| **7** | *jety* |
| **8** | *segiz* |
| **9** | *toguz* |
| **10** | *on* |
| **100** | *jüz* |
| **1000** | *ming* |

## TAJIK

Tajik, the state language of Tajikistan since 1989, belongs to the southwest Persian group of languages and is closely related to Dari (the principal language of Afghanistan) and Farsi (the language of Iran). This sets it apart from all the other Central Asian languages which are Turkic in origin. Tajik was formerly written in a modified Arabic script (similar to the Farsi alphabet) and then in Roman, but since 1940 a modified Cyrillic script has been used (see p482 and p484).

In Dushanbe most people speak Tajik and Russian. Uzbek is also spoken by a significant percentage of the population.

### Tajik Basics

| | |
|---|---|
| **Peace be with you.** | *assalomu aleykum* |
| **And peace with you.** (response) | *valeykum assalom* |
| **Hello.** | *salom* |
| **Goodbye.** | *khayr naboshad* |
| **Thank you.** | *rakhmat/teshakkur* |
| **Yes/No.** | *kha/ne* |
| **How are you?** | *naghzmi shumo?* |
| **I'm well.** | *mannaghz* |
| **Do you speak English?** | *anglisi meydonet?* |
| **I don't understand.** | *man manefakhmam* |
| **Where is ...?** | *... khujo ast?* |
| **How much?** | *chand pul?* |

| | |
|---|---|
| **airport** | *furudgoh* |
| **bus station** | *istgoh* |
| **doctor** | *duhtur* |
| **friend** | *doost* |
| **hospital** | *bemorhona/kasalhona* |
| **hotel** | *mekhmon'hona* |
| **police** | *militsia* |
| **restaurant** | *restoran* |
| **toilet** | *khojat'hona* |
| **train station** | *istgoh rohi ohan* |

| | |
|---|---|
| **bad** | *ganda* |
| **boiled water** | *obi jush* |
| **bread** | *non* |
| **expensive** | *qimmat* |
| **good** | *khub/naghz* |
| **meat** | *gusht* |
| **rice** | *birinj* |
| **tea** | *choy* |

| | |
|---|---|
| **Monday** | *dushanbe* |
| **Tuesday** | *seshanbe* |
| **Wednesday** | *chorshanbe* |
| **Thursday** | *panjanbe* |
| **Friday** | *juma* |
| **Saturday** | *shanbe* |
| **Sunday** | *yakshanbe* |

| | |
|---|---|
| **1** | *yak* |
| **2** | *du* |
| **3** | *seh* |
| **4** | *chor* |
| **5** | *panj* |
| **6** | *shish* |
| **7** | *khaft* |
| **8** | *khasht* |

| | |
|---|---|
| **9** | *nukh* |
| **10** | *dakh* |
| **100** | *sad* |
| **1000** | *khazor* |

## TURKMEN

Turkmen, the state language of Turkmenistan since 1990, has been described as '800-year-old Turkish'. It belongs to the Turkic language family, forming part of the southwestern group together with the Turkish and Azeri (spoken in Azerbaijan). In Turkmenistan virtually everyone speaks Russian and Turkmen (except for Russians, who speak Russian only). English speakers are generally only found in the tourist industry and at some universities.

There's been a significant infiltration of Russian words and phrases into Turkmen, especially in this century (particularly words to do with science and technology). Turkmen conversation is punctuated with Russian, to the extent that sentences may begin in Turkmen, then slip into Russian midway through.

Three different scripts have been used to write Turkmen; Arabic, Roman and Cyrillic. Arabic was the first, though little Turkmen was ever written in it (there's a popular style of calligraphy, often used on monuments, in which Cyrillic script is rendered in such a way that it almost resembles Arabic script). A modified Turkish-Roman alphabet was used until 1940 when the Cyrillic alphabet took over. On 1 January 1996, Turkmen Cyrillic was officially replaced by another modified Roman alphabet called Elipbi, and the changeover to this is complete.

### Turkmen Basics

| | |
|---|---|
| **Peace be with you.** | *salam aleykum* |
| **And peace with you.** (response) | *waleykum assalam* |
| **Hello.** | *salam* |
| **Goodbye.** | *sagh bol* |
| **Thank you.** | *tangyr* |
| **Yes/No.** | *howa/yok* |
| **How are you?** | *siz nahili?* |
| **Fine, and you?** | *onat, a siz?* |
| **I don't understand.** | *men dushenamok* |
| **Do you speak English?** | *siz inglische gepleyarsinizmi?* |
| **Where is ...?** | *... niredeh?* |
| **How much?** | *nyacheh?* |
| **airport** | *aeroport* |
| **bus station** | *durolha* |
| **doctor** | *lukman* |
| **friend** | *dost* |
| **hospital** | *keselkhana* |
| **hotel** | *mikmankhana* |
| **police** | *militsia* |
| **restaurant** | *restoran* |
| **toilet** | *hajat'hana* |
| **train station** | *vokzal* |

| | |
|---|---|
| **bad** | *ervet* |
| **boiled water** | *gaina d'lan su* |
| **bread** | *churek* |
| **expensive** | *gummut* |
| **good** | *yakhsheh* |
| **meat** | *et* |
| **rice** | *tui* |
| **tea** | *chay* |

| | |
|---|---|
| **Monday** | *dushanbe* |
| **Tuesday** | *seshenbe* |
| **Wednesday** | *charshanbe* |
| **Thursday** | *penshenbe* |
| **Friday** | *anna* |
| **Saturday** | *shenbe* |
| **Sunday** | *yekshanbe* |

| | |
|---|---|
| **1** | *bir* |
| **2** | *ikeh* |
| **3** | *uch* |
| **4** | *durt* |
| **5** | *besh* |
| **6** | *alty* |
| **7** | *yed* |
| **8** | *sekiz* |
| **9** | *dokuz* |
| **10** | *on* |
| **100** | *yuz* |
| **1000** | *mun* |

## UZBEK

Uzbekistan's three major languages are Uzbek, Russian and Tajik. Uzbek is the country's official language and, with 15 million speakers, it is the most widely spoken of the non-Slavic languages of all the former Soviet states. It belongs to the Turkic language family.

Uzbek was written in Roman letters from 1918 to 1941. Since then it has used a modified Cyrillic alphabet, but the country is now moving to a Roman alphabet. While the majority of signs are now in Uzbek Latin, there is still sufficient evidence of Cyrillic (including in menus) to make familiarity with it a good idea (see p482 and p484).

## Uzbek Basics

| | |
|---|---|
| **Peace be with you.** | *salom alaykhum* |
| **And peace with you.** (response) | *tinch berling* |
| **Hello.** | *salom* |
| **Goodbye.** | *hayr* |
| **Thank you.** | *rakhmat* |
| **Yes/No.** | *kha/yuk* |
| **How are you?** | *qanday siz?* |
| **Do you speak English?** | *inglizcha bila sizmi?* |
| **Where is ...?** | *... qayerda?* |
| **How much?** | *qancha/nichpul?* |

| | |
|---|---|
| **airport** | *tayyorgokh* |
| **bus station** | *avtobeket* |
| **doctor** | *tabib* |
| **friend** | *urmoq/doost* |
| **hospital** | *kasalhona* |
| **hotel** | *mehmon'hona* |
| **police** | *militsia* |
| **restaurant** | *restoran* |
| **toilet** | *hojat'hona* |
| **train station** | *temir yul vokzali* |

| | |
|---|---|
| **bad** | *yomon* |
| **boiled water** | *qaynatilgan suv* |
| **bread** | *non* |
| **expensive** | *qimmat* |
| **good** | *yakhshi* |
| **meat** | *gusht* |
| **rice** | *guruch* |
| **tea** | *choy* |

| | |
|---|---|
| **Monday** | *dushanba* |
| **Tuesday** | *seyshanba* |
| **Wednesday** | *chorshanba* |
| **Thursday** | *payshanba* |
| **Friday** | *juma* |
| **Saturday** | *shanba* |
| **Sunday** | *yakshanba* |

| | |
|---|---|
| **1** | *bir* |
| **2** | *ikki* |
| **3** | *uch* |
| **4** | *turt* |
| **5** | *besh* |
| **6** | *olti* |
| **7** | *etti* |
| **8** | *sakkiz* |
| **9** | *tuqqiz* |
| **10** | *un* |
| **11** | *un bir* |
| **100** | *yuz* |
| **1000** | *ming* |

**Also available from Lonely Planet:**
***Russian Phrasebook* and *Central Asia Phrasebook***

# Glossary

## ABBREVIATIONS

This glossary contains Arabic (A), Kazakh (Kaz), Kyrgyz (Kyr), Russian (R), Tajik (Taj), general Turkic (T), Turkmen (Tur), Uzbek (U) and English terms you may come across in Central Asia.

**-abad** (T) – suffix meaning 'town of'
**aiwan** – covered portico or vaulted portal
**ak** (T) – white
**ak kalpak** (Kyr) – felt hat worn by Kyrgyz men
**akimat** (T) – regional government office or city hall, also *aqimat*
**aksakal** (T) – revered elder
**akyn** (Kyr) – minstrel, bard
**ala-kiyiz (**Kyr) – felt rug with coloured panels pressed on
**alanghy** (Kaz) – square
**alplager** (R) – mountaineers camp, short for *alpinistskiy lager*
**apparatchik** (R) – bureaucrat
**apteka** (R) – pharmacy
**arashan** (T) – springs
**arenda** (R) – literally 'lease' or 'rent', usually referring to buses that make a trip only if there are enough passengers
**asalam aleykum** (A) – traditional Muslim greeting, meaning 'peace be with you'
**ASSR** – Autonomous Soviet Socialist Republic
**aul** (T) – yurt or herders' camp
**aviakassa** (T) – air ticket office
**avtobus** (R) – bus
**avtostantsia** (R) – bus stop or bus stand
**azan** (A) – Muslim call to prayer

**babushka** (R) – old woman; headscarf worn by Russian peasant women
**balbal** (T) – totemlike stone marker
**banya** (R) – public bath
**basmachi** (R) – literally 'bandits'; Muslim guerrilla fighters who resisted the Bolshevik takeover in Central Asia
**batyr** (Kyr & Kaz) – warrior hero in epics
**beg** (T) – landlord, gentleman; also spelt *bay* or *bek*
**berkutchi** (Kyr) – eagle hunter
**beshbarmak** (Kaz & Kyr) – flat noodles with lamb, horse meat or vegetable broth (served seperately)
**Bi** (Kaz) – honorific Kazakh title given to clan elders
**bishkek** (Kaz & Kyrg) – see *pishpek*
**bosuy** (Kyr) – see *yurt*
**bufet** (R) – snack bar selling cheap cold meats, boiled eggs, salads, breads, pastries etc
**bulvar** (R) – boulevard
**bulvary** (Kyr) – boulevard
**buzkashi** (T) – traditional pololike game played with a headless goat carcass (*buz*)

**caravanserai** – travellers inn
**chabana** (Kyr & Kaz)- cowboy
**chaikhana** (T) – teahouse
**chapan** (U/Taj) – traditional Uzbek/Tajik cloak
**chay** (T) – tea
**chaykhana** (T) – see *chaikhana*
**chong** (T) – big
**chorsu** (T) – market arcade
**choy** (U & Taj) – see *chay*
**choyhona** (T) – see *chaikhana*
**chuchuk** (Kaz) – see *kazy*
**chuchvara** (T) – dumplings
**CIS** – Commonwealth of Independent States; the loose political and economic alliance of most former member republics of the USSR (except the Baltic states); sometimes called *NIS*, for Newly Independent States
**CPK** – Communist Party of Kazakhstan

**dacha** (R) – a holiday bungalow
**dangghyly** (Kaz) – avenue
**darikhana** (Kaz) – pharmacy
**darya** (T) – river
**dastarkhan** (T) – literally 'tablecloth'; feast
**depe** (Tur) – see *tepe*
**dezhurnaya** (R) – floor-lady; the woman attendant on duty on each floor of a Soviet-style hotel
**dom** (R) – building
**dom otdykha** (R) – rest home
**dopy** (U) – black, four-sided skullcap embroidered in white and worn by men; also *dopi*, *doppe* or *doppilar*
**dutar** (T) – two-stringed guitar

**eshon (A)**- *Sufi* leader, also spelt *ishan*

**GAI** (R) – traffic police
**gastronom** (R) – state food shop
**geoglyph** – geometric pattern of stones, often used in astrological observations
**ghanch** (T) – carved and painted plaster
**gillam** (T) – carpet
**glasnost** (R) – 'openness' in government that was one aspect of the Gorbachev reforms
**gorod** (R) – town
**Great Game** – the geopolitical 'Cold War' of territorial expansion between the Russian and British empires in the 19th and early 20th centuries in Central Asia

**Hadith** (A) – collected acts and sayings of the Prophet Mohammed
**haj** (A) – the pilgrimage to Mecca, one of the five pillars of Islam, to be made by devout Muslims at least once during their lifetime
**hakimyat** (Kyr) – municipal administration building
**hammam** (A) – bathhouse
**hammomi** (U) – baths
**hanako** (U) – see *khanaka*
**hauz** (T) – an artificial pool
**hazrat** (A) – honorific title meaning 'majesty' or 'holy'
**Hejira** (A) – flight of the Prophet Mohammed and his followers to Medina in AD 622
**hoja** (U) – lord, master, gentleman (honourific title)

**ikat** (U) – tie-dyed silk
**IMU** – Islamic Movement of Uzbekistan
**IRP** – Islamic Renaissance Party; grouping of radical activists dedicated to the formation of Islamic rule in Central Asia
**Ismaili** (A) – a branch of *Shiite* Islam
**iwan** – see *aiwan*

**jailoo** (Kyr) – summer pasture
**jami masjid** (A) – Friday mosque
**jamoat khana** (Taj) – Ismaili prayer hall and meeting hall
**jihad** (A) – holy war
**jumi** (U) – Friday, see *jami masjid*

**kala** (T) – fortress
**kalon** (Taj) – great
**kara** (T) – black
**kassa** (R) – cashier or ticket office
**kazan** (T) – large cauldron used to cook plov
**kazy** (Kaz) – horse-meat sausage
**-kent** (T) – suffix meaning 'town of'
**khanaka** (A) – a *Sufi* contemplation hall and hostel for wandering ascetics; the room of an *eshon* in which he and other *Sufis* perform their *zikr*
**khanatlas** (U) – see *ikat*
**kino** (R) – cinema; also kinoteatr
**kochasi** (U) – street
**köchösü** (Kyr) – street
**kökör** (T) – *kumys* shaker
**kökpar** (Kaz) – see *buzkashi*
**kok** (T) – blue
**kolkhoz** (R) – collective farm
**köshesi** (Kaz & Karakalpak) – street
**koshk** (U & Tur) – fortress
**koshma** (Kaz) – multicoloured felt mats
**kozha** (Kaz) – see *hoja*
**kumys** (Kaz & Kyr) – fermented mare's milk
**kupeyny** (R) – 2nd-class or sleeping carriage on trains; also *kupe*
**kupkari** (U) – see *buzkashi*
**kurgan** (T) – burial mound
**kurort** (R) – thermal-spring complex
**kurpacha** (U) – colourful sitting mattress for a *tapchan*
**kvartal** (R) – district
**kymys** (Kyr) – see *kumys*
**kyzyl** (T) – red
**kyz-kumay** (Kyr) – traditional game in which a man chases a woman on horseback and tries to kiss her
**kyz-kuu** (Kaz) – see *kyz-kumay*

**laghman** (T) – noodles
**LOI** – letter of invitation
**lux** (R) – deluxe, though often a euphemism

**mahalla** (U) – urban neighbourhood
**Manas** (Kyr) – epic; legendary hero revered by the Kyrgyz
**manaschi** (Kyr) – type of *akyn* who recites from the Kyrgyz cycle of oral legends
**manty** (T) – small stuffed dumplings
**marshrutka** (R & T) – short term for *marshrutnoe and marshrutnyy avtobus*
**marshrutnoe** (R & T)- small bus or van that follows a fixed route but stops on demand to take on or let off passengers, with fares depending on distance travelled
**marshrutny avtobus** (R & T) – large bus that follows a fixed route but stops on demand to take on or let off passengers, with fares depending on distance travelled
**maydoni** (U) – public square
**mazar** (T) – tomb or mausoleum
**medressa** (A) – Islamic academy or seminary
**mihrab** (A) – niche in a mosque marking the direction of Mecca
**mikrorayon** (R) – micro region
**militsia** (R & T) – police
**minor** (T) – minaret
**MSDSP** – Mountain Societies Development Support Project
**muezzin** (A) – man who calls the Muslim faithful to prayer
**mufti** (A) – Islamic legal expert or spiritual leader
**mujaheddin** (A) – Muslim freedom fighter engaged in *jihad*
**mullah** (A) – Islamic cleric

**nan** (T) – flat bread
**Naqshband** – the most influential of many *Sufi* secret associations in Central Asia
**Navrus** (A) – literally 'New Days'; the main Islamic spring festival; has various regional transliterations (Nauroz, Nauryz, Nawruz, Norruz or Novruz)
**non** (U & Taj) – see *nan*

**oblast** (R) – province, region
**oblys** (Kaz) – province, region
**OVIR** (R) – Otdel Vis i Registratsii; Office of Visas and Registration

**pakhta** (T) – cotton
**pakhtakor** (T) – cotton worker
**panjara** (T) – trellis of wood, stone or *ghanch*
**perestroika** (R) – literally 'restructuring'; Gorbachev's efforts to revive the economy
**piala** (T) – bowl
**pishpek** (Kaz & Kyr) – churn for making *kumys*
**pishtak** – monumental entrance portal
**platskartny** (R) – hard sleeper train
**ploshchad** (R) – square
**plov** (T) – a rice dish with meat, carrots or other additions (traditionally prepared by men for special celebrations), also known as pilau
**pochta (R)** – post office
**pol-lux (R)** – semideluxe
**polyclinic** – health centre
**propusk** (R) – military border permit
**prospekt** (R & T) – avenue

**qala** (U) – see *kala*
**qymyz** (Kaz) – see *kumys*
**qyz-quu** (Kaz) – see *kyz-kumay*

**rabab** (T) – six-stringed mandolin, also *rubab*
**rabad** (T) – suburb
**rabat** (T) – caravanserai
**rayon** (R) – district

**samovar** (R) – urn used for heating water for tea, often found on trains
**samsa** (T) – samosa
**sary** (T) – yellow
**şayoli** (Tur) – street
**sharq** (Taj & U) – east
**shashlyk** (T) – meat roasted on skewers over hot coals
**shay** (Kaz) – see *chay*
**shaykhana** (T) – see *chaikhana*
**Shiite** (A) – one of the two main branches of Islam
**shubat** (Kaz & Taj) – fermented camel's milk
**shyrdak** (Kyr) – felt rug with appliquéd coloured panels
**skibaza** (R) – ski base
**SLLPCP** – Sustainable Livelihoods for Livestock Producing Communities Project
**SSR** – Soviet Socialist Republic
**stolovaya** (R) – canteen, cafeteria
**Sufi** (A) – mystical tradition in Islam
**suzani** (U) – bright silk embroidery on cotton cloth

**tapchan** (Taj) – tea bed
**tash** (T) – stone
**tebbetey** (Kyr) – round fur-trimmed hat worn by men
**telpek** (Tur & U) – sheepskin hat worn by men
**tepe** (T) – fort or fortified hill, also *depe*
**tim** (T) – shopping arcade
**toi** (T) – celebration
**Transoxiana** – meaning 'the land beyond the Oxus'; historical term for the region between the Amu-Darya and Syr-Darya rivers
**TsUM** (R) – *Tsentralny universalny magazin*; central department store
**turbaza (R)** – holiday camp typically with Spartan cabins, plain food, sports, video hall and bar, usually open only in summer
**Turkestan** – literally 'the Land of the Turks'; covers Central Asia and Xinjiang (China)

**UAZ** (R) – Russian jeep
**ulak-tartysh** (Kyr) – see *buzkashi*
**ulama** (A) – class of religious scholars or intellectuals
**ulitsa** (R) – street
**umuvalnik** (R) – portable washing basin
**univermag** (R) – universalny magazin; department store
**uulu** (Kyr) – meaning 'son of'

**viloyat** (U) – province
**vodopad** (R) – waterfall
**voksal** (R) – train station

**ylag oyyny** (Karakalpak)- see *buzkashi*
**yurt** – traditional nomadic 'house', a collapsible cylindrical wood framework covered with felt

**zakaznik** (R) – protected area
**zapovednik** (R) – nature reserve
**zhyostky** (R) – hard carriage on trains
**zikr** (A) – recitation or contemplation of the names of God; recitation of sacred writings; one part of traditional *Sufi* practice

# Behind the Scenes

## THIS BOOK

The 1st edition of this book was researched and written by John King, John Noble and Andrew Humphreys. Bradley Mayhew coordinated the 2nd edition. Richard Plunkett and Simon Richmond researched and wrote for that edition. The 3rd edition was again coordinated by Bradley Mayhew, who wrote all the front chapters, as well as Kyrgyzstan and Tajikistan. Also authoring were Michael Kohn (Kazakhstan and Uzbekistan), Paul Clammer (Afghanistan), and our anonymous Turkmenistan author. This 4th edition was yet again coordinated by Bradley Mayhew, who also researched and wrote the Tajikistan chapter, and all the front and back chapters. Other authors for this edition were John Noble (Kazakhstan), Greg Bloom (Uzbekistan), Dean Starnes (Kyrgyzstan), and another anonymous Turkmenistan author. Dr Trish Batchelor wrote the Health chapter. This guidebook was commissioned in Lonely Planet's Melbourne office, and produced by the following:

**Commissioning Editors** Sam Trafford, Tashi Wheeler
**Coordinating Editor** Trent Holden
**Coordinating Cartographer** Valentina Kremenchutskaya
**Coordinating Layout Designer** Katie Thuy Bui
**Managing Editor** Suzannah Shwer
**Managing Cartographer** Shahara Ahmed
**Assisting Editors** Elisa Arduca, Evan Jones, Kate Cody, Kate Evans, Craig Kilburn, Amy Thomas, Jeanette Wall
**Assisting Cartographer** Wayne Murphy
**Assisting Layout Designers** Clara Monitto, Wibowo Rusli, Cara Smith
**Cover Designer** Annika Roojun
**Project Manager** Eoin Dunlevy
**Language Content Coordinator** Quentin Frayne

**Thanks to** Sally Darmody, Carolyn Boicos, Erin Corrigan, Ryan Evans, Kate McDonald, Trent Paton, Averil Roberston, Lyahna Spencer, Celia Wood

### LONELY PLANET: TRAVEL WIDELY, TREAD LIGHTLY, GIVE SUSTAINABLY

#### The Lonely Planet Story

The story begins with a classic travel adventure: Tony and Maureen Wheeler's 1972 journey across Europe and Asia to Australia. There was no useful information about the overland trail then, so Tony and Maureen published the first Lonely Planet guidebook to meet a growing need.

From a kitchen table, Lonely Planet has grown to become the largest independent travel publisher in the world, with offices in Melbourne (Australia), Oakland (USA) and London (UK). Today Lonely Planet guidebooks cover the globe. There is an ever-growing list of books and information in a variety of media. Some things haven't changed. The main aim is still to make it possible for adventurous individuals to get out there – to explore and better understand the world.

#### The Lonely Planet Foundation

The Lonely Planet Foundation proudly supports nimble nonprofit institutions working for change in the world. Each year the foundation donates 5% of Lonely Planet company profits to projects selected by staff and authors. Our partners range from Kabissa, which provides small nonprofits across Africa with access to technology, to the Foundation for Developing Cambodian Orphans, which supports girls at risk of falling victim to sex traffickers.

Our nonprofit partners are linked by a grass-roots approach to the areas of health, education or sustainable tourism. Many projects we support – such as one with BaAka (Pygmy) children in the forested areas of Central African Republic – choose to focus on women and children as one of the most effective ways to support the whole community.

Sometimes foundation assistance is as simple as restoring a local ruin like the Minaret of Jam in Afghanistan; this incredible monument now draws intrepid tourists to the area and its restoration has greatly improved options for local people.

Just as travel is often about learning to see with new eyes, so many of the groups we work with aim to change the way people see themselves and the future for their children and communities.

## THANKS

### BRADLEY MAYHEW

'Awesome' Andre Ticheler was the perfect travel companion for a month in the Pamirs, as he has been in eastern Tibet, Mongolia, Everest and various other ridiculously remote locations across the world. In the words of one breathless Tajik female admirer, 'you are an awesome guy'.

Thanks to Marielle for all her help in Khorog and for showing me the Geisev Valley and to her and Yorali for a great trip up the Bartang Valley. Good luck with all your ecotourism ventures. Christophe Belperron and Ubaidullah were fantastic in Murghab and without them I'd never have got to Shaimak. Our driver, Ergash, was a trooper and didn't even complain when his axle fell off after a 4WD-destroying trip to Bazar-Dara.

Robert Middleton of www.pamirs.org was generous with his information – shame we couldn't travel together this time, Robert, but good luck with your own guidebook.

Rick Allen and Michael Davis of Great Game Travel and David Berghof of StanTours offered professional advice and much help. Lots of people helped with lifts, especially Caroline Glowka and Andre Fabian – thanks, guys. My co-authors on this project were very professional and a joy to work with.

Readers' letters were great, as always, so thanks to the dedicated band of hard-core 'stan travellers who wrote in with tips and advice. Thanks to Louise for detailed notes of her impressive trip.

Thanks as ever to my wife Kelli for holding the fort, repairing the fort and paying the fort's bills while I am away. Love you, honey.

### GREG BLOOM

It would be impossible to cover a place like Uzbekistan without help, and I received plenty, especially from my posse in Tashkent – Robert Gray, Leah Hoffman, Renate Quelle, Kevin Yamami and Gaye Ozyuncu. A special shout out to Gaye for her relentless club-crawling efforts and for storing my stuff. *Spacibo* to Kevin Glass of Tashkent International School for the countless tips and contacts and for babysitting my carpet. No less invaluable were the efforts of my posse in cyberspace – Airat Yuldashev, Murod Nazarov, Saad of Sogda Tours and visa guru David Berghoff – in answering my incessant emails on *Kupkari,* ancient Qurans and the like.

In the regions, thanks go to Andrea Leuenberger and Gulya Gaifull in Bukhara, to Abdulla in Khiva, and to Gulya in Termiz for sticking with me when things got dicey. Thanks to the fellow travellers who shared tips with me along the way, especially Daniel McCrohan and Spencer Harris. Thanks also to Anatoly Ionesov, Andrea Berg, Tim Molyneux, Margaret Shanafield, Komil, Boris Karpov, Denis Vikulov, Charles Rudd and Matteo Mode for their help at various stages of the game.

Thanks to Anna for keeping me sane on deadline, and to Batir and Raushania for making my trip possible.

### JOHN NOBLE

The warmth, hospitality and will to help of so many people in Kazakhstan – both permanent and shorter-term residents – made my research trip something really special. Extra special thanks to: Akylbek (Zhanaozen), Nathan Austin, Svetlana Baskakova, Seamus Bennett, David Berghof, Alex Briggs, Paul Brummel, Jay Chen, Summer Coish, Gregory Costanza, Jena English, Sue Faqueri, Gauhar at VSO, Gulyara in Aktau, Amanda Haase, Michael Hancock, Kaisar (Zhanaozen), Lucy Kelaart, Adam Kennedy, Folke von Knobloch, Zhuldyz Kydyrbaeva, Becky Long, Karla Makatova, Robert Manson, Sabir Mikhalyov and family, Danara Muratbaeva, Hilary Murphy, Criss Norris, Jared Novoseller, Nancy Otieno, Shain Panzer, Charlene Pena, Jessica Robertson, Kristin Ruger, Linda Schmitz, Dana Sadykova, Dorothy Seidel, Vladimir Shakula, Ainur Suleimenova, Akmaral Utemisova, Kazbek Valiev and Elisabeth Wilhelm.

### DEAN STARNES

A heartfelt thanks to all the people who patiently endured my terrible Kyrgyz and Russian, resisting the urge to clamp their hands over their bleeding ears while they tried to make out what I was asking. Special thanks to Daniyar Abdurahmanov of Osh Guesthouse, Nurdan Abdybek uulu of South Guest House and Almaz Kemelov who were tirelessly forthcoming with all manner of travel gems.

Another big thanks to the staff of CBT – Aigul Shabdanbekova, Asylbek Rajiev, Aisha Mambetalieva, Kubat Abdyldaev, Natalia Ovcharova and Tamta Shaburishvili – all of whom went above and beyond the call of duty.

Also in Kyrgyzstan thanks to Asel Karabakirova of Novimad, Marlis Chonorov of Kyrgyz Concept, Ian Claytor of Celestial Mountains and the staff of Mundunz Travel in Osh. Cheers to Maison du Voyageurs out of Bishkek for picking up a cold hitchhiker stranded on the road to Tash Rabat.

Big thanks to fellow travellers Tom Horovitch, Peter Caley, Liron Rosenbaum, Itay Blumenthal, Spencer Harris, Trent Milam, Brenda and Mike Parker, Rhonda Ferns, David Lawlor, Anna Brun-

**SEND US YOUR FEEDBACK**

We love to hear from travellers – your comments keep us on our toes and help make our books better. Our well-travelled team reads every word on what you loved or loathed about this book. Although we cannot reply individually to postal submissions, we always guarantee that your feedback goes straight to the appropriate authors, in time for the next edition. Each person who sends us information is thanked in the next edition – and the most useful submissions are rewarded with a free book. See the Behind the Scenes section.

To send us your updates – and find out about Lonely Planet events, newsletters and travel news – visit our award-winning website: **www.lonelyplanet.com/contact**.

Note: we may edit, reproduce and incorporate your comments in Lonely Planet products such as guidebooks, websites and digital products, so let us know if you don't want your comments reproduced or your name acknowledged. For a copy of our privacy policy, go to www.lonelyplanet.com/privacy.

ninghausen, Andrea Schneider, Tanja Homann, Manfred Grimpe, Anne Wieland, Robyn Garrard, Wilbuy Yen, Scott Reed, Asipa Jumabaeva, Daniel Maselli, Isaac Stone Fish, Michael Pareles and in particular Stephanie Wilkins, who accompanied me on my first jaunt to Central Asia.

It wouldn't be right not to acknowledge the legacy of work from previous editions and the help and assistance from commissioning editor Sam Trafford, coordinating author Bradley Mayhew and managing cartographer Shahara Ahmed.

Finally my biggest thanks are reserved for my family and Debbie who between them make coming home the best part of travelling and leaving the worst.

### TURKMENISTAN AUTHOR

A big thank you to my fellow authors Greg, John and Dean for reams of border and visa info and coordinating author Bradley for bringing it all together. In Turkmenistan, the journey was made all the more pleasurable by the generous Turkmen and expats who shared their stories. I dedicate this to you.

## OUR READERS

**Many thanks to the travellers who used the last edition and wrote to us with helpful hints, useful advice and interesting anecdotes:**

**A** Jon Abrahams, Mahina Ahmadova, Kim Alexandra, Maya Alexandri, James Anderson, Kamola Aripova, Gulnara Auketayeva, Mahmoud Aziz **B** William Beeman, Fabio Bertino, Ute Bletzinger, Rachel Bochenski, Michelle Boudreau, Dominique Bromberger **C** Ron Cameron, Steve Cope, Bruno de Cordier, Ben Cousins, Ann Curry **D** Mariana Dahan, Julie Duvivier, Hakon Dyrkoren **E** Tim Eyres **F** Farrokh Faridian, Joseph Fatula, Eli Feiman, Charles Frisby **G** Roger Gilboy, Mary Gough, Kevin Griffith, Ingrid & Emmerich Gruber, Gael Guichard **H** Habib Habibov, Sandra Harrison, Stephanie Heise, Robert Heiser, Jess Hemmings, Jack Hemsley, Stéphane Henriod, Stephanie Hockman, Anna-Clara Hollander **J** Gustav Jahnke, Rok Jarc **K** Elle Kay, Alice Keen, Filip Keysers, Lucie Kinkorova, Riccardo Klinger, Erkin Koshoev, Melanie Krebs, Uschi Kunkel, Jana Kvaltinova **L** David Larson, Tanja Lehmann, Valere Liechti, Harold Linder, Anja Lohse, Eve Lomasny, Helen Lunn **M** Robert Macdonald, Kent Maxwell, Hugh Mclean, Roberta Melchiorre, Anthony Melov, Sadie Melov, Norma Metcalfe, Peeters Michiels, Sarah Mueller, Iris Mundigl, Amanda Musker **N** Dominique Nadelhofer, Mariam Nassary, Steve Newcomer **O** Jan O'Neill, Carolyn Orcutt, Stephanos Orestis **P** Sam Palsmeier, Jean-Maire Parmentier, Michael Pedersen, Johan Pettersson, Katharina Posse, Alberto Postigo, Fernando de la Puente **R** Werner Racky, Barak Rinat, Jan Rohac **S** Samantha Sartain, Sjaan Schaap, Christine Schwarz, Jayne Sharp, Selina Short, Jack Simms, J Sims, Paul Skeet, Radek Skrivanek, Niels Smit, Nate Smith, Tony Solomun, Gerald Sorg, Theo Sudomlak **T** Jane Taylor, Maureen Taylor, Emma Tebbutt, Paul Tibbitts, Catherine Till, James Timmis, Joshua Tokita, Dagny Trentelman **U** Bahodur Umarov **V** Jas van Driel, Robert van Voorden, Luc Vandervelde, Frank Vlaardingerbroek, Gian Volpe, Folke von Knobloch **W** Bill Weir, Karyn Wesselingh, Brad Wicherson, Claire Wilkinson, Emily Wong **Y** Andrew Young **Z** Jennifer Zorko

## ACKNOWLEDGMENTS

Many thanks to the following for the use of their content:

Globe on title page © Mountain High Maps 1993 Digital Wisdom, Inc.

# Index

| ABBREVIATIONS | |
|---|---|
| Kaz | Kazakhstan |
| Kyr | Kyrgyzstan |
| Taj | Tajikistan |
| Tur | Turkmenistan |
| U | Uzbekistan |

INDEX

**000** Map pages
**000** Photograph pages

## G



## H

**000** Map pages
**000** Photograph pages

## N

INDEX

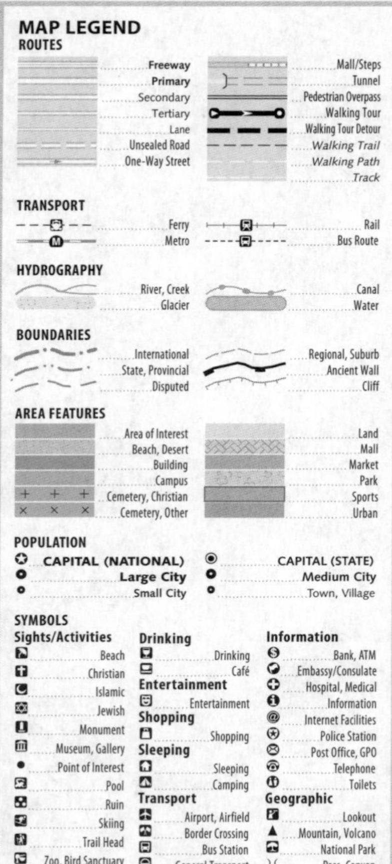


## LONELY PLANET OFFICES


### Australia
Head Office
Locked Bag 1, Footscray, Victoria 3011
☎ 03 8379 8000, fax 03 8379 8111
talk2us@lonelyplanet.com.au

### USA
150 Linden St, Oakland, CA 94607
☎ 510 893 8555, toll free 800 275 8555
fax 510 893 8572
info@lonelyplanet.com

### UK
72–82 Rosebery Ave,
Clerkenwell, London EC1R 4RW
☎ 020 7841 9000, fax 020 7841 9001
go@lonelyplanet.co.uk



**Published by Lonely Planet Publications Pty Ltd**
ABN 36 005 607 983





Cover photograph: Kyrgyz family portrait outside summer yurt, near Kochkor, Anthony Plummer/Lonely Planet Images. Many of the images in this guide are available for licensing from Lonely Planet Images: www.lonelyplanetimages.com.





Printed through The Bookmaker International Ltd.
Printed in China